# The History of the Norman Conquest of England, Its Causes and Its Results

# HISTORY OF THE NORMAN CONQUEST.

London

MACMILLAN AND CO.

*PUBLISHERS TO THE UNIVERSITY OF*

Oxford.

# THE HISTORY

OF THE

# NORMAN CONQUEST OF ENGLAND,

ITS CAUSES AND ITS RESULTS.

BY

EDWARD A. FREEMAN, M.A., Hon. D.C.L.

LATE FELLOW OF TRINITY COLLEGE

VOLUME IV.

THE REIGN OF WILLIAM THE CONQUEROR.

' Magna feres tacitas solatia mortis ad umbras,
A tanto cecidisse viro '—*Ovid Metam* v 191

Oxford:

AT THE CLARENDON PRESS.

M DCCC. LXXI

# PREFACE.

THE present volume contains the reign of William. I regret that the bulk to which the text has swelled has caused me to leave out several notes which were designed to have a place in the Appendix; but I believe that their substance will find a place as least as fitting among the more general disquisitions which I hope to give in the fifth volume.

Besides the friends whom I have so often thanked in earlier volumes, I have now to acknowledge the great help which I have received from several friends at the various places which I had to examine in order to give a full account of William's Western and Northern campaigns. I have to thank them alike for help on the spot and for suggestions as to the local maps and plans. At Exeter I was accompanied by Mr. W. A. Sanford, whose eye for any physical point is much keener than mine. At Lincoln I had much help from the Precentor, the Rev. Edmund Venables; at York from Archdeacon Jones and the Rev. James Raine, Canon of York; in the City and Bishoprick of Durham from the Rev. William Greenwell and Mr. W. H. Longstaffe of Gateshead; and at

Chester from the Dean and Mr. Hughes. And in speaking of my topographical researches, though I do not think that in the present volume I have had any direct help from Mr. J. R. Green, yet I have often felt the benefit of earlier inquiries of the same kind made in his company. I may truly say that it was from him that I first learned to look on a town as a whole with a kind of personal history, instead of simply the place where such and such a church or castle was to be found.

In the plans of towns, I have tried to show their extent as they must have stood in the days of William, and to mark such buildings as were then certainly or probably in being. But in such an attempt as this a good deal is necessarily left to conjecture. The map of the Fen country, illustrating the campaigns of Hereward, is grounded on the map in Professor C. C. Babington's Ancient Cambridgeshire, and I have to thank the Professor for most valuable help both in drawing the map and in personally going over the ground. I have to say the same of the plan of the town of Cambridge, which is also founded on his work. The general map of England, showing the gradual progress of William's conquest, is, as far as I know, a new attempt. Here again something must be left to conjecture. The Welsh boundary especially was very uncertain and fluctuating, and I cannot expect to have attained complete accuracy, but the map will at least show that all the shires on the March as they stand in Domesday took in certain districts which now do not belong to them. With regard to the other shires, I have not attempted to mark the small differences between their present and their Domesday boundaries, except in the extreme cases of the largest and smallest among them. Yorkshire was then far greater, and Rutland, which in truth was not a distinct shire, was still smaller than it is now. In making this map, I have to acknowledge many valuable hints from Mr. James Parker.

The present volume has taken a longer time in its composition than any of those that have gone before it, partly because of the interruption caused by the revision of the first two volumes for the second edition, partly because of the greater extent and difficulty of the work itself. The fifth and last volume will, like the first, consist partly of narrative and partly of dissertation. In it I trust to go thoroughly into the effects of the Norman Conquest on the later condition and history of England, and to carry on the narrative in the form of a sketch to the point which I designed from the beginning, the reign of Edward the First.

SOMERLEAZE, WELLS,
*May* 27, 1871

# CONTENTS.

## CHAPTER XVII

### THE FIRST DAYS OF WILLIAM'S REIGN
### December, 1066—December, 1067

#### § 1 *Character of the Reign of William*

| A.D | | PAGE |
|---|---|---|
| | Position of William at the time of his coronation, no armed opposition in any part of England | 3—4 |
| | Position of Eadwine and Morkere | 4 |
| | England not yet conquered | 5 |
| | Effects of the Coronation on the formal legality of his position | 5 |
| | Character of the resistance to William after his Coronation | 6—7 |
| | Legal fictions of his reign | 8—9 |
| | Their practical effect | 9 |
| | William's attempts at conciliation | 10 |
| | Results of the disturbance at the Coronation | 10 |
| | Inherent falseness of his position | 11 |
| | His beginnings compared with those of Cnut | 12—17 |
| | True character of his conquest | 13—14 |
| | Real extent of the transfer of lands | 14 |
| | Different positions of Danes and Normans in England | 16 |
| | Blending of Normans and English | 17 |
| | Unity of the Kingdom established by William | 18 |

#### § 2. *William's first Days in England.*
#### December, 1066—March, 1067.

| | | |
|---|---|---|
| Christmas, 1066-1067 | William withdraws to Barking | 19 |
| | Change of feeling among the English | 19 |
| | Submission of the Northern and Mercian chiefs | 20—22 |
| | Surrenders and confiscations of land | 22 |

## CONTENTS

| A D | | PAGE |
|---|---|---|
| | All land held to be forfeited | 23 |
| | *Folk-land* becomes *terra Regis* | 24 |
| | Cases of regrant | 25 |
| | General redemption of lands, the three Commissioners | 25—26 |
| | Harold's acts null and void | 27 |
| | Submission of Northern England only nominal | 28 |
| | William's charter to London | 29 |
| | His strict discipline and police | 30 |
| January—March, 1067 | William's first progress, his regrants and alms | 31—32 |
| | Case of Berkshire | 32—47 |
| | Patriotism of the Berkshire men | 33 |
| | Lands and family of Godric | 33—37 |
| | Comparison with Kent and Sussex | 34 |
| | Lands of the House of Godwine | 34 |
| | Illegal occupations of Froger and Henry of Ferrers | 37 |
| | Foreigners settled in Berkshire | 39—42 |
| | Small number of Englishmen who retained their lands | 42—44 |
| | Story of Azor the *Dapifer* | 44 |
| | Wigod of Wallingford wins William's favour | 45 |
| | His Norman sons-in-law | 46 |
| 1072 | Robert of Oily founds Oxford Castle | 46 |
| 1129 | Robert of Oily the younger founds Oseney Priory | 47 |
| | Causes of lack of resistance to the confiscation | 47—50 |
| | Confiscation familiar at the time | 50—52 |
| | Familiarity with the settlement of foreigners | 52—53 |
| | Permanent effects of the confiscation | 54—55 |
| | Land largely retained by its actual possessors | 56 |
| | Abbot Brand of Peterborough buys William's favour | 56 |
| | William's dealings with the New Minster | 57—59 |
| 1069 | Election of Abbot Wulfric | 59 |
| | Taxes and offerings | 59—60 |
| | William's gifts to foreign churches | 61—62 |
| | Harold's standard sent to Rome | 61 |
| | Extent of William's occupation of England | 63—65 |
| | Analogy between the position of William and Harold | 65 |
| | Building of castles | 66—68 |
| | Condition of Norwich | 67 |
| | William's foreign auxiliaries | 68—69 |
| | Vicegerency of Odo and William Fitz-Osbern | 69—73 |
| | Their special Earldoms | 70 |
| | Earls appointed for single shires, effects of the change | 70—71 |
| | Holders of subordinate commands | 73—74 |
| | William's policy towards the North, the Earls summoned to attend him to Normandy | 74—77 |

## CONTENTS

| A D | | PAGE |
|---|---|---|
| February 4, 1067 | Oswulf deposed, Copsige appointed Earl | 76 |

### § 3 *William's first Visit to Normandy*
### *March – December, 1087.*

| | | |
|---|---|---|
| March, 1067 | William sets sail for Normandy | 77 |
| | His English attendants or hostages | 79 |
| | Suppression of piracy | 80 |
| | His reception in Normandy | 80—81 |
| | His visits and grants to churches | 82 |
| | His probable consultations with Lanfranc | 82—83 |
| | English and German skill in gold-work and embroidery | 84—85 |
| April 8, 1067 | William keeps Easter at Fecamp | 86 |
| 990—1082 | Condition and history of the monastery | 87—90 |
| 1062 | Ralph of Montdidier, his marriage with King Henry's widow | 90 |
| | The English visitors | 91 |
| | Consecration of churches | 92—94 |
| May 1, 1067 | Saint Mary-on-Dive | 93 |
| July 1 | Jumièges | 93 |
| August 9 | Death of Archbishop Maurilius | 94 |
| | Lanfranc refuses the primacy | 95 |
| 1067—1069 | Primacy of John of Ivry | 96—98 |
| | Flourishing state of Normandy | 98 |

## CHAPTER XVIII.

#### THE CONQUEST OF WESTERN AND NORTHERN ENGLAND.
#### March, 1067—April, 1070.

| | | |
|---|---|---|
| | Great part of England still unconquered | 101 |
| | William's motives for leaving England | 101—103 |
| | Called back by the prospect of foreign invasion | 103 |

### § 1. *The Administration of Odo and William Fitz-Osbern*
### *March—December, 1067.*

| | | |
|---|---|---|
| | Oppressive government of the regents | 103—106 |
| March 11, 1067 | Revolt against Copsige, he is killed by Oswulf at Newburn; Norman praises of him | 106—108 |
| | Special oppression in Herefordshire and Kent | 108—109 |
| | Union of Welsh and English | 109 |
| August 15 | Eadric the Wild holds out, his alliance with Bleddyn and Rhiwallon, their ravages in Herefordshire | 110—111 |

| A.D. | | PAGE |
|---|---|---|
| | The Kentish outbreak, help sought from Eustace of Boulogne | 111—114 |
| | Unsuccessful attack on Dover, escape of Eustace and capture of his nephew | 114—118 |
| | Help sought in foreign lands, state of Germany and Denmark | 119 |
| | Close connexion of Swend with England, English invitations to him, presence of Eadric of Norfolk in Denmark | 119—122 |
| 1066—1093 | State of Norway; reigns of Magnus and Olaf Kyrre | 122 |
| | William's real danger from Denmark | 123 |

### § 2  The Conquest of the West.
### December, 1067—March, 1068.

| A.D. | | PAGE |
|---|---|---|
| December 6, 1067 | Matilda and Robert regents in Normandy | 123 |
| | William sets sail at Dieppe | 124 |
| December 7 | He lands at Winchelsea | 125 |
| December 6 | Christ Church burnt | 125 |
| | No open revolt in the conquered shires, but the West and North threatening | 126 |
| December 25, 1067—Jan 6, 1068 | William keeps Christmas at Westminster; further confiscations and taxations | 127—128 |
| | Eustace of Boulogne tried and condemned in absence | 128—129 |
| | His later reconciliation, his lands | 129—130 |
| | Death of Wulfwig, Bishop of Dorchester | 130 |
| | Exclusion of Englishmen from ecclesiastical preferment | 131 |
| 1067—1092 | Remigius, Bishop of Dorchester, afterwards of Lincoln, he is consecrated by Stigand | 132—133 |
| Autumn, 1067 | Oswulf slain by a robber | 133—134 |
| Christmas, 1067—1068 | Gospatric buys the Earldom of Northumberland of William | 134—135 |
| | William's negotiations with Swend and Adalbert of Bremen, mission of Abbot Æthelsige | 135—137 |
| 1070 | Later history of Æthelsige, his outlawry | 137 |
| | His return | 138 |
| | State of the West, zeal of the men of Exeter, their alliance with the neighbouring shires and towns | 138—139 |
| | Connexion of the Western movement with the House of Godwine, their lands in the West | 140—141 |
| | Gytha and her grandsons at Exeter, state of the family | 141—143 |
| | Volunteers from other districts, story of Blæcman of Berkshire | 143—144 |
| | The West unsupported by the North | 144 |

# CONTENTS

| A D | | PAGE |
|---|---|---|
| February, 1068 | William demands the submission of Exeter . | 145 |
| | Attempt at a compromise, republican schemes at Exeter, royal rights over the city . | 145—147 |
| | Position of the local Thegns and of the family of Harold . . . . . | 148 |
| | William's answer, he marches against Exeter . | 149 |
| | His employment of English troops . | 149—150 |
| | William's march, his harryings in Dorset, the magistrates of Exeter offer to submit | 151 |
| | The capitulation disowned by the citizens . . | 152 |
| | William besieges Exeter, description of the city . | 152—154 |
| | Insult offered to him by the besiegers; he blinds one of the hostages . . . | 155 |
| | Valiant defence of the city, it is taken by means of a mine . | 156 |
| | Gytha and her company escape to the Flat Holm, history of the Holms . | 157—158 |
| | Harold's sons take refuge at Dublin . | 159 |
| June, 1069? | Gytha withdraws to Flanders . . | 159 |
| | Gunhild dies at Bruges . | 159 |
| August 24, 1087 | Marriage and descendants of the younger Gytha . | 159—160 |
| | Surrender of Exeter . | 160 |
| | Foundation of the castle, increase of the tribute of the city . | 161—162 |
| | William's conquest of Cornwall . | 162—163 |
| | Settlement of the West, Englishmen who retained their lands; history of Eadnoth and his son Harding . . . . . . | 163—165 |
| | Story of Brihtric and Matilda . . . | 165 |
| | The Western Bishops undisturbed; alienation of the gifts of Gytha, history of the lands of Blæcman | 165—167 |
| | Grants to the Norman churches and to the Church of Rome . | 167 |
| | Other Norman grantees . | 168 |
| | Possessions of Robert of Mortain, Earl of Cornwall, his robbery of churches | 168—170 |
| | State of Cornwall, the British element revived by the Norman Conquest . . . | 170—173 |
| 1068—1069 | History of Gloucestershire and Worcestershire, oppressions of the Sheriff Urse; he is rebuked by Archbishop Ealdred . . | 173—175 |
| | Favour of Æthelwig of Evesham; Godric of Winchcombe entrusted to his keeping . | 176—177 |
| March 23, 1068 | Bristol subject to William . . . . | 178 |

# CONTENTS.

| A. D. | | PAGE |
|---|---|---|
| | Easter feast at Winchester . . . . | 178 |
| May 11 | Whitsun feast at Westminster, coronation of Matilda | 179 |

§ 3 *The First Conquest of the North.*
*Summer and Autumn, 1068.*

| | | |
|---|---|---|
| | Position and character of Eadwine and Morkere; a daughter of William promised to Eadwine | 179—182 |
| Summer, 1068 | Eadwine and Morkere revolt; rising in the North | 181 |
| 1067—1068 | Union of English and Welsh, civil war in Wales; death of Rhiwallon . . . . | 182—183 |
| | General gathering against the Normans; applications to Swend and Malcolm . . | 184 |
| | Eadgar the nominal head of the movement, action of the Northern Thegns . . . | 185 |
| | No effectual Scottish help given . . | 186 |
| | General zeal of the people, York the centre of resistance . . . . . | 186—187 |
| | William's first Northern march, question of the storm of Oxford . . . . . | 188 |
| | William at Warwick, submission of Ælfwine and Thurkill, history of the town and castle . | 188—192 |
| | March of Eadwine and Morkere; they submit to William and are restored to favour . | 192—193 |
| | The English army disperses, but a party withdraw to the North and occupy Durham . . | 193—194 |
| 1068—1069 | Eadgar, Gospatric, and others pass the winter in Scotland . . . . | 194—195 |
| | Question of the destruction of Leicester . | 196—197 |
| | William reaches Nottingham; history of the town | 196—199 |
| | William Peverel, his castles at Nottingham and in the Peakland . . . . | 200—201 |
| | York submits, history of the city . . | 201—203 |
| | Foundation of the first castle, William Malet appointed Sheriff . | 203—204 |
| | Submission of Archill and Æthelwine . | 205 |
| | First submission of Malcolm . . | 206 |
| | Extent of William's dominion in 1068 . | 206—207 |
| | His return march, he reaches Lincoln . | 208 |
| | History of Lincoln, effects of William's reign on the city . . . . . | 208—215 |
| | Comparatively favourable treatment of Lincoln and Lincolnshire . . . . | 213—216 |
| | Treatment of Stamford and Torkesey . | 216—217 |
| | Foundation of Lincoln castle . . | 217—218 |
| | Migration to the lower town, churches of Coleswegen . . . . | 218—219 |
| | William reaches Cambridge, early history of the town | 219—221 |

# CONTENTS

| A.D. | | PAGE |
|---|---|---|
| | Foundation of the castle and origin of the modern town | 221—222 |
| | William at Huntingdon, history of the town and foundation of the castle | 222 |
| | Heavy confiscations in Cambridgeshire and Huntingdonshire, oppressions of the Sheriffs Picot and Eustace | 223—224 |
| | Harold's sons return from Ireland; they attack Bristol in vain | 224—226 |
| | Their drawn battle with Eadnoth the Staller, death of Eadnoth, their ravages in the West | 225—227 |
| September? 1068 | Birth of the Ætheling Henry; his name, education, and character | 227—230 |
| c 1069 | Legend of Henry's birth at Selby, foundation of the Abbey | 230—231 |
| | Legend of the complaints of the Norman women; estimate of the story | 231—233 |
| | William sends away his mercenaries | 233 |

### § 4 *The Revolt and Final Conquest of the North*
#### 1069—1070

| | | |
|---|---|---|
| | Importance of the year 1069, final establishment of William's power | 234 |
| January, 1069 | He grants the Earldom of Northumberland to Robert of Comines | 235 |
| | Robert enters Durham, he is slain with his followers | 236—238 |
| | Revolt at York and slaughter of Robert Fitz-Richard | 238 |
| | Return of Eadgar, Gospatric, and others, they are received at York | 240 |
| | Siege of the castle; William hastens to York and defeats the insurgents | 240 |
| | The second castle built and intrusted to William Fitz-Osbern | 241 |
| | Legend of the miraculous defence of Durham | 241—242 |
| | Renewed revolt at York; the insurgents defeated by William Fitz-Osbern | 242—243 |
| c June 24 | Second enterprise of Harold's sons, their ravages in Devonshire | 243 |
| | They are defeated by Count Brian, no further mention of them | 244—245 |
| 1069 | Death of Diarmid of Dublin | 245 |
| | Story of the Counts of Stade | 246 |
| Autumn, 1069 | Swend at last sends help; description of his force | 247—248 |
| | The commanders, Osbiorn, Harold, Cnut, and Thurkill | 248 |
| | Probable objects of Swend | 249—250 |
| | William in the Forest of Dean | 251 |

## CONTENTS.

| A.D. | | PAGE |
|---|---|---|
| | Course of the Danish fleet, unsuccessful attempts in Kent and East-Anglia | 251—253 |
| September 8. | The fleet enters the Humber; it is joined by Eadgar and the English exiles | 253—255 |
| | Waltheof joins the Danes, his character and early history | 255—259 |
| | Confidence of the Norman commanders at York | 259—260 |
| September 11 | Stories of Archbishop Ealdred, his death | 260—266 |
| | Unlucky adventure of Eadgar in Lindesey | 266 |
| September 19 | The Danes and English march on York, the city fired by the Normans | 266—267 |
| September 21 | The Danes and English take York; exploits of Waltheof | 268—269 |
| | Capture of William Malet and Gilbert of Ghent | 269 |
| | Destruction of the castles | 270 |
| | The army disperses | 271 |
| | Movements in the West; sieges of Montacute and Exeter | 271—273 |
| | Movements in Staffordshire and on the Welsh border, Shrewsbury besieged by Eadric | 273—274 |
| | The revolts put down piecemeal | 275—277 |
| | Montacute relieved by Bishop Geoffrey | 278 |
| | Defeat of the besiegers of Exeter | 279 |
| | Eadric burns Shrewsbury and retires | 280 |
| | William marches northward, he surprises the Danes in Lindesey, they retreat into Holderness | 280—281 |
| | The two Earls Robert left in Lindesey, their successes against the Danes | 281—283 |
| | William conquers Staffordshire and marches to Nottingham | 282—283 |
| | His delay by the Aire; origin of Pontefract castle | 284—287 |
| | William enters York without opposition, and repairs the castles | 287 |
| | The great harrying of Northumberland; its deliberate and systematic character | 288—289 |
| | Legend of the deliverance of Beverley | 289—292 |
| | Details of the harrying; contemporary estimate of William's conduct | 292—295 |
| Dec. 25, 1069 | He keeps Christmas at York, settlement of Yorkshire | 295—296 |
| Jan. 6, 1070 | Grants to Alan of Britanny, foundation of Richmond | 296 |
| | Grants to Robert of Mortain and others | 297—298 |
| | Land retained by Englishmen, fall in its value | 298 |
| | English refuge at the mouth of the Tees | 299 |
| Dec 11—14, 1069 | Flight of Æthelwine and his canons from Durham to Lindisfarn | 299—301 |
| | General flight of the people | 302 |

## CONTENTS.

| A.D. | | PAGE |
|---|---|---|
| January, 1070 | William marches from York through Cleveland | 302 |
| | Submission and restoration of Waltheof and Gospatric, marriage of Waltheof and Judith | 303 |
| | William ravages the Bishoprick, submission of Archill and Eglaf | 304—305 |
| | William returns to York by Helmsley, Northern England finally conquered | 306—308 |
| February? | William's last march from York to Chester, difficulties of the road and mutiny of his troops | 308—311 |
| | Chester the last conquest; former history of the town | 311—314 |
| | Ravaging of Cheshire and the neighbouring shires, charity of Abbot Æthelwig | 315—316 |
| | Castles founded at Chester and Stafford | 317—318 |
| February— March? | William marches to Salisbury and reviews his army | 318—319 |
| 1069—1070 | The Danish fleet remains in the Humber; Osbeorn bribed by William | 319—320 |
| | The Conquest now practically accomplished | 320 |

## CHAPTER XIX.

### THE ECCLESIASTICAL SETTLEMENT OF ENGLAND
### 1070—1089.

| | | |
|---|---|---|
| | State of England in 1070; William in possession of the whole country, later revolts only local | 321—322 |
| | Gradual change in William's character | 322 |
| | His attempt to learn English | 323 |
| | Legend of the publication of the Laws of Eadward | 324 |
| | William's real legislation, renewal of Eadward's Law | 325—326 |
| | Blending of races, especially in the towns | 326—327 |

### § 1 *The Councils of the Year* 1070

| | | |
|---|---|---|
| February— March, 1070 | Plunder of the monasteries | 328—329 |
| April 4 | Easter Feast at Winchester, William crowned by the Papal Legates | 329—330 |
| | Schemes for the removal of English Prelates | 330—331 |
| April 11 | Trial and deprivation of Stigand, stories of his last days | 331—334 |
| | Deposition of Æthelmar | 334 |
| November 27, 1069 | Death of Brand of Peterborough, he is succeeded by Turold | 335 |
| | Æthelric seized and Æthelwine outlawed | 335—336 |
| April 6 | The church of Durham reconciled | 336 |

b

| A.D. | | PAGE |
|---|---|---|
| April | Æthelwine sails for Koln, but is driven back to Scotland . . . . . . | 337 |
| | Flight of Æthelsige, Scotland appointed Abbot of Saint Augustine's . . . | 338 |
| | Wulfstan demands the lands alienated by Ealdred; the decision delayed . . | 339—340 |
| May 23—31 | Whitsun Gemót at Windsor; appointment and history of Thomas of York and of Walkelin of Winchester | 340—343 |
| May 24 | The Legate Ermenfrid holds a synod; deprivation of Æthelric, appointment of Stigand of Selsey and Herfast of Elmham . . | 343—344 |
| May 30 | Walkelin consecrated by Ermenfrid . . . | 344 |
| | Lanfranc appointed to Canterbury, his scruples overcome by Herlwin . . | 345—347 |
| August 15 | Lanfranc receives the Archbishoprick from the King | 347 |
| August 29 | His consecration . . . | 347—349 |

### § 2 The Primacy of Lanfranc
### 1070—1089.

| | | |
|---|---|---|
| | Relations between William and Lanfranc . | 349—350 |
| | Relations between the two Archbishopricks, William's policy requires the subordination of York | 350—351 |
| | Lanfranc refuses consecration to Thomas unless he makes profession, compromise brought about by William . . . . . | 352—354 |
| 1071 | Lanfranc and Thomas go to Rome for their pallia; Lanfranc intercedes for Thomas and Remigius | 355—357 |
| April 8, 1072 | Easter Gemót at Winchester; settlement of the question between the Archbishopricks . | 357—359 |
| | Ecclesiastical scheme of Lanfranc; his works at Canterbury . . . . . | 359—364 |
| 1072—1079 | Rebuilding of Christ Church . . . | 361 |
| 1084 | His foundation of Saint Gregory's . . | 363 |
| 1072 | Encroachments of Odo on the lands of the see, Lanfranc recovers them on Penenden Heath, retention of English Law . . . | 364—368 |
| 1075—1076 | History of Rochester, death of Siward and episcopate of Ernost . . . . . | 369 |
| 1077—1108 | Episcopate of Gundulf, his reforms and buildings | 369—372 |
| 1070—1100 | History of York; primacy of Thomas . | 372—374 |
| 1093 | He consecrates Anselm, revival of the dispute between the Archbishopricks . . | 372—373 |
| | Works of Thomas at York . . . | 373—374 |
| 1051—1075 | Bishops of London, episcopate of William . | 374 |
| 1075—1085 | Episcopate of Hugh of Orival . . | 375 |
| 1086—1087 | Episcopate of Maurice, he begins to rebuild Saint Paul's . . . . . | 375 |

# CONTENTS

| A.D. | | PAGE |
|---|---|---|
| 1070—1098 | History of Winchester, episcopate of Walkelin; scheme for the substitution of canons for monks | 375—376 |
| 1046—1072 | History of Exeter, episcopate of Leofric | 378 |
| 1072—1103 | Episcopate of Osbern, his English tendencies | 378 |
| 1107—1136 | Foundation of the present cathedral by William of Warelwast | 378 |
| 1079 | History of Hereford, death of Walter | 379 |
| 1079—1095 | Episcopate of Robert, he rebuilds the church | 379 |
| 1075 | History of Wulfstan; his deposition designed by Lanfranc; legend of his appeal to Eadward | 379—383 |
| 1085 | Wulfstan's management of his diocese, foundation of Malvern Priory | 383 |
| 1084 | He rebuilds the church of Worcester | 384—385 |
| | He preaches against the slave-trade at Bristol | 385—387 |
| | Bond between Wulfstan and six other monasteries | 387—391 |
| 1077—1084 | Death of Æthelwig, Walter Abbot of Evesham | 387—388 |
| 1077—1095 | Ralph Abbot of Winchcombe | 388 |
| 1085—1087 | Death of Eadmund of Pershore, abbacy of Thurstan | 388 |
| 1072—1104 | Serlo Abbot of Gloucester, his reforms | 388—389 |
| 1089—1100 | He rebuilds Gloucester Abbey | 389 |
| | Councils held by Lanfranc, distinction between ecclesiastical and temporal assemblies | 391—393 |
| 1071 or 1072 | Deposition of Abbots, Wulfric of New Minster succeeded by Rhiwallon | 393 |
| 1078 | Deposition of Æthelnoth of Glastonbury | 394 |
| 1082—1083 | Thurstan Abbot of Glastonbury; his dispute with the monks and deposition by William | 394—397 |
| 1089—1090 | He buys his restoration of William Rufus | 398 |
| 1066-1077(?) | Frithric Abbot of Saint Alban's, legendary nature of his history | 398 |
| 1077—1088 | Paul Abbot of St Alban's; his reforms and buildings, he destroys the tombs of the English Abbots | 398—400 |
| | William's personal zeal in ecclesiastical matters, appointment of Abbots of Westminster | 401 |
| 1072(?) | Eadwine succeeded by Geoffrey | 401 |
| 1077 | Appointment of Vital, correspondence of William with John of Fécamp | 401—402 |
| 1070—1076 | William's vow to Saint Martin; beginning of the foundation of Battle Abbey | 402—404 |
| | Story of the building of the Abbey, the High Altar fixed on the site of the Standard | 404—409 |
| | Succession of Abbots; consecration of the church | 406—407 |
| | Exemption of the Abbey from episcopal jurisdiction | 409—410 |
| | Lanfranc's opposition to monastic exemptions, his dealings with Saint Eadmundsbury | 410—412 |
| 1088 | His dealings with Saint Augustine's, he forces Abbot Guy on the monks | 412—414 |

# CONTENTS

| A.D. | | PAGE |
|---|---|---|
| 1075 | Decree for the removal of Bishopricks, comparison of English and continental sees | 414—417 |
| 1075—1078 | Hermann removes the see of Sherborne to Salisbury | 418 |
| 1221 | Foundation of new Salisbury | 418 |
| 1078—1079 | Episcopate of Osmund | 418 |
| | Stigand removes the see of Selsey to Chichester | 418 |
| 1072—1085 | Peter removes the see of Lichfield to Chester | 419 |
| 1086—1117 | Robert of Limesey removes the see to Coventry, his ill-treatment of the monks and rebuke from Lanfranc, later history of the see | 419—421 |
| 1085 | Remigius removes the see of Dorchester to Lincoln | 421 |
| 1078 | Herfast removes the see of Elmham to Thetford | 421 |
| 1091—1119 | Herbert Losinga removes the see to Norwich | 422 |
| 1088—1122 | John of Tours removes the see of Wells to Bath | 422 |
| April 1, 1076 | Council at Winchester, prohibition of the marriage of the clergy, modification of the decrees of Hildebrand | 422—426 |
| 1076 | Mission of Thomas, Lanfranc, and Remigius to Rome, privileges confirmed to William | 426—428 |
| 1077—1078 | They return through Normandy; consecration of Saint Stephen's and Bec, death of Herlwin | 428—429 |
| | Wider separation of Church and State, and closer connexion with Rome | 430 |
| | Relations between Gregory and William, Gregory demands homage, but William refuses | 430—434 |
| 1079—1082 | Relations between Gregory and Lanfranc, Lanfranc summoned to Rome, his cautious language during the schism | 434—437 |
| | Exercise of the royal supremacy by William | 437—439 |
| | Un-English feelings of Lanfranc, his contempt for the English saints | 440—441 |
| 1078—1079 | Anselm Abbot of Bec, his visit to England, he convinces Lanfranc as to the martyrdom of Ælfheah | 441—444 |
| | William's disposal of ecclesiastical preferment | 445 |
| | Wimund of Saint Leutfred refuses preferment, his protest against the conquest of England | 446—448 |
| 1079—1099 | Later history of Wimund, he refuses the Archbishoprick of Rouen, but becomes Archbishop of Aversa | 448—449 |
| | Gulbert of Hugleville refuses lands in England | 449—450 |

## CHAPTER XX.

### THE REVOLTS AGAINST WILLIAM. 1070—1076

| 1070 | Complete establishment of William's authority, consolidation of the Kingdom | 451—452 |
|---|---|---|
| | Distinction between the revolts and the earlier resistance to invasion | 452—453 |
| | Classification of the revolts | 454 |

# CONTENTS

| A D | | PAGE |
|---|---|---|
| | § 1 *The Revolt of the Fen Country* 1070—1071. | |
| May, 1070 | Osbeorn at Ely, the fenland for Swend . | 454 |
| | Appearance of Hereward, legendary and historical notices of him . | 455—457 |
| November 27, 1069—April 4, 1070 | Death of Abbot Brand of Peterborough, succession of Turold . . . . | 457 |
| June 1, 1070 | Turold sets out to take possession, he reaches Stamford . . . | 458 |
| June 2 | Hereward plunders Peterborough, Turold reaches the monastery . . . | 458—461 |
| June 24 | Departure of the Danes . . | 461 |
| | Æthelric excommunicates the plunderers of Peterborough . . | 462 |
| June— August | Eadric submits to William . | 463 |
| | Revolt of the Isle of Ely under Hereward; description of the country . . . | 463—465 |
| April? 1071 | Revolt of Eadwine and Morkere; death and character of Eadwine . . . | 465—467 |
| | Morkere and others join the insurgents at Ely, early history of the Isle . . . | 468—471 |
| | William attacks the Isle, presence and death of William Malet . . | 471—473 |
| | Geography of the campaign, legends of Hereward | 473—475 |
| | Surrender of Morkere, Æthelwine, and others, imprisonment of Morkere . . . | 475—477 |
| 1071—1072 | Æthelwine imprisoned at Abingdon; his death . | 477—479 |
| 1071—1084 | Adelelm Abbot of Abingdon, his grants on military tenures . . | 478—479 |
| 1071 | Walcher succeeds Æthelwine at Durham, saying of Eadgyth at his consecration . . | 480 |
| | Submission of the monks of Ely . . | 480 |
| October, 1071 | William comes to Ely, his treatment of the monastery . . | 480—482 |
| 1076—1079 | Death of Thurstan; Abbacy of Theodwine . | 482 |
| 1079—1082 | Administration of Godfrey, he recovers the lands of the Abbey . . | 482—483 |
| 1082—1093 | Abbacy of Simeon, beginning of the present church | 483 |
| 1071 | Escape of Hereward, legends of his later life and death . . . . | 483—487 |
| 1073 | He accompanies William to Maine . | 485 |

§ 2 *The Affairs of the Welsh and Scottish Marches.*
1070—1074

State of the North, no more Earls of Deira or Mercia appointed, continuation of the Bernician Earldom 487—489

| A.D | | PAGE |
|---|---|---|
| | Earldom of Chester under Gerbod | 489 |
| 1071—1101 | Hugh of Avranches, Earl of Chester; special privileges of the Earldom | 489—491 |
| 1073—1088 | Robert of Rhuddlan, his wars with the Welsh | 490—492 |
| 1101 | Earl Hugh dies a monk, his friendship for Anselm | 493 |
| | Roger of Montgomery, Earl of Shrewsbury, privileges of the Earldom, treatment of Shrewsbury | 493—494 |
| 1082 | Murder of Mabel at Bures, good influence of Roger's second wife Adeliza | 494—495 |
| | History of Odelerius, his settlement at Shrewsbury | 495 |
| February 16, 1075 | Birth of Orderic, his English education | 495—496 |
| 1085 | Orderic sent to Saint Evroul, his abiding English feeling, lessons taught by his history | 496—498 |
| 1087—1094 | Earl Roger founds Shrewsbury Abbey at the suggestion of Odelerius, his death | 498—500 |
| 1081 | Earl Roger introduces Cluniac monks at Wenlock | 500 |
| 1071—1072 | Roger's wars with the Welsh, foundation of Montgomery Castle | 500—502 |
| 1067—1071 | Earldom of Hereford under William Fitz-Osbern | 502—504 |
| 1070 | His wars with the Welsh, his alliance with Caradoc the son of Gruffydd | 503 |
| 1070 | Malcolm ravages Northern England | 505 |
| | He receives Eadgar and his sisters at Wearmouth | 505—506 |
| | Gospatric invades Cumberland, increased cruelties of Malcolm | 506—508 |
| | Eadgar and his sisters remain in Scotland, marriage of Malcolm and Margaret, its lasting effects | 508—513 |
| April 3, 1071 | Walcher takes possession of the see of Durham | 513 |
| August 15, 1072 | William invades Scotland, he is accompanied by Eadric | 514—515 |
| | Malcolm does homage at Abernethy | 515—518 |
| November, 1072 | Legends of William's return, foundation of the castle of Durham | 518—522 |
| November, 1072 | Gospatric deprived of his Earldom, his later history and partial restoration | 522—524 |
| 1072—1075 | Waltheof Earl of Northumberland, his marriage with Judith and friendship with Walcher | 523—524 |
| 1073 | The sons of Carl murdered by order of Waltheof | 525 |

§ 3 *Dealings with Ireland* 1074—1087.

| | | |
|---|---|---|
| | William's designs on Ireland, ecclesiastical intercourse between England and Ireland | 526—528 |
| 1074 | Correspondence of Lanfranc with Irish Kings and Bishops, he consecrates Patrick to the see of Dublin | 528—529 |

## CONTENTS. xxiii

| A D. | | PAGE |
|---|---|---|
| 1085 | Donatus consecrated by Lanfranc, reforms in the Irish Church suggested by him | 529—530 |
| 1096—1140 | Later consecration of Irish Bishops in England, the Irish predisposed to the English connexion | 529—530 |

### § 4. *The Revolt of Maine* 1073

| | | |
|---|---|---|
| Christmas, 1070 | William Fitz-Osbern sent to Normandy | 531 |
| 1067—1070 | Affairs of Flanders, death of Baldwin of Lisle, reign of Baldwin of Mons | 531—532 |
| 1063 | Adventures of Robert the Frisian; his marriage and settlement in Holland | 532—533 |
| 1070 | War between Baldwin and Robert; death of Robert | 533 |
| | Regency of Richildis; she asks help of William Fitz-Osbern | 534—535 |
| February 20, 1071? | French and Norman intervention in Flanders, battle of Cassel, death of Count Arnulf and William Fitz-Osbern; imprisonment of Gerbod of Chester | 535—536 |
| | Philip makes peace with Robert, delay of Arnulf's German allies | 536—537 |
| | Division of the estates of William Fitz-Osbern | 537 |
| | Hostility between Normandy and Flanders, William abets Baldwin of Hennegau against Robert | 538 |
| May, 1074 | William's alleged designs on Germany, alleged invitation from Archbishop Hanno of Köln | 538—539 |
| | Other versions and estimate of the story | 539—540 |
| 1072 | William in Normandy, Synod of Rouen | 540—543 |
| 1069—1085 | State of Maine, episcopate of Arnold | 543—544 |
| 1066—1109 | Fulk Rechin of Anjou, his alleged intrigues | 544—545 |
| 1073 | Revolt of Maine, invitation to Azo and Gersendis and their son Hugh; action of Geoffrey of Mayenne and Bishop Arnold | 545—547 |
| | Azo in Maine, he leaves Gersendis and her son behind, relations of Geoffrey and Gersendis | 547—548 |
| | Municipal traditions in Gaul, the *Commune* of Le Mans | 548—552 |
| | War of the *Commune* with Hugh of Sillé, treason of Geoffrey | 552—554 |
| | Gersendis betrays the castle to Geoffrey; the citizens invite Fulk, who takes the castle | 554—556 |
| | William sets forth to recover Maine; his English troops | 556—558 |
| | Harrying of Maine; sieges of Fresnay and Sillé, surrender of Le Mans and submission of the country | 558—560 |
| | Fulk attacks La Flèche; he is joined by Howel and the Bretons | 561 |
| | Peace of Blanchelande, Robert does homage to Fulk for Maine | 561—564 |

## CONTENTS

### § 5. *The Revolt of Ralph of Norfolk*
### 1075—1076

| A.D | | PAGE |
|---|---|---|
| 1072—1074 | State of England, increased oppression, special complaints of the English women . . . | 564—568 |
| | Jealousy between William and Philip . | 568 |
| 1073 | William returns to England . . | 568 |
| 1074 | He goes back to Normandy . . | 568 |
| July 8, 1074 | Eadgar goes from Flanders to Scotland, Philip offers Montreuil to him . | 568—569 |
| | Eadgar sets sail for France, but is driven back | 569 |
| | His reconciliation with William . | 570—572 |
| | Dealings of William with Waltheof . | 572 |
| | Roger Earl of Hereford suspected of treason, Lanfranc's letters and excommunication . | 573 |
| 1075 | Ralph of Norfolk marries Emma sister of Roger; conspiracy at the bride-ale . | 574—578 |
| | Question of the complicity of Waltheof, his confessions to Lanfranc and William . | 578—579 |
| | Revolt of Ralph and Roger, the Bretons support Ralph, aid sought from Denmark . | 579 |
| | Roger defeated and taken prisoner . | 580—581 |
| | Ralph encamps at Cambridge, he flies to Norwich . | 580—581 |
| | Union of Normans and English; mutilation of the prisoners | 581 |
| | Ralph flies to Denmark and thence to Britanny . | 582—584 |
| | Norwich defended by Emma, its siege and capitulation . . . . | 580—584 |
| | William returns, arrest of Waltheof . | 585 |
| | The Danish fleet in the Humber; plunder of York Minster . . . . | 585—586 |
| December 19, 1075 | Death of Eadgyth, her burial at Westminster . | 587—588 |
| Christmas, 1075—1076 | Midwinter Gemót at Westminster; trial of the Earls and their followers . . . | 589 |
| | Ralph condemned by default; cruel punishment of the Bretons . . . | 589 |
| | Trial and condemnation of Roger, his imprisonment for life . . . | 590—592 |
| | Trial of Waltheof, enmity of his wife Judith, he is remanded to prison at Winchester . | 590—591 |
| | Confiscation of the lands of Ralph and Roger, grants to Roger the Bigod; no new Earls appointed . | 591 |
| | Continued imprisonment of Waltheof, his penitence | 593 |
| May 15, 1076 | His final trial and condemnation to death, injustice of the sentence . . . | 593—594 |
| May 31 | Beheading of Waltheof; he is looked upon as a martyr | 594—596 |

# CONTENTS

| A.D. | | PAGE |
|---|---|---|
| 700—715 | History of Crowland, story of Saint Guthlac | 597 |
| c 877 | Monastery destroyed by the Danes | 597 |
| 946—955 | Restored by Thurcytel | 597 |
| 1062—1086 | Ulfcytel Abbot of Crowland, gifts of Waltheof to the monastery | 598 |
| June 15, 1076 | Waltheof's body translated to Crowland | 599 |
| Christmas, 1085—1086 | Deposition of Ulfcytel, its probable grounds | 599 |
| 1086—1109 | Ingulf Abbot of Crowland, his real and legendary history | 600—601 |
| 1092 | Second translation of Waltheof, his miracles | 601—602 |
| 1109—1124 | Geoffrey Abbot of Crowland | 602 |
| 1124—1138 | Waltheof Abbot of Crowland, visit of Orderic | 603 |
| | Real and legendary history of Judith, her foundation at Elstow | 603—604 |
| c 1089 | Matilda, daughter of Waltheof, marries Simon of Senlis, her second marriage with David of Scotland, its results | 604—605 |
| | Estimate of the execution of Waltheof | 605—607 |
| | William's love of hunting, nature of hunting in early times | 608—609 |
| | Beginning of Forest Laws, legislation of William | 609—610 |
| 1070—1081 | Making of the New Forest, contemporary feeling | 611—613 |
| | Deaths of his children in the New Forest; a curse deemed to rest on his house | 613—615 |

## CHAPTER XXI

### THE LATER DAYS OF WILLIAM 1076—1087

§ 1 *Character of the Later Reign of William.*

| | |
|---|---|
| Quiet of England, William's unsuccessful warfare on the Continent | 616—617 |
| Character of William's government, his strict preservation of the peace | 617—619 |
| His fiscal and other oppressions | 620—622 |
| His revenue | 622 |
| He keeps up the meetings of the Witan | 623 |
| His legislation, legal relations between French and English | 623—624 |
| Laws against the slave-trade | 625 |
| Capital punishment forbidden, practice of mutilation | 625 |
| William's personal appearance, splendour of his court, his avarice | 625—626 |
| Practical despotism of his government | 627 |

## CONTENTS.

| A. D. | | PAGE |
|---|---|---|
| | Englishmen take service at Constantinople | 627—628 |
| April 1, 1081 | Accession of Alexios Komnênos; Robert Wiscard threatens the Eastern Empire, English reinforcements | 628 |
| June | Robert besieges Dyrrhachion | 629 |
| October | Alexios comes to its relief; his motley army | 629 |
| October 18 | Battle of Dyrrhachion, valour and slaughter of the English | 630—631 |
| | Alexios builds Kibôtos | 631 |
| 1083 | The English defend Kastoria against Bohemund | 631—632 |
| 1084 | Repulse of Bohemund and Brian of Britanny | 632 |
| | Permanence of the Warangian guard | 632 |

### § 2. *William's later Continental Wars.* 1076—1086.

| | | |
|---|---|---|
| | William's movements between England and Normandy | 633 |
| | He makes no grants to his children | 633—634 |
| April 5, 1075 | Easter at Fecamp, Cecily takes the veil | 634 |
| 1113—1127 | She becomes Abbess of Caen | 635 |
| 1076 | William besieges Dol, his motives | 635—636 |
| September 27, 1076 | Dispute about the Bishoprick, letter of Gregory to William | 636 |
| | Dol relieved by Alan and King Philip; peace with Britanny | 637 |
| 1077 | Peace with France | 638 |
| | Robert's disputes with his father | 638—642 |
| | War with Rotrou of Mortagne, quarrel of Robert and his brothers, he openly revolts | 642—643 |
| | Robert helped by Hugh of Neufchâtel; siege and capture of Raimalast | 643—644 |
| | Wanderings of Robert; Matilda sends him help, quarrel between her and William | 644—646 |
| 1079 | Philip sets Robert at Gerberoi | 646 |
| January, 1080 | William besieges Gerberoi; he is defeated and wounded by Robert | 647—648 |
| May 8 | William reconciled to his son, Gregory's letter to Robert | 649—650 |
| Autumn | Robert's expedition to Scotland, his final quarrel with his father | 650 |
| 1086—1090 | Constance marries Alan of Britanny; her death and character | 650—651 |
| 1080 | Marriage of Adela with Stephen of Chartres | 652—654 |
| 1074—1082 | Story of Simon of Valois, he refuses William's daughter and helps to reconcile Robert | 652—654 |
| | Betrothal of a daughter of William to Alfonso | 654—655 |
| November 3, 1083 | Death of Queen Matilda, her tomb and epitaph | 655—656 |

## CONTENTS

| A.D | | PAGE |
|---|---|---|
| 1083 | Revolt of Hubert of Beaumont, he defends Sainte-Susanne . . . | 656 |
| 1083—1086 | War of Sainte-Susanne, ill success of William; death of Richer of L'Aigle . . | 657—659 |
| 1086 | Hubert reconciled to William . . | 659 |
| July 17— August 4, 1077 | Death of Bishop Hugh of Lisieux, dispute as to his burial . . . | 659—660 |
| 1077—1100 | Gilbert Maminot, Bishop of Lisieux; his character . | 660—661 |
| 1079—1100 | Death of Archbishop John, the see of Rouen refused by Wimund, Primacy of William "Bona Anima" . . . . | 661 |
| 1086 | Council of Lillebonne; re-enactment of the Truce of God . . . . | 661—662 |

### § 3. *The Affairs of the Scottish and Welsh Marches.* 1078—1081

| | | |
|---|---|---|
| 1078 | Malcolm defeats Mælslæhta . | 663 |
| August, 1079 | Malcolm invades Northumberland . | 663 |
| 1071—1080 | Episcopate and Earldom of Walcher of Durham, his character . . . . | 663—664 |
| 1074 | Revival of monasticism in the North, Ealdwine and his companions come from Winchcombe, they repair Jarrow . . . | 665—666 |
| | Restoration of Whitby | 666 |
| 1078 ? | Foundation of Saint Mary's at York . | 666 |
| 1068 ? | History of Turgot, his escape from Lincoln, his favour with Olaf of Norway . | 667 |
| | He joins Ealdwine at Melrose and Wearmouth | 667—668 |
| | Monastic tendencies of Walcher, his dealings with Waltham . . . | 668—669 |
| | His favourites, Ligulf murdered by Gilbert and Leobwine, Walcher shelters the murderers | 669—671 |
| May 14, 1080 | Gemót at Gateshead, Walcher and his friends killed | 671—673 |
| | Fate of the murderers | 674 |
| | Odo sent to Northumberland, his cruelties and spoliations . . | 674—675 |
| Autumn, 1080 | Robert's expedition to Scotland, foundation of Newcastle-upon-Tyne . . | 675—676 |
| | Succession of the Earls of Northumberland, Alberic, Geoffrey, Robert of Mowbray . | 676—677 |
| 1080—1096 | William of Saint Carilef Bishop of Durham . | 677 |
| 1093 | Beginning of the present church . . | 677 |
| 1081—1085 | He substitutes monks for canons at Durham, Ealdwine and Turgot Priors . . | 677—678 |
| | Affairs of Wales, lands held by Meredydd and his son Gruffydd . . | 678—679 |

|  |  | PAGE |
|---|---|---|
| A D |  |  |
| 1079 | Victories and death of Trahaern | 679 |
| 1081 | William in Wales, his conquests and pilgrimage to Saint David's, history of Saint David's | 679—681 |
| 1080? | Foundation of Cardiff Castle | 680 |

### § 4 *The Later Legislation of William.* 1082—1086

|  |  |  |
|---|---|---|
|  | Character of the years 1082-1086 | 681 |
|  | Pride and oppression of Odo, he aspires to the Papacy | 681—682 |
| 1082 | William accuses and arrests him; his imprisonment at Rouen | 682—685 |
| 1082 | Famine in England | 685 |
| Christmas, 1083—1084 | Tax laid on the land | 685—686 |
| 1076 | State of Denmark, death of Swend Estrithson | 686 |
| 1076—1080 | Reign of Harold Hein | 686 |
| 1080—1086 | Reign of Saint Cnut, he prepares to invade England, contingent of Olaf Kyrre | 686—687 |
| 1085 | William returns to England, his mercenaries, he lays waste the coast | 688—689 |
| July 10, 1086 | Discontent of the Danish fleet, martyrdom of Cnut | 689 |
| Christmas, 1085—1086 | Gemót at Gloucester; the Great Survey ordered | 690—691 |
| January— July, 1086 | The Commission for the Survey, popular discontent and disturbances | 691—694 |
| May 24 | Whitsun Gemót at Westminster, Henry dubbed knight | 694 |
| August 1 | Gemot at Salisbury, all landowners become the men of the King; effect on later English history | 694—696 |
|  | Another tax laid on; William goes to Normandy | 696—697 |
|  | Eadgar goes to Apulia, Christina takes the veil | 697 |

### § 5 *The Last Days of William*
### *August—September,* 1087

|  |  |  |
|---|---|---|
|  | Physical phænomena of the years 1086—1087, miscellaneous events and deaths | 697—699 |
| 1087 | Dispute about the French Vexin, incursions of the French commanders at Mantes | 699—700 |
|  | William's sickness at Rouen, Philip's jest | 700—701 |
| August, 1087 | William invades the Vexin | 701 |
| August 15 | William burns Mantes, and receives his death-wound | 701—703 |
|  | He is carried to Saint Gervais, his sickness | 704 |
| August 14 | Death of Gulbert of Hugleville | 705 |
| August 24 | Death of Gunhild at Bruges | 705 |

# CONTENTS.

| A. D. | | PAGE |
|---|---|---|
| | Details of William's sickness, his repentance and disposal of his dominions | 706—709 |
| | His bequest to Henry | 709 |
| | He releases his prisoners | 710—711 |
| September 9 | Death of William | 711—712 |
| | General confusion at his death, neglect of his body, he is taken to Caen by Herlwin | 712—715 |
| | Reception of the body at Caen; fire in the town | 715—716 |
| | The burial of William, the ground claimed by Ascelin | 716—721 |
| | William's monument and epitaph | 721—722 |
| 1562—1642 | The tomb destroyed by the Huguenots and restored | 722—723 |
| 1742—1793 | The third tomb | 723 |
| 1802 | Present stone and inscription | 723 |
| | Summary | 723—724 |

# APPENDIX

| NOTE A | The Legal Fictions of William's Reign | 725 |
|---|---|---|
| B | The Confiscations of William's Reign | 725 |
| C | The Three Commissioners for Redemption of Lands | 725 |
| D | The King's Thegns | 727 |
| E | The Condition of Kent, Surrey, and Sussex | 727 |
| F | The Lands and Family of Godric | 728 |
| G | Wigod of Wallingford and Robert of Oily | 731 |
| H | Robert and Swegen of Essex | 736 |
| I. | Eadric the Wild | 738 |
| K | Castles and Destruction in Towns | 741 |
| L | The Earldom and Death of Copsige | 741 |
| M. | The Possessions of the Ætheling Eadgar | 744 |
| N | The Possessions of Count Eustace | 745 |
| O | The Earldom of Gospatric | 748 |
| P. | Æthelsige Abbot of Ramsey | 749 |
| Q | The Lands of Gytha and her Family in the West | 752 |
| R | The Children of Harold | 754 |
| S. | Eadnoth the Staller | 757 |
| T | Brihtric and Matilda | 761 |
| U. | The Possessions of Robert of Mortain in the West | 764 |
| W | The Condition of Worcestershire under William | 767 |
| X | The Titles of Queen and Lady | 768 |
| Y. | The Northern Campaigns of William | 768 |
| Z | The Submission of Oxford | 778 |
| AA | Thurkill of Warwick | 780 |

## CONTENTS.

|  |  | PAGE |
|---|---|---|
| BB | The Date of the Marriage of Malcolm and Margaret | 782 |
| CC. | The First Submission of Malcolm | 786 |
| DD. | The Expeditions of Harold's sons | 788 |
| EE | The Birth and Education of Henry the First | 790 |
| FF. | The Foundation Legend of Selby Abbey | 794 |
| GG. | William's Grants of Holderness | 798 |
| HH. | The Churches of Jarrow and Monkwearmouth | 800 |
| II. | Retention of English Names in Durham | 800 |
| KK. | The Laws of Eadward and William | 800 |
| LL | The Relations of the Provinces of Canterbury and York | 800 |
| MM | The Alleged Penance of William's soldiers | 801 |
| NN | Frithric Abbot of Saint Alban's | 802 |
| OO | The Legend of Hereward | 804 |
| PP. | Bishops Æthelric and Æthelwine | 812 |
| QQ. | The Connexion of Waltheof with the Conspiracy of Ralph | 813 |
| RR | The Siege of Dol and the Marriage of Constance | 816 |
| SS | The Battle of Gerberoi | 818 |
| TT | The Betrothal of William's Daughter to Alfonso | 820 |
| UU. | The Claim of Ascelin | 821 |

# ADDITIONS AND CORRECTIONS.

p. 19, note, for "William of Poitiers who," read "William of Poitiers, who "

p 24, l 20   The words about Ralph of Norfolk should be left out   See p. 727.

p 41, l 2, for "Regennbald" read "Regenbald" or "Reinbald "

p 64, l 10   For Eadric's title of "Child" see p 111.

p. 70, l 2 from bottom   Norfolk and Suffolk seem to have both been under the government of Ralph of Wader, but the two divisions of East-Anglia were only just beginning to be looked on as distinct shires

p. 94, l 17, for "schmatically" read "schismatically "

p. 118, note 3, for "quietum" read "quietem "

p. 124, note 1   In connexion with this should be taken William of Malmesbury's account (v 407), in which Roger appears as almost equalling Gulbert of Hugleville in his own person, though not as carrying his scruples so far as to forbid the enrichment of his sons, "Homo antiquæ simplicitatis et fidei, qui, crebro a Willelmo primo invitatus ut Angliam veniret, largis ad voluntatem possessionibus munerandus, supersedit, pronuncians, patrum suorum hæreditatem se velle fovere, non transmarinas et indebitas possessiones vel appetere vel invadere."

p. 130, l. 5, for "other shires in those western lands" read "other shires and in those western lands "

p. 143, l. 1   On the probability that Wulf had a twin brother, bearing the name of his father, see p. 756

p. 164, l. 4 from bottom   No part of Eadnoth's lands seems to have passed to his son   See p 759

p 170, note 2, for "tene" read "tenet "

p 178, l. 11.   That Bristol Castle was built during William's reign, possibly at the very end of it, appears from its appearing in 1088 as one of the great centres of revolt   See the Chronicle and Florence under that year, where the two Mowbrays "ferdon to Bricgstowe and hergodon and brohton to þam castele þa hergunge, and syððon foron út of þam castele and hergodon Baðon and eall þæt land þær abutan and eall Beorclea hyrnesse hi awæston "

p 192, note 1, for "NN " read "OO "

p. 214, note 6.   The "Turoldus" here spoken of is doubtless the Sheriff Thorold.   See p 472, note 3

p 257, note 2.   Compare the business spoken of in p. 21, note 5

xxxii ADDITIONS AND CORRECTIONS.

pp. 267-268, note 2. For "mala cepit, Eboracum" read "mala, cepit Eboracum."

p. 279, note 2. For "Comites, duos Guillelmum" read "Comites duos, Guillelmum."

p. 308, l. 4 from bottom, for "retain" read "retains."

p. 316, note 1, for "maximus" read "maximis."

p. 329, l. 10. So Ralph of Diss (X Scriptt. 531, cf. R. Wendover, ii. 287) says of Henry the Second in 1158, "Henricus Rex Anglorum, coronatus apud Wigorniam, post celebrationem divinorum coronam super altare posuit, nec ulterius coronatus est." Compare the story of Cnut in vol. 1 p. 483, and of Eadgar in Appendix BB of the second edition.

p. 331, note 2. I should have excepted one or two other Bishops, like Leofric of Exeter and Siward of Rochester, who were not deprived, but who died while the process of change was going on. But Wulfstan stands out conspicuously as the one Bishop—there were several Abbots—who survived all changes, and died in possession of his see long after.

For "appointments" read "the appointments."

p. 347, note 2, for "elegentibus" read "eligentibus."

p. 354, note 1, for "deberi" read "debere."

p. 357, l. 12. That is, Thomas claimed for the see of York the Primacy over Mercia as well as over Northumberland. Hereford alone, a diocese still partly Welsh, would have been left to Canterbury.

p. 367, note 2. Put a comma after "palum fixerit."

p. 371, side-note, for "Cambridge" read "Cambridgeshire."

p. 373, l. 3. The question was also raised by Thomas at the intended dedication of Remigius' church at Lincoln in 1092, when Thomas "illi contradicendo resistebat, affirmans eam in suâ parochiâ esse constructam." So says Florence, who goes on with a story which revives the old charge of simony against Remigius. William Rufus "pro pecuniâ quam ei Remigius dederat" bids the Bishops to dedicate the church, and Remigius dies before the appointed day "occulto Dei judicio."

p. 374, note 1. Put a semicolon after "repperit."

p. 382, note 3. Put a semicolon after "retrado."

p. 391, heading, for "Churches" read "Churchmen."

p. 402, note 3, for "in-finibus" read "in finibus."

p. 420, l. 4 from bottom. The words of William of Malmesbury (Gest. Pont. 310, Gest. Reg. iv. 341) are remarkable. In the Gesta Regum he clearly wishes to imply that there was no lawful removal of the see to Coventry, "Quinetiam moriturus, *parvi faciens scita canonum quibus edicitur pontifices in suis sedibus sepeliri debere,* non apud Cestram, sed apud Coventream se tumulatum in præcepit, suâ opinione relinquens successuris non indebitum calumniandi, sed quasi jus legitimum vindicandi." The words in Italics are left out in the Gesta Pontificum.

p. 422, note 1. William of Malmesbury seems here to be copying Florence, 1094, "Hereberhtus, qui cognominabatur Losinga, quod ei ars adulationis nuper egerat." The name without the explanation appears in the Chronicle of the same year, under the form of "Herbearde Losange." See his life and

## ADDITIONS AND CORRECTIONS

writings discussed in the preface to his letters in the series called Annales Monastici in the same volume with the letters of Osbert of Clare

p. 423, note 2, *dele* comma after "adds"

p. 444, side-note, for "change" read "changes"

p. 445, note 2. We have another witness to the same effect in the contrast drawn by William of Malmesbury between the ecclesiastical rule of the Conqueror and that of his successor (iv 314), "Tempore patris, post decessum episcopi vel abbatis omnes reditus integre custodiebantur, substituendo pastori resignandi, eligebanturque personæ religionis merito laudabiles; at vero, pauculis annis intercedentibus, omnia immutata."

p. 448, side-note, for "wealth of the country" read "wrath of the courtiers"

p. 449, l. 11. Yet the question might have been raised whether the acceptance of the see of Aversa did not imply complicity in the Norman Conquest of Apulia, and whether the Norman Conquest of Apulia was not as blameworthy as that of England. Perhaps longer possession and the specially Norman character of Aversa might be held to make a difference

p. 458, note 2, for "qui inter paludes" read "quia inter paludes"

p. 470, side-note, for "settlement" read "settlements."

p. 477, line 6, *dele* "with."

p. 478, note 5, for "Ib" read "Hist. Ab u. s"

pp. 482, 483, side notes, for "1076" read "1073," for "1079" read "1075;" for "1086" read "1082," for "1089" read "1082." See below, p. 824

p. 490, l. 10. Yet Roger of Poitou appears in the Chronicle (1093) under the form of "Rogger Peiteuin," and again in William of Malmesbury (v 396) with the reason for his surname—"quod ex eâ regione uxorem acceperat sic dictus"

p. 502, l. 9 from bottom. The castle of "Muntgumri" appears in the Chronicle, 1095, as taken by the Welsh

p. 502, l. 2 from bottom. On the date of William Fitz-Osbern's appointment as Earl, see above, p. 72. But I ought to have mentioned the grant of the Isle of Wight to him, at one date or the other. Orderic (521 D) couples it with the grant of the Earldom, "Rex Guillelmus . . . Willelmo dapifero Normanniæ, Osberni filio, insulam Vectam et comitatum Herfordensem dedit." The large Crown lands in Wight which appear in Domesday had doubtless been his. The union of Wight and Hereford under William Fitz Osbern is like the union of Arundel and Shrewsbury under Roger of Montgomery. It is quite in character with William's policy

p. 517, l. 5 from bottom. This is the "Dunechaldus, Regis Scottorum Malcolmi filius," whom we read of as being released—"a custodia laxatum"—on the death of William (see Florence, 1087, and below, p. 711) He is also the "Dunecan Melcomes cynges sunu" of the Chronicle under 1092, who appears with the same description in Florence, with the addition that "Regi Willelmo [Rufo] tunc militavit" Donald is Dufenal or Dufenaldus the brother of Malcolm. William of Malmesbury (v. 399) calls Duncan "filium Malcolmi nothum," which is hard on Ingebiorg

## ADDITIONS AND CORRECTIONS.

p. 520, l. 10. We find doubts as to the body of Saint Cuthberht raised again in 1104 by "quorumdam incredulitas abbatum." Florence in anno

p. 521, note 2. He appears in the Chronicle (1128) and in Florence (1094) as "Passeflambard."

p. 524, l. 5. I suppose that this Dolfin is the same who appears in the Chronicle under 1092 as holding Carlisle or its site, no doubt by the grant of Malcolm. He is driven thence by William Rufus.

p. 528, note 2. See above, p. 441.

p. 532, l. 1. It is hard to believe the statement of William of Malmesbury (v. 403) that William paid a yearly pension of three hundred marks to his father-in-law and his successor, "His ille illustres crebro retributiones refuderat, omnibus, ut ferunt, annis trecentas argenti marcas pro fide et affinitate socero annumerans. Ea munificentia, in filio Baldewino non imminuta, hæsit in Roberti Frisonis malitia."

p. 532, note 4, for "Galicia" read "Gallicia."

p. 537, l. 5. I need hardly except the small and doubtful case of the Priory of Carisbrooke in the Isle of Wight. Carisbrooke is not mentioned by that name in Domesday, but William Fitz-Osbern gave several churches in the island, and among them Bowcomb, by which is probably meant Carisbrooke (Domesday, 52, 52 b), to his foundation at Lyra. Carisbrooke before long (see Monasticon, vii. 1090-1091) became a cell to Lyra, but it is not clear that it was strictly speaking a foundation of William Fitz-Osbern.

p. 573, l. 1, dele "the" before "successor."

p. 575, note 2, for "vestram" read "vestrum."

p. 592, l. 7 from bottom. I do not feel quite satisfied about this life-long imprisonment of Roger. See p. 711.

p. 600, last line, for "in" read "among."

p. 604, note 4, for "Wadevi" read "Waldevi."

p. 620, l. 13, for "more pounds" read "more hundred pounds."

p. 629, note 1. I ought to have remarked that Alberic got his pun from William of Malmesbury, iv. 387, "Quum oppidani fiduciâ moenium jactitarent ideo urbem Durachium nominatum, quod contra omnes obsidiones imperterrita duraret, 'Et ego' (inquit) 'vocor Durandus, et eo usque in obsidione durabo quo civitati nomen auferam, ut non Durachium sed Mollicium amodo dicatur.'"

p. 638, note 3. William of Malmesbury (iv. 389) also puts the nickname into William's mouth, "Per resurrectionem Dei, probus erit Robelinus Curta Ocrea." His character of Robert is one degree better than that given by Orderic. After mentioning the nickname, he adds, "Hoc enim erat ejus cognomen, quod esset exiguus, cæterum nihil habens quod succenseres, quia nec illepidæ formæ, nec infaceti eloquii, nec virtutis imbecillæ, nec enervis erat consilii." He had just before said, "Natus in Normanniâ, spectatæ jam virtutis habebatur adolescens quando pater Angliam venit, fortitudinis probatæ, quamquam exilis corporis et pinguis aqualiculi."

p. 644, l. 5. We find a man of the same name and office—very likely a son—in the Chronicle, 1124, "þes kinges stiward of France Amalri."

p. 651, note 3, for "zeal of" read "zeal for."

p. 660, note 2, for "voluntate" read "voluntati."

## ADDITIONS AND CORRECTIONS.   xxxv

p 662, note 1. Fifteen years later, 1095, the Truce of God was confirmed by the higher authority of the Council of Clermont  Will Malm iv. 345; "Quod ab Adventu Domini usque ad octavas Epiphaniæ, et a Septuagesimâ usque ad octavas Paschæ, et a primâ die Rogationum usque ad octavas Pentecostes, et a quartâ feriâ occidente sole omni tempore usque ad secundam feriam oriente sole trevia Dei custodiatur "

p 670, l 1. This Ealdgyth would be a niece of Ealdgyth the daughter of Uhtred and mother of Gospatric  See p 134. I trust to go more fully into these pedigrees in my fifth volume

p. 676, l 2. The New Castle and the castle at Tynemouth ("se castel æt Tinemuðan") appear in the Chronicle, 1095, "Feorde se eorl [Robert of Mowbray] anre nihte ut of Bebbaburh towardes Tinemuðan ac þa þe innan þam *niwan castele* wæron his gewær wurdon "

p 677, note 3. On the character of this Bishop see the remarkable entry in the Chronicle (1088) recording his revolt against William Rufus, " Swa wæll dyde se cyng be þam biscope þæt eall Englaland færde æfter his ræde and swa swa he wolde, and he þohte to donne be him eall swa Judas Scarioð dide be ure Drihtene "  This is somewhat softened by Florence; " Eâ quoque tempestate Rex prædictus illius, ut veri consiliarii, fruebatur prudentiâ, bene enim sapiebat, ejusque consiliis totius Angliæ tractabatur respublica "

p 683, note 1  If by these words we are to understand an "aula regia" in Wight itself, we can hardly place it anywhere but at Carisbrooke  There must have been some royal dwelling-place in Wight, as William stayed there some time in 1086 (see p. 697), and Carisbrooke is most likely intended by the entry in Domesday (52 *b*) about a castle at Alwinestone  See Ellis, i 213

p. 710, last line, for " and Ælfgar " read " the son of Ælfgar "

p 711, note 1, for " Donald " read " Duncan."

p. 731, Note G. A better spelling of this name, according to its evident origin, would be *Wiggod*, and it is so spelled in the Worcester Chronicle, 1079  See p 818.

p 735, l. 3. On the works of Robert of Oily see Mr James Parker's just published History of Oxford, pp. 38 et seqq

p 735, l 10 from bottom, for " Hugh Grantmesnil " read " Hugh of Grantmesnil "

p 745, Note N. In the Chronicle for 1088 we read of " Eustatius se iunga " as engaged in the revolt against William Rufus.  For this Florence has " Eustatius junior, *Comes Bononiæ*," which sounds as if he looked on the elder Eustace as having died before 1088.

p 768, l. 15, after " Norman writers " add " and Englishmen writing in Latin "

p 773, l 13 from bottom, for " would probably " read " probably would "

p. 778, Note Z  For a full discussion of the reading and authority of the manuscripts see Mr. James Parker's History of Oxford, p. 36

p 791, l 8 from bottom  I should have mentioned that it is here that William of Malmesbury (v. 390) quotes the proverb which elsewhere (see vol ii p 274) has been put into the mouth of Fulk the Good of Anjou  Henry

xxxvi ADDITIONS AND CORRECTIONS.

"pueritiam ad spem regni literis muniebat, subinde, patre quoque audiente, jactitare proverbium solitus, 'Rex illiteratus, asinus coronatus'"

p 793, l. 4 On considering this matter again, I think it is an open question whether Mary meant that the English King, whether Ælfred or Henry the First, translated the Greek fables into Latin and then into English, or whether she simply meant that he translated them from Latin into English In the former explanation I followed Sir Francis Palgrave, but a good deal depends on the punctuation, which he and M de Roquefort give differently, and which is of course arbitrary But in either case, if we accept the reading *Henris*, the English education of Henry the First is equally asserted On the other hand, if all that is meant is a translation from Latin into English, one objection to Ælfred being the King intended is taken away But the knowledge of Greek is about an equal difficulty in either case.

p 797, l. 2, for "salutens" read "salutem"

p 800, l 1. For "plays" read "play." Florence also in the passage referred to speaks of Stephen as "filius amitæ filius" [Willelmi Rufi, sc ], which would make him the son of a sister of William His father appears in the Chronicle (1096) as "Eoda eorl of Campaine þæs cynges aðum," a word which leaves the question open

p. 810, l 12 from bottom, for "remarking" read "finding out."

# THE HISTORY

OF THE

NORMAN CONQUEST OF ENGLAND.

# CHAPTER XVII

THE FIRST DAYS OF WILLIAM'S REIGN.[1]

December 1066—December 1067

## § 1. *Character of the Reign of William.*

THE coronation rite was over, and the formal reign of William over England was to begin. As far as outward forms were concerned, he might be looked on as King over the whole land. He had indeed direct military pos-

*Position of William at the time of his Coronation*

---

[1] The chief thing to be noticed with regard to the authorities for these years is the loss of some of the most important. The Biographer of Eadward failed us at the death of his own hero or, at the outside, at the Battle of Stamfordbridge. With the Battle of Stamfordbridge also the Abingdon Chronicle comes suddenly to an end. The Tapestry takes us only to the flight of the light-armed at Senlac, and the poem of Guy of Amiens takes us only to the coronation of William. Wace again ceases to be of any value just at present, as he cuts the history of William very short between his coronation and his burial. We miss also Mr Kemble's great collection of Charters, which contains only a few documents later than the accession of William. The documents of William's reign are numerous and important, but we have to seek them where we can find them, in the Fœdera, in the Monasticon, in Hickes' Thesaurus, in the various local histories, anywhere in short where they may happen to be preserved. (A continuation, as well as a new recension, of the Codex Diplomaticus would be an unspeakable gain to historical scholarship.) And, while we lose so many of our old authorities, we are not reinforced by new ones of any importance. But several of our remaining authorities increase in value. Florence now definitely becomes an independent and, as we go on, a contemporary writer of the first rank. Orderic, born in 1075, does not reach that rank during our present period; still he had good means of information, and his value gradually increases. So does that of William of Malmesbury as he gets nearer to his own time. The value of Henry of Huntingdon on the other hand lessens. His main value has always consisted in the early traditions and fragments of early songs which he preserves, and his stock of

session only of certain of the southern and eastern shires. But it does not appear that any part of the land was at this moment actually in arms against him. Rival King there was none. The rival who had appeared against him for a moment had submitted to him and had been received to his favour. The chief men of a large part of England had submitted with him. Eadwine and Morkere indeed still held out,[1] but they seem to have been simply, after their manner, waiting to see what course events would take. At all events they did not venture on any armed opposition. And the consecration of William by the Northumbrian Primate might be looked on as some sort of guaranty, however weak, for the obedience of his province. The two chiefs of the national Church, the representative of the national kingship, the holiest Prelate in England, the chosen friend of the slain Harold, had all bowed to William and had become his men.[2] He had possession of the mightiest and of the most venerable of English cities. The metropolis of Æthelberht, the royal city of Ælfred, were alike his. He had been crowned in Eadward's church; he dwelt in Eadward's palace; and if London had been slow to submit, a fortress was now rising which would for ever fetter the hands of William's unwilling subjects. It might well seem that England was already William's in fact as well as in name. York, Gloucester, Exeter, had as yet not seen his face. But it might seem that all that was needed for their full possession was for the King to show himself before their gates in the friendly state of a peaceful progress. William, King

them now grows much smaller. The subsidiary sources, the local writers and the incidental notices in foreign authors, have to be attended to much as before. And the paramount importance of Domesday grows, I need hardly say, at every step as we draw near to the date of the Survey itself. The mass of personal and local detail which may be recovered from its incidental entries is utterly amazing.

[1] See vol. iii. pp. 547, 767.     [2] See vol. iii. pp. 529, 547.

of the English, King chosen, crowned, and anointed, might well give himself out as already master of the whole realm.

And yet we may be sure that there was none who knew better than the Conqueror himself how far the land still was from being conquered. William was King; but he knew well that in the greater part of his Kingdom his kingship as yet hardly existed in name. But he knew also how much he had gained by becoming a King. William knew, as well as Henry the Eighth himself, the inestimable advantage of having the letter of the law on his side. Since the homage at Berkhampstead, since the election and coronation at Westminster, William was no longer a mere foreign invader, a mere candidate or pretender to the Crown. He was, as far as outward ceremonies could make him, the King, the choice of the English people, the consecrated of the English Church. The greater part of his realm had still to be conquered; but he could go forth to its conquest in quite another character from that in which he had landed at Pevensey. Resistance to his authority would no longer be the defence of the country against an invader from beyond sea. It would be rebellion against a lawful King and an established government. In William's theory indeed, all resistance to his power, all refusal to acknowledge his rights, had been guilty rebellion ever since the death of Eadward.[1] But he could now put forth his pretensions with tenfold force. Those pretensions had now been acknowledged in the most solemn way. William was King; those who submitted to him were loyal subjects; those who might still withstand him were traitorous rebels. The King had still to win his Kingdom, but the King could win it far more readily than the mere Duke could have done. The might of the royal arm was to be tried only where the magic of the royal favour might fail to

[1] See vol iii p. 411

CHAP XVII. win. It could hardly fail but that many, whether individuals or whole districts, would be ready to submit to a King who claimed only the allegiance formally due to his Crown, while they would have fought to the death against one who came before them simply as a foreign invader or an unacknowledged pretender

*Character of the resistance to William after his Coronation*

The true way of looking at those important stages of the Conquest which followed William's coronation seems to be this. The opposition which William met with was in truth the stubborn resistance of a land striving to guard the last fragments of its freedom against the assaults of a foreign invader who was winning the land bit by bit. But in form it was resistance or rebellion against the lawful King and the established government of the land. This twofold aspect of the struggle greatly affected its character. The fall of Harold and his brothers, the lack of any one else able or worthy to stand forth at the head of the nation, had left the English people without a leader. The coronation of William cut them off from all hope of finding a leader. It cut them off from all hope of united national action. The coronation took place, as I have said, during a moment of apparent universal submission; if all England had not acknowledged William, no part of England acknowledged any one else. The struggle which followed was a reaction after a panic; it was the revolt of a people goaded to revolt by the oppression far less of William himself than of William's unworthy lieutenants. In all those parts of the country which had already submitted to the new King, it was strictly rebellion, however justifiable rebellion, against an established government. And even in those parts to which William's power had not yet reached, in those parts which he had to subdue by force after his coronation, the struggle bore a somewhat different character from that of simple national resistance to foreign invasion. When the men of Exeter or Chester bade defiance to

*A real national resistance plausibly represented as rebellion.*

*Distinction consequent on this character*

William, they were bidding defiance to the only *de facto* King and government in England. Their resistance was therefore local rather than national; each city and district fought for its own hand, not for the common freedom of the whole realm. A land therefore which resisted bit by bit was, in the nature of things, conquered bit by bit. The only way to make the least show of resistance to William on equal terms was again to proclaim the kingship of the puppet Eadgar, or to call on Swend of Denmark to come and claim the Crown of his uncle and his cousin. But neither Eadgar nor Swend ever obtained any general acknowledgement. The warfare waged in their names was only local warfare. William was the King; Eadgar and Swend were only pretenders—in the Latin phrase of the time, Tyrants.[1] In all this it is easy to see the immeasureable advantage which William gained from being the King in possession, however imperfect that possession was in many parts of the Kingdom. And it is quite possible that the fact that many of those who fought against William were really technically traitors, that they were breaking their plighted allegiance, that they were fighting against a King to whom they had sworn oaths and become his men, may have done not a little to unnerve the hearts and to weaken the arms of the later defenders of England.

Certain it is that, at the actual moment of William's coronation, there was no armed opposition to his authority in any part of England. In the districts which he had already subdued men had made up their minds to submit to what they could not help, and to make the best of a bad bargain. In the districts to which his arms had not reached men had, to say the least, not made up their minds

---

[1] William of Malmesbury (iu 248) says of York, " Ibi Rex Scotorum Malcolmus cum suis, ibi Edgarus et Marcherius et Weldeofus cum Anglis et Danis, *nidum tyrannidis* sæpe fovebant " On this use of the word, see vol 1. pp. 152, 396.

CHAP XVII

*Legal fictions of William's reign William held to be the successor of Eadward, and the reign of Harold ignored*

on any plan of resistance, nor had they chosen any chief in whose name they should resist. William's election and coronation were therefore, not only formally regular, but actually undisputed. In William's reading of the Law, the reign of Harold was an usurpation, and the new King was the lawful successor of his cousin King Eadward. He was the hereditary King, a form of words which however must not be pressed to the full extent of its modern meaning.[1] To put the rights of conquest offensively forward, to deal with his new subjects as with a conquered people, in no way fell in with his policy. The orthodox way of speaking under William, at least in his milder moments, was to look on the fight of Senlac as a sort of unhappy accident. The King had come to claim his Crown, and he was so unlucky as to be forced to overcome certain rebels and traitors before he could take possession of it.[2] In the official language of William's reign, his entry is always spoken of as if it had been an entry as peaceful as that of Charles the Second or George the First. Indeed the way in which the reign of Harold is ignored in the legal language of William's reign is an exact parallel to the way in which the Commonwealth and the rule of Cromwell are ignored in the legal language of the reign of Charles the Second.[3] The delicate euphemism, so common in Domesday, "When King William came into England," is exactly of a piece with the legal fiction by which the year sixteen hundred and sixty is

*Fictions of the same kind in later history.*

---

[1] See vol. iii. p. 682.

[2] In the somewhat suspicious (see Chapter xix.) foundation charter of Battle Abbey (Rymer, i. 4, Mon. Ang. iii. 244) William says, "Quum in Angliam venissem et in finibus Hasting' cum exercitu applicuissem contra hostes meos qui mihi regnum Angliæ injuste conabantur auferre." So in the Westminster charter quoted in Ellis, i. 312, and in the notes to Benoit, iii. 164 (see vol. iii. p. 684), "Angliam veniens, in ore gladii regnum adeptus sum Anglorum, devicto Haroldo Rege cum suis complicibus, qui mihi regnum, providentiâ Dei destinatum, et beneficio concessionis domini et cognati mei gloriosi Regis Edwardi concessum, conati sunt auferre." The odd thing is that the title of King is here given to Harold.

[3] On these legal fictions see Appendix A.

spoken of in Acts of Parliament as the twelfth year of King Charles. It is exactly of a piece with those strange pieces of regnal arithmetic which have given the world a Lewis the Eighteenth and a Napoleon the Third. In all these cases it was convenient to put the plainest facts of history out of sight. But there was probably no case in which the legal fiction told with more effect than it did in the case of William. No man seriously believed that Charles the Second became, in any practical sense, King of England from the moment when the axe fell on the neck of Charles the First. No man seriously believed that a Lewis the Seventeenth or a Napoleon the Second had ever really reigned over France. And in these latter cases all that was meant was to represent the incoming ruler as the heir of a remote predecessor; it was not meant to brand all the acts of all the intervening governments as null and void. But the legal fiction of the reign of William, like the legal fiction of the reign of Charles the Second, was intended to brand the acts of the alleged usurpation as null and void. And this system, fully and consistently carried out, had its effect. The legal fraud came admirably to the help of the religious fraud. While the Church systematically branded Harold as a perjurer, the Law systematically branded him as an usurper. The new King, ostentatiously, perhaps sincerely, gave himself out as no enemy, no conqueror, towards the English nation, but simply as the chastiser of the late usurper and his partizans. Such teaching, both legal and religious, did its work on men's minds at the time, as it has done its work on the pages of history ever since. When the event had bowed down men's minds to submission, they might even seek shelter in either the religious or the legal subtlety, as a kind of relief, as a sort of salve to their consciences in accepting the rule of the invader.

And of one thing we may be perfectly certain, that

*Practical effect of legal fictions*

CHAP. XVII
William not purposely an oppressor

His attempts to conciliate the English

Ill feeling arising from the disturbance at the Coronation

William did not come into England with any fixed purpose to play the tyrant in England. When he swore his coronation oath, he doubtless meant to keep it. William, as I have often said, though he stuck at no crime that would serve his purpose, was at no time one who rejoiced in crime for its own sake. His soul was far above the meanness of those petty tyrants who boast themselves that they can do mischief. Of wanton oppression for oppression's sake I do not believe that he was guilty at any time. And now, in the first moments of his reign, it was his policy as well as his disposition to make his government as acceptable as he could to his new subjects of every class. His interest forbade him, and his temper certainly did not urge him, to do them any kind of wrong or damage which he knew how to avoid. His difficulties lay wholly in his position. He had contrived to mount the English throne with every circumstance of formal legality. But he must have known that he had not mounted it with the real good will of the English people. He must have known that the sort of artificial eagerness with which his accession had been welcomed was almost sure to be followed by a reaction against him. And the untoward accident which had turned the day of his coronation into a day of havoc and sorrow had already done much to destroy his newly-won popularity.[1] The very first day of his reign had made Englishmen feel the insolence of his foreign followers. The very rite of his consecration had been disturbed by their irresistible passion for plunder and destruction. They had chosen that solemn moment to burn and harry, in sheer wantonness as it would seem, the houses and goods of Englishmen who were guilty of no crime against the new King, but who were at that very moment engaged in doing him the

---

[1] Ord. Vit. 503 D. "Angli factionem tam insperatæ rei dimetientes nimis irati sunt, et postea Normannos semper suspectos habuerunt, et infidos sibi dijudicantes ultionis tempus de eis optaverunt."

most loyal service. The deeds of wrong of that Midwinter Day were not forgotten. Men saw in them an omen of what the rule of the Norman would be. There can be no doubt that they did much to set the minds of Englishmen against the new King and his government.

And in truth the deeds of wrong of that day were in every way a presage of what the reign of William was to be. It had not been by William's order or by William's wish that any Englishman had suffered harm in his goods or in his person. But William had, of his own will, brought about a state of things in which it could not fail that Englishmen should suffer harm in their goods and in their persons. It was not at William's bidding that the Norman horsemen who guarded the approach to the West Minster had set fire to the houses of Englishmen. But it was wholly at William's bidding, and wholly through William's act, that Norman horsemen were ever called on to keep guard at the crowning of an English King. So it was throughout his reign William had no wish to oppress; but he had placed himself in a position in which oppression could not be avoided. He had no wish to make his reign a reign of terror; but the mere fact that he reigned at all left him no choice but either to cease from reigning or to make his reign a reign of terror. However he might disguise the fact by outward ceremonies and legal subtleties, he was in truth the Conqueror in every sense. He had won the land by force at the head of a foreign army, without the good will of a single English-born inhabitant of England. He had at once to reward the foreign army which in truth had made him King, and, if not to punish, at least to guard against the nation which had received him as King against its will. That army could not be rewarded except at the expense of the conquered nation. The nation could not be guarded against except by putting strangers in posts of dignity and authority. Here was the evil; the evil which

*CHAP XVII*

Oppression unavoidable in William's position

Difficulties arising from the presence of William's followers.

CHAP XVII drove William to become an oppressor against his will; but an evil which was wholly of his own creation. He had, of his own selfish ambition, attacked and subdued a people that had never wronged him. And that sin became its own appropriate punishment by driving him into sins of yet deeper dye

*Good beginnings of William, contrast with those of Cnut.*

And yet the beginnings of William were as good as the beginnings of a foreign conqueror could be. If we compare William with Cnut, the contrast between the first days of each is as favourable to William as the contrast between their last days is favourable to Cnut. The Danish conqueror began his reign with banishments and executions, some of which executions seem to have taken the form of simple murders.[1] But, after the submission of Berkhampstead, William does not seem to have shed a drop of English blood. Even before the submission, he does not seem to have been guilty of any slaughter except in what in his eyes would be held to be the lawful operations of war.[2] It is certain that the establishment of his power was not marked, like the establishment of the power of Cnut, either by assassinations or by judicial executions.[3] Some amount of banishment and confiscation does seem to have taken place, but, on the whole, William, at this stage of his reign, warred rather against the memory of the dead than against the lives or fortunes of the living. From the picture which

[1] See vol. 1. p. 456, and the whole account of the death of Eadric

[2] For the opposite evidence on this point, see vol III p. 554 But it is worth remarking that Florence, though he charges William with burnings and harryings after the submission at Berkhampstead, yet leaves out the words "homines interficere," which form part of his description of his earlier doings

[3] Nothing can be more exaggerated than the account quoted in vol. III p 640 from the Chronicle of Ekkehard, where we are told that William, immediately on his coronation, "mox omnes pene regni ejusdem præsules exsilio, nobiles vero morti destinavit" No Bishop or Abbot was banished before the flight of Æthelsige in 1070 (see Appendix P), and the death of Waltheof, nearly ten years after his coronation, is the only recorded political execution of William's reign.

his panegyrist gives us of his clemency and kindness to the vanquished[1] we must make the needful deductions. But it is plainly not without a certain groundwork of truth.

It is of the more paramount importance that the real position of William, and his real disposition at this time, should be thoroughly understood, because of the two extreme theories in opposite directions which have been maintained by the two most eloquent and popular writers on the subject. It is utterly unjust to look upon William as a mere successful adventurer, a mere chief of a hostile army encamped in a conquered country. It is utterly unjust to speak of his claim of legal right and his show of legal government as mere pretences to cover the violence of a successful brigand. On the other hand, we shall be tempted greatly to underrate the importance of the Conquest, greatly to mistake its true character, if we are led to look on it as little more than a change of dynasty. William was a foreign Conqueror, King in very truth only by the edge of the sword.[2] But the show of legal right by which he cloked his real position really did a great deal to change the character of that position. His position was different from the position of a King, even of foreign birth, who succeeds to a Crown by peaceful election or peaceful hereditary succession. But it was also different from the position of a mere invader, reigning by sheer military force. If we look at one picture, we may be led to think that the rights of Englishmen were as strictly regarded, that the laws of England were as strictly administered, during the reign of William as they

---

[1] See the whole passage in William of Poitiers (146), beginning "multa Lundoniæ, posteaquam coronatus est, prudenter juste clementerque disposuit." To some of the particular expressions I shall have to refer again; the general description makes William exhort his followers "nimium opprimi victos nequaquam oportere, victoribus professione Christiana pares, ne quos juste subegerint injuriis ad rebellandum cogerent."

[2] Cf. the words of the charter quoted in p. 8.

14                THE FIRST DAYS OF WILLIAM'S REIGN.

CHAP XVII. could have been during the reign of a native King. If we look at another picture, we may be led to think that all right and law were trampled under foot, and that the rule of William was a rule of simple brigandage. Neither of these pictures represents the real truth of the case. The laws of England were not formally or systematically abolished, the rights of Englishmen were not formally or systematically disregarded. What Englishmen suffered from was mainly that irregular, often undesigned, oppression which must take place when the laws of a conquered people are administered by their conquerors. Another point which has been the subject of much exaggeration is the transfer of lands and offices from Englishmen to Normans and other foreigners. This has sometimes been spoken of as if William had systematically divided the lands of England among his followers, as Guthrum and Hælfdene had divided the lands of East-Anglia and Northumberland.[1] Or rather it is spoken of as if the lands of England had been left open to a general scramble, in which every man in the invading army took whatever his right hand could seize upon.[2] It is perfectly true that, in the course of William's reign, all the greatest estates and all the highest offices in England were transferred from English to foreign owners. The transfer of land was certainly not so great as has often been fancied. The notion that every Englishman was turned out of hearth and home is a mere dream. The actual occupants of the soil remained very generally undisturbed. Still the transfer of land was very great, great enough to

*The old laws not abolished, but the spirit of their administration changed.*

*Real extent of the transfer of lands under William*

---

[1] See vol 1 p 50  The words in the Chronicles (876) are, "þy geare Halfdene Norðhanhymbra land gedælde þæt hie syþþan ergende and heora tilgende wæron," and in 880, "her for se here of Cyrenceastre on Eastengle, and gesæt þæt land, and hit gedælde"

[2] Take for instance the passage where Thierry (i. 269) begins to tell how "l'immense produit de cette spoliation universelle fut la solde des aventuriers de tous pays qui s'étaient enrôlés sous la bannière du duc de Normandie"

amount to the establishment in the land of a territorial aristocracy of foreign birth. And this transfer may undoubtedly be said to have been done systematically. But it was not done at a blow; it was done warily, gradually, and seemingly under the cover of legal form. There was no one moment of general confiscation or general plunder

In fact I have no doubt that William, at the time of his coronation, was thoroughly disposed to rule his new Kingdom as well as he had ruled his paternal Duchy. I have no doubt that he wished to do all that might be to identify himself and his dynasty with the land which he claimed to be his by lawful right. We shall find that, in order better to discharge the duties of an English King, he himself strove to learn the English language, and that his English-born son was brought up as an English Ætheling. But all these good intentions were thwarted by the inherent vice of his position. He could not maintain himself without the help of his Norman followers, and the presence of his Norman followers in England made it hopeless for him to try to reign in England as an English King. The example of Cnut, which so instinctively presents itself to our minds, could not fail to present itself to the mind of William himself.[1] No example could be more brilliant or more attractive. One foreign conqueror had already reigned in England as an English King, and had left behind him a name which lived in the memories of Englishmen side by side with the names of the noblest of their native princes. But the example was one that was altogether delusive. The position of William was wholly different from the position of Cnut. The difference was both personal and national. Cnut must have been really more at home in England than he was in Denmark. England was the prize of his first youthful warfare; the Crown of England was the first of the many

*CHAP XVII.*

Good disposition of William at the time of his Coronation

His intentions thwarted by his position

Misleading influence of the example of Cnut

Differences between the position of Cnut and that of William.

[1] See vol ii p 299, iii p 549.

16                    THE FIRST DAYS OF WILLIAM'S REIGN.

CHAP. XVII. crowns which were gathered on his brow,[1] and he was the son of a prince to whom Englishmen had given at least an outward and ceremonial homage as their King. At his age and under his circumstances, it was not hard for Cnut really to identify himself with his conquest, and to feel as an Englishman rather than as a Dane. But William entered England at a mature age, after a reign in his own land which had been but a few years shorter than his life, when his character and habits were already formed, and when, however much he may have wished, he could not identify himself with England as Cnut had done. But the national differences were still stronger. The Danes were the pupils and proselytes of the English. They were a kindred race, speaking a kindred tongue. They could claim no superiority over the English except the superiority of military success. And even in warfare the arms and tactics of the two nations were much the same. Whenever Danes and Englishmen had met in open battle, there had been no marked or lasting superiority on either side, and the final victory of Cnut had not been owing to any lack of prowess on the part of his enemy. In every other respect, the English, with their purer faith and higher civilization, stood ready to be the masters of those who had overcome them in mere warfare. With William's Normans the case was wholly different. To decide whether the Normans or the English of that age had made the more real advances in civilization would require that we should first define in what real civilization consists. A fair comparison of the two nations might perhaps lead us to say that each had points of real superiority over the other. But at all events there were the widest differences between them. Their language, their habits, their mode of warfare, their social and political feelings, were widely different. The native Normans, once the kinsmen of Danes

Different positions of the Danes and the Normans in England

[1] See vol. i. p. 404.

and Englishmen, had cast aside all outward signs of their kindred, and it must not be forgotten that a large part of William's followers were not native Normans, but adventurers gathered from every part of Gaul.[1] The success of William's invasion was a distinct triumph of one language, of one mode of warfare, of one social and political system, over another language, another mode of warfare, another social and political system. Under these circumstances it could not be that Normans and Englishmen should blend together under William as Danes and Englishmen had blended together under Cnut. Above all, it could not be that the Norman should, like the Dane, accept the conquered Englishman as his intellectual master. The result was that, while the rule of Cnut could daily become less Danish and more English, the rule of William was driven to become daily less English and more Norman. Cnut began with harshness, William began with clemency. But in the later days of Cnut, Danes had made way for Englishmen in all the great offices of the land, and Danes in their own land were beginning to complain of the promotions held by Englishmen in Denmark. By the end of William's reign, without any one act of general or violent expulsion, Normans had supplanted Englishmen in all the highest offices of Church and State. When William gathered his Witan to his great Gemót at Salisbury,[2] there was not a single English Earl, and only one English Bishop, to answer his summons.

In the end, I need not say, the conquerors and the conquered were blended together; and, when we look at the circumstances of the Conquest, we shall find that the wonder really is that they were blended together so soon as they were. But their perfect blending was not the work of a single life or of a single age. The process was doubtless hastened, silently and unwittingly, by that real kindred

*CHAP. XVII.*

*Cnut's rule became gradually milder, but William's gradually harsher*

*1086*

*Final blending of Normans and English its causes*

---

[1] Vol iii p 306      [2] Chron Petrib 1086

18    THE FIRST DAYS OF WILLIAM'S REIGN.

CHAP XVII
Effect of William's own policy.

between Norman and Englishman of which neither Norman nor Englishman dreamed at the time. But it was hastened also, and hastened perhaps in an equal degree, by the consummate policy of William himself. Whoever dwelt in the land, Englishmen, Normans, or any other, William was their master and moulded them to his will. A less discerning conqueror might have made simple havoc of all that he found established in the land which he conquered. A man of meaner mould might have indulged in mere paltry and wanton tyranny. But William neither changed one whit nor tyrannized one whit beyond what his position and his purposes demanded He knew how to use Normans against Englishmen, but he knew also how to use Englishmen against Normans, and he knew how to make the whole land his own and every man in it his subject.

The unity of the Kingdom finally established by William

His position as Conqueror, combined with that craft of the ruler in which none could rival him, enabled him to put the final seal to the work of Ecgberht, of Eadward, and of Æthelstan, to make England one united Kingdom, which, since his days, no man has ever dreamed of dividing.

§ 2. *William's first Days in England.*
*December* 1066—*March* 1067.

Effects of the tumult at the coronation

The violence of William's followers had changed the day of his coronation from a day of formal, and perhaps more than formal,[1] joy into a day of sorrow and wrath. The wrong done by the foreign soldiers who guarded the West Minster was not forgotten,[2] though there seems to have been no open outbreak at the time But it is a significant fact that, either at once upon his coronation or within a very short time after, William found it convenient to leave London—and we may suppose West-

---

[1] See vol III p 550        [2] See above, p 10

minster also—and to withdraw to Barking in Essex. This was a point from which he could easily appear in London at any moment, though he was removed for a while from the immediate neighbourhood of the city. And the reason is expressly given, that he waited till additional strength was given to the fortress which he had already begun to rear, the germs of the future Tower. That fortress was reared to guard against and to curb the high spirit—the historian adds, the fickleness—of the citizens of the proud and populous city.[1] The acclamations, not wholly insincere, which had greeted the first appearance of the Conqueror in his new character of an English King were already changed into murmurs of distrust. The English people—William doubtless already knew it—were only biding their time.

*William withdraws from London to Barking, while his fortress is building*

*Change of feeling among the English*

Still the formal investiture of William with the royal office was already beginning to do its work upon men's minds. Men who had waited to see what might be the course or the destiny of the mere invader, the mere

*Effects of the coronation.*

---

[1] The arrangement of William of Poitiers who, at this point is our chief authority, is always very confused. In this case he begins with the passage which I have already quoted (see above, p. 13), describing the King's conduct in London and his general designs and scheme of government, including much which could hardly have been done in a day. Presently we read (147), "Egressus e Londoniâ, dies aliquot in propinquo loco morabatur Bercingis," and the reason is added, "dum firmamenta quædam in urbe contra mobilitatem ingentis ac feri populi perficerentur. [On this beginning of Tower-building, see vol. iii p. 553.] Vidit enim in primis necessarium magnopere Lundonienses coerceri." With this as his motive, William would not stay very long in London or at Westminster. But how much of the various acts and designs which William of Poitiers seems vaguely to put between the coronation and the homage at Barking really belongs to William's first stay in London, how much to the stay at Barking, how much to the progress which followed, must be largely matter for conjecture. One grant of lands recorded in Domesday (ii 59) would seem to belong to the very first days of William's reign. Lands in Essex which had belonged to a certain Leofsuna appear as the property of Geoffrey of Mandeville, with the comment "Hoc manerium dedit Rex G quando remansit Londoniæ." One can hardly fancy that any later sojourn in London would be referred to in this marked way.

CHAP XVII

Submission of Eadwine, Morkere, and others.

candidate for the Crown, hastened to do their homage to the King chosen, crowned, and anointed. The Northern Earls themselves now saw that William was thoroughly determined to be King of the English in the fullest sense, and that he had no mind merely to displace the House of Godwine in the possession of Wessex and East-Anglia. Eadwine and Morkere therefore now made their way to Barking[1] to bow to the King whom the Primate of Northern England had already hallowed.[2] With them came a crowd of others of the great ones of the land who had as yet delayed their submission. They must have been chiefly the men of the North, the Thegns of Northhumberland and of those Mercian shires whose warriors had not marched to Senlac. The slaughter of Harold's own following must have left comparatively few men of note to come from Wessex and East-Anglia. And those among them who, from any cause, had not been in the battle, or who, having survived it, ventured to throw themselves on William's mercy, would probably have already made their submission either at Berkhampstead or at Westminster. Besides the two Earls, several names are mentioned, all of which seem to be Northumbrian.[3] Among them was the chief of the Northumbrian party, if there was any such Northumbrian party, which was

[1] On the reasons for accepting the account which places the homage of Eadwine and Morkere at this point, instead of placing it at the earlier submission at Berkhampstead, see vol iii p 767

[2] Will Pict 148. "Ibi veniunt ad obsequium ejus Edvinus et Morcardus, maximi fere omnium Anglorum genere ac potentiâ, Algardi illius nominatissimi filii" A singular expression of Orderic (511 A) sounds as if this submission was in a special way the work of Eadwine, who is spoken of almost as if he had brought Morkere with him against his will; "Eduinus Comes cum eo [Guillelmo] concordiam fecerat, eique *fratrem suum* et pene tertiam partem Angliæ subdiderat"

[3] William of Poitiers says simply, "alii complures nobiles et opibus ampli" He then mentions Copsige by name, but no one else The other names come from Orderic, 506 B

most opposed to the two Earls. The prudent Copsige,[1] once the lieutenant of Tostig in Northumberland, came now to become the man of William.[2] The others are described as Thurkill, Siward, and Ealdred, of whom the last two seem to have been descendants of Uhtred and great-nephews of King Eadward.[3] Eadric the Wild of Herefordshire, of whom we shall presently hear so much, is also placed in their company; but it seems far more likely that he did not submit till a much later time.[4] We know not whether it was now or later that Waltheof made his submission; but it could not have been long delayed, as he soon afterwards accompanied William in his voyage to Normandy.[5] Of Oswulf we do not hear till afterwards.[6] But there can be little doubt that, between Berkhampstead, Westminster, and Barking, all

*CHAP. XVII. Submission of Copsige and other men of the North.*

*of Waltheof.*

*The formal submission now complete*

---

[1] On Copsige or Coxo see vol ii p 484, and Appendix L  William of Poitiers speaks in this place (148) of his "singularis et fortitudo et probitas," and again in p 158, when recording his death, he says, " Prosapia et potentatu Anglus hic juxta præcelsus, magis animi singularitate prudentis et omnino honesti excelluit "

[2] Will Pict. 148  "In his erat Comes Coxo," but he clearly was not in possession of an Earldom at this moment

[3] Ord Vit 506 B  "Siwardus et Aldredus, filii Edelgari pronepotis Regis "  To answer this description, they must have been descendants of Uhtred by his third wife Ælfgifu, the half-sister of Eadward (see vol i p 358), but I cannot trace them in either of the genealogies given by Simeon, X Scriptt 80, 204 (pp 155, 91 of the Surtees edition by Mr. Hinde, which I shall quote for the future)  But all three names are found plentifully in Domesday  I know not whether this Ealdred is the same as either or both of the Ealdreds who appear in 149 b as "homo Morcari Comitis" and in 139 as "Teignus R E"

[4] On Eadric, see Appendix I

[5] In fact we hear nothing distinctly of Waltheof at all till the voyage to Normandy. His appointment to his Earldom is matter of inference (see vol ii. p 499), his presence or absence at Senlac is nowhere distinctly affirmed or implied (see vol iii p 424)  We only know that during the reign of Harold he was engaged in certain private transactions about land and money  " Hanc terram [Tooting in Surrey] accepit Wallef Comes de Swan post mortem Regis E , et invadiavit pro ii markis auri Alnodo Londoniensi." (Domesday, 32 )  The characteristic relations between the young noble and the rich citizen began thus early      [6] See Simeon, 91

CHAP XVII the surviving Earls, Prelates, and chief Thegns of England had become the men of the Conqueror. They craved—so the Norman writers tell us—William's pardon for anything that they had done, or even thought, against him, and threw themselves and all that they possessed on his mercy.[1] He received them graciously; he accepted their oaths of homage; he granted them their lands afresh, and held them in high honour.[2] At the same time, according to inveterate practice, he required hostages for their good faith, and the royal favour was not won, perhaps the royal presence was not entered, without a gift.[3]

*William's gracious reception of the new homagers*

This account of the surrender and regrant of the lands of Englishmen who submitted to William is worthy of special attention. If it stood by itself, it might be taken as simply meaning that commendation of the man and his land to the new lord which is implied in the act of homage. And, considering the circumstances under which that new lord had made his entry, it may well have been thought desirable to have every such act confirmed as solemnly as might be under the King's writ and seal. But when we take in the other evidence of different kinds, we shall perhaps be inclined to see in these almost casual words of the Norman panegyrist a deeper import even than this. The great confiscation of lands which is such a marked characteristic of William's reign was undoubtedly gradual. But when did it begin? There is, I think, every reason to believe that it began in the very first

*Surrender and regrant of lands*

*Confiscations of William's reign,*

---

[1] Will Pict 148. "Deprecantur veniam si quâ in re contra eum senserant, tradunt se cunctaque sua ejus clementiæ."

[2] Ib "Rex eorum sacramenta, ut postulaverunt, libens accepit, liberaliter eis donavit gratiam suam, reddidit eis cuncta quæ possederant, habebat eos magno honore"

[3] Chron Petrib 1066 "And menn guldon him gyld and gislas sealdon" This comes directly after the coronation, and no doubt at least takes in those who submitted at Barking

days of William's English reign. He had to reward his foreign followers, and, in conformity with his whole character and position, he had to reward them in some way which might be, formally at least, different from simple plunder and brigandage. His system of legal fictions easily supplied him with the means. He, King William, the lawful successor of his kinsman King Eadward, had been for a while hindered from receiving his Crown and exercising his royal authority He had even been met, when he came to take possession of his Kingdom, not with the welcome which was his due, but with an obstinate resistance in arms. Many Englishmen had fought against him; no Englishman, except an exile or two in his own train, had fought for him. Here was active treason in a large part of the nation, and at least passive complicity with treason in the remainder. The rights of the case, according to William's reading of the Law, were plain. According to its strict letter the lands of all such undutiful subjects were forfeited. William would have been justified in restoring Ralph of Norfolk[1] to his confiscated lands, and in seizing all the rest of the soil of England—save of course the lands of ecclesiastical corporations—for himself. But mercy and policy alike forbade such a course. Some favour was due to those who had not actually drawn the sword against the lawful heir; some perhaps was even due to those survivors of the fight on Senlac or the skirmish at Southwark who had atoned for their fault by a speedy submission. And besides this, the lands of most of those who had fought against him lay at his mercy, while the lands of many of those who now came in to give their submission could not be reached without another campaign. William could at once seize on the lands of any Kentish or South-Saxon Thegn or churl who had either died beneath the Standard or had

[1] See vol III p. 753.

lived to deal a blow in the *Malfosse*.[1] But the more part of the lands of Eadwine and Morkere and Waltheof and Copsige lay in regions to which William's arm had not yet reached, and to which, if he insisted on such an extreme stretch of severity, it never might reach. His course then was his usual one; he was debonair to those who submitted, and stark beyond measure to those who withstood him.[2] A less charitable way of putting it might be that he was debonair to those whom it might be dangerous further to provoke, and stark beyond measure to those who were already in his power. But in warring with these last he was in a great measure warring with the dead. The evidence that we have leads us to believe that the whole of the lands of those men, dead or living, who had fought at Senlac was at once dealt with as land forfeited to the King.[3] William thus had the means wherewith at once to enrich himself and to reward his followers. That the royal domain passed into his hands was the natural and legal result of his admission to the royal office. And now the final stroke was put to a change which had been gradually going on for some generations. The *folkland*, the common land of the nation, was now changed, fully and for ever, into *terra Regis*, the land of the King.[4] But besides what still remained as *folkland*, this great confiscation at once put into William's hands the greater part—all that lay within the shires which he already occupied—of the vast estates of Harold and his brothers, and of the great mass of the landowners, great and small, of southern and south-eastern England. It is not necessary to suppose that every rood of ground was actually seized, and either kept by the King or granted out to his foreign followers. There is distinct evidence that the actual occupiers of the soil, here as in other parts of

---

[1] See vol. iii. p. 503.  [2] See vol. ii. p. 169, iii. p. 537.
[3] See Appendix B.  [4] See vol. i. p. 102.

England, largely retained possession. Sometimes, when a great estate was confiscated, the widow and children of the former owner obtained a grant of some small portion of their heritage. In other cases the widow or daughter of the former owner was constrained to give herself and her lands to a foreign husband. In some cases Englishmen of high rank contrived to win William's personal favour, and to keep their lands and even their offices. A crowd of smaller Thegns and of well-to-do churls seem to have been left undisturbed. Either they had not been present in the battle, or they were looked on as victims whom William could afford to spare, or else they won his favour by timely submission or redeemed their lands by a payment to the new King. In some cases we distinctly read of men having their lands granted back to them, or of their buying them of King William for money. And yet we shall see that this process did not always secure them against the necessity of having in the phrase to "seek a lord" as a defender against illegal spoliation.[1]

But this last mentioned expression, of men buying their lands of the King, is most important, and is of much wider import than might seem at first sight. One of our national Chroniclers distinctly extends the phrase to all who did homage to William at or soon after his coronation.[2] And an entry in Domesday, which seems never to have received the attention which it deserves, distinctly speaks of a time when the English as a body redeemed their lands.[3] No date is assigned in the Survey to this event; but the two statements, taken together, can leave hardly any doubt that both refer to the same act, and that the general

---

[1] On all these cases see Appendix B.

[2] Chron. Petrib. 1066 "And menn guldon him gyld and gislas sealdon, and syððan heora land bohtan."

[3] This most important entry (Domesday, ii. 360) is quite incidental. Of some of the lands of Saint Edmundsbury we read, "Hanc terram habet Abbas in vadimonio pro xi marcis auri, concessu Engelrici, *quando redimebant Anglici terras suas*."

CHAP. XVII.

The three Commissioners, Bishop William, Ralph, and Engelric

redemption took place at the point of time which we have now reached, at the very beginning of William's reign. And by the help of another incidental notice in Domesday, it seems possible to recover the names of the Commissioners whom William employed in this somewhat delicate matter. They seem to show that William tried to give as little offence as might be to his new subjects in the course of a transaction which must have deeply grated on their feelings. He was represented by men, all of whom either were English by birth, or might, after long settlement in the land, be supposed to share in some measure the feelings of Englishmen.[1] The first was William, the Norman Bishop of London, the one foreign Prelate who had been allowed to return to his see after the great expulsion of strangers on the return of Godwine.[2] The others were Ralph the Staller, an old favourite of Eadward and a man who was at least born in the land,[3] and Engelric, a man seemingly of English birth, whose name is constantly found in the Survey of the eastern shires.[4] That these men all came from the same part of England is not wonderful. Essex, Suffolk, and Norfolk were precisely the parts of England which had come into William's hands without effort or resistance. His first English officials therefore came from those districts. And we may well remark the skill shown in the choice of men who were at once likely to be faithful to himself, and not likely to give special offence to the conquered people.

The theory of this memorable transaction was, as I have already said, that the whole soil of England, with the necessary exceptions of Crown and Church lands, was for-

---

[1] I get their names from a passage in Domesday (ii 367 b), which I shall discuss in Appendix C. It also refers to lands belonging to Saint Eadmundsbury. "Hanc terram invadiavit Abbas contra Barones Regis, scilicet W. Episcopum, Engelricum, et Radulfum Stalra."

[2] See vol ii p 345.   [3] See vol iii p 752, and Appendix C

[4] On Engelric, whose character, as far as regards the acquisition of land, seems to have been none of the best, see Appendix C.

feited. But strictly to carry out the sentence of forfeiture was alike unjust, impolitic, and impossible. A large portion of land was actually taken into the King's hands. The rest was redeemed by its owners. It was received as a fresh gift from the new lord, and received no doubt on various terms, according to the merits or demerits of each particular grantee. Some doubtless received their lands as a free gift; others, as we have seen, had to buy them back in the strictest sense of those words. Some received the whole, others a part; in some cases we are told that Englishmen received fresh grants beyond what they had inherited or received from earlier lords [1] But, amidst all this variety, it would seem that in all cases of lay estates the land was received as a fresh grant, which needed the writ and seal of King William as its witness. The date of legal memory went back only to the day when the forfeited land of England was redeemed of the reigning sovereign. In the case of ecclesiastical bodies, as not being liable to forfeiture, the rule was of course less stringent. In their case the writ and seal of King Eadward was of equal validity with the writ and seal of King William, and the grants even of earlier Kings could be put in as evidence. But it is plain that all acts done by the authority of the usurper Harold were held to be null and void [2]

We must not forget that, with regard to perhaps the greater part of these grants, William was granting away that of which he had no kind of actual possession. When he was restoring the lands of Eadwine and Morkere and Copsige, he was restoring lands most of which were quite beyond his grasp. No soldier of William's army had as yet set foot in Northumberland or Northern Mercia. But the policy of the transaction on both sides is obvious. The

CHAP. XVII.

Land henceforth held by a fresh grant from the King

Exception of ecclesiastical bodies

Harold's acts null and void

The land granted often not really in William's possession.

Policy of the agreement on both sides.

---

[1] Will. Pict 148 "Ejusdem liberalitatis dono acceperant Angli complures quod a parentibus vel prioribus dominis non acceperunt"

[2] On all these points see Appendix A and B

CHAP XVII. Northern Earls had found that there was no chance of William being satisfied with half a Kingdom; they knew by this time that he had made up his mind to be master of the whole land. If they did not submit, they would have to fight; and they thought it wiser to submit on favourable terms, rather than to run the risk of a struggle which might end in their utter destruction. To William, on the other hand, it was clearly a gain to receive even a nominal submission. It quite fell in with his whole policy of words and names and legal fictions to grant away lands of which he had never had a moment's possession. It was a bold stroke to convert, without stirring from London or Barking, the Earls of the Northumbrians and the Mercians into his lieutenants, and their lands into fiefs held by his grant. The formal submission might possibly prove to be a real one. And, if it did not, if Northumberland had after all to be conquered by force, the submission of its Earls, Prelates, and chief Thegns would put altogether a different colour on the conquest. If William had still to go forth on a Northern campaign, he would now be going forth to recover what was, in every legal form, his own. He would be going to chastise men who were not only rebels and traitors in some vague constructive sense, but who were actually men faithless to their lord, men who had rebelled against the sovereign to whom they had sworn oaths and from whom they acknowledged themselves to hold all that they had. With this formal submission William seems for the present to have been content. Eadwine, Morkere, and their companions had indeed to give gifts and hostages to the Conqueror, but they received all their lands and honours again, and were admitted to the full favour of the new King. Eadwine indeed seems really to have won William's personal regard, and he was further flattered by the promise, sincere or insincere, of the hand of one

Northern England left untouched for the present.

of the King's daughters.[1] The whole of Northern England was simply left as it was before; the old rulers, the old proprietors, were undisturbed, it does not seem that a single castle was built to keep Northumberland and Northern Mercia in check, or that a single soldier was sent to occupy or to spy out the land. All was trusted to the loyalty of William's new made vassals. The House of Leofric, the House of the old Northumbrian Earls, might alike seem to have lost nothing by the revolution which had enthroned a Norman instead of a West-Saxon in Winchester and London

Thus far did the Conqueror show himself mild and debonair to those parts of England which had not acted openly against him and which were as yet beyond his immediate grasp. Towards the districts which lay at his mercy, the districts whose men had followed Harold and his brothers, he began, if not to show himself beyond measure stark, at least to show that the forfeiture of the lands of the rebels was not to remain a dead letter. To the city of London he had, perhaps before he left Westminster for Barking, already granted a charter in the English tongue, that venerable parchment which may still be seen in the city archives with the cross traced by the Conqueror's own hand[2] By that charter he confirmed to the city all its rights, possessions, and customs, as freely as

*William's dealings with Southern and Eastern England*

*His charter to London.*

---

[1] Ord Vit 511 A. "Guillelmus Rex . filiam suam se in conjugem ei [Eduino Comiti] daturum spoponderat"

[2] The original is given by Riley, Lib. Cust ii. part ii. p 504, Stubbs, Select Charters, 79 "Willelm Kyng gret Willelm Bisceop and Gosfregð Portirefan and ealle þa burhware binnan Londone, Frencisce and Englisce, freondlice And ic kyðe eow þæt ic wille þæt get beon eallra þæra laga weorðe þe gyt wæran on Eadweides dæge kynges And ic wille þæt ælc cyld beo his fæder yrfnume æfter his fæder dæge And ic nelle geþolian þæt ænig man eow ænig wrang beode God eow gehealde" One or two words here look a little suspicious, but this copy, if not absolutely the original, is at any rate much older than the versions given by Mr Riley, vol ii part ii pp. 246, 247.

CHAP XVII they had been held in the days of his predecessor. Wanton innovation, needless disturbance of the regular order of things which he found established, formed no part of William's policy. But this very charter shows us a stranger, Godfrey by name, holding the office of Portreeve of the city. His English predecessors, Leofstan and Ælfsige,[1] had perhaps died in the battle, and William had taken care thus early to give them a successor of his own nation. And we must not forget that, while the charter of their rights was being granted to the citizens, the fortress of the Conqueror was rising above their heads. We can well believe that William did his best to shield his new subjects from the insolence of his foreign followers. The strict police of his reign began already; robbers, murderers, intruders on lands not legally granted, the spoilers of the traveller and the merchant, were kept in check, seemingly without regard to their rank or nation.[2] The leaders of the host were exhorted to gentleness and moderation; the inferior officers and common soldiers were kept in order by stringent proclamations.[3] William's military code not only forbade slaughter, plunder, and rape, but dealt with all breaches of chastity and temperance as military offences.[4] Courts martial were com-

*A foreign Portreeve in London.*

*William's strict police and military discipline.*

[1] A writ of Eadward is addressed to them in Cod. Dipl. iv. 214. Another Portreeve, Ulf, appears as a benefactor to Westminster in iv. 221 (see vol. ii. pp. 510, 568).

[2] Will. Pict. 147 "Latrociniis, invasionibus, maleficus, locum omnem intra suos terminos denegavit Portus et quælibet itinera negotiatoribus patere, et nullam injuriam fieri, jussit" "Invasiones," it should be remembered, is a kind of technical term for illegal occupations of land. The mention of the havens suggests the doings of the royal officers, who at all times needed careful keeping in check

[3] Ib. 146. "Suis primatibus dignâ se et gravitate præcepit, et diligentiâ suasit æquitatem" Part of William's sermon has been already quoted (see above, p 13) The historian then goes on, "Milites vero mediæ nobilitatis atque gregarios aptissimis edictis coercuit." The distinction reminds one of that drawn by Odysseus, Il. ii 188

[4] Will Pict 147 "Tutæ erant a vi mulieres quam sæpe amatores inferunt Etiam illa delicta quæ fierent consensu impudicarum infamiæ

missioned to visit all evil doers of every kind with severe punishment, and to show no favour to the native Normans above the auxiliaries from other parts of Gaul.[1] All these statements of the panegyrist we can, with the necessary deductions, fully accept. William, we need not doubt, honestly did his best to preserve peace in his Kingdom and discipline in his army. It was the more needful to do so while the work of legal spoliation was going on. The King now set forth on a progress, the object of which, there can be little doubt, was to visit and take possession of the forfeited lands.[2] In the course of that progress he came across no opposition; not a road was shut against him; not a man met him in arms. He was met only by suppliants, who implored and obtained his mercy, a mercy shown specially to those of low degree.[3] Mothers came forth with their children to work, and not unsuccessfully, on his pity.[4] This too we need not doubt, at least in the sense which the great Survey enables us to put upon it. Many a man once rich and powerful doubtless met William at some stage of his progress, and won from his mercy, perhaps under the name of alms, some fragment of his old possessions which would at least keep him from want or servile work. Now too it doubtless was that the crowd of smaller landowners, Thegns

*William's progress and occupation of the forfeited lands*

*His alleged clemency*

*Its real nature*

prohibendæ gratiâ vetabantur Potare militem in tabernis *non multum* concessit, quoniam ebrietas litem, lis homicidium solet generare Seditiones interdixit, cædem, et omnem rapinam, frænans ut populos armis, ita legibus arma"

[1] Will Pict 147. "Judices qui vulgo militum essent timori constituti sunt, simul acerbæ pœnæ in eos qui delinquerent decretæ sunt; neque liberius Normanni quam Britanni vel Aquitani agere permittebantur"

[2] Ib 148 "Inde progrediens diversas partes regni accessit, ordinando ubique *utilia sibi* et incolis terræ"

[3] Ib "Iter nullum obstruitur, occurrunt passim obsequentes aut explicantes Omnes ille clementibus oculis respexit, clementissimis plebem"

[4] Ib. "Sæpe vultu miserantem animum prodidit, jussit multotiens misericordiam, quum supplices conspiceret aut egenos, matres animadverteret voce et gestibus precari cum liberis"

of the lowest rank or churls of the highest, whom we find retaining their lands in the southern shires, came and begged the mercy of the new King, and were by his mercy deemed too insignificant to be disturbed.[1] And we can better understand the picture of William's clemency to the suppliant widows and orphans, when we turn to those entries in the great Survey which set before us the widows of men of all but the highest rank glad to find some small part of the forfeited wealth of their husbands and sons thrown back to them, perhaps burthened with some ignominious tenure, by the contemptuous pity of the Conqueror.

*Cases of Englishmen retaining their lands*

*"Alms" to widows and orphans*

We shall perhaps better understand the process which now went on through a large part of England, if we fix our eyes more minutely on the fate of some particular individuals, families, and districts about which we are able to gather an unusual amount of detailed information. Such a typical region is supplied to us by a district of which we may take Berkshire as the centre, but which also takes in parts of most of the adjoining shires. This district is one of those in which the Commissioners employed on William's Survey have been most bountiful in local and personal notices, while in some parts of England they give us little beyond dry lists of names. We are also able to draw a good deal of help from the detailed history of the great monastery of the district, the house of Saint Mary of Abingdon.[2] By these means we are able to call up a personal image of several men of the days of Eadward, Harold, and William, of some of whom we have heard already.

*Evidence of particular districts*

*Effects of the confiscation in Berkshire.*

It may be simply because our local details are specially

---

[1] See Appendix D
[2] The local History of Abingdon, "Chronicon Monasterii de Abingdon," edited by Mr Stevenson, forms two volumes in the series of Chronicles and Memorials

rich, but our evidence certainly sets before us the men of Berkshire as a race specially loyal to Harold and to England. Their shire had formed part of Harold's own Earldom, and we have already come across more than one instance in which his name is directly connected with the affairs of the shire. He appears on terms of friendship with the chief men of the district and, if not as himself a benefactor to the great local Abbey, yet as one who was ready to protect its rights and to forward its interests.[1] The local officer second in rank, the Sheriff Godric, is one of the chosen few whom we know by name as having given their lives for England in the great battle.[2] And it is plain that the glorious end of the local chief had been largely shared by the men of his shire. An incidental expression in the local history shows that for a man to have been a Thegn of Berkshire implied, almost as a matter of course, that he had died at Senlac.[3] Long after William's accession, the tenants of the Abbey are mentioned as being specially zealous in every form of revolt and resistance against the foreign government.[4] It is not wonderful then if the hand of William lay heavy on both the ecclesiastical and the temporal landowners of so stout-hearted a district. The vague laments of the local history[5] are fully borne out by the detailed evidence of

CHAP. XVII
The men of Berkshire among the foremost at Senlac.

Godric the Sheriff

Great slaughter of the Berkshire Thegns

Zeal of the tenants of Abingdon Abbey.

---

[1] See vol. ii. p. 42, and cf. vol. iii. p. 68.

[2] See vol. iii. pp. 426, 730.

[3] Hist. Mon. Ab. ii. 3. "Quæ possessiones [the estates held by the tenants of the Abbey] ab eis habitæ fuerant, quos Tainos dicunt, et in bello Hastingis occubuerant."

[4] Ib. i. 486, 493, speaking of a much later time, "Sed et homines abbatiæ Abbendonensis, *dum regis parti favere Willelmi debuerant*, animo et consultu mutati, armati, quo hostes regis ipsius consistere acceperant, gressum contenderunt." The writer's position should be noticed; he admires Harold and Godric, but he holds that submission was due to King William.

[5] Ib. "Nullius sacrorum liminum prospectûs reverentia, nulla fratrum desolatorum compassio. Extra per villas posthabito cujuslibet respectu, passim impensa vastatio."

VOL. IV. D

the Survey. There are not many parts of England in which the confiscation seems to have been more sweeping; none perhaps of the shires which formed William's first conquest, except the two where he first set foot, and where his hand fell heaviest of all, the old Kentish and South-Saxon lands.[1] There, as well as in some other shires which were conquered later, not a single Englishman was allowed to keep his lands on their old tenure, and only two English tenants-in-chief appear in the Survey. The confiscation in Berkshire was not so extensive as in these extreme cases, but among the more typical shires, where English tenancy-in-chief was not wholly forbidden, there are few where the number of Englishmen who retained their estates seems to have been smaller. Still, here as elsewhere, we find some instances of Englishmen who contrived to make their peace with the Conqueror, and we find the case of one man of high rank who seems to have risen to a special place in his favour.

The lands held by Harold and his family in Berkshire were not very extensive; still Harold himself, his mother Gytha, his sister Eadgyth, his brothers Tostig, Gyrth, and perhaps Leofwine, are all found as land-owners in the shire.[2] The lands of the Lady of course remained untouched till her death; those of Tostig—of no great extent[3]—no doubt fell in to the Crown at his outlawry in the days of Eadward. The estates of the fallen King and his loyal brothers were of course, in William's reading

---

[1] On the confiscations in Kent and Surrey, see Appendix E

[2] The lands of Harold in Berkshire will be found in Domesday, 57 b, 58, 59 b, 60, 62 b, 63 b In 58, 59, and 60 we find the names of his tenants and grantees, the last one perhaps being Eadnoth the Staller. Gytha and Gyrth occur together in 59 b, and Gyrth alone in 61 Tostig in 60 There is a Leofwine in 60 b, but he is not distinguished as "Comes." The estates of the Lady appear in 56 b, 57, 58, 60, 63 b, which last entry I shall have to mention again.

[3] Tostig's estate was reckoned at fourteen hides T. R. E., but at seven only at the time of the Survey

of the Law, forfeited by the treason of their owners, and they were no doubt at once seized into the King's hands. The greater part of them remained in the King's hands at the time of the Survey, but some portions had been granted out.[1] But a more special interest, in a view of this particular district, is awakened by the fate of the Sheriff Godric and his family. His name is so common that it is not always easy to distinguish his lands from those of less famous Godrics, but it is plain that his estates were large, both in his own shire and beyond its bounds, and that they were held by various tenures Some of his lordships were held of the Crown, one at least by a grant from Eadward himself,[2] others, as we have seen, were held of the Church of Abingdon, a happy accident to which we owe our better knowledge of the man and his deeds. But he also held other lands by virtue of his office as Sheriff, an office which he seems also to have filled in Buckinghamshire as well as in Berkshire. And with regard to these various possessions, the Survey has happily preserved a number of incidental details, which throw light on the manners of the time, and which, like all details of the kind, help us better to understand the men and the age with which we are dealing. Two hides of land in Buckinghamshire were held in absolute property by a maiden whose English name appears in so corrupt a form that it can only be guessed at. But besides this, she occupied half a hide of royal domain, which was granted to her by Godric the Sheriff for the term of his Sheriffdom, as her fee for teaching his daughter the special art of Englishwomen of those days,

*CHAP XVII.*

*Chiefly kept in the King's hands*

*Lands of Godric*

*Personal details of Godric*

---

[1] The greater estates of Harold in 57 b and 58 are all in the King's hands, some of the holders of smaller portions will be mentioned presently

[2] On the lands of Godric and all points connected with them, see Appendix F.

CHAP XVII the art of embroidery in gold.[1] This gift would, even in peaceful times, have reverted to the Crown at the death of Godric, but the freehold of the Englishwoman had equally passed away before the time of the Survey.[2] In another entry we find mention of a part of the royal domain in Berkshire which was used for the feeding of the Sheriff's horses.[3] How far either of these applications of the royal property was strictly legal, it might be hard to say; at any rate they illustrate the liberties which officers of every rank were in the habit of taking, whether by received custom or not, with the property of their masters.

*Charges against him of wrongful occupation*
*Lands of Godric granted to Henry of Ferrers*

Other entries however seem distinctly to charge Godric with wrongful occupation of portions of the King's land.[4] The lands of Godric himself were confiscated, and were granted out to a follower of William named Henry of Ferrers. This man, whose descendants held the Earldoms of Derby and Nottingham, was the son of Walkelin of Ferrers, one of the disturbers of the peace of Normandy in the days of William's childhood.[5] He had fought at Senlac,[6] and was rewarded with high offices and vast possessions in various parts of England. But he could also stoop to despoil those whom the Conqueror himself had spared. One obscure entry in the Survey illustrates the account given by the panegyrist of William's clemency to suppliant wives and mothers. A single hide of land seems

---

[1] Domesday, 149 "De his tenuit Aluuid puella II. hidas quas potuit dare et vendere cui voluit, et de dominicâ firmâ Regis E habuit ipsa dimidiam hidam, quam Godricus Vicecomes ei concessit quamdiu Vicecomes esset, ut illa doceret filiam ejus aurifrisium operari." What does "Aluuid" stand for? Ealhswith, Ealdgyth, or what? Of the English embroidery I shall have to speak again

[2] Her land was held by a tenant of Robert of Oily, of whom more anon.

[3] Domesday, 57 b "Henricus de Fereres tenet de hoc manerio XLIII. acras terræ quæ fuerunt in firmâ Regis T. R. E, sicut scira dicit Dicunt autem quod Godricus Vicecomes fecit ibi pascua equis suis, sed nesciunt quomodo"

[4] See Appendix F.

[5] Will. Gem vii 2, Ord Vit 522 D.

[6] Roman de Rou, 13498.

to have been left to the widow of the fallen Sheriff, to be held by the degrading tenure of feeding the King's dogs. Even of this she was in the end defrauded; even this small fragment of former wealth came into the hands of the rapacious stranger.[1]

 The process of confiscation is well worth studying. Almost every detail illustrates the way in which, in William's policy, wrong contrived to assume the mask of right, and how the plunder of the Conquest was gathered in with all the forms of a legal process. The process was strikingly like that which went on at the Dissolution of the Monasteries. The lands of Godric were granted to Henry of Ferrers, just as the lands of a dissolved monastery were granted to Seymour, Dudley, or Cranmer. In either case the new owner stepped into the exact position of the old one. He had a right to all to which the former owner had a right, and to nothing more. He had a claim to all his advantages, and he was bound by all his burthens. Godric became, in the technical sense of the Conquest, the *ancestor*[2] of Henry of Ferrers, and Henry might claim all that had lawfully been Godric's and nothing more. But it is not wonderful if an intruding soldier did not always bind himself by the strict letter of the Law. Some of Godric's possessions ought to have reverted to the Crown, others to the Abbey of Abingdon. Henry of Ferrers seized all, to the damage of Crown and Abbey alike. The Survey records the wrong in both cases, as it also records other wrongs either done to the King or done in the King's name to others. Thus we find that the Sheriff Froger,

---

 [1] Domesday, 57 *b*. "Henricus tenet ibi 1 bidam, quæ fuerat in firmâ Regis Godricus tenuit Aluricus de Taceham dicit se vidisse brevem Regis quod eam dederit feminæ Godrici in dono, eo quod nutriebat canes suos Sed nemo est in hundredâ qui brevem viderit præter Aluricum."

 [2] "Antecessor" is the regular technical term in Domesday, of which "ancestor," though now used only in the sense of "forefather," is simply a contraction. See Appendix A, and the Epistles of Lanfranc, 1 32, ed. Giles.

CHAP XVII  seemingly the Norman successor of Godric, in at least two cases converted to the use of the Crown the lands of Englishmen which had not been regularly confiscated.[1]

Losses of Abingdon Abbey.

The historian of the Abbey is naturally most eloquent on the wrongs of his own house, but, except the loss of the lands held of the Church by Godric and Thurkill,[2] those wrongs belong chiefly to the times of disturbance and oppression somewhat later, and not to the acts of William's first progress.

Nearly universal extinction of the smaller English landowners in Berkshire

In looking over the names of smaller owners in Berkshire, we are struck, as I have already said, by the almost universal extent of the confiscation. The number of landowners of the middle class, answering to our smaller gentry and richer yeomanry, must in King Eadward's days have been very large. Lordship after lordship had been held by three brothers, by two or by three Thegns, by one or two or three freemen,[3] the heritage of many such being swept in

---

[1] The unjust doings of Froger appear in Domesday, 57, 58. The Abingdon historian (i 486, 494) speaks of him as a special enemy to the Abbey, and rejoices over his disgrace and loss of office, which is not recorded in Domesday, but which we might have guessed from his not appearing there as a landowner "Itaque temporis illius rerum abbatiæ amissarum vel insinuatio vel computatio, non facile dictu Quarum executioni Frogerus tunc Berchesire vicecomes præcipuus efferebatur, sed ejusdem illo potentis hominis immoderatum super homines depressos progressum moderantis universa postea Dei vindicta coercuit, ut et jus quo efferebatur tyrannicum regiâ sibi justitiâ auferretur, et in despectum omnium inopiâ et stoliditate quoad vixit verteretur," etc

[2] The local History (1 484) records the commendation of Thurkill to the Abbey (see vol ii p 42), and adds, "hic quum in bello memorato occubuisset, terram, cujus dominationis investituram multo ante tempore quam bellum foret ecclesia in manus habebat, Henricus de Ferrariis sibi usurpavit, abbate invalido obstare" Then follows the lease to Godric (see vol iii p 731), with the special provision made to meet any case of forfeiture, "Quidquid tamen offensionis possessoribus forte accideret, ecclesia inde jacturam nullam incurreret" Then follows, "Itaque ipso cum prædicto viro pariter in bello occiso, idem Henricus de Ferrariis hanc villam cum alterâ suæ ditioni adjecit"

[3] In pp 62 b, 63, we find "duo taini tenuerunt in paragio," "tres liberi homines tenuerunt de rege Edwardo," "tres fratres tenuerunt de rege E. in alodio," "tres taini tenuerunt in alodio de rege E" There are other entries of the same kind

NORMANS SETTLED IN BERKSHIRE. 39

a mass into the hands of some insatiable stranger. Among those to whose grasp the lands and homes of Englishmen were thus handed over we come across many names familiar to us in our Norman history, to some of whom we should not grudge any amount of wealth and honour in their own land. The men whose exploits we could follow with delight below the steep of Arques or among the burning streets of Mortemer now meet us again in a less pleasing form as intruders in the shire which gave birth to Ælfred. William of Eu,[1] Ralph of Toesny,[2] and Ralph of Mortemer[3] now had their reward in the spoils of the conquered land. With them we find the aged Walter Giffard, who had refused to bear the standard at Senlac,[4] and Toustain the son of Rolf, in whose hands the sacred banner had been so truly guarded.[5] Other lands fell to the lot of kinsmen of the Conqueror himself, to his brother Robert of Mortain[6] and to his cousin Richard of Evreux.[7] Here we see the lands which Eudo of Rye, Eudo of Colchester, the worthy son of the faithful Hubert, received as the reward of his own and his father's loyalty.[8] Here we light on the names of Miles Crispin, of the house of the defenders of Tillières,[9] and of Hugh of Avranches, more famous in another quarter of England as the first Count Palatine of Chester.[10] The foreign allies and mercenaries of the host are represented by the names of Gilbert of Ghent[11] and Arnulf of Hesdin[12]

*Chap. XVII. Normans settled in Berkshire.*

*Lands granted to Flemish followers of William.*

[1] See Domesday, 61, and for his fate Ord Vit 704 C   He was the son of Count Robert   See vol iii p 118
[2] See Domesday, 62 b.   Vol iii pp 287, 465.        [3] Ib 62 b
[4] Ib 60    Vol iii pp. 129, 153, 465
[5] Ib 63    Vol iii p 465
[6] Robert of Mortain (60), wonderful to say, held only one lordship in Berkshire, and that was held of him by the Abbey of Preaux, the foundation of Humfrey de Vetulis   See Neustria Pia, p 520
[7] See Domesday, 60   Vol ii p. 210      [8] Ib. 61 b   Vol ii. p 249.
[9] Ib 61 b   Vol ii. p 204            [10] Ib. 60   Vol ii pp. 207, 291
[11] Ib 62   Vol iii p 312.
[12] Ib 62 b   Vol iii. p 714, where I ought not to have confounded Arnulf of Hesdin with his much smaller namesake of Ardres.

CHAP XVII.
Lands granted to Norman Churches and Churchmen, and to Battle Abbey

Nor was the Norman Church likely to be forgotten in the division of the plunder. An Englishman named Eadward and two nameless allodial holders were dispossessed in favour of the great house of Saint Peter on the Dive.[1] And the Norman Abbey which soon began to rise on English ground as a monument of English overthrow came in for the spoils alike of the spiritualty and of the temporalty of England. It might in William's view be fitting that a lordship which had passed from a nameless Thegn to Earl Harold should pass from him to Saint Martin of the Place of Battle;[2] but we may ask, even on William's own principles, why a monk from Marmoutiers should enjoy the spoils of a church and eight hides of land held in King Eadward's days by the English Abbess Leofgifu.[3] And among gifts to ecclesiastical bodies we also see gifts to at least two churchmen in their personal character. One is no less a person than Geoffrey of Mowbray, the famous Bishop of Coutances, he who had exhorted the Norman host on the night before the battle, and had asked their assent to the crowning of their Duke within the walls of the West Minster.[4] His lands and lordships reached into well nigh every corner of England, and probably among their firstfruits was a single Berkshire manor, the spoil of an Englishman whose name of Oda

Possessions of Bishop Geoffrey of Coutances

---

[1] Domesday, 59 b. "Abbas de Superdivâ tenet de Rege Peise. Duo alodiarii tenuerunt et potuerunt ire quo voluerunt. Ipse Abbas tenet II. hidas in Coserige. Edunardus tenuit de Rege E."

[2] Ib. 59 b. "Abbas de Labatailge tenet de Rege Bristoldestone. Heraldus comes tenuit tunc pre X hidis, quidam Tainus qui ante eum tenuit geldabat pro XV hidis, modo pro nihilo."

[3] Ib. 60. "Ipse Abbas tenet in Reddinges ecclesiam cum VIII hidis ibi pertinentibus, Leveva abbatissa tenuit." This would seem to be Leofgifu Abbess of Shaftesbury, of whom we hear in the Exon Domesday, 176, where we read of Combe in Somersetshire, "Abbatissa [Sancti Edwardi] habet I mansionem quæ vocatur Comba, quam tenuit Leveva abbatissa." See Ellis, ii. 160.

[4] See vol. iii. pp. 451, 559.

perhaps points to his being, like Thurkill of Kingston, of the stock of the Danes.[1] Regennbald too, the Norman Chancellor of Eadward, was not only confirmed in his former holding, but received also the estate of a free Englishwoman named Ælfgifu.[2] And with these we find the name of a man of unrecorded nationality, who doubtless owed the favour of William to his skill in an art specially adapted to enhance the splendour of a King's court, an art for which both natives and sojourners in England were specially famous.[3] Five Berkshire estates, four of which had been the property of an Englishman named Eadward, had passed into the hands of Theodoric the Goldsmith. He was doubtless one of those craftsmen from the Teutonic mainland whose presence in England had been encouraged by a constant tradition going back at least to the days of Eadgar.[4] Theodoric had been settled in England in King Eadward's time, and he had held lands in various shires both under the King and under Earl Harold. He now did not scruple to accept the confiscated lands of Englishmen at the hands of William.[5] He, and all the rest of

*CHAP. XVII.*
*Reinbald, Chancellor of Eadward.*

*Theodoric the Goldsmith.*

---

[1] Domesday, 58 b "Episcopus Goisfridus tenet Contone, Oda tenuit de Rege E"

[2] See vol ii p 359 Domesday, 63 "Reinbaldus de Cirecestre tenet de Rege Hacheborne, ipse tenuit de Rege E ... Isdem Reinbaldus tenet Estone Eileva quædam libera femina tenuit T R E"

[3] Will Pict 155 "Anglicæ nationis opera feminæ multum acu et auri texturâ [see above, p 36] egregie viri in omni valent artificio Ad hoc incolere apud eos Germani solebant talium artium scientissimi Inferunt et negotiatores, qui longinquas regiones navibus adeunt, doctarum manuum opera."   [4] See vol i. p 68

[5] The lands of Theodoric in Berkshire are given in p 63 All had been held T R. E. by an Eadward, save one estate whose owner is called Lanc He appears in Surrey, 36 b, as holding lands which he had himself held T R E ; and in Oxfordshire, 160 b, as holding lands which had belonged to his own wife. "Has ii terras uxor ejus libere tenuit T R E" I presume that he is also the Tedric who appears in Surrey, 36 b, as holding of Harold But there are several entries of this thoroughly Nether-Dutch name in various parts of England, and it is not likely that they all belong to the same person

CHAP. XVII. William's grantees, great and small, stepped each man into the place of one or more Englishmen who became his legal *ancestors*. As in the case of the confiscated lands of Godric and Thurkill, disputes sometimes arose as to the exact extent of the *ancestor's* property, and consequently as to the exact rights of his Norman successor. Questions of this kind, decided as they were by the common witness of the shire, are eminently characteristic of that system of spoliation cloked under legal forms and legal language which distinguished William's policy throughout.[1]

It is not to be supposed that all these sweeping confiscations took place at once. But they doubtless began during William's first progress, at all events in the cases of men who, like Thurkill and Godric, had actually died in arms against him. But in the end, small indeed was the remnant, in Berkshire at least, which any Englishman was able to keep for himself. In many other shires we find a large class of King's Thegns, bearing English names and holding small estates, which themselves or their fathers had held in the time of King Eadward. A long list of such is found in the neighbouring district of Wiltshire. But in Berkshire the list is indeed short. One Englishman alone holds a single hide of land which he had himself held under King Eadward.[2] This man, Eadward by name, is most likely the same who occurs as the predecessor of several Norman owners, a case no doubt where the Conqueror's clemency had allowed the former owner of a great estate to keep some small portion for his mere maintenance. Another Englishman, Ælfward, still held of King William the land which his father had held of the Lady Eadgyth; but he was of the same craft as Theodoric, and his skill doubtless pleaded

Small number of Englishmen who kept their lands.

[1] See Appendix A
[2] Domesday, 63 *b* "Edwardus tenet de Rege I hidam in Coserige, ipse tenuit in alodio de Rege E"

for him.¹ A few others occur who held land which in Eadward's days had belonged to other Englishmen, and of which it is mostly impossible to say whether it had passed by confiscation, by purchase, or by inheritance. But in one case it is recorded in a marked way that one Ælfsige of Faringdon held as a grant from King William an estate which had belonged to Earl Harold.² Another, Cola, held lands which had once belonged to two other Englishmen, and he was even bold enough to lay claim to property which was held by the powerful Robert of Oily.³ Still more to be noticed, as illustrating the boasted clemency of William, are the cases in which a string of women appear as keeping, under the title of alms from King William, the lands which they had held in full property under King Eadward.⁴

Other entries let us into the fact that men who retained their land were sometimes driven to commend themselves, to seek a lord, in order to win the protection of some powerful man.⁵ They thus sank, as far at least as those particular lands were concerned, from the rank of tenants-in-chief to the rank of mesne tenants. These commendations would doubtless not take place during the first stage of William's confiscations and renewed grants. Men

*marginalia:* CHAP XVII. Englishmen who received their own land as "alms". Cases of commendation.

---

¹ Domesday, 63 b " Alwardus aurifaber tenet de Rege Sotesbroc, pater ejus tenuit de reginâ Eddid " This is Shottesbrook, famous for its graceful collegiate church of the fourteenth century.

² Ib. "Alsi de Ferendone tenet Lierecote de dono Regis W, Heraldus tenuit. .. Isdem Alsi tenet de Rege dimidiam hidam quam Aluric quidam liber homo tenuit T R E"

³ The holdings of Cola come in page 63 b, but in 62 we read of two mills at Ardington, belonging to Robert of Oily, " Cola Anglicus calumniatur unum ex his molinis, sed Aluuin et Goduinus et Aluricus testificantur quod semper jacuit in Ardintone " But it should be noticed that the *antecessor* of Robert in this property was the same as one of the *antecessors* of Cola

⁴ Domesday, 63 b " Ibi habet Ældeva libera femina 1 hidam de Rege in elemosina, quam eadem tenuit T R E et quo vellet ire potuisset " The same entry follows of " Eddid quædam femina," and " Eldit quædam femina "

⁵ See Appendix B

44 THE FIRST DAYS OF WILLIAM'S REIGN.

CHAP XVII.  would begin to find them needful when oppression on the part of the strangers and discontent on the part of the natives had begun to take the shape of open violence on both sides. Then doubtless it was that a nameless Englishman, who, in King Eadward's days, "could go where he would," that is, who could commend himself to what lord he pleased or to no lord at all, commended himself for the sake of safety to the Bishop of the diocese, the Lotharingian Hermann. After Hermann's days his son Thored, whose name witnesses to the Danish descent of the family, renewed the commendation to Hermann's Norman successor Osmund.[1] Such a case doubtless did not stand alone; indeed we find one remarkable instance expressly recorded in the case of a man of much higher rank. Azor, the sewer or *dapifer* of King Eadward, held, among various estates in various places, one hide of land at Ardington. He met William at Windsor, and received the restoration of his land, confirmed by the royal writ. Yet at the time of the Survey Azor had been driven to hold this same land, no longer as a tenant-in-chief of the Crown, but as a tenant of Robert of Oily.[2] Here was a case of forced commendation without any claim of legal right Robert had no writ of King William to show. Simply by the right of the stronger, he had at once defrauded the King of

Commendation of Thored to Bishop Hermann.

Forced commendation of Azor to Robert of Oily.

---

[1] Domesday, 58 "Isdem Episcopus tenet de Rege I hidam et dimidiam, et Tori de eo. Pater Tori tenuit T R E et potuit ire quo voluit, sed *pro sua defensione* se commisit Hermanno Episcopo, et Tori Osmundo Episcopo similiter"

[2] Ib 62 "Isdem Robertus tenet unam hidam quam Azor dispensator R E tenuit, et cum eâ ire potuit quo voluit . . Hanc terram tenet isdem Azor de Roberto, sed homines de hundredâ testificantur eum de Rege debere tenere, quam Rex W apud Windesores ei reddidit et brevem suum inde ei dedit Robertus vero tenet injuste Nemo enim eorum vidit brevem Regis vel ex parte ejus hominem qui eum inde saisisset." We do not often get the history of a piece of land in such full and clear detail

his rights as Azor's immediate lord, and had further wronged Azor himself by reducing him to a lower rank in the territorial hierarchy.[1]

This mention of Robert of Oily leads us at once to the most remarkable instance in this district of an Englishman of rank retaining his lands under William. Besides Godric and Thurkill and the members of the house of Godwine, there are not many English names in the Berkshire Survey to which we can attach a personal idea. The two Stallers, Bondig and Eadnoth, both held lands in the shire. One certainly, the other possibly,[2] passed into William's service, yet at the time of the Survey the lands of both of them were distributed among foreign holders. Of the fate of Bondig we know nothing for certain, but it is strange that the lands of Eadnoth, who died fighting in William's cause, were not allowed to pass to his son.[3] A third Englishman of rank in the district knew better than all how to adapt himself to the new state of things. It is plain that Wigod of Wallingford, the kinsman and cupbearer of Eadward,[4] had made his submission to William and had been received into his full favour. There is therefore every reason to accept the tradition which represents him as having made his submission when William appeared in Berkshire before his coronation, and which makes it owing to Wigod's help that William was peacefully received and enabled to cross the Thames without opposition. Wigod seems to have retained so much influence in the new state of things that Englishmen of smaller account found it expedient to seek his protection by com-

*Case of Wigod of Wallingford.*

*His favour with William*

*Probability of his receiving William on his first march December, 1066.*

---

[1] See Appendix G

[2] That is, if we can believe in the Westminster writ in the Monasticon, i. 310, where "Willem King gret Bundi stallere and Sawold sirefen and alle mine thegnes on Oxnefordesue freondlice." For the lands of Bondig in Berkshire, see Domesday, 60 b, 72 b

[3] On Eadnoth, see Domesday, 58 b, and Appendix S

[4] See vol iii p 768 On Wigod and Roger of Oily, see Appendix G.

mendation. He died before the time of the Survey, but his lands, and much more than his lands, had passed to his Norman sons-in-law, Robert of Oily and Miles Crispin, otherwise Miles of Wallingford. This was of course the most honourable way which William could find of providing for his favourites. An English heiress, the widow or daughter of a landowner who had either died in the battle or had made timely submission to William, was given in marriage to some foreign adventurer, who thus, either at once or on the death of his father-in-law, was settled in an English estate without any formal wrong or confiscation. So now Robert of Oily and his sworn brother in arms, Roger of Ivry,[1] came, like other men, to make their fortunes, and received establishments in the border shires of Wessex and Mercia. The destiny of Robert, owing probably to his marriage with Wigod's daughter, was the more brilliant of the two. His possessions in Oxford and Oxfordshire were large, and six years after William came into England, he reared, to frown over the wasted and impoverished town, that keep of Oxford which plays such a part in the wars of the next age. One of its surrounding towers still stands, a relic of days when Oxford, unknown as a seat of learning, was famous as a border fortress. He and his English wife died childless, and his inheritance at Oxford passed to the son of his brother. But the younger Robert, like his uncle, married a wife whose English name of Eadgyth makes her English descent all but certain. Robert and Eadgyth left descendants, and we may thus believe that, in a strange and indirect way, some fragments of the lands and honours of England abode in the hands of men who, by the spindle side at least, were English. Some portions too of English soil were still held by men whose descent from the ancient stock was yet more direct

---

[1] See Appendix G.

than the descent of the sons of Norman fathers and English mothers. The merits of Wigod pleaded for his kinsfolk, and one at least of them deserved at William's hands the highest rewards of faithful and really honourable service. We shall see a son of Wigod, Tokig by name, die fighting at William's side against his rebellious son.[1] His name therefore finds no place in the Survey, and his inheritance doubtless went to swell the wealth of his sisters' husbands  But two nephews of Wigod are found in Domesday,[2] and one of them appears in close and significant neighbourhood with Guy of Oily, doubtless a kinsman of Robert. As for the younger Robert and his wife, their names live in local history as the founders of that great Abbey of Oseney which was for a moment the cathedral church of the Bishoprick whose throne is now hidden in the elder minster of Saint Fritheswyth.

<small>CHAP XVII. Wigod's son Tokig and his nephews. Robert of Oily the younger founds Oseney Priory. 1129.</small>

Such is the witness of a single district to that process of confiscation and distribution of land which was now carried on through a large part of southern and eastern England. We are inclined to wonder at first sight that such wholesale robbery could be endured for a moment, that every inch of ground was not disputed in arms, that every hedge was not defended as a palisade, that every field did not become a local and unrecorded Place of Battle. Several causes may help to explain the fact. Some of them are obvious enough. The English were for the moment thoroughly cowed. Their moral force was utterly broken, and in a large part of the country their physical force was utterly broken also. They had no leader, and in many districts, could Eadmund or Harold have come again, he could have gathered round him but a slender

<small>Causes of lack of resistance to the confiscation. The spirit of the people broken for the moment.</small>

[1] See Appendix G , and Chron. Wig 1079.
[2] See Appendix G.

48            THE FIRST DAYS OF WILLIAM'S REIGN.

CHAP XVII
Effects of the slaughter at Senlac

following. The land had not yet recovered from the mere carnage of the battle. Shires like Kent and Berkshire, whose men had been foremost at Senlac, were, for that very reason, less able than other shires to offer resistance after Senlac. If Wigod had had the heart to defend the bridge at Wallingford or to stand a siege within the walls of Oxford, he could no longer have summoned to his banner the Thegns and Housecarls who had gone forth to the war with Godric and Thurkill.

Effects of William's position as King

We may well forgive the surviving elders of this or that town or district if their feeling at the approach of the Conqueror was, "Behold, two Kings stood not before him, and how shall we stand?" And we must not forget that now, on William's second appearance in the shires along the Thames, William was the King. Resistance would no longer be resistance to a foreign invader, but rebellion against one whose authority, however acquired, was actually the only authority established in the country. Many, we may be sure, hastened to buy back their lands of the crowned King, who, three months before, would have been ready enough to lift their axes against the invading Duke. Herein we see how

Affectation of strict legality in the confiscations.

William's policy helped him no less than his arms. And his policy helped him again in the particular bounds which he set to his confiscations and in the way in which they were carried out. Everything, we may be sure, was scrupulously done according to the letter of the Law, as William chose to understand the Law. His panegyrist, who does not directly mention the confiscation, implies it, and he also implies its nature, when he tells us that William at this time gave nothing to any Frenchman which was unjustly taken from an Englishman.[1] This, we be sure, is strictly true in the sense in which it is meant.

[1] Will Pict 148 "Nulli Gallo datum est quod Anglo cuiquam injuste fuerit ablatum"

William, beyond all doubt, no less than Henry the Eighth, did everything in strictly legal form. We see that irregular seizures of land did take place, at least in after times. But we also see that, whether the injured party was the King himself, or a foreign settler, or a native Englishman, the wrong is in every case alike reported in the Survey as a wrong. We may be sure that no such illegal occupations were made by William's knowledge during his first progress, however soon they may have begun when his back was turned and when Odo and William Fitz-Osbern reigned in his stead. And there is no need to think that all the land, even in the southern shires, which the Survey shows to have passed from Englishmen to foreigners passed from them during the first months of William's reign. The confiscation began now as the punishment of the great treason done on Senlac, but it was continued from time to time as excuses were given for it by the various local risings and disturbances of later years. William no doubt at once seized the lands of Harold and his family, of Godric, Thurkill, and others whose estates were large, and who had been foremost in what he called rebellion. But many a man who appears in Domesday as holding under King Eadward, but whose lands had passed to another at the time of the Survey, must have had them granted back again by William in his first days and must have lost them on account of his share in some later insurrection. And it must be remembered that, in taking Berkshire as my type, I have purposely taken a strong case, and that there were other shires in which the proportion of land finally retained by Englishmen was much greater. But, in any case, whatever was done was done in a regular and legal way. And this must have done something to raise men's spirits again, and to lead them to put some sort of trust in the new government. It was plain that, though the rule of King William was

*Chap. xvii.*

Mere violent seizures not encouraged by William.

The actual confiscation and redistribution done gradually.

Effects of the outward conformity to Law.

VOL. IV.                E

likely to be stern and exacting, yet it was not likely to be, at any rate by King William's own will, a reign of mere lawless violence. At all events, not a drop of blood was shed, and that was something, when men looked back to the beginning of the days of Cnut. A vast extent of land was seized, but it was seized in all legal form; a large portion was granted out to foreign landowners, but that too was granted out in all legal form. For the rest, the Englishman who got back his land under King William's writ and seal, even if he had to pay a mark or two of gold for the favour, most likely went back to his house rejoicing. He had been in the mouth of the lion, and he had come forth unhurt. His good success with one who might have harried his lands with fire and sword, who might have doomed himself to death or bondage, must have made him, at least in these earlier days of William's reign, disposed to be thankful that his lot was not far harder than it was.

But there were other and deeper causes at work which made the change easier to work than it would be in our time, and which also made it seem less strange and monstrous than it would seem in our time. Nothing is more repulsive to modern ideas than the confiscation of private property under any circumstances. Except in a few extreme cases, except under a few special tyrannies, the tenure of a private estate lives through both domestic revolution and foreign conquest. No conqueror of our days would dream of confiscating the lands of every man who had served in the army which he had overcome. And in the internal affairs of civilized states there is a deep and growing feeling against confiscation in any shape, against punishing the children for the sins of the fathers, even against making the rights of the individual give way to the needs of the commonwealth. As for wrongs done by individuals to each other, it would be a thing unheard of in

England or in any other civilized country, for the lands of a private owner or of an ecclesiastical corporation to be seized without process of law by the steward of a neighbouring Duke or Earl. Now on all these points the circumstances and the feelings of the men of the eleventh century were wholly different from our own. Confiscation, a word which is so frightful a bugbear to most modern ears,[1] was nothing strange or monstrous to them. The name might be unknown; but they were familiar with the thing in all manner of shapes, just and unjust, legal and illegal. Confiscation was the received punishment for all manner of crimes, moral as well as political; it was the doom of the adulterer no less than the doom of the traitor.[2] Every revolution in the state, even every change analogous to what we should call a change of ministry, was not indeed, as in the fifteenth, sixteenth, and seventeenth centuries, accompanied by the slaughter of the defeated party, but it was commonly accompanied by their banishment and forfeiture. All the lands of the House of Godwine which William now seized on had been already seized and restored in the days of Eadward. Even women of the highest rank were no more secure than other folk. Eadgyth, who now sat at Winchester in queenly wealth and honour, had, in the days of her own husband, been driven thence despoiled of her lands and goods. Her predecessor Emma had twice undergone the same doom, once at the hands of an

*Confiscation an usual punishment,*

*and the usual result of a political revolution.*

*Case of Godwine*

*Cases of Emma and Eadgyth*

---

[1] "Confiscation" of course strictly means forfeiture to the royal Treasury, whether such forfeiture be just or unjust. In modern language the word always seems to be used in an odious sense, and it is even vulgarly used as a mere equivalent for robbery.

[2] See vol. i p. 341. Compare the entry in Domesday (1) among the customs of Dover and Kent; "De adulterio per totum Chent habet Rex hominem et Archiepiscopus mulierem." So Cod Dipl iii 145, in a deed of Eadgar, where a certain Ælfred loses lands held of the see of Winchester for adultery, "Is equidem insipiens, adulterans, stuprum, propriam religiose pactatam abominans, scortum diligens, libidinose commisit Quo reatu omni substantiâ peculiali recte privatus est" The whole story is curious

CHAP. XVII. enemy and once at the hands of a son. As for irregular and illegal occupations of land, made more commonly, it would seem, by the agents of powerful men than by the powerful men themselves, we have abundant instances of such deeds of wrong, alike in the days of Eadward and in the days of William. Men no doubt complained of such wrongs, and sought redress at the hands of the Law; but their complaints were often made in vain, and the Law was not always strong enough to punish the wrongdoer. In all these ways men had become accustomed to see land transferred from one holder to another in arbitrary, and often illegal, ways. After so great a revolution as that which had set William on the throne, a confiscation on a great scale was in truth a thing naturally to be looked for. It might be looked forward to with dread; it might be looked back upon with bitterness and with hopes of revenge. But it could not be looked on as anything strange or unnatural, when every man of mature years must have remembered the same process happening on a smaller scale at the outlawries of Osgod Clapa, of Swegen, of Godwine, and of Ælfgar.

Cases of illegal occupation by Reeves.

The confiscation a thing to be looked for under the circumstances

Special case of the settlement of foreigners

Such settlement familiar in that age

Case of the followers of Cnut

Nor was this aspect of the case essentially altered by the fact that William's confiscations were, to a great extent, confiscations of the lands of Englishmen for the behoof of foreigners. Even in this there was nothing new. Men had been used to the establishment of foreigners in the land, ever since the days when Hugh the French churl had shown himself so poor a defender of the walls of Exeter.[1] Old men might remember those later days when Danish Earls and Danish Thegns were established in England, and when English nobles and even English Æthelings died by the hands either of the hangman or of the assassin.[2] With such memories as these in their minds,

[1] See vol i p 346
[2] See above, pp 12, 17. Compare the words of William of Poitiers, 145;

they might be thankful that their present conqueror was satisfied with seizing on lands, and did not go on to shed blood.[1] Men whose memories did not go so far back as this could still remember to how great an extent English lands and honours had been parted out among the foreign favourites of Eadward. They could remember the evil deeds of the castle-builders in Herefordshire and the flight of the foreign Bishops through the eastern gate of London.[2] And of those foreign favourites some were still in the land, some still held English lands and honours. Robert the son of Wymarc, Staller and Sheriff of the East-Saxons, is perhaps not to be reckoned as an enemy of England. His unlucky counsel to William on his landing was forgotten or forgiven. His estates were largely increased by grants from the Conqueror, and were handed on to his son Swegen.[3] Regenbald the Chancellor[4] kept at once his temporal estates and his ecclesiastical benefices. And, worse than all, the original sinners of the Herefordshire border, Richard and his son Osbern, were still lords of English soil and holders of English offices, ready to play their part in the work of conquest which still had to go on. With such men as these already in the land, the establishment of William's foreign followers in England was simply a large addition made to a class whose presence Englishmen had already learned, if not to love, at least to endure.

Favourites of Eadward continued under William.

Osbern of Herefordshire.

In all these various ways, the first confiscations of William

---

"Nobilissimos tuorum [he is apostrophizing England] filiorum, juvenes ac senes, Chunutus Danus trucidavit nimiâ crudelitate, ut sibi ac liberis suis te subigeret. Hic [Willelmus] ne Heraldum vellet occubuisse."

[1] See vol. ii. p. 266.  [2] See vol. ii p. 331

[3] On Robert and Swegen see Appendix H

[4] For his Berkshire holdings, see above, p 41 He appears as "Rainbaldus presbyter" in Wiltshire, 68 b, Buckinghamshire, 146, Gloucestershire, 166 b The Buckinghamshire estate he had himself held T.R E, but the lands in Herefordshire, 180 b, which "Reinbaldus Canceler" had held T R E, had been exchanged with Earl William of Hereford, and were held by the King at the time of the Survey.

would not seem at the time either so strange or so hateful as a spoliation of the same sort would seem in our own day. But they must have caused much sorrow and awakened much indignation. For the moment men who had lost heart endured this along with the other scourges of the Conquest. Presently they strove to redress the wrong, but by that time the yoke of the stranger was too tightly fixed upon their necks.

Effects of the confiscation on the permanence of the Conquest.

There can be little doubt that it was to this great transfer of lands from Englishmen to strangers that the Norman Conquest of England owed its distinguishing character. This was the cause, more than any one cause, which made the Norman Conquest so thorough and so lasting in one point of view, so transitory, if we look at it from another. It was the master-piece of William's policy of outward legality. He did not remain a mere conqueror at the head of a foreign army, holding his new Kingdom by main force, and liable to be driven out whenever the whole nation should join together in one sudden and vigorous uprising. Himself, in his own reading of the Law, a lawful King, he would turn the followers by whose swords he had won his Crown into supporters of his throne, bearing a more lawful and peaceful character than that of mere foreign soldiers. The King by the edge of the sword changed himself in all outward show into a King according to the laws of England, and by the same process his foreign knights and men-at-arms were changed into English landowners, holding the soil of England according to English Law. He had his garrison in every corner of the land, but his garrison was formed of the chief lords of the soil and of the chief tenants who held under them.

Position of William's grantees in England.

Such a garrison was harder to drive out than any mere army. Each detachment of William's great army of occupation was weak and isolated; but in its very weakness and isolation lay its strength.  To have cut off every Norman lord and his Norman retainers throughout the length and breadth of England would have been a far harder work, and would have called for a far larger exercise both of concert and of secrecy, than to storm any fortress or to defeat any army in the field.  Something of the kind had been done in the great massacre of the Danes under Æthelred, but the Danes who were then cut off must have been gathered together in bodies at particular places.  They were not settled, each man in an English home, from one end of England to the other. Such a garrison as William planted in England could never be driven out, but for that very cause it soon ceased to be a garrison at all.  The Norman landowner held his lands on the same tenure and according to the same law as his English neighbour.  Each alike held them according to the ancient Law of England.  Each alike held them as a gift from the same hand, as a grant from the bounty of King William.  In a generation or two the stranger ceased to be a stranger.  The foreign spoiler, as he must have once seemed to English eyes, insensibly changed into the son of the soil, an Englishman who knew no home but England.  William divided the lands of England among his followers, to secure his own throne and to hold the people of England in his obedience.  The not remote descendants of those on whom he laid this duty became the champions of the land which their fathers had conquered, the men who stood forth to curb the pride of Kings who sat on William's throne, and to save the lands of England from being again parted out as the spoil of the Poitevin and the Brabançon.

The incidental witness of our authorities has thus enabled us to put together a picture of a part of William's policy, of which the chroniclers of his actions give us nothing

CHAP. XVII.

Land largely retained by its actual possessors

Dealings with the Abbeys of Peterborough and New Minster.

William's wrath at the election of Brand.

Reconciliation between the King and the Abbot,

beyond hints and dark allusions. We must however bear in mind that in this its first stage the confiscation probably extended only to those who had actually fought against William before his coronation. It is plain that the living who submitted for the most part retained their lands, even though their tenure might be changed and the restitution not made without a price paid to the new lord. Confiscation of this kind was mainly confiscation against the dead, though, as in all such cases, it was the living heir who really suffered. But how rigorous William deemed it his policy to be in pressing what he professed to look on as his right is shown by his dealings even with ecclesiastical bodies. Two of the greatest monasteries in England lay specially open to his wrath. We have seen how the Abbots of Peterborough and New Minster, Leofric the nephew of Earl Leofric and Ælfwig the brother of Earl Godwine, had given their lives in the cause of England.[1] And the brotherhood of either house was in William's eyes as guilty as its chief. Twelve monks of the New Minster had been found among the slain at Senlac,[2] and the convent of the Golden Borough had done a deed of treason well nigh as dark in William's eyes by sending the Abbot chosen in Leofric's place to seek the royal confirmation at the hands of the English Ætheling.[3] There seems to have been something specially galling to William in this quiet ignoring of his claims. The monks of Peterborough had not even waited to see what would be the final end of the strife. They had shut their eyes to the presence of the Conqueror in the land, and had dealt with the uncrowned Eadgar as already King. What followed is best told in the words of the local Chronicler. "When that King William heard that saying he was very wroth, and said that the Abbot had done despite to him. Then went good men between

---

[1] See vol. iii. pp. 426, 501.   [2] See vol. iii. p. 426.
[3] See vol. iii. p. 530.

## WILLIAM'S DEALINGS WITH PETERBOROUGH.

them and reconciled them, because that the Abbot was a good man. Then gave he to the King forty marks of gold for reconciliation."[1]

The wrath of William was thus turned away from the Golden Borough by a discreet employment of the wealth of Saint Peter. On the great house of Ælfred and Eadward his hand fell more heavily. Winchester, it will be borne in mind, bowed to William some while before his coronation,[2] so that he was the *de facto* ruler in the old royal city while Peterborough still looked to Eadgar as the lawful King-elect. Had the convent of the New Minster ventured on the choice of an Abbot, it must have been from William that he must have sought for confirmation. Either the monks were too utterly downcast at the fall of their country and of their own chief to risk such a step at such a moment, or else the election was directly hindered by the authority of the Conqueror. One is tempted to think that, in William's reading of the Law, the New Minster was held to fall by the treason of its Abbot, just as, in the days of Henry the Eighth, the Abbey of Glastonbury, which never surrendered, was held to fall by the attainder of Richard Whiting.[3] At all events no capitular election was allowed for three years, and the church remained all that time without an Abbot.[4] But this was not all.

*CHAP. XVII.*

*large price paid for William's pardon.*

*William's dealings with the New Minster.*

*No successor to Ælfwig elected.*

---

[1] Chron. Petrib. 1066 "Þa þe cyng Willelm geherde þæt secgen, þa wearð he swiðe wrað, and sæde þæt se Abbot him hæfde forsegon Þa eodon gode men heom betwenen, and sahtloden heom, forðan þæt se abbot wæs goddera manne Geaf þa þone cyng xl. marc goldes to sahtnysse" That this is the right time (see vol iii p 530) for this story is plain from what follows, "þa lifede he [Brand] litle hwile þæræfter, buton þry gear." Brand died (Chron Petrib 1069) November 27th, 1069 The only question then is whether William's dealings with Peterborough were not before his coronation But the use of the word *King* seems to forbid this

[2] See vol. iii. p. 540

[3] Compare the suppression of Leominster on account of the misconduct of Eadgifu See vol. ii p 89.

[4] See the reference in vol. ii p 644, and Mon. Angl ii 428-431

CHAP. XVII.
Confiscation of lands belonging to the Abbey.

A large part of the possessions of the monastery were seized by the new King—William the Tyrant, as the local historian emphatically calls him [1]—and granted out to his followers. A legend, conceived in the same spirit of grim pleasantry as so many other tales about the Conqueror, describes him as saying that he punished the crime of the Abbot by the confiscation of a barony and the crime of the twelve monks by the confiscation of an equal number of manors.[2] Nay more; the two minsters of Winchester, Old and New, stood in awkward neighbourhood to each other, so much so that the singing of the worshippers in the one is said to have disturbed the devotions of the worshippers in the other. The newer foundation was cabined, cribbed, and confined in a very narrow space between the cathedral church and the buildings of the city. William still further narrowed the dwelling-place of the monks of New Minster by seizing part of their precinct for the site of a palace for himself, the walls of which almost touched the west front of the church [3] Such a royal dwelling-place was specially needed in a city which, under William, recovered some of the dignity which it had lost under Eadward and Harold. The older palace of the West-Saxon Kings had become

William's palace at Winchester encroaches on the monastery.

---

[1] T. Rudborne, Hist. Maj. Wint ap Ang Sacr 1 249 "Wilhelmus Conquæstor illud ab ipso monasterio rapuit injuste et militibus suis tradidit. Consimili modo se habuit *Wilhelmus Tyrannus* aliis monasteriis et cæteris nobilibus Angliæ"

[2] In the document called "Destructio Monasterii de Hidâ" (Mon. Angl ii. 437, see vol. ii p 644) we read, "Anno regni suo tertio mare transiit, ducens secum ecclesiæ prædictæ thesauros, qui, in brevi rediens, dicti monasterii, videlicet pro Abbate baroniam unam et pro singulis monachis qui cum Abbate contra dictum Regem in bellum processerunt, singula feoda militum arripuit, militibus qui cum eo venerant conferendis." The date at least is wrong.

[3] See the *plan* in Edwards' Liber de Hydâ, p xli Of this palace no trace remains A royal house, as distinguished from a castle, of William's reign would have been a precious addition to our knowledge of domestic antiquities

the dwelling-place of the royal widows Emma and Eadgyth, and nothing could be further from William's purpose than in any way to disturb the relict of his revered predecessor and lord.[1] But William's wrath against the offending house seems gradually to have relaxed. In the third year he allowed the election of an Abbot, whose name of Wulfric moreover proclaims him to have been an Englishman, and whose deposition, three years later again, awakens an interest in his favour.[2] And it appears that some parts of the alienated lands were in the course of William's reign restored to the Abbey, and other lands granted to it, some of them expressly in exchange for the ground alienated for the building of the palace.[3]

*Election of Abbot Wulfric. 1069.*

*Partial restoration to the Abbey.*

Besides these seizures of landed property, William also possessed himself of great moveable wealth from various sources. The native Chronicler simply tells us that he laid a very heavy tax upon all men.[4] But the expressions

*Taxes and offerings received by William*

---

[1] In the Liber Winton (Domesday, iv 535) we read, "domus Emmæ Reginæ fuit quieta T R. E et modo est quieta." The palace kept the name of the first Old Lady who held it.

[2] See Edwards, Liber de Hydâ, xli , Appendix to Winchester Chronicle, Thorpe, i 386

[3] Edwards, ib ; Domesday, 43 Two of the new grants, Alton and Clere, are expressly said to have belonged to Eadgyth, who had a house at Clere—"ibi fuit aula " These grants therefore could not have been made till some years later, when the Lady was dead But Clere is expressly said to have been given as a recompense for the site of the palace ; " Hoc dedit ecclesiæ W. Rex pro excambio terræ in quâ domus Regis est in civitate." Of another place, Laverstock, we find this curious notice, "Ulveva *Beteslau* tenuit de abbatiâ usque ad obitum Post mortem ejus reddidit Rex W hoc manerium eidem ecclesiæ pro suâ animâ et uxoris ejus." The King therefore had some claim after the death of Wulfgifu. Was she one of the widows of men slain at Senlac, who were allowed to keep their lands as alms ? Of the mysterious and Slavonic-sounding name *Beteslau*, which seems also to have puzzled Mr Edwards, I can give no account.

[4] Chron. Wig. 1066 (just after the account of the coronation oath), "swa þeah leide gyld on mannum swiðe stið." William of Poitiers, on the other hand, says (147), "Tributis et cunctis ad regium fiscum reddendis

of writers on the other side may lead us to think that the legal subtlety of William had forestalled another device of later times, and that what those who paid looked on simply as a tax was clothed in the eyes of those who received it with the milder form of a *benevolence*. Cities and rich men made bountiful offerings to the new King.[1] So churches and monasteries were equally liberal to one whose fresh gifts abundantly made up for whatever he took away.[2] It is not perfectly clear whether these offerings are to be looked on as something distinct from the sums paid for the redemption of lands or as another way of describing them.[3] We hear also of the rich hoards of Harold, of the goodly things of various kinds gathered in his treasure-house, which the wide-spread commerce of England had brought together from all parts of the world.[4] These expressions of course fall in with those stories of Harold's greediness and parsimony of which we have heard already.[5] Here, as elsewhere, we need some less suspicious witness than that of Norman panegyrists and legend-makers before we see anything in these tales beyond a wise economy. Certain it is that, afterwards at least, no one laid himself more open to the

---

modum qui non gravaret posuit " This however, whatever truth we may choose to see in it, is probably meant to refer to regular and permanent taxation, while the words of the Chronicler suggest a single extraordinary payment.

[1] Will Pict 144 "Id munificentiæ studium adjuvit non modicus census, quem undique civitates et locupletes quique obtulerant novitio domino."

[2] Ib 155 "Abundantes ecclesiæ transmarinæ aliqua ei libentes quæ in Galliam transferret dederunt, quoniam ea multiplo redemit rebus aliis"

[3] On the redemption, see above, p 25 It is possible that the two Chroniclers may mean the same thing by two such different forms of expression

[4] Will Pict 143 "In hujus ergo Imperatoris [Regis Regum sc ] quasi tributum large erogavit quod Heraldi Regis ærarium avare inclusit. Terræ illi sua fertilitate opimæ uberiorem opulentiam comportare soliti sunt negotiatores gaza advectitia Maximi numero, genere, artificio, thesauri compositi fuerant, aut custodiendi ad vanum gaudium avaritiæ, aut luxu Anglico turpiter consumendi "   [5] See vol iii. pp. 422, 423, 629.

charge of greediness than William himself.[1] Now however, according to his own laureate, he showed nothing but bounty. Of the wealth which came into his hands from all these sources, part went to reward the companions of his warfare, but far more, we are told, to the poor and to monasteries and churches, seemingly in England as well as beyond sea.[2] But these last were naturally the chief objects of his thankfulness and bounty. First of all came the mother of all churches, the church to whose approval it might be almost said to be owing that he held the Crown of England at all. Words, we are told, would fail to describe the wealth, in gold and silver and precious objects of all kinds, which King William sent as his thank-offering to Pope Alexander.[3] The New Rome herself—a witness to the place which the New Rome still held in the minds of men—would have wondered at the gifts which the Conqueror poured into the lap of the Old.[4] One gift was precious above all, alike from its intrinsic value and as a record of the victory which had been won. In return for the consecrated banner which Toustain had borne beside him at Senlac, William now sent the fallen gonfanon of Harold, on which the skill of English hands had so vainly wrought the golden form of the Fighting Man.[5]

*chap xvii.*
William's distribution of his wealth

His gifts to foreign Churches

Harold's standard sent to Rome

---

[1] Chron Petrib 1087 "He wæs on gitsunge befeallan, and grædinæsse he lufode mid ealle" This is another story from what William of Poitiers tells us (146), "Nam, uti adversus libidines alias, ita adversus avaritiam invictum animum gerebat"

[2] Will. Pict 144 "Quorum partem ad ministros confecti belli magnifice erogavit, plurima ac pretiosissima egenis et monasteriis diversarum provinciarum distribuit"

[3] Ib. "Romanæ Ecclesiæ sancti Petri pecuniam in auro atque argento ampliorem quam dictu credibile sit."

[4] Ib "Ornamenta quæ Byzantium percara haberet in manum Alexandri Papæ transmisit"

[5] Ib "Memorabile quoque vexillum Heraldi, hominis armati imaginem intextam habens ex auro purissimo [see vol iii p 475], quo spolio

CHAP. XVII.

*Gifts to churches in various parts of Gaul.*

The churches of all the lands whence soldiers had flocked to his standard, or where prayers had been put up for his success, were enriched with the holy spoils of conquered England. The gifts which William bestowed on the smallest monastery were gifts which a metropolitan church would not have despised.[1] Golden crosses studded with jewels, precious vestments, chalices of gold, even ingots of the same costly metal,[2] were scattered at William's bidding through the churches of France, Aquitaine, Burgundy, and Auvergne.[3] But precious

*Gifts to the churches of Normandy.*

above all were the gifts which his own Normandy received from the hands of her son and sovereign. The colds and storms of January did not hinder him from sending messengers across the sea, who at once announced his elevation, and who with the news bore the thank-offerings of the King and Conqueror to the holy places

*Public joy in Normandy at William's coronation.*

of his own land.[4] Every loyal Norman heart beat high with joy at the news that Duke William had become a King.[5] He himself seems to have been eager

pro munere ejusdem Apostolici benignitate sibi misso par redderet; simul et triumphum de tyranno Romæ ulteriusque optatum pulcre judicaret."

[1] Will. Pict 144 "Splendide adornaret metropolitanam basilicam, quod minimum in his donis cœnobolum aliquod lætificavit."

[2] Ib "Aliæ cruces aureas admodum grandes insigniter gemmatas, pleræque libras auri vel ex eodem metallo vasa, nonnullæ pallia vel pretiosum aliud quid accepere" These things were evidently among the pretended gifts of the English monasteries which I have mentioned just before

[3] Ib. "Mille ecclesiis Franciæ, Aquitaniæ, Burgundiæ, necnon Arverniæ, aliarumque regionum perpetuo celebre erit Willelmi Regis memoriale." Benoît (37882) oddly changes Auvergne into Saxony;

"N'out en France riche moster,        Où il n'enveiast ses presenz
N'en Aquitaine n'en Borgoigne,        Riches e precios e jenz "
Ne par tot ci que vers Saissoigne,

[4] Will. Pict 144 "Munera quidem gratissima Normanniæ advenerunt a suo dulci nato, pio patre, festinante affectu missa, quum sævitia temporis atque maris, intrante Januario, esset acerrima "

[5] Ib. 145. "Nullus umquam illuxit ei [Normanniæ] dies lætior, quam quum certo rescivit Principem suum, *auctorem sui quieti status*, Regem esse." He goes on with much more in the same strain, but the words which I have put in Italics form William's real title to honour.

to visit his native land in all the glory of conquest and in all the splendour of his new rank. His first stay in England took up less than three months from the day of his coronation, less than six months from the day of his first landing at Pevensey.

*CHAP XVII.*
*He prepares to visit Normandy.*

But, before he ventured to leave his new Kingdom, William had to take measures for its government and defence during his absence. We must here remember his position. He was King over all England, inasmuch as there was no other King, inasmuch as the chief men of all England had outwardly become his men. But he was in actual possession of only a small part of the country. It is not easy to trace the exact extent of the fully conquered territory. The south-eastern shires, Sussex and the Earldom of Leofwine, were, I need not say, hopelessly in the grasp of the Conqueror. Kent and Sussex, above all, had not only seen the flower of their inhabitants cut off in the great battle; they had seen every inch of their territory, ecclesiastical estates alone excepted, portioned out among foreign masters. Not a rood of ground in those shires remained in the hands of an English tenant-in-chief of the King.[1] Westwards we have traced William in person as far as Wallingford, and by his representatives as far as Winchester. There is therefore no doubt as to the submission of Hampshire, Berkshire, and part of Oxfordshire; as to the town of Oxford itself the evidence is far from clear.[2] On the other hand Exeter, and with it Devonshire and Cornwall, was still untouched. In Herefordshire and on the Welsh border the state of things was very unsettled. The Norman colony, planted in that region by Eadward and so strangely tolerated by Harold, was still doing its

*Extent of his occupation of England*

*Districts still independent*

*State of Herefordshire*

---

[1] In Kent and Sussex we find none of the class of King's Thegns of whom I have already spoken in Berkshire. See above, p. 34, and Appendix E.     [2] See Appendix G., Z

64     THE FIRST DAYS OF WILLIAM'S REIGN.

CHAP. XVII work. Osbern, it will be remembered, had been Sheriff under Eadward, even when Harold was Earl of the shire,[1] and his father Richard, the old offender, still lived. Their own Richard's Castle was a ready-made outpost of the Norman King. And by some means, doubtless through Osbern's office of Sheriff, they were also in command of the city of Hereford, where, probably under Osbern's hands, a castle had now sprung up.[2] But the most powerful Englishman in those parts, Eadric the Wild, who bears the title of Child and is described as the son of Ælfric the brother of Eadric Streona,[3] had refused to submit,[4] and it is needless to say that no homage has been received from the Welsh Princes. Of the remaining shires of Harold's own Earldom, Gloucester, Somerset, Dorset, and Wiltshire, our accounts are less certain. Wiltshire had probably submitted along with Hampshire and Berkshire, but Somersetshire and Dorsetshire, there can be little doubt, still held out. In the central and northern part of England it does not seem that William had taken a single step to secure submission beyond receiving the homage of their Earls and reinstating them in their offices. In the East of England William's dominion was secured by the possession of Norwich, the chief town of the Earldom of Gyrth.[5] In short the state of things seems roughly to have been

Resistance of Eadric.

Somersetshire and Dorsetshire untouched.

East-Anglia occupied.

[1] See vol ii p. 346, and above, p. 53

[2] Florence (1067) speaks of the "Herefordenses castellani et Richardus filius Scrob" as the opponents of Eadric. I could almost have fancied that the words "Herefordenses castellani" referred to "the castle" in Herefordshire, that is Richard's Castle (see vol. ii. p. 138), but the words of the Worcester Chronicler, "þa castelmenn on Hereforda," seem to fix the meaning to the city itself. It is possible that Harold himself, during the Welsh war, may have found it expedient to build a castle at Hereford But it is just as likely to have been a work of Osbern himself during these first months of William's presence in England

[3] Fl Wig 1067. "Eo tempore exstitit quidam præpotens minister, Edricus, cognomento Silvaticus, filius Ælfrici, fratris Edrici Streonæ." See above, p. 21, and Appendix I.

[4] Ib "Se dedere Regi dedignabatur."          [5] See below, p. 67

on this wise. The battle of Senlac and his later cam- *Chap. XVII.* paigns and progresses had given William real possession *Analogy between* of by far the greater part of those regions of England *William's* which had been under the immediate government of the *position in January* House of Godwine. The south-western shires, the West- *1067 and* Saxon *Wealhcyn*, alone seem to have held out. William *Harold's in January 1066.* in short had stepped into the place of those whom he had himself overcome. He had become, as Harold had been, King in the fullest sense over the West-Saxons and the East-Angles. Over the districts ruled by the sons of Ælfgar he held, as Harold had held, a supremacy which the sons of Ælfgar were anxious to throw off at the first opportunity. This singular analogy between the position of Harold at the beginning of one year and the position of William at the beginning of the next is one which I have pointed out already.[1] I may add that both princes *Attempts* tried the same means, and that both tried them in vain, *of both Harold and* for securing the fidelity of the Northern Earls. The tie *William to secure the* of marriage or promised marriage was attempted in both *North by marriages* cases. But as the bridal of Ealdgyth brought no Northumbrian warriors to Harold's side at Senlac, so the promise of William's daughter to Ealdgyth's brother worked very little towards bringing the Mercian shires into practical submission to the Conqueror.

I have already shown that Harold's nominal dominion *William's* over Northumberland was changed into a reality by one *measures for the* of the most signal instances on record of the might of *security of the con-* persuasion.[2] We shall presently see that William's nominal *quered shires* dominion over the same country was changed into a reality only by fire and sword. And the dominion of William over the districts where his authority was really acknowledged had, before he could venture again to cross the sea, to be secured by means of which neither Harold nor any other English King was likely to dream. I have

---

[1] See vol. iii p. 59  [2] Ib. p. 61.

CHAP. XVII.
Rarity of castles in England.

Instances at Dover, Arundel, and perhaps Hereford

Castles built by William

already spoken of the extreme rarity of castles in England before the Norman Conquest, and of the general indignation which was awakened by the building of a single castle in Herefordshire by a single Norman adventurer.[1] Harold however had not scrupled to follow the Norman example in this matter in positions where the fortress would act, not as a centre of oppression against Englishmen, but as a defence against invading enemies. He had, as we have seen, built the famous castle at Dover;[2] it is possible that he had built one at Hereford,[3] and it seems likely that he had also built another at Arundel. Domesday at least bears its witness to the existence of a castle there in the days of King Eadward,[4] a solitary instance in the whole course of the Survey. But now the age of castle-building fairly set in. It was William's policy to keep the conquered land in check by commanding every town and every important point by one of these fortresses, which became in truth the fetters of England.[5] We have already seen him begin the work on the heights of Hastings,[6] and go on with it in the greatest city of the land.[7] And, as we follow his steps, we shall see that, at every stage of the Conquest, the building of a castle in a conquered town was ever the first work of the Conqueror's foresight. Most of the castles whose foundation is distinctly recorded naturally belong to places which came into William's hands in the course of later warfare. But

---

[1] See vol. ii p 138   [2] See vol iii p 536   [3] See above, p 64
[4] Domesday, 23. "Castrum Harundel T R. E reddebat de quodam molino XL solidos" See Appendix K
[5] Ord Vit 511 C (speaking however of a somewhat later time), "Rex igitur secessus regni providentius perlustravit, et opportuna loca contra excursiones hostium communivit" So Will Gem vii 42 "Rex autem monitus quidem prudentiâ, quâ consulere in cunctis Regi novit, immunita regni providissimâ dispositione perlustravit, ac ad arcendos hostium excursus tutissima castella per opportuna loca stabilivit, quæ militum electissimo robore et uberrimâ stipendiorum copiâ munivit"
[6] See vol. iii p. 409       [7] See above, p. 19.

there were castles in Southern and Eastern England also, and it is most likely that their foundation at least, if not their completion, was among the very first works of William's reign. In one case indeed we have distinct evidence of the fact. The borough of Norwich, not yet an episcopal city, was, as we have seen,[1] one of the chief among English towns, the chiefest by far in its own quarter of England, the capital of the Earldom held successively by Harold, Ælfgar, and Gyrth. It had now fully recovered from the damage which it had suffered in the wars of Swend and Ulfcytel.[2] The Norman panegyrist speaks of it as a noble and powerful city, inhabited by rich, daring, and he is pleased to add faithless, citizens.[3] In King Eadward's reign the burghers of Norwich had reached the great number of thirteen hundred.[4] It stood at no great distance from the sea which separated, or rather united, England and Denmark, and the citizens, like the rest of the men of East-Anglia, had no doubt a strong Danish element among them. Norwich was therefore a point which called for special attention at the hands of a conqueror whose Crown might at any moment

*CHAP XVII*

*Condition of Norwich, its wealth, population, and military importance*

---

[1] Vol i. p 350        [2] Ib p. 351.
[3] Will. Pict 148  "Guenta urbs est nobilis atque valens Cives ac finitimos habet divites, infidos, et audaces"  "Guenta" would of course, if there were no reason to the contrary, mean Winchester, *Venta Belgarum*, but the description given of its position shows that the Archdeacon must have taken a classical fit, and that he means *Venta Icenorum*, of which Norwich, though not exactly on the site, may fairly pass as a representative Benoît however, in translating William of Poitiers (37949), says,

"Guincestre ert mult noble cite," &c.

[4] Domesday, ii 116. "In Norvic erant tempore Regis E MCCCXX" The numbers had sadly dwindled at the time of the Survey  In 116 b we read, "Modo sunt in burgo DCLXV burgenses Anglici et consuetudines reddunt, et CCCLXXX bordarii qui propter pauperiem nullam reddunt consuetudinem, et in illâ terrâ quam tenebant Stigandus T R E manent modo ex illis superioribus XXXVIIII burgenses .. et in illâ terrâ de quâ Heroldus habebat socam sunt XV burgenses"

68                THE FIRST DAYS OF WILLIAM'S REIGN.

CHAP XVII  be threatened by a Scandinavian rival.¹ A fortress was
Building of the castle  therefore built within the walls of the city,² a fact which
at once shows that the city itself was already fortified, and that the new fortress was mainly intended as a curb upon the citizens themselves. Whether William's present work was really the beginning of the great fortress whose shell still survives, or whether all that was now done was to provide in a hasty way for the needs of the moment, is a question which may be left to local inquirers.
Other castles in South-Eastern England.  In the course of William's reign other castles arose within the limits of the territory which was already subdued, at Canterbury, Rochester, Bramber, Lewes, Carisbroke, Wallingford, and Windsor, the last being the most famous and abiding of all.³ Of most of these it is probable that the beginnings at least belong to this early stage of William's reign, but all or most of them have either perished or survive only in the form of representatives of later date  The present keep of Rochester above all is the noblest example of the Norman military architecture
Commanders from "Gaul" placed in the castles  of the next generation. In all these castles we are told that William placed trusty and valiant captains, who had come with him from Gaul, at the head of large forces of horse and foot.⁴ The expression "from Gaul" is remarkable. It is a witness to the importance of the force
Import of the phrase; importance of the  which William had drawn from lands beyond the bounds of his own Duchy. The foreign, especially the Breton,

---

¹ Will Pict. 149  "Danos in auxilium citius recipere potest  A mari, quod Anglos a Danis separat, millia passuum quatuordecim distat"

² Ib  "Hujus quoque urbis intra mœnia munitionem construxit"  So Ord. Vit. 506 B.  "Intra mœnia Guentæ opibus et munimine nobilis urbis et mari contiguæ, validam arcem construxit." This almost looks as if the famous castle of later times was now at least begun, though the words may merely refer to some temporary predecessor

³ On these castles, see Appendix K.

⁴ Will Pict. 148.  "Custodes in castellis strenuos viros collocavit, ex Gallis traductos, quorum fidei pariter ac virtuti credebat, cum multitudine peditum et equitum."

auxiliaries, must, at this stage of the Conquest, have been numerous and formidable, and we shall see that, later in his reign, William was well pleased to get rid of them. To encourage the commanders of these fortresses under the toils and dangers which, peaceful as the country seemed, it was assumed that they would still have to undergo, they were endowed by the King with wealthy fiefs.[1] It is now that we are assured that, among all William's grants of this kind, nothing was given to a Frenchman which was unjustly taken from an Englishman.[2] That is, as I have already explained it, William despoiled none of his new subjects, except those who, whether dead or alive, were, in his reading of the Law, justly liable to the penalties of treason.[3]

*CHAP XVII.*

*foreign auxiliaries at this time.*

*Grants of land to William's officers.*

Among these faithful servants of the Conqueror who were thus set to bear rule over Englishmen, or more truly to hold Englishmen in check, two claim special notice, both from the place which they have already held in our narrative and from the office which they were now called upon to fill. High above all those whom William put in places of trust, he chose as his special lieutenants and representatives in absence his brother and his chosen friend. The rule of the conquered land was entrusted to William Fitz-Osbern, the man who had done more than any other man to bring about the invasion of England,[4] and to Bishop Odo of Bayeux, who had had, next to the Conqueror himself, the greatest share in making the invasion successful. The panegyrist of William tells us that he knew his namesake, the son of Osbern, to be specially dear to the Normans and specially dreaded by the English.[5]

*The supreme command given to Bishop Odo and William Fitz-Osbern*

---

[1] Will Pict 148. "Ipsis opulenta beneficia distribuit, pro quibus labores ac pericula libentibus animis tolerarent"

[2] See the extract from William of Poitiers in p. 48

[3] See above, p 24

[4] See vol iii p. 296

[5] Will Pict 149 "Hunc Normannis carissimum, Anglis maximo terrori

70                THE FIRST DAYS OF WILLIAM'S REIGN.

CHAP. XVII Of Odo, on the other hand, we are told that, dear as he was to Normans and Bretons, even the English themselves were not such barbarians as to fail to appreciate him. They saw that, whether as Prelate or as temporal ruler, he was entitled not only to their fear but to their reverence and love.[1] These two specially favoured chiefs were invested with English Earldoms, and were entrusted with a general command over the whole of the conquered country. But, even at this early time, William began that policy of division which has affected the whole course of English history since. In the Northern part of England, where his power was purely nominal, he was constrained for a season to leave the successors of Leofric and Siward in possession of the vast governments held by their predecessors. But, within that part of the land which was really his own, William was not going to allow the growth of any power, even in the hands of those dearest to him, which had the faintest chance of becoming dangerous to his own. There was no longer to be an Earl of the West-Saxons or an Earl of the East-Angles, wielding the vast powers and ruling over the vast territory which had been held by the Earls of the Houses of Godwine and Leofric. Returning in this to earlier English practice, the Earl under William was to have the rule of a single shire only, or if two shires were ever set under one Earl, they were at least not to be adjoining shires. The results of this change have been of the highest moment. This one resolution of the Conqueror

*Earldoms given to William Fitz-Osbern and Odo William's policy with regard to Earldoms.*

*Earls appointed for single shires*

*Results of the change*

esse sciebat" He enlarges on William Fitz-Osbern's merits and on the friendship which had lasted between him and the Duke from their earliest days

[1] Will Pict 150 After a long panegyric on Odo, he winds up, "Libentes eidem obsequebantur, ut acceptissimo domino, Normanni atque Britanni. Nec Angli adeo barbari fuerunt, quin facile intelligerent hunc præsulem, hunc præfectum, merito timendum esse, venerandum quoque ac diligendum"

did more than any other one cause to make England an united Kingdom, and to keep it from falling asunder like France and Germany. The Duke of the Normans and the King of the English had widely different interests. William would not run the faintest chance of having such a feudatory in his own Kingdom as his own lord the King of the French had in William's own person. A Norman Earl of all Wessex, feeling himself in truth Earl by the edge of the sword, might well have forgotten that the Law of England looked on him simply as a magistrate accountable to the King and his Witan, and, under a King who showed the least weakness, he might have found opportunities of growing into a territorial prince. But William the Great never showed weakness in any matter, and in this matter he followed a course which cut off all fear of danger. An Earl of the West-Saxons might be dangerous to the power of the King and to the unity of the Kingdom; there was no such danger in a local Earl of Kent or Hereford. William thus took care that no one man in his Kingdom should be stronger than the King. Any one noble, however powerful, could be at once overcome. This secured the unity of the Kingdom in one way. In order to resist the royal power with any hope of success, the nobles had to combine with one another and to seek for the help of the people. Thus the Old-English parliamentary instincts which the Conquest for a while checked were again awakened and strengthened, and the unity of the Kingdom was secured in another way. It was precisely because William for a while overthrew English freedom, because he knew how to win for himself such a power as no King of the English had ever held before him, that in the end national unity and national freedom appeared again in more perfect shapes than they had ever taken in the days of our old insular independence.

*The royal power strengthened and the unity of the Kingdom furthered.*

CHAP XVII.
Odo Earl of Kent;
William Fitz-Osbern Earl of Hereford.

Their joint command;

the South under Odo, the North under William.

The firstfruits of the new system were seen in the appointment of Bishop Odo to the Earldom of Kent[1] and of William Fitz-Osbern to the Earldom of Hereford.[2] The immediate and permanent authority of both was thus confined within very narrow bounds; the wider commission which they also held was a mere temporary delegation of authority during the King's absence. In this last character they seem to have been joined together as co-regents, while each had his own special province within the limits common to both.[3] The South, which, we are assured, was, through its neighbourhood and intercourse with Gaul, somewhat less savage than the rest of the island, was put under the milder rule of the Bishop.[4] It was left to the new Earl of Hereford to keep watch against the still independent North, and Norwich, with its newly rising castle, was put under his special care.[5] These two extreme points of his province, Hereford on

[1] William of Poitiers (149) implies, without directly stating, Odo's appointment as Earl, "Castrum Doveram Odoni fratri suo commisit, cum adjacente orâ australi, quæ, nomine vetusto Cantium dicta, Galliam propius spectat." The Peterborough Chronicler also calls him Earl (1087), though without naming his Earldom, "He hæfde eorldom on Englelande." His Earldom is implied in the well-known story of his seizure by his brother's orders (Will. Malm. iii. 277, Ord. Vit. 647 C), and William of Malmesbury, just before telling it, says, "Odonem, quem ad episcopatum Baiocensem provexit Comes, Comitem Cantiæ Rex instituit," as Orderic directly after the story speaks of his "comitatus Cantiæ."

[2] From the language of Orderic (521 D) one might have thought that William Fitz-Osbern did not receive the Earldom till 1070, but Florence (1067) says expressly, "Willelmum filium Osberni, quem in Herefordensi provinciâ Comitem constituerat."

[3] The joint commission of Odo and William appears faintly in the Worcester Chronicle, 1066, "and Oda Biscop and Wyllelm Eorl belifen her æfter." It is more distinct in Florence, 1067; "Fratrem suum Odonem Baiocensem et Willelmum filium Osberni Angliæ custodes relinquens." So Will. Pict. 156. "Interea Baiocensis Præsul Odo et Willelmus Osberni filius præfecturas in regno, uterque suam, laudabiliter administrabant, interdum simul agitantes, modo diversi."

[4] Will. Pict. 149. "Cantium . . . Galliam propius spectat, unde et a minus feris hominibus incolitur . . . Consueverant enim merces cum Belgis mutare."

[5] See above, p. 67. The words of William of Poitiers (149), "Ibidem

the West and Norwich on the East, show plainly how far the real dominion of William reached towards the North. The two Earls were to be the royal lieutenants during William's absence, and they were specially bidden to be diligent in the great work of securing the obedience of the land by the building of castles.[1]

Besides these two great Viceroys, we also know the names of some of the subordinate captains who held commands under them. The few whose names appear in the history were all of pure Norman birth. The Castle of Dover, the chief fortress of the government of Odo, was entrusted to the immediate care of Hugh of Montfort.[2] Of him we have heard in two widely different characters on different sides of the sea. Dover, perhaps again arising from the ruin of the Norman fire, was given to the care of the man who had so well guarded the burning streets of Mortemer. The fortress raised by the forethought of Harold was put under the rule, not of one who had met his axe face to face, but of one of the evil four who had wrought the last brutalities upon his disabled body.[3] The fortress of Hastings had, from the very day when it began to arise, been placed under the command of Humfrey the brother-in-law of the more famous Hugh of Grantmesnil.[4] His son Robert,

[Guentæ] Willelmum reliquit Osberni filium præcipuum in exercitu suo, ut in vice suâ interim toti regno Aquilonem versus præesset," show that "Guenta" cannot be Winchester

[1] Fl Wig. 1067 "Castella per loca firmari præcepit"

[2] Will Gem vii 39 "Milites Odonis Baiocasini Præsulis atque Hugonis de Monteforti, quibus custodia Dorobernia credita erat" Will Pict 157 "Munitiones custodes Præsul Baiocensis atque Hugo de Monteforti"

[3] On the doings of Hugo of Montfort at Mortemer and Senlac, see vol iii pp 155, 287, 499.

[4] Ord Vit 512 B "Sororius ejus [Hugonis de Grantemaisnil] Unfridus de Telliolo, qui Hastingas a primâ die constructionis ad custodiendum susceperat." See also 600 C In 669 C we read of his son Robert, "Umfridus pater ejus fuit filius Amfridi de progenie Dacorum Adeliza

74  THE FIRST DAYS OF WILLIAM'S REIGN.

CHAP. XVII.

Hugh of Grantmesnil at Winchester

known afterwards as Robert of Rhuddlan, had been one of the Norman favourites of Eadward; he had received knighthood at his hands, and had held what one would think must have been the sinecure office of armour-bearer to the Saint.[1] To Hugh of Grantmesnil himself was entrusted the government, or at least the military command, of the old Imperial city and of a district which at least took in the whole of Hampshire.[2] As one Norman Hugh had been set by Emma to bear rule in her morning-gift of Exeter,[3] so now Eadgyth saw, perhaps without repining, her still nobler morning-gift of Winchester placed under the rule of another Norman Hugh of greater renown.

William's policy with regard to the North

Of the state of things in the Northern Earldoms we unluckily hear nothing. It was William's policy to remove from the country during his absence all those whose presence in it at such a moment might have been dangerous to his authority. An honourable pretext was not wanting. The chief men of England were called upon to accompany their new King on his visit to his dominions beyond the sea. Normans and Englishmen, now under the rule of one common sovereign, were to feel, if not as fellow-countrymen, at least as fellow-subjects. They were to become accustomed to the presence and companionship of one another, and each was to look on the land of the other as a land not wholly foreign.

---

vero mater ejus soror Hugonis de Grentemaisnil de clarâ stirpe Geroianorum." Was Humphrey a brother of Thurstan Goz, and therefore great-uncle of Hugh Earl of Chester? See vol. 1 p. 205

[1] See Ord Vit 666 C, 669 C, where we read of Robert, "Hic Eduardi Regis armiger fuit, et ab illo cingulum militiæ accepit"

[2] Ib 512 B "Hugo de Grentemaisnil, qui præsidatum Gewissorum, id est Guentanæ regionis, jam habuerat" The flourish about the Gewissi (compare a kindred flourish in a charter of Eadwig quoted in vol i p 622) need not make us carry Hugh's government beyond Hampshire. A large part of Wessex was still unconquered

[3] See vol i. p 346

We are expressly assured that those whom William took with him were not taken as captives, but as men high in his favour, as the men of highest dignity in his new realm, who were to be further honoured by being thus brought into the closest companionship with the royal person.[1] But, if they were not taken as captives, we are no less distinctly told that they were taken as hostages. William chose as his companions the men whose power he dreaded and of whose faithfulness he was doubtful. In their absence revolts would be less to be feared. For there would be no leaders of the first rank to head them, and regard for the safety of those who were in William's hands might keep back their friends from beginning disturbances which might be avenged on them.[2] In pursuance of this policy, William summoned three out of the four Northern Earls, Eadwine, Morkere, and Waltheof, to accompany him on his visit to his native Duchy. They could not well refuse. They may have seen through the real motives of the invitation, but on the surface everything was friendly and honourable. They could not have declined so flattering a request from the King whom they had just acknowledged, unless they wished to hurry on the open quarrel which it was their interest as well as his to stave off. Eadwine, Morkere, and Waltheof accordingly obeyed the summons.[3] Of Oswulf

*Eadwine, Morkere, and Waltheof called on to accompany him to Normandy*

[1] Will. Pict. 150 "Præsertim quum non traherentur ut captivi, sed dominum suum Regem proximi comitarentur, ampliorem ex hoc gratiam atque honorem habituri"

[2] Ib. "Abducere secum decreverat, quorum præcipue fidem suspiciebat ac potentiam, ... ut ipsis auctoribus nihil sub decessum suum novaretur, gens vero tota minus ad rebellionem valeret spoliata principibus. Denique eos potissimum, *veluti obsides*, in potestate suâ tali cautelâ tenendos existimabat, quorum auctoritas vel salus propinquis et compatriotis maximi esset." The Peterborough Chronicler (1067) puts all this into a very short formula; "Her for se cyng ofer sæ, and hæfde mid him *gislas* and sceattas"

[3] Ib. "Sic autem fuere subacti, ut obsequentissime facerent imperata."

CHAP XVII.
Apparent deposition of Oswulf.

we hear only incidentally, but it is plain that he must have given offence. If he had failed to appear at Berkhampstead or at Barking, to become William's man, and to receive his Earldom again at William's hands, that was quite ground enough, according to the code of the new reign, to deal with him as a traitor whose lands and honours were forfeited without further sentence. But as yet William exercised as little authority beyond the Tyne or the Humber as he exercised in the Orkneys.

Policy of William's dealings with Northumberland.

But it was politic to treat as his own the land which was one day to be his own. The day had not yet come when he could try the experiment of sending a foreign Earl and foreign soldiers into that distant and dangerous land. But it was prudent to make at least a show of authority even in the furthest corner of the land over which he claimed to be King. Such a show of authority might be made by granting the forfeited Earldom to an Englishman, and leaving him to take possession of it in William's name, if he could. Such an instrument was found in Copsige, the old lieutenant of Tostig. A partizan of Tostig would naturally be at feud with Oswulf, as one whom the favour of Tostig's enemy Morkere had restored to some share of the possessions of his forefathers.[1] William acted with speed. Early in the month of February Copsige was invested with the Earldom, and he at once set forth to take possession. We shall see hereafter how he fared on his errand.[2]

Copsige appointed Earl, February 4, 1067

Position of the Abbots Æthelwig and Æthelsige

Besides the Earls and Prelates who are spoken of as accompanying William, there are one or two other leading churchmen of whom we hear later in the story, and of whom we should have been well pleased to learn something at this particular moment. One of these is Æthelwig, the prudent Abbot of Evesham. High as he had

---

[1] See vol ii p 487
[2] See the next Chapter and Appendix L

stood in the favour of Eadward and Harold, he stood equally high in the favour of William. The annals of his house set him before us as one of the first of English Prelates to submit to the new order of things, and as being at a somewhat later time invested with large authority in several Mercian shires.[1] Another Prelate also, whose church lay in the Earldom of Waltheof, Æthelsige of Ramsey, who had borne to Harold in his sickness the miraculous message of comfort from his saintly predecessor,[2] was also soon after high in William's favour. He therefore probably was so already. The presence of Copsige, Æthelwig, and Æthelsige in the Earldoms of Morkere, Eadwine, and Waltheof respectively may possibly have been looked on as a guaranty for the preservation of order no less valuable than the absence of the Earls. But on all these points of detail we are left to conjecture.

### § 3. *William's First Visit to Normandy.*
### *March—December* 1067.

All was now ready for the royal voyage. The place chosen for the embarcation was the same which had been chosen for the landing six months before. In the course of the month of March the ships were ready at Pevensey, already most likely the lordship of William's brother, Robert of Mortain.[3] Those ships, the Norman panegyrist tells us, should have been adorned, in ancient fashion, with white sails, as bearing a conqueror to his triumph.[4] A

---

[1] See Appendix W.       [2] See vol iii p 359
[3] See Domesday, 20 *b*  I know not on what authority Thierry (i 273) says, "à Pevensey, lieu de débarquement de l'armée, les soldats normands partagèrent entre eux les maisons des vaincus." He refers to Domesday, 26, where there is not, and could not well be, anything of the kind
[4] Will Pict 150 "Stabant naves ad transmittendum paratissimæ, quas

large body of Englishmen of rank had assembled on the spot, either to accompany the King on his voyage or simply to do him worship on his departure.[1] And of those who were chosen for the former dangerous honour the first was Eadgar, the King of a moment, whom we are told that William had enriched with large gifts of land and enrolled among those who were dearest to him.[2] Another was Stigand the Primate, whom he had already made up his mind to remove from his office, but with whom he thought good to bear for a while, till his deposition could be brought about by proper Papal commission. Till this could be done, William deemed it prudent to show all honour to one whose authority stood so high among his countrymen.[3] The only other churchman of whom we hear by name is Æthelnoth, Abbot of Glastonbury, whose obedience to William's summons is the only sign which we have yet come across of any authority being exercised by the new King in the Western shires. That Æthelnoth, who was afterwards deposed from his Abbey, was already honoured by William's jealousy is a fact which may be set against the charges which are brought against him.[4] Among laymen the only one

vere decuerat albis velis more veterum adornatas esse Erant enim revecturæ, gloriosissimum triumphum nuntiaturæ, maxime optatum gaudium" Thierry (i 281) seems to think that the sails actually were white.

[1] Will. Pict. 150. "Convenit eodem multus Anglorum equitatus"

[2] See Appendix M

[3] Will Pict 147 "Pontificium Stigandi, quod noverat non canonicum, minime probabat, sed Apostolici sententiam exspectare melius quam properantius deponere existimabat Suadebant et aliæ rationes, ut ad tempus pateretur atque honorifice haberet illum cujus inter Anglos auctoritas erat summa" William of Malmesbury, Gest. Pont 36 (I quote henceforward from Mr Hamilton's new edition), especially marks the unwillingness of Stigand to go on this journey, "Nec multo post in Normanniam navigans sub velamine honoris renitentem secum traxit, ne quid perfidiæ, se absente, per ejus auctoritatem in Anglia pullularet"

[4] On Æthelnoth, see vol ii. p 361 Thierry (i 281) for Æthelnoth substitutes Frithric Abbot of Saint Alban's, for whose presence he quotes no authority I suspect it to be as mythical as most other stories about that Prelate. William of Poitiers (150) mentions no Prelate but Stigand, but

mentioned besides the Ætheling and the three Earls, is a Thegn of Kent, who bore the same name as the Abbot of Glastonbury.[1] Those however whose names are given us did not form the whole of William's English escort; many "good men," who are otherwise unrecorded, went with him. And, along with his English companions, no small amount of English treasure also found its way on board William's ships. We are assured that it was all honourably gotten and was designed to be honourably spent;[2] but the mention of it draws forth a glowing description of the wealth of England from our Norman informant. Gaul, in the widest extent of its three divisions, could not have furnished such wealth of gold and silver as William now brought from his new conquest, a conquest which is proudly contrasted with the petty exploits of the first Cæsar in the same island.[3] Some part of all

in a flourish a little way on (153) he speaks of "totius Britanniæ episcoporum primatem atque magnos in transmarinis cœnobiis abbates" Æthelnoth appears in the Worcester Chronicle, 1066, and in Florence, 1067

[1] The Ætheling and the three Earls are mentioned in the Worcester Chronicle, and by Florence and William of Poitiers, both of whom give a Latin equivalent for the "manege oðre gode men of Englalande" Florence mentions the Kentish Thegn Æthelnoth by name (" satrapam Agelnothum Cantuariensem"), distinguishing him from the Abbot, with whom Orderic (506 B) evidently confounded him He is most likely the "Alnod cild," "Alnod Chentiscus," "Alnod Cantuariensis" of Domesday See Appendix S

The Peterborough Chronicler (see above, p 75) puts the whole escort together under the head of "gislas" Oddly enough, he is literally translated in the Normanniæ Nova Chronica, 1067 "Willelmus Dux, et Rex Anglorum, eodem anno mare transiit, in Normanniam ducens secum *obsides et thesauros*"

[2] Will Pict 153 "Quod rectissimo jure acceperat, quod, ubi honestissimæ rationes postularent, expendere cogitabat" The panegyrist clearly had a lurking doubt as to the perfect righteousness of his master

[3] The comparison between William and Cæsar is drawn out at great length by the Archdeacon of Lisieux, pp 151-154 The passage with which we are here concerned comes near the end , "Attulit non aliquantulum vectigal, non rapinas, sed quantum ex ditione trium Galliarum vix colligeretur argentum atque aurum . Carri metalli abundantiâ multipliciter Gallias terra illa vincit Ut enim horreum Cereris dicenda videtur frumenti copiâ, sic ærarium Arabiæ auri copiâ"

80     THE FIRST DAYS OF WILLIAM'S REIGN.

CHAP. XVII this wealth was scattered among the companions of William's labours, while the fleet was still in the haven of Pevensey.¹ But enough was carried beyond sea to set on fire the minds of all those among William's countrymen who had tarried by their own hearths while the land which sent forth such goodly stores was in winning.

William's police by sea
Piracy probably specially prevalent at the moment

The voyage was prosperous, and it seems to have had the incidental good effect of securing the safety of seafaring folk of lower degree. A stop, we are told, was put to all piracy for a long time to come² The expression is remarkable; it might seem to imply that, since the great fleet of Harold had disappeared from the Channel, piracy had been specially rife. The Danish havens in Ireland were no doubt always full of men in whom the old Wiking spirit was strong, and who were ready to sail forth for fighting or plunder wherever either fighting or plunder was to be had. And it is quite possible that dispossessed Englishmen may have already begun, as we know that they did before long, to take service in any quarter which promised either a chance of restoration or a hope of vengeance on those who made restoration hopeless. For the present at least, it would seem that the southern coast of England, the coast which William's own fleet could immediately protect or coerce, remained unharried by either friends or enemies.

William's reception in Normandy

The haven at which William landed is not told us. But we have full, perhaps not exaggerated, accounts of the joy with which the Duke, now a King, was received in his native land. Few, in any time or place, are slow to pay their homage to a conqueror, and we must never forget that, within his own Duchy at least, few princes have been better entitled than William to the real love and thankful-

¹ Will Pict 150 "At milites repatriantes, quorum in tantis negotiis fideli operâ usus fuerat, largâ manu ad eumdem portum donavit, ut optimum fructum victoriæ secum omnes percepisse gauderent"

² Ib 151 "Transmissio hæc mare diu pacavit, piratâ omni procul fugato"

ness of their people. It was Lent; it was winter· but the return of William turned the gloomy season into days of summer festival.[1] Every town through which the Duke passed was crowded with men from the remotest parts of the Duchy, who pressed to set eyes once more on their own prince who had won such glory for himself and for the Norman name.[2] The pomp of his approach to Rouen, the assemblage of all ages, ranks, and sexes, carries back the classical imagination of the panegyrist to the triumphs of old Roman days. And it is worth noticing that, after he had just spent all his ingenuity in proving the exploits of William to be in every way greater than the exploits of Cæsar, he still seems to think that he is doing further honour to his own hero by likening his reception at Rouen to the reception of Pompeius at Rome.[3] At Rouen it probably was that he again met his beloved Duchess, who, though uncrowned, already, on Latin-speaking lips at least, bore the royal title.[4] Aided by the counsel of the wise and aged Roger of Beaumont, she had kept Normandy in peace and prosperity during her husband's absence,[5] and it needs no great flight of imagination to picture to ourselves the truest and purest source of joy in that proud entry, when, not the King or the Conqueror, but the faithful partner of so many cares, returned to the home which, almost alone

*His entry into Rouen*

*Regency of Matilda*

---

[1] Will Pict 154 "Dies erant hiberni, et qui pœnitentiæ quadragesimalis rigori vacant Ceterum ubique agebantur tamquam summæ festivi temporis feriæ: sol æstivâ serenitate lucidus videbatur, gratia dierum solitâ longe major" Is this merely metaphor, or was William really favoured by the weather?

[2] Ib "Minorum sive remotiorum locorum incolæ in urbes, aut alio ubi facultas conspiciendi Regem daretur, confluebant"

[3] Ib "Quum in metropolim suam Rothomagum introiret, senes, pueri, matronæ, cunctique cives spectatum processerant; conclamabant salutantes reducem, adeo ut civitas illa universa applaudere putaretur, sicuti Roma quondam Pompeio suo applaudens tripudiavit"

[4] Ib 155. "Optime quidem egerat in gubernaculo domina nostra Matildis, jam nomine divulgato Regina, etsi nondum coronata"

[5] See vol III p 384

82 THE FIRST DAYS OF WILLIAM'S REIGN.

CHAP XVII.

William and the Norman Church

His reception by the monks and clergy

His gifts to churches.

His visit to Saint Stephen's at Caen

His probable consultations with Lanfranc

among princely homes, supplied a model for lowlier homes to follow.

But besides his own household, besides his people at large, William, the champion of the Church, the Crusader against the perjured blasphemer, the reformer of the corrupt manners of the benighted island, stood in a more direct and special relation to the ecclesiastical foundations of his Duchy. He had felt the benefit of their prayers during his days of warfare; they were now in return to feel the benefit of his liberality in his day of triumph. Costly gifts had already been sent over the sea, and gifts yet more costly were now the witness of his personal presence. Regulars and seculars strove which should pay the highest honours to the returning hero.[1] And regulars and seculars alike were rewarded with such gifts as no King or Emperor had ever before lavished on holy men and holy places.[2] Some churches William visited in person; to others he sent his offerings.[3] One of the first objects of his personal pilgrimage was his own creation at Caen, his own house of Saint Stephen, which it had been one of his last acts before his voyage to England to place under the care of his chosen counsellor Lanfranc.[4] The two now met again; but no chronicler gives us the details of their meeting. We are left to picture to ourselves the mutual greetings of King and Abbot, and to conceive the more secret discourse of the man whose wit had planned the great enterprise and the man whose arm had so far guided it to success. But those

---

[1] Will. Pict. 154. "Monasteria certabant monachorum atque cleri quodam in adventu sui carissimi tutoris amphorem officiositatem impenderent." Mark the use of the word "monasterium" (see vol i p 472; ii pp 249, 441) as applied to churches of both classes

[2] Ib "Nullius umquam Regis aut Imperatoris largitatem in oblationibus majorem comperimus"

[3] Ib "Item quas ecclesias non præsentiâ suâ, muneribus visitavit iterum" "Iterum" must refer to the gifts sent now, as distinguished from those which had been already sent from England in January See above, p. 61.

[4] See vol iii p. 382

two men must have had other thoughts in their minds than any that were likely to occur to the minds of the mass of those who greeted the Conqueror on his return. To the shouting multitudes and to the rejoicing clergy the work no doubt seemed to be done, when their Duke returned from his island warfare in the guise of a triumphant King. But both William and Lanfranc must have known that the work was only begun, and that the real Conquest of England was still a thing of the future. To Lanfranc the Conqueror might not scruple to reveal the secret that the seeming King of the English was in truth King only over East-Anglia and part of Wessex. He had with him the Earls of the North and an Abbot of the West, but the West and the North were still wholly unsubdued That York and Exeter would one day be his, no less than London and Winchester, William could hardly doubt; but as to the way, the means, the time, of making his kingship a reality over the whole realm there was room for much of thoughtful consultation between the two subtle and daring minds which now again came together. And there was one point of still deeper personal moment to the Abbot of Saint Stephen's. William, we know, had, among the other objects of his undertaking, gone forth as a missionary to reform the corrupted Church of England. The chief Prelate, in William and Lanfranc's eyes the intrusive Prelate, of that corrupted Church, the Prelate already doomed in William's counsels, was now one of the most honoured among William's train, possibly a guest within the walls of Lanfranc's own Abbey.[1] Is it going too far to surmise

CHAP XVII

Presence of Stigand, Lanfranc probably fixed on as his successor.

[1] See above, p 78. William of Malmesbury (Gest Pont 37) is emphatic on the honours paid to Stigand in Normandy, "Inter quæ difficile dictu est quantis eum [Stigandum] exceperit officiis, dignanter ubicumque locorum assurgendo et contra eum in omnibus episcopatibus Normanniæ et abbatiis longâ serie pompæ procedi faciendo" But he adds pointedly, "Sed quidquid his tegebatur involucris erupit in clarum, veniente Angliam Ermenfredo, Sedunense Episcopo, legato Alexandri Papæ" See Chapter xix.

CHAP. XVII. that, during William's Lenten pilgrimage to Caen, it was fully arranged who should be the next to fill the throne of Augustine, and what should be the policy of the Primate who should step into the place of the already condemned schismatic?

But of all this the writers of the time tell us nothing. The meeting of William and Lanfranc would supply admirable materials for an Imaginary Conversation, but all that the historian can affirm with positive certainty lies on the surface The unfinished minster, not to be hallowed for another ten years,[1] was rising under the care of its great Abbot The gifts of William to his own house were splendid. To all the churches which he visited he gave costly vestments and ingots of gold;[2] would it be too wild a flight of fancy to deem that for the church of Saint Stephen was reserved that mighty ingot of all which Harold Hardrada had brought from the far East, and which had passed from the hands of the victor of Stamfordbridge into the hands of the victor of Senlac?[3] However this may be, the choicest wealth of England was poured forth before the altar of the protomartyr. Men gazed with wonder upon the rich spoils of the conquered island. They might look down on its inhabitants as barbarians; they might scorn them as unskilled in the tactics of the horseman, as lagging behind continental lands in the crafts of the sculptor and the mason. But there were other arts, arts of skill and adornment, in which England and other Teutonic lands were allowed to outdo the nations of the Romance speech. The women of England were renowned for the art which had wrought the Raven on the banner of Ragnar and the Fighting-Man on the banner of Harold. And the same

William's offerings at Saint Stephen's.

Skill of the English in the arts, especially goldwork and embroidery

---

[1] See vol. iii p 108

[2] Will Pict 154 "Quam pietatem ipse confestim lucro multiplici recompensavit, donans pallia, libras auri, aliaque magna altaribus et famulis Christi" See above, p 62.

[3] See vol. iii. p 341

## ENGLISH SKILL IN THE ARTS.

skill turned to more peaceful uses had adorned the gorgeous vestments with which Eadgyth had appeased the wrath of the saintly Abbot of Saint Riquier.[1] We have seen by what rich rewards the knowledge of that art was purchased for the daughters of Englishmen of high degree.[2] The men were no less skilful in workmanship of other kinds. And if insular skill was lacking in any point, the extended commerce of England with the kindred races of the mainland[3] was ready to supply it. The merchants of the Imperial havens brought goodly things of this kind among their precious wares, and strangers of Teutonic birth had settled in the land to practise the gainful crafts of the goldsmith and the moneyer.[4] All these arts William knew how to encourage in his new realm by rich gifts to their professors of whatever sex or nation.[5] And now the choicest of these fruits of the skill and commerce of England were scattered among the rejoicing churches of Normandy, the choicest of all finding their way to adorn the newborn minster at Caen. The gifts of William were such that natives of the

*Chap. xvii*

*English intercourse with Germany*

---

[1] See vol. ii. p. 536.

[2] See above, p. 35, for the reward given by Godric to the instructress of his daughter in the art of embroidery.

[3] See vol. i. p. 310.

[4] The whole description given by William of Poitiers (155) is most remarkable, "Anglicæ nationis feminæ multum acu et auri texturâ, egregie viri in omni valent artificio. Ad hoc incolere apud eos Germani solebant talium artium scientissimi. Inferunt et negotiatores, qui longinquas regiones navibus adeunt, doctarum manuum opera."

[5] On Theodoric and the other Berkshire goldsmiths see above, p. 41. Another of the same craft, "Otto aurifaber," or "Otho aurifex," appears in Essex (Domesday, ii. 97 b) and Suffolk (ii. 286 b). He does not seem to have had anything T. R. E., or to have been enriched by William to anything like the same degree as Theodoric; indeed at Sudbury he was merely a tenant of the King's demesne. He however left a family who kept on the ancestral craft in the form of mintmasters. See Ellis, i. 462. "Grimbaldus aurifaber" (Domesday, 74) was a King's Thegn in Wiltshire, and held lands which had been held by one Eadward. In the same page we find "Leviet" or "Leviede" (Leofgyth), a widow holding, among many other widows in Wiltshire, the land which her husband had held T. R. E. It is added, "Fecit et facit aurifrisium Regis et Reginæ."

lands where wealth and luxury most abounded, men used to the splendours of Byzantine Cæsars and Saracen Caliphs, might have found delight in beholding them.[1] This whole picture is a striking witness, not only to the early developement of the ornamental arts in England and in the kindred lands, but to the influence over men's minds which was still held by the realms and cities which, fallen as they were from their ancient power, still kept up the unbroken traditions of elder days. Constantinople and Bagdad[2]—perhaps rather Constantinople and Cordova—were still looked up to as the special homes of all that was most magnificent upon earth. The Greek and the Saracen, the two nations which, if last in the race of political freedom, were foremost in the race of material civilization, were instinctively appealed to as the natural judges of all that was rich and splendid. High and strange indeed was the calling of the Normans of those days. The sovereign of Normandy was bringing the wealth which Greeks and Saracens might wonder at from his conquered island in the Northern Ocean. Meanwhile other men of his own race were treading the path which was to lead them to grasp the wealth of Greeks and Saracens in their own land. As William turned to his own ends the skill of the continental and the insular Teuton, so his countrymen were soon to turn the skill of Greek and Saracen to their ends, in that other island of hardly less renown which the Norman won as his home and kingdom in the southern sea.

Easter now drew nigh, and William had appointed the festival to be kept in the ducal palace and monastery of Fécamp.[3] This year no crowning feast, no national

[1] Will Pict 154 "Transiret illac hospes Græcus aut Arabs, voluptate traheretur eâdem"

[2] It should be remembered that, in this age, Babylon means Bagdad Two hundred years later it meant Cairo.   [3] See vol. i p 280.

Gemót, was held in the royal hall or in the Old Minster of Winchester. After his own Saint Stephen's, no church in Normandy stood higher in William's favour than the great house of Richard the Fearless and Richard the Good. That house was now flourishing under its second Abbot John, William's special friend and counsellor.[1] But of the mighty pile which now commands the Fécamp valley, that huge length of nave which almost rivals our own Saint Alban's, that central tower so stately in its simple majesty, that Lady Chapel where the rich work of later days contrasts with the stern dignity of the thirteenth century, not a stone had yet arisen.[2] The monks of Fécamp still worshipped in the elder church of Richard the Fearless. That church had been built for secular canons, who, under Richard the Good, the patron and father of monks,[3] gave way to regulars from Saint Benignus of Dijon, that great Burgundian abbey which has become the cathedral church of a modern diocese.[4] Thence too came their first Abbot,

CHAP XVII.

Condition and history of the monastery

Secular Canons founded by Richard the Fearless 990

Monks substituted by Richard the Good 1001.

[1] We shall see him in this character in Chapter xix
[2] The earliest part of the existing church is due to William of Ros, Abbot from 1087 to 1107 See Ord Vit 832 A, who says of him, "Cancellum veteris ecclesiæ, quam Ricardus Dux construxerat, dejecit, et eximiæ pulcritudinis opere in melius renovavit, atque in longitudine et latitudine decenter augmentavit Navem quoque basilicæ ubi oratorium Sancti Frodmundi habetur eleganter auxit, opusque tandem consummatum a Guillelmo Archiepiscopo aliisque quatuor præsulibus xvii Kal Julii [1107] consecrari fecit" William, surnamed "Bona-anima," was Archbishop of Rouen from 1079 to 1110 Of the choir then consecrated one chapel remains in a very marked style of Romanesque
[3] Add ad Will. Gem, Duchèsne, 316 C "De Richardo filio primi Richardi dicitur, quod fuerat pater patriæ et maximi monachorum" See vol ii. p 223
[4] When I spoke of Fécamp in connexion with Richard the Fearless (vol i. p 280) I did not accurately distinguish between his first foundation, for secular canons, and the change to regulars which was afterwards designed by him and carried out by Richard the Good The mistake was, I hope, a pardonable one, considering that William of Malmesbury (ii 165), when speaking of Richard the Fearless, says, "Fiscannum cœnobium, quod ipse, aliquantis redditibus ampliatum, regulâ monasticâ per Willelmum quemdam

CHAP XVII.
William the first Abbot 1001-1031.

the renowned and holy William,[1] a native of Italy, who boasted of a descent from the ancient Lombard Kings and of being held at the font by the restorer of the Roman Empire. The godson of Otto and Adelaide[2] ruled his house in wisdom and sanctity; he enjoyed the special favour of Duke Richard, and he is said to have been the first Prelate in Normandy to shelter the banished Æthelred when he fled before the arms of the conquering Dane.[3]

Greatness of the monastery;

His church boasted, as it still boasts, of a relic holy beyond all relics, of that Precious Blood brought to its site by miracle,[4] which to this day draws thither crowds of votaries and pilgrims. At Fécamp both the founders of the church were buried, neither within nor without the pile which they had reared and enriched.[5] There too its second founder loved to keep the highest of the Church's festivals, and to honour rather than to abase himself by performing menial services to the holy inmates.[6]

its special connexion with the Ducal house.

In later days the house of the two Richards became the special home of those among their descendants who embraced the monastic life. There the

Abbatem Divionensem insigniverat." See the whole history in Neustria Pia, 210 et seqq , De Lincy, Essai Historique et Littéraire sur l'Abbaye de Fécamp (Rouen, 1840), pp 7 et seqq , 244 et seqq  Indeed I ought to have found out the change from Wace, who first (5873), speaking of the foundation of Richard the Fearless, says,

"Clers establi ki servireient,
E provendes dunt il vivreient"

But afterwards (5945 et seqq ) he goes on to tell about Abbot William and the monks coming from Dijon.

[1] For his history see the Chronicle of Saint Benignus in D'Achery, ii. 381, 386 ; cf Mabillon, Analecta, i 229

[2] So says the local Chronicle in De Lincy, p. 245, but was it according to Canon Law for a man and his wife to be sponsors to the same child ?

[3] Neustria Pia, p 213

[4] The whole legend is treated at length by M. De Lincy, p. 79 et seqq  He connects it with the story of the Saint Graal.

[5] See the story in Dudo, 156 D , Palgrave, ii 903.

[6] See Add ad Will. Gem., Duchèsne, 317 A.

unhappy Malger had passed his youthful years,[1] and there too dwelt perhaps the only members of the ducal house whose names are never mentioned in connexion with political strife, William the son of Richard the Good,[2] and Nicolas, the son of the third Richard, who left his cell at Fécamp to receive the abbatial staff of Saint Ouen.[3] There the young and pious Margaret, the last scion of the house of Maine, had found her grave, when she had escaped from the fear of earthly wedlock to the presence of a heavenly Bridegroom.[4] The reigning Abbot John, of Lombard birth like his predecessor, had now presided over the house for six and thirty years. He had received the second profession of Maurilius, the Primate who still for a short time longer filled the metropolitan throne of Rouen.[5] He had crossed the sea to get what he might at the hands of Eadward; the bountiful King had granted to his house a prospective interest in the lordship of Steyning in the South-Saxon land, but Godwine, not coveting the presence of strangers in his own special shire, had managed to convert the estate to his own use. Harold had been less austere or less grasping; he had not restored Steyning, but he had allowed the church of Fécamp to obtain other possessions in England. William, before he crossed the sea, had promised the restoration of the disputed lands, and the promise had been carried out in a charter granted by the new King, which most likely formed part of his oblations at the present Paschal feast.[6] In no part of William's dominions had he been more loyally served than within the monastic walls of Fécamp. One monk of Fécamp, Hugh Margot,

CHAP XVII.

Abbot John 1031–1082.

Gifts of Eadward to Fécamp, hindered by Godwine;

confirmed by William

Zeal of the Fécamp monks for William.

---

[1] See vol ii p. 210, iii p. 93.
[2] Will. Gem v 13.   [3] See vol i p 518, iii. p 380.
[4] See vol. iii p 213.   [5] See vol. iii p. 100
[6] On Steyning and the other English possessions of Fécamp, see Cod. Dipl iv 229, Neustria Pia, 223 I have enlarged on the subject in an Appendix (Note C.) to the second edition of my second volume.

90 THE FIRST DAYS OF WILLIAM'S REIGN.

CHAP XVII

had borne William's messages of warning and defiance to his rival.[1] Another, the almoner Remigius, had given a well-manned ship to share in the voyage from Saint Valery to Pevensey.[2] The house itself, and especially this last-named zealous member of the house, were now to reap their reward.

Great gathering at Fécamp

The Norman Prelates

Ralph of Valois or Montdidier,

his marriage with King Henry's widow. 1062.

The Easter Feast at Fécamp was attended by a goodly company of various nations. The knights and soldiers of William's army followed him thither, and a vast crowd of all orders came together to meet him. The Bishops and Abbots of Normandy were there, and a large body of the nobles of France. Foremost among these last was one who had greatly risen in renown and worldly rank since we last heard of him. Ralph of Montdidier, once the lord and the captive of Roger of Mortemer,[3] had risen to be a mighty Count, lord of Valois and Amiens and of the French Vexin.[4] He had, five years before, against the will of the young King Philip and of his guardian the Marquess Baldwin, married the Russian princess Anne or Adelaide or Agnes, the widowed mother of the King. Either on the ground of kindred between Ralph and her former husband or on that of the existence of an earlier Countess, the marriage was loudly denounced, and Ralph underwent more than one excommunication.[5] A princess brought up in Eastern Orthodoxy may perhaps have felt but little dread of Western anathemas, and William, with all his piety, may have felt some lurking sympathy for those who had drawn on

---

[1] See vol. III p 431.  [2] See vol III p 380

[3] See vol III pp 145, 157

[4] Will Pict 156 "Regis Francorum vitricus intererat hujus curiæ, Rodolphus præpotens Comes, multaque nobilitas Franciæ"

[5] Chron S Petri Vivi Senon 1060 (ap D'Achery, ii 476) "Rodulfus Comes consanguineus ejusdem Regis duxit uxorem in conjugio contra jus et fas, unde fuit excommunicatus." See Art de Vérifier les Dates, II. 701

themselves the censures of the Church for this particular CHAP. XVII. cause. At all events the excommunicated Count was received with all honour at the festival at Fécamp, and, as we are told that William exacted strict attendance at divine service from all his company,[1] we must infer that the assembled Prelates of Normandy did not shrink from his spiritual society. But chief among the guests The English visitors of the King-Duke were the companions, the hostages, whom he had brought with him from his island realm. To Eadgar, the momentary King, brought as a child from Hungary to England, a visit to Normandy was but a small episode in a life of wanderings. Eadwine and Morkere may possibly have been visiting the native land of their own mother.[2] But Waltheof the son of Siward, whose not remote forefather was held to have been a bear in a Norwegian forest,[3] was treading a land which his kindred had certainly never visited in any peaceful guise. Amid the splendours of the Easter feast the Abbot of Glastonbury might compare the church of Duke Richard with his own church reared by the great Dunstan, and with that primæval temple of wood which still lingered on from the days of the conquered Briton.[4] The older and wiser among the English visitors, the Primate above all, might see through the hollowness of the honours which were everywhere shown to themselves and their countrymen. But outwardly at least all was joy and festivity. The English visitors were the objects of universal at- Norman admiration of the tention, of universal admiration. The outward attractions of our countrymen had not lessened since Gregory English had beheld the angelic children of Deira in the Roman slave-market. The beauty of the English youth, the

---

[1] Will. Pict. 155. "Humiliter adstans ille choris ordinum religiosorum, ludicra intermittere, concurrere ad divina, militum plebisque turbas coegit."

[2] See vol. ii. p. 629, iii. p. 699.

[3] See vol. i. p. 586.

[4] See vol. i. p. 486.

92                THE FIRST DAYS OF WILLIAM'S REIGN.

CHAP XVII  long-haired children of the North, rivetted the eyes of the close-shorn Normans.[1]  And the wealth of England again dazzled all eyes at Fécamp, as at every other stage of William's Norman progress.  The robes of state of the King and his chief nobles, rich with the embroidery of gold wrought by English hands, made all that France and Normandy had beheld of the same kind seem mean by comparison.[2]  At William's Paschal feast the whole company, we are told, drank out of the spoils of England, cups of gold and silver, in number and goodliness such as no man had seen before, cups too made of the horns of the wild bull of the English woods, and tipped at either end with the same costly metals.[3]  The fame of the King of the English and of the wealth and splendour of his Kingdom was soon spread abroad through every land.[4]

Royal splendour of William.

Consecration of churches.

As soon as the Easter Feast was over, a whole round of ecclesiastical ceremonies and ecclesiastical cares pressed upon the mind of William.  As not uncommonly happened,[5] several great monastic churches, which had probably been finished some while before, were still waiting for consecration.  The piety of the Duke demanded that the ceremony should be no longer delayed.  The feast of Saint Philip and Saint James was fixed by his bidding

[1] Will Pict 156  "Curiose hi cum Normannis cernebant crinigeros alumnos plagæ aquilonalis, quorum pulcritudini Galliæ Comatæ formosissimi juvenes inviderent  Nec enim puellari venustati cedebant"  The introduction of Gallia *Comata* is happier than most of the Archdeacon's classical flourishes

[2] Ib.  "Regis autem regiorumque satellitum indumenta spectantes intexta atque crustata auro, quæque antea viderant vilia æstimavere"

[3] Ib  "Item vasa argentea sive aurea admirabantur, quorum de numero vel decore vere narrari possent incredibilia  His tantum ex poculis cœnaculum ingens bibebat, aut cornibus bubalinis metallo decoratis eodem circa extremitates utrasque"

[4] Ib  "Denique plurima hujuscemodi, competentia regali munificentiæ, notabant, quæ, reversi domum, ob novitatem prædicarent."

[5] See vol ii p 212

for the hallowing of the minster of Our Lady at Saint Peter on the Dive.¹ This was the great foundation of the pious Lescelina, the widow of Count William of Eu, the mother of his three sons, the valiant Robert, the holy Hugh, and the traitor William.² The first Abbot Ainard had been appointed one and twenty years before, and the minster, which has been wholly supplanted by work of later date, was now ready for consecration. The King was present at the ceremony, and the church on the Dive, like other churches, came in for its share of William's bounty.³ But it would seem that William's *Champ de Mai* was not held only for ecclesiastical purposes. We hear of a large gathering of men of all ranks, to whom certain decrees which the Duke had made for the good of his whole people were announced by the voice of the herald.⁴ Of this legislation, whatever was its nature and object, we should gladly learn some further details. A day two months later was devoted to a still greater ceremony of the same kind, the hallowing of a minster of still higher renown, one which still remains, though unhappily in ruins, to bear witness to the arts of those days and of days far earlier still.⁵ The church of Jumièges had been begun, seven and twenty years before, by that Abbot Robert whom the blind favour of Eadward had successively thrust into the episcopal chairs of London and Canterbury, and

CHAP. XVII.
Saint Mary (or Peter) on Dive. May 1, 1067.

William's legislation.

Consecration of Jumièges. July 1.

The church of Robert 1040-1058.

---

¹ Ord Vit 507 A "Celebratâ Paschæ sollennitate, Rex dedicari basilicam Sanctæ Mariæ super Divam præcepit." See Neustria Pia, p 498.

² See vol III pp. 117, 153

³ Ord Vit 507 A "Utramque [Dives and Jumièges] nimirum ex prædiis dominii sui largiter dotavit, suâque præsentiâ, dum sanctum mysterium celebraretur, devote sublimavit"

⁴ Ib. "Ipse cum magno cœtu optimatum et mediocrium Kal Maii reverenter interfuit, et utillima' totius populi commoditati edicta sub voce præconis promulgavit."

⁵ The existence at work of Merowingian days in the earlier and smaller church at Jumièges has been satisfactorily proved by M Bouet

94        THE FIRST DAYS OF WILLIAM'S REIGN.

CHAP XVII whom the indignant voice of the English people had driven from the office in which he had made himself the root of all evil.[1] Robert was now dead, and he had been buried in the church of his own rearing, but the consecrating rite had been delayed through the incumbencies of two Abbots, Godfrey, the immediate successor of Robert, and another Robert who now held the office.[2] The slender towers of Robert's west front, the massive and almost rude arcades of his nave, must have already looked antiquated at a time when the twin churches of Caen were rising in a more developed, a more strictly national, form of Norman art. It would seem that it was at William's express order[3] that the ceremony was now performed by Archbishop Maurilius, assisted by one or more of his suffragans.[4] With what eyes, we may again ask, did Stigand look on the works of the predecessor whom, in Norman belief, he had unjustly and schimatically driven from his throne? Again the Conqueror devoutly attended at the ceremony, and a share of the wealth of England fell to the lot of the church of Jumièges as well as to the house on the Dive and to his own Saint Stephen's.

Death of Archbishop Maurilius August 9

The consecration at Jumièges was the last official act of Maurilius. He fell sick and died within two months, and the metropolitan throne of Normandy was again vacant.[5] In the search for a successor the claims of one

---

[1] See vol ii. pp. 70, 120, 331, 335, 341    [2] See Neustria Pia, 309.

[3] Orderic (507 A) again uses the same expression, "Kal Julii ecclesiam Sanctæ Mariæ apud Gemmeticum dedicari præcepit, et ipse sacro mysterio veneranter adfuit." So William of Jumièges (vii 38), "Paullo post in Normanniam regressus, ecclesiam Sanctæ Mariæ in Gemmetico cum honore magno dedicari jussit."

[4] Orderic (u. s ) says, "Maurilius cum suffraganeis episcopis hanc dedicationem humiliter et devote perpetravit" But William of Jumièges (u s) mentions only Maurilius himself and Baldwin, Bishop of Evreux (1067 to 1071) See Bessin, Conc Rot Prov 374.

[5] Ord Vit 507 A, B "Paullo post, duodecimo episcopatus sui anno,

man stood forth beyond all comparison. There was one *Chap. XVII.* Prelate in Normandy who towered, as no Prelate had ever towered before, over the whole Church of the Duchy. Lanfranc, Abbot of Saint Stephen's, was called *Unanimous election of Lanfranc* by every voice to fill the highest spiritual place in his adopted country. The process of his election reads as if it were copied from our own side of the water in the days of Eadward. The church of Rouen chose Lanfranc as Archbishop by a canonical election; the Duke, the nobles, and the whole people of Normandy—we seem to be reading the acts of English Witenagemót—with one voice confirmed their choice.[1] But Lanfranc refused to bow *He declines the office* his shoulders to such a burthen; he was even zealous on behalf of another candidate, John, Bishop of Avranches.[2] When we look forward three years, and see how much heavier a burthen was then laid on Lanfranc's shoulders, we cannot avoid the suspicion that the refusal was preconcerted between the Abbot of Saint Stephen's and his sovereign and Founder. The votes of the Chapter of Rouen, the approval of the nobles and people, were

in lectum decubuit Peracto autem quidquid religioso Dei vernulæ competit V. Idus Augusti ad Deum (cui diu servierat) migravit Corpus vero ejus in Episcopali Ecclesia (quam ipse ante v annos Indictione I sanctæ Dei genitrici Mariæ dedicaverat) delatum est, et ante crucifixum honorifice tumulatum est" So Will Gem vii 38 On his church see vol iii p 101

[1] Ord, Vit 507 B "Post mortem antistitis sui Rotomagensis Ecclesia Lanfrancum Cadomensem Abbatem sibi Præsulem elegit, et Rex Guillelmus, cum optimatibus suis omnique populo, libentissime concessit" Vit Lanfr ed. Giles, 1 292 "Ea tempestate civitas Rothomaga viduata est sancto ac venerabili Archipræsule Maurilio, tum clerus omnis et populus congregati volebant substituendum eligere Lanfrancum"

[2] Ord Vit 507 B, C "Sed vir Deo devotus, et humilitate studens, tanti primatûs sarcinam refutavit, et sibi ad hunc apicem toto conatu Johannem Abrincatensium præsulem præferre sategit" Vit Lanfr ed Giles, i 292 "Verum toto conamine ille [Lanfrancus] tale onus devitabat subire, humiliter magis cupiens subesse quam præesse Nam abbatiam Cadomensem, quam invitus susceperat, libenter dimisisset, si extra animæ læsionem gravem facere valuisset" William of Jumièges mentions the appointment of John without mentioning the offer to Lanfranc.

96        THE FIRST DAYS OF WILLIAM'S REIGN.

CHAP. XVII doubtless given in good faith; but we may feel sure that the ducal confirmation was given only on the understanding that the Primacy of Rouen would be declined by the man who was already designed for the Primacy of Canterbury. On Lanfranc's refusal, the Bishop of Avranches, his favourite and doubtless the favourite of William, obtained the metropolitan see. John was a remote kinsman of the ducal house, being a son of that Rudolf of Ivry who won for himself so unenviable a fame in the early days of Richard the Good.[1] He was thus a man of a past generation, a cousin of the grandfather of the reigning Duke. An elder brother, Hugh, had held the see of Bayeux for forty years before the appointment of Odo, and had proved himself a troublesome kinsman and subject to William's father Robert.[2] In these two Prelates the male line of Asperleng and Sprota came to an end, but the stock was continued in females. Hugh of Montfort, who now held the command at Dover, was married to a niece of the new Primate,[3] and the more famous William Fitz-Osbern was the son of his sister.[4] Archbishop John was a rigid asserter of ecclesiastical discipline. In order to put his appointment beyond all cavil, an embassy was at once despatched to Rome to obtain the pallium for the new Primate, a step which is spoken of as if it were at once praiseworthy

*John, Bishop of Avranches 1060-1067, Archbishop of Rouen 1069-1079*

*His descent*

*Lanfranc sent to Rome to obtain the pallium for John.*

---

[1] Ord. Vit 507 C; Will. Gem vii 38. The latter writer goes on to give the whole history and pedigree of Rudolf and his descendants, including his killing a bear in the days of Richard the Fearless The tale is translated by Benoît (38071 et seqq). On Rudolf's suppression of the peasant revolt, see vol i p 284

[2] See vol 1 p 518. Hugh must surely have been very much older than John His episcopate and that of Odo fill up between them the almost unparalleled space of eighty-eight years, a speaking comment on the way in which, before William's reforms, preferments of this kind were given to mere boys See vol. ii pp. 209, 211 The occurrence of the name John in a man of his generation is itself remarkable See vol ii p. 211.

[3] Will Gem vii 38             [4] See vol ii p 194.

and unusual. But when we read that the messenger employed on this errand was no other than the Abbot of Saint Stephen's, and that he went at the Duke's special bidding, we cannot help suspecting that Lanfranc was sent to act as the mouth-piece of William towards Alexander and Hildebrand on other matters besides the grant of the pallium to the new Archbishop of Rouen.[1] The pallium was of course sent without difficulty, and Primate John ruled for ten years with great strictness and holy indignation against offenders of all kinds.[2] His zeal was that of another Phinehas, and it was specially displayed against the married clergy. In one synod which he held on this matter, the party of laxity had the upper hand, and the zealous Primate was driven out of the church amidst a volley of stones, crying aloud as he went that the heathen had come into God's inheritance.[3] It could hardly have been in the same cause that the monks of Saint Ouen's set upon him with force and arms

*John's zeal against the married clergy*

---

[1] Orderic (507 C) says, "Porro ut canonice fieret ista conjugatio, Romam adiit, prædictæ ordinationis licentiam ab Alexandro Papâ impetiavit sacrum quoque pallium, unde et ipsi et toti Normanniæ gloriandum erat, cum licentiâ deportavit" This becomes clear in the Life of Lanfranc (i 292), "Quod Rex advertens providit subrogare Johannem quem Abricatensium constituerat Pontificem, sed ut hoc canonice fieret, licentiam petendi gratiâ Romam direxit eumdem Abbatem Cadomensem Lanfrancum, qui onus hujusce legationis alacriter perferens *sicut ecclesiis cupiebat esse consultum* a Papâ Alexandro impetravit, sacrum quoque pallium, cum licentiâ hujus promotionis deportavit, unde et ipsi toti Neustriæ gaudium fuit" The words in Italics may cover a great deal It should be remembered that Malger had held the Archbishoprick without the pallium. See vol iii p 95

The journey seems to fill up the space between 1067 and 1069, from which the years of John as Archbishop are reckoned.

[2] Ord. Vit. 507 C "Hic ardore virtutum in verbis et operibus multipliciter fervebat, nimioque zelo in vitia ut Phinees sæviebat"

[3] Ib "Multum contra impudicos presbyteros pro auferendis pellicibus laboravit, a quibus, dum in synodo concubinas eis sub anathemate prohiberet, lapidibus percussus aufugit, fugiensque de ecclesiâ, 'Deus, venerunt gentes in hæreditatem tuam,' fortiter clamavit"

98         THE FIRST DAYS OF WILLIAM'S REIGN.

CHAP XVII when he was saying mass on the day of their patron.[1] But the Primate was, to say the least, unlucky who thus contrived to set both regulars and seculars against him. He was succeeded in the see of Avranches by an Italian named Michael, whose learning and piety are highly spoken of.[2] Here we have another instance of the discerning patronage which William was ready to extend on both sides of the sea to worthy men of any speech or any country except the proscribed natives of England.[3]

Michael, Bishop of Avranches 1067-1087

Flourishing condition of Normandy.

These ecclesiastical cares and other peaceful duties occupied William during the whole summer and autumn. Normandy is, as usual, described—and probably described with truth—as rejoicing and flourishing in the presence of its sovereign The peace and order which the watchful eye of William established throughout his Duchy are described in glowing terms.[4] From works of this kind, so

[1] Chron S Steph Cad 1073 (Duchèsne, 1017 D) "Invaserunt monachi Sancti Audoeni Johannem Rothomagensem Archiepiscopum, missam celebrantem in festivitate ejusdem sancti, cum armatâ manu virorum Unde judicatum est in concilio in eâdem civitate congregato, præsidente Rege Anglorum Willelmo, monachos hujus criminis reos per abbatias carceribus retrudi ad placitum Archiepiscopi"

[2] Ord Vit 507 D. "Michael, natione Italicus, eruditione literarum imbutus, studio religionis venerandus"

[3] Will Malms Gest Reg iii 240 "In locum illorum qui morerentur, cujuscumque gentis industriam, præter Angligenam, imposuit Exigebat hoc, ni fallor, indurata in Regem pervicacia, quum sint Normanni . in conviventes advenas naturali benignitate proclives"

[4] Ord Vit 509 B "Willelmus Rex, dum moraretur in Normanniâ, tranquillitati ejus in longum prospiciebat sollicitudine maximâ Justas leges et recta judicia ex consultu sapientum [mid minra witena geþeahte] divitibus et pauperibus æque sanxit, optimosque judices et rectores per provincias Neustriæ constituit . Omnibus tam advenis quam indigenis pacem in totâ terrâ suâ præconis voce propalavit, et super fures ac seditiosos patriæque quietis contemptores graves justasque ultiones rigide promulgavit" Cf vol ii pp 165, 172 William of Poitiers (156) also waxes eloquent on the same subject, but, oddly enough, he is driven to employ exactly the same words which he had already used more appropriately when describing the good discipline of William's army at the mouth of the Dive See vol. iii p 386

worthy of the higher parts of his nature, he was presently called away to occupations of quite another kind. While William was busied with ecclesiastical ceremonies at Caen and Jumièges, while he was displaying in Normandy the gifts of the wise lawgiver and the firm administrator, events were happening in England which showed, what he at least doubtless knew well enough, that his work in his island realm, instead of being ended, was hardly begun. It now became plain that, after the victory at Senlac, the homage at Berkhampstead, the coronation at Westminster, the kingship of William was still hardly more than a name, and the Conquest of England was still a thing of the future.

<small>CHAP XVII.

Imperfection of the conquest of England</small>

# CHAPTER XVIII.

THE CONQUEST OF WESTERN AND NORTHERN ENGLAND.[1]

March 1067—April 1070

William's position.

WE have now reached a stage in our history in which it is of special moment to bear in mind the peculiar nature of William's position as I have already set it forth. William had taken seizin of his Kingdom on the shore

[1] In the course of this Chapter we lose the help of William of Poitiers, whose work, as we have it, suddenly breaks off soon after William's return to England. He seems however to have brought his story to a good epic finish at the point when William's power was really established throughout the country (see Ord. Vit. 521 C). The substance of the latter part of his work is preserved to us by Orderic, whose own value also is constantly increasing. As the affairs of Northumberland are now of great moment, it is a great advantage to have the important insertions in the text of Florence which have been hitherto attributed to Simeon of Durham, but which have been lately subjected to a searching examination by a most competent Northumbrian critic, with whose writings I am sorry that I did not become sooner acquainted. Mr. J. H. Hinde, in his History of Northumberland—a book which is a model of what local histories should be, but what they very seldom are—and again in his Preface to the edition of Simeon of Durham published by the Surtees Society, argues that these insertions are not the work of Simeon, but of some unknown monk of Hexham, writing after the Scottish inroad in the time of David. The chief argument is the occasional contradictions, real or apparent, between these insertions and the History of the Church of Durham printed in the *Decem Scriptores*, which Mr. Hinde strongly maintains to be the work of Simeon, in opposition to the view which has assigned it to Turgot. I confess that, whether the author be Simeon or any one else, and whether he wrote at Durham or at Hexham, I set great store by a work which in any case is Florence adapted to Northern readers by the insertions of a Northern writer. And it adds something to my mind that the work was approved by so judicious a later compiler as Roger of Howden. I shall therefore,

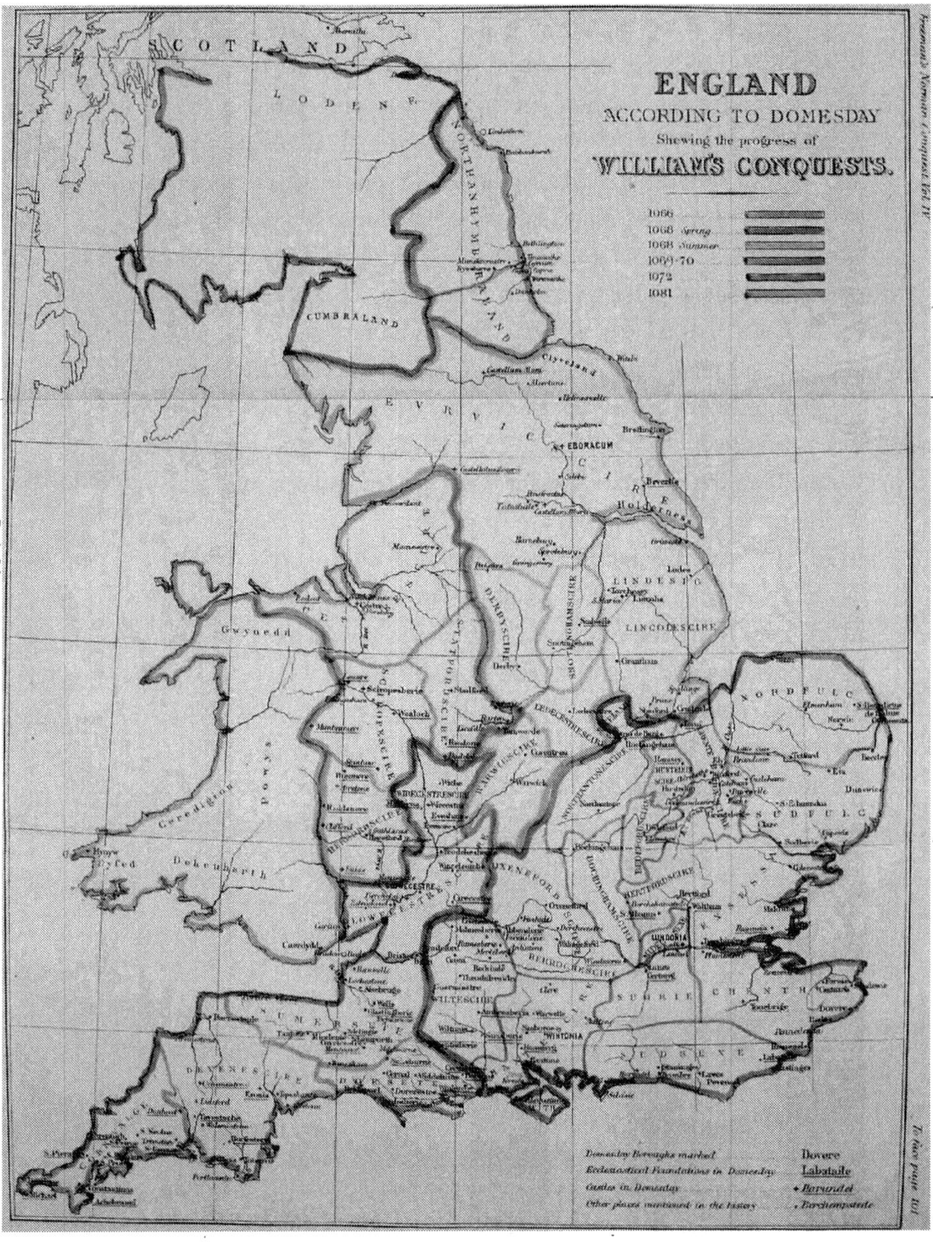


For the Delegates of the Clarendon Press.

of Pevensey,[1] he had been solemnly invested with the kingly office before the altar at Westminster; he had appeared as King and Conqueror before the eyes of his native subjects; he had actual possession of many shires of England, and he held in his power such among the chiefs of the rest of the land as seemed likely to endanger his dominion. He had now to establish his power over those parts of England where he was King only so far as that no one else was King And it was by the sword that his power was established. It was now, for more than half England, that the Conquest really began. And it was now that William reaped the fruit of his great victory and of his coronation. No rival King or leader acknowledged by the whole Kingdom appeared against him. The land was therefore conquered piecemeal, and William was enabled to use the force of one district to overcome the resistance of another. And, as the King, he had the great moral advantage of being able to brand all resistance to the establishment of his power as rebellion against a power already lawfully established.

CHAP. XVIII.

A large part of the land still to be conquered.

It is a natural question to ask why, when William must have seen that his hold over England was so imperfect, he should have left the country so long without the restraint of his own presence. He did not even come back at the first hearing of news which seemed to make his presence specially needful. In such a mind as William's we may be sure that many motives joined together. It was due to his own native Duchy, which had served him so loyally in his great undertaking, to show himself once more among his own people, and to thank and reward both his earthly and his heavenly helpers. Moreover, as the

William's probable motives for leaving England

Necessity of keeping up his popularity in Normandy.

without deciding the question of authorship, quote the enlarged Florence as Simeon, referring to Mr Hinde's own edition But I shall of course weigh the evidence for each of the statements which Mr. Hinde calls in question
[1] See vol III p. 405.

ruler of two states, it was impossible for him to dwell exclusively in either, and it was doubtless good policy to visit Normandy at this particular moment. His popularity in his native Duchy must now have been at its very highest, but anything which could be construed as neglect of his own land and people might have caused that popularity to cool as it had warmed. The visit to Normandy, the Easter-Feast at Fécamp, the ceremonies at Jumièges and on the Dive, were all signs that the King of the English was not puffed up by his new greatness, but that he was still the Duke of the Normans, loving his own land, labouring for its welfare, showing honour to its holy men and its holy places. And as his presence in Normandy was certainly politic, his absence from England may have been politic also. It was doubtless meant to be taken as a sign of confidence in his new subjects. King William, a righteous and merciful King, had dealt in all gentleness and tenderness with a people of whom well nigh every man was entangled in the guilt of treason. He had shown favour and honour to all who had not personally sinned against him; the noblest men of England had been chosen as his companions in his voyage, and they were now the objects of wonder and admiration to his subjects beyond the sea. A Conqueror who had shed no blood except in battle,[1] who had seized no man's lands or goods save with every legal formality, might affect to trust himself to the good will of his new subjects, and might profess to deem that his actual presence was not needed to secure their obedience. In his own heart he may not have been sorry to put their obedience to the test, to see what his chances really were of retaining the part of the land which he had already won, and of winning

[1] Unless we except the probable executions at Romney (see vol. iii. p. 534), and these were, after all, a military operation while the war still lasted. *King* William had certainly not put any man to death.

the rest to a more than nominal subjection. This policy <small>CHAP XVIII.</small>
enabled him directly to prove the disposition of the
people at large. The shires which had submitted were
free from the terror of his own presence, and the presence
in his train of the Earls of northern and central England
left the still independent districts to their own devices.
I do not believe for a moment that William purposely
put England into the hands of oppressive lieutenants,
in order that the people might be goaded into revolt.
But it is not unlikely that he may have wished to bring
matters to an issue and to learn what the temper of the
nation really was. It is possible that he was not sorry
when an imperfect and unsatisfactory state of things was
put an end to by the act of others, when he found that,
if he meant to be King at all, he must go on with the
work of conquest. The same kind of feeling may have *Reasons for*
led him not to hurry back at once on the first news of *delaying his return*
disaffection. Haste would have implied fear. It would
rather suit his purpose to deal with the isolated movements
which took place during his absence as trifles which his
lieutenants could easily put down, even if they were not
put down by the loyal English themselves. It was only *William*
when he found that the disaffected were intriguing for *called back by the*
foreign help, that there was a chance of his having to *prospect of foreign*
struggle for his Crown against Swend of Denmark or *invasion*
some other foreign King, that William thought that the
time was come to return to England with all speed.

§ 1. *The Administration of Odo and William Fitz-Osbern.*
*March—December, 1067.*

The new Earls of Kent and Hereford, Bishop Odo *Joint command of*
of Bayeux and William Fitz-Osbern, had been left, as we *Odo and*
have seen, in a joint general command in England. The *William Fitz-*
Bishop was charged with the special care of the South, the *Osbern.*

104    CONQUEST OF WESTERN AND NORTHERN ENGLAND.

CHAP. XVIII. region which was most thoroughly subdued, while the Seneschal had to keep watch against movements from Northumberland and the still unsubdued parts of Mercia.[1]

Norman praises of their administration.

Of the character of their administration the Norman panegyrist of William gives a glowing picture. They were models of loyalty towards their master, of harmony towards one another, and of just government towards those over whom they were set. Their example in all these respects was carefully followed by the subordinate commanders of the castles, whose building, in conformity with William's parting orders,[2] they were diligently pressing on.[3] The native Chronicler has another tale to tell. From him we learn how Odo Bishop and William Earl stayed in the land, and wrought castles wide among the people, and oppressed the poor folk, and how evil grew ever after.[4] Here is another speaking witness to the horror with which our fathers looked on the fortresses, the special badges of foreign rule, which were fast rising among them. And I think that we may see that a distinction is drawn between the rule of William himself and the rule of his oppressive lieutenants. At all events, the record, or rather the wail, of the native writer is more than borne out by the elaborate picture drawn by our one authority who is English, French, and Norman all at once. And in his

Opposite picture given by the English writers,

and by Orderic

[1] See above, p 72.    [2] See above, p 73.
[3] Will Pict 157 "Mutuo sese, Regem æqualiter, diligebant, affectu ardebant pari ad continendum in pace gentem Christianam, consilio alter alterius æquanimiter assentiebantur Æquitate utebantur maximâ, uti Rex præmonuerat, quâ homines efferi et inimici corrigerentur et benevoli fierent. Item præfecti minores, ubi quisque in munitionibus locatus fuerat, strenue curabat."
[4] Chron Wig. 1066. "And Oda Biscop and Wyllelm Eorl belifen her æfter [after King William's departure for Normandy], and *workton castelas wide geond þas þeode, and earm folc swencte*, and á syððan hit yflade swiðe. Wurðe gód se ende þonne God wylle." The words in italics are nearly the same as the Peterborough writer's description of William himself; "Castelas he lét wyrcean and earme men swiðe swencean" See vol. ii. pp 138, 192

version also the distinction between William and his unworthy representatives is plainly drawn. The two haughty chiefs whom he had left in command despised his orders, and laid every kind of oppression on the people. The English were insulted by the pride of the Normans. Their property and the honour of their women lay open to the attacks of the followers of the two viceroys, and no redress could be had from Earl or Bishop for any wrong that an Englishman suffered; if an injured man dared to bring a complaint before them, he was driven from the judgement-seat with scorn.[1] We must remember that the excesses here complained of were not the momentary excesses of soldiers whose blood is roused by the excitement of a battle or a storm. The land was now, at least nominally, at peace, and the oppression here described is the wearing, grinding, daily oppression of unrighteous rulers in time of peace. And the evils spoken of were just the evils which it was William's own great object, both in Normandy and in England, to put down. Wherever his personal authority was peaceably established, he had no mercy for the robber or the ravisher.[2] We may fully acquit William of any personal share in the evil deeds

*Oppressive government of Odo and William Fitz-Osbern.*

*Amount of the King's own responsibility*

---

[1] Ord. Vit. 507 D "Interea Normannico fastu Angli opprimuntur, et præsidibus superbis, qui Regis monitus spernebant, admodum injuriabantur. Odo nimirum Episcopus et Guillelmus Osberni filius nimiâ cervicositate tumebant, et clamores Anglorum rationabiliter audire, eisque æquitatis lance suffragari despiciebant. Nam armigeros suos immodicas prædas et incestos raptus facientes vi tuebantur, et super eos qui contumeliis affecti querimonias agebant, magis debacchabantur." This account of Orderic is very remarkable, because in this part of his work he is, in his main facts, following William of Poitiers. But he here deliberately leaves out William's panegyric on the two Earls and puts this widely different description of them instead. The passage has the same kind of value as the controversial passages of Florence (see vol. ii. p. 607; iii. p. 578), or as the places where Matthew Paris, following the narrative of Roger of Wendover, changes the political colouring.

[2] See the famous character in the Peterborough Chronicle, 1087, and vol. ii. p. 172.

of Odo and his fellow-viceroy; his share in the blame is that of not seeing how utterly unfit his brother and his dearest friend were for the trust which he placed in them. Yet perhaps no fitter deputies could be found. As throughout the whole story, wrong was its own punishment. The original sin of an unjust enterprise drove William against his will to become a tyrant and a favourer of lesser tyrants. Deeds were done under the shadow of his name which we may be sure that in his own heart he abhorred. For the lesser commanders, each safe in his own castle, faithfully followed the example of the two great viceroys, and ground down Englishmen of every degree both with illegal exactions and with insults which were probably more bitter than any injury.[1] While the new King's authority was wielded by men like these, any feelings which may have still lingered on from the momentary and factitious popularity which had greeted the day of William's crowning died utterly away.

But the first appeal to arms in England during William's absence was not provoked by any oppression on the part of his Norman lieutenants. It happened in a district which was far withdrawn from William's practical authority, and though his name was used by one party, the struggle was really a local struggle between Englishman and Englishman. Copsige, the newly appointed Earl of Bernicia or Northern Northumberland, must have set forth to take possession of his Earldom about the time that William was setting forth for Normandy.[2] What kind of force he headed we are not told, but it must have been a force of his own partizans, personal or local. Everything goes against the notion that any Norman troops could have made their way into the extreme North of England so early in William's reign.

[1] Ord Vit 507 D "Præfecti minores, qui munitiones custodiebant, nobiles et mediocres indigenas injustis exactionibus multisque contumeliis aggravabant"  [2] See above, p 76.

But, however Copsige found the means, it was only by force that he was able to dispossess the reigning Earl Oswulf.[1] The son of the old Earls had to lurk in woods and mountains till his day of vengeance came. He soon gathered together a band of outlaws,[2] and it presently became plain that popular feeling was on his side. Five weeks after William's grant,[3] a much shorter time therefore after Copsige could have actually appeared north of the Tyne, the new Earl was feasting in a place called Newburn. Then followed a scene to which we find several parallels in Northumbrian history. The partizans of Oswulf beset the house where Copsige was; he contrived to slip out secretly and to seek refuge in a neighbouring church. But his lurking-place was soon betrayed, the church was set on fire; the Earl, to escape the flames, tried to make his way out by the door, and was cut down on the threshold by the hands of Oswulf himself.[4] The victor in this struggle, a scuffle rather than a battle, again took possession of the Earldom, and held it for a few months.

*CHAP XVIII.*

*Copsige slain by Oswulf. March 11, 1067.*

By the Norman writers Copsige, or, as they call him, Coxo[5], is held up to honour as the martyr of his loyalty to the Norman King, and they are not sparing of the praises which, according to their views, were due to the one Englishman whom William found thoroughly faithful.[6] In

*Norman praises of Copsige.*

---

[1] Sim. Dun Gest Reg 1072, p. 91, ed. Hinde "Pulsus a Copsio de comitatu Osulfus."

[2] Ib. "Osulfus in fame et egestate silvis latitans et montibus, tandem collectis quos eadem necessitas compulerat sociis, Copsium in Nyweburne convivantem concludit"

[3] Ib. 92. "Quintâ hebdomadâ commissi sibi comitatûs iiii. Idus Martii"

[4] Ib "Qui [Copsius] inter tumultuantes turbas lapsus dum lateret in ecclesiâ proditus, incendio ecclesiæ compellitur usque ad ostium procedere, ubi in ipso ostio manibus Osulfi detruncatur."   [5] See vol. ii p 484

[6] Will Pict 158. "Sed ubi mentem firmiter in tenore boni fixam taliter dimovere nequeunt, comprovinciales ad invidiam concitavere, quam

108  CONQUEST OF WESTERN AND NORTHERN ENGLAND.

CHAP XVIII.
Copsige's probable policy

English ears, whether then or now, such praise might perhaps sound like a charge of the deepest treason. What Copsige seems to have done was to use the name of the Norman King as a means to carry out a personal scheme, most like to carry out a Northumbrian deadly feud. His act was an attempted betrayal of the country into the hands of an invader who had as yet not ventured to assert his claims in any practical form. It is not wonderful that Northumbrian feeling was aroused against him, and that his enterprise had only a momentary success. The day when William was really to subdue the most northern shire of England was still far distant.

Discontent with Odo and William Fitz-Osbern

Outbreaks in Herefordshire and Kent

Oppression possibly greater in those districts.

These Northumbrian disturbances had little effect on the general march of the events, and they had no immediate connexion with the outbreaks in other parts of England which were caused by the oppressions of Odo and William Fitz-Osbern. Of the general discontent at their administration, and of the outbreaks to which that discontent gave rise, we have accounts which enter a good deal into detail, but it is not easy to fix the exact order of events. But the general indignation of the people, and their readiness to seek for foreign help in any quarter, are plainly shown on all sides. And it is plain also that the two most formidable outbreaks took place in the districts immediately subject to the two Earls, in Herefordshire and in Kent. Under the immediate eye of the two viceroys oppression ought to have been less flagrant than in other places; but with rulers who systematically refused to listen to the complaints of the oppressed, it is possible that the grievances in the near neighbourhood of head-quarters may have been even greater

necessario placaret ab Rege deficiendo. Postremo augescente in dies malevolentiâ ipsorum, quum ille popularium odia, omnemque injuriam perpeti, quam integritatem fidei temerare mallet, per insidias oppressum interfecere Ita eximius vir suo casu quod majestas domini sui stare deberet asseruit"

than elsewhere. A local commander, perhaps of no great consideration in his own country, but who found his services at Senlac rewarded with an English estate and sometimes with an English wife, might, from the very beginning, be more inclined to identify himself with his new country than men of such high place in their own land as the Bishop of Bayeux and the Seneschal of Normandy. Kent and Herefordshire were moreover the two ends of William's real dominion, and they were the districts where foreign aid might most easily be found. Kent lay open to help from any enemies of William who might be found beyond the sea, and on the Herefordshire border the Welsh were always ready to step in on any pretext which promised a chance of fighting and plunder. We have seen that the old alliance between Ælfgar and Gruffydd had caused Eadwine to be accompanied by Welsh followers on his march to Northampton.[1] That alliance was doubtless still remembered. On the other hand, the reigning princes, Bleddyn and Rhiwallon, had received their kingship at the hands of Harold and had become his men.[2] They had therefore, if they chose, a fair right to give themselves out as his avengers or as assertors of the rights of his house. When English plunder was to be had, kinsmen and followers both of the Northern and of the Southern Gruffydd would be ready to answer either call. The unhappy thing was that, in those times, a movement for the deliverance of any district too often took the form of a general harrying of that district by friends and enemies alike. So it now was in Herefordshire. The land had not yet recovered, it had not fully recovered twenty years after, from the wasting warfare of Gruffydd the son of Llywelyn.[3] It was now to be wasted again. The most powerful, at any rate the most enterprising, Englishman

*Foreign help more easily found there.*

*Readiness of the Welsh to join in any English quarrel.*

[1] See vol ii p 490   [2] See vol. ii. p. 476
[3] See vol. ii. p 388

110    CONQUEST OF WESTERN AND NORTHERN ENGLAND.

CHAP XVIII
Eadric the Wild maintains his independence.

of those parts was Eadric, of whom we have already heard.[1] He held lands both in the north of Herefordshire and in Shropshire, and he had refused all submission to the new King. Here then, right in the teeth of the new Earl of Hereford, right in the teeth of the old enemies, Richard the son of Scrob and his son Osbern, lay an outlying piece of independent England which still needed to be conquered. None of the representatives of Norman rule in the district were slow to act in such a case. The garrisons of both fortresses, of Richard's Castle and of the castle of Hereford, made constant inroads on the lands of the refractory Eadric. The English Thegn and his followers, and whoever else may have joined him, stood manfully on their defence, and every Norman incursion was beaten back with loss on the part of the invaders.[2] At last, in the month of August, the English chief ventured on reprisals. He formed an alliance with the two Welsh Kings, and their combined forces entered the obedient[3] districts of Herefordshire. Eadric seems to have thought himself justified in dealing with lands which had submitted to the Normans as with an enemy's country. Bleddyn and Rhiwallon would of course have no scruples. The whole land as far as the Lugg, the river which flows by Leominster, was ravaged, and a vast booty was carried off by the combined English and Welsh forces.[4] The geographical limit thus given would take in the city of Hereford

Vain attempts of the Normans to subdue him.

He leagues with Bleddyn and Rhiwallon, and harries as far as the Lugg.
August 15, 1067.

---

[1] See above, pp. 21, 64.

[2] Flor Wig 1067 "Cujus [Edrici] terram, quia se dedere Regi dedignabatur, Herefordenses castellani [see above, p 64] et Richardus filius Scrob, frequenter vastaverunt, et quotiescumque super eum irruerant, multos e suis militibus et *scutariis* perdiderunt" On "scutarii," see Ducange in voc The word is the parent of *écuyer* and *esquire*

[3] I adopt the familiar phrase of the days of Philip the Second

[4] Flor Wig u. s "Idcirco adscitis sibi in auxilium Regibus Walanorum, Blethgento videlicet et Rithwalano, idem vir Edricus, circa Assumptionem S Mariæ, Herefordensem provinciam usque ad pontem amnis Luege, devastavit, ingentemque prædam reduxit."

itself. The town and its fortress were clearly not taken, but the Norman garrison was reduced to great straits.[1] Eadric himself retained his independence for at least two years longer. The impression which he made on the Normans is shown by the surname of the Wild or Savage which he bore among them.[2] Among the hills and woods of the border land, Eadric and his British allies could maintain themselves as easily against the Norman chivalry as Gruffydd had done against the English Housecarls, till the genius of Harold found out the way to bring the restless enemy to submission.[3]

This contest in Herefordshire was strictly a local war. It was an attempt, and an unsuccessful attempt, on the part of the invaders to subdue a district, however small, which had never submitted to William's authority. The outbreak in Kent, a shire where William's authority was fully established, was of course strictly a revolt. In the Herefordshire case, the strangers had simply to be kept out; in the Kentish case, they had to be driven out. It may possibly be owing to this difference that the exploits of Eadric are recorded by the English writers only, while the movement in Kent is narrated at some length by our Norman informants, but is wholly passed by in the national Chronicles. The attempt at deliverance in Kent was certainly planned with very little regard to its chance of success and with still less regard to the national honour. The Kentishmen sought for foreign help, but they sought it in a very different quarter from that in which it was sought by Eadric. However practically dangerous might be the presence of Bleddyn and Rhiwallon on

*Distress of the garrison of Hereford*
*Eadric remains unsubdued 1067-1069*

*Difference between the Herefordshire and Kentish outbreaks*

---

[1] Chron. Wig. 1067. "And Eadric cild and þa Bryttas wurdon unsehte, and wunnon heom wið þa castelmenn on Hereforda, and fela hearmas heom dydon."

[2] See Appendix I.    [3] See vol. ii p. 473.

112        CONQUEST OF WESTERN AND NORTHERN ENGLAND.

CHAP XVIII. English ground, no formal treason towards England was implied in an alliance with Under-kings of the English Empire against strangers who threatened Briton and Englishman alike. But the Kentish insurgents sought for help at the hands of a stranger who had done greater despite to Englishmen than any other man living, and for whose rule it would have been madness indeed to exchange the rule of William. Oppression must indeed have reached its height, men's minds must have reached that state when any change seems as if it must be a change for the better, when the men of Kent sent to ask for the help of Eustace of Boulogne in an attack on the castle of Dover. The man whose crime had been the beginning of evils, the man who had slaughtered the burghers of Dover in their streets and in their houses,[1] the man whose one exploit in the great battle had been to wreak a coward's spite on the corpse of the dead Harold,[2] was now called on to help to rid Dover of its Norman lords and to join in the siege of the fortress which Harold himself had reared. Perhaps, if we minutely study the story, we may see signs that the invitation was not shared in by the men of Dover itself, but it is plain that the men of the shire in general clutched eagerly even at so feeble a chance of help as this. What the object proposed by such an invitation could be is not clear; it was probably an act done in the mere frenzy of despair, without any rational reckoning of what was likely to come of it. We are told that the English, unable to have a native ruler, preferred one who was at least their neighbour and known to them.[3] It is possible that some vague sentimental feeling may have attached to the son-in-law of Æthelred;[4] otherwise one would have thought that

The Kentishmen ask help of Eustace of Boulogne

Objects of the invitation

---

[1] See vol. ii pp 131–133    [2] See vol iii p 499.
[3] Will Pict. 157. "Si erat serviendum non compatriotæ, noto servire atque vicino satius putabant"
[4] See vol. ii. p 131

what was known of William was, even now, better than what was known of Eustace. Men could hardly have dreamed that the Count of Boulogne could dispossess William of those parts of England which he had already conquered, or that the still unsubdued districts could be persuaded or compelled to receive him as their King. They could hardly have seriously thought that, if a foreign King had to be endured, they were likely to find a better King in a paltry coward and murderer than they already had in the great Conqueror. Most likely the reckonings of the men of Kent did not go so far afield. Anything seemed better than the rule of Odo and Hugh of Montfort. Eustace was at that moment the enemy of William,[1] and any enemy of William seemed for the moment to be the friend of England.[2] Eustace's own views were most likely not much clearer than those of his Kentish allies. He may, or he may not, have aspired to the Imperial Crown of Britain; but our hints rather set him before us as one who looked with jealousy on the Norman power, and who hoped, by obtaining possession of the strong fortress of Dover, to be better able to hold his powerful neighbour in check on both sides of the sea.[3] But, whatever may have been the views on both sides, the men of Kent patched up an alliance with their bitterest enemy.[4] It

*Probable views of Eustace*

---

[1] Will. Pict. 157 "Regi eâ tempestate Eustachius Comes Boloniæ adversabatur, qui filium de fide ante bellum in Normanniâ obsidem dederat" Cf vol iii. p 748 I do not know the grounds or circumstances of this quarrel between Eustace and William, or of the suspicion in which William seemingly held Eustace even before his expedition

[2] Ord Vit 508 B. "Olim cum eodem inimicitias ingentes habuerant, sed nunc, quia simultates inter eum et Regem insurrexerant . pacem cum illo fecerunt"

[3] Will Pict 157 "Equidem fore, si firmissimo loco hoc sit potitus cum portu marino, ut potentia ejus latius distendatur, sicque potentiam Normannorum diminutum iri" These words are put into the mouths of the English messengers, but they express the reasons why Eustace should accept the invitation, not why the English should send it

[4] Ib "Quia Normannos odere, cum Eustachio, pridem sibi inimicissimo, concordavere" See Ordenc in the passage last quoted.

114    CONQUEST OF WESTERN AND NORTHERN ENGLAND.

CHAP XVIII. was agreed that the Count of Boulogne should sail across
Scheme for putting Dover into his hands. with a fleet and with a fitting land force, and that the Kentishmen should be ready to do their best to make him master of the castle of Dover.[1]

Plan of the attack. However unwise the scheme of Eustace and the Kentishmen may seem in a wider aspect of things, the actual attack on the castle seems, as a military enterprise, to have been skilfully planned  Advantage was taken of a time when Bishop Odo, Viceroy and Earl, and Hugh of Montfort, the immediate commander of the castle, were both of them absent. They had gone beyond the Thames with the greater part of their forces.[2] This movement clearly shows that something was going on in other parts of England of which we should gladly learn more. It can hardly be that the forces which were meant to keep down the men of Kent were called away for the defence of Hereford against Eadric. While Dover was thus comparatively defenceless, Count Eustace was warned that the proper moment was come  He at once embarked in the fleet which he had made ready for the purpose, and crossed in the night with a band of picked knights. Horses, which could be of little use in attacking the castle on the cliff, were, with few exceptions, of which the Count's own horse was one, left behind.[3] The state of

Absence of Odo and Hugh

Eustace sails across.

---

[1] Will Pict 157. "Persuadent hi maxime qui Cantiam inhabitant, uti castrum Doveram invadat, ipsis utens adjutoribus." Ord. Vit. 508 B. "Multimodis Normannorum oppressionibus Angli ad rebellionem lacessiti, Boloniam legatos miserunt, et Eustachio Comiti, ut cum classe diligenter militibus et armis instructâ ad suscipiendam Doveram acceleraret, mandaverunt .  Munitionem Doveræ contra Regem illi tradere conati sunt " Orderic's account is founded on that of William of Poitiers, whose words he largely copies, but he also brings in matter of his own, and he gives quite a different turn to the personal conduct of Eustace

[2] Will. Pict. 157. "Accidit ut occasio temporis eventum rei quam affectabant promitteret. Abierant ultra flumen Tamisim primi munitionis custodes, Præsul Baiocensis atque Hugo de Monteforti, militum parte majori secum ductâ "  So Orderic, 508 C, in nearly the same words

[3] Will. Pict 157. "Eustachius itaque accepto nuntio Anglorum [" Can-

readiness in which Eustace kept himself, and the energy shown in his passage, should be noted. And it is important also to notice that, in his general plan at least, he seems to have risen above that superstitious trust in horses in all times and places which distinguished the French and Norman knights of those days.¹ It is even possible that his former experience in Dover itself may have taught him a lesson on this head. What we hear of Eustace now, just like what we hear of him at Senlac,² suggests the idea of a man who well understood the science of war,³ but who, like his stepson Ralph,⁴ was lacking in personal courage. He landed, and found a large English force gathered together to join him, the Kentishmen being the most forward of all. Within two days, if the siege should last so long, still larger reinforcements were looked for from the more distant parts of the country.⁵ It was however judged better to begin the attack at once; the two days which might bring together a larger English force might also bring back Odo and Hugh with their following. At day-break accordingly the attack was made.⁶ Our accounts show that the town itself had to be taken as well as the castle, and it was on the town that the first attack

*CHAP. XVIII.*

*Union of skill and cowardice in Eustace*

*Eustace and the English attack Dover.*

---

tiorum veredario" in Ord. Vit.], cum suis ad eos noctis conticinio transivit, ut incaute opprimeret castellanos ["classem paratam ascendit, noctisque conticinio, ut oppidum ex insperato præoccuparet, cum suis festinanter transfretavit" Ord. Vit.] Classem duxit militibus delectis oneratam ["milites multos secum duxit." Ord. Vit.], relictis equis præter admodum paucos."

¹ See vol. ii. p. 132.   ² See vol. iii. p. 748.
³ Will. Pict. 157. "Eum bellandi peritum atque in prælio felicem experimentis cognoverant." Does this mean at Dover itself, or at Senlac, or where?
⁴ See vol. ii. p. 388.
⁵ Will. Pict. 158. "Vicinia omnis adfuit armata [Orderic adds "maxime Cantiorum caterva, quæ toto nisu suffragari Eustachio erat conata"], auctior numerus ex ulterioribus accederet, si morâ biduanâ obsidio traheretur."
⁶ Will. Gem. vii. 39. "Eustachius . . . in noctis conticinio mare transfretans, diluculo cum copioso exercitu corum obsedit." This writer's account seems to be independent of the others.

116     CONQUEST OF WESTERN AND NORTHERN ENGLAND.

CHAP XVIII.
Stout resistance of the garrison and townsmen.

was made[1] Eustace and his English allies seem to have looked for an easy success But the garrison was found better prepared and in higher spirit for defence than they had deemed possible.[2] And it is plain that the townsmen were on the side of the garrison. Whatever might be the feelings of the rest of the shire, the men of Dover had no mind to see Count Eustace again within their walls. At every point which lay open to attack, the assailants were vigorously withstood, and a stout fight was kept up on both sides for several hours.[3] At last the heart of Eustace failed him, as it had failed him on the steep of Malfosse amid the twilight of Saint Calixtus[4] The assault must have begun to slacken, for he feared a sally of the besieged. He therefore ordered a retreat to the ships.[5] The evil which he thought to avoid now came upon him; the gates were thrown open by the townsmen, and a general attack on the part of the besiegers changed the retreat into a flight. In the last scene of the great battle the thought of Eustace had been that a new English host was coming to snatch the victory from the conquerors; so now the cry of Eustace and of his whole host was that the Bishop

Retreat of Eustace

Utter rout of his army.

[1] At this point William of Poitiers suddenly draws in his horns, so that his story reads like an abridgement of Orderic's, instead of Orderic's being, as it must be, an enlargement of William's Is it possible that Orderic, who clearly had William's account before him, had it in some form earlier and fuller than our present copies, from which William of Poitiers, like his namesake of Malmesbury, afterwards cut out parts through prudence?

The special mention of the town comes from Orderic (508 C), "Quum hostes vehementer impetum facere in *oppidum* molirentur, custodes ad defensandum reperti sunt, et ferventissime, qua locus poterat impugnari, restiterunt"

[2] Will Pict 158. "Ceterum custodiam invenerunt minus opinione remissam, plus metu ad defensandum validam."

[3] Ord. Vit 508 C. "Acerrime per aliquas horas diei utrimque certatum est"

[4] See vol. iii p 503 Cf p 483.

[5] Ord Vit. 508 C "Sed dum Eustachius diffideret, eruptionemque propugnatorum, quâ turpius abigeretur, timeret, receptui ad naves cani signa jubet"

of Bayeux was upon them at the head of a mighty army.[1] CHAP XVIII.
The loss was frightful, but, though the Norman horsemen
followed on the fliers, slaying and taking captives, yet the
smallest number of those who fell that day were those who
were slain by the sword. The terrible name of Odo
scattered them in all directions. Some, seeking to escape
the horsemen, strove to climb the steep heights on either
side of the town. But in their flight and hurry and
ignorance of the paths, the more part of them perished
by falling over the rocks. Some threw aside their arms,
and were dashed to pieces by the mere fall; others, in the
general confusion and entanglement, received deadly wounds
from their own weapons or from those of their comrades.
Some contrived to reach the coast unhurt, but, as they
crowded recklessly into their ships, the frail vessels sank,
and many of them perished.[2] The Count himself was Escape of Eustace
more lucky; he had indeed taken special care for his own
safety. He at least knew the way, if his comrades did not,
and for him a fleet horse was ready. He made fast for his
ship, where better order was kept than in the others, and so
saved himself from the general wreck of the undertaking.[3]

[1] Ord Vit 508 C "Denique oppidani confestim portas patefecerunt,
avideque et caute sequentes novissimos conciderunt Fugientes vero Baiocensem Episcopum cum agmine copioso subito supervenisse rati sunt"

[2] The description in Orderic (508 C, D) is very graphic, "Eâ formidine
velut amentes per aviæ rupis præcipitium se dejecerunt, et tali compendio
fœdius quam ense virorum perierunt .. Plerique abjectis armis, acumine
saxeo exanimati sunt, nonnulli telo suo se sociosque suos una labentes
necârunt, et multi letaliter vulnerati vel collisi spirantes ad mare devoluti
sunt Plures etiam qui ad puppes propere anhelant, dum salutis nimium
cupidi trepidant, suâque multitudine naves deprimunt, subito submersi
pereunt Equites Normanni quantos consectari possunt comprehendunt
vel occidunt."

[3] At this point William of Poitiers (158) begins again, "Eripiunt
velocitas equi, notitia tramitis, navisque paratior" But the accusative
"Eustachium," which is needed to explain who this lucky rider was, is left
to be supplied by Orderic, who also improves "equi" into "cornipedis."
William of Jumièges (vii 39) tells us how "Eustachius ad mare devertens,
cum paucis indecenter navigio aufugit"

William of Jumièges makes no mention of the townsfolk, and speaks

118        CONQUEST OF WESTERN AND NORTHERN ENGLAND.

CHAP XVIII.   His nephew, who had accompanied him, was less lucky,
Capture of    probably more valiant, and he became the captive of the
his nephew    pursuers.[1] As was natural, the horrors of the flight and
slaughter fell mainly on the French followers of Eustace.
His English allies knew the country, and, protected by
their own numbers, they contrived to baffle the smaller
bands which attempted to follow them.

An enterprise which had been planned in folly thus
ended in utter disgrace. While the sons of the soil,
British and English alike, could still hold their own on
the Herefordshire march, the attempt to rescue England
by an alliance with the basest foe of Englishmen had led,
General       as it deserved, only to signal discomfiture. Of the rest of
discontent    the land which was already conquered we hear nothing in
in other      detail. Our stories of oppression and discontent are per-
parts of      fectly general. But men were everywhere seeking either
England       to shake off the yoke or to escape it in their own persons.
Even where no open outbreak took place, local conspiracies
were everywhere rife.[2] Many left England altogether;
some sought a lasting home in foreign lands; others

only of the "milites Odonis Baiocasini Præsulis atque Hugonis de Monteforti," and how they, "liberalibus animis accensi, portas patefaciunt," &c
From this, and from the accounts of men falling headlong from the rocks,
we might have thought that the attack was made only on the castle  But
from the distinct mention of "oppidum" and "oppidani" in Orderic it
would seem that it was the town which was immediately assaulted. The
besiegers may have invested the town on all sides, from above as well as
from below, or footmen pursued by horse may have tried to escape by
climbing the heights on each side of the town

[1] Will Pict 158. "Nobilissimus tiro, nepos ejus, comprehensus est"
Of this nephew I can give no further account  I conceive him to have
been the son of Eustace's brother Lambert, who is described as Lord
of Sens, and who died in 1054  Eustace's other brother Godfrey was
Bishop of Paris, and his sister Gerberga, the wife of Duke Frederick of
Lotharingia, had only daughters  See Art de Vérifier les Dates, ii 761.

[2] Will Pict 157  "Angli neque beneficio, neque formidine satis coerceri
poterant, ut quietum serenam quam res novas ac turbidas mallent  Con-
surgere palam in arma non confidunt, sed *regionatim* de pravis conspira-
tionibus tractant, si quibus forte dolis prævaleant ad nocendum"  The
word "regionatim" explains the cause of the real conquest of England.

simply visited them to seek the means of their own restoration or of the deliverance of their country.[1] Englishmen, charged with the bidding of some section or other of their countrymen, were scattered over every corner of Europe where there was any chance of help being found. Some seem to have sought for allies in the old land of their fathers at the mouth of the Elbe and the Weser.[2] But the state of things during the sickly and licentious youth of Henry the Fourth did not offer much prospect of help from the Teutonic Kingdom. The King himself was, in the autumn of this very year, lying on a bed of sickness at Goslar,[3] and the troubles of Saxony and Thuringia, if they had not yet broken forth, were already festering in silence. There was another quarter in which such attempts were far more likely to be crowned with success. There was one foreign potentate to whom Englishmen might look as all but their countryman. The old West-Saxon dynasty had died out; its only representative was the King of a moment who was now tarrying in William's Norman court. The new West-Saxon dynasty had been cut off in the cause of England; besides the sons of the traitor Tostig, its only adult legitimate representative was the hostage Wulfnoth, who was tarrying either in William's court or in William's dungeon.[4] But the stock of the Northern kinsmen and conquerors of England still flourished in a prince who was united by the closest ties of blood alike

*CHAP XVIII*

*Movements after foreign help.*

*State of Germany.*

*Denmark the most promising quarter*

*Position of Swend Estrithson.*

---

[1] Will. Pict 157 "Ultro in exsilium aliqui profugiunt, quo extorres vel a potestate Normannorum sint liberi, vel aucti opibus alienis contra eos revertantur."

[2] I think we may infer this from the words of William of Poitiers (u s ), "Ad Danos, vel alio, unde auxilium aliquod speratur, legatos missitant," compared with the legend of Harold's German journey (see vol iii pp 515, 761), and with the various indications which we shall come across of the intercourse between England and Germany at this time

[3] Lambert, 1067 Henry fell sick on November 11th His life had been despaired of in a former sickness in May, 1066

[4] See vol iii pp 242, 674 I shall give, a little further on, some account of the state of the House of Godwine at this moment

with the House of Cnut and with the House of Godwine. Swend, the son of Ulf and Estrith, the nephew of Cnut, the nephew of Gytha, the brother of the murdered Beorn, the cousin of the fallen Harold, was, of all men not absolutely born of English parents on English soil, the man who was most called on to avenge the blood of his kinsmen and to break the chains of what he might almost call his country. Five-and-twenty years earlier, a party in England had sought to place him on the throne in preference to Eadward himself.[1] Since that time he had acted as the ally of England, as the friend of Godwine, and he had perhaps met with less of English thankfulness than his services deserved.[2] He had refused to abet the schemes of Tostig or to clutch at the crown which Tostig offered him.[3] He had equally refused to abet the enterprise of William, and Norman writers believed, though doubtless without foundation, that subjects of his had been among their foes on Senlac.[4] But now everything had changed since the day when Swend had refused to undertake at Tostig's bidding an enterprise which might befit the greatness of Cnut, but which was beyond the power of his own littleness. It was not now a solitary Englishman, banished by English justice, who asked him to attack a King of his own blood whom the free choice of the English people had honoured with their Crown. Englishmen were pressing to him from all quarters, to crave help against a foreign conqueror at the hands of one who might give himself out either as the heir of Cnut or as the avenger of Harold.[5] Things too had changed in another way. Since the day of Stamfordbridge Norway

---

[1] See vol. ii. pp. 9, 523.   [2] See vol. ii. pp. 91–93.
[3] See vol. iii. p. 330.   [4] See vol. iii. p. 746.
[5] Ord. Vit. 508 A. "Ad Suenum Regem Danorum dirigunt, atque ut regnum Angliæ, quod Suenus et Chunutus avi ejus armis obtinuerunt, reposcat expetunt." In the Legatio Helsini (of which more below) in Langebek, iii. 253, we read, "Contigit ut Danorum Rex, auditâ morte Haraldi consanguinei, venire in Angliam disponeret, ut et mortem ejus vindicaret et terram sibi subigeret quam dicebat suam esse."

was no longer threatening, and the prudence of Swend himself no longer needed to shrink from the risks of an English campaign. There is indeed no reason to believe the wild fable of a late writer that, immediately on William's coronation, Swend sent to require the new King to hold the English Crown of him as its lawful Over-lord [1] Such a piece of bravado would be quite out of character with the prudence which had enabled the Danish King to hold his own among so many storms. But now that Englishmen were bidding him to come and deliver England from the invader, there was no doubt that their requests were favourably listened to. And among the Englishmen who sought refuge in his Kingdom there was one especially who could give him the best information as to the naval resources of England. Eadric, the captain of King Eadward's ship, who had perhaps met Norman ships in naval warfare before the day of Senlac, had been outlawed at the coming of William, and was now an exile in the Danish Kingdom.[2] While he and other Englishmen were pressing Swend to action, there could be no doubt where the greatest hope for England, the greatest danger for William, now lay The whole North lay open to a Danish invasion at any moment. No Norman soldier had crossed the Humber; the brother Earls were with William in Normandy; the Northumbrian people, as yet unchecked by Norman castles and garrisons, would doubtless have welcomed the Danish King to put an end to what, as far as they were concerned, was a state of Interregnum. Even if Swend had hastened, even if the expedition which took place two years later had taken place at once, it would perhaps be too much to deem that William could have been driven out of England. But

*CHAP XVIII*

*Presence of Eadric of Norfolk in Denmark.*

*Northumberland ready for Danish help.*

*Swend loses the favourable moment*

---

[1] See the story in Knighton, 2343, and Appendix P
[2] On this Eadric from the East of England, see vol III p 717, and Appendix I

CHAP XVIII. there can be little doubt that, if such a course had been taken, the final conquest must have been long delayed. If Swend had come at once, William could never have occupied Northern England, except at the price of a hard struggle against the men of the land, supported by their kinsfolk from Denmark.

Aid sought elsewhere, specially in Norway.

Besides the Danes, we hear vaguely of what the Norman writers call other barbarous nations, as likely to take a part in disturbing William's possession of England.[1] The reference is doubtless to Norway, whither we shall see that William did, a little time later, find it worth his while to send an embassy,[2] no doubt with the object of warding off any danger from that quarter. But under the sons of Harold Hardrada, Magnus and Olaf surnamed Kyrre or the Tranquil, Norway, instead of threatening either Denmark or England, had well nigh itself fallen under the power of Swend.[3] The power of the Kingdom, as well as its reputation, must have been greatly lessened by the failure of the great expedition against England, and even by the mere slaughter of Stamfordbridge. Neither of the brother Kings inherited the enterprising disposition of their father. Olaf especially, who soon became sole King by the death of his brother, was much more occupied in maintaining peace and good order in his own Kingdom, than in disturbing the Kingdoms of others. Men who doubtless yearned for the days of his father called him in mockery Olaf the Bonde or Churl.[4] And whatever gratitude the sons of Harold

State of Norway after Harold Hardrada. [Magnus sole King, 1066-1067 Magnus and Olaf together, 1067-1069. Olaf alone, 1069-1093]

Peaceful character and reign of Olaf Kyrre.

---

[1] Ord. Vit. 509 C "Ex malevolentiâ Anglorum cum nisu Danorum aliarumque barbararum gentium, magnam cladem Normannis orituram intimabant"

[2] Sim Dun 1074 (p 95, Hinde) See Chapter xxi

[3] See Laing, III. 103

[4] Laing, III 108 "King Olaf Haraldsson was called by some Olaf Kyrre, but by many Olaf the Bonder, because he sat in peace, without strife within or without the country, and gave no reasonable cause for others to plunder in his dominions" Yet in the poem which Laing translates in

Hardrada may have felt for the merciful dealings of Harold of England after his great victory,[1] they could have had no motive to avenge his fall, or to disturb the reign of his conqueror. From Norway then there was no real hope for England, no real danger for William. The real hope, the real danger, was to be looked for wholly from Denmark. And it was evidently the news that English exiles were gathering at the Danish Court, and that King Swend was lending a favourable ear to their prayers, which made William suddenly break off his festive and devout sojourn in his native Duchy, to embark once more on the sea of troubles which still awaited him in his half-conquered island Kingdom.

*§ 2. The Conquest of the West.*
*December* 1067—*March* 1068.

When William had once determined on his return to England, he did not tarry long in carrying his purpose into effect. The Lady Matilda, a King's wife but not yet a crowned Queen, was again entrusted with the government of Normandy, but this time William's eldest son Robert was nominally associated with his mother.[2] He was still a boy; he could not have been above thirteen years old, and he was probably younger;[3] but his capacity

---

p 113, and the original of which is given in Johnstone, p. 228, he appears as a triumphant ravager of England,

"Orr er Engla þverrir
Olafi borinn solo"

He certainly was so in intent at a later time
[1] See vol iii p. 375.
[2] Ord Vit 509 C "Rex igitur Mathildi conjugi suæ, filioque suo Rodberto adolescenti principatum Neustriæ commisit, et cum eis religiosos præsules et strenuos proceres ad tuendam regionem dimisit."
[3] M Bouet (Saint-Etienne, p 8) places Robert's birth about ("environ")

124    CONQUEST OF WESTERN AND NORTHERN ENGLAND.

CHAP XVIII for government was most likely as great now as it ever was, and the real authority must have been left in the hands of his wiser parent. Matilda was still surrounded by a Council of Prelates and Barons; but it would seem that they were now deprived of the man who had acted as their President during William's first absence. The old and experienced Roger of Beaumont was called on to accompany his sovereign to his new Kingdom at this critical moment.[1] And later events show that William also brought back with him the English attendants or hostages who had been his companions in Normandy, and whom he could not venture to leave out of his sight in either country. Having made these arrangements, William hastened to the haven at the mouth of the Dieppe, which was then spoken of as lying near the town of Arques.[2] He passed by the scene of his exploits of fourteen years earlier,[3] and once more took ship for England. The month was December; the sea was stormy; but we are told that the prayers of the Norman Church, then engaged in keeping the festival of Saint Nicolas, kept its Prince safe from all dangers.[4] As in the September of the year

*Roger of Beaumont and the English hostages accompany William*

*William sets sail at Dieppe, December 6, 1067,*

---

1056, but I know of no evidence for the exact date. It could not have been before 1054

[1] Orderic (509 C) says, "Rex in illâ transfretatione Rogerium de Monte-Gomerici (quem tutorem Normanniæ, dum ad bellum transmarinum proficisceretur, cum suâ conjuge dimiserat) secum minavit." Here is a plain, though very strange, confusion between Roger of Montgomery and Roger of Beaumont. It was Roger of Beaumont who was left in charge in Normandy (see vol iii p 384), and Roger of Montgomery (see vol iii p 460) commanded the French contingent at Senlac.

[2] Ord. Vit 509 C "Sextâ nocte Decembris ad ostium amnis Deppæ ultra oppidum Archas accessit" On the name Deppa, see vol iii p 123

[3] See vol iii. pp 122-140

[4] Ord Vit u s "Primâ vigiliâ gelidæ noctis austro vela dedit . . Jam aura hiemalis mare sævissimum efficiebat, sed sancti Nicolai Myræorum Præsulis sollennitatem Ecclesia Dei celebrabat, et in Normanniâ pro devoto principe fideliter orabat. Omnipotentia ergo Dei . . benevolum Regem inter hiemales tempestates ad portum salutis cum gaudio dirigebat"

before, one night was enough for the passage, though the course taken, from Dieppe to Winchelsea, was longer than the course of the great fleet from the mouth of the Dive to Pevensey. On the morrow of the festival, William stood once more on English ground.[1]

CHAP XVIII. and lands at Winchelsea, December 7.

He came on a day of evil omen for England. The most venerated among the minsters of England, the mother church of the whole land, the church of Christ at Canterbury,[2] was on that Saint Nicolas' day burned to the ground The church, which had been simply damaged, but not destroyed, by the fire of Thurkill's Danes,[3] was now utterly wasted by the flames which lighted William back to complete his errand of conquest. That church, so men fondly deemed, was still the first building of Augustine and Æthelberht, which had been simply repaired and heightened under the primacy of Oda.[4] But the native fabric was now to be wholly swept away to make room for the work of the first of a line of foreign Primates. Men's minds must indeed have been impressed, when the return of the Conqueror was ushered in by the destruction of the ecclesiastical home of the nation at the very moment of his coming.

Christ Church at Canterbury burned, December 6

At the time of William's return no part of those shires

This is plainly from William of Poitiers, but the date is confirmed by our own Chroniclers.

[1] Ord Vit 509 C. "Mane portum oppositi litoris, quem Wicencsium vocitant, prosperrimo cursu arripuit"

[2] Chron Wig 1067 "Her com se kyng eft ongean to Englalande, on Sc̄e Nicolaes mæssedæge, and þæs dæges forbarn Cristes cyrce on Cantwarebyri"

[3] This is distinctly affirmed by Eadmer in the "Epistola ad Glastonienses," Ang Sac ii 225 "Ad hæc considerandum quia Ecclesia ipsa in passione beatissimi martyris Elphegi nec igne consumpta nec tecto aut parietibus diruta fuit. Violatam quippe fuisse et pluribus ornamentis spoliatam, ac supposito de foris igne ut concremaretur adorsam, novimus quo vesana manus Pontificem intus sese tuentem, quem mandaret exire, compelleret."

[4] See all the passages bearing on this point collected by Willis, Architectural History of Canterbury, 7, 8.

of England which had ever been really subdued was actually in arms against him. Eadric still held out on the Herefordshire march, but Eadric had never submitted at all. The Kentish revolt had met with the fate which it deserved. And if we believe the Norman writers, a party of order had been formed among all classes of Englishmen, who stood firmly by the Norman King against their rebellious fellow-countrymen. At its head was Ealdred the Northern Primate and several other Bishops, and they were supported by many others, Thegns, citizens, and churls, the wisest and most respected, we are assured, of their several orders, who had learned to practise the divine precept which bids men fear God and honour the King.[1] Wherever William had either himself appeared or had secured the district by the building of a castle, that is, generally throughout south-eastern England, his will, outwardly at least, was law.[2] He was received on his return by the English inhabitants, clergy and laity alike, with every formal sign of loyalty.[3] On the other hand there was the general, if hidden, feeling of discontent within the obedient districts; there was the imminent fear of an invasion from Denmark, and the threatening aspect of the still independent West and North.[4] William had need of all his arts of war and policy to triumph over the combination of so many enemies at once.

---

[1] Ord. Vit. 509 B. "Tunc Adeldredus Primas Eboracensis aliique Pontifices quidam utilitati regiæ intendebant, quia sapientis monitum scientes æquitati obtemperabant 'Time,' inquit, 'Deum, fili mi, et Regem' Tunc etiam aliquot sapientissimi civium urbanorum et nonnulli ex militibus ingenuis, quorum nomen et opes valebant, et multi ex plebeius contra suos pro Normannis magnopere insurgebant." This plainly comes from William of Poitiers

[2] Ib 509 D "Cunctæ urbes et regiones, *quas ipse adierat* vel præsidiis occupaverat, ad nutum ei parebant."

[3] Ib. "Adventui Regis Angli occurrerunt, ipsumque tam honorificentiâ monasteriali quam secularibus officiis sublimaverunt"

[4] Ib "Circa terminos regni occidentem aut plagam septemtrionalem

This new act of the drama began with the great ceremony, ecclesiastical and political, which habitually marked the Midwinter Festival. For the third successive year that festival was kept, not as it had been in past times and was again to be in later times, at Gloucester, but in the new seat of royalty at Westminster.[1] There, in the chosen dwelling of his revered predecessor, King William wore his Crown and gathered the Witan of England around him for counsel and for judgement. We hear much of the courtesy and honour with which he received the English Prelates and Thegns, with what readiness they were admitted to the royal kiss, how willingly their requests were granted and their counsels followed, and how by these generous arts many of the disaffected were won over.[2] After making the needful deductions, there is probably much of truth in this. Now, as ever, there were those to whom William found it prudent to be gentle, and those to whom he deemed it his wisdom to be harsh. It stands unmistakeably on record that William's return was accompanied by a confiscation and distribution of lands on so wide a scale that it could be said with indignant sarcasm that he gave away the land of every man.[3] The revolts and conspiracies

*CHAP XVIII*
William keeps Christmas at Westminster December 25, 1067— January 6, 1068.

The Midwinter Gemót

William's policy towards the English Thegns.

Second confiscation and distribution of lands

---

versus effrænis adhuc ferocia superbiebat, et Angliæ Regi, nisi ad libitum suum, famulari sub Rege Eduardo aliisque prioribus olim despexerat " This is largely true of the North, but hardly of the West

[1] Ord. Vit. 509 D "Ipse Lundoniæ Dominicam nativitatem celebravit " See vol iii p 66

[2] Ib. "Pontificibus Anglis proceribusque multâ calliditate favit Ipse omnes officioso affectu demulcebat, dulciter ad oscula invitabat, benigne, si quid orabant, concedebat, prompte, si nuntiabant aut suggerebant, auscultabat Desertores hujusmodi arte aliquoties reducuntur "

[3] Chron Petrib 1067 "And he geaf ælces mannes land þa he ongean com." Thomas Rudborne (Ang Sac 1 248) gives a rhetorical account of William's doings at this time in which, among a good deal of exaggeration, some expressions are worth notice , " Willelmus in Regem sublimatus pacifice tractabat nobiliores regni Angliæ, post fidelitatis juramentum ab ipsis sibi præstitum quamdiu fidem ei servabant, sed postquam rebellare cœperunt, homagiis iterum ab ipsis acceptis datisque obsidibus, omnibus,

CHAP XVIII.
Heavy tax laid on the country.

William's instructions to the French and Normans

which had happened during his absence would give ample excuse for such a measure. And the confiscation was further attended by one of those heavy imposts in money which to the feelings of those days were more hateful than confiscation. "The King set mickle geld on the poor folk."[1]

William was thus busy in half caressing, half coercing, his English subjects. Meanwhile the men of French and Norman birth who were about him were carefully warned of the state of the country, and bidden to be ever on their guard against the plots of the disaffected English.[2] And it also suited William's policy to give his subjects of both nations the spectacle of a great judicial pageant, to teach them that their King was no respecter of persons, and that no man of either race could safely revolt against him. This Midwinter Gemót of Westminster was made unusually impressive by a trial of which the like had certainly never been seen in England. Sentence of banishment and forfeiture had been over and over again pronounced against English Thegns, Earls, and even

qui ad regnum aspiraverant factus est terrori. Civitatibus quoque depositis et castellis propriisque ministris impositis, ad Normanniam cum obsidibus Angliæ et thesauris impretiabilibus navigavit. Quibus incarceratis et sub salvâ custodiâ deputatis, ad Angliam denuo remeavit, ubi commilitonibus suis Normannis qui in bello Hastingensi patriam secum subjugaverant *terras Anglorum et possessiones, ipsis expulsis, successive manu distribuit affluenti, et modicum illud quod eis remanserat, factus jam de rege tyrannus, sub jugo detrusit perpetuæ servitutis.* Et quum se viderat in sublimi elevatum et in fastu regni confirmatum, in alium virum subito est mutatus, nobiles terræ quos antiquus sanguis ex antiquo sublimaverat, proh dolor, exhæredando."

[1] Chron Wig 1067 "And her se kyng sette micel gyld on earm folc."

[2] Ord Vit 509 D "Pari sedulitate et sollertiâ *Guallos* nunc instruebat, nunc ut contra omnes dolos et insidias singulorum semper ubique parati essent clam Anglis admonebat." I think, with Maseres (209), that for "Guallos" we must read "Gallos." It seems impossible that intrigues with the Bret-Welsh can be meant, and, in Orderic, we can hardly understand "Gualli" of *Gal-Welsh.* See vol ii p 140

Æthelings  Once, in the midst of warfare, a general decree had been passed declaring every Danish King an outlaw.[1] But it was a new thing for a foreign prince to be formally put on his trial before an English court, and, as it would seem, to be condemned by default. Eustace of Boulogne was, in his County of Boulogne, a sovereign prince, owning no superior but his lord the King of the French. But by taking service in William's army he had become the man of the Duke of the Normans, and by receiving any grants of English lands, he became for them the man of the King of the English. As such, he had been guilty of treason against his lord, and for that crime he was arraigned, in ancient form, before the King and his Witan. It cannot be supposed that he appeared; but we know that the voices of the assembled Wise Men, French and English, were given against him, as they could hardly fail to be where all Kent might have been summoned to bear witness.[2] The sentence is not recorded, but according to all English precedent, it would be outlawry and forfeiture of all lands and honours within the Kingdom of England. But, at some later day, Eustace contrived to win back William's favour and to be reckoned among those who were most highly honoured by him.[3] He was enriched with lands,

*Eustace of Boulogne tried and condemned by the Gemót*

*Eustace's later reconciliation with William*

---

[1] See vol. 1 p. 405

[2] The trial and sentence are clearly implied by William of Poitiers (158), though he cuts the thing as short as he can, " Neque sententia erravit dicta consensu Anglorum et Gallorum, quâ de reatu convictus est "

[3] The caution of William of Poitiers (158) is amusing, " Equidem si rationes quæ ejus liti controversantur depromerem, Regis eum gratiam atque *Regis dono accepta beneficia* ex æquo et bono *amisisse* plane convincerem . Sed parcendum sentimus personæ multifariam illustri, Comiti nominato, qui reconciliatus nunc in proximis Regis honoratur " The words in Italics imply forfeiture  Orderic (508 D) of course changes the tense, "Non multo post Eustachius Consul Willermo Regi reconciliatus est, ejusque amicitiâ longo tempore postmodum perfunctus est  Erat enim idem Comes magnæ nobilitatis," &c  He goes on to speak of his pedigree and his children

130    CONQUEST OF WESTERN AND NORTHERN ENGLAND.

CHAP XVIII.  chiefly in those parts of England which were not in any
Lands held  dangerous neighbourhood to his foreign dominions  He
by his
widow and  himself was dead at the time of the Survey, but his widow
son
and son appear there as holders of lordships, both in various
other shires in those western lands which on the day of his
Their  sentence were still unconquered. The names of Ida and
estates in
Somerset  Eustace, the widow and the son of the coward of Boulogne,
the mother and the brother of the hero of Jerusalem, are
found as owners of English soil on spots which would
have a strange propriety if we could deem that they were
ever honoured with the sojourn of the mightiest of the
foes of Paynimrie. One of the western possessions of the
House of Boulogne lies nestling at the foot of the north-
western crest of Mendip, where the power of evil of the
old Teutonic creed has left his name in Count Eustace's
lordship of Loxton  Another, Kenwardston, the dowry of
the widowed Countess, crowns the wooded height which
looks full on that inland mount of the Archangel which
shelters the earliest home of Christianity in Britain.[1]

The see of  It was probably in the same Gemót that William for
Dorchester
vacant by  the first time exercised the power of bestowing an English
the death  Bishoprick on one of his own countrymen. The great see
of Wulfwig
of Dorchester, the greatest in extent of territorial jurisdiction among the Bishopricks of England, had become vacant,
seemingly during William's absence in Normandy, by the
death of its Bishop Wulfwig.[2] It was in this Christmas
session of the Witan that the vacancy would regularly be
filled. The death of Wulfwig at such a time might seem
of hardly less evil omen than the burning of Christ Church.
He was a living memorial of what Englishmen had done
and suffered in the cause of English freedom. He had, in
1052   the moment of deliverance from Norman influence, been

---

[1] On the estates of Eustace in Somerset and elsewhere, see Appendix N
[2] Chron. Wig and Fl Wig. 1067

raised to the seat which the Norman Ulf had disgraced and forsaken.[1] He was now taken away at the moment when such parts of his diocese as still retained their independence were about to be added to the dominion of the strangers. He died at Winchester, but he was buried in his own church, the last of the long line of Prelates who had not despised that lowly dwelling-place.

*Wulfwig the last of the bishops of Dorchester*

The appointment of his successor marked the beginning of a new æra. Since the flight of Robert and Ulf no man of French speech had been raised to an episcopal throne in England. The few men not natives of the island whom the policy of Harold had called to such high offices were men whom England could hardly look on as strangers, men from the kindred land of the Lower Lotharingia.[2] William of London alone, honoured equally by men of all races, had been allowed to hand on to the reign of William the worst tradition of the early reign of Eadward. What Eadward had done out of mere weakness and personal favouritism William was now to do out of systematic policy. The Prelacy of England was to be used as a means for rivetting the fetters of England. The rule which was strictly carried out through the rest of the century and the first half of the next now began. As the Bishopricks and Abbeys of England became vacant by the death or deprivation of English Prelates, men of Norman or other foreign birth were appointed in their room. For a long time to come the appointment of an Englishman to a Bishoprick is unknown, and even to a great Abbey it is extremely rare. In the case of the Primacy indeed the rule was so strict that the exclusion of Englishmen was extended even to men of Norman descent born in England, and for a hundred years after the Conquest, till the days of Thomas of London, no native of the Isle of Britain sat in the chair of Augustine. We have now to see the firstfruits of this system in the

*Long exclusion of Englishmen from high spiritual preferment*

[1] See vol ii pp 113, 117, 331  [2] See vol ii pp 80, 449

*Remigius of Fécamp appointed Bishop of Dorchester 1067-1092*

*Remigius consecrated by Stigand*

*His excuse of ignorance*

choice of a successor for Wulfwig. The great Bishoprick of Mid-England, a large part of whose diocese was not yet in William's power, was given to Remigius the Almoner of Fécamp, whose zeal and liberality in William's cause has been already recorded.[1] The voice of scandal ventured to breathe that neither the gift of Remigius nor the gratitude of William was wholly a free-will offering. It was in after times brought up as a formal charge against the new Prelate that, before the fleet had sailed from Saint Valery, an English Bishoprick had been promised as the price of the well-appointed ship which had been the contribution of the loyal almoner.[2] As yet however Remigius took possession of the see without objection, and it is specially to be noticed that the first Norman appointed by William to an English Bishoprick received consecration at the hands of Stigand.[3] Remigius himself, in his later profession to Lanfranc, declared that he did it unwittingly, that he went for the rite to the actual Metropolitan, without knowing the uncanonical and schismatical character which attached to all his official acts.[4] Yet we cannot forget the notoriety of Stigand's position, and the formal utterances of the Roman See against him.[5] We cannot forget that Englishmen, that Harold himself, had commonly avoided his ministrations, that English Bishops, Wulfwig among them,[6] had commonly been consecrated by other hands, that Harold and William alike had chosen the other Primate to perform the rite of their own crowning. The expulsion of Robert and the alleged usurpation of Stigand

---

[1] See above, p. 90.  [2] See the next Chapter.

[3] This fact appears from Remigius' own profession to Lanfranc, printed by Mr Dimock, Gir. Camb. vii. 151.

[4] Remigius in his profession repeats the Norman stories about Robert and Stigand, and adds, "Ego vero hujus negotii nec ex toto ignarus, nec usquequaque gnarus, ordinandus ad eum veni, professionem sibi suisque successoribus feci, curamque episcopalem de manu ipsius me consecrantis accepi." Ib. p. 152.

[5] See vol. ii. p. 466.  [6] See vol. ii. pp. 344, 466.

had even been put forward among the grounds for William's expedition against England.[1] It would be strange if nothing of all this had ever made its way to the cloister of Fécamp; it would be strange if Remigius, on coming to England, found no one, Norman or English, to warn him of the canonical risk which he was running. It is hard to avoid the belief that it was not so much the ignorance of Remigius as the policy of William which led to what all strict churchmen must have deemed a gross breach of ecclesiastical order. William was still temporizing with Stigand; the time for his degradation was not yet come.[2] It would be a great, perhaps an unlooked for, mark of his continued confidence for the King to direct the new Bishop of Dorchester to seek consecration from the still acknowledged Primate. When the day came, the friend of Lanfranc and Hildebrand could easily find means to set straight any past irregularity. At all events, Remigius was consecrated by Stigand, with the help of what assistant Bishops we are not told, and he made profession to the schismatic as his lawful Metropolitan. He took possession of his humble bishopstool, in a land where Wigod on one side and Robert of Oily on the other were ready to give him all needful help. There, we are told, he planned and began great works,[3] which were left unfinished when the further progress of William's conquests allowed him to remove his throne to a more lordly seat of episcopal rule.

*The application to Stigand more probably due to William's policy.*

*Remigius begins buildings at Dorchester.*

*The see removed to Lincoln.*

At the same Gemót William had also most probably the opportunity of again, nominally at least, bestowing an English Earldom. The second reign of Oswulf beyond the Tyne had not lasted long. In the course of the autumn he was slain, not however, as it would seem, in any political broil or at the hand of any avenger of Copsige. He died by the

*Oswulf slain by a robber. Autumn, 1067.*

---

[1] See vol. iii. pp. 282, 283.   [2] See above, p. 78.
[3] Will. Malm. Gest. Pont. 312. See the next Chapter.

134        CONQUEST OF WESTERN AND NORTHERN ENGLAND.

CHAP XVIII spear of a common robber, one of the brood who had escaped the heavy hands of Siward and Tostig, and the story reads as if he were killed in the act of trying personally to arrest the wrong-doer.[1] His death left the dangerous post open to the ambition of another Englishman of the highest rank. This was Gospatric the son of Maldred, who, by female descent at least, sprang of the noblest blood of Northumberland and even of the kingly blood of Wessex. For his mother Ealdgyth was the daughter of Uhtred by his third wife, the daughter of King Æthelred. And the words of our chief Northhumbrian guide seem to imply that this descent gave him some kind of right of preference to the Earldom.[2] This is a comment on the growing notion of hereditary right with regard to such offices, and it is further remarkable as showing that the notion of succession through females was already beginning to be entertained. We cannot suppose that it would have come into any man's head to propose a woman as a candidate for an Earldom, but men were clearly beginning to think that the son of an Earl's daughter had a better right to his grandfather's dignity than an utter stranger to his blood. Of the former life of Gospatric we know nothing, unless, as seems most likely, this is the same Gospatric who so gallantly jeoparded his life to save the life of Tostig on his return from his Roman pilgrimage.[3] He now went to William, probably at this Christmas feast at Westminster, and asked for the Earldom vacant by the successive deaths of Copsige and Oswulf. His claim,

Position of Gospatric

His connexion with the ancient Earls

Growing ideas of hereditary descent and female succession

Gospatric buys the Northumbrian Earldom

---

[1] Sim Dun Gest Reg 92. "Mox sequenti auctumno et ipse Osulfus quum in obvii sibi latronis lanceam præceps irrueret, illico confossus interiit"

[2] Ib "Nam ex materno sanguine attinebat ad eum honor illius comitatus Erat enim ex matre Algithâ, filiâ Uhtredi comitis, quam habuit ex Algivâ filiâ Agelredi regis Hanc Algitham pater dedit in conjugium Maldredo filio Crinani."

[3] See vol ii p 457

backed by a large sum of money, was successful,[1] but whether he took any practical steps to take possession of the lands beyond the Tyne we are not told. A thick veil shrouds the affairs of the extreme North for some time to come, and when we next hear of Gospatric, he appears in the same character as Eadwine and Morkere, as a dweller in William's court, but as one who had already begun to fear his enmity.[2]

*Christmas of William, 1067-1068.*

But William had other cares besides thus regulating the affairs of the obedient shires of England, and granting away the nominal government of shires which still remained to be subdued. He had to guard against the dangers which threatened him both from Denmark and from the still unsubdued West. In that quarter the determination not to admit his authority was every day assuming a character of more direct hostility. William had his remedy for both dangers. The intentions of the Danish King were to be sounded, and his purposes, if hostile, were to be staved off by the discretion and power of speech of an ambassador of English birth. For the defenders of Western England, the rebels as they were deemed in Norman eyes, William determined on the bold step of a winter campaign. To employ an Englishman as his ambassador to the Danish King was a clear stroke of policy on William's part. Such an ambassador would come, not from the Norman Conqueror, King by the edge of the sword, but from the lawful King of the English, the kinsman and successor of the saintly Eadward. The man chosen for this purpose was a churchman of high rank of whom we have already heard more than once. Æthelsige, Abbot of Saint Augustine's, had received the abbatial benediction, as Remigius of Dorchester had received

*William's negotiations with Swend.*

*Policy of choosing an English ambassador.*

*Mission of Abbot Æthelsige; his former history.*

---

[1] Sim Dun Gest Reg 92. "Quo [Osulfo] mortuo, Cospatricus, filius Maldredi filii Crinani, Willelmum Regem adiens multâ emptum pecuniâ adeptus est comitatum Northymbrensium."

[2] On the Earldom of Gospatric, see Appendix O.

136   CONQUEST OF WESTERN AND NORTHERN ENGLAND.

CHAP XVIII his episcopal consecration, at the hands of Stigand.[1] He had been further entrusted by Eadward in his lifetime with the government of the great house of Saint Bene't of Ramsey,[2] and legends went on to say that he had been chosen by the departed King to carry a message of health and victory from Eadward to his chosen successor.[3] No choice on William's part could have been better planned to make a moral impression on the minds of Danes and Englishmen. A Prelate who had been the fast friend both of Eadward and of Harold now appeared at the court of Swend as the representative of William. The whole life of Æthelsige is wrapped in confusions and contradictions, and the details of his embassy to Swend have come to us only in a legendary shape. But there is no need to doubt the fact of his mission, as the legend falls in most remarkably with several entries in the great Survey.[4] Æthelsige then sailed for Denmark and reached the court of Swend in safety. He was received with honour, and offered the gifts of William to the Danish King and his nobles. His stay was long; of the political details of his mission we have no accounts, but the course of events would seem to show that he succeeded in staving off for a while any interference of Swend in English affairs.[5] We may perhaps even guess that his mission was not confined to Denmark only. It is certain that William entered into negotiations with Adalbert, the renowned Archbishop of Bremen, once the guide of the tender years of the youthful Henry.[6] The Primate of the North was led by the gifts of William to do all that he could to keep Swend from disturbing

His reception in Denmark

William's negotiations with Adalbert of Bremen perhaps carried on through Æthelsige

---

[1] See vol. II p 454   [2] Ib p 455   [3] See vol III p 359.
[4] See Appendix P.
[5] Lectio ap Langebek, III 253 "Reverenter igitur a Rege Danorum receptus et habitus, non modico tempore apud eum mansit Tandem, quum negotia pro quibus missus fuerat ad placitum peregisset, licentiâ redeundi a Rege datâ, iter per mare cum sociis aggressus est"
[6] See vol III. p 307

the peace of England.[1] The legendary part of the story now follows. When Æthelsige set sail from Denmark on his return to England, his ship was well nigh lost in a storm. In answer to the prayers of the Abbot and his companions an angel presently appeared, and bade them keep the feast of the Conception—not yet declared to be immaculate—of our Lady. On his vow so to do, the storm ceased, and on his return the new festival was first established in the church of Ramsey, and from thence its observance spread over England and Christendom.[2]

*Legend of Æthelsige's return.*

Abbot Æthelsige is thus set before us as chosen for the second time to be the vehicle of a supernatural communication. And his real history is well nigh as marvellous as anything that legend could invent. It may be as well, at the expense of strict chronological sequence, to sketch the remainder of his strangely chequered life. At this moment he seems to have been as high in the favour of William as he had been in that of Eadward and Harold. Within two years he had lost the favour both of William and of his own monks at Saint Augustine's. The displeasure of the monks is said to have been caused by alienations of the lands of the monastery to Normans. The grounds of William's displeasure are not mentioned, but there is no doubt that the Abbot was outlawed, and that he took shelter in the land which he had so lately visited as William's ambassador. The strange thing is that, ten years later, he had, by some means or other, by some service doubtless at the Danish court, contrived to recover the favour of William. He was allowed to return, not to Saint Augustine's, which was in the hands of his Norman successor Scotland, but to Ramsey, where his place during his absence seems to have

*Later history of Æthelsige.*

*His outlawry and flight to Denmark 1070*

---

[1] Adam Brem. iii. 53 "Inter Suein et Bastardum [see vol. ii. p. 582] perpetua contentio de Anglia fuit, licet noster pontifex [Adalbertus, sc.] muneribus Willehelmi persuasus, inter Reges pacem formare voluerit."

[2] See the different versions in Langebek, iii. 253 et seqq., and Appendix P.

been taken by his predecessor Ælfwine.[1] His outlawry is recorded in the great Survey, but it is no less plain that, when the Survey itself was made, he was again Abbot of Ramsey. And to wind up all, as if purposely to make way for a new state of things, both Æthelsige and his successor at Saint Augustine's died in the same year as William himself.[2]

*State of the West.*

Meanwhile William was making every preparation for the campaign in the West. The shires of the *Wealhcyn* seem as yet to have retained perfect independence. The only sign of anything like an acknowledgement of William's kingship in those parts is the fact of the Abbot of Glastonbury being one of William's companions in his voyage to Normandy.[3] On the other hand, we are distinctly told that Exeter, the great city of Western England, had had no dealings whatever with the new King.[4] And it would seem that the attitude of the men of the West was now taking the form of something beyond a mere refusal to acknowledge the King who reigned in London and Winchester. Exeter was of course the centre of all patriotic action. The city had doubtless fully recovered from the misfortunes which fell on it in the days of Swend,[5] but it is quite possible that the memory of Hugh the French churl[6] had helped, along with later events, to make its inhabitants specially hostile to all men of French blood or speech. That hatred they are said to have shown in cruel and insulting treatment towards certain Norman knights who had been sent by William himself, and whom stress of weather had driven into their haven.[7] This may or may not imply that a

*Exeter the centre of the independent shires*

*Hatred of its citizens towards Frenchmen.*

---

[1] See vol. ii. p. 455
[2] See these points worked out in Appendix P
[3] See above, p. 78.
[4] Ord. Vit. 510 A " Regem alienigenam . cum quo antea de nullo negotio egerant " [5] See vol. i. p. 346 [6] See above, p. 52.
[7] Ord. Vit. 510 C "Militibus crudeliter et contumeliose illuserant, quos ipse de Normanniâ miserat et tempestas ad portum illorum appulerat."

force had been sent against the West while William was still in Normandy. At all events the city was at this moment perfectly independent and full of zeal for the national cause. The citizens of Exeter were rich, numerous, and valiant, and, at this stage at least of the story, all ranks joined in full purpose to withstand the stranger to the uttermost.[1] Like their brethren at Winchester, they stood in a special relation to the widowed Eadgyth,[2] as their forefathers had stood towards the widowed Emma. But the influence which the absent Lady could exercise at Exeter was far less than that which she could exercise in her own dwelling-place at Winchester.[3] The walls which Æthelstan had reared, and which Swend had at least partly overthrown,[4] had been repaired or rebuilt, and the city was again strongly fortified.[5] And now towers and battlements, and whatever was needed for defence against a siege, were carefully repaired, and new works added wherever any further strength could be given.[6] But it should be noted that we hear only of the defences of the city itself; Exeter did not as yet contain a castle. But the resistance of the West was not to be only the resistance of a single city, however great; the men of Exeter sent messengers to and fro to rouse the men

*Zeal and valour of all ranks.*

*Their relation to Eadgyth*

*They seek help from the neighbouring shires and towns.*

This incidental mention is just in the style of William of Poitiers (cf his account of Romney, vol iii. pp 410, 534), one would be well pleased to know the story more at large

[1] Ord Vit 510 A "Cives eam tenebant furiosi, copiosæ multitudinis, infestissimi mortalibus Gallici generis, puberes ac Senatus" One is tempted to read either "plebs et Senatus" or "puberes ac seniores" But the mention of "Senatus," it will be presently seen, is important. (In this suggestion I find myself forestalled in the excellent note of Maseres, p 210)

[2] In Domesday (100) twelve houses in Exeter appear as "liberæ ad numerum in ministeriis Eddid Reginæ"

[3] See vol iii p 541                [4] See vol i pp 338, 346

[5] "Operose munita," says Orderic

[6] Ord Vit 510 A "Pinnas ac turres et quæque necessaria sibi censebant in munimentis addebant vel restaurabant"

140 CONQUEST OF WESTERN AND NORTHERN ENGLAND.

CHAP XVIII of the neighbouring shires, and to call on their towns to enter into a league with Exeter against the foreign King.[1] Those shires, those towns, were now undoubtedly wholly English in feeling; they were probably by this time mainly English in blood. The Thegns and the citizens at all events would be so; the towns, we may be sure, like Exeter itself, had been from the beginning English colonies in the Celtic land. The memory of older distinctions would simply tend, as in some parts it tends to this day, to make local feeling a little stronger than elsewhere. But the patriots of Exeter were ready to welcome help from any quarter, and, among other quarters, they sought it among the strangers from distant lands whom the commercial importance of their city had brought to sojourn within their gates. Foreign merchants, if they seemed likely to be of use in the campaign, were pressed into the service, to take their part on behalf of the land to which they owed a temporary allegiance.[2] It was plain that to put down such a movement as this must be William's first work. The active hostility of the West was becoming more dangerous than the stubborn sullenness of the North or even than the chances of an invasion from Denmark.

The *Wealhcyn* now mainly English.

Connexion of the movement with the family of Godwine.

And there was another feature about the movement at Exeter which would make it specially hateful in William's eyes. The *Denalagu* might be ready to welcome Swend or to seek for a King in the House of Leofric. The name of Eadgar might kindle a sentimental feeling in any part of the Kingdom over which he had been for a moment chosen King. But the voice which came up from Exeter

---

[1] Ord Vit 510 A "Hi nimirum socios e plagis finitimis inquiete arcessebant ... alias quoque civitates ad conspirandum in eadem legationibus instigabant, et contra Regem alienigenam toto nisu se præparabant, cum quo antea de nullo negotio egerant"

[2] Ib. "Mercatores advenas bello habiles retinebant."

was a voice raised on behalf of the House of Godwine and Harold. Of that House we have heard nothing since Gytha, the mother of heroes, craved the body of her son on the morrow of the great battle.[1] But now the widow of Godwine was present in the city whose holy places she had enriched with offerings for the soul of her husband.[2] There was no part of England in which her own possessions and those of her children were larger than in the shires of Devon and Somerset. And it is in those shires only that we can trace in the Survey the names of those younger members of the family of whom so little record is to be found elsewhere.[3] The lands of the House of Godwine, at all events the lands of Harold, Gyrth, and Leofwine, had, wherever William's rule had reached, been forfeited to the behoof of the Conqueror and his followers. Here, in the free West, their revenues and the fighting power of their occupants were still ready to be used in the cause of England. The men of Somerset and Dorset had sent their contingents to Senlac; the men of Devonshire and Cornwall are not mentioned;[4] in the swift march of events between the two great battles the forces of such distant regions may easily, without any suspicion of backwardness or disloyalty, have failed to find their way to Harold's muster. But for this very reason those shires were better able to resist now; their noblest and bravest had not been cut off, like the noblest and bravest of Kent and Berkshire. The widow of the great Earl, the mother of the fallen King, was thus dwelling within the walls of a city where she was well known, in the midst of vast estates belonging to herself and her house. We may here stop and see what was at this moment the state of the

CHAP XVIII.

Presence of Gytha at Exeter

Great possessions of Harold and his family in the West

---

[1] See vol. iii p 512, cf p 519
[2] See vol. ii p 352 for her gifts to Saint Olaf's church at Exeter
[3] See Appendix Q and R
[4] See the list from Wace in vol iii p 423

142        CONQUEST OF WESTERN AND NORTHERN ENGLAND.

CHAP XVIII.  House of Godwine, as several of its members will flit before
State of     our eyes for a few moments. All the sons of Godwine were
the House
of God-      dead, save only Wulfnoth the hostage, who was in the
wine
Wulfnoth     hands of William.[1] Of Harold's other companion in his
the only     fatal voyage, Hakon the son of Swegen, no certain account
surviving
son.         can be given  I have ventured, rather doubtingly, to give
Hakon son    him his place among the warriors of Senlac[2]  He may
of Swegen
             have died there, or the conjecture[3] may be true which,
             without any further evidence, makes him the same as a
             Danish Earl Hakon of whom we shall hear later in the
The          history. Of the daughters of Godwine, Eadgyth was still
daughters
of God-      enjoying the honours of the Old Lady within the walls of
wine         her Imperial morning-gift. Ælfgifu, according to one
             version, was dead;[4] at all events there is no further
             account to give of her  Gunhild, alive and unmarried,
             was doubtless in attendance on her mother. In the third
             generation, besides the doubtful case of Hakon, the sons
             of Tostig were in Norway,[5] of any children of Gyrth and
The          Leofwine we hear nothing. But Harold had left behind
children of
Harold       him five children, who, as I have elsewhere suggested, were
Three sons   probably the offspring of Eadgyth Swanneshals.[6] Of their
and two
daughters,   mother we hear no more after her sad errand to Senlac.
probably
children of  If she really was the rich and fair Eadgifu of Domesday, her
Eadgyth      lands formed—most likely had already formed—a rich
Swan-
neshals      harvest for Norman spoilers. But her three sons, Godwine,
             Eadmund, and Magnus, of whom Godwine was a holder
             of lands in Somerset,[7] and her daughters Gytha and Gun-
             hild, will all call for momentary notice. Everything leads
             us to believe that the whole family were now gathered
             round their grandmother at Exeter  But there was an-
             other child of Harold who was most likely in a distant

---

[1] See above, p 119               [2] See vol iii p 476
[3] This is made by Lappenberg, Norman Kings, p 168 (Eng ed ), after Suhm.
[4] See vol iii pp 262, 703        [5] Ib p. 374
[6] Ib p 764, and Appendix R       [7] See Appendix Q.

part of England. There can be little doubt that Ulf, the son of Harold and Ealdgyth, was born after his father's death. It would follow that he was born at Chester, whither his mother had been sent for safety by her brothers.[1] As Chester was not yet in William's possession, the babe, whom the event of the great battle had hindered from being a born Ætheling, was probably dwelling with his mother within the Mercian Earldom. Sooner or later indeed he fell into William's clutches and remained a prisoner till the end of William's reign.[2] But we may believe that his captivity dated only from the fall of Chester rather than suspect that even Eadwine could stoop to the baseness of giving up his infant nephew as the price of the Conqueror's favour to himself.

*Ulf the son of Ealdgyth;*

*his captivity.*

The son of Ealdgyth united the blood of the two greatest houses in England, and, had his father's reign been as long as the heart of England had prayed for at his crowning, he might have been the second King of the House of Godwine. The sons of Harold who were within the walls of Exeter came of a lowlier and doubtful stock. But, as vigorous youths fast approaching manhood, they were better fitted to become the rallying point of a patriotic movement, and the probable stain on their birth could hardly be thrown in their teeth in the days of William the Bastard. The whole West was ready for defence, and volunteers flocked in from other parts. One recorded instance in such cases proves many unrecorded. Blæcman, a wealthy secular priest of Berkshire, a tenant of the Abbey of Abingdon, and himself founder of a goodly church in its neighbourhood, risked all his possessions, temporal and spiritual, to share the fortunes of the widow of Godwine.[3]

*Harold's sons at Exeter.*

*Volunteers from other districts.*

*Blæcman of Berkshire.*

---

[1] See vol. ii. pp. 511, 764.   [2] See Flor. Wig. 1067.

[3] Blæcman, Blacheman, Blachemannus, is spoken of in the History of Abingdon, i. 474, as "presbyter pecuniosus." By the leave of the convent he built a church, with buildings of a monastic pattern attached, on an island to the south of the monastery, which, from the dedication of the

CHAP XVIII. Such a man, we may be sure, did not stand alone; Exeter, the one great city of Southern England which remained free, was doubtless a city of refuge to many a patriotic heart from all the shires over which the House of Godwine had ruled. At no moment since the battle had the hopes of deliverance been higher. But, as usual, local and internal dissensions spoiled everything. England had no leader. If the North had risen now, if the Danish fleet had come now, their united forces might perhaps have driven William once more beyond the sea. But while Exeter was in arms, York did not stir, and when York did stir, Exeter had no longer the power of stirring. The grandsons of Leofric doubtless cared little for a movement on behalf of the House of Godwine. Had the son of Harold and Ealdgyth been a grown man, capable of leading armies, both the great divisions of England might possibly have gathered round one who united the blood of Godwine and the blood of Leofric. But the babe at Chester could give no strength to any cause, and Eadwine and Morkere

*The Western movement not supported by the North*

church to Saint Andrew, got the name of "Andresia" (Andreasege?) The buildings were "mirifice coaptata, picturis cælaturisque infra et extra ubique locorum delectabile visu subornata." He then "privatim se monachis ingerendo, tum auri argentique ostentu, tum facundi oris profusione," got a lease of three lordships from the Abbey. The writer seems to record the grant with some displeasure, but it was merely one of the usual leases. Blæcman was, as he is described in the local history (i. 484), "ecclesiæ homo effectus," just like Sheriff Godric. Of one of the places spoken of, Sandford in Oxfordshire, we also read in Domesday (156 b), "Blacheman presbyter tenuit ab ecclesiâ." The name, whether of the same person or not, is found in several other entries in the Survey. Another entry in Oxfordshire (160) doubtless belongs to our Blæcman. The connexion of Blæcman with the siege of Exeter comes from the local history, i. 483, 484. The passage runs thus, "Willelmus vero Angliæ diadema obtinuit. Cui dum quidam subjectionis fidelitatem sponderent, nonnulli exteras sibi sedes per alia regna consulti rati petere sese subducerent, Abbas Ealdredus, primorum sese sententiæ dedens, Regi fidelitatis sacramenta persolvit. At in posteriorum numero quum multi diverterent, tum et perempti Regis mater, secum in comitatu suo, una cum plurimis aliis, presbyterum Blachemannum habens, Angliam deseruit." If Blæcman accompanied Gytha in her flight, we may be pretty sure that he was with her at Exeter.

tarried in the Court of William till William's rule was as safe at Exeter as it was at Winchester and London.

In overcoming the hostility of the West, William acted as he always did act. Before he tried arms, he tried negotiation. In the great case of all, in his dealings with Harold himself, he did not strike a blow till all the powers of diplomacy had been thoroughly worn out between himself and his rival. In the course of his march after the battle, he had sent a successful embassy to Winchester,[1] and one of more doubtful issue to London.[2] So he now sent to Exeter to demand that the citizens should take the oath of allegiance to him as their lawful King.[3] He also, it would seem, required to be received in person within the city. William, on becoming full sovereign of Exeter, might have purposed, like Æthelstan, to celebrate and to secure his conquest by holding one of the solemn Gemóts of the year within its walls.[4] On the arrival of this message, we see the first signs of a wavering policy, of a division of feeling between different classes in the city. At Exeter, as everywhere else, the mass of the people were patriotic, but a fainthearted, if not a traitorous, faction soon began to show itself among those of higher degree.[5] The chief men, whether by those words we are to understand the local magistracy or generally the leading men who were gathered within the walls of the city, sent a temporizing answer to William. In so doing they showed that they as little understood the man with whom they were dealing as Robert the Staller had understood him when he counselled him to go back quietly from Hastings to Normandy.[6] In dealing with William the Conqueror there were only two

CHAP XVIII.

William negotiates

He demands the submission of Exeter

Attempt of the Exeter leaders to take a middle course.

---

[1] See vol III p 540
[2] Ib p 545
[3] Ord. Vit 510 A. "Rex ubi hæc certius comperit, primoribus civitatis jurare sibi fidelitatem mandavit"
[4] See vol. I p 338
[5] See the note in vol III p 332
[6] See vol III p 414

VOL. IV.                    L

choices, unconditional submission and resistance to the last. Submission would bring favourable terms. Resistance might be successful, and William moreover now and then showed that he could find it in his heart to honour a valiant enemy. The Wise Men of Exeter tried a middle course, a course which made success impossible; but their answer is most valuable as an illustration of the politics of the time. It shows the strength of local, as distinguished from national, patriotism; it shows the ideas of municipal freedom which were growing up; it shows, we may add, the chances and tendencies from which William saved England. The answer to William's summons, as reported by our Norman informants, ran thus, "We will take no oaths to the King, we will not receive him within our walls; but we are ready to pay to him the tribute which we have been used to pay to former Kings."[1] That is to say, they were ready to receive him as Emperor, but not as King. The words are exactly such as an Italian city might have used to a Teutonic Cæsar. We long to know whether such language came from the magistrates of Exeter only, or whether it was shared by the Thegns of the West in general. In the former case the object is plain; the aim of the Exeter patricians was to make their city an aristocratic commonwealth, like those of which the germs were already showing themselves within the continental Empire. Is it possible that, among the foreign visitors who gave

---

[1] Ord. Vit. 510 A. "At illi remandaverunt ei dicentes, Neque sacramentum Regi faciemus, neque in urbem eum intromittemus, sed tributum ei ex consuetudine pristinâ reddemus." It must be remembered that our only account of these most interesting negotiations comes from Orderic, who doubtless followed William of Poitiers. The short accounts in the Chronicles and Florence begin only with the actual siege. This is much to be regretted, as we should never have more gladly welcomed a record in our own tongue than in the report of these answers, which could not fail to preserve to us so many technical phrases of early politics.

*Importance of their answer*

*They are ready to pay tribute, but not to swear oaths or to receive William within their walls*

*Comparison with Italy and elsewhere*

*Probable wish to found an aristocratic republic, owning only an*

their help in matters of war, there were some who could give lessons to the rulers of Exeter in matters of Italian policy? Exeter was to be a republic, independent in all its internal affairs.[1] The Emperor of Britain might be Over-lord of the commonwealth; his protection might be bought, or his enmity might be bought off, by a payment in money. The burthens which had been laid on Exeter by former Kings had not been excessive. The city paid in money only when London, York, and Winchester paid, and the sum to be paid was a single half mark of silver, for the behoof of the soldiers, that is doubtless of the King's Housecarls.[2] The mention of Exeter in such company marks the high position that it held among the cities of England. When the King summoned his *fyrd* to his standard, by sea or by land, Exeter supplied the same number of men as were supplied by five hides of land.[3] These payments, these services, the commonwealth was ready to render to the new master who claimed its allegiance. But the men of Exeter would not, each citizen personally, become his men; they would not receive so dangerous a visitor within their walls; they would not, we may believe, be handed over as a morning-gift to any more widows of Kings, or again be exposed to the treason or the incapacity of Reeves commissioned by foreign Ladies. Such schemes were natural enough in a civic aristocracy, but they could hardly have been shared by the rural Thegns of Devonshire and Somerset.

[1] On the condition of Exeter at this time and its league with the other boroughs, see Palgrave, iii. 419, 426-429, and English Commonwealth, i. 645. There is perhaps a little exaggeration in the line which he takes, but it is a striking thought when he says, "But a little more, and England might have become the first Federal Commonwealth in Christendom."

[2] See below, p. 162.

[3] Domesday, 100. "Quando expeditio ibat per terram aut per mare, serviebat hæc civitas quantum v. hidæ terræ." So Exon, 80.

*Chap XVIII*
*Position of the local Thegns Their probable bearing towards a commonwealth*
*Position of the family of Harold.*

Still less were such schemes likely to be shared by Gytha and her grandsons. The sons of Harold might well dream of Kingdoms, greater or smaller, whether of England, of Wessex, or only of the *Wealhcyn*. But they would hardly aspire to be Consuls or Burgomasters of the Free Imperial City of Exeter. As for the ordinary Thegns of the country, we can hardly attribute to them such a degree of political foresight as to understand the probable results of the establishment of an independent commonwealth in the great Western city. Such a commonwealth, if it lived and prospered, was not unlikely to play the part which was afterwards played by Bern and Florence, which was, a few years later, played for a moment by Le Mans, and to constrain the neighbouring lords of the soil to become its citizens or its subjects. Exeter had already possessions beyond its own walls, which might easily form the germ of a subject district.[1] But, without supposing the Western Thegns to look so far afield as this, the scheme of establishing a commonwealth of Exeter could have no charm or interest for them. If they were fainthearted, they might seek their advantage in becoming William's men and buying back their lands of him.[2] If they were stout-hearted and hopeful, they might look forward to keeping William out of the Western lands altogether. But no half-measure offered any chance. A commonwealth of Exeter promised them nothing, and they could have no hope of admitting William as Over-lord without admitting him as immediate King. They could hardly have cherished any dream so wild as that of establishing the *Wealhcyn* as a separate principality like the Northern Wales, paying tribute to William as Basileus of Britain,

*No chance of founding a dependent principality in the West*

---

[1] Domesday, 100. "Burgenses Exoniæ urbis habent extra civitatem terræ xii carucatas quæ nullam consuetudinem reddunt, nisi ad ipsam civitatem."

[2] See above, p. 25.

but ruled by a prince of the House of Godwine, a prince who might himself be the man of the Over-lord, but whose personal vassalage should not be shared by his subjects.

But of all princes of his day William was the least likely to be entangled into middle courses or to be satisfied with a half-submission. He might be Duke of the Normans and Cæsar of the English;[1] but in either character he would be the immediate lord of every one of his subjects. He might be satisfied with maintaining the external superiority of his predecessors over the outlying provinces of his Empire, but within the Kingdom which his kinsman had bequeathed to him he would put up with nothing short of unreserved allegiance. He would have nothing to do with terms and reservations. His answer to the Exeter deputation was terse and to the purpose, "It is not my custom to take subjects on such conditions."[2] War of course followed; William marched with an army into Devonshire, an army drawn partly from the English inhabitants of the conquered districts. This was the first, but not the last, time in which William learned to employ English valour in his wars on both sides of the sea.[3] The policy of so doing was obvious; it was not a foreign conqueror who was marching against an independent city, it was the King of the English, at the head of his loyal Englishmen, marching against a city which refused him his lawful

CHAP XVIII

William's purpose to be immediate lord everywhere.

His answer to the Exeter deputation

He marches against Exeter

Englishmen in his army.

Policy of their employment.

---

[1] "Qui Dux Normannis, qui Cæsar præfuit Anglis," says Abbot Baldric in his verses on William. Duchèsne, Rer Franc Scriptt iv 257 A

[2] Ord. Vit 510 A "E contra sic eis remandavit Rex dicens, Non est mihi moris ad hanc conditionem habere subjectos"

[3] Ib. "Deinde cum exercitu ad fines eorum accessit, et primos in eâ expeditione Anglos eduxit" I do not see that this need mean—though the fact is not at all unlikely—that "the English were placed in the front of his army" (Lappenberg, 121, Eng tr) Surely it simply means that this was the first time that William used English troops.

150    CONQUEST OF WESTERN AND NORTHERN ENGLAND.

CHAP XVIII.  rights.    Nor is it wonderful that native Englishmen,
Explana-    even from the West-Saxon shires, were found ready to
tion of
their    march on such a service. A government in possession,
willingness
to serve    however unpopular, has vast advantages over a people
without leaders. If King William summoned the *fyrd*
in ancient form, under the same penalties which had been
decreed in the days of Æthelred,[1] the man, Thegn or
Churl, who dared to hold back must have been a man
of unusual boldness and vigour   And when soldiers are
once under arms, the blind instinct of military discipline,
and of what is called military honour, has too often been
found utterly to outweigh the higher biddings of moral
and political duty. If the soldiers of Cromwell and the
Buonapartes did not scruple to drive out Parliaments at
the bidding of their military chiefs, we cannot wonder
that William, now and at other times, found Englishmen ready to march at his bidding against those who
were fighting to deliver England. The thing was not
Earlier in- new. Swend,[2] Cnut, Harold Hardrada,[3] had always
stances of
service    found means to draw fresh forces from the districts of
under
con-    England which submitted to them. In the wars of Cnut
querors    the still stranger sight had been seen of West-Saxon
troops serving under the Danish Raven against a West-
Saxon Ætheling at the head of the forces of the *Denalagu*.[4]
So now, it was at the head of a host largely composed
of Englishmen that William set forth to win for himself
the great stronghold of English freedom in the Western
shires.

His line of march was, as usual, marked by ravage.[5]
His course naturally led him through Dorset, and it was

---

[1] See vol. i pp, 366, 415         [2] Ib 394
[3] See vol III p 352               [4] See vol i p. 414
[5] Chron Wig 1067 (after recording the tax, see above, p 128), " And þeahhwæðre lét æfre hergian eall þæt hi oferforon " This will at least include the Dorset harryings

no doubt now that the towns of that shire, Dorchester, Bridport, Wareham, and Shaftesbury, underwent that fearful harrying the result of which is recorded in Domesday. Bridport was utterly ruined, not a house seems to have been able to pay taxes at the time of the Survey. At Dorchester, the old Roman settlement, the chief town of the shire, only a small remnant of the houses escaped destruction.[1] These facts are signs that William followed the same policy against Exeter which he had followed against Le Mans[2] and against London[3] The boroughs of Dorset were doubtless among the towns which had joined in the civic league. Probably they stood sieges and were taken by storm. At any rate they were ruthlessly harried, in order at once to isolate and to frighten the greater city which lay beyond them. This policy did its work. As William drew near, the fear of him and his wrath fell on the patricians of the commonwealth of Exeter. At a distance of four miles from the city a second deputation met him, whose language was very different from that of the earlier message Nothing was now said of conditions; nothing was refused, all was abject submission to William's will. The men of Exeter craved for peace, their gates were open to receive the King, they would obey all his orders In pledge of their good faith, hostages, as many as William demanded, were at once given up.[4] And it would seem that William now made some special promises of favour which he afterwards failed to carry out.[5] We cannot

*CHAP XVIII.*
William's ravages on his march, ruin of the Dorset towns

William's policy the same as in earlier conquests

Its effect the magistrates of Exeter offer submission and give hostages

Alleged breach of promise by William

---

[1] On the details, see Appendix K
[2] See vol iii p 202          [3] Ib pp 533, 543
[4] Ord Vit. 510 B   "*Majores* mox, ut Regem cum exercitu appropinquare cognoscunt, obviam advenienti procedunt, pacem poscunt, portas ei patere dicunt, imperata quælibet se facturos promittunt, et obsides illico, quantos Rex jubet, adducuntur." This of course cannot mean that they went back to the city for hostages
[5] So it would seem from the short but weighty account in the Worcester Chronicle, which gives hints which we should be well pleased to see drawn

CHAP. XVIII

The capitulation disowned by the citizens at large.

The SIEGE of EXETER William draws near to reconnoitre, and finds the city prepared for defence

wonder that it was so, for, as soon as the messengers returned to the town, it speedily appeared that the act of the ruling body was not confirmed by the general feeling of the citizens. The capitulation was disowned, even regard for the safety of the hostages did not move men who had made up their minds not to yield.[1] After the deputation had withdrawn, and had left the hostages in the King's hands, no further marks of submission followed. The road was not thronged, as William probably looked to see it, by his new subjects pouring forth to welcome their sovereign. One might almost be led to think that acts of direct hostility followed on the part of the citizens. At all events, William saw that he was deceived, and we can hardly blame him for being filled with wonder and wrath.[2] With five hundred horsemen he rode forth to see the city, to judge of its site and its fortifications, and to find out what the enemy were doing.[3]

out at greater length The words are—after the harryings—" And þa he ferde to Defenascire, and besæt þa burh Exancester xviii dagas, and þær wearð micel his heres forfaren, ac he heom wel behet, and yfele gelæste, and hig him þa burh ageafon forþan þa þegenas heom geswicon hæfdon" The account seems hardly to follow chronological order, and this seems the most likely time for promises

[1] Ord Vit 510 B "Reversi ad concives, qui supplicia pro reatu nimis metuebant, nihilominus machinantur hostilia quæ cœperant, multisque pro caussis ad oppugnandum sese incitabant" These words by themselves would rather imply that those who made the capitulation were the same as those who disowned it. But the mention in the Chronicle of the treason of the Thegns, and the distinction which Orderic himself seems to draw between the "primores" now and the "municipes" a little later, seem to justify me in following Lappenberg in the view which I have taken in the text I see that Thierry and Mr St John take it in the same way, only it is hardly fair of Thierry to quote the words of Orderic so as to make "concives" the nominative cases

[2] Ord Vit 510 B. "Quod audiens Rex, qui ad quatuor milliaria consistebat ab urbe, irâ repletus est et admiratione"

[3] Ib. "Imprimis itaque Rex cum quingentis equitibus propere perrexit, ut locum et mœnia videret, et quid hostes ageret deprehenderet" Compare the five hundred horsemen sent against London (see vol iii p 542), but then William was not present in person

EXETER.

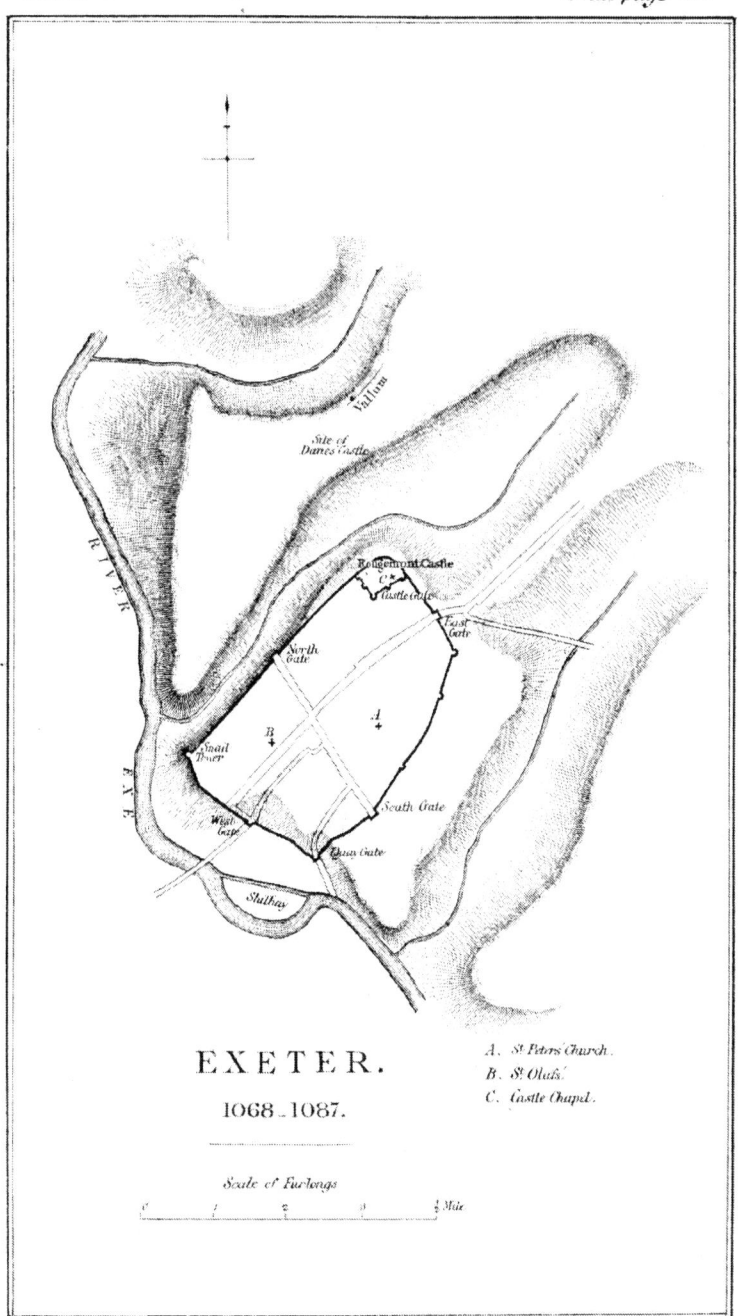

1068–1087.

A. St Peters Church.
B. St Olafs.
C. Castle Chapel.

The city to which William now drew near did not indeed rival the natural strength of Le Mans or Domfront, but it came nearer than most English towns to recalling somewhat of the character of those memorable scenes of his earlier exploits. Exeter is described by the most detailed historian of this campaign as standing in a plain,[1] and to one who looks down upon the city from the higher ground which surrounds it on nearly every side the description might not seem inappropriate. But the city really stands on a hill, and a hill, in some parts, of no inconsiderable steepness. The Exe flows to the south-west; at the northeast a sort of narrow isthmus connects the hill with a large extent of ground at nearly its own level. On either side of the isthmus a sort of ravine, stretching towards the river on each side, forms a kind of natural moat round the greater part of the city. On the isthmus, the most important point in the line of defence, stood the east gate of the city, one of the four which guarded the ends of the four main streets which still keep up the memory of the ground-plan of Roman Isca. The wall which, with a little care, may be traced through nearly the whole of its extent,[2] followed the crest of the hill, which is divided from the river by rich alluvial pastures, in those days most likely mere swamps. The defences were therefore

[1] Orderic (510 A) calls the city "in plano sita," and adds "a litore marino, quo ex Hibernia vel Britanniâ minore brevissimo aditur spatio, distans milliaria circiter duo" "Litus marinum" may, by a favourable construction, be taken to mean the shore of the estuary of the Exe, but the whole geography is confused.

[2] The walls of Exeter are well shown in the plans in Izacke's "Remarkable Antiquities of the City of Exeter" (London, 1724), and Jenkins's "History and Description of the City of Exeter" (Exeter, 1806) In April, 1870, I made the whole circuit of the defences in company with Mr W A. Sanford, and we were able to trace the wall nearly everywhere It has been greatly patched at various times, and shows a most remarkable variety in its masonry I do not feel at all certain that some portions of the foundation of Æthelstan's wall do not remain on the north side All the gates have been destroyed

not carried down to the water, except at the extreme southern point of the city, where a fifth gate, the *Quay Gate,* came between the Western and Southern Gates of the four main arms. Here then were the two main approaches for either friends or enemies. The Exe, not yet, as at a later time, bridled by weirs,[1] afforded free access from the friendly districts, and we hear nothing of any fleet being employed by William At the opposite end of the city, William's line of approach would lie by the isthmus leading to the East Gate which opened into the High-street. The ground is such that he and his horsemen would see but little of the town till they came into its near neighbourhood. To the left of the East Gate, just within the wall, stood the cathedral church of the newly translated Bishoprick, which has since given way to the building whose combined uncouthness of outline and perfection of detail makes it unique among English churches. To the right of the gate rose the high ground, which William's keen eye would at the first glance mark as the site of the future castle The river, the main source of the importance of the city, flowed out of sight on the other side, but on the right, soaring over the city and the intervening valley, rose the height of Penhow, where, sixty-seven years before, Swend of Denmark, driven back from the city, had found his revenge in a victory over the men of Devonshire and Somerset.[2] The new invader found the city as well prepared for defence as ever it had been against the earlier enemy. The gates were shut, and the whole range of walls and towers was thick with defenders.[3] According to one version, one of the besieged went so far as to offer to William and his followers an

---

[1] On the blocking of the river by the Earls and Countesses of Devon, see Oliver's "History of the City of Exeter," p 249    [2] See vol. 1 p 340
[3] Ord. Vit 510 B  " Portæ offirmatæ erant, densæque turbæ in propugnaculis et per totum muri ambitum prostabant "

insult as unseemly as it was senseless.[1] The wrath of William was now kindled to the uttermost. God, he said, would never help men who dared to treat him with such scorn.[2] The whole army now drew near; the siege was formed, and William began by striving to strike awe alike into his followers and into his enemies by an act in which the laws of war were strained to the uttermost. One of the hostages was brought close to the East Gate, and his eyes were put out in the sight of both armies.[3] We shudder at the cruelty; to the avenger of Alençon[4] the act most likely seemed at once politic and merciful. In the eyes of William it was a means by which Exeter might be won, as he loved to win his conquests, without further shedding of blood.[5] But the sight in no way bent the hearts of the

---

[1] Will Malm. iii. 248. "Unus eorum, supra murum stans, nudato inguine auras sonitu inferioris partis turbaverat, pro contemptu videlicet Normannorum." So Rog. Wend. ii. 4, Matt. Paris, 6, ed. Wats. There is however the question whether this story does not belong to Oxford instead of Exeter. See Appendix Z.

[2] Will. Malm. u. s. "Ipse audacius eam assilierat, protestans homines irreverentes Dei destituendos suffragio." Cf. vol. ii. p. 287.

[3] Ord. Vit. 510 B. "Denique regio jussu exercitus ad urbem admotus est, et unus ex obsidibus prope portam oculis privatus est."

[4] See vol. ii. pp. 287, 288.

[5] On the rights of hostages and the unlawfulness of putting them to death, see Grotius, De Jure Belli et Pacis, iii. 11. 18, Vattel, Droits de Gens, ii. 16 (vol. i. p. 190, ed. Leyden, 1758). This doctrine William would no doubt have readily accepted, even while reserving to himself the right of blinding or other mutilation short of death. See vol. ii. p. 266. Grotius refers to the conduct of Narses as described by Agathias. The reference is to the siege of Lucca in 553 (see Gibbon, vii. 395, ed. Milman). The defenders of the city failed to surrender at the time agreed on, so he *pretended* (if the story is to be believed) to put their hostages to death. His words are remarkable, ἐνίοις δὲ τῶν ἀμφ' αὐτὸν καὶ χρῆναι ἐδόκει τοὺς ὁμήρους διαφθαρῆναι, ὡς ἂν οἱ ἐν τῷ ἄστει ἀναθείεν καὶ ταύτῃ ποινὰς ὑφέξειεν τῆς ἀπιστίας· ὁ δὲ στρατηγὸς, γνώμῃ γὰρ ἅπαντα ἔπρασσε, καὶ οὐ λίαν τῇ ὀργῇ ξυνεχώρει, οὐκ ἐς τόδε ὠμότητος εἴη ὡς ἀποκτεῖναι τοὺς μηδὲν ὅ,τι καὶ ἠδικηκότας ἀνθ' ὧν ἕτεροι ἐπλημμέλουν. Agath. p. 23, ed. Paris.

Yet, if nothing might be done to the hostages, one wonders what hostages—so habitually given in that age on all occasions—were for

156    CONQUEST OF WESTERN AND NORTHERN ENGLAND.

CHAP XVIII.  
The defenders made more obstinate by the sight.  
Valiant resistance for eighteen days  

men of Exeter; they were rather stirred up to a yet more valiant defence of their hearths and homes.[1] The siege began, and was carried on with vigour on both sides for eighteen days. The besiegers kept up a constant attack on the walls; the defenders however stood their ground, and many of the assailants lost their lives.[2] William might have been beaten back from Exeter as Swend had been, if the military art of Normandy in William's days had not been many steps in advance of the military art of Denmark in the days of Swend. It was by undermining the walls that William at last gained possession of the city.[3] This was a mode of attack for which the men of Exeter were most likely not prepared They could hurl their javelins from the battlements; they could cleave the skull of any daring assailant who mounted a scaling-ladder; but a countermine would probably have been a refinement beyond their skill. William's mine advanced so far that part of the wall crumbled to the ground, making a practicable breach.[4] The hearts, not only of the magistrates but of the mass of the citizens, now at last gave way. To avoid the horrors of a storm, it was determined to submit unreservedly to the mercy of a prince who, to do him

The city at last taken by a mine

The citizens determine to surrender

---

[1] Ord Vit 510 B  " Pertinacia furentis populi nullo timore, nec ullâ reliquorum obsidum flectitur miseratione, sed acuitur ad defensandum se suosque lares totâ obstinatione."

[2] Chron Wig 1067  " Þær was micel his heres forfaren "

[3] Ord Vit 510 B.  " Rex autem fortiter urbem obsidione concludit, militari feritate invadit, et per plurimos dies obnixe satagit cives desuper impugnare et subtus murum suffodere "

[4] I infer this from William of Malmesbury (in 248)  " Urbem Exoniam rebellantem leviter (?) subegit, divino scilicet jutus auxilio, quod pars muralis ultro decidens ingressum illi patefecerit " This is of course on the supposition that " Exonia " is the right reading. It strikes me that William's story, allowing for a little legendary improvement, fits so well into Orderic's as to form an argument in favour of Exeter.

The expression of Florence " infregit " seems to fall in with this account

justice, had never ordered or allowed an indiscriminate massacre of unarmed suppliants.[1]

But there were still those in Exeter who scorned or feared to throw themselves upon the mercy of William. The mother of Harold was within the walls, and, as I have already conjectured, she was probably accompanied by all those members of the House of Godwine who were still free and still on English ground. Gytha left the city, evidently before the gates were thrown open,[2] with her went the wives of many good men,[3] and probably others of both sexes, for the presence of Blæcman the priest is distinctly recorded.[4] If her grandsons were with her, they no doubt accompanied her in her flight, though they did not share her final place of refuge. The means of escape were easy. William, superior to Swend in his other resources, had brought no ships to share in the attack on Exeter. The besieged therefore must have retained their communications with the river and the sea during the whole length of the siege. There was therefore nothing to hinder any who were minded to escape by water from so doing. When the breach in the wall showed that resistance was now hopeless, perhaps even while William was marching in triumph through the East Gate, it was still easy for Gytha, and those who chose to share her fortunes, to make their way by the Quay Gate to the still friendly stream. The widow of Godwine, the mother of Harold, was able

*Gytha and her company escape before the surrender.*

*Easy escape by means of the river.*

*Escape of Gytha and her following.*

---

[1] Ord Vit 510 C "Tandem municipes ingenti hostium instantiâ utile consilium coacti capiunt, ad deprecationem descendunt" Here I seem to see a vote passed by a general Assembly of the citizens (municipes) as distinguished from the earlier action of the "primores" only Cf on the constitution of London, vol iii pp 545–547

[2] Flor Wig 1067 "Gytha vero Comitissa, scilicet mater Haroldi Regis Anglorum, et soror [it should be "amita"] Suani Regis Danorum, cum multis *de civitate fugiens* evasit"

[3] Chron Wig 1067 "And her ferde Gyða ūt, Haroldes modor, and manegra godra manna wif mid hyre"

[4] See above, p 144.

CHAP XVIII. to sail away with her companions before the last stronghold of her children had bowed to the Norman as its lord. She and her immediate company either doubled the Land's End, or were perhaps able to find their way across a friendly country to the coast of Somerset. There they sought shelter on one of those two islands in the Bristol Channel, the Steep and the Flat Holm, which form such prominent objects in the view from either coast, and which can be seen even from the distant hills of Gloucestershire. To one of them Gildas, the one British chronicler of the English Conquest, had retired for solitude and meditation, till pirates from the Orkneys, forerunners of the Wikings of a later day, drove him to seek for refuge in the inland isle of Ynysvitrin.[1] In the days of the Danish invasions, a band of ravagers, flying before the arms of the men of Hereford and Gloucester, had sat on the lonely island till food failed them, when they sailed away to Dyfed and to Ireland.[2] And now Gytha and her companions, her daughter Gunhild and her granddaughter the younger Gytha, sought the same dreary refuge,[3] perhaps only till one more chance of restoration could be tried. For the sons of Harold sought the same place of shelter which their father had

*Marginalia:* Gytha and her company take refuge on the Flat Holm. Early history of the Holms. Settlement of Gildas on the Steep Holm. Their history in the Danish wars 915.

---

[1] Vita S Gildæ, p xxxviii Stevenson (the Life is attributed to Caradoc of Llancarvan), "Sanctus Abbas Cadocus et Gildas doctor optimus communi consilio adierunt duas insulas, scilicet Ronech et Echin Cadocus intravit proximiorem Walliæ [the Flat Holm], Gildas adjacentem Angliæ" [the Steep Holm]. After a description of their mortified life for seven years, we read of the "piratæ de insulis Orcadibus"—the description savours rather of the age of Caradoc than of the age of Gildas—who spoiled their goods and carried away their servants Then Gildas sailed to Glastonbury ("reliquit insulam, ascendit naviculam, et ingressus est Glastoniam") where King Meluas reigned "in æstivâ regione"—that is *Somerset*.

[2] See the Chronicles, 915 Winchester reads, "þa sæton hie ute on þam iglande æt *Bradanrelice*"—that is the *Flat* Holm, while all the other versions have "æt *Steapanreolice*" "Relic" or "Reolic" must be the same name as the "Ronech" of Caradoc

[3] Chron Wig 1067 "Her ferde Gyða út into *Bradanreolice*"—that is the Flat Holm—nearer the coast of Morganwg.

sought seventeen years before. King Diarmid still reigned in Dublin, and was still ready to give aid and comfort to English exiles.[1] It was perhaps not till this last hope proved as vain as all others that the sister of Ulf and widow of Godwine bade her last farewell to the land of her adoption.[2] She made her way to the old shelter in Flanders, and found a home at Saint Omer in very different case from the days when, in her former exile, she had come with her husband and her sons.[3] This is the last stage that we are allowed to see of her long and chequered life. Of her descendants we get a few more glimpses. Gunhild, the daughter of Godwine, already vowed to a virgin life, spent nineteen years of pious mortification in the land of banishment. From Saint Omer she passed to Bruges, from Bruges, according to all precedent, she went on to Denmark, where she was sure of an honourable welcome at the hands of her royal cousin. She afterwards returned to Bruges, and there died a few weeks before the death of the Conqueror at Rouen.[4] Her niece Gytha also found her way to the court of Swend. By his means she is said to have been given in marriage to the Russian prince Vladimir of Novgorod. To him she bore a son who was honoured with the name of his English grandfather, and daughters too, through whose inter-marriages

*CHAP XVIII*
*1051*
*The sons of Harold take shelter with Diarmid of Dublin*
*Gytha withdraws to Flanders. June, 1069?*

*Gunhild, daughter of Godwine, dies at Bruges, August 24, 1087*

*Marriage and descendants of Gytha, daughter of Harold.*

---

[1] Ord. Vit. 513 A. "Duo filii Heraldi Regis Angliæ, mœsti pro patris occisione suique propulsione, confugerant ad Dirmetum Regem Hiberniæ." See vol ii pp 154, 387

[2] Florence cuts the story short, "De civitate fugiens evasit et Flandriam petit." But her stay on the Flat Holm was not very short, as the Chronicle adds, "And þær wunode sume hwile and swa fór þanon ofer sǽ to Sĉe Audomare." This "some while" may possibly cover the space till the final discomfiture of her grandsons in June, 1069.

[3] See vol ii. p 151.

[4] The bones of Gunhild, and her sepulchral inscription written on lead, were first found in the church of Saint Donatus at Bruges in 1786. The church was destroyed in 1804, but the inscription and a single bone—like the one bone of William which escaped the Huguenot destroyers of Saint Stephen's—were preserved. I have given the inscription in Appendix L.

160    CONQUEST OF WESTERN AND NORTHERN ENGLAND.

CHAP XVIII the blood of Harold found its way into the veins of many of the princely houses of Northern Europe [1]

Surrender of Exeter.

But we must hasten back to the gates of Exeter. Gytha and her companions were gone, and those who had less personal reason to dread the wrath of William went forth to crave his mercy. The pageant which had greeted his eyes as he entered Le Mans [2] greeted them again as he entered the capital of Western England. The whole population poured forth to meet the Conqueror whom they were now forced to acknowledge as their sovereign. Along with the elders in age or rank came forth the goodly youth of Devonshire,[3] and the clergy of the city, bearing their sacred books and other holy things, to appeal to the religious element which was ever strong in the mind of William. The appeal was hardly needed; William's heart was not yet so hardened as to inflict the horrors of slaughter and plunder in mere wantonness. The prayer of the suppliants was heard, and they were assured of the safe possession of their lives and goods. Remembering perhaps the accident which had led to the destruction of Dover,[4] William secured the gates with a strong guard of men whom he could trust, in order to preserve the goods of the citizens from any breaches of discipline on the part of the common soldiers.[5] A free pardon was granted to the city; even

The citizens pray for mercy

They are favourably received.

Care of William to hinder accidental outrages

[1] See Appendix M
[2] See vol iii pp. 203–206.
[3] Ord. Vit 510 C "Formosissima juventus, majoresque natu [þa yldestan þegnas], cum clero gestante sacros libros et hujusmodi ornatum, ad Regem exeunt" On the "formosissima juventus" see above, p 91 Mr St John (ii 319) turns them into "numbers of the loveliest women of Devonshire" In the "majores natu," as ever, the notions of "old men" and "aldermen" run into each other
[4] See vol. iii p 537.
[5] Ord Vit u s. "Princeps moderatus humiliter prostratis clementer pepercit, confitenti populo reatus indulsit, ac si nescisset quod illi eidem

the wrongs, whatever they were, which had been done to his soldiers at an earlier time, were graciously overlooked.[1]

William was thus master of Exeter. His first step, as ever, was to secure his conquest by the building of a castle. In the north-east corner of the city, immediately within the walls, a site stood ready, such as the Normans loved for the building of their fortresses, a site admirably suited to keep the half-subdued citizens under the yoke.[2] A mound, probably a natural mound strengthened by art, which, from its Norman occupiers, received the name of Rougemont,[3] overlooked both the city and the surrounding country, and there William laid the foundations of the famous Castle of Exeter. The present remains are not imposing. The greater part of the buildings, including the collegiate church which arose within the walls,[4] have vanished, and unsightly modern buildings have intruded within the precinct. Still the gate which leads from the town, though a good deal disfigured, may well be of the time of William or of a time but little later. A better site for commanding the city, the opposite heights, and the valley which lies between, could not have been wished for. The command of the rising fortress was given to Baldwin of Moeles, a son of William's kinsman and early guardian Count Gilbert, and married, according to some accounts, to a kinswoman of

*Foundation of the Castle of Exeter*

*The castle entrusted to Baldwin of Moeles*

proterve restiterant. . . . Exonii gaudent, gratesque Deo referunt, quod post tot iras terribilesque minas spe melius alienigenæ Regi pacificati sunt Rex autem a rebus eorum abstinuit, et portas urbis valente fidâque custodiâ munivit, ne gregarii milites repente introirent et pecunias civium violenter diriperent"

[1] See above, p 138  It is now that Orderic mentions the story

[2] Ord Vit 510 C.  "Locum intra moenia ad exstruendum castellum delegit."

[3] *Rougemont, Rubens mons.* See Oliver, 181

[4] See its history in Oliver, 193.

162    CONQUEST OF WESTERN AND NORTHERN ENGLAND.

CHAP. XVIII. his sovereign.[1] Baldwin was left, with other men of fame and rank, to keep strict watch over the city whose conquest had cost William so dear. He was to hasten on with the completion of the castle, a process which, together with the other effects of the siege and the surrender, involved the destruction of forty-eight of the houses of the city.[2]

Increase of the tribute of Exeter.

Besides the building of the castle and the destruction which it involved, another penalty was inflicted upon the city. The patricians of the half-born commonwealth had offered to pay to William the tribute which had been paid to earlier Kings.[3] The money payment was now raised from an occasional half-mark of silver to eighteen pounds yearly. The rights of the Old Lady were not forgotten, and Eadgyth received two-thirds of the increased burthen laid upon her morning-gift.[4]

William marches into Cornwall and overcomes all opposition.

The amount of resistance which William met with in the West after the fall of Exeter is not clearly marked. There were movements which he had to put down; and the heavy destruction which fell on the town of Barnstaple in the north-western part of Devonshire, and the still heavier destruction which fell on the town of

---

[1] Ord. Vit. 510 C "Ibi Balduinum de Molis, filium Gisleberti Comitis, aliosque milites præcipuos reliquit, qui necessarium opus conficerent præsidioque manerent." On Baldwin, see Will. Gem. viii 37, Ord. Vit. 687 C, 694 D, which latter passage gives some details of his actions after death. The genealogy in Du Cange, 1085, gives him as his wife a daughter of an aunt of Duke William, whom Dr. Oliver (181) calls "Albreda the Conqueror's niece," but Orderic (687 C) seems to speak of her only as "bona uxor."

[2] Domesday, 100 "In hac civitate sunt vastatæ xlviii domus postquam Rex venit in Angliam." We may assume that these houses were destroyed to make way for the castle, though it is not expressly said that they were, as in some other places.    [3] See above, p. 146.

[4] Domesday, 100 "Hæc reddit xviii libras per annum. De his habet B[alduinus] vicecomes vi libras ad pensum et arsuram et Coluinus xii libras ad numerum in ministeriis Eddid Reginæ. Hæc civitas T R E non geldabat nisi quando Londonia et Eboracum et Wintonia geldabat, et hoc erat dimidia marka argenti ad opus militum." But even the tribute imposed by William was not large for so great a city, when we find that Tawton paid fifteen pounds and Brampton sixteen

Lidford,[1] might seem to show that those two boroughs were special scenes of resistance. Lidford lay on the road towards Cornwall, into which peninsula William now marched. Whatever may have been the zeal of their English landlords, the *Bretwealas* themselves had no special motive to struggle against one master on behalf of another, and whatever resistance William met with in that quarter was easily overcome.[2]

The conquest of Western England was thus complete, and the usual processes of confiscation and division of lands now began. I say began, for of course, neither here nor in any other part of the country, is it necessary to suppose that it took place altogether at once. In some cases it is plain that it did not. And here, as elsewhere, a few Englishmen of rank contrived to win William's favour and to keep their lands and offices. One of these perhaps was Aiulf, a man who appears as Sheriff of Dorset, and who may be the same as a landowner of the same name in the reign of Eadward.[3] A more certain case is

*Confiscation and division of lands*

*Englishmen who obtained favour*

*Aiulf?*

---

[1] Domesday, 100, Exon Domesday, 80 Dr Oliver (180) remarks that "this record shows that Lidford did not submit to the Conqueror until forty houses of the burgesses were demolished, nor Barnstaple until twenty-three houses were laid waste, a proof of the deadly hostility of the townsmen against the Norman invaders" The number of burgesses in Barnstaple T. R E was forty within the borough and nine without. Lidford had twenty-eight within the borough and forty-one without Lidford, once more populous than Barnstaple, is now a very inconsiderable place. No destruction of houses is spoken of in the other Devonshire towns

[2] Ord Vit. 510 C "Ipse postea in Cornu Britanniæ ulterius contendebat Composito ubique motu quem deprehendit, exercitum dimisit"

[3] The entries about Aiulf may lead to the belief that there were two persons of the name We have in Berkshire (63), Wiltshire (73), and Dorset (82 b, 83), an Aiulf, described as "Vicecomes" and "camerarius," holding lands all of which had belonged to English owners T. R E In Devonshire (116) there is an Aiulf in the same case without any official description. In Devonshire (109) there is an Aiulf who holds of Judhael of Totnes lands which he had himself held T R E Again, in Somerset (94) and in Devonshire (115 and 116) we find an Aiulf holding T R. E. whose

CHAP XVIII. that of Colwine, who stands at the head of a long list
Colwine. of English Thegns who appear as landowners at the time of the Survey. Most of them retained the lands which they had themselves held in the time of King Eadward. Colwine seems also to have been the representative of the
Large number of English Thegns in Devonshire. Lady in the city of Exeter.[1] This large number of Devonshire Thegns who retained their lands seems to show that the greater part of the shire submitted easily after the fall of the capital.[2] But the most remarkable man, and the official of highest rank, among those who
Eadnoth the Staller. won William's favour in the Western shires was Eadnoth, a man who seems to have risen by the favour of Harold, who had held the office of Staller under both Eadward and Harold, and who held large estates in various parts of England, but especially in the West. He became a zealous adherent of William and, as we shall presently see, died in his service. It is therefore almost certain that
Loss of his estates by his son Harding. he must have retained his lands; still only a small part of them passed to his son Harding, who, there is every reason to believe, was the ancestor of the great house of the Lords of Berkeley. Some pretext must therefore have

lands had passed to Norman owners. In Wiltshire (74) we find among the King's Thegns an Eadmund son of Aiulf holding lands which his father had held T. R. E. This last person can hardly fail to have been an Englishman, but, as he can hardly fail to have been dead at the time of the Survey, he can not well have been the Sheriff. It remains a question whether the Sheriff and the holder T. R. E. can be the same person. It should be noted that the Sheriff's largest estate, that in Dorsetshire, was partly an official and not a personal holding. After one of the entries (83) follows the comment, "hanc tenet Aiulf de Rege quamdiu erat vicecomes."

[1] Colwine appears in Domesday (118) as the owner of eight lordships, two of which had been held by himself, four by Godric, who may have been his father—possibly however an English *antecessor*—and two by women, Odeva (Eadgifu) and Briteva (Brihtgifu). On his office in Exeter, see p. 162, note 4.

[2] The largest owner is Godwine (118), who holds eleven lordships, three of which had been held by himself and the rest by Alestan (Æthelstan?), probably his father. Of one Thegn, Donne by name, we read (118), "hic tenuit de Rege E. et modo dicit se tenere de Rege Willelmo."

been found for defrauding Harding of his full succession; such a pretext was perhaps easily to be found in the case of a man who, we are told, was much more valiant with his tongue than with his sword.¹ Another Englishman, Brihtric by name, whose lands were scattered at least from Worcestershire to Cornwall, was less lucky than Eadnoth or even than his son. Of him we have already heard I have elsewhere² told the legend how, in the days of King Eadward, Brihtric had been sent as an ambassador to the Court of Flanders; how Matilda offered herself to him in marriage and was refused; how, when Brihtric was in William's power, she remembered the slight which he had put upon her, and stirred up her husband's wrath against him. Brihtric was seized at his house at Hanley in Worcestershire, on the very day when Saint Wulfstan had hallowed a chapel of his building. He was hurried to Winchester, and died in prison, when his lands were divided between Matilda and Robert Fitz-Hamon Such is the tale. It has thus much of corroboration from history, that a portion of the lands of Brihtric did pass to Matilda; but nothing more can be said.³

Among ecclesiastics neither of the two Western Bishops were disturbed, and the Abbot of Glastonbury, William's companion in his Norman voyage, was allowed to keep his place for several years. Both Gisa and Leofric held their sees for the rest of their days, and Gisa outlived William himself. The two great assertors of Lotharingian discipline⁴ were not likely to be foremost in the championship of English freedom. Gisa, a stranger by birth, found favour and help from the stranger King; he at last obtained a portion of the lands which had been disputed between him and Earl Harold. In his gratitude he learned to look on the overthrow of England as a

---

¹ On Eadnoth and Harding see Appendix S  ² See vol. iii. p 85
³ On Brihtric see Appendix T  ⁴ See vol. ii pp 84, 452

CHAP XVIII.
Topsham not restored to the see of Exeter.
Alienation of the gifts of Gytha.

small price to be paid for the addition of the lordships of Banwell and Winesham to the possessions of the see of Wells.[1] Leofric, who was at least of English or British birth, was less lucky; he never obtained the restitution of the lands at Topsham of which Harold was said to have deprived him.[2] Within the conquered city itself a small transfer of ecclesiastical property took place, which in William's eyes perhaps seemed specially appropriate The church of Saint Olaf in Exeter, the church of the Scandinavian saint which the Danish Gytha had enriched for the welfare of the soul of Godwine,[3] was, either now or at a later stage of William's reign, bestowed on the Abbey of the Place of Battle.[4] Another of Gytha's pious gifts, bestowed for the same cause on the Old Minster of Winchester, passed away altogether from the Church, and became part of the spoil of William's insatiable brother of Mortain.[5] As William could have no motive for despoiling the chief church of his own capital, and as we can hardly suspect him of going so far as to try to do Godwine an ill turn in the other world, this last alienation is more likely to be due to some usurpation on the part of Earl Robert than to any legal grant on the part of the King. Lastly, the fate of the lands of the patriotic priest Blæcman illustrates at once the confusion of tenure so common at the time and also

History of the lands of Blæcman.

[1] Historiola, ap Hunter, 18 "Præoccupante autem illum [Haroldum] judicio divinæ ultionis .... Dux victoriâ potitus, quum regni gubernacula post eum suscepisset, et a me de injuriâ mihi illatâ querimoniam audisset, Wynesham ecclesiæ resignavit, privilegio confirmavit," &c On Banwell, see vol. ii p. 639 This means that Winesham came into the King's hands by the forfeiture of Ælfsige I should like to know more of one "Johannes Danus" (Domesday, 89 b) who was also dispossessed in favour of the Bishoprick

[2] See vol. ii. p 549        [3] See vol ii p. 352

[4] Domesday, 104 "Ipsa ecclesia [de Labatailge] habet in Execestre ecclesiam Sancti Olaf."

[5] See vol ii p 352 The entry on Crowcombe in Domesday (91 b) is, "Ecclesia Sancti Suuithuni Winton tenuit T R E."

William's constant desire to do formal justice as he understood it. Blæcman's flight was, as usual, held to be equivalent to outlawry, and his estates were seized. But, just as Henry of Ferrers had seized, not only the freehold lands of Godric, but the lands which should have reverted to the King and to the Abbey of Abingdon,[1] so the lands held by Blæcman of the same abbey were seized with his other possessions, and it was only with much difficulty that Abbot Ealdred at last obtained their restitution.[2]

The conquest of the West opened a wider field than ever for the reward of William's followers and allies. The saints of Normandy and France were not forgotten. The metropolitan church of Rouen, the two Abbeys of Caen, and the Abbey of the Battle all came in for their share.[3] And later in his reign, when the death of the Lady Eadgyth put her lands also at his disposal, William bethought himself of making a more permanent offering than banners and treasures to that one among his allies who ranked highest both in heaven and earth. One lordship in Somerset, alone among all the lands of England, became the freehold of the Church of Saint Peter at Rome.[4] Among more earthly helpers, the Bishop who

[1] See above, p 37

[2] Hist Ab 1 484 "Ipso, ut dixi, ab Angliâ discedente, quæcumque illius fuerant, in manum Regis ut puta [utpote?] profugi, redacta sunt Quare Abbas magno cum labore prædictarum terrarum apud Regem obtinuit restitutionem"

[3] The church of Rouen held the two lordships of Ottery and Rovrige in Devonshire, the former the site of the well-known collegiate church Rovrige (Domesday, 104) was William's own gift out of the estate of a woman named Wulfgifu Ottery had been held by the church T R E, and, according to a document quoted in the Monasticon (vii 1118), it was a gift of Earl Odda, doubtless during his momentary Earldom over Devonshire in 1051–1052 (see vol. ii p 160) Both the Abbeys of Caen (Domesday, 104) held lands in Devonshire which had belonged to Brihtric, and Saint Stephen's had also lands in Somersetshire (91) For the possessions of Battle in Devonshire besides the church of Saint Olaf, see Domesday, 104

[4] Domesday, 91. "Terra Ecclesiæ Romanæ Ecclesia Romana beati Petri Apostoli tenet de Rege Peritone Eddid Regina tenebat T R E"

had played at Senlac and the Bishop who had fought, Geoffrey of Coutances and Odo of Bayeux, received grants in their personal and temporal character. The estates of the Earl of Kent in the West were not large, but among them was part of the spoil of the House of Godwine.[1] Geoffrey of Mowbray received an endless list of lordships in Somerset, together with smaller possessions in the other Western shires.[2] Fresh possessions fell, as we have seen, to the lot of Eustace of Boulogne when he recovered the favour of William,[3] and few of the leading followers of the Conqueror went without their share in the new distribution.[4] Baldwin, who had been left in command at Exeter, and who drew his name from the conquered city, received a vast estate lying wholly in the two shires of Devon and Somerset, in the former of which he held the office of Sheriff.[5] And there was one beyond all these, whose share of the spoils of England was greater than that of any other one man, and whose chiefest and richest rewards lay in the newly conquered lands. Robert, the son of Herlwin and Herleva, in whose favour William of Mortain had been despoiled,[6] who had received the very first fruits of the Conquest on the shore of Pevensey,[7] and whose

---

[1] Domesday, 87 *b* "Episcopus Baiocensis tenet Come et Sanson de eo. Leuuinus Comes tenuit T R E"

[2] See Domesday, 87 *b*-89 *b*, 102-103 *b*

[3] See above, p 130, and Appendix N

[4] Nearly all the familiar names, Earl Hugh, Walter Giffard, William of Eu, Ralph of Mortemer, Toustain the son of Rolf, and so forth, are found in Somerset or Devonshire, or both William of Moion has a single lordship in Devonshire (110) and a vast estate in Somerset (95 *b*-96 *b*), among the entries of which we read " ipse tenet Torre, et ibi est castellum ejus " This is Dunster.

[5] " Baldwinus de Execestre," " Baldwinus vicecomes," appears in Somerset (93), where he holds the historic lordship of Porlock His estates in Devonshire fill eleven columns of Domesday, 105 *b*-108 *b*. Among his many tenants French and English, but mainly French, we twice find his own wife, "uxor Baldwini tenet de eo "

[6] See vol ii. p. 292

[7] See above, p 77.

lands spread into well nigh every shire from Sussex to Yorkshire, now gathered in the richest spoil of all in the forfeiture of countless Englishmen within the Western shires.[1] To his Earldom of Mortain Robert now added the Earldom of Cornwall, and within his own shire he held a position to which only one or two other parallels can be found in the roll-call of the conquerors. Well nigh the whole shire was granted to him. The list of his possessions, lands of Earl Harold, of the Sheriff Mærleswegen, and of a crowd of smaller victims, is simply endless. Hardly any other landowners appear in Cornwall, except the Crown and ecclesiastical bodies. And the lands retained by the Crown are small compared with those in the hands of the Earl, and in favour of the Conqueror's brother the Church itself was not spared. The two great Cornish foundations, the two churches which laid claim to be looked on as the episcopal sees of the West-Welsh diocese, were both shorn of their wealth to glut the insatiable appetite of the new Earl. These were the church of Saint German, which bore the name of the missionary who had won back Britain from the Pelagian heresy,[2] and the more renowned house of Saint Petroc at Bodmin, a church which had won the favour of the West-Saxon conquerors,[3] and which had but lately yielded its episcopal rights to the capital of the West. Both alike were despoiled of many of their lordships to swell the vast possessions of Earl Robert.[4] Thus arose that great Earldom, and afterwards Duchy, of Cornwall, which was deemed too powerful to

*His Earldom of Cornwall.*

*His robberies of the churches of Bodmin and Saint Germans*

---

[1] See his Somerset estates in Domesday, 91 b-93, and those in Devonshire, 104 b-105 b. In Cornwall, with the exceptions mentioned in the text, he simply holds the whole shire, 121 b-125

[2] See Bæda, Hist Eccl 1 17 et seqq, Bædæ Chronicon, 189, ed. Stevenson

[3] See Mon Angl ii 459

[4] On the aggressions of Robert of Mortain on Church lands, see Domesday, 121, and Appendix U

be trusted in the hands of any but men closely akin to the royal house, and the remains of which have for ages formed the appanage of the heir-apparent to the Crown. But the lands of Robert in the West were not confined to his own Earldom. The lord of the waterfalls heaped together manor upon manor among the dashing streams of Devonshire and among the hills and islands of Somerset. And one spot came to him by an exchange with an ecclesiastical body, the possession of which, like the possession of Pevensey, seemed to mark him out as the very embodiment of the overthrow of England. The hill of Lutgaresbury, whence came the holy relic which had given England her war-cry and which had been the object of the life's devotion of her King,[1] now passed into the hands of one who was to wipe out its name and memory. The height, one of the peaked hills which form so marked a feature in the scenery of Somerset, was now crowned by a castle of the new Earl, which, under the French name of Montacute, became at once a badge of the presence of the stranger and an object of the bitterest hatred to the men of the Western lands.[2]

In tracing out the distribution of lands in the shires which fell into William's power after the surrender of Exeter, we are struck at every step by the all but utter absence, among the dispossessed landowners, of names suggestive of British origin. In Somerset, and even in Devonshire, this is not wonderful. Though much of British blood must have remained in those shires, and though their originally British character was not yet wholly

---

[1] See vol. i p. 590, ii p. 440; iii pp. 428, 480

[2] Domesday, 93 "Ipse comes tene in dominio Biscopestone, et ibi est castellum ejus quod vocatur Montagud Hoc manerium geldabat T R E pro ix. hidis, et erat de Abbatia de Adelingi, et pro eo dedit Comes eidem ecclesiæ manerium quod Candel vocatur" In 92 is another entry, "duo portarii de Montagud tenent de Comite Estuit"

forgotten,[1] they had no doubt by this time become to all outward appearance thoroughly English. Even in local nomenclature, the British names, though common as compared with their rarity in the purely Teutonic parts of England, are still decidedly exceptional. But Cornwall, I need not say, retained its British speech for ages after this time, the local nomenclature is mainly Celtic, and the local families profess to show in their surnames the evidence of their British origin.[2] It is therefore remarkable that even in Cornwall the landowners in the days of King Eadward seem by their names to have been almost wholly English. In an age when surnames were still unknown in Britain, we are of course not to look for "Tre, Pol, and Pen" among the owners of Cornish soil. But we might have looked for distinctively Welsh Christian names, and of them we find a few, but very few.[3] This is the more striking, as in other Cornish documents which survive, the number of Welsh names, though not overwhelming, is much larger than it is in Domesday.[4] The natural inference seems to be that Cornwall before the

*CHAP XVIII.*

*even in Cornwall.*

---

[1] Take such signs as the description of Odda's Earldom in 1051 (see vol ii pp 160, 564), the description of Devonshire and Somerset by the Biographer of Eadward in 1052 (see vol ii p 316), perhaps the words of Thietmar about Æthelstan's army in 1016 (see vol i. p 422)

[2] Every one knows the saying about "Tre, Pol, and Pen," but it is a saying which carries its own refutation with it  Tre, Pol, and Pen are now surnames, that is, they are the names of places adopted as surnames by their possessors or inhabitants  But the man who first took such a local name as a surname was just as likely to be of English or Norman as of Cornish descent

[3] We find a genuine Welshman in 120 b, Caduualant by name, who held Lancheroc in Cornwall T R. E of Saint Petroc  In 123 b we find Griffin holding lands T R E which at the time of the Survey were held of Earl Robert by Jovinus, and of the men in Domesday, 124-125, bearing the nondescript names of Briend, Offers, Hueche, Rabel, and Blohin, some may have been true Britons

[4] See the manumissions at the altar of Saint Petroc, Cod Dipl iv 308  We there find plenty of Gruffydds and other genuine Welshmen in the time of Eadgar and earlier

CHAP XVIII
The British element in Cornwall probably revived by the Norman Conquest

Norman Conquest was in much the same state as England after it. The land must have been mainly in the hands either of Englishmen or of Anglicized Britons. The Norman Conquest may very well have given the native element a fresh start. Nowhere was the dispossession of former landowners more complete. The whole shire passed into the hands of a few ecclesiastical corporations and of a few great proprietors, Earl Robert far outtopping all others. In Cornwall we find none of those King's Thegns, Englishmen who kept small estates or fragments of large ones, of whom there are so many in other districts. On Earl Robert's estates the names of the tenants are mostly French, but some are English, and a still smaller number are British[1] But now Briton and Englishman were at least brought down to the same level under their common master. The greater numerical strength of the Britons would give them an advantage over the strangers of either speech, just as the English in England proper had the same advantage over the Norman settlers. And it would be singular indeed if this result was in any way strengthened by what may pass as another, and the last, of the many migrations and counter-migrations which have gone on in various ages between Armorica and West-Wales The followers of one Alan of Britanny had once pressed into the greater Britain to seek shelter from Glorious Æthelstan against the attacks of Norman invaders.[2] The followers of another Alan now came to receive their share of the spoils of the land which had sheltered their forefathers from the hands of the descendants of their old enemy. A few Breton settlers in Cornwall and the other shires of the West may be discerned in the Survey.[3] And one

Breton settlers in the West

---

[1] Of Robert's English tenants several went on holding the lands which they had themselves held T R E  See Domesday, 124 b
[2] See vol 1 p 208, III p 459.
[3] Take for instance Aluredus Brito, who holds a large estate in Devon-

adventurer, bearing a name common in different shapes to Wales and Britanny, Judhael, who from his chief seat took the name of Judhael of Totnes, became the owner of a vast estate in Devonshire, and extended his possessions into the proper Cornwall also.[1]

The West was now conquered, and the distribution of its lands among the conquerors had at least begun. It was probably in this campaign also that Gloucestershire was fully subdued, though the accounts to which we have to trust are very imperfect. A castle was built at Gloucester, and its building of course involved a certain amount of destruction of houses, but the date of its foundation is not given, and the destruction is much smaller than in many other towns.[2] This looks as if the capital of the shire was at least not taken by storm. With regard to Worcestershire our information is in one way still scantier, while in another it is much fuller. There is no shire of whose condition during the Conqueror's reign we are able to put together a more vivid picture from the combined evidence of the Survey and of local records,[3] but we have no record of the date of its conquest. We find that the two shires were put under the care of a single Sheriff, Urse of Abetot, who stands conspicuous

CHAP XVIII
Judhael of Totnes

Conquest of Gloucestershire.

Gloucester Castle

State of Worcestershire

Oppressions of the Sheriff

shire (Domesday, 115 b, 116) So also Rualdus Adobed in Devonshire (114 b) suggests the Ruallus, that is Rhiwallon, of William of Poitiers, 110. See vol III p 233 He may not unlikely be the same man

[1] See his estates in Devonshire, Domesday, 108 b–110, and Cornwall, 125 We have met with the name in different forms, as Ioþwel, one of the Welsh princes who sought Eadward the Elder to Lord (see vol i p 129), Judwal, Juchil or Judethil, one of those who rowed Eadgar on the Dee (Fl Wig 973, Will Malm ii 148, 155), Juhel Berengar in Britanny in William Longsword's time (see vol i p 207), and we find Gyðiccæl as the name of a slave in Cornwall in Cod Dipl iv 313

[2] Domesday, 162 "Sedecim domus erant ubi sedet castellum quæ modo desunt, et in burgo civitatis sunt wastatæ xiii domus"

[3] Our accounts of the condition of the Worcestershire monasteries are so full, that I have thrown them together in another place (see Appendix W)

174         CONQUEST OF WESTERN AND NORTHERN ENGLAND.

CHAP XVIII.  among the most oppressive of his class, and whose hand
Urse of      seems to have fallen heavily on clerks and laymen alike.
Abetot.
Spoliations  Odo also, the insatiable Bishop of Bayeux, appears at a
of Odo.      later time among the spoilers of the Church in this district, and as he did not spare men of his own calling, neither did he spare men of his own nation. Among Englishmen we come across the well-known names of Saint Wulfstan the Bishop of the diocese, of the prudent Æthelwig of Evesham, and of Ealdred, who, though long since removed to a higher see, seems to stand towards the Worcester Bishoprick in a character strangely made up of guardian and spoiler.[1] In behalf of the rights of the church of Worcester he braved the terrible Sheriff himself. Urse of Abetot was only the chief of a whole band of Norman spoilers, who seem to have fallen with special eagerness on the lands of the Church in this particular shire. But the Sheriff was the greatest and most daring offender of all. He built his castle in the very jaws of the monks of Worcester, so that the fosse of the fortress encroached on the monastic burying-ground.[2] Church and castle must thus have stood side by side over-
Ealdred      looking the Severn. Complaint was made to the Arch-
rebukes
and curses   bishop, who came to the spot, examined the ground, and
Urse         rebuked the King's officer to his face. To a Latin or
1068–1069
             French speaker the name of Urse might have suggested an easy play upon words. To the English Prelate, who

[1] On Ealdred's spoliation of the church of Worcester, see vol. ii p. 467. Of his guardianship and benefactions I shall speak in Appendix W.

[2] Will Malm Gest Pont. 253 "Ursus erat vicecomes Wigorniæ a Rege constitutus, qui in ipsis pene faucibus monachorum castellum construxit, adeo ut fossatum coemeterii partem decideret." The castle of Worcester is utterly gone, but the site to the south of the church is still well known. From the story of Saint Wulfstan, to be told in the next Chapter, we may infer that Oswald's church, then standing, did not stand on exactly the same site as the church of Wulfstan, so that the castle may have been still nearer to the church than its site is now.

appears as addressing the Norman Sheriff in English verse, it seems rather to have suggested a happy rime.

"Hightest thou Urse?
Have thou God's curse"

is the vigorous bit of English which is preserved to us. The rest we have only in the Latin of the narrator, but he goes on to add, "and mine and all hallowed heads, unless thou takest away thy castle from hence; and know of a truth that thine offspring shall not long hold the land of Saint Mary to their heritage."[1] We hear of no repentance on the part of Urse, and yet, as in the case of the penitent Ahab, the evil that was to come on his house was kept back till the days of his son. In the days of King Henry, the Lion of Justice, Roger the son of Urse drew on himself heavy punishment at the hands of the King in whose days no man dared to hurt another.[2] A servant of the King was slain by Roger's order, and the lands of Saint Mary, along with his other possessions, passed away from the son of the first spoiler.[3]

This famous tale of course implies the complete submission of Worcestershire, but the tale is unluckily

---

[1] The way in which William of Malmesbury (Gest Pont 253), tries to explain the nature of a rime is curious. "Libertas animi ejus [Aldredi] in uno verbo emituit præclare, quod Anglice apponam, quia Latina verba non sicut Anglica concinnitati respondent . Ursum his verbis adorsus est, *Hattest þu Urs, have þu Godes lurs,* eleganter in his verbis sed dure nominum euphoniæ alludens, '*Vocaris,* inquit, Ursus, *habeas Dei maledictionem,*' et (quod Anglice non apposui) meam et omnium consecratorum capitum, nisi castellum hinc amoveris, et scias profecto quod progenies tua non diu de terrâ Sanctæ Mariæ hæreditabitur"

The apologetic way in which William quotes a few words of English reminds one of his difficulty about the names of the English shires see vol 1 p 382.

[2] See vol iii. p. 112

[3] Will Malm u s "Dixit ille implenda quæ nos videmus impleta Siquidem non multis annis filius ejus Rogerius paternarum possessionem compos, gravi Henrici Regis indignatione pulsus est, quod quemdam ex ministris regis præcipiti furore jussit interimi"

CHAP. XVIII.

Temporal jurisdiction conferred by William on Abbot Æthelwig

without an exact date. The mention of Ealdred however enables us to fix it to a time not later than the year following the taking of Exeter.¹ Nor can we give a date to the secular commission which, if we may trust the local history of Evesham, Æthelwig received at some time or other from William's hands. This commission clothed him with large authority in several shires, in some of which it is plain that, at the time of the fall of Exeter, William had no authority save such as he derived from the nominal submission of Eadwine. Æthelwig is described as chief ruler, or at any rate as chief judge, in no less than seven shires, Worcester, Gloucester, Oxford, Warwick, Hereford, Stafford, and Shropshire.² We naturally suspect exaggeration, but there is no reason to doubt either Æthelwig's early submission to William or his lasting favour with him.³ He appears as already trusted by the Conqueror in a story which not improbably belongs to the time which we have now reached, and which seems to preserve a record of the struggle which led to the Norman occupation of the two Hwiccian shires.⁴ We

¹ Ealdred died in September, 1069.

² Hist. Eves. 89. "Et quoniam Rex sapiens cognoverat eum virum prudentem, pene omnes hujus gentis homines saeculari sapientiâ praecellentem, commisit ei curam istarum partium terrae, videlicet, Wirecestrescire, Glouecestrescire, Oxenefordscire, et Wareuuickescire, Herefordscire, Stafordscire, Scrobschire, ita ut omnium hujus patriae consilia atque judicia fere in eo penderent. Et non solum in istis partibus, sed etiam per totam Angliam ubicumque veniebat, tam Franci quam Angli pro justissimâ lege tenebant quidquid ipse legibus saecularibus dicebat."

³ See above, p. 77, and Appendix W.

⁴ The doubtful language of the Winchcombe writer preserved in the Monasticon, ii. 302, preserves at least the tradition of a severe struggle in this district. "Si vero sint qui scribunt Winchecombensium et Persechorensium monasteria, tempore quo Willielmus Normannorum Dux sibi regnum subjugaverat, longe majora atque plura quam modo habuisse possessiones et dominia, sed quia minus caute sibi de futuris prospicientes, elegerunt eidem Willielmo Duci pro viribus resistere aut eum forte debellare, ideo dicunt eumdem Willielmum Regem, vehementer in eos commotum, abstulisse plurima ex eorum possessionibus, et ea pro suâ voluntate aliis piis locis contulisse. Verum an haec aliquid veritatis

get glimmerings of fighting on the borders of those shires, which ended in a Gloucestershire Abbot being entrusted to the safe keeping of his brother in Worcestershire. Godric, Abbot of Winchcombe, whose appointment to that monastery was recorded in an earlier Chapter,[1] is set before us as the leader of patriotic movements in that quarter. His opposition was thought of importance enough to call, not merely for deprivation or outlawry, but for personal restraint. The monastery was despoiled of many of its possessions; Godric himself was at first put in ward at Gloucester, and was afterwards entrusted to the milder keeping of Æthelwig, to whom also the care of the Abbey itself was entrusted for three years, till a successor for Godric was found in a Norman named Galand or Waland.[2] The exact date of these events is not to be fixed, and it must remain uncertain whether they were connected with the movement in the West which I have just recorded or with the movement in the North which I shall presently have to record. But it seems plain that Gloucestershire was fully subdued at some stage of the

*Warfare on the Hwiccian border*

*Resistance and imprisonment of Abbot Godric of Winchcombe.*

---

habeant, necne, cum ea in nostris antiquitatibus nusquam legerim, non ausim scribere. Memini tamen me, apud monasterium Eveshammensium, in eorum antiquissimis historiis olim legisse, Willielmum Ducem Normannorum, tunc Anglorum Regem, Godricum Abbatem Winchelcumbensem violenter tenuisse, ac in castro Gloucestriæ jussisse retrudi custodiendum, Winchelcumbenseque cœnobium Abbatis Eveshammensium moderationi commendâsse, et paulo post cuidam monacho ex Normannorum, ut creditur, genere, Galando nomine, illud idem Winchecumbense monasterium contulisse regendum. Quo reverâ fieri umquam haud potuit nisi (ut communis se habet fama) idem Willielmus Rex in Abbatem hujus loci fuisset vehementer exacerbatus." [1] See vol ii p 362.

[2] The account of Godric in the Evesham History (90) runs thus, "Rex Willielmus tollens Abbatem Wincelcumbensem, Godricum nomine, fecit constitui in captivitate apud Gloecestre, moxque huic Abbati, Ageluuio suam abbatiam commisit, quam fere per tres annos quasi propriam in cunctis gubernando servavit. Deinde Rex donavit illam cuidam Abbati Galando nomine, et eo post modicum tempus ex quo eam accepit defuncto, iterum isti Abbati Ageluuio committitur." In the next Chapter we shall come across a record of Godric's sojourn at Evesham

CHAP XVIII *year which we have now reached, and I have connected it with the Western movement because the subjugation of Gloucestershire is at least connected with it in idea.* The conquest of Gloucestershire put into William's hands the whole of the former Earldom of Harold, except the corner of Herefordshire which was still defended by Eadric the Wild One thing is certain, that the great merchant borough on the borders of Mercia and Wessex was in William's power, and was not disposed to revolt against him. The castle of Bristol is famous in the wars of the next century, but there is no record of its foundation in the Survey.[1]

*All Harold's old Earldom in William's hands*

*Bristol subject and loyal to William*

William, now conqueror of all southern and western England, returned to his southern capital and kept the Easter Feast, according to the custom of his predecessors, in the royal city of Winchester.[2] There might Eadgyth, while her mother, sister, and niece were seeking shelter in their lonely island, receive all the honours due to the widow of a King. Her lands in the West had been spared, and her royal home in her dower city was still hers. But she was not long to enjoy her position as the highest of her sex in England William now deemed that his Kingdom was secure enough for him to call on his wife to come and share his honours. An honourable embassy was sent to the Duchess-Regent in Normandy to invite her presence in England.[3] She came with a train of clerks and lords and noble ladies; and among the churchmen in her company one is specially recorded, Bishop Guy of Amiens,

*William keeps Easter at Winchester, March 23, 1068*

*Matilda comes to England*

---

[1] Bristol is simply mentioned in Domesday (163) under the head "In Bertune apud Bristou," "Hoc manerium et Bristou reddunt Regi c et x markas argenti, burgenses dicunt quod Episcopus G[oisfridus Constantiensis sc] habet xxxiii markas argenti et unam markam auri præt-r firmam Regis"

[2] Chron Wig 1067 "On þisan Eastron com se Kyng to Wincestre, and þa wæron Eastra on x Kal April" Ord Vit 510 C "Guentam ad vacandum illuc paschali festo rediit"

[3] Ord Vit u s "Guillelmus Rex legatos honorabiles in Neustriam direxit, et Matildem conjugem suam ad se venire præcepit"

the poet of the great battle.[4] His work was already written, perhaps as a laureate's offering at the great solemnity which was presently to take place. For at Pentecost King William, again walking in the steps of his predecessor, wore his Crown at Westminster. And there, in the church which had beheld his own anointing, though doubtless in far other guise than the wild tumult of the great Midwinter-day, the Lady Matilda was hallowed to Queen by Archbishop Ealdred. The law which had marked the crime of Eadburh by lessening the dignity of the wife of the West-Saxon King was now repealed or forgotten, and the consorts of English Kings have ever since shared equally with their husbands in all the honorary dignities and privileges of royalty.[1]

*William keeps Pentecost at Westminster*

*Matilda is crowned by Ealdred May 11, 1068*

### § 3. *The First Conquest of the North.*
### *Summer and Autumn,* 1068.

All for the moment now seemed quiet. William had assured his dominion over the West, and the chiefs of the North were still at his court in a character which did not greatly differ from that of hostages. Eadwine and Morkere were William's Earls over Mercia and Deira, as William Fitz-Osbern was his Earl over Herefordshire and Bishop Odo over Kent.[2] But it was his policy to

*Position of Eadwine and Morkere*

[4] Ord. Vit. 510 C "Protinus illa mariti jussis libenter obedivit, et cum ingenti frequentiâ virorum ac nobilium feminarum transfretavit In clero qui ad divina ei ministrabat, celebris Guido Ambianorum Præsul eminebat, qui jam certamen Heraldi et Guillelmi versifice descripserat" See vol iii pp xxvi 136, 377

[1] Chron Wig 1067 "And sona æfter þam com Mathild seo *hlæfdie* hider to lande, and Ealdred arcebisceop hig gehalgode to *cuéne* on Westmynstre on Hwitan Sunnan dæg" Ord Vit 510 D "Adelredus Eboracorum metropolitanus, qui maritum munxerat, Matildem ad consortium regni honoris die Pentecostes anno ii regni præfati Regis munxit" On the use of the words "Queen" and "Lady," see Appendix X

[2] There is an English writ of William (Mon Ang 1 301) on behalf of Westminster addressed to "Leofwine B and Edwine Eoill and alle tha thegnas in Staffordescire" This may be a nominal exercise of authority

CONQUEST OF WESTERN AND NORTHERN ENGLAND.

CHAP XVIII

*A daughter of William promised to Eadwine, but the marriage delayed*

*Possible influence of Norman prejudice*

keep them away from their Earldoms, and to hold them immediately under his own eye. Eadwine seems to have really won his personal regard, and he had tried to win him over by a promise, whether sincere or designedly illusory, of the hand of one of his daughters. Her name, whether Matilda or Agatha, I do not pretend to determine, but there seems every reason to believe that, whatever may have been the objects of William, a real attachment had sprung up between the Norman maiden and the young and handsome English Earl. But, whenever Eadwine asked for his bride, some excuse was always found to delay the accomplishment of his wishes. It is to be noticed that this breach of faith is distinctly attributed, not to William's own designs, but to the bad counsel of some of his Norman advisers[1] There is something grotesque in the notion of William the Great being led astray, like Æthelred or Eadward, by the arts or the advice of any man. But it is quite possible that a feeling of contempt towards the conquered nation, which William assuredly did not share, may have already grown up among William's Norman followers. Eadwine, we are told, had won the love of William's courtiers as well as of William himself.[2] Still they may have looked on a marriage with the native Earl of

now, or it may belong to the short time in 1070-1071, between the real conquest of Staffordshire and the last revolt of Eadwine The writ is followed by another addressed to Archbishop Ealdred, Bishop Wulfstan, Earl William (Fitz Osbern), and all the Thegns in Gloucestershire and Worcestershire

[1] Ord Vit 511 A "Guillelmus Rex, quando Edumus Comes cum eo concordiam fecerat [see above, p 20] . filiam suam se in conjugem ei daturum spoponderat, sed postmodum fraudulento consultu Normannorum concupitam virginem et diu exspectatam denegavit nobilissimo juveni" The same language is used afterwards (521 A) with regard to William's treatment of Morkere, "Rex Guillelmus, consilio pravorum male usus, laudi suæ damnum ingessit"

[2] When Orderic (521 B) records the death of Eadwine, "formosissimus juvenis Eduinus Comes," he adds, "auditâ per Angliam Eduini morte, luctus ingens non solum Anglis sed etiam Normannis et Francis ortus est, qui eum velut socium et amicum seu cognatum cum multis fletibus planxerunt"

the Mercians as unworthy of a daughter of the conquering King of the English. And to a prejudice of this kind William may have found it needful to show some deference. But it is quite as likely that it was William's own policy which led him to try to keep Eadwine still more dependent upon himself by constantly promising and never fulfilling. However this may be, the marriage was delayed, and the anger of Eadwine was further kindled against William. The position of the two brothers must have been irksome and degrading enough in any case, and the further wrong done to Eadwine brought matters to a head. The sons of Ælfgar, the Normans say, openly rebelled.[1] The view of the people of their Earldoms would doubtless be that they at last came back to head them against a foreign invader to whom, though they had submitted, their people never had.

At this moment then, when the West had just submitted, the North rose. As yet no step had been taken for its practical subjugation, and the men of Mercia and Northumberland had now their natural chiefs to head them. There was little in the past career of Eadwine and Morkere to give any good ground of hope for any undertakings begun under their lead. But in Northumbrian eyes the acts by which they had undone England, their successive betrayals of Harold and Eadgar, and, still more, their earlier share in the revolt against Tostig, might seem praiseworthy assertions of the independence of Northern England. Absence too and distance would work their usual work. The forced presence of the Earls in William's court would look like imprisonment; their visit to Normandy would look like banishment. They might thus seem entitled

CHAP XVIII

Indignation of Eadwine

Revolt of the two brothers

Rising in the North Summer, 1068

Position and character of Eadwine

---

[1] Ord. Vit 511 A. "Eodem anno egregii juvenes Eduinus et Morcarus, filii Elfgari Comitis, rebellaverunt, et cum eis multi alii ferociter insurrexerunt, quorum motus Albionis regnum vehementer turbaverunt .. Eduinus .. iratus cum fratre suo ad rebellionem incitatus est."

On the different accounts of these events, in no way contradictory to each other, but every one strangely imperfect, see Appendix Y.

182   CONQUEST OF WESTERN AND NORTHERN ENGLAND.

CHAP XVIII to claim somewhat of the honours of confessors in the national cause. Add to this that, politically worthless as Eadwine clearly was, he plainly possessed many of those superficial attractions which often have a stronger influence on men than the highest wisdom and virtue. His high birth and office, his handsome person and winning address, combined, we are told, joined with a large share of the piety of the age, won for him a wide-spread popularity among the English people.[1] The monks, the clergy, and the poor joined in daily prayers for the welfare of the two Earls,[2] and, when they made their way from William's court to their own Earldoms, the flame broke out in the whole northern region of the island.

Union of English and Welsh

1055

1065

Civil war in Wales Winter, 1067-1068

The movement headed by the Mercian Earls is specially spoken of as a common movement of English and Welsh.[3] The league between Ælfgar and Gruffydd the son of Llywelyn[4] seems never to have been forgotten. Welsh allies had joined the revolted Northumbrians in their march to the Gemóts of Northampton and Oxford.[5] It is not clear what amount of understanding may have existed between Eadric of Herefordshire and the Mercian Earls; but we have seen Eadric powerfully supported by the reigning Welsh Princes Bleddyn and Rhiwallon.[6] Bleddyn had now, by the result of a civil war, become sole sovereign of at least all North Wales. Bleddyn and Rhiwallon,

---

[1] Ord. Vit. 511 A "Fervens adfectus erat præfatis fratribus erga Dei cultum et bonorum reverentiam hominum. Erat eis ingens pulcritudo, nobilis et ampla cognatio, late valens potentatus et nimia in eos popularium dilectio." So at a later stage (521 B); "Idem [Eduinus], ut supra dictum est, fuerat ex religiosâ parentelâ natus, multisque bonis deditus, prout poterat inter tanta sæcularium curarum impedimenta positus. Corporis pulcritudine in multis millibus eminebat, et clericorum atque monachorum pauperumque benignus amator erat."

[2] Ib 511 A "A clericis et monachis crebra pro illis fiebat oratio et a turbis pauperum quotidiana supplicatio."

[3] Ib. "Eum magna pars Anglorum et Gualorum sequuta est."

[4] See vol ii p 387     [5] See vol ii p 490

[6] See above, p 110

whom the English make brothers of Gruffydd,[1] appear in the Welsh Chronicles as sons of Cenwyn,[2] and we find them about this time engaged in a war with two of their countrymen, described as Meredydd and Idwal, sons of Gruffydd.[3] A battle took place at Mechain in Powys, in which the brother princes were victorious. Idwal fell in battle, and Meredydd, flying from the field, died of the cold,[4] a description which seems to fix this campaign to the same winter which beheld William's return from Normandy. But the victory was purchased by the death of Rhiwallon, and the struggle seems in some way to have led to a division of the great dominion of Gruffydd the son of Llywelyn. Bleddyn reigned alone in Gwynedd and Powys, but Deheubarth or South Wales is spoken of as being under the rule of another Meredydd, the son of Owen the son of Etwin, one of a house of which we heard in the days of Æthelred.[5]

The language of the one writer who narrates these events in any detail seems to describe the holding of an assembly which must have been designed as a general Gemót of the Empire, at which the chief men of Wales as well as of

*Battle of Mechain, death of Rhiwallon, Bleddyn sole Underking*

*Holding of a Gemót, presence of the Welsh*

---

[1] See vol ii p 476. Orderic, it may be remembered (see vol ii p 630), makes Bleddyn a son of Gruffydd and Ealdgyth, he now remembers the supposed kindred, and speaks of Eadwine and Morkere as Bleddyn's uncles (511 B); " Blidenus Rex Guallorum *ad avunculos suos* suppetias venit."

[2] They are so called under 1068 both in the Annales Cambriæ and in the Brut y Tywysogion, but the Brut under 1073 seems to speak of Bleddyn as Gruffydd's brother."

[3] Idwal in the Annales, Ithel in the Brut. Here are further forms of the name spoken of in p 173

[4] Ann Camb 1068 "Bellum Methein inter filios Kenwin, scilicet Bledin et Ruallo et filios Grifini, scilicet Maredut et Idwal, in quo filii Grifini ceciderunt, Idwal bello, Maredut frigore, Ruallo etiam filius Kenwin, occisus est." So Brut y Tywysogion in anno

[5] The Brut says, "Bleddyn, son of Cynvyn, held Gwynedd and Powys, and Maredudd, son of Owain, son of Edwin, held South Wales" [Deheubarth] (On Etwin see vol i p 313.) The Annals say simply, "Bledin in regnum successit." It should be remembered that the Welsh writers do not mention the investiture of Bleddyn and Rhiwallon by Harold

184    CONQUEST OF WESTERN AND NORTHERN ENGLAND.

CHAP XVIII

*Great general gathering against the Normans*

*Possible concert with the sons of Harold,*

*with Swend of Denmark;*

*with Malcolm of Scotland.*

England appeared.[1] The grievances of the whole country were strongly set forth, and it was determined to seek for help in every quarter. Messengers were sent to every part of England to stir up the people. They of course went openly to the parts which were still independent, and they sent secretly to the shires which were already under the yoke.[2] The resolution to defend or to recover their ancient freedom was widely spread and firmly fixed in the hearts of Englishmen.[3] Nor was the chance of foreign aid neglected. It is not clear whether it was in concert with this Northern movement that the sons of Harold and their Irish allies presently attempted to return. The only difficulty in the way of such a supposition is the rivalry which had so long reigned between the House of Leofric and the House of Godwine. But however strong this motive might be in the hearts of Eadwine and Morkere, there is no need to believe that it would be shared by their followers in general. We seem also to get glimpses of further applications to Swend of Denmark,[4] and there can be no doubt that it was as a part of this same general movement that communications were opened with Scotland which led to a chain of events of the highest moment in the history of both Northern and Southern Britain.

Our history just at this time has to be put together in so piecemeal a way that it is not easy to arrange events in their exact order, or even always to assign their proper share in them to each of the actors  It is not, for instance, perfectly

---

[1] Ord Vit. 511 B  " Blidenus  .  venit, secumque multitudinem Britonum adduxit  Congregatis autem in unum multis Anglorum et Guallorum optimatibus, fit generalis querimonia de injuriis et oppressionibus quibus intolerabiliter Angli affligebantur a Normannis et eorum contubernalibus "—that is, the foreign mercenaries

[2] Ib  " Legationibus quoscumque poterant per omnes Albionis terminos in hostes clam palamque stimulabant "

[3] Fit ex consensu omnium *pro vendicandâ libertate pristinâ* procax conspiratio et obnixa contra Normannos conjuratio "

[4] Hist Ab i 493  " Pars gentem Danorum ut Angliam appeteret illicere."

clear what was at this moment the position of Eadgar, the Ætheling, the momentary King. But on the whole it seems most probable that he was the nominal head of the movement, and that whatever was done was done in his name as the King already lawfully chosen.¹ Such a doctrine might not be acceptable to the sons of Harold; it might not be acceptable to Swend of Denmark; it might not be acceptable in their heart of hearts to the two Earls by whom the Ætheling had already been once betrayed. But there was no one round whom so many varying interests and associations could gather as round the last representative of the House of Cerdic. Whatever the brother Earls may have done, the Northumbrians in general seem to have accepted Eadgar in good faith. They were perhaps not without a remembrance of that earlier Eadgar, who had found his way to the West-Saxon throne by Northumbrian help, and whose name abode on Northumbrian tongues as the embodiment of just and good government, till his memory was overshadowed by the more recent memory of the Danish Cnut.² At the head of the Northern movement stood Gospatric, who had, not many months before, been invested by William with the Bernician Earldom.³ William's jealousy seems up to this time to have kept him idle in his court along with his fellow-Earls of the house of Leofric, while the province which he nominally held under the Norman King still retained its perfect independence. Next in rank to Gospatric was the Sheriff Mærleswegen, whom Harold had left to command the North after the great day of Stamfordbridge,⁴ and who now jeoparded the distant possessions which he held in William's latest conquest of Cornwall⁵ Hardly lower in local esteem than these great chiefs was Archill, who is described as one of the

*Position of Eadgar, probably the nominal head of the movement.*

*Action of the Northern Thegns.*

*Gospatric.*

*Mærleswegen.*

*Archill.*

---

¹ On the order of events, see Appendix Y.
² See vol i. pp 67, 462
³ See above, p 134
⁴ See vol iii p 421.
⁵ See above, p 169

most powerful Thegns of Northumberland,[1] and whose vast estates stretched, if not, like those of Mærleswegen, from Yorkshire into Cornwall, yet from Yorkshire into the South-Mercian shire of Warwick.[2] King Malcolm too accepted the alliance of the insurgents, and a powerful Scottish army was summoned for an English expedition.[3]

But either Malcolm lingered in his preparations, or else the whole movement had fallen through before his troops could be got together. For we have to tell the same tale which we have ever to tell in the English history of these years, save when a born King of Men, an Eadmund or a Harold, stands forth as the leader of a people worthy of him. As in the days of Æthelred, as in the days of the Interregnum, as at the siege of Exeter, the zeal and courage of a whole people were again brought to nought by the cowardice and selfishness of incompetent leaders. The blood of the nation was thoroughly roused. Every town which was as yet unchecked by a Norman fortress or a Norman garrison looked well to its ramparts and made ready for resistance. The metropolis of Northern England set the example. What Exeter was in the West, York was in the North. It was the centre of every patriotic movement,[4] where all the mild piety of Ealdred strove in vain to keep down the burning zeal of its eager citizens.[5] But it was not the towns only; every defensible spot, woods, marshes,

---

[1] Ord. Vit. 511 C. "Archillus potentissimus Nordanhimbrorum."

[2] See Ellis, ii. 41.

[3] Ord. Vit. 511 D. "Malcolmus licet ab Anglis requisitus fuerit, et validam expeditionem [fyrd] in eorum auxilium paraverit."

[4] The declamation of William of Malmesbury (iii. 248) is in truth a noble panegyric on the city, "Eboracum, unicum rebellionum suffugium ibi enim Rex Scotorum Malcolmus cum suis, ibi Edgarus et Marcherius et Weldeofus cum Anglis et Danis, nidum tyrannidis sæpe fovebant, sæpe duces illius [Willelmi] trucidabant." Mark the use of *tyrannis*. See vol. i. pp. 152, 269.

[5] Ord. Vit. 511 B. "Eboracensis civitas ardentissime furit, quam sanctitas Pontificis sui sedare nequit."

mouths of rivers, were all seized upon and strengthened in readiness for an attack.[1] Men thought it shame to dwell at such a time under the shadow of a house. The wild men, the *savages*, as the mocking tongues of the Normans called them, dwelled of their own choice in tents and lurking-places, lest their strength should grow rusty among the comforts of their own roof-trees.[2] All this is credible enough; but it is hard to fix the chronology, and it is almost harder to believe the tale of a general conspiracy throughout England to massacre all the Normans during the penitential solemnities of Ash Wednesday. The plot, we are told, failed through the sudden return of the great warrior, who is thus conceived as being absent from England at the time when he was winning his great successes in the West. The malecontents, it is added, withdrew into the inaccessible North, and there for a while withstood the royal power.[3] That such a tale as this is wholly legendary it is hardly needful to prove.

Thus matters stood in northern and central England not very long after William had brought over his Queen to enjoy the honours of royalty in the conquered land. News was presently brought to the King that the folk in the North were gathered together, and that they would stand

---

[1] Ord. Vit. 511 B. "Seditiosi silvas, paludes, æstuaria, et urbes aliquot in munimentis habent." The "urbes aliquot" would doubtless take in all the walled towns of the independent shires.

[2] Ib. C. "Plures in tabernaculis morabantur, in domibus, ne mollescerent, requiescere dedignabantur, unde quidam eorum a Normannis *silvatici* cognominabantur." See above, p. 111, of Eadric of Herefordshire.

[3] Will. Gem. vii. 40. "Ipse vero in regnum remeans Anglicum, iterato plurimos ejusdem gentis repperit, quorum levia corda ab ejus fidelitate prævaricatrix conspiratio averterat. Conjuraverant enim latrunculi per totam patriam, quatinus milites, quos ad tuendum regnum reliquerat, in capite jejuni nudis vestigiis, quo solet usu pœnitens Christianorum religio, ad ecclesiam festinantes incautos ubique perimerent, et sic ipsum a Normanniâ regredientem levius e regno proturbarent." He then goes on to speak of their taking up a position at Durham, which I shall have to speak of presently.

188    CONQUEST OF WESTERN AND NORTHERN ENGLAND.

CHAP XVIII against him if he came.[1] Possibly the presence of Ealdred at York, so soon after the great ceremony at Westminster, and his attempts to check the patriotic movement by pious exhortations, may have been the firstfruits of the message. But at any rate William was not slow to follow with other weapons. His course was his usual one, to seize the towns and other important points and to strengthen them with castles.[2] One version, a version resting more on inference than on direct authority, would lead us to think that at this time Oxford still held out, that the town was taken by storm, and that the fearful devastation recorded in the Survey was the result.[3] If such was the beginning of William's first Northern campaign, we can well understand the terror-striking effect of such a blow dealt at such a moment. But the direct evidence for a siege of Oxford is so weak that the tale cannot be relied on with any certainty. The first place where William's presence is distinctly recorded is Warwick. That town was one of the series of strongholds by which the renowned Lady of the Mercians, the daughter of Ælfred, had sought to put a bridle in the mouth of the Danish invader.[4] It lies at no great distance from the obedient districts, and it is even possible that it may have already been in William's power. The property and influence of his friend Abbot Æthelwig of Evesham stretched into the shire, and William found in Warwickshire at least one Englishman of rank and wealth ready to play the part of Wigod in Berkshire. Thurkill of Warwick

William's first Northern campaign Summer, 1068
Building of castles
Question as to the storm of Oxford
William at Warwick.
Foundation of the town by Æthelflæd 915

---

[1] Chron. Wig. 1067 "Þa kyðde man þan kyninge þæt þæt folc be norðan hæfdon heom gegaderad togædere, and woldon him ongean standan, gif he come"

[2] Ord Vit 511 C. "Rex igitur secessus regni providentius perlustravit, et opportuna loca contra excursiones hostium communivit." It is now that Orderic makes that remark on the lack of castles which I quoted long ago See vol. ii p 140.

[3] On the date of the taking of Oxford, see Appendix Z

[4] Chron Wig 915 "Her on þison geare wæs Wærincwic getimbrod." Florence (in anno) adds that it was founded "in fine auctumni"

appears in the Survey as one of the very few Englishmen retaining or possessing estates which put them at all on a level with William's great Norman grantees. He was the son of Ælfwine, who seems to have been Sheriff at the time of William's entry, and who evidently made his peace with the Conqueror.[1] Thurkill kept his lands, which were largely increased by royal grants out of the confiscated estates of less lucky Englishmen. For among his possessions a small part only had been held by his father in King Eadward's days; the greater part had been the property of various English owners, among whom we discern Earl Eadwine, another Eadwine described as the Sheriff, and the greater name of Hereward. It is painful, on looking through the Warwickshire Survey, to compare the vast estates of Thurkill with the two or three other Thegns of the shire who retained some small fragments of their property.[2] It is plain that here, as elsewhere, the men of the shire at large were patriotic, and paid the penalty in the confiscation of their lands. The one loyal man, the one prudent man, the one traitor, as he would be called in the mouths of his more stout-hearted countrymen, reaped his reward, in retaining his wealth and honours, and in adding to them alike at the cost of a less successful fellow-traitor and at the cost of men better than himself.

William thus held Warwick, and we can hardly doubt that he held it through the adherence, either now or at some earlier time, of the Sheriff Ælfwine and his son.

*Chap XVIII.*

*Probable adhesion of Ælfwine the Sheriff*

*Lands of his son Thurkill*

*Few English Thegns in Warwickshire.*

*William's conquest of Mercia begins.*

[1] On Ælfwine and Thurkill, see Appendix AA

[2] See Domesday, 244, 244 b Two women hold land in "alms," Eadgyth who kept her own estate, and Leofgifu the nun, whose lands had been held T. R. E. by Godgifu, widow of Leofric Ælfsige, Ordric, and Godwine had kept their lands, though those of Ordric were waste Ælfric had lands which had been held by Wichig The only one remaining holder is Leofwine, who holds two very small estates Of one we read, "Hic Leuuinus emit ab Aluuino fratre suo" He may have been the Sheriff's brother. These men are not given the title of Thegn They are the only English tenants *in capite*, though of course there are English under tenants

He had now passed out of those lands, West-Saxon, East-Anglian, and Mercian, which had been for a longer or shorter time under the rule of the House of Godwine. He had entered those strictly Mercian lands over which the House of Leofric had, since their great rise under Cnut, always retained at least a superiority. Warwickshire had perhaps been held as a subordinate government by Ralph and Odda, but the Hwiccian lands had reverted to the rule of Leofric or his son,[1] and William was now setting forth to establish his effective supremacy over the Earldom of Eadwine, the old realm of Offa and Cenwulf. He was in truth setting forth to conquer a new Kingdom. And, unless we accept the version which represents Oxford as being stormed during the campaign of this year, Warwick was the firstfruits of his conquest. The new possession had to be guarded in the usual way. Whatever bulwarks survived from the days of Æthelflæd were deemed worthless in the recent advance of the defensive art. Warwick could be safely guarded only by a castle of the newest Norman pattern. Yet in this case at least the works of the defender of England have proved more lasting than the works of her Conqueror. The new town which arose at the bidding of the Lady of the Mercians, stood on a slightly rising ground at a small distance from the sluggish stream of the Warwickshire Avon. For the defence of her new creation, the Lady reared between the town and the river one of those vast artificial mounds which played so important a part in the early history of fortification. Whatever works, whether of stone or of timber, crowned or surrounded it in its first estate have utterly passed away, and the crest of the artificial hill is crowned by defences of a far later date than the days of either Æthelflæd or William. But the mound itself still remains, a monument of the wisdom and energy of

*Foundation of Warwick Castle*

[1] See vol. ii. pp. 563-565.

the mighty daughter of Ælfred, while the keep of William has so utterly perished that its very site can only now be guessed at. Most likely it stood in the void space between the mound, the gateway, and the later castle, whose picturesque turrets and battlements hang so proudly over the river at its feet. At all events, it was now that that famous fortress took its beginning. Either because the town passed peaceably into the hands of the Conqueror, or because the site of the fortress stood more than usually isolated from the town, the building of the castle seems to have involved a far smaller destruction of houses than was commonly the case elsewhere.[1] Thus arose the renowned castle of Warwick, famous alike in legend and in history, the seat of the mythical Guy and of the historical King-maker.[2] And, though the actual work of William himself has vanished, yet his foundation abides, one of the few fortresses of his day which have lived on through all changes and all rebuildings, and which still remain the dwelling-places of noble owners. With the guardianship of the new fortress no man of English birth, not even the loyal Ælfwine, might be trusted. He might retain the civil administration of the shire, but the military command of the castle could be safely entrusted only to Norman hands. The new castle was placed in the keeping of Henry, the younger son of Roger of Beaumont.[3] A great

CHAP XVIII

Its later history

---

[1] The only destruction in the town of Warwick recorded in Domesday is that of four houses belonging to the Abbey of Coventry, which are entered in p 238 as "vastæ propter situm castelli"

[2] The legend of Guy, which may be found at large in Knighton (X Scriptt 2324), is placed in the days of Æthelstan There is in the popular mind an invincible tendency to identify this mythical hero with Earl Richard Neville The confusion is possibly helped by the existence of a real Guy Earl of Warwick in the days of Edward the Second See the so called Walsingham, i 130, ed Riley

[3] Ord Vit 511 C " Rex itaque castrum apud Guarevicum condidit, et Henrico Rogeri de Bellomonte filio ad servandum tradidit "

192    CONQUEST OF WESTERN AND NORTHERN ENGLAND.

CHAP XVIII
The castle entrusted to Henry of Beaumont

The Earls of Warwick.

1499

March of Eadwine and Morkere.

They submit to William.

estate in the shire also fell to Henry's elder brother, Robert, Count of Melent, who, at the head of the French auxiliaries, had been the first to break down the English palisade at Senlac.[1] His son, Robert Earl of Leicester, became in the female line the forefather of the great Simon;[2] and from Henry's son, Roger Earl of Warwick, came, through various intermarriages, the long line of inheritors of his Earldom. The coronet of the house of Beaumont passed on to Beauchamps, Nevilles, Plantagenets, till the last of the old stock, the last direct descendant of the Angevin Kings, was cut off to appease the jealousy of the first Tudor and to allay the fears of a King of distant Aragon.[3]

This vigorous beginning of the campaign did its work. Our accounts are strangely imperfect, but, such as they are, they lead us to think that Eadwine and Morkere were actually marching at the head of an army to meet the invader, and that, as they drew near to Warwick and learned the occupation and defence of the town, they shrank from meeting the Conqueror in arms, and, without a blow, submitted and craved his pardon.[4] They were again received to favour, and it may be that the hopes of a royal bride were again dangled before the eyes of

---

[1] See Domesday, 239 b-240 b The English owners are mainly unknown persons, but one lordship had belonged to Earl Eadwine, and Hereward appears as under tenant of lands which had been his own See Appendix NN. On the history of the family, see Will Gem. vii 4, viii 40, 41 On Robert's exploits at Senlac, see vol. iii pp. 384, 488

[2] See vol ii p 200

[3] The King-maker, Richard Neville, was Earl of Warwick only in right of his wife Isabel Beauchamp, but, through her, the female descent from Henry of Beaumont went on to Isabel Duchess of Clarence and her children, Edward Earl of Warwick, the victim of Henry the Seventh, and Margaret, Countess of Salisbury (mother of Reginald Pole), the victim of Henry the Eighth

[4] Ord Vit. 511 C " Tunc Eduinus et Morcarus cum suis anceps prœlii discrimen præpendentes, gratiam Regis petierunt "

Eadwine. But we are told, and we can well believe it, that the favour at William's hands to which the sons of Ælfgar were now received was a favour only in name.[1] But the policy of receiving them even to apparent favour did its work. In the next struggle for Northumbrian independence Eadwine and Morkere had no share. They seem to have fallen back into their former position of hangers-on at the court of the Norman King.[2] They doubtless retained the rank and title of their Earldoms, but William disposed of the shires and fortresses of Mercia and Northumberland according to his will, and Englishmen of stouter hearts disputed his possession of them, without the will of the sons of Ælfgar being taken into account on either side.

*CHAP XVIII*
*Eadwine and Morkere again reconciled to William.*

*They remain in William's court.*

Thus, for the second time within a few months, chances of deliverance brighter than any that had offered themselves since William's coronation were utterly thrown away. During the course of the spring and summer of this year, far more than the half of England must have been in arms against William. But there was no one moment when all his enemies were in arms against him at once. The West rose and the North rose, but the North did not rise till the West was overcome. The West was betrayed by the Exeter patricians; the North was betrayed by the Mercian Earls. Their army no doubt dispersed on their submission. Any army of those days which found itself cheated of all chance of either fighting or plunder was pretty sure to disperse, even if its leaders did not forsake it. The mass of the followers of Eadwine and Morkere went, each man to his own home, to see their homes conquered in detail. The more resolute spirits determined on retiring to

*Want of concert and steadiness in the resistance to William*

*The army disperses,*

---

[1] Ord. Vit. 511 C. "Specie tenus obtinuerunt"
[2] This will appear from the way in which their final revolt in 1071 is spoken of in all our accounts

CHAP XVIII.
but a party withdraw to the North and occupy Durham

Strength of the position of Durham

the extreme North, and there organizing a separate resistance. They left Mercia and Southern Northumberland to their fate, and occupied the stronghold of the Bernician Bishoprick.[1] No spot could be better chosen for such a purpose than the peninsular height on which the happy choice of Ealdhun had placed the minster of Saint Cuthberht[2] and the humbler home of episcopal rule which preceded the mighty castle of William of Saint Carilef and Hugh of Pudsey. The mound on which the later keep of the episcopal fortress still stands may well have been called into play at this time, if not in times earlier still. Commanding the neck of the peninsula, guarded on three other sides by the river which flows by the foot of the well nigh perpendicular hill, a fort on or near this point would make the ecclesiastical precinct secure against all attack. At all events, Durham was put into a state of such vigorous defence that its independence was not threatened for the present. As for the rest of the land, William had only to march on and take possession.

Eadgar and his sisters, Gospatric, and Maerleswegen flee to Scotland

But meanwhile a company of Englishmen of higher rank sought a shelter yet further to the North than that which had been chosen by the defenders of Durham. King Malcolm of Scotland had already promised his help to the patriots, but before his help was forthcoming, the whole scheme had broken down through the desertion of the brother Earls But the Scottish King might still show his good will to the cause in another way. Two of the chief men of the North had chosen a different course from

---

[1] Will Gem vii. 40 "Repentinum magni debellatoris formidantes adventum, furtim, ut festinum magni terroris consilium suasit, fugâ lapsi in quamdam partem Cumberlondæ comitatûs, aquis pariter et silvis inaccessibilem, se contulerunt, et firmissimo vallo castrum erexerunt, quod propriâ linguâ Dunelmum nuncupârunt" This follows the passage quoted in p. 187, the geography breaks down at once, on the chronology see Appendix Y

[2] See vol 1 p 321.

that followed by the sons of Leofric. One of them was a man of birth even more lofty than their own and of equal nominal rank. When Eadwine and Morkere bowed to the Conqueror and returned to their luxurious ignominy in his court, Gospatric, with a nobler spirit, set forth to seek a shelter in Scotland till the day might come when he could again serve his country. With him went the Sheriff Mærleswegen and many others of the best men of the North. They took with them the nominal leader of the enterprise, Eadgar the Ætheling, with his mother Agatha and his sisters Margaret and Christina.[1] They set sail, at what haven we are not told, and reached the court of Dunfermline in safety.[2] Malcolm received the exiles as favourably as he had, two years before, received Tostig.[3] The whole party abode under his protection through the whole winter,[4] planning no doubt new schemes for the deliverance of the land which the sons of Ælfgar had forsaken. The shelter given by Malcolm was valuable in itself, and in the end the sojourn of the English exiles at the Scottish court led to events memorable in the history of both countries. Not only did Scotland stand ready as a land where English exiles were ever welcome, but greater results still came when at a later time one of the company was prevailed on to accept the land of refuge as a permanent dwelling place.[5]

We return to the progress of the Conqueror. The next

---

[1] On the movements of Gospatric and Mærleswegen, see Appendix Y

[2] The Chronicles simply say "comon [foran, Petrib] to Scotlande" But Florence adds "navigio Scottiam adierunt" If they could once reach a port, they were doubtless safer from William by sea than by land

[3] See vol III p 327

[4] "On Malcholomes cyninges gryð," says the Worcester Chronicler See vol ii pp 151, 154

[5] On the date of the marriage of Malcolm and Margaret, see Appendix BB

CHAP XVIII
William's course from Warwick to Nottingham

No mention of Coventry or Leicester

History of Leicester.

Alleged destruction of Leicester

point at which we hear of him is Nottingham. But Nottingham is a long way from Warwick; and, if no blow was struck in all the region between those two towns, there must at any rate have been many peaceful submissions. Coventry, with Earl Leofric's minster, and Leicester, the capital of the intervening shire, are not mentioned; but the submission of those towns and of the neighbouring country must have happened on this march. That we hear nothing of Coventry is perhaps not wonderful. The town does not appear in the Survey as a borough; its name has not yet been mentioned in English history, except as the site of the great monastery which was soon to grow into an episcopal church. But the omission of Leicester raises questions of quite another kind. Unlike Coventry, the town had played a considerable part in early history; it was one of the famous Five Boroughs, and it had been fortified, no less than Warwick, by the Lady of the Mercians.[1] It was now a town of at least equal importance with Warwick. If Warwick sent ten, Leicester sent twelve, of its burghers whenever the King called forth his *fyrd*[2] Are we to suppose that the contingents of these towns were pressed to follow William's banner, as the men of the North had in times past followed Swend to the conquest of southern England? Or is it possible that, in the case of Leicester at least, no power was left either to follow or to resist? While we have no evidence either way on which we can rely with confidence, one of those secondary and local records which sometimes contain fragments

---

[1] Chron 918, 942, 943
[2] Domesday, 230, 238 This was in case of an expedition by land. When the King went to war by sea, Leicester gave the use of four pack-horses as far as London ("mittebant ei iiii equos de eodem burgo usque Londoniam ad comportandum arma vel alia quæ opus esset"), while Warwick sent either four sailors (" batsueins," *boatswains*) or four pounds in money ("iiii libras denariorum") Why was Warwick held more capable of finding sailors than Leicester?

of authentic tradition, suggests, in a perfectly casual way, that a doom fell upon Leicester which might, doubtless with some exaggeration, be spoken of as utter destruction.[1] And this incidental hint may perhaps draw some indirect confirmation from the highest evidence of all. The Survey contains no account of a castle at Leicester, though one undoubtedly arose there before long, nor does it contain any account of destroyed or wasted houses. But then it contains no mention at all of English burghers or English freeholders within the borough.[2] The whole town had passed into the possession of strangers. The shire too is one of the districts on which the hand of confiscation fell heaviest. Only two or three English landowners of the smallest class retained their lands. In Nottinghamshire, on the other hand, the number of King's Thegns, keeping lands which they had held in the days of King Eadward, is remarkably large,[3] though there are also many entries of lands as waste. This difference plainly points to some unrecorded difference in the circumstances of the conquest of the two shires, and it may be that Leicester earned its overthrow by a defence worthy of a borough which was to give its name to the greatest of England's later worthies. Of the chief town of the next shire our notices are clearer

*Extensive confiscations in Leicestershire*

*Great number of King's Thegns in Nottinghamshire.*

---

[1] In the History of the Foundation of Leicester Abbey in the Monasticon, vi 466, the narrative begins, "Robertus Comes Mellenti, veniens in Angliam cum Willielmo Duce Normanniæ, adeptus consulatum Leycestriæ, ex dono dicti Ducis et Conquæstoris Angliæ, *destructâ prius civitate Leicestriæ* cum castello et ecclesiâ infra castellum, tempore prædicti Conquæstoris, reædificavit ipsam ecclesiam Sanctæ Mariæ infra castellum."

[2] There are many English under-tenants, but of tenants *in capite* there seem to be only three, Aschil, Raven, and Turchil—all seemingly of Danish descent—among the "servientes Regis" in p. 236 b.

[3] See Domesday, 292 b, 293. On 294 the list goes on with the Thegns of Rutland, so strangely treated as an appendage to Nottinghamshire. One entry (293) shows William in a somewhat amiable light, "In Wareshope tenet quidam cæcus i. bovatam in eleemosynâ de Rege." But he might have been blinded by the royal order. Cf. vol III p. 107.

CHAP. XVIII.
Importance and early history of Nottingham.

The main importance of Nottingham was drawn from its position near the Trent, the great southern tributary of the Humber. The town stood on the great highway to the North, both by land and water, and to keep open and guard the communications both ways was the great public duty laid upon its burghers.[1] The river flows at some distance from the original town, which stands on a hill divided by a slight depression from a steep rocky height to the west, at the foot of which runs the smaller stream of the Leen. Nottingham, like Leicester, was a member of the Danish Confederacy, and its defence had been a special object of the care of Eadward the Elder. Its acquisition indeed seems to have been the crown of his conquests in central England. He visited Nottingham twice, and at each visit he secured his conquest by a fortress. His first occupation of Nottingham was followed by the final submission of all Mercia, English and Danish, and its incorporation with the West-Saxon Kingdom. His second visit was followed within the same year by that great Commendation of the states north of the Humber which first made the West-Saxon King to be Lord of all Britain. The position of Nottingham in truth made it in some sort the key of Northumberland, and the great object of Eadward's fortifications was to secure the river. On the former of his two visits he secured the borough by a fortress on the left bank of the Trent;[2] on the second he added another

Fortifications of Eadward the Elder 922-924

[1] Domesday, 280 "In Snotingeham aqua Trentæ et fossa et via versus Eboracum custodiuntur, ita ut si quis impedient transitum navium, et si quis araverit vel fossam fecerit in viâ Regis infra duas perticas, emendare habet per viii libras" The importance of the navigation of the Trent comes out also in the Charter of Henry the Second to Nottingham in Rymer, 1 41, and Stubbs' Select Charters, 159 The burgesses were entitled to tolls from those who used the river, but it is also ordered, "Iter de Trenta liberum esse debet navigantibus quantum pertica una obtinebit ex utraque parte fili aquæ"

[2] Chron. Wint 922 "Þa fór he þonan to Snotingaham, and gefór þa burg, and het hie gebetan and gesettan, ægþer ge mid Engliscum

fortress on the opposite bank, and joined the two together by a bridge.[1] All traces of Eadward's works have vanished. But their site is doubtless marked by the picturesque mediæval bridge which is now giving way to a modern successor. This important post the men of Nottingham had to hold; no further military service is spoken of; yet, besides merchants, we hear of horsemen or knights as forming a chief element in the population of Nottingham.[2] Two churches are recorded in the Survey, but Nottingham never became the seat of any great ecclesiastical foundation. Of the submission of this important post we get no details; but it was at the head of his army that William appeared before the town,[3] and its possession was at once secured by the foundation of a castle.[4] The site which William chose for the fortress which was to overawe the

*Nottingham submits to William*

*Foundation of the castle.*

mannum ge mid Deniscum, and him cierde eall þæt folc to þe on Mercnalande geseten wæs, ægþer ge Denisc ge Englisce." This entry follows immediately on the commendation of the Welsh princes See vol i p 60

[1] Chron Wint 924 "Her on þysum gere foran to middum sumera, fór Eadweard cyning mid fierde to Snotingaham, and het gewyrcan þa burg on suð healfe here eas, ongean þa oþre and þa brycge ofer Treontan, betwix þam twam burgum" Then follows the entry of the fortification of Bakewell and the Peak land, and then that of the commendation of Northumberland, Scotland, and Strathclyde

[2] In Domesday we read of "domus mercatorum" and of "domus equitum," the latter being seemingly a numerous class. Were they the remains of an old Danish patriciate? See vol i p 64 "Eques," whatever its meaning, is a most unusual word Du Cange (in voc) quotes a charter of Philip of France in 1050 (I do not understand the date), in which "duo equites" are granted along with "duo rustici" But these Nottingham "equites" rather suggest the *cnihtenagild* of London.

[3] Flor Wig. 1068. "Rex Willelmus cum exercitu suo Snotingaham venit."

[4] Chron. Wig 1067 "He for þa to Snotingaham and worhte þæt castel" So Florence, "Ubi castello firmato Eboracum perrexit" Ord Vit 511 C. "Deinde Rex Snotingheham castrum construxit et Guillelmo Peverello commendavit" The building of the castle is not distinctly mentioned in Domesday, but we read (280), "Willelmo Pevrel concessit Rex x acras terræ ad faciendum pomœrium" This would seem to be the town wall, as the "fossatum burgi" is mentioned just above.

borough was one which would have been less eligible for Eadward's objects of protection. The castle of Nottingham was now reared on the highest point of the great rock overhanging the town. A new town spread itself over the lower ground between the castle and the older borough.[1] In such a case the building of the castle did not involve any destruction of houses; but the borough suffered under the foreign government. The number of its burghers dwindled, while the amount of royal revenue drawn from the town was increased.[2] The command of the new fortress was placed in the safe hands of William Peverel, a Norman adventurer of unknown origin, who became one of the greatest landowners in this and the adjoining shire.[3] From Nottingham his name has passed away; a modern house, now itself a ruin, occupies the site of the Conqueror's fortress. But the name of Peverel is inseparably bound to another of his possessions. In the wild Peakland of Derbyshire, where the huge mass of Mam Tor rises over the valley of the southern Derwent, a height of less elevation than some of its fellows, but of singular steepness of ascent, overhangs the huge cavern which bears the name of the Devil's Hole. On its highest point, standing on the very edge of a perpendicular cliff, where the fosses of Arques and

---

[1] Domesday, 280 "Hugo vicecomes, filius Baldrici in terra comitis in novo burgo statuit xiii. domus quæ antea non fuerant, apponens eas in sensu veteris burgi"

[2] See Ellis, ii 476, Domesday, 280 "T R E reddebat Snotingham xviii libras; modo reddit xxx libras et x libras de monetâ" Another grievance was the interference with the burgesses' right to fish in the river, "In aquâ Trente soliti erant piscari, et modo querelam faciunt, eo quod piscari prohibentur"

[3] William Peverel's estates in Derbyshire appear in Domesday, 276, and those in Nottinghamshire in 287, 288 This is the William Peverel whom an utterly uncertified and almost impossible scandal calls a natural son of the Conqueror. See vol iii p 656, and Ellis, 1 466, 467. Ranulf Peverel is a real man, but he is far more likely to have been a brother of William than a reputed father. On Engelric, the alleged maternal grandfather of William Peverel, see above, p. 26

Old Sarum were needless and impossible, William Peverel reared his castle of Peak Forest,[1] the true vulture's nest of a robber-knight. It is the worthy fellow of those other fortresses which freedom has left as forsaken ruins on so many of the heights where the young Rhine runs through the land of the Three Leagues. The still existing keep most likely belongs to a slightly later age, but, as in so many other cases, it fairly represents the position and general style of the first building. Romance unites with history to make the name of Peverel of the Peak cleave to a spot where the frowning fortress of the invader seems almost a natural finish for the wild height on which it is reared

William had thus passed, seemingly without a blow being struck, certainly without anything to be called a battle, through the heart of Mercia. He was now so far on Northumbrian ground that he was within the province and diocese of the Northumbrian Primate, perhaps even within the jurisdiction of the Northumbrian Earl.[2] His last conquest commanded the approach by land and by water to the still independent North. The defection of the Earls, the actual approach of the Conqueror in person, did what all the preaching of Ealdred had failed to do. The Northumbrian metropolis trembled, as the Kentish metropolis had trembled two years before.[3] At what stage of the march between Nottingham and York we know not, but seemingly before William appeared beneath the walls, certainly before any hostile steps had been taken, an embassy from York drew near with the keys of the city, and with hostages for the good faith of the

---

[1] Domesday, 276. "Terram castelli in Pechefers Willelmi Pevrel tenuerunt Gernebern et Hundinc" On the date of the present castle, see Mr Hartshorne's paper in the Archæological Journal, v 214, where also may be seen some account of the doings which went on in it even as late as the reign of Henry the Fourth.

[2] See vol ii p 560   [3] See vol iii p 539.

202    CONQUEST OF WESTERN AND NORTHERN ENGLAND.

CHAP. XVIII citizens.[1] The submission was accepted; but William put little trust in the promises which were made to him, and he determined to take every means to secure the city which was his greatest conquest since the sub-
Early history of York. mission of London. The old Eboracum lay on the left bank of the Ouse, at a point where the course of the river is towards the south-east. At a short distance below the Roman city it receives the waters of the Foss, a stream flowing from the north-east, and which therefore forms a sort of peninsula with the greater river. But even in Roman times a suburb had arisen on the right bank of the Ouse, and the Anglian and Danish city, a city which in the tenth century is said to have numbered more than thirty
Extension of the Roman city thousand inhabitants,[2] had spread itself far beyond the Roman walls, both on the right bank and in the direction of the confluence of the rivers. The minster of Saint Peter, the metropolitan church of Northumberland, stood within the ancient circuit, but the new foundation of Saint Olaf, the burying-place of Siward,[3] lay beyond the walls, not far from their south-west corner, where a Roman multangular tower still remains. And in the newer parts of the city

[1] Ord. Vit. 511 C. "Hæc Eboracenses ut audierunt, extimentes maturatâ deditione vim declinaverunt, Regique claves civitatis cum obsidibus dederunt."

[2] The manuscript Life of Archbishop Oswald, quoted by Mr. Raine (Fasti Eboracenses, i. 123), says, "Est civitas Eboraca metropolis totius gentis Northanimbrorum, quæ quondam erat nobiliter ædificata et firmiter muris constructa, quæ nunc dimissa vetustate, quæ tamen gaudet de multitudine populorum, non minus virorum ac mulierum, exceptis parvulis et pubetinis, quam xxx millia in eâdem civitate numerati sunt, quæ medicabiliter repleta et mercatorum gazis locupleta qui undique adveniunt, maxime ex Danorum gente." I need hardly say that very little trust is to be put in such statistics. In the time of King Eadward the city was divided into six "scyræ," besides the "scyra" of the Archbishop. One of the six at the time of the Survey was waste because of the castles, "Una ex his est vastata in castellis." In the other five were 1418 inhabited houses, besides 189 in the shire of the Archbishop.

[3] See vol. ii. p. 375.

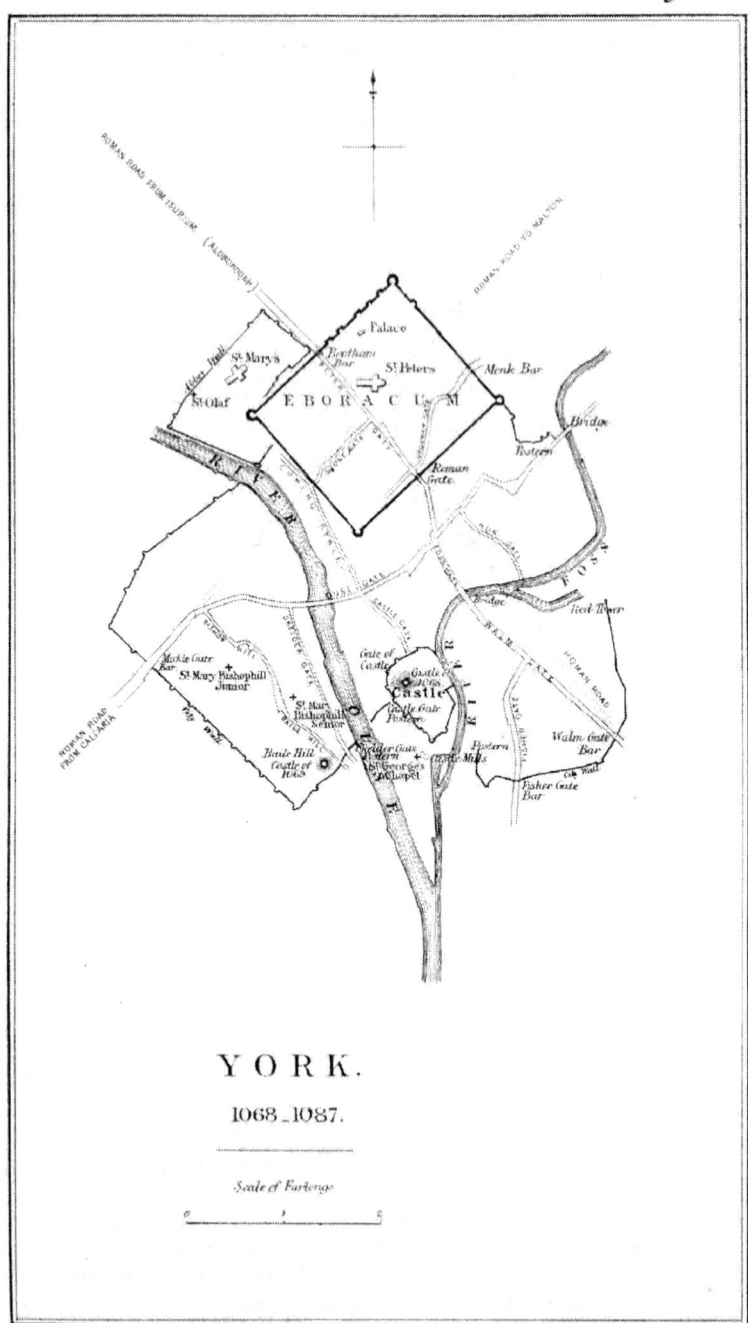

YORK.

1068–1087.

other churches had sprung up,[1] witnessing to the growth of population beyond the ancient precinct, a growth which may well have been one of the causes of that neglect of the older fortifications which is said to have happened at a somewhat earlier time.[2] The wealth and importance of the city largely depended on its trade. This was chiefly carried on with the kindred people of Denmark, to whom the broad stream of the Ouse offered an easy access. To control this great city William took the usual means of founding a castle. He chose a site where a high mound suggests that it had been used for purposes of defence in earlier times, and which is not unlikely to have been the site of the old Danish tower of York, famous in the wars of Æthelstan.[3] It was on the peninsular ground between the Ouse and the Foss, on the mound which is now crowned by the later fortress known as Clifford's Tower, that William planted his new fortress. The position commands one main passage of the Ouse, and the waters of the Foss may, then as now, have washed the outworks of the castle. Thus the first castle of York arose, the castle on the left bank of the river, but which, distant as it was from the elder walls of Eboracum, was, then as now, held to be within the bounds of the city.[4] Five hundred picked knights were set to guard

William builds his first castle on the left bank of the Ouse.

---

[1] The church of Saint Mary Bishophill Junior, on the right bank of the river, has a tower which may possibly have been rebuilt in later times. But, if so, it must have been rebuilt out of materials not later than the time of William. Parts indeed of it seem to be fragments of Roman work, with which the neighbourhood—the Roman suburb—abounds.

[2] See note 2 on last page.

[3] Will. Malm. ii. 134. "Ethelstanus castrum quod olim Dani in Eboraco obfirmaverunt ad solum diruit, ne esset quo se tutari perfidia posset."

[4] Ord. Vit. 511 C. "Ipse tamen, quia fidem illorum suspectam habuit, *in urbe ipsâ* munitionem firmavit, quam delectis militibus custodiendam tradidit." He afterwards, as we shall see, mentions the building of the second castle. This minute statement seems to outweigh the words of the English writers, which in strictness would imply that both of the York castles

CHAP XVIII
The three commanders, Robert Fitz-Richard, Gilbert of Ghent, and William Malet

the fortress, under the command of at least three trusty captains. One of them, Robert Fitz-Richard, we know only from his fate in the next year.[1] Of the others one was the Flemish adventurer, Gilbert of Ghent;[2] the other was a man whose name must always awaken a certain sympathy in English hearts, William Malet, who had borne the body of Harold to its first hasty burial on the rocks of Hastings.[3] He received the office of

Lands and offices of William Malet

Sheriff,[4] and he was at once rewarded with large grants of lands in the shire. This is shown by several passages of the Survey, which speak of lands as having been held by William Malet before the revolt of the next year.

Probable confiscations

This of course implies confiscations at this particular time. But among the names of those English owners whom we can certainly say were dispossessed at this moment, there are none to which we attach any idea.[5] It appears that William also at this time made gifts to

---

were built at once. So Chron. Wig. "He for swa to Eoferwic and þær worhte *twegen castelas*." And Florence, "Eboracum perrexit, ibique duobus castellis firmatis, quingentos milites in eis posuit."

[1] See below, p. 238.

[2] See vol. iii. p. 312. For his lands, not large, in Yorkshire, see Domesday, 326.

[3] See vol. iii. pp. 466, 514. William and Gilbert both appear in the history of the next year.

[4] Sim. Dun. 1069, p. 85. "Willielmo Malet qui tunc vicecomitatum gerebat." So Domesday, 374. "Vivente Willelmo Malet et vicecomitatum tenente in Euruic."

[5] In the Clamores de Evruicscire in Domesday, 373-374, we find several entries speaking of lands as being held by William Malet "antequam castellum captum fuisset," "donec invasum est castellum," "donec fractum est castellum," "quamdiu tenuit castellum de Euruic," "usque Dani ceperunt illum." The names of the former possessors are given, including a long string of Danish names in Holderness. But the only one (373) which awakens any personal interest or curiosity is a woman named Asa—it is hard to see what English name can be meant—who had been, on what ground we are not told, divorced or separated from her husband Beornwulf. All her lands which she held in her own right "ut domina," free from all control of her husband, were given to William Malet. Cf. p. 51.

the church of Saint John at Beverley, and confirmed gifts of his predecessor Eadward to the same church.[1]

The confiscations which are implied in the grants to William Malet are not likely to have stood alone, but in other cases there is not the same means of distinguishing between forfeitures made now and forfeitures made at a later time. We must however suppose that, as Eadwine and Morkere were now again in the King's nominal favour, their lands were spared for the present. And it is certain that, while William was at York, he received the submission of some other men of importance, whose lands would, according to his usual policy, be restored to them either wholly or in part. Thus Archill, the great Northumbrian Thegn,[2] deemed it hopeless to resist, now that the Earls had forsaken the cause and the capital of the Earldom was in the hands of the Conqueror. He came to York; he was received into the King's peace, and gave his son as a hostage.[3] And he was followed by another homager of higher rank, who appeared on the errand of one higher still. Durham still held out; but, as Ealdred had hallowed William and his Queen long before York had

*Grants to Saint John of Beverley.*

*Position of Eadwine and Morkere.*

*Submission of Archill,*

*of Bishop Æthelwine.*

---

[1] In Domesday, 373, the Canons of Beverley claim "donum Regis W et confirmationem." This however might be at any time in his reign, but in two other cases the date of the grant seems to be distinctly fixed to William's first appearance at York. Thus we read in 373 b, "in Risbi habuit Gamel iiii carucatas terræ, quas vendidit Ældredo Archiepiscopo T R W. De hac terrâ jacuit olim soca in Welleton, sed Thomas Archiepiscopus habet brevem Regis W, per quem concessit ipsam socam quietam Sancto Johanni de Beureli Similiter de iiii carucatis terræ in Walchinton pertinebat soca ad Welleton, sed Rex W donavit eam quietam Eldredo Archiepiscopo, testante wapentaco, qui brevem Regis inde vidit et audivit" So again in 374 lands are witnessed to belong to Saint John "per homines de Treding [the Riding] et per donum Regis W quod dedit Sancto Johanni tempore Ældredi Archiepiscopi" It is added, "de hoc habent canonici sigillum Regis Edwardi et Regis Willelmi."

[2] See above, p 185

[3] Ord Vit 511 C "Archillus . cum Rege concordiam fecit, eique filium suum obsidem tradidit"

## CONQUEST OF WESTERN AND NORTHERN ENGLAND.

CHAP. XVIII

submitted, so Æthelwine, the Bishop of Durham,[1] came to William's court at York, and was received into his favour.[2] But he did not come only in his own name. He bore a commission from King Malcolm, whose Earldom of Lothian formed part of his diocese, and he arranged terms of peace between the Conqueror and the Scottish prince.[3] We know not their exact nature; but it is plain that they implied the recognition of William's supremacy, and that they did not involve the surrender or expulsion of the English exiles The Bishop returned to Scotland, and thence came back to York with ambassadors from the King of Scots. They brought Malcolm s acceptance of the proposed terms, and swore fealty to William in their master's name.[4]

*Æthelwine negotiates between William and Malcolm*

*First submission of Malcolm*

*Position of William in 1066 and in 1068 compared*

*Extent of his real and nominal dominion at the two points of time.*

Thus gradually the power of William advanced. His position was now widely different from what it had been at the time of his coronation less than two years before. His dominion was far more extensive than it was then. But, within the limits of his possessions at the two points of time, his position at the earlier and at the later point had many analogies with one another. When he was crowned at Westminster, he held actual possession of only a small part of the land; over more than half England he was King only by virtue of the formal homage of its chiefs. With the dependent members of the Empire he had entered into no relations whatever. In London and Winchester he was King in every sense; at Exeter and York

---

[1] On Æthelwine, see vol II p 408

[2] Ord Vit 511 D "Præsul quoque Dunelmi Regis in gratiam accessit"

[3] Ib "Pro Malcomo Rege Scotorum pacis mediator intervenit, et acceptas conditiones in Scotiam detulit"

[4] Ib "Malcomus . . auditâ . legatione pacis quievit, et cum Præsule Dunelmi nuntios suos ovanter remisit, per quos Guillelmo Regi fidele obsequium juravit" On Mr E W Robertson's objections to this important passage, see Appendix CC.

Orderic follows with a panegyric on the peace-loving temper of the Scots, which the local history of Durham would hardly bear out

he was King only in name; at Dunfermline he was not even a nominal over-lord. In the two years that had since passed, Exeter and York had come into his actual possession; but there were still lands and cities which stood to him now as Exeter and York had stood to him in those days. Bernicia was now what all Northumberland had been then, Durham was as independent now as York had been; the homage of Æthelwine had brought with it as little practical submission on the part of his flock as the earlier homage of Ealdred. So too he had now received the nominal homage of Malcolm of Scotland, but as yet it was purely nominal, and the two Kings had not even seen one another face to face. Now as before, William was satisfied for a while with taking seizin as it were by these nominal submissions, of which he would know how to make use when the time came. York was the most northern point at which he thought it expedient for the present to appear in person, and to confirm his dominion by fortresses and garrisons. Scotland, Bernicia, and the north-western shires of Mercia, were still left in their precarious independence. A large district, still unsubdued, lay between the line of his late march northwards and the East-Anglian shires which he had won by the great wager of battle on Senlac. On that district he deemed it prudent firmly to fix his yoke before he risked any more enterprises in the extreme North. He therefore returned by a road lying to the east of that which had taken him by Warwick and Nottingham. And on his southward, no less than on his northward, march, each important point on his progress was secured as it submitted by the building of a castle.[1]

[1] The Worcester Chronicler, after mentioning the castles at Nottingham and York, adds vaguely, "and on Lincolna and gehwar on þan ende" So Florence, "in civitate Lindicolinâ aliisque locis castella firmari præcepit" Orderic (511 D) is more definite, "Rex posthæc in reversione suâ Lincoliæ, Huntendonæ, et Gruntebrugæ castra locavit, et tutelam eorum fortissimis viris commendavit"

208    CONQUEST OF WESTERN AND NORTHERN ENGLAND.

CHAP XVIII
William at Lincoln
Greatness of the city

Its Danish aristocracy of the Twelve Lawmen.

Their power and hereditary succession

Priests among their number.

The first recorded point of his homeward march was Lincoln. That borough, soon to become a city, was then one of the greatest in England.[1] It boasted eleven hundred and fifty inhabited houses[2] A member, doubtless the foremost member, of the Danish civic Confederation, it still retained a Danish patriciate of twelve hereditary Lawmen. Had the royal power ever fallen as low in England as it did in Germany and Italy, the ruling burghers of Lincoln might have stood forth as an oligarchy not less proud, and even more narrow, than their brethren of Bern and Venice. It is only the peculiar character of English history, the steady advance of the whole realm, as opposed to the more brilliant developement of particular cities, which hindered the descendants of Swarting the son of Grimbold and Swartbrand the son of Ulf from handing on names as memorable in history as the names of Erlach and of Foscari. The Lawmen of Lincoln enjoyed the rights of territorial lords. All twelve were clothed with the judicial powers of *sac* and *soc*, and one among them, whether by seniority or by hereditary right, further enjoyed the profitable privileges of *toll* and *team*.[3] And it is to be noticed that three of these great officers were men in holy orders. The list does not begin, like an ancient charter, but ends like a modern commission of the peace,

---

[1] William of Malmesbury (Gest Pont 312) calls it "Lindocolinam civitatem, unam ex populosioribus Angliæ, emporium hominum terrâ marique venientium" See also vol ii p 512  Henry of Huntingdon (M H. B 693 D) quotes the line,

"Testis Lincoliæ gens infinita decore."

[2] Domesday, 336. "In civitate Lincoliâ erant tempore Regis Edwardi novies centum et lxx. mansiones hospitatæ  Hic numerus Anglice computatur i centum pro cxx"  See Ellis, i 148, ii 466

[3] Domesday, 336  "In ipsâ civitate erat xii Lageman, id est, habentes sacam et socam, Hardecnut, Suartin filius Grimboldi, Ulf filius Suertebrand, qui habuit thol et theim, Walraven, Aluuold, Britric, Guret, Ulbert, Godric filius Eddevæ, Siwardus presbyter, Leuuine presbyter, Aldene presbyter" I presume that *Ealdhun* is the name intended by the corrupt form *Aldene*

with the names of the clerical members of the body, the priests Siward, Leofwine, and Ealdhun. It would seem that they did not sit by virtue of their ecclesiastical benefices, but that their ecclesiastical character was simply incidental and personal. It is certain that one left a widow and that another was succeeded by his son.[1] Besides its Lawmen, Lincoln also contained citizens who, in the country at large, were of yet higher dignity. Mærleswegen the Sheriff, Earl Morkere, Earl Harold himself, held houses in the borough, and within their precincts they held the same rights of jurisdiction as the civic aristocracy.[2] Private burghers also had their halls, and many houses were held of them by their fellow-citizens of lower degree.[3] The rights both of burghership and of clanship were strictly enforced, and grants, even to religious houses, of property within the borough were denounced as illegal.[4]

*Possessions of Earls and others in the city*

---

[1] Domesday, 336 "Ulnodus presbyter loco Siuuard presbyteri, Buruolt loco patris sui Leuuine, qui modo est monachus, Leduuinus filius Revenæ loco Aldene presbyteri" Of "Ulnodus" we shall hear in a later note It would seem that the son succeeded the father quite irrespective of his character, lay or clerical Mark also that the priest who became a monk was civilly dead

[2] The "mansiones" of Mærleswegen, Morkere, and Harold all appear in Domesday, 336 The two Earls had sac and soc, Mærleswegen, it would seem, had not. We then read, "Rogerus de Busli habet 1 mansionem Suen filii Suave cum sacâ et socâ, Judita comitissa habet 1 mansionem Stori sine sacâ et socâ"

[3] Domesday, 336 "Tochi filius Outi habuit in civitate xxx mansiones præter suam hallam, et 11 ecclesias et dimidiam, et suam hallam habuit quietam ab omni consuetudine, et super alias xxx. mansiones habuit locationem, et præter hoc de unâquâque unum denarium, id est landgable." Tokig's thirty houses had at the time of the Survey passed to Bishop Remigius "in ecclesiâ Sanctæ Mariæ." They therefore probably stood on the site of the present prebendal houses

[4] Certain lands belonged to the church of All Saints Of these the Survey (336) goes on to say, "Hanc ecclesiam et terram ecclesiæ et quidquid ad eam pertinet habuit Godricus filius Gareuinæ, sed, eo facto monacho, Abbas de Burg obtinet. Burgenses vero omnes Lincoliæ dicunt quod injuste habet, quia nec Gareuine nec Godricus filius ejus, nec ullus alius, dare potuerunt extra civitatem nec extra parentes eorum nisi concessu Regis Hanc ecclesiam et quæ ibi pertinent clamat Ernuin presbyter hereditate Godrici consanguinei sui"

VOL. IV      P

CHAP XVIII.
Common land

Rights of the King

Position of Lincoln

The minster and the castle

The community, like that of Exeter, had its lands lying without the city walls, lands which seem to have been apportioned among the magistrates and chief burghers.[1] The King had a mint in the borough, which brought him in seventy-five pounds yearly.[2] But whether he was entitled to any forfeitures or other profits within the walls seems to have been matter of controversy.[3] We hear nothing of military service; it would almost seem as if a yearly tribute of thirty pounds, twenty as usual to the King and ten to the Earl of the shire, redeemed the borough from all claims on the part of any external authority.[4]

Such a community as this, strengthened further by the alliance of the other members of the Danish Confederation, had claims yet higher than those of Exeter to rank as an independent commonwealth. And no town in England occupied a prouder site, or might consider itself more safe against all assaults. Yet no town in England has more utterly changed its outward garb than the Colony of Lindum[5] has changed in every leading feature since the day when William came to demand its submission. Now, throughout a vast district around the city, the one great feature of the landscape is the mighty minster, which, almost like that of Laon,[6] crowns the end of the ridge, rising, with a

---

[1] Domesday, 336. "In campis Lincoliæ extra civitatem sunt xii carucatæ terræ et dimidia." The Survey goes on to mention their present and former owners, several of whom were among the Lawmen.

[2] Ib. 336 b. "Moneta vero reddit lxxv. libras."

[3] Ib. 336. Of the thirty houses which had belonged to Tokig we read, "Super has xxx mansiones habebat Rex thelonium et forisfacturam, ut burgenses juraverunt. Sed his jurantibus contradicit Vluiet presbyter, et offert se portaturum judicium quod non ita est sicuti dicunt."

[4] Ib. 336 b. "T. R. E. reddebat civitas Lincolia Regi xx. libras et Comiti x. libras. Modo reddit c. libras ad numerum inter Regem et Comitem."

[5] The ending *coln*, the same of course as Colonia Agrippina, *Köln*, is, as far as I know, peculiar to Lincoln in English local nomenclature.

[6] There is however this difference, that at Laon the hill runs east and west, while at Lincoln it runs north and south, so that the minster stands as it were against the grain.

steepness well nigh unknown in the streets of English towns, above the lower city and the plain at its feet. Next in importance to the minster is the castle, which, marred as it is by modern changes, still crowns the height as no unworthy yokefellow of its ecclesiastical neighbour. The proud polygonal keep of the fortress still groups well with the soaring towers, the sharp pointed gables, the long continuous line of roof, of the church of Remigius and Saint Hugh. The slope of the hill and the long line of road at its foot are covered by the buildings of the city, its houses, many of them presenting forms dear to the antiquary,[1] the Guildhall over its southern gate, the dark arch which spans the polluted river, the tall square towers of those churches of the lower town, whose tale, we shall soon find, comes more deeply home to us than anything else in the local history. When William drew near, minster, castle, houses, churches, had not yet come into being; all alike are direct memorials of his coming. One alone among the many antiquities of the city was already there to meet the eye of the Conqueror, to remind him of conquerors as far removed from his age as he is himself now removed from ours. The Danish borough had more than one predecessor. The height on which it stands, the promontory of Lincoln,[2] is part of that long line of low hills, stretching through a large part of Central and Eastern England, which seems like a feeble rival of the loftier ranges of the West. At this point the range is broken by a depression which, if it were worthy of the name, might pass as the valley of the Witham. Thus is formed the promontory of Lincoln, looking

*Effects of William's reign on Lincoln.*

---

[1] Especially the Jews' House, and one or two other twelfth-century houses on the slope, and the building called John of Gaunt's Stables, more properly called Saint Mary's Guild, near the church of Saint Peter-at Gowts. John of Gaunt (see Mr. Nichols in the Lincoln Volume of the Institute, p 277) held the Earldom of Lincoln, and had a house in this part of the city.

[2] "Sub promontorio Lincolniæ" is Henry of Huntingdon's (M. H. B. 760 D) description of the site of Stow-in Lindesey

down upon the river to the south of it. Vale and ridge alike are traversed by those great roads which abide as the noblest relics of the days of Roman dominion. The steep is climbed by the united line of the Ermine Street and the Foss Way, which last again diverged from the eastern gate of the Roman city. But the Roman was not the first to occupy the spot. His road, after climbing the hill, cuts through an earlier town to the north of the present city, of which the dyke and foss are still easy to be seen. The road itself, the Ermine Street, notwithstanding all the centuries which have passed since it was first traced out and paved, is still distinguished from a yet older track by the name of the New Street. And the New Street leads to the New Port, the Roman arch of massive stones which still remains the entrance to the city from the north.

The Roman town, the Colony of Lindum, arose to the south of this more ancient site, on the very brow of the hill. Fragments of the wall still remain, and the site of the southern gate is still marked at a point but a little way down the steep descent. In the later days of Roman occupation, a fortified suburb seems to have spread itself down the slope of the hill, from the southern gate to the banks of the Witham. The Danish town still occupied the Roman site, gathering round at least two churches whose names have been preserved. An earlier Saint Mary's seems to have already occupied some small portion of the site of the present minster,[1] and the memory of Paullinus, the Apostle of Lindesey no less than of Deira, was cherished in a church whose present mean representative preserves a trace of the ancient dedication in its corrupted name of Saint Paul.[2] Here then on its hill-top, with the Witham,

---

[1] The earlier existence of Saint Mary's church appears from the words in Domesday, 336, "Sancta Maria de Lincoliâ, in quâ nunc est episcopatus."

[2] Bæda, ii 16. The present insignificant church of Saint Paul, or Saint Paullinus, is traditionally said to represent the church there spoken of

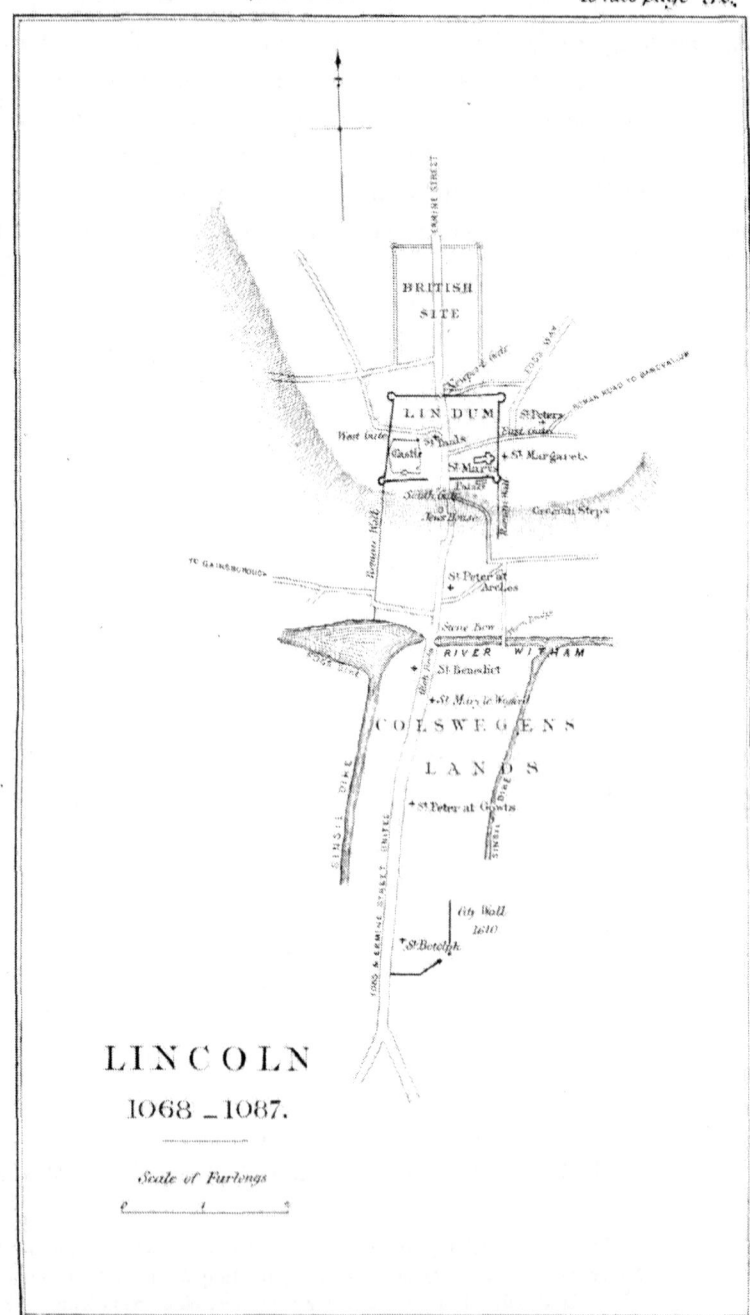

Freeman's Norman Conquest. Vol. IV.    To face page 212.

LINCOLN
1068–1087.

Scale of Furlongs

For the Delegates of the Clarendon Press.

then an important highway of merchandize, at its feet, dwelled the rich and proud commonwealth, which, holding such a position, might have been expected to withstand the invader as manfully as Domfront, Le Mans, or Mayenne. But not one word has been preserved to us either of the negotiations or of the warlike operations by one or other of which Lincoln must have been won. We have no such records of the fall of the Danish commonwealth as we have of the fall of the great city of the West All that we can say is that William, advancing from the North, was able to attack the town from the point where it gained little advantage from its site, and that the still abiding Roman gate was doubtless the scene of the Conqueror's triumphal entry, whether that entry was the result of a successful attack or a peaceful submission.

CHAP XVIII.
No details of the taking of Lincoln

Lincoln thus came into William's hands, and we may be led to believe that it came into his hands without any very serious resistance. We may infer this from the fact that the treatment which it received from him was on the whole favourable. The amount of tribute was largely raised,[1] but the civic constitution remained untouched. The numbers and powers of the magistrates, and even their hereditary succession, remained under King William as they had stood under King Eadward. The son succeeded to his father's office, and one Norman only, Peter of Valognes, had found his way at the time of the Survey into the ranks of the Lincoln Lawmen [2] One of the priestly members of the magistracy must in some way have given offence, as a payment of forty shillings had been laid upon him as a fine, probably for the redemption of his land or office. But even he had a successor of his own nation and calling, who however stands charged with wrong-doing

The constitution of the city not disturbed by William

---

[1] See p 210, note 4

[2] Domesday, 336 " Petrus de Valonges loco Godric filii Eddevæ " The other Lawmen are Danish or English, several sons having succeeded their fathers between 1068 and 1086

CHAP. XVIII. towards the widow of his predecessor.[1] That the houses and jurisdictions of Harold, Morkere, and Mærleswegen passed to Norman owners is in no way wonderful.[2] It is more remarkable to trace how many Englishmen, both in the city and in the shire, who retained their lands, how many were even further enriched by grants from the Conqueror, too often, it is to be feared, at the expense of less fortunate or more patriotic countrymen. Besides a good number of Thegns of less degree,[3] several Englishmen, as Colegrim,[4] Coleswegen,[5] Ælfred of Lincoln,[6] and two men of the name of Northman,[7] appear as holders of large estates alongside

*Englishmen who kept their lands in Lincolnshire.*

---

[1] Domesday, 336 "Aliam carucatam T R E habuerunt Siuuard presbyter et Outi, et vi acras terræ quas tenet Ulviet presbyter, nunc habet Alfnod medietatem hujus carucatæ et Norman filius Siuuard presbyteri alteram medietatem Hanc vero prædictam medietatem istius terræ et uxorem Siuuardi presbyteri invasit Unlof presbyter, dum erat in saisitione Regis, propter xl solidos quos ipsemet Rex imposuerat super Siuuardum presbyterum" In the former column, in the list of the Lawmen, we find "Ulnodus presbyter loco Siuuard" The strange name Unlof of the other entry must surely be the "Ulnodus" (Wulfnoth or Ulfnoth) of this

By the Charter of Henry the Second to Lincoln (Rymer, i 40, Stubbs, Select Charters, 158) the citizens are to keep "omnes libertates et consuetudines et leges suas quas habuerunt tempore Eadwardi et Willelmi et Henrici Regum Angliæ, et gildam suam mercatoriam de hominibus civitatis et de aliis mercatoribus comitatus, sicut illam habuerunt tempore prædictorum antecessorum nostrorum Regum Angliæ melius et liberius" But there is no mention of Lawmen

[2] Domesday, 336 Ralph Pagenel held the "mansio" of Mæileswegen with sac and soc, Earl Hugh that of Earl Harold, and Earnwine the priest, though an Englishman (see above, p 209, note 4), that of Earl Morkere, with the note, "Sic de Rege tenet sicut Morcar habuit, ut ipse dicit"

[3] Ib 370 b-371 b "Terra Sortebrand et aliorum Tainorum" Most of the names are English or Danish, but among them we several times find "Ernuinus presbyter," doubtless the same who had Harold's house in the city But in one case with the addition, "In eleemosyna Regis" Another entry is worth notice, to a small holding of one Chetel is added, "wasta est, Waldinus habuit, sed Rex reddidit Anglico"

[4] Ib 370          [5] Ib 356 b, 357 b

[6] Ib 357 b-358 b So in the city (336 b), "Aluredus nepos Turoldi habet in toftes de terra Sybi quam Rex sibi dedit" See Mr. J. G Nichols in the Lincoln Volume of the Archæological Institute, 255

[7] "Norman de Adreci" appears in 361 b, and "Normannus Crassus," a much smaller holder, in 362.

of the great Norman grantees. Among these last we have the usual difficulty in finding out whether the confiscations which provided for them were made now or at a later time. But, sooner or later, Earl Hugh,[1] Ralph of Mortemer,[2] William of Percy,[3] Walter of Eyncourt,[4] Ilbert of Lacy,[5] Henry of Ferrers,[6] Ivo Taillebois, famous in local history or legend,[7] and a crowd of other foreign adventurers, were established at the expense of the Danish Thegnhood of Lindesey, Kesteven, and Holland, as their forefathers had, in the days of Ingwar and Hubba, been established at the expense of earlier Anglian owners. A few names awaken curiosity without satisfying it. The element of foreign adventure in William's host was largely represented in Lincolnshire. Besides the well-known names of Earl Alan[8] and Gilbert of Ghent,[9] we find Baldwin of Flanders,[10] Ralph of Saint Valery,[11] two Bretons, Oger[12] and Waldin,[13] and three other men of uncertain race described as Waldin the engineer,[14] Heppo the *balistarius*,[15] and

CHAP XVIII

Norman grantees

---

[1] Domesday, 349    He comes next after Alan, and several of his lordships had belonged to Earl Harold    Coleswegen appears as his tenant

[2] Ib 363    He holds five lordships, two of which had belonged to Copsige, and three to Eddeva, whether "Eddeva pulcra" or not there is no sign    [3] Ib 353 *b*

[4] Ib 361    Under one of his lordships is the entry, "Hoc manerium tenuit Tori T. R. E et Norman post eum eodem tempore, sed homines patriæ et de wapentac nesciunt quo pacto habuit, quia nullum servitium inde viderunt illum facere"    [5] Ib 353 *b*.

[6] Ib    The estates of Ilbert and Henry are but small.

[7] Ib 350-351 *b*    I shall have more to say of him when I come to the story of Hereward

[8] Ib 347    He stands first of the lay landowners, and Colegrim appears more than once as his tenant    One entry in 347 *b* is curious, "Terram Eculf habebat Willelmus Blundus eo die quo Ernuinus presbyter captus fuit et ante."    I can give no account of this arrest of Earnwine

[9] For his lands in Lincolnshire see Domesday, 354 *b*-356, and on his Earldom and his successors see Mr Nichols' paper already referred to

[10] Domesday, 370    Compare 337    [11] Ib 364 *b*
[12] Ib 364 *b*    [13] Ib 365
[14] Ib 365 *b*    "Waldinus ingeniator"
[15] Ib 369    "Heppo balistarius"

CHAP. XVIII Odo the crossbowman.[1] Of these last, men who had clearly raised themselves by proficiency in the more intellectual branches of warfare, we should be better pleased to learn something more than of many of their fellow-adventurers of higher rank and fame

Lincolnshire comparatively well treated.

On the whole then the amount of land and of authority which remained in English or Danish hands in Lincolnshire and the Lincolnshire boroughs is very remarkable. It is plain that Lincolnshire submitted more peaceably, and was dealt with more tenderly, than most parts of the Kingdom. Stamford, the town next in account after the local capital, fared only less well than Lincoln itself. Of its twelve Lawmen, nine were undisturbed,[2] and Lawmen and burghers retained a large portion of their common land beyond the town walls.[3] Stamford, like Lincoln, had been a member of the Danish Confederacy, and, like its allies, it fills a prominent place in the wars of Eadward the Elder and his son Eadmund. In William's days, as now, the town stood in two shires. Of its six wards, five were in Lincolnshire and one in Northamptonshire.[4] The fortress of Eadward stood on the southern side of the river,[5]

Condition of Stamford,

---

[1] "Odo arbalistarius." Domesday, 365 b.

[2] Domesday, 336 b. "In Stamford T. R. E. erant xii Lagemanni, qui habebant infra domos suos sacam et socam et super homines suos, præter geld et heriete et foris facturam corporum suorum de xl oris argenti et præter latronem. Hoc idem modo habent, sed non sunt nisi novem."

[3] Ib. "Terram arabilem extra villam in Lincolescire habet Rex dc. acras. Lagemanni et burgenses habent cc et lxxii acras sine omni consuetudine." On the other hand, five houses had been destroyed for the castle, and the money payment had been largely raised. "T R E dabat Stanford xv libras, modo dat ad firmam l libras, de omni consuetudine Regis modo dat xxviii libras."

[4] Ib. "Ibi fuerunt et sunt vi. custodiæ, quinque in Lincolescyre et sexta in Hantunescyre, quæ est ultra pontem."

[5] Chron. Wint. 922. "Her on ðyssum gere, betweox gangdagum and middansumera, for Eadweard cing mid firde to Steamforda, and het gewyrcan þa burg on suð healfe þære eas, and þæt folc eal ðe to þære norþerran byrig hierde him beah to and sohtan hine him to hlaforde."

but now the town was overawed by a Norman castle on the Lincolnshire side, which however involved the destruction of five houses only.[1] Torkesey, a place now utterly insignificant, but which then seems to have ranked next after Lincoln and Stamford, suffered far more severely than either, so as to suggest the idea that William met with some serious resistance at this point. The position of the town on the Trent, where it still commands a ferry, made it a place of importance on the great Northern road, and its two hundred and thirteen burgesses had the honourable duty of conducting the King's commissioners down the river on their way to York.[2] But at the time of the Survey the burgesses had sunk to one hundred and two, and a hundred and eleven houses stood waste.[3] To return to Lincoln itself, the Survey contains several entries which have a special interest. One burgher of Lincoln, Ulfkill or Ulfcytel by name, received a grant of land without the city as the price, or part of the price, of a ship which he sold to the King.[4] Another grant of the same kind has had a higher and more lasting importance. A castle was of course raised at Lincoln as well as elsewhere, and at Lincoln, unlike Nottingham, the strongest site was to be found within the city itself. The mound which now supports the polygonal keep of the next age may have supported some earlier fortress; it doubtless supported the fortress

---

[1] Domesday, 336 b. Of a hundred and forty-one houses in the five Lincolnshire wards we read, "Modo totidem sunt, præter v quæ propter opus castri sunt wastæ."

[2] Ib 337 "Hoc autem eorum erat ut, si legati Regis illuc venirent, homines ejusdem vici cum navibus suis et aliis instrumentis navigationis usque Eboracum eos conducerent."

[3] Ib. "Modo habet Rex in dominio, et sunt ibi cii burgenses manentes Wastæ sunt vero cxi mansiones."

[4] Ib 336 "Ex his [of the carucates spoken of in p 210, note 1] dedit unam Rex Willelmus cuidam Vlchel pro unâ navi quam ab eo emit Ille vero qui navim vendidit mortuus est, et hanc carucatam terræ nullus habet nisi Rege concedente."

which was now reared by William. The building of the castle and its outworks involved the destruction of a large number of houses. One hundred and sixty-six dwellings perished to make room for it,[1] and we can hardly doubt that the building of the minster a few years later must have involved further destruction. Of seventy-four other waste houses we find a most remarkable entry, assuring us that their forsaken state was not owing to any oppression on the part of the King's officers, but to fires and other ordinary accidents of human life.[2] By these various means no small portion of the burghers of Lincoln, who had once held houses on the height, were driven from their former homes and had to seek dwellings where they could. For a small part of them a dwelling-place was found in a manner which forms one of the most interesting pieces of local history in England. Without the city, at the foot of the hill, beyond the stream of the Witham, lay a waste piece of land which had never been dwelled upon by man. This the King granted to his English favourite Coleswegen. A new town began to arise. At the time of the Survey thirty-six inhabited houses, inhabited doubtless by men who had lost their homes on the height, formed part of the estate of Coleswegen. For the use of his tenants he built two churches, the most striking portions of which still remain. They still bear witness, in their tall slender towers and windows of the more ancient fashion, that, even while the Norman castle and the Norman minster were rising above their heads, Englishmen could still build in earlier and more national forms of art. Reared as they were after King William came into England, the works of Coleswegen, the towers of Saint

---

[1] Domesday, 336 b. "De prædictis wastis mansionibus propter castellum destructæ fuerunt clxvi."

[2] Ib. "Reliquæ lxxiv wastatæ sunt extra metam castellam, non propter oppressionem vicecomitum et ministrorum, sed propter infortunium et paupertatem et ignium exustionem."

Peter-at-Gowts and Saint Mary-le-Wigford still reproduce that style of building which Wilfrith and his contemporaries had brought from Rome, and which so long remained the common heritage of Western Christendom. I hardly know of any works of man which speak more strongly to the heart than these two stern and unadorned, yet stately, towers, reared, in the days of bondage, by an Englishman who, by whatever means, contrived to hold up his head among the conquerors of England, and to win no small share of the honours which belong to the founders of new temples of God and of new dwelling-places of man.[1]

Of the places through which William passed on his march southward from Lincoln two only are mentioned, Huntingdon and Cambridge. Cambridge, not yet famous as the seat of a great University, was a borough of considerable importance, though not attaining to the measure of Exeter, Lincoln, or Norwich. The town of Cambridge, or, in the language of those days, Grantbridge—the Roman Camboritum—then stood wholly on the left bank of the river Cam or Grant. The alternative name of the river is still not wholly forgotten. The extent of the Roman town can be easily traced.[2] It is something like

*William at Cambridge*

*Origin of Camboritum, Grantbridge, or Cambridge*

---

[1] Domesday, 336 b "Colsuen habet in Lincoliâ civitate iv toftes de terrâ Cole nepotis sui, et extra civitatem habet xxxvi domos et ii ecclesias, in quibus nihil adjacet, quas hospitavit in wastâ terrâ quam Rex sibi dedit et quæ numquam ante hospitata fuit." This entry seems to make it absolutely certain that the towers of Saint Mary le-Wigford and Saint Peter at-Gowts were built by Coleswegen between the years 1068 and 1086 Of the importance of this fact in the history of architecture I shall speak in my fifth volume When I first saw Lincoln in 1847, traces could still be seen of the Romanesque north aisle of Saint Peter-at-Gowts, before 1866 they had vanished Hard by is a house which must be late in the twelfth century, but whose windows bear the impress of the earlier work of Coleswegen The name Wigford is worth notice The church stands near the present bridge, which may have been preceded by a ford, and *wig* may well point to some battle in the Anglian conquest of the district, perhaps to that which made Lindum an English possession.

[2] On the early history of Cambridge, see Professor C C Babington's

that of Lincoln in small. The original town occupied the end of a positively small, but in that flat region, considerable, ridge of higher ground overlooking the river at its feet. Like so many other Roman sites, Camboritum seems to have been utterly overthrown and forsaken in the havoc of the English Conquest. In the seventh century the town is spoken of as lying desolate; it was there, among the shattered remains of Roman skill, that a marble sarcophagus was sought to receive the remains of the virgin Queen and Abbess Æthelthryth. Sexburh, her sister and successor in the rule of the holy house of Ely, thought good to translate her body to a place of higher honour in the church which she had founded.[1] No stone fit for such a purpose could be found in the land of flats and fens, but the ruins of the Roman town still remained as a quarry where all who would might seek materials for their own buildings. But in process of time, as civilization and the art of defence advanced, the Roman site, like so many other Roman sites, was again occupied, and at the beginning of the tenth century Grantbridge had once more grown up to enough of importance to give its name to a shire in the new nomenclature of Mercia.[2] In the wars of Swend the town, like other towns, was burned.[3] But to a wooden town—and in that part of

Ancient Cambridgeshire, published in the Transactions of the Cambridge Antiquarian Society, p 3.

[1] Bæda, iv. 19 "Quum sedecim annis esset sepulta, placuit eidem abbatissæ levari ossa ejus, et in locello novo posita in ecclesiam transferri, jussitque quosdam fratribus quærere lapidem, de quo locellum in hoc facere possent, qui ascensâ navi (ipsa enim regio Elge undique est aquis ac paludibus circumdata, neque lapides majores habet), venerunt ad civitatulam quamdam desolatam, non procul inde sitam, quæ linguâ Anglorum Grantacæstir vocatur, et mox invenerunt juxta muros civitatis locellum de marmore albo pulcerrime factum, operculo quoque similis lapidis aptissime tectum"

[2] The first mention of Cambridge in the Chronicles is in 921, when it is in the hands of the Danes The first mention of the shire is in 1010 See vol 1 p 378   [3] Chron 1010 See vol. 1. p 380

CAMBORITUM.
Grantbridge.
CAMBRIDGE.
1068 — 1087.

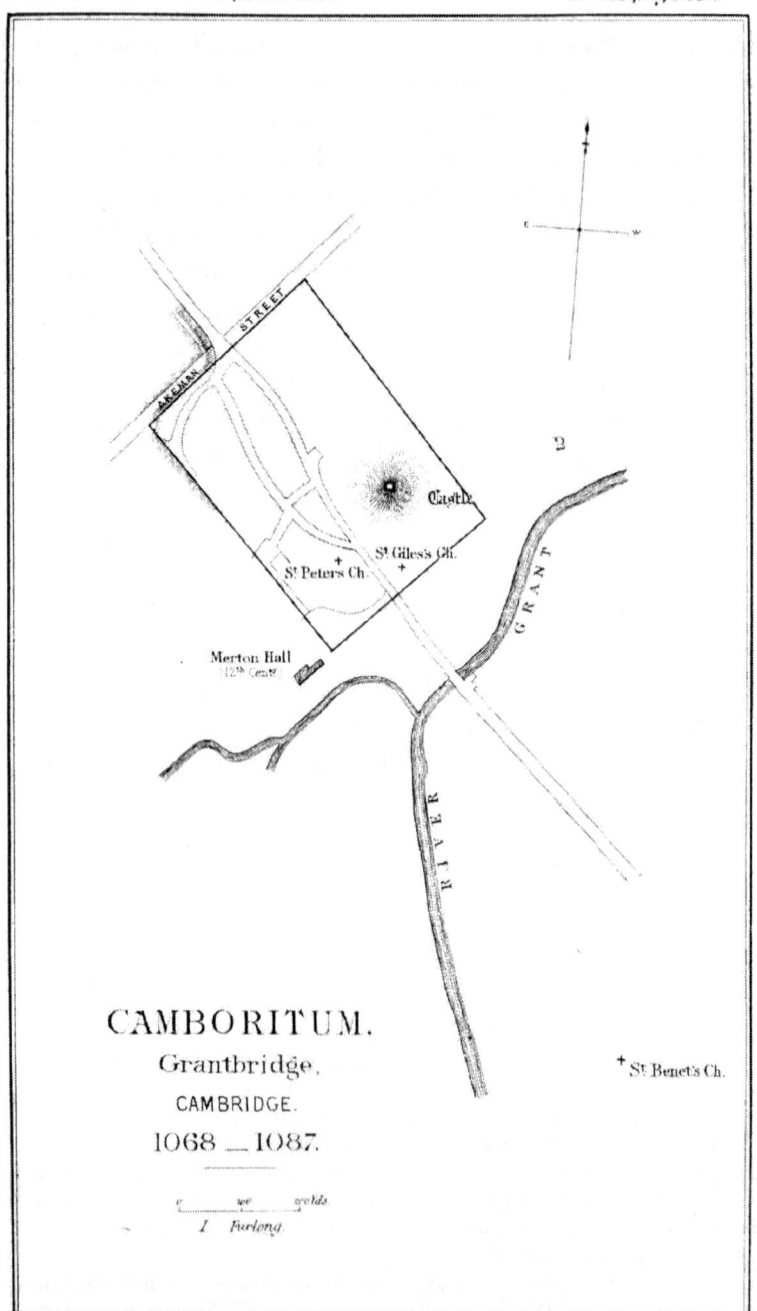

England towns must have been even more completely wooden than elsewhere—a destruction of this sort was a mere passing misfortune. In William's day Grantbridge was again a town of four hundred houses, divided into twelve wards, and ruled by Lawmen after the manner of Lincoln and Stamford.[1] No details of its siege or submission are given. A castle was of course built:[2] it arose on a mound, partly natural, partly artificial, which still marks the site of the Norman fortress, as it doubtless marked that of some earlier English predecessor. But all actual traces of either have utterly passed away. The building of the castle immediately involved the destruction of twenty-seven houses, and, either now or in the wars which followed in the neighbourhood, a large number of other dwellings became waste.[3] But this havoc seems to have led to even more important consequences at Cambridge than it led to at Lincoln. At Lincoln the driving out of the former inhabitants led only to the extension of the city by the formation of a suburb at the foot of the hill. At Cambridge the river and the marshy ground beyond it had to be passed. On this new site a new town arose, the town first of monasteries and then of colleges, adorned by the minster of Saint Radegund and the minster of Barnwell, and far more famous as the dwelling-place of that renowned University which has so deeply stamped its mark on the intellect of England and

*Its condition in William's time.*

*Building of the castle.*

*Origin of the modern town and University.*

---

[1] Domesday, 189. "In hoc burgo fuerunt et sunt decem custodiæ." We presently hear of the "harieta Lagemanorum."

[2] Ord. Vit. 511 D. "Rex post hæc in reversione suâ Lincoliæ, Huntendonæ, et Gruntebrugæ castra locavit, et tutelam eorum fortissimis viris commendavit." The Worcester Chronicle (1067) simply says, after mentioning the castles at York and Lincoln, "And gehwar on þan ende." So Florence, "In civit. te Lindicolinâ aliisque locis castella firmari præcepit."

[3] Domesday, 189. "Pro castro sunt destructæ xxvii domus." The number of waste houses in each of the ten wards is entered separately, amounting in the whole to fifty-three out of four hundred, besides those destroyed for the castle.

the world. But, unlike the case of Lincoln, it would seem that the exiles who were driven from the higher ground of Cambridge had rather to enlarge an earlier settlement beyond the river than absolutely to found a new one. The ancient tower of Saint Bene't, the most venerable monument in Cambridge, clearly points to an age earlier than that of the churches of Coleswegen at Lincoln, and shows that a site which was destined to become so famous had already become the dwelling-place of man.

*William at Huntingdon*

*Early history of the town*

The town of Huntingdon was, then as now, one of much less account than Cambridge, and one that would seem to be of purely English origin. As at Cambridge, no trace remains of the fortress reared by William beyond the mounds which no doubt mark the old *Huntersdown* which gave the town its name. They rise well above the stream of Ouse, and look forth on the old Roman site of Durolipons or Godmanchester on its opposite bank.

*Fortifications of Eadward the Elder 921*

They mark also, no doubt, the site of the fortress restored by Eadward the Elder in the course of his Danish wars.[1] On Huntingdon too, as on Cambridge, and also on both the shires named after the two boroughs, the hand of confiscation pressed far more heavily than it did on Lincoln and Lincolnshire.[2] Here again chronology fails us. One part at least of Cambridgeshire played a most

---

[1] Chron. Wint. 921. "Þy ilcan siþe for se here of Huntandune and of Eastenglum, and worhton þæt geweorc æt Tæmeseforda, and hit budon and bytledon, and forleton þæt oþer æt Huntandune .. þa for oþer ut, and gefor þa burg æt Huntandune, and hie gebette and geedneowade, þær heo ǽr tobrocen wæs." There was therefore an older fortress.

[2] Neither in Cambridgeshire nor in Huntingdonshire do we find any Englishmen keeping large estates like those of Colegrim and Coleswegen in Lincolnshire. In Cambridgeshire we do not even find any of that smaller class of King's Thegns of whom we have so often heard, and in Huntingdonshire we find only some four or five (207 *b*) who keep lands which themselves or their fathers had held T. R. E.

important part in later struggles against William, and it is impossible to say to which date the main spoliation is to be referred. One thing is plain, that, either now or at a later time, both shires were put into the hands of most unscrupulous Sheriffs. Picot bore rule in Cambridgeshire and Eustace in Huntingdonshire, and the amount of wrong wrought at their hands seems to have far surpassed the ordinary measure of havoc.[1] Among the other sins of Picot, the Survey charges him with depriving the burgesses of Cambridge of their common land.[2] Yet he too appears as an ecclesiastical benefactor. A church and monastery of regular canons arose at his

---

[1] The Sheriff Picot appears in Domesday, 189, 190 b, 193 b, 197, 200, 201 b. In one of these places (190) he is charged with an "invasio super Regem," in 193 b he seems engaged in a very doubtful transaction with Earl Roger, and in the entries of his own lands (201 b) we find a whole string of parcels of land held by him which belonged to various churches. Picot also appears in the Historia Eliensis (249, 251, Stewart), and in pp. 266, 267 we get the characters of the Sheriff himself and of one of his agents. Picot was "genere Normannus, animo Gætulus," and a vast number of hard names follow. In the next page the like measure is dealt to Gervase, "cui dominus ejus jam dictus Picotus, tamquam cæteris fidelion, pro suâ pravitate totius vice-comitatûs negotia commiserat." We shall also hear of him in Chapter xix. Eustace is charged in p. 202 with an "occupatio" in Cambridgeshire, in 228 with another in Northamptonshire on the church of Ramsey, and the entries in his own town and shire are full of complaints against him. In the town of Huntingdon in 203 there are several, both from churches and from private English owners. The complaint from the representatives of a former English Sheriff is quite pathetic, "Habuit Aluricus vicecomes T R E. unam mansionem quam W. Rex postea concessit uxori ejus et filiis. Eustachius modo habet, quam pauper cum matre reclamat." In the entries of Eustace's own lands (206 b) we find English owners, and also the Countess Judith, complaining of his seizures. Other cases occur in 208, to one of which we get a date. A small piece of land, "tertia pars dimidiæ hidæ," belonging to the Abbey of Ely was seized by Eustace in 1071–1072, doubtless while the exploits of Hereward were going on, "Sic Abbas habuit T R E et post adventum W. Regis v. annis, hanc Eustachius vi de ecclesiâ rapuit et retenuit."

[2] Domesday, 189. "Burgenses .. reclamant super Picotum vicecomitem communem pasturam sibi ab eo ablatam." A complaint about Picot's mills follows.

224    CONQUEST OF WESTERN AND NORTHERN ENGLAND.

CHAP XVIII.  bidding in honour of Saint Giles within the bounds of
Picot's foundation at Cambridge    the old Camboritum,[1] and, strangely as the building has been disfigured in later times, some small relics of the work of the rapacious Sheriff still survive  The evil deeds of Eustace of Huntingdon stand out still more clearly in the Survey. But of the town with which his name is connected we should specially like to hear more. It lay within the Earldom of Waltheof, and its history is shrouded in the darkness which surrounds all the doings of its Earl till he breaks forth into full light
State of Northamptonshire.   in the course of the next year. As to the other shire which formed Waltheof's Earldom, Northamptonshire, and as to its capital, history is equally silent. But the Survey shows that here also, whether now or at a later time, the yoke was pressed very heavily both on borough and shire [2]

Return of Harold's sons from Ireland    While William was thus bringing the greater part of Mercia and Northumberland under his rule, an attempt was made to shake the dominion which he had established over Wessex. We have seen how, early in the year, the sons of Harold had escaped to Ireland, and had found shelter with the same prince who had once sheltered their

---

[1] On Picot's foundation of Saint Giles in Cambridge, see Monasticon, vi 83, 86  The foundation for a Prior and six regular canons was made in 1092 at the prayer of his wife Hugolina  There is an incidental notice of her marriage in Domesday, 197, " Has terras tenet Picot vicecomes de Roberto Gernon in maritagio feminæ suæ "  The Priory of Saint Giles was moved in 1112 to Barnwell, outside the town, where it grew and flourished

[2] At Northampton (Domesday, 219) sixty burgesses had shrunk up to forty-seven, the remaining houses being waste, but forty more had appeared in the new town (" in novo burgo ").  All the freeholders mentioned in the town are strangers, and among all the large owners in the shire, even among the tenants of the church of Peterborough, very few English names are found  Two priests, Godwine and Leofwine, appear in 222 b as " eleemosynarii Regis," and in 229 we get a short list of Thegns, among whom are two with the Danish names Olaf and Oslac

father, King Diarmid of Dublin.¹ It was not hard to find the means of raising and manning a fleet in the Danish towns on the east coast of Ireland. So, before the first year of their banishment was out, three sons of the fallen King, Godwine, Eadmund, and Magnus,² appeared, exactly as their father had done sixteen years before,³ to attempt to win their way back into their native land by force. How far this was done in concert with the leaders of the Northumbrian movement we can only guess. But things look as if all the enemies of William had agreed to do their best to shake his power, each in those parts of the island where his influence was strongest. Harold's sons, just as their father had done, chose for their field of operations those shires of the West where the cause of their house had been defended longer than anywhere else. Their fleet, which is said to have numbered fifty-two ships,⁴ was manned no doubt partly by Danes from Ireland, partly by English exiles. At the head of this force they sailed up the Bristol Channel. But either they had not taken warning by the error of their father, or they looked on a land under Norman rule as an enemy's country, or else the natural love of plunder in the breasts of the Wikings from Ireland could not be overcome. The usual, but invariably fatal, mistake was made; the deliverers began by ravaging the land far and wide.⁵ After thus harrying the coast as they went, they sailed up the Avon to Bristol, the port whence

*They sail up the Bristol Channel, and attack Bristol,*

---

¹ See above, p. 159, and vol. ii. p. 154.

² On the sons of Harold engaged in this attempt, and on the authorities for the story, see Appendix DD.

³ See vol. ii. pp. 315-319, 596-598.

⁴ So at least say the Winchester Annals, Ann. Mon. ii. 28. The Chronicler and Florence do not mention the number.

⁵ Chron. Wig. 1067. "Com an Haroldes suna ... mid scyphere into Afenan muðan unwær, and hergode sona ofer eall þone ende." Florence does not mention these earlier harryings, nor the attack on Bristol.

VOL. IV. Q

CHAP XVIII
but are beaten off by the burghers

their father had sailed to the land whence they now returned.[1] They at once assaulted the city. Whatever were the feelings of the burghers of Bristol towards the House of Godwine, they not unreasonably thought that to have their town sacked by Irish Danes would be worse than to live under the peace of King William. They fought manfully against the besiegers, and drove them off without their being able to carry off anything as a memorial of their attack on Bristol.[2] But, loaded with the spoil which they had gathered in the neighbourhood, they returned to their ships and sailed to some point of the coast of Somerset which is not more fully described.[3] There they landed, and the story of their father's landing at Porlock was acted over again. Under the circumstances of their landing, it is not wonderful that they found the shire unfriendly, or that Eadnoth, once their father's Staller, preferred his lately sworn allegiance to the Norman King to any feelings of regard for the sons of his old master. Eadnoth, as King William's officer, met the sons of Harold in arms at the head of King William's new subjects, the local *fyrd* of Somerset.[4] Many good men were slain on both sides.[5] This form of words commonly refers to the

They ravage Somerset

They are met by Eadnoth the Staller,

---

[1] See vol ii p 154
[2] Chron Wig 1067 "Foron þa to Brycgstowe and þa burh abrecan woldon, ac seo burhwaru heom heardlice wið feaht, and þi hi ne mihton of þære burh naht gewinnan, hi foron þa to scypan mid þan þe hi gehergod hæfdon"
[3] Ib "And swa hi foron on Sumersæton and þær upp eodon." Here the narrative of Florence joins in, "de Hibernia redeuntes in Sumersetaniâ applicuerunt"
[4] Ib. "Eadnoð Stallere heom wið gefeaht" Flor Wig "Eadnothus, qui fuit Haroldi Regis Stallarius, occurrit cum exercitu." William of Malmesbury (iii 254) is fuller on William's policy on this head; "Anglıgenam exercitum et ducem objecit, Normannos feriari permittens, ingens sibi levamen providens, utrilibet vincerent." Yet it is clear that William's interest needed the repulse of Harold's sons
[5] Ib "Eadnoð . wearð þær ofslagen and manege gode menn on ægðre healfe"

rank of the persons spoken of,[1] and it would seem to imply that such English Thegns as were left in the shire did not scruple to obey the summons of Eadnoth. The result seems to have been a drawn battle. Eadnoth fell in the fight, and his son, as we have seen, failed to retain the inheritance which might have seemed the due reward of his father's services.[2] Godwine and his brothers sailed away, and, after further harryings in Devonshire and Cornwall, made their way back to Ireland.[3] All that King Harold's sons had done towards the recovery of their father's Kingdom had been to be beaten back by English burghers, to harry three English shires, and to lose a large part of their own force in an indecisive battle against Englishmen.[4]

*who is killed in battle*

*They ravage Devonshire and Cornwall, and sail back to Ireland.*

At some stage of this year, and seemingly not later than the month of September, an event took place which may have had the effect of making the foreign dynasty seem one degree less foreign in the eyes of Englishmen. At some time after her coronation Queen Matilda gave birth to the fourth and youngest son of the Conqueror, most

*Birth of Henry the First. September (?) 1068.*

---

[1] Cf. Mr. Grote's remarks on the analogous use of ἀγαθός and ἐσθλός. ii 88, iii 62

[2] Florence says of the sons of Harold, "illi potiti victoriâ," but William of Malmesbury puts the victory on the other side, "Nec eum cogitatio lusit, nam utrique Angli, aliquamdiu digladiati inter se, palmam otiosam Regi refudere, advenæ Hiberniam fugati, regni, maximâ sui clade, nomen inane victoriæ, amisso duce, mercati Vocabatur is Ednodus," &c It is now that William goes on to speak of Harding See above, p. 45, and Appendix S.

[3] Chron Wig. 1067. "And þanon aweig foron þe þær to láfe wæron" Compare the use of the same formula with regard to William's army after Senlac, vol iii p 533.

[4] Here may come in the curious comments of the Winchester Annalist (Ann. Mon ii 28), "Godwinus, Haroldi Regis filius, patrem vindicare cupiens, cum lii. navibus Angliam venit, et multa mala Regi et regno intulit, de regno tamen postremo expulsus est In hoc autem maxime ibi profecit, quod interemptis sodalibus de eorum victu et pollicito præmio minus reddebatur sollicitus" Compare the story of Antigonos and Dēmētrios in Plutarch, Dem 40

228          CONQUEST OF WESTERN AND NORTHERN ENGLAND.

CHAP XVIII  likely the youngest of all his children. Born on English
Henry       ground, the son of a crowned King and Queen, the babe
alone of
William's   was a born Ætheling, and was marked out from his birth
sons an
English     as a future King of the English.[1] There can be little
Ætheling    doubt that, as the chances of deliverance from the foreign
            yoke grew weaker and weaker, English feeling began to
            attach itself to that one among the Conqueror's children
            who alone could be looked on as in any sense an English-
            man. William no doubt, designed from the beginning
Analogy     that it should so attach itself. His policy with
with Ed-
ward the    regard to his English-born son was probably much the
Second in   same as that of Edward the First with regard to his
Wales
            British-born son.[2] The very name of the young Ætheling
The name    is worth notice. He was called Henry, a name strange to
Henry
            England, almost equally strange to Normandy, but a name
            of genuine Teutonic ring.[3] If to Norman ears it might
            suggest the French King who had been William's ally at
            Val-ès-dunes and his enemy at Varaville, to English ears it
            might rather suggest the reigning German King and his
            father the renowned Emperor, close alliance with whom
            had ever been the policy of England. The choice of such
            a name, a name hitherto unknown in the ducal house, but
            which was to become one of the most famous among the
            royal names of England, may well have been a sort of com-
            promise between the purely Norman and the purely English

[1] See Appendix EE.

[2] Whatever we make of the familiar legend, there is no doubt that Edward the Second was born at Caernarvon (though not in the tower of his own building), and it is not likely that he was born there without a reason See N. Trivet, 309 ; Lingard, ii 522, Greatest of Plantagenets, 138; Williams' Hist of Wales, 421.

[3] There are very few Henries in Domesday, besides the well-known Henry of Ferrers In English the name occurs as Heinric, Henric, Heanrig, Henrig, later as Henri and Heanri In the first two forms it is looked on as a real Teutonic name, the last two are attempts to represent the French sound, the middle two may perhaps throw some light on the process of softening the final *g*

nomenclature. Henry then, the one royal-born son of his parents, the one who, by English Law, would have a claim to a distinct preference at the next vacancy of the throne, was brought up with special care. He was taught all the learning of the age; his proficiency became wonderful among contemporary princes, and Henry the Clerk, as men called him, retained his taste for letters through the whole course of a long life and an eventful reign.[1] And there is little doubt that one among the branches of learning which were instilled into the young Ætheling was a knowledge of the speech and the literature of the land in which he was born. The youngest son of the Conqueror showed a knowledge of two tongues, one of which must have been as unusual as the other, when, most probably as a youthful exercise, he translated the fables which bore the name of Æsop from the Greek tongue into the English. That such was the case rests on the authority of the well-known poetess, Mary of France, who used the English translation of King Henry as the groundwork of her own version in her own tongue.[2] And, in his later life, though at some periods of his reign his policy became mainly foreign, yet he never wholly threw aside the character of an Englishman. In his first marriage with Eadgyth of Scotland the green tree first began to return to its place.[3] The son of that marriage was freely spoken of as an English Ætheling,[4] and the first marriage of his sister Matilda with the Emperor Henry the Fifth was a continuation of the policy which had given the daughter of Eadward the Elder to Otto the Great and the daughter of Cnut to the Emperor Conrad.[5] And the King who, with his English Queen, had been mocked by Norman courtiers as Godric and Godgifu, filled her place with a second bride, in the person of Adeliza of Lowen, sprung from those lands

CHAP XVIII.
Careful education of Henry.

His love of letters

His knowledge of Greek and English

Henry's policy largely English

---

[1] See Appendix EE  [2] Ib  [3] See vol iii pp 12, 39
[4] See Appendix EE  [5] See vol i pp 63, 252, 479, 505

230    CONQUEST OF WESTERN AND NORTHERN ENGLAND.

CHAP XVIII  kindred in blood and speech with England, a close connexion with which, if it was part of the policy of William, had been equally part of the policy of Godwine.

Legend of Henry's birth at Selby

The place of birth of a prince who was to be so renowned cannot be fixed with certainty. A local tradition, for which I can find no confirmation among contemporary writers, places it at Selby in Yorkshire.[1] No place would at first sight seem more unlikely; it is the very unlikeliness of the tale which suggests that it must have some groundwork of truth. The tradition at once connects itself with the fact that it was just about this time that the great Abbey to which Selby owes its fame made its first feeble beginnings.[2] The most perfect of the monastic churches of Yorkshire, still, with some mutilations, retained in use as a parish church, is older than the more famous Cistercian minsters which it has survived, and which now remain only in ruins. The foundation legend is full of marvels and miracles, but we may trust it so far as to believe that the house of Saint German at Selby was a colony from his more famous house at Auxerre.[3] According to the legend, the monastery began in a way more characteristic of earlier times, in the settlement of a single hermit in the wilderness This was Benedict, a monk of Auxerre, who planted himself in solitude among the wild forests by the Ouse. He won the notice and favour of several powerful men, and at last of King William himself; his hermitage grew into a monastery, he himself grew into the first Abbot of the new house, and, as usual, a town grew up around the Abbey. The presence of Matilda in

Foundation of Selby Abbey c 1069

Legend of its origin

---

[1] See Monasticon, iii 485 As usual, a building of much later date than Henry's time was shown as his birth-place

[2] Sim Dun 1069 (83 Hinde) "Cœnobium Sancti Germani de Selebi sumpsit exordium"

[3] The legend, on which I shall have something to say in Appendix FF, will be found at length in Labbe's Bibliotheca, i 594

Northumberland at such a time is in itself unlikely; her presence at such a spot as Selby then was is unlikelier still. It is indeed possible that William may have brought his wife into Northumberland, as Edward brought his wife into Wales, in order that the expected Ætheling might be not only an Englishman, but a native of that part of England which had cost his father most pains to win. But in that case we should have looked for his birth, not in some hut or cell in the wilderness, but in the renowned capital of the province. If Henry really was born at Selby, his birth there could only have been the accidental result of some visit of curiosity or devotion to the spot where the newly founded monastery was just beginning to rise.

*Possibility of Henry's birth in Northumberland*

William was thus comforted amidst his toils by the presence of his wife, whose almsdeeds, we are told, ever wrought mightily for him in the day of battle.[1] Many of his comrades however had not the same advantage. While they were fighting and receiving the reward of their fightings, their wives still tarried in Normandy. Fearful, so we are told, of the dangers of the sea, fearful of the dangers of a land which seemed to be wholly given up to war and tumults, the Norman ladies feared to trust themselves in England. But the long absence of their husbands soon became more than they could bear; they sent, so the story runs, messengers saying that, if their lords did not speedily come back, they would be driven to seek out other consorts for themselves.[2] The Norman warriors were torn asunder by the force of two contending ties. Could they

*The Norman women complain of the absence of their husbands, their alleged messages and threats.*

---

[1] Ord. Vit. 513 A. "Eleemosyna, cui quotidie hæc hera insistebat, marito agonizanti in procinctu bellico plus quam fari nôrim succurrebat."

[2] Ib. 512 A. "His temporibus quædam Normanniæ mulieres sævâ libidinis face urebantur, crebrisque nuntiis a viris suis flagitabant ut cito reverterentur, addentes quod, nisi reditum maturarent, ipsæ sibi alios conjuges procurarent." Orderic tells the tale at length, not without some touches of humour.

*Some of the Normans return home*

forsake their King in his hour of need? But could they tamely abide in a strange land while their wives were throwing themselves into the arms of other men? The domestic duty or interest prevailed; the offers made by the King of lands and honours, of greater lands and honours still when the whole Kingdom should be subdued, had no effect on men whose hearths were thus threatened.[1] Hugh of Grantmesnil left his command in Hampshire;[2] Humfrey of Tilleul left his guardianship of the fortress of Hastings,[3] to revisit the wives whose importunate clamours thus called for them. They and many others crossed over into Normandy, leaving their King and their comrades to their fate, and leaving their English lands and honours to the King's mercy.

*Elements of truth and falsehood in the story*

That this story is not true in all its details is shown by the fact that our informant, the monk of Saint Evroul, goes on to say that those who now returned to Normandy forfeited for ever the lands and honours which they left behind in England.[4]

*Hugh of Grantmesnil retains his English honours*

Now in the case of Hugh of Grantmesnil this is notoriously false. He appears, not only in Domesday, but in the historian's own pages, as retaining his English possessions, including his Sheriffdom of Leicestershire, and as dying in England long after the death of the Conqueror.[5] And it is specially strange that the historian of Saint Evroul should, even by a momentary slip or a mere inaccuracy of expression, go so far wrong

---

[1] Ord Vit 512 A. "Rex inter tot bellorum motiones secum milites suos retinere cupiebat, et terras cum redditibus et magnis potestatibus eis amicabiliter offerebat, et majora dum totum regnum ab adversariis undique liberatum esset promittebat"

[2] See above, p 74     [3] See above, p 73

[4] Ord. Vit 512 B "Deinde famulari lascivis dominabus suis in Neustriam reversi sunt, sed honores quos jam nactos hâc de caussâ reliquerunt, ipsi vel hæredes eorum numquam postea recuperare potuerunt"

[5] He appears as Sheriff of Leicester in p 600 B (cf 522 C, 602 B), he dies in England in 1098 in 716 D. The beauty of his wife Adelaide, daughter of Ivo of Beaumont, is witnessed in 691 D

in the case of one of the founders of his own house.[1] CHAP.XVIII.
The story too has in itself a mythical air; it seems to be a modified form of a tale which turns up in various times and places.[2] Yet legends of this kind commonly grow round a certain kernel of truth. And such a kernel there most likely is in this tale also. Some of William's followers, perhaps Hugh of Grantmesnil himself, may have forsaken him for a while at this stage of his enterprise. That their return to Normandy was owing to the importunities of their wives would be an obvious jest at the time, and would be easily mistaken for a piece of true history.

*Similar tales elsewhere*

*Probable origin of the story.*

Nor is it unlikely that desertions of this kind were in some way connected with the fact which the historian goes on to record, that William at this time dismissed the mercenary part of his army, loading them with rewards and allowing them to go where they would.[3] Such an act, at such a time, when William's power was still so insecure, seems to point to mutinies and discontents of some kind or other. And nothing would be more likely to awaken the jealousy of the mercenaries than if the native Normans either received or took to themselves the privilege of returning to their own land.

*William sends away his mercenaries*

---

[1] See vol ii p 232

[2] The Norman women here simply threaten what the women in some other stories do The Scythian women in Herodotus (iv. 1) consort with their slaves during the twenty-eight years' absence of their husbands The Polish women do the same during the absence of Boleslaus the Second and his army at Kief in 1076 See Dlugoss, i 280 (ed Leipzig, 1711), Chron Polono-Silesiacum, Pertz, xviii 559 In these cases the husbands return and take vengeance But the story of the origin of the Partheneiai, the founders of Tarentum, in Strabo, vi 3 (vol ii p. 45), and Justin, iii 4, is essentially the same, and a tale of the like sort seems implied in the legend of the foundation of the Italian Lokroi See Polybios, xii 5 et seqq

[3] Ord Vit 512 C " Rex, perspectis importunitatibus terræ, solidarios milites convocavit, omnesque regali munificentiâ pro militari servitute muneratos domum abire benigne permisit "

## § 4. *The Revolt and Final Conquest of the North.*
## 1069–1070.

*Importance of the year 1069*

*William's power then finally established*

We have now reached one of the most eventful years of William's reign, the year which may be said to have finally made him master of all England. His power was already spread over the greater part of the Kingdom. The extreme north of Northumberland and some districts in the north-west of Mercia alone remained unsubdued. But William's hold was as yet far from firm over a large part even of those shires where he had personally appeared to receive submission and where he had planted castles to secure his conquests. And the state of the country every-

*Wretched state of the country*

where was wretched. The old powers had been broken down by William's conquest, and William's own power was not yet so firmly established as to give his subjects of either race that protection which it certainly was his wish to give to both alike. Englishmen and Normans were preying on one another, and, as so constantly happens, natural powers of destruction followed in the wake of the havoc which was wrought by man. Whatever escaped the sword fell into the jaws of hunger and pestilence.[1] Such is the picture given us in our most detailed narrative of these times. The prophecy of the dying Eadward had been fulfilled; fiends had indeed stalked through his land.[2]

Where William kept the Christmas Feast of this year we are not told; according to the practice of the more settled

---

[1] Ord. Vit. 512. "Multimodis desolationibus Anglia nimis attrita est, et tam ab indigenis quam ab alienigenis valde aggravata est. Incendia, rapinæ, et quotidianæ cædes miseram gentem invaserunt, percusserunt, dejecerunt, et conquassaverunt. Adversa fortuna miseros tam victos quam victores muscipulâ suâ irretivit, nunc ense, nunc fame, nunc peste, irreverenter præcipitavit, prout omnipotens arbiter unicuique dispensavit."

[2] See vol. iii. p. 11.

years of his reign it would be at Gloucester. Wherever the place was, it was no doubt the result of the deliberations of the Midwinter Gemót that an attempt was made to subdue the extreme North, or rather to deal with it as with a land already subdued. The Earldom of Northumberland in the narrower sense of the name was vacant by the flight of Gospatric, and the office, with the task of subduing the country, was entrusted to one of William's own followers, seemingly one of the adventurers from Flanders. This was Robert of Comines, on whom all our authorities bestow the title of Earl,[1] and who now, in the course of January, set forth on the perilous task of taking possession of a district where William's own presence and William's armies had not yet been seen. He commanded a body of troops which is variously reckoned at five, seven, and nine hundred. We have, as in some other cases, the further difficulty that it is not perfectly clear whether the numbers take in his whole force or only those among them who were of knightly rank.[2] His course lay through Durham, a city which had not as yet submitted, and which we have seen was a stronghold of the independent English.[3] We are told that the general feeling in the country was

*Midwinter Gemót at Gloucester? 1068-1069*

*The Earldom of Northumberland beyond the Tyne granted to Robert of Comines*

*Durham still unsubdued*

---

[1] Orderic (512 C) says, "Guillelmus Rex Dunelmensem comitatum Rodberto de Cuminis tradidit," but Simeon (1069) says distinctly, "misit Rex Wilhelmus Northymbris ad *Aquilonalem plagam Tinæ* Comitem Rodberto cognomento Cumin." The Chronicles (1068) simply say, "Willelm cyng geaf Rodberde Eorle þone eorldom on Norðymbraland." On the new use of "Northumberland" in the narrower sense, see vol. 1 p. 585, vol. 11 pp. 483, 487. At any rate the expression of Orderic need not imply that Robert was invested with a special Earldom of Durham, of the land between the Tees and the Tyne.

"Rodbertus de Cuminis" I take to have drawn his name from the same place as the historian Philip. It has become Comyn, Cumin Cumming, and is one of the names which has come to be looked on as "Scotch."

[2] "*Milites* quingenti," says Orderic, "septingenti *homines*," according to Simeon, "ix hund *manna*" in the Chronicles. Are these different reckonings, or the same?

[3] See above, p. 187.

236 CONQUEST OF WESTERN AND NORTHERN ENGLAND.

CHAP XVIII

*Robert received by Bishop Æthelwine.*

in favour of flight, but that the severity of the winter, heightened by a deep fall of snow, made flight hopeless. The men of the district therefore determined to meet the invader, and either to slay him or to perish themselves.[1] The new Earl drew near to Durham, where he had one friend in the city, in the person of the Bishop Æthelwine. That prelate, as we have seen, had made his peace with William at York,[2] and he now came, with more reason, to act towards Robert of Comines the part which Robert the son of Wymarc had acted towards William himself.[3] He met the new Earl on his way, and warned him not to think of entering the city.[4] Robert made light of the warning; he marched on, dealing with the land through which he marched as an enemy's country, and even slaying some of the tenants or bondmen of the church of Saint Cuthberht. He entered Durham with his force, and we read of no opposition to his entrance. The Bishop perhaps prevailed thus far with his fellow-citizens, or perhaps the site of his episcopal dwelling made him practically master of the military position. Certain it is that Robert was admitted into the city, and that he and his immediate followers were lodged in the Bishop's own house, the doubtless far lowlier forerunner of the fortress which, side by side with the minster, looks down on the encircling stream of the Wear. But it was soon shown that, if the prudence of Æthelwine led him to receive a visitor stained with such outrages as those of which Robert had been

*Robert enters Durham*

---

[1] Sim Dun Hist Dun iii 15. "Quem illi ubi advenientem audierant, omnes relictis domibus fugere parabant Sed subito nivis tanta nimietas, tantaque hiemis obvenit asperitas, ut omnem eis fugiendi possibilitatem adimeret Quapropter omnibus idem fuit consilium ut aut Comitem exstinguerent aut simul ipsi caderent" Id Hist Regg. 1069 (84 Hinde). "At illi omnes in unam coacti sententiam, *ne alienigenæ domini subderentur,* statuerunt aut illum interficere aut ipsi simul omnes in ore gladii cadere"

[2] See above, p 206    [3] See vol iii p 414

guilty, his flock, within and without the city, were not like-minded with him. They had no mind to receive a Norman Earl, an Earl whose approach to his intended capital had been marked by slaughter and devastation. As Robert had begun, so he went on; received as he was by the Bishop with all honour, he allowed his men to deal with the town as with a place taken by storm.[1] The spirit of the people was now aroused. The news spread during the night, and towards morning the gates of Durham were burst open by the assembled forces of Northumberland. A general massacre followed. In the houses, in the streets, the Normans were everywhere slaughtered.[2] No serious resistance seems to have been offered except in defence of the Bishop's house, where the Earl and his immediate companions withstood their assailants so manfully that they were driven to have recourse to fire. The palace was burned; the Earl and his comrades all died, either by the flames or by the sword. One man alone contrived to escape with his life, and he was wounded.[3] But, even amid the slaughter of their enemies, the men of Durham found time to think of their patron

*Outrages of his followers*

*Massacre of the Normans.*

*Resistance at the Bishop's house*

*The house is burned and Robert and his party slain.*

---

[1] Sim Dun Hist Regg 84 "Dunelmum cum multa militum manu ingressus permisit suos hostiliter ubique agere, occisis etiam nonnullis ecclesiæ rusticis, susceptus est autem ab Episcopo cum omni humanitate et honore" So Hist Dun ii 15, "Intravit Dunelmum cum septingentis hominibus ubique per domos hostiliter agentibus"

[2] Sim. Dun Hist. Regg 94 "At Northymbri totâ nocte festinantes Dunelmum summâ vi diluculo per portas irrumpunt et socios Comitis imparatos ubique locorum interficiunt Atrociter nimis res geritur, prostratis per domos et plateas militibus" So in the Durham History, "Tanta denique fuit interfectorum multitudo ut omnes plateæ cruore atque cadaveribus replerentur" Compare Orderic, 512 C, "Primâ vero nocte cives collecti sunt et ipsum cunctosque milites, præter duos fugâ illapsos, mactaverunt Fortissimi viri nequiverunt defendere se, oppressi tempore, dolo, multitudine."

[3] Sim Dun. Hist Regg 1069 "Domum Episcopi, in quâ Comes fuerat susceptus, aggrediuntur pugnantes, sed quum non ferrent jacula defendentium, domum cum inhabitantibus concremaverunt." The account in the

saint and of his minster The flames which destroyed the Bishop's palace all but seized on the neighbouring western tower of the church, the last finish of the building, which Eadmund had added to the work of the founder Ealdhun. But, owing, we are told, to the prayers of the people, the wind changed, the flames turned away from the tower, and the church of Ealdhun and Eadmund was spared to give way to the grander conceptions of Norman architects.[1]

*Escape of the church*

The blow struck at Durham was at once followed by a blow struck at York.[2] As Durham, which had never submitted, refused to give up its freedom, York, which had submitted, was aroused to make an effort to win its freedom back again. The citizens rose, and slew one of the Norman commanders, Robert the son of Richard, with many of his companions.[3] That this was done with the distinct intention of throwing off all allegiance to the Norman King is shown by their immediately welcoming, most likely inviting, his English rival. The descendant of the West-Saxon Kings had small chance of winning back the Kingdom and the royal city of his fathers, but he was to have another momentary reign in the Kingdom and city which had cost his fathers so much pains to win and to keep in hand. The Ætheling Eadgar ventured to leave his shelter in Scotland, and the whole force of Northumberland—the word being here no doubt

*Revolt at York and slaughter of Robert Fitz-Richard.*

*Eadgar returns from Scotland*

Durham History is to the same effect, except that it is not said to be the Bishop's house One escaped, according to Simeon, two, according to Orderic

[1] The escape of the tower, "turris occidentalis quæ juxta stabat," appears in the Durham History only It was seemingly a single western tower See vol i pp. 496, 565

[2] On the succession of events during this campaign, see Appendix Y

[3] Ord Vit 512 C "Non multo post Rodbertus Ricardi filius, Eboracensis præsidii custos, cum multis peremptus est" No other writer mentions this outbreak, but it seems needed to account for what comes after

again used in the wider sense—was gathered to him. For with him came the local chiefs, Mærleswegen and the banished Earl Gospatric,[1] whose lead was no doubt followed by the Northumbrian people in general. Of Eadwine and Morkere we hear nothing; they were most likely still half guests, half prisoners, in the court of William. But it is plain that the chiefs and people of the North no longer trusted them; the career of the house of Leofric in those regions was over. The new scheme was the restoration of the West-Saxon Ætheling by the might of Northumberland and the kindred help of Denmark The policy of the scheme is obvious. Mærleswegen, Gospatric, Archill, and the rest would never agree to submit to any one of their own number; they might all agree to yield a nominal submission to a prince who was indifferent to their local feuds, and in whose name each of them might hope to govern. But the choice of Eadgar as chief clearly points to at least a hope of driving William wholly out of the island. The heir of Cerdic could never be satisfied with a Northumbrian Kingdom, he could never sit down quietly to reign at York while Winchester was in the hands of the Norman Bastard. If left to themselves, Eadgar and his advisers would probably have waited for the Danish succours which did come in the course of the year. But the present moment could not be lost; the advantage of the movements at Durham and York was not to be thrown away. The spirit and confidence of the people was high, and

*CHAP XVIII*

*Eadgar supported by Gospatric and Mærleswegen. Their policy.*

*General spirit of the Northumbrian people*

---

[1] Orderic (512 C) at this point waxes classical, and talks of "Marius Swevus [Mærleswegen], Gaius Patricius [Gospatric, see vol ii p 457], Edgarus Adelinus, aliique potentes et factiosi" The Chronicles (1068) say simply, "Sona þæræfter [after the movement at Durham] Eadgar Æðeling cóm mid eallum Norðhymbrum to Eoforwic, and þa burhmenn ["portmen" in the Peterborough Chronicle] wið hine gnðedon." But Eadgar would never have got "all the Northumbrians" together without the guidance of some of the great men of the country

the oppressions which everywhere went on kindled the national indignation more and more. Men who had sworn oaths and given hostages to the foreign King recked little both of their oaths and of the safety of their surviving friends, as they thought of the lands from which they had been driven and of the kinsmen and countrymen who had fallen by the hands of the strangers.[1]

*Eadgar received at York, siege of the castle*

In such a frame of mind the assembled forces of Northumberland, with the young Eadgar at their head, drew near to the walls of York. The citizens at once welcomed the English King, joined his forces, and began a general attack on the newly-built castle.[2] The command was now held by William Malet, who at once sent to King William, saying that, unless help came with all speed, he should be driven to surrender.[3] William was not likely to risk the loss of his northern capital; the need called for his full force and his own presence. He came with all speed at the head of an overwhelming power;[4] his march must, as a military exploit, have been the fellow of the great march which carried Harold from London to Stamfordbridge. He came, and his vengeance was fearful. He burst upon the besiegers of the castle, slew, captured, or put to flight the whole party, harried the town, and in some way or other did dishonour to the metropolitan

*Message of William Malet to King William*

*March of William to York*

*He defeats the insurgents*

---

[1] Ord Vit 512 C "Fiducia deinceps Anglis crevit contra Normannos, a quibus videbant nimium vexari suos collegas et amicos. Fides, sacramentum, et salus obsidum vilia fuerunt iratis pro amissis patrum suorum prædus et occisis parentibus et compatriotis"

[2] Ib "Consociatâ manu civium ac finitimorum, munitionem Regis in Eboraco impugnare ausi sunt"

[3] Ib "Willelmus cognomento Maletus, præses castrensis, Regi denunciavit se defecturum nisi maturum fessis conferat auxilium"

[4] Chron Wig 1068. "Wyllelm kyng com suðan on unwær on heom mid geotendan here," or, as Peterborough has it, "mid eallan his fyrde" Ord Vit. 512 "Rex ocius advenit"

church of Saint Peter, most likely by showing small heed
to its rights of sanctuary.¹ York was a second time
subdued, and this time a second yoke was added. One
castle had not proved check enough for the turbulent city;
William therefore took the same steps to curb York which
Eadward the Elder had taken either to curb or to defend
Nottingham. One castle already commanded the left
bank of the Ouse; another now arose on its right bank,
on the mound which still bears the name of the Bail
Tower, just within the later walls of the city. The
navigation of the river and, with it, the direct communication between the Danes of York and the Danes of
Denmark, was thus brought altogether under Norman
control. The new fortress however, one which has always
remained quite subordinate to the elder, must have been
a hasty structure of wood or of the roughest kind of
masonry. For we read that it was built during the
King's sojourn of eight days. It was however thought
needful to entrust it, for a time at least, to a leader
of the highest rank. No less a person than the Earl
of Hereford, the famous William Fitz-Osbern, was left
in command of the new tower.² York was thus secured for a while; but the power of Saint Cuthberht,
so local legends told, rescued the more guilty city of
Durham from William's wrath. The King sent troops,
under a commander whose name is not mentioned, to

*and builds a second castle at York.*

*Legend of the miraculous defence of Durham*

---

¹ Chron. Wig. 1068 "Hi aflymde, and þa ofsloh þa þe ætfleon ne mihton, þæt wæron fela hund manna, and þa burh forhergode, and Sce Petres mynster to bysmere macede, and ealle þa oðre eac forhergode and forhynde" So the Peterborough Chronicle more briefly, and without any mention of the minster Ord Vit 512 C "Rex .. in obsidentes ruit, nec ulli pepercit Multi capti, plerique interfecti, cæteri sunt fugati"

² Ord Vit. 512 D "Rex autem dies octo in urbe morans alterum præsidium condidit, et Guillelmum Comitem Osberni filium ad custodiendum reliquit"

242     CONQUEST OF WESTERN AND NORTHERN ENGLAND.

CHAP XVIII avenge the death of Earl Robert.[1] They went as far as Alverton, and, in the common course of things, they would have reached Durham the next morning. But a great darkness came upon them, so that they could not see the way before them.[2] Presently one came among them who told them that the city against which they were marching had a saint who dwelled in it, who was ever its defender, and who suffered no man to harm it.[3] When the invaders heard this, they turned back again, and the men of Durham, who had been marked out for the slaughter, heard at the same time that a host had been sent against them, and that, by the help of Saint Cuthberht, the host had been turned away.[4]

The truth probably is that William was satisfied for the present with the recovery of York, and thought it wiser to leave Durham for a while untouched. He went away in triumph to keep the Feast of Easter, according to custom, at Winchester.[5] His back was no sooner turned than the English again rose, and attacked both the new fortress and the old. Something followed which seems to have deserved the name of a battle, or at least of a skirmish. Earl William, we are told, fought against

Renewed revolt at York and defeat of the insurgents.

---

[1] Sim Dun Hist Eccl Dun iii 15. "Rex Wilhelmus graviter offensus, ducem quemdam cum exercitu ut ejus mortem ulcisceretur, direxit."

[2] Ib "Quum autem ad Alvertoniam venissent, et jam mane facto Dunelmum profecturi essent, tanta nebularum densitas orta est ut vix adstantes sese alterutrum videre, viam vero nullo modo valerent invenire." A story of the same kind is told of certain Northmen who sought to plunder the Abbey of Saint Remigius at Rheims The origin of all tales of the kind is doubtless to be found in the blindness of the Syrians in 2 Kings vi 18

[3] Sim Dun Hist Eccl Dun iii 15 "Homines illos quemdam in suâ urbe sanctum habere qui eis semper in adversis protector adesset, quos nemo impune, illo vindicante, lædere umquam valeret "

[4] Ib "Hi vero ad quos interficiendos missi fuerant nihil ex hostibus, antequam reversi fuissent, agnoverunt "

[5] Ord. Vit 512 D. "Ipse vero lætus Guentam rediit et Paschale festum ibi celebravit "

the insurgents in a certain dale, of the position of which we should like to know more. The English were again defeated; some were killed, others taken, and the rest put to flight.[1]

Thus it was that the strength of England was frittered away in petty local struggles and enterprises. Never once, after the day of Saint Calixtus, did the whole nation show an united front to the invader. After the defeat at York, while King William was on his way back to Winchester, his rival Eadgar again went back to his shelter in Scotland.[2] He could not have been there long before another enterprise was risked in the West. Two of the sons of Harold, which of the three we are not told, appeared again at midsummer off the north coast of the Western peninsula, at the head of sixty-four or sixty-six ships.[3] They sailed up the mouth of the Taw, and their followers seem, in the true Wiking spirit, but with less than the old Wiking caution, to have spread themselves over well nigh the whole of Devonshire, plundering as they went. According to one account, they attacked Exeter itself; but, if so, the defences of Rougemont were too strong for them, or the zeal of the citizens in their cause was quenched. They might not unnaturally be less ardent on the behalf of the exiles, now that they appeared at the head of foreign pirates, than they had been when Harold's sons were defending the last stronghold of English freedom in the West. The extent of their harryings may be partly traced by an entry in the local Domesday, which

*Second enterprise of two sons of Harold c June 24, 1069*

*They sail up the Taw and harry a large part of Devonshire*

---

[1] Ord. Vit. 512 D. "Rursus Angli post Regis discessum contra utrumque præsidium congregati sunt, sed, Guillelmo Comite cum suis viriliter in quâdam valle dimicante, non prævaluerunt, sed, pluribus eorum captis seu trucidatis, alii fugâ mortem distulerunt."

[2] Chronn. Wig Petrib "And se Æðeling fôr eft ongean to Scotlande"

[3] Sixty-four in the Worcester Chronicle and Florence, sixty-six in Orderic (513 A) and William of Jumieges (vii 41)

shows that they reached points in the central and southern parts of the shire, far away from their first landing-place.[1] They were met in arms, most likely on their return towards their ships, by Brian, son of Count Odo of Britanny, who bears the title of Earl, and by another leader described as William Waldi, whom I cannot further identify.[2] The force under these captains was not small;[3] they came on the plunderers unawares, and fought with them two battles in one day[4] This is a comment on the disorderly way in which the irregular force which followed the sons of Harold had spread themselves over the country. The Breton Earl probably fell in with two detachments at different points, each of which separately he found it easy to overcome. The slaughter was terrible; seventeen hundred men are said to have been killed, and, as usual, the loss fell heaviest on the "best men," whether by that name we are to understand English exiles of rank or chief men among the Danes of Ireland.[5] Nightfall alone, we are told, hindered the plunderers from being utterly cut off. As it was, the

---

[1] On the geography of this expedition, see Appendix Y.

[2] Ord Vit 513 A. "Protinus illis Briennus, Eudonis Comitis Britanniæ Minoris filius, et Guillelmus Gualdi cum armis obvii fuerunt" "Breon eorl," as the Worcester Chronicle calls him, was the son of Odo the brother of Howel and of the Alan who fought at Senlac, and cousin of the late Count Conan. See vol iii. pp. 230, 231, 313 He appears in the Suffolk Domesday (ii 291) as "Comes Brienus," but he must have been dead before the Survey, as his lands are held by Earl Robert of Mortain.

[3] Chron Wig 1068 "Breon eorl com on únwær heom togeines mid unlytlan weorode and wið gefeaht"

[4] Will Gem vii 41. "Briennus . cum eis sub die unâ duobus prœliis manum conseruit." So Orderic, "duobus uno die conflictibus"

[5] Ib. "Cæsis vero mille et septingentis bellatorum cum nonnullis regni proceribus reliqui e certamine fugientes navium præsidio necis excidium, utcumque evaserunt" Are these "regni proceres" English exiles or men serving under Brian? The expression certainly falls in singularly with that of the Chronicler, "and ofsloh þær ealle þa betstan menn þe on þam lyðe wæron"

two sons of Harold, with a small remnant of their followers, escaped in two ships to the friendly court of King Diarmid.[1]

This crushing overthrow quenched for ever the hopes of the House of Godwine. Of the sons of Harold we hear no more. The family which in two generations had risen from obscurity to the highest pitch of greatness was in the third generation, so far as history is concerned, utterly wiped out. Of the band of sons who had gathered round Godwine in the march from Beverstone[2] and in the Gemót of London,[3] the captive Wulfnoth alone remained. All the rest had been cut off. But of that generation we at least know the end. Of the next we know only that male descendants of Tostig,[4] that female descendants of Harold,[5] lived on in Northern Europe. But in English history they have no longer a place. The Earl who delivered England from the stranger, the King who died as her champion against the stranger, have left behind them a name better than that of sons and daughters, but of their sons and daughters themselves no trace abides in the land which they loved and guarded. Godwine, Eadmund, and Magnus now vanish from our story. A time of confusion followed in Ireland, and their protector King Diarmid lost his life in the very year of their second enterprise.[6] Possibly they were cut off in these foreign broils

*No further mention of Harold's sons.*

*No further traces of the House of Godwine in English history.*

*Death of Diarmid. 1069*

---

[1] Ord. Vit 513 A "Horrendam multitudinem in eam paucitatem redegerunt ut residui duabus scaphis subtracti aufugerent et Hiberniam luctu replerent At, nisi nox prœlium diremisset, ne nuntius quidem cladis repatriavisset" So Will Gem vii 41 "Qui profecto, nisi nox prœlium diremisset, omnes mortis novaculâ abrasi fuissent" The Chronicler is much to the same effect, "þa oðre lytlan werode to scypum ætflugon, and Haroldes sunas foron eft to Yrlande ongean"

[2] Vol ii p 141     [3] See vol ii p. 333.
[4] See vol iii p 374     [5] See above, p. 160.
[6] See Chronicon Scotorum, 1069, Ann Camb 1070; Brut y Tywysogion, 1070, where he is described as "terrible to his foes, friendly to his countrymen, and gentle towards pilgrims [pererinyan] and strangers"

CHAP XVIII — while men were still fighting for England at York and Ely. At all events their career on English soil was over

Gytha leaves the Flat Holm for Flanders.

It was probably after this final overthrow of her grandsons that Gytha at last left the shelter of her rock in the Bristol Channel, and betook herself to a surer refuge beyond sea.[1] Of those many wives of good men[2] who shared her banishment we seem to get a glimpse in a story preserved by a German historian.[3] An English matron and her three daughters, sailing away from what was now the land of bondage, had the ill luck to suffer shipwreck in the County of Stade near the mouth of the Elbe. That county was then held by the Margrave Udo as a fief of the church of Bremen.[4] The laws of his coast were at least as inhuman towards shipwrecked persons as the laws of the coast of Ponthieu.[5] The helpless beings who escaped the waves were doomed to become the bondmen of the lords of the soil.[6] This custom was enforced against the English lady, and her daughters became the bondswomen of the Margrave's wife. The harshness of their lot was however greatly lessened in practice. The daughters found husbands, and their sons were carefully brought up and promoted to offices of trust.[7] One of the grandsons of the banished Englishwoman, Frederick the son of Reinhold, after a strange and discreditable career,

One of her companions probably wrecked in North Germany.

Frederick Count of Stade 1123-1135.

---

[1] See above, p 158.  [2] See above, p. 157.

[3] The story is found in the Annales Stadenses, Pertz, xvi 320, which I should not have been likely to explore save for the reference in Lappenberg, Norman Kings, 114.

[4] Pertz, u s "Prædictus Udo tenuit Stadensem Comitatum ab ecclesiâ Bremensi in beneficio."

[5] See vol. iii p 222

[6] Pertz, u. s "Friderici avia et mater de Angliâ navigantes in comitatu Stadensi naufragium passæ sunt, et, secundum prisci juris rigorem, tam homines quam res regiæ ditioni sunt mancipati"

[7] Ib. "Filii favorabiliter a Dominis educati sunt, et adultis collata administratio et dispensatio quarumdam villarum"

died as the reigning Count of the land into which his ancestress had found her way in so strange a sort.[1]

We again flit from the West to the North. Ever since the accession of William, England, Northern England at least, had been looking for help from the once hostile land of Denmark. All this while King Swend had been coming, perhaps to assert his own rights, at all events to avenge the blood of his kinsfolk who had died at Senlac. At once the nephew of Cnut and the nephew of Gytha, he might, for lack of more distinct representatives, pass as the champion of the house of the West-Saxon Earls no less than of the house of the Danish Kings.[2] And now at last, in the autumn of this present year, three years after England had been for the last time invaded by a Scandinavian enemy, her shores were approached by a Scandinavian fleet bearing men who at least gave themselves out as her friends. In August, less than two months after the final discomfiture of the sons of Harold in the West, two hundred and forty ships, commanded by men of their own blood, nephews and grand-nephews of Gytha, drew near to the eastern havens of England. The numbers in all these statements are utterly uncertain; we therefore have no trustworthy means of judging whether the efforts of Swend

*Swend at last sends help. Autumn 1069.*

*Description of his force.*

---

[1] Frederick and his brother Ulric are said to have got rich by robbing and drowning in the Elbe three Danish Bishops who were passing through the country. When the County passed to a minor heir, Henry, Frederick acted as regent in his name, and afterwards bought his freedom and the possession of his County from the Emperor Henry the Fifth. After many successes and reverses he was finally, on the death of Henry—by poison as was alleged—in 1123, formally invested with the fief by Adalbert the Second, Archbishop from 1123 to 1148.

[2] Ord. Vit. 513 B. "Multotiens enim pecuniis Anglorum et obnixis precibus fuerat sollicitatus, et ruinâ suorum qui nuper in Heraldi conflictu occisi fuerant motus: quinetiam proximâ cognominatione [cognatione?] ad regni cupiditatem incitatus, utpote nepos Eduardi Regis, Hardecunuti filius." A pedigree was seldom more utterly mistaken; Swend, son of Ulf the son of Thorgils and of Estrith the daughter of the elder Swend, was sister's son to Cnut, brother's son to Gytha, cousin alike to Harthacnut and to the sons of Godwine, but he had not a drop of blood in common with Eadward

to deliver England were or were not greater than the efforts of Harold Hardrada to subdue her. Writers on the Norman side strain all their powers of language to set forth how Swend drained the whole strength of his realm and of many surrounding realms. The whole might of Denmark was gathered together; auxiliaries in the cause of England came from the kindred lands of Friesland and Saxony. All this may be believed; but we begin to have our doubts when we hear of warriors coming from Slavonic Poland, and from the still heathen land of Lithuania.[1] The fleet was commanded by Osbeorn, the son of Ulf and Estrith, the brother of King Swend and of the murdered Beorn, who had himself once been an Earl in England, but who had been banished six and twenty years before at the election of Eadward.[2] With him came his nephews, Harold and Cnut, the sons of King Swend,

*His alleged foreign allies*

*Commanders of the fleet, Osbeorn, Harold, Cnut, and Thurkill*

---

[1] Ord Vit 513 B, C "Hic [Suenus] ingenti potentiâ pollebat, universas regni sui vires contrahebat, quibus a vicinis regionibus et amicis auxilia magna coacervabat. Adjuvabant cum Polenia, Frisia, necne Saxonia Leutecia quoque pro Anglicis opibus auxiliares turmas mittebat In eâ populosissima natio consistebat quæ, gentilitatis adhuc errore detenta, verum Deum nesciebat, sed ignorantiæ muscipulis illaqueata, Guodeven et Thurum, Freamque, aliosque falsos Deos, immo dæmones, colebat Hæc gens terrâ marique prœliari perita erat, quam Suenus cum Rege suo sæpe vicerat suæque ditioni subegerat"

My small stock of Northern history and geography here quite breaks down. As Orderic's Leutecia cannot well be Lutetia Parisiorum, nor yet Leodium or Luttich, nor yet Lausitz, I can find no name the least like it nearer than Lithuania The Lithuanians undoubtedly remained heathens long after this time, and we must remember that Sembia or Sambia, seemingly in Eastern Prussia, was (see vol 1 p 504) reckoned among the Kingdoms of Cnut. But I know of no conquests of Swend in those parts, and I cannot believe that Lithuanians worshipped our Teutonic Gods Still it is hardly fair to expect Orderic to be a comparative mythologist, and one would be well pleased to number the last speakers of verbs in $\mu\iota$ (see Lord Strangford's Remains, 1. 6) among our helpers

It must have been from the Polish contingent that some of Sir Walter Scott's characters learned to call on Czerni Bog, the Black God of the Slaves. Godescalc was too good a Christian for the purpose

[2] See vol 11 p 63 He appears as "Beornus comes" in the Winchester Annals, 1069, where he is further inaccurately made the son of Swend

both of whom in turn came to wear the Danish Crown, CHAP.XVIII.
while Cnut won also the crown of martyrdom on those [Harold King 1074 -1081. Cnut 1081 -1086.]
easy terms on which it was often adjudged to royal candi-
dates.[1] We hear also of an Earl Thurkill and of two
Danish Bishops as having a share, therefore doubtless a
command, in the expedition.[2] One would be well pleased
to know what instructions the leaders of the fleet received
from the wary prince who sent them. They undoubtedly came to deliver England, to help those who were
striving to free her from the yoke of her foreign King.
But what form was the deliverance to take? Was the Possible scheme of Swend.
attempt to be made on behalf of Eadgar, once the King-
elect, on behalf of Swend's kinsmen the sons of Harold, or
on behalf of Swend himself? In Eadgar Swend could
take no interest; in his eyes he would be simply the
representative of a family which had displaced his own.
In young Godwine, or in any other of Harold's sons, he
might well take a kinsman's interest, and it is quite possible Probable concert with Harold's sons.
that the two expeditions, from Ireland and from Denmark,
were planned in concert. But, if so, they had failed to act
in concert, and the last hopes of the House of Godwine
had been smitten to the ground in Western England
before the Danish deliverer had appeared in the East.
The discomfiture of the sons of Harold may well have
been felt as a serious check to Swend's plan of operations;
it may even have brought about a change in his main

[1] Chron. Petrib. and Florence, 1087.

[2] The Worcester Chronicle (1069) gives the list as "þreo Swegenes suna kyninges . and Esbeorn Eorl and þurkyl Eorl." Peterborough leaves out "þreo" and does not mention Thurkill. Florence has "Suani Regis Danorum filii Haroldus et Canutus, et patruus eorum Esbernus Comes, et Comes Turkillus." Orderic (513 B) gives the list thus, "In illâ tempestate Suenus Rex Danorum magnam classem Danis et Anglis accuratissime instruxit, duosque filios suos et Osbernum fratrem suum, Pontificesque duos, Comitesque tres dilectissimos præfecit, et in Angliam misit." The Peterborough Chronicle under 1070 gives us the name of one of the Bishops, "Christien þa Densce biscop." The later characteristic royal name of Denmark is already coming in.

250  CONQUEST OF WESTERN AND NORTHERN ENGLAND.

CHAP XVIII.

Swend's probable personal objects.

Adhesion of Eadgar

Swend's objects embraced all England

Connexion between the invasion and movements in the West

objects. All hopes of joint action were at an end, Swend could no longer be looked on as bound to support men who had so utterly failed to support themselves. His object, now at least, cannot fail to have been to restore the monarchy of Cnut in one form or another. As far as we can dive into Swend's mind, one may be inclined to think that his caution and experience must have taught him that it was hopeless to attempt to place the two crowns of England and Denmark upon the same brow. But one of Swend's many sons might well become the stock of a new dynasty, a dynasty which to Northern England would be in every way welcome, while in Southern England it would be at least preferred to the rule of the Norman. We can however well believe that the schemes of Swend, whatever they were, were not so distinctly chalked out, but that they were liable to change according to the chances of war, and according to the reception which they might meet with in England. We may perhaps also infer that, whatever Swend's objects were, they were not very clearly made known, and that, at any rate, no purposes irreconcileably hostile to the claims of Eadgar were publicly announced. For we shall presently find the Ætheling acting in concert with the Danish invaders. And Eadgar at least must have hoped for the Crown for himself. If he had only to choose between two masters, he could have no motive for preferring Swend to William.

But in any case it is plain that Swend's objects, whatever they were, took in the whole of England, and were not merely confined to its northern portion. And we may feel sure that it was generally known throughout England that a Danish invasion was preparing. The movements which took place in various parts of the country before the year was out, if not actually planned in concert with the Danish King, were doubtless at least undertaken in the hope of being supported by Danish help. William had to struggle against enemies in the West as well as in the North, and this danger from various points may account for the place where we next hear of him, one which otherwise seems somewhat strangely chosen. When the Danes actually drew near, William was engaged in hunting in the forest of Dean, in the part of Gloucestershire west of Severn.[1] Fond as William was of the craft of the woods, he was the least likely of all men to let his sport stand in the way of his interest. Strangely chosen as the place seems for a prince who had to withstand the invasion of an enemy on his eastern coast, it was a good central point for watching the movements which soon broke forth on each side of him, and which had most likely already given signs of their coming.

*William in the forest of Dean*

*Probable motives for his presence there.*

The Danish fleet did not at once make for that part of England where it was most sure of a hearty welcome. It might have seemed the wisest as well as the most direct course if the deliverers had steered straight to the mouth of the Humber. Instead of so doing, whether by the orders of King Swend or by the discretion of their immediate commanders, they began their work by a series of attacks on various points in the south-east of England In these, as it turned out, they simply lost time, strength, and credit.[2] Their first attack was on Dover, where Harold's castle on the rock had been so vainly assaulted by Count Eustace.[3] We have not the same detailed account of this enterprise as we have of the former one, and we hear nothing of the feelings either of the men of Dover or of the men of Kent in general. But it seems that Odo,

*Course of the Danish fleet*

*Unsuccessful attack on Dover,*

---

[1] Ord Vit 513 C. "Rex autem Guillelmus tunc in Danâ silvâ erat, ibique pro more venatui vacabat."

[2] From the Chronicles and Florence we learn nothing of the course of the Danish fleet till its appearance in the Humber, the accounts of these unsuccessful attempts in other parts of England come from Orderic, who is probably following William of Poitiers

[3] See above, p 114.

252    CONQUEST OF WESTERN AND NORTHERN ENGLAND.

CHAP XVIII or Hugh of Montfort, or whoever was in immediate command, was able to drive back the invaders with the troops which he found at his disposal.[1] A like repulse followed on an attempt which was next made on Sandwich.[2] The Danes now sailed northward for the once Danish land of East-Anglia. As the fleet of the earlier Thurkill had done fifty-nine years before, they entered the estuary of the Stour and Gippen, and landed near Ipswich, not far from the scene of Ulfcytel's battle of Ringmere.[3] This time we are distinctly told that they betook themselves to plunder, and that they were driven back with the loss of thirty men, not by a Norman garrison, but by the people of the country.[4] It is plain that we are here reading, not of any serious attempt on the part of the whole fleet, but of an isolated repulse which fell on some isolated, perhaps unauthorized, band of plunderers. An attempt on Norwich which followed was a much more important enterprise, and one much more likely to have been deliberately planned. One of the reasons which led William to place that great city for a time under the command of his trustiest friend was the ease with which succours from Denmark might be received there.[5] But William Fitz-Osbern was no longer in command in the East; his services had been called for in the West and in the North, wherever in short the power of his friend was most in danger. The man who now commanded at Norwich, and who was already or soon afterwards invested

and on Sandwich

A plundering party defeated near Ipswich

Attack on Norwich repulsed by Ralph of Wader

[1] Ord. Vit 513 C. "Appulsos Doveram regiorum militum occursus reppulit"

[2] Ib "Itidem apud Sandguicum abacti sunt, sed a Normannis repulsi sunt"

[3] See vol 1 p 378

[4] Ord Vit u s. "Nacti opportunitatem egrediendi apud Gepesuicum in prædam diffusi sunt, sed *provinciales* congregati triginta necaverunt et reliquos in effugium coegerunt" The "provinciales" seems here to stand in contrast to the "Normanni" and "regni milites" of the other entries          [5] See above, p 67

with the East-Anglian Earldom, was the renegade native of the shire, Ralph of Wader.[1] We do not read that matters came so far as to an actual assault on the city; it would rather seem that Ralph attacked the Danes while they were still in disorder, perhaps while they were scattered in search of plunder. Some were slain by the sword; others perished in the waters of the river, of the Yare or the Wensum; the remnant were driven in shameful flight to their ships.[2]

The beginnings of the expedition were thus very far from auspicious. But it should be borne in mind that, of all these Kentish and East-Anglian skirmishes, we have only Norman accounts. As the fleet drew near to what must have been all along the main object of the enterprise, we again get the help of our own writers.[3] Early in September the fleet entered the Humber.[4] The day of its appearance was exactly the third anniversary of the day when King Harold of England had been driven to disband the troops with which he was guarding the southern coast;[5] it must have been very near the third anniversary of the day when the Landwaster of Harold of Norway was first seen in the same waters.[6] But now the Raven of Denmark came on an errand of deliverance, and men flocked from every side to welcome English exiles and Danish

*CHAP XVIII*

*The fleet enters the Humber.*
*September 8, 1069*

---

[1] See vol iii pp 459, 751.

[2] Ord. Vit 513 C. "Egressos Northguici ad similem discursionem Radulfus de Guader invasit, et multis ferro, multis aquâ, vitam ademit, et reliquos turpiter navigium arripientes in pelagus abire compulit"

[3] The accounts in the Chronicles and in Florence give the same general facts, but Florence attends much more strictly to chronological order That his account is copied by Simeon with only a few additions is the best proof of its trustworthiness

[4] "Betwyx þam twam Sēa Marian mæssan," says the Peterborough Chronicle (1069) "Ante Nativitatem S Mariæ" in Florence.

[5] See vol iii p 338

[6] The battle of Fulford was fought on September 20 See vol iii p 350

254          CONQUEST OF WESTERN AND NORTHERN ENGLAND.

CHAP XVIII. allies. All Northumberland rose to meet them, and men
The English join the Danes. came even from distant shires to join the muster. As in so many other cases, the Norman Survey preserves to us the name of a single man, who was doubtless only one man
Scalpin of Essex. among many. A former Housecarl of King Harold, attached to him doubtless in the early days of his East-Anglian government, whose name in French ears sounded as Scalpin, left the lands in Essex which William had allowed him to keep and died at York as an outlaw.[1] Men too of higher rank and fame pressed to join the host
The fleet joined by Eadgar and the English exiles. of the deliverers. While the Danish fleet was still in the estuary, it was joined by a reinforcement of ships, sailing no doubt mainly from the havens of Scotland, which carried the exiles who had taken refuge at the court of Malcolm.[2] They had been already joined by many of the chief men of the land, who eagerly threw off their

[1] In Domesday, ii 59, among the lands of Geoffrey of Mandeville in Essex, we find the following entry, "Istud quoque manerium T R E dedit Esgarus Haroldo, et Heroldus iterum dedit cuidam suo huscarlo nomine Scalpino, et iste Scalpinus dedit uxori suæ in dote, videntibus iibus hominibus, scilicet Rogero Marescalco et quodam Anglico Et hoc testatur hundreda, quod audierunt recognoscere Scalpino, et postquam Rex venit in hanc terram tenuit ipse, donec ivit ubi mortuus fuit in Ebroicâ in utlagariâ"

"Ebroica" ought to mean Evreux, but the name is often confounded with "Eboracum," and Evreux would be a strange place of shelter for an English exile. One can hardly doubt that Scalpin, or whatever his real name was, fought and died in this Yorkshire campaign But the entry has an interest of another kind, the grant of lands by Esegar to Harold would seem to connect itself with the transfer of Tofig's Waltham estate to Harold See vol. ii p 441

[2] That the English leaders came by sea is distinctly implied by Florence, 1069, "Suani . filii . . . in ostio Humbræ fluminis applicuerunt, ubi eis clito Eadgarus, comes Waltheofus et Marleswein, multique alii, cum classe quam congregaverant, occurrerunt" The chronology of Orderic (513 D) is less clear, though he well describes the nature of the great estuary, "Jam Adelinus, Guallevus, Siguardus, aliique præpotentes Angli ad Danos contulerant se. Perventum est ad Humbræ lati fluminis ostium" Wherever Waltheof and some of the others got their ships, those which brought Eadgar and his companions must have come from Scotland.

allegiance to William. A band of men of the noblest blood of England, the descendants of ancient Kings and ancient Earls, were gathered together on board the fleet of confederated Denmark and Northumberland. Thither came the Ætheling Eadgar, once more to try the chances of the last representative of the House of Cerdic. Thither came Gospatric with the forces of his Northern Earldom, the men of the still independent England beyond the Tees, proud no doubt of the slaughter of their would be Norman Earl, prouder probably that the aim of Saint Cuthberht had been stretched forth to save them from the wrath of William himself.[1] Thither came the exiled Mærleswegen to win back his own, and Archill, who thus jeoparded all that he had gained by his former submission to the stranger.[2] Thither came Siward the son of Æthelgar, repenting of the homage which he had done to the newly crowned Conqueror in his court at Barking.[3] Thither came the four sons of Carl, the treacherous slayer of Earl Ealdred in the lawless days of the sons of Cnut.[4] And thither came the representative of the house most hostile to theirs, the grandson of the murdered Earl, cloaking his deadly feud while they marched together on their common enterprise. Waltheof the son of Siward, the Earl of Northampton and Huntingdon, came now to join the

---

[1] Chron Wig 1069 "And heom com þær togenes Eadgar cild and Waldþeof eorl and Mærleswegen and Gospatric eorl mid Norðhymbrum and ealle þa landleoden" On Gospatric, see above, pp 134, 195

I conceive that "Norðymbrum" is here to be taken in the narrower sense, as it seems to be opposed to the "landleoden," that is doubtless the men of Yorkshire, and perhaps those of Lindesey. To the list already given by Orderic (note 2 on the last page) he afterwards adds, "Gaius Patritius [Gospatric], Marius Suevus [Mærleswegen], Elnocinus [whom I cannot identify], Archillus, et quatuor filii Karoli"

[2] See above, p. 205

[3] See above, p 21 I suppose he is the same as the Siward Bearn of whom we shall hear presently.

[4] See vol. i p 586

256        CONQUEST OF WESTERN AND NORTHERN ENGLAND.

CHAP XVIII. forces which were leagued to deliver the land of his fathers.[1]

Previous career and character of Waltheof. Difficulties and contradictions in his character.

I have more than once incidentally noticed that a certain obscurity hangs over the actions of Waltheof up to this moment. An obscurity of the like kind hangs over his whole character. As the victim of the Norman King, as the last Englishman who held a high secular office under his government, as the one man whom, in the whole course of his reign, William sent to the scaffold on a political charge,[2] he won the abiding love of Englishmen. And that love took the usual form; in accordance with the invariable feeling of the age, the patriot was enrolled, by the popular voice at least, in the list of saints and martyrs. Yet, when we look at the recorded acts of Waltheof, it is not very easy to see why he should have drawn to himself in so high a degree either the love of his own people or the fear or hatred of the Norman. His political conduct was lacking in steadfastness; his reputation as a soldier rests wholly on a single display of personal strength and personal daring; his government of his Earldom was stained by at least one frightful crime, and the two or three acts of his private life which ooze out from incidental sources are, if not specially criminal, at least not specially honourable. His liberality to the Church is undoubted,[3] and the accounts

[1] It is worth notice that the words of the Peterborough Chronicler, "þa ferde se eorl Walþeaf ut," are the same as those that are applied in 1067 to the going out of Eadgar and the others. Waltheof "went out," he left William's court, allegiance and protection, and joined the outlaws and insurgents. It is essentially the same expression as " being *out* in the '45"

[2] See vol ii p 266.

[3] Orderic (536 B) thus describes his general character, "Erat idem vir corpore magnus et elegans, et largitate, et audaciâ multis millibus præstans Devotus Dei cultor sacerdotum, et omnium religiosorum, supplex auditor, Ecclesiæ pauperumque benignus amator, pro his et multis aliis charismatibus quibus in ordine laicali specialiter fruebatur a suis et ab extens

which we have of his later days seem to point to a tenderness of conscience, to a feeling of more than formal religion, which we should hardly have looked for in a man whose hands were undoubtedly stained with innocent blood. Yet on the other hand, even with regard to ecclesiastical property, we find him engaged in one of those transactions of doubtful honesty, which were of no very deep dye according to the practice of the time, but which, like some of the doings of Eadward himself,[1] are not exactly what we should look for in a saint and martyr. The benefactor of Crowland stands charged, on what seems to be trustworthy evidence, of detaining lands to which Saint Peter of the Golden Borough had a lawful claim.[2] Altogether we hardly see why, apart from his

*His dispute with Peterborough Abbey*

qui Deo placita diligere nôrunt multum diligebatur." Afterwards, in 542 C, he speaks of Waltheof's gifts to the church of Crowland, and the help he gave in rebuilding the minster

[1] See vol. ii p 551

[2] This is the business referred to in vol ii p 374 The gifts of Godgifu, the step-mother of Waltheof be it observed, not his own mother Æthelflæd, to the Abbey of Peterborough were detained by Siward after her death for his own life by consent of the convent, "Deprecatus est Siwardus Comes Abbatem Leofricum et fratres ut quamdiu viveret posset habere supradictas villas, et post illius decessum reverterentur ad monasterium" On the death of Siward however the lands were still not made over to the Abbey An agreement was made in the presence of Eadward ("facta est conventio ante Regem Eadwardum inter Walðeof filium supradicti Comitis et Leofricum Abbatem"), by which Waltheof received five marks of gold, and was to keep one of the lordships for life, while the other went at once to the Abbey After the death of Eadward—the usual Domesday euphemism for "during the reign of Harold"—this agreement was broken by Waltheof, seemingly by his taking possession of both lordships, "Hoc actum est apud Regem publice, sed post mortem Regis fracta est conventio ab ipso Walðeofo" Afterwards, moved by penitence, he himself came to the monastery and gave the lands to Saint Peter on the condition that he himself should keep them for life It was especially provided that they should not be forfeited by any act of their temporary owner, "nec terras proprio reatu perdere potest" The story is given in a deed printed in Cod. Dipl. iv. 265, which was evidently drawn up while Waltheof was still in possession, but the lands spoken of, Ryhall and Belmesthorp in

CHAP XVIII death, he should have so specially commanded the love of his countrymen. We hardly see why William should first have raised him to a degree of rank and personal favour high above all other Englishmen, and then have so heavily visited in him an offence far lighter than many offences which he had forgiven.

*Probable balance of qualities in his character.*
But in the men of those days much inconsistency of character must be looked for, and must be excused. Waltheof was clearly not a deliberate and systematic traitor, like Eadric or Eadwine. Neither was he a hero like Harold, whose very greatness leads us, whenever he goes astray, to judge him by a harsher rule than that by which we judge meaner men.[1] We shall perhaps best understand the contradictions in the character of Waltheof, if we look on him as a man governed mainly by impulse, a man in whom noble and generous elements were but little strengthened by real stability of purpose. In such a man in such an age we need not wonder that particular acts of crime could go along with early good impressions which never wholly forsook him.[2] In such a man we do not wonder at much political wavering and inconsistency; we do not wonder at finding that the daring of the mere soldier did not rise into the higher courage either of the general or of the statesman. But, whatever judgement we pass upon Waltheof, it is at this stage that his historical life begins. His presence or absence at Senlac is, as we have seen, utterly doubtful.[3] The only fully ascertained act of his former life is that he accompanied William on his first voyage to Normandy.[4] It is plain

Northamptonshire, appear in Domesday (228) in possession of Waltheof's widow Judith without any account of their former history.

[1] See vol ii p. 319

[2] When in prison he daily repeated the Psalms of David, "quos in infantiâ didicerat," so says Orderic, 536 B

[3] See above, p. 21, and vol iii. p. 424.

[4] See above, p. 75

that he had retained his Earldom, and the silence of all our authorities seems to show that he had taken no share in any of the earlier movements against William. But now the son of Siward, the heir of Ealdred, brought the strength of his great name and the might of his strong arm, backed doubtless by the force of the two shires over which he ruled, to join the men of his native Earldom in welcoming the deliverers of England.

It is not plain at what stage of its voyage the tidings of the approach of the Danish fleet was brought to King William in the forests of Gloucestershire. The only historian who tells us anything in detail about his movements makes him hear the news immediately after the unsuccessful attack on Norwich. But we can hardly doubt that earlier messengers must have told him of the appearance of the Danes off Dover, Sandwich, and Ipswich. But their repulse from Norwich, and no doubt other movements also, now made William see where the real danger from the invaders lay. The revolt of Waltheof, whether he set forth from William's own presence or from his own home at Northampton, was of itself the most marked sign of what was coming. It was York and all Northumberland that was threatened. Still William did not leave his quarters in the West; he was doubtless carefully watching the movements which were soon to break out on each side of him. But he sent a messenger to York, bidding his garrisons there stand firmly on their defence, and call at once for his own presence if it should be needed. As we hear no more of William Fitz-Osbern, he had doubtless left what could have been meant only as a temporary command [1] The Norman commanders in York were William Malet the Sheriff and the Fleming Gilbert of Ghent. They either overrated the strength of their

[1] See above, p 241

CHAP XVIII

Confidence of William Malet and Gilbert of Ghent.

own walls and of their own troops, or else they greatly underrated the force which was coming against them. They sent word to William that they could hold out for a whole year without calling on him for further help.[1] This message, it appears, was actually sent after Waltheof, Eadgar, and the rest had joined the Danish fleet in the Humber.[2] York was seemingly about as well guarded now by its Norman oppressors against Scandinavian deliverers as it had been guarded three years before by its chosen Earl against Scandinavian invaders.

Stories of Archbishop Ealdred.

But the news which fell so lightly on the ears of the Norman commanders in York told a very different tale in the ears of the English Archbishop. Ealdred, the Primate who had crowned both Harold and William, has appeared in our history as one who had done his best to keep his province in the obedience of the foreign King.[3] But his later days are surrounded by a crowd of stories, in some at least of which it is hard not to suspect the presence of a legendary element. One tale has already shown him, in his character of guardian of the church of Worcester, as withstanding the terrible Sheriff of that shire, Urse of Abetot.[4] Another tale more directly concerns his later diocese, and, if it ever happened at all, it could not have happened long before the time which we have now reached. In this story Ealdred appears clothed with a higher mission, as daring to rebuke, not a subordinate officer, however high in rank, but the mighty Conqueror himself. Ealdred, we are told, was present in his metropolitan city on one of the feasts of the Church, by which must be meant either

---

[1] Ord. Vit 513 C "Illic [in Danâ silvâ] audito adventu Dacorum, statim nuntium direxit Eboracum, monens eos ut sese cautius in eos præpararent, ipsumque, si forte necessitas posceret, advocarent Remandaverunt custodes præsidiorum non indigeri subventu ejus ad annum."

[2] Orderic adds, "*Jam* Adelinus &c ad Danos *contulerant* se."

[3] See above, p 186.      [4] See above, p 175

the Christmas of the last year, or the Easter or Pentecost of the present.[1] A large stock of all manner of good things was being brought into the city from the episcopal lands in its neighbourhood. It chanced that the Sheriff— William Malet must be meant—was at that moment going out of York with a large company. At a short distance from the city he met the Archbishop's horses and waggons bringing in wheat and other meats for the feast. The Sheriff asked the drivers who they were, and for whom they were bringing those good things. They answered that they were the servants of the Archbishop, and were bringing in the things which were needful for his service. The Sheriff, caring little for the Archbishop or his servants, bade his own followers seize on the whole of the stores and carry them to the King's storehouse in the castle. When the news was brought to Ealdred, he sent messengers, clerks and citizens, to the Sheriff, and bade him restore the stolen property and make good the loss to Saint Peter and to himself as his Vicar. Otherwise he would at once go on to wield his spiritual weapons against him.[2] As no satisfaction was to be had, but as the Archbishop's messengers were driven away with threats and insults, the high-spirited Primate made up his mind to go at once and lay his complaints in person before the King. He went to London, where William then was. His coming is said to have caused some stir in the city,

*Pentecost, 1069?*

*Ealdred plundered by William Malet*

*William Malet refuses restitution.*

*Ealdred goes to London*

---

[1] T. Stubbs, Act Pont Ebor X Scriptt 1703 "Morabatur in unâ sollennitatum Eboraci" If there be any truth at all in the story, the feast must be one of the three mentioned in the text, as they are the only three of the greatest festivals of the Church which come between William's first occupation of York in 1068 and Ealdred's death in 1069

[2] Ib. "Ille sine morâ legatos cum clericis et civibus post vice-comitem dirigens, mandavit ei ut sua sibi redderet et Sancto Petro sibique ejus vicario satisfaceret, alioquin sciret ipsum de tam contumeliosâ injuriâ deinceps pontificaliter acturum" There is a certain satisfaction to English feeling in finding the Vicar of Saint Peter not at Rome but at York.

and the Norman Bishop William, with a crowd of clergy and people, came to meet him with all due honour. They went first to pray in the episcopal church of Saint Paul, and then to the Abbey of Saint Peter, hard by which William was dwelling in Eadward's palace of Westminster.[1] Ealdred entered the royal presence in his pontifical robes, and with his staff in his hand. William rose to greet him with the kiss of peace, but the English Primate refused the greeting; he stood still, and spoke to William in words such as the Conqueror was not wont to hear. "Hear me, King William. When thou wast a stranger, and when God in his wrath against the sins of our nation granted to thee to win with much blood the Kingdom of all Britain,[2] I hallowed thee to King, I gave thee my blessing, and set the crown upon thy head. Now, because thy deeds call for it, I give thee my curse instead of my blessing, as to a persecutor of the Church of God, an oppressor of her ministers, as one who hast broken the promises and oaths which thou didst swear to me before the altar of Saint Peter." William, we are told, trembled, as he had once before trembled in the presence of the man who now stood before him.[3] He fell—can we believe the tale?—at the feet of Ealdred and asked what he had done that such a sentence should pass upon him. The great men who

---

[1] T Stubbs, 1703 "Moxque episcopus illius civitatis cum multitudine cleri et populi ei, ut tanto debeat pontifici, obviam pergens orationis gratiâ, primo ad ecclesiam Sancti Pauli, deinde ad ecclesiam Sancti Petri Westmonasterii ubi Rex erat, eum honorifice comitatus est." The King's presence at Westminster seems to point to Pentecost as the feast intended If so, it must be the Pentecost of 1069

[2] Ib "Audi, inquit, Willhelme Rex, quum esses alienigena, et Deo permittente nostræque gentis superbiam puniente, regnum Britanniæ, quamvis multo cum sanguine, obtinuisses, ego te in Regem consecravi et coronam capiti tuo cum benedictione imposui"

[3] Ib 1704 "Ad hæc verba Rex tremefactus procidit ad pedes ejus, humiliter efflagitans ut in quo tam gravem sententiam meruisset aperiret" Cf. vol iii p 560

stood around began to assail the Primate with threats, and to cry out that the man who offered such an insult to the King should be at once banished from the realm.[1] They bade him at once raise the King from the ground, but Ealdred answered, "Good men, let him lie there; he lies not at my feet, but at the feet of Saint Peter, who has done wrong to Saint Peter's Vicar."[2] He then raised William from the ground, he told him his wrongs, and graciously accepted the royal prayer that his blessing might not be turned into a curse. Ealdred went home in safety and honour, and one of the highest nobles of William's court was sent with letters by virtue of which everything, even to the cords which tied the sacks of corn, was faithfully restored to the Archbishop, and from that day no man dared to wrong him any more.[3]

Such is the tale of Ealdred's daring, as it stands in the local records of the church of York. The tale hangs lamely together, but the scene in the King's court is boldly conceived, and, though no doubt romantic in its details, it at least bears witness to the abiding English spirit of those who loved to conceive the Norman Conqueror grovelling at the feet of a man of English birth. In what can hardly fail to be another version of the same tale, the conduct of Ealdred is clothed with a higher moral

*Estimate of the tale*

---

[1] T. Stubbs, 1704 "Ipsum merito de medio debere tolli, vel in exsilium extra regnum expelli, qui tanto Regi tantam injuriam irrogasset" "De medio tolli" is an idea fitter for the time of Stubbs than for the time of Ealdred He carries on his history only to 1373 Could he have lived to see the fate of Archbishop Scrope?

[2] Ib "Sinite, inquit, boni viri, sinite illum jacere, non enim jacet ad pedes Aldredi sed ad pedes Petri apostoli Debet enim experiri Petri potentiam, qui non est veritus Petri vicario irrogare injuriam" Is not this story formed after the model of the legendary humiliation of Frederick Barbarossa before Alexander the Third? See Milman, Latin Christianity, iii 536

[3] Ib "Itaque ab illo die nullus potentium ausus fuit aliquam sibi vel suis injuriam inferre vel contumeliam"

264    CONQUEST OF WESTERN AND NORTHERN ENGLAND.

CHAP XVIII  dignity, as he steps in to avenge not a private wrong of his own, but the general oppression of his people. It is hard however to fit in the tale with the known chronology of William's reign. As long, we are told, as the new King ruled with any show of moderation, so long Ealdred showed towards him the reverence due to a King.[1] But when he laid an unbearable tax on the people, then Ealdred sent messengers to remonstrate. We are not told whether this refers to any of the general exactions of which we have already heard, but which could hardly have touched Ealdred's diocese, or whether we are to suppose some special local burthen levied after the conquest of York.[2] In either case the messengers of the Archbishop were driven away with scorn. Ealdred then put forth a solemn curse against the King and all his offspring. He had once, he said, blessed him wrongfully, he would now curse him rightfully.[3] The news of the anathema was brought to William, devotion or policy moved him; he sent messengers to Ealdred, craving that the curse might be taken off. But before they could reach the presence of the English Primate, his soul had passed away from this world. There was no voice to speak the words of absolution, and

*In another version Ealdred withstands the imposition of a tax*

*Ealdred pronounces a curse on William, and dies before it is taken off.*

---

[1] Will. Malm. Gest Pont X 252 After mentioning the oath which William had sworn to Ealdred at his coronation (see vol iii. p 560), including a promise "quod se modeste erga subjectos ageret, et æquo jure Anglos quo Francos tractaret," he goes on, "itaque illum quamdiu erga suos temperiem habuit, dilexit ut prolem, veneratus est ut Regem." One would like to know the number of months or weeks that this feeling lasted

[2] Ib. "Sed quum importabilis tributi pensum a provincialibus exigeret, convenit eum per legatum antistes" On William's early exactions, see above, pp 22, 59, 128 The word "provinciales" looks as if it referred to Ealdred's own part of England, but it does not amount to absolute proof

[3] Ib "Non moratus ille maledictionis telum in illum in omnem ejus vibravit progeniem, præfatus posse se maledictionem dare merito qui benedictionem dedisset immerito."

we are left to suppose that the curse of Ealdred took its effect in the misfortunes which clouded the later days of William, and in the mysterious doom by which all the male descendants of his house were swept from the earth within seventy years after Ealdred had placed the Crown of England on his brow.[1]

Whatever may be the exact amount of truth and falsehood in these tales, their real value lies in their showing the strength of popular feeling, and not only the strength but the permanence of local popular feeling. All the faults and doubtful actions of Ealdred were forgiven; York and Worcester alike were ready then, and ages after, to canonize the Prelate who had dared to defy the stranger in the cause of his Church and country. And such tales could hardly have gained popular belief, unless there had been something in Ealdred's real conduct to form a groundwork for the story. We need not believe that William really crouched at the feet of Ealdred; we need not even believe that Ealdred put forth a formal curse against William. But we can hardly doubt that some remonstrance against wrong, some expression of sorrow for his own hasty acknowledgement of the invader, was uttered by the English Primate in his last days. At all events, we know that his heart was smitten with fear and sorrow at the coming woes which the struggle which was about to begin was sure to bring upon his people. The man who had traversed well nigh the whole of the known world on errands of policy and devotion, the man who had stood before Pope and Cæsar, and who

[1] In this version the death of Ealdred seems to be attributed to grief caused by these dealings with William, "Verumtamen prævenerat nuntios mors antistis, qui ex ægritudine animi, ut plerumque fit, contracto morbo decubuerat et obierat"

On the difficulties arising from a Bishop dying or resigning before he had withdrawn a malediction, see the story of the Emperor Andronikos Palaiologos and the Patriarch Athanasios, Finlay, Byz Emp ii 471.

had placed the Crown on the head alike of Harold and of William, could not bear up against the sorrows which were in store. His strength gave way, and he prayed to be taken away from the evil to come. His prayer was heard. The English and Danish fleets had already met in the Humber, but their banners had not yet been seen beneath the walls of York, when a tomb within the minster of Saint Peter closed on the body of the last Primate of Northhumberland of the old stock.[1]

Meanwhile the confederate fleets were in the Humber. The only recorded detail of what befel them there is a single anecdote, telling how the Ætheling Eadgar left the main body with a small company, the crew of a single ship, to plunder on the coast of Lindesey. They were attacked by the Norman garrison at Lincoln; the whole party, save the Ætheling and two comrades, were taken; the ship, forsaken by those who were left to guard it, was seized and destroyed.[2] Such an adventure was an evil omen; but it was nothing more. The fleet sailed on; we are not told at what point of the Ouse the troops disembarked,[3] but it is plain that the most obvious approach to York from any convenient landing-place would lead them along the left bank of the river, over the former battle-ground of Fulford.[4] This road would bring them

---

[1] The Worcester Chronicle (1069) seems to put the death of Ealdred before the Danish fleet entered the Humber, but it is plain, from the more careful order of Florence, that it happened between their appearance in the Humber and their approach to York.

[2] Ord. Vit. 513 D "Adelinus ibi [in ostio Humbræ] seorsum ab sociâ turbâ cum quibusdam suorum prædatum ierat Quos insiliens familia Regis e Lincolniâ cepit omnes, exceptis duobus cum Adelino elapsis, et navim confregit quam custodia pavens deseruit"

[3] I do not know that the words of Florence, "Danica classis supervenit," need imply that they actually sailed up to York, and the description in the Chronicles is that of an army marching by land

[4] See vol iii p 350

at once upon the elder of the two castles. It was indeed guarded by the stream of the Foss, but, even if the bridge did not already exist, the crossing of so small a stream was a hindrance which might easily be overcome. It is plain that the castles were the first object of attack, and, if the fleet or any part of it did sail up to York, it would be the castles which they would first come upon as barring their course. Before the Danes reached the city, the whole country poured forth to join their banners. Men went on with all joy, walking and riding. A host that could not be numbered, pressing on with one heart and one soul, came within sight of the warders of the Norman castles.[1] Their captains had boasted that they could defend themselves for a whole year without help from William; but they soon found that such a boast was vain indeed. They looked for a siege, and their first thought was to hinder the besiegers from filling up the ditches of the castle and so finding a more ready approach to the walls. Lest the houses near the castle should be used for this purpose, the Normans had recourse to their favourite element. They set fire to the houses in their own immediate neighbourhood. The flames spread, the greater part of the city was destroyed, and the fire even seized upon the metropolitan church in the opposite quarter.[2] Whether

*CHAP XVIII*

*General zeal of the people*

*The city fired by the Normans September 19, 1069.*

---

[1] The description in the Worcester Chronicle (1069) is most graphic. The Ætheling and the Earls and Thegns have come, "and ealle þa landleoden, ridende and gangende [compare Rolf's surname of *Ganger*], mit unmætan here, swiðe fægengende, and swa ealle anrædlice to Eoferwic foron."

[2] The Worcester Chronicler would seem to imply a wilful desecration of the minster, "And ærþan þe þa scypmenn þider comon, hæfdon þa Freciscan þa burh forbærned, and eac þæt halie mynster Sc̃us Petrus eall forhergod and forbærned." But Florence seems to make the burning of the minster accidental. "Normanni qui castella custodiebant, timentes ne domus quæ prope castella erant adjumenta Danis ad implendas fossas castellorum essent, igne eas succendere cœperunt, qui nimis excrescens totam civitatem invasit, monasteriumque Sancti Petri cum ipsâ consumpsit."

268    CONQUEST OF WESTERN AND NORTHERN ENGLAND.

CHAP XVIII  
The Danes and English reach York September 21.

this sacrilege was intentional or unwitting, it was speedily avenged. Two days later, while it would seem that the flames were still blazing, but while the city was not yet wholly destroyed, the host drew nigh which was to save it from its foreign masters.[1] The Earls Waltheof and Gospatric, and the chief Thegns who had joined the army, led the way; the whole force of Denmark and North-

The garrisons sally and are cut to pieces

humberland followed. The garrisons ventured on a sally, and a fight followed within the walls of the burning city.[2]

Personal exploits of Waltheof

And now it was that, for one moment, Waltheof the son of Siward and Æthelflæd stood forth as the hero of deeds which handed down his name in the warlike songs of the tongues of both his parents. We hear again the old ring of the lays of Brunanburh, of Maldon, and of Stamfordbridge,[3] as we listen to the tale which speaks of the giant form of the Northumbrian Earl, his mighty arms, his sinewy breast; how he stood by the gate as the enemy pressed forth, and how, as each Norman drew nigh, a head rolled on the earth beneath the unerring sweep of the Danish battle-axe.[4] Three thousand of the

---

The Winchester Annalist (28) somewhat unfairly transfers the blame of the burning to the Danes, "Beornus Comes [see above, p 248] post alia quæ regno intulit mala cepit, Eboracum et interfecit viros, et domos combussit"

[1] Flor. Wig 1069 "Sed hoc ultione divinâ citissime in eis vindicatum est gravissime Nam priusquam tota civitas esset combusta Danica classis supervenit feriâ ii."

[2] Ord Vit 513 D. "Castellani obviam eis inconsultius exeunt, et intra urbis mœnia infeliciter confligunt. Non valentes resistere multitudini omnes interimuntur aut capiuntur"

[3] The account in William of Malmesbury, iii 253, which appears again in the Vita et Passio Waldevi Comitis (Chron Angl Norm iii 111), as plainly comes from a ballad as anything in Henry of Huntingdon. We have also the verses of Thorkill Skallason which I shall quote directly.

[4] Will Malms u s "Siquidem Weldeofus in Eboracensi pugnâ plures Normannorum solus obtruncaverat, unos et unos per portas egredientes decapitans, nervosus lacertis, torosus pectore, robustus et procerus toto corpore, filius Siwardi magnificentissimi comitis, quem Digera Danico vocabulo, id est fortem, cognominabant."

strangers died that day[1] A hundred of the chiefest in rank were said to have fallen among the flames by the hand of Waltheof himself, and the scalds of the North sang how the son of Siward gave the corpses of the Frenchmen as a choice banquet for the wolves of Northhumberland.[2] The tale stirs the blood like the tale of the last victory of Harold by the banks of Derwent. In either case we mourn that the strength, and valour, and victory of Englishmen brought no lasting safety to their country. But Harold did all that mortal man could do, and yielded only to a destiny that was too strong for him. The men who smote the Normans in the gate at York threw away the victory that they had gained by the inveterate habits of plunder and lack of discipline.

*Fruitlessness of the victory*

But for the moment all seemed triumphant The Norman garrison of York was utterly cut off. Of the men who had held city and shire in dread a few only were saved alive as prisoners. Among these were the two commanders, Gilbert of Ghent and William Malet, together with William's wife and two children.[3] The two

*Gilbert of Ghent and William Malet spared as prisoners*

---

[1] Flor. Wig. 1069 "Plus tribus milibus ex Normannis trucidatis" The two Chroniclers say only, "fela hund manna Frenciscra þær ofslogon"

[2] The story in the Saga of Harold Hardrada (Johnston, 218, Laing, iii 95) about Waltheof burning a hundred Frenchmen in a wood after the battle of Senlac seems to me to be simply moved to this fight among the burning ruins at York Anyhow the verses of Thorkill Skallason are spirited,

"Hundrat let í heitom        Frett er at firdar knátto
Hirdmenn iofurs brenna       Flagd viggs und kló liggia
Sóknar yggr enn seggiom      Imleitom fechz áta
Svido kvelld var þat elldi.  Ols black vid hræ Fracka"

This ἑκατομφονία of Waltheof is more easily to be believed than the two thousand men killed by William, see vol iii p 509

[3] The Peterborough Chronicler says, "And þa heafodmen hæfdon on beandon" In Florence and Simeon (85, Hinde) we get the names, "Willelmo Malet [qui tunc vicecomitatum gerebat, Sim ] cum suâ conjuge et duobus liberis [et Gileberto de Gant, Sim ] aliisque per paucis vitæ reservatis" The captivity of William Malet is also mentioned in Domesday (374). It

270   CONQUEST OF WESTERN AND NORTHERN ENGLAND.

CHAP XVIII
The castles destroyed

castles were broken down.[1] An enlightened policy might perhaps have bidden the victors to spare the fortresses, and to turn them to their own purposes against the enemy. But every passion of the moment pleaded the other way. Wherever a Norman castle had been reared, it was the object of the bitterest of all hatred, as the living embodiment of the foreign yoke. We now look on those massive square keeps, wherever they are left to us, as among the most venerable and precious of the antiquities of our land. And venerable and precious they are, now that they stand in ruins as the memorials of a time which has for ever passed away. But when those towers were still newly built, when their square stones were still in their freshness, when the arches of their doors and windows were still sharp and newly cut, they were to our fathers the objects of a horror deeper even than that with which France in the moment of her uprising looked on the Bastille of her ancient Kings. They were the very homes of the Conquest; within their impregnable walls the foe was sheltered; from their gates he came forth to spread fear and havoc through the streets of the city, or through such surrounding lands as still owned an Englishman for their master. In the eyes of the men of those days the castle was an accursed thing, to be swept away from the earth by the stroke of righteous vengeance, as when liberated Syracuse swept away the citadel from which her Tyrants had held her in thraldom.[2] On the very day on which the army

English feeling towards the castles

is said of certain lands in Holderness that William held them "usque Dani ceperunt illum."

[1] Chron Petrib "And þa castelas gewunnan" Chron Wig "And þone castel tobræcon and towurpan" The distinction of the castles is mentioned several times in Domesday, (298), "primo anno post destructionem castellorum, (373), "antequam castellum captum fuisset," "donec invasum est castellum," "donec fractum est castellum"

[2] Plut Timoleon, 22 "Ἐκήρυξε τῶν Συρακουσίων τὸν βουλόμενον παρεῖναι μετὰ σιδήρου καὶ συνεφάπτεσθαι κατασκαπτομένων τῶν τυραννικῶν ἐρυμάτων.

reached York the two castles were broken down.[1]  We are not to suppose that the whole of the massive walls of two Norman keeps could be razed to the ground in the afternoon of a day of battle.  But they were doubtless dismantled, breached, and left in a ruined state, so that they could not, for some while at least, be again used as places of defence.[2]  Thus, between friends and enemies, York had become a mass of ruins.  Churches and houses had fallen before the flames kindled by the Normans; the Norman castles had fallen before the hammers and crowbars of liberated Englishmen.  No attempt seems to have been made to occupy the city, or to defend the Roman walls which had not utterly perished.  The work of the moment had been done; the enemy had been swept from the earth; till another day of battle should come, there seemed to be no work on hand save to enjoy the plunder which had been won.  The Danes went back to their ships with their booty; the men of Northumberland, following the common instinct of irregular troops after either a victory or a defeat, went away every man to his own home.[3]

*The Danes and English leave York.*

*The Danes go to their ships, and the English disperse.*

The news of the fall of his castles at York, of the slaughter of their garrisons, and of the capture of their commanders, was presently brought to King William in the West.  He had work on his hands there also.  It is plain that the tidings of the coming of the Danish

*Various movements in the West*

'Ως δὲ πάντες ἀνέβησαν, ἀρχὴν ἐλευθερίας ποιησάμενοι βεβαιοτάτην τὸ κήρυγμα καὶ τὴν ἡμέραν ἐκείνην, οὐ μόνον τὴν ἄκραν, ἀλλὰ καὶ τὰς οἰκίας καὶ τὰ μνήματα τῶν τυράννων ἀνέτρεψαν καὶ κατέσκαψαν."

[1] Flor Wig 1069.  "Castellis eodem die fractis."

[2] Ord Vit 513 D "Castella desolata patent"  I do not know that the words of the English writers need imply more than this

[3] The fullest account is in Simeon's expansion of Florence (85), "Naves Dani cum innumeris manubiis suasque sedes repetierunt Northhymbri"  On the custom of irregular armies dispersing after a battle, see vol 1 p 426

272    CONQUEST OF WESTERN AND NORTHERN ENGLAND.

CHAP XVIII fleet had led to risings in various parts of England, even in shires far away from the banks of the Humber and the shores of the German Ocean. While William was in the Forest of Dean, war again broke out north and south of him. Devonshire and Somerset rose once more, and there were hostile movements in Staffordshire and Shropshire, a district which must have remained very imperfectly subdued up to this time. The men of the West had castles to fight against as well as the men of Yorkshire. I have already told how William's insatiable brother, Robert of Mortain, now Earl of Cornwall and lord of vast estates in all the Western shires, had raised a fortress for the defence of his new possessions. He had raised it on the very height which had beheld the finding of the Holy Rood of Waltham.[1] From the peak which had now taken the name of Montacute, the fortress of the stranger Earl looked down like a vulture's nest on the surrounding hills and on the rich valleys at its foot. Of the castle itself not a stone is left; the present ornaments of the spot, the graceful tower of the parish church, the rich gateway of the fallen priory, the mansion of the latest days of English art, are all things which as yet had no being. But the wooded height still covers the fosses which marked the spot which the men of Somerset and Dorset in those days looked on as, above all others, the house of bondage. In the further West the fortress which had grown up on the Red Mount of Exeter[2] held the men of the once proud commonwealth in fetters. The men of all the Western shires rose by a common impulse. Their zeal now, after so many defeats and harryings of their country, shows how deeply the sons of Harold had erred in trusting to the help of foreign plunderers, instead of boldly throwing themselves on the

The castle of Montacute.

The castle of Exeter

General movement in the Western shires

[1] See above, p 170.            [2] See above, p 161.

patriotism of the people of the *Wealhcyn*. No names of leaders are given us, the movement seems to have been a thoroughly popular one. We read how the West-Saxons of Somerset, Dorset, and the neighbouring districts besieged the castle of Montacute.[1] Meanwhile the men of Devonshire, strengthened by a large force of the Britons of Cornwall, the immediate victims of Robert of Mortain, appeared in arms beneath the walls of Rougemont.[2] To the north, Staffordshire was in arms, and though this is the only movement of which we get no detail, it must have been one specially to be dreaded, as it was the only one which it needed the presence of William himself to quell. On the Welsh border again, the men of both races, British and English, had risen with a common zeal against the common enemy. There the Normans had to strive, not against revolters eager to shake off their dominion, but against men whose necks had never yet been bent to their yoke. The centre of defence in that region was the town of Shrewsbury, once, under the name of Pengwern, the capital of the Welsh Kingdom of Powys, but which the victories of Offa had changed from a bulwark of the Briton against the Englishman into a bulwark of the Englishman against the Briton.[3] No site could be more important, none better fitted either for resistance or for dominion. The town stands on the right, the Welsh, bank of the Severn; but a bold bend of the river makes it occupy a strong peninsular site, which may call to mind the more famous peninsular sites of Bern and Besançon. A narrow isthmus commands the

CHAP XVIII

The men of Somerset and Dorset attack Montacute

The men of Devonshire and Cornwall attack Exeter

Movement in Staffordshire

Movement on the Welsh border

Position of Shrewsbury

---

[1] Ord Vit 514 A "Eo tempore Saxones Occidentales de Dorsetâ et Summersetâ cum suis confinibus Montem Acutum assilierunt"

[2] Ib. "Idem apud Exoniam Exoniensis comitatûs habitatores fecere, et undique coadunatâ turbâ ex Cornu Britanniæ. Nam supremi fines Anglorum occidentem versus et Hiberniam Cornu Britanniæ, id est Cornuallia, nuncupantur."

[3] See vol. 1. p 39, Williams' History of Wales, 11, 116

whole country on both sides of the river, and this neck of land, rising steep above the stream, had doubtless been chosen in earlier, as well as in later, times as the site of the stronghold which was to keep the border land in awe. At what time this important post had fallen into the hands of the Normans we are not told; but it is plain that Shrewsbury was now held by a Norman garrison, and a Norman garrison commonly implied at least the beginnings of a Norman castle. It may be then that Shrewsbury was already bridled by some hasty forerunner of the fortress which was soon to become the centre of the power of the united house of Montgomery and Belesme. At all events, Shrewsbury was now in William's obedience, and a motley host was gathered to assault this new outpost of the strangers Besiegers gathered from all parts, and the English inhabitants of the town itself eagerly joined them in their attack on the Norman fortress. Thither came Eadric the Wild, who had never bowed to the Norman King, with the forces of his own still independent corner of Herefordshire. Thither came the men of still unconquered Chester, where the widow of Harold was perhaps still dwelling with her child, after the treason of her brothers and the overthrow of her step-sons. And from within the Cambrian frontier the subjects of Bleddyn, now the sole King of Gwynedd and Powys, flocked to the call of their old ally. The united forces of so many districts and races now laid siege to the fortress which had arisen on the bank of the great border stream.[1] Meanwhile York was falling, or had already fallen, and the Danish fleet was

---

[1] Ord Vit 514 A. "Gualli et Cestrenses praesidium Regis apud Scrobesburiam obsederunt, quibus incolae civitatis cum Edrico Guilda, potenti et bellicoso viro, ahisque ferocibus Anglis auxilio fuerunt" Rhiwallon, it will be remembered, had died in the civil war (see above, p 183), so that Bleddyn was now sole King

still in the Northumbrian waters. The power of William was threatened on every side, and one might be tempted to think that it needed something like his star to guide him to victory when so many foes were leagued against him.

We should be glad of fuller details than we have of the steps by which all these movements were put down. The account in our single narrative is given with a good deal of confusion [1] But we see that all were put down, and that they were put down without any great difficulty. The story of these campaigns is in many respects the story of the reign of Æthelred over again. There is far from being the same cowardice and treason. We meet with English leaders who are perhaps somewhat hasty in making their peace with the Norman, but we do not read either of armies forsaking their leaders or of leaders forsaking their armies. The rule of Cnut, of Godwine, and of Harold had clearly raised the moral and military tone of the nation. But there is the same local isolation, the same incapacity to form any combined plan of operations, the same general helplessness in the absence of any one chief of the type of Eadmund and Harold. Whatever attachment men had to Waltheof, to Eadric, to the sons of Harold, was mainly local. Eadgar, the one man who might on sentimental grounds have become the centre of loyalty to the whole nation, was utterly unfit for command. Add to this that, while the patriotic English had to struggle with enemies among whom the military science of the age was carried to its highest pitch, their own military resources must have fallen back even below what the resources of the country had been in the days of Æthelred.

*The revolts put down piecemeal*

*State of national feeling*

*Improvement since Æthelred's days*

*Local isolation of the English insurgents*

*Their lack of disciplined soldiers*

---

[1] Our only account of these Western campaigns comes from Orderic (514), who doubtless follows William of Poitiers. The English writers mention only the march against York

276                CONQUEST OF WESTERN AND NORTHERN ENGLAND.

CHAP XVIII  As in the days of Æthelred, there was no national standing
army  In his days the force of the Housecarls had not
yet come into being, and now that force had been swept
away from the earth. Earls like Waltheof and Gospatric
no doubt kept a certain number of armed followers con-
Destruc-  stantly in their pay. But that noble army which had
tion of the
Housecarls  been called into being by Cnut and brought to perfection
at Senlac  by Harold, the army which had overthrown Macbeth and
Gruffydd and Hardrada, had died, man by man, around
the fallen King on Senlac. There was no longer an
English force of which men said in other lands that any
one man therein was a match for any two elsewhere. In
these later enterprises everything had to be trusted to
such a force as the towns and shires could supply of
Compari-  themselves at a moment's call. There was also another
son be-
tween the  wide difference between the two cases. The opposition
resistance
to the  to the Danes was the work of a regular government, which,
Danes and  weak and vicious as it was, was defending territory which
the resist-
ance to the  was actually in its own possession  The opposition to
Normans  the Normans was driven to take the form of isolated
revolts against an established government. It was at most
the defence of isolated pieces of territory in which it
could hardly be said that there was any regular government at all. The men of each district had to rise, how
they could, against those who were in the actual possession
of power in their own districts, and they had little means
of communication with their brethren who were engaged
All the in-  in the same struggle in other parts of the country. They
fluences of
govern-  had to strive against the forms of Law and against the
ment and
discipline  influence of property—Law which was now administered
now on the  by the officers of a foreign King, property which had
Norman
side  passed away into the hands of foreign owners. It was
no longer as in the two great campaigns of Harold,
when the tried and disciplined soldiers of England were
matched against the tried and disciplined soldiers of other

lands It was not even as when the levies of each district CHAP.XVIII.
were called out at the bidding of a power which could
inflict summary penalties on all defaulters. The cowardly,
the sluggish, the prudent, could hold aloof, and would
be serving those actually in power by holding aloof. None
would take part in these desperate enterprises but the
brave and zealous, who were prepared to risk everything
in the cause of freedom. And they had to make the risk,
when the odds, if not of actual numbers, at least of
discipline and regular command, were all on the other
side. An united effort of the whole nation was now
impossible; the last chance of such an effort was lost when
Eadwine and Morkere drew back and left the faithful men
of London to their fate.[1] There was now no room for anything beyond local, desultory, and in truth hopeless, efforts.
The force of the strangers in each district was commonly
strong enough to put down the insurgents in that district.
And it was even possible, by means of those powers which The force
every established government has at its disposal,[2] to use district
the native force of the obedient districts against the dis- employed
tricts which were at any moment in revolt. another.

So it proved at this moment, when so many distant Isolation
parts of England were in arms against William at the same several
time. The forces of the West, of the North, and of the movements
shires on the Welsh border, if they had only been brought in 1069.
together by a common effort under a competent leader,
would have formed a host which it would have cost
William himself some pains to overthrow. As it was,
the disjointed attempts of the insurgents were easily put
down in detail. We do not even hear that the men of
Dorset and Somerset thought of joining their forces with
the men of Devonshire and Cornwall. The besiegers of
Montacute and the besiegers of Exeter were crushed

---

[1] See vol. iii. p. 531.   [2] See above, p. 150.

separately. And in both cases they were partly crushed by English hands. A force was brought to the relief of Montacute under the command of Bishop Geoffrey of Coutances, whose vast grants of land in the West were directly threatened by the insurrection. Against the men of Somerset and Dorset he led the men of London, Winchester, and Salisbury.[1] These words would doubtless take in detachments from the Norman garrisons of those cities. But when we consider the nature of the force which Eadnoth led against the sons of Harold,[2] and of that which William himself led to the first siege of Exeter,[3] it can hardly fail but that Geoffrey also commanded the *fyrd*, the legal English levy, of those towns and of the surrounding shires. The force thus raised was, we are told, especially under the Divine protection,[4] whether because they had a Bishop to their captain is not more fully explained. We have no details of the march or of the operations of the warlike Prelate. We are only told that the force under Geoffrey attacked the English who were besieging Montacute; that they slew some, took others prisoners, and put the rest to flight. The prisoners, according to the martial law of the eleventh century, were punished by mutilation;[5] in the more polished days of Elizabeth or James the Second these forerunners of the followers of Monmouth would hardly have escaped the gibbet or the quartering-block. The suppression of the other revolts is recorded with equal lack of detail, and withal with a good deal of confusion. Earl Brian, whom we have already heard of as defeating

---

[1] Ord. Vit. 514 A. "Guentani, Lundonii, Salesberii, Gaufredo Constantiensi præsule ductore, supervenerunt."

[2] See above, p. 226.   [3] See above, p. 149.

[4] Ord. Vit. u. s. "Divino nutu impediti sunt."

[5] Ib. "Quosdam peremerunt, partim captos mutilaverunt, reliquos fugiverunt."

the second attempt of Harold's sons,[1] again appears on the stage. With him is coupled an Earl William, whether the same who had been his companion in the former campaign or the more famous William Fitz-Osbern of Hereford is not so clear as we could wish. Our single account seems to send the same pair of commanders at once to the relief of Exeter and to the relief of Shrewsbury.[2] But we can at least see, what is perhaps the most important fact in the whole history of the campaign, that the citizens of Exeter were no longer on the patriotic side. With the Norman garrison of the Red Mount within their walls, the actual pressure brought upon them was not small; in such a case they may well have been tired of enterprises which brought so little fruit, and they may have been well pleased to accept a season of peace even at the hands of the stranger. The spirit of the proud commonwealth was so changed that its burghers, so far from giving any help or comfort to the insurgents, seem to have actively joined in driving them back. The defenders of Exeter, a name which most likely takes in both the foreign garrison and the English citizens, made a vigorous sally, and drove away the besiegers from the walls. The flying insurgents were met by the forces of

*Chap. XVIII. Action of Brian and William Fitz-Osbern.*

*The citizens of Exeter favour William.*

*Defeat of the besiegers of Exeter.*

---

[1] See above, p. 244.

[2] Ord. Vit. 514 A, B. "Exoniæ cives Regi favebant, non immemores pressurarum quas olim passi fuerant. Protinus ubi Rex hæc accepit, Comites, duos Guillelmum et Briennum, laborantibus subvenire præcepit. Verum priusquam illi Scrobesburiam pervenissent, urbe combustâ hostes discesserant, defensores quoque Exoniæ subito eruperunt et impetu in se obsidentes abegerunt. Fugientibus obvii Guillelmus et Briennus grandi cæde temeritatem punierunt." From this account, taken literally, we should certainly think that the same two commanders were sent both to Exeter and to Shrewsbury. But this is unlikely, and almost impossible. Brian however was very likely to be sent to relieve Exeter, and William, if William Fitz-Osbern be meant, was very likely to be sent to relieve Shrewsbury. One is tempted to suspect that two distinct expeditions under William and Brian have been rolled by Orderic or by William of Poitiers into a joint expedition under the two.

the two Earls, and paid, we are told, the forfeit of their rashness by being smitten with a great slaughter.

The hopes of the West were thus crushed once more. The hopes of the shires on the Welsh border were crushed no less utterly, but it is not equally easy to follow the march of events. The besieging force of Eadric, English and Welsh, disappeared from Shrewsbury, after, it would seem, burning the town.[1] The movement at Stafford, that one of the three which William looked on as calling for his own presence, still remained to be put down. But as yet he had not time to attend to it. The danger in the North, where the Danes were actually in the land, where the castles of York had been broken down, and the city itself was little more than a heap of blackened ruins, was the greatest danger of all. William knew when to pause, and he knew also when to act with speed and energy. The over confidence of his commanders in York had for once led him astray, and the fall of the capital of the North had been the result. As soon as the news came, he was moved with grief and wrath,[2] and he at once set forth to avenge the blow which he had not been able to hinder. The nature of the force which he took with him showed that speed was the main object. It is mentioned in an emphatic way that it was a force of cavalry.[3] Before William could reach the North, the Danish fleet had with-

---

[1] See the last note.

[2] Ord. Vit. 513 D. "Securo Regi casus suorum nuntiatur, terribilitas hominum major quam sit amplificante famâ refertur, et quod cum ipso dimicaturi confidenter præstolentur. Rex ergo tam dolore quam irâ conturbatur, ac ad hostes cum exercitu properare conatur." If we may trust the Winchester Annalist (Ann. Mon. ii. 28), William showed his wrath towards his defeated servants in the same way in which he had shown it to his defeated enemies at Alençon, "Multi de castello latenter egressi rem infaustam Regi nuntiârunt, quare manus dexteræ et nasi sunt amputati, ad infidelium terrorem, et in manifestum judicium, quod commissum sibi castellum infideliter custodierant."

[3] Ib. 514 A. "Ipse illuc cum equitatu contendit."

drawn into the Humber, and the ships had been drawn up on the coast of Lindesey.[1] William and his horsemen followed them. The crews were evidently scattered over the country, which William seems to have scoured with his horse. Some were overtaken and slain in the marshes of the district, others were driven out of various lurking-places, of which we have no distinct account, but which would seem to have been some kind of rough and hasty fortresses, which William deemed it needful to level with the ground.[2] But the mass of the invaders made their way to their ships, and crossed over to the Yorkshire side of the estuary. There they were safe for the present. William had no naval force in those waters; so the Danes were left for awhile to devise plans by which they might avenge both themselves and their comrades.[3]

William had thus done all that could be done with the means immediately at his disposal. If he had not crushed the invading host, he had at least made them feel the force of his hand, and he had shown with what speed he could appear even in those parts of his Kingdom where his presence was least looked for. As he had no immediate means of reaching the Danes in Holderness, he himself went back to put down the insurgents who still held their ground at Stafford. In Lindesey he left two trusty captains to guard that coast against any attacks from the Danes on the other side of the Humber. One of these was his brother Robert, Count of Mortain and now of Cornwall, who was thus soon called away from his new estates in the West, and who must have been fighting in the flats of Lincolnshire at the very time that the

[1] Ord Vit 514 A "Illi vero metu magni bellatoris in Humbram aufugiunt, et ripæ quæ Lindissem attingit applicant"

[2] Ib "Nefarios quosdam in paludibus pene inaccessibilibus repperit, gladioque punnit, et aliquot latibula diruit"

[3] Ib "In ripam alteram evadunt Dani, opperientes tempus quo se sociosque suos possent ulcisci"

282    CONQUEST OF WESTERN AND NORTHERN ENGLAND.

CHAP. XVIII insurgents were besieging his own castle on the peaked hill in Somerset. With him was joined in command another kinsman, Robert Count of Eu, the loyal son of William and Lescelina, now enriched with vast estates in the South-Saxon land, and who held one of the first fruits of the Conquest as guardian of the castle on the rocks of Hastings.[1] William meanwhile made his way, no doubt with all speed, to put down the enemies to the south-west whom he had been obliged to bear with for a season. He appeared at Stafford, and there is none of his exploits of which we should be better pleased to have full details.

William's conquest of Staffordshire. Our one account, if vague and brief, is still emphatic. By an easy success he wiped out many of the factious party.[2] But the effects of the blow were lasting; many entries in the Survey show how deeply both the town and the shire of Stafford suffered, and how much lies hid under the few and pithy words of our story. The wasted houses of the town, the wasted lands of the shire, the vast scale on which the confiscation was carried out, show that Staffordshire must have been the scene of vigorous resistance, and that it was therefore marked out for special vengeance.[3]

Severe dealings with the town and shire.

[1] See Domesday, 18
[2] Ord. Vit. 514 B "Rex interim apud Estafort quam plurimos factiosarum partium facili proventu delevit." Here Orderic—can it be William of Poitiers?—stops to comment on the general state of things; "In tot certaminibus sanguis utrinque multus effunditur, et tam inermis quam armata plebs diversis infortuniis hinc inde miserabiliter concutitur. Lex Dei passim violatur et ecclesiasticus rigor pene ab omnibus dissolvitur Cædes miserorum multiplicantur, animæque cupiditatis et iræ stimulis stimulantur ac sauciantur, et catervatim hinc inde ad inferna raptantur, damnate Deo, cujus judicia esse justissima comprobantur."
[3] Domesday, 246 "In burgo de Stadford habet Rex in suo dominio xviii burgenses et viii vastas mansiones, præter has habet Rex ibi xxii. mansiones de honore Comitum, harum v sunt vastæ, aliæ inhabitantur." Of the houses belonging to other lords, all foreigners, ninety-five were inhabited and thirty-six waste. The entry of "wasta" often occurs in the shire, especially in a long list of Crown lands in 246 There are no large

The western and central shires were thus subdued; Chester alone, the north-western angle, so to speak, of Western England, still remained independent. But the more pressing dangers of the North at least won for this untouched fortress of English freedom the gloomy privilege of being devoured the last. For the present, William took up his quarters at Nottingham, a town which, as we have seen, he had strongly fortified in his first Northern march.[1] This was an excellent central position from which to watch at once Lindesey, York, and Chester, as well as to guard against any movements which might even now arise in the newly conquered districts. While William was putting down the movement at Stafford, his commanders had not been idle on the banks of the Humber. The people of the land were doubly the friends of the invaders. They were bound to the subjects of Swend by the old tie of the common Danish blood which formed so large an element amongst the inhabitants of Lindesey; they were bound too by their good wishes for the success of their helpers in the common cause. The joyful season of Christmas was drawing near, and the men of Lindesey called their Danish friends to join them in the feasts with which they enlivened the gloom of winter. The Danes landed, and shared in the entertainments of their English hosts. But the Norman Earls came upon them, when they were unprepared, in the moment of festivity. The hospitable board was stained with blood, and the Danes were driven back with much slaughter to their ships.[2] But it was

*William marches to Nottingham*

*Action of the Earls against the Danes in Lindesey*

English landowners, but there is a list of Thegns at the end, among whom we find the Northumbrian Gamel. See vol. ii. p. 483.

[1] See above, p. 109.

[2] Ord. Vit. 514 B, C. "Dani aliquamdiu delituere. Verum postquam tuta sunt, opinati conviviis provincialium (quæ vulgo firmam appellant) illecti ad terram egrediuntur. Ambo Comites ex improviso eos invadunt, epulas cruore confundunt, instant trepidis, ad naves usque cædendo fugientes persequuntur."

presently rumoured that feasting on a grander scale and on a more important spot was thought of. The Danes, and no doubt their English friends also, were purposing to keep the Midwinter Feast at York.[1] This, as well as what follows, shows either that some considerable part of the city must have escaped the flames, or else that, as so often happened in those days, the damage had already begun to be repaired by the rebuilding of houses which were mainly of wood.[2] To hinder this enterprise, or again to surprise his enemies in the moment of rejoicing, William set forth from Nottingham. He marched as far as the banks of the Aire. That stream flows from the high lands which so long divided the Northumbrian Angles from the Northern Welsh, and finds its way into the Ouse below the hermitage which was perhaps already growing into the minster of Selby, hard by the spot which was in after times to become the site of the palace and minster of Howden. The spot itself where William reached the stream is marked out as lying in the neighbourhood of one of the most famous castles reared by those whom the event of that campaign was to set as lords over Northern England. It was near the place where Ilbert of Lacy raised that renowned fortress, the scene of the martyrdom of Thomas of Lancaster[3] and of the mysterious death of the deposed Richard,[4] which, most likely from the incident of this very march, received the Romance name of Pontefract. The fortress however, all whose remains seem to

---

[1] Ord. Vit. 514 C "Divulgatur iterum eosdem latrunculos Eboracum ad venire, qua natalem Dominicum celebrent, seseque ad proeliandum præparent." [2] See vol. i pp. 380, 395.

[3] On the execution of Thomas of Lancaster "extra villam de Ponte Fracto," see Walsingham, i. 165, ed. Riley, and Rymer, ii. 493, and on the miracles wrought at his tomb, see the other writ in ii. 525.

[4] I am not bound to determine the manner of death of Richard the Second, but I suppose that we may safely use the words of Walsingham (ii. 245), "Clausit diem extremum apud castrum de Ponte Fracto."

be of much later date, does not, like so many others, overhang a river at its feet. The actual spot of William's encampment is to be looked for among the mills and wharfs and factories of the modern town of Castleford. That name shows itself to be of a later date than the foundation of Ilbert, while at the same time it marks the spot as having been used as a place for crossing the river in much earlier times. The stream is now spanned by a bridge, but, if that bridge had any predecessor in the days before William, it had been broken down by the enemy.[1] The Aire at this point is now navigable, at all events for the keels of the country, but it is described as being at the time of William's coming impassable alike by boats and by fording.[2] We need not however take this as implying more than the incidental condition of the stream during the winter months. William, we are told, rejected the counsels alike of those who proposed a retreat and of those who suggested the repair of the bridge. The bridge might supply a means of passage for the enemy, or an attack might be made upon them while they were still engaged in the work.[3] William preferred to remain idle for three whole weeks on the right bank of the Aire,[4] while, as the story implies, the left bank

*William's delay at Castleford*

*He refuses to rebuild the bridge*

[1] The name Pons Fractus, though it is not found in Domesday, must have been known to Orderic, probably to William of Poitiers. It exists in English only in its Romance form. It is therefore almost certain that the name was given soon after the place was brought into notice by this incident in William's march. It therefore follows that a bridge was actually broken down at the time. The difficulty arising from the distance between the town and castle of Pontefract and the possible site of any real *pons fractus* is equal in any case.

[2] Ord. Vit. 514 C. "Properans illo Rex e Snotingeham, præpeditur ad Fracti-pontis aquam impatientem vadi, nec navigio usitatam." *Fractus Pons*, as distinguished from the more usual *Pons Fractus*, shows the name in a state of transition from a description to a proper name.

[3] Ib. "Reditum suadentibus non acquiescit, pontem fieri volentibus id opportunum non esse respondet, ne hostis repente super eos irrueret, et inferendæ cladis occasionem in ipso opere haberet."

[4] Ib. "Tres hebdomades illic detinentur."

286        CONQUEST OF WESTERN AND NORTHERN ENGLAND.

CHAP XVIII was lined by at least a detachment of the insurgents and their allies. This is not exactly in the spirit of Brihtnoth;[1] we may add that it is not in the spirit of William himself.

Lisois finds a ford

The tale goes on to say that all this while a valiant man named Lisois[2] was carefully seeking for a ford both above and below the camp.[3] At last, after much search over difficult ground, a ford was found. Lisois, at the head of sixty horsemen, crossed it in the teeth of a party of the enemy on the other side. The English tried to hinder the passage of Lisois and his men, but they were themselves defeated and dispersed.[4] On the next day Lisois

William and his army cross the river

returned to the camp with the good news. The army marched to the spot; they forded the river at the point which he showed them, and thence made their way towards York, through woods, marshes, hills, and valleys, along a narrow track through which two could not go abreast.[5] This description, as well as the evident distance of the ford from Pontefract, seems to show that, if the tale is to be trusted, the ford must be looked for in the hilly country far up the river, and that the march to York must have been made by a roundabout course indeed. It is perfectly easy to understand that fords which were available in summer would be useless when the stream was swollen by the

[1] See vol. 1. p 300

[2] The only notice of this Lisois which I can find in Domesday is in ii 49 b, where he appears in possession, but seemingly illegal possession, of a small holding in Essex Half a hide was held by "ii franci homines," "quam occupavit Lisoisus, quia unus illorum utlagavit"

[3] Ord. Vit 514 C " Denique Lisois, audax miles, quem de Monasteriis agnominabant, flumen summopere attentabat, et vadum supra infraque quæritabat"

[4] Ib " Per multam demum difficultatem locum transmeabilem deprehendit, et cum lx magnanimis equitibus pertransivit, super quos hostium multitudo irruit, sed his acerrime repugnantibus non prævaluit."

[5] Ib " Postero die Lisois reversus prodit vadum, nec mora, traducitur exercitus Itur per silvas, paludes, montana valles, arctissimo tramite qui binos lateraliter ire non patiebatur"

floods of winter, and that the means of crossing had to be looked for at a great distance from the camp. But it must have been no small obstacle which caused William to lose so much time at such a moment, and to reach the object of his march by such a roundabout and difficult way, when the Roman road leading straight over the flat country from Pontefract to York lay invitingly before his eyes. It is hard to avoid the suspicion that some part of the seemingly wasted time was spent in those negotiations with the Danish commander which afterwards led to the utter and shameful failure of his whole enterprise.[1]

*Probable negotiations of William with the Danes*

At last William for the third time drew near to York. I wish we could believe the tale of a later writer, who tells us that he met with a valiant resistance, and that the city was taken only by storm with the slaughter of thousands of men.[2] But it seems plain that he entered the city or its ruins, and found no man to withstand him. The Northumbrians had gone each man to his home after their first great success,[3] and we hear nothing which shows that their forces had been again brought together. Of the Danes we are expressly told that the news of their flight was brought to William before he had reached the city.[4] His first object was once more to secure its possession. A force was left at York, with orders to begin at once with the repair of the castles, which were once more to hold the

*William reaches York and enters without opposition*

*The castles of York repaired*

---

[1] This is the probable suggestion of Sir Francis Palgrave, iii 455

[2] This seems to be the meaning of Matthew of Westminster (1069), if that is the right name, "Eboracum, ubi fuit Danorum receptaculum, potenter cum ibi inventis expugnavit, et multa milia hominum ibidem interfecit" This is wrought up by Thierry into a picture of a dearly bought victory on the part of the Normans after a long defence of which the "Roi Edgar" seems to be the hero.

[3] See above, p 271

[4] Ord Vit 514 C. "Eboraco appropinquatum est, sed Danos aufugisse nuntiatum est"

288                CONQUEST OF WESTERN AND NORTHERN ENGLAND.

CHAP XVIII  metropolis of the North in subjection.[1] And now came
The great  that fearful deed, half of policy, half of vengeance, which
harrying of
Northum-   has stamped the name of William with infamy, and which
berland    forms a clearly marked stage in the downward course of
his moral being. He had embarked in a wrongful undertaking, but hitherto we cannot say that he had aggravated
the original wrong by reckless or wanton cruelties. But,
as ever, wrong avenged itself by leading to deeper wrong.
The age was a stern one, and hitherto William had
certainly not sinned against the public opinion of the age.
Hitherto he had been on the whole a merciful conqueror.
He had shown that he belonged to another type of beings
from the men who had wasted his own Duchy in his childhood, and from the men on whom Siward and Tostig had
striven to put some check within the land which he had
now won.[2] Siward and Tostig were both of them men of
blood, stained with the guilt of private murder, from
which we may be sure that William would have shrunk
at any time of his life. But we may be no less sure that
Siward and Tostig, harsh as they were, would have shrunk
from the horrors which William now proceeded deliberately
Its delibe-  to inflict on Northern England. The harryings of which
rate and
systematic   Sussex and Kent had seen something on his first landing [3]
character.   were now to be carried out, far more systematically, far
more unflinchingly, through the whole of Yorkshire and
several neighbouring shires.[4] The King took the work

[1] Ord Vit 514 C. "Rex tribunos et præsides cum armatorum manu, qui restaurarent in urbe castella, direxit, et alios nihilominus in ripâ Humbræ, qui Danis resisterent, reliquit."
[2] See vol. ii p 381                    [3] See vol. iii. pp 411, 534.
[4] The great harrying of the North is mentioned briefly but emphatically in the Chronicles, 1069, "Þa se kyng þis geaxode, þa for he norðward mid ealre his fyrde þe he gegaderian mihte, and þa scire mid ealle forhergode and aweste." So Florence, "Quod ubi Regi innotuit Willelmo, exercitu mox congregato, in Northymbriam efferato properavit animo, eamque per totam hiemem devastare, hominesque trucidare, et multa mala non cessabat

of destruction as his personal share of the conquest of Northumberland. He left others to build his castles in York; he left others to watch the Danish fleet in the Humber; but he himself went through the length and breadth of the land, through its wildest and most difficult regions, alike to punish the past revolts of its people and to cripple their power of engaging in such revolts for the time to come. That all who resisted were slain with the sword[1] was a matter of course, Harold had done as much as that in his great campaign against Gruffydd.[2] But now William went to and fro over points a hundred miles from one another,[3] destroying, as far as in him lay, the life of the earth. It was not mere plunder, which may at least enrich the plunderer; the work of William at this time was simple unmitigated havoc. Houses were everywhere burned with all that was in them; stores of corn, goods and property of every kind, were brought together and destroyed in the like sort; even living animals seem to have been driven to perish in the universal burning.[4] The authentic records of the Conquest give no hint of any exceptions being made or favour being shown in any part of the doomed region. But local legends as usual supply their tale of wonder. Beverley was saved by the interposition of its heavenly patron, the canonized Archbishop John.[5] The

*William's personal share in the devastation.*

*Utter destruction of property of all kinds*

*Legend of the preservation of Beverley*

agere." Fuller details come from Orderic, the Evesham History, and other sources

[1] Ord. Vit 514 D " Plerosque gladio vindice ferit, aliorum latebras evertit, terras devastat, et domos cum rebus omnibus concremat "

[2] See vol ii. p 474

[3] Ord Vit u. s " Spatio centum milliariorum castra ejus diffunduntur "

[4] Ib " Jussit irâ stimulante segetibus et pecoribus cum vasis et omni genere alimentorum repleri, et igne injecto penitus omnia simul comburi, et sic omnem alimoniam per totam regionem Trans-humbranam pariter devastari "

[5] On the history and legends of Saint John of Beverley (Bishop of Hexham 687-705, of York 705-718, died 721), see Bæda, v 2-6 We

VOL. IV.   U

CHAP XVIII. King had pitched his camp seven miles from the town, when news was brought that the people of the whole neighbourhood had taken shelter with all their precious things in the inviolable sanctuary which was afforded by the frithstool of the saint [1] On hearing this, some plunderers, seemingly without the royal orders,[2] set forth to make a prey of the town and of those who had sought shelter in it. They entered Beverley without meeting with any resistance, and made their way to the churchyard, where a vast crowd of people was gathered together.[3] The leader of the band, Toustain by name [4]—not, let us hope, the son of Rolf, the standard-bearer of Senlac [5]—marked out an old man in goodly apparel with a golden bracelet on his arm.[6] This was doubtless the badge of his official rank, or the prize which Harold or Siward or some other bracelet-giver [7] had bestowed as the reward of good service against Scot or Briton or Northman. The Englishman fled within the walls of the minster. The sacrilegious Toustain, sword

*Miraculous discomfiture of Toustain.*

get another instance of his worship in the account of the Battle of the Standard in Richard of Hexham, X Scriptt 321, where his banner is brought forth, along with those of Saint Peter of York and Saint Wilfrith of Ripon.

[1] The legend is told by Ælfred of Beverley, 129, ed. Hearne  Beverley was the "unicum asylum"  The Normans hear "omnem illius regionis populum illuc ad pacem Sancti venisse, et omnia pretiosa sua secum de tulisset." The allusion is plainly to the famous *Frithstool*

[2] Ib  " Quidam milites rapinis assueti Beverlacum armati petierunt "

[3] Ib  " Ad septa cœmiterii, quo territa totius populi multitudo confluxerat, ausu temerario progrediuntur "

[4] Ib " Primicernus Turstinus "

[5] See above, p 39

[6] Al Bev. u s  " Quemdam veteranum pretiosius indutum, auream in brachio armillam ferentem."

[7] Compare in the Song of Brunanburh the description of Æthelstan as "beorna beahgifa," and again in the Song of Maldon (Thorpe, Analecta, 132) ;

"Heton ðe secgan,
þæt þu most sendan raðe
beagas wið gebeorge."

# LEGEND OF BEVERLEY.

in hand, spurred his horse within the consecrated doors [1] CHAP XVIII
But the vengeance of Saint John of Beverley did not slumber. The horse fell with its neck broken, and Toustain himself, smitten in his own person, his arms and legs all twisted behind his back, no longer seemed a man but a monster.[2] His affrighted comrades laid aside all their schemes of plunder and slaughter, and humbly implored the mercy of the saint [3] They made their way back to William and told him the tale of wonder. The King had already shown himself a friend to the church of Saint John,[4] and now, fearing the wrath of the saint, he summoned the chief members of the Chapter before him, and again confirmed all their possessions by charters under the royal seal.[5] He added new grants of land and precious gifts for the adornment of the minster,[6] and, what was of

William confirms the rights of the College.

---

[1] Al Bev 129. "Extracto quo erat præcinctus gladio, per medium plebis attonitæ, super emissarium furens senem persequitur . intra valvas ecclesiæ jam pene fugiendo exstinctum insequitur"

[2] Ib. " Ecce equus in quo sederat fracto collo corruit, et ipse, facie jam deformi post tergum versâ manibus pedibusque retortis, velut monstrum informe omnium in se mirantium ora convertit " It is curious to see how Thierry (1 319) waters down the miracle, "son cheval, glissant sur le pavé, s'abattit et le froissa dans sa chute " Of course this is likely enough to have been the kernel of truth in the legend, but no man has a right to tell the tale in this shape as if it were undoubted fact. On stories of this kind, see the profound remarks of Professor Stubbs in his Preface to *De Inventione*, XXVII-XXIX.

[3] Ib "Stupefacti et exterriti socii ejus, projectis armis et depositâ ferocitate, ad impetrandam Sancti Johannis misericordiam convertuntur "

[4] See above, p 205

[5] Ib "Rex, auditâ virtute gloriosi confessoris, verensque similem ultionem de ceteris, accersitis ad se majoribus ecclesiæ, quæcumque priorum Regum vel principum libertate eidem ecclesiæ fuerant collata, regiâ auctoritate et sigilli sui munimine confirmavit" The chief of these former benefactors was Æthelstan, the second founder of the church in its secular shape. See the legend in Bromton, X Scriptt. 838. I suspect that this present confirmation is a legendary version of the earlier one in Ealdred's time.

[6] Ib. "Ne ipse prædecessorum suorum munificentiis esset impar, præfatam ecclesiam pretiosis donis decoravit, et possessionibus ampliavit"

U 2

CHAP XVIII
He removes his camp.

more immediate value than all, that there might be no further danger of the peace of Saint John being broken, he at once broke up his camp by sound of trumpet, and removed his head-quarters to a place far removed from the hallowed spot.[1]

General desolation of the country

The lands of Saint John of Beverley were thus, according to the local legend, spared amid the general havoc, and remained tilled while all around was a wilderness.[2] The long abiding traces of the destruction which was now wrought were its most fearful feature. The accounts of the immediate ravaging are graphic and terrible enough, but they are perhaps outdone in significance by the passionless

Entries in Domesday

witness of the great Survey, the entries of "Waste," "Waste," "Waste," attached through page after page to the Yorkshire lordships which, seventeen years after, had not recovered from the blow.[3] Indeed we may be inclined to ask whether Northern England ever fully recovered from the blow till that great developement of modern times which has reversed the respective importance of the North and the South. For nine years at least no attempt was made at tilling the ground; between York and Durham every town stood uninhabited; their streets became

[1] Al. Bev. 129 "Ne exercitûs sui vicinitate pax ecclesiæ ab eo firmata dissolveretur, sonantibus per exercitum classicis statim a loco recessit, et valde procul inde tentoria figi præcepit"

[2] Bromton, X Scriptt 966 "Nec terra aliqua erat culta, excepto solo territorio beati Johannis Beverlaci, nam ibi quidam Regis miles, collo equi sui fracto et facie propriâ retortâ, vindictam incurrebat"

[3] I take at a venture pp 305, 305 b. After a long string of places we read, "omnia wasta præter Engelbi" After another such list, "omnes sunt wastæ excepto Wirueltun" The entry of "wasta" occurs also in twenty-four other places in those two pages These are on lands belonging to the two great Earls Robert and Hugh The destruction however was not spread quite equally over the whole land. In pp 319, 319 b, the fatal word occurs only nine times Among the places which escaped we find the names of "Barneburg" and "Sproteburg" Sprotburgh has its frithstool as well as Beverley, and it is hard that it has not also its legend

lurking-places for robbers and wild beasts.¹ Even a generation later the passing traveller beheld with sorrow the ruins of famous towns, with their lofty towers rising above the forsaken dwellings, the fields lying untilled and tenantless, the rivers flowing idly through the wilderness.² At the time the scene was so fearful that the contemporary writers seem to lack words to set forth its full horrors. Men, women, and children died of hunger; they laid them down and died in the roads and in the fields, and there was no man to bury them.³ Those who survived kept up life on strange and unaccustomed food. The flesh of cats and dogs was not disdained, and the teaching which put a ban on the flesh of the horse as the food of Christian men was forgotten under the stress of hunger. Nay, there were those who did not shrink from keeping themselves alive on the flesh of their own kind.⁴ Others, in the emphatic words of our old records, bowed their necks for meat in the evil days. They became slaves to any one who would feed

CHAP XVIII.

Long abiding traces of the ravages.

State of the country at the time.

Utter wretchedness of the survivors

Men sell themselves for slaves

---

¹ Sim Dun Gest Regg 1079, p 85, Hinde "Interea ita terrâ cultore destitutâ, lata ubique solitudo patebat per novem annos Inter Eboracum et Dunelmum nusquam villa inhabitata, bestiarum tantum et latronum latibula magno itinerantibus fuere timori"

² Will Malm iii 249 "Itaque provinciæ quondam fertilis et tyrannorum nutriculæ incendio, prædâ, sanguine, nervi succisi, humus per sexaginta et eo amplius milliaria omnifariam inculta, nudum omnium solum *usque ad hoc etiam tempus*, urbes olim præclaras, turres proceritate suâ in cœlum minantes, agros lætos pascuis, irriguos fluvus, si quis modo videt peregrinus, ingemit, si quis superest vetus incola, non agnoscit" Are we to see in these heaven-reaching towers the tall slender unbuttressed steeples of our earliest Romanesque?

³ Sim Dun u s "Erat horror ad intuendum per domos, plateas, et itinera cadavera humana dissolvi, et tabescentia putredine cum fœtore horrendo scaturire vermibus Neque enim superat qui ea humo cooperiret, omnibus vel exstinctis gladio et fame, vel propter famem paternum solum relinquentibus"

⁴ Flor Wig 1069 "Normannis Angliam vastantibus, in Northymbriâ et quibusdam aliis provincus anno præcedenti, sed præsenti et subsequenti fere per totam Angliam, maxime per Northymbriam et per contiguas illi provincias, adeo fames prævaluit, ut homines equinam, caninam, cattinam, et carnem comederent humanam"

them, sometimes, when happier days had come, to be set free by the charity of their masters.[1] Before the end of the year, Yorkshire was a wilderness. The bodies of its inhabitants were rotting in the streets, in the highways, or on their own hearthstones; and those who had escaped from sword, fire, and hunger, had fled out of the land.

*Contemporary estimate of William's conduct.*

The harrying of Northern England was a deed which was denounced by men not indisposed to make the best of William's deeds as a deed on which the wrath of God was sure to follow.[2] To his own conscience it was perhaps reconciled by the thought that, after all, he had shed no

---

[1] There is a most remarkable document in Cod. Dipl. iv. 263, in which a lady named Geatflæd sets free several persons, who are mentioned by name, with the striking addition, "and ealle þa men þe heonon heora heáfod for hyra mete on ðám yflum dagum." Mr. Kemble (Saxons in England, i. 196), who mentions other examples of the practice, refers this deed to a time "as late as the Norman Conquest." From the words which follow, in which Gospatric is mentioned, the document would seem to belong to the year 1070. Geatflæd sets free another party of slaves, who are described as "þa men þe heo þingede æt Cwæspatrike." All the names are English or Danish. This example illustrates the general description of Simeon of Durham (85), "Alii in servitutem perpetuam sese venderent, dummodo qualitercumque miserabilem vitam sustentarent."

[2] Ord. Vit. 514 D, 515 A. "Nusquam tantâ crudelitate usus est Guillelmus, hic turpiter vitio succubuit, dum iram suam regere contempsit, et reos innocuosque pari animadversione peremit ... In multis Guillelmum nostra libenter extulit relatio sed in hoc quod una justum et injustum rabidæ famis lanceâ æque transfixit, laudare non audeo. Nam dum innocuos infantes juvenesque vernantes et floridos canitie senes fame periclitari video, misericordiâ motus miserabilis populi mœroribus et anxietatibus magis condoleo, quam frivolis adulationibus inutiliter studeo. Præterea indubitanter affero quod impune non remittetur tam feralis occisio. Summos enim et imos intuetur omnipotens Judex, et æque omnium facta discutiet ac puniet districtissimus vindex, ut palam omnibus enodat Dei perpetua lex." This passage is valuable, even if it be simply the comment of Orderic, whose sense of right and wrong was keen enough. But it becomes of tenfold value, if we can believe that he copied it from William of Poitiers. It would show that there were bounds beyond which even that abandoned flatterer refused to follow his hero

blood except in open fighting. He had spared the lives of rebels whom a less merciful prince might have doomed to the slaughter. His vengeance fell only on the lands and goods which were his own lawful forfeit, and if their former owners died of hunger through their loss, that was no guilt of his. All this, all that had gone before, all that was to come after, was to be done and suffered that William might win and wear the Crown which the choice of those whose gift it was had given to another. And, as if in mockery, William decreed to show himself in all the pomp of kingship in the midst of the land which he had wasted. He would remind men that all that he had done was not the act of a lawless invader overcoming his foreign enemies, but the act of a lawful King subduing the rebels who had again and again risen against him, who had slain his garrisons and broken down his castles. The Christmas Feast was this year to be kept, not in the new minster of Eadward at Westminster or of Ealdred at Gloucester,[1] but amid the ruins of the houses and churches of the wasted metropolis of the North. The Crown which Ealdred had placed on William's head was to be worn in his own city, when there was no Northumbrian Primate to do his duty to his King, and only the blackened walls of the minster to be the scene of the ceremony. Still the form was gone through, doubtless with such diminished splendour as the circumstances allowed. The Crown and all the other badges of royalty were brought from Winchester, the army was left encamped without the city, and King William, not King Eadgar or King Swend, held the Christmas Feast in York.[2] It was doubtless at this grim

CHAP. XVIII

Probable estimate of William himself.

He holds the Christmas feast at York. 1069-1070

---

[1] See vol. ii. p 435

[2] Ord Vit 515 A, B "Inter bella Guillelmus ex civitate Guentâ jubet adferri coronam, aliaque ornamenta regalia et vasa, et dimisso exercitu in castris Eboracum pergit, ibique Natale Salvatoris nostri concelebrat." This is confirmed by the Worcester Chronicle, 1069; " And se kyng wæs þone midwintres dag on Eoferwic "

CHAP XVIII
Settlement of Yorkshire

Grants to Alan of Britanny

Richmond Castle

Ecclesiastical foundations at Richmond

Midwinter Gemót that the main settlement of Yorkshire took place. It must have been now that the Breton Alan received that vast grant of land which placed him at the head of the nobles of the North.[1] In one of the most picturesque spots of that land of dales and streams, on a height overlooking the rocky bed of the dark Swale, he reared the castle which, under its French name of Richmond, so long remained as a link between the English Earldom and the Breton Duchy.[2] A hall, a keep, a chapel, either of this or of the next age, survive to tell of the proud state of its early lords, but how much of them is actually the work of the first founder may remain a problem for the architectural antiquary.[3] Under the shadow of the castle a town, as usual, arose, and the borough of Richmond gained importance enough to give its name to new ecclesiastical and temporal divisions of the surrounding country.[4] The bounty of the Earls and their followers surrounded the castle with ecclesiastical foundations. A stately parish church arose on the

[1] In Domesday, 309, Alan appears as third among the lay landowners in Yorkshire, after the Earls Hugh and Robert, but his estate is the largest of the three.

[2] The descent of Duchy and Earldom may be studied in Dugdale's Baronage, 46, and in the Art de Vérifier les Dates, ii. 897 et seqq. See also Gale, Registrum Honoris de Richmond, the Preface and the Genealogical Tree. It is enough to remember the regrant of the Earldom to Duke John in 1268, and the descent from him of the famous Arthur, the Constable of France, in the fifteenth century.

[3] I cannot find any authentic dates for the different parts of the castle of Richmond, one of the finest Norman buildings in the kingdom. Gale attributes the building of the great tower to Conan, the fourth Earl, 1145–1171. It would seem to be of late Norman date, but retaining an earlier entrance. The hall overhanging the river struck me as possibly earlier than the keep. The original chapel is very small and plain. Both hall and chapel stand quite apart from the keep, showing how completely, at all events in castles of this palatial kind, the keep was merely an occasional place of defence.

[4] The name of "Richmondshire" is familiar; see Gale, and Whitaker's History passim. Richmond also gives its name to an Archdeaconry.

slope of the hill, and a Benedictine Priory, a cell to Saint Mary of York, crowned the opposite height beyond the river. At a short distance from the town, among the woods by the river side, arose in the next age the Præmonstratensian Abbey of Saint Agatha of Easby, and the tall slender tower of the still later Franciscan church might almost seem in its general proportions to recall the architecture of an earlier day.[1] Another Yorkshire borough arose on the estate of another of William's followers. Ilbert of Lacy became lord of the lands where William's host had tarried on their Northern march, and, on the nearest convenient spot to the presumptuous river, the incident of the campaign was commemorated in the name of his castle of Pontefract or the Broken Bridge.[2] Another grantee was William of Percy, the founder of a great name, whose genuine bearers soon passed away, but which has been, like that of the Cæsars, artificially handed on to later times.[3] The still more renowned name of Robert of Bruce also appears in the Survey, but his lands were a later

*Chap XVIII*

Lands of Ilbert of Lacy, origin of Pontefract

---

[1] The Priory of Saint Martin was founded about 1100 by Wymar, *dapifer* to the second Alan, and a chief benefactor was " Roaldus filius Roaldi, filii Alani, constabularii Richmundiæ" Earl Conan himself was also a benefactor  Mon Angl in 601, 602  Roaldus [Rhiwallon] was also the first founder of the Abbey of Easby  Mon. Angl vii. 921  The Franciscan Friary was founded in 1258. Mon. Angl viii 1545  The tall slender tower of the fifteenth or sixteenth century is, as usual, inserted between the nave and choir of the elder church  Easby is well known for its noble refectory, of the church but little is left

[2] See above, p. 284

[3] The Percies, who seem to have a mythical genealogy before they landed in Normandy, most likely came from Percy in the Cötentin  The genuine line became extinct in the third generation with William, the son of William's second son Richard  See Dugdale's Baronage, 270, and Hartshorne, Feudal and Military Antiquities of Northumberland, 285. His daughter Agnes, in Henry the Second's time, married Joceline, son of Godfrey, Duke of Brabant or Lower Lotharingia, a descendant by female succession of Charles the Great, in whose line, and afterwards in those of Seymour and Smithson, the artificial house of Percy has been continued to our own time

298   CONQUEST OF WESTERN AND NORTHERN ENGLAND.

CHAP XVIII
Other Norman grantees

gift from the Conqueror.¹ These are names specially belonging to Northern history; but William's immediate kinsfolk and friends did not fail to come in for their share. Earl Harold's lands at Coningsburgh passed to William of Warren.² A vast estate, the reward doubtless of his services in Lindesey, fell to the insatiable Earl of Mortain and Cornwall.³ One Drogo of Bevere, whose legendary history I shall discuss elsewhere, obtained a grant of the peninsula of Holderness.⁴ Still many English Thegns retained their lands under the Crown,⁵ while others had to hold them of Norman lords. This is specially the case with the lands of Ilbert of Lacy, which were largely held by their former owners,⁶ while on the lands of Earl Robert they seem to have been almost wholly dispossessed in favour of his foreign followers. But, after the frightful havoc of this winter, lands in Yorkshire could have been of little value to any man, native or stranger. Through page after page of the Survey the same frightful entry of "Waste" constantly meets the eye, and a more attentive study will show many a lordship which had once kept up the hall of more than one English Thegn, but from which only the barest shadow of profit could now be wrung for its Norman owner.⁷

Retention of land by English tenants

Fall in the value of land

---

[1] Domesday, 332 b "Hic est feudum Rotberti de Bruis, quod fuit datum postquam Liber de Wintoniâ scriptus fuit"

[2] Domesday, 321 Coningsburgh and its appurtenances seem to have been the only possessions of William of Warren in Yorkshire.

[3] Domesday, 305–308 b

[4] See Appendix GG

[5] Domesday, 330 b, 331 b.

[6] In pp 316 b, 317 b, will be found a long list of English tenants of Ilbert, many of them holding lands that had formerly been their own To be sure, many of the lands are waste

[7] Thierry quotes the passage in Domesday, 315, where we read of a Yorkshire estate, " Duo Taini tenuerunt per ii maneria Ibi sunt ii. villani cum i carucâ Valuit xl solidos, modo iiii solidos " In the same page are other similar entries Sacroft, which had been held by five English possessors, and was worth four pounds, was now held of Ilbert by

Yorkshire was thus conquered. William had made a wilderness and he called it peace. Nor can we doubt that order reigned in York while the King wore his Crown at the Midwinter Feast in his Northern capital. As soon as the holy season was over, more warfare, more havoc, was to begin. With William the time when Kings go forth to battle was not bounded by any limits of the seasons, and in the extreme North of England there were still foes to be overcome and lands to be wasted. In some remote corner, seemingly near the mouth of the Tees, in an inaccessible spot surrounded by marshes, a daring band still defied his power. They held out in a fastness stored with rich plunder, and deemed that there at least they were safe from all attacks.[1] The lands of the future Palatinate of Durham were also unsubdued. Since the overthrow of Robert of Comines, no Norman had appeared within the franchises of Saint Cuthberht. But the land of the saint was already a wilderness. Bishop Æthelwine and his priests had already fled. Frightened at the horrors which were going on south of the Tees, they determined to leave the church and city on the height above the Wear, and to seek safety once more for themselves and for the body of their patron in his own holy isle of Lindisfarn. No one was more eager in recommending this course than the Earl Gospatric. Whether out of zeal for their preservation or from any less worthy motive, he himself undertook the keeping of the more precious part of the moveable ornaments of the church during their absence.[2] The

*Marginalia:* CHAP XVIII. William's Midwinter campaign January, 1070. English refuge by the mouth of the Tees. Flight of Æthelwine and his Canons from Durham December 11, 1069. Gospatric counsels their flight.

---

a certain Robert, was entered as waste and valued at twenty pence. The next place, Tornevre, held by four Englishmen, had been worth four pounds, and was now worth ten shillings.

[1] Ord Vit 515 B "Rursum comperit hostile collegium in angulo quodam regionis latitare, mari vel paludibus undique munito." The position of this place of shelter is marked by the course of William's march, when he set forth to reduce it.

[2] Sim Dun Hist Dun Eccl iii 16 "Hic enim Gospatricus hoc maxime

Bishop and his clerks then set forth. Four days were taken up with the march, the first of which led them to the mouth of the Tyne, at the point where its waters are joined by those of the northern Don. There, on the banks of the inlet locally known as the Slake of Jarrow, still stood the venerable church of the monastery where Bæda had dwelled, and where we may still see the massive walls and narrow windows of the choir in which he worshipped.[1] Since the first Danish invasions Jarrow seems to have no longer existed as a monastery, but the church was at least so far preserved that it was able to give a night's shelter to Æthelwine and his companions[2] The next day's march carried them to a place called Bethlington, in the land beyond the Tyne. In this district the venerable fugitives were exposed to the persecutions of a powerful man of that country, whose name Gilmichael points to his Scottish birth or descent. He vexed them on their course in every way, hindering their passage, plundering the goods which they bore with them, and seemingly doing personal despite to the holy men themselves[3] Notwithstanding all these difficulties, on the fourth day, towards evening, they reached the coast of the mainland opposite to the Holy Island. A miracle enabled them to reach the goal of their journey more

dederat consilium, ut fugientes ecclesiam relinquerent, et ipse maximam ornamentorum ejus partem secum abduxerat"

[1] On the state of Jarrow and Monkwearmouth at this time, see Appendix HH

[2] Sim. Dun Hist Dun Eccl iii 15 "Primâ quidem nocte in ecclesiâ Sancti Pauli in Gyrvum, secundâ in Bethlingtun, tertiâ in loco qui Tughala dicitur, mansit "

[3] Ib 16 "In fugâ memoratâ quâ cum sancti patris corpore ad prædictam insulam fugerant, quidam ultra amnem Tinam præpotens Gillomichael, per contrarium, id est puer Michaelis, appellatus, nam rectius puer diaboli nuncuparetur, multas fugientibus injurias irrogavit, iter eorum impediendo, ipsos affligendo, prædas ex eis agendo, et quodcunque mali poterat faciendo " On these Gaelic names beginning with *Gil*, see Miss Yonge's History of Christian Names, ii 113

speedily. The tide, which was full when they reached the coast, ebbed at once to allow them to cross, as the waters by Mount Klimax made way for the passage of Alexander.[1] As soon as they were safe on the island, the waters came back, so that no pursuers might overtake them.[2] A single aged clerk was sent back to Durham to see how matters fared in the church and city. On the way, in the visions of the night, he beheld Saint Cuthberht and the holy King Oswald, and he was warned by them that the judgements of another world had already overtaken the wicked Gilmichael, whom he had so lately seen flourishing and boasting that he could do mischief. He was warned too that woes would fall on Gospatric also for his timid, perhaps sacrilegious, counsel.[3] The priest sought the Earl and told him of the divine threatenings. Gospatric hastened with naked feet to the Holy Island, and craved pardon for that in which he had offended. But on him vengeance came in this world; the loss of his Earldom and all the troubles which befel him were his punishment.[4]

[1] See the story in Arrian, i. 26 2, 3, Plut Alex 17, and compare the comments of Josephus, Antiq ii 16. 5

[2] Sim Dun Gest Regg 86 "Circa vesperam, quum plenum undique mare advenientibus prohiberet ingressum, ecce, subito sui recessu liberum præstitit introitum, ita ut nec festinantes aliquanto tardius sequerentur fluctus marini, nec tardantes aliquanto citius præcurrerent Quum autem terram attigissent, ecce, refluum mare, sicut ante, totas arenas operuerat." The story is told at greater length and more dramatically in the Durham History, iii. 15

[3] See the whole story in the Durham History, iii 16 The words of Saint Cuthberht about Gospatric are, "Væ tibi, Gospatrice, væ tibi, Gospatrice, ecclesiam meam suis rebus evacuâsti et in desertum convertisti"

[4] Sim. Dun. Hist Dun Eccl iii 16 "Cujus [Gillomichaelis] tormenta intolerabilia Comiti Cospatrico, sed et ea quæ de illo a prædicto sancto audieram dum referrem, pavens ille intremuit, moxque nudis pedibus ad insulam, ubi sanctum corpus fuerat, incedens, veniam eorum quæ in eum deliquerat precibus et muneribus petivit Verumtamen postea numquam ei fuerat idem qui prius status honoris, expulsus enim de comitatu, multas quamdiu vixit adversantium rerum importunitates et afflictiones pertulit"

302        CONQUEST OF WESTERN AND NORTHERN ENGLAND.

CHAP XVIII.
General flight of the people

William sets forth from York January, 1070

His march through Cleveland to the Tees

The Earl and the Bishop had fled, and the mass of the people of the Northern diocese followed the example of their chiefs. They sought shelter among hills and woods, and wherever shelter was likely to be found.[1] None stayed in their dwellings save those who from any cause lacked the means of flight. The camp of refuge by the mouth of the Tees was well stocked with provisions, and was fondly deemed to be impregnable.[2] Against this stronghold, at once the nearest and the most dangerous of the spots held by those whom he called rebels and outlaws, William now set forth on his January march.

His march led him through a rugged and difficult country, which, we are told, had never been crossed by an army, and where a road of twenty feet wide among the hills was the only means of approach.[3] The geography shows that the country intended must be the hilly district of Cleveland, which lies on the direct road for one marching from York to any point at the mouth of the Tees.[4] William pressed on, and drew near to the head-quarters of the enemy, who took flight by night at his approach. He followed them to the banks of the river, by a road whose ruggedness was such that the King himself had often to march on foot.[5] On the banks of the river he made a halt of fifteen days,[6] during which space he received the sub-

---

[1] Sim Dun. Gest Regg 86 "Regis exercitus . vacuis ubique domibus, solam invenit solitudinem, indigenis fugæ præsidium quærentibus, vel per silvas et abrupta montium latitantibus"

[2] Ord Vit 515 B " Prædam abundantem contraxerant, securi agitabant, nullam sibi vim nocere putabant"

[3] Ib "Unicus aditus per solidum intromittit, latitudine tantum viginti pedum latens."

[4] On the geography of this march, see below, p. 306, note 2, and Appendix Y On Cleveland, see vol III p. 347

[5] Ord Vit. u s "Rex ardens infestos sibi hostes ad flumen Tesiam insequitur, et avia prorumpit, quorum asperitas interdum peditem eum ire. compellit"

[6] Ib "Super Tesiam sedens quindecim dies transegit"

mission of the two most powerful among his English enemies. Waltheof came in person; Gospatric appeared by proxy. They again swore oaths to him and became his men, William even consenting to receive the oath of Gospatric, as he had received the oath of King Malcolm,[1] at the hands of his messengers.[2] Both Earls were reinstated in their Earldoms, and no doubt in all their possessions Waltheof indeed was more than restored to his former place; he was admitted to the King's highest favour, and was allowed to mingle his blood with the princely blood of Normandy and Ponthieu. A daughter of William had been only promised to Eadwine; a niece of William was actually given to Waltheof. The elder Adelaide, the whole sister of William, the daughter of Robert and Herleva, the wife of Ingelram of Ponthieu, was by him, as we have seen, mother of two daughters, Adelaide and Judith.[3] Both were provided for in England. Adelaide became the wife of Odo of Champagne, who in the end became possessed of the Earldom of Holderness.[4] The other sister became the bride of the English Earl of Northampton and Huntingdon.[5] Of her later career, and of her children, we shall hear again.

But the submission of the Earl of the Northumbrians

---

[1] See above, p 206

[2] Ord Vit 515 B "Ibi reconciliati sunt Guallevus præsens et Gaius Patricius absens, sacramento per legatos exhibito" So both the Chronicles under 1070 "Her se eorl Walþeof griðede wið þone cyng" Mr. Hinde (Hist. North 1 179) remarks that Gospatric "felt himself safer in his rocky citadel of Bamborough than at the court of a sovereign to whom he had given such frequent provocation"

[3] See vol ii pp 587, 588        [4] See Appendix GG.

[5] Waltheof is made by Orderic (534 D) to say at the bride-ale, "Guillelmus Rex fidem meam, ut major a minori, jure recepit, ac ut ei semper fidelis exsisterem, in matrimonium mihi neptem suam copulavit." In 522 C we read more distinctly, "Rex Guillelmus Guallevo Comiti, filio Siwardi potentissimo Anglorum, comitatum Northantoniæ dedit, eique Judith neptem suam, ut firma inter eos amicitia perduraret, in matrimonio conjunxit, quæ duas filias speciosas marito suo peperit"

CHAP XVIII.
William's ravages in the Bishoprick of Durham

Burning of the church of Jarrow

State of Durham.

was not allowed to insure safety or pardon for the land over which he ruled. We must suppose that the submission of Gospatric was not accompanied by any general submission of the chiefs and people of his Earldom. Whatever may have been the case with the land beyond the Tyne, the land between the Tyne and the Tees, the special inheritance of Saint Cuthberht, was doomed to a harrying as remorseless as that which had fallen on Yorkshire itself. To take seizin, as it were, of the conquered land, the host of William was spread over the whole country on its errand of destruction.[1] The materials for slaughter were few, as the inhabitants had everywhere fled, but their houses and churches stood ready for the favourite Norman means of destruction. We are specially told that the church of Jarrow, which had so lately sheltered Æthelwine and his canons, was now destroyed by fire.[2] But we shall soon find reason to see that, as in so many other cases, the destruction could not have gone beyond the burning of the roof and other woodwork. We are not told whether the minster of Durham received any damage in its fabric; but the great church of Ealdhun, forsaken by its Bishop and his clergy, with the sound of divine worship hushed within its walls, became a place of shelter for the poor and weak and sickly, who lay there dying of disease and hunger.[3] Thus at last William had possession of the city which had so long withstood the attacks of Scot and Norman alike. But he had possession only of a city without citizens, and of

---

[1] Sim Dun Gest Regg 86 "Interea regis exercitus etiam per loca quæque inter Tesam et Tine diffusus"

[2] Ib "Tunc et ecclesia Sancti Pauli in Girvum flammis est consumpta" See Appendix HH

[3] Ib "Dunelmensis ecclesia, omni custodiâ et ecclesiastico servitio destituta, spelunca erat pauperum et debilium et ægrotantium, qui, quum fugere non poterant, illuc declinantes fame ac morbo deficiebant"

a land so utterly wasted that it finds no place in the great Survey. *CHAP. XVIII*

This last named fact, that the shires north of Yorkshire are not entered in Domesday, makes it hard to complete our picture of the state of the most northern parts of England after their conquest. It is possible that so much had been done in the way of ravage that it was hardly needful to follow it up with so elaborate a system of confiscation as elsewhere. It is certain that, both within the limits of our own history and in later local annals, men bearing unmistakeable English and Danish names, but still holding high local position, appear in the Bishoprick of Durham in greater numbers than elsewhere.[1] And it is clear that, along with the two Earls, some of the leading men of Yorkshire made their submission to the Conqueror and were received into some measure of favour. Among these we may probably reckon Archill. He is said to have been sent into banishment at some stage of William's reign;[2] but it is clear from the Survey that he was pardoned at last. He must however have been heavily mulcted, as he kept only a very small portion of his great estate.[3] We hear too incidentally of one Eglaf, a Housecarl, whose name speaks his Danish descent, but who is said to have risen high in William's favour.[4] Of Eadwine and Morkere, at this stage of our story, we hear not a word. It is plain that

*Durham and Northumberland not entered in the Survey.*

*Retention of English and Danish names in Durham.*

*Submission of Archill.*

*Favour of Eglaf.*

*Position of Eadwine and Morkere.*

---

[1] See Appendix II

[2] Sim Dun de Obsessione Dunelmi, 157, ed Hinde "Postea Willelmo Rege veniente in Angliam ipse Arkillus fugiens exsul factus est" I presume that the Archill of Domesday is the same as the "Arkil filius Ecgfrith" of Simeon, the last of the three husbands of Sigrid the granddaughter of Bishop Ealdhun

[3] He appears as a tenant in capite in Domesday, 331, 331 *b*. All his estates had been held by himself T R E, but the amount is but small.

[4] Simeon in his History (89) speaks casually of "Eilaf huscarl apud regem præpollens honore," whom he classes among "principales viri"

VOL IV      X

306   CONQUEST OF WESTERN AND NORTHERN ENGLAND.

CHAP XVIII. they took no part in the revolt, and the events of the following years show that they were still in William's court, though doubtless quite as much his prisoners as guests. Still we cannot suppose that their lands were confiscated as yet, while they were still in the King's allegiance and in his apparent favour. Had Morkere to look on during the conquest and desolation of the Earldom of which he does not seem to have been formally deprived?[1] And where was Eadwine when William went forth to overcome the special home of his house, the last citadel of independent England?

William returns to York.

Difficulties of the march by Helmsley.

For we are now drawing near to the end. One more march through the wilds of Northumberland put William in complete possession of the land whose native rulers had again bowed to him. From the Tees he returned to York by way of Helmsley,[2] and the chronicler of his march now becomes specially eloquent on the difficulties of the passage. Some change in the weather may have made those difficulties even more frightful than they were on his march northwards. We now read how his course led him through hills and valleys, where the snow often lay while neighbouring districts were rejoicing in the bloom of spring.[3] Through that wild region William now

---

[1] We shall see, two years later, that Eadwine and Morkere were then still courtiers of William, and the Earldom of Gospatric took in only Northumberland in the narrower sense, the Earldom of Oswulf

[2] In the text of Orderic (515 C) William is now carried to Hexham, an impossible piece of geography See Appendix Y I thankfully accept the correction of Mr Hinde (Hist North i 178); "On this route he [Orderic] places Hexham (Hagustald), doubtless in mistake for Helmsley (Hamelac), which is on the direct line from the lower valley of the Tees to York, and reposes under the dreary summits of the Hambleton range, to which the above description unquestionably refers" I have for once been content to take Mr Hinde's word for the character of the district This Helmsley must be distinguished from Gate Helmsley, which figures in the history of Stamfordbridge See vol iii p 356

[3] Ord Vit 515 C "Mense Januario Rex Guillelmus Haugustaldam revertebatur a Tesiâ, viâ quæ hactenus exercitui erat intentata, quâ

made his way amid the cold and ice of winter. It needed the bidding and the example of a leader who was ever the foremost, and who shrank from no toil which he laid upon others, to keep up the spirits of his followers.[1] The march was toilsome and dangerous; the horses died in crowds; each man pressed on as he could, thinking only of his own safety, and recking little of his lord or of his comrade.[2] At one point William himself, with six horsemen only, lost his way, and had to spend a night in utter ignorance of the whereabouts of his main army.[3] A chance attack from some band of wandering outlaws might possibly have delivered England. It might at least have undone the work of the Conquest, and thrown the conquerors into utter anarchy and confusion. But the fortune of William once more carried him safe through all dangers. He reached York, and there he finally settled the affairs of the city and shire.[4] We should be well pleased to know all that may possibly lurk in so vague a phrase Some confiscations, some giants of land, are doubtless implied; but we know that he restored the castles, and he most likely took other measures for the restoration of the city, a large part of which must still have been a ruin. William's work north of the Humber was now done. The land was thoroughly conquered, but it was thoroughly conquered only because it was thoroughly wasted. The strength and the life of

crebro acutissima juga, et vallum humillimæ sedes, quum vicinia serenitate vernâ gaudet, nivibus compluuntur"

[1] Ord Vit 515 C "At ille in acerbissimo hiemis gelu transivit, animosque militum confirmavit suâ alacritate."

[2] Ib. "Illud iter difficulter peractum est, in quo sonipedum ingens ruina facta est Anxius pro suâ quisque salute exstitit, dominique parum aut amici meminit"

[3] Ib "In eâ difficultate Rex cum senis tantum equitibus aberravit, et noctem integram ubinam essent quos ductabat ignarus exegit"

[4] Ib "Eboracum reversus complura illic castella restauravit et urbi ac regioni commoda ordinavit"

308    CONQUEST OF WESTERN AND NORTHERN ENGLAND.

CHAP XVIII the whole district and its people had been broken by his merciless policy. We shall still hear of one or two local outbreaks in Northumberland, we shall hear of inroads in which the Scot ate up the little that the Norman had spared. But we shall hear of no more battles or sieges in which William had still to strive to win or to keep the Northern portion of his Kingdom. William was now lord of Northumberland; but, in being lord of Northumberland, he was lord only of a wilderness.

*Northern England finally conquered.*

One corner of England now alone remained to be conquered. Chester was still untouched, and it would seem that there were still movements throughout the north-western shires of Mercia which it needed William's own presence and all his energy to put down. He was now fully minded to finish the work which he had begun. He would not show himself again at Rouen or at Winchester in any character but that of the undisputed master of all England. He set forth therefore on yet another march, the last and most fearful of the marches of this wonderful winter campaign. Between York and Chester lay the wild region of southwestern Yorkshire, a portion of that great hill range which so long sheltered the Briton of Strathclyde from the invading Angle, the range which, sometimes rising, sometimes sinking, unites the Peakland of Derbyshire with the mountains of Westmoreland and Cumberland. The Peakland is in winter preeminently a land of ice and snow, but it is hardly possible that William's line of march can have led him so far to the south. He must rather have passed through a land which in later times has been filled with some of the busiest seats of English industry, but which still retain many signs to show how rugged a land it must have been in a winter in William's day. Densely peopled settlements of man alternate with spots of rural beauty which here and there rise into somewhat

*Chester still holds out*

*William's last march, February? 1070*

*Difficult character of the country between York and Chester*

of the grandeur of the wilderness. It is a land of hills and dales and streams, the hills here and there almost swelling into mountain-peaks.[1] Through this land, then no doubt an utter waste, William's army, after all its earlier toils, had to force its way amid the cold of February. As he was making ready for this last enterprise, he was met by what we now hear of for the first time in his history, a mutinous temper on the part of his own troops. They had had enough of marchings to and fro in the depth of winter, and now they were called on to set forth on another march which threatened dangers and difficulties yet greater than any of those which had gone before it. They feared the roughness of the country through which they had to pass, the cold and storms of the winter, the lack of provisions, the fierceness and daring of the enemy with whom they would have to strive.[2] This last source of dread, at any rate, does no small honour to the men of North Wales and North-western Mercia. These feelings, it would seem, were felt most deeply and expressed most loudly by those parts of William's army which were neither Norman nor English. We hear of these complaints mainly as the complaints of the Bretons, the Angevins, and the men of Maine.[3] Now it will be remembered that in an earlier stage of the war, soon after his first expedition to the North, William had dismissed all his mercenary soldiers.[4] If the Angevins had not

*Mutinous spirit of his troops*

*Special disaffection of the Bretons, Angevins, and Cenomannians*

[1] I am thinking mainly of the country between Huddersfield and Manchester, which lies pretty well in the direct line for a march from York to Chester.

[2] Ord. Vit. 515 C. "Deinde movit expeditionem contra Cestrenses et Guallos, qui, præter alias offensas, nuperrime Scrobesburiam obsederunt. Exercitus autem, qui dura toleraverat, in hoc itinere multo duriora restare timebat. Verebatur enim locorum asperitatem, hiemis intemperiem, alimentorum inopiam, et hostium terribilem ferocitatem."

[3] Ib. C, D. "Andegavi, Britones, et Cenomanni servitiis, ut dicebant, intolerabilibus oppido gravabantur, unde pertinaciter a Rege missionem petentes conquerebantur." [4] See above, p. 233.

been mentioned, we might have thought that the men of Maine, who were now William's own subjects, and the Bretons, who were in some sort his vassals, were not reckoned among the mercenaries. But it is hard to see how any troops from the rival land of Anjou could have been serving in William's army in any character but that of private adventurers.[1] Still we can understand that mere geographical neighbourhood might keep together the forces of North-western Gaul, after those from more distant regions had sought their dismissal. On the other hand, it is easy to believe that new swarms of strangers had flocked to William's banners to take their chance of a share in the spoils of England. At all events, it was the men of Anjou, Maine, and Britanny who took the lead in the mutiny. They demanded their dismissal; they complained of the hardship of following a lord who was ever aiming at some new enterprise of boundless ambition, and was ever laying on his subjects orders too hard to be carried out.[2] William, we are told, kept the example of his model Cæsar before his eyes. He did not stoop to entreat the mutineers or to win them over by promises.[3] He set forth at once, bidding the faithful and valiant to follow him; as for cowards and weaklings, he recked little whether they followed him or not.[4] This kind of dealing told on the troops. They marched on, making their way among high hills and deep valleys, across rivers swollen by the winter's rain, and bottoms which the same season had

William's dealings with the mutineers

Difficult march to Chester

---

[1] See vol. iii. p. 314.

[2] Ord. Vit. 515 D. "Sui nimirum ad expurgationem depromebant non posse domino semper nova et immoderata audenti nimiaque præcipienti obsequi."

[3] Ib. "Rex autem constantiam Julii Cæsaris in tali necessitate sequutus est, nec eos multo precatu seu novis promissis retinere dignatus est."

[4] Ib. "Audacter inceptum iter iniit, fidasque sibi cohortes se sequi præcepit; desertores vero, velut inertes pavidosque et invalidos, si discedant, parvi pendit."

PLAN OF CHESTER.
1070–1087.

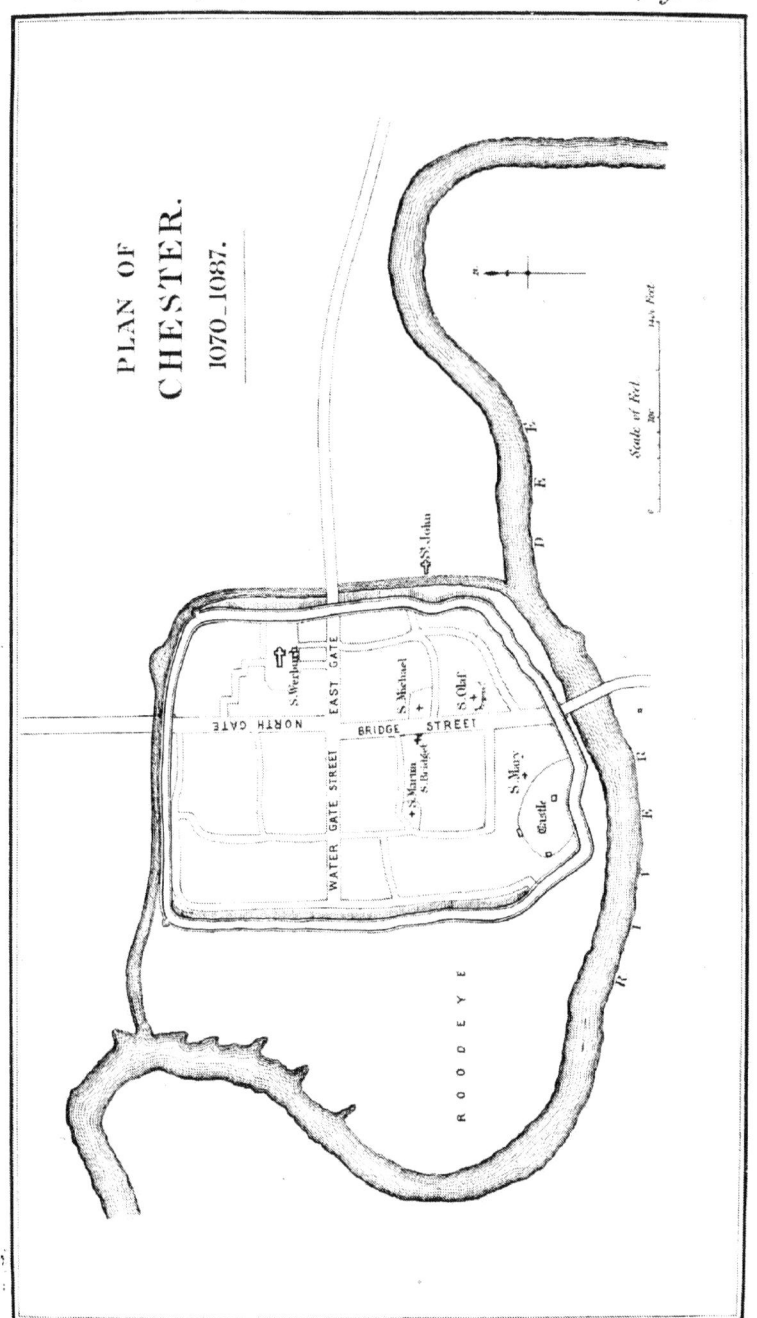

changed into well nigh impenetrable marshes. Storms of rain and hail troubled them on their march. Horsemen and footmen were brought to a level, as the horses of the knights were swallowed up or swept away by the treacherous swamps.[1] King William himself had often to lead the van on foot, and to give help with his own hands to those whose strength was failing.[2] But all dangers were at last overcome. To have led his army safely through so strange and wearisome a trial speaks more for William's gifts as a leader of men than to have won the prize on the stricken fields of Val-ès-dunes and Senlac.

*Personal energy of William.*

At last the fearful march was over. William and his host came down into the rich pastures of the land which in after days was known as the Vale Royal of England.[3] Here was the one great city which had not yet bowed to his might, the one still abiding home of English freedom. All the other great seats of royal, ecclesiastical, and municipal power were already his. William was King at Winchester and London, at Canterbury and York, at

*William enters Cheshire*

*Chester the last conquest*

---

[1] Ord. Vit. 515 D. "Indefessim itaque pergit viâ equiti numquam ante expertâ, in quâ sunt montes ardui et profundissimæ valles, rivi et amnes periculosi, et voraginosa vallium ima. In hâc viâ gradientes sæpe nimio vexabantur imbre, mixtâ interdum grandine. Aliquando præstabant cunctis usum equi in paludibus evecti."

[2] Ib. "Ipse Rex multoties pedes cunctos agiliter præcedebat, et laborantes manibus impigre adjuvabat."

[3] Ib. "Tandem exercitum incolumem usque Cestram perduxit." For Chester and Cheshire see the description given by William of Malmesbury, Gest. Pont. 308. "Cestra Legionum Civitas dicitur, quod ibi emeriti legionum Julianarum resedere. Collimitatur Aquilonalibus Britannis. Regio farris et maxime tritici, ut pleraque aquilonalium, jejuna et inops, pecorum et piscium ferax. Incolæ lac et butyrum delicias habent, qui ditiores sunt carnibus vivunt, panem hordeicium et siliginium pro magno complectuntur. Transmittitur a Cestrâ Hiberniam revehunturque civitati necessaria, ut quod minus natura soli habet labor negotiantium apportet." Henry of Huntingdon also (M. H. B. 693 D) speaks of "Hibernis Cestria propinquans."

312        CONQUEST OF WESTERN AND NORTHERN ENGLAND.

CHAP XVIII Glastonbury and Peterborough, at Exeter and Lincoln. But he was not yet King at Chester. The old City of the Legions, the river on which Eadgar had been rowed by vassal Kings, the minster where the English Basileus had knelt with his vassal Kings around him, the walls from which men could look out on the land which Harold had added to the English realm [1]—all still were free, standing untouched amid surrounding bondage, like a single perfect column standing unhurt amid the shattered ruins of a forsaken temple. The twelve judges of the city had in old times sat in the name of the King, the Bishop, and the Earl.[2] They must now, in the utter break-up of all national authority, have wielded a power as little amenable to any jurisdiction beyond their own gates as the rulers of any Italian city which barely stooped to own a nominal lord in the Teutonic Cæsar. By ancient right the men of the whole shire were bound to repair the walls and the bridge of the local capital,[3] and we cannot doubt that, in the course of the three years during which Chester had maintained its independence of the invader, the labour of the surrounding lands had been willingly given to strengthen the last national stronghold. There is no point in William's history at which we should more gladly welcome the minutest details than in this, the last stage of the real Conquest of England. But not a detail, not an anecdote, is preserved; we know only the results. The work which had begun at Pevensey was brought to an

Municipal constitution of Chester

Its local privileges

Lack of details of the Cheshire campaign

[1] See Note SS in the second edition of vol ii

[2] Domesday, 262 b "T. R E . erant xii judices civitatis, et hi erant de hominibus Regis et Episcopi et Comitis Horum si qui de hundret remanebat die quo sedebant sine excusatione manifestâ x solidos emendabat inter Regem et Comitem." Various other rights of the Earl and the Bishop are mentioned, the latter being the more remarkable, as the see was not yet at Chester.

[3] Ib "Ad murum civitatis et pontem reædificandum de unâquâque hidâ comitatûs unum hominem venire præpositus edicebat. Cujus homo non veniebat, dominus ejus xl solidos emendabat Regi et Comiti"

end at Chester, and we can see that it was not brought to an end without hard fighting. William had to put down by force the hostile movements of what was now specially the Mercian land.[1] We know not whether the city surrendered or was taken by storm; we know not by what operations the shire and the adjoining lands were conquered. But a siege of Chester would have put the military art of the time to as hard a trial as the siege of Exeter. The Roman town, beneath whose walls the heathen Æthelfrith had unwittingly fulfilled the warnings of Augustine to the stubborn Britons,[2] had been left by him as Ælle and Cissa had left Anderida.[3] In the Danish wars of Ælfred the walls still stood, no longer surrounding any dwelling-place of man, but still capable of being turned to a defensive purpose in the warfare of the time.[4] By the watchful care of the Lady of the Mercians Chester had been again called into being as a city and fortress;[5] and it was probably by her that the circuit of the Roman wall was extended to take in the mound on which the Norman castle was now to supplant her earlier stronghold.[6]

*Submission of the shire and city*

*Defences of Chester, their history*

*Victory of Æthelfrith 605-613*

*Desolation of the city. 605-907*

*Restoration by Æthelflæd 907*

---

[1] Ord. Vit. 516 A. "In totâ Merciorum regione motus hostiles regiâ vi compescuit."

[2] See the Chronicles, 605, 606, Florence, 603, Hen Hunt M H B 715 B, who calls Æthelfrith's victory "bellum bellorum maximum."

[3] See vol. iii p 403

[4] In 894 the Danish army pursued by the English took refuge within the ruined site of Chester. The way in which the place is spoken of by the Chronicler is remarkable, "Þæt hy gedydon on anre wæstre ceastre on Wirhealum, seo is Ligeceaster haten." It is curious to find the future proper name of the city used as an appellative, "a waste chester." Florence is more distinct, "Civitatem Legionum, tunc temporis desertam, quæ Saxonice Legeceaster dicitur, priusquam Regis Ælfredi et Ætheredi subreguli exercitus, qui illos insequutus est, assequi poterant, intrant." The fugitives were able to defend the "geweorc," as the Roman walls are called, very successfully.

[5] Chron 907 "Her wæs Ligceaster geednoewad." Florence (908) is fuller, "Civitas quæ Karlegion Britannice, et Legeceaster dicitur Saxonice, jussu Æthercdi Ducis et Ægelfledæ, restaurata est."

[6] For this hint I have to thank the local antiquary Mr. Hughes

314          CONQUEST OF WESTERN AND NORTHERN ENGLAND.

CHAP XVIII
The walls of Chester.

The minsters of Saint John and Saint Werburh

Position and strength of the city.

Fall of Chester

The mediæval walls of Chester are more perfect than those of any other English city, and traces of their Roman forerunners still remain, enough to show that, except at this point, the line of the Roman fortification was strictly followed. Their circuit takes in the minster of Saint Werburh, then a secular, but soon to become a monastic house, and which the changes of the sixteenth century have made the seat of the modern Bishoprick. The minster of Saint John, the church chosen for the devotions of Eadgar, also a house of secular canons, soon to become one of the cathedral churches of the Mercian diocese, lies on the east side of the city, without the walls.[1] The fortifications which William had to reduce were doubtless those of the old Cæsars as strengthened by the Mercian Lady. They took in a space which in those days must have been peninsular, as it is plain that the flat land which now lies between the river and the west wall of the city, known locally as the *Rooddee,* was covered by water long after William's time.[2] The bridge on the south side was commanded by the fortress of Æthelflæd, as it has since been by the later castle, and the whole city must have stood as a compact square, well defended both by nature and art. How this our last national stronghold fell we know not, but we know that it did fall, and that, as usual, a Norman keep soon rose on the old mound to act as a curb on the conquered city. And we know that the resistance which William met with in this

---

[1] On Saint Werburh's church at Chester and its change to a Benedictine Abbey by Earl Hugh in 1093, see Mon Angl ii 370, and the entries of the lands of its Warden (custos ecclesiæ) and Canons in Domesday, 263. The entries about Saint John's are in the same page, but are put among the lands of the Bishoprick, though the Bishoprick is still spoken of as "Sanctus Cedde," from its ancient seat at Lichfield    See also Mon Angl. viii 1447.

[2] This is clear from the local name of the Water-gate, which is no longer deserved   I believe however that a geologist would not stand in need of this argument

his last conquest was enough to lead him to apply the same stern remedy which he had applied north of the Humber. A fearful harrying fell on city and shire and on the lands round about.[1] From Cheshire, Derbyshire, Staffordshire, Shropshire, men young and old, women and children, pressed southwards in search of a morsel of bread. It is pleasant to learn that many of them found some measure of food and shelter at the gates of the Abbey of Evesham. The prudence of Abbot Æthelwig, and the favour which he contrived to keep at the hands of three successive Kings, had at least not quenched his will to help the distressed, while the yet untouched wealth of his Abbey allowed him the means as well as the will. The houses, the streets, the churchyard, of Evesham were crowded with homeless wretches who, well nigh dying of hunger before they reached the hospitable spot, had barely strength to swallow the food which the bountiful Prelate offered them.[2] Every day, five, six, or more of the fugitives died and were buried by the pious care of the Prior Ælfric, to whose immediate guardianship the sufferers were entrusted.[3] Nor was the bounty of Æthelwig

*Ravaging of Cheshire and neighbouring shires*

*Charity shewn to the sufferers by Abbot Æthelwig of Evesham*

*Mortality among the fugitives*

---

[1] Hist. Evesh. 90. "In primis temporibus sui regni Rex Wilhelmus fecit devastari quasdam sciras istis in partibus, propter exsules et latrones qui in silvis latitabant ubique et maxima damna pluribus hominibus faciebant, videlicet Eoveruuicscire, Ceastrescire, Scrobscire, Stafordscire, Deorbiscire."

[2] Ib. "Maxima multitudo senum, juvenum, mulierum, cum parvulis suis, famis miseriam fugientes, dolentissime huc veniebat, quos omnes ille vir miseratus pro posse suo alebat. Plures namque diu absorpti durissimâ fame, dum cibum avidius sumerent, moriebantur. Jacebant miseri homines per totam villam, tam in domibus quam deforis, necnon et in cœmeterio isto languidi, huc antequam venirent fame consumpti, et idcirco ut cibum corporis sentiebant plurimi vitâ deficiebant."

[3] Ib. 91. "Facta est magna mortalitas multo tempore de talibus hominibus, ita ut quotidie fere quinque vel sex homines, aliquando plures, miserabiliter morientes a Priore hujus loci sepeliebantur." The local historian goes on to describe at some length the arrangements made by

confined to those only who, in the very depth of the evil days, amid the cold and hunger of this fearful winter, craved for alms to sustain their lives. Many a man of higher rank, whom the confiscations of William had driven from the lands and home of his fathers, found shelter and help in the holy house of Saint Ecgwine.[1] But little was the help which all the Prelates and Thegns of England, had every one been as openhanded as Æthelwig, could have given to relieve the distress of a whole people[2] A hundred thousand human beings, no small portion of the inhabitants of England in those days, are said to have died of cold and hunger in the winter which made William full King over the whole land.[3] The figures are probably a mere guess; they can hardly rest on any trustworthy statistics; we know not whether they are meant to apply to Northumberland only or to all the shires which William harried. Such was the price to be paid for William's conquest. As the painter of his portrait tells us, he was so stark that he recked not either of men's

*Alleged depopulation of the country.*

the Abbot and Prior Ælfric for the relief of the sufferers, and especially for the care of the children

[1] Hist Evesh 92 "Et non solum talibus pauperibus, sed etiam pluribus nobilibus ad eum confugientibus, paternâ hæreditate omnique substantiâ miserabiliter sublatâ Rege Willielmo jubente, factus est refugium et adjutor piissimus in maximis necessitatibus." The writer goes on to mention other charitable acts of Æthelwig, especially his custom when travelling of making his followers give up their cloaks—which however were restored twofold—to any whom they met by the way in want of clothing This reminds one of the stories told of Kimôn by Plutarch (Kim. 10), and of the story told by William Fitz-Stephen (Giles, S. T C 191) of Henry and Thomas

[2] Compare Burke's description of the suffering caused by Hyder Ali's devastation of the Carnatic, "The alms of the settlement in this dreadful exigency were certainly liberal, and all was done by charity that private charity could do But it was a people in beggary, it was a nation that stretched forth its hands for food"

[3] Ord Vit 514 D "Unde sequenti tempore tam gravis in Angliâ late sævit penuria, et inermem ac simplicem populum tanta famis involvit miseria, ut Christianæ gentis, utriusque sexûs et omnis ætatis, homines perirent plusquam centum millia"

sufferings or of their hatred.[1] He had but won his own, and amidst all the woes of the wasted land, he could still give his thanks and offer his gifts to God and Saint Martin and to all the saints of Normandy and Gaul, who had blessed his holy work with success, and had girded him with strength to chastise the perjurer and the rebel.

But, at whatever cost, England was conquered. William had yet to struggle against revolts both among the conquered English and among his own people. But the land was won; there was no longer any portion of English ground which could still refuse submission to an invader; future struggles were simply revolts against a government which was now in full possession. The fall of Chester was the last scene of the long battle the first blows of which had been struck when, well nigh four years back, Tostig had first harried English ground by William's licence.[2] We ask, but we ask in vain, whether Ealdgyth and her child were within the walls of the captured city, and whether it was now that William gained possession of the young heir of the House of Godwine, whose life, as long as William lived, was to be the life-in-death of a Norman prison.[3] To questions like these no certain answer can be given. We know only that the land was won, and we know by what means the land which had been won was to be kept. The castle which was built to defend what was left of Chester was entrusted, with the rank of Earl, to the King's own step-son the Fleming Gerbod[4] William then marched again to Stafford, and took the same means as at

*CHAP XVIII*

England now fully conquered.

Question as to Ealdgyth and Ulf

The castle of Chester built and entrusted to Gerbod the Fleming as Earl.

[1] Compare the famous description in the Peterborough Chronicle, 1087.
[2] See vol iii p 324
[3] See Flor Wig 1087, where he records the liberation of Ulf after William's death. Cf above, p 143
[4] Ord Vit 522 A "Cestram et comitatum ejus Gherbodo Flandrensi jamdudum Rex dederat." On Gerbod, see vol iii p 647

CHAP XVIII
A castle built at Stafford

William marches to Salisbury February —March? 1070

He reviews his army

552

Chester, by the foundation of a castle, to keep that dangerous town and shire also in order. The later castle of Stafford stands at some distance from the town, but the probability of the case may lead us to accept the local tradition which speaks of an earlier castle in the town itself, which from an entry in Domesday[1] would seem to have been built and destroyed before the end of William's reign. The castles both of Chester and Stafford were guarded by competent garrisons, and were well furnished with provisions.[2] The King then marched across the conquered country to Salisbury. The royal head-quarters were doubtless fixed within the mighty trenches of elder days, on the hill fort where yet another Norman castle was no doubt already rising, and where the Norman minster was soon to rise. The great plain which is now covered by the modern city was well suited for a final gathering and review of the victorious army. On that ground, more than five hundred years before, had Cynric the West-Saxon won one of those great fights, each of which marks a stage in the change of Britain into England.[3] And now William's host gathered on the same spot, to mark the last stage of the change by which England was not indeed changed into Normandy, but was driven to accept the Norman as her master. The Conqueror now gave great gifts to the men who had shared his toils, gifts which, we are told, were reward enough even for all that they had

---

[1] In Domesday, 248 *b*, it is said of one of the lordships of Henry of Ferrers, "ad hoc manerium pertinuit terra de Stadford, in quâ Rex præcepit fieri castellum, quod modo est destructum." Local Staffordshire writers also speak of a castle in the town, distinct from that on the somewhat distant height. An unavoidable accident drives me to speak of Stafford from much older and vaguer recollections than those which I can bring to bear on most of the places mentioned in this Chapter.

[2] Ord. Vit. 516 A. "In reversione suâ apud Estafort alteram [munitionem] locavit, milites et almonias abunde utrobique [at Chester and Stafford] imposuit."

[3] See vol. i. p. 349.

gone through. The conquerors of York and Stafford and Chester, the men who had laid waste English homes and fields, and who had forced their way through the frozen hills and valleys of Cleveland, received from the mouth of their sovereign the praises due to their deeds. They were at once dismissed with all thanks and honour And those who had forsaken William's banners, or who had quailed under the toils of his marches, received no heavier punishment than to lose their share in the rewards of their comrades, and to be themselves kept under arms for forty days longer.[1] When William could thus send away the troops whom he could really trust, and could keep himself surrounded only by discontented mutineers, it was plain that England was conquered.

*His rewards and punishments*

It remained only to get rid of the Danish allies who had promised so much, and had done so little, for the deliverance of England. Osbeorn and his fleet stayed during the whole winter in the Humber, beyond the reach of William's arms,[2] but not beyond the reach of his arts. Osbeorn was perhaps in his heart not over zealous on behalf of a land from which he had once been driven into banishment.[3] At some stage of this memorable winter William contrived to send a secret message to the Danish Earl, and to win him over by the promise of a large sum of money. He was to sail away when winter was over, and he was to be allowed in the meanwhile to plunder the English coast, on condition that he did not come to any actual engagement

*The Danish fleet remains in the Humber 1069-1070*

*Osbeorn bribed by William*

---

[1] Ord Vit. 516 A "Perveniens inde Salesburiam præmia militibus ibi pro tantâ tolerantiâ largissime distribuit, bene meritos collaudavit, et cum gratiâ multâ dimisit Desertores autem ad dies xl. ultra discessum commilitonum per indignationem retinuit, eâque pœnâ delictum quod pejus meruit castigavit"

[2] Chron Wig. 1069 "And þæt hð læig ealne winter innan Humbre, þær se kyng heom to cuman ne mihte"

[3] See vol ii p 63

with the King's forces [1] These terms, to his disgrace and final ruin, he agreed to. He seems however to have done his best to cheat both sides, Norman and English alike. We shall see in the course of the next year that William's licence to plunder was somewhat liberally construed, and that the time during which the Danish fleet was to be allowed to tarry in English waters was prolonged far beyond the time on which William might fairly reckon. In the course of the next two years we shall still hear of the doings alike of English revolters and of their Danish allies. So, somewhat later, we shall hear of the doings of Breton, Cenomannian, and even Norman revolters. Still the Conquest was now really over. After the fall of Chester no integral part of the English Kingdom remained unsubdued. William was full King over all England. What remained still to be done, as far as the whole island was concerned, was for the new King of the English to establish somewhat more than the external over-lordship of his predecessors over all the lands which had formed part of their island Empire. Within England itself, what was still to be done was for the priest to follow in the track of the warrior, for the wiles of Lanfranc and Hildebrand to build up a power against which William himself could hold his own, but before which his weaker descendants had for a while to bend.

---

[1] Flor Wig 1069 " Interea nuntius ad Danicum comitem Esbernum missis spopondit se clanculo daturum illi non modicæ summam pecuniæ, et permissurum licenter exercitui suo victum sibi circa ripas maris rapere, eâ tamen interpositâ conditione, ut sine pugnâ discederet peractâ hieme Ille autem, auri argentique nimis avidus, non sine magno dedecore sui petitis concessit" Orderic (515 B) gives us only a rhetorical account of the sufferings of the Danes and of their return to Denmark, not a word about the dealings between William and Osbeorn. Here at least Orderic is following William of Poitiers

## CHAPTER XIX.

### THE ECCLESIASTICAL SETTLEMENT OF ENGLAND.[1]

A.D. 1070—1089

ENGLAND was now fully conquered; the authority of William was now acknowledged in every corner of the realm. We shall hear almost immediately of fresh resistance against William's authority; but resistance now takes the form of the revolts of a subdued people; it is no longer the defensive warfare of a people whose independence was attacked but was not yet overthrown. William had done his work of conquest, and his reign over the land which he had won was now to begin. Things had greatly changed since his crowning on the great Midwinter-Day. The realm of which he had then taken a formal possession was now truly his, but it had become his only by the sword. The dream of a peaceful reign, under which England might flourish as Normandy had done, had passed away

*State of England in 1070*

*William in possession of the whole country*

---

[1] For the ecclesiastical history of William's reign, which I have endeavoured to deal with as a whole in the present Chapter, several sources become of importance besides those to which we have trusted all along The various local histories, being mainly the histories of monasteries, are of course of special value for this purpose. The Lives and Letters of Lanfranc are now of increased importance, and not least among them the short Latin Annals of his life which are attached to the Winchester Chronicle. Eadmer in his two Histories, Historia Novorum and Vita Anselmi, is now of primary importance, and William of Malmesbury's Gesta Pontificum, which I can now quote in the new edition of Mr. Hamilton, becomes a book of great value

VOL. IV. Y

for ever. William had been driven to make his reign thus far a reign of terror, a reign of slaughter, exile, confiscation, and ravage. A large part of the lands of England had been laid waste; a larger part still had been portioned out among foreign owners. Yet for a moment there was peace; comparative peace indeed, if only the peace of utter subjection, set in from this time for the rest of William's reign. Revolts indeed were to go on, but they were all purely local revolts. There was never again a moment when any large portion of the land was in arms at once, when, as during the last year, warfare was going on at once at Exeter, at Chester, at Durham, and at Norwich. For a moment the sword was sheathed; no element of disturbance seemed to be left in the land except the Danish fleet in the Humber. The conquerors and the conquered alike had a moment's breathing-time.

But in dealing with the acts of such a man as William, the personal position, the personal intentions, of the man himself are of hardly less moment than the condition and the temper of armies and nations. We can hardly doubt that William had changed for the worse since the day of his crowning Everything since that time had tended to draw out the worse features of his character and to throw the better ones into the shade. He had become harder, more unscrupulous, more reckless of human suffering. But the harshness of William's rule never sank into mere purposeless tyranny, into mere delight in oppression. He never wholly lost the feeling that he owed a duty towards God and man Even now he was capable of honest endeavours to do his duty towards the realm which he had won at the cost of so much of crime and sorrow. It was about this time that he gave one most conspicuous instance of his wish, even now, to rule in England as an English King. It was his business as King to hearken to the complaints of his subjects, to do right and justice among them according to the laws of the Kings who had gone before him. It was his duty to go, like Ælfred and Cnut, through the shires and cities of his Kingdom, and to see with his own eyes that those who ruled in his name refused, sold, or delayed justice to no man.[1] But this duty could not be thoroughly done by a King who knew not the tongue of his people, who had to hear their complaints and to pronounce his own judgements through the mouth of an interpreter. William then, at the age of forty-three, in all the pomp of kingship and the renown of victory, again bowed his neck to the yoke of the schoolmaster. As Charles the Great had striven in his later years to learn the art of writing,[2] so now William the Great strove, we cannot doubt with all honesty of purpose, to master the tongue of his English subjects.[3] In neither case were the efforts of the royal student crowned with any great measure of success. The vague rhetoric of our informant leaves us with no very clear notion as to the real extent of William's English scholarship. We are told that he found his age an hindrance, and that, as we might have expected, other affairs called him away from his studies.[4] We may feel sure that the Conqueror never learned to address an English Assembly like Godwine; but we may be allowed to believe that he learned English enough to understand the simple formulæ of his

*He tries to learn English*

*Probable extent of his studies*

---

[1] I need hardly quote the 29th chapter of the Great Charter, "Nulli vendemus, nulli negabimus, aut differemus justiciam vel rectum."

[2] The description given by Eginhard (Vita K. 25) of Charles's attempts to write is well known, "Parum successit labor præposterus ac sero inchoatus." But I doubt whether it is always remembered that his attempts to write prove that he could read.

[3] Ord. Vit. 520 D. "Anglicam locutionem plerumque sategit ediscere, ut sine interprete querelam subjectæ legis posset intelligere, et scita rectitudinis unicuique, prout ratio dictaret, affectuose depromere."

[4] Ib. "Ast a perceptione hujusmodi durior ætas illum compescebat, et tumultus multimodarum occupationum ad alia necessario adtrahebat."

own charters. And the fact that he made even an attempt in his own person to acquire the English tongue wholly wipes away the legendary notion of his striving to abolish its use,[1] and makes it all but certain that English formed part of the education of his English-born son.[2]

It is certain that this year, the fourth year of William, left behind it a special and a favourable memory in popular belief. The traditions of a later age told how King William, in his fourth year, summoned the Witan of the land to declare what the ancient laws of England were. He had already, we are told, remembering his own Scandinavian descent and that of his Norman followers, decreed that the customs of the Denalagu should be observed throughout his realm. But the people of England cried with one voice for the Laws of good King Eadward and for none other. Twelve men therefore were, by the writ of King William, chosen in each shire, who declared on oath before the King what the Laws of King Eadward were. Those Laws were then put into the shape of a code, and were published by the order of King William as the only Law of his Kingdom.

No one who fully takes in the history and the legal formulæ of this age can accept this story as it stands. No one can believe that the large extant codes which bear the names of Eadward and William were really put forth in their actual shape by either of those Kings.[3] On the other hand, there is little doubt that we have some genuine pieces of William's legislation surviving, though it would seem that ordinances put forth at various times and places have been put together as if they formed a continuous statute.[4] And among these there are some enactments which we may, almost with certainty, refer to this par-

---

[1] See the false Ingulf, 71, Gale  [2] See Appendix EE
[3] On the alleged Laws of William and Eadward, see Appendix KK
[4] The seemingly genuine Laws of William have been last printed by Professor Stubbs, Select Charters, 80 See Appendix KK

ticular period of William's reign It followed almost as a matter of course that, in this passing moment of peace, when William was for the first time undisputed master of England, he should mark his new position by some formal act of reconciliation between his old and his new subjects. To "renew the Law" of some revered prince after a time of war or disturbance was a process familiar both in England and in Normandy. Harold Blaatand had renewed the Law of Rolf in Normandy,[1] and Harold the son of Godwine had renewed the Law of Cnut in Northumberland.[2] But a still closer parallel is supplied by that great Gemót of Cnut's early reign in which Danes and Englishmen formally made up their differences, and united in the renewal of the Law of Eadgar.[3] So it was quite in the order of things that William should, especially at this particular moment, ordain the formal reconciliation of his Norman and his English subjects, and decree the renewal of what was doubtless already beginning to be spoken of as the Law of Eadward. There is little doubt that we have the actual text of these two ordinances, ordinances most probably passed in the Easter Gemót of this year, and which not unlikely preserve to us, with the needful changes, the words of the earlier ordinances of Cnut. In the same language as the first among the laws of the Danish conqueror, William now bids his subjects throughout his Kingdom to worship one God and to keep one true Christian faith; and if he does not venture, like his predecessor, to bid them love William King with right truthfulness, he ordains that there shall be peace and mutual security between Englishmen and Normans.[4] The Laws of Eadward are renewed

CHAP XIX Reconciliation of English and Normans, and renewal of Eadward's Law

Language of the decrees,

borrowed from those of Cnut

---

[1] See vol 1 p 244    [2] See vol. 11. p 499.
[3] See vol 1 p 462.
[4] Select Charters, 80 "In primis quod super omnia unum vellet Deum

William's changes

Provision for the safety of William's Norman followers

Intercourse between Norman and English now begins

William's strict police

as touching the holding of lands and all other matters whatsoever, but a reservation is made for such changes as the reigning King had made for the good of the people of the English.[1] This reservation was indeed a dangerous one. But once granting the position of William in England, some changes in, or additions to, the ancient laws could hardly be avoided. We cannot blame him for providing for the defence of his Norman followers against any irregular violence on the part of the discontented English.[2] This provision, the germ which afterwards grew into the famous law of *Englishry*,[3] can hardly fail to belong to this early stage of William's legislation. Other provisions which regulate the relations between men of the two races within the Kingdom more probably belong to a later date.

It was quite in the spirit of this legislation that William at this moment did what he could to encourage harmony and good feeling, intermarriage and intercourse of all kinds, among all his subjects, French and English. And now that actual warfare had for a while ceased, the land began to feel the benefit of that stern police which, in

per totum regnum suum venerari, unam fidem Christi semper inviolatam custodiri, pacem et securitatem inter Anglos et Normannos servari" It is impossible to doubt that this is borrowed from the opening of the Laws of Cnut quoted in vol 1 p 481

[1] Select Charters, 81. "Hoc quoque præcipio et volo, ut omnes habeant et teneant legem Edwardi Regis in terris et in omnibus rebus, adauctis iis quæ constitui ad utilitatem populi Anglorum" This reservation is made again in the renewal of the Laws of Eadward by Henry the First See Florence, 1100; "Legem Regis Eadwardi omnibus in commune reddidit, cum illis emendationibus quibus pater suus illam emendavit"

[2] Ib 80 "Volo ut omnes homines quos mecum adduxi, aut post me venerunt, sint in pace meâ et quiete Et si quis de illis occisus fuerit, dominus ejus habeat infra quinque dies homicidam ejus, si potuerit, sin autem, incipiat persolvere mihi xlvi marcas argenti quamdiu substantia illius domini perduraverit Ubi vero substantia defecerit, totus hundredus in quo occisio facta est communiter persolvat quod remanet"

[3] See vol 1 p. 493.

William's hands, dealt out speedy justice on the robber, the murderer, and the ravisher.[1] In the towns especially the two races began to dwell peaceably together; French merchants were seen with their wares in the streets of English boroughs, and French burghers began to form a part of their permanent inhabitants. Their English neighbours began in some degree to adopt their dress and manner of life, and we may be sure that each found it needful to gain some knowledge of the others' language.[2] The process had begun through which, a hundred years later, it had become impossible, except in the highest and lowest ranks, to distinguish Englishmen from Normans.[3] This process, busily at work among the smaller Thegnhood, was still more busily at work in the towns, and it bore its noblest fruit when the marriage of Gilbert of Rouen and Rohesia of Caen gave birth to Thomas of London.[4]

This year then of comparative peace, as it was certainly

---

[1] Ord. Vit. 520 C, D. "His temporibus, opitulante gratiâ Dei, pax in Angliâ regnabat, et securitas aliquanta, procul repulsis latronibus, habitatores terræ refovebat .. nemo prædari audebat, sed unusquisque sua rura tuto colebat suoque compari (sed non per longum tempus) hilariter applaudebat." We must not forget that "latrones" most likely means, to some extent at least, English patriots. Still there is no doubt as to the real efficacy of William's police. See above, p. 30, and vol. ii. p. 172.

[2] Ib. D. "Civiliter Angli cum Normannis cohabitabant in burgis, castris, et urbibus, connubiis alteri alteros mutuo sibi conjungentes. Vicos aliquos aut fora urbana Gallicis mercibus et mangonibus referta conspiceres, et ubique Anglos, qui pridem amictu patrio compti videbantur Francis turpes, nunc peregrino cultu alteratos videres." "Mangones" is here doubtless to be taken in the widest sense, but it is not to be forgotten that it would still be applicable in the narrower meaning.

[3] Dialogus de Scaccario, i. 10. "Jam cohabitantibus Anglicis et Normannis, et alterutrum uxores ducentibus vel nubentibus, sic permixtæ sunt nationes, ut vix discerni possit hodie, de liberis loquor, quis Anglicus, quis Normannus sit genere, exceptis duntaxat adscriptitiis qui villani dicuntur."

[4] See the Lambeth Life of Thomas (Giles, ii. 73) "Gilbertus cognomento Becchet, patriâ Rotomagensis. habuit uxorem Roesam, natione Cadomensem." Yet Thomas himself (Epp. iii. 286) speaks of his parents as "cives Londonienses" without a hint of their foreign origin.

328    THE ECCLESIASTICAL SETTLEMENT OF ENGLAND.

CHAP. XIX
Ecclesiastical importance of the year 1070

not wholly bare of military events, was probably not bare of important political events. Still it is in its ecclesiastical aspect that it stands out most clearly in our annals; it was itself a year of special moment in our ecclesiastical history, and it is still more important as witnessing the beginning of the systematic policy of William and Lanfranc in ecclesiastical matters.

§ 1. *The Councils of the Year* 1070.

This specially ecclesiastical year, in which William was to show himself to the world mainly in the character of a reformer of the Church, began, strangely yet characteristically, with an act which, in a less pious prince than William, might have been set down as a gross breach of all ecclesiastical privilege. Many wealthy Englishmen, mainly, we may suppose, those who had suffered outlawry or confiscation of lands, had sought to save at least their moveable wealth by placing large sums of money in the safe-keeping of various monastic bodies. But the thresholds of the English saints proved no safe-guard against the Norman King. Early in the year, in the course of Lent, while he was still at Salisbury or before he reached Salisbury, William caused all the monasteries of England to be searched, and all deposits of this kind to be carried to the royal treasury. It always has a grotesque sound when the deeds of William the Great, like those of smaller men, are either excused or aggravated by throwing the blame on evil counsellors; but we are told that of this particular deed the Earl of Hereford, William Fitz-Osbern, was the chief adviser.[1] It may have been deemed that

Englishmen entrust their wealth to the monasteries.

William searches the monasteries and carries off the money February–March, 1070

The design attributed to William Fitz-Osbern

[1] Both Chronicles (1071 Wig , 1070 Petrib ) record this search and spoliation, but they give no hint as to its special motive; " And þæs on Lengten se cyng let hergian ealle þa mynstra þe on Englalande wæron." Florence (1070) adds the cause, and mentions William Fitz-Osbern as the adviser, " Willelmi Herefordensis Comitis et quorumdam aliorum consilio, tempore Quadragesimali, Rex Willelmus monasteria totius Angliæ perscrutari, et

the holy places were rather purified than profaned by easing them of the worldly wealth of rebels and traitors. The season of penitence having been spent in this charitable work, William could better give his mind to the great schemes of ecclesiastical reform whose carrying out was to begin on the Easter festival.

At that festival the usual Gemót was held at Winchester, and the King wore his Crown with the usual pomp. This public wearing of the Crown was in some sort a religious ceremony, a continuation, as it were, of the original rite of consecration, and the Crown itself was placed on the royal head by one of the chief Prelates of the land.[1] In this case the rite received a special dignity and significance from the position of those by whom it was performed. Pope Alexander had sent three Legates to the court of his obedient and victorious son Ermenfrid, Bishop of Sitten, a man already well known both in England and in Normandy, whom we have already seen as the

*Easter Feast at Winchester April 4, 1070.*

*Presence of the Papal Legates Ermenfrid of Sitten*

pecuniam, quam ditiores Angli, propter illius austeritatem et depopulationem, in eis deposuerant, auferri et in ærarium suum jussit deferri." William Thorn, the historian of Saint Augustine's, asserts that, not only money, but the charters to which William had sworn, and which he had now broken, were carried off (X Scriptt 1787), "Wilhelmus videns se in sublimi positum et in regni solio confirmatum, subito ad alium virum mutatus, de Rege factus est tyrannus Wilhelmus Conquæstor dictus in multis promissa violavit, monasteria totius Angliæ perscrutari fecit, et pecuniam simul et chartas, in quarum libertatibus nobiles Angliæ confidebant et quas Rex in arcto positus observaturum se juraverat, ab ecclesiis ubi in securo jacuerant auferri præcepit, et in ærarium suum deferri." It must not be forgotten that this writer had his head full of the legendary confirmation of the franchises of Kent

[1] As the Winchester Annalist remarks under the year 1073, "Sciendum est quod quolibet anno dum quietus fuerat ter coronari consueverat Rex, *Wigorniæ* ad Natale, Wintoniæ ad Pascha, Londoniæ ad Pentecosten." This of course comes from the Peterborough Chronicle, 1087, "þriwa he bær his cynehelm ælce geare." But we see that the ceremony was a sort of repeated coronation So it is called by Benoît (39141), when describing the Christmas Feast at York (see above, p 295).

"A Everwic fu corone,
A la sainte Nativité"

330    THE ECCLESIASTICAL SETTLEMENT OF ENGLAND.

CHAP XIX.
1055.
1062.

Papal representative at the courts both of William and of Eadward,[1] now came a third time, accompanied by two other Legates, the Cardinal Priests John and Peter,[2] at once to congratulate the Conqueror on the temporal success of his holy enterprise, and to help him in carrying out his ecclesiastical schemes for the subjugation and reformation of the benighted islanders.[3] They came at William's own prayer,[4] and one at least of them tarried with him a whole year  They were honoured by him, we are told, as the Angels of God, and they helped him with their advice and authority in many matters in many places.[5] Their first function was the ceremonial one of placing the Crown on William's head at the Easter Feast, a sort of confirmation by Papal authority of the consecration which had been long ago performed by Ealdred in the West Minster.[6] This ceremony done, a ceremony far from lacking significance or importance, King and Legates turned themselves to the more serious business which lay before them.

William crowned by the Legates.

Schemes of ecclesiastical policy

This was no other than the beginning of William's great scheme for gradually remodelling the Church of England, as he had already gone far to remodel the State of England. It was the policy of which we have already seen the first-fruits in the appointment of Remigius of

---

[1] See vol ii p 461 , iii p 96.

[2] Orderic, 516 A, mentions Ermenfrid only by name, adding, "et duos canonicos cardinales " Florence adds their names, "presbyteros Johannem et Petrum, cardinales sedis apostolicæ "    [3] See vol iii p 284

[4] Ord Vit. 516 A. " Ex petitione ipsius Alexander Papa tres idoneos ei ut clarissimo [carissimo?] filio legaverat vicarios."

[5] Ib "Apud se ferme annuo ferme spatio retinuit, audiens et honorans eos tamquam angelos Dei. In diversis locis, in plurimis negotiis, sic egere, sicut indigas canonicæ examinationis et ordinationis regiones illas dinovere." From Florence we learn that only Ermenfrid could have stayed so long as a year  John and Peter went back before Pentecost

[6] Ib "Guillelmus Rex Dominicam Resurrectionis in urbe Guentâ celebravit, ubi Cardinales Romanæ Ecclesiæ coronam ei sollenniter imposuerunt" Vita Lanf. (Giles, 1 292) "Eum in paschâ, coronam regni capiti ejus imponentes, in Regem Anglicum confirmaverunt "

## DEPRIVATION OF ENGLISH PRELATES.

Fécamp to the see of Dorchester.[1] The great places of the Church of England were to be filled by Normans or other strangers whom William could trust. Englishmen were to be wholly shut out from the rank of Bishop and but sparingly admitted to that of Abbot.[2] But William was no more inclined to act hastily in this matter than in any other. As ever, he was disposed to walk warily and was careful to have the letter of the law on his side. It would not have suited his purpose to make a wholesale deprivation of the English Prelates. But as Bishopricks and Abbeys became vacant, fitting occupants of foreign birth were to be found for them,[3] and there was no objection to quicken the succession by depriving, one by one, those English Bishops or Abbots against whom any plausible accusation could be brought. These two processes were to be first of all applied to the two highest ecclesiastical posts in England. The metropolitan chair of York was regularly vacant by the death of Ealdred; that of Canterbury was to be made vacant by the deprivation of Stigand.

*CHAP. XIX.*
*English prelacies to be filled by strangers.*
*The change made gradually*
*The two Archbishopricks*

We have already seen that the ecclesiastical position of the Archbishop had been looked on as doubtful from the time of his nomination to the primacy by the voice of liberated England in that Mickle Gemót which drove his foreign predecessor from his ill-gotten throne.[4] Ermenfrid,

*Ecclesiastical position of Stigand*

---

[1] See above, p 132

[2] Fl Wig 1070 "Operam dante Rege ut quamplures ex Anglis suo honore privarentur, in quorum locum suæ gentis personas subrogavit, ad confirmationem scilicet sui quod noviter adquisierat regni " We shall find however that a distinction, and not an unnatural one, was made between the case of Bishops and that of Abbots An Abbot was not clothed with the same high temporal powers as a Bishop From this time we shall see that no Englishman was appointed to a Bishoprick, and that the English Bishops, with the exception of Wulfstan, were gradually deprived In the case of Abbots the deprivations of Englishmen were many and appointments were few, but the rule was not absolutely inflexible.

[3] See above, p 131

[4] See vol ii pp 331, 335, 341, and on the ecclesiastical position of Stigand, p 605

332    THE ECCLESIASTICAL SETTLEMENT OF ENGLAND.

CHAP XIX.
1062

William's double-dealing towards him.

Canonical charges against Stigand. April 11, 1070.

His defence

the present Legate, had, on his former visit to England, been the bearer of a Papal missive against him.[1] Yet William had hitherto treated him with studied honour;[2] he had consecrated the only Bishop who had been appointed since his accession,[3] and, if he had not been allowed to pour the consecrating oil on William's own head, he had filled the second place in the ceremony of his coronation.[4] But his hour was now come; he could now be deposed, not by the mere arbitrary will of the King or by the sentence of a purely English or Norman Assembly, but by the full authority of the Head of Western Christendom. As usual, all kinds of vague and improbable charges were brought against him;[5] but the canonical grounds on which he was formally condemned were three. He had held the see of Winchester along with the Archbishoprick.[6] He had taken the Archbishoprick during the life-time of Robert, and he had used at the mass the pallium which Robert had left behind.[7] He had obtained his own pallium from the usurping Pontiff Benedict the Tenth.[8] Stigand was heard in his own defence; but his defence seems to have consisted of arguments which would have more weight in the minds of Englishmen than in those of William and Ermenfrid. He appealed to the faith of the King who had so long treated him as a friend; he protested against the iniquity of his sentence, and apparently against the autho-

---

[1] See vol. ii p 466
[2] See above, p 78.
[3] See above, p 132
[4] See vol iii p 558
[5] Ord Vit 516 B "Stigandum pridem reprobatum anathemate deposuerunt Perjuriis enim et homicidiis inquinatus erat, nec per ostium in archipræsulatum introierat"
[6] See the charges in full in vol ii p 605
[7] That Robert left his pallium behind is a point insisted on with glee by the Peterborough Chronicler. See vol. ii p 331 The consequences were not then foreseen.
[8] See vol. ii p 432.

rity of his judges.¹ Such a defence was of course in vain; he was deprived of both his Bishopricks, and, if not absolutely imprisoned, he was at least kept under some measure of restraint under the King's eye at Winchester.² It seems however that he retained some of his private property,³ enough at least to give him the means of better fare and clothing than those of an ordinary prisoner. Legend was of course busy with the end of such a career

*CHAP. XIX.*
*His deprivation and imprisonment*

---

¹ Will. Malm. Gest Pont 37 "Qui [Ermenfridus] ad voluntatem Regis coacto concilio, Stigandum deposuit fidem Willelmi appellantem, et violentiam reclamantem"

² Florence simply says of the deposed Prelates in general, "Nonnullos, tam episcopos quam abbates, quos nulla evidenti [sic] causa nec concilia nec leges seculi damnabant, suis honoribus privavit, et usque ad finem vitæ custodiæ mancipatos detinuit, suspicione, ut diximus, tantum inductus novi regni" The language of William of Malmesbury (u s), speaking of Stigand only, is only one degree less strong as to the injustice of the deprivation, "Et quamvis ille se blande excusans præceptum Papæ objectaret, non tamen opinionem affectatæ depositionis exclusit, quod eum toto ævo in vinculis Wintoniæ habuerit." The "vincula" of William, who is copied by several later writers, are more distinct than the "custodia" of Florence Gervase (Act Pont Cant X Scriptt. 1652) speaks of him as "in carcere trusus," and adds, "in ergastulo regio apud Wintoniam mortuus est" The Winchester Annalist (29) has a more curious story He records his deprivation under 1070 and under 1072, adding, "Hoc anno Stigandus, qui dudum Archiepiscopus, jussu Regis captus et in Wintoniæ oppido positus est, ubi, etsi invitus, luit quidquid in archiepiscopatu deliquit" This seemingly refers to the tale of Stigand's escape to Ely

³ Domesday, 38 "Ipse Rex tenet Menes, Stigandus Archiepiscopus tenuit T. R E ad opus monachorum, et post quamdiu vixit habuit" This in some sort confirms the account of Stigand's position given by the Winchester historian, Thomas Rudborne, following his "Auctor de Concordantus sub litterâ S" (Angl Sacr 1 250), "Habuit Willelmus eum in salvâ custodiâ, viz in castro Wyntoniæ, infra quam custodiam diverteret quo vellet, sed extra limites ei non liceret. Honestissime enim cum eo tractavit, dimittens ei in pace omnes thesauros auri et argenti et aliarum rerum quos ante depositionem suam habebat, et nihil ex omnibus accepit Rex quamdiu Stigandus viveret Attamen Stigandus ne minimum nummum ex omnibus divitiis super semetipsum expendere voluit Eo vero defuncto, assignavit Rex Willelmus corpus ejus sepeliri in ecclesiâ cathedrali Wyntoniæ, et crucem magnam ex argento cum duabus imaginibus in thesauro ipsius Stigandi inventam, ex omnibus pretiosissimis divitiis quam Rex invenerat ecclesiæ Wyntoniensi pro animâ Stigandi solummodo transmisit"

334        THE ECCLESIASTICAL SETTLEMENT OF ENGLAND.

CHAP XIX
Legends of his last days.

as his. He lived in his prison the life of an ascetic. His friends, especially his neighbour the Lady Eadgyth, prayed him to indulge himself somewhat more both in food and in clothing. He answered with the most solemn oaths that he had not a penny or a penny's worth to supply his wants. Whether either the Old Lady or any other friend did anything to help him in his need we are not told. But the tale goes on to say that, after Stigand's death, a mass of treasure was found hidden underground, and that round the deposed Primate's neck was a key, which was found to open a private writing-case, in which were papers wherein the tale and weight of the whole hoard were accurately entered.[1]

Deprivation of Æthelmær of Elmham. [1047–1070]

The fall of the Primate carried with it that of his brother Æthelmær, whom he had promoted to the Bishoprick of the East-Angles,[2] a Bishoprick which he had once held himself.[3] We are not told what crimes were laid to his charge besides those of being an Englishman and a brother of Stigand. One probable ground of accusation may however be inferred from an entry in

[1] This tale appears in William of Malmesbury (Gest. Pont. 37), "Ibi Stigandus tenui victu vitam toleravit, quod ei parum de fisco inferebatur, et ipse ingenitâ mentis duritiâ nihil de suo inferri pateretur. Quin et hortantibus amicis, et præcipue Reginâ Edgithâ, Edwardi Regis relictâ, ut se delicatius vestiret et pasceret, per omne sanctum pejerabat non se habere nummum nec valens  Huic sacramento soliditatem veri abfuisse probavit ingens vis opum post mortem ejus in subterraneis specubus inventarum  Ad quarum indictum ut veniretur auxilio fuit clavicula collo examinati dependens, quæ familiaris scrinii esset custos.  Ea seræ immissa manifestavit per cartas inventas et qualitatem metallorum et quantitatem ponderum "  This became the stock passage for later writers to copy. Gervase however (Gest Pont Cant X Scriptt. 1652) tells it in a form which seems to be original, "Siquidem eodem mortuo, clavis parvula in secretis reperta est, quæ serâ cubicularis scrinii, appositâ innumerabilum thesaurorum dedit indicium. Cartæ quidem inventæ sunt in quibus notata erat et metallorum qualitas et ponderum quantitas quæ per omnia prædia sua compilata defoderat."
[2] Will Malm. Gest Pont 150  "Stigandus evaluit, ut sibi Australium Saxonum episcopatum restitueret, et Orientalium Anglorum fratri Ethelmero adquireret."        [3] See vol. ii pp. 64, 65

the Survey, by which it appears that the East-Anglian Prelate had a wife.¹ We are told also that several Abbots were deposed,² but it is hard to identify more than one who was deposed at this particular Gemót. It is probable that our informant had in his mind the general system of deprivation of both Abbots and Bishops which went on from this time, rather than any special acts of this Easter Assembly. It is certain however that one great Abbey was at this moment vacant by death and another by forfeiture, and it would appear that the Norman successors of the English Prelates were appointed in this Council. Brand of Peterborough, the Abbot who had been confirmed by the Ætheling Eadgar,³ died while William was engaged on his Northumbrian campaign.⁴ The vacant post was given to one Turold, of whose exploits, military rather than ecclesiastical, we shall presently hear.⁵ William's vengeance fell also on an inmate of the Golden Borough, who might have seemed likely to be perfectly harmless. This was Æthelric, who had once been Bishop of Durham, but who had long ago given up his see and had retired to spend the remnant of his days in the monastery.⁶ About this time,

*Chap. xix Deprivation of Abbots*

*Death of Brand of Peterborough November 27, 1069 Succeeded by Turold*

*Seizure of Æthelric, late Bishop of Durham [1042–1056]*

---

¹ Domesday, ii 195  "Hoc manerium accepit Almarus cum uxore suâ antequam esset Episcopus, et postea tenuit in episcopatu" Æthelmær, like most other people, French and English, is charged in Domesday with something in the way of *invasiones* In the same page where his wife is mentioned we read, "Hemesbi tenuit Algarus Comes T R E et Alwius emit Stigandus abstulit et dedit Almaro fratri suo, sed hundred nescit quomodo ex illo fuit in episcopatu" Another entry in p 200 is more curious After the account of the outlawry and flight of Eadric the naval captain (see above, p 121), it is added, " Episcopus Almarus invasit terram " But if Æthelmær was Eadric's next heir, or, as he very likely was, his lord, his occupation of the forfeited land of an outlaw would be an *invasio* in the Domesday sense

² See above, p 333, note 2  ³ See vol iii p 530
⁴ Chron Petrib 1069. "And on þisum ilcan geare forðferde Brand Abbot of Burh on v Kal Decembr." This is one of the earliest instances of the modern idiom "Abbot *of* Burh"
⁵ See the next Chapter  ⁶ See vol ii p 407

336    THE ECCLESIASTICAL SETTLEMENT OF ENGLAND.

CHAP XIX. and seemingly by a decree of this Easter Assembly, he was seized and led to Westminster; what was his fate there we are not told. His offence, whatever it was, had doubtless some connexion with the career of his more active brother Æthelwine, his successor in his Bishoprick. It seems, as far as we can make anything out of our chronology, that this Prelate was outlawed by another decree of this Council.[1] The charge would seem to have been a charge of sacrilege, or of complicity with sacrilege. During the flight of the Bishop and his Canons from Durham the great crucifix of the church had been left behind, as being too heavy to carry away. Soon after their flight, when the Normans reached the city, it was thrown down by some of the invaders, and robbed of the ornaments with which it had been enriched by Tostig and Judith. William, on reaching Durham, whether moved by piety or by covetousness, expressed no small indignation. He found out the offenders, and sent them to the Bishop and Chapter, seemingly in their retreat at Lindisfarn, calling on them to sit in judgement on the sinners, and to visit them with ecclesiastical censures. No censure however followed; Æthelwine may have doubted whether it would in the end be safe to excommunicate the soldiers of the Conqueror. In the course of Lent the Bishop and his Canons returned to Durham, and, at the very time when the Council was sitting at Winchester, the church of Durham was solemnly reconciled after its desecration, and the body of Saint Cuthberht was set back again in his shrine with all honour.[2] It must have been

*Outlawry of Æthelwine of Durham*

*His alleged connivance at sacrilege*

*The Church of Durham reconciled. April 6, 1070*

---

[1] On the dealings with these two brother Bishops, see Appendix PP.

[2] The story is told in the Durham History, iii 15. "Instante autem Quadragesimâ, tranquillitate redditâ, sacrum corpus Dunelmum reportaverunt, atque reconciliatâ solenniter ecclesiâ vii. Idus Aprilis, cum laudibus intrantes ecclesiam suo in loco illud reposuerunt. Invenerunt autem imaginem Crucifixi in solum dejectam, et a suo ornatu quo a Comite supradicto, videlicet Tosti, et ejus conjuge fuerat vestita, omnino spoliatam Hanc enim solam ex ornamentis post se in ecclesiâ reliquerant, ob hoc

just at this time that the sentence of outlawry was pronounced against Æthelwine, and there is no other visible motive for it except his disobedience to the royal order. No charge could better fall in with William's policy; the English Prelate had failed to show that zeal on behalf of his own church and its possessions which he, the Conqueror, had not forgotten, even in the midst of his Northumbrian warfare. If sacrilege was the crime of Æthelwine, he soon added to it, at least in the eyes of William. He saw that England was no longer a place for him, he took a large part of the moveable treasures of his church and set sail for Koln. Stress of weather however drove him back to Scotland, where he passed the winter.[1] He was thus enabled to have a share in the exploits and

*Æthelwine sets sail for Koln, but is driven back to Scotland April, 1070*

videlicet quod difficile in fugâ portari poterat, simul sperantes quod propter illam majorem loco reverentiam hostes exhibere vellent Verum quidam illorum supervenientes, quidquid in eâ auri et argenti vel gemmarum invenerant, penitus abstrahentes abierunt Quo facto Rex graviter indignatus jussit eos perquisitos comprehendi, et comprehensos ad episcopum et presbyteros, eorum judicio puniendos, perduci At illi, nihil triste eis facientes, permiserunt illæsos abire " The same story is told by Roger of Howden (i 120), some of whose expressions sound as if he had got the tale from some other quarter than Simeon , " Imago Crucifixi, quæ sola de ornamentis ecclesiæ remanserat, quoniam non facile, pro sui magnitudine, a festinantibus poterat asportari, auro suo et argento est spoliata, detrahentibus Normannis Rex autem quum non longe esset, agnoscens ecclesiæ solitudinem et Crucifixi exspoliationem, graviter satis tulit, ipsosque qui hoc fecerant perquiri præcepit, nec multo post eosdem ipsos sorte sibi obvios habuit, quos, quum publicam viam declinare conspicerat, illico intellexit homines mali alicujus esse conscios, qui protinus comprehensi aurum et argentum, quod de Crucifixo tulerant, ostenderunt. Quos statim ad judicium episcopi et eorum qui cum illo erant, jam de fugâ regredientium, transmisit, sed illi a reatu absolutos impune dimittunt."

[1] Sim Dun Hist Dun iii. 17 " Reportato in Dunelmum, sicut jam dictum est, beatissimi confessoris corpore, Egelwinus xv sui episcopatûs anno, partem thesaurorum ecclesiæ secum asportans, Angliam relicturus navem ascendit Sed quum jam cupito itinere versus Coloniam navigaret, vento repulsus in Scotiam ibidem hiemavit " This flight was evidently the consequence of the outlawry recorded in the Chronicles Simeon records the events which happened in the North , the Chronicler records, though imperfectly, the acts of the Council

338    THE ECCLESIASTICAL SETTLEMENT OF ENGLAND.

CHAP. XIX

Flight of Abbot Æthelsige

Scotland Abbot of Saint Augustine's 1070–1087

sufferings of the next year. Another Prelate who took nearly the same course was in worldly fortune more prosperous. It was now in all probability that Æthelsige, the pluralist Abbot of Ramsey and Saint Augustine's, who had been William's own ambassador at the court of Swend,[1] left England and again sought the shores of Denmark, this time in the character of an exile.[2] His Kentish office at least was dealt with as forfeited, being the other Abbey which was filled about this time, and most probably in this Council. A Norman monk of the name of Scotland was forced on the unwilling brotherhood of Saint Augustine's.[3] He did something however to retrieve the scandal of his appointment by great works in the way of building, and by recovering many of the lost estates of the church, some of them of William's own seizing.[4]

It must have been a striking episode among the acts

---

[1] See above, p 135.    [2] See Appendix P.

[3] W Thorn X Scriptt 1787 " Anno Domini quo supra, comperto quod Egelsinus sic in Daciam fugerat, suamque ecclesiam absque licentiâ Regis petitâ aut obtentâ dereliquerat, prædictus Rex monasterium Sancti Augustini cum omnibus internis et externis appendiciis confiscavit, et eidem monasterio quemdam monachum nomine Scotlandum, natione Normannum, in abbatem præfecit, monachis Augustiniensibus, tum propter Regis tyrannicam potentiam, tum propter sui monasterii ex omni parte depressionem multiplicem, licet non sine mentis amaritudine, ad tempus hoc tolerantibus "

[4] Ib. 1787, 1788. " Scotlandus multa et magna laude digna temporibus suis fecisse scribitur  Terras et possessiones a monasterio injuste ablatas, regio fultus auxilio, multas, licet non omnes, recuperavit Quasdam de novo perquisivit, quasdam absque consensu conventûs alienavit " He had just before said that in the time of Æthelsige some Normans had seized (" violenter occupaverunt ") lands belonging to the monastery, while Æthelsige had granted away others through fear ("timore compulsus, invitis suis fratribus, concessit "). Plumstede and Fordwich are specially spoken of as places recovered from Bishop Odo, who claimed them as having belonged to Godwine, his predecessor in the Kentish Earldom.  Both places appear in Domesday (12) as possessions of the abbey; and of Fordwich we read, " Hujus burgi duas partes dedit Rex E. Sancto Augustino, tertiam vero partem, quæ fuerat Godwini Comitis, Episcopus Baiocensis concessit eidem sancto annuente Rege W " But in 6 b among the possessions of Odo we find, " Abbas Sancti Augustini tenet de Episcopo Baiocensi Plumestede "

of this Assembly, in which so many English Prelates were deprived of their dignities, when one of their number boldly stood forth to assert the rights of his see. While others saw the King's purpose and trembled lest the stroke might fall upon them, the holy Bishop of Worcester arose and demanded the restitution of the estates of which Ealdred, on his translation from Worcester to York, had defrauded the church which he had left.[1] The lands were now, during the vacancy of the see of York, in the King's hands, and Wulfstan called both on the King and on the other members of the Assembly to do justice to his church.[2] We may feel certain that, in this and in every other action of his life, Wulfstan acted with perfect single-mindedness But the man whom Harold had chosen as his fellow-worker when Northumberland was to be won over by persuasion[3] could not have been absolutely wanting in worldly wisdom. He could not have been the mere model of childish innocence and simplicity which his monastic admirers are inclined to make of him. Wulfstan was no doubt conscious that, even from William's point of view, no charge could be brought against him. He was also no doubt equally ready to run any risk in maintaining a right whose maintenance was really the discharge of a trust.[4]

[1] See vol. ii p 467
[2] Flor Wig 1070 "In hoc itaque concilio, dum cæteri trepidi, utpote Regis agnoscentes animum, ne suis honoribus privarentur timerent, venerandus vir Wulstanus, Wigornensis episcopus, possessiones quamplures sui episcopatûs ab Aldredo Archiepiscopo, dum a Wigornensi ecclesiâ ab Eboracensem transferretur, suâ potentiâ retentas, quæ eo tunc defuncto in regiam potestatem devenerant, constanter proclamabat, expetebat, justitiamque inde fieri, tam ab ipsis qui concilio præerant quam a Rege flagitabat "
[3] See vol iii p 62
[4] We are often unpleasantly struck, in reading the history of ecclesiastical bodies, with the eagerness, almost greediness, shown by them in the assertion and retention of every kind of temporal right But it must in fairness be remembered that the right of the members who form the corporation at any given time is not absolute, they are trustees for their successors and the corporation itself We may be sure that this was the

340        THE ECCLESIASTICAL SETTLEMENT OF ENGLAND.

CHAP XIX But he probably knew also that a claim of right on behalf of an ecclesiastical foundation was exactly the kind of cause in which both conscience and policy would lead William to do justice. Nor would he forget that the chief of the Papal Legates was an old friend of his own. Eight years back Ermenfrid had been his guest at Worcester, and had raised his voice on his behalf in the Gemót at Gloucester.[1] The claim was made and listened to; but the answer of William and Ermenfrid was discreet. They could not judge without hearing both sides; they had heard the claim of Worcester; they had not heard the defence of York; the church of York was dumb, having no shepherd to speak for her; when the Northern Archbishoprick should again be full, both sides should be heard and the case decided.[2]

1062.

The decision put off till the church of York should be full

The appointments to the two metropolitan sees were not formally made at the Easter Council. We cannot doubt that William had long ago settled in his own mind who should be the successor of Stigand.[3] Still it was seemly to wait, to take time for deliberation, and not to let it go forth to the world that Stigand had been condemned, and his successor fixed upon, before he had been called on for his defence. The appointments to the vacant sees were therefore delayed till the next great Festival and the next regular Gemót. This was the Feast of Pentecost; but the meeting usual at that season was held, not,

Whitsun Gemót at Windsor May 23–31, 1070

feeling of Wulfstan in his pertinacious assertion of his right to temporal possessions. - Personal greediness could have no place in such a mind as his.

[1] See vol ii pp 464, 465

[2] Flor. Wig 1070. "Quia Eboracensis ecclesia, non habens pastorem qui pro eâ loqueretur, muta erat, judicatum est ut ipsa querela sic remaneret quousque, archiepiscopo ibi constituto qui ecclesiam defenderet, dum esset qui ejus querelæ responderet, ex objectis et responsis posset evidentius ac justius judicium fieri. Sicque tunc ea querela ad tempus remansit"

[3] See above, p. 84.

## GEMÓT OF WINDSOR. 341

according to rule, at Westminster, but at the royal seat of Windsor.[1] This is a place of which we begin first to hear in the days of Eadward,[2] and which became of increased importance under William. Either now or later in his reign, a castle, the germ of the present royal dwelling, arose there, and its defence seems to have been a special burthen laid upon the landowners of Berkshire.[3] There, instead of close under the walls of London, the Assembly was held in which the thrones of Augustine and Paullinus were again filled by men of foreign blood and Roman speech. On the Pentecostal day itself, King William, doubtless by his writ and seal like his predecessor King Eadward, granted two of the vacant sees to Norman priests.[4] York, regularly void by the death of Ealdred, was granted to Thomas, Treasurer of the church of Bayeux and chaplain to the King. Winchester, void by the deprivation of Stigand, was granted to Walkelin, another royal chaplain, who is also said, like so many

*CHAP XIX*

*Windsor Castle.*

*William grants the sees of York and Winchester to Thomas and Walkelin May 23*

---

[1] Ord Vit 516 A, B "Maxima vera ac utillima synodus Windressoris celebrata est anno MLXX ab incarnatione Domini" He however confounds the acts of this Council with those of the Easter Council at Winchester. Florence carefully distinguishes them

[2] Eadward's grant of Windsor to the church of Westminster is mentioned in his writ, Cod Dipl iv 227, and in the spurious charter, iv 178, he also dates a charter there in iv. 209.

[3] In Domesday, 56 b, Windsor appears as held by the Crown both T. R E and T. R. W. without any mention of the rights of the church of Westminster The place is also mentioned in 62, 62 b The Buckinghamshire Thegn, Leofwine of Newham, had also (151 b) to find "ii loricatos in custodiam de Windessores," and in the Abingdon History, ii 3, we read how the same duty was laid upon that monastery, "Tunc Walingaforde et Oxenforde et Wildesore, cæterisque locis castella pro regno servando compacta. Unde huic abbatiæ militum excubias apud ipsum Wildesore oppidum habendas regio imperio jussum"

[4] Orderic, 516 B, says only "constituti sunt nominandi præsules Normanni duo regii capellani Guaschelinus [Gualchelinus?] Guentanorum et Thomas Eboracorum, unus in loco depositi, alter defuncti" But Florence brings in the royal grant more distinctly, "Die Pentecostes Rex apud Windesoram venerando Baiocensi canonico Thomæ Eboracensis ecclesiæ archiepiscopatum, et Walcelino suo capellano Wintoniensis ecclesiæ dedit præsulatum."

342    THE ECCLESIASTICAL SETTLEMENT OF ENGLAND.

CHAP XIX. other people, to have been a kinsman of the King.[1] Both appointments, like most of William's ecclesiastical appointments, did him honour, and that of Thomas may even have been prompted by a wish to make some slight amends to a part of the Kingdom which had been so deeply wronged. Thomas, a native of Bayeux, as well as a canon of its church, had sought for learning beyond the bounds of Gaul and even beyond the bounds of Christendom. Like his Metropolitan Maurilius,[2] he had studied in the schools of Saxony and other Teutonic lands, and there he may possibly have learned enough of the kindred tongues to make him not wholly incapable of communicating with his English flock.[3] But his love of knowledge had carried him into the South as well as the North, he had crossed the Pyrenees, and had come back to Bayeux full of all the learning of the Spanish Saracens.[4] His diocesan Odo, who made up somewhat for his own misdeeds by generous promotion of merit in others,[5] placed Thomas in the Treasurer's stall in the church of his native city[6] This was an office for which one who had studied in the land of the goldsmith's craft[7] might be supposed to

Character and history of Thomas Archbishop of York. 1070–1100

[1] I do not find the kindred of Walkelin to William anywhere except in Thomas Rudborne, Ang Sac 1 255, "Walcelinus, vir magnæ litteraturæ, doctor in theologiâ egregius, in studio Parisiacensi cathedram ascendit magistralem, consanguineus *enim* [the logic is not very clear] erat Wilhelmi Conquæstoris et natione Normannus."

[2] See vol III p 99

[3] T. Stubbs, X Scriptt 1705 "Thomas senior, qui Baiocis oriundus, in Gallus eruditus, ardore discendi in Germaniam profectus, omnem Saxonum et Teutonum scholam est perscrutatus"

[4] Ib "Inde per Franciam reversus Normanniam, perrexit ad Hispanias. Ibique multa alia quæ alibi non potuit addiscens, pectus suum Hispanicarum fecit armarium scientiarum"

[5] See vol II. p 211

[6] T Stubbs, u. s. "Tandem ad natale solem reversus, magnifici viri Odonis Baiocensis episcopi familiaritatem nactus, tum propter morum elegantiam, tum propter multimodam scientiam, Baiocensis ecclesiæ ab eodem episcopo assecutus est thesaurariam."

[7] See above, p 41.

be specially fit. The character of Thomas stood high in every way, and he has left a special name behind him in the history of his own church as the restorer alike of its fabric and of its discipline.¹ The name of Walkelin of Winchester is of less renown, but he too bears a good report in local history, and his work may still be seen in the solemn transepts of Saint Swithhun's, and even in some sort in the mighty nave of Edington and Wykeham²

*CHAP. XIX.*

*Walkelin Bishop of Winchester 1070–1098*

William had thus on the Pentecostal Sunday exercised the ancient right of an English King to bestow the great benefices of the English Church. On the morrow an ecclesiastical Synod—such bodies are now beginning to be distinguished from the general Gemóts of our forefathers—was held by Ermenfrid, who was now the only Legate in England, his two colleagues having already gone back to Rome.³ Here we are told that several Abbots were deposed, and also one Bishop, Æthelric of Selsey. We are not told what his offence was, but our English informant commits himself in this, as in other cases, to the assertion that the sentence was uncanonical.⁴ Of Æthelric personally we know nothing, except that at a later time both William and Lanfranc did not scruple to make use of his knowledge of the ancient laws of

*Ermenfrid holds a synod May 24*

*Æthelric of Selsey deposed*

---

¹ See the account of his works in T Stubbs, 1708 I shall have to mention them again

² On the episcopate of Walkelin, see below, p 375

³ Flor Wig 1070 "Cujus [Regis] jussu mox in crastino prædictus Sedunensis episcopus Armenfridus synodum tenuit, Johanne et Petro præfatis cardinalibus Romam reversis"

⁴ Ib. "In quâ synodo Agelricus Suthsaxonum pontifex non canonice degradatur . abbates etiam quamplures sunt degradati " It is worth noting that the deposition of Æthelric seems not to have been satisfactory to Pope Alexander In one of his letters to William (Giles, 1 31) he says, " Caussa Ebrici [Ethrici ?], qui, olim Cicestrensis ecclesiæ præsul dictus, a suppositis legatorum nostrorum depositus est, non ad plenum nobis tractata videtur " The cause was entrusted to the further hearing of Lanfranc (see Will Malm Gest Regg in 293, where the name stands as " Alricius"), but it does not appear that Æthelric was ever restored

England.[1] For the present however the deposed Bishop of the South-Saxons was kept in ward at Marlborough.[2] His see was granted to one Stigand, whom it was hardly needful for any writer to distinguish from the deposed Primate.[3] The name is Norman as well as English, and it is just possible that the Bishop of Selsey, soon to be of Chichester, is the same person as the guardian of Margaret of Maine.[4] The East-Anglian Bishoprick, vacant by the deprivation of Æthelmær, was given to Herfast, the royal chaplain whose lack of learning had been long before exposed by Lanfranc in his cell at Bec.[5] One at least of the new Bishops, Walkelin of Winchester, was at once consecrated by the Legate.[6] The consecration of the Northumbrian Primate was delayed. The chronicler of his own church tells us that it was because, owing to the flight of Æthelwine, there was no Bishop of his own province to perform the ceremony.[7] But it is hard to see how an Archbishop of York, whose nominal jurisdiction reached to the Orkneys,[8] but who

---

[1] In the famous cause on Penenden Heath, of which more in the next section.

[2] Flor Wig 1070 "Quem [Agelricum] Rex sine culpâ mox apud Mearlesbeorge in custodiâ posuit"

[3] Ib "Quibus degradatis, Rex suis capellanis, Arfasto East Anglorum et Stigando Suth-Saxonum, dedit episcopatum" William of Malmesbury (Gest Pont 205) thinks it needful to add, "Stigandus, non ille qui postea fuit episcopus Wintoniensis et archiepiscopus Cantuariensis"

[4] See vol iii p 213    [5] See vol iii. p 104

[6] Flor Wig 1070 "Quia Dorubermiæ archipræsul depositus, et Eboracensis erat defunctus, jussu Regis, in octavis Pentecostes ab eodem Armenfrido, Sedunensi episcopo, ordinatus est Walcelinus."

[7] T Stubbs (1706) records the flight of Æthelwine, and adds, "Sic factum est, ordinatio ipsius per tres fere menses delata est, eo quod Eboracensis ecclesia illo tempore suffraganeos a quibus ordinari possit non habebat." The position of the Scottish Bishops as supposed suffragans of the see of York comes out more distinctly in the Appendix to the Winchester Chronicle under the year 1080. Archbishop Thomas consecrates William Bishop of Durham with the help of suffragans of the see of Canterbury, "Jubente Rege et Lanfranco consentiente . . . eo quod a Scottorum episcopis, qui sibi subjecti sunt, habere adjutorium non potuit."

[8] See Appendix LL.

had practically only a single suffragan at Durham, could ever have been canonically consecrated by Bishops of his own province. We cannot doubt that the real reason for the delay was that it suited William's policy that the new Primate of York should be admitted to his office by no hands but those of the new Primate of Canterbury.

The purpose which William had doubtless formed long before was now carried into effect. It was formally decreed by the King and the whole Assembly[1] that the vacant metropolitan throne should be filled by the Abbot of Saint Stephen's. But Lanfranc was not at hand either to receive the Archbishoprick at the King's hands or to receive the ecclesiastical sacrament at the hands of the Bishops of his intended province. The Legate Ermenfrid, with another Legate named Hubert, of whom we have not before heard, but who henceforth takes a leading part in all the ecclesiastical doings of William's reign, was commissioned to bear the news to the Primate-elect and to obtain his consent to his promotion.[2] A Synod of the Norman Church was held on the occasion, in which the Bishops, Abbots, and nobles of the Duchy were gathered together.[3] All pressed on Lanfranc the duty of accepting the office to which he was called; the Legates demanded his obedience in the

*Lanfranc appointed to Canterbury*

*The Legates sent to invite him*

*Synod of the Norman Church*

---

[1] Vita Lanfr (Giles, i 293). "Cogitanti Regi de hac re et proceres regni consulenti, convenientissimo fine, in Lanfranco quievit, quatenus uberrimum luminare in hac arce elatum, nebulas undique pravitatum et caligines dilueret, saluberrimo fulgore cuncta honestans"

[2] So Lanfranc says in his letter to Alexander (Giles, i. 19), "Legati tui, Hermenfredus videlicet Sedunensis Episcopus atque Hubertus Sanctæ Romanæ Ecclesiæ cardinalis, in Normanniam venerunt" He appears elsewhere (Will Malm iii 298) as "sanctæ Romanæ Ecclesiæ subdiaconus" and "lector," and under Hildebrand he becomes the chief means of communication between Rome and Normandy and England.

[3] Ib. "Episcopos, abbates, ejusdemque patriæ nobiles convenire fecerunt" So in the Life (i 293), "Quum igitur Sedunensis episcopus invitaret eum ad regimen pontificale, denuntians in consilio episcoporum et abbatum Normanniæ petitionem regis simulque voluntatem suam, et reliquorum sedis apostolicæ legatorum" It must have been in this Synod, if ever at all, that the Norman Prelates pronounced censures on the Norman soldiers who had fought at Senlac or taken any share in the war See Appendix MM.

346    THE ECCLESIASTICAL SETTLEMENT OF ENGLAND.

CHAP. XIX
Lanfranc refuses the offer

name of the Apostolic See.[1]   Lanfranc of course set forth, in the style usual on such occasions, his own general unfitness for so great a post, and he added other objections which were a good deal more to the purpose, his ignorance of the English tongue and of the manners and customs of the barbarous islanders.[2] Still to this it would have been easy to answer that the scholar of Pavia had once been as great a stranger in Normandy as he would be in England, and that, if he were out of place on an English archiepiscopal throne, he must be equally out of place in the chief stall of a Norman abbey. But all objections were overruled. Queen Matilda and her son Robert urged his acceptance of the post; their urgings however took the form of prayers; what Lanfranc seems to have been specially moved by was the interposition of one in whom

His scruples are overcome by Herlwin

he still acknowledged a right to command. Herlwin, the Abbot of Bec, who had first received him to the monastic life, bade him, by virtue of his old authority as a spiritual father, not to shrink from the sphere of duty to which he was called.[3] Lanfranc yielded to the combined prayers and commands of all Normandy. With a heavy heart, as he himself tells us, he forsook the monastic life which he

---

[1] Ep Lanfr (Giles, 1 19) "In eorum præsentiâ, ut Cantuariensem Ecclesiam regendam susciperem ex apostolicæ sedis auctoritate præceperunt"

[2] Ib. "Adversus hoc imbecillitas mearum virium, morumque indignitas prolata in medium nihil profuit excusatio incognitæ linguæ gentiumque barbararum nullum apud eos locum invenire prævaluit" The biographer (1 293) gives another reason, "Perspectum namque vel indubitatum tenebat, simul ire non posse negotium archipræsulis et otium monachi Ad hoc sui provectum solito despiciebat, atque extimescebat onerosissimum gubernaculum." This comes partly from Orderic, 520 A.

[3] Ord. Vit 520 A "Abbas Herlwinus imperat, cui obsecundare velut Christo solebat Regina cum filio principe precatur, majores quoque ideo collecti studiose hortantur" The word "princeps" applied to Robert, which the biographer leaves out, is remarkable I know no instance of its use at this time in the vulgar sense, it is therefore probably applied to him as being joined with his mother in the government of the Duchy. See above, p 123

loved above all other lives,[1] he crossed the sea; on the Feast of the Assumption he received the Archbishoprick at the King's hands,[2] on the Feast of the Decollation of Saint John Baptist he was consecrated to what his continental admirers looked on as the post of Chief Pontiff, Patriarch and Pope of the nations beyond the sea.[3]

*He comes to England. Lanfranc receives the Archbishoprick August 15, 1070*

The ceremony was performed at Canterbury,[4] in the metropolitan church. That church had been burned nearly three years before.[5] It had doubtless been patched up so as to allow the monks to keep up their regular services, but it could hardly have been in a fitting state for so great a rite as the consecration of a Metropolitan, and that a Metropolitan who was, in some sort, the beginner of a new line. But in point of attendance of the higher ecclesiastics of the realm there was no lack. The Archbishop-elect was received with all honour by both the convents of the city, by the monks of his own church, and by those of the rival house of Saint Augustine.[6]

*His consecration at Canterbury August 29*

*Reception of Lanfranc at Canterbury*

---

[1] Ep Lanfr (Giles, i 20) He prays Alexander to release him from his Archbishoprick, "Abrupto per eamdem auctoritatem hujus necessitatis vinculo absolvatis, vitamque cœnobialem, quam præ omnibus rebus diligo, repetendi licentiam concedatis"

[2] Flor Wig 1070 "Rex    archiepiscopum constituit Cantuariensis ecclesiæ" The Appendix to the Winchester Chronicle is remarkable for the Old-English constitutional language, "Lanfrancus Cadomensis abbas, compellente Rege Willelmo et jubente Papa Alexandrâ, Angliam venit, et primatum regni Anglorum in ecclesiâ Cantuariensi suscepit, elegentibus eum senioribus ejusdem ecclesiæ cum episcopis et principibus, clero et populo Angliæ, in curiâ Regis"

[3] See vol 1 p 626, and the still stronger expression of Pope Urban (Will Malm Gest Pont 100), "Includamus hunc [Anselmum] in orbe nostro quasi alterius orbis papam," and of the Worcester Annalist (1102), "Anselmus Papa"

[4] Chron Wint (1070) "He wæs gehaded on Kal Septembris on his agenum biscopsetle" This explains the words of Florence, "et in festivitate Sancti Johannis Baptistæ die Dominicâ, archiepiscopum consecrari fecit Cantwariæ" The Feast of Saint John intended is that of the Decollation, not of the Nativity See also Vit Lanfr (Giles, i 300), and Will Malm Gest Pont 39      [5] See above, p 125

[6] Chron. Wint App 1070 "Quum autem Cantuariam venisset, obviam

348    THE ECCLESIASTICAL SETTLEMENT OF ENGLAND.

CHAP XIX.
His consecrators

Variety of their birth and spiritual descent

For the actual rite of consecration eight[1] Bishops of his province were assembled. Four were absent, among whom the absence of the sainted Bishop of Worcester is the most remarkable. But all who did not appear in person signified their assent by messengers and letters, and gave reasons which excused their absence.[2] The eight who joined in the rite presented a singular variety, alike in their birth and origin and in the sources of their episcopal commission. William of London, the actual celebrant, was a man of Norman birth, consecrated by the Norman Robert, but who had received his see from Eadward and had been restored to it by the good will of Godwine or Harold.[3] His countryman, Walkelin of Winchester, had just been consecrated by the Papal Legate Ermenfrid, and so, it is to be supposed, had Herfast, the new Bishop of the East-Angles, and Stigand, the new Bishop of the South-Saxons. Gisa of Wells and Hermann of Sherborne were, like William, members of the Old-English hierarchy, though of foreign birth. But Gisa had been consecrated at Rome by Pope Nicolas; Hermann alone had received his consecration from a Primate at once of English birth and of undoubted canonical position.[4] Nor

ei processit honorabiliter conventus ecclesiæ Christi, conjuncto sibi toto conventu Sancti Augustini, cum electo ejusdem ecclesiæ Abbate Scotlando"

[1] Chron. Wint 1070 " He wæs gehaded .. fram eahte biscopum his underðioddum " So the lists in Vit Lanfr (Giles, i. 300), Will Malm. Gest Pont. 39, Gervase, Act Pont X Scriptt 1653, reckon eight bishops. Florence does not give a full list, but says, "Consecratus est ab episcopis Gisone Wyllensi, et a Waltero Herefordensi, . . . Hermannus etiam episcopus . . . cum quibusdam aliis ejus interfuit consecrationi" Walter's name is not found elsewhere

[2] Chron. Wint 1070. " Þa oþre þær næron þurh ærendrakean and þurh gewrite atiwdon hwi hi ðær beon ne mihton " This is translated in the Life of Lanfranc (Giles, 1 300) and William of Malmesbury (Gest Pont 39), " Cæteri qui absentes fuerunt caussas suæ absentiæ, tam legatis quam litteris, ostenderunt "          [3] See vol ii. pp 161, 345.

[4] Hermann, appointed in 1045 (see vol ii. p 79), must have been consecrated by Eadsige, or by some other English Bishop acting in his name.

was the line of the deprived Stigand left unrepresented in the admission of the man who supplanted him. Two of the ministering Prelates had received the episcopal order at his hands, Siward of Rochester in the days of King Eadward[1] and Remigius of Dorchester since King William came into England.[2] By the hands of these eight Lanfranc, the scholar of Pavia, the teacher of Avranches, the monk of Bec, the Abbot of Caen, was received into the episcopal order and placed in the patriarchal see of Britain.

### § 2. *The Primacy of Lanfranc.*
### A.D. 1070—1089.

Another stage of the Conquest was thus accomplished. The Crown of England had been won by the greatest of living warriors and statesmen, and now the highest place in the English Church was filled by the most renowned of living scholars, the ablest—though not the most renowned —of living ecclesiastical rulers. But at that moment the fame of Abbot Lanfranc was most likely equal to that of Archdeacon Hildebrand, and we may doubt whether the Primate who lived and died honoured by all men and successful in all his undertakings did not show a higher power of adapting means to ends than the Pope who loved righteousness and hated iniquity and for his reward died in exile.[3] At that moment it might well seem that the two foremost men of the mainland of Western Christendom had crossed over together to rule as Pope and Cæsar in

---

[1] See vol ii p. 433.   [2] See above, p 132.
[3] Paul. Bernfried ap Murat iii 348 "Ubi in extremo positus erat, ultima verba ejus hæc fuerunt, 'Dilexi justitiam et odivi iniquitatem; propterea morior in exsilio.' Quod contra quidam venerabilis Episcopus respondisse narratur, 'Non potes, Domine, mori in exsilio, qui in vice Christi et Apostolorum ejus divinitus accepisti gentes hæreditatem et possessionem terminos terræ '"

350    THE ECCLESIASTICAL SETTLEMENT OF ENGLAND.

CHAP XIX
Their harmonious government in England

the island which men looked on as another world. And truly William and Lanfranc ruled together in their island Empire as no Pope and Cæsar ever ruled together in the Imperial city itself.[1] It is certainly to the honour of William, it is perhaps not altogether to the honour of Lanfranc, that no serious difference seems ever to have arisen between the two illustrious colleagues. Lanfranc does not stand charged with direct complicity in any of William's particular acts of oppression, but we never hear of his protesting against them, and he may fairly be looked on as sharing the responsibility of William's general system of policy. Each had to keep down the conquered nation by his own special arms, and the hardness of the priest was ready to go hand in hand with the hardness of the warrior.

Consolidation of England under William.

The great object of William was to bring the whole land into direct submission to his own power, a process in which he thoroughly succeeded, and which first made England that consolidated and indivisible Kingdom which it has ever since remained. The ecclesiastical shape of this process was to secure the more complete submission of the Northern metropolis to the Southern. The position of the Archbishops of York was an anomalous one. There is no doubt that, in the original scheme of Gregory the Great, the two Metropolitans of Britain were meant to hold an equal rank and to have ecclesiastical jurisdiction over a territory of nearly equal extent.[2] The Province of York is smaller than the Province of Canterbury simply because political causes kept the Northumbrian Primate from exercising any effective authority north of the Tweed

Ecclesiastical side of the process

Position of the Archbishops of York
Intended extent of the two provinces

---

[1] Brevis Relatio (Giles, 10) "De Rege vero Willelmo et Lanfranco Archiepiscopo dicebant multi qui tunc erant, quod tales duo simul in unâ terrâ non invenirentur, quales essent Rex Willelmus et Lanfrancus suu Archiepiscopus"

[2] See Appendix LL

and the Solway. Scotland was meant to form part of the sheepfold whose centre was at York, just as Wales was meant to form part of the sheepfold whose centre was at Canterbury. Wales was in the end ecclesiastically subdued; Scotland never was subdued to any practical purpose, and the result was that the Archbishops of York were left with a vast region under their diocesan care, and with the single suffragan see of Durham under their metropolitan jurisdiction. But the diocese and province of York was, as events had shown, exactly the part of England where the authority of William and the unity of the monarchy were most likely to be threatened. It was always possible that some insurrection of the inhabitants, or some invasion from Denmark, might set up an opposition King in the Northumbrian capital. It was a point of some moment to cut off such a pretender from the means of obtaining any ecclesiastical sanction for his claims. An Archbishop of York who retained any claim to be independent of the see of Canterbury might consecrate a King of the Northumbrians, and the King of the Northumbrians might grow into a King of all England.[1] An Archbishop of York who had professed canonical obedience to the Church of Canterbury could not venture on such an act without drawing on himself the charge of ecclesiastical as well as civil rebellion. It was needful then for the joint schemes of William and Lanfranc that the first ecclesiastical act of the new epoch should be the full submission of the new Primate of York to the new Primate of

*Scotland designed to be under York.*

*Political position of the York province.*

*Danger of an independent Metropolitan in Northumberland.*

*Thomas to make profession of obedience to Lanfranc.*

---

[1] T. Stubbs, X Scriptt. 1706. "Porro utile esse ad regni integritatem et firmitatem ut Brittania uni quasi Primati subderetur, alioquin contingere posse ut de exteris gentibus, quæ Eboracum navigio venientes regnum infestare solebant, unus ab Eboracensi Archiepiscopo et ab illius provinciæ indigenis Rex crearetur, et sic regnum turbatum scinderetur." This is one of the things which, according to the York writer, the wily Lanfranc "persuasit novo et credulo Regi."

Canterbury. Thomas of Bayeux was to receive his consecration at the hands of Lanfranc and to make profession of canonical obedience to him.

It was no doubt with this object that, when the other newly appointed Bishops were consecrated by the Legate Ermenfrid, the elect of York remained without consecration.[1] Thomas now came to Canterbury and sought consecration at the hands of Lanfranc. All things were ready for the ceremony; the Archbishop and the assistant Bishops were in their places before the altar of Christ Church; but, before the actual performance of the sacramental rite, Lanfranc demanded a profession of canonical obedience. In the eyes of writers in the interest of Canterbury the Southern Primate was only asserting the undoubted right of his church; our solitary Northern informant looks on him as the subtle deviser of new and unheard of pretensions[2] Thomas refused the demand. The writers on the rival side are charitable enough to say that the refusal was not prompted by pride or perverseness. The elect of York was a stranger in England and knew not the customs of the realm. He had also listened too much to the words of flatterers—possibly of Northumbrian patriots[3] Lanfranc was inexorable; he bade the assembled Bishops and monks take off their vestments; the assembly broke up, and Thomas went away unconsecrated[4] Little

---

[1] See above, p 344

[2] T. Stubbs, X Scriptt. 1706 "Iste est Lanfrancus qui primus omnium ab Eboracensi Archiepiscopo professionem exegit, suisque successoribus hoc idem exigendum exemplum dedit"

[3] Will Malm Gest. Pont. 39. "Hoc autem ignorantiâ magis quam spiritûs elati pertinantiâ faciebat Novus enim homo et Anglicæ consuetudinis penitus expers, verbis adulatorum plus æquo et bono fidem exhibebat"

[4] I follow the zealous Canterbury writer, who tells the tale in our own tongue (Chron. Wint. 1070); "On þam geare Thomas, se wæs gecoran biscop to Eferwic, com to Cantwarebenrg þæt man hine ðær gehadede efter þan ealdan gewunan Da þa Lanfranc crafede fæstnunge his gehersumnesse mid aðswerunge, þa forsoc he and sæde þæt he hit nahte so donne. Da

however as Thomas might have learned of English Law, he had learned enough to know who was the Supreme Governor of the Church of England. His first appeal was to the King.[1] William, it is said, was at first indignant at the refusal of Lanfranc. He deemed that the claim of Canterbury was one not founded on plain truth and reason, but was something devised by the subtle learning of Lanfranc.[2] But within a few days the Archbishop of Canterbury came to the King's Court and set forth his own case. His hearers from beyond sea were convinced by his arguments; those of English birth bore witness that all that he claimed was in accordance with the ancient laws of the land.[3] The whole controversy illustrates William's position; it marks his strong spirit of technical legality, his freedom from any design of formal innovation on the laws and customs of England. William heard the disputants and gave judgement. The abstract question he deemed too weighty to be decided all at once. Still it was absolutely necessary to come at

*CHAP. XIX.*

*He appeals to the King*

*William's alleged displeasure at Lanfranc's demand.*

*Lanfranc asserts his right*

*William brings about a compromise.*

gewraðede hine se arcebisceop Lanfranc, and bebead þam biscopan ðe þar cumene wæran be ðas arcebisceop L. hæse þa serfise to donde, and eallan þan munecan þæt hi scoldan hi unscrydan, and hi be his hæse swa didan Swa Thomas to þam timan agean ferde buton bletsunga"

[1] Chron Wint App 1070 "Thomas non sacratus abscessit, Regem adiit, et de Lanfranco querimoniam fecit"

[2] Will Malm. Gest Pont. 40 "Rex audiens graviter accepit, existimans Lanfrancum injusta petere et scientiâ magis litterarum quam ratione et veritate confidere" The York writer (X Scriptt 1706) goes a step further, "Thomas exactionem Regi rettulit, qui primo moleste accipiens mandavit archiepiscopo ut absque professione eum consecraret" This is a perfectly natural Northumbrian view, but it seems quite inconsistent with the general relations between William and Lanfranc, and it is strange to find it in one who, like William of Malmesbury, wrote within the Province of Canterbury

[3] Will. Malm u s "Paucorum dierum spatio evoluto, Lanfrancus ad curiam venit, a Rege audientiam postulavit, redditis rationibus ejus animum mitigavit, transmarinis qui aderant suæ parti justitiam adesse suasit et persuasit Angli enim qui rem noverant assertionibus ejus per omnia constantissime testimonium perhibebant"

VOL IV.    A a

354    THE ECCLESIASTICAL SETTLEMENT OF ENGLAND.

CHAP. XIX.

Thomas to make personal profession to Lanfranc

Consecration of Thomas.

Lanfranc receives the pro-

once to a settlement of some kind, and not to leave the Church of York, at such a time, any longer without a pastor. The practical mind of William decreed a temporary compromise. Thomas should make a written profession to Lanfranc personally, pledging himself to full canonical obedience. But he should not be bound to do the like to any successor of Lanfranc, unless in the meanwhile the matter had been thoroughly sifted, and the respective rights of the two metropolitan churches formally defined by a competent tribunal.[1] Thus far Thomas was content to yield. With some unwillingness, he returned to Canterbury, made the required profession, and went away a consecrated Bishop.[2]

Soon after, seemingly before the year was out, Lanfranc received professions of canonical obedience from those

[1] Vita Lanfr (Giles, 1 301), Will Malm. Gest Pont 40 "Itaque regio edicto, communique omnium decreto, statutum est ad praesens deberi Thomam ad matrem totius regni ecclesiam redire, professionem scribere, scriptam legere, lectam inter examinandum in praesentiâ episcoporum Lanfrauco porrigere, in quâ praeceptis quidem ejus in omnibus quae ad Christianae religionis cultum pertinent se obtemperaturum absolute, nullâ interpositâ conditione, promitteret, successoribus vero ejus non ita, nisi prius vel coram vel in episcopali concilio competens ei ratio redderetur, quâ antecessores suos Dorobernensis ecclesiae primatibus id fecisse et facere debuisse evidentissime comprobaretur." This would seem to be the right version, as coming between the two extreme statements on each side The Continuator of the Winchester Chronicle misplaces the event by putting the consecration after the journey to Rome, and adds that Thomas yielded all that Lanfranc asked ("eal þæt se arcebisceop æt him crafede eadmedlice gefylde") So Gervase (X Scriptt 1653); "Decretum est tandem ut Thomas Cantuariam rediret, et inter sacrandum debitam ecclesiae Cantuariensi et Lanfranco faceret professionem" T Stubbs, on the other hand (X Scriptt 1706), makes William threaten Thomas with banishment both from England and Normandy if he does not make at least a personal profession, ("si non saltem personalem Lanfranco faceret professionem") He yielded to the unreasonable wrath ("irrationabilis ira") of the King, but he took special care not to make a written profession ("cartam professionis neque ipse scripsit, neque scribi fecit, nec a Cantuariis scriptam legit vel Lanfranco tradidit").

[2] Will Malm. Gest. Pont 40 "Igitur rediit, quae jussa sunt implevit, sacratus abscessit"

Bishops of his province who, in the days of the usurpation of Stigand, had received consecration from various other Archbishops or from the Pope.[1] Our informant, in mentioning these two classes, forgets to add a third, namely those, including the Norman Bishop of Dorchester, who had been consecrated by Stigand himself.[2] It was now that Remigius made that remarkable profession which I referred to at an earlier stage,[3] and Wulfstan that no less remarkable one which I referred to at an earlier stage still.[4]

The next year both the newly consecrated Archbishops went to Rome for their pallia. Lanfranc was received by Alexander with special honour. Contrary to all custom, the Pope rose to meet him, and bestowed on him, not one pallium only, but two, the second, it would seem, being a special badge of personal favour.[5] Yet some incidents in the story might make us think that we were reading over again the stories of earlier days. Alexander dealt with Thomas of York pretty much as Nicolas the Second had dealt with Ealdred when Earl Tostig went on pilgrimage.[6] He dealt with Remigius pretty much as Leo the Ninth had dealt with an earlier Norman Bishop of Dorchester, the unbishoply Ulf.[7] The

---

[1] Chron. Wint. App. 1070 "Nec multo post Lanfrancus ab omnibus Anglici regni episcopis professionem quæsivit et accepit." William of Malmesbury (Gest Pont 40) adds, "Qui diversis temporibus, diversis in locis, ab aliis archiepiscopis vel a Papâ tempore Stigandi sacrati sunt."

[2] See above, p 132   [3] Ib.   [4] See vol ii. p. 607

[5] Chron Wint App. 1071 "Secundo anno ordinationis suæ Romam ivit, quem Papa Alexander in tantum honoravit ut ei contra morem assurgeret, et duo pallia ob signum præcipui amoris tribuit, quorum unum Romano more ab altare accepit, alterum vero ipse Papa, unde missas celebrare consueverat, suâ manu porrexit." So Will Malm Gest Pont 40. The Life (Giles, 1 302) puts a special reason into the Pope's mouth, "Non ideo assurrexi ei quia archiepiscopus Cantuariæ est, sed quia Becci ad scholam ejus fui, et ad pedes ejus cum aliis auditor consedi." For a list of his schoolfellows, see Charma, Lanfranc, p 17, and the notes, p 43 et seqq

[6] See vol ii p 456.   [7] Ib p. 117

356        THE ECCLESIASTICAL SETTLEMENT OF ENGLAND.

CHAP XIX. Pope, or his great adviser, was minded to deprive both Thomas and Remigius of their Bishopricks. Thomas stood charged with no offence of simony or plurality; but he was the son of a priest. This was nothing wonderful or disgraceful either in English or in Norman eyes; but in a court where Hildebrand was the presiding spirit, it would doubtless be held that the son of a priest came within the scope of those canons which forbade ecclesiastical dignities to those who were not born in lawful wedlock. The appointment of Remigius lay open to cavil on stronger grounds. The gifts which the loyalty of the almoner of Fécamp had made to the Duke, when he was about to set forth on his great enterprise, were affirmed to have amounted to a simoniacal bargain of which the see of Dorchester was the price[1] The policy of these charges is plain. It was expedient to show that the acts even of so loyal a son of the Church as William were liable to be called in question, and that breaches of ecclesiastical rule were not to be overlooked even in him. But it was no less expedient to deal tenderly with one who was at once so dutiful and so powerful. In William's case the Church was satisfied with asserting principles without rigorously carrying them into practice Alexander showed himself no more inflexible than Nicolas and Leo. The matter was referred to the judgement of Lanfranc, and by his decision both Thomas and Remigius were allowed to keep their Bishopricks.[2] The rings and staves of which they

Charge of simony against Remigius

The matter referred to Lanfranc, who restores them

---

[1] Will Malm Gest Pont 65 "Denique ambos itineris sui comites, Thomam Archiepiscopum Eboracensem et Remigium Episcopum Lincoliensem, baculis et annulis exspoliatos, quod primus esset filius presbyteri, secundus pro auxiliis Willelmo venienti Angliam præbitis factus esset episcopus, divinum munus bellicosis laboribus nundinatus, precibus suis restituit officio." On the gifts of Remigius to William, see above, p. 90, and vol iii p. 380.

[2] Ib. "Papa enim, pondus facti a se rejiciens, in eum considerationem transfudit, bene an secus fieret Redderet ipse investituras si vellet, sin

had been deprived—rings and staves which they had *chap xix.* received from the King of the English in an Assembly of his Witan—were restored to them again by the hands of the Primate. We know not whether it was before *Thomas* or after this intercession on the part of his rival that *asserts the right of* Thomas craved for a decision by Papal authority of the *his see,* point in dispute between the Churches of York and Canterbury. He pleaded that, by the ordinance of Gregory the Great, the two Primates were to be of equal authority, and that a simple personal precedence was to belong to him whose consecration was of older date.[1] But Thomas *and claims* claimed more than this. He asserted that three Bishop- *jurisdiction over three* ricks of the province of Canterbury, Dorchester, Lichfield, *suffragan sees of* and Worcester, belonged of right to his own metropolitan *Canterbury* jurisdiction.[2] Alexander declined to decide either question; both should be heard and decided in England by a Council of the Bishops and Abbots of the realm.[3] With affairs in this state the three Prelates returned to England

The cause was heard and decided in the course of the next year. It appears to have been twice heard, in the regular Paschal and Pentecostal Gemóts. The former was *The Easter Gemót at* held, according to ancient use, at Winchester, while the *Winchester* latter was held, like one of the meetings two years before,[3] *April 8,* in the now favourite royal dwelling-place of Windsor *1072* The two meetings are evidently confused in our several

---

minus, faceret quod commodum sciret Ita illi de manu Lanfranci baculos et annulos recipientes, lætum ad patriam cum eodem moliti sunt reditum " It is almost needless to say that nothing of this sort is to be found in the loyal Yorkist Thomas Stubbs [1] See Appendix LL

[2] Will Malm Gest Pont. 40. "In cujus [Alexandri Papæ] præsentiâ Thomas calumniam movit de primatu Dorobernensis ecclesiæ et de subjectione trium episcoporum, Dorcensis sive Lincoliensis, Wigorniensis, Licitfeldensis, qui nunc est Cestrensis " So Vita Lanfr 302

[3] Ib 41 "De quâ re et de tribus Episcopis multis hinc inde verbis prolatis, decrevit Alexander Papa oportere hanc caussam in Anglicâ terrâ audiri, et illic totius regni episcoporum et abbatum testimoniâ et judicio diffiniri."

[3] See above, p 340

accounts; but it would seem that the matter was first heard at Winchester before a purely ecclesiastical assembly, but that the final decision was given at Windsor in a general Gemót of the whole realm.[1] The Bishops and Abbots and the great men of the laity were all assembled,[2] the Papal Legate Hubert was present,[3] and the King himself, presiding, like his predecessors among his Witan, adjured all present to hear and determine according to right between the two illustrious disputants.[4] The cause was argued. From the side of Canterbury we have a minute account of the pleadings, as detailed by Lanfranc himself to the Pope. On the side of York no record is preserved of the pleadings, except so

*Trial of the cause between Lanfranc and Thomas*

---

[1] Besides the account in the Gesta Pontificum, we have Lanfranc's own letter to Pope Alexander (Giles, i. 23), and the formal decree of the Assembly with the signatures (Vit Lanfr. Giles, i. 303 ; Will Malm Gest Regg iii 298) In this document the two hearings are distinctly brought out, while Lanfranc's letter might have implied only a single hearing at Winchester , " Ventilata est hæc causa prius apud Ventanam civitatem in Paschali solemnitate, in capellâ regiâ quæ sita est in castello, postea in villâ regiâ quæ vocatur Windlesor, ubi et finem accepit in præsentiâ Regis, episcoporum, abbatum, diversorum ordinum, qui congregati erant apud curiam in festivitate Pentecostes "

[2] Lanfranc himself, in his letter to the Pope (23), plainly sets forth the mixed character of the Assembly , " Quibus de rebus, vos, sicut sanctum prudentemque pastorem decuit et oportuit, per scriptum sententiam promulgâstis, quatenus conventus Anglicæ terræ, episcoporum, abbatum, cæterarumque religiosi ordinis personarum, utriusque partes rationes audiret, discuteret, definiret , factumque est ita Convenerunt enim ad regalem curiam apud Wentanam civitatem in Paschali sollemnitate episcopi, abbates, cæterique ex sacro ac laicali ordine quos se de actione morumque probitate par fuerat convenisse inprimis adunati sunt a nobis ex vestrâ auctoritate per sanctam obedientiam " Mark the mention of the laity, of whom there is no mention in the words attributed to Alexander. The Pope wished the matter to be judged by a Convocation, but it was judged by a Parliament

[3] On Hubert, see above, p 345

[4] Ep Lanfr 24 " Deinde regia potestas per semetipsam contestata est eas per fidem et sacramentum quibus sibi colligati erant quatenus hanc caussam intentissime audirent, auditam ad certum rectumque finem sine partium favore perducerent. Utrumque omnes concorditer susceperunt, sese ita facturos sub præfatâ obligatione spoponderunt "

far as they may be guessed from the points insisted on by Thomas at the Roman Court. The History of Bæda was put in as evidence; so were a long series of letters from various Popes,[1] and the decision of the Assembly was given wholly in favour of the Kentish metropolis. The Humber was to be the boundary of the two provinces,[2] a boundary clear enough as between Holderness and Lindesey, less clear if we go up to the higher course of the Trent or the Ouse. This sentence of course confirmed the right of Canterbury to archiepiscopal authority over the three disputed dioceses; but the claim of York over them was even now not quite silenced.[3] As to the church of York itself, the inherent precedence of Canterbury was acknowledged; Thomas and his successors were to make profession, not only to Lanfranc personally, but to him and his successors. A zealous Canterbury writer adds, in a somewhat mocking strain, that, lest the Primate of York should be left altogether without suffragans, he was allowed to receive the profession of the Bishop of Durham.[4] He was doubtless allowed to receive the profession of the Scottish Bishops also, if it were to be had.

*Pleadings on the side of Canterbury. Decision in favour of Canterbury.*

*One suffragan left to York.*

The undisputed ecclesiastical reign of Lanfranc now began. His actions as the second man in the realm, as

*Ecclesiastical schemes of Lanfranc.*

---

[1] See Ep Lanfr 24-26, and more fully Will Malm. Gest. Pont 44-65, and Appendix LL

[2] Will. Malm Gest Pont 65 "Succubuit tantis rationibus Thomas, et placitum ad moderationem transferrens, libenter conditioni concessit animum, ut ulterior ripa Humbræ fluminis esset principium suæ diœcesis, citerior esset limes parochiæ Cantuariensis"

[3] See below, p 372

[4] Gervase, Act Pont Cant X Scriptt 1653 "Attamen pro bono pacis Lanfrancus sponte concessit Thomæ ut Dunelmensis episcopus de cetero sibi profiteretur et ut suffraganeus obediret, ut vel sic, uno saltem decoratus episcopo, nomen archiepiscopi obtineret" He adds maliciously, "Legimus tamen episcopos Eboracenses nonnullos sine pallio toto vitæ suæ tempore prædictam Eboracensem rexisse ecclesiam"

CHAP XIX. William's viceroy when he was out of England, will be recorded at other stages of this volume. The general effects of his administration, the closer connexion with the Papacy, the reform or revival of monasticism, the impulse given to learning, results all of them in which the personal agency of Lanfranc had no small share, will be better discussed when we come to a final survey of the results of the Norman Conquest. At present I purpose to go on with a sketch of the acts of his primacy, and of the great, though gradual, revolution wrought by him in the Church of England alongside of the revolution which William was working in the State. William was distributing lands and granting out Earldoms, in such sort that, without any one moment of violent change, the native nobility of the land was gradually supplanted by strangers. Lanfranc meanwhile was doing the same work among the Bishops and Abbots of England. We may be sure that no act of such moment as the appointment or removal of a Prelate—unless possibly in the small dependent see of Rochester—was ever made without William's personal authority and approval. Still Lanfranc appears throughout as the immediate actor in all these matters. Meanwhile the series of ecclesiastical Councils held by him get more and more clearly distinguished from those common Assemblies of the whole realm which men of old had looked on as failing in their duty if they did not take order in all causes and over all persons, ecclesiastical and civil, within the English realm.[1]

Gradual removal of English Prelates.

William's supremacy

Personal agency of Lanfranc

[1] See vol 1. p 405. We begin to see the division between the two classes of assemblies in such an expression as that (see above, p 343) of the Legate holding a synod on the morrow of the assembly held by the King So in 1085 (Chron Petrib in anno) we find the King holding his court for five days, and then the Archbishop holding his synod for three days more Here are the beginnings of the anomalous position of the two Convocations in England, half ecclesiastical synods, half estates of the realm, each character hindering the effectual working of the other

But besides his general care over the whole Church and realm, Lanfranc was a diligent Bishop over his own city and diocese. His most pressing local cares were the rebuilding of the metropolitan minster, and the restoration of its monks to their full number and the re-establishment of canonical discipline among them. As for the material fabric, whatever the fire had spared of the church which Oda had repaired and raised[1] was now swept away to make room for the last improvements which the building-art had received beyond the sea. Lanfranc took as his model the church which he had left at Caen,[2] and which still lacked somewhat of completion.[3] Prudent, like his master, Lanfranc took care not to lay himself open to the reproach which lights on those who begin to build and are not able to finish. The church of Canterbury, as designed and carried out by him, was not one of those vast piles whose building was necessarily spread over several generations. His whole work was done in the space of seven years, a space whose shortness amazed his own generation.[4] The ancient church, with its two apsidal ends and its basilican ranges of pillars, now gave way to a minster of the received Norman type, with two towers, one of which was standing within the present generation, flanking its western front, and with the central lantern rising, as usual, over the choir with its supporting

*CHAP XIX*
*Lanfranc's administration of his diocese*
*He rebuilds the metropolitan church 1072-1079*
*Changes in the plan of the new church.*

---

[1] See above, p 125 See all the evidence in Willis's Canterbury, 13, 14
[2] See the comparison between the two churches in Willis, 65
[3] See vol iii pp 108, 382
[4] Eadmer, Hist Nov 8 (Selden) "Ædificavit. ecclesiam, quam spatio septem annorum a fundamentis ferme totam perfectam reddidit" William of Malmesbury also (Gest Pont 69) remarks on the speed with which Lanfranc's work was done, "Ædificia ecclesiæ cui sedebat vorax flamma ante non multum consumpserat, cumulabantque ruinam aggeres parietum, disjecta tectorum Ille, deturbatis veteribus fundamentis, suscitavit in ampliorem statum omnia, ignores majore pulcritudine an velocitate." So Eadmer also (7) says of the monastic buildings, " domos ad opus monachorum necessarias citato opere consummavit "

362        THE ECCLESIASTICAL SETTLEMENT OF ENGLAND.

CHAP. XIX. transepts.[1] The building thus raised was enriched with every ornament known to the age; the vaulting of large spaces with stone had not yet been ventured on, but all the skill of the goldsmith and the painter was lavished on the adornment of the rich ceilings of Lanfranc's minster.[2] And, if the Primate was careful for the material temple, he was no less careful for the welfare and discipline of its ministers. The monks of Christ Church, Earls rather than monks in the stateliness of their following, lived, we are told, the life of laymen in all things, except that the vow of chastity was still observed.[3] Dice, banquets, raiment softer than the rule of Saint Benedict allowed, the joys of torture and slaughter so dear to the saint upon the throne, formed, so Norman reformers gave out, the delights of the English brotherhood in the days of Stigand.[4] All this was

*He reforms his monks and increases their number.*

---

[1] The description of Gervase (De Combustione, X Scriptt 1293) clearly points out the position of the choir under the tower, "Turris in medio ecclesiæ maximis subnixa pilariis posita est, sicut in medio circumferentiæ centrum .. ab hac versus occidentem navis vel aula est ecclesiæ subnixa utrimque pilariis octo, hanc navem vel aulam finiunt duæ turres sublimes . . pulpitum vero turrem prædictam a navi quodammodo separabat ... prædicta magna turris crucem habebat ex utroque latere, australem scilicet et aquilonalem." This "pulpitum," it is plain from his description, was the rood-screen across the western arch of the lantern, but, when the choir was rebuilt by Prior Conrad, it would seem that the stalls were placed in the eastern limb, for Gervase says (1294), "De turre in chorum per gradus plurimos ascenditur"

[2] Will Malm Gest Pont 69 "Jam vero ex abundanti est dicere, quantum ibi ornamentorum congesserit, vel in palliis et sacratis vestibus, in quibus, cedente materiâ, manus aurificum vincebat expensarum pretium, vel in diversicoloribus picturis, ubi lenocinante splendore fucorum ars spectabilis rapiebat animos, et pulcritudinis gratia sollicitabat oculos ad lacunaria"

[3] Ib 70 "Monachi Cantuarienses, sicut omnes tunc temporis in Angliâ, secularibus haud absimiles erant, nisi quod pudicitiam non facile proderent."

[4] Ib. "Canum cursibus avocari, avium prædam raptu aliarum volucrum per inane sequi, spumantis equi tergum premere, tesseras quatere, potibus indulgere, delicatiori victu et accuratiori cultu, frugalitatem nescire, parsimoniam abnuere, et cetera id genus, ut magis illos consules quam monachos pro frequentiâ famulantium diceres."

changed, but not suddenly. Lanfranc knew better than at once to put new wine into old bottles, and the sinners were gradually led by his mild rebukes to forsake the error of their ways.[1] He also largely increased the numbers of the society. The monks of Christ Church were raised by him to a body of not less than a hundred and fifty, and they were placed under the more regular government of a Prior.[2] He rebuilt the archiepiscopal palace in the city, besides building houses on many of his rural lordships.[3] He built hospitals for the poor and sick of both sexes, and founded the church of Saint Gregory the Apostle of the English, served by a body of regular canons—the first, it would seem, of that order who had been seen in England—whose duty it was to minister to the souls and bodies of the brethren and sisters[4] In all these good

*His buildings and charitable foundations*

*Saint Gregory's at Canterbury founded 1084*

---

[1] Will Malm Gest Pont i 70 "Sciebat enim, artis artium, id est regiminis animarum, peritissimus, consuetudinem a naturâ esse secundam, a repentinâ morum conversione teneriores exacerbari animos Quapropter blandis monitionibus per intervalla temporis, nunc illa, nunc ista subtrahens, cote virtutum rudes exacuebat ad bonum mentes, eliminabatque ab eis vitiorum rubiginem "

[2] Gervase, Act Pont. Cant. X Scrippt 1654 " Processu temporis centum monachos apposuit, sic prudenter instituens ut in ecclesiâ Christi monachi essent septies xx vel centum et l, quibus ordinem scripsit, Priorem instituit "

[3] Eadmer, Hist Nov 8 " Ædificavit et curiam sibi " Gervase, Act Pont Cant 1655 " In maneriis ad archiepiscopum pertinentibus ecclesias et domos honestas ædificavit " Of one of these buildings we find a somewhat suspicious notice in Domesday, 3 b, " Ad hoc manerium [Estursete] pertinuerunt T R. E. in civitate lii. masuræ, et modo non sunt nisi xxv, quia aliæ sunt destructæ in novâ hospitatione archiepiscopi "

[4] Will Malm Gest Pont 72 " Extra urbem Cantuariam in aquilonali parte lapideas domos omnibus egenis, in occidentali parte regiâ valetudine fluentibus ligneas locavit, canonicis etiam apud Sanctum Gregorium regularibus institutis, qui eis divina facerent officia, divisis pro varietate sexuum habitaculis, sumptibus provisis, ministris delegatis " The distinction of the two classes of buildings in wood and in stone should be noted. Compare the buildings of Bishop Avesgaud of Le Mans, vol ii p 607, 2nd ed, Gervase, Act Pont Cant 1655 " Ecclesiam Sancti Nicolai ad occidentem civitatis et hospitale fecit leprosorum, in quibus ecclesiis clericos instituit, ut prædictis ægrotis vivis et defunctis spiritualia

CHAP XIX

*His private good works*

works the King helped and favoured him, as also in his efforts for the spread and reform of monasticism in the country generally.¹ And besides these public acts, we hear much also of his private alms,² alms in which his abundant bounty did not always wait till it was called upon. Lanfranc freely offered help wherever it was needed, and he strove that his left hand should not know what his right hand did³

*He recovers the estates of his see*

But if Lanfranc was bountiful in spending, he was no less careful in recovering the property in regard to which he was trustee for his church and his successors. One famous case of his zeal in the recovery of the lost possessions of his see has become familiar as an example of the jurisprudence of the age.⁴ The King's brother, Bishop Odo, had, in his temporal character of Earl of Kent, usurped divers possessions and rights belonging to the Archbishop.⁵ To these Lanfranc made his claim, and the

*Encroachments of Odo.*

ministrarent, victualia quoque eisdem ægrotis et redditus assignavit" The word "clerici" as applied to *regular* canons should be noted

¹ Will Malm Gest. Pont. 72 "Hujusmodi tempore Willelmi majoris insistebat operibus, non multas de his quæ ab eo petenda putâsset repulsas passus Nam ad ceteros minus civilis, illi erat affectuosus et dulcis"

² The writer of the Brevis Relatio (Giles, 9) records a not very happy play upon Lanfranc's name, "Propter largitatem itaque animi ejus dicebant quidam merito eum vocatum esse Lanfrancum, id est ferentem cor largum, eo quod largus et bonus erga omnes homines fuit"

³ Will Malm Gest. Pont 71. "Ultroneus juvenibus offerre denarios, quibus necessitudinum propriarum inopiæ occurrerent Si datum fortuitu excideret, geminare, idque clam aliis esse præcipere"

⁴ The famous scene on Penenden Heath, "congregatio illa famosa nobilium Angliæ et seniorum [þa yldestan þegnas], quæ ex præcepto Regis facta est apud Pinnindene," as Gervase (Act Pont Cant 1655) calls it, is also recorded in the Appendix to the Winchester Chronicle as "magnum placitum in loco qui dicitur Pinenden" But the fullest account is found in Bishop Ernulf's Rochester History, Anglia Sacra, 1 334.

⁵ The pompous opening in which Ernulf records this fact is worth noticing, "Tempore magni Regis Willelmi, qui Anglicum regnum armis conquisivit et suis ditionibus subjugavit, contigit Odonem Baiocensem Episcopum et ejusdem Regis fratrem multo citius quam Lanfrancum Archiepiscopum in Angliam venire, atque in comitatu de Cant. cum magnâ

King commanded the matter to be heard, in ancient English form, before the Scirgemót of Kent. He further bade that Englishmen known to be well versed in the Laws of England should be specially summoned.[1] Such a provision was not needless. When the King's men, French and English, were gathered together, the result might be different in a shire like Kent, which had been utterly given over as a prey to the spoiler,[2] and in a shire like Lincoln, where English Thegns and Lawmen still held their own in considerable numbers.[3] The Assembly met in the ancient meeting-place of the shire on Penenden Heath,[4] and the pleadings on the two sides occupied the whole shire for three days.[5] In this case the natural presidents of the Assembly, the Bishop and the Earl,[6] were themselves the litigants; the court was therefore held by Geoffrey of Mowbray, Bishop of Coutances, who appears on more than

Lanfranc's suit on Penenden Heath. 1072.

potentiâ residere, ibique potestatem non modicam exercere. Et quia illis diebus in comitatu illo quisquam non erat qui tantæ fortitudinis viro resistere posset, propter magnam quam habuit potestatem, terras complures de archiepiscopatu Cantuarberiæ et consuetudines nonnullas sibi arripuit, atque usurpans suæ dominationi adscripsit."

[1] Anglia Sacra, i. 335. "Præcepit ergo Rex comitatum totum absque morâ considere, et homines comitatûs omnes Francigenas, et præcipue Anglos in antiquis legibus et consuetudinibus peritos in unum convenire."

[2] See above, p. 34.    [3] See above, p. 214.

[4] Domesday, i. "Si fuerint præmoniti ut conveniant ad sciram, ibunt usque ad Pinnedennam, non longius." See Furley's Weald of Kent, 187, 237, 268. Compare the meetings of the Berkshire Scirgemót at Cwichelmeshlæw, vol. i. p. 360.

[5] Anglia Sacra, i. 335. "Et quoniam multa placita de diratiocinationibus terrarum et verba de consuetudinibus legum inter Archiepiscopum et prædictum Baiocensem Episcopum ibi surrexerunt, et etiam inter consuetudines regales et archiepiscopales quæ primâ die expediri non potuerunt, eâ caussâ totus comitatus per tres dies ibi fuit detentus."

[6] We find Lanfranc and Odo acting together in this character in Domesday, 2. A reeve named Bruman had levied T. R. E. certain dues belonging to the Abbey of Saint Augustine, "qui postea T. R. W. ante Archiepiscopum Lanfrancum et Episcopum Baiocensem recognovit se injuste accepisse, et sacramento facto juravit quod ipsæ ecclesiæ suas consuetudines quietas habuerunt R. E. tempore, et ex inde utræque ecclesiæ in suâ terrâ habuerunt consuetudines suas, judicio baronum Regis qui placitum tenuerunt."

one other occasion in the character of Justiciary.[1] A crowd of men of rank and authority, French and English, appeared in that mixed character, at once judges and witnesses, which marks the jurisprudence of the age. But special weight was attached to the witness of Æthelric, the deposed Bishop of the South-Saxons, an aged man, specially learned in the laws of the land. He was, by the King's special order, brought—perhaps from his prison at Marlborough—in a car or waggon like a Merowingian King, to declare to the Assembly what the ancient customs of England were.[2] The Assembly heard and determined, on grounds, we are told, so strong and clear that from that day no man ever dared to call in question one jot or one tittle of its decision.[3] Divers lands of the see were recovered from Odo and his followers and from other unjust occupants. Among them we specially mark Hugh of Montfort, already known at Senlac and at Dover,[4] and Turold of Rochester, whose dwarfish form still lives in the Tapestry of Bayeux.[5] A third was Ralph, described, possibly from some physical defect of the same kind, as *Curva-spina* or *Curbespine*, who appears in the Survey as a special despoiler

---

[1] Ang Sac 1. 335. "Huic placito interfuerunt Goisfridus Episcopus Constantiensis, qui in loco Regis fuit et justitiam illam tenuit"

[2] Ib " Ægelricus Episcopus de Cicestrâ, vir antiquissimus et legum terræ sapientissimus, qui ex præcepto Regis advectus fuit ad ipsas antiquas legum consuetudines discutiendas et edocendas in unâ quadrigâ" No one would have guessed from this description that Æthelric had ceased to be Bishop of any see, and that, while he was Bishop, his see was at Selsey and not at Chichester He is spoken of again in nearly the same way when his cause, of which we have already heard (see above, p 343), was finally settled in the Council of 1076, "Fratris nostri Ailrici, Cicestrensis quondam Episcopi, caussa canonice definita et ad finem perducta est" Wilkins' Concilia, i 367

[3] Ang Sac u s "In illâ die quâ ipsum placitum finitum fuit non remansit homo in toto regno Angliæ qui aliquid inde calumniaretur neque super ipsas terras etiam parvum quidquid clamaret"

[4] See above, p. 73.

[5] "Turoldus de Hrovecestrâ," as he appears in Ernulf See vol iii p 568 So in Domesday, 6 b, 7, we find " Radulfus filius Turaldi de Rovecestre" as a tenant of Bishop Odo in Kent

of women.[1] The Archbishop moreover succeeded in defining the King's rights over his own lands, which were narrowed to certain cases touching the safety and good maintenance of the King's highway.[2] He established in return divers rights of his own over the lands of the King and the Earl, such especially as touched the good morals and the souls' health of his flock.[3] The decree of the local Gemót was laid before the King, by whom it was approved and confirmed, and it was seemingly sanctioned with all solemnity by a general Council of the whole realm.[4]

*Rights of the King and the Archbishop.*

[1] "Radulfus de Curvâ spinâ" in Ernulf. We find him in Domesday (2) as holding the houses in Canterbury which had belonged to Harold's mistress, whether Eadgyth Swanneshals or any other (see vol. iii. pp. 763, 764), "Radulfus de Curbespine habet iv mansuras in civitate quas tenuit quædam concubina Heraldi." He appears again in 9 b, "Radulfus de Curbespine tenet de Episcopo [Odone] unum jugum in Berfrestone Ibi una paupercula mulier reddit iii denarios et unum obolum." The name *Curbespine* may be hereditary, as in Orderic (550 D) we find a "Robertus de Curvâ-spinâ, strenuus miles," father of Gilbert Mammot, Bishop of Lisieux, and perhaps of this Ralph.

[2] The royal rights are thus defined in the Winchester Appendix, "Lanfrancus diratiocinavit, se suamque ecclesiam omnes terras et consuetudines suas ita liberas terrâ marique habere, sicut Rex habet suas, exceptis tribus, videlicet, si regalis via fuerit effossa, si arbor incisa juxta super eam ceciderit; si homicidium factum vel sanguis in eâ fusus fuerit, in iis qui deprehensus, et ab eo pignus acceptum fuerit, Regi enim dabit, alioquin liber a Regis exactoribus erit." They are given more fully by Ernulf, 335, but to the same effect. Compare also the customs of Canterbury in Domesday, 2, "Si quis infra has publicas vias intus civitatem vel extra foderit vel palum fixerit sequitur illum præpositus Regis ubicumque abierit et emendam accipiet ad opus Regis."

[3] Ernulf, Ang Sacr i 336 "Etenim ab illo die quo clauditur Allelujah usque ad octavas Paschæ, si quis sanguinem fuderit, Archiepiscopo emendabit. Et in omni tempore tam extra Quadragesimam quam infra quicumque illam culpam fecerit quæ Cildwite vocatur, Archiepiscopus aut totam aut dimidiam emendationis partem habebit, infra Quadragesimam quidem totam et extra aut totam aut dimidiam emendationem. Habet etiam in eisdem terris omnibus quæcumque ad curam et salutem animarum videntur pertinere." *Cildwite* is the fine paid by the father of an illegitimate child. On other penalties of this kind see above, p. 51.

[4] Ib "Hujus placiti multis testibus multisque rationibus determinatum finem postquam Rex audivit, laudavit, laudans cum consensu omnium principum suorum confirmavit, et ut deinceps incorruptus perseveraret firmiter præcepit."

CHAP. XIX.
Illustration of William's character and position.

This is one of the moments in his history which set before us the mixed character of William on its brightest side. He could at all times play the tyrant when so it suited his policy. In course of time he even learned to play the tyrant at the mere bidding of his own pleasure. But when no such motive led him astray, no prince was more ready than William to reign as a just King over his people. In this present matter Ælfred or Cnut could have done no more than William did. He appears as not only willing, but anxious, that justice should be done, even against his own brother. He steps in, not as a partizan of either disputant, but as a supreme power, careful to provide that the lawful judges should have the means of judging fairly between both disputants. Above all, the story shows that nothing was further from his thoughts than to root out the Laws of England and to bring in some foreign code of his own devising in their stead. The matter is judged by the lawful English Court, assembled in its ancient place of meeting. It is judged according to the ancient Laws of England, as set forth by the mouths of those who knew them best, those whose memories could go furthest back into the days of the holy Eadward and the righteous Cnut. If men of foreign birth were present, if they even presided in the Assembly, it was not as men of foreign birth that they were there. Geoffrey of Mowbray and his companions were present in the Gemót at Penenden as men who held English lands according to English Law. They were present as the officers of a King of the English who, on that day at least, fully carried out the oath which he had sworn, to rule his Kingdom as well as it had ever been ruled by any of the Kings of the English that were before him.[1]

Retention of English Law

Having thus sketched the state of the metropolitan

[1] See vol iii p. 560

church, I will run briefly through the history of the chief Bishopricks and Abbeys of England, as they were affected by this memorable primacy. A few events which had a direct bearing on general history will be kept for their proper place in chronological order.

*Chap XIX. Sketch of the chief churches of England under Lanfranc.*

Next to his own church of Canterbury, the chief object of Lanfranc's care was the little dependent Bishoprick of Rochester. The nomination to this see lay in his own hands [1] The English Prelate Siward, who had a share in the consecration of Lanfranc, was allowed to keep his see for life.[2] He was followed in quick succession by two monks of Caen, Ernost and Gundulf,[3] the latter of whom has left a great name behind him in the history of military architecture. He was the architect of the great work of the Conqueror, the mighty Tower of London,[4] he built also his own tower

*Rochester. Death of Bishop Siward 1075. Ernost Bishop. 1076. Gundulf Bishop 1077-1108.*

---

[1] All our authorities emphatically point to this peculiar position of the Rochester Bishoprick Thus in the Appendix to the Winchester Chronicle we read, "Sexto anno dedit Hernosto monacho, in capitulo ecclesiæ Christi, ecclesiam Rofensem regendam, quem et Lundoniæ sacravit..... Hernostus hoc ipso anno ab hâc vitâ migravit. Septimo anno, Gundulfo modo ecclesiam Rofensem tradidit, quem etiam Cantuariæ sacravit" See also Gervase, Act Pont Cant 1654 Will. Malm. Gest Pont 136, "Has miserias corrigere volens, sapientissimus Lanfrancus Archiepiscopus Arnostum quemdam monachum pontificem loco dedit Sed eo veloci morte præerepto, Gundulfum æque monachum induxit" But the other side may be seen in the "Libellus" of the Rochester monks, Ang Sac 1. 384

[2] Ann Roff Ang. Sac i. 342 "Anno MLXXV. Sywardus Roffensis Episcopus obiit, cui successit Arnostus, Beccensis monachus" Florence inadvertently puts this under 1070, seemingly wishing to clear off the histories of several Bishops at once

[3] There is a special Life of Gundulf in Anglia Sacra, ii 273. He was a native of the Vexin, first a canon of Rouen, then a monk of Bec, who moved to Saint Stephen's with Lanfranc

[4] On the building of the Tower of London see Mr G T Clark in Old London, 97, 98 As a direct authority for Gundulf's share in the work he refers to the "Conventio inter Gundulfum Episcopum et Eadmerum Anhande burgensem Londoniæ," in Hearne's Textus Roffensis, 212, "Dum idem Gundulfus, ex præcepto Regis Willielmi Magni, præesset operi magnæ turris Londoniæ, et hospitatus fuisset apud ipsum Ædmerum" The name *Tower*, and not *Castle*, belonged to Gundulf's fortress from the first See the Peterborough Chronicle, 1097, 1100, 1101

VOL. IV.   B b

370   THE ECCLESIASTICAL SETTLEMENT OF ENGLAND.

CHAP. XIX
Architectural works of Gundulf

He rebuilds Rochester Cathedral, and substitutes monks for canons

Marriage of the canons

at Malling,[1] and in the days of William Rufus he built a royal castle in his own city, which in the next age gave way to one of greater enrichment, which now forms one of the noblest ruins of Romanesque defensive work.[2] But he also, no doubt in partnership with his patron, rebuilt his cathedral church [3] and reformed the discipline of its ministers. At the death of Siward, we are told, it was in a wretched state. It was still served by secular canons, of whom only four were left, and those living in the same poverty in which we are told that their brethren at Wells were found at the coming of Gisa.[4] We gather from another source that they were commonly married, that their wives and children were legally recognized, and that moreover both husbands and wives remained on good terms with the monks who supplanted them.[5] These, under the care of Lanfranc

---

[1] See Old London, 97.

[2] A dispute between the Bishop and William Rufus about the manor of Hedenham in Buckinghamshire was compromised by the Bishop, as a skilful architect, undertaking to build the King a castle, "quatenus pro pecuniâ, quam pro concessione manerii exigebat, Episcopus Gundulfus, quia in opere cæmentarii plurimum sciens et efficax erat, castrum sibi Hrofense lapideum de suo construeret" (Ang Sac i. 338.) So presently we read, "Igitur hoc pacto coram Rege inito, fecit castrum Gundulfus Episcopus de suo ex integro totum, costamine, ut reor, lx librarum." The whole story is curious.

[3] Ernulf (Ang Sac i. 337) speaks only of Gundulf's share in the work, "xxxi. annis inibi superstes exsistens, ecclesiam S Andreæ, pene vetustate dirutam, novam ex integro, ut hodie apparet, ædificavit, officinas quoque monachis necessarias, prout loci necessitas pati potuit, omnes construxit" But Gervase, Act Pont. Cant. 1665, distinctly attributes the work to Lanfranc, "Ecclesiam Sancti Andreæ Roffensis, quam Rex olim fundaverat Ethelbertus, renovavit, consummavit, quam etiam preciosis ornamentis et monachis ditavit"

[4] Ang Sac i. 339 "Et quum non amplius in introitu episcopatûs sui quam quinque invenisset in ecclesiâ S Andreæ canonicos, die quâ sæculo præsenti decessit plusquam sexaginta monachos, bene legentes et optime cantantes, in servitio Dei et apostoli sui Deum timentes et super omnia amantes, reliquit" William of Malmesbury (Gest Pont 72) speaks of the canons of Rochester, just like those of Wells, as "ipsi quotidiani panis egentes."

[5] This appears from a curious set of entries in Ang Sac. i. 340, from

and Gundulf, grew to the number of fifty, and the rule of Saint Benedict flourished in the church of Saint Andrew of Rochester. Lanfranc also won back for his vassal church a lordship in the distant shire of Cambridge, a lordship which had belonged to Earl Harold, and whose grant is recorded in a writ of William in the English tongue.[1] The story illustrates the state of things in the days when English Law had to be administered by foreign officers. The Bishop of Rochester claims the land of King William; the King refers the matter to the lawful tribunal, the Scírgemót.[2] But through fear of the Norman Sheriff Picot, of whom we have already heard,[3] the English witnesses gave a false verdict that the land belonged to the Crown. Complaint was made to Bishop Odo, who had been present at the first hearing, and who, like his brother, was not disinclined to do justice when his own interest was not concerned. The *venue* was changed; the case was heard again in London

*Lanfranc recovers the estates of the see in Cambridge.*

*Unjust dealing of the Sheriff Picot.*

*The wrong redressed by Odo.*

which it is plain that neither the English nor the Norman clergy had any scruple about marrying, and moreover that the monks did not think them very wicked for so doing

[1] The writ given by Ernulf (Ang Sac i 336) is addressed to Erfast Bishop and Baldwin Abbot (see vol ii p 585, 2nd ed ), Picot Sheriff, Robert Malet, " and ealle þa þegenas þæt þis gewrit to cymð " It grants to Lanfranc the land at Fracenham, " swa full and swa forð swa Harold hit fyrmest hæfde þæs deges þe ic fyrmest fram ofer sæ com [it is curious to see this familiar Domesday formulary in the English tongue and in the first person] and swa swa Þurbearn and Goti of Harolde heolden " The land which Ernulf (339) describes as " terra quæ erat de Fracenham et jacebat in Giselham " appears in Domesday (190 b) under the latter name It is held by the Bishop of Rochester " sub Archiepiscopo Lanfranco." There is no mention of Harold or of Goti, but besides " Wulwinus venator Regis E ," we read that " xii soci habuerunt i hidam sub Turberto [doubtless the Thurbearn of the writ], qui omnes dare et vendere potuerunt "

[2] Ernulf, Ang Sac i 339 " Rex præcepit ut omnes illius comitatûs homines congregarentur, et eorum judicio cujus terra deberet rectius esse probaretur "

[3] See above, p 223

## 372     THE ECCLESIASTICAL SETTLEMENT OF ENGLAND.

CHAP. XIX.

Thomas Archbishop of York 1070-1100

He consecrates Anselm

1093

Revival of the question as to profession,

before a general Assembly of the realm, and the land was adjudged to the Bishoprick.[1]

In the metropolitan see of York Thomas of Bayeux sat with all honour for thirty years, outliving Lanfranc and William and William's successor. The old dispute between the two metropolitan sees was not fully healed. It fell to the lot of Thomas to consecrate the successor of Lanfranc, the holy Anselm. It was held at York that the profession which Thomas had made to Lanfranc personally was now utterly cancelled as regarded his successor,[2] and it would seem that the southern province yielded so far as that Anselm should be consecrated, not as Primate of all Britain, a title which would have reduced York to a mere suffragan rank, but with

---

[1] The story is told at large by Ernulf, and it is a good illustration of the way in which English Law was carried out by the Norman rulers. The Scirgemót first, for fear of the Sheriff, declares the land to belong to the King ("illi autem congregati terram illam Regis esse potius quam B. Andreæ timore Vicecomitis affirmaverunt"). But Odo has his doubts; he therefore requires that twelve members of the assembly should be chosen to confirm the sentence on oath. Twelve men, six of whose names are given, being again threatened by the Sheriff, take the oath ("illi autem quum ad concilium secessissent, et inibi a Vicecomite per internuntium conterriti fuissent, revertentes verum esse quod dixerant juraverunt'), and the land remains in the King's hands. The Bishop of Rochester, hearing of this decision, complained to Odo, and two of the jurors on being examined confessed the perjury. The story then goes on, "Denique mandavit Vicecomiti, ut reliquos obviam sibi Londoniam mitteret, et alios duodecim de melioribus ejusdem comitatûs, qui quod illi juraverant verum esse confirmaverant. Illuc quoque fecit venire multos ex melioribus totius Angliæ baronibus, quibus omnibus Londoniæ congregatis, judicatum est, tam a Francis quam ab Anglis, illos omnes perjuros esse, quandoquidem ille, post quem alii juraverant, se perjurum esse fatebatur. Quibus tali judicio condemnatis, Episcopus Hrofensis terram suam, ut justum erat, habuit." The rest of the story should be read as an illustration of the custom of ordeal.

[2] T. Stubbs, X Scriptt. 1707. Thomas is made to say, "Quum duo tantum sint metropolitæ in Britanniâ, alter super alterum esse non potest. Si timore vel amore et juvenili consilio personaliter et indebite alicui me subjeci, liberatus sum, in Primatem neminem consecrabo."

the vaguer title of Metropolitan.[1] The question too about the diocese of Dorchester or Lincoln also rose again. On the death of Remigius, Thomas objected to the consecration of his successor Robert Bloet as Bishop of Lincoln. He might be Bishop of Dorchester, like his predecessors; but Lindesey, part of the spiritual conquest of Paullinus,[2] was of ancient right subject to the metropolitan authority of York.[3] This claim came to nothing, and Thomas found better scope for his energies in the reform of his own church. The minster of Saint Peter, like that of the southern metropolis, was found by Thomas a blackened ruin.[4] Yet it would seem that the ancient church was not utterly destroyed, and that the work of Thomas was rather to repair than actually to rebuild.[5] But of the works either of Thomas or of his predecessors nothing remains beyond a few fragments embedded in the crypts which support the vaster and more splendid fabric of later days. With regard to the constitution of his church, his career was a memorable one in local and even in general history. It forms a good illustration of the habits and feelings of Englishmen with regard to the position of the secular clergy. The church of York had been

*CHAP XIX.*

*and as to the jurisdiction of Lindesey. 1093.*

*Works of Thomas at York.*

*Restoration of the minster*

*His reforms in the constitution of the Chapter*

---

[1] T Stubbs, X Scriptt 1707 We read first, "Scriptâ petitione et lectâ ut eum in Primatem totius Britanniæ consecraret, et Thomas discessit, et se pontificalibus exuit" This was evident retaliation for the behaviour of Lanfranc towards Thomas himself, see above, p 352 But Thomas is presently pacified by Anselm and Walkelin of Winchester, and it is agreed that "quod scriptum erat, 'in Primatem,' minime lecto et ex toto abraso, petitione correptâ ut in metropolitanum Cantuariensem consecraretur" The Worcester Annals under 1092 remark, "Tunc primo vocati sunt Cantuarienses archiepiscopi, qui prius totius Angliæ metropolitani vocabantur"

[2] See T Stubbs, X Scriptt 1707
[3] See above, p 357
[4] See above, p 267.
[5] See Willis, Architectural History of York, 13–16 This seems to be borne out by the words of T Stubbs, X Scriptt 1708, "Ecclesiæ recoopertæ et juxta possibilitatem suam restructæ" On the other hand, he says afterwards (1709), "Ecclesiam quæ nunc est a fundamentis fecit."

374          THE ECCLESIASTICAL SETTLEMENT OF ENGLAND.

CHAP. XIX. served by seven canons only, and, after the desolation of Northumberland, but three were found at their post.[1] Thomas recalled those who had fled, and increased the number of the body. He at first followed the example of Gisa at Wells[2] and Leofric at Exeter,[3] in introducing the Lotharingian discipline. He built a dormitory and refectory, and made his canons live in common under the superintendence of a Provost.[4] He probably lived to find that this system did not suit the habits of Englishmen at York any more than it did at Exeter. Wiser advisers afterwards led him to introduce the system which was gradually introduced into the secular cathedrals of England. He divided the estates of his church into prebends, thus allotting to each canon his separate maintenance. He also founded the dignities of Dean, Precentor, and Treasurer. The office of Chancellor or Master of the Schools he had already introduced while the church was under the Lotharingian discipline.[5] The work of Thomas in this respect still lives. The constitution of the church of York, as laid down by him, still remains nearly unaltered, and in no church in England have the original rights of the whole capitular body been so little encroached on by the growth of a residentiary oligarchy.

He first brings in the Lotharingian discipline,

but afterwards withdraws it

He founds the dignities and prebends

William Bishop of London 1051–1075.

In the church of London no change was needed. Bishop William lived on, honoured by men of both races, and leaving behind him a memory which was long cherished

---

[1] T. Stubbs, X Scriptt. 1708. "De septem canonicis, non enim plures fuerant, tres tantum repperit, ceteri vel mortui erant, vel metu vel desolatione patriæ exsulabant"

[2] See vol ii. p 84            [3] See vol ii. p. 452.

[4] T Stubbs, u. s "Canonicos quos invenit, restituit, dispersos revocavit, et aliquos addidit, refectorium et dormitorium refecit, præpositum constituit, qui cæteris præesset, et eos procuraret"

[5] Ib 1709. "Annis plurimis canonicis communiter vescentibus, quorumdam consilio placuit archiepiscopo de terrâ Sancti Petri, quæ adhuc multum vastata erat, singulas præbendas partiri Tunc quidem statuit decanum, thesaurarium, cantorem, nam magistrum scholarum ante statuerat"

among the burghers of his city.[1] Two Bishops succeeded him in the days of Lanfranc and King William. Hugh of Orival is an obscure name enough,[2] but his successor Maurice was memorable for beginning the mighty pile of old Saint Paul's. But, unlike his Metropolitan, he began it on a scale which made it in the end the vastest of the minsters of England, but which also put it utterly out of the power of its first founder to finish it.[3]

*Hugh of Orival Bishop 1075-1085 Maurice Bishop 1086-1107*

At Winchester Bishop Walkelin survived his metropolitan and his sovereign. He too began a church perhaps hardly second in size to that of London, that great minster where his transepts still remain well nigh untouched, and where even his gigantic nave cannot be said to have utterly vanished.[4] He was less fortunate in his attempt to reconstruct the constitution of his church, than in renewing its material fabric. While several other Bishops were displacing their secular canons to make room for monks, Walkelin became the leader of a counter party among the Prelates, whose object was to displace the monks of cathedral churches in general, and even to make this change in the metropolitan church itself.[5] They argued that the

*Walkelin Bishop of Winchester 1070-1098.*

*Scheme for removing monks from cathedral churches.*

---

[1] See his epitaph, set up by the "Senatus populusque Londinensis," in Godwin's Catalogue of Bishops.

[2] Will. Malm. Gest. Pont. 145. He underwent the fate of Origen, but for the health of his body and not of his soul.

[3] Ib. "Magnanimitatis certe ipsius est indicium basilica beati Pauli quam inchoavit Londoniæ . . quia igitur Mauritius erat mentis immodicus, laboriosi operis impensam transmisit ad posteros."

[4] Ann. Wint. 1079 "Walkelinus Episcopus a fundamentis Wintoniæ cœpit re-ædificare ecclesiam." The monks removed from the old church to the new in 1093. "Sequenti vero die, jussu domini Walkelini Episcopi, cœperunt homines primum vetus frangere monasterium, et fractum est totum in illo anno, excepto portico uno et magno altari." See Willis, Winchester, 17, 33, 35.

[5] Eadmer, Hist. Nov. 10 "Super hæc suis quoque et eisdem ferme diebus, omnes circiter qui ex clericali ordine per Regem Willielmum in Angliâ constituti Pontifices erant, monachos qui in nonnullis episcopatibus Angliæ ab antiquo vitam agebant, inde eliminare moliti sunt, et Regem ipsum in hoc sibi consentaneum effecerunt. Namque pari voto,

376          THE ECCLESIASTICAL SETTLEMENT OF ENGLAND.

CHAP XIX. metropolitan Chapter, above all, had duties laid upon it which were quite inconsistent with the monastic profession, and which could be better discharged by the more worldly experience of the secular clergy.[1] Modern leaders will probably be convinced by their arguments, arguments whose weight was admitted by the clear and sagacious mind of William himself.[2] The party which followed Walkelin's lead is said to have numbered in its ranks all the Bishops who were not themselves members of the monastic order. Walkelin himself was so sure of the success of his schemes that he had, with the King's good liking, forty canons ready in the garb of their office to take possession of the stalls of Saint Swithhun's.[3] Nothing was needed but the consent of the Archbishop,[4] and Walkelin and his party seem to have thought that what the King approved Lanfranc would not venture to gainsay.[5] But from Lan-

The scheme hindered by Lanfranc.

simili conamine, uno consensu, concordi animo, Pontifices quos religionis ordo non sibi astrinxerat eniti cœperunt quatenus saltem de primatu Cantuariensi monachos eradicarent, intendentes se hoc facto facillime alios aliunde exclusuros"

[1] Eadmer, Hist. Nov 10. " De illis etenim, potioribus, sicut eis videbatur, rationibus ad id agendum fulciebantur, partim ob sublimitatem Primatis sedis, quæ dispositioni et correctioni ecclesiarum per suas personas quâque, per Angliam invigilare habet, partim ob alias multiplices causas quarum exsecutio, juxta quod ipsi confingebant, magis clericorum quam monachorum officium spectat "

[2] Ib  " Deductus est in sententiam istam Rex et alii principes regni "

[3] Ib. " In quo tamen se effectu potituros certi exstiterant, ut Walchelinus Episcopus adunatos pene quadraginta clericos, canonicorum more tonsurâ ac veste redimitos, haberet, quos, ejectis monachis, Wentanæ ecclesiæ cui præsidebat mox intromitteret " So Will. Malm. Gest. Pont 71  " Jam enim episcoporum livor increverat, volentium ab episcopalibus sedibus monachos, clericis immissis, extrudere. Auctor hujus factionis fuit Walkelinus Wentanus, ad cætera bonus, sed in hoc ad pravum consiliis susurronum flexus, plus xl<sup>ta</sup> canonicos cappis et superpelliciis ornaverat "

[4] Eadmer, u s  " Sola mora hæc peragendi, nondum requisita ab Archiepiscopo Lanfranco licentia fuit."

[5] Ib.  " Ut autem eam dicto quoque citius impetraret, nulla menti ejus [Walkelini] dubitatio inerat, sed aliter ac sibi mens sua spoponderat exitus rei provenit "

franc, the father and lover of monks, no consent to any such scheme was to be had.[1] The Primate appealed to Pope Alexander. He obtained from him a bull censuring in the strongest terms the scheme for the humiliation of the monastic order,[2] and decreeing that the church of Canterbury should remain served by monks, as the blessed Augustine had founded it.[3] The design for the like change in the church of Winchester was equally brought to nought. There also all innovation was forbidden by Papal decree.[4] The canons whom Walkelin had gathered together had to go back to their homes without taking possession of their expected prebends,[5] and the discipline which had been

---

[1] " Se arwurða muneca feder and frouer Landfranc arcebisceop," says the Peterborough Chronicler in recording his death in 1089.

[2] The bull is given in Eadmer, 10, and Lanfranc's Letters, Giles, i. 27. Its language shows that the Papal gift of scolding was as vigorous then as it is now. 'Accepimus a quibusdam venientibus de partibus vestris ad limina sanctorum Apostolorum Petri et Pauli, quod quidam clerici, associato sibi terrenæ potestatis, laicorum videlicet, auxilio, diabolico spiritu repleti, moliuntur de ecclesiâ S Salvatoris in Dorobernia, quæ est metropolis totius Britanniæ, monachos expellere et clericos inibi statuere, cui nefario operi molitionis suæ hoc adjicere conantur, ut in omni sede episcopali ordo monachorum extirpetur, quasi in eis non vigeat auctoritas religionis."

[3] The bull of Alexander professes simply to confirm an earlier one of Boniface the Fifth, which orders, " ut vestra benignitas in monasterio Dorobernensi civitate constituto, quod sanctus doctor noster Augustinus, beatæ memoriæ Gregorii discipulus, Sancti Salvatoris nomini consecravit licenter per omnia monachorum regulariter viventium habitationem statuat, apostolicâ auctoritate decernentes, ut ipsi vestræ salutis prædicatores monachi monachorum gregem sibi associent, et eorum vitam sanctitatum moribus exornent."

[4] Will Malm Gest Pont 71 "Regem in sententiam traxerat [Walkelinus], et tantum moræ in medio ut archiepiscopi consensum eliceret, is quominus haberetur, nihil dubitandum At ille auditum facinus exhorruit, et tot potentum excogitatas machinas, ut casses aranearum, solo intuitu dissolvit, quinetiam, ne idem auderent posteri, egit ut Alexander Papa scriptis inhiberet."

[5] Eadmer, 10 "Ergo et clerici qui succedere monachis fuerant per Walchelinum collecti, et in sua dimissi sunt, et monachi qui cedere clericorum præjudicio quodam damnati erant, gratiâ Dei et instantiâ boni Lanfranci, pristinæ conversationis in suâ ecclesiâ compotes effecti sunt."

378    THE ECCLESIASTICAL SETTLEMENT OF ENGLAND.

CHAP XIX. brought into the Old Minster by the zeal of Eadgar and Æthelwold remained untouched till the general dissolution of monastic bodies.[1]

Leofric Bishop of Exeter 1046-1072

Leofric, the first Bishop of Exeter, the Prelate who had brought in the [Lotharingian] discipline,[2] kept his Bishoprick for life. A Briton or Englishman whose feelings were mainly foreign, he was followed by a stranger who had learned to feel as an Englishman. Osbern, a son of the faithful guardian of William,[3] a brother of the famous Earl of Hereford, had, like others of his nation, crossed the sea to enjoy the favours and bounty of the good King Eadward.[4] But, unlike most of those who came on that errand, he adopted the manners and feelings of Englishmen. Amongst other signs of this tendency, he forbore to destroy the works of his predecessors to make room for buildings in the now prevailing style.[5] The beginnings of the Norman cathedral of Exeter, with the two massive towers which still remain, are due to his successor William of Warelwast in the days of Henry the First.

Osbern Bishop 1072-1103.

William of Warelwast Bishop 1107-1136.

The see of Hereford remained in possession of its Lothar-

---

[1] Will. Malm. Gest. Pont. 72. "Magnum id et laudandum, ut quod sedula sanctorum benignitas tempore Regis Edgari inchoaverit ista labefactam non permiserit" Notwithstanding his offence against his order, William of Malmesbury elsewhere (Gest Regg ii 269) gives Walkelin a splendid panegyric, "Cujus bona opera, famam vincentia, vetustatem oblivionis a se repellent quamdiu ibi sedes episcopalis durabit."

[2] See vol. ii p 54.

[3] Will Malm. Gest Pont. 201. "Successit Lefrico Osbernus Regis Willelmi tempore, natione Normannus, frater Willelmi præcellentissimi Comitis" His consecration in London is recorded in the Appendix to the Winchester Chronicle

[4] Ib. "In Angliâ sub Eduardo Rege liberaliter et domestice conversatus, quippe qui cognationem regiam vicino attingeret gradu."

[5] Ib "Unde in victualibus et cæteris rebus ad Anglicos mores pronior, parum Normannorum pompam suspiciebat, consuetudines domini sui Regis Eduardi efferens, et quum per alios exhiberentur cum assidentibus manu et gestu aggaudens. Ita pro more antiquorum præsulum, veteribus contentus ædificiis, liberalis animo et castus habebatur corpore"

ingian Bishop Walter. Thirteen years after William's coming it became vacant by his death, a death which, if the scandal of the time spoke truly, was a strange and shameful one. Walter died by the hand of a woman in the defence of her chastity.[1] His successor, another Lotharingian, Robert by name, was the chosen friend of Saint Wulfstan, and, like most other Norman Bishops, the rebuilder of his cathedral.[2] The sainted Bishop of Worcester himself survived both King and Metropolitan, and remained for many years the only Bishop of English birth in England.[3] We are told that, in one of the early Councils of William's reign, the two Archbishops conspired together against the Englishman, or at least attacked him at once from their several points of view. Thomas, as we have already seen,[4] claimed him as a suffragan; Lanfranc despised him as a simple

CHAP XIX
Death of Walter Bishop of Hereford 1079
Robert Bishop of Hereford 1079-1095
Position of Saint Wulfstan

---

[1] William of Malmesbury (Gest Pont 300) tells the story doubtingly ("nisi fama mentitur"), and adds that the King did all that might be to hinder the scandal from getting wind ("rumor criminis et ultionis totam pervagatus Angliam Regis quoque aures attigit Ille dignitate regiâ credulitatem dissimulans, ne vel cæteri disseminarent gravissimo coercuit edicto" The way in which Thierry deals with this Prelate is amusing In ii 21 the Lotharingian Bishop appointed by Eadward in 1062 becomes one of "une nuée d'aventuriers partis de la Gaule" under William Of these adventurers he tells us "la plupart affichèrent dans leur nouvel état l'immoralité la plus dehontee"—an utter calumny as regards the Prelates appointed by the Conqueror—then comes "l'un d'eux fut tué par une femme à qui il voulait faire violence," with a reference to the story of Walter, of all places in the world, in Knighton, X. Scriptt 2347 A few pages on (28) Walter comes to life again as an English patriot, "Flamand de naissance, le seul parmi les étrangers, evêques avant la conquête, qui se soit montré fidèle à la cause de sa patrie adoptive" See vol. ii p 81.

[2] Will Malm Gest Pont u s "Robertus Lotharingus ibi ecclesiam tereti ædificavit schemate, Aquensem basilicam pro modo imitatus suo" If so, all traces of his building have perished The present Romanesque work at Hereford follows the common type of English and Norman minsters, and has not the faintest likeness to the church of the Great Charles

[3] Wulfstan died in 1095, twenty years after the death of Siward of Rochester (see above, p 369), sixteen after that of Walter, Siward being the last surviving Bishop of English birth and Walter the last of English appointment          [4] See above, p 357.

380    THE ECCLESIASTICAL SETTLEMENT OF ENGLAND.

CHAP. XIX
Lanfranc meditates his deposition.
1075.

His acquittal and friendship with the two Archbishops

Legend of his appeal to Eadward,

and ignorant man, unable, it would seem, to speak any language but his own.[1] His deposition seemed hardly to be avoided; but he went forth in his simple faith, taking no thought what he should speak when he was brought before Kings and rulers.[2] His faith had its reward, he came forth triumphant over all his enemies. He not only kept his see, but Thomas was glad of his help as a native in administering his vast and desolate diocese;[3] Lanfranc too was glad to send him to visit the newly-conquered diocese of Lichfield, the Bishoprick of which was vacant, and in whose half-subdued districts no Norman Prelate as yet ventured to risk himself.[4]

In after days legendary writers drew a striking picture of the King and his Council assembled in the West Minster before the tomb of the holy Eadward.[5] The foreign King

---

[1] Will Malm Gest Pont 284 "Sub seniore Willelmo inclamatum est in eum a Lanfranco de litterarum inscientiâ, a Thomâ Eboracensi archiepiscopo quod ei subjici deberet ex antiquo jure" In the account in the Life of Wulfstan (Ang Sac ii 255) Lanfranc does not appear as an enemy of Wulfstan

[2] Vita Wlst 256. "Tandem jussus exire ut strictiori consilio responsum poliret, cum paucis secum egressis horam nonam incœpit et percantavit. Illis porro referentibus ut alia magis quam psalmos curaret, et id propter quod venerat expediret, respondit, ' Stulti nescitis quod Dominus dixit, Dum steteritis ante Reges et præsides, nolite cogitare quomodo aut quid loquamini Dabitur enim vobis in illâ horâ quid loquamini '"

[3] Will Malm Gest Pont 285 "Ita datâ benedictione monacho, minimæ facundiæ viro, sed Normannicæ linguæ sciolo, rem obtinuit, ut qui suæ diœcesis ante putabatur indignus regimine ab Archiepiscopo Eboraci suppliciter rogaretur ut suas [sic] dignaretur lustrare, quo ipse pro timore hostium vel sermonis ignorantiâ cavebat accedere" The epithet "minimæ facundiæ vir" sounds odd, when we think of Wulfstan's journey to York in company with Harold, described by the same writer in his Life of Wulfstan

[4] Vita Wlst 256 "In eodem concilio apud Pedridan habito episcopatûs ei Cestrensis a Lanfranco Archiepiscopo visitatio commissa est Ea enim provincia, quæ tres habet pagos, Cestrensem, Crobernensem, Tefordensem [I presume that Shropshire and Staffordshire lurk under these two strange names], erat adhuc propter longinquitatem Normannis inaccessa, et propter barbariem impacata."

[5] The story first appears in Æthelred of Rievaulx (X Scriptt. 406), who

and Primate called on the English Bishop to give up his staff and ring. He was, they said, a simple and unlearned man who knew not the French tongue, and who could be of no use in the counsels of the King.[1] Wulfstan arose, staff in hand. He knew his own unworthiness; he would willingly give up his staff, but he would not give it up to Lanfranc, from whom he had not received it; he would give it up to the holy Eadward who had given it to him. Wulfstan walked to the tomb of Eadward and spoke to his dead master; "Thou knowest, most holy King, how unwillingly I took this burthen upon me, and how it was thou who didst constrain me thereto. The choice of the monks was not wanting, nor the petition of the people, nor the consent of the Bishops and nobles, but it was thy will which stood forth chief above all.[2] Lo, now there is a new King, a new Law, a new Primate, who puts forth new decrees. They charge thee with error, who didst make me a Bishop;[3] they charge me with presumption

is followed by Roger of Wendover (ii 52) and Matthew Paris (20 Wats) In the Historia Anglorum (i 53) it is given in a much shorter form, and also in Bromton (X Scriptt 976), who gives one or two touches of his own. The story is partly designed in honour of Eadward, but there is also a clear intention to make out the English Prelates to have been bolder assertors of the national freedom than they really were It comes in short from the same mint as the stories of Archbishop Ealdred (see above, p 260) and Abbot Frithric (see Appendix NN) The strong assertion of the royal supremacy which breathes throughout the story shows that its beginnings at least must have been of early date The Council is said to have been that of 1075, in which the removal of the Bishopricks from small towns was ordered

[1] R Wend ii 52 "Apud hunc archiepiscopum beatus Wlstanus simplicitatis et illiteraturæ accusatus, et quasi homo idiota, qui linguam Gallicanam non noverat nec regiis consiliis interesse poterat, ipso Rege consentiente et hoc dictante, decernitur deponendus" Bromton, whose wording is different, adds, "Ut sic aliquem Normannicum loco ejus subrogarent"

[2] Ib 53 "Licet fratrum non deesset electio, plebis petitio, voluntas episcoporum et gratia procerum, his tamen omnibus tua præponderabat auctoritas, tua magis voluntas"

[3] Ib. "Te erroris arguunt qui me pontificem fecisti"

in that I obeyed thee. Yet will I not resign my staff to them, but I will give back to thee the charge which thou didst give me."[1] He raised his hand, he struck the staff on the tomb, and spake again; "Take it, my Lord O King, and give it to him whom it shall please thee." He went back and took his seat, no longer among the Bishops, but as a simple monk among the monks. But at the touch of Wulfstan's staff the solid marble had yielded, and the badge of rule which Eadward had given remained safe in Eadward's keeping. The unbelieving Primate, like his English predecessor by the dying bed of Eadward,[2] put no faith in the wonder done before his eyes. He bade his chaplain and creature, Gundulf of Rochester, take the staff from the tomb. The staff yielded not, and in one version of the story Wulfstan turned to the King himself; "A better than thou gave it me, take it away if thou canst."[3] The Primate tried; the King himself tried; but the staff remained fixed in the tomb till Wulfstan was fully confirmed in his see, till King and Primate had craved his forgiveness. Then, at Wulfstan's prayer, the holy Eadward loosened his hold, and the staff which would yield to no other hand at once gave way to the touch of its lawful owner.

*Witness of the legend to the royal supremacy.*

Whatever we make of this legend, whatever we make of the whole story of the intended deposition of Wulfstan, the tale at least shows from whom, alike in the days of Eadward and of William, an English Bishop was held to receive his episcopal office. Wulfstan does not appeal to

---

[1] R Wend 11. 53. "Non illis, qui exigunt quod non dederunt, sed tibi baculum resigno qui dedisti, tibi curam eorum dimitto quos mihi commendâsti" The *regale* could hardly be more strongly set forth.

[2] See vol. iii p 12.

[3] Bromton (X Scriptt 976) alone gives this speech, and he puts it doubtingly at the end of the story, "Dixerat Regi, ut quidam aiunt, dum baculum figeret, 'Melior te hunc mihi dedit, cui et retrado, avelle si poteris'"

Pope or Council, to any ecclesiastical laws and canons. His appeal is from the Norman King to his English predecessor. But what, if more prosaic, is far more certain, is, that in an Assembly of the realm under the King's own presidency,[1] Wulfstan won back from Archbishop Thomas the twelve lordships of which Ealdred had robbed the see of Worcester. Lanfranc zealously abetted Wulfstan's cause, and the malicious rumours of the time said that he abetted it out of his grudge against his brother Metropolitan.[2]

This storm over, the saintly Bishop was left to rule his diocese in as much peace as the presence of the Sheriff Urse[3] and men of his stamp would allow. Many tales, whether historical or legendary, bear witness to his faith and piety, his zeal in the discharge of his official duty, his severity against evil-doers, the reverence in which he was held by men of both races alike. The cathedral monastery of Worcester especially flourished under his care, and grew both in its revenues and in the number of its monks.[4] At no great distance from the city, at the foot of the range of hills which bound the shire and diocese to the west, the priory of Malvern, the work of the holy Ealdwine, arose under his patronage.[5] But

*CHAP. XIX*

*Wulfstan's management of his diocese*

*Flourishing state of Worcester monastery under him.*

*Foundation of Malvern Priory 1085*

---

[1] The York version in T. Stubbs, 1708, 1709, runs thus, "Ipse vero dono Regis aliquamdiu xii. villas habuit quas Aldredus de Wygornensi episcopatu retinuerat, sed eas molimine Lanfranci et Rex abstulit." The Worcester version appears in Florence, 1070, who is careful to mark that York had now (see above, p. 340) a pastor to speak for her (" episcopo jam consecrato Thomâ, qui pro Eboracensi loqueretur ecclesiâ "). The restitution was made (" Deo donante ac Rege concedente"), and the authority by which it was done was the highest possible; " Querela . coram Rege ac Dorubermæ Archiepiscopo Landfranco et episcopis, abbatibus, comitibus, et primatibus totius Angliæ, Dei gratiâ adminiculante, est terminata "

[2] Will Malm. Gest. Pont 285. " Quum Lanfrancus Archiepiscopus constanter assisteret caussæ, urgens videlicet æmulum primatûs et potentiæ " [3] See above, p. 174

[4] See the entry in Domesday, 173 b, " Crescente congregatione T R W "

[5] Ann Wig 1085 " Major Malvernia fundata est per Alwinum

CHAP. XIX. Wulfstan's greatest work was in his own city. Unlike the Norman-born but English-minded Bishop of Exeter,[1] he yielded to the fashion of the day, and destroyed the church of his holy predecessor Oswald to make room for a building on a greater scale, and more in accordance with the prevalent taste of the times.[2] Of the work of Wulfstan in the minster of Worcester some portions still abide above ground, and his crypt remains untouched, showing that the style of the day could assume forms of lightness and elegance which seem strange to one used to the massive undercrofts of York and Gloucester. But when the work was done, when the monks had taken possession of the new church, when the work of the blessed Oswald began to be unroofed and pulled down, the holy Wulfstan stood and wept[3] The bystanders asked him why he did not rather rejoice at being the means of carrying so great and holy a work to its completion.[4] The Bishop forthwith made answer; "Our predecessors, whose monuments we deface, rather (I doubt) to set up the banners of our vain glory than to glorify God, they indeed (quoth he) were not acquainted

*Rebuilding of Worcester Cathedral 1084.*

*Wulfstan weeps at the destruction of the old church.*

monachum." A somewhat fuller account is given by William of Malmesbury, Gest Pont, 286, 296 Ealdwine had a companion named Guy, another instance of Norman and Englishman working together

[1] See above, p 378

[2] Ann. Wig 1084. "Inceptio operis Wigorniensis monasterii per sanctum Wulstanum." Vita Wlst. 263. "Tunc autem et novam ecclesiam perfecit, nec facile invenias ornamentum, quod eam non decoraverit. Ita erat in singulis mirabilis et in omnibus singularis."

[3] The story is told by William of Malmesbury in the Life of Wulfstan, 262, and in Gest Pont 283. The words in the latter place are, "Quum ecclesiæ majoris opus, quod ipse a fundamentis inceperat, ad hoc incrementi processisset ut jam monachi migrarent in illam, jussum est veterem ecclesiam, quam beatus Oswaldus fecerat, detegi et subrui Ad hoc spectaculum stans sub divo Wlstanus lacrimas tenere nequivit "

[4] Will Malm. Gest. Pont 283 "Modeste a familiaribus redargutus, qui gaudere potius deberet, quod se superstite tantus ecclesiæ honor accessisset ut ampliatus monachorum numerus ampliora exigeret habitacula "

with such stately buildings, but every place was a church sufficient for them to offer themselves a reasonable, holy, and lively sacrifice unto God. We contrariwise are double diligent in laying heaps of stone, so to frame a material temple, but are too negligent in setting forward the building of that lively temple the Church of God."[1]

Yet there was no Prelate of his own or of any other day who had less need than Wulfstan to charge himself with neglecting the spiritual temple of God in order to build up heaps of stones. I pass by his zeal against the married clergy and other matters of purely ecclesiastical concern.[2] I will rather dwell on one side of his character which sets him before us as an unflinching assertor of the eternal principles of right. One act of Wulfstan's life, to which I have already incidentally referred in an earlier volume,[3] places him high among the apostles of humanity. Notwithstanding the repeated legislation of the days of Æthelred and Cnut, the Bristol slave-trade still went on. Indeed we may believe that, in the first years of the

CHAP XIX.

He preaches against the slave-trade at Bristol

---

[1] I have given the speech of Wulfstan in the vigorous though somewhat free translation of Bishop Godwin in his Catalogue of Bishops It is curious to see how, while he preserves the general sense, he translates some of the ideas as well as the words into those of the sixteenth century But William of Malmesbury does not put exactly the same words into Wulfstan's mouth in his two works. In Gest Pont 283 they stand thus, "Ego longe aliter intelligo, quod nos miseri sanctorum opera destruimus, ut nobis laudem comparemus Non noverat illa felicium virorum ætas pompaticas ædes construere, sed sub qualicumque tecto seipsos Deo immolare subjectosque ad exemplum attrahere Nos e contra nitimur ut animarum neglegentes accumulemus lapides"

[2] Vita Wlst 263 "Uxoratos presbyteros omnes uno convenit edicto, aut libidini aut ecclesiis renuntiandum pronuntians" Wharton remarks on this that marriage was not forbidden to the parochial clergy till 1112, so that Wulfstan's severity in this respect must have applied to the canons only. But as both the cathedral and the other great churches of the diocese were in the hands of the regulars, Wulfstan would have found no great scope for his energies in dealing with the canons only

[3] See vol 1 p 365, vol ii p 153 The story is told by William of Malmesbury both in the Life of Wulfstan, 258, and less fully in the Gesta Regum, iii 269

VOL. IV.  C C

Conquest, when men bowed their necks for meat in the evil days,[1] the wicked traffic in human flesh became more rife than ever. Men, we are told, went the length of uniting lust, cruelty, and greed; they sold their female slaves when they were with child by themselves.[2] Such a state of things could in no way give strength to William's throne or help in any way to carry out the schemes of his policy. William therefore was as zealous against the evil practice as his predecessors. But the evil practice was too deeply rooted even for William's power.[3] The saint of Worcester therefore devoted himself to the good work of reclaiming the men of the merchant borough which then formed the furthest point of his diocese. He went repeatedly to Bristol; he stayed there two or three months at a time, and preached every Sunday against the great sin of the place.[4] The habit which had been too strong for Cnut and William gave way—at least for a season—to the exhortations of Wulfstan The burghers of Bristol became convinced of their sin; they forsook their unlawful gains and became an example in such matters to the other trading-towns of England.[5] So far indeed did their newly-born zeal carry

*Reformation of the burghers*

---

[1] See above, p 293.

[2] Vita Wlst 258 "Homines enim ex omni Angliâ coemptos majoris spe quæstûs in Hiberniam distrahebant, ancillasque prius ludibrio lecti habitas jamque prægnantes venum proponebant Videres et gemeres concatenatos funibus miserorum ordines et utriusque sexûs adolescentes, qui liberali formâ, ætate integrâ, barbaris miserationi essent, quotidie prostitui, quotidie venditari"

[3] Ib. "Ab his Wulstanus morem vetustissimum sustulit, qui sic animis eorum occalluerat, ut nec Dei amor nec Regis Willelmi hactenus eum abolere potuissent" It should be remembered that one of the alleged Laws of William, which I shall have to mention afterwards, which is probably quite genuine in its substance, is as strong against the slave-trade as those of any of the older Kings See Stubbs, Select Charters, 81.

[4] Ib "Sciens enim cervicositatem eorum non facile flecti, sæpe circa eo duobus mensibus, sæpe tribus, mansitabat, omni Dominicâ eo veniens et divinæ prædicationis semina spargens"

[5] Ib. "Quæ adeo per intervalla temporum apud eos convaluere, ut non solum renuntiarent vitio, sed ad idem faciendum cæteris per Angliam essent exemplo"

them, that one stiff-necked sinner, who refused to hearken to the repeated entreaties and arguments of the Bishop, was driven from the town by his fellow-burghers with the loss of his eyes.[1]

*Spiritual bond between Wulfstan and other Prelates*

With regard to Saint Wulfstan, there is a document in which he is concerned which throws a good deal of light on the relations between English and Norman churchmen just at this time. It is a sort of bond of spiritual confederation between the Bishop of Worcester and his monks and the monks of six other monasteries, some of them in his own diocese and some in other parts of England.[2] The members of the league, after Wulfstan himself, are the famous Abbot Æthelwig of Evesham, Wulfwold of Chertsey, Ælfsige of Bath, Eadmund of Pershore, Ralph of Winchcombe, and Serlo of Gloucester. Of these Prelates two only, Ralph and Serlo, were foreigners, and all the English Abbots mentioned kept their Abbeys for life. Æthelwig lived on in all honour, continuing his career of wisdom and munificence, till the eleventh year after the Conquest. His architectural works were less splendid than those of some contemporary Prelates; but he bestowed much on his church in many ways, and he gave up part of his paternal estate in the vain attempt to recover

*Death of Æthelwig. 1077.*

---

[1] Vita Wlst. 258. "Denique unum ex suo numero, qui pertinacius obviaret præceptis Episcopi, vico ejectum, mox luminibus orbavere. In quâ re devotionem laudo, sed factum improbo, quamvis semel vitiatis agrestium animis nulla queat obsistere vis rationis."

[2] The document is printed by Mr Hart in the Preface to the Gloucester History, iii. xviii. He however confounds Saint Wulfstan with the elder Prelate of that name, who brought in the monks at Gloucester (see vol. ii p. 435). Yet one would have thought that no man could have fancied that a document in which men plight their faith to William and Matilda could belong to the days of Cnut. The date must come between 1072, when Serlo became Abbot of Gloucester, and 1077, when Æthelwig died. The document is in English, and begins thus, "On Drihtnes naman Hælendis Cristes, is þæt Wulstan biscop on Drihtnes naman hæfð geræðd wið his leofan gebroðra þe him getreowe synd, for Gode and for worulde." Then follow the names of the Abbots, with the addition of "Ælfstan Decanus on Wigraceastre."

## 388   THE ECCLESIASTICAL SETTLEMENT OF ENGLAND.

CHAP. XIX

Walter
Abbot of
Evesham
1077–1084

Ralph
Abbot of
Winch-
combe
1077–1095
Eadmund
Abbot of
Pershore,
died 1085
Thurstan
1085–1087
Serlo
Abbot of
Gloucester
1072–1104

part of the lands of the Abbey from the rapacious Urse.[1] On his death, the Abbey was granted to a Norman chaplain of Lanfranc, Walter, a monk of Duke Robert's house at Cerisy,[2] who carried on great buildings with the money which Æthelwig had gathered together,[3] but who lost a large part of the estates of his church in a contention with the all-powerful Bishop of Bayeux.[4] It helps to bring more fully home to us the nature of the times with which we are dealing when we find the signature of Æthelwig followed by that of his guest or captive Godric, the deposed Abbot of Winchcombe,[5] and at a little distance by that of Ralph, the actual Norman Abbot of that Church. His English neighbour, Eadmund of Pershore, kept his office till his death late in William's reign. He was succeeded by the Norman Toustain or Thurstan, a monk of Gloucester, and was buried with all honour by the reigning Norman Abbot of that house.[6] This was Serlo, who succeeded to the Abbey on the death of his predecessor Wulfstan, who died on that distant pilgrimage to Jerusalem in which he followed the example of his benefactor Archbishop Ealdred.[7]

---

[1] Hist. Eves. 95. Of Acton in Worcestershire, "Hæc fuit terra patris sui, has duas villas dedit Ursoni pro Beningurthe quam injuste occupavit, sicut medietatem iterum postea fecit, et omnes tres injuste detinet."

[2] Ib. 96. He was "literis tam liberalibus quam grammaticis undecumque eruditissimus." On the Abbey of Cerisy, see vol. i. p. 529.

[3] Ib. 97. "Maxime de pecuniâ quam Agelumus abbas ad hoc opus reliquerat."   [4] Ib.

[5] See above, p. 177.

[6] Flor. Wig. 1085 "A venerabili Glawornensi abbate Serlone sepultus est honorifice."

[7] Hist. Mon. Glouc. i. 9. "Wilstanus Jerosolimam profectus, obiit peregrinus anno Domini millesimo septuagesimo secundo, prælationis suæ decimo quarto, et anno regni Regis Edwardi filii Regis Egelredi, decimo septimo." This is a curious confusion of chronology. There can be no doubt that 1072 is the right date, giving Wulfstan an incumbency of fourteen years from his appointment in 1058, but the chronicler heedlessly added a regnal year which belongs to the pilgrimage of Ealdred in 1058–1059. See vol. ii. pp. 436, 437. Serlo was at first a secular priest, a canon of Avranches; he then became a monk of Saint Michael's Mount

## BOND BETWEEN WULFSTAN AND THE ABBOTS. 389

Serlo fills a great place in the annals of his house, alike as the reformer of its discipline and as the man who began the great minster which still remains. In the former point, notwithstanding all the zeal of Ealdred and the three Wulfstans,[1] Gloucester had sunk so low that Serlo found in his monastery only two monks of full age and eight young novices.[2] He is also described as recovering to his church some of the possessions of which it had been defrauded by Ealdred, and the local writer records with triumph the deep contrition with which Archbishop Thomas gave back the ill-gotten gains of his predecessor to their lawful owners.[3] His architectural works rest on surer evidence. After eleven years from its beginning, the minster of Gloucester, or at least its eastern portions, the massive piers and arches now so strangely hidden by the net-work of a later age, stood ready for consecration in the last year of the eleventh century.[4] Of the Abbots beyond Wulfstan's diocese who signed the document, Wulfwold of Chertsey is remarkable only for his death being thought worthy of a record in the national

*CHAP. XIX.*
*His reforms*

*His buildings at Gloucester 1089-1100*

*Death of Wulfwold Abbot of Chertsey 1084*

("monachus in ecclesiâ Sancti Michaelis Monte Tumbâ," see Max Muller, Chips, iii 351), then "quinto anno conversionis suæ" he became Abbot of Gloucester

[1] On the three Wulfstans who figure in Gloucester history during this century, see vol ii p 669, 2nd ed

[2] Hist Mon Glouc i 10 "Ibi duos tantum perfectæ ætatis monachos et circiter octavos juvenes parvos inveniens"

[3] Ib. 11, 12 "Hæc acta sunt in præsentiâ domini Serlonis Abbatis in capitulo monachorum, multis præsentibus et gaudentibus" We hear how Thomas came, "se ipsum graviter inculpando, pectus tundendo, genu flectendo, qui injuste eas [villas] tamdiu tenuerat" This is placed in 1095 It is not wonderful that we hear nothing of this in the historian of York, but it is hard to reconcile the story with the statement of the Gloucester historian himself that some of the disputed lands were not recovered till the time of Abbot Hamelin, who succeeded in 1148, when we hear of another restitution

[4] The first stone was laid on Saint Peter's Day, 1089 It was consecrated by Samson Bishop of Worcester and other prelates, July 15, 1106 Hist. Mon Glouc. i 11, 12

CHAP XIX. Chronicles,[1] which however leave us to find from other sources that he too had a Norman successor, Odo by name.[2] The remaining Prelate, Ælfsige of Bath, is known only as the last independent Abbot of that church before its union with the Bishoprick of Somerset.[3]

*Friendly relations of English and Norman churchmen*

The document to which the names of these Prelates are subscribed is chiefly interesting as showing the friendly relations which existed at the time between churchmen of Norman and of English birth. Wulfstan himself had won the special regard of his Norman neighbours,[4] and he lived on terms of greater intimacy than we might have looked for with the worldly Bishop Geoffrey of Coutances.[5] So we here find the heads of these great monasteries, some Norman, some English, but presiding over brotherhoods almost wholly of English birth,[6] binding themselves together, without respect of birth or birth-place, in the closest spiritual fellowship. They bind themselves to be

---

[1] Chron Petrib 1084 "Her on þisum geare forðferde Wulfuuold abbod on Ceortesege on þam dæge Kl Mai"

[2] Ann. Wint 1084 "Wluuodus Abbas Certesiæ dimisit, morte præventus, abbatiam Odoni" Does this mean a death-bed nomination in Odo's favour?

[3] His death is recorded by Florence, 1087, "Abbas Bathoniensis Alsius decessit" His name is found in some of the deeds of manumission in Cod Dipl. vi 209.

[4] Fl. Wig 1088. "Normanni .. diligebant eum [Wlstanum] valde."

[5] It was to this Prelate, who reproved the saint for the meanness of his attire, that Wulfstan made the famous answer, which to our ears does not sound either specially witty or specially reverent, "Crede mihi, sæpius cantatur Agnus Dei quam cattus Dei" Vit Wlst Ang Sac. ii 259. Geoffrey recommended that "pelles sabelinas vel castorinas vel vulpinas .. vel saltem cattos indueret" Wulfstan, in his lamb-like innocence, clave to his lambskins "Crede mihi," it should be noticed, was the holy man's substitute for an oath, "nam hic mos jurandi episcopo inoleverat," says William in his other account in Gest Pont 283

[6] The lists of the subscribing brethren at Evesham, Chertsey, and Bath are added to the list Most of the names must be English; all of them may be. The possible exceptions are Godefrith, Regnold, Ulf, Benedict, and Hærlewine. The names for the most part go in pairs, Godefrith and Theodred, Regnold and Eadric.

obedient to God, Saint Mary, and Saint Benedict,[1] and to their own Bishop,[2] as well as to be loyal to their worldlord King William and to Matilda the Lady.[3] Among themselves the seven monasteries were to be as though they were but one monastery; their inmates are to have one heart and one soul;[4] and they bind themselves to certain special acts of devotion and charity.[5] The whole document breathes that spirit of simple piety, of earnest love towards God and man, which breathes in most of the ancient records of the native English Church. And it is not unpleasing to find Prelates of foreign birth so readily taking their places alongside of the men of the conquered nation with whom they were brought into spiritual alliance

One chief feature of this memorable primacy was the number of Councils held by the Archbishop year after year,[6] Councils which, as has been already said, were

*Terms of the document*

*Councils held by Lanfranc*

---

[1] Hist Mon Glouc III xviii "Ðæt is þæt we willað gehyrsume beon Gode and Scā Marian and Scē Benedicte"

[2] Ib xix "And nu is þara abboda cwydrædene þæt hig willað beon Gode gehyrsume and heora bisceope, to heora gemænelicum þærfe" How does this apply to Chertsey? Or does it mean to the Bishop of the diocese, whoever he may be? The passage seems to point to a time when monasteries were just beginning to seek exemptions from episcopal jurisdiction.

[3] Ib "And we willað urum worulde-hlaforde Willelme cininge and Mahthilde þære hlæfdian holde beon, for Gode and for worulde"

[4] Ib "Þæt is, we willað beon on annesse, swylce ealle þas vii mynstras syn an mynster, and beon swa hit her beforan awriten is, quasi cor unum et anima una"

[5] Ib Besides singing masses, each Abbot was to wash, feed, and shoe one hundred poor men, "And an C þærfendra manna gebaðige, and þa fedan, and ealle þa gescygean" Clothes are not spoken of, but shoes are, a point to be noticed

[6] A list of these Councils is given in the Latin Life of Lanfranc attached to the Winchester (now Canterbury) Chronicle They were held in the years 1071, 1074, 1075, 1076, 1078, 1081, 1086, at different places, Winchester, Gloucester, and London That is to say, they were held at the same time as one of the regular Gemóts of the year

CHAP XIX. beginning more and more to assume a purely ecclesiastical character, unknown to earlier English usage.[1] In earlier days ecclesiastical and temporal causes had been heard, and ecclesiastical and temporal decrees had been passed, in the same assemblies, local and national. The practice of separating ecclesiastical and temporal affairs had even been solemnly condemned by a formal decree of a national Gemót.[2] But this state of things was altogether opposed to the theories of ecclesiastical propriety which were held both by Lanfranc and by William. The episcopal laws which had been hitherto in force in England were now declared by King William and his Witan to be bad and contrary to the sacred canons.[3] The Bishops were now forbidden to bring any cause which involved questions of Canon Law, or questions concerning the cure of souls, before the ancient courts of the shire and the hundred. Hitherto the Bishop had presided alongside of the Ealdorman, and the men of the shire had given judgement in matters alike ecclesiastical and temporal.[4] The Bishops were now to hold courts of their own, in which alone matters of ecclesiastical concern were to be judged, and in which every man was bound to appear when summoned, no less than in the court of the civil magistrate.[5] Here we have the be-

---

[1] See above, p 360.  [2] See vol i. p. 405.
[3] The writ is given in Selden's Eadmer, p 167 ; Thorpe's Laws and Institutes, i 495, Stubbs, Select Charters, 82 The censure on Old-English Law runs thus, " Sciatis vos omnes et cæteri mei fideles qui in Angliâ manent, quod episcopales leges, quæ non bene nec secundum sanctorum canonum præcepta usque ad mea tempora in regno Anglorum fuerunt, communi concilio, et consilio Archiepiscoporum meorum et cæterorum Episcoporum et Abbatum, et omnium principum regni mei, emendandas judicavi "
[4] The enacting part of the writ goes on , " Propterea mando et regiâ auctoritate præcipio, ut nullus Episcopus vel Archidiaconus de legibus episcopalibus amplius in hundret placita teneant , nec caussam quæ ad regimen animarum pertinet ad judicium sæcularium hominum adducant."
[5] The writ ends, " quicumque secundum episcopales leges, de quacunque caussâ vel culpâ interpellatus fuerit, ad locum quem ad hoc Episcopus

ginnings of those specially ecclesiastical tribunals which, with lessened powers, have survived to our own day. The best that can be said for them is that, in the dark days of oppression, their claim to judge the causes, not only of ordained persons, but of all who bore any ecclesiastical character, and even of the poor, the fatherless, and the widow, did something to place the most helpless part of the population under the rule of a milder jurisprudence than that of the courts of the Norman Kings and their officers.

The ecclesiastical courts were thus one fruit of the policy of William and Lanfranc. Another fruit was, not the absolute beginning but the confirmation of the usage occasional in earlier times, of holding a Convocation as a distinct body from the Parliament. In one case we are distinctly told that, after the King and his Witan had sat for five days, the Archbishop and his clergy sat for three days more [1] And it seems that, in this instance at least, Bishops were chosen in the purely ecclesiastical assembly, though, as the choice in every case fell on the King's clerks, the King's will could not have been without its influence. In several of these Councils one chief matter taken in hand was the deposition of English Abbots. In the very first of these synods which is recorded, Wulfric, the newly chosen Abbot of the New Minster, was deposed to make room for a successor whose name of Rhiwallon witnesses to his birth in the lesser Britain. This assembly was held at Winchester In another, held in London five years later,[2]

*CHAP XIX*

Distinction of ecclesiastical and temporal assemblies.

Gloucester, Midwinter, 1085

Election of Bishops in ecclesiastical assemblies

Deposition of Abbots Wulfric of New Minster 1071 or 1072

elegerit et nominaverit, veniat, ibique de caussâ suâ respondeat, et non secundum hundret, sed secundum canones et episcopales leges rectum Deo et Episcopo suo faciat "
[1] Chron Petrib 1085
[2] App Chron Wint " Octavo anno concilium Londoniæ celebravit, in quo Ailnodum, Glastingensis cœnobii Abbatem, deposuit " But the discord between Thurstan and the monks is placed in the Peterborough Chronicle under 1083, and William of Malmesbury in his Glastonbury

394    THE ECCLESIASTICAL SETTLEMENT OF ENGLAND.

CHAP. XIX.
Æthelnoth of Glastonbury 1078

Appointment of Thurstan 1082

His disputes with the monks 1083

Æthelnoth of Glastonbury, William's companion on his first voyage to Normandy,[1] was set aside for a Norman successor. In this choice at least William and Lanfranc did not display their usual discretion. The new Abbot, Thurstan by name, made himself memorable by giving occasion to a local disturbance, a minute account of which has been thought worthy of a place in the national Chronicles. His doings illustrate the worst side, as the League of the Worcester Abbots illustrates the best side, of the strangers who were now set to rule over the churches of England. The monks, we are told, were in every way well disposed towards him, and prayed him oft that he would deal gently with them, as they were loyal and obedient to him.[2] But the new Prelate, a monk of Lanfranc's own house at Caen,[3] despised the English brethren, and insisted on innovations in the service of the Church according to the newest fashions of Normandy. The monks of Glastonbury were called on to cast aside the immemorial Gregorian chants, and to adopt a new way of singing which had been lately devised by one William of Fécamp.[4] One day the monks were gathered

---

History (330) places the accession of Thurstan in 1082, without any mention of the deposition of Æthelnoth. It is hardly like the policy of Lanfranc to leave the Abbey vacant for five years.

[1] See above, p. 78.

[2] Chron. Petrib. 1083. "Ærest hit com of þæs abbotes unwisdome, þæt he misbead his munecan on fela þingan, and þa munecas hit mændon lufelice to him, and beadon hine þæt he sceolde healdan hi rihtlice and lufian hi, and hi woldon him beon holde and gehyrsume. Ac se abbot nolde þæs naht, ac dyde heom yfele and beheot heom wyrs."

[3] Will. Malm. Ant. Glast. 330. "Turstinus quem Willelmus, ex Duce Normanniæ factus Rex Angliæ, ex monacho Chadomensi Abbatem constituit." So Florence, 1083.

[4] Ib. 331. "Inter cætera etiam Gregorianum cantum aspernatus, monachos compellere cœpit ut, illo relicto, cujusdam Willelmi Fiscanensis cantum discerent et cantarent. Hoc ægre accipientes, quippe qui jam tam in hoc quam in alio ecclesiastico officio secundo [secundum?], Romanæ ecclesiæ morem insenuerant, insuper mores ejusdem, tamquam alienigenæ

together in the chapter-house, rather, it would seem, to receive their Abbot's orders on this and other matters than for any purpose of free debate. The monks were stubborn; the Abbot was fierce and threatening. At last he called for his Norman archers, who presently entered the chapter-house all harnessed as if for battle.[1] What followed cannot be so well told as in the words of the Chronicler; "Then were the monks sore afeared of them, and wist not what to do, and fled hither and thither. And some went into the church, and locked the door after them, and they went after them into the minster, and would drag them out, for that they durst not go out. And a rueful thing there happened that day;[2] for the Frenchmen brake into the choir, and shot towards the altar, where the monks were, and some of the knights[3] went up to the up-floor,[4] and

*The monks killed and wounded in the church*

---

nec de gremio ecclesiæ canonice instituti, molestius forsitan tolerabant." The Chronicle does not mention this particular grievance about the change in the manner of singing, but it appears in Florence, whose words are partly followed, partly not, in the fuller account in the Glastonbury History. So Orderic, 523.

[1] Chron Petrib 1083. "Anes dæges se abbot eode into capitulan, and spræc uppon þa munecas, and wolde hi mistukian, and sende æfter læwede mannum, and hi comon into capitulan on uppon þa munecas full gewepnede." This story shows that they were archers, but in William of Malmesbury (Hist Glast 332) they become "milites et satellites sui phalerati." These are evidently the same persons of whom William speaks in his very rhetorical account in Gest Pont 197, how the Abbot "terras et pecunias in *lecatorum* suorum abusus consumpsit." "Lecator" = *lecher*, is plainly used as a mere vague term of abuse, but it misled the writer of Bromton's Chronicle (973) into saying that Thurstan "res ecclesiæ *lenocinando* consumpit."

Florence's description of Thurstan as himself armed, and as doing much of the mischief with his own hands, is doubtless to be taken only in the sense that "qui facit per alium facit per se."

[2] Chron Petrib 1083. "Ac reowlic þing þær gelamp on dæg." Compare the words in 1087 about the death of William, "reowlic þing he dyde, and reowlicor him gelamp."

[3] Ib. "Sume of þam cnihtan." Not *knights* in the sense of *chevaliers*, which, as we see under 1086, would be "rideras," but most likely the younger men of the party, as Mr Thorpe takes it.

[4] Ib. "Uppon þone uppflore," a most speaking description of a great

shot downwards with arrows towards the halidom,[1] so that on the rood that stood above the altar stuck on many arrows. And the wretched monks lay about the altar, and some crept under it, and cried with yearning to God, craving his mildness,[2] for that they could get no mildness from men. What may we say, but that they shot sorely, and that others brake down the doors there, and went in, and slew some of the monks to death, and many wounded therein, so that the blood came from the altar upon the grees and from the grees upon the floor.[3] Three were slain to death and eighteen were wounded."[4]

*Illustration of the state of the times supplied by this story*

It is needless to say that scenes of blood and sacrilege like this formed no part of the schemes of ecclesiastical reformation designed by William and Lanfranc. But the story shows how easily, in such a state of things, a man of ungoverned temper placed in a position of authority

Romanesque triforium William of Malmesbury has "solaria inter columnas erecta," which would well describe the triforia at Romsey and Saint Frithswyth's, and in the far older church of Saint Martin at Angers

[1] Chron Petrib. 1083. "Toweard þam haligdome," the sacrarium or presbytery.

[2] Ib. "Gyrne cleopedon to Gode, his miltse biddende, þa þa hi ne mihton nane miltse æt mannum begytan." Surely the English tongue was now at the full height of its power

[3] Ib. "Swa þæt þet blod com of þam weofode uppon þam gradan, and of þam gradan on þam flore " For "gradan" I use the later form "grees," which so oddly survives in the "*Grecian* Stairs" at Lincoln

[4] William of Malmesbury (in the Glastonbury History) adds some marvellous details One of the monks seized on the great rood as a defence, and the blood, which in the Chronicle simply flows from the wounded monks, now flows miraculously from the rood itself ("sed providente Deo, sagitta imaginem Dominicam in cruce defixam subtus genua vulnerans, sanguinis rivulum ex eadem produxit, qui de altari usque ad gradus de gradibus usque ad terram descendens, ultionis divinæ terrorem infaustis viris incutiebat ") The actual sinner of course dies at once, and various degrees of punishment light on his comrades None of these wonders are to be found in the Chronicles, or Florence, whom William to some extent copies, nor yet in William's own shorter accounts in the Gesta Regum and Gesta Pontificum Neither are they in the Winchester Annals, nor in Bromton, who follows Florence with some verbal changes, and who had the account in the Gesta Pontificum before him

could give occasion to horrors which he himself perhaps as little really wished for as his superiors. A foreign Prelate, with foreign soldiers at his command, might easily be hurried into deeds which could not have happened either in the England of Eadward or in the Normandy of William. And if such measure was dealt out by churchmen to one another, we may guess what deeds were done in many a new-built donjon towards men who had not the same means as the monks of Glastonbury of handing down their wail to posterity. As in most wars and revolutions, the greatest evils of the Norman Conquest were not those which were done by the regular authority of the Conqueror himself. The cruellest blows were those which were dealt by the more violent and base-minded among his followers, to whom a state of things for which he was responsible had given the power of working deeds of evil which even his mighty arm could not always redress.

The upshot of this story is remarkable, as showing the difference between the Conqueror and his immediate successor. William heard the cause between the Abbot of Glastonbury and his monks. Neither side was pronounced to be wholly guiltless, but the greater blame was declared to rest with the Abbot. Thurstan was removed from his office, and sent back in disgrace to his cell at Caen. Of the monks, several were sent to other monasteries, to be kept under some degree of restraint, the exact nature of which we are left to guess.[1]

*The Abbot censured and banished by William*

---

[1] Will Malm Ant. Glast 332 (partly following Florence) "Regi demum Willelmo primo querelâ super hoc delatâ, dum maxima fuisse patuit Abbatis culpa, ab eodem Rege in Normanniam ad monasterium unde venerat redire compulsus est inglorius, de monachis vero quamplures per episcopatus et abbatias jussu Regis *custodiendi* disperguntur" The Winchester Annalist (1083) uses very strong language, "Abbas autem, quasi in testimonium innocentiæ excusso caputio, quum dignus esset vel igne cremari vel suspendi patibulo, ad claustri sui columnam Cadomi unde venerat, jussu Regis reversus est"

CHAP. XIX
He buys his restoration from William Rufus
1089-1090

Frithric, Abbot of Saint Alban's 1066-1077?
Legendary nature of his history.
1072.

Paul appointed Abbot by Lanfranc 1077

But as soon as the great King was dead, Thurstan, by the help of his kinsfolk, and of the more prevailing eloquence of a bribe of five hundred pounds of silver, obtained from William Rufus his restoration to the office of which he had shown himself so unworthy.[1]

Another great monastic house was also supplied by Lanfranc with a ruler in the year of the deposition of Æthelnoth Frithric, who held the Abbey of Saint Alban at the time when King William came into England, is a man whose history has become almost wholly mythical, and the details of his story I shall therefore examine elsewhere.[2] It is certain that he still held his Abbey at the time of the settlement of the dispute between the two Archbishops.[3] But five years later the Abbey had become vacant, and the way in which it was bestowed is everywhere spoken of as the Primate's own personal act. The great foundation of Offa was put under the rule of a Norman monk from Saint Stephen's, Paul by name, a near kinsman of his patron, and whom the scandal of the time

---

[1] Will. Malm. Ant. Glast. 332 "Rege tamen mortuo, idem Turstinus, auxilio parentum suorum, abbatiam Glastoniæ a filio suo Willielmo dicto Rufo quingentis libris argenti dicitur redemisse, et monasterium aliquot annis occupans et per ejusdem possessiones pervagatus, longe ab ipso, ut dignus erat, misere vitam finivit." This is partly copied from Florence, who however says nothing about the "auxilia parentum." In the Gesta Pontificum (197) William adds the comment, "Impudens et infamis, qui, tanti sacrilegii conscius, ausus sit iterum loco quem violaverat intrudi." Notwithstanding all this, in the Glastonbury History he winds up his account by speaking of Thurstan's "fervor religionis, nonnulla pietas in Deo, multa providentia in sæculo."

The restoration of Thurstan must have been one of the first acts of William Rufus, as his name is added to the (manuscript) grant of the town of Bath to Bishop John de Villulâ in 1090.

There is a letter from Lanfranc to Thurstan (Giles, i. 77). It is short and pithy, and chiefly consists of advice to make his peace as fast as he can both with God and with the King.

[2] See Appendix NN.

[3] "Ego Fridericus Abbas Sancti Albani consensi," occurs among the signatures. Will. Malm. iii. 298.

affirmed to be his son.¹ He ruled as a great and magnificent Prelate, reforming the discipline and increasing the revenues of his house,² and raising that gigantic minster which, for size at least, if not for beauty, has remained the wonder of all succeeding ages. The ruins of Roman Verulam had long formed a quarry for the works of the neighbouring Abbey;³ and it was mainly out of bricks taken from that inexhaustible source that Paul, aided by the purse of Lanfranc, reared the vastest and sternest temple of his age.⁴ His gifts to his house were bountiful,⁵

---

¹ Gest. Abb S Alb 1 51 " Paulus Abbas, natione Neuster, consanguinitate Archiepiscopo Lanfranco propinquus (et, ut quidam autumant, filius), monachus fuit Cadomensis ecclesiæ Hic ecclesiam Beati Albani suscepit regendam, procurante dicto Archiepiscopo Lanfranco, qui eumdem Paulum filiali dilexit amore " Eadmer, Hist Nov 8 " Quid referam de abbatiâ Sancti Albani, quam intus et extra ad nihilum fere devolutam ipse, ut suam, instituto ei bonæ memoriæ Paulo Abbate, a fundamentis reædificavit, et intus magnâ religione, foris multarum rerum donatione auxit, honestavit, ditavit " Gervase, Act Pont Cant 1655 " Ecclesiam etiam Sancti Albani quam Rex Ine [Offa] fundaverat olim, restauravit et ibidem monachos instituit " So 1658 " Præcepit Rex ut . . abbatia Sancti Albani, quam Lanfrancus et antecessores ejus habuerant, ad alodium Cantuariensis ecclesiæ perpetuo jure transiret." So the Worcester Annals under 1093 remark , " Rex Willelmus concessit Anselmo abbatiam Sancti Albani in alodium "

On the possibility of Lanfranc having been married before his monastic profession, see Hook's Archbishops, ii 80. Compare Lingard's remarks on the wife and son of Cardinal Campeggio, iv 508

² See the details in the Gesta Abbatum, i 53–60

³ The details of the state of the ruins of Verulam in the Gesta Abbatum, 1 24, 25, contain matter interesting to the geologist and the comparative mythologist The passage with which we are concerned runs thus, " Tegulas vero integras, et lapides quos invenit [Ealdredus Abbas] aptos ad ædificia, seponens, ad fabricam ecclesiæ reservavit Proposuit vero, si facultates suppeterent, dirutâ veteri ecclesiâ, novam construere; propter quod terram in profunditate evertit ut lapideas structuras inveniret "

⁴ Gest Abb 1 53 " Paulus Abbas, quum jam Abbas undecim annis exstitisset, infra eosdem annos totam ecclesiam Sancti Albani, cum multis aliis ædificiis, opere construxit lateritio, Lanfranco efficaciter juvante ; qui, ut dicitur, mille marcas ad fabricam contulit faciendam "

⁵ The most interesting among these gifts is a collection of twenty-eight books, all seemingly ecclesiastical (58) One wishes to see the " duos textus, auro et argento et gemmis ornatos "

yet he did not fail, any more than Thurstan at Glastonbury, to show the insolence of the conquering race towards those over whom he was set to rule. But while Thurstan shed the blood of living men, Paul was satisfied with doing despite to the memory of the dead. In rebuilding the minster, he swept away the tombs of his English predecessors, many of whose names were held in the deepest reverence, affirming that they were rude and ignorant barbarians, unworthy of any respect.[1] Yet even this contumelious stranger could have borne witness that the barbarous people showed him no little kindness in carrying out his mighty works. Among the Abbot's plans was the replenishing of the tower of the minster with bells.[2] Two of these were, so the story went, the gift of Ligulf, a rich Thegn of the neighbourhood, and his wife.[3] The wealth of Ligulf consisted largely of flocks of sheep and goats. Of these he sold many, and with the price bought a bell, and when he heard its music in the minster-tower, he rejoiced and said merrily in his native tongue that his sheep and goats bleated sweetly.[4] The other bell was the gift of his wife, who, when she heard her husband's gift and her own ringing in concert, rejoiced in so happy a figure of their lawful marriage and mutual love.[5]

[1] Gest Abb i 62 "Tumbas venerabilium antecessorum suorum, Abbatum nobilium, quos rudes et idiotas consuevit appellare, delevit, vel contemnendo eos quia Anglicos, vel invidendo, quia fere omnes stirpe regali vel magnatum præclaro sanguine fuerant procreati" Matthew Paris goes on especially to rebuke him for omitting to translate the body of King Offa to the new church This is in direct contradiction to the legend of Offa's burial in the Vitæ Offarum (Wats, ii 32)

[2] Gest Abb. i 60

[3] Ib "Quidam de nobilibus Anglicis, hujus patriæ partes inhabitans nemorosas, Lyolf nuncupatus" I cannot find him in Domesday.

[4] Ib 61. "Emit unam campanam, quam quum audisset suspensam in turri, tunc novam, sonare, jocose ait Anglico idiomate, 'Eja, quam dulce blaterant capræ meæ et balant oves'"

[5] Ib. "Uxor illico aliam adquisivit, quæ duæ dulcissimam copulam reddiderunt. Quam quum audisset mulier, dixit, 'Non credo hanc copu-

In these cases the Primate was the chief mover, but instances are not lacking to show the personal, and evidently conscientious, interest which William himself took in ecclesiastical affairs. No church in the realm had higher claims on his reverence than the newly-reared minster of his lord and predecessor, where that lord and predecessor slept amid the reverence of both races, and where he himself had been changed from a Duke into a King.[1] We have no record of the first avoidance of the Abbey of Westminster, but we can hardly conceive that Eadwine, the Abbot appointed by the sainted King himself, was disturbed in his possession by his founder's kinsman and successor. He probably died during the first years of William's reign, as the great award between the two Primates bears the signature of his Norman successor Geoffrey.[2] The next vacancy gave rise to a correspondence which does William honour. He mused long as to the choice of a fit person to fill the office. At last, by the advice of Lanfranc and the other chief men of his realm, he pitched on Vital, a monk of Fécamp, who was the Abbot of his grandmother Judith's foundation of Bernay.[3] He had raised that house from such lowly beginnings to so high an estate that the discerning eyes of the King and the Primate marked him out, notwithstanding his

*Personal zeal of William in ecclesiastical matters*

*History of Westminster*

*Abbot Eadwine.*

*Geoffrey Abbot in 1072*

*William appoints Vital, Abbot of Bernay 1077*

---

lam favore carere divino, qui me viro meo legitimo matrimonio et fœdere dilectionis mutuæ copulavit.'"

[1] William sets forth his own feelings towards Westminster in his letter to Abbot John of Fécamp, of which I shall speak presently in the passage quoted in vol III p. 555

[2] Will Malm Gest Regg III 298. "Ego Gosfridus Abbas cœnobii Sancti Petri, quod non longe a Londoniâ situm est, consensi."

[3] Chron Petrib 1076 "On þisum geare .. se cyng geaf Westmynster Vithele [Fiþele, Wig 1077] abbode, se wæs ǽr abbot on Bærnege." He is spoken of by Orderic (491 D) as "Bernaicensium Abbas" in the account of the endless disputes about his own monastery. See vol. II. p. 234 On Vital's chronology, see Neustria Pia, 401, on Bernay, see vol. I. p. 508

402    THE ECCLESIASTICAL SETTLEMENT OF ENGLAND.

CHAP. XIX
His correspondence with Abbot John of Fécamp

own unwillingness, as the fittest man for the higher place now vacant in England. On this matter the King writes to John, the Italian Abbot of Fécamp,[1] the ecclesiastical superior of the house of Bernay, and the answer of that Prelate, giving his canonical sanction to the wishes of the King, may pass as a model of a style at once respectful and independent in addressing a superior.[2] In weighing the mixed character of William it would be utterly unfair not to let the relation in which he stood to men like Lanfranc, John, and Vital reckon for something, even against those dark passages of his history which I have already recorded and those darker passages still which I have yet to record

William's vow to Saint Martin 1066

But besides acting the part of a nursing-father to the churches which he found already existing in the conquered land, the Conqueror had also to discharge the vow which, in the great crisis of his life, he had made on the height of Telham to the Apostle of the Gauls.[3] If William was

[1] See vol. III p. 100

[2] The connexion between Fécamp and Bernay appears from the charter of Duke Richard the Good, quoted by Mabillon, I 223, and printed at length in Neustria Pia, 398–400. So in the letters in Mabillon (i 220). William asks John that the translation of Vital, "quod de eo communi consilio meorum providi procerum," may be made " licentiâ tuâ et bonâ voluntate et conventûs fratrum " The Abbot answers, "Ego Johannes, vester totus in Domino, humiliter vobis suggero et litteris significo, quoniam moleste acciperem quod frater noster Domnus Vitalis sine licentiâ nostrâ de abbatiâ ad abbatiam migraret, nisi quod vos diligo et vestra consilia honorare volo Idcirco laudo et confirmo quod vestra regalis sancivit auctoritas" The whole letter should be read

[3] See vol III p 457, and the alleged foundation charter of the Abbey, Mon Angl III 244, Rymer, I 4 "Quum in Angliam venissem, et infinibus Hastingiæ cum exercitu applicuissem contra hostes meos, qui mihi regnum Angliæ injuste conabantur auferre, in procinctu belli, jam armatus, coram baronibus et militibus meis, cum favore omnium, ad eorum corda roboranda, votum feci ecclesiam quamdam ad honorem Dei construere pro communi salute, si per Dei gratiam obtinere possem victoriam" But this charter is suspicious It is signed by William Fitz-Osbern, who died in

not to prove himself as faithless to the Saints as ever Harold had been, the hill of Senlac must needs be crowned with the holy house which should be the memorial of that day's strife and victory. And it was to be no mere memorial, no mere thank-offering; the prayers and masses which were to be offered there were to go up to heaven for the souls' health of all, Norman and English alike, who had given up their lives in the day of the great slaughter.[1] But even in discharging his vows to the Saints, even in his charitable work for the souls of friends and enemies, William chose his own time. Still the Apostle of the Gauls was not a person to be trifled with. Ages before, Hlodwig, in the first zeal of his conversion, had been hurried into the irreverent comment that Saint Martin, good friend as he was in time of need, was one who took good care not to be defrauded of his rights.[2] The vow of William was not forgotten, but it certainly was delayed.[3] He held perhaps that the thank-offering for his victory

1071, and also by Gundulf Bishop of Rochester, who was not consecrated till 1077, and by Maurice Bishop of London, who was not consecrated till 1086.

[1] Brevis Relatio (Giles, 8) "In eo loco, ubi Willelmus, tunc Comes Normannorum postea vero Rex Anglorum, abbatiam construi præcepit ob memoriam hujus pugnæ et absolutionem omnium peccatorum illorum qui ibi interfecti sunt." Liber de Hydâ, 294 "Abbatiam in loco qui nunc Bellum dicitur, eo quod Anglos ibi bello superavit, in remissione peccatorum omnium illic defunctorum a fundamentis instituit." Matthew Paris (12, ed Wats) goes so far as to mention the soul of Harold personally, "Quo in loco monachos instituit, ut pro animâ Regis Haroldi et aliorum ibidem occisorum divina celebrarent."

[2] See the tale in Gesta Regum Francorum (Duchesne, i 704-5) Hlodwig wishes to redeem the horse which he had given to Saint Martin when starting on his campaign against the Goths He offers a hundred shillings, the horse will not stir Another hundred, and the horse comes away, "Tunc cum lætitiâ Rex ait, 'Vere beatus Martinus bonus est in auxilio, sed carus in negotio.'"

[3] Chron de Bello, 6 "Quia multis et innumeris præoccupatus negotiis, regnum in brevi *unire* ac pacificare nullatenus quiverat, plura diutius necessario omisit, quæ maturius exsequenda proposuerat."

404   THE ECCLESIASTICAL SETTLEMENT OF ENGLAND.

CHAP XIX. was not due till his victory was more complete than it had been on the morrow of the battle, or even on the day of his crowning. The exact date of the beginning of the work is uncertain, but it did not happen till William could fairly call England his own.[1] He was often reminded of his promise by William *Faber*, the monk of Marmoutier, who, at the moment of his vow, had procured that it should be made to the great Saint Martin, and not to any meaner patron.[2] At last he gave his monitor a commission to begin the foundation alike of the material and of the spiritual temple. In the form of that commission the grim pleasantry characteristic of William and his nation rose into something like a poetical conception. The house which was to commemorate the Conquest was to be raised on the very spot where the Conquest had been won, the brotherhood which was to be the sign that England had been subdued by the arms of Gaul should be brought from no meaner spot than the greatest house that bore the name of the Gaulish Apostle.[3] The *Faber* accordingly hastened to his home at Marmoutier, and thence brought four of his brethren to form the beginnings of the new society. They looked at their new dwelling-place, but the site prescribed by the King's order pleased them not. To men who had spent their days at Marmoutier, with the rocks above their heads and the mighty Loire at their feet, the hill of Senlac would offer but small attractions. The spot was high and bleak; the hill was waterless;

*Margin notes:* Beginning of the foundation of Battle Abbey. 1070–1076. William orders William Faber to begin the buildings, and to bring monks from Marmoutier. The monastery to be built on the site of the battle. Monks brought from Marmoutier. Their dislike to the site.

---

[1] Chron de Bello, 6 "Per plurimum enim temporis ad municipiorum expugnationem atque ad rebellium subjugandam cervicositatem sollicitus animum occupavit et vires."

[2] Ib 7 "Willelmo Fabro horum mentionem studiosius inculcante." See vol iii p 458

[3] Ib "Eidem monacho, ut optaverat, Rex, quia ad manum habebatur, operis fabricam committens, præcepit quatenus *in antefato congressionis loco*, accitis secum suæ ecclesiæ aliquibus fratribus, opportunum festinaret fundari monasterium."

the nature of the ground was unsuited to receive the vast and varied buildings of a great monastery.[1] They better liked a lower spot towards the western slope of the hill, a spot which, to men who had been themselves in the fight, would be more suggestive of Norman mishap than of Norman victory.[2] There they actually began to build houses for their dwelling-place,[3] and they then sent to the King, who had begun to take a lively interest in the work, praying that the unfit site which he had chosen might be exchanged for one so far better suited for the purpose.[4] But the mind of the Conqueror, when once fixed, was not easily turned. He was as little likely to give up his purpose of building his minster on the most appropriate spot as to give up his struggle for his wife or for his Kingdom. The King was wroth at the request; he again bade that his church should be built on no spot but that where he had won his crowning mercy. The high altar of the Abbey of Saint Martin should stand nowhere but on the spot where the Standard of the Fighting Man had been pitched on the day of Saint Calixtus.[5] The monks, in their prosaic mood, pleaded

*CHAP. XIX.*

*They begin to build on another site.*

*William insists on the site of the battle.*

*The high altar on the site of the Standard.*

---

[1] Chron. de Bello, 7. "Qui memoratum belli locum considerantes, quum ad tam insignem fabricam minus idoneum, ut videbatur, arbitrarentur." So soon after they complain "quod locus ille ubi ecclesiam fieri decreverat, uti in colle situs, arenti glebâ, siccus et aquarum foret indigus."

[2] Ib. "In humiliori non procul loco, versus ejusdem collis occidentalem plagam, aptum habitandi locum eligentes." This could not have been far from the spot where so many Normans were cut in pieces in an early stage of the battle. See vol. iii. p. 490.

[3] Ib. "Ne nil operis agere viderentur, mansiunculas quasdam fabricaverunt."

[4] Ib. We now hear of "Regis animus sollicitus de fabricæ provectu."

[5] Ib. "Quod quum Rex percepisset, indignatus refugit, ociusque jussit in eodem loco quo hoste prostrato sibi cesserat triumphus basilicæ fundamenta jacere." So Will. Malm. Gest. Pont. 207. "Cœnobium . . . Sancti Martini de Bello, quod Rex Willelmus fundavit et provexit in loco ubi, Angliam debellaverat, multa ibi et pretiosa quum vivus tum moriturus delegans. Altare ecclesiæ est in loco ubi Haroldi pro patriæ caritate occisi cadaver exanime inventum est."

the lack of water on the hill. William answered merrily that, if God gave him long life enough, there should be a readier flow of wine in his new house than there was of water in any other abbey in England.[1] They pleaded the lack of building-stone in the neighbourhood. William's answer was prompt and practical; ships were at once sent off to Caen to bring as much stone as might be needed from the quarries of Allemagne.[2] The work began; the foundations were laid on the appointed spot, and the high altar rose on the site of King Harold's Standard.[3] But the work was still delayed; William, with his hands full of other matters, had no time to visit the spot in person;[4] the craftsmen employed were skilful but dishonest; the foreign monks themselves were less zealous than they should have been.[5] The first Abbot, Robert Blanchard, was drowned on his return from a voyage to Marmoutier immediately on his appointment.[6] Under the second Abbot, Gausbert, also a monk of the parent house, the works went on more speedily and the number of the brethren increased.[7] But even now the

---

[1] Chron. de Bello, 7 "Quinque obniti non præsumentes, aquarum penuriam caussarentur, verbum ad hæc memoriale magnificus Rex protulisse fertur, 'Ego,' inquit, 'si, Deo annuente, vita comes fuerit, eidem loco ita prospiciam, ut magis ei vini abundet copia quam aquarum in aliâ præstanti abbatiâ'"

[2] Ib 8. A tale is added how, while the stone was bringing from Normandy—"a Cadomensi vico"—a neighbouring spot was revealed to a devout matron, where a rich quarry was found

[3] Ib "Jactis ergo fundamentis præstantissimi, ut tunc temporis habebatur, operis, secundum Regis statutum altare majus in eodem loco quo Regis Haraldi signum, quod Standard vocant, coriuisse visum est, provide statuunt." So Chron. Petrib 1087 "On þam ilcan steode þe God him geuðe þæt he moste Engleland gegán, he ærerde mære mynster, and munecas þær gesætte, þæt hit well gegodade"

[4] Ib "Innumeris irretitus negotiis, nec locum præ dolore intimo adire, nec de codem quæ proposuerat, hujusmodi forte dilationibus circumventus, exsequi valuerit."

[5] Ib. The details are curious.    [6] Ib.

[7] Ib, and also p. 23 "Statuit conventum ad minus lx monachorum

building was far from going on with the same swiftness
with which Lanfranc had rebuilt his metropolitan church
in the space of seven years.¹ The founder never saw the
finishing of his work. It was not till twenty-eight years
after the great battle, till twenty years at least after the
beginning of the foundation, that the fully completed
Abbey of Saint Martin was hallowed, not in the presence
of William the Great, but in that of his unworthy son.²

*Consecration of the church. 1094*

Thus arose the great monastery on which William, in
the spirit in which he had fixed upon his site, gave the
name of the Abbey of the place of Battle.³ Around the
monastery a town arose,⁴ and the solitude which once had
reigned around the hoar apple-tree of former days⁵ gave way

*The Abbey of Battle.*

*Growth of the town.*

---

ibidem congregari, proponens eamdem ecclesiam quum dedicari faceret, in tantum ditare ut conventûs ejusdem omni tempore numero septiesviginti monachorum existeret 'Sed homo proponit, Deus autem disponit.' Nam id perficere, proh dolor, morte quæ Regi æque imperat ut mendico, præventus nequivit"    ¹ See above, p 361

² Chron Petrib 1094, and Florence

³ Chron de Bello, 9 "Rex igitur magnificus inchoati operis non indevotus, ad victoriæ suæ perpetuandam memoriam ipsum locum Bellum memoriter per succedentia tempora nominari censuit" So Will Malm. Gest Regg in 267 "Alterum monasterium Hastingis ædificavit Sancto Martino, quod cognominatur de Bello, quia in eo loco principalis ecclesia cernitur ubi inter consertos cadaverum acervos Haroldus inventus fuisse memoratur" The usual title is "ecclesia Sancti Martini de Bello," "ecclesia de Bello," or, as we have seen in English, "þæt mynster æt þære Bataille" The fuller form, "Abbas Sancti Martini de loco Belli," appears in Domesday, 11 b, but it is commonly called in the Survey "ecclesia de Labatailge" Compare the church of Batalha in Portugal. The verses of Robert of Gloucester, ii 368, must not be forgotten —

"Kyng Wyllam byþo3te hym ek of þe volc, þat was verlore,
And aslawe eke þoru hym in bataylc byuore
Þere, as þe batayle was, an abbey he let rere
Of Seyn Martyn, vor her soules, þat þer aslawe were,
And þe monckes wel y nou feffede wyþoute fayle,
Þat ys ycluped in Engelond, abbey of þe batayle"

⁴ Chron de Bello, 17 "Homines ipsius villæ ob ejusdem loci per maximam excellentiæ dignitatem, burgenses vocantur" The Chronicle goes on to describe their customs

⁵ See vol iii p 443

to the busy sights and sounds of the temporal and spiritual life of the age. We might wish that the spot had for ever remained a wilderness, that no sign of man's hand, save some massive stone, some simply-sculptured cross, had ever marked the place where the martyrs of England fell. And as it is, we look on the small remains of William's minster which still crown the hill of Senlac with other feelings from those with which we look elsewhere on the fallen temples and altars of former days. At Glastonbury and Crowland we curse the work of greed and barbarism and sacrilege; as we trace out the length and breadth of the Abbey of the Battle, we can rejoice that the spot where Harold fell is again open to the light of day and the winds of heaven. And yet it is among the remaining buildings of the Abbey that we find the most speaking witness that is left us of the ebb and flow of defeat and victory on the day of the great battle. The site of the Standard fixed the site of the high altar, and the site of the high altar fixed the site of the other buildings of the Abbey. Strangers from Marmoutier, to whom the place itself was a penance, would have no mind to fix their cloister and other buildings on the chilly northern side of the minster. And on the south, the nearness of the Standard to the slope of the hill gave but little room for the erection of the complicated group of buildings which surrounded the cloister of a great Benedictine house. The great dormitory, a building in its present state of a later age, was thus driven over the slope, and had to be borne aloft on the vastest and tallest of those underlying vaults with which the wisdom of ancient builders provided for health and safety.[1] Those

---

[1] Vaults of this sort are constantly found under the main portions of monasteries and other buildings, and they are constantly shown as cloisters, dormitories, anything but what they are One of the earliest and best that I know is that which supports the hall of the episcopal palace at Angers, the prototype of that at Wells.

vaults, gradually lessening in height with the ascent of the hill, mark a spot only less hallowed to the hearts of Englishmen than the site of the Standard itself. They mark the spot where William and Odo made their second and fiercest onslaught, the spot where Gyrth and Leofwine died for England.[1]

The foundation of Battle Abbey is important also in another point of view. If it did not begin, it certainly did much to promote, that system of exemption from the ordinary jurisdiction of the Bishops at which the monastic bodies were now constantly aiming. The special pledge of obedience to diocesan authority contained in the bond of Saint Wulfstan and the confederate Abbots was most likely not without a special meaning at that particular time.[2] In the case of Battle, independence of the Bishop of the diocese was asserted from the very beginning.[3] In local belief, it had even formed part of the Duke's original vow upon the hill of Telham.[4] The warfare with the Bishops of Chichester forms a large part of the local history. It was the greatest of local triumphs when Stigand, the Prelate who moved the South-Saxon Bishoprick to its later site, had to forego his claim to summon the second Abbot

*Exemption of the Abbey from episcopal jurisdiction. Growth of such exemptions.*

---

[1] See vol. iii. p. 485.    [2] See above, p. 391.
[3] The story of the dispute with the Bishop of Chichester is given in the Chronicon de Bello (25, 26). In the foundation charter the words run, "Sit libera et quieta in perpetuum de omni subjectione Episcoporum et quarumlibet personarum dominatione, sicut ecclesia Christi Cantuariæ." In the other charter in the Monasticon, iii. 245, William is made to say, "Ita ut libera et quieta in perpetuum ab omni subjectione et dominatione et querelâ Majoris Monasterii et aliarum personarum exactione permaneat, sicut ecclesia Christi Cantuariensis, et sicut mea dominica capella, et signum Anglicæ coronæ per quam ego regno, et successores mei Reges regnum Angliæ debent obtinere." All this has a very suspicious sound, but the signatures are not impossible, like those of the other charter. They are those of Peter Bishop of Chester, Hermann Bishop of Salisbury, William of Warren, Bernard Newmarch, the founder of Saint John's Priory at Brecknock—a cell of Battle—and Abbot Gausbert himself.
[4] See vol. iii. p. 458.

410       THE ECCLESIASTICAL SETTLEMENT OF ENGLAND.

CHAP. XIX.
Gausbert, second Abbot, 1076-1095, blessed at Battle

Gausbert to receive the benediction in the cathedral church, and himself came to Battle and performed the ceremony before the high altar of the probably temporary church of the monastery.[1] The house of Battle had also to defend its independence against another claimant. The elder house of Saint Martin asserted the rights of a parent over the younger foundation. But William protected his own creation against the claims of the Abbot of Marmoutier, no less than against the claims of the Bishop of Chichester.[2] The house whose independence was thus carefully guarded against intruders from all quarters was richly endowed with lands and temporal rights, and the list of its early tenants and officers affords a valuable study of the customs and nomenclature of the time.[3]

Independence of Battle on Marmoutier

Endowments of the Abbey

Lanfranc's opposition to monastic exemptions

It would seem that Lanfranc by no means willingly gave in to a system by which episcopal authority and the common order of the Church were so thoroughly undermined, as when the Abbey of Battle was released from all ordinary jurisdiction on the part of the Bishop of Chichester. Charters of exemption were now constantly obtained by the monastic bodies. A few generations later the evil

---

[1] The story is told at length in the Chronicon de Bello, 25, but the gist of it is found in the charter, Mon Angl iii 245, "Primum Abbatem Gausbertum in eodem monasterio de Bello Stigandus Episcopus Cicestrensis benedixit"

[2] See Chron de Bello, 27, 28, where William is described as waxing very fierce against the claims of Marmoutier, "Quamobrem commotus Rex, omnes qui secum aderant Majoris Monasterii monachos remittere præcepit, ipsique interminatus, 'Per splendorem Dei' inquit (hoc enim assueverat juramento), 'si hâc de causâ mare transieris, aut illuc ulterius ieris, in perpetuum Angliam, ad abbatiæ meæ custodiam, non repedabis'"

[3] The list of names is given in Chronicon de Bello, 12-16. A few are French, but far more are English. Among the latter we may notice "Æilricus Child," where Child can hardly be a title of honour. The names Russellus and Herodes, in the same page, have an odd sound alongside of Goldwine, Eadwine, Siward, and other intelligible persons. "Ælfuinus Abbat," in p 15, should also be noticed.

spread still further; the independence which had been obtained by the regulars was envied and imitated by the seculars, and the authority of the Bishops began to be specially set at nought in those churches which were specially their own.[1] Each diocese was thus cut up into a group of distinct ecclesiastical jurisdictions, some of them subject to the authority of the Ordinary and others holding him at defiance. Lanfranc, if a monk, was also a Bishop, and he seems to have done what he could to stop the innovation. He was severely taken to task by Pope Gregory for abetting, or at least not restraining, Herfast, Bishop of Thetford, in certain acts which were looked on as breaches of the privileges of the house of Saint Eadmund.[2] At a later time we find him exhorting the same Prelate, among other precepts moral and ecclesiastical, to observe the privileges of that illustrious Abbey.[3] But the tone of

*Dealings of Lanfranc and Herfast with Saint Eadmundsbury.*

---

[1] Compare the disputes of Archbishops Baldwin and Hubert with the monks of Christ Church, so graphically told by Professor Stubbs in the Preface to his Epistolæ Cantuarienses, and the long controversy between Robert Grosseteste and his refractory Chapter of Lincoln, which will be found in Dr Shirley's edition of his Letters

[2] Epp. Lanfr 23 (Giles, i 44) "Non minimâ admiratione dignum ducimus quâ fronte, quâ mente, Arfastum dictum Episcopum sanctæ Romanæ Ecclesiæ illudere et beatæ memoriæ Alexandrum prædecessorem nostrum, ejusque decreta contemnere patiamini . fraternitatem vestram confidenter deprecamur, ut viâ nostrâ Arfasti nugas penitus compescatis, et Sancti Edmundi Abbatem contra decretum decessoris nostri inquietari nullo modo sinatis" Still more curious is the way in which Gregory speaks of the King, "Guilielmum Regem, carissimum et unicum filium sanctæ Romanæ Ecclesiæ, precibus nostris et viâ nostrâ super his admonere dilectionem vestram precamur, et ne Arfasti vanis persuasionibus acquiescat, in quo sua singulis prudentia supra modum diminuta et contracta ab omnibus cognoscitur"

[3] Epp Lanfr 26 (Giles, i 47) "Postpositis aleis, ut majora taceam, ludisque sæcularibus, quibus per totam diem vacare diceris, divinas litteras lege, decretisque Romanorum Pontificum sacrisque canonibus præcipue studium impende" This letter is headed "Lanfrancus Hereberto," but as Herbert Losinga did not become Bishop till 1091, I have no doubt, with Dean Hook (ii 154), that the letter was really addressed to Herfast The letters of Lanfranc contain other references to the affairs of the Abbey, and especially to Abbot Baldwin's skill in medicine (See Epp 20, 21, 22, and

Lanfranc is remarkable; he does not at all take up the high line of Gregory; he simply exhorts Herfast to conform strictly to the existing Law, and to make no claims over the monastery which were not justified by the example of his predecessors.[1] Nearer home the Primate was more vigorous still in putting down all pretensions which were inconsistent with his full episcopal and metropolitan authority. The Abbey of Saint Augustine was one of those great monasteries in or close to episcopal cities which seem to have been designed as special thorns in the side of the diocesan. The writers of the house asserted that it had enjoyed the fullest exemption from all external jurisdiction from the very beginning of things.[2] They charge Lanfranc with having obtained from the Norman Abbot Scotland concessions which destroyed the ancient independence of the monastery.[3] On the death of Scotland, which did not happen till after the death of the Conqueror, the Primate

*Lanfranc's dealings with Saint Augustine's*

*His alleged violation of the privileges of the Abbey 1088.*

---

vol ii pp 446, 585, 2nd ed ) We must also remember that Herfast was an old acquaintance of Lanfranc (see vol iii p 104)

Baldwin, after all, was a Frenchman I know not how I came to overlook the decisive passage in Florence (1097), "Baldwinus, *genere Gallus*, artis medicinæ bene peritus " He is there called "eximiæ vir religionis "

[1] Epp Lanfr 26 (Giles, 1 47) "Ad præsens præcipio tibi ne in his rebus Sancti Edmundi aliquid appetas, nisi id ab antecessoribus tuis appetitum fuisse certis documentis ostendas "

[2] W Thorn, X Scriptt 1790 "A tempore enim beati Papæ Gregorii ac sancti patris Augustini hæc illius summæ matris ecclesiarum specialis filia et spiritualis alumna regni Anglorum cœnobiali dignitate et monachili religione primariâ gratiâ omnipotentis Dei, qui libertate vult filios suos frui et non ut fiat cum servis tributariis, ac sanctione sancti patris Gregorii cæterorumque Romanorum pontificum necnon beati Augustini, omnique ecclesiasticâ pace honore ac libertate usa est, nec ullus unquam præsulum sive alia persona eam inquietare ausa est "

[3] Ib 1791 "Lanfrancus hanc ecclesiam apostolicam persequi incepit, et dominium quod super eam juste habere non potuit, ut aliquo modo obtineret per se et suos complices machinari non destitit Hic ergo postquam aliquot annis dignitate archiepiscopali functus est, Abbatem Scotlandum quasi in magnæ amicitiæ familiaritatem, sibi in dolo associavit, ut sub umbrâ hujus mutuæ dilectionis quod sæpius optabat celerius adipisceretur Erant autem quasi compatriotæ," &c

went still further. He gave the abbatial benediction to a certain Guy, who must have been nominated either by himself or by the new King.[1] He then went to Saint Augustine's, strengthened by the secular arm in the person of Odo, Bishop and Earl,[2] and required the brethren to receive Guy as their Abbot. On their refusal the Archbishop installed Guy by his own authority, and intrusted him with the government of the church.[3] The mass of the monks seceded, like the Roman Commons, and found their Sacred Mount near the church of Saint Mildthryth.[4] But as the hour came which was commonly spent in the refectory, the more part of them, pressed by hunger, gave in and submitted to Guy as their Abbot.[5] But on those who resisted the hand of the Primate was heavy. Ælfwine the Prior and others were condemned to terms of imprisonment of different degrees of length and severity,[6] and one, who

*CHAP XIX*
*He names Guy Abbot 1088*

*Resistance and secession of the monks*

*Punishment of the refractory monks*

---

[1] Chron Wint App "Widonem ecclesiæ Sancti Augustini Abbatem Cantuariæ in sede metropoli examinavit atque sacravit"

[2] Ib "Associato sibi Odone Baiocensi Episcopo, fratre Regis, qui tunc Cantuariam venerat"

[3] Ib "Venit itaque Lanfrancus, adducens Abbatem, et quum monachos pertinaciter videret resistere, nec ei velle parere  Lanfrancus cum suis Abbatem honorifice introductum in sede locavit, et ecclesiam commendavit"

[4] Ib "Quum omnibus rite peractis domum rediret, nuntiatum est ei monachos qui exierant sub castro, secus ecclesiam Sanctæ Miltrudæ, consedisse."

[5] Ib "Horâ autem refectionis, quum esurirent plures ex iis, pœnitentes suæ pertinaciæ, ad Lanfrancum miserunt, et ei omnem obedientiam promiserunt  Quibus continuo pepercit, mandans ut redirent, et professionem suam præfato Abbati se servaturos sacramento confirmarent  Itaque redierunt, et se deinceps fore fideles et obedientes Widoni Abbati super corpus beati Augustini juraverunt" Compare the momentary and partial submission of the Fellows of Magdalen College in 1687 Macaulay, ii 299 It does not appear whether the dinner-hour, which has before now influenced parliamentary divisions, had the same effect at Oxford which it had at Canterbury

[6] Ib "Priorem ejusdem ecclesiæ, nomine Ælfwinum, et alios quos voluit, cepit  et Cantuariam claustrali custodiâ servandos protinus transmisit, eos vero qui fortiores et caput scandali exstiterant in castellum duci, ibique in carcere custodiri præcepit  Qui vero remanserant

414    THE ECCLESIASTICAL SETTLEMENT OF ENGLAND.

CHAP XIX

Possible origin of the disturbance.

Part taken by the citizens of Canterbury 1089

confessed a design to kill the new Abbot, was publicly scourged and expelled from the city. This man bore the Scottish name of Columban, and the only other person mentioned by name, besides the Prior Ælfwine, is an English Ælfred.[1] This certainly looks as if national as well as ecclesiastical jealousies had something to do with the matter.[2] And it looks the more so as, when the dispute went on after the death of Lanfranc, the monks in their attacks on the Abbot were vigorously supported by the men of the city.[3]

Decree for the removal of Bishopricks 1075.

The mention of the various monastic houses, some of which were deeply interested in the series of Councils held by Lanfranc, has led me away from the succession of the Councils themselves In one of them, held nine years after William's first entry into England, a measure was taken which has had an important influence on the later history of the English Church, and which is still more important as an illustration of its earlier state. This was the decree by virtue of which several of the Bishopricks of England were removed from their former seats, which in some cases were small and insignificant places, to cities of greater importance. This was a decree which could hardly have been needed in Gaul, Spain, or

cepit Lanfrancus, et per ecclesias Angliæ divisit, constrinxit, donec eos obedientiam profiteri coegit"

[1] Chron Wint App. "Æluredum, unum ex illis, vagantem fugiendo cepit, et Cantuariæ in sede metropoli, cum quibusdam sociis illius, qui Abbati malum moliti sunt, ferro compeditos, multis diebus rigorem ordinis in claustro discere fecit " The affair of Columban happened the next year. His punishment is thus described , " Præcepit itaque Lanfrancus ut ante portas beati Augustini, spectante populo, ligaretur nudus, flagellis afficeretur, deinde, præciso capitio, ab urbe pelleretur"

[2] See Hook, Archbishops, ii 159.

[3] The story is given at length in the Winchester Appendix The Abbot was nearly killed , the refractory monks were scourged, as for the citizens, "cives, qui Abbatis curiam armatâ manu intraverant, capti; et qui se ab ejus impugnatione purgare non poterant oculos amiserunt "

# ENGLISH AND CONTINENTAL BISHOPRICKS.

Italy, and it points to a distinction between the ecclesiastical condition of England and that of continental countries which goes back to the earliest days of Christianity in each. As usual, differences in ecclesiastical arrangements were owing to differences in social and political condition. When Christianity was first preached in the Romanized lands of the West, it was, just as during its still earlier preaching in the East, mainly preached to and received by the inhabitants of the cities. How slow the Gospel was in reaching the dwellers in the open country is plain from the name of *pagan* or countryman being familiarly used to express those who clave to the gods of the elder faith.[1] Under the Roman municipal system, hardly less than among the commonwealths of ancient Greece, the city was the hearth and home and centre of all public and private life. In such a state of things the ecclesiastical arrangements and divisions could hardly fail to conform themselves to the existing civil arrangements and divisions. The seats of ecclesiastical authority were naturally fixed in the same spots as the seats of temporal authority; the limits of two jurisdictions were marked by the same boundaries, and the Bishop had his almost exclusive home in the city from which he took his name. An ecclesiastical map of France, as the dioceses stood before modern changes, faithfully reproduces the map of Roman Gaul.[2] But when,

*Chap XIX. Contrasts between English and continental episcopacy*

*Greater importance of the cities on the continent*

*Coincidence of ecclesiastical and civil divisions.*

---

[1] Our Teutonic word *hæðen*, *heathen*, *Heide*, has an origin closely analogous, but not quite identical. The distinction points to the difference in the condition of the Teutonic and the Romanized lands of which I am speaking in the text. The idolater is not the *paganus*, the man of the country as opposed to the man of the city; he is the *heathen*, the man of the *heath* or wilderness, as opposed to the man both of the city and of the cultivated land.

[2] The changes made in the episcopal arrangements, chiefly of southern Gaul, in the fourteenth century must be remembered, as well as those made in the nineteenth and a few in intermediate times. The earlier changes consisted chiefly in the division of dioceses, as the last changes

in the case of Britain, the Gospel was, for the first time in the West, accepted by a land beyond the limits of the Empire, its preachers had to deal with a wholly different social and political state. In this aspect, the Celtic and the Teutonic portions of the island may be classed together. In neither were the cities dominant, and in both the ecclesiastical arrangements adapted themselves to this fact.[1] The Bishop did not become, in the almost exclusive sense in which he did in the Romanized lands, the Bishop of the city; in some dioceses there was hardly anything to be called a city at all. The extent of the Bishop's jurisdiction was marked out by the extent of the temporal jurisdiction of some King or Ealdorman, but, like the King or Ealdorman, he was essentially the Bishop, not of a city, but of a district or rather of a tribe. Hence, both in England and in other parts of the British Islands, the titles of Bishops were for a long time more commonly territorial or tribal than local, and in the case of some of the Celtic Bishopricks the territorial style is kept on to this day.[2] The Bishop had indeed his see, his *Bishopstool*, his ordinary dwelling, in some particular church of his diocese. This was his cathedral church, the church which was specially his own, where he was surrounded by the monks or canons who were his immediate companions and fellow-workers. But this his special home was not always placed in the greatest town

consisted chiefly in their union. Several churches, as Toulouse, Alby, and Paris, have also been at different times raised from diocesan to metropolitan rank.

[1] Far be it from me to plunge into the mysteries of early Celtic ecclesiastical history, Coarbs, Lay Abbots, and what not I speak of the Irish and Scottish Bishopricks as they appeared when they had assumed an intelligible territorial shape

[2] It is so with the Bishopricks of Meath, Ossory, Galloway, Ross, Argyll, the Isles, Caithness, and Sodor and Man. The Scandinavian Bishoprick of Orkney follows the same rule See Appendix M in the second edition of my second volume

in his diocese. In some cases, as at Saint David's and Lindisfarn, the seat of the Bishoprick seems to have been designedly placed in an inaccessible spot, as if it were rather meant to be the place of the pastor's occasional retreat from his more active duties than to be the constant centre of them. This state of things went on at least till the end of the tenth century. Then it was that the see of Saint Cuthberht was translated to what speedily became the city and fortress of Durham.[1] But Ealdhun created church and city by a single act, and his probable motive was the greater safety of the site which he chose. The systematic removal of Bishopricks from smaller towns to greater belongs to a later time.

This peculiar position of the English Bishops was no doubt reckoned in foreign eyes among those errors of the barbarous islanders which it was the mission of William to reform. The beginning of change, in this respect as in most others, showed itself in the days of Eadward. The same feeling which shows itself in the decree of Lanfranc's Council shows itself also in Leofric's translation of the united sees of Devonshire and Cornwall to the great city of Exeter.[2] We can hardly doubt that this change, as well as the changes which Leofric made in the internal constitution of his church, was prompted by his Lotharingian education. Under William and his successor a long series of changes of the same kind were made. In a Council held at Saint Paul's in London,[3] it was ordered, with the King's sanction, that episcopal sees should be removed from villages or small towns to cities.[4] Three

---

[1] See vol i p 321      [2] See vol ii p 83
[3] Will Malm. Gest Pont 66 All the Bishops of England were present, save Walcher of Durham, who had a canonical excuse for absence Rochester was vacant
[4] Ib 67 "Ex decretis summorum pontificum Damasi et Leonis, necnon ex conciliis Sardicensi et Laodicensi, in quibus prohibetur episcopales sedes in villis exsistere, concessum est regiâ munificentiâ et synodali auctoritate

418    THE ECCLESIASTICAL SETTLEMENT OF ENGLAND.

CHAP. XIX. Bishopricks were at once removed by virtue of this decree.
Hermann removes his see to [Old] Salisbury. 1075-1078.
The Lotharingian Hermann, who had united the sees of Sherborne and Ramsbury, now followed the example of Leofric, and removed the seat of the united diocese to the hill-fortress of the elder Salisbury.[1] The choice of such a position was strange, and its evil consequences were felt till the day when Richard Poore came down from the hill into the plain, and, like Ealdhun, founded at once a church and a city which supplanted their elder neighbours.[2]

Foundation of New Salisbury 1221.

Death of Hermann 1078.
Hermann, old as he was, began vigorously to build a church on the unpromising spot which he had chosen; but he only began, and he left his work to be finished by his successor, the famous Osmund, a name renowned in liturgical history.[3] At the same time Stigand of Selsey removed the seat of the South-Saxon Bishoprick from the site which Æthelwealh had granted to Wilfrith[4] to the town, once the Roman Regnum, which had taken the name of one of the earliest Saxon conquerors in Britain. Cissa the son of Ælle, one of the destroyers of Anderida,[5] had given his name to Cissanceaster or Chichester, a city which has retained its episcopal rank ever since the days of Stigand. Here again the choice seems strange, at least if the central position of the city

Osmund Bishop of Salisbury 1078-1099

Stigand removes the see of Selsey to Chichester.

History and position of Chichester

episcopis de villis transire ad civitates, Herimanno de Siraburnâ ad Serisberiam, Stigando de Selengeo ad Cicestrum, Petro de Licitfelde ad Cestrum." Florence must be mistaken when (1070) he makes the removal of the see to Salisbury happen before the consecration of Lanfranc.

[1] See vol i p. 349, vol ii p 406

[2] Ann Wav. 1217 "Ricardus . . . cujus consilio et auxilio nova ecclesia Saresberiæ novo in loco incepta est, ecclesiâ veteri infra castelli moenia sitâ prius effractâ atque submotâ" Richard became Bishop of Salisbury in 1217 The actual building of the church began in 1221, see the Tewkesbury Annals in anno

[3] Will Malm Gest Pont 183 He goes on to speak of the excellent state of the church of Salisbury during the administration of Osmund Hermann's death is recorded in the Chronicles under the year 1078, with the description which I quoted in vol ii p. 406

[4] Bæda, Hist Eccles iv. 13        [5] See vol iii p. 402.

was to be at all thought of as well as its size.[1] The third see which was forsaken was that of Lichfield, the seat of the holy Ceadda. To modern eyes few episcopal sites in England are more attractive than that where, after all the havoc wrought by war and barbarism, the three spires still rise in all their grace above the silver pool at their feet. But few places were further removed than Lichfield from the continental ideal of an episcopal city.[2] Instead of the church crowning the highest point of a great city like Bourges or Le Mans, a small town had gathered itself outside the episcopal precinct, as it had gathered itself outside the monastic precinct at Crowland and Evesham. Such a site was at once condemned, and by virtue of the new decree, Peter Bishop of Lichfield moved his dwelling-place to William's last conquest of Chester, and placed his throne in the minster of Saint John without the walls of the city.[3] But this change was not a lasting one; the next Bishop, Robert of Limesey,

*See of Lichfield*

*Peter Bishop of Lichfield, 1072-1085, removes the see to Saint John's at Chester*

---

[1] Will. Malm. Gest. Pont. 205. "Stigandus, a Willelmo Rege ibi factus episcopus, mutavit sedem in Cicestram, diœcesis suæ civitatem, prope mare, ubi antiquitus et Sancti Petri monasterium et congregatio fuerat sanctimonialium." Compare the removal of the nuns of Exeter by Leofric, vol. ii. p. 84. One wonders that Stigand did not fix his see at Lewes, where the great Priory of Saint Pancras, the foundation of William of Warren and Gundrada (see vol. iii. p. 645), arose soon after. See the Bermondsey Annals, 1077.

[2] William of Malmesbury (Gest. Pont. 307) thus describes the place. "Licitfeld est villa exigua in pago Statfordensi, longe a frequentiâ urbium Nemorosa circa regio, rivulus aquæ propter fluit. Ecclesia angusto situ erat, antiquorum virorum mediocritatem et abstinentiam præferens. Locus pudendus nostri ævi episcopis, in quo episcopalis dignitas diversari deberet Ibi, ut prædictum est, sanctissimus Cedda et sedit et obiit."

[3] Ib. 309. "In eâdem civitate, ut dixi, fecit Petrus episcopus sedem in ecclesiâ Sancti Petri, positis pauculis canonicis." There can be no doubt however that the church meant is that of Saint John, see above, p. 314.

I gather from Lanfranc's letter to Pope Alexander (Giles, i. 22) that Peter's English predecessor Leofwine was excommunicated for being married and for refusing to appear at a Synod, and that he then resigned his Bishoprick. But there is no distinct mention of this either in the Gesta Pontificum or in the local History.

420        THE ECCLESIASTICAL SETTLEMENT OF ENGLAND.

CHAP XIX
Robert of Lımesey, 1086-1117, removes the see to Coventry
His rapacious dealings with the monks of Coventry
He is rebuked by Lanfranc

again removed the see to Earl Leofric's minster at Coventry.[1] He is said to have been instigated to the step by the vast wealth and splendour of that house, which he wished to make his own by annexing the Abbey to his Bishoprick.[2] We learn, on the evidence of the Primate himself, that the way in which Robert took possession partook strongly of the nature of a raid or a storm. Lanfranc, who kept up a diligent correspondence with his suffragans and rebuked them sharply on occasion, rebukes Robert with special sharpness, not only for his irreverent treatment of his own metropolitan letters,[3] but also for his dealings with the monks of Coventry. He had entered their dormitory by force; he had broken open their chests, taken away their horses and other property, pulled down their houses and carried off the materials to his manors, and lastly, quartered himself and his following on the monastery for eight days.[4]

Coventry the head church of the diocese
Diocese of Coventry and Lichfield.

Restitution is ordered; yet Coventry remained the head church of the diocese,[5] and in the course of the next century Chester seems to have been well nigh forgotten as an episcopal see. The churches of Coventry and Lichfield were now acknowledged as joint seats of the Bishop-

[1] Will. Malm Gest Pont 309  "At vero successor ejus Rotbertus iterum sedem in Coventreiam migravit"  See vol II pp 414, 415. He goes on to speak of the splendour and wealth of the monastery.

[2] Ib 310  "Hoc Rotbertus inhians ex ipsis ecclesiæ gazis accepit, unde Regis occupationes falleret, unde Romanorum aviditati irreperet."

[3] Epp Lanfr 32 (Giles, i 51)  "Litteras ante paucos dies tibi transmisi, et eas vix susceptas legere despexisti, et cum magnâ indignatione, sicut mihi dictum est, super quoddam sedile eas projecisti"

[4] Ib  "Clamorem fecerunt ad me tam abbas quam monachi ejus, quod dormitorium eorum per vim introisti, arcas eorum fregisti, et equos et omnes proprietates quas habebant rapuisti. Insuper domos eorum destruxisti, et materias earum ad tuas villas asportari præcepisti. In ipso quoque cœnobio cum famiļiâ tuâ, consumens bona monachorum, octo dierum moram fecisti"  Compare also the account of his doings given by William of Malmesbury, Gest Pont 310

[5] See the letter of Bishop Rowland Lee to Lord Cromwell praying for the preservation of the church of Coventry, Mon Angl III 199

rick of north-western Mercia.[1] The dissolution of the monasteries swept away Coventry; modern arrangements have even removed the city into another diocese, and the old home of Ceadda is now again, as it was in the earliest times, the only seat of his successors.

*Suppression of Coventry 1539 Lichfield the sole see 1836.*

But these three changes, made by the immediate orders of the Council of London, were not the only changes of the kind which were made during this reign and the following one. First of all, Remigius, the monk of Fécamp, the Prelate of Dorchester, the man of small stature but of lofty soul,[2] removed the seat of his episcopal rule to the lordliest spot within his diocese. He forsook the old home of Birinus by the winding Thames, guarded by its Roman dykes and looking up at the mighty hill fort of Sinodun. He placed his church and throne among yet prouder relics of early times,[3] side by side with the castle which was already rising to curb the haughty burghers of wealthy and famous Lincoln. Herfast of Elmham too translated the see of the East-Angles to Thetford, the town so famous and so unlucky in the Danish wars.[4] His next successor but one, the famous Herbert, who has left behind him so mixed a

*Remigius translates the see of Dorchester to Lincoln. 1085*

*Herfast translates the see of Elmham to Thetford. 1078*

---

[1] Lichfield was not wholly forgotten even under Robert of Limesey, who (Will Malm. Gest. Pont. 311) "magnarum apud Licetfeld ædificationum inchoator exstitit." So we read in the local History (Ang. Sac. i. 443) of the great things done at Lichfield in the next age by Roger of Clinton, Bishop from 1128 to 1148. From the election of his successor, Walter Durdent, the agreement or disagreement of the Canons of Lichfield and monks of Coventry in the election of the Bishop is carefully noted, without any mention of the Canons of Chester. Nor must we forget the momentary substitution of Canons for monks at Coventry by Bishop Hugh Nonant in 1190, a subject on which Richard of the Devizes (65, 66) is very eloquent. See also Ang. Sac. i. 436.

[2] Will. Malm. Gest. Pont. 313. "Quod eo jocundius erat, quia ipse pro exiguitate corporis pene portentum hominis videbatur. Luctabatur excellere et foris eminere animus, eratque

　Gratior exiguo veniens e corpore virtus,

quem ideo natura compegisse putaretur, ut sciretur beatissimum ingenium in miserrimo corpore habitare posse."

[3] See above, p. 212.　　　　[4] See vol. i. pp. 351, 380.

422    THE ECCLESIASTICAL SETTLEMENT OF ENGLAND.

CHAP. XIX
and Herbert Losinga [1091–1119] from Thetford to Norwich. 1101.

character and so ambiguous a surname,[1] removed it yet again. He chose as his dwelling the Eastern rival of Exeter and Lincoln, and raised the rich and populous Norwich to the rank of a city.[2] Lastly, but not till the Great William was no more, another foreign Prelate was found to undo the work of Gisa in the Bishoprick of Somerset.

John of Tours [1088–1122] translates the see of Wells to Bath 1088

John, a learned physician from Tours,[3] was the successor of the reforming Lotharingian. He, like Peter at Lichfield, despised his little city at the foot of Mendip. He swept away the works of his predecessor, and left the Canons of Wells in the poverty from which his predecessor had raised them. He then moved his throne to the Abbey of Saint Peter at Bath; the line of independent Abbots was merged in that of the Bishops; and John himself ruled alike as spiritual and temporal lord in the old Roman town which had beheld the crowning of Eadgar the Peaceful.[4]

Council at Winchester, April 1st, 1076.

In another Council held at Winchester, in the year following that which decreed the translation of the Bishopricks, a variety of canons were passed, some of which must be taken in connexion with the great ecclesiastical movement which was going on throughout Europe. We must never forget that, while Lanfranc ruled at Canterbury,

---

[1] William of Malmesbury here uses nearly the same words in the Gesta Regum (iv 338) and in the Gesta Pont (151), " Herbertus, cognomento Losinga, quod ei ars adulationis impegerat, ex abbate Ramesiensi emit episcopatum Thetfordensem, patre quoque suo Roberto, ejusdem cognominis, in abbatiam Wintoniæ intruso" I do not see how this Robert can be the same as " Robertus Lotharingus " (Gest. Pont. 300), " venerandus vir Robertus" (Fl Wig 1079), the great friend of Saint Wulfstan, who became Bishop of Hereford in 1079. See above, p 379

[2] After going to Rome, and getting his staff restored, " domum reversus, sedem episcopalem transportavit ad insignem mercimonus et populorum frequentiâ vicum, nomine Norwic." (Gest. Reg. iv. 338, Gest Pont. 151.) On Norwich, see above, p 67

[3] On John of Tours, see Gest Pont. 194, Historiola, 22  I have spoken more fully of Bath and Wells matters in my History of the Church of Wells, p 35 et al

[4] See vol. i p. 68.

Hildebrand ruled at Rome. We shall presently see that, in some most important points, the Primate of all Britain had fallen away from that rigid standard of perfection in Roman eyes which had been reached by the monk of Bec.[1] Still the ecclesiastical legislation of Lanfranc is the legislation of Hildebrand, only slightly modified and with a little of its overbearing harshness softened down. The two main objects of the great Pope, two objects which in his idea could hardly be kept asunder, were the subjection of the civil to the ecclesiastical power, and the establishment of the clergy as a distinct order, animated by one universal corporate spirit, and cut off from those ties of citizenship and kindred which bind men together in earthly bonds. The great means to this end was absolutely to forbid marriage to the clergy of every grade. An exaggerated reverence for virginity had been growing up in the Church from the beginning, and it reached its full height when Eadward was deemed a saint for his real or supposed breach of his first duty as a King. This feeling fell in with the politic views of Gregory. In a Council held at Rome two years before the time which we have reached in our English narrative, the marriage of the clergy was forbidden more strongly than it had ever been forbidden before; married priests were commanded to separate from their wives, and the laity were warned that the sacraments lost their effect when administered by the hands of men who transgressed this new and stern commandment.[2] The

CHAP. XIX.
Relations between Lanfranc and Hildebrand

Objects of Hildebrand

Prohibition of the marriage of the Clergy.

Decrees of the Council of Rome March 9, 10, 1074

---

[1] See below, p 434

[2] So it would appear from the theological argument of Sigeberht (in anno, Pertz, iu 362) He gives the decree of the Synod thus, "Gregorius Papa celebratâ synodo simoniacos anathematizavit, et uxoratos sacerdotes a divino officio removit, et laicis missam eorum audire interdixit" He adds, that this was "novo exemplo et, ut multis visum est, inconsiderato præjudicio contra sanctorum patrum sententiam," and goes on to argue that the unworthiness of ministers hindereth not the effect of the sacraments He is followed by Roger of Wendover (ii 13) and by Matthew Paris

## 424 THE ECCLESIASTICAL SETTLEMENT OF ENGLAND.

CHAP XIX

Frequency of clerical marriage in England

Distinction made by Lanfranc between parochial and capitular clergy

Marriage absolutely forbidden to Canons

Analogy in Elizabeth's reign.

English Council re-enacted the acts of that of Rome in a considerably milder shape. In England and in other Teutonic lands, no less than in the Churches of the East, the habit of clerical marriage had taken far too deep root to be got rid of in a moment. Lanfranc set to work warily. He drew a distinction which was afterwards drawn again in a modified shape in the days of Queen Elizabeth. The parochial and the collegiate clergy were not treated exactly according to the same measure. The Canons of cathedral and other capitular churches were first dealt with. Of the prevalence of marriage among this class we have already seen several instances.[1] The practice was of course the greatest of all obstacles in the way of those reforming Bishops who sought, sometimes to replace their Canons by actual monks, sometimes to bring them under the intermediate rule of Chrodegang. To the capitular clergy then marriage was absolutely forbidden, without reserve or exemption, and those who were already married were called on to separate from their wives. The decree of the Synod on this head is brief and pithy, " Let no Canon have a wife."[2] So in the days of Elizabeth, when the marriage of the clergy was neither allowed nor forbidden, but winked at, the parish clergy were let alone, but wives and children were not allowed to appear within either cathedral closes or academical

---

in his greater work (ed Wats, 9), but in the Historia Minor (Madden, 1 18) the theological argument is left out. See Milman, iii 118. Lambert (1074, p 163 of the lesser Pertz) tells us how the decrees were received in Germany, and how " vehementer infremuit tota factio clericorum, hominem plane hæreticum et vesani dogmatis esse clamitans " The chief argument was that Hildebrand's rule was fit only for angels and not for men, and that the German clergy were men and not angels

[1] See especially the account of the Canons of Rochester in p 37; and on Waltham compare vol ii p 444

[2] Wilkins, Concilia, 1 367 " Decretum est ut nullus canonicus uxorem habeat

colleges.[1] So now a milder rule was applied to the parochial clergy than that which was brought to bear on their collegiate brethren. Vested interests at least were respected. It was distinctly ordered that the married priests who were scattered up and down the country in towns and villages should not be called on to leave their wives.[2] This relaxation of the edicts of Gregory showed the practical good sense of Lanfranc and those who acted with him, but it amounted to giving up the point as a matter of principle. If, as Hildebrand taught, no saving grace could be bestowed by the ministrations of a married priest, a large part of the people of England were doomed to go without valid sacraments for years to come. The more distant future indeed was carefully provided for. Those priests who were not already married were strictly forbidden to marry, and the Bishops were no less strictly warned against ordaining married men.[3] And other rules were laid down with regard to the marriages of the laity,[4] which seem to show that the Danish custom, or some kindred form of laxity, still prevailed. Men were forbidden to give their daughters or kinswomen in marriage without the blessing of the Church They were warned

*CHAP XIX*

*Parish priests not to leave their wives*

*Marriage forbidden for the future.*

*Secular marriages forbidden to the laity*

---

[1] See Queen Elizabeth's order prohibiting the residence of women in colleges, printed in Archbishop Parker's Correspondence (edit Parker Society), p 146  Her Majesty did not go quite so deep into the matter as Hildebrand, but she held, perhaps not without reason, that when "chief governors, prebendaries, students, &c do keep particular household with their wives, children and nurses, no small offence groweth to the intent of the founders and of the quiet and orderly profession of study and learning"

[2] Concilia, 1 367   "Decretum est ut . . sacerdotes in castellis vel in vicis habitantes habentes uxores non cogantur ut dimittant "

[3] Ib   "Non habentes interdicantur ut habeant, et deinceps caveant episcopi ut sacerdotes vel diaconos non presumant ordinare nisi prius profiteantur ut uxores non habeant "

[4] On this I have spoken more at length in an Appendix (Note X ) to the second edition of my first volume  In the next Chapter we shall come across something of the same kind in Ireland

426    THE ECCLESIASTICAL SETTLEMENT OF ENGLAND.

CHAP XIX that such unions were not lawful marriage, but mere fornication.¹ Other provisions had reference to the state of the times and to the new legislation by which William had separated the ecclesiastical and temporal courts.² It was ordained that no priest in town or country should have any burthens laid on his ecclesiastical benefice other than the living had been charged with in the days of King Eadward.³ Such a provision might well be needed to protect English priests alike against Norman Bishops and against Norman patrons. Another ordinance denounced excommunication, with its attendant temporal penalties, against all who should neglect any summons which cited them to appear in the newly established courts of the Bishops.⁴ The cause of Æthelric, the deposed Bishop of the South-Saxons, of which we have heard more than once without any very clear account of its nature, was now finally heard and decided.⁵

*The ancient burthens on Church livings not to be increased*

*Summonses to the Bishops' courts enforced*

*Case of Bishop Æthelric*

*Lanfranc, Thomas, and Remigius go to Rome. 1076.*

It is worthy of special notice that, soon after this important Synod, within the course of the same year, Lanfranc, again accompanied by Thomas of York and Remigius of Dorchester, paid a visit to the threshold of the Apostles.

---

¹ Concilia, i 367. "Præterea statutum est ut nullus filiam suam vel cognatam det alicui absque benedictione sacerdotali, si aliter fecerit, non ut legitimum conjugium sed ut fornicatorium judicabitur"

² See above, p 392

³ Concilia, u s. "Statutum est ne aliquis clericus civilis vel rusticus de beneficio ecclesiæ aliquod servitium reddat præter illud quod fecit tempore Regis Edwardi'

⁴ Ib "Laici vero, si de crimine suo accusati fuerint, et episcopo suo obedire noluerint, vocentur semel, et iterum, et tertio, si post tertiam vocationem emendare noluerint, excommunicentur, si autem post excommunicationem ad satisfactionem venerint, forisfacturam suam, quæ Anglice vocatur *oferhyrnesse* seu *lahslite*, pro unâquâque vocatione episcopo suo reddant." On *lah-slit* and *oferhyrnes* see Schmid's Glossary. Good examples of the latter will be found in p. 146 of Schmid in the Laws of Æthelstan

⁵ See above, p 360

They would doubtless report to Pope Gregory the acts CHAP XIX. of the Synod at Winchester, how it had been found impossible to carry out the Roman decrees in their fulness, and how the perverseness of the stiff-necked islanders had made some relaxation of their strictness unavoidable. But, at that particular moment, Hildebrand himself might well be willing to purchase the allegiance of the Crown and Church of England by allowing the parish clergy of England to keep their wives for life. It was the great year of Synods and Diets, the year when the two swords 1076. clashed with all their might, the year when the sun and moon of the Christian firmament strove eagerly to eclipse each other, when the successor of Augustus took upon him to depose the successor of Peter, and when the successor of Peter took upon him more effectually to depose the successor of Augustus.[1] At such a moment the presence of Import of the three English Prelates was doubly welcome; it was a their visit in that sign that, whatever storms might vex the Church in year. Italy and the Teutonic Kingdom, the island Empire at least and its mighty sovereign remained firm in their allegiance to the mother and mistress of all Churches. Lanfranc, Thomas, and Remigius appeared at Rome, not Their mission from to pay a mere ecclesiastical homage, but in the further William character of ambassadors from the King of the English.[2] They were, as they well might be, received with all

---

[1] See vol III. p 274 The wonderful letters which passed between the Pope and the King, and the formula by which the German Bishops renounced the obedience of Hildebrand, are given at length in Bruno de Bello Saxonico, pp 57–79 of the smaller Pertz. Whatever may be thought of the reasoning on either side—and the Pope's assertion that no King ever worked miracles sounds odd so soon after the death of Eadward—there can be no doubt that the superiority in the style of controversy is on the side of Hildebrand

[2] Ord Vit 548 C. "Legationes Guillelmi Regis, quas antistites jam dicti cum muneribus detulerunt, Papa clerusque Romanus gratantissime susceperunt."

honour by the Pope and the Senate of Rome.¹ By this last name it may be safer to understand the ecclesiastical College of Cardinals, than the body which still remained as a shadow of the earlier Empire and of the still earlier Commonwealth. The wealth of England was, as ever, lavished on the greedy Romans, and the bounty of the three Prelates drew forth no less admiration than their eloquence and learning.² In their character of ambassadors the three Bishops were thoroughly successful They brought back to William the confirmation of certain privileges which his predecessors on the English throne had enjoyed before him, and for which he stooped so far as to ask the Papal approval.³ What these privileges were we should have been glad to learn. William, as a matter of fact, always exercised the right of investiture in all its fulness. Can it be that the right which was so sternly denied to the King of Germany and Italy was formally allowed to the ruler of the other world beyond the sea?

The three Bishops came back to England by way of Normandy, but they did not reach even Normandy till the next year. We should gladly learn where and how they spent their winter, for that winter was the winter of Canosa.⁴ However that may be, in the course of the next year they came back to the dominions of the prince whose throne stood firm while the thrones of Pope and Cæsar were rocking to and fro. As if in gentle mockery of the storms elsewhere, that year was in Normandy a

---

¹ Ord Vit 548 C "A domno Gregorio Papâ Senatuque Romano honorificentissime suscepti sunt"

² Ib "De divitiis Anglicis larga munera *cupidis Romanis* ubertim dederunt, suâque sic largitate cum facundiâ geminâque scientiâ mirabiles Latus visi sunt" We already hear the voice of Thomas of London and of Matthew Paris

³ Ib D "Papa clerusque Romanus .. privilegia quæ per eos petierat [Guillelmus Rex], antecessoribus suis olim concessa libenter annuerunt."

⁴ See Lambert, 1077, p 257 of the smaller Pertz

year of peace, specially given up to ecclesiastical cere- | Chap xix
monies. The King-Duke, his Queen, their sons Robert | Consecration of
and William, the Primates of Canterbury and Rouen, | churches in Normandy
and a crowd of Prelates of less degree, took part in a
series of dedications of cathedral and monastic churches.[1]
The episcopal churches of Evreux and Bayeux were among
the minsters now hallowed.[2] Two other ceremonies followed in which the Primate of Britain had a nearer
personal interest. The minster of Saint Stephen, the | Consecration of Saint Stephen's,
work of William, the home of Lanfranc, now stood ready
for consecration.[3] The rite was done in the presence of
William and Lanfranc, and the stones on which they
gazed are there to bear witness to this day. And yet
another rite, in a spot still more dear, called for both
the presence and the personal ministrations of the English
Primate. The minster of Bec, the work of the still living | of Bec. October 23, 1077.
Herlwin, was next to be hallowed. And there, in the
home which had beheld his first conversion, the monk
whom Herlwin had welcomed to the fold, the Prior whose
learning had made Bec one of the wonders of the world,
now came in all the pomp of the Patriarch of the lands
beyond the sea, to hallow the church which the friend
and guide of his youth had at last brought to perfection.
He knew not perhaps that he came also to hear the *Nunc* | Death of Herlwin August 20, 1078.
*dimittis* of the man whose simple virtues stand in such
strange yet pleasing contrast with the intellectual giants
who pressed into his spiritual household.[4]

---

[1] Ord Vit 548 D "Tunc basilicæ plures in Normanniâ cum ingenti tripudio dedicatæ sunt, ad quas Rex et Regina cum filiis suis Roberto atque Guillelmo [the English Ætheling was perhaps left in his own island] et ingenti frequentiâ optimatum et populorum affuerunt " Cf above, p. 92, and vol ii p 212

[2] Ib On Odo's work at Bayeux, see vol ii p 212

[3] Ib See vol iii p 109 382

[4] Ib, and more fully Will Gem vi 9, for both the dedication and the death of Herlwin See vol ii p 222. Orderic (549 A) adds, " Venerabilis Herluinus Abbas, dedicatâ Beccensi ecclesiâ, valde gavisus est, visoque quod

CHAP XIX.
The English Church becomes less national under Lanfranc
Widened separation of Church and State, and closer connexion with Rome
Safeguard of William's personal character.

Such were some of the most striking scenes, such were some of the most important ecclesiastical changes, which marked the primacy of Lanfranc. All his changes tended to weaken that thoroughly national character which had belonged to the English Church in earlier days. All tended to widen that distinction between the spiritual and temporal powers which in the days of our insular freedom was hardly known. All tended to bring the English Church into closer dependence on the see of Rome. But while William wore the Crown which he had won, there was no fear lest the most devout among the royal sons of the Roman Church should ever degenerate into her abject slave. Not a jot of the supremacy which had been handed on to him from his predecessors would the Conqueror wittingly give up. In the very year when Lanfranc, with the authority of William, was calmly decreeing that Lichfield should yield its episcopal rank to Chester, Gregory, without the authority of his sovereign, was decreeing that no Bishop or Abbot should receive his ring and staff from any temporal lord.[1] Such thunderbolts might hurl the lord of Germany and Italy from his throne; against the lord of Normandy and England they were harmless. Not a trace is seen of any attempt on Gregory's part to seek any change in the law of England by which the Prelates of England received the badges of their office from the royal hand. What King Eadward had freely done King William went on doing no less freely. William was

1075

Dealings of Gregory with William

vehementer in hoc sæculo desideraverat, ulterius inter mortales commorari dedignatus est." See also Vit Lanfr (Giles, i. 276), Chron Bec (ib. 200). It is now that Lanfranc gets his magnificent title of "reverendus gentium transmarinarum summus Pontifex"

[1] See the words of the decree in Abbot Hugh's Verdun Chronicle (Pertz, viii 412), "Si quis deinceps episcopatum aut abbatiam de manu alicujus loicæ personæ susceperit, nullatenus inter episcopos vel abbates habeatur," &c Compare also the later decrees of 1078 in p. 423.

throughout his reign the favoured son of the Roman Church. He did not absolutely reach perfection in the eyes of Gregory, but he came so much nearer to it than other princes that he deserved to be treated with special tenderness. Something was to be allowed to a King who neither destroyed churches nor sold them, who made laymen pay tithe and made priests forsake their wives, and who refused all invitations to join in any schemes contrary to the interests of the Holy See.[1] One of Gregory's first acts on his accession was to profess his special affection for William, and at the same time to exhort him to a more punctual payment of the money due to the Church of Rome.[2] Later in his reign, Gregory thought it needful to expound to William, by help of the usual metaphors and comparisons, how far the power of Pontiffs stood above the power of Kings.[3] But no serious dispute ever arose

*Special favour shown to William*

[1] Ep Greg vii 5, ap Labbe, Concilia, x 281. "Rex Anglorum, licet in quibusdam non ita religiose sicut optamus se habeat, tamen in hoc quod ecclesias Dei non destruit [the New Forest was perhaps not heard of at Rome] neque vendit, et pacem justitiamque in subditis suis moderari procurat, et quia contra Apostolicam Sedem, rogatus a quibusdam inimicis crucis Christi pactum inire, consentire noluit, presbyteros uxores, laicos decimas quas detinebant, etiam juramento dimittere compulit, cæteris Regibus se satis probabiliorem ac magis honorandum ostendit Unde non indignum debet existimari potestatem illius mitius esse tractandam atque respectu probitatis ipsius, subditorum et eorum quos diligit negligentias ex parte fore portandas." The letter is addressed to Hugh Bishop of Die in the Province of Vienne in the Royal Burgundy, a Prelate employed by Gregory on many of his missions

[2] Ib 57. "Hæc, carissime, tibi inculcamus quia inter Reges te solum habemus quem præ aliis diligere supra scripta credimus" He then mentions the Peter-pence, "Rebus Sancti Petri quæ in Angliâ colliguntur sic te ut tuis invigilare admonemus sic liberalitati tuæ ut tua committimus ut pium et propitium debitorem Petrum reperias et eum tibi ex debito subvenire admoneas quem sibi multa te tribuisse non latebit" The *Romscot, Romescot, Rompænig, Pecunia Romana, Denarius Sancti Petri*, the *heorð-pænig*, as it is called in the Laws of Eadgar, is mentioned in a crowd of enactments from the Peace of Eadward and Guthrum onwards

[3] Ib 246 "Credimus prudentiam vestram non latere, omnibus aliis excellentiores apostolicam et regiam dignitates huic mundo ad ejus

between two men each of whom could respect the other, and each of whom knew that the other could be useful for his purposes. Once only Gregory went too far, and he then found that the loyal son of the Church was not prepared to be its slave or its vassal. Even then Gregory did not ask that William should give up the right of investiture, though he made a claim which was bolder still. At some time in William's reign of which we do not know the exact date, a Legate from Rome, Hubert of whom we have already heard, had come to England on two errands. He again demanded a more regular payment of the Peterpence. And he made a far more daring demand; he asked that the King of the English should profess himself the man of the Bishop of Rome.[1] Some vague notion that such a profession was due may well have floated in the minds of Popes and Cardinals ever since Alexander had sent the ring and banner to bless the invasion of England.[2] But whatever external claims Gregory ventured to assert over the Kingdom of England, they were wholly external claims. He claims a suzerainty over the realm, but he makes no claim to control the lawful powers of King and Witan in its internal government. The answer of William was short and simple, and breathed in its fulness that spirit of deference to precedent which has ever been

---

regimina omnipotentem Deum distribuisse Sicut enim ad mundi pulcritudinem oculis carneis diversis temporibus repræsentandam solem et lunam omnibus aliis eminentiora disposuit luminaria, sic ne creatura, quam sui benignitas ad imaginem suam in hoc mundo creaverat, in erronea et mortifera traheretur pericula, providit ut apostolicâ et regiâ dignitate per diversa regeretur officia Qua tamen majoritatis et minoritatis distantiâ religio sic se movet Christiana, ut cura et dispensatione apostolicæ dignitatis post Deum gubernetur regia"

[1] Ep Lanfr. 10 (Giles, 1 32) "Hubertus, legatus tuus, religiose pater, ad me veniens ex tuâ parte, me admonuit, quatenus tibi et successoribus tuis fidelitatem facerem, et de pecuniâ quam antecessores mei ad Romanam Ecclesiam mittere solebant melius cogitarem."

[2] See vol III. p 321.

the life and soul of English Law. The money he would pay; his predecessors had paid it. Owing to his absence in Gaul, it had been for three years irregularly gathered; he therefore bound himself to see that all arrears were faithfully paid in. But the claim of fealty was another matter; that he had never promised and his predecessors had never paid.[1] But he craved the prayers of the Pontiff; he was ready to show to Gregory the same affection and obedience which he had ever paid to the Pontiffs who had gone before him.[2]

When we read this memorable letter, we are struck with the calm daring of the man who could thus at once brave and refute the mighty Hildebrand without a word of threatening or railing, without a word that the Pontiff himself could look on as undutiful or irreverent. The simple dignity, the crushing logic, of these few words of William the Great form a marked contrast to the foul calumnies and wild invectives which the partizans of Pope and Cæsar were hurling at one another in other lands. But to Englishmen the letter has another and a deeper interest. It shows how thoroughly William held himself to have stepped into the position of the Kings of whom he professed himself to be the lawful successor. He claims all their rights, but not more than their rights. What they paid he will pay, what they never paid he will never pay. With the Crown of the island Empire William had, in the face of foreign powers, assumed the spirit

---

[1] Epp Lanfr 10 "Unum admisi, alterum non admisi Fidelitatem facere nolui, nec volo, quia nec ego promisi, nec antecessores meos antecessoribus tuis id fecisse comperio" He then goes on to promise the more regular payment of the money The date of the letter is not clearly marked It cannot be earlier than 1076, as it was only in 1073 that William's frequent absences from England began

[2] Ib "Orate pro nobis et pro statu regni nostri, quia antecessores vestros dileximus, et vos præ omnibus sincere diligere et obedienter audire desideramus"

434    THE ECCLESIASTICAL SETTLEMENT OF ENGLAND.

CHAP. XIX. which became one who wore it. The words of William to Hildebrand are as truly English as the words of Tostig to Nicolas.[1] When we see the honour and freedom of England thus guarded as truly as the noblest of earlier or later Kings could have guarded it, we may for a moment forget that it was a foreign conqueror who so worthily discharged one at least of the duties of an English King.

Share of Lanfranc in the correspondence

The question naturally arises how far the answer of William to the demands of Gregory was also the answer of Lanfranc. It is certain that, at or immediately after the time of this memorable correspondence, Lanfranc was

Lanfranc rebuked by Gregory

rebuked by Gregory for lack of reverence towards the Apostolic See, and the words of his answer seem to imply that the Primate of all Britain was charged with having, on the strength of the dignity of his see and its distance from the common centre, set himself up as in some measure independent of the Bishop of Bishops at Rome.[2] It is certain also that Lanfranc professed that he had advised the King to make a different answer from that which he actually made, but that the King refused to listen to

Lanfranc's view of Papal supremacy

his counsels.[3] But it is also certain that Lanfranc's language is as guarded as language can be. In professing his devotion to the Pope, he makes no promise of unlimited submission, but simply of a legal obedience bounded

---

[1] See vol ii p 458.

[2] Epp Lanfr 11 (Giles, 1 32) "Litteras . suscepi, in quarum fere omni contextu paternâ me dulcedine reprehendere studuistis, quod, in episcopali honore positus, sanctam Romanam Ecclesiam vosque ob ejus reverentiam minus diligam quam ante honoris ipsius susceptionem diligere quondam solebam Ego, teste conscientiâ meâ, in memetipso intelligere non possum, quid vel corporalis absentia, vel locorum tanta intercapedo, aut ipsa qualiscumque honorum sublimitas in hac parte vindicare sibi quidquam praevaleat, quin mens mea praeceptis vestris in omnibus et per omnia, secundum canonum praecepta, subjaceat "

[3] Ib " Domino meo Regi suggessi, suasi, sed non persuasi."

by the canons [1] So too he leaves it perfectly vague what the advice which he gave to William really was, and for further information he refers the Pontiff to the King's own letters and messages.[2] Language like this addressed to a Pope, and that Pope Hildebrand, certainly suggests that Lanfranc's feelings went along with the King and not with the Pontiff, and that if he in any sense advised William to yield to Gregory's demands, the advice was purely formal advice, given merely to enable Lanfranc to tell Gregory that he had given it.[3] So much of double-dealing as is implied in conduct of this kind is certainly not inconsistent with the ecclesiastical morality of the time. In two other letters, both of them later than the joint visit of the two Archbishops and Remigius, Lanfranc is severely rebuked by Gregory for failing to appear at the threshold of the Apostles. In the first letter it is implied that the hindrance came from the King, and Lanfranc is bidden to use all means for bringing William to a better frame of mind.[4] In the second letter Lanfranc

*Lanfranc rebuked for not coming to Rome 1079*

---

[1] "Secundum canonum præcepta" in the extract just above.

[2] Epp. Lanfr. 11 (Giles, 1. 32). "Cui autem voluntati vestræ omnifariam non assenserit, ipsemet vobis tam verbis, quam litteris innotescit."

[3] See Hook, Archbishops, ii. 141.

[4] The letter is given in Labbe, Concilia, xii. 450; Jaffé, Monumenta Gregoriana, 367, where it is referred to 1079, March 25. Gregory complains of Lanfranc's not often coming to Rome ("venire ad nos non multum curavit fraternitas tua"), and then uses this remarkable language about William, "Certissime compertum habemus, adventum tuum vel metus Regis, ejus scilicet quem inter cæteros illius dignitatis specialius semper dileximus, vel maxime tua culpa nobis negavit. Et te quidem, si vel prisci amoris memoria superesset vel debita matri Romanæ ecclesiæ dilectio in mente remaneret, non debuit aliquis aut mundanæ potestatis terror, aut cujusquam personæ superstitiosus amor, a conspectu nostro retrahere. Illum vero si contra apostolicam sedem novus arrogantiæ tumor nunc erigit, sive contra nos ulla libido seu procacitas jactat, tanto gravius feremus, quanto eum dilectione nostrâ indignum se fecisse constituit." Lanfranc is bidden to reform William, "ei diligenter aperiendo et constanter admonendo ne contra matrem omnium Romanam ecclesiam quid injustum præsumat neve quid a religiosâ potestate alienum petulanter audeat, et neque tuam neque

CHAP. XIX

Lanfranc summoned to Rome by Gregory. 1082?

Schism of Wibert or Clement 1080

Cautious language of Lanfranc.

is charged with disobeying repeated invitations to appear at Rome, and he is even threatened with removal from the episcopal office if he does not appear within the current year.[1] It is not however at all clear that either the rebuke or the threat had the effect of bringing the English Primate to the threshold of the Apostles. And it is even more important to note that, when the right of Gregory to the Papal throne was again called in question, when King Henry had given him a successor in the person of Wibert or Clement,[2] and had received the Imperial Crown from the Pontiff of his own making,[3] Lanfranc again uses the most cautious language, and declines to commit himself either way. England, he tells a correspondent, had neither rejected Gregory nor recognized Clement; the matter had still to be examined; both sides had still to be heard and a decision to be come

alicujus devotionem ab apostolicæ sedis visitationem ulterius coercere attentet." Lastly he tells him, " Decet fraternitatem tuam negligentiæ suæ excessus sapienter corrigere atque ad apostolicam sedem quantocius properare "

[1] The letter, given in Labbe, Concilia, xii 53, is there assigned to 1081, but by Jaffé (Mon. Greg 494), though doubtfully, to 1082 After rejecting all excuses about distance and the difficulty of the way, Hildebrand goes on to use some rather strong language, "Quare apostolicâ tibi auctoritate præcipimus, ut, postposita occasione vel inani formidine, datis inducis quatuor mensium, postquam hæc nostra mandata ad notitiam tuam pervenerint in præsentis anni festo omnium sanctorum Romæ adesse procures et satagas, et inobedientiæ tuæ reatum per tantum temporis supportatum emendare non ulterius negligas Quod si nec adhuc te mandata apostolica moverint, sed ea dissimulans in contemptu durare malueris, et periculum inobedientiæ incurrere non erubueris, quod est quasi scelus idololatriæ, testante beato Samuele, a beati Petri gratiâ scias te procul dubio removendum, et ejus auctoritate omnino feriendum, ita videlicet, ut si infra prædictum spatium ad nos non veneris, ab omni sis officio episcopali suspensus "

[2] Sigebert, 1079 (Pertz, vi 364) Otto of Freisingen (Annals, vi 36), in recording the appointment of Wibert, gives a general picture of the times which is well worth turning to

[3] For the coronation of Henry at Easter, 1084 or 1085, see the authorities collected by Struvius, 1 389

to after hearing them.¹ Meanwhile he declines to join his correspondent in any disrespectful language towards Gregory or in any extraordinary praises of Clement.² On the other hand, he cannot believe that the Emperor —he does not deny him the title—can have taken so weighty a step without good reasons, or that he can have won so great a victory without the manifest help of God.³ It is plain that both the Cæsar and the Pontiff of the island Empire had fully made up their minds to hold their own, and that all the obedience which Rome was likely to win from William, or from Lanfranc under William's rule, did not go beyond a decent ceremonial reverence.

In fact there was no time when the royal supremacy in matters ecclesiastical was more fully carried out than it was in the days of the Conqueror. If William was pre-eminently Defender of the Faith, he was no less pre-eminently Supreme Governor of the Church throughout his dominions. In all causes and over all persons was that supremacy asserted. Alongside of all that we hear of William's zeal and piety, we hear another voice complaining of his aggressions on ecclesiastical privileges, and of the new customs which he brought over from Normandy for the more complete subordination of the ecclesiastical state to his will.⁴ On that will, we are told, all things

*Effectual exercise of the royal supremacy by William*

*Charge of ecclesiastical innovations against him*

---

¹ Epp Lanfr 65 (Giles, i 80) "Nondum enim insula nostra priorem refutavit, nec utrum huic obedire debeat sententiam promulgavit Auditis utrimque causis, si ita contigerit, perspicacius quid fieri oporteat provideri valebit"

² Ib "Non probo quod Papam Gregorium vituperas, quod Hildebrandum eum vocas, quod legatos ejus spinosulos nominas, quod Clementem tot et tantis præconiis tam propere exaltas."

³ Ib "Credo tamen quod gloriosus Imperator sine magnâ ratione tantam rem non est aggressus patrare, nec sine magno auxilio Dei tantam potuit victoriam consummare"

⁴ Eadmer Hist Nov 6 "Usus ergo atque leges quas patres sui et ipse

438    THE ECCLESIASTICAL SETTLEMENT OF ENGLAND.

CHAP XIX
No Pope to be acknowledged or Papal letters to be received without the King's consent
The King's confirmation needed for the decrees of Synods
The King's officers not to be excommunicated without his leave
How far these were innovations

divine and human were made to depend.[1] Among these innovations we hear that he would have no Pope acknowledged within his dominions without his consent, and that no Papal letters or bulls were allowed to have any force or currency in his realm, unless they were first seen and approved by himself.[2] When the Archbishop summoned a national Council, its decrees had no force until they were confirmed by the King; it might almost seem that no matters could be even debated without the royal licence.[3] Nor did William allow any of his Barons or officers of state to be excommunicated or subjected to any ecclesiastical censure without his consent.[4] All these things are complained of as innovations on earlier English practice. And in a certain sense they were so. The supremacy of William was not greater in extent than the supremacy of Eadward, but it was exercised in a different way. Under the native English Kings the Church and

in Normanniâ habere solebant in Angliâ servare volens, de hujusmodi personis episcopos, abbates, et alios principes per totam terram instituit, de quibus indignum judicaretur, si per omnia suis legibus, postpositâ omni aliâ consideratione, non obedirent, et si ullus eorum, pro quâvis terreni honoris potentiâ, caput contra eum levare auderet, scientibus cunctis unde, qui, ad quid, assumpti fuerint " This is somewhat in the style of Queen Elizabeth's famous letter to Bishop Cox of Ely

[1] Eadmer, Hist Nov 6  " Cuncta ergo divina simul et humana ejus nutum exspectabant."

[2] Ib  " Non ergo pati volebat quemquam in omni dominatione suâ constitutum Romanæ urbis Pontificem pro Apostolico, nisi se jubente, recipere, aut ejus litteras, si primitus sibi ostensæ non fuissent, ullo pacto suscipere "

[3] Ib  " Primatem quoque regni sui, Archiepiscopum dico Cantuariensem scu Dorobernensem, si coacto generali Episcoporum concilio præsideret, non sinebat quidquam statuere aut prohibere nisi quæ suæ voluntati accommoda et a se primo essent ordinata "

[4] Ib  " Nulli nihilominus Episcoporum suorum concessum iri permittebat ut aliquem de Baronibus suis seu ministris sive incesto sive adulterio sive aliquo capitali crimine denotatum publice, nisi ejus præcepto, implacitaret aut excommunicaret aut ullâ ecclesiastici rigoris pœnâ constringeret "  The practical effect of this stretch of the secular power would probably be very different under William the Conqueror and under William Rufus

the State of England had been absolutely the same thing;[1] decrees in temporal and spiritual matters were made by the same authority; Kings, Earls, and Bishops were elected and deposed by the same all-ruling assembly. Under William all things were tending towards a separation between the ecclesiastical and the temporal power. The Archbishop now held his Synod as a body distinct from the great Gémot of the realm. It almost necessarily followed that the King should assert a distinct authority over ecclesiastical matters in a shape which gave him the aspect of an external, and even a hostile, power. In this sense it was a novelty for the King to control the action of a distinct ecclesiastical body, or distinctly to signify his personal will in ecclesiastical matters. The alleged changes of William became matters of fierce debate from the days of his son onward. But all of them became part and parcel of the Law of England. The supremacy established by William was essentially the same as the supremacy which was contended for by Henry the Second, and finally established by Henry the Eighth. But it is easy to see the weak point of his policy. William, like many other great rulers, established a system which he himself could work, but which smaller men could not work. Under weaker and baser Kings evils showed themselves which under his rule had no place. Under a weak King the distinct ecclesiastical body could assume a degree of independent power which it could not assume in earlier days. Under a wicked King the ecclesiastical powers which William used, on the whole, for good could be, far more easily than under the elder system, perverted into means of oppression and corruption.

But the brighter side of the combined policy of William and Lanfranc must not blind us to the fact that they

[1] See vol. 1. p. 406.

*Margin notes: The supremacy exercised in a new way by William. Changes consequent on the separation of jurisdictions. Controversies from William Rufus onward. Claims of Henry the Second, 1164, of Henry the Eighth, 1534. Weak points of William's system. Darker side of William and Lanfranc.*

440    THE ECCLESIASTICAL SETTLEMENT OF ENGLAND.

CHAP. XIX
Appointment of foreigners.

William's appointments commonly good in themselves.

Un-English feelings of Lanfranc.

His cosmopolitan position.

were, after all, rulers whom force alone imposed on an unwilling people. While William was asserting the rights of the English Crown, he was using its powers to fill all offices of trust, temporal and spiritual, with men of other lands and other tongues. From his own point of view most of his appointments were wisely and conscientiously made; but every Norman Bishop and Abbot was none the less a badge to show that England was a conquered land. And in some cases at least, either William and Lanfranc were mistaken in the men of their choice, or else those men were corrupted by the temptations of their position. Against Thomas of York and Osmund of Salisbury we must set Prelates like Robert of Chester[1] and Thurstan of Glastonbury,[2] and we must not forget that Lanfranc himself did in some degree tread in their ways in the matter of Saint Augustine's.[3] Lanfranc never became a naturalized Englishman, like Osbern of Exeter; he did not advance so far in the same path as Thomas of York. Perhaps his character, hard if lofty, his devotion to interests spread over a field far wider than the Isle of Britain, hindered him from ever thoroughly throwing himself into any purely local or national position. His destiny made him first Norman and then English, but we may suspect that he never heartily assumed either character. In his eyes Normans and English alike were simply instruments for carrying out designs in which Normandy and England seemed but as small specks on the globe. An Italian born, a lawyer of the Empire, a devotee of the Papacy, he brought with him into England a contempt for the barbarous islanders. That contempt he never got over, even when his position drove him to throw aside his former devotion to Rome, and to appear in some sort as the champion of England.

[1] See above, p. 418
[2] See above, p 394.
[3] See above, p 412.

The man who could defend the rights of our island,[1] of CHAP. XIX. its King and of its Primate, himself showed, in his own dealings with Englishmen, too much of the spirit in which his creature had plucked down the tombs of the English Abbots of Saint Alban's.[2] His favour to the monks, combined with his sterling personal virtues, won him the veneration of all English writers, except those who belonged to foundations, like York and Saint Augustine's, with which he had been actually at war.[3] Yet an admiring monk of his own house has left a tale on record which shows how little reverence the stranger Primate felt for the holiest of his native predecessors, and how he was brought to a more worthy frame of mind by another stranger more righteous and better than he. We must for a moment go back to the old home of Lanfranc, to the house which in that generation might seem the chosen nursery of English Metropolitans.

His contempt for the English saints.

The long life of the founder and first Abbot of Bec[4] had at last ended. Herlwin had at last raised a church worthy of the fame of his house, and his most renowned disciple, the Primate of all Britain, had performed the great rite of its hallowing.[5] The next year after this completion of his labours Herlwin went to his rest,[6] and his staff passed to the Prior of his house, the holy Anselm of Aosta.[7] The English possessions of the Abbey caused the new Abbot, in the first year of his appointment, to visit the island of which fourteen years later he was to

Anselm Abbot of Bec 1078-1093

He visits England 1078-1079.

---

[1] Mark the words "insula nostra" in the letter of Lanfranc quoted in p. 437. In the next chapter we shall find him speaking of "nos Angli."

[2] See above, p 400.   [3] See above, pp 351, 412.
[4] See vol ii p 216   [5] See above, p 429   [6] Ib
[7] Will Gem vi 9 "Paucis interpositis diebus electus est Abbas Anselmus pro eo, qui tunc erat Prior ejusdem loci." See more details in Eadmer, Vit Ans i 5

become the chief shepherd.[1] He had much discourse with the Primate, his old friend and brother, on the many matters which were of common interest to both. The converse of Lanfranc and Anselm sets before us a remarkable and memorable pair. The lawyer, the secular scholar, met the divine and the philosopher; the ecclesiastical statesman stood face to face with the saint  The wisdom, conscientious no doubt, but still hard and worldly, which could guide Churches and Kingdoms in troublous times, was met by the boundless love which took in all God's creatures of whatever race or species. The talk of the two friends fell on the ecclesiastical state of England. Lanfranc, as yet unused to the habits and feelings of his flock, was bent on changing many things, some, our English informant tells us, for good reasons, others simply of his own arbitrary will.[2] Amongst other things, the Italian Primate took on him to doubt as to the holiness of some of the English saints and martyrs.[3] A native of a Lombard city, used to fellow-citizens but not to fellow-countrymen, familiar with the local strife of city and city but not with the national struggles of a whole people, Lanfranc doubtless found it hard to understand the feeling which, in the minds of Englishmen, made religion and patriotism but two sides of the same thing, and which gave the honours of martyrdom to men who died in fight against the

---

[1] Eadmer, Vita Anselmi, i 5 40  "Habebat præterea cœnobium plures possessiones in Angliâ, quas pro communi fratrum utilitate necesse erat per Abbatis præsentiam nonnumquam visitari  Ipso itaque suæ ordinationis anno Anselmus in Angliam profectus est"  He goes on to speak of his conferences with Lanfranc.

[2] Ib 42  "Erat Lanfrancus adhuc quasi rudis Anglus, necdumque sederant animo ejus quædam institutiones quas repererat in Angliâ, quapropter quum plures de illis magnâ fretus ratione, tum quasdam mutavit solâ auctoritatis suæ deliberatione"

[3] Ib.  "Angli isti inter quos degimus instituerunt sibi quosdam quos colerent sanctos  De quibus quum aliquando qui fuerint, secundum quod ipsimet referunt, mente revolvo, de sanctitatis eorum merito animum a dubietate flectere nequeo"

heathen invader. Even the reverence paid to the holy ÆIfheah was unintelligible to him. Ælfheah might have been a saint; Lanfranc could not bring himself to look on him as a martyr. He had not died for the faith of Christ; he had only died rather than pay a sum of money which could not be raised save by doing wrong to his people.[1] In the eyes of Lanfranc, the lawyer and administrator, it was no martyrdom to die, not for faith but for charity, not for a theological dogma but for righteousness and mercy. He laid his doubts before the father of dogmatic theology, and from him he learned that dogma did not come before righteousness. If Christ was truth, He was also righteousness; it was as holy a thing to die for righteousness as to die for truth.[2] The Baptist died, not on behalf of a theological proposition, but on behalf of the eternal laws of right and wrong.[3] So did Ælfheah. He died for righteousness as John died for truth, for the truth which he spoke forth at his own peril[4] In the judgement of Anselm, the English Primate was as true a martyr as the Forerunner of the Saviour[5] Lanfranc, with a noble frankness which redeems his earlier prejudices, confessed his error, and declared himself convinced.

CHAP XIX.

He consults Anselm

Argument of Anselm on behalf of Ælfheah

Lanfranc convinced by Anselm.

[1] Eadmer, Vita Anselmi, 1 § 43 "Hunc [Elfegum] non modo inter sanctos verum et inter martyres numerant, licet eum, non pro confessione nominis Christi, sed quia se pecuniâ redimere non voluit, occisum non negent . Quam [pecuniam] nullo pacto poterat habere nisi homines suos eorum [pecuniâ] spoliaret et nonnullos forsitan invisæ mendicitati subjugaret, elegit vitam perdere quam eam tali modo custodire" Lanfranc followed the version in the Chronicles See vol. 1 p 388

[2] Ib 44 "Christus veritas et justitia sit, qui pro justitiâ et veritate moritur pro Christo moritur, qui autem pro Christo moritur, ecclesiâ teste, martyr habetur"

[3] Ib "Beatus Johannes Baptista non quia Christum negare, sed quia veritatem tacere noluit occisus est"

[4] Ib "Beatus Elfegus æque pro justitiâ ut beatus Johannes passus est pro veritate"

[5] Ib "Cur ergo magis de unius quam de alterius vero sanctoque martyrio quisquam ambigat, quum par caussa in mortis perpessione utrumque detineat?"

CHAP XIX.
Ælfheah retains his honours
Comparison of Lanfranc and Anselm.

Saint Ælfheah retained all his honours,[1] and he still keeps his place in the English Kalendar. The man who thus defended the cause of the English martyr was himself to sit in his seat, and thence to rebuke sin in Kings and nobles in the true spirit of the Baptist.[2] Lanfranc, with all his great qualities, lived and died among us as a stranger. His worthier successor, from the moment when he first set foot on our land, won the rank of an adopted Englishman by standing forth as the champion of the saints of England. Stranger as he was, he has won his place among the noblest worthies of our island It was something to be the model of all ecclesiastical perfection; it was something to be the creator of the theology of Christendom; but it was something higher still to be the very embodiment of righteousness and mercy, to be handed down in the annals of humanity as the man who saved the hunted hare[3] and stood up for the holiness of Ælfheah.

Twofold aspect of Lanfranc's administration
Points of reform.
Dark side of his change.
The foreign Prelates.

Looked at, not from a purely English but from a more general point of view, the primacy of Lanfranc, that is, the ecclesiastical administration of William, was certainly a time of advance and reform. The standard of the English Church, intellectual and moral, was, in a cosmopolitan aspect, undoubtedly raised In a strictly national point of view, the case is quite different. The foreign Prelate might be, as a rule, a man of higher

---

[1] Eadmer, Vita Anselmi, 1 5 44 "Firmâ ratione tuâ edoctus beatum Elfegum ut vere magnum et gloriosum martyrem Christi deinceps me colere et venerari ex corde, gratiâ Dei juvante, confido." He then goes on to speak of the honours retained by Saint Ælfheah, at Lanfranc's order, in the church of Canterbury

[2] Anselm, unlike some assertors of ecclesiastical rights, could denounce moral as well as ecclesiastical offences See his discourse with William Rufus in Eadmer, Hist Nov 24.

[3] The two stories which I quoted in my second volume (p 25) from John of Salisbury's Life of Anselm are told also in the earlier Life by Eadmer, ii 3 27

culture than his English predecessor, but he could not have the same sympathy with his flock and with their subordinate pastors   And the reforms of Lanfranc were purchased by much of wrong and hardship in particular cases. We are significantly told that the outrages of Thurstan at Glastonbury did not stand alone.[1]  And, though William's hands were undoubtedly clean from all stain of simony,[2] yet even in his reign, and still more in the reigns of his sons, Bishopricks and Abbeys were turned into the rewards of purely temporal service.[3]  This is an evil which will ever beset every Church whose offices carry with them enough of temporal wealth and dignity to become objects of temporal ambition.  And this evil would assume its worst form in days when services done to the King would commonly mean services done against the people.  Men complained that Prelates were hurled from their seats at the royal will, with small attention either to natural justice or to the forms of the Canon Law.  The English Abbot—it is the inmate of a Norman monastery who speaks—was put aside to make way for one who was not an Abbot but

*Disposal of ecclesiastical offices*

*Unjust deposition of English Prelates*

---

[1] Ord Vit 523 D. "Conventio et profectus fiebat inter commissos greges et archimandritas hujusmodi, qualis inter lupos et bidentes sine defensore solet fieri   Quod facile probari potest ab his qui interfuerunt in Turstino Cadomensi et conventu Glestomensi "

[2] We may, I think, fairly accept the statement of William or Orderic in the death-bed speech (658 C), " Ecclesiasticas dignitates nunquam venum dedi, simoniam detestatus semper refutavi"   He goes on to add, " In electione personarum vitæ meritum et sapientiæ doctrinam investigavi, et, quantum in me fuit, omnium dignissimo Ecclesiæ regimen commendavi," and quotes the examples of Lanfranc and Anselm in proof   Compare the statement of Gregory quoted in p 431, and the words of the Hyde writer (294), " Episcopos et Abbates     absque ullâ consideratione pecuniæ aut nummi susceptione, sed solo divinitatis amore studiose cœpit ordinare "

[3] Ord Vit 523 C, D   " Nonnulli ecclesiastici viri, qui sapientes et religiosi videbantur, regali curiæ pro dignitatibus cupitis obnixe famulabantur, et diversis assentationum modis non sine dedecore religiosæ opinionis adulabantur .    Clerici et monachi nunc terreno principi pro talibus stipendiis inhærebant, et pro temporali commodo multiplex servitium, quod divino cultui non competit, indecenter impendebant"

a Tyrant.[1] In such a state of things one man at least of the conquering race was found to denounce the oppression of England and her native Church and to refuse for himself all share in her spoils. This was Wimund, a Norman monk of the Abbey of Saint Leutfred,[2] who crossed the sea at William's bidding, but who listened unmoved to the royal wish that he should abide in the conquered land and share in the rich benefices which were falling to the lot of others.[3] Wimund turned away from temptation, but he did not turn away in silence. Like the Elias of either dispensation, he dared to speak the truth before princes. Pressed by the King to accept some rich Bishoprick or Abbey, he spoke out his mind before William and his lords. The learning of Wimund was famous; yet we need not believe that he gave the illustrious assembly a complete sketch of universal history, from Nabuchodonosor to Rolf, to prove that Kingdoms are not eternal, and that the power of this world often passes speedily away.[4] But we seem to hear his genuine words when he says that God hates robbery for burnt-offering, and will not accept those who make oblations of the spoils of the poor.[5] He asked by what

*Marginalia:* Protest of Wimund of Saint Leutfred. He refuses preferment in England. His speech before William. He rebukes the oppressors of the English Church and nation

---

[1] Ord. Vit. 523 D. "Prisci Abbates sæcularis comminatione potestatis terrebantur, et sine synodali discussione de sedibus suis injuste fugabantur, pro quibus stipendiarii, non monachi, sed tyranni, contra sanctorum scita canonum intrudebantur"

[2] Ib 524 A. On the history of this monastery, "Crux Heltonis," "Crux Sancti Leufredi vulgo La Croix Saint Leufroy," in the diocese of Evreux, see Neustria Pia, 346

[3] Ib. "Regio jussu accersitus, pontum transfretavit, et oblatum sibi a Rege et proceribus regni onus ecclesiastici regiminis omnino repudiavit"

[4] The speech, whether his own composition or Wimund's, is given at length by Orderic, 524-526 Leaving out these parts, which are merely one of the usual displays of irrelevant learning, the speech is thoroughly worthy the occasion, and we may hope that it fairly represents the substance of what Wimund really said

[5] Ord Vit 524 C "Dicit enim scriptura, 'Immolans ex iniquo, oblatio est maculata.' Et paulo post, 'Qui offert sacrificium ex substantiâ pauperum quasi qui victimat filium in conspectu patris sui.'"

law he could be justified in holding a place of authority among men of whose tongue and manners he was ignorant.[1] With what face could he bear rule among men whose friends and kinsfolk his countrymen had slain with the sword, or had deprived of their heritage and condemned to banishment, to unrighteous imprisonment, or to intolerable slavery?[2] He bade them search the scriptures, and see whether there was any law by which the Lord's flock ought to receive their shepherds at the hands of conquering enemies.[3] How could he, one of an order whose profession it was to forsake the world and to give up all worldly wealth, become a sharer in the spoils which had been won by war and bloodshed? He trembled as he looked on England lying before him as one vast spoil, and he shrank from the touch of its wealth as from a burning fire.[4] He went on to warn the King and his nobles of their danger. He reminded William that none of his fathers had worn a royal crown, that the Kingdom had come to him by no hereditary right, but by the gift of God and the favour of Eadward, to the prejudice of the Ætheling Eadgar and of others who were nearer than himself to the royal stock.[5]

---

[1] Ord. Vit. 524 B. "Omnibus vigili mente perlustratis, non video quâ lege digniter præesse valeam illorum cuneo quorum extraneos mores barbaramque locutionem nescio."

[2] Ib. "Quorum patres carosque parentes et amicos occidistis gladio, vel exhæredatos opprimitis exsilio, vel carcere indebito, vel intolerabili servitio."

[3] Ib. "Scrutamini scripturas, et videte si quâ lege sancitur ut Dominico gregi pastor ab inimicis electus violenter imponatur."

[4] Ib. C. "Hæc et his similia divinæ legis præconia pertractans expavesco, et totam Angliam quasi amplissimam prædam dijudico, ipsamque cum gazis suis, velut ignem ardentem, contingere formido."

[5] Ib. 525. "Nullus patrum tuorum ante te regale stemma gessit, nec hæreditario jure tantum decus tibi provenit, sed gratuitâ largitione omnipotentis Dei et amicitiâ Eduardi consanguinei tui. Edgarus Adelinus, aliique plures ex lineâ regalis prosapiæ orti, secundum leges Hebræorum aliarumque gentium propinquiores sunt hæredes diadematis Anglici." This assertion of the right of Eadgar, to say nothing of the pedantic reference to the laws of the Hebrews, seems more in character with Orderic and his generation than with Wimund.

He spoke in friendship. He bade them think of the judgement to come, lest the prosperity of this world should lead only to weeping and gnashing of teeth in the next. For himself he would go back to Normandy; he would leave the spoils of England to those who loved the rubbish of this world, and he would himself strive after the reward which Christ had promised to the poor in spirit.[1]

<small>William's generous treatment of Wimund</small>

It is to the honour of William that he bore such a rebuke as this with patience, and let the man who dared to utter it go back to his Norman monastery in the full enjoyment of his favour.[2] But baser hearts were filled with wrath at the man who had preferred the poverty of the monk to the wealth of the Bishop, who had denounced the conquest of England as robbery, and had charged every foreign Bishop and Abbot who held an English prelacy with the crime of robbery in his own person.[3] Some time later, the metropolitan throne of Rouen became vacant by the death of Archbishop John.[4] William, consulting the better part of his nature, offered the vacant post to Wimund. But the baser spirits whom Wimund had rebuked clamoured against him, though against a man of such virtue and learning they had nothing to say beyond the convenient charge that he was the son of a priest.[5] Rather than become a subject

<small>Wealth of the country</small>

<small>Death of John Archbishop of Rouen. 1079</small>

<small>William offers the see to Wimund</small>

<small>Opposition of Wimund's enemies</small>

---

[1] Ord. Vit. 525 D. "Normanniam cum vestrâ licentiâ redire dispono, et opimam Angliæ prædam amatoribus mundi quasi quisquilias derelinquo."

[2] Ib 526 A. "Admiratus Rex cum proceribus suis insignis monachi constantiam, supplex ac devotus impendit ei decentem reverentiam, et competenter honoratum jussit eum remeare in Neustriam"

[3] Ib "Auditum est passim . . quod ipse monachilem pauperiem divitiis Episcoporum præposuerit, et quod obtentâ Angliæ in præsentiâ Regis et optimatum ejus rapinam appellaverit, et quod omnes Episcopos vel Abbates qui, nolentibus Anglis, in ecclesiis Angliæ prælati sunt rapacitatis redarguerit"

[4] See above, p 96.

[5] Ord. Vit 526 A. "Æmuli ejus, quos idem vituperaverat, ne Archipræsul fieret quantum potuerunt impedierunt. In tanto viro nil objiciendum invenerunt, nisi quod filius esset presbyteri." See above, p 356

of strife, Wimund determined to forsake his country, and obtained leave of his Abbot Odilo to visit foreign lands.¹ Beyond the bounds both of Normandy and England, he found patrons who could appreciate his merit, and offers of preferment which he could accept with a good conscience. Gregory the Seventh raised him to the rank of Cardinal; Urban the Second bestowed on him the Archbishoprick of Aversa  There, in a Norman city founded on Italian soil,² he at last found a place where he could undertake the care of the souls of men without putting his own soul in jeopardy.

*Wimund declines the Primacy and goes into Italy*

*He is made Cardinal by Gregory, and Archbishop of Aversa by Urban the Second 1088-1089*

While such men as Wimund were to be found among the priesthood of Normandy, it is with delight that we also find at least one equally noble assertor of truth and righteousness among her gallant chivalry  Herlwin did not stand alone in practising the highest Christian virtues beneath the harness of the Norman warrior.³ In English eyes the noblest of the men who followed William must ever be Gulbert of Hugleville, the son of that valiant Richard who had fought so well for his Duke in the ambush of Saint Aubin⁴  A kinsman of William, he had married Beatrice of Valenciennes, who is described as a kinswoman of the Duchess Matilda.⁵ The ties of loyalty and kindred had led him across the sea in the following of his cousin and sovereign. He led his men to William's standard; he fought by his side against the English axes; he shared in all the toils by which England was brought under William's hand.⁶ And when the land was at peace, when

*Gulbert of Hugleville refuses lands in England*

---

¹ Ord Vit 526 B "Ille ab omni avaritiâ purgari volens, et inter exteros paupertate premi quam inter suos dissensiones fovere malens"

² Ib "Hæc urbs tempore Leonis IX Papæ a Normannis qui primo Apuliam incoluerunt constructa est."

³ See vol ii p 218          ⁴ See vol iii p 132

⁵ Ord Vit 606 D "Mathildis Reginæ consobrina erat" She is described as "Beatrix, filia Christiani de Valencenis illustris tribuni"

⁶ Ib "Præfatus heros consanguineus Ducis semper ei fidelis fuit,

VOL IV.          G g

450    THE ECCLESIASTICAL SETTLEMENT OF ENGLAND.

CHAP. XIX.  William was firmly fixed upon his throne, he turned away, refusing lands and honours in the conquered island, and went back to his Norman home, choosing rather to hold with a good right the modest heritage of his fathers than to stain his hands with wealth which was won only by wrong and robbery.[1]  Without forsaking the world like Herlwin, he waged the harder strife of living in the world the life of a Christian man.  Content with their own, Gulbert and Beatrice spent the rest of their days in prayer and almsdeeds, and left behind them a name worthy of higher honour than most of those whose renown is more widely spread.[2]

His later life.

Such were the main results of the ecclesiastical administration of William, carried out by the acute and far-seeing statesman whom he had called from his cell at Bec to be the sharer in his counsels on both sides of the sea. We have now to go back and to take up the general history of William's reign, from the time when he could first be said to be really master of England, to the time when his fortunes began to fade away into the gloom of his later days.

et cum illo præcipua cœtibus suis stipatus in bello Anglico discrimina pertulit."

[1] Ord. Vit. 606 D  "Verum postquam regnum pacatum est, et Guillelmus regnavit, Gulbertus, Rege multas in Angliâ possessiones offerente, Neustriam repetiit, legitimâque simplicitate pollens de rapinâ quidquam possidere noluit. Suis contentus aliena respuit"

[2] Ib. "Cum religiosâ conjuge  . diu vixit, et eleemosynis ac orationibus aliisque bonis operibus usque ad finem laudabiliter studuit."  See more of his good works in 604 C, D, 605 A

## CHAPTER XX.

### THE REVOLTS AGAINST WILLIAM.[1]

#### 1070—1076.

A SPACE of about three years and a half from the time of his first landing at Pevensey had made William master of England. The event of the fight of Senlac gave him possession of the south-eastern portion of the Kingdom. Then, after about a year of comparative peace, two years of ceaseless warfare, beginning with the campaign against Exeter, gave him possession of the whole land from Cornwall to the Scottish border. He was now in every sense King. Not only was there no rival King acknowledged by any part of the country, but William's authority was as fully established everywhere as the authority of any government could be in those times. His Earls and Sheriffs bore rule in every part of England. All land, whether it had been granted out to a stranger or was kept by its former owner, was held by his grant. The tributes and other services due from the boroughs of England were paid to him. and in

Position of William in 1070

1066

1068-1070

Complete establishment of his authority

---

[1] Our authorities for this period remain much the same as before. We have the Worcester and Peterborough Chronicles, Florence and his Northumbrian interpolator, and Orderic, besides the usual subsidiary writers. And as much of this Chapter is concerned with the exploits of Hereward and Waltheof, the mass of mythology which has grown round their names in the false Ingulf and elsewhere has to be tested by the evidence of history.

many cases they had been increased by his authority. The Church was as much under his command as the State; he hurled Bishops from their Bishopricks and Abbots from their Abbeys,[1] and appointed whom he would in their stead. He was fully King; he was perhaps more truly King than any King who had gone before him. No King had ever had the whole land, and those who bore rule in every corner of it, so thoroughly under his control. The process by which William had gained his power was harsh and wrongful; it had inflicted unutterable wretchedness on the whole land; parts of the land it had turned into a wilderness. The way in which his power was used was systematically stern, occasionally cruel. But the Kingdom which he had won gained in the end from his winning of it. It was William's conquest and William's rule which fixed for ever that England should remain a Kingdom one and indivisible.

From this time then whatever opposition William had still to face took the form of revolts or insurrections. Those who now fought against him were no longer striving to keep something which they had, but striving to win back something which they had lost. Their right so to do I should be the last to dispute. The right to resist an oppressive, above all a foreign, government is the groundwork of all freedom. It is undoubtedly a right to be exercised with the greatest caution, and only in the extremest cases. A hopeless revolt, where success is impossible and where failure only increases oppression, is undoubtedly a crime. But we must remember that many an enterprise which seems hopeless to men who look at it calmly from a distance does not seem hopeless to those who are engaged in it. And we must also remember that in the eleventh century men's local feelings were at

---

[1] Chron Petrib 1087 "Biscopas he sætte of heora biscoprice and abbodas of heora abbodrice"

least as strong as their national feelings. An enterprise which was wholly hopeless as an attempt to drive William out of the land was not necessarily hopeless as an attempt to win back the independence of some particular district. From our point of view we should look on the lasting dismemberment of the Kingdom as a greater evil than its misgovernment at a particular time. We should argue that to assert a precarious independence for a particular district could lead only to making the bondage of the whole land heavier The men of the eleventh century did not look at matters in this light. They would have been best pleased to shut out the stranger from every corner of the land. But failing this, it was in their eyes a worthy object to rescue any corner of the land from his grasp. From their own point of view then, the men who, in the cause of England, revolted against William were as worthy of English sympathy as those who at an earlier stage withstood him. But we must bear in mind the historical difference between their several positions. The defence of Exeter was resistance to a foreign invader; the defence of Ely was a revolt against a *de facto* King of the land.

The time with which we have now to deal is marked by several revolts against William's authority both in his insular and in his continental conquests. And the same time brings us also to the extension of William's power in Britain beyond the limits of the English Kingdom. We have now to see his assumption of the Imperial as well as the royal authority. But during this period his strife is wholly with his own discontented subjects and vassals. This character distinguishes it in a marked way from a later period, in which he had to struggle at once against his own feudal lord and against foes in his own household. The wars and revolts of this time are often

454    THE REVOLTS AGAINST WILLIAM.

CHAP. XX.

Revolt of the Fenland 1070-1071
Troubles in Northumberland and Scotland. 1070-1072
Revolt of Maine. 1074.
Fate of Waltheof 1075-1076

closely connected with one another; still it is easy to arrange them in several well-defined groups. There is the revolt of the fen country, which has made the name of Hereward immortal. Partly contemporary with this, and closely connected with it, are the renewed troubles of Northumberland and Scotland. We then cross the sea to trace the revolt of Maine, and its recovery chiefly by English arms. We lastly come to the abortive conspiracy which led to the great personal crime of William's reign, the execution of Waltheof.

§ 1. *The Revolt of the Fen Country.*

1070–1071.

Osbeorn and Christian at Ely May, 1070
The men of the fen country join them.

Kingship of Swend probably designed.

We must now go back to the last stage of William's great Northern campaign. The Danish fleet under Earl Osbeorn and Bishop Christian was, by the agreement with William, allowed to pass the winter in England and to plunder the coasts.[1] It was stretching this licence to the uttermost when they appeared in the waters of Ely in the month of May.[2] The people of the district at once flocked to them, believing that they would win the whole land. The Chronicler speaks of them as the English folk of all the fenland; but the Danish blood was strong in those parts, and we can quite understand that here, no less than in Yorkshire, the followers of Christian and Osbeorn would be welcomed as countrymen.[3] We hear nothing of Eadgar or his cause; the impression which

[1] See above, p 319

[2] The plunder of Peterborough, presently to be spoken of, took place on June 2  The first appearance of the fleet in those parts would therefore doubtless be in May

[3] Chron. Petrib 1070 "Þa comen into Elig Christien þa Densce bisceop and Osbearn eorl, and þa Densce huscarles mid heom, and þet Englisce folc of eall þa feonlandes comen to heom, and wendon þæt hi sceoldon winnon eall þæt land"

the story gives us is that the men of the fenland were ready to receive Swend as King.¹ At this moment we hear for the first time of one whose mythical fame outshines all the names of his generation, and of whom the few historical notices make us wish that details could be filled in from some other source than legend. Suddenly, without preparation or introduction of any kind, we find ourselves face to face with the renowned but shadowy form of Hereward. With no name has fiction been more busy.² One tale, the wildest of all, has made the famous outlaw a son of the great Earl Leofric. Romancers probably did not stop to think that this was to make him a brother of Ælfgar, an uncle of Eadwine and Morkere, an uncle by marriage of King Gruffydd and of King Harold.³ In truth, nothing whatever is known of his parentage; there is no more evidence for making him the son of an unknown Leofric of Bourne than there is for making him a son of the renowned Earl of the Mercians. Both the voice of legend and the witness of the great Survey agree in connecting Hereward with Lincolnshire, but they differ as to the particular spot of the shire in which he is to be quartered. Legend also has forgotten a fact which the document has preserved, namely, that the hero of the fenland did not belong wholly to Lincoln-

*Appearance of HEREWARD*

*Legendary accounts of his birth and exploits*

*His property in Lincolnshire and Warwickshire.*

---

¹ Yet, uncomfortable as it is to depart from the Chronicles, I confess that I know not how to accept the statement of the Peterborough Chronicler (1070) that Swend came this year in person into the Humber, "Þa on þam ilcan geare com Swegn cyng of Denmarcan into Humbran." Nothing however is said to have followed his appearance. We directly after hear of the coming of Osbeorn and Christian to Ely.

² Besides the account in the false Ingulf, we have the Gesta Herewardi Saxonis, published in M. Francisque Michel's Chroniques Anglo-Normandes, which is essentially the same which has been worked into the Liber Eliensis published by Mr. D. J. Stewart in 1848. There are also some notices in Geoffrey Gaimar.

³ I shall examine the chief statements of the mythical accounts, as well as the few authentic notices of Hereward which we have, chiefly in Domesday and the Chronicles, in Appendix OO.

shire, but that he was also a landholder in the distant shire of Warwick. But the Survey has preserved another fact with which the legendary versions of his life have been specially busy. Hereward, at some time it would seem before the period of his exploits, had fled from his country.[1] But the date and cause of his flight, whether he had drawn on himself the wrath of Eadward, of Harold, or of William, is utterly uncertain. On such a foundation as this a mighty superstructure could not fail to be piled up. The banished hero is of course carried into various parts of the world, and is made to work various wonderful exploits, possible and impossible In one tale he encounters in Northumberland a mighty bear, who, it is plainly insinuated, was near akin to Earl Siward and his son Waltheof.[2] In another he is brought across a native prince of Cornwall, whose name Domesday has forgotten to record among the long list of English land-owners who held the West-Welsh peninsula in the days of King Eadward.[3] But Ireland and Flanders were such common resorts of English exiles that the tales which carry Hereward into those countries have distinct probability on their side. And if any one chooses to believe that he came back from Flanders in company with a Flemish wife, such a belief in no way contradicts history. But leaving fables and guesses aside, we know enough of Hereward to make us earnestly long to know more. There is no doubt that he defended the last shelter of English freedom against the

---

[1] See Appendix OO

[2] No smaller pedigree can be inferred when we read (Chron. Ang.-Norm ii 7) of "illum maximum ursum qui aderat, quem incliti ursi Norweye fuisse filium, ac formatum . pedes illius et caput ad fabulam clavorum affirmabant, sensum humanum habentem, et loquelam hominis intellectricem, ad doctum ad bellum; cujus igitur pater in silvis fertur puellam rapuisse, et ex eâ Biernum Regem Norweye genuisse" (See vol i pp 468, 586 ) The editor remarks, "locus est corruptissimus"

[3] See above, p 171.

might of William. His heart failed him not when the hearts of the noblest of the land quaked within them. Our most patriotic Latin annalist adorns his name with the standing epithet with which he adorns the name of Harold,[1] and our native Chronicler records his deeds in words which seem borrowed from the earlier record of the deeds of Ælfred.[2]

The authentic narrative does not tell us in what relation Hereward stood to the movement on the part of the fenmen of which Ely was the centre. Neither can we make out the exact position of Abbot Thurstan of Ely and his monks. Thurstan was the friend and nominee of Harold,[3] so that the legend which represents him as active in the revolt has probability on its side; but nothing can be said for certain. Our authentic accounts at this stage deal less with the monastery of Ely than with the not far distant monastery of Peterborough. The death of Brand, the Abbot who had succeeded the patriot Leofric, has been already recorded,[4] as well as the appointment of his successor in the Easter Gemót of the past year. He was of course a stranger, but his Norman name, Turold,[5] a form of the Danish Thorold, was a name still familiar in that part of England, one which had been borne by an English Sheriff who is recorded as a benefactor of the house of Crowland.[6] He is spoken of by the local Chronicler as a very stern man,[7] and the known details of his earlier history fully bear out the character. He was a monk of

CHAP. XX

Position of Abbot Thurstan and the monks of Ely

Death of Abbot Brand November 27, 1069

Turold appointed Abbot of Peterborough April 4 ? 1070.

---

[1] "Herewardus vir strenuissimus" says Florence (1071), like "strenuus Dux Haroldus." See vol ii pp 393, 537.

[2] The words in the Chronicles, 1071, "buton Herewarde ane," repeat those in 878, "butan þam cyninge Ælfrede."

[3] See vol iii p 69  [4] See above, p 335

[5] Chron Petrib 1070 "Se cyng hæfde gifen þæt abbotrice an Frencisce abbot, Turolde wæs gehaten"

[6] See above, p 214 and Domesday, 346

[7] Chron Petrib 1070 "He wæs swiðe styrne man."

458    THE REVOLTS AGAINST WILLIAM.

CHAP XX.
His former career at Malmesbury.

Fécamp, who had been placed by William over the Abbey of Malmesbury, its English Abbot Brihtric having been translated backwards to the less important Abbey of Burton.[1] His rule at Malmesbury was tyrannical, and the story runs that William picked him out, as being more of a soldier than a monk, as the fittest man to rule the great house of Peterborough, now that it was threatened by Hereward and his fellow outlaws in the fens[2] In conformity with his character, he is now described as coming at the head of an armed force of Frenchmen to take possession of his monastery.[3] He had reached Stamford,

He comes with an armed force to Stamford June 1 ? 1070
Hostile feelings of the neighbourhood.

when he heard of the state in which he was likely to find the house over which he was set to rule. In the eyes of English outlaws or patriots, a monastery under the command of a Norman Abbot, especially of an Abbot who came surrounded by a foreign military force, was looked on as part of the enemy's country.[4] One of our few notices of Hereward's earlier life sets him before us as one not specially remarkable for respect towards ecclesiastical property,[5] and his feelings against the foreign Prelate would doubtless be still more bitter, if the legend has any ground

[1] Will Malm Gest Pont 420 " Willelmus . Rex . . Turoldum quemdam Fiscamnensem monachum, qui eum magnis demeruerat obsequiis, viventi Brihtrico intrusit. Verumtamen postmodum rem perperam factam intelligens, dolensque se ambitione festinantis circumventum, dono abbatiæ de Burhtunâ exsulantis damnum consolatus est "

[2] Ib " Idem Turoldus, dum tyrannidem in subjectos ageret, ad Burh a Rege translatus est, abbatiam opulentam, sed tunc quæ a latrunculis, duce quodam Herewardo, infestaretur, qui inter paludes sita erat ' Per splendorem' inquit ' Dei, quia magis se agit militem quam abbatem, inveniam ei comparem, qui assultus ejus accipiat Ibi virtutem suam et militiam experiatur, ibi prœlia proludat ' "

[3] Chron Petrib 1070 " He wæs cumen þa into Stanforde mid ealle hise Frencisce menn "

[4] This feeling is plainly set forth in the words with which the Chronicler brings in his notice of the appointment of Turold , " Þa herdon þa munecas of Burh sægen þæt heora agene menn woldon hergon þone mynstre   þæt wæs forðan þet hi herdon sæcgen þet se cyng," &c

[5] See Appendix OO

for speaking of him as a nephew of the late English Abbot Brand.[1] The news came to the monks of Peterborough that a motley force, made up of outlaws, of their own men, and of the Danish allies, was coming to harry the monastery. This, says the Chronicler, was Hereward and his gang.[2] This is the first mention of Hereward's name in authentic history, but it is a mention which shows that his name was already well known at Peterborough. While the gang was on its march, a prudent churchward, Yware by name, acting by the counsel of the monks,[3] took out of the minster such books and other moveable articles as he could, to preserve them from robbery. He then before daybreak sent word to Turold, asking for his peace and protection, and telling him that the outlaws were coming.[4] This was not the way either to stave off or to soften the coming attack. The outlaws had now fair ground for looking on the monks as traitors to the national cause, and for giving out that whatever they did was done as good service to the monastery itself, which was betrayed by its present inmates.[5] Early in the morning the outlaws came with many ships, and the monks at first strove to keep them from entering the monastic precinct. Thus provoked, they took to the weapon so familiar to their Norman enemies; they set fire

CHAP. XX.

Hereward heads the outlaws and the men of the monastery

They march to Peterborough

Yware hides the treasure and sends word to Turold

June 1, 1070

Hereward plunders the monastery

June 2, 1070

---

[1] So the false Ingulf in Gale, p. 70; Gesta Herewardi, Chron Ang-Norm ii 39

[2] Chron Petrib 1070 "þæt wæs Hereward and his genge" These seem to be specially the rebellious tenants of the Abbey, "heora agene menn," but we directly after hear of "þa utlaga" and of "þa Denesce menn" as having a share in the work.

[3] Ib "Þa wæs þære an cyreceward, Yware wæs gehaten" Presently, after mentioning the articles removed and the message sent to Turold, the Chronicler adds, "þæt he dyde call be þære munece ræde" On the meaning of this passage and the force of the word þæt, see Mr Earle's note, Parallel Chronicles, p 348

[4] Ib "And ferde sona ær dæg to þone abbot Turolde, and sægde him þæt he sohte his griðe, and cydde him hu þa utlages sceolden cumen to Burh"

[5] Ib "Sægdon þæt hi hit dyden for ðes mynstres holdscipe"

460                THE REVOLTS AGAINST WILLIAM.

CHAP. XX  to the monks' houses and to the whole town, and all was burned save one house.[1] By the same means they made their way through the Bolhithe Gate, the southern gate of the monastery, and the monks now sought for their peace and protection.[2] But it was too late. The whole band, outlaws, Danes, and vassals, whether loyal or rebellious, burst into the minster. They climbed up to the great rood and carried off its ornaments of gold;[3] they climbed up the steeple, and carried off the gold and silver pastoral staff[4] which was there hidden.[5] Shrines, roods, books, vestments, coined money,[6] treasures of every kind, were carried away to the ships and were taken to Ely. The monks were all scattered abroad—an act which seems to be specially attributed to the Danish allies—all save one sick brother in the infirmary.[7] This fact seems at once to speak well for the health of the brotherhood, and to mark the respect which even the outlaws showed to buildings and persons that might specially claim their forbearance. Presently came Abbot Turold with a hundred and sixty armed Frenchmen. The enemy had already set sail, and he found only the one sick monk, and the empty church standing

Turold reaches Peterborough June 2.

---

[1] Chron. Petrib 1070 "þa lægdon hi fyr on and forbærndon ealle þa munece huses and eall þa tun, buton ane huse" On the Norman passion for setting fire to everything, see vol. i p 224, vol iii pp. 155, 560

[2] Ib. "þa comen hi þurh fyre in æt Bolhiðe geate, and þa munecas comen heom togeanes, beaden heom grið"

[3] Ib "Ac hi na rohten na þing, geodon into þe mynstre, clumben upp to þe halge rode, namen þa þe kynehelm of ure Drihtnes heafod, eall of smeate golde, namen þa þet fotspure þe wæs undernæðen his fote, þæt wæs eall of read golde"

[4] See vol ii p. 437, for the hallowing of this steeple

[5] Chron Petrib u s. "Þæt hæcce þe þær wæs behid, hit wæs eall of gold and of seolfre"

[6] The Chronicler specially mentions "swa manega gersumas on sceat" Something had perhaps escaped the pillaging of last Lent

[7] Chron. Petrib u s "Beleaf þær nan butan ân munec, he wæs gehaten Leffwine Lange, he læi seoc in þa sacræman in." "Secræ man," it is written by Mr Earle

in the midst of the blackened ruins of the monastery. But the brotherhood gradually assembled, and divine service was again begun in the minster after ceasing for one week.[1]

At this point the Chronicler places a reconciliation between the two Kings, William and Swend.[2] But we may suspect that nothing really happened beyond some further negotiation between William and Osbeorn, and perhaps a further bribe to the Danish Earl. At all events, soon after their exploit at Peterborough the Danes sailed away from Ely, and, after showing themselves for two days in the Thames, they sailed towards Denmark,[3] laden with the wealth which the faithless vassals of Saint Peter had helped to carry away from his minster. But, as the tale evidently implies, their sacrilege was not to go unpunished. While they were in the midst of the sea a mighty storm arose and drove the ships hither and thither, some to Ireland, some to Norway, some to their own shores of Denmark. These last landed at a King's town whose name seems to have been unknown to our Chronicler. The treasures of Peterborough, including the precious staff, were placed in the church of the town, but, through the drunkenness of its guardians, the church and all that was in it was burned in the night, and the relics of the wealth of the Golden Borough were lost for ever.[4] Osbeorn, who had

*Divine service restored June 9*

*Alleged reconciliation of William and Swend.*

*Departure of the Danes. June 24, 1070*

*Fate of the plunderers of Peterborough*

---

[1] Chron Petrib 1070 "And þus se abbot Turolde com to Burh, and þa munecas comen þa ongean, and dydan Christes þeudom in þære cyrce, þæt ær hæfde standen fulle seofeniht forutan ælces cynnes riht"

[2] Ib "Þa twegen kyngas Willelm and Swægn wurðon sæhtlod"

[3] Ib "Þa þæs sumeres com þet hð norðan of Humbran into Tæmese, lagon þær twa niht, and heoldan syððon to Dænmercan" The way in which this is brought in shows plainly that the account of Hereward's doings is a local insertion in an earlier Chronicle, which must have been nearly the same as the extant Worcester Chronicle See Earle, Parallel Chronicles.

[4] The name of the town is left a blank The account then goes on, "Þa syððon þurh heora gemelest and þurh heora druncenhed on an' niht forbærnde þa cyrce and eall þet þær innæ wæs Þus wæs se mynstre of Burch

so shamefully betrayed the hopes of England, and who had brought his great expedition to such a pitiful end, met with an angry reception from his brother King Swend. He was banished from Denmark on account of the bribe which he had taken from William.[1] A spiritual censure also fell upon the English offenders. Bishop Æthelric, seemingly from his prison at Westminster, put forth an excommunication against all who had any share in the plunder of Peterborough[2] It is hard to see on what principle of Canon Law a Bishop without a diocese could claim to exercise any such jurisdiction. But the long sojourn of Æthelric at Peterborough may have been felt to give him some kind of control over the house and its belongings. His censure of the offenders may even have been required by William as an act of policy; it certainly would have a deeper effect on the minds of the men of the fenland than any censure put forth by Abbot Turold or Bishop Remigius.

After this exploit, which the most zealous patriotism can hardly bring itself to look on as glorious, we hear nothing of the doings of the revolted English during the remainder of the year or during the following winter. Our only notice belongs to quite another part of Eng-

forbærnd and forhærgod, Ælmihtig God hit gemiltse þurh his mycele mildhertniesse "

[1] Flor Wig 1070 "Imminente autem festivitate S Johannis Baptistæ comes Esbernus, cum classe quæ in Humbræ flumine hiemaverat, Danemarciam adiit, sed frater suus Rex Danorum Suanus, illum, propter pecuniam, quam contra voluntatem Danorum a Rege Willelmo acceperat, exlegavit "

[2] Chron. Petrib 1070. "þa herde Ægelric biscop þet gesecgon, þa amansumede he ealle þa men þa þæt yfel dæde hæfden don " The Worcester version would seem to place the excommunication before the plundering, and to make it refer to some earlier wrong done to Æthelric himself personally, " And man hergade þæt mynster æt Burh, þæt wæron þa menn þe se biscop Ægelric ær amansumade, *forþon þe hi namon þær eall þat he ahte* "

land. Eadric the Wild, the hero of the western march, now made his submission to the King.¹ This event is mentioned immediately after the retirement of the Danish fleet, and in a way which might suggest that the two things were in some way connected. Perhaps Eadric thought that, with the failure of Danish help, all hope for England had passed away, and that there was nothing to be done but to make what terms he could with the Conqueror. For the next year our accounts, though not easy to reconcile, are comparatively full, and the Norman account is decidedly more discreditable to William than the English. And the renewed troubles of this year seem to be spoken of as the beginning of a new and worse state of things, a state of greater wretchedness for the conquered.² The centre of the insurrectionary or patriotic movement was the Isle of Ely. It is therefore almost certain that the Isle had been held by the insurgents ever since the appearance of the Danish fleet in those waters in the summer of the year before. No part of Britain could be more easily defended. Before the great works of drainage which have changed the course of the rivers and wholly altered the face of the

*Eadric the Wild submits to William. June— August, 1070.*

*Norman and English versions of the events of the year 1071.*

*Revolt of the Isle of Ely.*

*Description of the country.*

---

¹ Flor. Wig. 1070 "Vir strenuissimus Edricus, cognomento Silvaticus, cujus supra meminimus, cum Rege Willelmo pacificatur." The submission of Eadric is placed between the departure of Osbeorn in June and the consecration of Lanfranc in August.

² Orderic's account of the defence of Ely and the fate of Eadwine and Morkere (521) follows immediately on the description of the momentary reconciliation of English and Normans (see above, p 327) A little way on (523), after describing the events of the year 1071, he gives a special picture of Norman oppression Now with the death of Eadwine the History of William of Poitiers ended, and Orderic was from that point left to his own guidance The favourable picture of Norman rule may therefore come from William, and the unfavourable one may be Orderic's own But the account of the Conqueror's dealings with Eadwine and Morkere also comes within the range of the Archdeacon of Lisieux, and the tone of this account, while trying to clear William in some degree by throwing blame on evil counsellors, is on the whole decidedly unfavourable to him.

464      THE REVOLTS AGAINST WILLIAM.

CHAP XX. country, the Isle of Ely was strictly an island. It is a tract slightly raised above the level of the surrounding wateis, and at the point where the great minster still stands it may be said to rise to the dignity of a hill.[1] The only means of approach weie the roads of Roman and earlier date, roads which, in such a country, necessarily took the form of causeways. The great Akeman Street led straight to Ely from William's newly built castle of Cambiidge,[2] while another road, of uncertain date, led from his other fortress of Huntingdon,[3] itself connected with Cambridge by the Roman Via Devana. But the main approach was not by either of these great roads, but at a point called Aldreth, a corruption of the name of the patron saint Æthelthryth, where the ancient course of the Ouse, now shallow indeed, is crossed by a causeway and

Approach to the Isle at Aldreth

---

[1] On the geography of this district see Professor C. C Babington's Ancient Cambridgeshire, and the map  I learned much from a personal examination of the ground between Cambridge and Ely in June, 1870, in company with the Professor and with Mr Bonney of Saint John's College

A vivid description of the whole country, of which the Ely fenland is only a part, is given by Orderic (537 D), but it is copied from the Life of Saint Guthlac by Felix of Crowland, whom Orderic has oddly confounded with Felix Bishop of the East-Angles (537 A), who died in 647 (Bæda, ii. 15, iii 30) in the century before Guthlac lived  The extract is given in Wright's Biographia Britannica Litteraria, i 248  "Est in mediterraneorum Anglorum Britanniæ partibus immensæ magnitudinis acerrima palus, quæ a Grontæ fluminis ripis incipiens, haud procul a castello quod dicunt nomine Gronte, nunc stagnis, nunc flactiris, interdum nigris fusis vaporibus et laticibus, necnon crebris insularum nemoribus intervenientibus, et flexuosis rivigarum ab austro in aquilonem mari tenus longissimo tracta protenditur.",
An Old-English version, said to be by Ælfric, follows, which begins thus, "Ys on Bretone lande sum fenn unmætre mycelnysse þæt on-ginneð fram Grante ea naht feor fram þære cestre ðy ylcan nama ys nemned Granteceaster"  The remarkable thing is that Camboritum, which in Bæda's day was still "a waste chester" (see above, p 313), is spoken of as if it were an actual town  Felix and Bæda were contemporary, but Felix must have been the younger man, and it is just possible that the town may have been set up again before he wrote.

[2] See above, p 221            [3] See above, p 222

THE FENLAND
IN THE ELEVENTH CENTURY.
ILLUSTRATING THE CAMPAIGN
OF HEREWARD.

Scale of Miles

*Little Ouse*

Brandon

Burwell
Exning
ICKNIELD WAY
DYKE

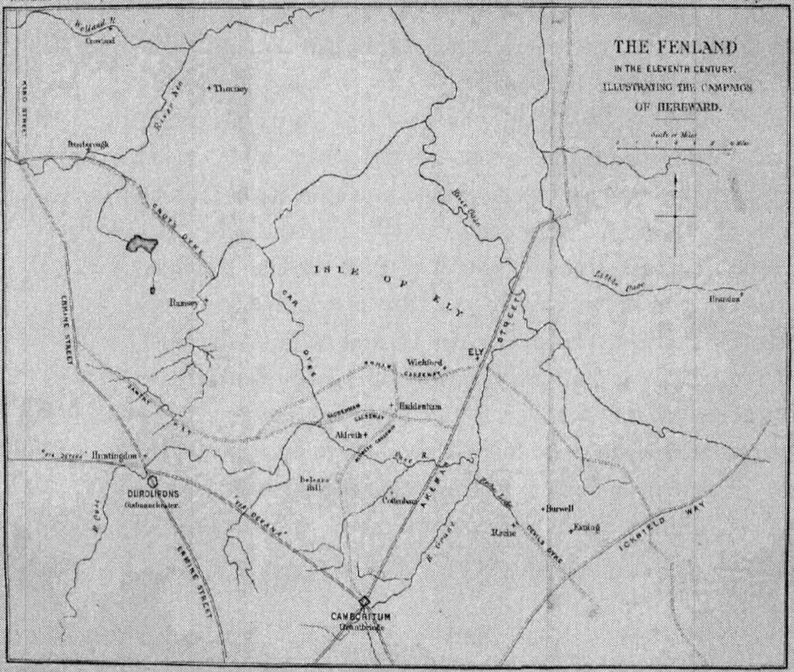


For the Delegates of the Clarendon Press.

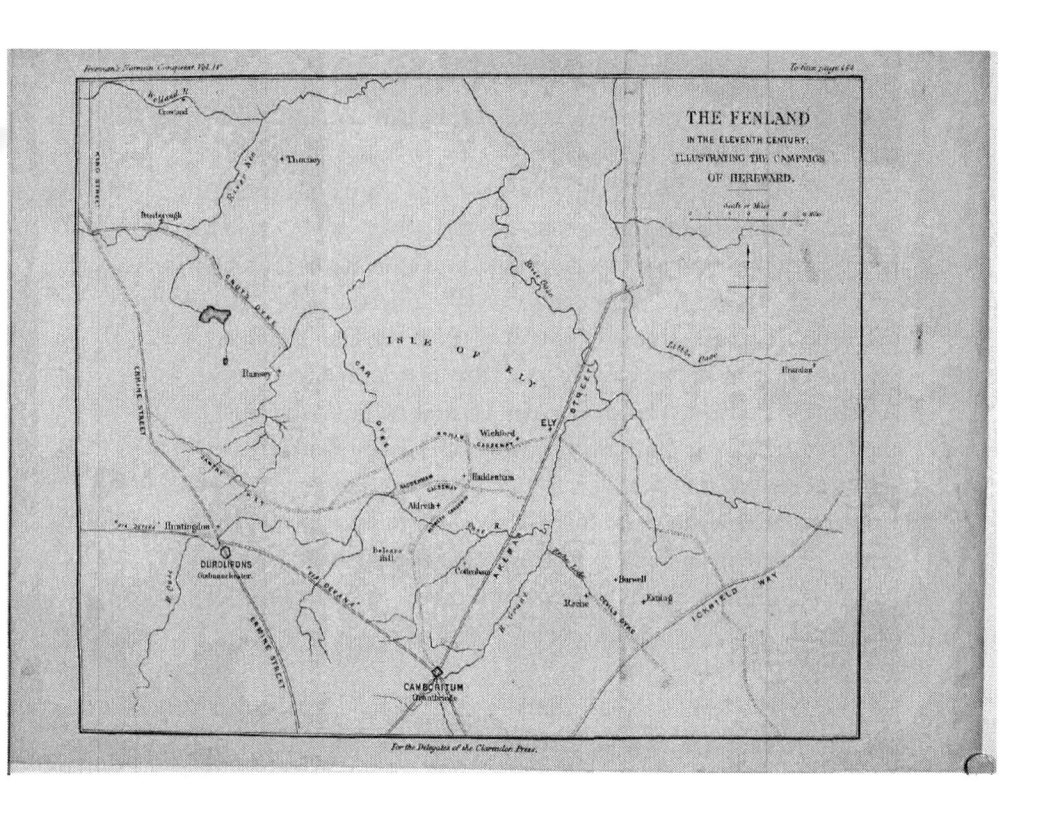

bridge.[1] As the causeway cuts through what seems to be a British site, the camp which bears the strange name of Belsar's Hill, it can hardly fail to be itself of Roman work.[2] It was here that the Isle was most accessible to an enemy, and the course of the river was further protected by a causeway forming an angle with that by which the bridge is approached.[3] Within the Isle then, in a position as strong in its way as if it had stood on the height of Laon or Lincoln, the revolted inhabitants of the fen district, probably with Hereward as their chief, had remained without interruption during the winter. In the course of the next year an altogether new turn was given to affairs when the force of the outlaws was strengthened, if strengthened it was, by the accession of several men of higher rank and renown from other parts of England.

*Hereward in the Isle.*

While the conquest of Northern England was going on, Eadwine and Morkere, whose treason had blighted the first attempt at resistance within their own Earldoms,[4] were dwelling in William's court in a character which we may call at pleasure that of guests, prisoners, or hostages. At last they felt dissatisfied with their condition. Bad men, we are told, stirred up strife between them and the King.[5] William, so runs another account,

*Position of Eadwine and Morkere*

---

[1] On Aldreth causeway, see Ancient Cambridgeshire, p. 49 In the Gesta Herewardi (57) the place is called "Abrehede .... ubi minus aquis et palude præcingitur [insula]" In the Ely History, 229, it is "Alrehethe, ubi aquæ insulæ minus latæ sunt" The bridge, when I was there, looked very much as if it had been broken down by Hereward and not mended since.

[2] See Ancient Cambridgeshire, 49

[3] Haddenham Causeway, called from a village in its course, with a large and striking church, but containing nothing of early date.

[4] See above, p 192.

[5] Ord. Vit 521 A. "Rex Guillelmus, consilio pravorum male usus, laudi suæ damnum ingessit"

VOL. IV.   H h

CHAP XX.
They leave William's court and revolt April? 1071

English and Norman accounts of Eadwine's death.

thought to change their state of honourable restraint into one of actual dungeons and fetters. They now left his court and openly revolted.[1] We have no details of their doings, but they seem to have engaged in vague and purposeless attempts at insurrection, which could not fail to come to nothing. They wandered about in woods and fields[2] till they parted company. Eadwine attempted to reach the friendly court of Scotland,[3] but he was slain on his way thither. The English account simply says that he was basely slain by his own men.[4] The Norman version is fuller. The English traitors, three brothers, followers of the Earl and admitted to his special favour, betrayed him to the Normans.[5] In what part of England he was overtaken we are not told, but it must have been somewhere not very far from the coast, as an unusually high tide hindered him from crossing a river.[6] This description would suit many spots in his own former Earldom, and still more in that of his brother. It is therefore in vain to guess where Eadwine's last, and nearly

[1] Flor. Wig 1071. "Comites Edwinus et Morkarus, quia Rex Willelmus eos in custodiam ponere voluit, latenter e curiâ ejus fugerunt, et aliquamdiu contra illum rebellaverunt"

[2] Chron Wig 1072, Chron Petrib 1071 "Her Eadwine eorl and Morkere eorl hlupon út and mislice ferdon on wuda and on feldon" This must be the time to which Orderic really refers when he says (521 B) that Eadwine "sex mensibus a Scotis et Guallis vel Anglis auxilia sibi quæsivit," but he wrongly places the wanderings and death of Eadwine after the surrender of his brother The six months may possibly help us to a date for Eadwine's revolt—six months before the surrender of Ely in October See below, p 480

[3] Flor. Wig 1071.

[4] Chron Petrib. 1071. "Eadwine eorl wearð ofslagen arhlice fram his agenum mannum" The Worcester Chronicle and Florence leave out the adverb.

[5] Ord Vit 521 B. "Interea tres fratres, qui ei familiares præcipuique satellites erant, Normannis eum prodiderunt."

[6] Ib. "Ad hoc facinus exæstuatio marina Normannos adjuvit, quæ ad rivulum quemdam Eduinum morari coegit, eique fugam penitus ademit."

his first, passage of arms may have happened.¹ At the head of twenty horsemen the Earl gallantly withstood the attacks of a party of Normans, till he was slain, as it would seem, by the hands of the three traitors.² They brought his head to William, hoping of course to win his favour, but, as such traitors have usually been dealt with from the days of David onward, their reward was outlawry instead of honour.³

Thus died the Earl of the Mercians, the grandson of Leofric and Godgifu, the brother-in-law of Harold. The historian who records his death waxes eloquent on his high birth, his personal beauty, his piety, his bounty to the clergy and the poor.⁴ The news of his death, we are told, caused grief throughout all England, not among the English only, but among the Normans and French, who wept for him as for a comrade or a kinsman.⁵ Of the feelings of the royal maiden who, like so many other royal maidens, had been made the sport of her father's policy, we hear nothing. William himself—it is the last of his acts recorded by his panegyrist—shed tears over Eadwine's lifeless head.⁶ All this may be; Eadwine doubtless had many winning personal qualities, and knew how to make himself the ornament and darling of a court. But all this does not relieve him from the guilt of betraying every cause which he undertook, and breaking his faith to every lord to whom he plighted it. Those were days in which men both drew and sheathed their swords somewhat hastily;

*CHAP XX*
*He is betrayed and killed by his own men*

*His character.*

---

¹ On the question whether Eadwine ever entered the Isle of Ely, see Appendix OO

² Ord Vit 521 B "Tres fratres ipsi eumdem cum xx equitibus toto nisu sese defendentem occiderunt"

³ Ib. C. "Proditores, qui pro favore illius ei caput domini sui deferebant, severus in exsilium expulit."

⁴ See above, p 182.

⁵ See above, p 180.

⁶ Ord. Vit 521 C "Rex Guillelmus, compertâ proditione quâ sæpe fatus Merciorum Consul perierat, pietate motus flevit"

468                THE REVOLTS AGAINST WILLIAM.

CHAP XX. they were days in which oaths were lightly taken and lightly broken. But even in those days it must have been a special preeminence in evil to have been faithless alike to Eadward, to Harold, to Eadgar, and to William.

Morkere joins the insurgents at Ely

The surviving son of Ælfgar, Morkere, still perhaps holding in name the Earldom to which he had been called in Eadward's days by the Northumbrian rebels,[1] seems hitherto to have acted mainly under the influence of his brother.[2] Now that Eadwine was dead, he showed, for a while at least, a higher spirit. He joined the outlaws in the Isle, which had now become the resort of the more daring spirits from every part of England. Legend indeed has peopled the Camp of Refuge, as it has been romantically called, with a crowd of persons who undoubtedly were not there. We hear of Earl Eadwine, notwithstanding his death, of Archbishop Stigand, notwithstanding his imprisonment at Winchester,[3] of Abbot Frithric of Saint Alban's, whose name at once plunges us into an atmosphere of myth.[4]

Legend of the Camp of Refuge

Presence of Siward Barn and of Bishop Æthelwine.

But there is no doubt as to the presence of Morkere,[5] of the Northumbrian Thegn Siward Barn,[6] and of Æthelwine Bishop of Durham, who left his shelter in Scotland to share the dangers of his countrymen.[7] And there can be little doubt that the life and soul of the defence was Hereward himself. Though we cannot venture to accept a single

Position of Hereward

---

[1] See vol. II. p. 485      [2] See above, p 20.
[3] See above, p 333         [4] See Appendix NN.
[5] Chron Wig 1072; Petrib 1071 "And Morkere mid scype gewende to Helig, and þær com Ægelwine biscoep and Sigwarð Barn, and fela hund manna mid heom" Florence (1071) adds, "*Herewardus vir strenuissimus,* cum multis aliis" Simeon (1071. 89, Hinde) adds of Æthelwine and Siward, "de Scottiâ renavigantes illo advenerant" The account of Orderic (521 A) must be taken for what it is worth; "Rex Guillelmus .... fraudulenter inclitum Comitem Morcarum in Eliensi insulâ conclusit, sibique confœderatum et nil mali machinantem vel suspicantem obsedit"
[6] See above, p. 21.        [7] See above, p 337.

detail of his legendary history as matter of historical fact, yet the mere abundance of such details shows the impression which he made on the popular imagination. His legendary prominence makes it pretty certain that, even if Hereward was not the formal leader of the defenders of the Isle, it was on the strength of his heart and arm that the hopes of the defence mainly rested. And one of those incidental notices which in the history of these times often prove so much, shows that the spirit which was kindled by the revolt of the Fenland spread itself into shires far away from Peterborough and Ely. A party of the valiant men of Berkshire, tenants of Saint Mary of Abingdon, set forth to join the new champions of England. They were surprised on their march by a body of the King's troops, and underwent various punishments for their rebellion.[1] The one instance of such zeal which happens to be recorded was doubtless not the only instance that took place; brave or desperate men from various parts of England doubtless pressed to join in the defence of the spot which now alone was truly England. And if legend is allowed to count for anything, none of the warlike guests of Saint Æthelthryth showed greater zeal in the common cause than the monastic indwellers of her island. Monks and warriors sat side by side in the refectory, the chief leaders being honoured with a place at the table of the Abbot, while weapons of war hung from the walls and the roof, that the comrades, lay and spiritual alike, might at once spring to their harness at any call of sudden need.[2] Everything bade fair for a long defence; men might deem that, though the rest of

*Unsuccessful march of the Berkshire men.*

*Alleged zeal of the monks of Ely*

---

[1] See above, p 33   The writer adds, "Circumventi in itinere captique incarcerantur, et satis misere affliguntur"

[2] Gesta Herewardi, 64   A Norman spy gives the report of the doings in the refectory, and adds, " Hoc nempe mihi præ cunctis unum et valde mirificum est de illis omnibus quod percipi, monachos loci illius pene omnes tam præclaros in militiâ esse quod nedum penitus ante audivi, nec ipso in aliquo alio loco numquam expertus sum"

the land might submit to the Norman, yet the Isle of Ely might long remain independent English ground.

With hopes like this it is impossible not to sympathize; yet, from our calmer point of view, we can see that the cause of England could not really be served by thus defending a single spot of ground while the rest of the land was conquered. The Fenland was, of all parts of Britain, one of the best suited for the last remnants either of a vanquished nation or of a vanquished political party to hold out against their enemy to the last. There is reason to believe that some isolated spots in this wild region had been held by remnants of the old Celtic inhabitants for ages after East-Anglia and Mercia had become English ground.[1] It is even possible that, here and there, an outlying British settlement may have lingered on to the days of William, and that Hereward, as well as Eadric on the other side of England, may have found allies among the descendants of those whom his fathers had displaced. In after days the land which had thus sheltered the last relics alike of British and of English independence sheltered the last relics of the party which had fought for the freedom of England by the side of Simon of Montfort.[2] But a remnant of this kind, holding a spot like the Isle of Ely, could never be more than a community of outlaws. It was not even as if any substantive and considerable part of the country, a land like Northumberland or the

---

[1] A passage from the History of Ramsey, c 86, to which I have already referred in vol 1. p 477, certainly seems to point to the existence of British robbers in the Fenland as late as the time of Cnut The English tenants of an oppressive Danish Thegn are made to say, " Quousque alienigenæ istius vitam *donandam gratis Britonibus latronibus* continuis noctium excubiis ad nostrum dedecus et damnum conservamus?"

[2] The holding of the Isle of Ely by Simon's followers is mentioned by all the historians of Henry the Third, see for instance Rishanger, 44, ed. Riley The Royalist Wikes (Ann Mon. iv 204, 207) has of course many hard words for the patriots

*Wealh-cyn*, or the whole of East-Anglia, had contrived to retain its independence. A district of this kind might have kept a real political being and a real national existence, just as Wales and Scotland did. But the independence of the Isle of Ely could have meant nothing more than a constant *guerrilla* warfare in its own neighbourhood, and a constant source of discontent and suspicion through the rest of the Kingdom. We admire, we sympathize with, the followers of Hereward and the followers of the younger Simon; but, in the general interest of England, we can hardly lament that their efforts were not crowned with success.

One thing is plain, that William looked on the revolt of the Fenland as something which needed all his energies of craft and force to put down. He called forth both land troops and a fleet, which last must have been chiefly manned by English sailors.[1] Legend speaks of William of Warren, now Earl of Surrey,[2] the husband of the King's step-daughter, as taking a leading part in this expedition. His chief object was to avenge his brother Frederick, who is said to have been slain by Hereward at an earlier time.[3] We also hear much of Ivo Taillebois,

CHAP XX

William attacks the Isle with a great force

Alleged deeds of William of Warren,

and Ivo Taillebois

---

[1] Chron Wig 1072, Petrib 1071 "Ac þa se kynge Wyllelm þis geahsade þa bead he ut scypfyrde and landfyrde and þæt land call utan embsette and brycge worhte and scypfyrde on þa sæ healfe." So Flor. Wig (1071), "Sed hoc audito Rex cum butsecarlis in orientali plagâ insulæ omnem illis exitum obstruxit, et pontem in occidentali duorum milliariorum longum fieri jussit" The last time we heard of the "butsecarli" was when they were so eager to fight for Eadgar and against William. See vol III pp 525, 531

[2] See Orderic, 522 C  It is true that in 680 C, speaking of William Rufus, he says, "Guillelmus Rex Guillelmum de Guarennâ Comitem Suthregiæ constituit," but this can hardly be the first grant.

[3] See vol. III p 647  The incidental mention of Frederick's lands at Trumpington in Domesday (196 b) and in Norfolk (II 165 b, 170 b) seems to show that he was dead at the time of the Survey  This falls in with the story of his being killed by Hereward, which is found in the Gesta, 46, 54, 61, and in the somewhat better authority of the Liber de Hydâ, 295, "Here-

who has become one of the most prominent figures in the legendary history, and who appears in the Survey as the owner of large estates in the neighbouring land of Holland.[1] Romance endows him with the marriage and heritage of the mythical Lucy, the long-lived and often-wedded daughter of Earl Ælfgar,[2] and therefore, according to one version, the niece of Hereward himself. History shows that there is so much of truth in the myth that Ivo really had a wife, certainly not a daughter of Ælfgar, but still of English parentage, who on Norman lips was spoken of as Lucy, much as Eadgyth the daughter of Malcolm had her name changed to Matilda.[3] Legend describes Ivo, possibly with truth, as a bitter enemy of the monks of Crowland;[4] it is more certain that the Priory of Spalding counted him among its benefactors.[5] And an incidental passage of the Survey may lead us to think that the one Norman who must ever claim most interest in the eyes of Englishmen was among the assailants of the last stronghold of independent England. William Malet, who had borne the body of Harold to his first burial[6] and who had been the prisoner of the

*His real and imaginary marriages.*

*Presence and death of William Malet.*

wardus . . inter cætera scelera sua, Fredericum germanum Comitis Willelmi de Warenniâ, genere et possessionibus insignitum, nocte quâdam in domo propriâ fraudibus circumventum occidit Pro cujus nece tantæ inter ipsum et prædictum Willelmum vitæ sunt discordiæ ut nullâ satisfactione nullâ regiâ [sic] potuerint quiescere "

[1] See his lands in Lincolnshire, in Domesday, 350–351 b.

[2] See vol ii p 631.

[3] Mr. Nichols has made it clear, in the Lincoln Volume of the Archæological Institute, 255, that Ivo's wife Lucy was a kinswoman at once of William Malet and of the Sheriff Thorold, the alleged brother of the famous Godgifu, who seems to appear as Ivo's *antecessor* in p 351. Some enterprising genealogist may perhaps find here the key to the mysterious description of William (see vol iii. p. 466) as "partim Normannus et Anglus" The younger Lucy, the Countess, was her daughter by Ivo

[4] See the false Ingulf, Gale, 74.

[5] See the Monasticon, iii. 206, 215 et seqq, and the Chronicle of John of Peterborough (nearly as mythical as Ingulf himself) under the years 1052 and 1074.    [6] See vol iii p. 514.

Danes after the taking of York,[1] had escaped or had been redeemed from his captivity, and now came to fight and die in the marshes of Ely.[2] Thus much is handed down to us in the great record; but romance, so busy with the names of other actors, Norman and English, has perversely forgotten to hand down to us a single tale of the deeds or the fate of the *compater Heraldi*.

Our authentic narratives describe William as attacking the Isle on both sides, bringing his ships to bear on the eastern side, while he made his assault on the western by means of a bridge.[3] The legendary accounts, utterly confused as they are as to the chronology and as to the actors, are the work of men who knew the country, and, like many other legendary accounts, they seem trustworthy as far as the geography is concerned. They thus enable us more exactly to fix the position of the operations which our soberer authorities point to more vaguely. The castle of Cambridge was, as might be expected, the royal head-quarters;[4] but the energy of William carried him to every point at which his presence could be needed. We find him in one tale directing his naval operations against the eastern part of the Isle from Brandon,[5] a

*Geography of the campaign*

*William's head-quarters at Cambridge.*

---

[1] See above, p 269

[2] The second volume of Domesday contains a crowd of references to the death of William Malet at some time before the date of the Survey; see pp 294, 334 b, 373 b, 380 b, 407, 440, 441, 442 b, 444 In three other entries things get more distinct In 247 we read of land being held "die quo pater R. Malet ivit in servitium Regis" In 332 b we read of lands in Suffolk "ex hoc erat sesitus Willelmus Malet quando ivit in servitium Regis ubi mortuus est" Lastly, in 133 b we find lands in Norfolk claimed by Robert Malet, who "dicit quod pater suus eam tenuit quando *ivit in maresc*, et hoc testatur hundret, et tamen non tenebat eâ die quâ mortuus fuit" This certainly looks to me as if William had been killed in the campaign in the Fenland.

[3] See the quotation from Florence in p. 471

[4] Hist Eli 237 "Rex .. ad castrum Cantebrigiæ secessit," after the defeat of the witch Afterwards (246) the monks go to Cambridge to pay their fine.

[5] In one of the legendary exploits of Hereward (Gesta, 70) he goes "ad

town on the Little Ouse, the stream whose bed has in later times received the waters of its greater namesake. Elsewhere we hear of attacks made by water from Reche, a point to the south-east of the Isle on the famous Devil's Dyke, and commanding a stream called Rechelode, which joins with the Grant or Cam a little above its junction with the old Ouse.[1] But the great interest of the campaign gathers round the bridge or causeway which William made at the accessible point of Aldreth. Stones, trees, hides, materials of every kind, were employed in the work;[2] stone especially was brought by water from Cottenham, a point in the direction of Cambridge, commanding a tributary of the old Ouse.[3] Here then the chief exploits of Hereward and his companions are placed. He more than once defeated the attempts of the Normans to enter the Isle by the causeway,[4] and a more wonderful tale is told how, by the advice of Ivo, a witch was placed in a wooden tower to overcome the resistance of the English by her spells, and how Hereward contrived to burn tower, pythoness, and all.[5] Tales again are told of the various disguises in which he made his way into the King's camp

Regis curiam apud Brandune" So in Hist Eli 229, "Rex ... ad Brandunam recessit." The Great Ouse anciently ran into the sea at Wisbech; it now follows the course of the Little Ouse to Lynn. See Ancient Cambridgeshire, 69

[1] Gesta, 65, Hist Eli 233.

[2] Gesta, 57 "Latitudo ibi iiii stadiorum extenditur, ubi adductis instrumentis et structuris lignorum et lapidum et ex omni genere struis, aggregationem in palude viam, licet nimis sibi perinutilem et angustam, straverunt ad magnum quippe flumen apud prædictum locum, scilicet Abrehede, etiam in aquâ maximas arbores et trabes conjunctas collocaverunt, subterius connexis pellibus bidentium integre et versipelles excoriatis et aere plenis infusis, ut onus supereuntium melius sustentaretur et pondus"

[3] Hist Eli. 236. "Cotingelade" at least implies Cottenham.

[4] The tale is told at length in the Gesta, 58.

[5] The story of the witch is given in the Gesta, 68–76, Hist. Eli. 234–237. In the former (75) she appears as "phithonissa mulier."

to spy out the hostile forces,[1] and of the way in which he harried the places which remained in the King's obedience.[2] What amount of truth there may be in each particular story it is impossible to guess, but the places spoken of quite fall in with the more general description of the Chroniclers, and we can have little doubt that the main struggle took place on the Ouse by the approach of Aldreth, and that many a gallant feat of arms was done on its dreary banks by the last champions of England.

The amount of time over which the struggle was spread is greatly exaggerated by the legendary writers, who bring the defence of the Isle of Ely into connexion with the still distant rebellion of Ralph of Norfolk.[3] But it is plain from the authentic accounts that the reduction of the Isle was not a work of any long time, and that the whole campaign took place in the course of the year following the departure of the Danish fleet. Those accounts read as if the hearts of Morkere and his companions failed them when they found themselves hemmed in both by land and by water.[4] The Norman version, on the other hand, tells of false promises and inducements held out to the Earl, by which he was led to throw himself on the King's mercy at a time when it was yet open to him either to have still defended the Isle or to have made his way out by water into the high seas.[5] The local legend, which is clearly

*Length of the defence exaggerated in the legends.*

*Surrender of Morkere, Æthelwine, and the rest*

---

[1] He goes as a potter, Gesta, 69, as a fisherman, ib 74
[2] Hist Eli 233  Seven men from the Isle burn Burwell
[3] See Gesta, 77, Hist Eli 239, and Appendix OO.
[4] Chron Wig 1072, Petrib 1071  "And þa utlagan þa ealle on hand eodan, þæt wæs Egelwine bisceop and Morkere eorl, and ealle þa þe mid heom wæron"  So Florence, 1071, "Illi, ubi se viderunt sic esse conclusos, repugnare desistebant"
[5] Ord Vit 521 A  "Versipelles inter eos nuntii discurrerunt, et dolosam conditionem nequiter pepigerunt, scilicet ut se Comes Regi redderet, eumque Rex pacifice ut fidum amicum susciperet. Obsessus nempe diu poterat sese ibidem inaccessibilitate loci defendere aut, nimiâ vi accidente,

wrong in bringing both Eadwine and Morkere into the Isle, and still more wrong in making both of them escape,[1] is probably right in attributing the surrender of the Isle to the treachery of the Abbot and monks, whose patriotism failed them when William seized on all the lands of the monastery beyond the borders of the Isle itself.[2] At all events it is certain that the greater part of the defenders of Ely came into William's hands. They were dealt with as he thought good.[3] According to William's constant rule,[4] no life was taken, but at Ely, as at Alençon, the Conqueror felt no scruple against inflicting punishments which to our notions might seem more frightful than death itself. Some were shut up in the horrible prison-houses of those days; others were allowed to go free after their eyes had been put out or their hands cut off.[5] Morkere himself, to judge from the English accounts, surrendered himself to the King's mercy. According to the Norman version, he surrendered on a promise of being received to the King's peace, which was broken by William through fear of the dangers which might happen to the realm if Morkere were allowed to remain at large. In either case, he was

per circumfluens flumen usque ad oceanum navigio diffugere Sed ille falsis allegationibus simpliciter adquievit, et cum suis ad Regem pacifice de insulâ exivit"

[1] See Appendix OO.

[2] The story is told in the Gesta (78), and more fully in the Ely History (240) In the former version Abbot Thurstan at first patriotically flees along with the Earls, and takes the treasures of the church with him. As the escape of the Earls is undoubtedly mythical, the escape of the Abbot is most likely no less so

[3] Chron Wig 1072. "And se kyng nam heora scypa and wæpna and manega sceattas, and þa menn ealle he toc and dyde of heom þæt he wolde." In Peterborough, 1071, "þa men he ateah swa swa he wolde." We may compare the words of William of Poitiers in describing the vengeance of William at Romney, see vol. iii p 534.

[4] See above, p. 53

[5] Flor Wig 1071 "Comitem cæterosque per Angliam divisos, partim custodiæ mancipavit, partim, manibus truncatis vel oculis erutis, abire permisit"

put into ward, but as he was entrusted to the keeping of Roger of Beaumont, it may be that the dungeons and fetters of which we hear are only a figure of speech.[1] He remained a prisoner in Normandy all the rest of the days of the Conqueror, and obtained but a single moment of freedom at his death.[2]

*His momentary release 1087.*

The like bondage, the like momentary glimpse of freedom, was the fate of Siward Barn.[3] In the case of Bishop Æthelwine earlier services may have been allowed to count against his later enmity. He was simply committed to the care of Abbot Ealdred of Abingdon,[4] and we have seen that this kind of custody did not involve any special hardship.[5] He reached the Abbey, it would almost seem, about the time when the tenants of the house were making their gallant but vain attempt to carry help to the defenders of Ely.[6] Their fault was visited on their lord the Abbot, who was first imprisoned in the castle of Wallingford, and then, like Æthelwine himself, transferred for the rest of his life to the milder custody of Bishop Walkelin at Winchester.[7]

*Imprisonment of Siward Barn*
*Bishop Æthelwine in ward at Abingdon*
*Imprisonment of Abbot Ealdred*

---

[1] Ord. Vit 521 A, B "Rex metuens ne Morcarus injurias sibi et compatriotis suis nequiter illatas ulcisceretur, et per eum aliquæ seditiones in regno Albionis implacabiles orirentur, illum sine manifesto reatu vinclis injecit, omnique vitâ suâ in ergastulo coercuit et cautelæ Rogerii oppidani Belmontis mancipavit"    [2] See Flor Wig 1087    [3] Ib

[4] Both Chronicles mention the sending of Æthelwine to Abingdon and his death soon after; "Þone bisceop Egelwine he sende to Abbandune and he þær forðferde sona þæs wintres" Florence, who gives a somewhat different account under the last year, here translates the Chronicles. See Appendix PP. So the local History of Abingdon (i 485, 493), "Talibus tentatis quum diversi ordinis et dignitatis viri se commiscuissent, tum episcopus Dunelmensis quoque, Ægelwinus nomine, inter eos qui capti sunt inventus, et Abbendoniam missus, in captione ibi ad suæ mortis degens diem obiit"    [5] See above, p 388

[6] The passage quoted in p 33 follows immediately on the last extract.

[7] Hist Mon Ab i 486 "In illorum etiam dominum, id est, Abbatem Ealdredum, qui et Brichwinus dictus est (binomius enim erat), Regis inimicitia est perlata, adeo ut absque dilatione, ejus præcepto, apud

The King then granted the Abbey of Abingdon to a Norman monk from Jumièges, who however bears the singularly English-sounding name of Adelelm or Æthelhelm.[1] His task was a difficult one, and one in which he seems to have had to trust about equally to English tongues and to Norman swords. The King's officers were constantly doing damage to the house by exactions of various kinds, in withstanding which the eloquence and legal knowledge of certain of his English monks stood him in good stead.[2] On the other hand, the necessities of the times, and the revolts and conspiracies which were still everywhere going on—especially, we may be sure, in so English-hearted a district as Berkshire— made it unsafe for even an Abbot to go about without a military guard.[3] He had also to send men to take a share in the defence of the newly-built castles of Oxford, Wallingford, and Windsor,[4] and moreover to provide for the defence of his own monastery.[5] The arms of soldiers

castellum Walingafordense in captione poneretur. Aliquanto autem post tempore a prædicto loco eductus, in manu Wintoniensis Episcopi Walchelini servandus committitur, apud quem mansit quoad vixit." In the other version, in p. 493, Walkelin is not mentioned, and we read more distinctly of Ealdred as "pastorali potestate nudatus."

[1] A writ in his favour in ancient form, addressed by William to Lanfranc, Robert of Oily, and others, opens the second volume of the Abingdon History. In different manuscripts of the History his name is written Athellelmus and Adelelmus That he came from Jumièges appears from the Appendix to the Abingdon History, ii 283. We there hear how he gave lands of the Abbey to his kinsfolk, and how he mocked at the English saints, calling them "rusticos," &c., much in the style of Paul at Saint Alban's He of course suffered a miraculous punishment, which reminds one of that of Arius

[2] See the very curious account in Hist Ab. ii. 2. There is a letter of Lanfranc to Adelelm (Giles, i 72) in which he pleads with the Abbot for some monks who had offended him.

[3] Hist Ab. ii. 3. "In primordio autem sui adventûs in abbatiam, non nisi armatorum septus manu militum alicubi procedebat"

[4] See above, p. 341.

[5] Ib "Taliter regni tumultuantibus caussis, domnus Adellelmus Abbas locum sibi commissum munitâ manu militum secure protegebat"

from beyond sea[1] were therefore as needful to him as the legal subtleties of Godric the monk and Ælfwine the priest of Sutton. At first he simply hired mercenaries;[2] afterwards, when things had got rather more quiet and when military tenures were being generally introduced among the occupants of ecclesiastical property, the lands which had been formerly held of the Abbey by English Thegns on an English tenure were granted out to Norman knights on a tenure strictly military.[3] This process, which went on at other places as well as at Abingdon, marks a stage in that gradual advance of feudal ideas in England which has been sometimes mistaken for the formal enactment of a Feudal System. As for Abbot Adelelm, he continued to play a certain part in public affairs during the rest of William's reign. His prisoner, the deposed Bishop of Durham, died in the year following his first imprisonment.[4] His successor was neither Norman nor English, but one of that intermediate class whom both Harold and William found it convenient sometimes to favour. He was Walcher, a Lotharingian of Luttich,[5] in whose appointment we may

*He grants out land on military tenures*

*Illustration of the growth of Feudalism*

*Death of Æthelwine 1072*

---

[1] Hist. Ab. ii. 3. "Tali in articulo hujus fortunæ milites transmarini in Angliam venientes favore colebantur præcipuo."

[2] Ib. "Primo quidem mercenariis in hoc utebatur."

[3] Ib. "His sopitis incursibus, quum jam Regis edicto in annalibus annotaretur quot de episcopiis, quodve de abbatiis ad publicam rem tuendam milites (si forte hinc quid caussæ propellendæ contingeret) exigerentur, eisdem donativis prius retentis, Abbas mansiones possessionum ecclesiæ pertinentibus inde delegavit, edicto cuique tenore parendi de suæ portionis mansione." Then follows the passage about the Thegns who died at Senlac, quoted in p. 33. Among these military tenants were doubtless the kinsfolk of whom the writer of the Appendix complains.

[4] See above, p. 477.

[5] "Genere Lotharingus," says Florence, 1072. Simeon (1071. 89, Hinde), more definitely, "de clero [mark the monk's view of things] Leodicensis ecclesiæ," and adds, "Invitatus namque ab ipso Rege venerat ad illum, prosapiâ clarus, honestus moribus, divinæ ac sæcularis scientiæ gratiâ præditus." To the same effect in Hist. Eccl. Dun. iii. 18, where he is said to be "de gente Hlothariorum"—it is pleasant to see so old a form of the name abiding—and it is noticed that "ab ipso Rege eligitur."

480        THE REVOLTS AGAINST WILLIAM.

CHAP. XX.  perhaps discern the influence of Harold's surviving sister.
Walcher    He was consecrated at Winchester, but by the hands of his
Bishop of
Durham.    own Metropolitan.¹ The Lady Eadgyth was present at
1071–1080  the ceremony, and as the Bishop-elect, a man of tall stature,
           with white hair and a rosy countenance, was brought before
           his consecrators, the Lady, reminded perhaps of the outward
Saying of  presence of her departed lord, exclaimed, "Here we have
Eadgyth
at his con- a goodly martyr." Later events caused the words of the
secration. widow of the saint to be looked on as a prophecy.²

           The monks of Ely—so runs the local history or legend—
Submission were punished as they deserved for their treason. The
of the
monks of   tale carries Thurstan and his companions as far as Warwick
Ely.       to make their submission to the King.³ There can be no
           doubt that they did submit, and that their submission
William    destroyed the hopes of the defenders of the Isle. A
comes to
Ely        picturesque tale describes William as coming to Ely, as
October    entering the minster, but as not daring to draw near to
27, 1071.
           the shrine of the virgin patroness of the spot. He was
           too well aware of the wrongs which he and his had done
           to the patrimony of Saint Æthelthryth; so, like the
           humble publican, he stood afar off, and offered a mark
           of gold on the altar.⁴ Strange to say, while the King

    ¹ This appears from the statement of Archbishop Ralph in his letter to
Pope Calixtus (X Scriptt 1744), that Thomas consecrated three Bishops of
Durham, but none of them at York, compared with what follows.
    ² Will Malm Gest Pont. 272. "Prædictum id ab Edgithâ Reginâ,
relictâ Regis Edwardi. Quæ quum vidisset Walkerium Wintoniæ ad
consecrandum duci, cæsarie lacteolum, vultu roseum [compare the description of Eadward in vol ii p. 27], staturâ prægrandem, 'Pulcrum,'
ait, 'hic martyrem habemus,' conjecturâ vidclicet immoderatæ gentis ad
præsagiendum inducta" William seems to have been as incredulous as to
the prophetic powers of Eadgyth as Stigand was as to those of her husband.
See vol. iii p 12.                         ³ Hist. Eli. 241.
    ⁴ Hist Eli. 245. "Ad monasterium denique veniens, longe a sancto
corpore virginis stans, marcam auri super altare projecit, propius accedere
non ausus, verebatur sibi a Deo judicium inferri pro malis quæ sui in loco
patraverant."

was in the church, the monks were in the refectory. Their untimely meal was broken in upon by Gilbert of Clare, who asked whether they could not dine at some other time, when King William was actually present in the minster.¹ They left the board and rushed into the church; but the King was gone.² His work had been done even in that short visit. He had marked out the site for a castle within the monastic precinct, and he had already given orders for its building by the work of men pressed from the three shires of Cambridge, Huntingdon, and Bedford.³ Aldreth too, the key of the Island, was to receive a garrison of foreigners faithful to the King.⁴ Meanwhile the monks followed William to Wichford, a place at a short distance from Ely on the road to Aldreth. There, by the intercession of Gilbert, who had aroused them in the refectory, they were admitted to an audience. With some difficulty they were allowed to purchase the King's peace by a fine of seven hundred marks of silver —no bad interest for the one mark of gold which the King had offered to Saint Æthelthryth. On the appointed day the money, raised by the sacrifice of many of the ornaments of the church, was brought to the King's officers at Cambridge. But, alas, through some fraud of the moneyers, the coins were found to be of light weight.⁵

*CHAP. XX.*

*A castle built at Ely*

*Aldreth garrisoned*

*Fines laid on the Abbey.*

*Spoliation of the church ornaments to pay the fine*

---

¹ Hist Eli 246 "O miseri et vecordes, num aliâ vice prandere non liceret, dum Rex apud vos est et in ecclesiâ consistit?" On the importance of the dinner-hour in monastic revolutions, see above, p 413.

² Ib "Quo dicto, relictis mensis, ad ecclesiam omnes cucurrere, sed Regem non invenere"

³ Ib. 245. "Ipse autem, præsidio intra septa monachorum delocato, et qui id opus conficerent de Cantebrigiæ, Huntedoniæ, et Bedefordiæ comitatu constituit, et electis militibus quos de Galliâ traduxerat commisit"

⁴ Ib. "Similiter castello de Alrehede [al. Aldrehethe] fidelibus Gallis munito, viâ regressus est quâ intravit" This would take him by Wichford.

⁵ Ib 246 "Dolo nummulariorum dragma fraudata minus recti ponderis examinata invenitur habuisse" "Dragma" seems to be simply the Greek δράγμα = *manipulus*. It would seem as if the ornaments were actually coined down in the monastery.

William was wroth; his peace should be refused to them altogether. At last his forbearance was purchased by a further fine of three hundred marks, the raising of which involved the loss of ornaments yet more holy and precious than those which had been already sacrificed.[1] The deposition of Abbot Thurstan was at least discussed in William's councils;[2] but in the end he was allowed to retain his office till his death six years later, when another raid was made on the precious things of the monastery.[3] The next Abbot, Theodwine, a Norman monk from Jumièges, brought about the restoration of some of the lost goods. After a short incumbency of three years Theodwine died, and the affairs of the monastery were prudently administered for a time by a monk named Godfrey, who was afterwards removed to the Abbey of Malmesbury.[4] In his day a final settlement of the rights and property of the Abbey was made, and the record of it gives us another of those glimpses of the jurisprudence of the age which seem to bring us specially

*Death of Thurstan 1076*
*Theodwine Abbot of Ely. 1076-1079.*
*Administration of Godfrey 1079-1086.*
*He recovers the lands of the Abbey 1080*

---

[1] The list (Hist Eli 247) is worth preserving, "Totum quod in ecclesiâ ex auro et argento residuum fuit, insuper imaginem sanctæ Mariæ cum puero suo sedentem in throno, mirabiliter fabrefactam, quam Ælfsinus Abbas [second Abbot, from 981 to about 1016 See Hist Eli pp 174, 178, 194, 197] fecerat de auro et argento, comminutum est, similiter imagines sanctarum virginum [Ætheltbryth and the other virgin saints of the place] multo ornatu auri et argenti spoliatæ sunt, ut pretium pecuniæ exsolvi queat." One is reminded of the reckoning of the ways and means of Athens in Thucydides, ii 13, where we find the sacred offerings, public and private, counted as a source of revenue, and specially the gold on the statue of Athênê, περιαιρετὸν ἅπαν, like that of Saint Ætheltbryth. The local writer adds mournfully that, after all the sacrifices made by the monks, "nihilominus speratæ quietis fiduciâ caruerunt."

[2] Hist Eli 248  Compare the story of Saint Wulfstan in p 379

[3] Ib  This happened both at Ely and at Wentworth  Some of the things seized and taken to the King's treasury at Winchester were the gifts of "bonorum executor Stigandus Archiepiscopus" (see vol iii p 70), words pleasant to read in 1076

[4] On Theodwine—a very English sounding name—and Godfrey, see Hist Eli pp 248-251

near to the men whose acts we are studying. In a court of five neighbouring shires presided over by Bishop Odo, among the members of which we discern many familiar names both Norman and English,[1] the liberties of the house of Saint Æthelthryth were finally settled and confirmed by writ of the King.[2] A new phase in the history of the Abbey now begins; the next Abbot, Simeon, the brother of Bishop Walkelin of Winchester, began the building of a new church. Of that church the massive and stately transepts still remain, a worthy portion of that wonderful pile which, raised soon after Simeon's day to cathedral rank, came gradually in vastness of scale and variety of style to surpass all the existing episcopal churches of England.[3]

Such were the results of the short revolt and defence of the Isle of Ely, as far as concerns the highest in rank among its defenders. But there were stouter hearts shut

*Simeon, born 993? Abbot 1089-1093. Beginnings of the present church*

---

[1] Hist Eli 251 Four Abbots appear, Baldwin of Saint Eadmund's, Wulfwold of Chertsey (see above, p 389), Ulfcytel of Crowland (of whom more below), and Ælfwold of Saint Benet of Holm, once Harold's guardian of the East-Anglian coast (see vol iii p 717) Ælfwold, so John of Oxenedes (293) tells us, on account of his favour with Harold, "a Willelmo Conquæstore non parva sustinuit discrimina" Yet he kept his place into the days of William Rufus, and died Abbot in 1089, having been appointed by Eadward in 1064 Among the lay names—"plurimi milites probati Francigenæ et Angli"—besides "Vicecomites Picot, Eustachius, Radulfus, Walterus," two at least of whom are well enough known, we find "Vicecomites Harduuinus, Wido, Wimer, Wihumer, Odo, Godricus, Norman, Colsuein, Godwinus" Could there have been so many English Sheriffs in 1080? The holding of high office by Godric of East-Anglia (see Appendix C) and Colswegen of Lincoln (see above, p 218) is not unlikely

[2] The King's writ is given in Hist Eli 252 The "barones" there mentioned are Bishop Geoffrey, Abbots Baldwin, Ælsi (doubtless Æthelsige of Ramsey), and Wulfwold, Ivo Taillebois, Peter of Valognes, Sheriff Picot, and some others with Norman names This throws great doubt on the English Sheriffs

[3] On his work, see Hist Eli 253 There was much disputing about his accepting the benediction from Remigius Compare about Battle, above, p 409

484                THE REVOLTS AGAINST WILLIAM.

CHAP XX    up within the Isle than those of Bishop Æthelwine and Earl
           Morkere   All else had yielded; the King, we are told,
           and all his host had entered the Isle and had come as near
Hereward   to the Abbey as Wichford,¹ when Hereward, with a small
escapes by band of comrades like-minded with himself, disdained sub-
water      mission. Untouched and unhindered, they made their way,
           in the ships which they kept ready armed and guarded, to
           the open sea in the neighbourhood of the East-Anglian
Legends    Wells.² With his escape from the Isle the certain history
of his later
life       of Hereward ends, but legend goes on to tell how he still
           led the life of an outlaw, how he still remained the terror
           of the Normans, and from the wood by his supposed ances-
           tral home at Bourne harried at pleasure the lands of nine
           shires, as far as the distant town of Warwick.³ The Abbey
           of Peterborough, under its Norman Abbot, was an object

    ¹ Gesta, 79  " Subjungens etiam Regem esse apud Wycheford prope
unius stadii cum omni suo exercitu "
    ² Ib  " Repente hoc fecit cum suis navibus quas habebat bene armis
munitas ad custodiendas aquas in circuitu insulæ, in quoddam mare *wide*
vocatum juxta Welle secessit, magnum et spatiosum lateribus aquarum et
liberos exitus habens "  " Mare *wide* vocatum " is, I suppose, simply the
" great and wide sea "
    Authentic history quite bears out the legend as regards the escape of
Hereward  All surrendered, say both the Chronicles, " buton Herewarde
ane, and calle þa þe mid him woldon, and he hi æhtlice ût lædde "  So
Florence , " Omnes, excepto Herewardo viro strenuissimo, qui per paludes
cum paucis evasit, Regi se dedebant "  Neither authority gives any further
account of him
    ³ According to the legend (Gesta, 81) Hereward first " in Brunneswald
transivit, et similiter in magnis silvis Northamtune *exhabitavit*, terram
igne et ferro devastans "  Then we are told that the forces of nine shires
were brought against him, but seven only, even counting Lincoln and
Holland as separate shires, are mentioned  The others are Northampton,
Cambridge, Leicester, Huntingdon, and Warwick.  I presume that the
Hyde writer mixed together these more inland exploits of Hereward with
the defence of Ely, when he said (295) that " Herewardus tentans rebellare,
conductâ undique validâ manu, mediterranea Angliæ loca. in quorum
paludibus delitescebat, die et nocte cæde et rapinâ complebat "  The
mention of Warwick also, which we should hardly have looked for, must
be taken in connexion with the Domesday entries about Hereward in that
shire

of his special hatred. Turold, it is said, was once made prisoner and was driven to redeem himself at an incredible price;[1] and we hear of a second raid on the monastery itself, unless indeed this is simply the earlier one moved by the licence of legend out of its proper place. As to the end of the hero, reports differ. The two chief versions agree in marrying him to a rich Englishwoman named Ælfthryth, who had made her own peace with the King and obtained his peace also for her husband or lover.[2] In one tale, after some further exploits and the refutation of some slanderous charges, he wins William's favour, and dies quietly in the King's peace.[3] Another version gives his life a more tragic end. The French poet, who gives the fullest account of his later days, represents William as practising towards him nearly the same policy which earlier in his reign he had practised towards other Englishmen whose power and influence he dreaded. William on his first voyage to Normandy took with him the chief Earls and Prelates of England,[4] and we shall presently see Eadric of Herefordshire, now reconciled with William, accompany the King in his expedition against Scotland.[5] It was another instance of the same policy when William, if I rightly understand a somewhat difficult passage, took Hereward with him among the Englishmen who helped to

*His dealings with Turold of Peterborough*

*His marriage with Ælfthryth*

*His reconciliation with the King.*

*He accompanies William to Maine. 1073*

---

[1] Gesta, 84. But who can believe in a ransom of thirty thousand pounds?

[2] The story, as told in the Gesta, is clearly made up of two distinct versions. The name Ælfthryth, in the corrupt form "Alfued," comes from Gaimar.

[3] This version is found in the Gesta, 89-98. The whole story thus winds up, "Herewardus igitur, miles insignis et in multis locis expertus et cognitus, a Rege in gratiam susceptus, cum terris et possessionibus patris sui multis postmodum vixit annis, Regi Willelmo fideliter serviens ac devote compatriotis placens et amicis, ac sic demum quievit in pace, cujus animæ propitietur Deus. Amen."

[4] See above, pp. 75-78.   [5] See the next section.

win back the revolted County of Maine.¹ In this version, as in the other, it would seem that the English hero had really won the favour of the Norman King, nor is William himself charged with any double dealing towards Hereward after his submission  But the King's peace could not make him safe against the violence and treachery of smaller men. He still remained exposed to the hatred of men of the conquering race, men perhaps who had suffered from his prowess, men at all events whose deeds were as lawless as any of his own during his days of outlawry. He had to keep watch within and without his house, and to plant guards when he was at his meals. Once his chaplain Æthelward, on whom this duty fell, slumbered at his post. A band of Normans now attacked Hereward. He armed himself in haste; his spear was broken, his sword was broken; he was driven to use his shield as a weapon; fifteen Frenchmen lay dead by his single arm, when four of their party got behind him and smote him in the back.² This stroke brought him to his knees. A Breton knight,

[margin: Gaimar's legend of his death.]

---

[1] This I take to be the meaning of the obscure passage in Geoffrey Gaimar, Chron Ang.-Norm 1 22–23,

"Vers lui ala od mult de gent,
Triwes avoit tut veirement,
Au roi se devoit acorder,
*Dedenz cel mois passer la mer*
*Devoit pur guerroier Mansaus,*
Qui ont au roi tolet chasteaus

Il i avoit ainceis este,
Walter del Bois avoit mate,
Et dan Geffrei cil de Meine
Tint en prison une simeine
Ereward, qui doit aler en pees,
D'or et d'argent avoit meint fes"

[2] Ib 26,

"Od s'espée iiij. en occist,
Dès qu'il fiert le bois retentist,
Mès donc brusa le brant d'ascer
Desus l'elme d'un chevalier,
Et il l'escu en ses mains prist,

Si en fiert qe ij Franceis occist,
Mès iij vindrent à son dos
Qui l'ont feru par mi le cors,
Od iiij lances l'ont féru ;
N'est merveille s'il est chéu"

We are again reminded of the fate of Harold (see vol iii p 499), and of that of Patroklos, Il xvi 806,

". . . ὄπιθεν δὲ μετάφρενον ὀξέι δουρὶ
ὤμων μεσσηγὺ σχεδόθεν βάλε Δάρδανος ἀνήρ,
Πανθοΐδης Εὔφορβος"

Ralph of Dol, a retainer, it would seem, of the despoiler of Godric's widow,[1] now rushed on him, but Hereward, by a last effort, once more wielded his buckler with deadly effect, and the Englishman and the Breton fell dead together.[2] Another Norman, Asselin by name, now gave the last stroke; he cut off the head of the English hero, and swore by God and his might that so valiant a man he had never seen, and that, if there had been three more in the land like him, the Frenchmen would have been slain or driven out of England.[3]

CHAP. XX.

Such is the tale, a tale worth the telling, but all that certain history can say is that a Hereward, most likely the hero of Ely, appears in Domesday as a holder of lands in the shires of Worcester and Warwick under Norman lords.[4]

Notices of him in Domesday

### § 2. *The Affairs of the Welsh and Scottish Marches.*
### 1070—1074

Our last notices of Northumberland left Gospatric restored to the Earldom over the desolated land of the

State of the North

---

[1] Gaimar, Chron Ang Norm 1 26,

"C'il out à non Raol de Dol,    De Tuttesbire estoit venuz"

Tutbury was the castle of Henry of Ferrers  See above, p 37

[2] Gaimar, u s ,

"Ore sont amdui mort abatuz    Et Ereward et li Breton"

[3] Ib ,

"Mès Alselin le paroceist        Que onques si hardi ne fut trove ,
Cil de Ereward le chef prist,    Et s'il eust éu od lui trois,
Se jura Dieu et sa vertu         Mar 1 entrassent li François,
Et li autre qui l'ont véu        Et s'il ne fust issi occis,
Par meinte foiz l'ont fort jure, Touz les chaçast fors del païs"

This version seems to be followed by the Hyde writer (295), "Post multas denique credes atque seditiones, multa pacis fœdera cum Rege facta et temerarie violata, quâdam die cum omnibus sociis ab hostibus circumventus miserabiliter occubuit"

[4] On the lands of Hereward, see Appendix OO

488                THE REVOLTS AGAINST WILLIAM.

CHAP XX    ancient Bernicia.¹ Of the spiritual chief of the district,
           Bishop Æthelwine of Durham, we have heard as leaving a
           safe shelter in Scotland to share the perils of the defenders
           of Ely, and as at last dying in ward in the distant
           monastery of Abingdon.² At York Thomas of Bayeux was
           beginning that career of ecclesiastical reform which has
           won him an honourable place in local history.³ But the
           Earldom of which his metropolitan city was the head now
           came even nominally to an end by the revolt and imprison-
No Earl of ment of Morkere. No Earl of Southern Northumberland,
Deira
appointed. of Deira or Yorkshire, was ever again appointed, and from
Name of    this time the name of the ancient Kingdom became defi-
North-
humber-    nitely confined to its Northern portion. The Northern
land be-
comes fixed metropolis was clearly looked on as a post which could
to Ber-    not be safely put under any local ruler. It must be placed
nicia
           under the direct authority of the King and his immediate
           officers. But Northumberland in the new sense, as a
           border land constantly exposed to Scottish inroads, called
           for a governor who should hold some amount of inde-
The Ber-   pendent power. For a while longer we shall see that
nician
Earldom    William still entrusted this great command to English
retained.  holders of the ancient local families. At a later stage
           of his reign the Northumbrian Earldom, like other
           Earldoms, was held by strangers, but the presence of
           an Earl of some kind in Northumberland was found to
           be always needful.
End of the    The rebellion and death of Eadwine, like the rebellion
Mercian
Earldom    and imprisonment of Morkere, brought the Earldom of
           Mercia to an end as well as that of Deira. It was
           probably at this time that the great Earldoms on the
           north-western border towards Wales were finally settled.⁴

           ¹ See above, p 303    ² See above, p 479    ³ See above, p. 372
           ⁴ I think we may infer this both from the probability of the case and
           from the expressions of Orderic (521 D), the beginnings of his perfectly
           independent narrative after the loss of William of Poitiers, " Rex Guil-

The Earldom of Hereford, held by William Fitz-Osbern, had been formed within the Earldom of Harold, but Eadwine probably kept his nominal jurisdiction over Chester and Shrewsbury till his last revolt.[1] These two important border districts were formed into Earldoms which had more of the character of separate principalities than it was the usual policy of William to allow Chester, the final conquest of the great Northern campaign, was, as we have seen, first entrusted to the King's step-son, the Fleming Gerbod.[2] But the new Earl was soon tempted to take a part in the wars of his own country, where he suffered a long imprisonment.[3] By his departure his English Earldom seems to have been looked on as vacated. It was now granted to Hugh of Avranches, the son of Richard, the grandson of the traitor Thurstan.[4] The dignity, as held by him, was clothed with special privileges All the land in the shire, with the exception of that held by the Bishop, belonged to the Earl in the first instance,[5] and its actual possessors held it of him as their lord. In Cheshire proper therefore there were no King's Thegns, nor any immediate tenants-in-chief of the Crown of any kind, nor were any lands held by the King himself in demesne. But in certain

*Chap. xx.*
Earldom of Hereford under William Fitz-Osbern 1067–1071

Earldom of Chester under Gerbod 1070–1071.

Hugh of Avranches Earl of Chester 1071–1101.

State of the County Palatine

lelmus, dejectis, ut diximus, Merciorum maximis Consulibus, Eduino scilicet interfecto et Morcaro in vinculis constricto, adjutoribus suis inclitas Angliæ regiones distribuit" He goes on to speak of the Earldoms, reckoning however that of William Fitz-Osbern, in which he is doubtless wrong

[1] See above, p 179    [2] See above, p 317
[3] Ord Vit 522 A   "Cestram et comitatum ejus Gherbodo Flandrensi jamdudum Rex dederat, qui magna ibi et difficilia, tam ab Anglis quam a Guallis adversantibus, pertulerat " Of his share in the Flemish troubles we shall hear in the fourth section of this Chapter
[4] Ib   "Interea Rex Cestrensem consulatum Hugoni de Abrincis, filio Ricardi cognomento Goz, concessit " See vol ii pp. 205, 291
[5] Domesday, 262 b   " In Cestrescire tenet Episcopus ejusdem civitatis de Rege quod ad suum pertinet episcopatum. Totam reliquam terram comitatûs tenet Hugo Comes de Rege cum suis hominibus "

490        THE REVOLTS AGAINST WILLIAM.

CHAP. XX.
State of the Thegns between Mersey and Ribble

outlying dependencies of the shire we find a different state of things. In those days Lancashire did not exist as a shire; its northern portion formed part of the vast shire of York, while its southern portion, described in the Survey as the Land between the Mersey and the Ripple, had been Crown land under King Eadward, and was held under him by a crowd of petty Thegns, who, by the nature of their tenures, seemed to have been raised but little above the rank of churls or even of serfs.[1] These lands had been granted by William to Roger of Poitou, but at the time of the Survey they were again held by the Crown. Robert of Rhuddlan also, King Eadward's armour-bearer,[2] held of the King a district bearing the vague but sounding title of North Wales, the boundaries of which it was perhaps discreet not to define more exactly.[3] With these exceptions, the whole of the Cheshire of the Survey, a district much larger than the present shire, formed what may be fairly called a principality in the hands of the Palatine Earl. If the privileges of the Earls of Chester had not been exceptional, if all the Earldoms of England had been of the same nature as theirs, England could never have remained an united Kingdom, but must have split in pieces like France and

Robert of Rhuddlan holds North Wales

Privileges of the Palatine Earls

---

[1] Domesday, 262 b. "Terram inter Ripe et Mersham tenuit Rogerius Pictaviensis. Modo tenet Rex." The fuller account of these lands comes in 269 b. The number of landholders T. R. E. is very great. Their holdings were very small and their burthens very heavy. "Omnes isti taini habuerunt consuetudinem reddere ii oras denariorum de unâquâque carucatâ terræ, et faciebant pro consuetudine domos Regis et quæ ibi pertinebant, sicut villani." Their services and tenures are described at length, and are exceedingly curious. I shall most likely have to speak of them again in my fifth volume.

[2] See above, p. 74. See the fuller account of his early life in Ord. Vit. 670 A.

[3] Domesday, 269. "Rotbertus de Roelent tenet de Rege Nortwales, ad firmam pro xl. libris, præter illam terram quam Rex ei dederat in feudo et præter terras episcopatus." Presently we read, "Omnis alia terra est in silvis et moris, nec potest arari."

the Empire.¹ But it is plain that William allowed these exceptional privileges only on the exposed frontiers of his Kingdom, where it was specially needful to strengthen the hands of the local ruler. The Earl of Chester had to wage a constant war with the Welsh,² and in this work Earl Hugh found an able helper in Robert, who bears the title of Marquess in its primitive sense, as one of the first Lord Marchers of the Welsh borders.³ On the site of King Gruffydd's palace of Rhuddlan, the palace which was burned by Harold as the earnest of his great Welsh campaign,⁴ a castle and town arose,⁵ from which the Marquess Robert carried on for fifteen years a constant warfare with his British neighbours.⁶ At last, in the year after the death

*Hugh's wars with the Welsh*

*Robert of Rhuddlan's wars with the Welsh 1073-1088*

*The castle of Rhuddlan*

---

¹ See vol i p 322
² Ord Vit 522 A "Qui [Hugo] cum Rodberto de Rodelento et Rodberto de Malo-passu, aliisque proceribus *feris* multum Guallorum sanguinem effudit" The second of the two Roberts has left his name to the town of Malpas
³ Ib. 670 A "Robertus princeps militiæ ejus et totius provinciæ gubernator factus est" He is directly after called "bellicosus Marchio" and "Robertus Marchisus," "Marchisus audax"
⁴ See vol ii p 470
⁵ Ord Vit 670 A "Decreto Regis oppidum contra Guallos [ἐπιτείχισμα] apud Rodelentum constructum est, et Roberto, ut ipse pro defensione Anglici regni barbaris opponeretur, datum est" Domesday, 269 "Hugo Comes tenet de Rege Roelend. Ibi T R E jacebat Englefield, et tota erat wasta  Eduinus Comes tenebat  Quando Hugo Comes recepit, similiter erat wasta  Modo habet in dominio medietatem castelli quod Roelent vocatur, et caput est hujus terræ" Presently we read, "Rotbertus de Roelent tenet de Hugone Comite medietatem ejusdem castelli et burgi," and again, "In ipso manerio Roelent est factum noviter castellum, similiter Roelent appellatum [some castles, like Rougemont at Exeter, bore names different from those of the towns where they stood]  Ibi est novum burgum" The wasted state of the land was handed on from the wars in Eadward's day  Cf vol ii p 388
⁶ Orderic (670 B) describes his warfare at large, how he followed the enemy through "silvas et paludes et per arduos montes" He then adds, "Quosdam comminus ut pecudes irreverenter occidit, alios vero diutius vinculis mancipavit, aut indebitæ servituti atrociter subjugavit  Christicolæ non licet fratres suos sic opprimere, qui in fide Christi sacro renati sunt baptismate" He goes on to speak of Robert's "superbia et cupiditas,

CHAP. XX.
Death of Robert of Rhuddlan 1088.
Bad character of Earl Hugh

of the Conqueror, the lord of Rhuddlan was himself cut off by the arms of another Gruffydd.[1] His chief, Earl Hugh, survived his valiant lieutenant many years. Of him our chief authority draws a most unfavourable picture. He resembled the great King in whose stead he ruled only in his personal corpulence[2] and in his love of war and hunting; in his nobler qualities he had no share. Given up to excess of every kind, he left behind him a large spurious offspring of both sexes;[3] and we are told that he was at once greedy and lavish, but never liberal.[4] In his devotion to the sports of the field he laid waste his own lands, and he paid more regard to hunters and falconers than to either the priest or the husbandman.[5] Against this assemblage of vices it may be a small matter to set that he substituted monks for canons in the church of Saint Werburh,[6] and rebuilt the minster, where he

quæ per totum orbem mortalium possident pectora." The brotherhood of Norman and Welshman was doubtless better understood at Saint Evreux than it was at Rhuddlan.

[1] His death is described at length by Orderic (670 C, D). It was followed we are told by "nimius luctus Anglorum et Normannorum." In common warfare with the Briton the conquerors and the conquered seem to have forgotten their differences.

[2] Ord. Vit. 522 A. "Ventris ingluviei serviebat, unde nimiæ crassiciei pondere prægravatus vix ire poterat."

[3] Ib. B. "E pellicibus plurimam sobolem utriusque sexûs genuit, quæ diversis infortuniis absorpta pene tota periit."

[4] Ib. A. "Hic non dapsilis, sed prodigus erat, non familiam secum, sed exercitum semper ducebat."

[5] Ib. "Ipse terram suam quotidie devastabat, et plus aucupibus ac venatoribus quam terræ cultoribus vel cœli oratoribus applaudebat." This picture is curiously borne out by Domesday. In 263 b we read of the former small estate of a free Englishman, "Wasta fuit, et est modo in forestâ Comitis," in 269, "Hanc silvam habet Comes in forestâ suâ positam," and, more emphatically than all, in 268 b, "Harum xx. hidarum omnes silvas habet Comes in forestâ sua positas. Unde maneria sunt multum pejorata." The entry also "aira accipitris" seems to occur more commonly on Hugh's lands than in other parts of the Survey.

[6] See above, p. 314. Orderic (671 A) makes the curious remark that "Deo monachorum gregem inter belluinos cœtus nutriebat."

himself in his last days put on the monastic garb,[1] and where portions of his work still remain. Yet one would think that there must, after all, have been some good thing in the man who, at least in his later days, chose the holy Anselm as the physician and guardian of his soul.[2]

*He becomes a monk and dies 1101*

*His friendship for Anselm*

To the south of the Palatinate of Chester lay the other great Earldom which was held by Roger of Montgomery. William's earlier conquests had given him his reward in the South, in the possession of Chichester and of that fortress of Arundel which, raised before King William came into England, is held to have kept to this day the special virtue of bestowing the rank of Earl upon its holder.[3] Besides these southern estates, Roger, after the fall of Morkere, received as a further grant the Earldom of Shropshire, with the peninsular town of Shrewsbury[4] as its capital. In that town and shire he held rights only less extensive than those which Earl Hugh held in Chester and Cheshire. In Shropshire there were no Crown lands and no King's Thegns; all the land, except what was held by ecclesiastical bodies and by a very few Norman owners, was held by the Earl and his men.[5] Of Earl

*Roger of Montgomery, Earl of Shrewsbury*

*His estates in Sussex*

*Arundel Castle.*

*He receives the Earldom of Shrewsbury*

*Privileges of his Earldom.*

---

[1] Ord Vit 787 B "Hugo Cestrensis Comes in lectum decidit, et post diutinum languorem monachatum in coenobio quod idem Cestriæ construxerat suscepit, atque postriduum, vi Kal Augusti, obiit"

[2] Eadmer, Vit. Ans ii 1 "Adjuratus ab Hugone Cestrense Comite multisque aliis Anglorum regni principibus, qui eum animarum suarum medicum et advocatum elegerant"

[3] Ord Vit 522 B "Rex Guillelmus Rogerio de Monte-Gomerici in primis castrum Arundellum et urbem Cicestram dedit" On Arundel Castle, see above, p 66.

[4] Ib "Postea comitatum Scrobesburiæ, quæ in monte super Sabrinam fluvium sita est, adjecit"

[5] After the small list of tenants-in-chief in Domesday, 252, we read, "Comes Rogerius quod reliquum est tenet cum suis hominibus" So in p 254, "Ipse Comes Rogerius tenet de Rege civitatem Sciropesberie et totum comitatum et totum dominium quod Rex E ibi habebat" Earl Roger had no less a tenant than Earl Hugh himself We read in the same

Roger a far better character is handed down to us than of his brother chiefs at Chester and Hereford, but it must be borne in mind that the writer who gives it to us was bound by an hereditary attachment to his memory.[1] It is plain, on the other hand, that the English burgesses of Shrewsbury bitterly complained of the grievances which they underwent under his rule. The building of the castle, and that of the Abbey which we shall presently have to speak of, the devastation of several houses from unknown causes, and the establishment in the town of French burgesses, who seem not to have been subject to the same taxes as their English neighbours, had greatly lessened the tax-paying power of the borough; yet the same tribute was exacted which had been paid in the days of King Eadward.[2] At the same time the burgesses of Shrewsbury might rejoice that they were in less evil case than their brethren in other towns whose tribute was actually raised.[3] And possibly the two pictures given us of Earl Roger may in some degree be explained by the influence for evil and for good of his two successive wives. For his first wife, it will be remembered, he had the heiress of Belesme, the cruel Mabel.[4] She at last met with the reward of her misdeeds. In her town of Bures by

*Marginalia:* CHAP XX. Complaints of the men of Shrewsbury. Influence of his successive wives. Murder of Mabel. 1082.

---

page, "Hugo Comes tenet Rogerio Comite in Walis terram de Gal." It is added, "T R E fuit wasta, et quando Hugo recepit similiter."

[1] Ord. Vit. 522 B "Hic sapiens et moderatus et amator æquitatis fuit, et comitatem sapientum et modestorum dilexit." He goes on to mention the good influence on the Earl's mind which was exercised by three clerks, his own father Odelerius, of whom more anon, and two others called Godebald and Herbert.

[2] Domesday, 252. "Dicunt Anglicenæ burgenses de Sciropesberie multum grave sibi esse quod ipsi reddunt totum geldum sicuti reddebatur T. R. E., quamvis castellum Comitis occupaverit li masuras et alii l masuræ sint vastæ, et xliii Francigenæ burgenses teneant masuras geldantes T R E, et abbatiæ quam *facit* ibi Comes dederat ipse xxxix. burgenses olim similiter cum aliis geldantes."

[3] See above, pp. 162, 200, 216.

[4] See vol. ii p. 196.

the Dive the Countess was reposing herself after her bath,[1] CHAP XX.
when she was slain by four brothers who were among the
many whose inheritances she had taken away by wrong
and robbery.[2] The death of his cruel helpmate, and the His second wife, Adeliza
virtues of his second wife, Adeliza the daughter of Everard
of Puisat, of the noblest blood of France,[3] wrought, we His monastic foundations
are told, for good upon the character of Roger. Already
a bountiful benefactor of monks in Normandy,[4] he became
in England a still more renowned patron and founder.

It is this last character of Earl Roger which indirectly
connects him with one of our most valuable authorities for
the history of these times. Among his followers was History of Odelerius of Orleans
Odelerius the son of Constantius, a priest of Orleans.
He was the Earl's chaplain and confessor, to whom His settlement at Shrewsbury
he gave a wooden church which stood in a suburb of
Shrewsbury beyond the Severn.[5] The French clerk had
married an English wife, and was the father of at least The father of Orderic
three English-born sons. One, seemingly the eldest, re- Birth of Orderic February 16, 1075
ceived the English name of Orderic;[6] another bore the

[1] The story of the death of Mabel is told at length by Orderic (578 B)
The chief murderer, with his brothers, "noctu ad cameram Comitissæ
accessit, ipsamque in municipio super Divam, quod Buris dicitur, in lecto
post balneum deliciantem, pro recompensatione patrimonii sui ense detruncavit." Her son Hugh tried in vain to overtake the slayers of his mother,
but they had warily broken down the bridges, and so escaped and made
their way to Apulia

[2] Ord Vit 578 B

[3] Ib D "Adelaisam Ebrardi de Pusacio, qui de nobilissimis Francorum
proceribus erat, filiam." He adds, "sequens a priori matrona dispar
moribus exstitit Nam maturitate et religione viguit, virumque suum ad
amorem monachorum et defensionem pauperum frequenter incitavit"
"Pauperes," in the case of Roger and Adeliza, may be translated *Englishmen*. [4] See Will Gem vii 22.

[5] Ord Vit 579 C, D. "Illic [beyond the east gate of Shrewsbury]
nimirum lignea capella priscis temporibus a Siuuardo consanguineo condita
fuerat"

[6] The truer English form of the name would be *Ordric*, like the Abbot
of Abingdon mentioned in vol iii p 731, and *Ordricus* is the form in his
own text, but his editors seem to have established the use of the longer
form, analogous to the received forms of the names Theodoric and Frederick

French name of Everard, while the youngest was called after the saintly Benedict, the father of Western monasticism.[1] The young Orderic received his name from the priest who baptized him in the church of Ettingsham near the Severn.[2] At the age of five years he learned the first rudiments of letters from the priest Siward, his maternal kinsman, in the church by the gate of Shrewsbury which was then or afterwards held by his father.[3] And, if we take his own words literally, his education was so strictly English that he did not understand the native tongue of his own father.[4] At the age of ten years, the young Orderic, called in religion Vital,[5] was sent as a tender exile, as he calls himself, from the furthest parts of Mercia, to serve God in a monastery beyond the sea.[6] This was that famous house of Ouche or Saint Evroul,

---

[1] See below, p 499.

[2] Ord Vit 548 A. "Apud Ettingesham in ecclesiâ Sancti Eattæ Confessoris, quæ sita est super Sabrinam fluvium, per ministerium Ordrici sacerdotis sacro fonte renatus sum." So again 924 A, where he adds, "mihi ejusdem sacerdotis, patrini scilicet mei, nomen indidisti"

[3] Ib 924 A "Quum quinque essem annorum, apud urbem Scrobesburiam scholæ traditus sum, et prima tibi servitia clericatûs obtuli in basilicâ sanctorum Petri et Pauli Apostolorum. Illic Siguardus insignis presbyter per quinque annos Carmentis Nicostratæ literis docuit me, ac psalmis et hymnis aliisque necessariis instructionibus mancipavit me" In 548 A it stands thus, "Siuua[r]do nobili presbytero literis erudiendis a genitore traditus sum" I presume that this Siward is the same as "Siwardus consanguineus" spoken of before He must have been a kinsman of Odelerius' English wife.

[4] In 924 C he says that, when he reached Normandy, "linguam, ut Joseph in Ægypto, quam non noveram audivi" The Normans are "exteri," but they show him no little kindness

[5] Ib "Nomen Vitalis pro Anglico vocamine, quod Normannis absonum censebatur, mihi impositum est."

[6] In 547 C he is "de extremis Merciorum finibus decennis Anglhgena huc advectus, barbarusque et ignotus advena," in the next page, "de Angliâ in Normanniam tenellus exsul, ut æterno Regi militarem, destinatus sum," and again in 924 C, "decennis itaque Britannicum mare transfretavi, exsul in Normanniam veni, cunctis ignotus neminem cognovi" Dunstan or Ælfheah could hardly have been a better Englishman than this son of a French settler

## HISTORY OF ORDERIC.

which owes no small part of its fame to his presence within its walls. There he spent the rest of his days, recording the acts of Norman saints and Norman heroes, but never losing the feelings of an Englishman, never forgetting his love for the land in which he was born.[1]

This personal history of Orderic is one which deserves our closest attention. Nothing shows more clearly how the foreign settlers in England mingled with the natives, and how their sons came to look upon themselves as Englishmen. The father of Orderic indeed, a Frenchman in the strictest sense, would not be open to any feelings which were distinctively Norman. But Normans and Frenchmen, both speaking the tongue of the conquerors, formed one class as distinguished from the conquered English, and, if there be anything in blood, a man from Orleans, whether his descent were Roman, Gaulish, or even Frankish, was much further removed from Englishmen than a man from Bayeux or Coutances. Yet this foreign priest clearly lived on terms of equality and friendship with the people from among whom he chose his wife, and to one of whom he trusted his son for education. To Orderic himself it seems never to have occurred, any more than it occurred to Thomas of London, that he was anything but an Englishman. His sojourn from childhood in a Norman monastery, his necessarily greater familiarity with the speech and manners of Normandy, never wiped out the English spirit from the heart of one who was born of an English mother on English soil. And Orderic the Englishman, as he loves to call himself,[2] could hardly have looked on his father, or even his father's patron, as an enemy of Englishmen.

We may remark also that, though Orderic often makes

CHAP. XX.

Lessons taught by the history of Orderic

The sons of the foreign settlers become English

Abiding English feeling of Orderic

---

[1] He once at least visited England, as we shall see further on
[2] "Vitalis Angligena" is his description throughout. See especially 547 B, and the end of his History, 924, 925

VOL IV.  K k

use of the common phrases of abuse towards the married clergy and their wives, though he lets us know that to be the son of a priest was looked on as a disqualification for ecclesiastical dignities,[1] yet he speaks of his own birth and his own parents without any feeling of shame. It is clear that Odelerius was a father of whom no son had need to be ashamed, and it is equally clear, from the position which he held and the influence which he exercised, that his neighbours, French and English, did not look on his married household as a matter of reproach. He was the right hand man of Earl Roger in his pious undertakings, and it was at his suggestion that the great Abbey of Shrewsbury first arose. The town which formed the capital of Roger's Earldom was a very stronghold of the secular clergy. At the time of the Conquest Shrewsbury contained no monastery, but several well-endowed foundations of secular canons stood within its walls.[2] The ordinary process would have been to drive the seculars out of one of these churches, as Earl Hugh did at Chester,[3] and to call this process a new foundation. Instead of this, Odelerius offered his own church as the groundwork of the new foundation.[4] The Earl made his vow before the altar

---

[1] See above, p 448

[2] The possessions of the churches of Saint Mary, Saint Michael, Saint Chad (Ceadda), Saint Alkmund (Ealhmund), and Saint Julian are all recorded in Domesday (252 b, 253). Of Saint Mary's, and the curious story about one of its canons, we have already heard, see vol ii p 550, 2nd ed The land there spoken of had, by the time of the Survey, come into the hands of Earl Roger, and it is added, " Vasta est et vasta inventa est," and of one possession of Saint Alkmund we read, " Comes Rogerius abstulit ecclesiæ" Otherwise none of these foundations seem to have been touched by the Conquest. Those of Saint Mary and Saint Chad remained independent collegiate churches with Deans down to the Dissolution Saint Julian and Saint Michael seem (Mon Angl viii 1464) to have got attached to the College of Battlefield founded by Henry the Fourth [3] See above, p 492

[4] Orderic (581 C) says that the monastery was founded " in fundo patris mei," evidently meaning the church of Saint Peter in which his father was

of Saint Peter, and made his gift by the symbolical CHAP XX
offering of his gloves [1] The Abbey gradually arose in the 1087-1094
Foregate of Shrewsbury,[2] but the endowment which it
received from its founder seems not to have been magnificent.[3] Odelerius himself was, according to his means, Gifts of Odelerius
a more bountiful benefactor than the Earl. He commended all that he had to the new monastery,[4] and both
himself and one of his sons became monks within its

priest So in Domesday (252 b) we read, "In Sciropesberie civitate *facit* [the present tense marks the work as still going on] Rogerius Comes abbatiam, et eidem dedit monasterium [mark the vague use of the word as applied to a parish church, see vol. 1 p 472, vol 11 p 441] Sancti Petri, ubi erat parochia civitatis" So in the foundation charter (Mon Angl iii 519) Roger speaks of his foundation as being made "in suburbio civitatis Salopesberiæ, in ecclesiâ sanctorum Apostolorum Petri et Pauli, quæ antiquitus ibi fundata erat" The local history printed in the Monasticon (iii 518) is to the same effect, and it presently adds, "locus ille in quo supradicta ecclesia fundata est fuit de hæreditate cujusdam militis, cui nomen Siwardus," and it is added that Roger gave Siward other lands to procure his consent and participation in the foundation If the description of Siward as "miles" is correct, "Siwardus consanguineus" and "Siwardus presbyter" (see above, p 495) must be two different people The nave of the church now standing, which must be of the age of Roger, or very little later, represents the wooden church of Odelerius, in the same way in which what is called Saint Joseph's Chapel represents the "lignea basilica" at Glastonbury

[1] Ord Vit 581 A. "Ad ecclesiam B Petri Apostoli abiit, ibique se abbatiam constructurum palam testibus multis devovit, totumque suburbium, quod extra portam orientalem situm est, Sancto Petro donavit, et super aram per chirothecas suas donationem posuit"

[2] Roger speaks in his charter of "vicum illum totum qui dicitur *Biforiete*," and in the local history (Mon Angl iii 517) "vicus ipse *Biforietta* vocatur quod nos linguâ Gallicâ *ante portam* dicimus" The place is still called the Abbey *Foregate*

[3] Ord Vit. 581 B "Terris ac redditibus *mediocriter* locupletavit" So Will Malm Gest Pont 305; "Scrobbesberiense recens est omnino, a Rogerio Comite de Monte Gomerico constitutum Ibi monachos locavit ex Sagio, angusto prorsus victu et amictu, sed qui has ærumnas spe futuræ mercedis lætis animis parvipendunt"

[4] Ib 580 D He first promises to spend fifteen pounds ("libras sterilensium") on the buildings of the monastery, and then follows one of those curious grants or commendations with a reservation, of which we have seen so many We read that "quod promiserat ex integro complevit"

K k 2

500        THE REVOLTS AGAINST WILLIAM.

CHAP XX.   walls.¹ The house however was always spoken of as the
Roger      work of the Earl. He placed in it an Abbot and monks
brings
monks      from his own monastery of Saint Martin of Seez,² and
from Seez
His death  there, when he died seven years after the death of the
and burial Conqueror, he was buried with the honours of a founder.³
1094
           Shrewsbury however was not the only place in his Earl-
           dom where Earl Roger appeared as a benefactor of monastic
Early      bodies. Wenlock in Shropshire had been in early times
history of
Wenlock    the seat of a house of nuns founded by the holy Mildburh,
           one of those virgin saints of royal birth in whom inde-
           pendent England had been so fruitful.⁴ The house, de-
           stroyed by the Danes, was, in some shape or other, restored
Roger in   by the bounty of Earl Leofric;⁵ and now under Earl Roger
troduces
Cluniac    the holy place of Saint Mildburh became a monastery of
monks      the Cluniac order, an order which had been lately intro-
1081
Introduc-  duced into England, and whose first-fruits were then
tion of the rising in the great foundation of William of Warren and
Cluniac
order into Gundrada at Lewes.⁶
England.
1077          But the cares of Earl Roger were not devoted wholly
Roger's    to ecclesiastical concerns. The position of his Earldom
wars with
the Welsh. involved constant dealings with his Welsh neighbours.

¹ Ord Vit 581 B "Datis ducentis libris argenti Deo Benedictum
filium suum ibidem obtulit, et ipse post obitum Rogerii Comitis monachilé
schema suscepit" He was then sixty years old
² See the charter, Mon Angl iii 519 (See Will Gem vii 22; Neustria
Pia, 577 )                               ³ Ord Vit 581 B.
⁴ Will Malm Gest. Pont 306, Gesta Regum, i 76, ii 216, where we
read of the wonderful discovery of her burying-place at the time of Earl
Roger's foundation.
⁵ Flor Wig 1057, Will. Malm Gest Regum, ii 196 It is plain from
Domesday, 252 b, that Leofric's foundation, whatever its nature, went on
till the changes made by Roger, "Ecclesiam Sanctæ Milburgæ fecit Rogerius
Comes abbatiam Ipsa ecclesia tenet Wenloch et tenuit T. R E" And the
same is said of all its other possessions, save one, of which we read, " Ipsa
ecclesia tenuit Godestoch Comes Rogerius dedit capellanis suis, sed ecclesia
debet habere." (Did Odelerius profit by this misappropriation ?) It is plain
that Roger did nothing except change the foundation and rebuild the church.
⁶ Will Malm Gest Pont. 306 On the Cluniac order, and its introduction into England, see Mon Angl v. 1, 72.

Under the later Earls of the House of Leofric the relations between Wales and Mercia, whatever we say of those between Wales and England, had commonly been friendly.[1] But the new Earls of the Mercians of the House of Montgomery[2] deemed it their business, now that England was conquered, to complete their work by the further conquest of Wales. The Welsh princes were ever fighting among themselves, and the Norman Earls, as English Earls on the same border had done before them, not uncommonly found it answer their purpose to help one party in the divided land against another. Earl Roger, with the aid of various valiant men whose names are duly recorded, was constantly at war with his dangerous neighbours. Chief among them was Warren the Bald, the husband of his niece Aimeria, who commanded at Shrewsbury,[3] and his own son Hugh, who, as the Welsh Chronicles witness, carried his wasting arms as far as the lands of Ceredigion and Dyfed.[4] But the chief border possession of the House of Montgomery was that to which they transferred the name which they had themselves borrowed from the ancestral hill in the land of

*Relations between the Welsh and the House of Leofric*

*Feuds among the Welsh princes*

*Invasions of Wales.*

[1] This is shown in the marriage of Gruffydd and Ealdgyth, in the help given by the Welsh to the Northumbrian revolt, and in more than one instance since the coming of William. See above, pp. 109, 182.

[2] "Rogerius Merciorum Comes" appears in Orderic, 667 B, but in 768 A the two Hughs, he of Chester and Roger's son and successor, appear more accurately as "duo Consules quibus Merciorum præcipue regio subjacet." In the same spirit (671 A) he calls the Bishop of Chester or Coventry "Merciorum Episcopus."

[3] Ord. Vit. 522 B. "Warinus Calvus, corpore parvo sed animo magno." Is this the "Warinus" the "antecessor" of the Sheriff Rainald who gave lands to Saint Peter for his soul? (Domesday, 254.)

[4] Ann. Camb. 1071. "Franci vastaverunt Keredigiaun." On this, to fill up the cup of misfortune, follows, "Menevia vastata est a gentilibus et Bangor similiter." 1072 "De Mungumeri Hugo vastavit Keredigiaun." Brut y Tywysogion, 1071, 1072. "Then, a year after that, the French ravaged Ceredigion and Dyfed. Then, a year after that, a second time the French devastated Ceredigion." The Welsh word for "ravaged" and "devastated" is the same.

502                    THE REVOLTS AGAINST WILLIAM.

CHAP. XX. Lisieux.[1] The castle of Shrewsbury was indeed a fortress raised to curb a conquered town and district, but it was also the seat of the civil government of a ruler who seems not wholly to have lacked the wish to do judgement and justice. But the second seat of the power of Earl Roger was, no less than the fortress of William Peverel in the Peakland, a simple vulture's nest on a crag. The site on which it arose was not a conquest of the Earl's own; it was already an English possession, and in King Eadward's days the neighbouring land had been held by three Englishmen, free from all taxes, as a mere hunting-ground in the wilderness.[2] But when Earl Roger's fortress had crowned the height, a town arose at its base, which in the tongue of the conquered Cymry bore, from some follower of the Earl, the name of *Tre Baldwin*. But on Norman and English lips castle and town took the name of their founder; and, in the later division of Wales, the name of Montgomery passed from the town to the newly formed county. No other man among the conquerors could boast so truly as Earl Roger that he called the land after his own name.

Foundation of the Castle of Montgomery Before 1072

William Fitz-Osbern, Earl of Hereford 1067–1071.

To the south along the British border lay the lands held by the great oppressor, William Fitz-Osbern, Earl of Hereford.[3] His tenure of his Earldom was short, and, as regards

---

[1] Domesday, 254 "Ipse Comes construxit castrum Muntgumeri vocatum"

[2] Ib "Adjacent Li hidæ et dimidia quas tenuerunt Seuuar, Oslac, Azor, de Rege E quietas ab omni geldo ad venandum eas habuerunt."

[3] There is something very striking in the tone, half of lamentation, half of triumph, in which Orderic (536 A) moralizes over the career of William Fitz-Osbern, "Vere gloria mundi ut flos fœni decidit et arescit, ac velut fumus deficit et transit. Ubi est Guillelmus Osberni filius, Herfordensis Comes et Regis vicarius, Normanniæ dapifer, et magister militum bellicosus? Hic nimirum primus et maximus oppressor Anglorum fuit, et enormem causam per temeritatem suam enutrivit, per quam multis millibus ruina miseræ mortis incubuit. Verum justus Judex omnia videt, et unicuique prout meretur digne redhibet Proh dolor ! ecce Guillelmus corruit,

Englishmen, his conquests were never complete, for the submission of Eadric did not take place till the dominion and life of Earl William had come to an end. But on the Cymry his short reign allowed him to make some fearful inroads. The Norman version makes him overthrow Welsh Kings by wholesale, Rhys, Cadwgan, Meredydd, and others who are not named.[1] The native chronicles of Wales make matters a little clearer. The names of all three princes appear in the Welsh history of the time, but it is the fate of Meredydd which we can most clearly connect with the arms of William Fitz-Osbern. We have seen Meredydd the son of Owen established in South Wales after the civil war in which Rhiwallon fell, and which broke up the arrangements which had been made by Harold after the fall of Gruffydd the son of Llywelyn.[2] But Caradoc the son of Gruffydd the son of Rhydderch, the same who had destroyed Harold's house at Portskewet,[3] now leagued himself with the French, that is evidently with the Earl of Hereford, and their united forces overthrew Meredydd on the banks of the Rumney.[4] We have here reached the beginning, though only the beginning, of that great Norman settlement in South Wales which was a few years later to make Morganwg, above almost every other part of the Isle of Britain, a land of Norman knights and Norman castles. But this work was to be done by other hands than those of William Fitz-Osbern. His career

*His wars with the Welsh*

*Meredydd defeated and slain by Caradoc and Earl William. 1070*

audax athleta recepit quod promeruit. Ut multos ense trucidavit, ipse quoque ferro repente interiit."

[1] Ord. Vit. 521 D. "Rex Guillelmus .. eum cum Gualterio de Laceio aliisque probatis pugilibus contra Britones bellis inhiantes opposuit. Horum audacia Brachanianuos primitus invasit, et Guallorum Reges Risen et Caducan ac Mariadoth, abosque plures prostravit."

[2] See above, p. 183.

[3] See vol. ii. p. 480.

[4] Ann. Camb. 1070. "Maredut filius Owini a Cradauc filio Griffid et a Francis occisus est super ripam Remny." So Brut y Tywysogion to the same effect.

was the shortest of any among William's chief followers; it was confined to the actual years of the Conquest. It is therefore no wonder that all that we hear of him relates to his military exploits, and that he does not, like his neighbour at Shrewsbury, appear in England either as an ecclesiastical founder or as a civil ruler. We hear of his liberality, but it was a liberality shown towards soldiers only, and one of which the more discerning mind of his master did not approve.[1] We hear of his legislation in his county of Hereford, but his only recorded ordinance is one which narrowly limited the penalties for offences committed by members of the favoured class.[2] But, as he had been the earliest friend of William, he retained his confidence to the last. From his warfare on the Welsh border he was called away to give the help of his counsel to Queen Matilda in her regency of the Norman Duchy,[3] and from thence he went to lose his life in that Flemish warfare of which it will be better to put off our notice until we have finished the survey of our own island.

*Earl William's military legislation*

*His death in Flanders 1071*

From the West we turn again to the North. Our best authority for Northern affairs[4] describes King Malcolm as

---

[1] William of Malmesbury (Gest. Reg. iii 256) ventures to say of him, "Siquidem .. Willelmus filius Osberni, principibus optimis comparandus fuerit, haud scio an etiam præponendus." He goes on to say, "Erat in eo mentis animositas quam commendabat manûs pene prodiga liberalitas, unde factum est ut militum multitudine, quibus larga stipendia dabat, hostium aviditatem arceret, civium sedulitatem haberet; quare pro effusis sumptibus asperrimam Regis offensam incurrit, quod gazas suas improvide dilapidaret."

[2] Ib. "Manet ad hanc diem in comitatu ejus apud Herefordum legum quas statuit inconcussa firmitas, ut nullus miles pro qualicumque commisso plus septem solidis solvat; quum in aliis provinciis, ob parvam occasiunculam in transgressione præcepti herilis, viginti vel viginti quinque pendantur."

[3] See below, § 4.

[4] On the invasions of Malcolm, and Mr Hinde's objections to the statements of the Northern interpolator, see Appendix QQ.

choosing the year of the completion of the Conquest, when William had withdrawn from the wasted lands of York and Durham, for another attack on a land which seemed already to have been given up to utter ruin. He passed through Cumberland, still part of his own dominions, into Teesdale,[1] and thence into Cleveland, and thence again northwards into the patrimony of Saint Cuthbeiht. The little that the Normans had left was now devoured by the Scots; men lost all that they had, and some of them lost their lives as well;[2] churches were burned along with the men who had taken shelter in them.[3] Malcolm had reached the mouth of the Wear, and was there riding backwards and forwards, enjoying the sight of the sufferings which his followers were inflicting on the wretched English,[4] and above all the destruction of the church of Saint Peter by fire.[5] While he was thus engaged two pieces of news were brought to him. The ships which bore the English exiles from conquered York had put in at the haven of Wearmouth.[6] They seem to have tarried awhile with the Danish fleet;[7]

CHAP XX.

Malcolm invades Northern England. 1070.

He ravages Cleveland and Durham

His ravages at Wearmouth

Eadgar and his sisters reach Wearmouth

---

[1] Sim Dun 1070, p 87 "Per idem tempus infinita Scottorum multitudo, ducente Malcolino Rege per Cumbreland traducta, versus orientem divertens, universam Tesedale et ejus finitima loca ultra citraque feroci vastavit depopulatione"

[2] Ib "Depopulata Clyvelande ex parte, repentina depopulatione occupat Heurtternysse, indeque per terras Sancti Cuthberti ferociter discurrens, omnes omnibus rebus, nonnullos etiam ipsis privat animabus"

[3] Ib

[4] Ib "Quum circa ripas fluminis equitaret, deque altiori loco suorum crudelia in miseros Anglos facinora prospiciens, tali spectaculo animos et oculos pasceret"

[5] Ib "Tunc et ecclesiam Sancti Petri Apostolorum principis in Weremuthe flammâ suorum, ipso inspectante, consumpsit" See Appendix HHH

[6] Ib "Nuntiatum est illi clitonem Eadgarum suasque sorores, regiæ stirpis puellas decoras, pluresque alios prædivites de suis sedibus profugos in illum portum applicuisse navibus"

[7] At least we have nowhere else to put them during the winter of 1069 Most likely they stayed with the fleet as long as it kept in the Humber, and parted company with the Danes as soon as they sailed towards Ely. This is in fact implied in the words of the next extract

CHAP. XX.  but if they had accompanied them in all their doings along the eastern coast, we should most likely have heard of it. At all events, ships drew near to the haven of Wearmouth, bearing the Ætheling Eadgar, his mother Agatha, his sisters Margaret and Christina, along with Siward Barn, Mærleswegen, and others, who were once more seeking a shelter at the court of Malcolm after the final ruin of their hopes in England.[1] They could hardly have expected to find their intended host in the very act of ravaging their native country; but his savage occupation in no way lessened his friendly feelings towards them. In his eyes perhaps England was already so completely the Kingdom of William that the friend of Eadgar was bound to deal with it as with the land of an enemy. The man who was feasting his eyes with the ruin of Wearmouth hastened to show all courtesy to the guests who were entering its haven.

Malcolm's friendly reception of the exiles.

He met them in person; he gave them his fullest peace, and bade them dwell in his realm as long as it might please them[2] They sailed on towards Scotland; he went on with the harrying of Northumberland For, while he was still at Wearmouth, another piece of tidings had been brought to him. While he was ravaging the land of Saint Cuthberht, Gospatric, William's Earl in Northhumberland, had burst into Malcolm's Cumbrian province,

Gospatric invades Cumberland.

---

[1] Sim Dun 1070, p 86 "Fuerant ibidem eo tempore et aliæ naves nonnullæ, quarum ductores erant clito Eadgarus cum matre Agathâ et duabus sororibus Margaretâ et Christinâ, Siward Barn, Marlessuein, Alfwinus filius Normanni, et alii quamplures, qui post expugnationem castellorum Eboraci, *Danis in sua revertentibus,* quoniam eis auxilio fuerant, indignationem Regis sibi metuerant, Scotiam ire profugi parabant, ibique navigationem prosperam præstolabantur " I can give no further account of Ælfwine the son of Northman The "aliæ naves" are opposed to that which carried Bishop Æthelwine

[2] Ib p 87 "Datis ergo dextris venientes ad se benigne alloquitur, eisque cum suis omnibus regni sui habitationem quamdiu vellent cum pace donavit firmissimâ "

had harried the land with fire and sword, and had returned with great spoil to the old fortress of Northumbrian Kings and Earls at Bamborough.[1] That post he held as his head-quarters, strengthening himself against any attack, and ever and anon making vigorous sallies against the invaders.[2] When the news of Gospatric's inroad into Cumberland was brought to Malcolm at Wearmouth, he was filled with wrath, and issued orders, such as we may be sure that William never gave, and which remind us of the worst deeds of the apostate Swend[3] and of the heathen invaders before him. From that day forward none of English race were to be spared; the remnant that the Norman had left were to pay for the exploit of their Earl by death or by hopeless slavery.[4] The word was given, and it was carried out to the letter by the ruthless marauders to whom it was addressed. The old men and women were slaughtered, as our local informant puts it, like swine for the banquet.[5] The Scots are even charged with renewing one of the most fiendish cruelties of the heathen Danes, that of seeking their sport in tossing little children on the points of their spears[6] Young men and maidens,

*Malcolm's increased cruelties*

---

[1] Sim Dun 1070, p 87 "Inter has Scottorum vastationes ac rapinas Gospatricus Comes . . . accitis auxiliatoribus strenuis atroci depopulatione Cumbreland invadit Peractâ cæde et incendio, cum magnâ prædâ revertitur, seque cum sociis in munitionem Babbanburch firmissimam conclusit"

[2] Ib "Ex quâ sæpius prorumpens vires hostium debilitavit."

[3] See vol 1. p 395

[4] Sim Dun 1070, p 88 "Auditis ille (quum adhuc flammâ suorum ardentem Sancti Petri ecclesiam spectaret) quæ Cospatricus in suos fecerat, vix præ furore seipsum ferens, jussit suis ut nulli Anglicæ gentis ulterius parcerent, sed omnes vel necando in terram funderent vel captivando sub jugum perpetuæ servitutis abducerent"

[5] Ib "Senes et vetulæ, alii gladiis obtruncantur, alii, *ut porci ad esum destinati*, lanceis confodiuntur"

[6] Ib "Rapti ab uberibus matrum parvuli in altum aere projiciuntur, unde recidentes lancearum acuminibus excipiuntur hastilibus confertim solo infixis, hâc crudelitate pro ludorum spectaculo delectabantur bestiis

*CHAP XX.*
*English captives driven into Scotland*

and all who were of age and strength to be useful in slavery, were driven in fetters to the land of bondage.[1] Many sank through fatigue, some of them never to rise again; those in whom life was left found no pity, but were driven on all the more unsparingly by the ruthless bidding of Malcolm.[2] Thus, we are told, was Scotland filled with English slaves of either sex. There was not a village, there was not even a house, so poor but an English captive was there to be seen in thraldom.[3]

*The English exiles reach Scotland*

While Malcolm was thus making his fearful march homewards, rich with the human spoil of England, the English exiles had reached his land in safety by sea. To some at least of the party it was only a momentary shelter.

*Æthelwine and Siward Barn go to Ely 1071*

Siward Barn and Bishop Æthelwine soon left Scotland to share the fortunes of their countrymen among the fens of Ely.[4] But the Ætheling and his family paid Malcolm a longer visit, and one of the company was now at last persuaded to accept the land of refuge as a permanent home. Margaret, the sister of Eadgar, had perhaps been betrothed to Malcolm in the days of King Eadward.[5] He had perhaps begun to yearn after her from the time of her first

*Eadgar and his sisters remain in Scotland.*

---

crudeliores Scotti." Of this particular form of cruelty we hear again in the invasion of the Scots under David in 1138, when it is specially attributed to the savages of Galloway, see Æthelred of Rievaux, X Scriptt 341; Hen Hunt Scriptt p Bædam, 222 Simeon adds the curious reflexion, "Sic innocens ætas cœlum adscensuras, inter cœlum pendens et terram, emittit animas"

[1] Sim Dun 1070, p 88 "Juvenes et juvenculæ, et quicumque operibus ac laboribus idonei videbantur, ante faciem hostium vincti compelluntur, ut perpetuo exsilio in servos et ancillas redigantur."

[2] Ib "Horum quædam dum plusquam vires ferrent currendo ante ora compellentium fatigarentur, illico ruentes in terram, eumdem locum casûs et mortis habebant Hæc Malcolmus considerans, nullis miserorum lacrimis, nullis gemitibus, flectebatur ad misericordiam, sed potius jussit ut amplius perurgerentur eundo."

[3] Ib "Repleta est ergo Scotia servis et ancillis Anglici generis, ita ut etiam usque hodie nulla, non dico villula sed nec domuncula, sine his valeat inveniri."

[4] See above, p 468        [5] See Appendix BB

visit.[1] At all events, the marriage of the Scottish King with the sister of the English Ætheling was now not long delayed. Malcolm's first wife, Ingebiorg, the widow of Thorfinn,[2] the mother of the two young Earls who had tarried with the Norwegian fleet at Riccall,[3] must have been removed in some way, and for Margaret's sake we may hope that she was removed by death rather than by divorce.[4] But the eagerness for the match was wholly on Malcolm's side. He indeed might well be bent on such an alliance. Margaret was indeed a banished wanderer; but both her personal merits and the splendour of her descent set her far above such wives as the Kings of Scots had hitherto taken to share their thrones. None of Malcolm's predecessors had ever had the chance of wooing a bride whose fathers were the whole line of West-Saxon Kings, and whose mother's kin went up to the Cæsars who bare rule over Rome.[5] But both the sisters of Eadgar were inclined to a religious life. Christina we shall see again as the stern Abbess of a famous English monastery, and Margaret's prayer at this time was to serve the mighty Lord through this short life in pure maidenhood.[6] She herself, her brother, and all her companions at first utterly refused

*CHAP XX.*
Malcolm seeks Margaret in marriage.
Question as to his former wife Ingebiorg.

Margaret's refusal and final unwilling consent.

---

[1] Chron Wig 1067 "Da begann se cynge Malcholm gyrnan his [Eadgares] sweostor him to wife, Margaretan"

[2] See vol III p 344  [3] Ib pp 357, 375

[4] See Appendix BB

[5] The English Chronicler descants with evident pride on Margaret's doubly royal kindred, " Of geleaffullan and æðelan cynne heo wæs asprungon, hire fæder wæs Eadward æðeling, Eadmundes sunu kynges, Eadmund Æþelreding, Æþelred Eadgaring, Eadgar *Eadreding* [it should be *Eadmunding*], and swa forð on þæt cynecynn, and hire modor cynn gæð to Heinrice casere, þe hæfde anwald ofer Rome " Henry the Second ought to be meant, but some of the reflected glory of Henry the Third seems to be thrown back on him.

[6] Chron Wig. 1067,

" Þæt heo on mægðhade  On þisan life sceortan,
Mihtigan Drihtne  On clænre forhæfednysse
Mid lichoman here heortan  Cweman mihte."

510                THE REVOLTS AGAINST WILLIAM.

CHAP. XX. to hearken to the King's suit. But the love of Malcolm was not to be withstood. He dealt with her brother till he said Yea; for in truth he durst not say otherwise, seeing they had come into his power.[1] In fact the marriage-vow of Margaret to Malcolm seems to have been plighted as unwillingly as the homage-vow of Harold to William. But the results in the two cases were widely different. It was a good day indeed for Malcolm and for Scotland when Margaret was persuaded or constrained to exchange the easy self-dedication of the cloister for the harder task of doing her duty in that state of life to which it had pleased God to call her. Margaret became the mirror of wives, mothers, and Queens, and none ever more worthily earned the honours of saintship. Her gentle influence reformed whatever needed to be reformed in her husband,[2] and none laboured more diligently for the advance of all temporal and spiritual enlightenment in her adopted country.[3] The wife of Malcolm played a part not wholly unlike the part played by the earlier wives of Æthelberht and Eadwine, an influence the opposite to the evil influence of the Norman Emma. There was indeed no need for Margaret to bring a new religion into Scotland, but she gave a new life to the religion which she found existing

*She marries Malcolm.*

*Her influence on her husband,*

*and on Scotland generally.*

*Her ecclesiastical changes*

---

[1] Chron Wig 1067 "And he [Eadgar] and his menn ealle lange wiðcwædon and eac heo sylf wiðsoc, and cwæð [then follows the poem] Se kynge befealh georne hire breðer, oð þæt he cwæð *ia* wið, and eac he elles ne dorste, forþan þe hi on his anwald becumene wæron."

[2] Ib "Se kyng hi þa underfeng, þa hit hire unþances wære, and him gelicade hire þeawas, and þancode God þe him swylce gemæccean mihtiglice forgeaf, and wishce hine beþohte swa he full witter wæs, and awende hine sylfne to Gode, and ælce unsiuernysse oferhogode." So Sim. Dun 88, "Cujus studio et industria Rex ipse, deposita morum barbarie, factus est honestior atque civilior.

[3] Ib " Deos foresprecene cwén seoððan on þam lande manege nytwyrðe dæda gefremede Gode to lofe, and eac on þa kynewisan wel geþeh, eallswa hire gecýnde wæs " On Saint Margaret, see Palgrave, iv 315 et seqq , part of the admirable chapter on Scottish affairs which is one of the gems of his work

there, and she made changes in various points where the traditions of the Scottish Church still differed from the received practice of Western Christendom.[1]  She became the correspondent of Lanfranc,[2] and her Life was written by the holy Prior and Bishop Turgot.[3]  And to turn from the personal and ecclesiastical aspect of the marriage to its historical and political side, no royal marriage was ever more important in its results for both of the countries concerned.  It was through Margaret that the old kingly blood of England passed into the veins of the descendants of the Conqueror;[4] it was in her daughter, the heiress of her virtues, that the green tree began to return to its place.[5]  And in the land of her adoption the mission of Margaret was to put the finishing stroke to the process which was fast making Scotland English.  The Kings of Scots had already learned that their English Earldom of Lothian was in truth the most valuable portion of their

CHAP. XX.

Impulse given to English influences in Scotland

---

[1] From the words of the Chronicler one might almost have thought that Margaret had to work on a heathen bridegroom, just like her Frankish and Kentish predecessors  And certainly, to judge from what we have seen of him on his Northumbrian raid, Malcolm would seem to have been personally a far more unpromising subject than Æthelberht or Eadwine  In the Chronicles Malcolm is "vir infidelis," Margaret is sent "þone kyng gerihtan of þam dweliande præðe, and gebēgean hine to beteran wege, and his leode samod, and alegcean þa unþeawas þa seo þeod ær becode"  On the nature of these "unþeawas," see Mr E W Robertson, i 149  His whole account of Malcolm and Margaret should be read  See also Innes' Scotland in the Middle Ages, 85 (though an unheard of exploit is there attributed to Margaret's father), and Burton's whole chapter beginning i 378

[2] See the letter of Lanfranc to her, Giles, i 59, but it contains no historical information  He sends to her a certain Goldewinus, who from his name may be supposed to be an Englishman

[3] The Life of Margaret by Turgot, printed in Mr Hinde's edition of Simeon, is one of the most interesting pieces that we have as a personal and ecclesiastical biography, but it throws little light on the marriage as a mere piece of history

[4] The descent of the Conqueror's sons from Ælfred seems to have been forgotten  See vol i p 23, ii p 304

[5] See vol iii pp 11, 30

dominions. Malcolm's sojourn in England, his close relations with Siward and Tostig, doubtless helped on the spread of English influences in Scotland.[1] And the coming of Margaret and the English exiles who followed in her train finally settled the matter Lothian, and the neighbouring lands which, like Fife, soon became as English as Lothian, became, as I said near the beginning of this work,[2] the historical Scotland. The Kings of Scots who sprang from Malcolm and Margaret were Englishmen, speaking English, often bearing English names,[3] ranking as the highest among English nobles,[4] and not wholly without hopes of the English Crown Just at the moment when England became in some measure French, Scotland became thoroughly English. The Celtic portion of Northern Britain became, like the Celtic portion of Southern Britain, a troublesome appendage which it cost much pains to keep in even nominal allegiance. The Scotland so formed, the Kingdom of Dunfermline and Edinburgh, remained an English state, speaking the purest surviving form of the English language, and whatever was other than English in it came from that irrepressible Norman influence which passed from the Southern England into the Northern. At last another marriage, the marriage of another English

---

[1] See Palgrave, iv. 311

[2] See vol. 1 p 140 Much on this head is to be found in the writers whom I have referred to in the last few notes, though I cannot say that Mr Robertson's Appendix, "On the Theory of Displacement" (ii 484), is so clear as the writings of his fellows I presume that his object is to show that Lothian did not *begin* to become English at this time—a point on which there can be no doubt Mr Innes (88) quotes the signatures of two charters of Duncan the stepson, and Edgar the son of Margaret All the names are English or Danish Cf Palgrave, iv. 334.

[3] See the list in Palgrave, iv 341, with his comments. Of eight children five have English names—Eadward, Eadmund, Eadgar, Æthelred, and Eadgyth The others are Alexander, David, and Mary. Not one is Scottish Alexander reminds one of Constantine and Gregory at an earlier time.

[4] See Will Malm v 400, Hist Nov i 3

Margaret—widely different as was the sister of Henry the Eighth from the sister of Eadgar Ætheling—completed the work which the earlier marriage began. In three generations, after exactly the space of a hundred years, the descendants of the second Margaret contrived to place themselves by an alleged hereditary right[1] on the throne which the immediate descendants of the elder Margaret had striven in vain to win.

CHAP. XX

1603.

The next year, probably the year of the marriage of Malcolm and Margaret, was the year of the revolt and re-conquest of the Isle of Ely. William was fully occupied in that quarter till a late stage of the autumn,[2] and no step could at once be taken to revenge the Northumbrian inroad of Malcolm. All that we hear of the North during the year which was so busy in the East is the reception of the new Bishop of Durham, the Lotharingian Walcher, in his diocese. The King's English favourite, Eglaf the Housecarl, and other men of note, led the new Prelate as far as York. He was there met at the King's bidding by Gospatric, the Earl of his diocese, and was led to his cathedral city, where at Midlent he took possession of the chair of Saint Cuthberht,[3] the first man of foreign birth who had sat there since the days of the Scottish missionaries in the first infancy of the Northumbrian Church.

1071.

Walcher takes possession of the see of Durham April 3, 1071

During the former part of the next year William's presence was needed in his own Duchy,[4] but in the

---

[1] It should always be remembered that the Stewarts, reigning in defiance of the lawful settlement of Henry the Eighth's will, were simply usurpers, except so far as popular acquiescence in their succession might be held to be equivalent to a popular election. It was by an Act of Parliament passed in the reign of her last elected King that the Crown of England was first made hereditary.

[2] See above, p. 480.

[3] Sim. Dun. 1071 (89 Hinde). On Eglaf or "Eilaf Huscarl," see above, p. 305.

[4] See below, § 4.

VOL. IV.  L l

514           THE REVOLTS AGAINST WILLIAM.

CHAP. XX.
William's expedition against Scotland.
August 15, 1072.
His motives

autumn his hands were free, and in the month of August he set forth against Scotland with a mighty force both by land and sea.[1] He went at once to avenge the special wrongs which his Kingdom had suffered at the hands of Malcolm,[2] and to assert in a practical shape his claim to the Imperial rights of his predecessors over the whole Isle of Britain.[3] Nothing else was now lacking to the perfection of William's Conquest. England was his own; the subjugation of the restless Britons might be left to the Earls of the border; but the subjugation of the greatest vassal of the Empire, the only vassal of undoubted kingly rank, was an enterprise which called for his own presence and for his

Division of the land and sea forces
Eadric accompanies William.

full force. The fleet was sent to beset the whole coast,[4] while he himself set forth with the land army. Among his following came Eadric the Wild, the hero of Herefordshire, who had been admitted to the King's peace about two years before.[5] We are not told whether Eadric's presence was the result of his new-born loyalty, or whether he was called on to follow William into Scotland as Hereward was perhaps called on to follow him into Maine.[6] At all events, it is plain that the position which Eadric held in William's host was, outwardly at least, one of high

Aspect of the war in the eyes of Englishmen.

honour.[7] And the present warfare of William was one in which the most patriotic Englishman might serve him without scruple. The Scot was more foreign than the

[1] Chron Ab 1073, Petrib 1072 "Her Willelm cyng lædde scipfyrde and landfyrde to Scotlande" So Florence, who gives the date "post Assumptionem S Mariæ"

[2] Sim Dun 1072 (89, Hinde) "Graviter namque Rex Scottorum Malcolmus eum offenderat, quia, ut supradictum est, anno præterito regni sui terminos atrociter depopulatus fuerat"

[3] Flor Wig. 1072. "Ut eam suæ ditioni subjugaret"

[4] Chron. Ab. 1073, Petrib. 1072 "And þæt land on þa sæ healfe mid scipum ymbe læg"

[5] See above, p 463        [6] See above, p. 486

[7] Flor. Wig 1072. "Habens in comitatu suo Edricum cognomento Silvaticum" The valiant Englishman was received as the Conqueror's personal *Gesið*.

Norman, and, whatever evils the Norman had done, the Scot had done worse. Malcolm might give himself out as the champion—some day perhaps to be the heir—of the Old-English kingly house; he might be the protector of Eadgar, the husband of Margaret; but just at that time Englishmen would be far more likely to look on him simply as the last and most brutal ravager of Northumberland, and they might look on William as, for the nonce at least, the avenger of that great wrong. Never would Englishmen be so ready to acknowledge William as their lawful King as when he was about to lead them forth against the old enemy of England. Men to whom it was pain and grief that William should be King of the English would, now that he was King of the English, be ready to do him loyal service in asserting the rights of the English Crown over its foreign vassals. Men might for a moment forget Senlac and York and Ely, as they followed the standard of a King who might seem to be leading the hosts of England to another Brunanburh.

But the Scottish campaign of William was not destined to be marked by any special feat of arms. His march might pass for a repetition of the march of Cnut thirty-five years before.[1] Whatever resistance William met with he easily overcame;[2] but there is nothing to show the Norman, any more than the Danish, Conqueror had to assert his rights over Scotland at the expense of a pitched battle. William marched through Lothian, the English Earldom held by the Scottish Kings; he crossed the Forth,[3]

*CHAP. XX.*

*William in Scotland.*

*No armed opposition.*

---

[1] See vol. i. p 497
[2] I presume, with Lingard (1 466), that this is the meaning of the difficult words of the Chronicles, "and he þær naht ne funde þæs þe heom þe betere (bet, Petrib ) wære." But see Thorpe, ii 179
[3] This seems to be Mr Earle's explanation (Parallel Chronicles, 348, 349) of the other difficult passage which goes just before in the Chronicles, "and his landfyrde æt þæm gewæde inn lædde," or in Worcester, " himsylf

516

CHAP. XX. and found himself in the proper Scotland. He pressed on through the Celtic lands over which, under the gentle influence of Margaret, civilization was just beginning to spread itself. He came near to the broad estuary of the Tay, the stream flowing down from that wilder northern land whose mountain rampart fringes the distant landscape at the furthest point to which William's mission as Conqueror led him. This was at Abernethy, the more southerly spot of that name, a spot said to have once been a dwelling-place of the Pictish Kings, but which is now a mean village, though still keeping the name of a burgh. The town lies on the slope of a low range of hills looking down on the wide Tay and on the loftier hills beyond it, and its houses cluster round a structure which has but one fellow within the Isle of Britain. The round bell-tower, its shape, it may be, borrowed from distant Ravenna, but clothed with a distinctive character of its own, had been the favourite form of ecclesiastical tower in Ireland from the earliest times,[1] and it remained so for a hundred years or more after the days of William. But this characteristic fashion of the Scots of Ireland seems never to have been prevalent among the Scots of Britain. Two examples alone remain in our island. One, the probable work of Kenneth, is

*He reaches Abernethy.*

*The Round Tower*

mid his landfyrde ferde inn ofer þæt wæð." The words of the Waverley Annals, referred to by Mr Earle, and which, as usual, translate the Peterborough Chronicle, are " exercitum suum per terram apud *Scotwade* introduxit " " *Inn* lædde," William was not " inn," he had not reached the genuine Scottish realm, till he crossed the Forth. So Æthelred of Rievaux, X Scriptt 340, "Angliæ victor Willielmus per Laodonam, Calatriam, Scotiam, usque ad Abernith penetraret " What is " Calatria ?"

[1] The Irish round towers cannot be better described than they are by Giraldus, Top Hib. ii 9 (vol ii. p 92, ed Dimock), " turres ecclesiasticæ, quæ more patriæ arctæ sunt et altæ, necnon et rotundæ " After the labours of Dr Petrie, it is needless to prove to any rational being that the "ecclesiasticæ turres " are "ecclesiasticæ turres " But it is as well to remark that the usage, which was ancient in the time of Giraldus, still went on in his own day. Some of the round towers are as old as an "ecclesiastica turris" is likely to be, others date only from the twelfth, or even the thirteenth, century

attached to the cathedral church of Brechin;[1] the other still stands, its upper portion seemingly rebuilt soon after William's day, but with the lower part of its primitive fabric still untouched, at the spot where William and Malcolm met face to face. The King of Scots came to Abernethy, and, under the shadow of the old Scottish tower, he became the man of the Conqueror, now, like the Kings who had gone before him, not only King of the Angles and Saxons, but Lord of the whole Empire of the Isle of Albion. As the elder Malcolm had bowed to Cnut, so the younger Malcolm now bowed to William. The vassal was received into the peace of his lord, and he gave hostages for his good faith, the young Donald, his son by the dead or forsaken Ingebiorg, being among them.[2] No further details are given; but we may suspect that among the terms of peace was a demand on William's side that Eadgar should be no longer sheltered in Scot-

*Malcolm becomes the man of William.*

*Malcolm gives his son Donald as a hostage.*

*Possible removal of Eadgar.*

---

[1] I have to thank Mr Stuart for the hint that the entry in the Pictish Chronicles (Johnston, 143), "Hic [Kenneth, Eadgar's Kenneth] est qui tribuit magnam civitatem Brechne Domino," gives the date of the foundation of the church and tower of Brechin. The Brechin tower is purely Irish; at Abernethy the upper part, which has plainly been rebuilt, shows Norman touches.

[2] Chron Wig 1073, Petrib 1072. "And se cyng Melcolm com and griðede wið þone cyng Willelm, and gislas sealde, and his man wæs." Florence cuts the formula of submission shorter, but adds the place, "Rex Scottorum Malcolmus, in loco qui dicitur Abernithici, occurrit [Willelmo] et homo suus devenit." So Will. Malm Gest Reg iii 250, "Malcolmus, antequam ad manus veniretur, se dedidit." Æthel Riev X Scriptt 340, "Bellicosus ille Malcolmus deditione factus est noster." Yet to become the man of a lord is not a Roman deditio. Mr. Robertson (i 137, ii 401), on the strength of the account in Florence, 1091, tries hard to make out that Malcolm simply did homage for twelve lordships in England and a pension of twelve marks of gold. Mr Burton (i. 409) looks the matter in the face, but it is odd to make Florence borrow from Æthelred. But I have to thank Mr Robertson for sending me to the passage bearing on the matter in the Ulster Annals, 1072, Johnston (69). In the version of Johnston the King's son—doubtless Donald—is made to be among the hostages, but in the Latin text in O'Conor, iv 343, it appears thus, "Franci profecti sunt Albaniam, et abstulerunt Regem Albaniæ secum obsidem."

518    THE REVOLTS AGAINST WILLIAM.

CHAP XX. land. We next hear of him in Flanders, two years later, when he was still out of the King's peace;[1] and no other time or cause for his removal from Scotland seems so likely. William had thus gained every formal point, and he had doubtless really made a deep impression on the Scottish King and his subjects by his arms and by his personal presence. The scene at Abernethy was the crowning day of William's fortune. He was for a moment undisputed lord, without a dog moving his tongue against him, from the Orkneys to the Angevin march. The Bastard of Falaise, Duke, King, and more than King, gave the law, not only at Rouen and at Winchester, but at Dunfermline and at Le Mans. How long such undisturbed supremacy lasted we shall presently see. The oaths of Malcolm were kept much as the oaths of Scottish Kings commonly were kept. His pledge of homage to William bound him about as much as his pledge of sworn brotherhood to Tostig.[2] William no doubt knew as well as any man that it would be so. But he had no motive or excuse for tarrying any longer within the dominions of his Northern vassal. The Lord of all Britain, having received the homage and the hostages of the Scottish King, turned his face southward and came back to England with his host.[3]

The highest point of William's fortune.

William Lord of all Britain

He returns to England.

Legendary accounts of his march
He reaches Pons Ælii, Monkchester, or Newcastle-on-Tyne

The march of William from Scotland was marked by important events in the history of Northumberland. A legendary tale, recording one of the usual ecclesiastical miracles, enables us to trace out part of his course. He came back by the site which had been the Pons Ælii of Roman days, and which was to become the great haven of Newcastle-upon-Tyne. In William's day the Roman name

[1] See below, p 568, and Chron. Wig. 1074, Petrib. 1073.
[2] See vol. ii. pp. 385, 460
[3] Chron. Wig. 1073, Petrib 1072 "Se cyug ham gewende mid ealre his fyrde."

had been forgotten, and the beginnings of the New Castle did not arise till a later stage of his reign. The place was known by the less famous name of Monkchester.[1] The Roman bridge too had vanished, and those wonderful works of modern skill which carry one of the great highways of Britain over the broad stream of Tyne had as yet no later forerunner. The stream was high, and crossing by any means was impossible.[2] The tale goes on to tell how William was obliged to tarry on the left bank of the river, and how his followers, used to live by rapine,[3] plundered the country round, and especially sacked Tynemouth, where such stock of food as was left after two harryings had been carefully stored up.[4] After this third scourge had fallen on the unhappy land, William made his way to Durham. He there began the building of the famous castle, designed in this case, not as the dwelling of King or Earl, but as a place where the foreign Bishop who had been sent as a shepherd over the turbulent land of Bernicia might be in safety against the probable attacks of his hostile flock.[5] Thus arose the huge fortified palace

*CHAP. XX.*

*Plunder of Tynemouth.*

*William reaches Durham, and founds the castle.*

[1] This story comes from a life of Saint Oswine published by the Surtees Society in their volume of Miscellanea Biographica, 1838. It begins in p 20, "Quodam tempore quum Rex ille victoriosissimus Willelmus, qui Normannis Angliam in manu forti subjugavit, cum exercitu valido a Scotia reverteretur, circa locum qui nunc Novum Castellum dicitur, quondam vero Monecestre dicebatur, fixit tentoria super Tynam fluvium"

[2] Vita Oswini, 21. "Contigerat enim tunc temporis fluvium ipsum adeo esse derivatum ut transvadari nusquam posset, nec pontis qui modo cernitur adminiculo pateret transitus. Hujus igitur necessitatis occasione, Rex inibi nonnullam fecerat moram"

[3] Ib. "Normanni de rapinâ vivere assueti"

[4] The legend of the "tribunus militum" Robert and his horse, illustrating the power of Saint Oswine, is worth reading.

[5] Sim Dun 1072, p 93 "Eodem tempore, scilicet quo Rex reversus de Scotiâ fuerat, in Dunelmo castellum condidit, ubi se cum suis episcopus tute ab incursantibus habere potuisset" Another, and not very intelligible, notice of William's return from Scotland is found in Domesday, 298, in the city of York, "De unâ mansione Uctred cujusdam dicunt burgenses W de Perci asportâsse sibi in castellum postquam de Scotiâ rediit Ipse vero

of the episcopal Princes of Durham, a wondrous change indeed from the hermit cell of Aidan and Cuthberht, or even from such a dwelling as may have satisfied the lowlier state of Ealdhun and Æthelwine. William probably built only what was necessary for the Prelate's defence; the most striking part of the vast and varied pile is perhaps the pillared chapel of William of Saint Carilef, the successor of the Bishop now established by the Conqueror. Strange tales were told of William's sojourn at Durham. The King had his doubts whether the body of Saint Cuthberht were really there, and he had furthered determined, if on examination it should prove not to be there, to put to death a crowd of Prelates and other great men who were gathered together to keep the festival of All Saints.[1] This is a strange tale to tell of a prince who had indeed harried Northumberland and mutilated his prisoners at Ely, but who had at least abstained from taking the lives of his most dangerous enemies. Bishop Walcher was saying mass, and the King was present in the minster, minded at once to carry out his irreverent purpose.[2] Straightway, on the November day, he was smitten with an intolerable heat. He rushed from the church, he forsook the costly banquet which had been made ready for the festival, and rode with all speed, but with what object it is not very clear, as far as the banks of the Tees.[3]

Willelmus terram ejusdem Uctred negat se habuisse, sed per Hugonem vicecomitem domum ipsius dicit se in castellum tulisse primo anno post destructionem castellorum " That is in 1070 instead of 1072.

[1] Hist Eccl. Dun. iii. 19 "Jam enim disposuerat ut, si sanctum ibi corpus inventum non esset, nobiliores et natu majores universos obtruncari praeciperet." The date is fixed when " Rex supradictus de Scotiâ, quo cum exercitu venerat, rediens Dunelmum intravit." The story is also told by Roger of Howden (i 126, Stubbs)

[2] Ib "In ipsâ Omnium Sanctorum festivitate praedicto episcopo missam celebrante, Rex quum id quod animo conceperat jamjamque perficere vellet "

[3] Ib "Festinans de ecclesiâ exire, relictoque quod ingenti copiâ

Of such a tale as this it is not easy to see the groundwork. William was not a scoffer; the work of jeering at English saints was more in the line of his Abbots;[1] and no man was less likely to order a massacre after the fashion of a Babylonian despot. Another tale is, to say the least, better conceived. William designed to violate the privileges of Saint Cuthberht by laying an unusual tax on the men of his patrimony. His instrument in this evil work was one Ralph or Randolf, in whom we may be tempted to see the famous Flambard.[2] He appears as the author of all evil in the next reign, but he ended his days as a magnificent Prelate on Saint Cuthberht's throne, and atoned for his misdeeds by rearing the mighty nave of Saint Cuthberht's minster. If the two men are the same, the future Bishop of Durham was now enabled to bear witness in his own person to the wonder-working powers of his predecessor In the night before the day on which the tax was to be levied, Saint Cuthberht appeared to the oppressor in his sleep; he smote him with his pastoral staff, and warned him that if he did not speedily depart out of the holy region a worse thing should befall him. When Ralph awoke in the morning, he could not stir from his bed. He told his tale to all who came near him; he pledged himself that, if he escaped

*CHAP XX.*

*He designs to tax the Bishoprick*

*His agent Ralph (Flambard ?)*

*Vengeance of Saint Cuthberht on Ralph*

præparatum fuerat convivio, equum confestim ascendit, et quousque ad Tesam veniret in cursum urgere non cessavit."

[1] See above, p 400

[2] Hist Eccl Dun ii 20 "Post tempus aliquod quemdam vocabulo Ranulphum illo miserat, qui ipsius Sancti populum Regi tributum solvere compelleret" Ralph Flambard appears by that name in Domesday in the town of Oxford (154), at Middleton in Oxfordshire (157), where he appears among a list of "clerici," and in three entries in the New Forest (51), from one of which it would seem that Eadward had the credit of bringing him into England. Two of the holdings belonged to English owners T R E, but of one we read, "Isdem Ranulfus tenuit in ipsâ villâ i hidam, et pro tanto se defendebat T. R. E." I presume that he is also the Ranulfus Flamme in Hampshire (49) who holds lands that had been held of Earl Godwine by one Thored

alive, he would do no more wrong to Saint Cuthberht or his people. He implored the saint's forgiveness and made a costly gift at his shrine. All was in vain, as long as he tarried within the forbidden borders. He was carried in a litter through the Bishoprick; but his pains increased till he passed its borders, when he was again made whole. The King, struck by the miracle, confirmed all the privileges of Saint Cuthberht and all the ancient customs of his people, and made further offerings at his shrine and added to the possessions of his ministers.[1]

The value of this tale is that it sets before us the strength of local feeling in those days, the strong attachment to all local customs and privileges, and the way in which William commonly respected them. So to do was an obvious part of his policy. A foreign prince who respected the privileges of Saint Cuthberht would be looked on with more kindly eyes than a native prince who disregarded them. On the other hand, we may perhaps see in both these stories signs that the frightful severities of William's rule in the North had gained him a worse name there than in other parts of the Kingdom, and that he was remembered as a sort of bugbear who might be made the subject of any tale of oppression or extortion

I turn from legend to history. Bishop Walcher now began his episcopal reign in his new fortress side by side with Ealdhun's minster, and it was William's pleasure to give him a new temporal yoke-fellow. Gospatric was deprived of his Earldom, on charges heavy enough in

---

[1] Hist Eccl. Dun. iii 20 He restored Billingham, "quam violentia malignorum abstulerat," and gave it, "pro suâ suorumque filiorum salute, ad victum in ipsâ ecclesiâ Sancto Cuthberto ministrantium" It is added, " Leges quoque et consuetudines ipsius sancti, sicut antiqua Regum auctoritas stabilierat, ipse quoque suo consensu et auctoritate confirmavit, et illibatas ab omnibus servari præcepit."

William's eyes, but which William had fully forgiven three years before. He had had a share in the slaughter of the Normans at York, and, though not present in person, he had been an accomplice in the earlier slaughter of which Robert of Comines had been the victim.¹ Whatever may have been the truth of this latter charge, there was no doubt about the former; but it was a charge which told equally against the Earl whom William chose to succeed him. William was not yet prepared again to try the experiment of sending a stranger to rule that distant and turbulent province. He bestowed the Earldom of Northumberland on an Englishman, and one who, like Gospatric, came by female descent from the ancient Earls and Kings of the land. The government of Northumberland was given to Waltheof the son of Siward and Æthelflæd, and it is clear that his descent was looked upon as giving him at least a preference for the succession to the Earldom.² He was already Earl of Northampton and Huntingdon, already probably the husband of the King's niece Judith.³ Gospatric became an exile, and flitted to and fro between the two common homes of exiles, Scotland and Flanders. The old quarrel between him and Malcolm was forgotten; both were enemies of William. The Scottish King made the banished Earl a grant of Dunbar and other lands in Lothian till better times should come.⁴ The better times

*marginalia:* CHAP. XX. Gospatric deprived of his Earldom. November, 1072. Waltheof Earl of Northumberland 1072–1075. His marriage with Judith. Gospatric received by Malcolm. His possessions in Scotland.

---

¹ Sim Dun 1072, p 89 "Rediens inde [from Scotland] Willelmus Cospatricum comitatûs honore privavit, imponens illi quod consilio et auxilio affuisset eis qui Comitem cum suis in Dunelmo peremerant, licet ipse ibidem præsens non fuisset, et quia in parte hostium fuisset quum Normanni apud Eboracum necarentur '

² Ib p 93 "Dejecto ab honore Cospatrico, Waltheovus in comitatum sustollitur, ei ex patris ac matris prosapiâ debitum  Fuerat enim Siwardi Comitis filius ex filiâ quondam Comitis Aldredi Ælfledâ ".

³ See above, p 303

⁴ Sim. Dun 1072, p 92 "Fugiens ad Malcolmum non multo post Flandriam navigio petit  Cui post aliquantum tempus Scottiam reverso, donavit ei Rex supradictus Dunbar cum adjacentibus terris in Lodoneio,

seem to have come in the case of Gospatric, as they came in the case of Abbot Æthelsige,[1] during the reign of William himself. Gospatric, though fallen from his ancient wealth and honours, appears in the Survey as a considerable landowner,[2] and his three sons, Dolfin, Waltheof, and Gospatric, have their place in the local history of Northern England.[3] His successor Waltheof at once contracted a close friendship with the new Bishop of Durham. Whatever measures Walcher took for the souls' health of his flock, Waltheof was ready to carry out with the strength of the secular arm.[4] It is to be hoped that Walcher did not in return lend his spiritual sanction to the one recorded act of Waltheof's Northum-

---

ut ex his, donec lætiora redirent tempora se suosque procuraret" I really do not see the inconsistency which Mr Hinde (p 86) sees between this statement and the account of the former enmity between Malcolm and Gospatric The enemy of an enemy has his own offences easily forgiven, and the relations between Malcolm and Gospatric do not greatly differ from those between Malcolm and Tostig Besides, the two stories which are said to be inconsistent both come from the same authority, that of the Northern interpolator.

[1] See above, p 137.

[2] The lands of Gospatric in Yorkshire appear in Domesday, 330, but to a large part is added the fatal entry "wasta," and in one case "non colit" He also held largely as a tenant of Earl Alan, see 309 b, 310 b, 311 b In some cases he held under Alan what he had himself held T. R E ; in others he held lands which had belonged to Archill, which was also the case with some of the lands which he held of the King.

[3] See Mr Hinde's note, p. 92, and Dugdale's Baronage, 54 We also find in Orderic, 543 D, " Guallevus Angligena Crulandensis cœnobii monachus frater Gospatritii de magna nobilitate Anglorum," who became Abbot of Crowland in 1124. " Walthef filius Gospatrici," " Gospatricius, filius eorumdem," and "Alanus filius Waldevi " all appear, along with nearly every one else in Yorkshire, French and English, among the benefactors of Saint Mary's Abbey at York. Mon Aug iii 550. Alan the son of Waltheof illustrates the law by which English names gave way to French

[4] Sim. Dun 1072, p 93 "Fuerunt autem amicissimi sibique mutuo acclines Walcherus Episcopus et Waltheovus Comes Unde una cum Episcopo et in synodo presbyterorum residens, humiliter et obedienter prosequebatur quidquid pro corrigendâ in suo comitatu Christianitate statutum ab Episcopo fuisset "

brian government. With all his piety and patriotism, the spirit of Northumbrian deadly feud was deeply rooted in the heart of the new Earl. Long before his own birth, in the days of Harthacnut, his mother's father, Earl Ealdred, had been treacherously murdered by his sworn brother Carl.[1] What was the fate of the murderer himself we are not told, whether the justice of Siward or Tostig had reached him or whether Law was found too weak to strike so powerful an offender. But his crime was now to be visited on those who were guiltless of it. The old tragedy was acted over again. Thurbrand had slain Uhtred; Uhtred's son Ealdred had slain Thurbrand; Thurbrand's son Carl had slain Ealdred, and had slain him in contempt of the tie of sworn brotherhood. Whether any such formal tie existed between Waltheof and the sons of Carl we know not; but they had at least fought at his side against the Norman in the great march upon York, and even a crime of their own doing might well have been forgiven to fellow-soldiers in such a cause. But Waltheof could not forgive the death of the grandfather whom he had never seen. The sons of Carl, whose estates would seem to have been left to them by William, were feasting in the house of their elder brother at Seterington in Yorkshire. A party of young men, sent across the border by the Earl of the Northumbrians, came upon them, as the Normans came on Hereward, when they were thus unarmed and unsuspecting. The whole family, all the sons and grandsons of Carl, were cut off, save one son, Sumorled, who chanced not to be present, and another, Cnut, whose character had won him such general love that the murderers themselves could not bring themselves to slay him.[2] The

*CHAP XX.*

Deadly feud between the descendants of Ealdred and Carl.

The sons of Carl murdered by order of Waltheof 1073

---

[1] See vol i p 586.
[2] The story is told by Simeon of Durham in the enlarged Florence, 1073, p 93, and more fully in the tract De Obsessione Dunelmi (157), "Comes Waltheof missâ multâ juvenum manu, avi sui interfectionem gravissimâ

chap. xx. slayers returned to their master with the spoils of their victims,[1] and the ancient crime of Carl was thus avenged by a still deeper crime on the part of Waltheof.

### § 3. *Dealings with Ireland.*
### 1074—1087.

*William's alleged design on Ireland.*

William might now fairly call himself master of the whole Isle of Britain. England was his immediate Kingdom; Scotland had acknowledged his over-lordship; the Welsh princes, technically the vassals of the English Crown, instead of harrying the English border, were now being gradually brought into subjection by the Earls on the Western frontier. It was not wonderful if, in such a case, the dream should present itself to William's mind that he might also win that other great island of the Western sea over which the dominion of the Cæsars themselves had never reached. A most remarkable passage of the English Chronicles shows that William did, at least in his later days, entertain the hope, not only of making Ireland his own, but of making it his own by peaceful means. "If he might yet two years have lived, he had Ireland with his wariness won, and that without any weapons."[2] Such an exploit might, with a little pardonable exaggeration, have

*Expectation of a peaceful conquest.*

clade vindicavit. Erant namque filii Carl convivantes simul in domo fratris sui majoris in Seteringetun non longe ab Eboraco, quos inopinate qui missi fuerant præoccupantes sævâ clade simul peremerunt, præter Cnutonem, cui pro insitâ illi bonitate vitam permiserunt. Sumerlede, qui usque hodie superest, ibi non aderat." The writer was evidently thinking of the sons of Job (Job i. 18). Lands held by Sumorled T. R. E. appear in Domesday, in Huntingdonshire, 206 *b*, Lincolnshire, 340 *b* (together with Archill, held by the Bishop of Durham), 351 *b*, 356 *b* (held by Colswegen), 371, Yorkshire, 300 *b*. Cnut appears as a holder T. R. E. in many places in Yorkshire and elsewhere, but there is nothing special about the entries.

[1] De Obs. Dun. 157. "Deletis filiis et nepotibus Carli reversi sunt, multa in variis speciebus spolia reportantes."

[2] Chron. Petrib. 1087. "Gif he moste þa gyt twa gear libban, he hæfde Yrlande mid his *werscipe* gewunnon, and wiðutan ælcon wæpnon." I follow the happy explanation of Mr. Earle (Parallel Chronicles, 353).

really been attributed to his great-grandson.[1] Throughout William's reign, things were tending towards a closer union between England and Ireland, and towards the establishment of at least one form of English supremacy. Putting aside the mythical claims of Eadgar and Cnut to Irish victories and Irish dominion,[2] we have hitherto had to do with Ireland as a land whence Danish auxiliaries came to the help of their countrymen in England, as the great market for English slaves, and as one of the lands where English exiles of every party were sure to find welcome. But now we see distinct signs of a wish among at least one class of the inhabitants of Ireland to place themselves under the spiritual jurisdiction of the English Primate. This movement began among the Danish settlers in the cities of the East coast, but it is plain that it spread from them to some at least among the native Irish. Among the Danes such a movement was natural; they were recent proselytes to Christianity, and they had of course embraced it in the form usual among the Churches of the West. They stood in fact towards the native Celtic Church in much the same relation in which the English on their first conversion had stood towards the native Celtic Churches in Britain. While strict diocesan episcopacy was the rule of all other Churches, in Ireland, besides the more regular tribal episcopate, imaginary Bishops were endlessly multiplied without any effective jurisdiction. Such a practice would naturally seem something strange and heterodox in the eyes of the Scandinavian converts. In such a case it was natural to strengthen the ties between themselves and the Church of the neighbouring island, whose Metropolitan claimed to be Patriarch of all the nations beyond

*Chap. xx. Conquest of Henry the Second. 1171. Ecclesiastical intercourse between England and Ireland.*

*The Danish settlers drawn towards England*

*Differences between the English and Irish Churches*

*Peculiar nature of Irish Episcopacy*

---

[1] There was then, if we may believe Giraldus (Exp. Hib. i. 34, vol. v. p. 280, Dimock), one peaceful moment in Irish history, "silente insulâ in conspectu Regis, et tranquillâ jam pace gaudente"

[2] See vol. i. p. 66, ii. p. 154

the sea. A movement accordingly began, which had the effect of largely assimilating the Irish Church to the English model, even before the political conquest under Henry the Second. It began by applications made to Lanfranc by several Kings and Bishops, both Danish and Irish; and we cannot doubt that the spiritual connexion thus formed was one of the chief means by which William hoped to bring the island under his dominion without slash or blow. The Primate's first correspondent was an Archbishop of Dublin whose name is variously Latinized into Donatus and Domnaldus.[1] The answer of Lanfranc[2] relates wholly to ecclesiastical matters. The death of his correspondent brought Lanfranc into a closer connexion with the Church of Ireland. He was called on to consecrate the successor of Donatus. Patrick the Bishop-elect came over to England with letters from the clergy and people of Dublin,[3] and also from a potentate to whom Lanfranc gives the sounding title of King of Ireland.[4] In him we may recognise that Godred who played a part against England in the fight at Stamfordbridge.[5] The Bishop was con-

---

[1] He is addressed (Ep Lanfr 1 54) as "venerandus Hiberniæ Episcopus Domnaldus." I presume that this is the Dunan or Donatus described as Archbishop of the Galls, that is of the Danes, and as Archbishop of Dublin, both of Irish and Danes, whose death is recorded in all the Irish Annals under 1073 or 1074 See Four Masters, ii. 906, 907, Chronicon Scotorum, 290, 291, Tigernach, ap. O'Conor, ii. 309

[2] The letter is addressed to the Bishop, "et iis qui sibi litteras transmiserunt." The expression "nos Angli," used by Lanfranc, should be noticed.

[3] Ep Lanfr 1 57. The superscription of the letter runs thus, "Venerando sanctæ Cantuariensis Ecclesiæ Metropolitano Lanfranco clerus et populus Ecclesiæ Dublinensis debitam subjectionem." They speak of "Ecclesia Dublinensis, quæ Hiberniæ insulæ metropolis est." The Patricius of the Latin correspondence appears in the Irish Annals as Gillaphadraig or Gilpatrick

[4] Ib 61. Lanfranc addresses his letter "glorioso Hiberniæ Regi Gothrico," and speaks of Patrick, "quem, carissime fili, excellentia vestra ad nos consecrandum transmisit"

[5] See vol. iii. p 346. This Godred or Gothric is therefore a different

secrated in London, and the English writers do not fail to record that he made his profession to Lanfranc.[1] The Primate, in his letter to the King, acknowledges him as a faithful and orthodox son of the Roman Church, and earnestly exhorts him to correct various abuses in his Kingdom, especially the laxity which prevailed as to many points touching marriages and divorces.[2]

*Lanfranc consecrates Patrick Archbishop of Dublin 1074 His letter to Godred.*

Archbishop Patrick was drowned in the tenth year of his episcopate,[3] and his successor—Donach, Donnghus, or Donatus—was also consecrated by Lanfranc.[4] His successor Samuel was consecrated by Anselm,[5] and the consecration of Irish Bishops to the sees of Dublin, Waterford, and Limerick by the hands of the English Primate occurs at intervals up to the time of the conquest under Henry the Second.[6] Lanfranc had also another Irish correspondent in a King of native blood, who plays a great part after the death of Diarmid,[7] and whose name is given in various forms ranging from Toirdhealbach ua Briain to

*Death of Patrick 1084. Donatus consecrated by Lanfranc 1085 Samuel consecrated by Anselm 1096 Correspondence of Lanfranc and Terlagh.*

person from Gothfraigh, King of the Galls or foreigners, whose death is recorded in the Chronicon Scotorum under 1072, Tigernach, 1075

[1] App Chron. Wint 1074. "Patricium Dubliniæ civitati in Hibernia sacravit Episcopum Lundoniæ, a quo et professionem accepit, et litteras ei deferendas Regibus Hiberniæ, dignas valde memoriæ, contradidit" This most likely means the extant letter to Gothric, see also Gervase, X Scriptt 1654.

[2] Ep Lanfr 1 61. "In regno vestro perhibentur homines seu de propriâ, seu de mortuarum uxorum parentelâ conjuges ducere, alii legitime sibi copulatas pro arbitrio et voluntate relinquere, nonnulli suas aliis dare, et aliorum infaudâ commutatione recipere"

[3] Four Masters, ii 981, Ann Ult 1084, ap. O'Conor, iv. 349

[4] W. Stubbs, Reg Sacr Angl 23 His death by pestilence is recorded by the Four Masters (ii 949) under the year 1095, by the name of Donnghus Bishop of Ath-Cliath

[5] See Eadmer, 34 He was however a monk of Saint Alban's

[6] After Samuel, we find (Eadmer, 36) Malchus of Waterford, a monk of Winchester, in 1096, who was recommended to Anselm by King Murchadh and his son Diarmid, Gregory of Dublin in 1121, and Patrick of Limerick in 1140 See W. Stubbs, Reg. Sacr. Angl 24, 26, 28

[7] See above, p 245

VOL IV. M m

530        THE REVOLTS AGAINST WILLIAM.

CHAP XX  the more easily uttered Terence O'Brien.¹  A deep affection
Reforms  towards him is professed by the English Primate,² but he
suggested
by Lan-  is exhorted to make great reforms in his realm. He is
franc    warned to get rid of the practice of irregular marriages,
of simony, and of the evil customs by which Bishops were
consecrated by one Bishop only, and several Bishops were
consecrated for the same place.³

Influence   This ecclesiastical intercourse with Ireland forms a
of these
events on  curious episode in the joint reign of William and Lanfranc.
later
history   It should be noticed that the name of the King of the
English is never found in any of the Primate's letters to the
Irish Kings and Prelates. The wariness of William may
have deemed it more discreet to keep for a while out of
notice, till the habit of submission to the Pope of the island
world might lead men's minds to submit to its Cæsar
also. We may be tempted to wish that William had lived
two years longer to undertake a work which he would
most likely have done more thoroughly than it was done
The Irish  by those who came after him. At any rate there can be
predis-
posed to   little doubt that the friendly intercourse of Lanfranc with
the English Godred and Toirdhealbach was the first step towards the
connexion
1171       submission of the Irish Princes to the English King at
Dublin and towards the submission of the Irish Church
to the English model at Cashel.⁴

¹ See the various Irish Annals collected in the Notes to the Four
Masters, 1073, where a strange legend is told of him  The intermediate
form Terlagh seems to be recognized  Lanfranc addresses him as "magnificus
Hiberniæ Rex Terdeluacus"
² Ep Lanfr. i 62  Patrick had spoken so highly of him "ut,
quamvis vos numquam viderimus, tamquam visos tamen vos diligamus, et
tamquam visis ac bene cognitis vobis salubriter consulere et sincerissime
servire cupiamus"  The flattery is at least well turned
³ Ib 63  "Quod episcopi ab uno episcopo consecrantur. Quod in villis
vel civitatibus plures ordinantur. Quod infantes baptismo sine chrismate
consecrato baptizantur. Quod sacri ordines per pecuniam ab episcopis
dantur."
⁴ See Giraldus Cambrensis, Exp Hib. i 33-35, vol v. pp 278-283, ed.
Dimock.

### § 4. *The Revolt of Maine.*
### 1073.

We must now turn for a while to William's dominions on the mainland, where we shall soon see the strange sight of French-speaking revolters against his authority brought back to their allegiance by the axes of his English subjects. But, before things came to this stage, the man who, after William himself and Odo, had played the foremost part in the conquest of England, lost his life beyond sea in a quarrel which was neither English nor Norman. William Fitz-Osbern had ever been the man whom William had most trusted, and whom he had ever chosen for those posts which called for the highest displays of faithfulness, daring, and military skill. Some danger, domestic or foreign, must have threatened the Norman Duchy when William took away this trusted friend from his command on the Welsh border, and sent him to help the Duchess Matilda in her government.[1] Of revolts in the Duchy itself we hear nothing at this time, but the commotions which were soon to arise on the side of Maine, Anjou, and Britanny may have already begun to cast their shadows before them. If so, the Earl of Hereford can hardly have fulfilled the special errand on which he was sent. For he at once turned his thoughts and his energies to the opposite side of the Duchy. A dispute was there raging in which the personal feelings of Matilda were doubtless deeply engaged, but in which it could hardly be said that the interests either of England or of Normandy were directly touched. Baldwin, the mighty Marquess of Flanders, whose name we have so often come across in

*William Fitz-Osbern sent to Normandy. Christmas, 1070*

*Affairs of Flanders*

*Death of Baldwin 1067*

---

[1] Ord. Vit. 526 C. "Anno quinto regni sui Guillelmus Rex Guillelmum Osberni filium misit in Normanniam, ut cum Mathilde Reginâ tueretur provinciam" As the fifth year of William begins December 25, 1070, his stay must have been very short. The order was probably given in the Midwinter Gemót

CHAP XX. our history, died in the year following that in which his Norman son-in-law had received the Crown of England.[1]

*Reign of Baldwin of Mons 1067-1071.*
He was succeeded by one of his sons, another Baldwin. It was the custom of the rulers of Flanders never to divide their dominions among their children. One son, at the father's choice, succeeded to the whole of his dominions, while the others might, if they choose, win settlements for themselves after the manner of the Wikings of the further North.[2]

*Adventures of Robert, son of the elder Baldwin.*
Either in conformity with this custom or because he had personally drawn on himself the displeasure of his father, another son of Baldwin, Robert, had left his country to seek for an establishment in foreign lands[3] He then went, like Harold Hardrada, through various adventures in Southern Europe. The strangest tale of all is that which tells how the Warangian guards at Constantinople offered him the Empire of the East, and how the reigning Emperor, by putting guards along the rivers which gave access to his dominions, hindered the design.[4]

*His establishment and marriage in Holland. 1063.*
Thus baffled in the East, Robert betook himself to lands nearer his native Flanders Either by force or by persuasion he established himself in Friesland, a name which, in the geography of the time, takes in Holland and Zeeland. There he married Gertrude, the widow of Count Florence,

---

[1] Ann. Elnonenses, 1067 (Pertz, v. 13). "Kal Sept obiit Balduinus Comes Insulæ sepelitur."

[2] Lambert (1071, p. 85 of the smaller Pertz) describes the custom at length, including the rule " ut unus filiorum, qui patri potissimum placuisset, *nomen patris acciperet*" He adds, " Hoc scilicet fiebat, ne, in plures divisâ provinciâ, claritas illius familiæ per inopiam rei familiaris obsoleret."

[3] Lambert (86) makes Baldwin appoint his son of the same name as his heir, and send Robert forth on his travels; " Ille patri adquiescens, assumptâ secum multitudine, qua regio prægravari videbatur, navem ascendit." But Orderic (526 C) gives the story another turn, " Rodbertus primogenitus jamdudum patrem offenderat, a quo repulsus et ejectus ad Florentium Ducem Fresionum, patris sui hostem, secesserat."

[4] After some unlucky adventures in Galicia and elsewhere, Lambert adds this alleged piece of Byzantine history, which it is still harder to verify than the exploits of Harold Hardrada

and became the guardian of her son the young Count, a bearer of that noble Gothic name which in the Low Countries was gradually cut short from Theodoric into Dirk.¹ From his settlement in this country he obtained— some say through the contempt of his father—the surname of Robert the Frisian.² On the death of the elder Baldwin one version makes a war at once arise between the two brothers. The new Count of Flanders, Baldwin the Sixth, is said to have attacked Robert without provocation in his Frisian dominions, and to have fallen in battle against him.³ However this may be, it is certain that Baldwin died after a short reign, leaving his son Arnulf under the regency of his mother Richildis of Hennegau, now for the second time a widow.⁴ This was in truth the age of the ascendency of widows. To a long list both in our

*His surname of "Frisian"*

*War between Baldwin and Robert.*

*Death of Baldwin. 1070.*

---

¹ Orderic (526 D) makes him marry the daughter of Florence But William of Malmesbury (iii 256) more accurately says, " patre superstite Comitissam Frisiæ uxorem nactus, Frisonis cognomen accepit " See Ubbo Emmius, Rer Fris Hist (Lugd Bat 1616), 94 , Art de Verifier les Dates, iii 5. 198. Lambert seems to stand alone in making his settlement the result of a war

² Ord. Vit u s  " Flandrensis Dux vehementer iratus infremuit, Fresionem eum præ irâ cognominavit, et eum omnino extorrem denuntians, Arnulfum juris sui hæredem constituit "

³ Lambert tells the story of this war at great length, and gives a graphic tale how the troops of Baldwin were defeated, and how he himself died like Hasdrubal. But neither William of Malmesbury, nor Orderic, nor Sigebert (Pertz, vi 362) gives any hint of Baldwin dying in battle, or of there being any war between him and Robert at all  See also Ubbo, p 95, Oudegherst, Chronique de Flanders, 89 *b*; Art de Vérifier les Dates, iii 5

⁴ Will. Malm iii 256  "Superstitibus duobus liberis, Arnulfo et Baldwino, de Richilde uxore, quorum tutelam Regi Francorum Philippo, cujus amitæ filius erat, et Willelmo filio Osberni commendaverat "  But all the local writers make Richildis act as regent.  Orderic does not mention her, and Lambert only incidentally

Richildis was Countess of Mons or Hennegau in her own right, and her dominions passed to her second son by Baldwin, who bore his father's name, see below, p 528.  She had before been married to Hermann, Count of Valenciennes.  See Chron S Andreæ, Pertz, vii. 533 , Gest. Ep. Cam. ib 492

own and in other lands,[1] this story enables us to add the names of Gertrude and Richildis. But the Countess-Regent of Flanders soon set the whole country against her by the tyrannical measures of her short regency.[2] Robert the Frisian presently invaded Flanders, but he invaded it at the request of a powerful party in the country, who were disgusted with the misgovernment of the Countess, and who abjured all allegiance to her and her sons.[3] In this strait, Richildis sought for political and military help at the hands of the two over-lords of the great Marchland, King Philip at Paris and King Henry at Luttich.[4] Herself, and seemingly a sort of crown-matrimonial over Flanders and Hennegau, she offered to the Earl of Hereford and Regent of Normandy, already named by her husband as one of the guardians of his children.[5] William Fitz-Osbern felt his heart kindled at the prospect of promotion to princely rank and of warfare of a more brilliant kind than an Earl of Hereford could wage at the expense of his British neighbours. And, mature widower as he must have been, we have hints that Richildis

---

[1] Emma, Matilda, the two Ealdgyths (the wife of Eadmund Ironside and the wife of Harold), Agnes of Poitiers, and Anne of Russia.

[2] See Ubbo, 95, Oudegherst, 92 *b*, Art de Vérifier les Dates, iii 5.

[3] William of Malmesbury (iii 256) says distinctly, "Illa femineo fastu ampliora sexu spirans novaque a provincialibus tributa exigens, in perfidiam illos excitavit, misso quippe propter Robertum Frisonem nuntio ut supplicantis patriæ habenas acciperet, omnem fidelitatem Arnulfo, qui jam Comes dicebatur, abjurant." He adds however, "Nec vero defuere qui pupilli partes fulcirent, ita multis diebus Flandria intestinis dissensionibus conturbata." Lambert and Orderic record the invasion but not the invitation.

[4] Orderic (526 D) mentions only the intervention of Philip, but Lambert (88) distinctly speaks of an application to Henry, "Filius Balduwini.... assumptâ matre suâ, ad Regem Teutonicorum Heinricum Leodii... venit, opemque ejus adversus patrui violentiam supplex imploravit." But he goes on to speak of Mons as if it had been the dowry of Richildis from her first husband, instead of her inheritance from her father.

[5] Will. Malm. iii 256. "Libens id munus suscepit Willelmus, ut, fœderatis cum Richilde nuptiis, altius nomen sibi pararet."

herself, as well as her possessions, had charms for him,[1] and that he went forth as a true knight-errant to wage war for his lady. He set forth with a light heart, looking on the conquest or defence of Flanders as a mere knightly sport. At the head of ten knights only he joined the force which Philip was making ready for the defence of his cousin.[2] We know not whether we are to count among them an adventurer of equal birth and rank with Earl William himself, over whose descent and actions a thick veil seems to be purposely thrown by all contemporary chroniclers. But it is certain that Gerbod, Earl of Chester, the son of Queen Matilda, invited by those among his countrymen whom he had left as his representatives in his office of Advocate of Saint Bertin, obtained William's leave to take a part in the Flemish war.[3] The French army, strengthened by the small Norman contingent, entered Flanders. Earl William went carelessly about from castle to castle, till Robert, who had better learned the lesson never to despise an enemy, found an opportunity for a sudden and decisive attack. In the battle of Cassel, the French army was utterly defeated with great slaughter; King Philip fled; the Earl of Chester was taken captive

CHAP. XX

He joins Philip's muster with ten knights.

Presence of Gerbod of Chester.

Battle of Cassel February 20, 1071?

---

[1] Will. Malm. iii. 256. "Totus in amorem mulieris concesserat." Thierry (ii. 59) makes wonderfully short work of the Countess Richildis and the revolutions of Flanders, "Guillaume fils d'Osbert, le premier des seigneurs normands, périt de mort violente en Flandre, où, pour l'amour d'une femme, il s'était engagé dans des intrigues politiques."

[2] Ord. Vit. 526 D. "Ille cum decem solummodo militibus Regem adiit, et cum eo alacriter, *quasi ad ludum,* in Flandriam accessit."

[3] I conceive this to be the time referred to by Orderic (522 A) when he says that Gerbod, "legatione coactus suorum quos in Flandriâ dimiserat, et quibus hereditarium honorem suum commiserat, eundi citoque redeundi licentiam a Rege acceperat." The Hyde writer (296), often inaccurate but always independent, seems to place the expedition of Gerbod after the suppression of the revolt of Ralph of Norfolk. After recording the bride-ale and its consequences, he adds, "Quo tempore Comes Cistrensis decessit Gerbodo, frater Gondradæ Comitissæ, Flandriamque veniens, inimicorum præventus insidiis miserabiliter periit."

*Chap xx.*
*Death of Arnulf and William Fitz-Osbern*
*Robert makes peace with Philip*
*Delay of the German allies of Arnulf.*

and endured a long imprisonment; the young Count of Flanders and the Earl of Hereford were slain.[1]

After this decisive defeat, the King of the French was glad to patch up a peace with the conqueror and to recognize his claim to the County of Flanders.[2] Meanwhile a German army was actually on the march to help the young Arnulf. King Henry had bidden Theodwin Bishop of Luttich,[3] and Godfrey Duke of Lotharingia,—son of the Godfrey of whom we have already heard[4] and possessor of the doubtful privilege of being one of the husbands of the Great Countess,[5]—to march with the forces of the Lotharingian Duchy to the support of Arnulf. Perhaps they tarried on the way; at all events they did not enter Flanders till Arnulf was dead and till Robert had made peace with Philip. Neither Duke nor Bishop had a mind to enter on a war with France

---

[1] Ord Vit 526 D, Will Malm (iii. 256), whose account is highly picturesque Lambert, oddly enough, does not mention the battle at all. Orderic places it "Dominico Septuagesimæ x Kal Martii," that is in 1071, when Easter fell on April 24 The short Chronicon Lyrense, the annals of William's own foundation (Bouquet, xii 776), places it on Septuagesima Sunday, 1072 Both our Chroniclers record the fact, Worcester under 1071, Peterborough under 1070, "And Baldewine Eorl forðferde, and his sunu Arnulf feng to rice, and Willelm Eorl sceolde ben his gebeald, and Franca Cyng eac, and com þa Rodbriht Eorl and ofsloh his mæg Arnulf, and þone Eorl and þone Cyng aflymda and his men ofsloh fela þusenda"

The fate of Gerbod comes from Orderic, 522 A; "Ibi [in Flandris] adversâ illaqueatus fortunâ in manus inimicorum inciderat, et in vinculis coercitus mundanâque felicitate privatus, longæ miseriæ threnos depromere didicerat" The Hyde writer is clearly wrong in killing him. The industry of Mr. Stapleton has found out documents of his dated long after, and which show that he was in the end reconciled to Robert the Frisian See Archæological Journal, iii 18, 19

[2] Ord Vit. 527 B "Rodbertus Fresio totam sibi Flandriam subegit et fere xxx annis possedit, amicitiamque Philippi Regis Francorum facile promeruit" So Will Malm. iii. 257.

[3] Lambert, 1071.

[4] See vol ii p. 97

[5] He was "præstantis animi adolescens, sed gibbosus" Lambert, 1069.

with his own resources, and they accordingly went back without striking a blow.[1]

CHAP. XX.

Such was the end of William's chiefest and earliest friend. His body was carried off and borne to his own home in Normandy. Though no ecclesiastical foundation preserved his name in England, two monasteries had arisen at his bidding on his Norman estates. One was at Lyra, in the diocese of Evreux, where his wife Adeliza was already buried; the other at Cormeille, in the diocese of Rouen, which was his own resting-place.[2] The policy of William divided his inheritance. In rewarding his own comrades, he had been obliged to make the same men great on both sides of the sea, but he did not wish that state of things to continue beyond the first generation. The Norman estates of William Fitz-Osbern passed to his eldest son William; the Earldom of Hereford and all that he held in England was granted to his second son Roger, by whom, as we shall presently see, it was soon lost as the punishment of a reckless treason.[3]

Norman monasteries founded by William Fitz-Osbern.

His estates divided between his sons

William succeeds in Normandy, Roger in England

The effects of the wild enterprise of William Fitz-Osbern long survived him. His intermeddling in Flemish affairs brought about a state of hostility between Normandy and the country which, ever since William's marriage, had been its closest ally. Robert the Frisian

Wars between Normandy and Flanders.

---

[1] Lambert, 1071, p 88 There is something not wholly satisfactory in his whole story, still it at least hinders us from accepting Orderic's statement (526 D) that the Imperial troops actually fought on Robert's side in the battle of Cassel, " Rodbertus Fresio exercitum Henrici Imperatoris cuneis suis sociavit "

[2] See Orderic, 527 A. On Lyra, founded about 1045, and the legend of its foundation, see Neustria Pia, 534 On Cormeille, see p 595 Emma, the daughter of William Fitz-Osbern, the heroine of the famous bride ale, is also spoken of as its foundress

[3] See Ord Vit 527 A, Will Malm iii 255 Orderic enlarges on the grief of the Normans at William's death, " Normannorum maximum strenuitate baronem valde omnes planxerunt qui largitates ejus et facetias atque mirandas probitates noverunt "

538                THE REVOLTS AGAINST WILLIAM.

CHAP XX  reigned for many years in Flanders, and he remained
the firm ally of Philip of France and the enemy of
William   William of Normandy. We hear of constant warfare
abets Bald-
win of Hen- between the two countries, but no details are given, except
negau
against    that William found it his interest to support Baldwin of
Robert    Hennegau, the brother of the slain Count Arnulf, in a
series of attacks on his uncle in Flanders.[1] Later in
1085.    William's reign we shall find Flanders and Denmark in
enmity against him[2] For the present we are tempted
to ask, whether this warfare of William in the Marchland of Gaul and Germany had anything to do with a
strange and isolated report which meets us in the German
William's  history of the time. Three years after the death of William
alleged
design on  Fitz-Osbern, King Henry was setting forth on an expe-
Germany.
May, 1074. dition against the Hungarians, and had advanced on his
Alleged   march as far as Regensburg. He was there met by the
invitation
of William news that the Archbishop of Koln, the famous Hanno,
by Hanno  had invited William the Bastard, King of the English, to
Arch-
bishop of invade the Eastern realm, and that he was already on
Koln
his march with a vast army to take possession of the
royal seat at Aachen.[3] The news was thought serious
enough to call the King away from his Hungarian ex-
Dealings  pedition. Hanno was with some difficulty admitted to
between
Hanno    clear himself by oath, and was again received into the
and King
Henry    King's friendship. If Hanno was to be believed, nothing

[1] Ord. Vit 527 B "Porro inter Normannos et Flandritas recidiva dis-
sensio prodit, et propter necem fratris Reginæ aliorumque affinium et
maxime pro casu Guillelmi Comitis diu perduravit" William of Malmesbury (iii. 257) more distinctly marks the action of Baldwin, "Robertus
nihil quod deploraret suo tempore vidit, licet Baldwinus frater Arnulfi,
qui in Hanoeâ provincia et castello Valentianis comitatum habuit, Regis
Willelmi auxilio plures assultus faceret."

[2] See Chron Petrib 1085 I shall speak of this in the next Chapter

[3] This is the passage of Lambert (1074, p 159) referred to in vol ii.
p 582, "Quum Ratisponam venisset [Rex Heinricus], insequuta est eum
legatio familiarium ejus nuntiantium quod Willehelmus cognomento *Bostar*,
Rex Anglorum, ab Archiepiscopo Coloniensi vanâ pollicitatione illectus, cum
magno exercitu adventaret, regni sedem Aquisgrani occupare paratus"

had ever passed between him and William; yet, even after *Henry fortifies Aachen against William* his reconciliation with the Archbishop, Henry deemed the danger from England or Normandy so formidable that he took up his quarters at Aachen, and devoted himself to strengthening the defences of that quarter of the Kingdom against the expected barbaric invasion [1]

Such is the story of William's relations with Germany, *Estimate of the story* as told by the contemporary chronicler whom no incompetent judge has placed at the head of all the historians of the middle ages.[2] It is hard to say what amount of truth there might have been in the rumour. While William was warring on the borders of the Empire, it is likely enough that Hanno may have tried to win his help for some of his own ambitious schemes. But we can hardly think that William, with England and Normandy on his hands, really dreamed of repeating in the elder minster of the Great Charles the same crowning rite which he had already received in the minster of Eadward. And it will be well to compare this *Version of Bruno.* version of the tale with that which is given by the Saxon enemy—perhaps calumniator—of Henry. In this picture *Henry asks William and other Kings for help* the King, in his despair and wrath against the Saxons, seeks for allies in every quarter. Besides nearer neighbours, he craves help of Swend of Denmark,[3] of his own uncle Duke William of Aquitaine,[4] and of the potentate to whom the

---

[1] The whole story in Lambert is most curious. The parts which most concern us are where Hanno (p 159) protests "se non ita rationis expertem vel communis commodi neghgentem esse ut in ultionem privatæ injuriæ patriam suam *barbaris* prodere velit," and where we read, a little way on (p 161), how Henry "hoc modo reconciliatus Archiepiscopo, Aquasgrani perrexit, et adversus ea, quæ de irruptione *barbarorum* fama vulgaverat eam regni partem, quantum poterat, communivit." As *barbarus* literally translates *walsch*, we may hope that William's Norman subjects are meant

[2] Milman, iii 168

[3] Bruno, Bell Sax 36 "Regem Danorum promissionis juramento confirmatæ commemorat, seque illi daturum cuncta quæ sit pollicitus affirmat." I do not know whether this refers to any promise more definite than Swend's vassalage to the Empire, see vol ii p 98

[4] Agnes, the mother of Henry, was the sister of the reigning Duke

540 THE REVOLTS AGAINST WILLIAM.

CHAP XX. German writer, loyal to his country, if not to its King, will give no higher title than that of Ruler of Latin France.[1] But he also prays William King of the English to come to his help, promising that he will give him the like help back again, should he ever need it.[2] William is made to answer that he had won his realm of England by force, and that he fears lest, if he ever set foot out of it, he might never find his way back into it again.[3] The actual terms of the answer are impossible, as William was actually beyond the sea, in his native Duchy, at the time when Henry's application is said to have been made. Yet the general sentiment is one more in character with the genius of the Conqueror than dreams of winning for himself the Crown of the Cæsars, a crown which assuredly no cousin had ever bequeathed to him.

*Refusal of William*

*Doubts as to Bruno's story*

*William in Normandy early in 1072*
Our speculations as to this curious and isolated piece of history, of which none of our Norman and English authorities make any mention, have carried us on some years beyond the proper stage of our narrative. It appears that the state of things in Normandy and the neighbouring countries called William beyond sea in the former part of the year of his Scottish expedition. What he did in a political or military way we are left to guess from the vague description that the lovers of peace rejoiced at his

William, otherwise called Guy and Geoffrey (see vol ii p 595, vol iii. pp 137, 309) He is made by Bruno to give a very sensible answer to Henry's petition for help, " Ille tantas Francigenarum, Nortmannorum, vel Aquitanorum virtutes inter se et illum esse respondit, ut nullo ingenio per tantam fortitudinem cum exercitu transire potuisset "

[1] Bruno, Bell. Sax. 36. " Philippum, *Latinæ Franciæ rectorem*, multis pollicitationibus sollicitat ut, antiquæ memor amicitiæ, sibi quandocumque vocatus fuerit in auxilium veniat"

[2] Ib " Willehalmum gentis Anglicæ Regem hac conditione suum vocavit in auxilium, ut ei vicem redderet æquam, si se uniquam haberet necessarium."

[3] Ib " Ille respondit se terram illam bellorum violentiâ pervasisse, et ideo, si reliquerit eam, ne posthac recipiatur in eâ, formidare "

coming, while the sons of discord and those whose evil consciences accused them trembled at the approach of the avenger.[1] Peace, in the sense which the word bore in those days, was the great object of William's government; but peace meant one thing in Normandy and another in England. Queen Matilda too was deeply moved by the misfortunes which had fallen on her house and country, so that the presence of William at Rouen was called for on domestic as well as on political grounds.[2] But we hear nothing in detail except of his holding certain Assemblies, temporal and spiritual, and, as usual, the acts of the ecclesiastical Convocation are preserved at far greater length than those of the temporal Parliament. Of the latter we only hear that William gathered together the great men of Normandy and Maine, and exhorted them to the practice of peace and righteousness.[3] But of the Synod of Rouen, held this year by Archbishop John, we have the acts at length, and it is worth notice that the non-resident Bishop of Bayeux left the cares of his Kentish Earldom to take sweet counsel with his spiritual brethren in Normandy.[4] The Prelates also, as well as the lay nobles, received abundance of good advice from the careful nursing-father of the Norman Church.[5] They presently

*Holding of an Assembly.*

*Synod of Rouen. 1072*

*Presence of Odo.*

*William's exhortations.*

---

[1] Ord. Vit. 527 B. "Audito undique Regis adventu, pacis amatores lætati sunt, sed filii discordiæ et fœdi sceleribus ex conscientiâ nequam adventente ultore contremuerunt." William was at Ely in October 1071 (see above, p. 480); he set out for Scotland in September 1072. We hear nothing of him in Britain between those two points, so we have the first half of 1072 for these Norman affairs.

[2] Ib. A.

[3] Ib. B. "Cænomannensium et Normannorum majores congregavit, et omnes ad pacem et justitiam tenendam regali hortatu corroboravit."

[4] Ib. C, 529 B. The Bishops Hugh of Lisieux, Robert of Seez, Michael of Avranches, and Gilbert of Evreux were also present, besides various Abbots. Geoffrey of Coutances is not mentioned. It might not have been safe for William, Odo, and Geoffrey to leave England all at once.

[5] Ib. 527 B. "Episcopos et ecclesiasticos viros admonuit ut bene

went on to carry out the intentions of their sovereign in the form of a series of minute and strict ecclesiastical canons. As might be looked for under the primacy of John of Ivry, the most rigid laws were enacted against all marriage and concubinage on the part of the clergy,[1] without any of that relaxation of strict discipline which the milder wisdom of Lanfranc found needful in England a few years later.[2] Still we do not hear that any inquiry was made into the parentage of that other John, who, if not the son of the Bishop of Bayeux, was at all events the son of the Earl of Kent.[3] There are other provisions touching marriages among the laity,[4] and about various minute ecclesiastical points. But it is worth notice that the Norman Church found it needful to put on record a profession of its orthodoxy in the profoundest mysteries of the faith,[5] and it passed one canon, the observance of which

---

viverent, ut legem Dei jugiter revolverent, ut Ecclesiæ Dei communiter consulerent, ut subditorum mores secundum scita canonum corrigerent, et omnes caute regerent."

[1] Ord. Vit. 528 C. "De sacerdotibus et Levitis et subdiaconibus qui feminas sibi usurpaverunt, Concilium Luxoviense observetur, ne ecclesias per se neque per suffraganeos regant, nec aliquid de beneficiis habeant." The Archdeacons are strictly to carry out the canon. It is plain that no distinction is made between the collegiate and the parochial clergy. The Council of Lisieux referred to is said (Bessin, 61) to be that of 1055, in which Malger was deposed (see vol. iii. p. 96).

[2] See above, p. 424.

[3] See vol. ii. p. 211. Possibly Odo drew the same distinction between his ecclesiastical and temporal functions which was drawn by Archbishop Robert of Rouen, see vol. ii. p. 181. At all events William afterwards knew how to draw it for him.

[4] No one was to marry within the seventh degree of kindred; people were to marry fasting; a man whose wife entered religion could not marry during her life time (compare the story of Hereward), and there is a curious provision (Ord. Vit. 528 D), "Ne aliquis qui, vivente suâ uxore, de adulterio calumniatus fuerit, post mortem illius umquam de quâ calumniatus fuit accipiat. Multa enim mala inde evenerunt, nam plurimi de caussâ hac suas interfecerunt." Did Archbishop John look forward as far as the sixteenth century?

[5] They profess (Ord. Vit. 527 C) their faith in the mystery of the Trinity according to the first Four General Councils.

might be useful, however difficult, in any age, namely, that great care should be taken as to the character and qualifications of those who were appointed Deans.[1] Such were the results of the archiepiscopal vigour of the Primate John. Whether it was in this synod that his zeal provoked the party of laxity to put him in danger of the fate of the protomartyr we are not distinctly told.[2]

CHAP XX
Appointment of Deans

The latter part of this year was devoted by William to the affairs of Scotland and Northumberland, but in the course of the next year he had again to cross the sea to stop the revolt of that noble city and county which, next to England itself, was his most precious conquest. Since the capture of Mayenne ten years earlier[3] we have heard little of Le Mans or of Maine. We have indeed heard of the zeal of Bishop Vulgrin in promoting the expedition against England,[4] and we have seen a knight of Maine show but doubtful loyalty to the Conqueror in the crisis of the great battle.[5] Vulgrin had now been dead four years. His successor Arnold was a Norman by birth, a native of the land of Avranches, but who had long been settled in the Cenomannian diocese, and who had held the post of Chancellor under Vulgrin and under his predecessor Gervase.[6] On the death of Vulgrin he

Revolt of MAINE

1063

Arnold Bishop of Le Mans. 1069-1085.

---

[1] Ord Vit 528 C  "Oportet etiam ut tales Decani eligantur, qui sciant subditos redarguere et emendare, quorum vita non sit infamis, sed merito præferatur subditis"  I presume that this takes in both urban and rural Deans.

[2] See above, p 97
[3] See vol iii p 211
[4] See vol iii p 379
[5] See vol iii p 487
[6] See his Life in Mabillon, Vetera Analecta, 312*. He was brought up by his uncle Robert, "grammaticus sapiens ac religiosus," and who had been diligent "sacrorum librorum instructione seu dirutarum ecclesiarum restauratione."  On his death his nephew succeeded him in his office, "et scholarum regimen . . prudentissime gubernavit"  I take the office to have been that of Chancellor of the church. Compare the father and son who held the same post at Waltham, vol ii pp 443, 444

was chosen by the clergy and people to succeed him.[1] We hear nothing of the rights of the King of the English, who was now Count of the Cenomannians, or of the more legal rights of the King of the French.[2] The only opposition to Arnold's appointment came from some of his own flock, who brought the same objection against him which was brought against Thomas of York, that he was the son of a priest. But on an appeal to Rome the objection was set aside by Pope Alexander;[3] Arnold was consecrated Bishop, and largely devoted himself to the great work of building Saint Julian's minster.[4] But more anxious secular cares soon pressed upon him. A Norman by birth, he was a loyal subject of William, and, soon after his election to the episcopate, the Cenomannian city and the whole Cenomannian land began to revolt against William's authority.

The beginning of mischief is by Norman writers attributed to the reigning Count of Anjou. This was the famous Fulk Rechin, one of the nephews and successors of Geoffrey Martel,[5] who had, in the very year in which

---

[1] Vet. An. 313.* "Clerus et populus Cenomannensis ipsum in Episcopum elegerunt."

[2] See vol. iii. p. 194. The right of advowson had clearly reverted to the King after the death of Geoffrey.

[3] Vet. An. 313.* "Papa apostolicâ auctoritate rescripsit, quod *videlicet in Christo spiritualiter renato generatio carnalis nihil posset officere*, quominus ad sacerdotium promoveri deberet, si nullus eo melior in ecclesiâ illâ poteriri reperiri." This answer is notable on two grounds; the principle on which it goes would seem to remove all the disabilities of illegitimate birth in the case of a baptized man, and it would also seem to narrow the choice of the electors of the Cenomannian Bishop to the members of the Cenomannian chapter.

[4] See vol. iii. p. 205. On reading over again the accounts in the Analecta, I am inclined to think that the shell of the present nave is older than Vulgrin, and that the work both of Vulgrin and Arnold was confined to the choir and transepts. Vulgrin's work was badly built and fell down, so that Arnold had to begin again. He finished the choir and laid the foundations of the transepts with their towers.

[5] See vol. iii. p. 180.

William came into England, overcome and imprisoned his brother Geoffrey the Bearded.[1] Fulk, we are told, mourned at seeing Maine, in the hands of William, altogether cut off from Angevin rule and Angevin influence.[2] But it does not appear that any party in the Cenomannian state as yet cast its eyes towards Anjou in search of a ruler or a deliverer. The thoughts of the men of Maine went back to the line of their ancient princes. The male line of Herbert Wake-dog was extinct, no fruit had come of the empty bethrothal of Robert and Margaret;[3] but sons of the other daughters of Hugh, the other sisters of the younger Herbert, were still to be found both at their own gates and in distant lands.[4] The more distant and more powerful deliverer was first appealed to; the claims of the house of La Flèche were put aside till the next generation, and the patriots of Maine, chiefs and people alike, sought their defender against the Norman yoke in Hugh the son of Gersendis and the Marquess Azo.[5] It was perhaps the rejection of his more obvious claim which caused John of La Flèche, the husband of the third sister Paula, the father of the famous Helias, to cleave steadily to the Norman side.[6] A few among the Cenomannian nobles took the same course,[7] but, as a rule, the whole County revolted. The city and its immediate neighbourhood

CHAP XX.
His alleged intrigues
State of the House of Maine.
Hugh, son of Azo and Gersendis
John of La Flèche takes the Norman side

---

[1] See vol III p 314

[2] Ord Vit 532 C. There is a strange silence on Cenomannian affairs at this time in our Angevin authorities, not excepting Count Fulk himself.

[3] See vol III. pp 199, 213     [4] See vol III p 197

[5] Vet An 314* "Cenomannensium proceres una cum populo ab ipsius Regis fidelitate unanimiter defecerunt, et mittentes in Italiam, Athonem quemdam Marchisium cum uxore et filio, qui vocabatur Hugo, inde venire fecerunt" Orderic makes no mention of the application to Azo

[6] Ord Vit 533 B  "Johannes de Flecchia potentissimus Andegavorum .. Normannis adhærebat."

[7] Ib 532 D

546

CHAP. XX
General revolt of the County.
The Normans driven out of Le Mans.

took the lead. Soldiers, citizens, peasants, joined in one patriotic impulse. The castle which held the city in bondage was stormed,[1] and in the joy of recovered freedom a terrible vengeance was taken on the Normans. Humfrey, the King's Seneschal, was killed in the storm of the castle, of the other Normans some shared his fate, others were put in bonds or driven out of the land.[2]

The city had, in the days of William's conquest, been well nigh the last part of the province to be subdued; it was now the first to assert its freedom. But presently the whole country rose. The Normans, looked on by all men as a common pest, were everywhere attacked[3]

Importance of Geoffrey of Mayenne.

Geoffrey of Mayenne, the man who had been the last to submit to William at the time of his first invasion,[4] was not likely to be wanting at such a time. He was clearly the life and soul of the movement at its present stage.[5]

Bishop Arnold goes to England;

Among the few who were faithful to William was naturally the Norman Bishop Arnold. As soon as the revolt broke out, he at once left the city, and crossed the sea to his sovereign in England.[6] We may be led to think that it was from Arnold that William, now at the height of his power and glory in his island Empire, first heard that his noblest conquest on the mainland had fallen away from him. The Bishop was received with all honour, but his stay in England was not long. As soon as he was

[1] Ord. Vit. 532 C. "Seditiosi cives et oppidani confines gregariique milites in exteros unanime consilium ineunt, arcem urbis et alia munimina [see vol III pp 206, 207] viriliter armati ambiunt, et Turgisum de Traceio Guillelmumque de Firmitate aliosque Regis municipes expugnant et ejiciunt."

[2] Vet An 314\*; Ord Vit u s

[3] Ord Vit 532 D "Regio tota turbatur, et ibidem Normannica vis obfuscatur ac pene ab omnibus, *quasi generalis lues,* passim impugnatur"

[4] See vol III p. 212

[5] Ord Vit u s. The special importance of Geoffrey will be shown presently    [6] Vet. An 314\*

gone, the revolters began to seize and plunder all the episcopal houses and possessions. It was an act of courage, and one which must have been done as an act of duty, when Arnold alleged the spoiling of his goods as a reason for returning to his flock, and obtained the King's licence to do so. He went back laden with royal gifts.¹ But the men of Le Mans had at first no mind again to receive the partizan of their enemy within their walls. The Bishop was for a while driven to take up his abode in the monastery of Saint Vincent without the city, till his clergy found means to reconcile him with the citizens, and he was again allowed to fill his throne in Saint Julian's.²

*CHAP XX*

*and returns*

*The Bishop and the citizens reconciled*

Meanwhile the first revolution was accomplished. The Marquess Azo had listened to the call of the Cenomannian nobles and people. He appeared in the land, accompanied by his wife Gersendis, the daughter of the ancient Counts, and by their son Hugh, who was called to reign over the province from which William had been driven. For a while he met with nothing but success. But little resistance was made to Azo's claims, and that little was overcome, partly by force, partly by gifts.³ But the Marquess and the citizens did not long agree. His money, which he had lavishly spent, began to fail him, and he therefore began, says the local writer, to taste the fickleness of the men of Le Mans, who gradually fell away from their attachment to him.⁴ Azo accordingly went back into Italy, leaving Gersendis and her son under the care of Geoffrey of

*Azo comes to Maine,*

*his first successes.*

*Disagreement between him and the citizens*

*He goes back, leaving Gersendis and Hugh*

---

¹ Vet An. 314*

² Ib 315* "Quum cives sui *odio Regis Anglici* nequaquam eum in civitatem paterentur intrare." Compare the description of William as "Anglıgena Rex" in Ord. Vit 655 D.

³ Ib. "Cunctâ regione tam vi quam muneribus adquisitâ"

⁴ Ib "Atho Marchisius .. cognitâ levitate Cenomannensium, quum jam, deficiente pecuniâ quam in eis initio copiose erogaverat, fidem quoque ipsorum erga se pariter deficere persensisset, reversus est in Italiam"

548                THE REVOLTS AGAINST WILLIAM.

CHAP XX        Mayenne.¹ The choice of a guardian proved both per-
Relations      sonally and politically unlucky. Geoffrey, so the scandal
of Ger-
sendis and     of the time said, made himself too acceptable to the
Geoffrey.      Marchioness in the absence of her husband,² and it is still
               more certain that he showed himself quite unfit to deal
               with a high-spirited people like the citizens of Le Mans.
Position of    He could fight manfully for his own hand; he could
Geoffrey.
               loyally discharge a vassal's duty to his lord; he could
               strive—we need not doubt, with an honest zeal—to free
               his country from the yoke of a stranger; but a spirit
               was now arising which struck straight at all the claims
               and all the prejudices of the lords and Prelates of those
               days, and, when tried by that harder test, he fell away.
Municipal      The spirit of municipal independence had never quite
traditions
in Gaul        died out in the Roman municipalities of Gaul. In the
               South there can be little doubt that traditions of this
               kind were never extinct; and even in the North there
               may have been faintly abiding memories of the days when
Position of    the cities of the Empire, allies or colonies of the one ruling
cities in
Roman          commonwealth, knew no King but Cæsar and no master
times          but the Law. The rule of Cæsar and of his lieutenants may
               have been oppressive; the Law which they administered
               may have been harsh and extortionate; still the rule of
               Rome was a rule of Law, and the subject commonwealths
               of the Empire still proudly cherished the shadow of repub-
               lican freedom. And, if the traditions of civic independence
               thus lingered within the Roman towns, the traditions of
               a more equal, a more widely-spread, form of freedom

---

¹ Vet An 315* "In manu Gaufridi de Meduanâ, viri nobilis et *versuti admodum ingenii*, uxorem cum filio derelinquens." William of Poitiers (see vol III. p. 208) gives Geoffrey the same epithet

² The local writer at this point says scoffingly that Geoffrey was "hujus [Gersendis] tutor et quasi maritus effectus," and further on (285) he speaks of the "illicita familiaritas quæ jam inter eos male succreverat" It should be remembered that Gersendis had been put away by her first husband. See vol III p 196

lingered also beyond their walls. The great peasant revolt in Normandy shows that the memory of the old Teutonic democracy, which lived on in Schwyz and in Friesland, had not wholly died away even within the bounds of Gaul.¹ These twofold memories worked together within the next century or two to bring about that great birth of freedom which established alike the rural democracies of Switzerland and the Free Imperial Cities of other parts of the Empire. Within the dominions of the French King and his vassals the growth of civic freedom was less perfect. No French or Norman or Aquitanian city ever reached the full rank of an independent commonwealth; none attained that measure of freedom which Florence and Genoa kept for so many ages, which Bern and Zurich have kept to our own day, which Massalia, the city which had once braved the might of Cæsar, so nobly defended against Charles of Anjou.² But even in France and its vassal states the growth of municipal life was one of the most marked features of the next age,³ and the French towns, under the name of *Communes*, won for themselves a degree of local freedom which discerning Kings found it their wisdom to foster, as a counterpoise to the overbearing power of the territorial nobility. Than the name of *Communes* no name was more hateful and more fearful to feudal lords and feudal churchmen.⁴ And we

CHAP XX.
Traditions of the Teutonic communities.
Republican movements in the Empire,
less successful in France.

Defence of Marseille against Charles of Anjou 1262

Growth of the Communes

---

¹ See vol 1 p 282

² On the destruction of Massalian freedom, see the Chronicle of William of Nangis, 1262, D'Achery, III 40. But Charles, on taking the city, beheaded a large number of the chief citizens, and the historian applauds an act done "secundum rigorem justitiæ." Neither the princes nor the chroniclers of the eleventh century had sunk so low as this

³ This whole subject may be studied in Thierry's History of the *Tiers État*, a far more trustworthy work than the more famous one with which I have more commonly to do See also his account of the *communes* of Le Mans and Cambray in the fourteenth of his *Lettres sur l'Histoire de France* But one does not see what place Cambray has in a work bearing that title

⁴ The words of Abbot Wibert of Nogent in his Life in Bouquet, xii, 250,

550                THE REVOLTS AGAINST WILLIAM.

CHAP. XX.   have now reached the time when that name was first heard
Le Mans    in Northern Gaul, when the two principles of municipality
the first
Commune    and feudalism met as enemies, if not for the first time
in North-
ern Gaul.  north of the Alps, at all events for the first time north of
Roman      the Loire. On the old Cenomannian height, girded by the
traditions
of the city. walls of Constantine and by the narrower circuit of the
           Old Rome[1]—in the city whose traditions had canonized
           the impersonation of municipal right alongside of the
           patron saint of its ancient Bishoprick — in the city
           which reverenced alike the name of Julian and the name
           of Defensor[2]—the old flame had never wholly died out,
           and it may well have been kindled into fresh life by some
           of the latest visitors from southern lands. Azo, a prince,
           came to rule as a prince in Maine no less than in Liguria.
Possible   But the men who came in his train could tell the burghers
influence
of Italian of Le Mans that a spirit was rising in their own land
examples.  which was soon to shake the power of Marquesses and of
           Emperors.[3] What was tried in vain at Exeter was tried
           also at Le Mans, with more lasting, but still only with
           temporary, success. When the exactions of Gersendis and
           Geoffrey could no longer be borne, the burghers left off
           putting their trust in princes, and sought for means which
           should put it beyond the power, either of their present
           masters or of any other, to bring them again under the
           yoke.[4] The local historian, with a strange mixture of

are well known; "Communio autem, novum ac pessimum nomen, sic se habet, ut capite censi omnes solitum servitutis debitum dominis semel in anno solvant, et, si quid contra jura deliquerint, pensione legali emendent; cæteræ censuum exactiones quæ servis infligi solent omnimodis vacent. Hac se redimendi populus occasione susceptâ, maximos tot avarorum hiatibus obstruendis argenti aggeres obdiderunt, qui, tanto imbre fuso, sereniores redditi, se fidem eis super isto negotio servaturos sacramentis præbitis firmaverunt."

[1] See vol. iii. p. 204.            [2] See vol. iii. p. 187.
[3] Compare the possible influence of Italian examples at Exeter, above, p. 147.
[4] Vet. An. 315*. "Consilium inierunt, qualiter ejus [Gaufredi] pravis

admiration and horror, tells us how the citizens of Le Mans made a *Commune*, how they bound themselves by mutual oaths to maintain their new-born freedom, and how they constrained the nobles of the land, with Geoffrey at their head, to share unwillingly in the civic oath.[1] We seem to be reading the history of an Italian republic, not the history of a city within any part of the dominions of William the Norman. The tale goes on to tell us of the crimes by which the new-born commonwealth disgraced its freedom, crimes which, to say the least, were not worse than the crimes of the princes of their age. In one respect indeed, if it be true that the new republic sent men to the gallows for small offences, the hands of William were cleaner than the hands of his revolted subjects. But the man who had wrought his vengeance at Alençon and at Ely, who had seared out the eyes of the hostage before the gates of Exeter,[2] had little reason to complain if the young republic did not rise in those matters above the standard of contemporary princes.[3] It was a saying far older than the days of William, that a people which has just won its own deliverance is tempted to be stern to those whom it has overcome.[4] We hear too of the impiety of the citizens in disregarding the Church's hallowed seasons, how they took castles in Lent, and even in the holy week

CHAP XX.
Foundation of the Commune
Geoffrey and the nobles swear to it
Alleged crimes of the new commonwealth
Their disregard of holy seasons

conatibus obsisterent, nec se ab eo vel quolibet alio injuste opprimi paterentur."

[1] Vet An 315* "Factâ conspiratione quam *communionem* vocabant, sese omnes pariter sacramentis adstringunt, et ipsum Gaufridum et ceteros ejusdem regionis proceres, quamvis invitos, sacramentis suæ conspirationis obligari compellunt"

[2] See above, p 155

[3] Vet An 315* "Conjurationis audaci innumera scelera commiserunt, passim plurimos sine aliquo judicio condemnantes, quibusdam pro causis minimis oculos eruentes, alios vero (quod nefas est referre) pro culpâ levissimâ suspendio strangulantes" The shrinking from the infliction of death otherwise than in battle is characteristic of the age

[4] Æsch Sept c Theb 1035 τραχύς γε μέντοι δῆμος ἐκφυγὼν κακά.

of the Passion.[1] In so doing the republicans undoubtedly sinned against the Truce of God; but they must share the blame with the Kings and Princes who kept their Paschal Feast on the stricken fields of Barnet and Ravenna.[2]

A great expedition followed, in which the men of the Commonwealth found how small was the worth of the extorted oaths of nobles, and how well the virtues of chivalry could agree with treachery towards the burgher and the peasant. A Cenomannian noble, Hugh by name, held the castle of Sillé, lying north-west of the city, at about an equal distance from Le Mans and Mayenne. He had refused allegiance to the Commonwealth, and had dealt with it as an open enemy.[3] Orders were accordingly sent through the whole country for a general march against his castle. Not a word is told us as to either the political or the military arrangements of the Republic, but the army which set forth against Hugh was evidently a general levy of the population of the country.[4] This fact suggests matter for thought In the first moment of recovered freedom, before disputes and differences had had time to arise, the people of the country at large gladly obeyed the orders which were sent forth to them from the capital. But the Cenomannian commonwealth would have displayed a wisdom shared with it by no other city-commonwealth save Rome and Athens, if it had found out any way of permanently

[1] Vet An 316*. "Castra vicina diebus sanctæ Quadragesimæ, immo Dominicæ passionis tempore, irrationabiliter succendentes."

[2] We may add Towton, fought on Palm Sunday in 1461, and some less famous Easter fights before and after

[3] Vet An. u s "Quibusdem injuriis adversum se conjuratorum animos irritâsset" Silliacum or Sulliacum is Sillé-le-Guillaume in the department of Sarthe

[4] Ib "Subito per totius regionis populos legatos miserunt, contra præfatum Hugonem, qui sanctis instructionibus obsistebat, tumultuosæ multitudinis agmina concitantes" The sneering tone of the writer at this stage should be noticed, as, before long, he begins to talk patriotically about "nostri"

attaching the country at large to the civic rule. To communicate equal rights to whole provinces, to place their villages and smaller towns in some higher position than that of subject districts, is an honour which has been reserved for the commonwealths of modern Switzerland. But for the moment all was harmony. The army of the Republic, if it recked little of holy seasons, at least put on the aspect of a religious procession. Bishop Arnold, unwillingly no doubt, but probably in accordance with the terms of his late reconciliation, sanctified the host with his presence and that of his clergy. The priests of the several churches marched at the head of their flocks, carrying their crosses and banners. In this sacred array, the host, full of eager zeal, pressed on to the attack of Hugh's castle.[1] But they had an enemy among them. Geoffrey had obeyed the summons to arms; he had come with his own following, probably from Mayenne on the opposite side of the besieged fortress, and he had pitched his camp hard by that of the civic army. But the Lord of Mayenne had not come with an honest heart to fight for burghers against a brother noble. He entered into a treasonable correspondence with Hugh, and a plan of action for the morrow was agreed on between them.[2] In the morning the garrison of the besieged castle made a sally; the army of the Commonwealth was taken by surprise, but they had time and courage left to make themselves ready for battle. But suddenly a false rumour was spread through the camp that the city itself had been betrayed to the enemy. The countrymen who had flocked

*CHAP. XX.*
*Relations of city commonwealths to the surrounding country*

*Presence of Bishop Arnold and his clergy.*

*Treason of Geoffrey of Mayenne*

*Rout of the besiegers*

---

[1] Vet An 316* "Congregato exercitu, Episcopo et singularum ecclesiarum presbyteris præcuntibus, cum crucibus et vexillis ad castrum Silliacum furibundo impetu diriguntur."

[2] Ib "Quum haud procul a castro consedissent, Gaufridus . ipsorum comitatui fraudulenter adjunctus, non longe ab eis castra posuit, et clam cum hostibus per internuntios colloquutus, ad dissipandos conjuratorum conatus modis omnibus laborabat."

to the civic standard around the banners of their own parishes at once threw down their arms and fled. The rest of the army, nobles and commons alike, soon followed their example, and the local historian gives us a graphic description of the rout. The pursuers do not seem to have been specially blood-thirsty, but crowds of the fugitives died by pressing into the rivers or crushing one another to death in the narrow paths. Men of all ranks, scattered about the fields, were taken like fawns, not only by soldiers but even by women, and it would seem that it was a female captor who made a prize of the chief shepherd of the Cenomannian Church.[1] Bishop Arnold was undoubtedly made a prisoner, and put into ward, but the piety of Hugh of Sillé presently released him and let him go home with all honour.

*Capture and release of the Bishop*

This great blow may be said to have sealed the ruin of the new-born republic. A defeat after a stout resistance might have been a strengthening discipline, but such a defeat as this only discouraged the hearts of the men of Le Mans and made them ridiculous in the eyes of their enemies. The city, says the local writer, full of sorrow and fear, was tossed to and fro like a ship without a rudder.[2]

*Effects of the defeat*

Geoffrey of Mayenne no longer dared to show himself at Le Mans; he sent the young Hugh back to his father in Italy, and betook himself to his castle of La Chartre on the Loir, close to the Angevin march.[3] Gersendis

*Hugh sent back to Italy*

---

[1] Vet. An. 316* "Quanti capti, quanti vulnerati, quanti a semetipsis in torrentibus et in semitarum angustiis oppressi atque exstincti sunt, non est opusculi præsentis evolvere. Et, ut de cæteris taceam, tam nobilibus quam ignobilibus, quos non solum milites sed et mulierculæ passim per agros velut damulas pro arbitrio capiebant, ipse quoque episcopus, proh dolor, ab ipsis comprehensus et custodiæ mancipatus est."

[2] Ib. "Civitas nostra, in luctu et tremore posita, huc atque illuc, velut navis absque gubernaculo, ferebatur."

[3] Ib. 285 "Utpote sibi male conscius, cives suspectos habens, Hugonem quidem puerum ad patrem in Italiam dimisit; ipse vero ad castrum quod Carcer vocatur secessit."

remained in the city; but the scandal of the time reported that she could not live without her lover, and that her whole mind was given to devising schemes for betraying Le Mans to Geoffrey.[1] At last, on a Sunday, some traitors in the interest of the Countess admitted the Lord of Mayenne with eighty knights into a fortress hard by the cathedral church, that is doubtless into the castle which had been built by William on his first entrance.[2] Hostilities followed between the citizens and the newcomers.[3] Fire, the favourite means of destruction, was freely used on both sides. The citizens called the neighbouring nobles to their help, and they called in one deliverer more dangerous than all in the person of Count Fulk of Anjou.[4] Such a step amounted to giving up all hopes of maintaining their republican freedom; it must have been a mere measure of despair. The Commonwealth was something to fight for; even the native dynasty was something to fight for; but if Le Mans was to acknowledge a foreign master, it is hard to see how the rule of Fulk promised better than the rule of William. But the help of the Count and of the nobles served the immediate purpose of the citizens All the engineering resources of the age were brought to bear upon the besieged fortress.[5] As

*The castle betrayed by Gersendis to Geoffrey*

*The citizens invite Count Fulk*

*Geoffrey besieged in the castle.*

[1] Vet An 285 "Gersendis in civitate remansit, quæ videns Gaufridum, propter nequitiam suam civibus exosum, non facile in eorum amicitiam posse redire, quum ejus absentiam sustinere non posset, cœpit machinari qualiter ei traderet civitatem"

[2] The fortress is described as "quædam arx civitatis, quæ juxta matrem ecclesiam sita erat," see vol iii p 206 The betrayal on Sunday, "quâdam die dominicâ," was perhaps to punish the disregard of the citizens for the holy seasons of the Church

[3] Vet An 285 "Cœpit [Gaufridus] hostiliter agere, et in perniciem civium totis nisibus anhelare"

[4] Ib "Totius regiones proceres, et præcipue Fulconem Andegavorum Comitem, subito convocârunt" There is something strange in this mention of the Count of Anjou as if he were simply the chief among the ordinary nobles

[5] Ib. "Telis et diversorum generum machinis expugnantes"

in the slaughter of the Normans at Durham,[1] the minster —where we may conceive that the works of Bishop Arnold were for a while at a standstill—narrowly escaped the flames which were used to dislodge the enemy from towers and houses in its immediate neighbourhood.[2] Geoffrey, by connivance with a party among the besiegers, escaped by night.[3] His followers, deceived of the further succours which he had promised them, finding their provisions fail, and feeling their walls quake beneath the strokes of the battering-engines, surrendered themselves and the fortress to Count Fulk.[4] Oddly enough, from this point Fulk vanishes for a season from the story. He at least did not hinder the citizens from taking a vengeance at once practical and symbolical on the fortress which had kept them in bondage. They did not indeed, like the Northumbrians at York,[5] rase the whole of the hated prison-house to the ground. They at once gratified their wrath and took measures for their future safety. The inner parts of the castle were pulled down to a level with the walls of the city, but the outer walls were allowed to stand, and to form part of the public defences.[6]

But the prince whose works were thus overthrown was already on the march to recover what he had lost. He who as a babe would not leave hold of the straw

---

[1] See above, p 237

[2] Vet An 285 "Duæ turriculæ eidem arci proximæ" are specially mentioned.

[3] The local writer is emphatic on the fears of Geoffrey, "Gaufridus perterritus, quorumdam nostrorum consensu de munitione latenter egressus, imminens periculum nocturnæ fugæ beneficio tremebundus evasit"

[4] Vet An 286. "Quum, deficientibus alimoniis, munitionem quoque crebris machinarum ictibus cernerent conquassari, tandem necessitate coacti, sese et munitionem Fulconi Comiti tradiderunt."

[5] See above, p 270

[6] Vet An 286 "Cives irâ commoti, ac sibi in futurum præcaventes, interiorem partem ejusdem munitionis muro civitatis coæquaverunt, exteriores parietes ad urbis præsidium integros relinquentes."

which he had once clutched[1] was not likely, as King and Conqueror, to allow the noblest prize of his earlier warfare to abide in any hands but his own. King William of England crossed the sea with a mighty host to win back the revolted city and province. We read with mingled feelings that the host which he led consisted largely of his English subjects,[2] and that, in English belief at least, it was mainly by English valour that the land was won back to William's allegiance.[3] Stranger than all is the thought, probable at least if not certain, that the captain of the English bands was no other than the most stout-hearted of living Englishmen, even Hereward himself.[4] As William took Eadric to witness and share in the subjugation of Scotland,[5] so he took Hereward to witness and share in the subjugation of Maine. We feel a kind of regret, a kind of shame, that valour which might have been used to free England from the yoke of William was used in quarrels in which England had no concern, to bring other nations under his yoke. But the same causes which enabled William to employ English troops to bring other Englishmen into bondage[6] would apply with tenfold force when they were summoned to serve the King in his wars beyond the sea. The mere love of adventure would stir up many to whom life in conquered England had become irksome. And many too, now that English prowess had been so discredited in the world, might rejoice in the opportunity of giving the men of the mainland a sample

*CHAP. XX.*

*His force largely composed of English.*

*perhaps commanded by Hereward.*

*Motives of the English soldiers.*

---

[1] See vol ii p 180
[2] Chron Wig 1074, Petrib 1073 "On þisum geare Willelm cyng lædde Engliscne here and Frencisce ofer sæ, and gewan þæt land Mans" English troops serving out of England and not for any English object are not called *fyrd*, but *here*, like the Danish invaders of old.
[3] Flor Wig 1073 "Rex Anglorum Willelmus civitatem quæ vocatur Cinomannis, et provinciam ad illam pertinentem, maxime Anglorum adjutorio quos de Angliâ secum duxerat, sibi subjugavit"
[4] See above, p. 486      [5] See above, p 514
[6] See above, p 150.

558          THE REVOLTS AGAINST WILLIAM.

CHAP. XX. of what Englishmen still could do. And men to whom all who spoke the foreign tongue were the same might feel that they were in some strange way paying off their own wrong when they harried the lands of Frenchmen, even if it were in the cause of the Norman King and with Normans to their fellow-soldiers.[1] The minds would be few indeed which could raise themselves to the thought that the cause of Maine and the cause of England were in truth the same.

With his mixed host then, of horse and foot, of Normans and English, William set forth to win back his lost city and province. The plan of his campaign was the same as the plan of his campaign in the same land ten years before.[2] The land was to be ravaged; the outlying towns and castles were to be taken; the city itself was to be devoured last. The amount of ravage, and the share which the English troops had in it, is emphatically dwelled on by the English Chroniclers. "The land of Mans they mightily wasted, and vineyards fordid, and boroughs burned, and mightily the land they wasted and brought it all into William's hands, and then they went home to England."[3] Norman and Cenomannian writers give us a few more details. The campaign began by the siege of the castle of Fresnay, which shows that William entered Mans by way of Alençon. Under its walls William girt the belt of knighthood on a man who was to win an

*Plan of the campaign*

*The land wasted and the city isolated*

*Siege of Fresnay*

*Knighthood of Robert of Belesme*

[1] Matthew Paris (Hist. Angl. i. 18, Madden) brings out this motive—perhaps all the more because he has somehow read "Normanniam" for "Cenomanniam"—' Normannis vicissitudinem nacto tempore non immerito reddiderunt."    [2] See vol. iii. p. 202.

[3] Chron. Wig. 1074, Petrib. 1073. "And hit [þæt land Mans] Englisce men swyðe amyrdon, wingeardas hi fordydon, and burga forbærndon, and swyðe þet land amyrdon, and hit eall abegdon Willelme [þan kyninge, Wig] to handa, and hi syððon ham gewendon to Englalande." Roger of Wendover (ii. 13) adds, "Omnem provinciam debiliorem multo post tempore reddiderunt." We have no Cenomannian Domesday to mark the entries of "wasta."

infamous renown, Robert the son of Earl Roger and of the cruel Mabel, who bore the name of Robert of Belesme, and in whom, along with the name of his mother's house, the evil deeds of his mother and her kindred seemed to revive.[1] The fields and vineyards round the castle were wasted in the usual sort, till Hubert its lord, finding resistance hopeless, surrendered the fortress and his other fortress of Beaumont, and received a royal garrison in each.[2] Thence the Conqueror moved south-westwards to Sillé, the castle which had so lately borne the attack of the republican forces. Hugh of Sillé, the enemy at once of King and Commonwealth, must have fought for Fulk or for Gersendis, or perhaps only for his own hand. But the terror of William's ravages and the example of his neighbour at Fresnay warned him against any obstinate resistance. He came forth; he craved for peace and obtained it.[3] The inhabitants both of the towns and the country began to take the same course, the monks and clergy being foremost in preaching submission[4] At last the host of William drew near to the city itself. He encamped by the Sarthe, and sent a message, calling on the men of Le Mans, as he had called on the men of Exeter, to avoid the horrors of a storm, to escape bloodshed and fire-raising, by a timely and peaceful submission[5] The next day the magistrates of Le Mans made their way to the royal presence. The Norman version simply tells how they

*Chap. XX.*

*Surrender of Fresnay and Beaumont.*

*Siege and surrender of Sillé*

*William encamps near Le Mans*

*The city surrenders*

---

[1] Ord. Vit 532 D On some of his later doings, see 707

[2] Ib Hubert bore the title of Viscount (Ord Vit 648 C), whence his two castles are still called Fresnay-le-Vicomte and Beaumont-le-Vicomte The local writer (Vet An 286) mentions the garrison, " Positi in ejusdem castri munitione custodiis "

[3] Ord Vit 533 A

[4] Ib "Omnes oppidani ac pagenses cum clericis et omnibus religiosis pacificum Marchionem decreverunt digniter suscipere illiusque ditioni legitimæ gratanter colla submittere" It takes a little thought to recognize the King and Conqueror in the garb of a peaceful Marquess

[5] Ib See above, p 145

560        THE REVOLTS AGAINST WILLIAM.

CHAP. XX. brought the keys of the city, how they threw themselves on William's mercy and were graciously received by him.[1] The local writer speaks in another tone. The interview between the King and the magistrates of Le Mans is described by a word often used to express conferences—in a word *Parliaments*—whether between prince and prince or between princes and the estates of their dominions.[2] They submitted themselves to William's authority as their sovereign, but they received his oath to observe the ancient customs and *justices* of the city.[3] Le Mans was no longer to be a sovereign Commonwealth, but it was to remain a privileged municipality. Thus this noble city came a second time into William's hands without shedding of blood. After the fall of the capital, the rest of the County had no heart to hold out. The banners of the other towns and districts pressed into William's camp, not as ensigns of defiance, but to swell the forces of the King, who received all his suppliants graciously, and sent them back to dwell and sport each man in peace under his own vine.[4]

It retains its privileges.

General submission of Maine.

Movements of Fulk of Anjou.

During this whole campaign we have heard nothing of Fulk of Anjou. He and Geoffrey of Mayenne both vanish from the scene after the taking of the castle by the combined forces of the Count and the citizens. But Maine was no sooner brought again under William's

---

[1] Ord. Vit. 533 A.

[2] Vet. An. 286. "Proceres civitatis egressi cum Rege de pace colloquium habuerunt." *Colloquium* is the word constantly used by Lambert of Herzfeld for a Diet or Parliament

[3] Ib. "Acceptis ab eo sacramentis, tam de impunitate perfidiæ, quam de conservandis antiquis ejusdem civitatis consuetudinibus atque justitiis, in ipsius ditionem atque imperium sese et sua omnia dedederunt." We see here that "dedere" in these times did not imply the fulness of a Roman "deditio." The "justitiæ" are the rights of jurisdiction, "haute justice," and the like. See Du Cange in voc.

[4] Ord. Vit. 533 B. "Exinde in domo suâ et sub vite suâ morari et ludere, si libet, quietè permissi sunt." The importance of the vines in Maine appears throughout the story.

power than we hear of him as seeking to disturb an order of things the establishment of which he seems to have done nothing to hinder. His wrath was mainly kindled against John of La Flèche and the other Cenomannian Barons who had stood firm in their allegiance to the King[1] He marched against La Flèche, a border post about midway between Le Mans and Angers, and drove its lord to ask help of William. The King sent a force under the command of two Barons of the land of Auge and Hiesmes, William of Moulins and Robert of Vieuxpont.[2] The war now took a more important form. Fulk gathered a greater host, and besieged John in La Flèche. His forces were presently swelled by a large reinforcement of Bretons, under the reigning Count. Conan, who died so opportunely on the eve of William's great expedition,[3] had been succeeded by the husband of his sister Hadwisa, who bore the name of Howel, the renowned lawgiver of the insular Britons. Norman and Angevin had alike been enemies of Britanny, but the wrongs received at Norman hands were the more recent, and Howel and his subjects pressed eagerly to join in the attack on William's ally.[4] Again, as in Harold's march to Dol and Dinan, Norman and Englishman went forth side by side against the *Bretwealas* of the mainland. For King William summoned to his standard his subjects of all races, Norman, English, and others, and gathered so great a power that men said

CHAP XX

He attacks La Flèche

William sends a force to defend La Flèche

Fulk joined by the Bretons under Count Howel

William gathers his forces, French and English

---

[1] Ord. Vit 533 B "Fulco Comes noxio livore nequiter infectus est, et contra quosdam Normannis faventes insurgere conatus est Tunc ei Johannes de Flecchiâ potentissimus Andegavorum præcipue infensus erat, quia Normannis adhærebat." Fulk marches against La Flèche "cum ferratis agminibus"

[2] Ib We have heard of Moulins before in vol iii p 137 See Stapleton, i. cxxxiii, cxxxiv, and on Vieux Pont, i clxxii, ii cclxiv

[3] See vol iii p 316

[4] Ord Vit 533 C On his descent, see Art de Vérifier les Dates, ii 897, and the pedigree in Mrs Green's Princesses, i 25.

VOL. IV.          O O

562   THE REVOLTS AGAINST WILLIAM.

CHAP XX.   that sixty thousand horsemen rode forth to the war.[1]
But no war followed. The Breton and Angevin host
had, if we can at all trust the geography of the story,
Fulk approaches the Norman border   left the siege of La Flèche for greater undertakings. It
was on the older border of Normandy and Maine, in the
debateable land of Bruère, that the two armies met face
to face.[2] But for once the Roman Church stepped in
Efforts of a Cardinal (Hubert?) for peace   to hinder and not to promote bloodshed. A Cardinal
Priest whose name is not given, but in whom we may
be tempted to see the ubiquitous Hubert, was by some
chance on the spot, charged probably with some of the
many letters which went to and fro between William
and the Holy See. He and some well-disposed monks
used their influence to bring about peace between the
contending princes and to hinder the shedding of Christian blood.[3] They were helped in their praiseworthy undertaking by several of the Norman Counts and nobles,
among whom we specially hear of Roger—I presume the

[1] Ord. Vit 533 C "Guillelmus Rex, ut tantam multitudinem girâsse suos agnovit, regali edicto Normannos et Anglos iterum excivit, aliasque sibi subditas gentes, ut fortis magister militum, conglobavit, ac, ut ferunt, sexaginta millia equitum contra hostiles cuneos secum adduxit" The number seems incredible, especially as William was not likely to repeat the blunder of Ralph, and to make the English as a body serve as "equites."

[2] The peace, according to Orderic (533 D), was made in "loco qui vulgo Blancalanda vel Bruena dicitur." This (see Stapleton, i. lxxvii) is on the borders of Normandy and Maine, in the district added to Normandy by William's conquest of Domfront This seems to show that the Angevin army had got so far north But I do not understand Orderic's story when he says (533 C), "Andegavenses et Britones, comperto Regis et agminum ejus adventu, non fugerunt, sed potius Ligerim fluvium audacter pertransierunt, et transvecti, ne timidiores spe fugiendi segnius præliarentur, scafas suas destruxerunt" The burning of ships has a legendary sound, and for *Ligerim* we should perhaps read *Lederim*, the *Loir* instead of the *Loire* Only a very small part of an Angevin and Breton host could need to cross the Loire for an invasion of Normandy.

[3] The mediators are simply described as "quidam Romanæ ecclesiæ Cardinalis presbyter et religiosi monachi." They were present "divino nutu" Cf the mediation of the Cardinal of Perigord before the battle of Poitiers  Froissart, c. 161

Earl of Shrewsbury—and of William of Evreux, grandson of the famous Robert, Archbishop and Count.[1] After many efforts, the messengers of peace at last succeeded in their good work.[2] Terms of peace were agreed upon, terms which, together with the peaceful disposition of the Norman leaders, seem to show that William could not have been very confident of victory. The rights of the Count of Anjou over Maine were virtually acknowledged, though means were taken to hinder their taking any practical shape. Under the elder arrangement with Herbert, Maine was to pass to William's eldest son Robert, as the inheritance of his betrothed wife Margaret.[3] That scheme had passed away; but Robert was again chosen as the nominal ruler of Maine. He received from Fulk a grant of all the rights over the County which were claimed by the House of Anjou, and for this grant he performed a formal act of homage to his new lord.[4] Each prince, unlike some renowned princes in later times, honourably stipulated for his own adherents. John of La Flèche and all the subjects of the Count of Anjou who had taken the side of William were to be received to the full favour of Fulk, and the partizans of Fulk in the Cenomannian city and county were to be received to the full favour of William.[5] Such was the Peace of Blanchelande or Bruère. Its terms secured William in full immediate possession of Maine, but it opened a door to any amount of future questions and cavillings. The treaty however did

*Peace of Blanchelande.*

*Robert does homage to Fulk for Maine.*

---

[1] Ord Vit 533 C "Guillelmus Ebroicensis et Rogerius aliique comites strenuique optimates" William of Evreux had succeeded his father Richard in the County, see vol iii p. 287. We are told that these nobles, "sicut erant prompti et audaces ad legitimos agones, sic nimirum perhorrebant per superbiam et injustitiam subire conflictus detestabiles" It is hard to see why this struggle was more detestable than others

[2] Ib. D.   [3] See vol iii p 199

[4] The homage seems to have been a merely formal one, "Rodbertus Fulconi debitum homagium, ut minor majori, legaliter impendit"

[5] Ord Vit. 533 D

CHAP. XX.
Maine still discontented.

secure peace between Normandy and Anjou during the remainder of the days of William.[1] But nothing could overcome the rooted dislike of the Cenomannian people to the rule of the Norman. Even during William's lifetime partial revolts took place,[2] and, when the great King was gone, the unconquerable hatred which the stout-hearted city and province bore to the sway of any foreign master showed itself under new leaders.[3]

## § 5. *The Revolt of Ralph of Norfolk.* 1075–1076.

Internal state of England.
1072–1074

We have but slight notices of the internal state of England during the years which were mainly taken up with the affairs of Scotland, Flanders, and Maine. But there is some reason to believe that the suppression of the revolt at Ely led to increased harshness, if not on the part of William himself, at least on that of the Normans established in England. It will be remembered that the time immediately following the completion of the Conquest is described as a time of unusual peace and harmony between the two races, a time when William himself, if not his followers, was trying to establish a state of things in which Norman and Englishman might sit down side by side as fellow-subjects.[4] In such pictures there is always some truth and some exaggeration. We must therefore look both for some truth and for some exaggeration in an opposite picture which is given us of the state of things immediately following the submission of Ely. We are

---

[1] Ord Vit 533 D. "Hæc nimirum pax . . . inter Regem et præfatum Comitem . . . omni vitâ Regis ad profectum utriusque provinciæ permansit"

[2] See the next Chapter.

[3] The long struggle between Helias and William Rufus is fully described by Orderic and by the local writer in the Lives of Bishops Howel and Hildebert.

[4] See above, p. 326.

told how the Normans, puffed up by their good fortune, oppressed the English in all manner of ways, how they deemed that they might do whatever they would, how they forgot that it was not by their own merits, but by the hand of God, that they had overcome a nation greater and richer and more ancient than themselves. We hear too that the originally low estate of many of the strangers who were suddenly raised to rank and wealth in England was specially galling to the natives. We hear too, above all, of the complaints of the English women. We hear of the sad estate of noble matrons who, having lost their husbands and all their friends, thought it better to die than to live. We hear of the sufferings of noble maidens who, handed over to be the sport of coarse and low-born ruffians, were left to weep for their shame and sorrow. In these last vague complaints we may perhaps venture to class together a variety of wrongs, ranging from unwilling marriages to actual violence. The whole picture is worthy of special study, especially when contrasted with the earlier one.[1] And with regard to the complaints of the women, there is an independent witness from another quarter. We are told that, when the Great William first conquered this land, many of his followers, proud of their success, and

*CHAP. XX.*

*Increased oppression of the Normans.*

*Special complaints of the English women.*

---

[1] The picture given by Orderic (523 B, C) of the state of things at this time is worth transcribing in full, "Adeptis itaque nimiis opibus quas alii aggregârant, Normanni furentes immoderate tumebant, et indigenas divino verbere pro reatibus suis percussos impie mactabant . Nobiles puellæ despicabilium ludibrio armigerorum patebant, et ab immundis nebulonibus oppressæ dedecus suum deplorabant Matronæ vero elegantiâ et ingenuitate spectabiles desolatæ gemebant maritorum et omnium pene amicorum solatio destitutæ magis mori quam vivere optabant Indociles parasiti admirabantur, et quasi vecordes e superbiâ efficiebantur, unde sibi tanta potestas emanâsset, et putabant quod quidquid vellent sibi liceret Insipientes et maligni cur cum totâ contritione cordis non cogitabant, quod non suâ virtute, sed Dei gubernantis omnia nutu, hostes vicerant, et gentem majorem et ditiorem et antiquiorem sese subegerant, in quâ plures sancti prudentesque viri Regesque potentes micuerant, multisque modis domi militiæque nobiliter viguerant"

deeming that they might follow their own lusts in all things, dealt according to their will, not only with the goods of the conquered, but with the matrons and maidens who came in their way. Many of them therefore took shelter in the monasteries of virgins, to protect themselves from shame under the veil. But when more orderly times came, the question was brought before Father Lanfranc, whether women who had thus taken the veil simply to preserve their chastity were thereby bound for ever to a monastic life. The matter was debated in one of the Councils held by the Primate, and the more reasonable and less rigid view prevailed. Such women were to be held in high honour for the zeal which they had shown in the defence of their chastity, but the obligations of the religious life were not to be forced upon them against their wills.[1] As the date of this one among Lanfranc's many Councils is not told us, we cannot say with certainty to what time of William's reign this account refers;[2] but we have heard

[1] Eadmer, Hist Nov 57 "Quando ille magnus Wilhelmus hanc terram primo devicit, multi suorum, sibi pro tantâ victoriâ applaudentes omniaque suis voluntatibus atque luxuriis obedire ac subdi debere autumantes, non solum in possessiones victorum, sed et in ipsas matronas et virgines, ubi eis facultas aspirabat, nefandâ libidine cœperunt insanire Quod nonnullæ prævidentes et suo pudori metuentes, monasteria virginum petivere, acceptoque velo sese inter ipsas a tantâ infamiâ protexere. Quæ clades, quum postmodum sedata et, pro temporis qualitate, pax rebus data fuisset, quæsitum ab eodem patre Lanfranco est quid de his quæ tali refugio suam pudicitiam servaverunt ipse sentiret, essentne videlicet constringendæ in monasterio velum tenere quod acceperant, necne At ipse quæstionem ipsam consilio generalis concilii taliter solvit ut eis pro castitate, quam se tam manifestæ rei ostensione amare testatæ fuerant, debitam magis reverentiam judicaret exhibendam quam ullam servandæ religionis continentiam, nisi propriâ illam voluntate appeterent, violenter ingerendam."

[2] I do not know that the word "primo" in the extract just given from Eadmer need bind us to place the injuries complained of in the very first days of the Conquest, or to fix the decision on the question to one of the earliest of Lanfranc's Councils Any time in the first half of William's reign would seem to answer Eadmer's description, and the passage which I have quoted from Orderic would seem to fix it to the time which we have now reached

something of the strict discipline which William, in the first days of the Conquest, meted out against all offenders against female chastity,[1] and we hear of it again in the portrait of his last years drawn by the native Chronicler.[2] At no time during William's reign is oppression of this and of other kinds likely to have been more rife than in the days which immediately followed the recovery of Ely. The revolt, the first revolt after the actual conquest of the whole country, must have greatly kindled the wrath of William and his Normans, and must have strengthened the belief which they professed to hold, that no Englishman could be trusted.[3] And it was also just at this time that William's followers in England began to be more often relieved from the restraint of his personal presence. It was immediately after the fall of Ely that William began that series of absences on the Continent of which we have just been describing some of the fruits. While William was holding synods in Normandy and waging war in Maine, the state of things in England must have been pretty much the same as it was under the first regency of Odo and William Fitz-Osbern. It would indeed seem that at this time the chief power during William's absence was placed in the hands of Lanfranc, and Lanfranc at least cannot be suspected of abetting or winking at excesses which sinned against every rule alike of morality and of ecclesiastical law. But we may doubt whether the hand of the monk of Pavia, subtle as was his brain and sage as were his counsels, would always be strong enough to control the rude soldiers who had risen to wealth and power. We may well believe that these years, the central years of William's reign, were among the darkest times for

CHAP. XX.

Increased oppression following the fall of Ely.

Effects of William's absence on the Continent

Alleged regency of Lanfranc.

---

[1] See above, p 30  [2] Chron Petrib. 1087
[3] Will Malm iii 254  "Inde propositum Regis fortassis merito excusatur, si aliquando durior in Anglos fuerit, quod pene nullum eorum fidelem invenerit"

568    THE REVOLTS AGAINST WILLIAM.

CHAP. XX. England, till the worst days of the Conqueror began to be looked back to with regret under the fouler oppression of his son.

Jealousy of King Philip against William

The visits of William to the Continent, and the large amount of his attention which had to be given to continental affairs, connect themselves closely with all the events of this period. We have heard nothing of Philip of France during the course of the war in Maine, but we may be sure that he watched the success of his mighty vassal with no small jealousy, and we must remember that, besides the hereditary rivalry between Paris and Rouen, Philip was now the firm friend of William's enemy in Flanders.[1] He now tried to raise up an enemy to William in the last representative of the Old-English kingly house.

1073.
1074.

Eadgar in Flanders

After the conquest of Maine, William came back to England, but in the next year he crossed to Normandy again,[2] and his constant neighbourhood probably stirred up the French King to schemes against him. Eadgar, after the marriage of his sister to Malcolm, had gone, with what object we are not told, to Flanders. The disturbed state of the country may have offered charms to an idle spirit of adventure, and Robert the Frisian was doubtless ready with a welcome for any enemy of William. From Flanders he had gone to Scotland on a visit—clearly his first visit to his sister after her marriage—when she and her husband received him with "mickle worship."[3] While at the court of Malcolm, Eadgar received a letter from the King of the

Eadgar in Scotland July 8, 1074

---

[1] See above, pp 536, 537

[2] Chron. Wig: 1075, Petrib 1074 "On þisum geare for Willelm cyng ofer sæ to Normandig" This implies his return after the Cenomannian campaign of the year before

[3] Chron Wig 1075 "Eadgar cild cóm of Fleminga lande into Scotlande on Sće Grimbaldes mæsse dæg, and se kynge Malcholom and his sweoster Margareta hine underfengon mid mycclan weorðscype" This visit to Flanders is not mentioned by Florence and the Peterborough Chronicler, who carry him at once from Scotland to Normandy

ADVENTURES OF EADGAR.

French, praying him to come to him, and offering to him the castle of Montreuil, where he might dwell and make inroads upon his enemies.[1] This offer to Eadgar of the old border-fortress of Flanders and Normandy, so famous in the wars of an earlier time,[2] was certainly not unconnected with Eadgar's sojourn in Flanders and with the warfare between William and Robert the Frisian. Nothing could better suit the interests of the enemies of Normandy than to place the English Ætheling, the rival King, probably at the head of a band of English exiles, in a position where he could so well abet any schemes of the Count of Flanders against their common rival. Eadgar caught at the opening thus offered to him. He set forth for France by sea, with the full favour of Malcolm and Margaret, who loaded him and his followers with gifts of all kinds, more especially furs, and among them the precious spoils of the ermine.[3] But their voyage was not prosperous; the Chronicler gives us a graphic description of the fierce storm which drove the ships ashore, seemingly on some part of the English coast. For we are told that some of the party were seized by the Frenchmen, a name by which we must here assuredly understand Normans in England and not subjects of Philip of Paris.[4] Eadgar however and his chief comrades contrived to make their way back to Scotland, some on horseback and some on foot, but both in very evil case.[5] Malcolm seems to have

*CHAP. XX. Philip offers Montreuil to Eadgar.*

*Joint policy of Philip and Robert of Flanders.*

*Eadgar sets sail for France, but is driven back by a storm*

---

[1] Chron. Wig. 1075 "On þære ilcan tide sende se kyng of Francrice Filippus gewrit to him, and bead him þæt he to him cóme, and he wolde geofan him þone castel æt Mustræl, þæt he mihte syððan dæghwamlice his unwinan únðancas dón" [2] See vol 1 p 227.

[3] Various kinds of skins are mentioned On the ermine see Mr Earle's note, p 349 But there were also " mycclageofa and manega gærsama .. on gyldenan faton and on seolfrenan"

[4] Chron Wig 1075 "And his men eac wurdon sume gelæhtæ of Frencyscan mannan"

[5] Ib "And his ferestan menn ferdon eft ongean to Scotlande, sume hreowlice on fotan gangende and sume earmlice ridende"

570            THE REVOLTS AGAINST WILLIAM.

CHAP XX  taken the storm for an indication of Providence that
He sends William was not to be withstood. For he counselled his
a message
to Nor-  brother-in-law to send to the King in Normandy and
mandy and
is recon- ask for his peace. Eadgar obeyed; he sent messengers
ciled to
William  into Normandy; they were favourably received by
William, and an embassy was sent to bring the Ætheling
to the King's court to receive the King's peace in
person.[1]

Policy of    The policy of this course was clear. Eadgar was be-
William  ginning to show that he could be dangerous. His establishment at Montreuil as a tool in the hands of Philip and
Robert was far more to be dreaded by William than anything that he could do in England. But it was not safe
to leave him at large. Whether in England, Scotland, or
Flanders, he might always be made use of by any enemy.
The wisest thing from William's point of view was to keep
him in that kind of honourable captivity in which no one
knew better than William how to keep those whom he
feared.[2] A prison was not needed for Eadgar; it was
enough to bring him to William's court, and to watch him
Eadgar's carefully under the guise of honour. There is something
journey to
Normandy. ludicrous in the picture of his journey. Eadgar once more
set out for the Continent, but this time not by sea, and this
time as William's friend and guest, not as the vassal and
soldier of Philip. Malcolm and Margaret again loaded him
with costly gifts—their former presents had been lost in the
storm.[3] He seems to have been looked on as remaining their

---

[1] Chron Wig. 1075 "Da gerædde se kynge Malcholom him þæt he
sende to Wyllelme cynge ofer sæ and bæde his gryðes, and he eac swa dyde,
and se cynge him þæs getiðade and æfter him sende"

[2] See above, pp 75, 193. So Will Malm iii 251; "Ultro solitus
erat quoscumque Anglos suspectos habebat, quasi honoris caussâ, Normanniam ducere, ne quidquam se absente in regno turbarent"

[3] Chron Wig 1075. "And se kynge eft Malcolm and his sweostor
him and eallon his mannan unarimede gærsama geafon, and swiðe weorð-
lice hine eft of heora gryðe sendon" These passages, together with the

guest till he reached Durham. There he was met by Hugh the son of Baldric, who had succeeded William Malet in the Sheriffdom of Yorkshire, and whose name figures in the foundation legend of Selby Abbey. Hugh attended him through the whole length of England, and across the sea into Normandy. At every castle on the road the Ætheling was honourably received, and meat and fodder were provided for him and his train. At last he found himself, as he had found himself six years before, a guest in William's Norman court.[1] He was received with mickle worship, and he became a permanent hanger-on of the King. He received such rights as the King gave him,[2] including lands in England of no great extent,[3] and a pension of a pound of silver daily. He lived in Normandy quiet, contented, and despised,[4] till just before the end of

*Eadgar reconciled to William. His grants and pensions*

account of the vast spoils taken by Siward in his Scottish warfare (see vol ii p 365), contrast strangely with later descriptions and proverbs about the poverty of Scotland

[1] Chron. Wig. 1075 "And se scirgerefa of Eoferwic com him togeanes æt Dunholme, and ferde ealne weig mid him, and let him findan mete and fodder æt ælcan castelle þær hi to comon, oð þæt hig ofer sæ to þam kynige coman" The Peterborough writer leaves out the details of the journey

[2] Ib. "And se kyng Wyllelm mid micclan weorðscype þa hine underfenge, and he wæs þær þa on his hirede, and toc swilce gerihta swa he him gelagade" So Chron Petrib. 1074, "And Eadgar cild com of Scotland to Normandige, and se cyng hine geinlagode, and ealle his men, and he wæs on þes cynges hyrede, and nam swilce gerihta swa se cyng him geuðe" Florence (1073) is to the same effect, "Clito Eadgarus de Scottiâ per Angliam venit in Normanniam, et cum Rege se repacificavit"

[3] "Terra Edgari Adeling" appears in Hertfordshire, Domesday, 142, the whole amount is less than eight hides It had been held T R E by various small English owners, among whom we discern several men of Esegar the Staller, one described as "Alnod Teignus Stigandi Archiepiscopi." It was held of Eadgar by one Godwine, doubtless the father of "Robertus filius Godwini, miles audacissimus," who went with Eadgar to the Crusade, and whose exploits and martyrdom are described by William of Malmesbury, iii 251

[4] Will Malm iii 251. "Receptus ergo Edgarus et magno donativo donatus est, pluribusque annis in curiâ manens, pedetentim pro ignaviâ et, ut mitius dictum sit, pro simplicitate contemptui haberi cœpit. Quantula

William's reign, when we shall suddenly hear of him as beginning a career of fitful activity, which went on through a large part of the reigns of William's sons.

Thus it was that William could afford to deal with the man who was most directly his personal rival. But Eadgar was to be dreaded only on account of his great name, and of the use which others might make of him; his personal qualities could not give William one moment of uneasiness. It was in a different way that he dealt with the man who was less directly his rival, but who, with all his faults, was far more likely than Eadgar to be some day the leader of successful opposition to foreign rule. We have now reached what we may fairly call the turning-point of William's reign, the tragedy of the fate of Waltheof. For once in his reign, William was to stain his hands with blood, blood not shed on the field of battle, but by a mockery of a judicial sentence, blood which, as far as the cause for which it was shed was concerned, was innocent. Nothing but the keenest conviction of danger could have led William to this marked deviation from his usual policy, that policy which, in his own eyes and in the eyes of his age, was a policy of mercy. Waltheof, at this moment, held as high a position as any man in the realm after the King himself. He held a position which was shared by no other Englishman save one, and that one to whom one almost shrinks from giving the name of Englishman, the renegade and half-caste Ralph of Wader. And now, by a strange chain of events, by a strange tale of rashness and folly, Waltheof and Ralph alike were to fall from their high places, to leave England without an English Earl, and to have as the partner in their ruin the

enim simplicitas ut libram argenti, quam quotidie in stippendio accipiebat, Regi pro uno equo perdonaret." I do not know the story here alluded to

son and the successor of the most cruel oppressor of Englishmen.

We have seen that Ralph of Wader, the son of Ralph the Staller of Eadward's days by a Breton mother, had received the Earldom of East-Anglia as the reward of his treason to his country. We have seen him acting vigorously in William's interest when the first Danish fleet which professed to come to deliver England tried to effect a landing in his Earldom.[1] At the other end of England, William Fitz-Osbern, after losing his life for the sake of Richildis or her dominions, had been succeeded in his Earldom of Hereford by his younger son Roger. The character of Roger is vaguely set before us in an unfavourable light, though in the eyes of Englishmen it might not have been thought any special blame that he did not walk in the steps of his father.[2] But there is more distinct evidence against him than this. Three letters are extant, addressed to him by Lanfranc, in which he stands charged not only with acts of doubtful fidelity to the King, which are but vaguely hinted at, but with denials of justice and unlawful invasions of the property both of the King and of other men. The letters are conceived in a tone of great personal affection. Roger is conjured by the memory of his father to turn from the error of his ways; he is implored to come in person to the Primate and receive his fatherly counsel. But in the third letter, as he still remains obstinate, sentence of excommunication is pronounced against him, an excommunication from which he is not to be released till he has thrown himself on the King's mercy and made restitution both to the King and to all others whom he had wronged.[3] It is plain from these letters that the

*CHAP XX.*

*Ralph of Wader, Earl of East-Anglia.*

*Roger, Earl of Hereford.*

*Lanfranc's letters to Roger*

*His excommunication.*

---

[1] See above, p. 252

[2] He was, according to William of Malmesbury (iii 255), "detestandæ perfidiæ juvenis, nec moribus patrissans"

[3] Ep Lanfr 47, p. 66 "Ab hoc vinculo anathematis absolvere te non

574                THE REVOLTS AGAINST WILLIAM.

CHAP. XX.   loyalty of Roger toward the King was not a little doubtful
for some time before the final outbreak.

Ralph marries Emma, daughter of William Fitz-Osbern.

A marriage contracted, as it would seem, in express defiance of the royal orders, was the immediate occasion of the rebellion. Earl William had left a daughter, Emma by name,[1] who was sought in marriage by the Earl of Norfolk. William, for whatever reason, forbade the match. But, taking advantage of his absence, the two Earls carried out their scheme, and Roger of Hereford gave his sister in marriage to her suitor.[2] The wedding-feast—the bride-ale, as our forefathers called it—was kept with

---

possum, nisi misericordiam domini mei Regis requiras, sibique et aliis quorum res injuste prædatus es justitiam facias." One or two passages in the letters give us vague hints of the suspicions that were arising against Roger. In the first letter (p. 64) we read, "Dominus noster Anglorum Rex salutat vos et nos omnes, sicut fideles suos, in quibus magnam fiduciam habet, et mandat ut, quantum possumus, curam habeamus de castellis suis, ne, quod Deus avertat, inimicis suis tradantur." And in the second letter (p. 65), "Auditis de te quæ audire nollem, doleo quantum dicere non possum, neque enim deceret ut filius Willelmi Comitis, cujus prudentia et bonitas et erga dominum suum et omnes amicos suos fidelitas multis terris innotuit, infidelis diceretur, et de perjurio vel fraude aliquam infamiam pateretur, imo conveniret potius, ut filius tanti viri imitator patris existeret, et omnis bonitatis et fidelitatis aliis exemplum præberet." Another passage in the first letter is also remarkable; "Item mandavit Rex, ne sui vicecomites aliqua placita in vestris terris teneant, quoadusque ipse male transeat, et inter vos et ipsos vicecomites per semetipsum causas vestras audiat."

[1] Will. Gem. vii. 25, viii. 15. The former passage gives William Fitz-Osbern only one daughter, while the latter, from which we get the name Emma, gives him two.

[2] Both the Chronicles (Worcester, 1076, Peterborough, 1075) make William approve the marriage and something more, "On þissan geare Wyllelm cyngc geaf Raulfe eorle Wyllelmes dohter Osbarnes sunu." But I cannot help looking on the words of Florence (1074), "Herefordensis Comes Rogerus, filius Willelmi ejusdem pagæ Comitis, East-Anglorum Comiti Radulfo, contra præceptum Regis Willelmi, sororem suam conjugem tradidit," as having the force of a correction. On the marriage see also the passages of William of Jumièges just referred to. Orderic (534 A) does not mention the marriage, but brings in the two Earls as "duo potentissimi Anglorum Comites, Rogerius Herfordensis et sororius ejus Radulfus Nortwicensis."

great splendour at Exning in Cambridgeshire,[1] and the Chroniclers tell us, in one of the last metrical or riming efforts to be found in their pages,

*The bride-ale at Exning 1075.*

> "There was that bride-ale
> To many men's bale"[2]

A great company of Bishops and Abbots and other great men was gathered together, and Ralph had specially got together the Bretons, the countrymen of his mother, who had received settlements in England.[3] At the feast men began to talk treason. They took rede how they might drive their Lord the King out of his Kingdom.[4] Among the guests was Waltheof, Earl of the neighbouring shires of Huntingdon and Northampton, and the point both of importance and of obscurity in the story is that it is not clear to what extent he lent an ear to the rash counsels of his companions.[5] One historian, using the licence familiar to classical and mediæval writers, puts speeches into the mouths of Waltheof and his tempters, which modern ingenuity has thrown into a highly dramatic shape.[6] All sorts of contradictory charges are brought

*Presence of Waltheof and others*

*Conspiracy against William.*

---

[1] The Chronicles say, "Þa lædde he þæt wif to Norðwic," but again I see a correction in the words of Florence (1074), "In Grantebrycgensi provinciâ, in loco qui Yxninga dicitur."

[2] Chron. Petrib. 1075,

> "Þær wes þæt bryd eala
> Mannum to beala"

Or, as Worcester reads the second line, "Þæt wæs manegra manna bealo"

[3] See below, pp 584, 589

[4] Chron Wig 1076 "Ðær wæs Rogeer eorl and Walþeof eorl, and biscopas and abbodas, and ræddon þær þæt hi woldon heora kynehlaford of his cynerice adrifan." Peterborough uses the form, one degree less loyal, "Hi woldon þone cyng gesettan ut of Englelandes cynedome"

[5] My narrative is put together from the Chronicles, Florence, and Orderic, of whom the last, writing under an inspiration from Crowland, is the most distinctly favourable to Waltheof. For the versions of other writers see Appendix RR

[6] Orderic (534) gives the supposed speech at length, but he does not say that it was made at the bride-ale, which is clearly implied by the Chronicles and Florence. It is curious to see how the speech has been

CHAP XX
Charges against William

against William. His bastardy is raked up against him; his very birth made him unworthy to be a King, and it would clearly be a work pleasing to God to get rid of him.[1] He had spoiled William of Mortain,[2] and poisoned Conan,[3] Walter, and Biota.[4] He had unjustly seized the noble Kingdom of England, and had murdered or driven into exile its lawful heirs.[5] This at least was a strange charge, when the Ætheling was living in mickle worship in William's court. To the companions of his victories he had paid no such honour as he ought; some he had put to death like others; to others, after their wounds, he had given nought but barren lands — such as the pastures of Herefordshire and the corn-lands of Norfolk —and those wasted by the ravages of the enemy.[6] All men hated him; many would rejoice at his death. No time could be better than the present; William was beyond the sea; the greater part of his host was with him; he was overwhelmed with cares and wars and rebellions and discords in his own family; no one believed that he would ever come back. The English were a peaceful race, fonder of feasts and ales than of

dramatized by Thierry (ii 61), who puts each charge into the mouth in which it seems most appropriate.

[1] Ord Vit 534 A "Degener, utpote nothus, est qui Rex nuncupatur, et in propatulo divinitus monstratur quod Deo displicet dum talis herus regno præsidet"

[2] Ib B. See vol ii p 292

[3] Ib See vol iii p 316      [4] Ib. See vol iii. p 207.

[5] Ib "Nobile regnum Angliæ temere invasit, *genuinos hæredes injuste trucidavit* vel in exsilium crudeliter pepulit."

[6] Ib. The mention of death of course shows how purely fanciful the picture is, but one charge is curious; "Vulneratis victoribus steriles fundos et hostium depopulatione desolatos donavit, et eisdem postmodum restauratos, avaritiâ cogente, abstulit seu minoravit." Does it mean that, when a grantee of William had brought the wasted land into tillage, the King took it away from him again? The charge has a certain likeness to the charge brought by the Peterborough Chronicler (1087), that in letting his demesne lands he would take them away from the first tenant, if another offered a higher rent

battles; yet they would rise in such a cause to avenge the blood of their kinsfolk.[1] Then the two Earls, Ralph and Roger, turn specially to Waltheof. The time was come for him to win back what he had lost, and to take vengeance for the wrongs which had been done to him.[2] The losses and wrongs of Waltheof are perhaps not very easily seen; still even the Earl of three shires and husband of the King's niece might be tempted by offers which might possibly give him the Crown itself, and which would at all events enlarge his Earldom to a third part of England. The land was to be brought back to the same state in which it was in the days of good King Eadward. All power was to be in the hands of the three, Roger, Ralph, and Waltheof. One should be King, the other two should be Earls.[3] Here we probably get a glimpse of the real intentions of the conspirators. The centralizing system of William, the effective power which he had given to the Crown in every corner of the land, was likely enough to be irksome to his Earls, French and English alike. Ralph, Roger, and Waltheof, great as they were, were far from being so great as Godwine, Leofric, and Siward had been. Their Earldoms were of smaller extent, their authority within them was far more carefully narrowed. England had, under Cnut, under Eadward, under William, made so many steps in the direction of unity. It was now proposed to make her take a step backwards. Waltheof was called on, in the name of English patriotism, to join in a scheme

*marginalia:* Ralph and Roger appeal to Waltheof. Alleged scheme of the conspirators. Irksomeness to the Earls of William's centralization. The Earls less powerful under William than under Eadward.

[1] Ord. Vit. 534 C. "Angli sua solummodo rura colunt, conviviis et potationibus, non proeliis, intendunt, summopere tamen pro suorum exitio parentum ultionem videre concupiscunt."

[2] Ib. D. They address him, "O strenue vir," which in Thierry becomes "homme de cœur," his English translator turns it into "valiant *Saxon*," a description hardly justified by Waltheof's mixed descent, Danish, Anglian, and ursine.

[3] Ib. C. "Volumus ut status regni Albionis redintegretur omnimodis sicut olim fuit tempore Eduardi piissimi Regis. Unus ex nobis sit Rex, et duo sint Duces, et sic nobis tribus omnes Anglici subjicientur honores."

VOL. IV.          P p

578       THE REVOLTS AGAINST WILLIAM.

CHAP XX  which promised such gains to his own oppressed nation.[1]
The conspiracy not favoured by the English in general
Waltheof may have been tempted by such offers; it is certain that the English people were not. They would gladly have exchanged King William for King Eadgar or for King Swend. They had no mind to exchange him for King Ralph or King Roger; nor had they any mind to clothe Ralph, Roger, or even Waltheof, with any power which might disturb the good peace which King William made in this land.[2]

Alleged answer of Waltheof
The narrative which we have just been following makes Waltheof answer in an edifying sermon, in which all the usual scriptural examples are hurled at the heads of his tempters. He is William's man, William's Earl, the husband of William's niece; he will never break his faith and turn traitor.[3] Moreover, by a somewhat doubtful statement of English Law, he tells them that by that Law the traitor is condemned to lose his head.[4] Other accounts set him before us as unwillingly beguiled into a consent to the conspiracy, but as presently repenting.[5] It is certain that he had no share in the open rebellion

Question of his consent to the conspiracy.

---

[1] Ord Vit 534 D  "Eja nobilis heros, consultus observa tibi generique tuo commodissimos omnique genti tuæ, quæ prostrata est, salutiferos"

[2] See vol ii p 172

[3] Ord Vit 534 D. "Guillelmus Rex fidem meam, ut major a minori, jure recepit ac, ut ei semper fidelis exsisterem, in matrimonium mihi neptem suam copulavit Locupletem quoque comitatum mihi donavit et inter suos familiares convivas connumeravit" The words in which the homage is described are not such as we should have looked for in the case of a mere subject  See above, p 563

[4] Ib 535 A. "Anglica lex capitis obtruncatione traditorem mulctat, omnemque progeniem ejus naturali hæreditate omnino privat"

[5] The story as told by Florence (1074) runs thus, "Magnam conjurationem, plurimis assentientibus, contra Regem Willelmum ibi fecerunt, Comitemque Waltheofum, suis insidiis præventum, secum conjurare compulerunt, qui, mox ut potuit, Lanfrancum Dorubernensem Archiepiscopum adiit, pœnitentiamque ab eo pro facto, licet non sponte, sacramento accepit, ejusque consilio Regem Willelmum in Normanniâ degentem petiit, eique rem ex ordine gestam pandens, illius misericordiæ ultro se dedit."

## WALTHEOF'S CONFESSION.

which followed. He hastened to Archbishop Lanfranc, doubtless as to a spiritual father, but perhaps also as being for the time a temporal superior. He told him of the unlawful oath which he had taken against his will. When the breaking of a constrained oath would be to William's advantage, the guilt of perjury was a far slighter matter than when its breaking was to William's damage. The oath of Harold was to be kept at all hazards; its violation could be atoned for only by his own overthrow and that of his Kingdom. But in the case of Waltheof an unwilling oath might lawfully be broken; all that Lanfranc required of his penitent was to go through certain ecclesiastical penances, and to go and confess the whole matter to the King against whom he had sinned. Waltheof crossed the sea and sought the presence of William. He did not come empty-handed; when he craved the King's forgiveness he offered rich gifts as the price of his mercy.[1] It is not quite clear whether the pardon was formally given, but it is certain that William made light of Waltheof's share in the matter, that the Earl abode in Normandy till the King's return, and that till the King's return he suffered no punishment or restraint.[2]

*His confession to Lanfranc*
*The oath of Waltheof and the oath of Harold*
*Waltheof goes to Normandy and confesses to the King*
*William's favourable treatment of him.*

Meanwhile the Earls of Hereford and Norfolk—strange predecessors of nobler bearers of the same titles[3]—were in open revolt against the King. Ralph made the most of his twofold descent. As a Breton, he called on the Bretons in England, perhaps on those beyond sea, to join in the enterprise. As an Englishman, born and ruling in one of the Danish districts of England, he sought for the help of a Danish fleet.[4] The Bretons flocked

*Revolt of Ralph and Roger*
*The Bretons in England join Ralph*
*He asks help from Denmark.*

---

[1] Chron Wig 1076 "And Walðeof Eorl ferde ofer sæ and wreide hine sylfne and bæd forgyfenysse and bead gærsuman"

[2] Ib "Ac se kynge let lihtlice of oð þæt he com to Englalande"

[3] See vol ii. p 291, iii 466

[4] Chron Wig 1076, Petrib 1075 "Rawulf Eorl and Roger Eorl wæron

580    THE REVOLTS AGAINST WILLIAM.

CHAP. XX. to his standard; the Danes came, but came too late for his purpose. Both the Earls went to their Earldoms, and gathered together such forces as they could muster, a large portion of the forces of Ralph being Breton or other mercenaries.[1] He set out towards the point where he was to meet the Earl of Hereford, and marched as far as Cambridge. But the movement met with no favour from men of either race. The King's men, French and English, answered willingly to the call of the royal officers, and served zealously against the rebel Earls. A summons to the King's court, issued to the Earls by the Justiciaries William of Warren and Richard the son of Count Gilbert, had no effect, and the campaign, if we may call it so, began.[2] The chief commands were in the hands of ecclesiastics of both races, and the progress of the war was carefully announced by the Primate to the King. The movement of Roger in the West seems to have been left to be dealt with by the forces of the district. Two English Prelates, Bishop Wulfstan and Abbot Æthelwig, appeared in strange union with Urse, the rapacious Sheriff of Worcestershire. The whole force of the country followed them; the Earl of Hereford was hindered from crossing the Severn,[3] and

*Ralph's mercenaries.*
*He encamps at Cambridge.*
*The people in general support the King.*
*The Earls disobey the summons of the Justiciaries.*
*Prominence of churchmen in the campaign.*
*Wulfstan and Æthelwig march against Roger.*

---

hofdingas æt þisan unræde, and hi speonon heom to þa Bryttas, and sendon eac to Denemarcon æfter scyphere"    [1] See below, p. 584.

[2] Ord. Vit. 535 A, B. "Guillelmus de Warennâ et Ricardus de Benefactâ, filius Gisleberti Comitis, quos Rex præcipuos Angliæ justitiarios constituerat in regni negotiis, rebellantes convocant ad curiam Regis. Illi vero præceptis eorum obsecundare contemnunt, sed proterviam prosequi conantes in regios satellites prœliari eligunt."

[3] The Chronicles say only, "Rogcer ferde west to his eorldome and gaderade his folc þan cynege to unþearfe he þohte, ac hit wearð heom seolfan to mycclan hearme," or, as Peterborough puts it, "ac he wearð gelet." Florence gives us the names of those by whom he was let; "Sed Herefordensi Comiti, ne, Sabrinâ transvadato, Radulfo Comiti ad locum destinatum cum suo exercitu occurreret, restitit Wlstanus Wigornensis Episcopus cum magnâ militari manu, et Ægelwius Eoveshamnensis Abbas cum suis, ascitis sibi in adjutorium Ursone Vicecomite Wigornæ et Waltero de

the sequel shows that he was himself taken prisoner. The movement in East-Anglia was clearly looked on as more dangerous. Besides William of Warren and Robert the son of William Malet, the two warlike Bishops, Odo of Bayeux and Geoffrey of Coutances, led forth a vast host of both races to attack the Earl of Norfolk at Cambridge.[1] For once the Norman castlemen and the English landfolk were fighting side by side with a good will;[2] neither looked for any good from an insurrection got up in the personal interest of two turbulent Earls. Ralph did not dare to meet the host which came against him at Cambridge. Lanfranc was soon able to announce to the King that the rebel Earl had taken to flight, that the King's men, French and English, were pursuing him, and that they trusted that in a few days his whole company would be killed or taken or driven out of the land.[3] Happy were those who came in for the last of these three alternatives. The justice of the Norman Bishops was as sharp now as it had been in earlier days in the West.[4] They acted on the principle of Eastern rulers, "Slay them not, lest my people forget it;"[5] that the prisoners might be marked and remembered, the right foot of each was

*CHAP. XX*

*Odo and Geoffrey of Coutances march against Ralph*

*Union of Normans and English*

*Flight of Ralph*

*Lanfranc's despatches*

*Mutilation of the prisoners*

---

Laceio cum copiis suis, et cætera multitudine plebis" Thierry (ii. 62) makes Roger assemble " beaucoup de Gallois des frontières " This seemingly comes from R. Wendover (ii 15), "Wallensibus sibi confœderatis," but this is simply a misunderstanding of the "Bryttas" of the Chronicles Thierry has also some details of the campaign for which I cannot find the authority

[1] Flor Wig 1074 "Prope Grantebrycgiam castrametanti"

[2] Chron Wig 1076, Petrib 1075 "Rawulf eac wolde mid his eorldome forðgán, ac þa castelmenn þe wæron on Englalande, and eac þæt landfolc heom togenes comon, and hi ealle geletton þæt hi naht ne dydon"

[3] Ep Lanfr 37 (Giles, 1. 56). "Rodulphus Comes, immo Rodulphus traditor, et totus exercitus ejus in fugam versi fuerunt, et nostri cum infinitâ multitudine Francigenarum et Anglorum eos insequuntur, et ante paucos dies, sicut mihi mandaverunt principes nostri, aut ipsi perjuri de terrâ vestrâ per mare fugient aut eos vivos vel mortuos habebunt"

[4] See above, p 278.         [5] Psalm li 11.

cut off[1] Ralph fled to Norwich, the capital of his Earldom. The castle which William had begun to build at a very early stage of his reign[2] was in his possession. Its building had involved the destruction of a large number of the houses of the city.[3] But, to make up for this loss, the King and the Earl between them had founded a new town, a French town, on what had been the common land of the English burghers.[4] It might seem from some dark entries in the Survey that some even of the English inhabitants of the city took the part of the rebel Earl. Still, according to the most trustworthy account, Ralph did not dare to stand a siege of Norwich in his own person.[5] He took ship and sailed to Denmark, to hasten the coming of the Danish fleet.[6]

[1] Orderic (535 B), who seems to make more of actual fighting than Florence does, tells the story thus, "Guillelmus et Ricardus [whom Florence does not mention] exercitum Angliæ coadunant, acriterque contra seditiosos in campo qui Fagaduna dicitur dimicant. Obstantes vero Dei virtute superant, et omnibus captis, cujuscumque conditionis sint, dextrum pedem *ut notificentur* amputant." Florence's version is, "Ipse suos conatus infirmari cernens, multitudinem resistentium veritus, ad Northwic clanculo refugit et, castello suæ conjugi militibusque suis commendato, ascensâ navi de Angliâ ad minorem Brytanniam fugit, quem fugientem adversarii illius insecuti, omnes quos de suis comprehendere poterant vel interemerunt vel diversis modis debilitaverunt." [2] See above, p. 67.

[3] Domesday, ii 116 b "In illâ terrâ de quâ Heroldus habebat socam sunt xxv burgenses, et xvii mansuræ vacuæ quæ sunt in occupatione castelli, et in burgo clxxx mansuræ vacuæ in hoc quod erat in socâ Regis et Comitis, et lxxxi in occupatione castelli."

[4] Ib 118. Under the head of "Franci de Norwic in novo burgo" we read, "Tota hæc terra burgensium erat in dominio Comitis Radulfi, et concessit eam Regi in commune ad faciendum burgum inter se et Regem."

[5] This appears from the passage of Florence just quoted, so also in the Chronicles, "[Rawulf] wæs fægen þæt he to scypum ætfleah, his wif belaf æfter in þam castele." Orderic however (535 B) first describes the flight of Ralph and the siege, and adds, "Radulfus autem de Guader, ut sese sic inclusione constrictum vidit, et nullum adjutorium a suis complicibus speravit, munitionem suam fidis custodibus caute commisit, et ipse proximum mare ingressus Daciam pro auxiliis navigio adiit."

[6] I accept the flight to Denmark, though resting on the authority of Orderic only, as it so exactly falls in with what went before and what follows. The Chronicles do not tell us whither he sailed; Peterborough,

Meanwhile the woman whose marriage had been the immediate cause of all this disturbance was showing a nobler spirit than either her brother or her husband. When the Earl of Norfolk took ship from Norwich, he left the castle in charge of his newly married Countess.[1] Emma boldly stood a siege in which all the engineering skill of the age was brought to bear for the space of three months upon the still new fortress of Norwich.[2] And she held out till she obtained terms of capitulation from the besiegers which might be looked on as comparatively favourable.[3] Lanfranc could announce to the King in his next despatch that the castle of Norwich had surrendered, and that, in the Primate's own energetic language, the Kingdom was cleansed from the filth of the Bretons.[4] Ralph, it is to be supposed, had some Norman and some English followers, but of their fate we hear nothing, except from a statement in the Survey which shows that some of Ralph's partizans in the city had to seek dwellings elsewhere.[5] This however, though it may

*Norwich defended by Emma.*

*Siege and capitulation of Norwich.*

*Terms granted to the Bretons.*

to the passage before quoted, adds, that he "for to scipe æt Norðwic" Florence (see the first note on the last page) mentions his flight to Britanny. He doubtless went there in the end

[1] See the passage in the Chronicles just quoted So also Florence, "Castello suæ conjugi militibusque suis commendato" Orderic does not mention the Countess at this stage.

[2] Orderic (535 B) gives the full details of the siege, how the walls were attacked "crebis assultibus variisque machinationibus," and that "per tres menses"

[3] Chron Petrib 1075 "And his wif wæs innan þam castele, and hine heold swa lange þæt man hire griÐ scalde"

[4] Ep Lanfr 38 (Giles, 1 57). "Gloria in excelsis Deo, cujus misericordiâ regnum vestrum purgatum est spurcitiâ Britonum."

[5] It seems plain from Domesday (ii 117 b) that some of the English citizens of Norwich were involved in Ralph's fall, "De bursensibus qui manserunt in burgo de Norwic abierunt et manent in Beccles villâ Abbatis Sancti Edmundi xxii et vi in Humilgar, H̄ et dimiserunt burgum. Et in Torp Regis i et in terrâ Rogerii Bigot i et sub W de Noies i et Ricardus de Seint-Cler i Isti fugientes et alii remanentes omnino sunt vastati, partim propter forisfacturas R comitis, partim propter arsuram, partim propter geltum Regis, partim propter Walerannum" In connexion

584   THE REVOLTS AGAINST WILLIAM.

CHAP XX have been the indirect result, was not likely to be the formal effect of the terms of capitulation. Among the Bretons, who must have been a considerable body, those who had lands in England were promised safety in life and limb, and were allowed forty days to get them out of the Kingdom, to which they were not to come back without the King's leave.[1] The mercenaries who had no land, but who had followed Earl Ralph for pay, were by dint of many entreaties admitted to the same terms, but the shorter time of a month was given them to leave the King-

Occupation of Norwich. dom.[2] The castle was occupied by two of the captains of the besiegers, Bishop Geoffrey and Earl William of Warren. With them was joined Robert Malet, a son of the famous William, who appears in the Survey as one of the great landowners of East-Anglia.[3] The garrison which they commanded consisted of three hundred men-at-arms, and a body of *balistarii* and other engineers[4] Norwich was thus held in safe keeping till the King's return. The Countess Emma, who had so valiantly defended the city, was received to the same terms as her followers. She made her way to Britanny, and was presently joined there by her husband.[5]

Thus there was once more peace in the realm of King

with this entry we may note the expression of Orderic (535 C), "Vicarii Regis Guillelmus et Ricardus *municipes oppidi* [though those words do not always bear a civic meaning] ad deditionem coarctant" There is nothing wonderful in Ralph having a party in his own capital, though his schemes were not approved by the country at large.

[1] Ep Lanfr 38 (Giles, i 57)

[2] Ib "Qui Rodulpho traditori et sociis ejus sine terrâ pro solidis servierunt, ad hoc faciendum unius mensis spatium multis precibus impetraverunt"

[3] On Robert Malet, see above, p 473, and for his lands in East-Anglia, see Domesday, ii 153-156

[4] Ep Lanfr 38 (Giles, i 57) "Trecenti loricati, cum balistariis et artificibus machinarum multis"

[5] Chron. Wig 1076, Petrib. 1075 "And heo þa utferde of Englalande, and ealle hire menn þe hire mid woldon" So Florence. Orderic (535 C), "Expulsus itaque cum uxore suâ Britanniam repetiit." This is Orderic's only mention of the heroine. Lanfranc does not speak of her at all.

William.[1] But it was known that the dealings of Ralph with the Danish court had not been in vain, and that a Danish fleet was then on its voyage. Lanfranc, as a watchful guardian of the realm, strictly charged Bishop Walcher to keep the new castle of Durham safe against their attacks.[2] Presently the King himself, whose presence had been earnestly asked for by his lieutenants,[3] came back to England. He brought with him Earl Waltheof, but not as yet as a prisoner. But soon after William's landing, Waltheof was arrested.[4] It is possible that this step may have been caused by the actual appearance of a fleet of two hundred Danish ships in the Humber. Such an invasion would naturally bring up again the memory of Waltheof's old exploits, and none the less that one of the leaders of the Danish fleet was Waltheof's old companion in arms. Swend had, as well nigh the last act of his life, once more sent his son Cnut, the future King and saint, together with an Earl named Hakon, as the commanders of the fleet.[5] At such a moment it might well

*William's return.*

*Arrest of Waltheof*

*The Danish fleet in the Humber.*

*Its commanders, Cnut and Hakon.*

[1] Ep Lanfr 38 (Giles, 1 57). "Omnis strepitus bellorum, miserante Deo, in Anglicâ terrâ quievit " So more emphatically in 21 (1 49), "Nos expulsis Britonibus et sedatis omnibus bellis, in tantâ tranquillitate vivimus ut, postquam Rex mare transiit, tranquillius nos vixisse nequaquam meminerimus "

[2] Ib 28 (1 49) "Dani, ut Rex vobis [Walchero] mandavit, revera veniunt castrum itaque vestram hominibus et armis et alimentis vigilanti curâ muniri facite." [3] Ord Vit 535 C

[4] Chron Petrib 1075 "And se cing syððan com to Englalande, and genam Roger Eorl his mæg and gefestnode hine, and Walþeof Eorl he genam eac " Worcester inserts here the account of Waltheof's voyage to Normandy, quoted in p 579. Roger's captivity is described in Worcester by the words " and sette on *prisun*"—foreign names being needed for foreign objects—and the arrest of Waltheof is mentioned in the words "and hine let syððan tacan " Flor. Wig 1074 " His gestis, Rex auctumnali tempore de Normanniâ rediens, Comitem Rogerum in custodia posuit, Comitem etiam Waltheofum, *licet ab eo misericordiam expetierat*, custodiæ tradidit."

[5] Chron Wig 1076, Petrib 1075 "And sona æfter þam comon eastan of Denmearcan cc scipa, and þæron wæron twægen heafodmenn, Cnut Swægnes sunu [Cynges, Wig ] and Hacun Eorl " This is the Hakon whom Lappenberg (see above, p. 142) identifies with Hakon the son of

586              THE REVOLTS AGAINST WILLIAM.

CHAP XX. seem that Cnut's old fellow-soldier, the man who had cloven so many Norman skulls before the gate of York Castle, was not a man who could be safely left at large in England. Waltheof was therefore put in ward as well as Roger, and the two Earls awaited their public trial in the Midwinter Gemót.[1]

The Danes at York

Meanwhile the Danes were once more in the Humber. We hear nothing of their reception by the people at large; we hear nothing of any resistance which they may have met with from the King's commanders in Yorkshire. On the other hand, we hear of no exploits on their part, of no battles fought, of no Norman fortresses destroyed or taken. It is plain that the two castles of York did not hinder the Danes from sailing up the Ouse, but it is equally clear that all that they did at York was an useless act of sacrilege, followed, so the story runs, by one of the usual judgements. "They dared not hold fight with William King, but they went to York, and brake Saint Peter's minster, and took therein mickle wealth, and so went away. And all died that were of that rede, that was Hakon Earl's son and many others with him."[2] Thus the metropolitan church of the North, rising from its ruins under the care of Archbishop Thomas, suffered again, though doubtless far less severely than it had suffered in the last days of Ealdred.[3] According to one version, the land to which the Danish fleet sailed

They plunder the minster.

---

Swegen the son of Godwine. But could Hakon, who must have been born about 1047, have had a son of the age which is implied directly after?

This Danish inroad is mentioned only in the Chronicles  The Danish writers, as usual, give no help          [1] See note 4 last page.

[2] Chron Wig 1076 "And ne dorston nan gefeoht healdan wið Willelme Cynge, ac ferdon to Eoforwic, and bræcon Sc̃e Petres mynster, and tócon þærinne mycele æhta, and foron swa aweg, ac ealle þa forferdon þe æt þam ræde wæron, þæt wæs Hacones sunu Eorles, and manege oðre mid him" Peterborough does not mention the sacrilege or its punishment.

[3] See above, p 267

after leaving York was Flanders.[1]  Cnut was, now or later, the husband of Count Robert's daughter,[2] both were enemies of William, and a meeting of the two princes might be sought on both sides for the devising of future schemes against him.

CHAP XX

While the two Earls were in prison, awaiting the meeting of the usual Midwinter Assembly, an event took place which, though it was of no political importance, yet marks the severing of another tie between the older and the newer England. The Lady Eadgyth, the daughter of Godwine, the sister of Harold, the widow of Eadward, died in the month of December, in her palace at Winchester.[3] While all the rest of her family were either slain or wandering to and fro in foreign lands, she had kept all her lands and honours, and, as Queen Matilda was almost always in Normandy, she must have practically kept something more than the usual rank of the Old Lady. We have seen reason to think that her heart was Norman rather than English;[4] still Englishmen must have felt that their land became somewhat less English by the loss of one who, though of English birth, still sat in the highest place among the conquerors. The age of Eadgyth it would be hard to fix exactly. If she was, as seems not unlikely, the eldest child of Godwine and Gytha,[5] she must have now been about fifty-five years old. In that comparatively short space she had seen mighty changes in England and in the world. Born

Death of Eadgyth December 19, 1075

Her position under William

Changes during her lifetime.

---

[1] Chron Petrib. 1075  "Ac heoldon ofer sæ to Flandran"

[2] Edla, Ethela, or Adela  See Knytlinga Saga, c 30; Ælnoth Hist. S Canuti, Langebek, iii 344, Will Malm. iii 257, and Chron Petrib 1085  "Cnut heafde Rodbeardes dohter"

[3] Chron Wig 1076, Petrib 1075, Flor. Wig. 1074  "And Eadgyð seo hlæfdie [hlæfdig, Petrib ] forðferde, seo wæs Eadwardes cynges geresta, seofon niht ær Xpes mæssan, on Wincestre"

[4] See vol iii p 635.    [5] See vol ii p 555.

in the early days of Cnut, she had seen the troubles of the reigns of his sons; she had shared in the royalty of the restored English kingly house; she had shared in one overthrow of her own family, and she had beheld another more utter overthrow in which she did not share. The sister of Harold holding the highest place among her sex at the court of William must have been a strange sight in the eyes both of Englishmen and of Normans. And the mention of Eadgyth suggests the momentary thought of other Englishwomen who, like herself, survived the bondage of their country. Godgifu, the widow of Leofric, was living after King William came into England;[1] and we ask, with still deeper interest, what were the latter days of her granddaughter, the widow of Gruffydd and of Harold. But as to both Godgifu and Ealdgyth history tells us nothing; it is Eadgyth alone whose death is recorded in the national annals. Of the details of her last days we have no account, save the half legendary statement that on her deathbed she protested her innocence of the personal scandals which had been raised against her.[2] The honours which William had shown her in her life-time followed her in death. "The King had her brought to Westminster with mickle worship, and laid her with Eadward King her lord."[3] There the two, so strangely joined in life, lay side by side in death, till the day came when the growing honours of the saint called for his translation from the side of a mortal and sinful woman to a higher place in his own temple.[4]

The Midwinter Gemót now came together, this time

---

[1] See vol ii p 632       [2] Will Malm ii 197.
[3] Chron. Wig. 1076, Petrib. 1075. "And se cynge hig let bryngan to Westmynstre mid mycclan weorðscype, and leide heo wið Eadwarde cynge hire hlaforde" Cf Will Malm iii 273
[4] See vol iii p. 39

also not at Gloucester, but in Eadward's old home at Westminster. The funeral rites of Eadgyth, the masses and offerings for her soul, doubtless formed part of the ecclesiastical side of the solemnity. But that Gemót had to do other work, which was in a more practical way to cut off the England of William and Matilda from the England of Eadward and Eadgyth. There was no longer an English Lady; there was soon to be no longer an English Earl. Ralph of Norfolk, who, traitor alike to England and to William, was still a son of the soil, had fled to the land of his mother. His more famous brother Earl, the son of Siward and Æthelflæd, the descendant by his mother's side of the long line of Bernician Earls and Kings, was a prisoner awaiting his trial. The King and his Witan sat in judgement, as in William's day they had sat in judgement upon Eustace,[1] as in the old time they had sat on Ælfgar and on Godwine. The traitors, so many as were within reach, were brought up for trial. Ralph, like Eustace, was condemned in his absence. It would have been vain to pronounce any sentence on him save the accustomed English sentence of outlawry and confiscation of lands.[2] But a heavier vengeance fell on some of his meaner accomplices. "There man fordoomed all the Bretons that were at the bride-feast at Norwich. Some were blinded, some were driven from the land, and some were put to shame. So were the King's traitors brought low."[3] Let us at least hope that those who were entitled to the benefit of the capitulation at Norwich did not come in for the heaviest of these sentences.

*Midwinter Gemót at Westminster. 1075-1076.*

*Trial of the Earls and their followers*

*Ralph condemned by default*

*Cruel punishments of the Bretons.*

[1] See above, p 129
[2] Ord Vit 535 C "Radulfus de Guader Comes Northguici Angliâ perpetualiter exhereditatus est"
[3] Chron Wig 1076, Petrib 1075 "Se kynge wæs þa þone midwinter on Westmynstre, þær mon fordemde ealle þa Bryttas þe wæron æt þam brydlope æt Norðwic Sume hi wurdon geblende, and sume wrecen of lande, and sume getawod to scande Þus wurdon þæs kyninges swican genyðerade."

590                THE REVOLTS AGAINST WILLIAM.

CHAP XX.        The other two Earls, Roger and Waltheof, were in safe
Trial and   keeping, and appeared in person before the Assembly.
condemna-
tion of     Roger, as may be supposed, had no defence to make against
Roger       the charge of treason. His sentence, according to Norman
            Law, was confiscation of lands and perpetual imprison-
Trial of    ment.[1] The case of Waltheof was one of more difficulty;
Waltheof    on no showing had he taken any active share in the
            rebellion; whatever his offence was, he had done what he
            could to repair it by a speedy confession, and the King's
            own treatment of him while in Normandy might have
            been taken as an earnest that no very heavy punishment
Enmity of   was in store for him. But Waltheof had his worst enemy
his wife
Judith.     on his own hearth; the tie which bound him most closely
            to William proved to be the very snare in which he was
            entangled. His foreign wife, for what reason we are not
            told, sought his destruction. It is plain that William
            himself was not disposed to deal harshly with him, but
            Judith stood forth as the accuser of her husband in the
            ears of her uncle. The Earl was charged before the
            Assembly with having been a favourer and accomplice
Waltheof's  of the late rebellion.[2] His defence was that he had indeed
defence.    heard the scheme of rebellion proposed, but that he had in
            no way consented to so wicked a design.[3] Such at least
            is the version of the historian who gives us the fullest
            narrative, but it is a version which overlooks the oath
            to the conspirators, which, willingly or unwillingly, there
            can be little doubt that Waltheof had taken. However
            this may be, there can be little doubt that the Gemót

---

[1] Ord. Vit 535 D "Secundum leges Normannorum judicatus est, et amissâ omni hereditate terrenâ in carcere Regis perpetuo damnatus est"

[2] Ib 536 B "Gallevus Comes ad Regem accersitus est, et per delationem Judith uxoris suæ accusatus est, quod prædictæ proditionis conscius et fautor fuerit dominoque suo infidelis exstiterit."

[3] Ib 535 B "Ille intrepidus palam recognovit quod proditorum nequissimam voluntatem ab eis audierit, sed eis in tam nefandâ re nullum omnino consensum dederit."

TRIAL AND DEFENCE OF WALTHEOF.  591

came to no definite conclusion as to his sentence. He was *CHAP XX.*
remanded to prison at Winchester—a straiter prison, we *He is remanded*
are told, than he had been in before his trial.[1] *to prison at Winchester.*
The outlawry of the Earls of Norfolk and Hereford
placed their estates and offices at the King's disposal, and *The lands of Ralph*
the death of the Lady threw her lands also into his hands. *and Roger confiscated.*
To enrich his followers was no longer so important an
object with William as it had once been, the needs of the
royal exchequer were now the first object. Still portions
of the forfeited lands were granted out.[2] In East-Anglia *Grants to*
especially a large part of the lands of Ralph went to *Roger the Bigod*
enrich the founder of that great House of Bigod which
some generations later was to succeed to his Earldom.[3]
But vast portions of the lands of the two Earls and of the
Lady were kept in the King's own hands,[4] and no new *No new*
Earls were appointed to the vacant Earldoms. The later *Earls appointed.*
history of the two chief rebels was strangely contrasted.
Ralph, banished from England, flourished in his mother's *Later line*
land of Britanny. He lived to take the Cross at the *of Ralph Wader*
preaching of Pope Urban, to set forth as a Crusader in
the train of William's eldest son, and to die, along with
his heroic wife, on their way to the Holy City.[5] His son

[1] Ord. Vit 535 B " Super hac confessione judicium indagatum est et, censoribus inter se sentientibus, per plures inducias usque in annum protelatum est " Florence (1074) says, " Comites Waltheofum et Rogerum, *judiciali sententiâ damnatos,* arction custodiæ mancipavit " I think we may accept the fuller version in Orderic, which does not suppose any inaccuracy in Florence, except in extending the words in Italics to Waltheof.

[2] Some lands which Ralph had given to Saint Benedict, seemingly of Ramsey, had come into the hands of William of Warren See Domesday, ii. 158, 158 b.

[3] For the lands of Roger the Bigod, see Domesday, ii 173-190. Roger died in 1107 The first Earl was his younger son Hugh, created Earl of the East-Angles by Stephen in 1140 See R Howden, i. 203 Stubbs, where he appears as " Hugo consul de Est Angle " See Dugdale's Baronage, 132.

[4] But we must not forget the remarkable application of one part of the lands of Eadgyth See above, p 167

[5] Ord. Vit 535 C " In viâ Dei pœnitens et peregrinus cum uxore suâ obiit."

592   THE REVOLTS AGAINST WILLIAM.

CHAP XX.
His children.
Imprisonment of Roger.
His insolence to the King.
He dies in prison.
His sons.
Continued imprisonment of Waltheof.

succeeded to his Breton estates of Wader and Montfort,[1] and his daughter was restored to England by a marriage with Earl Robert of Leicester.[2] While Ralph was doing something in his last days to wipe out the memory of his manifold treasons, his accomplice Roger pined out the rest of his days in prison. If William had any mind to release him, his own conduct effectually cut off all hopes. He is described as constantly reviling and murmuring against his sovereign, and in one case offering him the most marked insult. One year at the Easter Feast, when the King made gifts to his lords, he sent a gift also to his imprisoned kinsman, a gift of goodly raiment, of silks and costly furs.[3] Roger piled up the King's presents in a heap and at once set fire to them. The news was brought to William. "The man is too proud," said he, "who does such scorn to me; but, by the splendour of God, he shall never come out of my prison in my days."[4] William kept his word, and his successor kept it after him; Roger the son of William Fitz-Osbern died in prison, and when our informant wrote, his two sons, Reginald and Roger, were striving, by good service to Henry the First, to merit the restoration of some part of their father's possessions.[5]

But a deeper interest attaches to the fate of the Earl who was waiting his final sentence in his prison at Winchester. Waltheof remained for months in his bonds, but

[1] Ord. Vit 535 C.
[2] Ib 875 D, Will Gem. viii. 15  Orderic calls her Amicia, and the continuator of William, Itta  See Dugdale's Baronage, p 68
[3] Ord Vit. 535 D  "Regalia ornamenta, chlamydem, sericamque interulam, et renonem de pretiosis pellibus peregrinorum murium "  Compare the gifts made by Malcolm and Margaret to Eadgar, p. 569
[4] Ib 536 A  "Multum superbus est, qui hoc mihi dedecus fecit, sed, per splendorem Dei, de carcere meo in omni vitâ meâ non exibit." William's characteristic oath should be noticed.
[5] Ib. He adds, " Guillelmi progenies eradicata sic est de Angliâ ut nec passum pedis, nisi fallor, jam nanciscatur in illâ."

## WALTHEOF IN PRISON.

they were months of deep penitence. One sin at least CHAP. XX
we know that Waltheof had upon his soul for which the His penitence
deepest penitence could not be too deep. We may hope
that the tears with which he bewailed the sins of his past
life to Lanfranc and other Prelates were tears of honest
repentance for the blood of the sons of Carl.[1] Daily,
we are told, he repeated the whole psalter which he had
learnt by heart in his childhood.[2] Lanfranc himself bore
the strongest witness to his innocence of the crime which
was laid to his charge, and to the genuineness of his penitence for his real misdeeds.[3] But all availed him not.
Norman enemies feared his release, and hungered after Plots against him
his lands and honours.[4] His cause was again argued,
seemingly in the Pentecostal Gemót of the next year, His final trial
which would be held, according to custom, at Westminster. Pentecost [May 15], 1076
This time sentence of death was pronounced. He had
listened to the proposals of men who were plotting the
King's life. He had not at once opposed them, nor had
he revealed to his sovereign the danger in which he stood.[5]
On these grounds, grounds which, according to any version He is condemned to death
of the story, were utterly frivolous, the English Earl was
doomed to die. Whatever may have been the letter of the

---

[1] See above, p. 525.

[2] See the description of his penitence given by Ordenc (536 B) and Florence (1075), and see above, p. 256.

[3] Flor. Wig 1075 "Cujus memoriam volucrunt homines in terrâ delere, sed creditur vere illum cum sanctis in cœlo gaudere, prædicto archipræsule piæ memoriæ Landfranco, a quo, confessione factâ, pœnitentiam acceperat, fideliter attestante, qui et impositi criminis, supradictæ scilicet conjurationis, illum immunem affirmabat esse, et quæ in cæteris commisisset, ut verum Christianum, pœnitentialibus lacrimis deflevisse, seque felicem fore si post exitum vitæ illius felici potiretur requie."

[4] Ord Vit 536 C "Prævalens concio æmulorum ejus in curiâ regali coadunata est," and directly after, "Normanni qui . sibi prædia ejus et largos honores adipisci cupiebant"

[5] Ib "Eum post multos tractatus reum esse mortis definitum est, qui sodalibus de morte domini sui tractantibus consenserit, nec eos pro herili exitio perculerit, nec apertâ delatione scelerosam factionem detexerit"

594 THE REVOLTS AGAINST WILLIAM.

CHAP. XX.
Unprecedented nature of the sentence
Its injustice

law in either country, such an execution was without a precedent for years past either in England or in Normandy. It was specially unprecedented in the reign of a prince whose boast had hitherto been that he had never taken human life except in the operations of warfare. And strangest of all was the unequal balance of justice which spared the life of the man who had compassed the death of the King and openly levied war against him, and which doomed him to die whose crime at the utmost was not to have been zealous enough in revealing and hindering his schemes. But Roger was a Norman, Waltheof was an Englishman; and the time had now come when the final seal was to be put to the work of the Conquest. Englishmen had been slain on the field of battle; they had lost their lands; they had been banished from their country; they had suffered bonds and cruel mutilations; but as yet the sword of the headsman had not been called into play against them. But now the Englishman highest in birth and rank, the one remaining Earl of the blood of the conquered, was to die, and to die, as the conquered deemed, the martyr of his country.

Beheading of Waltheof.
May 31, 1076

When the sentence was once passed, its execution did not linger. The order was brought to Winchester, and early on the last morning of May, while the citizens were still in their beds, Earl Waltheof was awakened by the summons of death. It was feared that, if men knew the deed that was doing, they would rise up to rescue the champion of England from the hands of his enemies.[1] For the same reason doubtless he did not suffer within the city. A public execution within the walls of Winchester would have been too great

---

[1] Ord. Vit. 536 C "Nec mora, Guallevus a Normannis, qui evasionem ejus valde timebant . . . extra urbem Guentam, dum adhuc populus dormiret, mane ductus est in montem ubi nunc ecclesia Sancti Ægidii Abbatis et Confessoris constructa est."

a risk, and we may be sure that William, even in this his darkest day, would have shrunk from stooping to anything like private murder. The Earl was led forth to die on one of the downs which overlook the city, on the hill which, when our historian wrote, was marked by the church of the confessor Saint Giles. He came forth arrayed with all the badges of his Earl's rank. When he reached the place of martyrdom, he distributed them as gifts or relics among a few clerks and poor men who had heard of what was doing and had come together to that sight. And then he knelt him down and prayed, with sobs and tears of penitence, for a longer time than seemed good to those who thirsted for his blood. The headsmen feared lest, if they lingered longer, the news should get abroad, lest the Earl's countrymen should rise, and lest they should perish in his stead. The Earl had fallen on his face in the fervour of his devotions. "Rise," they said, "we must do the bidding of our master." "Wait yet," said Waltheof, "a little moment; let me at least say the Lord's Prayer for me and for you." He rose, he knelt down, he lifted his eyes to heaven, he stretched forth his hands, and spoke the prayer aloud till he came to the words "Lead us not into temptation." Tears then stopped his voice. The headsman would tarry no longer; the sword fell, and the head of the last English Earl rolled on the ground.[1] Men said that the severed head was heard to finish the prayer, and distinctly

---

[1] I have here done little more than translate the graphic and affecting narrative of Orderic (536 C, D). Florence (1075) says only, "Comes Waltheofus, jussu Regis Willelmi, extra civitatem Wintoniam ductus, indigne et crudeliter *securi* decapitatur." Orderic makes the instrument of death not an axe but a sword, "Carnifex . . exempto *gladio* fortiter feriens caput Comitis amputavit." The Chronicles are still briefer, "Her wæs Walþeof eorl beheafdod on Wincestre on Sc̄e Petronella mæssedæg." The feast of Saint Petronilla—daughter of the Apostle Peter—comes, according to the Art de Verifier les Dates (i 76), on May 31. If so, Orderic's date of April 30 must be a slip, and the sentence must have been passed at Westminster at Pentecost, not at Winchester at Easter (March 27).

CHAP. XX. to utter the words "Deliver us from evil."[1] The work was done. The man whom William and his Normans feared was taken out of their path, and his body was at once meanly buried upon the place of martyrdom. By this time the men of Winchester had risen from their beds, and had heard what a deed had been done without the walls of their city. But it was now too late; men and women now could do no more than raise a wail of fruitless sorrow for the hero and martyr of England.[2]

*Grief of the people*

But the history of Waltheof, like the history of Eadward, goes on after his death. The instinct of Englishmen, in whose minds religion and patriotism ever went side by side, saw in the murdered Earl, not only a martyr in the wider sense of the word, but a veritable saint. His great crime was forgotten — perhaps a deed of blood wrought in Yorkshire may never have been heard of at Winchester — and men's thoughts dwelled only on the unrighteousness of his sentence and on the piety of his later days. The circumstances of his death fell in with the popular feeling. The tears and sobs of Waltheof's last moments would have been deemed unbecoming in a patriot of the seventeenth century. But the model of the days of Waltheof was not the proud Roman despising or defying death, but the humble Christian, conscious of heavy sins, and fearful lest aught should have been left undone which was needed to make his peace with his Creator. The belief in Waltheof's sanctity spread through the land. His praises were sung, not only in England, but in the land of his Danish fathers. Englishmen, it was there significantly said, held him for a saint; but a poet who had known him in life chose rather, in commemorating his death at William's

*Waltheof deemed a martyr*

*Characteristic feelings of the time*

[1] Ord Vit 537 A "Caput, postquam præsectum fuit, cunctis qui aderant audientibus, clarâ et articulatâ voce dixit, Sed libera nos a malo, Amen."
[2] Ib.

bidding, to sing of his worldly virtues more than of his holiness.[1]

But there was one place above all in England where the name of the martyred Earl was precious both in life and death. On an island in the dreariest spot of the fens of Holland stood the monastery of Saint Guthlac of Crowland.[2] Thither that holy hermit had, in the days of Æthelred of Mercia, fled from the world to wage endless war with the foul spirits which assailed him in the wilderness, and to appear from time to time as the rebuker and adviser of Kings.[3] As elsewhere, the hermitage grew into a flourishing monastery, which, like so many others, perished in the Danish invasions.[4] In the days of King Eadred the house of Saint Guthlac was restored by a clerk of royal race named Thurcytel, who became the first Abbot of the new foundation, and who passed on his office, by a kind of hereditary succession, to two successors of his own kindred.[5] In the days of King Eadward Crow-

*Crowland Abbey.*

*Story of Saint Guthlac 700–715*

*Monastery destroyed by the Danes c 877.*

*Restored by Thurcytel 946–955*

---

[1] Heimskringla, iii 168 (Copenhagen, 1783) "De Engelske holde hannem for hellig Sva seger Þórkell,

"Víst hefir Valþióf hraustan      Satt er at síd muno letta
Vilhiálmr sá ei raud málma      snarr enn minn var harri
hinn er haf skar sunnan      deyrr eigi milldingr mærri
bællt í trygd of vælltan      mann-dráp á Englandi"

See above, p 269, for Thorkell's other song on Waltheof's exploits at York.

[2] The trustworthy history of Crowland, out of which the narrative of the false Ingulf seems to have grown, is given by Orderic, 537 et seqq The true form of the name is *Cruland, Croland, Crowland Croyland* is a form still unknown on the spot, and it is not found in ancient English writers In Domesday however we have *Croiland* and *Cruiland* Was this form owing to a devout pun, *quasi Croixland*?

[3] See Ord. Vit 539 D

[4] Ib 541 B. Every one knows the legendary but highly interesting story in the false Ingulf It may have some foundation in fact, but if so, it is strange to find no mention of it in Orderic

[5] Ib 542 A "Turketelo defuncto, Egelricus nepos ejus successit, et, completo vitæ suæ cursu, alii Egelrico, qui de cognatione ejus erat, abbatiam Crulandiæ dimisit"

land was one of the five monasteries which owned the rule of Leofric, the mighty Abbot of the Golden Borough.[1] At his bidding the government of the dependent house was given to a monk of his own monastery, Ulfcytel by name.[2] He began a new church, and in that work he was much helped by his neighbour the Earl of Northampton and Huntingdon, who gave to the house of Saint Guthlac the precious gift of the lordship of Barnack. This is a spot renowned for its tower as old or older than Waltheof's days, and also for the well-known quarries than which no gift could be more acceptable to a Prelate engaged in great architectural works.[3] The name of Waltheof was therefore well nigh as beloved at Crowland as the name of Harold was at Waltham. His fate was doubtless heard of there with a still deeper feeling of sorrow than it was heard of in other parts of England. And one feature in the tale came specially home to the hearts of the monks of Crowland. The hero had been buried without any of the honours due to his rank and character, seemingly without any religious service at all. The body of Waltheof, as soon as the breath was out of it, was covered with the green sod on the spot where he had died.[4] Another rumour spoke of a yet more unworthy burial in the highway.[5] But Waltheof's faithful bedesmen at Crowland could no more bear that the body of their benefactor should lie in unhallowed ground upon the downs of Hampshire than the bedesmen of Harold

---

[1] See vol. ii p 349

[2] Ord. Vit 542 C " Ulfketulus Burgensis ecclesiæ monachus Crulandiæ regimen a Rege Eduardo, jubente Leofrico Abbate suo, suscepit "

[3] Ib Barnack was given "ad hoc opus," for building the church.

[4] Ib 537 A. "Ibi in fossâ corpus ejus viliter projectum est, et viridi cespite festinanter coopertum est "

[5] M. Paris, 1 20 "Rex Willielmus præcepit Weltheofum Comitem in Wintoniâ decollari et extra civitatem in bivio sepeliri" (Compare the legend of Godwine in vol. ii p 612) This writer had no notion of the real scene of the execution.

could bear that his body should lie in unhallowed ground upon the rocks of Sussex.[1] And the monks of Crowland had a more powerful intercessor with William than the canons of Waltham had. Judith, whether to save appearances, or really smitten with remorse by the blow which had made her a widow, joined in the prayer of the convent, and William gave leave to Abbot Ulfcytel to remove the body of his benefactor. Fifteen days therefore after the martyrdom of Waltheof came his first translation. The body, still fresh and bleeding —so the tale ran—was borne to Crowland among the tears of many, and was there reverently buried in the chapter-house [2]

*The body translated to Crowland June 15, 1076*

But a subordinate part, however honourable, of the monastic buildings of Crowland, was soon deemed too mean a resting-place for the relics of the martyr of England. Abbot Ulfcytel kept his office for nearly ten years after the death of Waltheof. He was then deposed by Lanfranc in one of his Councils. We know not the formal ground of his sentence, but we are given to understand that his real crime was the crime of being an Englishman. There is therefore nothing unlikely in the uncertified tale or tradition that the charge was one of superstition and idolatry, witnessed by the unauthorized miracles which the Abbot allowed to be wrought at the tomb of the English Earl. Ulfcytel, on this view, was a fellow-sufferer with Sôkratês; he was punished for the introduction of strange saints whom King William did not find it convenient to acknowledge.[3] However this

*Deposition of Ulfcytel. Midwinter, 1085-6.*

[1] On the analogy between the burials of Harold and Waltheof, see vol. iii p 519.

[2] Ord Vit. 537 A, 542 C The translation was made "rogatu Judith et permissu Regis" The body was "adhuc integrum cum recenti cruore, ac si tum idem vir obisset"

[3] This is the well-known story of the false Ingulf (Gale, 73), who makes Ulfcytel be deposed on the accusation of Ivo Taillebois and others in the

Appointment of an English successor.

may be, it is certain that the wonder-working powers of Waltheof began to be blazed abroad a few years later. The appointment of Ulfcytel's successor was one of the few instances in William's reign of the appointment of an Englishman to a high office. The new Abbot was Ingulf, a name which has become too well known through the forged History of Crowland which bears his name, and which was so long mistaken for a genuine monument of the eleventh century.[1] No genuine historical writings of Ingulf are extant; but Ingulf himself must have been a remarkable man. An Englishman by birth, he had attached himself to William's fortunes; he had become his Secretary, so that we may very likely have some genuine pieces of his composition in the English writs of William's reign.[2] He

first assembly held in London after Waltheof's translation. The date is utterly wrong, for it is certain that Ulfcytel was not deposed till the Gloucester Assembly of 1085–1086 (see App Chron. Wint.) Orderic also (542 C) seems not to have known how many years passed before the deposition; "Post non multum temporis præfatus Abbas, quoniam Angligena erat et Normannis exosus, ab æmulis accusatus est, et a Lanfranco Archiepiscopo depositus et Glestoniæ claustro deputatus est." But here is no formal charge, and it is not at all unlikely that the false Ingulf may be reporting the genuine tradition of the house when he says that the "debita reverentia sancto martyri habita" was by his accusers turned into a charge of "idololatria" The story in short forestalls the later saying,

"De par le roi, defense à Dieu
De faire miracle en ce lieu"

[1] I need hardly, at this time of day, go about to disprove the genuineness of the so-called Ingulf A writer who misdates his own appointment by ten years, who finds Alexios Komnênos reigning at Constantinople at some time before King William came into England, and who makes William receive his death-wound at Le Mans instead of at Mantes, must, if contemporary, have been singularly careless For a cloud of evidence of other kinds, see Mr Riley's paper in the Archæological Journal, vol xix (1862), p. 32

[2] Ord. Vit 542 C "Ingulfus Fontinellensis monachus Abbatiam Crulandiæ dono Guillelmi Regis recepit, et xxiv annis per plurimas adversitates rexit Hic natione Anglicus erat, scriba Regis fuerat" There is nothing here to imply, as is asserted in the false history, that Ingulf attached himself to William during his visit to England in 1051. He is far more likely to have been one of the many Englishmen who entered William's service after his coronation.

had afterwards made the pilgrimage to Jerusalem, and had entered on religion in a Norman monastery, the famous house of Saint Wandrille. There he had risen to the dignity of Prior, and thence, by William's gift, he was promoted to the abbatial stall of Crowland.[1] His first act was to crave the King's mercy for his predecessor Ulfcytel had been committed to safe-keeping in the distant monastery of Glastonbury. At Ingulf's prayer, he was allowed to come back and end his days in the house of Peterborough where he had dwelled in his youth.[2] Ingulf, sickly in body but vigorous in mind, ruled the church of Crowland for twenty-four years.[3] He repaired the damage done by a fire to the church and the other buildings of the monastery, and he gave a fresh attraction to the restored building by removing into it the body of one who was beginning to be looked on as the local martyr. Waltheof was not a canonized saint, whose relics could be exalted in a shrine for a worship publicly recognized. But he might be laid in the founder's place of honour by the high altar. Thither the body was translated, a body which, so the legend told, was found, sixteen years after death, still whole, with the severed head joined again to the trunk, and with only a thin line of red to show where the headsman's sword had fallen.[4]

CHAP XX

Ingulf Abbot of Crowland 1086-1109

Second Translation of Waltheof. 1092.

---

[1] Ord Vit 542 D "Hierusalem perrexerat, unde reversus Fontinellam expetiit, et a viro eruditissimo Gerberto ejusdem coenobii Abbate monachilem habitum suscepit, sub quo jam in ordine instructus prioratum administravit Hunc ab Abbate suo Rex, qui prius eum noverat, requisivit et Crulandensibus præposuit" We here see where Ingulf really got his learning, not at Westminster or at Oxford Saint Gerbert, Abbot of Saint Wandrille from 1062 to 1089, was a German by birth and a great philosopher See Neustria Pia, 169

[2] Ib "Postquam Crulandiæ regimen habuit, prædecessori suo precibus benevolis apud Guillelmum Regem subvenire sategit"

[3] Ib "Gravi morbo podagræ detentus, diu ante mortem suam languit, sed vivaci animo subditis prodesse non desiit"

[4] Ib. "Corpus Guallevi Comitis de capitulo jussit in ecclesiam transferri, et aquam, unde ossa lavarentur, calefieri Sed postquam sarcophagi

CHAP XX.

1265.
1322.

Geoffrey Abbot
1109-1124

Miracles of Waltheof

Further miracles, miracles of healing, were of course wrought at the tomb of the translated hero, as in after days they were wrought by the relics of Earl Simon of Leicester and Earl Thomas of Lancaster.[1] And, seemingly after a lull, they began again in the reign of the next Abbot Geoffrey, whose work in repairing or rebuilding the minster may have needed some such special sanction.[2] In his day, more than a generation after the Conquest, Englishmen still rejoiced in the mighty works of the national hero.[3] An unbelieving Norman monk, who maintained the martyr to be a traitor justly punished for his crimes,[4] was sternly rebuked by his Abbot, a Frenchman from Orleans, who was therefore less open to purely Norman prejudices [5]

opertorium revolutum est, corpus xvi. dormitionis suæ anno integrum, sicut in die quo sepultum fuerat, et caput corpori conjunctum, repertum est. Filum tantummodo, quasi pro signo decollationis, rubicundum viderunt monachi et laici quamplures qui adfuerunt"

[1] Ord Vit 543 A In the second volume of the Chroniques Anglo-Normandes (p 131) there is a special tract, "Miracula Sancti Waldevi Gloriosi Martyris" Most of them are wrought for the benefit of persons with English or Danish names, but among them (141) is "quædam materfamilias religiosa, Athelis nomine, pago Normannico oriunda" Compare the analogous tract, "Miracula Simonis de Montfort," in Halliwell's Rishanger, p 67, and for Thomas of Lancaster see his Office in Wright's Political Songs (Camden Society), 268, and the document in Rymer, ii 525, about his alleged miracles, the counterpart of those of Waltheof

[2] It sounds strange to read directly after the passage just quoted (Ord. Vit 543 B) that under Geoffrey "ad tumbam Guallevi Comitis miracula demonstrari primitus cœperunt" These "more first miracles" of Earl Waltheof really remind one of " more last words of Mr Baxter"

[3] Ord Vit 543 B " Auditis rumoribus Angli valde lætati sunt, et Anglicæ plebes ad tumulum sancti compatriotæ, quem a Deo jam glorificari signis multiplicibus audiunt, tam pro gaudio novæ rei quam pro suis necessitatibus deprecaturi frequenter adcurrunt."

[4] Ib " Quidem de Normannis monachus, nomine Audinus, vidit, vehementer stomachatus advenientes derisit, et præfato Comiti cum irrisione detraxit, dicens quod nequam traditor fuerit, et pro reatu suo capitis obtruncatione mulctari meruerit "

[5] Ib C. " Dulciter eum, quia extraneus erat, redarguit " The Frenchman seems to have been quite naturalized in England, though the Norman was not Geoffrey had been a monk of Saint Evroul, and was a personal friend of Orderic

Nor was he merely rebuked by an earthly superior; divine vengeance presently smote the scoffer with sickness and death, while the faithful Abbot was rewarded with a vision in which he was assured that he who had been only an Earl on earth was now a King in heaven.[1] At last, the old times might seem altogether to have come back when, on the death of Geoffrey, the Abbey of Crowland received as its ruler a man of the noblest English blood, and bearing the martyr's name.[2] The hero had now to find his poet; the monks of Crowland needed an epitaph for the local saint, and Abbot Waltheof and his convent called in the aid of the monk of Saint Evroul, Orderic or Vital the Englishman, who had visited their house in the days of Abbot Geoffrey.[3] The historian undertook the task, and told in such hexameters as the age could produce, how Waltheof, the valiant and the devout, the son of the Danish Siward, died by the sword at the bidding of Norman judges.[4]

*Waltheof Abbot of Crowland 1124-1138*

The widow of Waltheof, Judith, appears in the Survey as holding large estates, especially in Northamptonshire, estates which had partly belonged to her husband, partly to other English owners.[5] She appears in monastic history

*Estates held by Judith.*

---

[1] See the story, and a wonderful hexameter or "monadicon," in Orderic, 543 C

[2] See above, p 524. Abbot Waltheof, I am sorry to say, was deprived in 1138 Mon Ang ii 101

[3] See Ord Vit 537 A. To this visit we owe Orderic's account of Crowland, which he wrote at the request of the Prior Wilsinus [Wulfsige?] See above, p 497

[4] Orderic gives the verses in pp 543, 544. "Danigenæ Comitis S[i]wardi filius audax" has his virtues recorded, and then we read of him as "denique judicibus Normannis ense peremptus" There is quite another epitaph in Chron Ang -Norm ii 123, where Judith is compared to Herodias and Job's wife,

"Hæc accusavit, Rex credidit, et tibi mortem
Intulit, assignans cum damnatis tibi sortem."

[5] Judith's estates in Huntingdonshire are given in Domesday, 217, those

604                THE REVOLTS AGAINST WILLIAM.

CHAP. XX
Her foundation at Elstow

Story of Simon of Senlis.

Matilda, daughter of Waltheof, marries Simon of Senlis c 1089.

as the foundress of a house of nuns at Helenstow or Elstow near Bedford,[1] a place more famous in later times as the birth-place of John Bunyan. Legend has much more to tell of her. Like Cnut at the tomb of Eadmund,[2] she offered a splendid pall at the tomb of her husband, but the gift was thrown back again by unseen hands.[3] Her uncle the King wished to give her in second marriage to a valiant man called Simon of Senlis, who does not appear in the Survey, but who in the story is already Earl of Northampton. But Simon was lame, and Judith preferred widowhood to a lame husband. The Earldom of Huntingdon and the other possessions of Judith were granted to Simon; she herself fled from the wrath of William to Hereward's refuge in the marshes of Ely; and Simon, instead of Judith the widow of Waltheof, received as his wife the martyr's daughter Matilda. The details about Judith are purely mythical, but there is no doubt that a daughter of Waltheof did marry Simon of Senlis, and conveyed to him the Earldoms of Northampton and Huntingdon.[4] Simon was the founder of the castle of

in Bedfordshire, 206 *b*, Northamptonshire, 228 Waltheof himself appears as the former owner of many of the Northamptonshire estates, but only once or twice in the other shires This gives the impression that most of the lands were personal grants to herself The former owners are various, including King Eadward, Earl Gyrth, and men of Earl Harold. Judith had also possessions in other shires, but none, it should be noticed, in Yorkshire, where her husband's estates were so large.

[1] See Mon Angl III 411, and Judith's gifts in Domesday, 206 *b*, 217.
[2] See vol I p 487
[3] See the false Ingulf, Gale, 72
[4] Compare the real account in Orderic, 702 C, and the Continuator of William of Jumièges, viii 37, with the stories in the false Ingulf, 72, and in the tract " De Comitissâ " which follows the Vita et Passio Wadevi Comitis in the Chroniques Anglo-Normandes, ii 123. The History of Saint Andrew's Priory at Northampton in the Monasticon, v 190, makes Simon " de Seynlyz," the son of " Raundoel le Ryche," come over into England with William at the beginning, but, as Simon is not to be found in Domesday, and as a " Symon Comes " signs the grant of Bath to John de Villulâ in 1090 (see above, p 398), it would seem that Simon came into

Northampton, and of the neighbouring Priory of Saint Andrew,[1] and he died on his way back from a pilgrimage or crusade to Jerusalem.[2] Of the marriage of Simon and Matilda came three children, a younger Simon, a younger Matilda, and a younger Waltheof, who became Abbot of Melrose.[3] But the daughter of the martyred Earl, after her first husband's death, consoled her widowhood with a loftier marriage. She became the wife of David of Scotland, one of the sons of Malcolm and of the holy Margaret, and who himself became one of the most renowned princes who ever wore the Scottish Crown. Through this marriage came the long connexion between the Earldom of Huntingdon and the royal house of Scotland, and through it too the blood of Waltheof, and thereby of the long list of his forefathers, human and otherwise, passed into the veins of the later Kings of England, and also, if genealogists are to be trusted, into those of many of their subjects.[4]

CHAP. XX.

Children of Simon and Matilda

Second marriage of Matilda, to David of Scotland [King 1124–1153]

Connexion between the Scottish Kings and the Earldom of Huntingdon.

The death of Waltheof is the turning-point in the history of William. As men generally look at the acts of princes, it was the greatest crime of his life. In an abstract view of morality, to attack an unoffending nation in the assertion of an imaginary right, to lay waste whole provinces by fire and sword, to slay by the lingering death of cold and hunger thousands more than are slain in the short struggle of the battle-field, and to do all

Character of the execution of Waltheof.

England and married Waltheof's daughter in the very last years of William the Conqueror or in the first years of William Rufus. Of Waltheof's other daughters, Judith married the younger Ralph of Toesny, and the third, who is nameless, married Robert the son of Richard. Will Gem viii 37.

[1] The date of 1084 is commonly given to this foundation (see the first document in Mon. Angl. v. 190), but, as the Priory does not appear in Domesday, the date is more likely to be 1108.

[2] Mon. Angl. v. 190.

[3] Chroniques Anglo-Normandes, ii. 126.

[4] On the succession of the Earldom of Huntingdon, see Chroniques Anglo-Normandes, ii. 128; Dugdale's Baronage, 59.

this in pursuit of a purely personal ambition, is a greater sin against humanity than to shed the blood of a single innocent man. And yet such are the inconsistencies of our nature that it needs a worse man to do the lesser crime. An unjust war and all that is involved in an unjust war, the harsh measures of repression which are needed to keep a Crown once unjustly won, can all be more easily cloaked under fair pretences, their real character can be more easily hidden from both doers and beholders, than can be done with the unrighteous slaughter of a single man. In this sense, the execution of Waltheof was a blacker deed than the invasion of England and even than the devastation of Northumberland. Yet even now William's love of formal justice did not forsake him. Even now we may feel sure that he would have shrunk from using the bowl or the dagger to get rid of the man whom he dreaded. Waltheof died in the sight of the sun, by the sword of the headsman, by the formal sentence of what was formally a competent court. William may even now have persuaded himself that he was but letting the law take its course, that he was but executing a righteous vengeance on a traitor righteously condemned. But so to persuade himself needed a yet stronger effort of the mighty power of self-delusion than to persuade himself of the righteousness of his former deeds. Never before had William sent an enemy to the scaffold. He had pardoned men who had over and over again rebelled against him; he had visited other traitors with outlawry, with bonds, with mutilation, never with death. And the man whom he chose for his one victim was innocent, or, even if in some measure guilty, he had redeemed his fault by a speedy penitence. Yet he had to die, while the life of his far more guilty comrade was spared. Never was legal execution more truly judicial murder; never was innocent blood more ruthlessly shed to escape a possible political danger. Such a deed needed a worse man than was needed for any of William's earlier deeds. And William now was a worse man than he had been when he set foot on the Mora to attack a people who had never wronged him. Crime, as ever, had punished itself by leading to greater crime. And now the more open punishment followed. With the death of Waltheof the days of William's glory and prosperity came to an end. From that day the Conqueror made no more conquests. His presence on the battle-field no longer carried with it the overthrow of his enemies; his presence beneath the walls of a besieged fortress no longer involved its speedy capture or surrender. William had to struggle against enemies at home and abroad; and now he found foes in his own household. The blood of Waltheof was avenged by the bonds of Odo and by the parricidal thrust of the spear of Robert. The punishment of crime came in the best and purest relation of his life, when, after so many years of faithful partnership, strife at last arose between William and the wife of his bosom. Eleven years of life and kingship were still to be his, but they were to be years of toil and trouble, years of warfare without glory, years clouded over with every form of public and private sorrow.[1]

Closely connected in idea with the death of Waltheof, and most likely not far distant from it in date, was that other great crime of William which, in the eyes of the

---

[1] The reflexion is that of Orderic, 544 A, "Pro interfectione Gualleri Comitis Guillelmus Rex a multis reprehensus est, et multis contra eum insurgentibus, justo Dei judicio, multa adversa perpessus est; nec umquam postea diuturnâ pace potitus est. Ipse quidem contra omnes (quia animosus erat) viriliter restitit, sed prosperis eventibus ad votum, ut antea, non tripudiavit, nec crebris victoriarum titulis exultavit. In tredecim annis, quibus postmodum vixit, armatorum aciem de campo non fugavit, nec oppidum obsidens bellicâ virtute cepit. Omnipotens arbiter omnia juste disponit, nullumque facinus impunitum relinquit, quia hic aut in futuro seculo omnia punit."

men of his own age, joined with the slaughter of the English Earl to bring down the wrath of God upon him and upon his house. The love of the sports of the field, which may be taken for granted in every man of that age of whom the contrary is not expressly recorded, seems to have reached its height in William and his sons. We must remember that in those days hunting had, in many parts even of our own island, not yet wholly lost its original character of defensive warfare with the wild beasts. Scottish traditions speak of the bear as still lingering on in the eleventh century,[1] and it is certain that, at all events in the less cultivated parts of Britain, the wolf still survived to prey on the flocks, and the wild boar to ravage the fields, of men who were striving to turn the wilderness into a fruitful field.[2] The stag and the roe, in northern Britain even the rein-deer,[3] were still untamed rangers of the wilderness, whose flesh was sought for as food, and whose haunts might be profitably cleared for the service of man. In such a state of things hunting might be a sport, as war might be a sport, but it was something more. It was always a

---

[1] I am sorry that I have nothing to quote on behalf of this statement beyond a vague Scottish tradition. The last bear is said to have been killed T. R. E. but no original authority is quoted. Is there any confusion with Osbeorn the son of Siward and his ancestors—his *forebears*?

[2] The boar appears in the passage of the Peterborough Chronicle which I shall presently quote. That wolves remained in England long after, at all events in the shires bordering on Wales, is plain from a writ of Edward the First in 1281 (Rymer, i. 591), in which Peter Corbet is commissioned to destroy wolves in the shires of Gloucester, Worcester, Hereford, Shropshire, and Stafford, "Lupos cum hominibus, canibus, et ingeniis suis capiat et destruat modis omnibus quibus viderit expedire." This proves more by a great deal than the possibly poetical mention of wolves by Guy of Amiens (see vol. iii. p. 510) and by the Scandinavian poet who commemorates the exploits of Waltheof (see above, p. 269).

[3] Orkneyinga Saga, 384. "Þat var siþr Jarla nær hvert sumar at fara yfer á Katanes oc þar upp á merkr at veida rauddýri edr *hreína*." I have to thank Mr Dawkins for this reference, and for other hints as to the *fauna* of Britain. The date of the story is about 1159.

business; it might often be a duty. The hunting of Ælfred is recorded, not as a sport but as a serious employment, along with the cares of war, government, and study.[1] In the story of the tribute of wolves' heads imposed by Eadgar on the Welsh prince Judwal, the original and lawful object of hunting, the getting rid of noisome beasts, not their artificial preservation, is set forth with perfect clearness.[2] In the records of the great Survey we find constant mention of various services to be rendered in the royal huntings, huntings which were doubtless part of the King's pleasure, but which were also plainly looked upon as a serious business to be pursued for the public good.[3] In the legislation of our later Kings we begin to find penalties for trespasses on the royal forests, but they are combined with an express acknowledgement of the right of every man to slay the wild beasts of the field on his own ground.[4] It was in William's age, and

*Example of Ælfred and Eadgar*

*Beginning of forest laws*

*Laws of Cnut*

[1] Asser, M H B. 486 A "Interea tamen Rex, inter bella et præsentis vitæ frequentia impedimenta, necnon Paganorum infestationes et quotidianas corporis infirmitates, et regni gubernacula regere et omnem venandi artem agere, aurifices et artifices suos omnes, et falconarios et accipitrarios, canicularios quoque, docere, et ædificia supra omnem antecessorum suorum consuetudinem venerabiliora et pretiosiora novâ suâ machinatione facere, et Saxonicos libros recitare," and so on through the whole string of Ælfred's literary and pious employments

[2] Will Malm ii 155 "Qui etiam omnis generis feras sanguinis avidas ex regno exterminare cogitaret, Judvaloque Regi Walensium edictum imposuerit ut sibi quotannis tributum trecentorum luporum pensitaret" The same distinction as to the *motive* of different forms of hunting is drawn out more at large in a remarkable letter of Peter of Blois, 56 (vol 1 p 166, Giles), where hunting "gratiâ voluptatis" is pronounced to be "ex ipsâ inventione suâ damnabilis"

[3] The *stabilitio*, so often spoken of in Domesday, is described by Kelham, 338, "One man went from every house to the stands or his station in the wood, viz for driving deer to a stand, in order to shooting them, or into buck-stalls, or deer-hays, for taking them" Compare the remarks of Mr Earle, Parallel Chronicles, 366, beginning with the words, "The nature of the hunt here imagined is totally different from that of our day. Now-a-days men hunt for exercise and sport, but then they hunted for food, or for the luxury of fresh meat"

[4] On the laws of Cnut, see vol i p. 482

610                  THE REVOLTS AGAINST WILLIAM.

CHAP XX. largely by William's own act, that what had once been
Change in necessary warfare with savage enemies finally changed
William's
time      into a mere sport, in which pleasure is sought in the
Exclusive- wanton infliction of suffering and death. It was then too
ness of his
legislation that what hitherto, whether sport or business, had been
          the sport or the business of every man, became the ex-
          clusive enjoyment of the King and of those whom he
          might allow to share it. It is plain that with William
          a new period in these matters begins. In other princes
          we incidentally hear of their hunting in the course of
Feeling of some story or legend; in William and his sons, as in
the time
          Eadward, it is specially mentioned by the writers of the
          time as a marked feature of their character, and in their
          case it is always mentioned with horror. It is plain that
          William's excessive love of hunting, the cruel laws by
          which his savage pleasures were fenced in, the pitiless
          havoc of which he was guilty to find means for their
          gratification, were something which was new to English-
          men. Our native Chronicler tells us how "he set mickle
          deer-frith, and laid laws therewith, that he who slew
          hart or hind that man should blind him. He forbade
          the harts and so eke the boars, so sooth he loved the
          high deer as though he were their father. Eke he set
          by the hares that they should fare free His rich men
          moaned at it and the poor men bewailed it; but he was
          so stiff that he recked not of their hatred; but they must
          all follow the King's will, if they would live or have their
          land or their goods or well his peace[1]" It was the

[1] Chron Petrib 1087 "He sætte mycel deor frið, and he lægde laga þearwið, þæt swa hwa swa sloge heort oððe hinde, þæt hine man sceolde blendian, he forbead þa heortas swylce eac þa baras, swa swiðe he lufode þa heah deor swilce he wære heora fæder, eac he sætte be þam haran þæt hi mosten freo faran His rice men hit mændon, and þa earme men hit bece- orodan, ac he wæs swa stið þæt he ne rohte heora eallra nið, ac hi moston mid ealle þes cynges wille folgian, gif hi woldon libban, oððe land habban, oððe eahta, oððe wel his sehta"

The "mycel deor-frið," a word which it is hard to express in modern

making of the "mickle deer-frith" which was the crown- CHAP XX.
ing wrong of all. It was not enough for William to
seek the delights of slaughter in those spots where the
uncleared land still harboured the beasts of the field. He William
did not scruple to lay waste the land which was already lays waste
the land
brought into man's possession, to uproot the dwellings for his
sport.
of man and the temples of God, in order to find a wider
field for the gratification of his lust of bloodshed. Heavy
was the guilt of the harrying of Northumberland; but
the harrying of Northumberland was at least done at
the dictate of a cruel policy, and not in the mere wantonness of sport. Heavy as the guilt of that deed was,
it was lighter than the guilt of the making of the New
Forest. Each deed marks a new and a lower stage in the
downward course.

The exact date of this devastation of a large tract of Making of
the New
fertile country is not recorded, but it cannot have been Forest
very far from the time which we have now reached. It 1070-1081
is not at all likely that William found leisure for such a
business during the actual progress of the Conquest. On
the other hand we not only find the Forest duly described
in the Survey,[1] but we come across an incidental mention
of it at an intermediate time which shows that the work
had been fully done within a few years after the death
of Waltheof.[2] The favourite dwelling-place of William Winchester
William's
when in England was Winchester. Under Eadward and capitals
Harold the old West-Saxon capital had in some degree

English, doubtless means chiefly, but perhaps not exclusively, the New
Forest Deor is now gliding from its older and wider meaning of *Thier*,
θήρ, *fera*, into its later special meaning of harts and hinds

The fatherly relations between William and the high deer were perhaps
measured by the relations between him and his eldest son.

[1] The New Forest entries take up pp 51-51 *b* in Domesday

[2] I refer to the death of William's son Richard, which seems (Ord Vit
573 C) to have happened about 1081 Whenever it happened, the New
Forest must have then been in full force

R r 2

lost its position.[1] Westminster had become the chief home of Kings, while Winchester was handed over to their widows. The death of Eadgyth, by which her rights over the city reverted to the King, was perhaps not without its influence in making Winchester again more distinctly the royal dwelling-place No other among the great cities of the Kingdom was so well suited to be the dwelling-place of a King who ruled in Normandy as well as in England. But in Hampshire, then no doubt the most civilized and best cultivated part of the Kingdom, it may well have been that either natural or artificial hunting-grounds were less extensive than in the wilder regions in the North or on the Welsh border. To find room therefore for William's sport, a fertile district, thirty miles in extent, was deliberately laid waste.[2] In the days of Eadward and the Kings before him it had been a flourishing land, full of the habitations of men, and thick set with churches where the worship of God was duly paid.[3] At William's bidding men were driven from their homes,

*He lays waste a large part of Hampshire*

---

[1] See vol iii p 65
[2] Will. Malm iii. 275 "Nova Foresta . locus est quem Willelmus pater, subrutis ecclesiis, desertis villis per triginta et eo amplius milliaria, in saltus et lustra ferarum redegerat" Ord Vit 781 A "Nunc Silva . vide lector, cur Nova vocitata sit Ab antiquis temporibus ibi populosa regio erat, et villis humanæ habitationi competentibus abundabat Copiosa vero plebs Suthamptonæ pagum solerti curâ obnixe colebat, unde australis provincia Guentanæ urbi multipliciter campestri ubertate serviebat Guillelmus autem primus, postquam regnum Albionis obtinuit, amator nemorum, plus quam lx parochias ultro devastavit, ruricolas ad alia loca transmigrare compulit, et silvestres feras pro hominibus, ut voluptatem venandi haberet, ibidem constituit" See also M Paris, i 29, Madden
[3] Florence (1100), after mentioning the death of William Rufus "in Novâ Forestâ quæ linguâ Anglorum Ytene nuncupatur," goes on to say, "Nec mirum, ut populi rumor affirmat, hanc proculdubio magnam Dei virtutem esse et vindictam Antiquis enim temporibus, Eadwardi scilicet Regis et aliorum Angliæ Regum prædecessorum ejus, eadem regio incolis Dei cultoribus et ecclesiis nitebat uberrime, sed jussu Regis Willelmi senioris, hominibus fugatis, domibus semirutis, ecclesiis destructis, terra ferarum tantum colebatur habitatione, et inde, ut creditur, causa erat infortunii"

their houses were pulled down, their churches were rooted up, and the fruitful land became a wilderness. The historians of both races raise their indignant wail over the homes of man which were changed into the lairs of wild beasts. The great Survey calmly gives us the names of the Englishmen who were driven forth from their wasted homes, and show how a few of them were allowed to retain some small scraps of land beyond the limits of the sacred precincts of William's sport.[1] There, we are told, amid the desolation which he had wrought, the Conqueror would gladly have spent his life,[2] rejoicing in the slaughter of the lower animals during the short intervals of the slaughter of mankind. But we are told also that the scene of William's greatest crime was the scene of the heaviest blows which were dealt upon his house. A curse seemed to brood over the region from which man had been driven to make room for the wild beasts. The wilderness which William had made was fatal to his sons and to his sons' sons.[3] His second son Richard, a lad of great promise, not yet girded with the belt of knighthood, was cut off in the New Forest by a sudden and mysterious stroke, while the wearied stag was fleeing for its

CHAP. XX

Language of contemporary writers

Evidence of the Survey.

The New Forest held to be fatal to his family.

Death of his son Richard.

---

[1] Take one instance in Domesday, 51 *b*, "Filii Godrici Malf habent de Rege Mintestede. Pater eorum tenuit de Rege E. Tunc se defendebat pro iii hidis et dimidiâ. Modo non habent filii ejus nisi dimidiam hidam, quæ geldavit pro unâ virgatâ. Alia terra est in forestâ." *Foresta*, it must be remembered, is *wilderness* rather than *wood*. So we find more than once such entries as "Silvam habet Rex in forestâ, ubi manebant vi homines."

[2] Will. Malm. iii. 275. "Ibi libenter ævum exigere, ibi plurimis omitto quod diebus, certe mensibus, venationes exercere gaudebat."

[3] William of Malmesbury goes on to say, "Ibi multa regio generi contigere infortunia, quæ habitatorum præsens audire volentibus suggerit memoria." He then mentions the death of William Rufus and the two Richards. Florence and Orderic speak to the same effect, and Orderic adds (781 A), "Multiformis visio quibusdam terribiliter apparuit, quibus consecratas ædes pro educatione ferarum derelictas Dominus sibi displicere palam ostendit."

life before him.[1] Another Richard, a natural son of William's eldest son Robert, died in the same forest by a chance stroke of one of his followers.[2] And how the Conqueror's son and successor, the second and baser William, perished —by whose stroke none knew—on the site of one of the churches which his father had levelled with the ground,[3] will come before us at a later stage of our story. Our age shrinks, and is often wise in shrinking, from seeing the visible hand of God in the punishments which seem, even on earth, to overtake the sinner. The age of William was

*Marginal note: Of Richard the son of Robert*

---

[1] William of Malmesbury (iii 275) says of him, "Ricardus magnanimo parenti spem laudis alebat, puer delicatus, ut id ætatulæ pusio, altum quid spirans" Of his death he says, "Tradunt cervos in Novâ Forestâ terebrantem tabidi aeris nebulâ morbum incurrisse" Orderic's account (573 C) is more intelligible, "Dum prope Guentam in Novâ Forestâ venaretur, et quamdam feram caballo currente pertinaciter insequeretur, ad sellæ clitellam valido corili ramo admodum constrictus est et letaliter læsus" The Continuator of William of Jumièges (viii 9) tells the story the same way, and adds, "Ferunt multi quod hi duo filii Willelmi Regis in illâ silvâ judicio Dei perierunt, quoniam multas villas et ecclesias propter eamdem forestam amplificandam in circuitu ipsius destruxerat"

There is a most remarkable story in Domesday, 141, 141 b, of lands in Hertfordshire restored by William to their ancient owner as an offering for Richard's soul, but again, it would seem, brought wrongfully into dependence on a Norman lord, "In Teuuinge tenet Aldene de Petro [" de Valongies," see above, p 213] v hidas et dimidiam . Hoc manerium tenuit isdem Aldene Teignus R. E et vendere potuit. Sed W Rex dedit hoc manerium huic Aldene et matri ejus *pro animâ Ricardi filii sui*, ut ipse dicit et per brevem suum ostendit Modo dicit Petrus quod habet hoc manerium ex dono Regis "

I do not understand the title of " Beorniæ Dux " on Richard's tomb at Winchester

[2] This Richard was one of two sons whom Robert had by a priest's daughter in the time of his wanderings See the story in Orderic, 780 D. Of his death Florence (1100) says, " Dum et ipse in venatu fuisset, a suo milite sagittâ percussus interiit " Orderic (780 C) gives the same account more in detail William of Malmesbury (iii 275) adds, " Vel, ut quidam dicunt, arboris ramusculo equo per transeunte fauces appensus," which seems a confusion with the death of the other Richard.

[3] Flor Wig 1100. " In loco quo Rex occubuit priscis temporibus ecclesia fuerat constructa, sed patris sui tempore, ut prædiximus, erat diruta"

less scrupulous. The men of his own day, even men who were ready to do at least justice to whatever was good in his mixed character, saw in the life of William a mighty tragedy, with the avenging Atê brooding over the sinner and his house. Up to a certain stage every scheme of his brain prospered, every stroke of his hand was crowned with victory. At length he reached the highest pinnacle of earthly greatness, all foes within and without his realm were laid helpless at his feet. Then came the crisis of his fate. The pride of greatness and victory overcame him. They led him on to those deeds of greater wrong by which the Avenger, as in the tales of old Hellas, was wont to punish earlier deeds of lesser wrong. From the invasion of England William had gone on to the harrying of Northumberland; from the harrying of Northumberland he had gone on to the judicial murder of Waltheof and to the desolation of Hampshire for his own wanton pleasure. On the guilt followed the punishment. William's later days of domestic trouble, of shame and defeat, the disgraces of his arms, the mysterious deaths of his offspring, events which have no parallel in the history of his earlier days, were, so men then deemed, so many strokes of the sword of the Avenger to requite the blood of Waltheof and the ruined homes and churches of Hampshire. To speculations beyond his range the historian can say neither Yea nor Nay. It is enough that, at the moment of Waltheof's death, William had reached the summit of his power, and that, after the death of Waltheof, the historian of his reign has only to pass with a swifter course through the dreary years of his later life to the days of his awful death and his more awful burial.

## CHAPTER XXI.

### THE LATER DAYS OF WILLIAM.[1]

#### 1076—1087.

§ 1. *Character of the later Reign of William.*

<small>Character of the years 1076–1087</small>

THE latter half of William's reign has no claim to take up at all the same space in our history which has been given to the former half. The Conquest of England was now over; there was no longer any hope of throwing off the yoke. The dream of delivering or conquering England had not passed out of the minds of the Kings of the North, but, if Englishmen still looked for help from this quarter, they were again doomed to disappointment. Of revolts on the part of the whole nation, or of any large portion of it, we hear nothing. A single riot, in which an unpopular governor was murdered, takes the place of campaigns like those of Exeter, York, and Ely. Of foreign warfare, within and without the Island, there is no lack, but the warfare of these years is for the most part desultory and inglorious. On the Continent William had to struggle with another revolt

<small>Hope of deliverance passed away</small>

<small>General quiet of England</small>

<small>William's unsuccessful continental warfare</small>

---

[1] There is little to remark on the authorities for this Chapter, which are the same as those with which we have been dealing for some time. We may however note that the value of Orderic increases at every step, and that Wace, whose company we have so long lost, joins us again at the very end of our story.

in the unconquerable land of Maine; he had to struggle with his own undutiful son and with his jealous overlord. He had to fight with the Briton on both sides of the sea, to flee before the *Bretwealas* of the mainland, and to win no very glorious laurels over those of our own Island. A renewed inroad of the Scottish King was but feebly avenged, and a more threatening attack from the joint powers of Denmark and Norway was staved off by policy rather than by arms. A petty campaign here one year, another petty campaign there the next, fill up the last days of William's life till we come to the death-blow in the burning streets of Mantes, to the fruitless penitence of Saint Gervase, to the hardly purchased tomb within his own Saint Stephen's.

<small>CHAP XXI

Relations with Scotland and Denmark</small>

On the other hand, these last eleven years were the years when William was undisputed master of England. It was during these years that the Conquest finally took root. It was now that the relations between the conquerors and the conquered finally fixed themselves It is to these later days of William, days, as far as England is concerned, of government rather than of warfare, that the general pictures of his reign which are given us by the native Chronicler must mainly belong. That picture sets before us, not a state of warfare, but a state of settled government, a government strict, harsh, often oppressive, but a government which had its bright side, and whose merits even those who suffered from it were ready to admit. It is to these more settled times that we must chiefly look both for the wrong which was done in William's days under the form of law, and for the strict justice which was dealt out to more vulgar offenders. Each picture alike is eminently characteristic of William. But the remarkable thing is that, among all the complaints which are made of the oppression and unrighteousness of the times, the moan of the English Chronicler

<small>William undisputed master.

Blending of the two races

Picture of William's government

Its good and bad sides</small>

never takes the shape which it certainly would have taken in our own day. We have the picture of an oppressed nation, but there is not a word to hint that that oppressed nation was what it is now the fashion to call an oppressed nationality. We hear of the hardness of the King, of the wrongdoings of the rich and of the sufferings of the poor, but there is no reference to the one obvious cause of all these griefs, that the poor were the conquered natives of the soil, while the King and the rich men were the strangers who had conquered them. King William was "a very wise man and very rich, and more worshipful and stronger than any of the Kings who had gone before him."[1] But the obvious distinction which we should at once draw between King William and the Kings who had gone before him is nowhere formally drawn. A man who drew his whole knowledge of William and William's acts from this memorable portrait would not learn from it, any more than he would learn from Domesday, that William was a foreign Conqueror.[2] It is plain that William and his acts had made the deepest impression on the man who had looked on him and had dwelled in his court.[3] There was something about William that was awful and wonderful and unaccustomed; but the man who describes him nowhere uses such language as a modern writer could not fail to use in speaking of a stranger who had won the Crown by the edge of the sword. We must not infer that the feeling of nationality was unknown to our forefathers of the eleventh century. Other passages of the Chronicles show plainly enough what their feeling was towards Frenchmen, out-

---

[1] Chron Petrib 1087 "Se cyng Willelm þe we embe specað wæs swiðe wis man, and swiðe rice, and wurðfulre and strengere þonne ænig his foregenggar wære"

[2] The passage quoted in p 406 would not imply more than that William had won the Crown in battle, like Edward the Fourth or Henry the Seventh.     [3] See vol ii p 165

landish men, and the like.[1] But it is plain that the feeling of nationality, though really felt, was in a manner latent, that it had not taken that definite and formal shape which in truth in most countries it did not fully take till quite modern times. And we must again remember how in everything Cnut had paved the way for William. The causes which made it possible for Cnut to reign in England as a national sovereign, and which made it impossible for William to do the like, were causes which the men of the eleventh century could not be expected fully to understand.

*Foreign conquest not new*

Three points in William's government stand out prominently in this wonderful picture, and all of them are fully borne out by the recorded acts of his life. He was strict and merciless in preserving the peace of the land. He favoured the clergy and promoted ecclesiastical reform He was guilty of great oppression, chiefly in the way of extortion and fiscal demands, but oppression which was largely cloked under the forms of law. On the first of these heads I have spoken several times already. It passed into a proverb that a man might go safely through William's Kingdom with his bosom full of gold.[2] "No man durst slay other man, had he never so mickle evil done to the other."[3] And if robbery and murder were thus vigorously put down, the third chief form of violence, outrages on female chastity, met with a speedy and fitting punishment.[4] In all this there was much to William's real honour, much

*Characteristics of William's rule*
*Strict preservation of the peace,*
*favour to the clergy,*
*oppression under the forms of Law*
*Safety of life and property under William*
*Punishment of rape*

---

[1] See the passage quoted in vol ii pp 327, 336, and again under 1088

[2] See vol ii p 172 R Wendover (ii 24) developes this into "puella"—M. Paris (ii 29) adds " virguncula "—" auro onusta "

[3] Chron Petrib 1087 " Nan man ne dorste slean oðerne man, næfde he næfre swa mycel yfel gedón wið þone oðerne " Here again we feel the power of the negative words (see vol ii pp 332, 336), and, I may add, of the double negative

[4] Ib. " Gif hwile carlman hæmde wið wimman hire unðances, sona he forleas þa limu þe he mid pleagode " The Chronicler clearly approves of the mutilation

*Chap XXI.*
*Ecclesiastical reforms.*

which hindered him from being looked on with unmixed hatred. The second point would also in those days go far to balance the darker side of his rule. Stark as he was to those who withstood his will, he was mild to the good men who loved God.[1] His days were a time when churches were built, when monasteries were reformed, when the rule of Saint Benedict was strictly followed, and when men carefully discharged the duties belonging to their order.[2]

*The forest laws*
*The castles*
*Fiscal oppression*

But there was a dark side to the picture. There were the forests and the forest laws.[3] There were the castles and the oppression which followed on them.[4] There was the heavy taxation. "The King was so very stark, and took of his subjects many marks of gold and more pounds of silver, that he took by right and with mickle unright of his landfolk for little need. He was into covetousness fallen, and greediness he loved withal."[5]

*Oppression of the Reeves*
*"Unlaw"*

Then there was the old complaint, made more grievous no doubt under foreign rule, of the doings of the King's Reeves. There was the grasping way in which William made money out of those lands of the Crown which under him finally ceased to be the lands of the people.[6] This state of things was what our fathers called *unlaw*, a state of things where law was on the mouths of men in power, but where law

---

[1] See vol. ii p 169.

[2] Chron Petrib 1087 "Eac his land wæs swiðe afylled mid munecan, and þa leofodan heora lif æfter Scs Benedictus regule, and se Xpendom wæs swilc on his dæge, þæt ælc man hwæt his hade to belumpe folgade, se þe wolde" [3] See above, p 610.

[4] See above, p 270, and vol ii p 192.

[5] Chron Petrib u s "Se cyng wæs swa swiðe stearc, and benam of his underþeoddan manig marc goldes and ma hundred punda seolfres, þet he nam be rihte and mid mycelan unrihte of his landleode for littelre neode. He wæs on gitsunge befeallan, and grædinæsse he lufode mid ealle" These words seem to show that William's habits of exaction at least grew upon him in his later days This is probably what later writers, like Matthew of Westminster (1083), meant by saying that he became a tyrant ("factus avarior et de Rege tyrannioi") after the death of Matilda.

[6] See above, p. 24

itself became the instrument of wrong. In such a state of things it was not wonderful if all classes, the conquered as well as the conquerors, shared in a general corruption, that "little righteousness was in this land amid any men."[1] The bright and the dark side of William's government, his strict police and his extortions and confiscations, were doubtless not unconnected with each other. Many a man whose lands had been forfeited, or who had been ground to the earth by William's taxation, may have taken to unlawful courses, and may have swelled the ranks of those thieves and murderers whom it was William's honest object to put down on both sides of the sea. The picture given of William's fiscal exactions is graphic and pithy; "The King and the headmen loved much and overmuch covetousness on gold and on silver, and they recked not how sinfully it was gotten, if only it came to them. The King gave his land so dear to bargain as it might be dearest; then came some other and bade more than the other had given, and the King let it to the man that bade him more; then came the third and bade yet more, and the King let it to that man's hands that bade most of all, and he recked not how very sinfully the reeves got it of poor men, nor how many *unlaws* they did. And as man spake more of right law, so man did more *unlaw*. They reared up unright tolls, and many other unright things they did that are hard to reckon."[2] We must bear in mind that many of these reeves were Englishmen,[3] and the annals of all nations bear witness that an enslaved people always suffers more deeply from those

*Alleged corruption of manners.*

*William's dealings with his tenants*

*Oppression by English Reeves.*

---

[1] Chron Petrib 1087 He excepts only the monks, and some only of them, "Buton mid munecan ane þær þær hi wæll ferdon"

[2] Ib The latter part is most emphatic, "Se cyng .. ne rohte na hu swiðe synlice þa gerefan hit begeatan of earme mannon, ne hu manige *unlaga* hi dydon Ac sua man swyðor spræc embe rihte lage, sua mann dyde mare *unlaga* Hi arerdon unrihte tollas, and manige oðre unriht hi dydan, þe sindon earfeþe to areccenne" [3] See Appendix C.

622          THE LATER DAYS OF WILLIAM.

CHAP XXI of its own blood who take service under the conquerors than it suffers from the conquerors themselves. English reeves serving under William were not likely to be among the most scrupulous or high-minded of Englishmen, and they would have better opportunities than strangers for carrying on that kind of oppression which clokes itself under the forms of law. For it is clearly oppression of this kind which is laid to the charge of William and his officers, not deeds of open violence, which it would have been altogether against William's principle and policy to encourage.

William's vast revenue

By these various means William wrung out of the unhappy nation a revenue which made him richer and mightier than all his predecessors One statement fixes his regular daily income at the incredible sum of more than a thousand and sixty pounds of silver.[1] The exaggeration is manifest, it is not unlikely to be a proverbial exaggeration mistaken for a serious piece of arithmetic; but it shows the popular belief as to the boundless wealth which William gathered together. The vast tracts of land held by the Crown, which were let, as we have seen, to tenants who were made to pay the uttermost farthing, the tributes of the towns, and occasional taxes or benevolences, filled William's coffers, while his outgoings were comparatively small. His followers had been rewarded with grants of lands, and the feudal tenures of those lands, combined with the old English law of *trinoda necessitas*, supplied him with an army almost without cost.

His outgoings small

Way of rewarding smaller dependents

Dependents of a lower class, old soldiers who had been less lucky than their comrades, Englishmen on whom

[1] Ord. Vit 523 B  " Ipsi Regi, ut fertur, mille et sexaginta libræ sterlensis monetæ, solidique triginta et tres oboli, ex justis redditibus Angliæ per singulos dies reddentur, exceptis muneribus regis et reatuum redemptionibus, aliisque multiplicibus negotiis quæ Regis ærarium quotidie adaugent " The place of this statement in the narrative shows that it is meant to apply to William as well as to Henry

William had looked with a more merciful eye than usual, could be provided for, without drawing on the royal purse, by quartering them on some monastery, or on some grantee who took their maintenance as part of his tenure.[1] William was doubtless the wealthiest prince of his time, and he kept up his royal state with fitting dignity. The national Assemblies prescribed by English Law were carefully held at the accustomed places and seasons, and doubtless with more than the accustomed splendour. "He was very worshipful, thrice he bare his kingly helm each year, so oft as he was in England. At Easter he bare it at Winchester, at Pentecost at Westminster, at Midwinter at Gloucester; and then were with him all the rich men over all England, Archbishops and suffragan Bishops and Abbots and Earls and Thegns and Knights."[2] The body thus gathered together kept their old constitutional name of the Witan,[3] and pieces of their legislation are preserved to us both in the records of the Chronicles and in the extant text of the documents themselves. Most of these statutes evidently belong to these later and more settled years of William's reign. The ordinance for taking the Great Survey, and that other ordinance which decreed that every man in the land should be the man of the King, both appear in the national Annals.[4] Others of William's

CHAP XXI

The regular Gemóts kept up by William,

at Winchester, Westminster, and Gloucester

Name of Witan goes on

Instances of William's legislation

[1] See the very curious story in Hist Ab ii 6 of one Hermer, a knight of the Abbey (see above, p 478), who was taken by pirates and seemingly lost his hands He had no lands, and he asked the King for a means of maintenance, "Cui Rex compatiens abbati mandavit debere se hujusmodi homini tantum terræ aliquorsum providere, qua quamdiu vixerit possit sustentari" The Abbot granted him an estate which he held for the rest of his days See also another story in Domesday, 218 b A King's Reeve named Osgeat, doubtless an Englishman, held lands in Bedfordshire which "tenuit i. sochemannus T R E., quem Rex W cum terrâ hac prædicto præfecto commendavit, ut quamdiu viveret victum et vestitum ei præberet"

[2] Chron Petrib 1087 "Eic he wæs swyðe wurðful, þriwa he bær his cynehelm ælce geare, swa oft swa he wæs on Englelande," &c See above, p. 329

[3] See Chron Petrib 1085, 1086

[4] Ib

624                    THE LATER DAYS OF WILLIAM.

CHAP. XXI   ordinances regulated the relations between the French
Legal rela- and English inhabitants of the country. The two races
tions be-
tween       appear on terms of legal equality, but, as in the settle-
French and
English     ment of the Teutonic tribes within the Roman Empire,
Each re-    each race was, for some purposes, allowed to retain the
tain their
own Law     use of its own Law. Frenchmen who had settled in
Eadward's
Frenchmen   England in King Eadward's days, and who had become
count as    naturalized English subjects, were counted as English-
English
            men.[1] Other Frenchmen, William's own followers or those
who had come into the land during his reign, were allowed
to keep some of their national customs with regard to the
trial of judicial causes. In cases of appeal, at all events
where there was no convincing evidence, the Law of each
nation allowed a reference to the direct judgement of God
English     But in England this reference took the form of the ordeal
practice of
ordeal      of water or of hot iron,[2] while in Normandy it took the
Norman      form of wager of battle. William recognized both modes
practice of
wager of    of trial. When a man of either race was appealed by
battle      a man of his own race, they no doubt followed their own
Regula-     Law. But special provisions are made for the case of a
tions of
appeals     man of either race appealing a man of the other race. If
between
French and  a Frenchman appealed an Englishman, the Englishman
English     had the choice of either mode of trial. In the case of an
Englishman appealing a Frenchman and declining both
ordeal and battle, the Frenchman might purge himself
by oath.[3] Two other pieces of William's legislation are

---

[1] W. Stubbs, Select Charters, 80. "Omnis Francigena qui tempore Regis Edwardi propinqui mei fuit in Angliâ particeps consuetudinum Anglorum, quod ipsi dicunt *onhlote* et *anscote*, persolvatur secundum legem Anglorum. Hoc decretum sancitum est in civitate Claudiâ." As no Gloucester Gemót was held in the earlier times of William, this statute must belong to the time which we have now reached

[2] See for instance the minute directions about the ordeal in the Laws of Æthelstan, ii. 23 (Thorpe, i. 210; Schmid, 144), and the legend of Emma, vol. ii. p. 568.

[3] See the statute in W. Stubbs, Select Charters, 81. "Decretum est ut, si Francigena appellaverit Anglum de perjurio aut murdro, furto,

worthy of still more special notice. The hateful trade in human flesh, in its cruellest form of selling men into foreign lands, the sin against which Saint Wulfstan preached to the burghers of Bristol,[1] is forbidden by William, as it had been forbidden by earlier Kings. Confiscation of lands and goods is the punishment denounced against him who shall sell a man out of the land.[2] In this enactment William acted as a just and merciful King, and he no doubt believed that he was acting as a just and merciful King in the enactment which follows it. Following out his own general practice throughout life, William altogether forbade the punishment of death. No man was to be hanged or otherwise put to death for any crime whatever. But instead of death William ordained punishments which, according to modern notions, were worse than death. The man whose crimes deserved death, but whose life William's mercy spared, was doomed to the horrible penalties of blinding—blinding in its most frightful form—and of fouler mutilation still.[3]

*Law against the slave trade*

*The punishment of death forbidden, but mutilation ordered*

Of the man himself our one personal portrait clearly belongs to his later years. William's height was tall, but not excessive; he was neither a giant like Harold Hardrada nor a small man like Eadgar and Cnut. His countenance was stern; the fore part of his head was

*William's personal appearance*

homicidio, ran, quod Angli dicunt apertam rapinam quæ negari non potest, Anglus se defendat per quod melius voluerit, aut judicio ferri aut duello .. Si Anglus Francigenam appellaverit et probare noluerit judicio aut duello, volo tamen Francigenam purgare se sacramento non fracto"         [1] See above, p 385

[2] Stubbs, Select Charters, 85 "Ego prohibeo ut nullus vendat hominem extra patriam super plenam forisfacturam meam."

[3] Ib "Interdico etiam ne quis occidatur aut suspendatur pro aliquâ culpâ, sed eruantur oculi et testiculi abscindantur Et hoc præceptum non sit violatum super forisfacturam meam plenam" This was the most brutal way of tearing out the eyes, that indulged in by Robert of Belesme, and to which Henry the Second at least confessed a tendency (see Henry of Huntingdon's story in Anglia Sacra, ii 698, and William Fitz-Stephen, Giles, i 271), for other and milder ways, see Ducange in *Abacinare*

## THE LATER DAYS OF WILLIAM.

<small>His corpulence</small>

<small>Splendour of his court</small>

<small>His avarice</small>

bald; whether standing or sitting his look was worshipful and kingly. Such he appears in the Tapestry; such he is described by one who may have looked on the great King with childish wonder. But in his latter days his majestic figure was disfigured by excessive corpulence.[1] Still, unwieldy as he became, he never lost the power of motion like Henry the Eighth; he was able to mount a horse to the end of his days. At the times of the three great yearly Assemblies William appeared in all his glory. All the great men of his realm were gathered together, not only for counsel on the affairs of the Kingdom, but to join in their sovereign's royal feasts, when the ambassadors of foreign lands came to see his magnificence, and when William showed himself affable and courteous and bountiful to all.[2] Yet perhaps it is not without significance that the historian who gives us this splendid picture goes on immediately to speak of his avarice and extortions in words hardly differing from those of the native Chronicler.[3] So too it is immediately after describing William's care in regularly summoning the constitutional Assemblies of the Kingdom that the native Chronicler himself goes on to tell us "how stark the King was, and how no man durst do anything against his will; how he had Earls in bonds that did against

---

[1] Will Malm. iii. 279. "Justæ fuit staturæ, immensæ corpulentiæ, facie ferâ, fronte capillis nuda, roboris ingentis in lacertis . . . magnæ dignitatis sedens et stans, quamquam obesitas ventris nimis protensa corpus regium deformaret." So he appears in Orderic (656 A) as "pinguissimus Rex Guillelmus."

[2] Ib. "Omnes eo cujuscumque professionis magnates regium edictum accersiebat, ut exterarum gentium legati speciem multitudinis apparatumque deliciarum mirarentur. Nec ullo tempore comior aut indulgendi facilior erat, ut qui advenerunt largitatem ejus cum divitiis conquadrare ubique gentium jactitarent."

[3] Ib. 280. "Sola est de quâ nonnihil culpetur pecuniæ aggestio, quam undecumque captatis occasionibus, honestas modo et regiâ dignitate non inferiores posset dicere, congregabat." He goes on to make some curious excuses for William's extortions.

his will, how Bishops he set of their Bishopricks and Abbots of their Abbeys, how he had Thegns in prison, and how at last he spared not his own brother." [1]

In this last picture some of the best and some of the worst acts of William's reign are mingled together; but all join to set before us the picture of a government far stronger, far more arbitrary, than anything that England had ever seen before. William strictly followed constitutional forms, because he could afford to do so, and yet could none the less wield a power which in his hands amounted to a practical despotism. King of the English according to the Law of England, he extended the royal power in its greatest fulness over all his subjects of either race; personal lord of every man in his Kingdom, feudal superior of his tenants-in-chief, military commander alike of his feudal followers, of his hired soldiers, and of the old constitutional force of the Kingdom—in one or other of these various characters William contrived to wield a power such as no other prince in Europe wielded, save only the Caliph at Cordova and the Cæsar at Byzantium. And, by a strange turning about of events, one of William's brother despots became in some sort his rival. Among the Englishmen who at various times during William's reign sought fresh homes in foreign lands, not a few made their way to the New Rome, and there, in the service of the Eastern Emperors, they not uncommonly had the satisfaction of meeting the kinsmen of their conquerors in open battle.

*Strength and practical despotism of his government*

*Englishmen take service at Constantinople.*

The movement towards the East probably began in the very first days of William's reign. No career was more attractive to a banished Englishman, especially to a native

[1] In the Peterborough Chronicle (1087) the description of the yearly Assemblies is at once followed by the words, "Swilce he wæs eac swyðe stearc man and reðe swa þæt man ne dorste nan þing ongean his willan don," &c

### THE LATER DAYS OF WILLIAM.

CHAP. XXI

of the Scandinavian parts of England, than the career which was offered by that Warangian guard to which the exploits of Harold Hardrada must have given redoubled fame throughout Northern Europe.[1] But the chief migration in this direction plainly took place in the later days of William, when the revolutions of Eastern Europe opened a fresh and specially attractive career to Englishmen. Men who found it vain to strive any longer against the Normans in their own land found a tempting field on which they might meet Normans in arms in lands beyond the sea. An Emperor had risen to power, whose fame, somewhat disproportionate perhaps to his exploits, has been far more widely spread through Western Europe than that of most of the Byzantine Cæsars. And he was the special foe of the Normans. Alexios Komnênos had barely been crowned in Saint Sophia[2] when the Eastern Empire was invaded by the Normans of Apulia under the command of their famous Duke Robert Wiscard, who by writers in distant lands has been strangely mistaken for an English King.[3] But on the shores of Epeiros, no less than on the shores of Sussex, the Norman had to meet Englishmen in battle before he could lay any claim to the name of Conqueror. The danger of the Empire, and the prospect of fighting under its banners against Norman enemies, had clearly drawn a new reinforcement of English warriors to the side of Alexios.[4] Robert

Accession of Alexios Komnênos April 1, 1081

Robert Wiscard threatens the Eastern Empire

English reinforcements.

---

[1] See vol. ii. pp. 75 et seqq.

[2] See his daughter Anna, Alex. iii. 1, Finlay, Byz. Emp. ii. 63

[3] The first invasion of Robert Wiscard is described in the third and fourth books of Anna, in the fourth book of William of Apulia in Muratori, vol. v, and in the third book of Geoffrey Malaterra in the same volume. See also William of Malmesbury, iii. 262, Gibbon, c. lvi (x. 278, Milman), Finlay, ii. 88. It is the Polish historian Dlugoss (i. 45) who, under the year 1056, speaks of Henry the Fourth as "a Roberto *Angliæ Rege* Româ pulsus"

[4] This seems to me quite plain from the account of Orderic (508 A), though he has placed it quite out of chronological order, at the very begin-

crossed the Hadriatic and besieged Dyrrhachion, the city whose later name had wiped out the memory of the more ancient Epidamnos.[1] Alexios came to its relief at the head of one of those gatherings of men of all races, tongues, and creeds, which were wont in those days to fight side by side around the eagles of the Eastern Rome With Greeks disguised under the name of Romans and Slaves disguised under the name of Macedonians,[2] came Mahometan Turks fighting in Europe for the throne which they threatened in Asia,[3] Paulician heretics whom persecution had changed from a religious sect into a warlike tribe,[4] and Franks, men of Latin speech and faith, fighting against men of their own tongue in the cause of the rival Church and Empire.[5] And

*CHAP XXI.*
*Robert invades the Empire and besieges Dyrrhachion June, 1081*
*Alexios comes to the relief of Dyrrhachion October, 1081.*
*His motley army*

... ning of William's reign The English exiles "militiæ Alexii Imperatoris Constantinopolitani sese audacter obtulerunt, . contra quem Rodbertus Wiscardus Apuliæ Dux cum suis omnibus arma levaverat Exsules igitur Anglorum favorabiliter a Græcis suscepti sunt, et Normannicis legionibus, quæ nimium Pelasgis adversabantur, oppositi sunt" Now the English exiles can no more have joined Alexios in 1067 than Ingulf (Gale, 74) can have been presented at his court at some time between 1051 and 1066 And Orderic gives so minute and accurate a description of the state of things that he can hardly have used the name of Alexios in mere carelessness Englishmen had doubtless been joining the Warangian force all along, but a special reinforcement went in 1081

[1] On the history of the name Dyrrhachion, see Mr E. B James in the Dictionary of Geography Both Anna and William of Apulia keep the correct form of the name—Anna indeed once (i 7) speaks of Epidamnos— but in Geoffrey Malaterra it has become Duracium, the modern Durazzo, a form which provoked a pun on the verb *durare* See Alberic, 1081

[2] Μακεδόνες and Θετταλοί appear in Anna, iv. 4 On their Slavonic descent, see Finlay, ii. 55

[3] Anna, iv. 4 οἱ περὶ τὴν Ἀχριδὼ οἰκοῦντες Τοῦρκοι

[4] The Μανιχαῖοι of Anna See Finlay, ii 79

[5] Anna, ii 3 τῶν Φραγγικῶν ταγμάτων ὁ Πανουκωμίτης καὶ Κωνσταντῖνος ὁ Οὐμπερτόπουλος, ἐκ γένους τὴν ἐπωνυμίαν λαχών. The French-speaking people are in Anna's style Φράγγοι, Κελτοί, Λατῖνοι, just as in Orderic and William of Apulia the Byzantines are Græci, Achivi, Danai, Pelasgi, Thraces, anything When we read such a sentence as ἐδίωκον οἱ Λατῖνοι τὸ Ῥωμαικὸν στράτευμα, we seem carried back to the days of the Decii or of the Tarquins

Constantine Humbertopoulos (Humbertidés or Humberting) is said

CHAP. XXI  
The English Warangians.

Their axes

Battle of Dyrrhachion October 18, 1081.
Defeat of Alexios

among this strange assemblage were men of whom we read with a thrill of mingled joy and sorrow that they were deemed the bravest and most faithful of all who were gathered under the banners of Augustus.[1] Byzantine and Norman accounts agree in setting before us the Warangians, the English, the Barbarians of the Isle of Thoulê, as the force in which, among all their varied bands, the Eastern Cæsars put their firmest trust.[2] Beneath the walls of Dyrrhachion, as on the height of Senlac, they bore the two-handed Danish axe, and at Dyrrhachion, no less than on Senlac, the Norman writers themselves bear witness to the terrible effect with which the Danish axe was wielded.[3] The battle was lost; the Cæsar of the East fled before the Norman invader,[4] as his momentary ally, the Cæsar of the West, was to do before many years had passed away.[5] But England at least lost no honour on that fatal day. For a while the Normans gave way before the Warangian charge. When a sudden flank attack threw the

to have been a discontented nephew of Robert Wiscard   See Finlay, ii. 72.

Somewhat later, about 1087, we find Flemish auxiliaries fighting for Alexios   See Anna, vii 7

[1] Gauf Mal iii. 27 (Muratori, v. 584) "Waringi, in quibus Imperatori maxima spes victoriæ fuerat."

[2] We appear in the actual description of the battle (Anna, iv. 6) as οἱ πεζῇ βαδίζοντες [cf our oldest character in Prokopios, Bell Goth iv 20] βάρβαροι, οἱ πελεκυφόροι   Elsewhere (ii 9) we are οἱ ἐκ τῆς Θούλης Βάραγγοι, οἱ πελεκυφόροι βάρβαροι   The commander of this contingent was Nabitês (vii 3, ὁ ἄρχων Βαραγγίας Ναμπίτης)   I wish I could identify him or his name   That this contingent was English seems plain from the mention of Thoulê, but Geoffrey Malaterra says still more directly (iii 27, p 584), "Angli quos Waringos appellant, ab Imperatore *primitias congressûs expetentes.*"

[3] Gauf. Mal u s "Angli . . . caudatis bipennibus, quibus hoc genus hominum potissimum utitur, infestissime instantes, nostris admodum importuni primo esse coeperunt." Cf vol. iii p. 474

[4] Anna describes her father's flight in iv 7. Even in flight however he did some prodigies of valour

[5] See vol i p 171   On the dealings of Alexios with the ῥὴξ 'Αλαμανίας 'Ενέριχος, see Anna, iii 10, v. 3

victorious and wearied English into confusion, the main body of the axemen died, like King Harold's Housecarls, around their standard [1] The remnant retreated and made a stand in and around the neighbouring church of Saint Michael, but the beloved Norman means of destruction was brought against them, and they died, as the Normans were said to have died at York,[2] crushed and scorched amid the ruins of the burning temple.[3] For others who had not joined in the march to Dyrrhachion, or who entered the service after the battle, Alexios began to build on the other side of the Propontis the city of Kibôtos, their ark of refuge, whose name on French-speaking lips was degraded into *Chevetot*.[4] But as the Normans, Robert himself and his son Bohemund, continued to harass the Empire, Alexios recalled the English to the Imperial city, and made them the special guards of his person and palace [5] They served in later stages of the war. Kastoria, besieged by Bohemund, was, after a gallant defence, surrendered to him by three hundred

*CHAP XXI*
Valour and slaughter of the English.

Alexios builds Kibôtos for the English

They become the Imperial bodyguard

Bohemund takes Kastoria. 1083.

[1] Anna, iv 6 ἐπεὶ δὲ οἱ πελεκυφόροι καὶ αὐτὸς ὁ τούτων ἀρχηγὸς ὁ Ναμπίτης δι' ἀπειρίαν καὶ θερμότητα ὀξύτερον βεβαδικότες [cf. vol iii pp 481, 489], ἱκανὸν τῆς Ῥωμαϊκῆς παρατάξεως ἀπέστησαν, σπεύδοντες συμβαλεῖν ἐν ἴσῳ θυμῷ τοῖς Κέλτοις (καὶ γὰρ οὐχ ἧττον ἐκείνων περὶ τὰς μαχὰς καὶ οὗτοι ἐκθυμότεροί εἰσιν καὶ τῶν Κελτῶν ἐν τούτῳ τῷ μέρει μὴ ἀποδέοντες) κεκοπιακότας τούτους ἤδη καὶ ἀσθμαίνοντας ὁ Ῥομπέρτος θεασάμενος, καὶ τοῦτο ἀπό τε τῆς ὀξείας κινήσεως τοῦ τε διαστήματος βεβαιωθεὶς καὶ τοῦ ἄχθους τῶν ὅπλων, τινὰς τῶν τούτου πεζῶν ἐπέσκηψε κατ' αὐτῶν εἰσπηδῆσαι οἱ δὲ προκεκμηκότες ἤδη μαλακώτεροι τῶν Κελτῶν ἐφαίνοντο πίπτει γοῦν τὸ τηνικαῦτα τὸ βάρβαρον ἅπαν [cf vol iii p 501]

[2] See above, p 269

[3] Anna, iv 6 οἱ Λατῖνοι πῦρ κατ' αὐτῶν ἀφέντες, σὺν τῷ τεμένει πάντας κατέκαυσαν The account in Geoffrey Malaterra (iii 27) is not quite the same, "Alii quantum capacitas permittebat subintrabant, alii tantâ multitudine tecta superscandunt ut pondere ipsa tecta dissoluta consubruantur, illos qui subintraverant opprimentes, conclusi pariter suffocarentur"

[4] Ord Vit 508 B "Augustus Alexius urbem quæ *Chevetot* dicitur Anglis ultra Byzantium cœpit condere"

[5] Ib. "Nimium infestantibus Normannis eos ad urbem regiam reduxit, et eisdem principale palatium cum regalibus thesauris tradidit"

CHAP. XXI.
His repulse 1084
Repulse of Brian of Britanny
Permanence of the Warangian guard
1204.

Warangians who guarded it;[1] and we can hardly deem that English warriors were absent when Bohemund himself was driven to retreat beyond the Hadriatic,[2] and when Brian, the same Brian of Britanny who had overcome the sons of Harold on their second raid in Devonshire, was compelled to surrender the city which Bohemund had won, and to withdraw his forces beyond the limits of the Empire.[3] The race of the English exiles flourished in the land of their adoption; their axes were again lifted against French-speaking foes when renegade Crusaders stormed and sacked the capital of Eastern Christendom; and, long after the days of Alexios Komnênos and of Alexios Mourtzouflos, they still formed the chosen body-guard of the Byzantine Emperors, and they still clave to the use of their Northern weapon and their Northern tongue.[4]

---

[1] Gauf. Mal. iii. 29 "Trecenti Waringi in eâdem urbe habitabant, custodes ab Imperatore deputati, quorum præsidio et opere non minimum defensabatur" See Anna, v 5, who does not mention the Warangians at Kastoria, Finlay, ii 97

[2] Anna, v 6, 7, Finlay, ii 99

[3] Anna, vi. 1, Finlay, ii 99 Mr Finlay identifies him with the Brian of whom we heard above, p 244 Anna (v 6) calls him Βρυέννιος, an easy source of confusion, but she adds, Λατῖνος δὲ οὗτος τῶν ἐπιφανῶν, ὃν καὶ κονοσταῦλον [Constable] ὠνόμασαν

[4] Ord. Vit 508 B. "Hâc itaque de caussâ Saxones Angli Ioniam expetierunt, et ipsi ac hæredes eorum sacro Imperio fideliter famulati sunt, et cum magno honore inter Thraces Cæsari et Senatui Populoque cari usque nunc perstiterunt" This passage is a good illustration of the use of the word Saxones as applied to Englishmen It is an ornamental archaism, a bit of the grand style, just like "Ionia" and "Thraces" and "Senatus Populusque"

Orderic carries our Warangians only to the reign of Kalo-Jôhannes. On their presence at the Crusading siege, see vol i p 577 As late as 1325 John Kantakouzênos (Hist 1. 41) speaks of οἱ τοὺς πελέκεις ἔχοντες Βάραγγοι προσαγορευόμενοι, and Gibbon (capp. liii lv., vol. x. pp 122, 213, Milman) quotes Kôdinos, whom I have not at hand, for the statement that, down to the very end of things, they spoke English—κατὰ τὴν πάτριον αὐτῶν γλῶσσαν, ἤγουν Ἰγκλινιστί We must remember that any distinctions between English and Danish would disappear in the latitude of Constan-

But, while Normans and Englishmen were thus striving together in distant lands, the rule of William in England was never seriously threatened. These later years of his life were years of comparative defeat and disgrace; but the ill successes of William were all undergone in other lands. The single Northumbrian outbreak hardly amounted to a rebellion, and a Scottish inroad, fearful as the scourge must have been to those who had already suffered so much, in noway endangered the safety of William's throne.

CHAP XXI
William's hold on England not weakened.

### § 2  *William's later Continental Wars* 1076—1086

The years immediately following the suppression of the revolt at Ely were years in which William was constantly passing to and fro between his insular and his continental dominions. He was ever and anon called back to England by some urgent political need, but at this time he made Normandy his chief dwelling-place, and Queen Matilda seems not to have left the country at all [1] But from this point the domestic events, and especially the domestic quarrels, in William's family begin to form an important part of our narrative  Of William's many sons and daughters not one obtained any grants of land in England.[2] Yet he made at least one grant to reward

William's movements between England and Normandy.

No grants made by William to his children.

---

tinople  Compare the mention of English as the tongue of Rolf Ganger See vol. 1 p 191.

[1] On William's movements in the years 1072-1076, see above, pp. 513, 543, 568.  There is no mention of Matilda accompanying him on any of his visits to England

[2] This remark is made by Sir H. Ellis, 1 321  It is also implied in Robert's discourse with his father in Orderic  This is a remarkable contrast to the accumulation of lands in the family of Godwine. The difference is that between a King and an Earl

634        THE LATER DAYS OF WILLIAM.

CHAP. XXI. service done to one of his daughters,[1] and his son William seems, characteristically enough, to have found a possession for himself by an act of sacrilegious spoliation.[2] William seemingly feared that his sons might become his rivals. He therefore gave them no political appanages, not even any landed estates. He wished to keep them in the state of dependent and, because dependent, dutiful children. They had no claim upon him for rewards; he had no need of them as instruments, he therefore systematically forbore to bestow on them any share of the wealth and power and official dignity which he bestowed on his friends and his brothers.

The first of the family of whom we now hear we hear of simply as vanishing from political and domestic life The vow which William made at the consecration of his wife's church, before he set forth on his great expedition,[3] was now fulfilled. In the year of the rebellion of the Earls William again kept the Easter Feast at Fécamp, and now his eldest daughter Cecily made her vows and received the habit of religion at the hands of her distant kinsman Archbishop John.[4] She passed her life in her mother's monastery, a pattern of virtue and learning, and of submission to the rule of her order. On the death of the first Abbess, Matilda, whose rule over the sisterhood was

Easter Feast at Fécamp April 5, 1075 Cecily takes the veil

---

[1] Domesday, 49 " Goisfridus Camerarius filiæ Regis    tenet de Rege pro servitio quod fecit Mathildi ejus filiæ "

[2] Ib. 77, of lands in Dorset, "W filius Regis tulit ab ecclesiâ sine consensu Episcopi et monachorum," that is the Bishop of Salisbury and the monks of Sherborne

[3] See vol III pp 383, 395

[4] Ord Vit 548 B   " Anno ab Incarnatione Domini MLXXV indictione xiii Guillelmus Rex Fiscanni sanctum Pascha celebravit, Cæciliamque filiam suam per manum Johannis Archiepiscopi Deo consecrandam obtulit " In Will Gem VII 26 we read, "Ibi [at Caen] Cæcilia virgo filia ejus Deo consecrata est et in servitio Dei diu commorata est " This probably refers to the ceremony in 1066, it seems impossible to set aside so distinct a statement as that of Orderic

prolonged for forty-seven years, Cecily succeeded to her office, and held it with honour till her own death fourteen years later.[1]

*CHAP. XXI.*
*Cecily Abbess 1113-1127.*

The next daughter of William of whom we hear was destined to a widely different fate from that of her eldest sister. While Cecily studied and prayed, served and ruled, in her monastery, Constance earned a fame no less pure by living an useful and honourable life in the rank in which she was born. Her first mention connects itself with the very beginning of William's later and darker days. After the beheading of Waltheof William again crossed the sea to Normandy, and we presently hear of him as besieging the Breton city of Dol.[2] He had been seen under its walls in earlier times; but then he had come as a deliverer, and Harold had come as his fellow-soldier. The warfare of William alone was less lucky than the warfare of William and Harold together. At the earlier time he came successfully to relieve Dol when besieged by the Breton Count. It was now the Breton Count whose forces came successfully to relieve Dol when besieged by William.

*Constance, wife of Alan of Britanny, betrothed 1076? married 1086, died 1090.*

*William besieges Dol. 1076.*

The motives of William for attacking the city which now was visited by its almost only gleam of good luck are not very clear. Our chief informant makes it a simple aggression on the part of William. He wished to extend his power, and to win back the rights over Britanny which had belonged to the Dukes of the Normans who had reigned before him.[3] It is possible that some of the rights which

*His motives.*

---

[1] Ord. Vit. 548 C. See also Will. Gem. viii. 34; Will. Malm. iii. 276, "Cæcilia, Cadomensis Abbatissa, *vivit*," R. Wend. ii. 26, Neustria Pia, 662, Mrs. Green, Princesses, i. 10.

[2] The siege of Dol appears in both Chronicles (Wig. 1077, Petrib. 1076), and Florence (1075), "And Wyllelm cynge for ofer sæ, and lædde fyrde to Brytlande and besæt þone castel æt Dol." Orderic (544 B) is fuller

[3] Ord. Vit. 544 B. "Guillelmus Rex, cupiens fines suos dilatare, sibique Britones, ut sibi obsecundarent, sicut olim Rolloni et Willermo aliisque Ducibus Normannicis servierant, volens subjugare, cum ingenti exercitu Dolense

CHAP. XXI.
Disputes as to the Bishoprick of Dol.
Letter of Gregory to William September 27, 1076.

William sought to regain were of an ecclesiastical kind. It is certain that about this time he received a letter from Pope Gregory, charging him to do nothing on behalf of Juhel, Bishop of Dol, who had been deposed by his authority. Another Bishop, Ivo, had been consecrated to the see by the Pope's own hands.[1] This certainly looks as if the Bishoprick of Dol, like the Primacy of Rheims at an earlier time,[2] had become an object to be fought for with temporal weapons. A still more obvious motive is suggested, if we could believe the statement of one of our own writers that Dol was at this time a possession or shelter of the fugitive Earl Ralph.[3] Nothing would be more natural than a campaign undertaken in the hope of seizing the fugitive, or at least of chastising the city and the land where he had taken refuge. However this may be, William besieged Dol with a great host, and pitched his camp, full of all the splendours of his wealth, beneath the walls of the city. The defenders of Dol trembled at his threats, and at the oath which he swore not to go away unless as a conqueror.[4] But the conscience of William had now, like the consciences of Harold and Waltheof, to bear the burthen of an unfulfilled oath. William went away from Dol, and he did not go away

Possible presence of Ralph of Wader at Dol

William besieges the town;

his threats

---

oppidum obsedit." William of Malmesbury (iii 258) confesses his ignorance of the cause, "Dum nescio quâ simultate irritatus manum illuc militarem duxisset"

[1] See Gregory's Letter of September 27, 1076 (Jaffe, Mon Greg 541). Juhel had been deposed for simony, marriage, and portioning his daughters, like Ealdhun (see vol i p 358), with episcopal lands. William is exhorted " ne       tam scelesto homini .   ulterius auxilium præbeas neve scelerum ejus te participem facias';" but we are not told exactly what he had done.

[2] See vol 1 pp 220, 230.

[3] Flor Wig 1075 " Post hæc mare transito Rex in minorem Brytanniam suam movit expeditionem, et *castellum Radulfi Comitis*, quod Dol nominatur, obsedit." But I know of nothing elsewhere to connect Dol with Ralph

[4] Ord Vit. 544 B. "Nec se inde discessurum, nisi munitionem obtineret, cum juramento asseruit"

as a conqueror. It was there indeed that he met his first defeat. Alan Fergant, son of the reigning Count Howel,[1] came to the relief of the besieged city, and with his forces were joined the forces of the common overlord of William and Alan. King Philip of France, now the firm ally of Robert of Flanders,[2] came to wage war on the island King who, on Gaulish ground, was still his man. The Bretons stood their ground manfully till the royal forces came.[3] William was then driven to retreat, if not to flight, by the united forces of King and Count. He left behind him men and horses and countless treasures, tents with rich furniture, vessels, arms, spoils of all kinds, to the value, men said, of fifteen thousand pounds.[4] At Crowland it was doubtless whispered with bated breath that the vengeance for the blood of Waltheof had begun.

But with William a new position had only the effect of enabling him to show his genius on a new field. His first defeat gave him his first opportunity of improving a defeat. Attacked on so many sides, it was his policy to disarm his enemies, and he began by disarming the enemy who was least powerful and most isolated. Alan was won over by the same arts which had been successfully practised on Eadwine. Peace was made; by one of its terms the hand of William's daughter Constance was promised to the son of the Breton Count; but the actual marriage was not

---

[1] Orderic (544 B) describes the relief brought by Alan, calling him "Comes Britanniæ," which he was not till 1083. See Appendix RR.

[2] See above, p 538.

[3] Chron Wig 1077, Petrib 1076 "Þa Bryttas hine heoldon þæt se cyng com of Francland" [" Francrice," Wig ] So Florence, 1075 Orderic and William of Malmesbury (iii 258) do not bring Philip to Dol.

[4] Chron Wig 1077, Petrib 1076 "And Willelm þanon for, and þær forleas ægðer ge men ge hors, and feola his [unarimede, Wig] gersuma" The details are from Orderic, who describes William as "territus," and adds, " pacem iniit, et confestim non sine magno rerum damno recessit " Florence speaks out more boldly, " Tamdiu obsedit, donec Francorum Rex Philippus illum inde fugaret."

638                THE LATER DAYS OF WILLIAM.

CHAP XXI celebrated till ten years later.¹ To keep a dangerous neighbour in this way dependent on him was a game which exactly suited William's policy; but it was a game which it was not safe for William himself to carry too far.

Peace with France 1077

In the course of the next year William also made peace with the King of the French; but the English Chronicler significantly remarks that the peace held but a little while.² For about this time the good faith of Philip was exposed to a temptation which seems to have been too powerful to be withstood. William was now beginning to find his foes in his own household  The curse of his later years was the disobedience and open rebellion of his eldest son Robert. The young man had some showy qualities which won him, if not friends, at least partizans. He was a daring soldier, a skilful archer, open of hand, bold and free of speech. But the personal portrait of him is not attractive. Short and fat, with a heavy face, the eldest-born of the Conqueror was known by the nick-names of *Gambaron* and *Curt-hose*.³ Of the higher qualities of his father, of his genius for war and government, he had not a trace.

Character of William's eldest son Robert

Robert declared William's successor in Normandy Before 1066

In his first quarrel with his father Robert was not without a plausible grievance. At some time before the invasion of England, and again during an attack of sickness at some later time, William had declared Robert his successor in the Norman Duchy, and had made his chief vassals do

---

¹ See below, p 650, and Appendix RR

² Chron Petrib 1077  " Her on þisum geare wurdon sæhte Franca cyng and Willelm Englalandes cyng, *ac hit heold litle hwile* "

³ Ord. Vit 545 C  " Erat loquax et prodigus, audax et in armis probissimus, fortis certusque sagittarius, voce clara et libera, lingua diserta, facie obesa, corpore pingui brevique statura, unde vulgo *Gambaron* cognominatus est et Brevis-ocrea "  This last name was given him by his father (664 C). *Gambaron* is explained (Roquefort, Glossaire de la Langue Romane), " Jambe courte, sobriquet donné a Robert, Duc de Normandie, parce qu'il avoit de grosses jambes sans mollets, et toutes rondes "

homage and swear fealty to him. One or other of these two settlements had been further confirmed by the King of the French as Overlord.[1] In both the settlements of Maine also it was rather to Robert than to William himself that the County was made over. At the conclusion of the last treaty with Fulk of Anjou, Robert had actually done homage for Maine, as for his own possession.[2] William however seems to have looked upon both these acts as mere securities for Robert's final succession, and he had not the faintest intention of giving up any part of his dominions during his life-time. He no doubt thought that he had done quite enough for his son when he joined him with his mother in the regency of Normandy during his absence.[3] We may further believe that William, though he might not be prepared to go the length of disinheriting his eldest son, did not wish so ill to his subjects as to give them Robert for their ruler before his time. Robert however took a different view of matters. He was stirred up by his own ambition and by the suggestions of evil companions to call on his father for an immediate provision.[4]

*CHAP. XXI.*

*Maine twice settled on Robert 1063, 1073.*

*Robert demands an immediate provision*

---

[1] Ord Vit 545 C "Guillelmus Princeps ante Senlaicum bellum, et post in quâdam suâ ægritudine, Robertum primogenitam sobolem suam fecerat suum hæredem, et jussit omnes optimates ei facere homagium et fidelitatem At illi gratanter imperante adquieverunt" The sickness of William here spoken of took place at Lillebonne (573 B), but the date is not given No one puts forth the grant so strongly as our own Worcester Chroniclei in his very last entry (1079), from which we also get the confirmation by King Philip Robert revolted "forþan þe his fæder ne wolde him lætan waldan his eorldomes on Normandige, þe he sylf and eac se kyng Filippus mid his geþafunge him gegyfen hæfdon, and þa þe betst wæron on þam lande hæfdon aðas him gesworon and hine to hlaforde genumen" He is abridged by Florence, 1077

[2] See above, p 563, and vol iii p 199

[3] See above, p 123

[4] I have here to put together two accounts in different parts of Orderic, in the fourth book and in the fifth (pp 545, 569). Both evidently refer to the same time, but it seems hopeless to fix the exact date Our one landmark is that the battle of Gerberoi is fixed by both Chronicles and Florence to the year 1079 Orderic (570 C) talks of Robert wandering

We hear of the abject state of dependence and poverty in which his father kept him, a reference we may suppose to the fact which has been already mentioned, that he had received no share whatever in the spoils of England.[1] His comrades exhorted him to demand a share of the Kingdom of England, or at all events the possession of Normandy and Maine. They reminded him of the promise of such a grant which his father had made long ago.[2] A dialogue is attributed to William and Robert, in which, among the conventional scriptural and classical allusions, some sayings highly characteristic of the Conqueror seem to be preserved. Robert asks for Normandy, which he says that his father had granted to him before the invasion of England. William answers that the request is inconsistent; Normandy is his hereditary possession, which he will not give up while he lives; England he holds through the strength of Normandy.[3] Robert has nothing to answer, except to ask what he is to do, and how he is to find the means to give anything to his followers.[4] "Be

*Dispute between William and Robert*

in various parts of the world for about five years, which would seem to fix the date of his first rebellion to about the year 1074 But in the story of the quarrel between the brothers at L'Aigle William and Henry are spoken of as "milites" But in 1074 Henry, the only one of William's children whose birth we can fix exactly, was only six years old, and he was not "dubbed to rider" till 1086 (See below, p 694) Florence again distinctly places the beginning of the rebellion in 1077, and this date has the force of a correction, for Florence is here following the Worcester Chronicle, which places the rebellion and the battle of Gerberoi in 1079. I think then that we may take 1077 as the probable date for the beginning of the quarrel between Robert and his father

[1] See Ord Vit 545 C, 569 C. "In ingenti paupere degis," say Robert's companions, and they go on at some length in the same strain

[2] Ord Vit. 545 C "Debitos honores, principatum videlicet Cænomannorum et Neustriæ" 569 C "Partem regni Albionis, aut saltem ducatum Normanniæ"

[3] Ib 569 D. "Incongruum est, fili, quod poscis Per virtutem Normannicam obtinui Angliam. Hereditario jure possideo Normanniam, ipsamque de manu meâ dum advixero non ejiciam."

[4] Ib "Quid meis clientibus tribuam?"

obedient to me in all things," answers William, "and share my dominions everywhere with me." Robert says that he will not be for ever his father's hireling, he wants something of his own that he may pay his own servants. To that end he asks for nothing short of the Duchy of Normandy. William reminds him of the duties of sons towards their fathers, and gives him a lecture on Rehoboam and the evil of listening to young and foolish counsellors. He would do better to consult wise men, experienced nobles, or learned scholars like the two Archbishops, Lanfranc at Canterbury and William at Rouen.[1] "My lord the King," says Robert, "I did not come here to hear sermons, of which my tutors gave me more than enough when I was learning grammar."[2] Will his father give him what he asks for, or not? He has made up his mind that he will not stay any longer in Normandy as his servant. William again answers that he will not give up his native Duchy of Normandy, that he will not give up the Kingdom of England which he has won with such toil. God had given him the Kingdom and God might perhaps take it away from him, but he himself would give it up to no man. He seems even to have pleaded a religious scruple; he had been crowned and anointed King, and he could not give up the Crown which the ministers of Christ had placed upon his head.[3] His purpose was fixed; while he lived, he

*William refuses to give up anything while he lives*

---

[1] Ord. Vit. 570 A. "A Guillelmo et Lanfranco Archiepiscopis, et aliis sophistis maturisque proceribus inquire consilium". The mention of Archbishop William shows that the dialogue is supposed to be held at some time after 1077, but if we are to admit a wandering of five years, or even of one year, this date is impossible

[2] Ib A, B. "Huc, Domine mi Rex, non accessi pro sermonibus audiendis, quorum copiâ frequenter usque ad nauseam imbutus sum a grammaticis"

[3] Ib B "Capiti meo a vicariis Christi sacrum diadema celebre impositum est, et regale sceptrum Albionis ferre mihi soli commissum est Indecens igitur est, et omnino injustum, ut quamdiu vitalibus auris perfruar, parem mihi vel majorem in ditione meâ quempiam patiar"

would not endure any one as his superior or his equal in any part of his dominions.

*Robert leaves Normandy.*

Robert, we are told, went away likening himself to Polyneikês, and hoping that he might somewhere find his Adrastos.[1] It would seem however that he did not at once plunge into open rebellion. But bitter wrath grew between father and son, and a trifling accident soon fanned Robert's discontent into a flame. William was now at war with Rotrou, Count of Mortagne in Perche, that border land, the nursery of the house of Belesme,[2] which formed part of the Norman diocese of Seez, but which owned the temporal superiority of France.[3] Rotrou bore a bad character as a plunderer of the church of Chartres, and was divinely smitten for his crime.[4] William, accompanied by his three sons, had marched as far as L'Aigle in the diocese of Evreux, not far from Ouche on the one hand and Verneuil on the other. This was the lordship of Richer, whose father Eginulf had died in the *Malfosse* of Senlac.[5] The King and his two younger and more dutiful sons,[6] William and Henry, were quartered in one house; Robert lodged in another. The two lads came to their elder brother's quarters, and began to play at dice in the solar or upper room, to make a great noise, and at last to throw water on Robert and his companions who were below. Robert, stirred up by two of the party, Ivo and Alberic of Grant-

*War between William and Rotrou of Mortagne 1077?[2]*

*Quarrel between Robert and his brothers at L'Aigle.*

---

[1] Ord Vit 570 C.

[2] This seems to follow from the words of Orderic (546 B), that William "cum Rotrone Mauritaniensi Comite pacem fecit" (see below, p 644), which imply an earlier state of war    [3] See vol ii p 183.

[4] Ord Vit 546 B "Animadversione divinâ obsurduit, et sic ad mortem usque surdus permansit"

[5] See vol iii p 504

[6] Ord Vit. 545 D "Guillelmus Rufus et Henricus patri favebant, viresque suas fraternis viribus æquas arbitrantes, indignum ducebant quod frater eorum solus habere patrium jus ambiebat, et agmine clientum sibi obsequente par patri æstimari peroptabat" Directly after, their playing at dice is said to be "sicut militibus moris est"    But see above, p 640.

mesnil, the sons of the Sheriff of Leicestershire,[1] rushed upstairs to avenge the insult. The King smoothed down matters for the moment, but in the night Robert decamped with his comrades, and made an attempt to seize the ducal castle at Rouen. But he was baffled by the faithfulness of its commander, the King's cup-bearer, Roger of Ivry, whom we have already heard of in England.[2] Robert was now at the head of a band of exiles, numbering among them several men of the noblest houses in Normandy. Among them we find the sons of the two great Earls of the Welsh border, William of Breteuil, the son of the fallen Earl of Hereford, moved perhaps by wrath at the bonds of his brother, and Robert of Belesme, the son of Earl Roger of Shrewsbury and of the cruel Mabel, the man who was so faithfully to reproduce the crimes of his mother and his mother's house. With these we find the son of another famous man, Ralph of Conches or Toesny,[3] the son of the elder Ralph, renowned at Mortemer and at Senlac. These and others of the young nobles of Normandy took up the cause of Robert, and forsook their solid possessions for the vain hopes he held out to them.[4] William seized their lands, and with his usual grim pleasantry, employed their revenues in hiring mercenaries to fight against them.[5]

Robert and his companions soon found protectors. Hugh of Neufchâtel, lord of the border-castles of Neufchâtel, Sorel, and Raimalast, was the husband of the younger Mabel, the sister of Robert of Belesme. He received the

*CHAP XXI.*

*Robert's attempts on Rouen defeated by Roger of Ivry.*

*Robert's companions*

*Robert helped by Hugh of Neufchâtel,*

---

[1] See above, p 232
[2] See above, p 46
[3] On the younger Ralph, see above, p 605
[4] Ord Vit 546 B "Oppida divitesque fundos pro inani spe et promissis floccipendendis reliquerunt" A longer list of Robert's companions is given in 570 C One is "Rodbertus de Molbraio," seemingly the future Earl of Northumberland
[5] Ib "Rex . de reddituibus eorum stipendarios dimicantes contra eosdem remuneravit"

CHAP. XXI.
and by King Philip.

Siege and capture of Raimalast.

Robert's wanderings.

exiles, and his castles became their head-quarters for ravaging Normandy.[1] And it would seem that Robert was already beginning to receive direct encouragement from the common Overlord of all, King Philip at Paris. An officer of the King's court, his *dapifer* Aimeric, was present in Hugh's castle of Raimalast. That castle was now besieged by William in company with an unexpected ally. The fief of Raimalast owned Rotrou of Mortagne as its immediate lord; William made peace with him, took him into his pay, and led him with him to attack the fortress of his vassal.[2] One day Hugh and his French ally ventured with three knights without the walls of the castle. Four knights of the King's set upon them, and presently the body of Hugh was carried off, and laid on a horse, as the historian says, like a hog.[3] Gulfer the son of Hugh at once made peace and submitted to William.

The fall of his immediate protector seems for a while to have checked the hopes of Robert. He wandered through various lands, betaking himself to the court of his uncle in Flanders, and to other princes and nobles of Lotharingia, Swabia, Aquitaine, and Gascony, among whom Udo Archbishop of Trier is specially mentioned.[4] Many of the princes whom he visited gave him large sums of money,

---

[1] Ord. Vit. 546 A. "Hugo ... municipia sua pro depopulandâ Neustriâ patefecit."

[2] Ib. B. "Rex Guillelmus hunc pretio conduxit, secumque ad obsidionem, quia Raimalast de feudo ejus erat, minavit."

[3] I accept Mr. Thorpe's explanation (Lappenberg's Anglo-Norman Kings, 176) of the text of Orderic. The words used with regard to Hugh of Neufchâtel should be noticed, "Cadaver infausti prædonis, velut occisum suem, super equum sustulerunt, et delatum ante mapalia Rogerii Comitis, contra quem diu hostiliter sævierat, projecerunt." Hugh was therefore at variance with his father-in-law.

[4] Orderic (570 D) calls both Count Robert and Archbishop Udo the "avunculi" of Robert. See vol. iii. p. 657. The Worcester Chronicler (1079) mentions the visit to Flanders, "Her Rodbert þæs cynges sunu Willelmes hleop fram his fæder to his eame Rotbryhte on Flandron, forþan þe his fæder ne wolde him lætan waldan his eorldomes on Normandige."

but all that he got he squandered on his worthless companions of both sexes. He remained as poor as ever, and plunged into debt to supply his needs.[1] Two sons however were born to him in the course of his wanderings, of one of them, Richard, I have already spoken as one of those among William's offspring who met their doom amid the haunted shades of the New Forest.[2]

Robert however had still one friend in his own country and in his father's house. He was the darling son of his mother, and now the doom of sorrow which brooded over William's house took a new form, by stirring up the first strife between William and his Queen. Matilda, without her husband's knowledge, sent large sums of gold and silver and other precious things to her banished son. William heard of it, and sternly forbade her. But the tenderness of the mother prevailed over the duty of the wife, and Matilda again sent her gifts to Robert. William again rebuked her. She, his companion whom he loved as his own soul, was spending his wealth on his enemies who sought his life, and was arming and strengthening them against him.[3] Matilda could only plead the love which she bore to one who is as usual mistaken for her first-born son.[4] If Robert were dead and lying buried seven feet deep below the earth, she would gladly shed her blood to bring him to life again. How could she enjoy wealth while her son was lacking all things? Such hardness was far from her heart, and she dared to add that her husband ought not to lay such commands upon her.[5]

The wrath of William was kindled,[6] but the constant

[1] See the graphic description in Orderic, 570 D  [2] See above, p 614
[3] Ord Vit 571 A "Collateralis mea, quam velut animam meam diligo, quam omnibus gazis et potestatibus in toto præfeci regno meo"
[4] Ib  She is made to call him "primogenitam progeniem meam"
[5] Ib B  "Nec vestra debet hoc mihi jubere potentia" The whole speech, whether genuine or not, is well conceived
[6] Ib. "His auditis Rex ferus expalluit, et in tantum ira ejus efferbuit," &c

CHAP XXI.
William threatens Matilda's messenger

love of so many years pleaded for his disobedient wife. But towards her agent he felt no scruples. One Samson, a Breton, had carried messages and gifts from Matilda to her son. William gave orders to seize and blind him. But the Queen's friends warned him of his danger; he fled to the house of Saint Evroul, where Abbot Mainer sheltered him, and where he put on the monastic garb for the salvation alike of soul and body.[1]

Philip takes Robert's part
Robert at Gerberoi.
1079

The quarrel between William and his son was soon to come to a crisis. Robert now came, doubtless not for the first time, to the King of the French, and craved for some effectual help. Philip accordingly quartered him in the castle of Gerberoi[2] in the district of Beauvais, near the borders of Normandy and France. The fortress was strong, both by its position and by its artificial defences. Our historian adds that it was always held by two lords of equal right, and that it was the custom of the place to welcome all exiles and fugitives, whencesoever they might come. Robert was welcomed by the two commanders, one of them nameless, the other the *Vidame* Helias, a different person doubtless from the famous Helias of La Flèche.[3] They acted zealously on Robert's behalf; mercenary soldiers crowded to Gerberoi from all quarters; men of higher rank from various parts of Gaul were drawn by the vain promises of Robert; even many men from Normandy itself, including some who

[1] Ord. Vit 571 B "Monachicum schema pro salvatione corporis et animæ salubriter indutus est" This Samson, "Reginæ veredarius," can hardly be the same person as the Samson who in Orderic (531) recommends Howel for the see of Le Mans, which did not become vacant till 1085

[2] "Gerberracum" in Orderic, "Gibboracum" in William of Malmesbury, "Gerborneð" in the Peterborough Chronicle, "Gerbotbret" in Florence. "Gerberoi" is the present name

[3] Ord Vit. 572. "Helias Vicedominus cum compari suo exsulem gratanter regium suscepit, illique suisque complicibus auxilium in omnibus spopondit Moris enim est illius castri ut ibidem duo pares domini sint, et omnes ibidem fugitivi suscipiantur, undecumque advenerint"

had hitherto borne a good character for loyalty, joined their fortunes with those of the exiles. Such a state of things in a fortress so near his border called for William's personal energy to put an end to it.[1] He accordingly gathered his forces, garrisoned the border fortresses of Normandy, and took means to keep the plunderers from Gerberoi in check. At last, when the Christmas Feast was over, William, to whom all seasons were alike when there was work to be done, set forth to besiege the castle in person. His force, English, Norman, and mercenary, had many skirmishes with the defenders of the fortress. Among those defenders, Robert's French allies are especially mentioned;[2] yet there is an extant charter from which it would seem, if words have any meaning, that King Philip himself, by whose authority Robert was quartered at Gerberoi, was personally present in the camp of the besiegers.[3] The policy of Philip was never very steadfast, but such a sudden change as this almost passes the bounds of belief. It is more certain that in this siege one specially memorable personal encounter took place. William, who had passed unhurt through the nine hours' storm of the great battle,[4] who, as far as we know, had never received a wound in any earlier or later fight, had now, for the first time, to turn his back on an enemy

CHAP. XXI

William begins the campaign.

William besieges Gerberoi. January, 1080.

Question of Philip's presence

William's first wound.

---

[1] Ord. Vit. 572 C. "Quod tam prope limitem suum hostes sui sedem sibi elegerant indignum duxit, nec sine terribili calumniâ diutius pertulit"

[2] Ib C, D "Hinc Normanni et Angli reguique auxiliares de finitimis regionibus acriter insistebant, illinc Galli et vicini hostes Roberto cohærentes fortiter resistebant."

[3] The document is a charter of Saint Quentin, printed in Bouquet, xii 604, Gallia Christiana, x, Instrumenta, 247, see also Prevost's edition of Orderic, ii 387 It bears the signatures of the Kings Philip and William, and is dated, "Actum publice in obsidione prædictorum Regum videlicet Philippi Regis Francorum et Willelmi Anglorum Regis, prope Gerberodum, anno Incarnati Verbi MLXXVIII anno vero Philippi Regis Francorum XIX" Compare the mention of Philip's ambassadors in p 649

[4] See vol iii p 508

in personal conflict, and to retreat, defeated and wounded, in a struggle beneath the walls of a paltry border fortress. And William's first wound came from the hand from which a wound is most bitter. Father and son met face to face in the battle  The parricidal spear of Robert pierced the hand of his father; an arrow at the same moment struck the horse on which he rode, and William the Conqueror lay for a moment on the earth, expecting death at the hands of his own son. A loyal Englishman sped to his rescue—a survivor of Senlac or Ely might well have fought for William in such a quarrel. Tokig, the son of Wigod of Wallingford, fighting on horseback in Norman fashion, sprang down and offered his horse, like Eustace at Senlac, to the fallen King. At that moment the shot of a crossbow gave the gallant Thegn of Berkshire a mortal wound, and Tokig gave up his life for his sovereign beneath the walls of Gerberoi, to the increase of the estates of his Norman brothers-in-law at Wallingford and Oxford. In this fierce exchange of handstrokes the younger William, the dutiful son, the future tyrant, was also wounded in the defence of his father. With difficulty the King and his sons retreated—an English writer ventures to say that they fled—before the face of the victorious rebel, leaving many of their followers dead on the field, and many prisoners in the hands of Robert.[1]

It is hard to conceive a blow more grievous than this. The King, the captain, the father, were all alike cut to the quick. Before Dol William had first learned what it was to flee before an enemy; at Gerberoi he underwent the most humiliating personal overthrow, and that at the hands of his own subjects and his own son. It is plain that the siege of Gerberoi was raised, and that the defeat was a real and serious blow; for directly afterwards we

[1] On the different accounts of this battle, see Appendix SS  On Tokig and his family, see above, p 45, and Appendix G

find William back again at Rouen, and the wisest heads of Normandy are soon debating, not how they might carry on the war, but how they might make peace between the King and his son.[1] Robert himself, in the moment of victory, went off again to Flanders.[2] He was not incapable of generous feeling, and he may have been struck with remorse for his crime. Or perhaps the men who flocked to Gerberoi on the faith of his empty promises may have begun to forsake him. At any rate we next find some of the chief men of Normandy, among them the old Roger of Beaumont, Roger Earl of Shrewsbury, and Hugh of Giantmesnil, whose sons had been the original authors of the mischief, pleading with William on behalf of his son. They admit his crime, but they set forth his youth and his penitence; they pray William not to thrust away the returning suppliant, and they venture also to plead for their own sons and other kinsmen who were involved in Robert's rebellion.[3] William at first was stern; he set forth his own wrongs as prince and father, wrongs such as no Duke of the Normans had ever undergone before. He complained especially of Robert's crime in stirring up foreign enemies against him.[4] At last however the constant entreaties of his nobles, the exhortations of his Bishops and other pious men, the entreaties of the Queen, the mediation of the Ambassadors of the King of the French and of other neighbouring princes,[5] at last moved

*The nobles of Normandy plead for Robert.*

*William reconciled to his son.*

[1] Ord. Vit. 572 D.

[2] Chron. Wig. 1079. "And Robert eft gewende to Fleminga lande." This is the last entry in this Chronicle. A sentence following it, expressing indignant weariness at Robert's conduct, is broken off, "Ne wylle we þeh her na mâre scaðe awritan þe he his fæder ge    ." The Peterborough writer is henceforward our only guide in our own tongue.

[3] Ord. Vit. 572 D, 573 A. Robert's penitence is strongly asserted.

[4] Ib. 573 A. "Gallos et Andegavenses cum Aquitanis et innumeris aliis in me terribiliter excivit. Omne genus humanum, si potuisset, contra me commovisset, et me vobiscum trucidâsset."

[5] Ib. B. "Legati Regis Francorum nobilesque vicini et amici." The last can hardly mean William's own subjects.

William's stern heart. He yielded, and received his son and his companions. The succession to the Duchy was secured to Robert on the same terms as before,[1] and a short time of peace followed. During this interval Pope Gregory addressed a letter to Robert, rejoicing that he had come to a better mind, and enlarging on his special duty to a father who had won so much for his heirs to inherit[2] It must also have been during this short time of reconciliation that Robert was sent on an expedition against Malcolm of Scotland, of which we shall hear presently, and in which he did not, to say the least, gain any special glory.[3] It was perhaps partly owing to William's disappointment at this further ill success that disputes again broke out between father and son. Robert refused to follow his father or to obey him in anything. Fierce remonstrances and reproaches on William's part followed, and Robert again went away into France with a small body of companions.[4]

From the rebellion of William's son we may turn to the marriages of his daughters. Constance, betrothed to Alan of Biitanny soon after the flight of William from

---

[1] Ord Vit 573 B See above, p 638

[2] Epp Greg VII ap Labbe, Conc. xii. 520, Jaffé, Mon. Greg. 420. "Insuper monemus et paterne precamur ut menti tuæ semper sit infixum quam forti manu, quam divulgatâ gloriâ, quidquid pater tuus possideat ab ore inimicorum extraxerit [this was true of Normandy, no less than of England], sciens tamen se non in perpetuum vivere, sed ad hoc tam viriliter insistere ut *hæredi alicui* [a discreetly vague phrase] sua dimitteret" Hubert was of course the letter-carrier between Gregory and Robert

[3] See the next Section

[4] Ord Vit 573 B "Denuo post aliquod tempus, paucis sodalibus fretus, a patre recessit, nec postea rediit, donec patei *rediens* Albericum Comitem, ut ducatum Neustriæ reciperet, in Galliam ad eum direxit" I do not understand this last allusion I suppose the Earl Alberic spoken of is the same whom we shall presently meet with in Northumberland, but I can make out nothing of this mission to Robert If for "rediens" we might read "moriens," the passage would be intelligible

Dol, appears several years later in attendance upon her mother.[1] In the end however she became Countess of the Bretons, though she did not long survive her marriage[2] Some accounts make her a model of every virtue; others hint that she, or her husband under her influence, pushed a rigid justice to such extremes that the angry people of Britanny conspired and took her off by poison.[3] She died childless, and Alan married Hermengarde, the daughter of Fulk of Anjou and the divorced wife of William the Ninth of Aquitaine.[4] Conan the son of Alan and Hermengarde renewed the connexion with William's house by a marriage with a natural daughter of Henry the First, and some generations later, through the chances of female succession, the County of Britanny became the heritage of the son of another Constance, that unhappy Arthur who has been so often mistaken for the lawful heir of England.[5]

*Her character and death 1090*

*Descendants of Alan.*

---

[1] Orderic (603 A) mentions a visit of Queen Matilda, accompanied by her daughter Constance, to the monastery of Saint Evroul. This was immediately after the granting of a charter to the house by William, which bears date in 1081

[2] On the dates, see Appendix RR

[3] Will Malm iii 276 "Constantia, Comiti Brittanniæ Alano Fergant in conjugium data, austeritate justitiæ provinciales in mortiferam sibi potionem exacuit" This is really in no way inconsistent with the account of Orderic (544 C), "Amatores æquitatis in Britannia multum exsultarent, si de fortunatâ progenie laudabiles sibi heredes impetrarent, qui genuinâ bonitate indomitis Britonibus justitiæ libram insinuarent, eosque secundum normam divinæ legis et humanæ rationis ire cogerent" An over strict justice like that of Tostig is quite consistent with the piety, charity, and zeal of the public good of which he goes on to speak. Benoît (42111) tells us,

"Mult par ert sage e afaitée
E proz e large e enseigniée"

And directly after,

"Kar trop ert bele, sage e proz"

The continuator of William of Jumièges (viii 34) records her marriage an death without giving her any character

[4] Ord Vit 544 C, Benoit, 42121.

[5] See vol 1 p 116

*CHAP. XXI.*

*Marriage of Adela with Stephen of Chartres 1080*

Another daughter, Adela, fills a higher place in history. She became the wife of Stephen Count of Blois and Chartres, the son of the third Theobald. By him she was the mother of Stephen King of the English, and of another son of higher personal renown, Henry, the famous Bishop of Winchester, the friend of Thomas of London, the founder of the Hospital of Saint Cross and of the Lady Chapel at Glastonbury.[1] As the wife of Count Stephen, Adela holds perhaps the highest place among the princesses of her generation.[2]

*Story of Simon of Valois 1074-1082*

As the daughter of William, she perhaps concerns us more as being most probably the subject of a romantic tale which introduces us to the highly remarkable son of a somewhat insignificant father. Ralph of Montdidier and of Valois, the stepfather, but not the friend, of King Philip,[3] was succeeded by Simon, his son by an earlier wife, Adela.[4] He, we are told, had been brought up at the court of William,[5] and he inherited from his father a state of war with his neighbour and lord the King of the French. He was a devout man, who consulted Pope Gregory in all his doings, and whom the Pontiff entrusted to the special care of Hugh Bishop of

---

[1] See Willis, Glastonbury

[2] Will Malm. ii 276 "Adala, Stephani Blesensis Comitis uxor, laudatæ in sæculo potentiæ virago, noviter apud Marcenniacum sanctimonialis habitum sumpsit." She died in 1137, having lived to see her son a King. For a full picture of her life and character—in every way admirable—and for her correspondence with Saint Anselm and Hildebert Bishop of Le Mans, I must refer to her Life by Mrs. Green

[3] See above, p 90

[4] See Art de Verifier les Dates, ii 703. The death of Ralph and succession of Simon in 1074 is recorded by Hugh of Fleury (Pertz, ix 390). There is a contemporary Life of Simon in Mabillon, Act Sanct Ord S Ben Sæc. vi. part 2 (vol viii.) p 374, Bouquet, xiv 37, from which a great deal is borrowed by Alberic of Trois-Fontaines, 1074-1082 There is a shorter notice of him by Wibert Abbot of Nogent, in D'Achery's edition of his works, 467, and Bouquet, xii. 236

[5] Bouquet, xiv 39 "Rex Anglorum potentissimus, Willelmus nomine, qui eum nutrierat"

Die.[1] One of the points on which he consulted Gregory was because his conscience was smitten on finding that his father had died excommunicate, and was buried at Montdidier, a place to which he had no lawful right. At the Pontiff's bidding, Simon had the remains of his father moved from this unjust possession to the church of Crepy, where he might at least sleep in ground which was lawfully his own. In the process of the translation Simon looked upon the face of the corpse, and, horror-struck with the sight, he made up his mind to devote himself to God.[2] For a while he was satisfied with living a pious life in the world, and presently his chief vassals pressed him to marry. He was married, or at least betrothed, to Judith, the daughter of Hildebert, or rather Robert, Count of Auvergne; but he took the first opportunity to persuade his bride to leave him and enter religion.[3] Presently he is summoned to Normandy by William, who tells him that his daughter is sought in marriage by Alfonso of Spain and by Robert of Apulia. But he would rather give her to Simon, in memory of the days when he had been brought up in his court.[4] Simon pleaded the kindred

He removes the body of his father.

---

[1] Bouquet, xiv. 38. The details of the dealings with Gregory are curious. The Pope sent him back absolved, "Adhibens etiam boni testimonii et summæ auctoritatis custodiam, Hugonem scilicet Diensem Episcopum, qui tunc legationis in Galliis functus est officio, Abbatemque Cluniacensem [Hugonem]." On Hugh, see above, p. 431.

[2] This striking incident is told by Wibert (Bouquet, xii 237), "Quo ante delationem detecto, et sub oculis filii ad nudum revelato, quum potentissimi genitoris quondamque ferocissimi tabidum attendisset corpus, ad contemplationem miseræ conditionis se contulit."

[3] Bouquet, xiv 38. The tale is very strikingly told. The Life calls her the daughter of Hildebert, but the reigning Count of Auvergne was named Robert. See Bouquet's note, and Art de Vérifier les Dates, ii. 354.

[4] William is made to say (Alberic, 1076), "Nutrimentum meum quod in te, augmentari cupiens, neglectis nuntiis Regis Hispaniarum Effunsi et Roberti Principis Apuliæ, tibi filiam meam quam quærebam tradere in uxorem prælegi." The original Life is fuller, but to the same effect. This

654                    THE LATER DAYS OF WILLIAM.

CHAP. XXI.  between himself and Queen Matilda, and craved leave to consult the Pope about the matter. He at once went and made his monastic profession; the Count became a Saint, and the fame of his holiness was spread throughout all Europe. He once more appears in connexion with the history of William, when he came to join his entreaties to those of the Norman nobles who strove to set Robert and his father at one again.[1] Dying at Rome a few years later, he received the unwonted honour of being buried among the Popes, and his tomb was adorned with special gifts by the Queen whose daughter he had refused.[2]

He helps to reconcile William and Robert

His death. 1082

Whatever faith we may put in this story, there is no doubt as to the marriage of Stephen and Adela. The proposals of the Count of Chartres are said to have been made through Geoffrey of Chaumont, of whom we have already heard as one of the adventurers from other lands who had followed William to the conquest of England.[3] The betrothal took place at Breteuil, and the marriage was celebrated at Chartres.[4] But it should be noticed that one version of the story of Simon brings before us that daughter of William, whoever she was, who was betrothed, but never married, to Alfonso of Spain. This, I am inclined to think, was the same daughter who

Proposals of Stephen made through Geoffrey of Chaumont

The marriage at Chartres

Alleged betrothal of William's daughter to Alfonso

wooing on the part of Robert Wiscard seems rather apocryphal, but I believe it is just possible

[1] Bouquet, xiv. 40. "Anglorum Regem et Reginam, qui eum nutrierant, visendi gratiâ Normanniam usque properavit, illucque perveniens contra filium, Robertum nomine, Regem dimicantem invenit, qui utrique compassus, pace reformatâ, pestilentiæ malum a regione fugavit."

[2] All this is given in full in the Life, and is copied by Alberic, but it is not found in Wibert.

[3] So we are told in the Liber de Castro Ambasiæ in D'Achery, iii. 277 He is said to have brought Adela to Chartres, and to have afterwards mainly dwelt at Stephen's court. On this Geoffrey, see vol. iii. p. 314.

[4] Ord. Vit. 573 D. Stephen sought for the marriage "cum Guillelmo Rege firmare volens amicitiam." See also Hugh of Fleury (Pertz, ix. 391), but he does not fix the date.

had been promised to Eadwine.[1] I do not pretend to fix her name; it was forgotten while two of her sisters and the King her brother were still living.[2] The story runs that the memory of her English lover still lived in her heart, that she prayed that she might never be joined to the Spaniard, that her prayer was heard, that she died on the journey, that her body was brought back and buried at Bayeux, and that, as one story adds, her knees were found to have grown hard by the length and frequency of her prayers.[3]

The blows were now falling heavily on the house of William. His eldest son was in open rebellion, and had barely escaped the guilt of parricide. A daughter had died, seeking death rather than a marriage which she hated. It was about the same time that his second son, the young Richard, met with his mysterious death in the New Forest, the first of the victims which the ruined homes and churches of Hampshire were to call for from the hearth of their destroyer.[4] And now a heavier stroke than all was to come upon the falling Conqueror. His wife, for whom in his youth he had so long waited and struggled, who had been for so many years the partner of his cares and counsels, but whose company he had of late so often had to sacrifice to the needs of his policy, had during these gloomy years for the first time withstood and disobeyed him, and now she was taken from him for ever. After a long sickness Queen Matilda died, and died, as was to be expected, a pious and edifying death. She was of course buried in her own church at Caen, where her eldest daughter was already a professed nun and was one day to

*Misfortunes of William's family.*

*Death of Queen Matilda November 3, 1083*

---

[1] See vol. iii. p. 661 I have there adopted the suggestion of Mrs Green that the betrothal of one daughter to Eadwine has been confounded with the betrothal of another daughter to Harold

[2] See Will. Malm. iii 277.

[3] See Appendix TT      [4] See above, p. 613

656  THE LATER DAYS OF WILLIAM.

CHAP. XXI
Her tomb and epitaph

be a renowned Abbess.¹ A tomb rich with gold and gems marked Matilda's resting-place, and an epitaph of letters of gold, in the hexameters of the day, told of the splendour of her birth and of her second marriage, of her foundation of the church in which she lay, and of the bountiful hand with which she had ever distributed of her wealth to the wants of the poor and needy.²

Revolt of Hubert of Beaumont. 1083.

The grief of William was deep and lasting. He was a mourner till the day of his death.³ But he had straightway to turn from his domestic sorrow to grapple with another revolt, and to see his arms undergo another check.⁴ There were spirits in the conquered land of Maine who could never bring themselves to submit to the Norman yoke. Chief among these was the Viscount Hubert, the lord of Beaumont and Fresnay, of the resistance of whose castles we heard in William's last Cenomannian campaign.⁵ Hubert had again offended the King, and the dispute grew till at last Hubert openly rebelled.⁶ He left Beaumont and Fresnay, and established himself in his hill fortress of Sainte-Susanne, planted on an inaccessible rock by the river Arne, a tributary of the Sarthe.⁷ Followers flocked to him, and from his fastness he spread havoc over those parts of the County which clave to their allegiance to William.

Hubert defends Sainte-Susanne 1083-1086

---

¹ See above, p. 634.

² See the epitaph in Orderic, 648 A. The verses most to her honour are,

"Hæc consolatrix inopum, pietatis amatrix,
 Gazis dispersis pauper sibi, divis egenis."

³ Will. Malm. iii. 273. "Lacrimis per multos dies ubertim prosecutus, amissæ caritatem desideraverit, quin et ex eo tempore, si credimus, ab omni voluptate descivit."

⁴ Ord. Vit. 648 B. "Post obitum gloriosæ Mathildis Reginæ Willelmus Rex pene iv annis quibus supervixit, multis procellis tribulationum contra eum insurgentibus vehementer laboravit."

⁵ See above, p. 558.

⁶ Ord. Vit. 648 B. "Quibusdam parvis occasionibus Regem prius offendit, sed postmodum in majus crescentibus," &c.    ⁷ Ib. C.

The walled towns and the capital itself were harassed,[1] and those who were entrusted with their defence sent urgent messages to their King, Duke, and Count to come to their rescue.

But the days were gone when Domfront and Alençon, when Dover and Lincoln, had yielded to the dread of William's name. He came, and he saw that the work was too much for him. Sainte-Susanne was not to be taken.[2] There were no means of besieging the castle; William confined his plans to doing something to check the ravages of Hubert. For this purpose he built and garrisoned a counter-fortress in the neighbourhood.[3] The weightier affairs of Normandy and England called William away from the beleaguering of a single Cenomannian stronghold,[4] or it may be that he was fain to leave to others an enterprise in which so little glory was likely to be won. The chief command was given to William's promised son-in-law, Alan of Britanny, and the war was deemed important enough to call for the services of many of the chief men both of England and Normandy. We hear of the presence of the two Williams, the Earls of Surrey and Evreux, of Richer of L'Aigle, of the Breton Hervey, who held a high command,[5] but we hear of them only through their ill luck. All were killed, wounded, or taken prisoners. One man whose name is familiar to us seems to have been more fortunate. Robert of Oily was

*CHAP XXI.*

*The castle not besieged, but a post in the neighbourhood garrisoned*

*Ill luck of the Normans, commanded by Alan of Britanny*

---

[1] Ord Vit 648 B "Custodes Cænomannicæ urbis et circumjacentium oppidorum infestationibus Huberti frequenter lacessiti sunt"

[2] Orderic (648 D) says expressly, "Castrum Sanctæ Susannæ, quod inaccessibile erat præ rupibus *et densitate vinearum quibus circumdabatur*, obsidere nequivit, nec hostem qui intus erat ad libitum coarctare valuit, quia fortiter sibi procurabat et amplos aditus habebat"

[3] See vol ii p 264 for the like at Brionne The ἐπιτείχισμα in this case is called "municipium"

[4] Ord Vit 648 D "Pro magnis regni negotiis in Neustriam rediit"

[5] Ib. 649 D "Herveus Brito, quem magistrum militum constituerat"

there, and his services in the war were such as to be rewarded by the King with a further grant of lands in Oxfordshire.[1] In a war which was spread over three years the advantage seems to have been always on the side of Hubert. Warriors flocked to him from Burgundy, where he had a family connexion,[2] from Aquitaine, and from other parts of Gaul. And we are told that, though the royal camp was better supplied with the signs of wealth and materials of luxury, the defenders of the rebel castle were fully the equal of the King's forces, not only in daring but in actual numbers.[3] Hubert and his comrades were enriched by the ransoms of the chief men of Normandy and England.[4] Not a few among them lost their lives. The end of Richer of L'Aigle is worth the telling. On a November day, a party of Normans were attacking the followers of Hubert. A beardless boy, hidden behind a thicket, struck Richer with an arrow beneath the eye. The comrades of the baron seized him and were about to put him to death, but the dying Richer gathered such strength as he had left to bid them for God's sake to spare

*Grant to Robert of Oily*

*Death of Richer of L'Aigle.*

---

[1] In Domesday, 158 b, it is said of Ludwell in Oxfordshire, "hanc dedit Rex W Roberto apud obsidionem Sanctæ Susannæ" A much more mysterious Domesday entry may also be connected with this war Certain lands of Oswald, a Thegn of Surrey (36 b), were said by Bishop Odo to be liable to a yearly payment either of two marks of gold or of two hawks—a singular alternative. It is added, "Et hoc per concessionem Abbatis fratris Osuuoldi, scilicet pro bello quod contra Gaufridum parvum facere debuit" I can throw no light on this forerunner of Sir Geoffrey Hudson, unless he has anything to do with one "Machiellus de Guitot filius Godefridi parvi" (Ord. Vit. 649 C), who was killed in this war. He was fighting on William's side, but his father may have been among the rebels.

[2] Ord. Vit 648 D.

[3] Ib. "Regis familia . . . divitiis, epulis, ac bellicis sumptibus præstabat; sed castrensis cuneus eis virtute ac multitudine æquiparari satagebat"

[4] Ib The last words of the description are emphatic; "Tribus annis Hubertus Normannis restitit, et, inimicorum opibus locuples, invictus permansit."

him, for that his own sins deserved death. The boy was let go, and Richer having, for want of a priest, confessed his sins to his comrades, died before he could be carried back to William's fortress.[1] A tale of generosity like this does something to relieve the weariness of this wretched border warfare.

The struggle went on, but wholly to the advantage of Hubert; Earl William of Warren, Gilbert the brother of Richer, and others who were seeking to avenge his death, got only wounds for their pains. Count William of Evreux was taken prisoner. At last the Normans, finding that all their attempts were vain and that their forces were daily lessening, laid the plain state of the case before King William in England. Hubert was not to be conquered; valour and luck were alike on his side. They exhorted the King to make peace, and peace was granted on the fullest terms. Hubert crossed over to England, he received the pardon of William for his past offences, he was confirmed in all his possessions and rights, and remained ever after his faithful subject.[2]

The war of Sainte-Susanne brings us very near to the last stage of William's life. But before we survey the great legislative acts of his latest years in England, one or two ecclesiastical events in Normandy may well be mentioned. The famous Bishop Hugh of Lisieux had died in the year which had been marked by the dedication of so many Norman churches.[3] A strange warfare was waged

CHAP. XXI.

Hubert reconciled to William. 1086.

Death of Hugh Bishop of Lisieux July 17, 1077.

---

[1] I have pretty well translated the story in Orderic, 649 A He adds a panegyric on Richer which, from this his one recorded act, we can believe to be fully deserved.

The "municipium" of a former extract has now become "urbs"

[2] The date seems to be marked by the war occupying the time between the death of Matilda in 1083 and the Survey in 1086 In Orderic, 649 D, the latter follows at once, introduced with "his temporibus."

[3] See above, p 429, and on Bishop Hugh, vol iii p 118.

over his body between his canons and the nuns of a monastery of his rearing,[1] while his metropolitan, the austere Primate John, was smitten with a divine judgement for refusing befitting honours to his deceased suffragan.[2] But the point of real importance is the choice of his successor, a choice in which William might seem not to have shown his usual care for spiritual things. Gilbert Maminot, who was now placed on the throne of Lisieux, was a man of eloquence and of varied worldly knowledge. He was skilled in the physical sciences, and especially in the art of medicine, and he made his church a centre of learning of this kind. He was bountiful and charitable, and did strict justice in all temporal matters. But to the spiritual care of his flock he took little heed; for the church and its services he had no love. Hunting, hawking, dice, worldly cares, studies, and amusements of all kinds, filled up his time. The historian hints that he might have said yet worse things of him, if he had not been withheld by his respect for one at whose hands he had himself received the order of subdeacon.[3]

The choice of Gilbert Maminot for a great ecclesiastical office is worth notice. He was clearly a man by no means lacking in merit. He ought not to have been made a

---

[1] See the story in Orderic, 550 B, and for the Abbey of Saint Mary at Lisieux see Neustria Pia, 583. Each party claimed to bury him, and unless their chronicler belies them, the strength of speech of the devout virgins carried them beyond the bounds of Latin or French, "Æternâ morte puniatur qui *soma* patris nostri filiabus suis auferre conatur." William heard both sides, " sed regalis censura fragilior magis sexui compatitur."

[2] See the story in Orderic, 550 B, C. The Archbishop was struck dumb, and remained so to the end of his days, so that he had to stand by while Hugh's successor was consecrated by Michael Bishop of Avranches.

[3] See the long picture of him given by Orderic, 550 B, 551 A. It is perhaps all summed up in one sentence, " Scientiâ litterarum et facundiâ pollebat, divitiis et deliciis indesinenter affluebat, propriæ voluntati et carnis curæ nimis serviebat." A list is given of the eminent men in the chapter of Lisieux at this time, including our old friend the Archdeacon William of Poitiers. On the parentage of Gilbert see above, p. 367.

Bishop; but in an age when the Church monopolized learning and science of all kinds, there was no way of promoting such a man except by making him a Bishop. The appointment was quite unlike those appointments in the days of William's minority, when ecclesiastical preferments were turned into mere provisions for younger or illegitimate members of the reigning house. It had more in common with those appointments of a somewhat later day, when Bishopricks and other ecclesiastical offices were made the rewards of statesmen and diplomatists. But whatever we say of this appointment to the see of Lisieux, in the next great ecclesiastical office which William bestowed he consulted the strictest ecclesiastical propriety. Two years after the death of Hugh of Lisieux the Primate died,[1] and William, as I have already mentioned,[2] at once offered the vacant post, the greatest spiritual preferment in his continental dominions, to Wimund of Saint Leutfred, the daring monk who had denounced his conquest and refused his offers in England. When Wimund, from the noblest motives, refused the offered promotion, William again sought for a man of real ecclesiastical merit. The successor of John, canonically elected, as we are told, was William, called the Good Soul, who had succeeded Lanfranc in the Abbey of Saint Stephen, and who now ruled the church of Rouen for thirty-one years.[3] His chief act was the holding of a council at Lillebonne in the second year of his primacy, in which, besides a great number of enactments of the usual kind, the Truce of God was once more solemnly ordained.[4] Ecclesiastical censures are denounced against all violators of the truce, and the secular power is

CHAP. XXI.

Death of Archbishop John. 1079

William offers the Archbishoprick to Wimund.

William "Bona Anima," Abbot of St Stephen's 1070–1079, Archbishop of Rouen 1079–1110

Council of Lillebonne. 1080

---

[1] Ord Vit 551 B. His epitaph is given, which does not mention his loss of speech, but does speak of his "lingua diserta."

[2] See above, p 448.

[3] Ord Vit 551 C, Chron S Steph in anno

[4] See vol. ii. p 241

called in to strengthen the hands of the Bishop.[1] The need for the re-enactment of this ordinance, which is said to have been carefully observed in the more prosperous years of William's reign,[2] was probably owing to the confusions which had begun to arise now that William's power was defied by his own subjects.

### § 3. *The Affairs of the Scottish and Welsh Marches.* 1087–1081.

*Comparative quiet of England.* While the affairs of Normandy were in this confused state, and while the arms of William met with little but defeat, England remained comparatively quiet. For several years we hear nothing of the greater part of the country. In some years the Chronicles are an absolute blank. Quite towards the end of William's reign we shall come to a time of great legislative activity; but, for about six years after the death of Waltheof, the internal history of England consists of a single outbreak, for it hardly amounted to an insurrection, in the most northern Earldom of England. But along the Marches, Scottish and Welsh, the usual warfare went on.

We have heard nothing of Malcolm since he counselled his brother-in-law Eadgar to make his peace with William.[3] We now first come across his name in a mutilated passage of our Chronicles which records a success which he gained over a competitor within his own Kingdom. Mælslæhta or Malsnechtan, a son of

---

[1] Ord. Vit. 552 A. " Pax Dei, quæ vulgo Trevia dicitur, sicut ipse Princeps Guillelmus eam in initio constituerat, firmiter teneatur, et per singulas parochias dictis excommunicationibus renovetur." The respective functions of the Bishop and the Viscount (Regis Vicecomes) are then described By another clause (553 D) penalties are denounced against priests who shall excommunicate any one without the licence of the Bishop, " præter Treviæ Dei infractores et latrones "

[2] See vol. ii. p 241.   [3] See above, p 570.

Lulach, and therefore a representative of the claims of Macbeth or of Gruach, had been again in rebellion, but he was now overthrown by Malcolm. The King took Mælslæhta's mother, and all his best men, and all his cattle, and he himself hardly escaped.[1] This victory doubtless raised the strength and spirit of Malcolm, and two years later he ventured on another inroad into England. He crossed the border in the August of the year in which William and Robert were fighting before Gerberoi. He harried all Northumberland as far as the Tyne, and went back after slaying many hundreds of men and carrying off great spoil in captives, money, and treasures of every kind.[2] The gentle influence of Margaret may have reformed the personal conduct and the internal government of Malcolm, but his neighbours of England reaped but little benefit from the change.

*Malcolm defeats Mælslæhta. 1078.*

*Invasion of Northumberland by Malcolm August, 1079*

This new blow, like Malcolm's former inroad into England, was not at once avenged. William took no measures against the Scottish King until he was called on to chastise a domestic disturbance as well as a foreign invasion. The episcopate of Walcher of Durham is known to us in some detail. We have seen that

*Episcopate of Walcher of Durham 1071–1080.*

---

[1] Chron. Wig. 1078 "And her Malcholom kynge gewann Mælslæhtan modor [a blank follows in the manuscript] and ealle his betstan menn and ealne his gærsuman and his orf, and he sylf uneaðe ætbærst" The parentage of this pretender comes from the Annals of Ulster (O'Conor, iv. 350), which record his death under 1085, with the title of King of Moray; "Maelsnectai mac Lulaigh ri Muineb" See Mr E W Robertson, i. 139, without whose reference I should hardly have searched the Ulster Annals on such a point On Lulach see vol ii p 366

[2] Chron. Petrib. 1079 "On þisum geare com Melcolm cyng of Scotlande into Englelande betwyx þam twam Marian mæssan mid mycclum fyrde, and gehergode Norðhymbraland oð hit com to Tine, and ofsloh feala hund manna and ham lædde manige sceattas and gersuma and menn on heftninge." This is specially marked to be in the same year as Gerberoi Florence is to the same effect, but curiously enough this entry is left out by Simeon, though this expedition is reckoned among the five attributed to Malcolm in the insertion under 1093

a close friendship existed between him and Earl Waltheof,[1] and after the execution of the English Earl, the temporal care of the Northumbrian Earldom was placed in the hands of its Lotharingian Bishop.[2] His government was hardly such as we should have looked for from a man chosen by William to rule a turbulent border province. He appears as amiable but weak, as one whose chief fault, like that of Eli, to whom he is expressly compared, was that of not doing enough to chastise the excesses of those who acted in his name.[3] Himself a secular priest, he became the reviver of the monastic life in his diocese; and foreigner as he was, we find natives as well as strangers both enjoying and abusing his favour. It was as a favourer of monks in a land where the religious life had wholly died out that his episcopate has left its most lasting memory. Since the great Danish invasion monks had been unknown north of the Humber; the old monasteries had fallen beneath the rage of the heathen, and till Selby became the dwelling-place of the holy hermit of Auxerre,[4] they had found no successors.[5] Of the fallen state of the once famous houses of Jarrow and Wearmouth we have

---

[1] See above, p 524.

[2] Sim Dun. 1075 (Hinde, p 98) "Waltheovus Comes decapitatur. Post quem cura comitatûs committitur Walchero Episcopo" William of Malmesbury (Gest Pont 271) seems to have fancied that he was appointed Earl at an earlier time, "Superpositus est adhuc viventi [Egeluuino] Walkerus, qui esset Dux pariter provinciæ et Episcopus, frenaretque rebellionem gentis gladio et formaret mores eloquio"

[3] See his character in the Durham History, iii 23 We hear of the evil deeds of his Archdeacon and some of his knights, who are charged with both robbery and murder. [4] See Appendix FF

[5] Sim Dun 1074 (p 94) "Postquam sævissima paganorum devastatio gladio ac flammâ ecclesias ac monasteria in cineres redegerat, deficiente pene Christianitate, vix aliquæ ecclesiæ, et hæ virgis foenoque contextæ, sed nulla uspiam monasteria per cc annos reædificabantur, tepescente paullatim fidei religione, cultu vero religionis penitus deficiente, monachorum nomen erat provincialibus inauditum. In stuporem vertebantur, quum quemlibet monachilis habitûs et vitæ forte conspicerent." So to the same effect, but more briefly, in the Durham History, iii 21

## REVIVAL OF MONASTICISM IN THE NORTH.

already heard.[1] But it now came into the hearts of certain monks in a distant shire, who had read in Bæda how full Northumberland once was of holy places, to set forth on a missionary enterprize to the benighted land. The leader of them was Ealdwine, who forsook a high position as Prior of the great house of Winchcombe to go forth and revive religion in the North. In the neighbouring house of Evesham he found two brethren like-minded with himself, Ælfwine a deacon, and Regenfrith, seemingly a lay brother.[2] The three set forth on foot, with an ass to carry their books and vestments. In this guise they reached York, and prayed the Sheriff of the shire, Hugh the son of Baldric,[3] to guide them to Monkchester, the future Newcastle.[4] But as Monkchester in no way answered to its name, they were glad to accept the invitation of Bishop Walcher, who offered them the ruined monastery of Jarrow for their dwelling-place. There they patched up the dismantled church, and built a poor dwelling-place for themselves beneath its walls.[5] The pious example spread, a few of the natives of Northumberland, and a larger number of proselytes from Southern England, joined the humble brotherhood.[6] The Bishop, marking their zeal

*CHAP. XXI*

*Three monks come from Winchcombe and Evesham 1074.*

*Ealdwine Prior of Winchcombe*

*They repair the church of Jarrow*

---

[1] See above, pp 300, 304, 505, and Appendix HH.

[2] See the Durham History, in 21, and by the Northumbrian interpolator under 1074 Regenfrith—Reinfridus—is described as "ignarus litterarum."

[3] See above, p 571 The Sheriff is not mentioned in the Durham History

[4] See both our authorities, and Mr Hinde's note, p 94 The Durham History adds, "Locus, licet ad episcopatum Dunelmensem pertineat, juris tamen Northanhymbrorum Comitis habetur." In 1074 Waltheof was still living

[5] Hist Eccl. Dun iii 21 "Culmen de lignis informibus et fœno superponentes, divinæ servitutis officia ibidem celebrare cœperunt Factâque sub ipsis parietibus casulâ ubi dormirent et manducarent, religiosorum eleemosynis pauperem vitam sustentârunt"

[6] Ib "Pauci de ipsâ Northanhymbrorum provinciâ, plures vero de australibus Anglorum partibus."

CHAP. XXI. and energy, gave them the lordship of Jarrow and other possessions, the revenues of which enabled them to build the tower and monastic buildings which still remain.[1] It is to the fortunate poverty of the house of Jarrow that we owe that Bæda's choir is still left to us.

Spread of monasticism in Northumberland.

But the flame, when once kindled, spread far more widely. The restored house of Jarrow became the cradle and centre of a whole crowd of monastic foundations. Ælfwine remained in the dwelling-place of Bæda as Prior of the revived monastery. But Regenfrith, now, we may presume, no longer ignorant of letters, went forth as the reviver of the monastery of Whitby, once, under the older name of Streoneshalh, the holy house of Hild, the daughter of the Bretwalda Oswiu.[2] From Whitby sprang another famous house; under the care of Earl Alan, and under the government of its first Abbot Stephen, the church of Earl Siward at Galmanho[3] grew into the great Abbey of Saint Mary without the walls of York.[4] Ealdwine himself became the master of a more famous disciple. Turgot, in after days Prior of Durham, Bishop of Saint Andrew's, and biographer of the holy Queen Margaret, was an Englishman of noble birth in

Foundation of Whitby.

[Hild, Abbess of Streoneshalh, died 680.]

Foundation of Saint Mary's at York 1078?

Adventures of Turgot.

---

[1] Hist Eccl Dun iii 21. They were given when Walcher "eos ecclesiam ipsam reædificare et destructa monachorum habitacula videret velle restaurare," "ut et operam perficere et sine indigentiâ ibi possent vivere."

[2] Bæda, iii. 24, iv 23 For the later foundation, see Mon Angl i 406, especially the documents in 1 409, 410 Regenfrith is here made a "miles strenuissimus," who comes into Northumberland "in obsequio Domini sui Willelmi Bastard Regis Anglorum," and who is struck with remorse at the desolation of so holy a place. In the list of benefactors in p 411 we are struck by the number of English and Danish names, as Uhtred the son of Thurkill, Uhtred the son of Gospatric, and his son Thorfin, and others.

[3] See vol ii p. 375

[4] See the History of Abbot Stephen in Mon Angl iii 545 In 1088 the house found a strange benefactor in William Rufus The date of the foundation, 1078, comes, it would seem, from an interpolator of the interpolator. See Mr Hinde's note, p 98 In 1074 we read, "de ecclesiolâ factum nobile cœnobium."

the parts of Lindesey. Already, it would seem, a priest, he was given to William as one of the hostages for the obedience of his shire.[1] Kept in ward in the castle of Lincoln, he escaped by dint of a bribe to his keepers, and made his way to a Norwegian ship in the haven of Grimsby. In that very ship certain ambassadors from King William to King Olaf of Norway[2] had already taken their passage. The hostage had been sought for in the ship by the King's officers, but the friendly Northmen kept him hidden till the ship had actually sailed. Then the hostage for whom such search had been made suddenly appeared before the astonished eyes of the envoys. They called on the sailors to turn back again, that the King's fugitive might be delivered up to him. The Northmen refused, and William's ambassadors had to put up with the company of the man who was fleeing from William's prison. The English priest was received in Norway with all honour, and the pious King Olaf took him as his master in divine things.[3] But the heart of Turgot was ever and anon stirred by calls to the monastic life. At last, enriched with the gifts of the friendly Norwegian King, he set sail to return to England. His ship was wrecked; his treasures were lost; he himself barely reached the shore of Northumberland with his life. He went to Durham, and told the Bishop his wish to enter religion. Walcher entrusted him to the care of Ealdwine

CHAP. XXI.

His escape from Lincoln. 1068?

His favour with Olaf of Norway.

He joins Ealdwine.

---

[1] Sim Dun 1074 (p. 95, ed Hinde) "Is, prosapiam trahens de genere Anglorum non infimo, unus erat inter alios qui, nuper subjugatâ Normannis Angliâ, obsides pro totâ Lindeseiâ in Lindicolono castro custodiebatur." This must, I suppose, be placed soon after the taking of Lincoln in 1068. The rest of the story comes from the interpolated Florence

[2] See above, p 122 The ambassadors go in a merchant-ship, "navem mercatoriam . in quâ navi etiam legati Willelmi Regis Norwegiam mittendi subvectionem sibi paraverant "

[3] Sim Dun u s. "Audito quod clericus de Angliâ venisset, quod magnum tunc temporis videbatur, eum ad discendos psalmos quasi magistrum sibi exhibuit "

at Jarrow,[1] and presently Ealdwine and Turgot set forth and dwelled at Melrose, within the dominions of Malcolm. Here they suffered persecution at the hands of the Scottish King, who is even said to have threatened them with death, because they refused to swear fealty to him.[2] At the bidding of Bishop Walcher they came back, and were placed by him at Wearmouth, where, under their care, the old church of Benedict Biscop, ruined in the wars of Malcolm, became again a place of Christian and monastic devotion.

Thus the religious life once more took root and flourished in the most northern parts of England. Bishop Walcher himself thought of making the monastic profession in his own person, and of setting monks instead of seculars to be the immediate ministers of Saint Cuthberht. He even began to raise monastic buildings around the cathedral church, from which the canons were not as yet driven.[3] We know not whether he had any schemes of the like sort with regard to a seat of the secular clergy more recent but hardly less venerable in the eyes of Englishmen than the church of Saint Cuthberht himself. William had made a gift to the Lotharingian Bishop of Earl Harold's lordship of Waltham, in order that he might have a home in the neighbourhood of London when he was called on to attend the Great Councils of the realm.[4] The college

---

[1] At this stage the account in the Durham History (iii 22) comes in Turgot appears without any account of him, Walcher entrusts him to Ealdwine, and for a while "sub magisterio Aldwini clericus inter monachos degebat"

[2] Hist Eccl Dun ib "Graves ab illo injurias pertulerunt et persecutiones, pro eo quod, *evangelicum præceptum servantes*, jurare illi fidelitatem noluerunt." Did they refuse to take any oath?

[3] Ib "Positis fundamentis monachorum habitacula ubi nunc habentur Dunelmi construere cœpit"

[4] De Inv 22 "Walcherius Dunelmensis Episcopus, cui dederat eam [villam Walthamensem] . . illustris Rex Willelmus ut haberet ibi domicilium quum vocaretur a remotis ubi habitabat partibus ad concilium" The

went on undisturbed in its foundation, though robbed, it is said, of part of its moveable wealth,[1] and though the Bishop of Durham himself is charged with taking possession of a portion of its lands.[2]

But the ecclesiastical schemes of Walcher were all cut short by the fate which was brought upon him by the errors of his temporal government. Chief among his unworthy favourites were one Gilbert, a kinsman, and therefore doubtless a countryman, of his own, and his chaplain Leobwine, of whose descent or birth-place we hear nothing.[3] Gilbert had the general care of the Earldom under the Bishop;[4] Leobwine too was trusted by him in affairs both ecclesiastical and temporal.[5] A third evil counsellor was Leofwine, the Dean of Durham, of whose English birth there can be no doubt. Another English friend of the Bishop was a man of another stamp. This was Ligulf, a Thegn of the noblest blood of

*Durham History* says that William granted him Waltham "cum ipsius nobili ecclesiâ quæ canonicorum congregatione pollet." But this is hardly borne out by Domesday, ii. 15 b, where the lands of the Bishop and those of the College are entered separately. See Professor Stubbs' note, and the remarks in his Preface, p. xix.

[1] That is, if we believe the story of William's spoliations of Waltham in the *Vita Haroldi* (Chron. Ang.-Norm. ii. 162), but this is most likely a confusion with those of William Rufus recorded in the chapter of *De Inventione* just quoted.

[2] This appears from the charter of Matilda the Queen of Henry the First, printed in Professor Stubbs' Appendix to *De Inventione*, pp. 53, 54, where she restores "illas duas hydas et dimidiam de Northlandâ, quas Walcherus Episcopus invide de ecclesiâ abstulit."

[3] See Florence, 1080, where the tale is told at length; it is copied by Simeon with a few additions. The two accounts by William of Malmesbury, Gest. Reg. iii. 271 and Gest. Pont. 271, are to the same effect. The form "Leo*b*winus" should be noted, as it looks like a High-Dutch form of our own Leofwine, with which in some MSS it gets confounded. See R. Howden, i. 135, Stubbs. The Durham History does not give the names of any of the offenders.

[4] Fl. Wig. 1080. "Gilebertus, cui præsul, quia suus propinquus exstitit, comitatum Northymbrensium subregendum commiserat."

[5] Ib. "In tantum exaltaverat ut et in episcopatu et in comitatu fere nil sine illius arbitrio agitaretur."

## 670   THE LATER DAYS OF WILLIAM.

CHAP. XXI    Northumberland, who had married Ealdgyth, a daughter of Earl Ealdred and sister of Æthelflæd the mother of Earl Waltheof.[1] By her he had two sons, Uhtred and Morkere, the latter of whom, while still a child, had been placed by his cousin the Earl under the care of the monks of Jarrow, and the trust was accompanied by a gift of the church and lordship of Tynemouth.[2] Ligulf held, or had held, great estates, which the lack of a Bernician Domesday hinders us from identifying. But we are significantly told that, to escape the insults and violence of the Normans in the open country, he had

*His favour with Walcher.*    taken up his abode in the city of Durham.[3] He was there admitted to the close friendship of the Bishop, and was consulted by him in all matters touching his temporal government.

*Enmity of Leobwine.*    The favour in which Ligulf was held aroused the envy of the chaplain Leobwine, who took every opportunity of thwarting and insulting him, even in the Bishop's presence. One day, at a Gemót held by the Bishop, the insolence of Leobwine provoked a harsher answer than usual from the insulted Thegn. The chaplain took counsel with Gilbert, and prayed his colleague to

*Ligulf murdered by Gilbert at the instigation of Leobwine.*    avenge him by speedily putting Ligulf to death. Gilbert consented, and, at the head of a band of soldiers in the Bishop's service, slew Ligulf in the night in his own house, together with most of his household.[4] Walcher heard the

---

[1] The family details come from Simeon; in Florence, "Liulfus"—a softer form than Simeon's "Ligulfus"—is only "nobilis generosusque minister."

[2] Sim. Dun 1080 (p. 99, Hinde). See Waltheof's charter in Mon. Angl. i 236.

[3] Flor. Wig. 1080 "Quia ubique locorum Normanni incessanter eâ tempestate operam dabant suæ feritati, cum suis omnibus ad Dunholme se contulit, quia Sanctum Cuthbertum corde sincero dilexit" This is copied by Simeon, but it is curious that he leaves out the account of certain visions with which, according to the monk of Worcester, Saint Cuthberht favoured his votary. So also William of Malmesbury in both accounts.

[4] Ligulf's house seems now to be conceived as not being in the town.

tale; he expressed his sorrow by his words and gestures, CHAP XXI.
and warned Leobwine that he had ruined him.[1] The Walcher protests his
Bishop took shelter in the castle, and sent forth mes- innocence.
sengers to announce that he was himself guiltless of the
blood of Ligulf, and that he was ready to make solemn
oath to that effect.[2] On this assurance the kinsfolk of the A Gemót to be held.
murdered man exchanged promises of peace[3] with the
Bishop, and it was agreed that the whole matter should
be brought before a general Gemót of the Earldom to be
held at Gateshead,[4] a place on the south side of the Tyne,
which the works of modern skill have well nigh joined
on to the town of Newcastle on the opposite bank. But
before the assembly met, men learned that the acts of the
Bishop were not strictly in agreement to his words. He Walcher's favours
had received both Gilbert and Leobwine to their former to the murderers.
favour and former place in his household.[5] Men now fully
believed that it was really by the Bishop's own orders that
Ligulf had been slain.

The assembly met, a gathering of the whole people of Gemót at Gateshead,
Northumberland, with the hereditary chiefs of the land at May 14, 1080.
its head.[6] One of them bore the name of Waltheof, a name
which speaks his kindred with the ancient Earls. Another

---

Gilbert goes, "et episcopi et ejusdem Leobwini militibus in unum coadunatis, ad villam ubi tunc Liulfus morabatur" Mark that the chaplain had "milites" of his own.

[1] Flor. Wig. 1080 "Me et te omnemque familiam meam tuæ linguæ peremisti gladio"

[2] Ib "Se necis Liulfi conscium non fuisse, quin potius ejus occisorem Gilebertum omnesque socios ipsius de Northymbriâ penitus exlegàsse, ac paratum fore semetipsum purgare secundum judicium pontificale." That is, by oath, neither by battle nor by ordeal

[3] Ib. "Pace ad invicem datâ et acceptâ."

[4] Ib. "In loco qui dicitur ad Caput Capræ." So the Durham History.

[5] Ib "Ut prius, in suam gratiam familiamque recepit"

[6] At this point the Durham History joins us. The account there (iii. 23, 24) is written far more strongly in Walcher's interest than that of Florence. The Assembly is described as "qui ultra Tinam habitaverant universi natu majores [þa yldestan þegnas] cum infinitâ totius populi multitudine in pessimum adunati consilium."

was Eadwulf, surnamed Rus, the son of Uhtred, the son of Gospatric, the son of that Earl Uhtred who, seventy-four years before, had delivered Durham from the Scots.[1] The Gemót was held, according to ancient English custom, in the open air. But the Bishop, fearing the vast and excited crowd, took his place in the church along with his chosen followers, the guilty men being among them. Between him and the people outside messengers went to and fro.[2] This refusal to meet his flock face to face would no doubt do much to stir up their minds still more fiercely against him. Men had no mind for the usual formalities and discussions. A cry was raised in the English tongue, seemingly from the mouth of Eadwulf, "Short rede, good rede, slay ye the Bishop"[3] The slaughter began. All those outside the church who were known to be the Bishop's friends were cut down, a few alone escaping by flight. Walcher then bade his kinsman Gilbert, who, as the actual murderer, was the most hateful of all, to go forth and by his death turn away the wrath of the people. He went forth, a body of knights following in the hope of defending him, but all fell beneath the swords and javelins of the armed

---

[1] The name of Waltheof comes from the Durham History, that of Eadwulf from Simeon, 1072

[2] Flor. Wig. 1080 "Semel et iterum de suis quos voluit pro pace facienda foras ad eos misit" This is somewhat differently told in the Durham History, "Declinans episcopus tumultum, ecclesiolam ipsius loci intravit, ubi convocatis ad se populi primatibus, de utriusque partis utilitate ac mutuâ amicitiâ tractavit Quo facto, episcopo cum paucissimis suorum in ecclesiâ remanente, omnes qui advocati fuerant quasi consilio loquuturi, egrediuntur." Roger of Wendover (ii 17) gives the whole account in a spirit most hostile to Walcher, and paints him as a mere fiscal oppressor who bought the Earldom of William He now says, "Episcopus nimis crudeliter respondit, quod de nullâ injuriâ vel calumniâ ipsis justitiam exhiberet, antequam sibi libras quadringentas monetæ optimæ numerâssent"

[3] I do not scruple to borrow this from R Wendover; "Unus ex illis, cujus arbitrium omnes exspectabant [this must be Eadwulf], præcipitanter patriâ linguâ dixit, 'Schort red, god red, slea ye the bischop.'"

Gemót, except two English Thegns whose kindred blood pleaded for them.[1] The Dean Leofwine and other clerks also went forth. But they were slaughtered as well as their lay comrades, the evil deeds of Leofwine outweighing any respect for his English blood.[2] At last the Bishop bade the first author of the whole evil, Leobwine himself, to go forth,[3] but he refused. The Bishop then himself went forth to the door of the church and pleaded for his life. The raging people refused to listen. The Bishop, like Cæsar, wrapped his face in his mantle and fell beneath the swords of his enemies, the actual death-blow, it is said, being dealt by the hand of Eadwulf.[4] A fierce cry was now raised for Leobwine; but the guilty man still tarried. The church was now set on fire, and presently Leobwine, already scorched by the flames, came forth. A thousand spears were ready to meet him, and the man who had plotted the death of Ligulf fell hewn in pieces by the countrymen of his victim. The slayers of the Bishop now hastened to Durham, in the hopes of slaying also those of his men whom he had left in the castle. But the works of Norman engineers were too strong for them; after a siege of four days they grew weary of the attempt, and were scattered abroad every man to his own home.[5]

*Walcher killed*

*The church burned and Leobwine killed.*

*Vain attack on Durham Castle by the murderers*

---

[1] William of Malmesbury (iii 271) makes Gilbert go out "ultro, ut suo periculo vitam domini mercaretur."

[2] I follow the details in Florence, the account in the Durham History makes no one come out till the church is on fire. The Bishop's companions then come forth "humiliter, peccata sua confessi perceptâ benedictione." Walcher himself dies last, "præ januis pacem prætento ramo offerens," says William of Malmesbury. The Winchester Annalist (1080) comments, "Ne solus decederet, sed haberet itineris comites, centum viros validos truncatis capitibus cum illo quo tendebat mittebant."

[3] Flor Wig 1080. "Intellexit illorum furorem nullâ ratione iri mitigatum quivisse, nisi caput et auctor totius illius calamitatis occideretur Leobwinus."

[4] Sim Dun 1072, p 91. "Eadulfus . . ducem se exhibuit eorum qui Walcherum episcopum occiderunt, ipseque dicitur suâ illum interfecisse manu." [5] Hist Eccl Dun iii 24.

VOL. IV.   X X

*Fate of Waltheof and Eadwulf*

Vengeance did not fail to light on them in this world and in the next. Eadwulf was killed by a woman, perhaps his own wife;[1] Waltheof was killed by his wife's brother; but before he died, one had been raised from the dead to announce that a place in the lowest pit of hell was standing ready for him.[2]

The murder of Walcher is one of those acts which it is alike impossible to wonder at and to justify. The Bishop, himself most likely guilty of nothing worse than culpable weakness, had stirred up the passions of the whole country against him, and his life was the forfeit. But the blood of a Bishop, in whatever cause it might be shed, was always sacred, and Walcher, without being canonized, was looked upon as a kind of martyr. His body was carried to Durham by the pious care of the monks of Jarrow, and was hurriedly buried in the chapter-house.[3] But it was not enough that the memory of Walcher should be reverenced; his blood had to be avenged. His death was an act which no government could pass over, but it was eminently a case for smiting the leaders and sparing the commons. But William entrusted the punishment of the rebellious district to his brother Odo, and the Bishop took, if not a heavier, at least a meaner vengeance than the King himself would have taken. The land, already so often harried, was harried yet again as a punishment for the slaughter of its pastor. Men who had had no share in the disturbance were mutilated, and even, contrary to William's own invariable rule, beheaded. Others redeemed their lives from false charges by the payment of money.[4] These

*Burial of Walcher.*

*Odo sent to Northumberland*

*His cruelties and spoliations.*

---

[1] Sim Dun 1072, p 91 "Mox ipse a feminâ occisus"

[2] See the whole story of this Waltheof in this world and in the next, and of the rising again of Eadwulf of Ravensworth, in the Durham History, iii. 23.   [3] Hist Eccl Dun iii 24

[4] Hist Eccl Dun iii 24 "Dum mortem episcopi ulciscerentur, terram pene totam in solitudinem redegerunt" Florence and after him the Interpolator speak to the same effect. The Durham History calls the

were doubtless the deeds of the Earl of Kent, who went away after leaving a guard in the castle. But meanwhile the Bishop of Bayeux had cast a longing eye on the treasures of Saint Cuthberht, and he carried off a pastoral staff of rare workmanship and material, for it was wrought of sapphire.[1]

Having thus chastised the Northumbrians, William deemed it time to chastise Malcolm of Scotland also. In the autumn the King's eldest son Robert, now for a moment reconciled to his father,[2] was sent against Scotland with an army, in which were many of the great men of the realm, and among others Abbot Adelelm of Abingdon. No battle was fought, but, according to one account, Malcolm met Robert somewhere in Lothian, renewed his homage, and again gave hostages.[3] This story may perhaps be a confused repetition of the scene between Malcolm and William at Abernethy. It seems certain that Robert reaped no special glory in his Scottish expedition. His march was chiefly memorable from the fact that on his way back he stopped at the place which had hitherto been Monkchester, and there, opposite to the scene of Walcher's murder, laid the foundation of a fortress to guard the stream and curb the turbulent people. From that fortress, rebuilt in the next age with all the improvements of the later days of Norman art, the momentary dwelling-place

*Robert sent against Malcolm Autumn, 1080*

*Foundation of Newcastle*

---

persons killed and mutilated "miseros indigenas, qui suâ confisi innocentiâ domi resederant."

[1] Hist Eccl Dun iii. 24 "Baculum pastoralem materiâ et arte mirandum, erat enim de sapphiro factus."

[2] See above, p 650

[3] Hist Ab ii. 9. "Rex filium suum Robertum majorem natu Scotiam suâ vice transmisit, cum quo et plures Angliæ primates, quorum unus Abbas Athelelmus fuit, præcipiens eis pacem armave offerre, pacem si obtemperantia sibi spondeatur, sin aliter, arma. Verum Rex ille Lodonis occurrens cum suis, pacisci potius quam prœliari delegit. Proinde ut regno Angliæ principatus Scotiæ subactus foret obsides tribuit." On this passage see Mr E W Robertson, i 143, ii 481, and Appendix CC.

676                THE LATER DAYS OF WILLIAM.

CHAP. XXI. of Ealdwine took the name which it has ever since borne of Newcastle-upon-Tyne.[1]

Succession of the Earls of Northumberland. Alberic.
On the death of Walcher the spiritual and temporal administration of Northumberland were again separated. The Earldom was first given to a certain Alberic or Aubrey, of whom little is known. He was found unfit for so difficult a post; he either resigned it or was removed from it, and went back into Normandy.[2] His name appears in the Survey as a past but not a present owner, which however need not imply more than the necessary loss of the lands attached to the Earldom.[3] It would seem that William then once more tried the temporal government of a Bishop, but a Bishop of a very different class from the feeble Walcher. The Bishop of Coutances,

Geoffrey Bishop of Coutances?
Geoffrey of Mowbray, who had smitten the men of Somerset and Dorset before Montacute, was sent to curb the men of Northumberland.[4] He, after a while, resigned his thankless office to his nephew Robert of Mowbray, a proud, stern, and gloomy man, who inherited the temporal pos-

Robert of Mowbray.

[1] Sim Dun 1080, p 100 "Rex Willelmus auctumnali tempore Rodbertum filium suum Scotiam contra Malcolmum misit Sed quum pervenisset ad Egglesbreth, nullo confecto negotio reversus, Castellum Novum super flumen Tyne condidit" This may simply mean that there was no battle, but the Abingdon version is most likely exaggerated.

[2] Ib 1072, p 92 "Rex dedit illum honorem Albrio. Quo in rebus difficilibus parum valente patriamque reverso, idem Rex Rodberto de Mulbreio dedit comitatum Northymbrensem" A strange legend about this Alberic will be found in Bromton (X Scriptt 1255), which illustrates the way in which Eastern Europe was ever present to the minds of the men of the eleventh century We have heard of Alberic in the story of Robert, see above, p 650. He becomes "Aluredus" in Ann Wint 1080.

[3] Wherever Alberic's name occurs in Domesday, it is always "tenuit," not "tenet" See especially Oxfordshire, 157 b, and Warwickshire, 239 b.

[4] So Dugdale (Baronage, 56) infers from the account of the foundation of Saint Mary's at York, Mon Angl iii. 546, where we read of "Godefridus Constantiensis Episcopus, qui eo quoque tempore Northanhumbrorum consulatum regebat" The date 1088 does not agree, as Robert of Mowbray was certainly Earl in that year. But is it not more likely that there is a confusion as to the date, than that Geoffrey should have acted as deputy to his nephew, as Mr Hinde (p. 92) suggests?

sessions of his uncle.[1] In the next reign he forfeited his honours by rebellion, and the Northumbrian Earldom came under the immediate government of the Crown.[2]

The vacant Bishoprick William bestowed on a namesake of his own, who, from a secular priest in the church of Bayeux, had become a monk and Prior in the monastery of Saint Carilef, now Saint Calais, in the diocese and county of Maine.[3] To him we owe the beginning of that mighty pile which supplanted the church of Ealdhun, and whose building forms one of the great landmarks in the history of architecture.[4] His buildings however were not begun till after the death of the Conqueror; but while William still lived he carried out the great ecclesiastical change in his church which Walcher had only designed. At the bidding of King William and Queen Matilda, Bishop William crossed the Alps to consult Pope Gregory on the affairs of the church of Durham. It was decreed that the canons[5] should give way to monks, and, as the revenues of the see were not enough to support three monasteries, that the houses of Jarrow and Wearmouth, lately founded on the episcopal lands, should be merged in the new cathedral monastery.[6] The scheme was carried

*CHAP XXI.*
1095

William of Saint Carilef Bishop of Durham Appointed November 5, 1080, consecrated January 3, 1081, died January 1, 1096.

Church of Durham begun. 1093.

Monks substituted for canons at Durham 1081–1085

---

[1] See the graphic description given of him by Orderic, 703 B.

[2] Sim Dun 1072, p 93 "Eo capto Rex junior Willelmus, hodieque Rex Henricus Northymbriam in suâ tenet manu"

[3] Hist Eccl Dun iv. 1, Will. Malm. Gest Pont 272. He was consecrated at Gloucester by Archbishop Thomas Sim Dun 1080, p 101 The local historian gives him an admirable character; William of Malmesbury is less favourable. He was "potens in sæculo et oris volubilitate promptus, maxime sub Willelmo Rege juniore"

[4] Of the importance of Durham in this point of view I shall have to speak in my fifth volume. On William's works, see Hist Eccl. Dun iv 8, and the following tract on the Bishops of Durham, X Scriptt 61

[5] They were, according to the local historian (iv 3), "nomen tantum canonicorum habentes, sed in nullo canonicorum regulam sequentes," that is, of course, the rule of Chrodegang. Their Dean seems to have been married

[6] Hist Eccl Dun iv 2 "Quia episcopatûs parvitas ad tria monachorum cœnobia non sufficeret" There is something odd in the complaint of

CHAP. XXI
Ealdwine and Turgot Priors

out; the monks of the two monasteries were removed to Durham, and Jarrow and Wearmouth sank into cells.¹ Bishop William had no feeling against employing Englishmen in the highest ecclesiastical offices in his gift. Ealdwine became the first Prior of the new monastery, and he was succeeded in his office by Turgot. Another Englishman of the name of Leofwine was the Bishop's secretary.² The lands of the monks were now separated from those of the Bishop,³ and the great Priory of Durham began and flourished⁴ The canons had the choice of resignation or making the monastic profession. All departed save the Dean, who was hardly persuaded by his son, already a monk, to become one of the new body.⁵ Everything shows how stoutly the English clergy, collegiate as well as parochial, clave to their separate married households.

Affairs of Wales.

Lastly, we must turn our eyes to the Welsh border. It would be vain to try to describe the endless civil wars within Wales itself, or to reckon up all the momentary Kings of the various rival dynasties. Some of them, as we have seen, did not scruple to call in Norman or English allies against each other, but such alliances were commonly short lived. Caradoc the son of Gruffydd had been allied with William Fitz-Osbern against Meredydd the son of Owen. Another

poverty as applied to the see of Durham, but Saint Cuthberht had as yet neither coal mines nor temporal principality

¹ See Mon Angl 1 502.

² Hist Eccl Dun. iv. 3. Ealdwine (iv 7) died April 12, 1087, when the Bishop appointed Turgot "communi fratrum consilio"

³ Ib. The monks' lands were to be "omnino ab episcopi servitio et ab omni consuetudine liberæ et quietæ ad suum victum et vestitum" This is alleged to have been the ancient privilege of those " qui Deo coram Sancti Cuthberti corpore ministrant." See the Bishop's charter in Mon. Angl 1 236, if it be not made up out of the Durham History

⁴ See King William's charter confirming all the arrangements, Mon. Angl 1 237, and that of Archbishop Thomas in R. Howden, 1 137, Stubbs.

⁵ Hist Eccl. Dun iv 3. We read of the Canons, "Illi de ecclesiâ exire quam taliter ingredi maluerunt."

Meredydd too enjoyed the favour of both Williams, King and Earl, and received lands in Herefordshire which had belonged to Earl Harold and other Englishmen. And at the time of the Survey those lands were held, not indeed by Meredydd himself, but by his son Gruffydd.[1] The most powerful prince in Wales during these years seems to have been Trahaern the son of Caradoc—not the Caradoc of whom we have so often heard—who is said to have avenged the blood of Bleddyn on Rhys of South Wales. Trahaern was himself killed in a battle with Rhys the son of Tewdwr the son of the slain Rhys.[2] And we might almost infer from the Welsh writers that it was this event which in some way led to the presence of William himself in Wales. They tell us that in the same year William the Bastard, King of the Saxons, French, and Britons, made his way to the shrine of Saint David, as they would have us believe, as a peaceful pilgrim.[3] The date must be wrong, for in the year of Gerberoi William was otherwise employed. But the English Chroniclers place two years later a great expedition of William himself into Wales, in which he freed many hundred men—captives no doubt carried off in the inroads of the Britons—and other writers speak of his subduing the country.[4] Something no doubt was

*CHAP. XXI*

*Lands held by Meredydd son of Bleddyn and his son Gruffydd.*

*Trahaern, son of Caradoc*

*His death. 1079.*

*William in Wales 1081*

*His conquests.*

---

[1] See the lands of "Grifin filius Mariadoc" in Domesday, 187 b. In one entry we read, "Comes W dedit Mariadoc Regi," and in another, "Rex W condonavit geldum Regi Mariadoc et postea filio ejus." I conceive that this is Meredydd the son of Bleddyn, who is mentioned in the Brut y Tywysogion, 1100, and his son Gruffydd in 1113, p 140. But, if so, Meredydd was not dead at the time of the Survey; he must therefore have given some offence and lost his lands, though they were kept by his son. Another Gruffydd, or the same, appears in 180 b as "Grifin puer," and a Madoc in 187 b.

[2] See Ann Camb. 1073, 1076, 1079; Brut y Tywysogion, under the same year, Williams, Hist of Wales, 185, 186. It should be noticed that Trahaern had Scottish, or more likely Irish, allies.

[3] In the Brut (1079) William appears as "Gwilim vastard, vrenhin y Saeson ar Freinc ar Brytanyeit," but in the Annals we simply read, "Willem Rex Angliæ causâ orationis Sanctum David adiit."

[4] Chron Petrib 1081 "On þisum geare se cyng lædde fyrde into

680                THE LATER DAYS OF WILLIAM.

CHAP. XXI. done towards that end by the foundation of the castle
Foundation of Cardiff, a foundation through which the immediate
Cardiff dominion of William was carried from the Usk to the
Castle. 1080? Taff, and the beginnings were made of that great occupation of South Wales which went on so vigorously
William's during the next reign[1] Yet though a pilgrimage to
pilgrimage to Saint Saint David's was certainly not William's only motive in
David's. History of entering Wales, we can well believe that both policy and
Saint David's devotion led him to make his way to the distant home of the
1011 British saint and to make his offering at his shrine. The
Ravages of church of Saint David's has not come under our notice since
pirates. 1078. it was wasted by Eadric seventy years before the visit of
William.[2] Since then it had suffered a series of misfortunes;
it had been more than once sacked by heathen invaders,
one invasion, in which the Bishop Abraham was killed,
having happened only a short time before William's own
coming.[3] In the next generation, the Norman conquest of
South Wales at least secured Saint David's from enemies

Wealan and þær gefreode fela hund manna " William's visit to Wales is also alluded to in Domesday, 31 *b* A King's Reeve is said to have held lands " quando fuit Rex in Wales, et postea, donec Episcopus Baiocensis in Chent perrexit " It was therefore before Odo's arrest in 1082 R Wendover (ii 20) has, " Rex Anglorum Willelmus in Walliam duxit exercitum copiosum, et eam sibi subjugavit, et a regulis illis homagia et fidelitates accepit " He places it in 1079, but calls it the same year as Thurstan's disturbance at Glastonbury, that is 1083, so does Henry of Huntingdon (Script p Bed. 212), but he places both in 1081, "Wilhelmus Rex anno decimo quinto duxit exercitum in Walliam, et eam sibi subdidit." So the Waverley Annals, but under 1080, adding, " multi ex utráque parte perierunt." So Winchester, 1081, " Rex Walliam sibi subjugavit, et de Walensibus, licet celeres sint cuisores et labi soleant de inimicorum manibus, multitudo innumerabilis capta et *in modum porcorum* [see above, pp 507, 644] occisa est. Ex hoc nunc, licet inviti, fatentur Anglos se in omnibus esse præstantiores " See Lappenberg, 182 This seems borne out by the language of the Chronicler, 1087, " Brytland him wæs on gewealde, and he þærinne casteles gewrohte, and þet manncynn mid ealle gewealde." Compare Will Malm in 258, and Hist Ab ii 10.

[1] Brut y Tywysogion, 1080         [2] See vol i. p. 384
[3] Ann Camb. 1078. " Menevia a gentilibus vastata est, et Abraham a gentilibus occiditur "

of this kind, but the British Church now lost its last trace of independence, and the succession of Norman Bishops of Saint David's begins.

<small>Bernard, first Norman Bishop. 1115</small>

### § 4. *The later Legislation of William.* 1082–1086.

We are now drawing near to the end of William's reign. In its latest years English affairs again received that share of attention at his hands which they had in some measure lost since the death of Waltheof. The continuous history of England during these years begins with a great act of justice on the part of the King. The pride and oppression of Odo, Bishop and Earl, had grown to such a height that William's policy and his better nature both led him to put a stop to them. The special atrocities which had distinguished Odo's chastisement of Northumberland, the extortion of bribes from innocent men, the wholesale execution of men whether innocent or guilty, were deeds such as William in his worst moments had never yet either done or approved. And now a fit of ambition of a still wilder kind seized on the mind of Odo. It was a small matter to rule England and Normandy, when, at least in his dreams, the lordship of the whole world offered itself to him [1] A soothsayer had prophesied that the successor of Hildebrand on the Papal throne should bear the name of Odo or Otto [2] So, some ages later, a prediction of the same kind foretold that the successor of Leo the Tenth should bear the name of Hadrian. In both cases a vain ambition was roused in the breast of a prelate who had in one way or another a footing in England, and in both cases the prediction was fulfilled

<small>Character of the years 1082–1086.</small>

<small>Pride and oppression of Odo.</small>

<small>He aspires to the Papacy</small>

---

[1] Ord Vit 646 D. "Odo .. qui cum fratre suo Guillelmo Rege Normannis dominabatur et Anglis, parvi pendens potestates et divitias regni occidentalis, nisi jure Papatûs dominaretur latius et omnibus terrigenis." [2] Ib.

in the person of another. Hadrian de Castello sought the death of Pope Leo in order to vacate the throne which, when it was vacated, was filled by Hadrian of Utrecht. We do not find that Odo of Bayeux conspired the death of Gregory the Seventh, but it seems certain that he took measures during Gregory's life to secure his own succession to the Pontificate which in the end fell to the lot of Otto of Ostia, the famous Urban the Second.[1] He sent to Rome; he bought himself a palace there, he filled it with goodly furniture, and spent large sums in winning favour on the spot.[2] He even designed to cross the Alps at the head of something very like an army. Many of the Normans both in England and in Normandy, among them the Earl of Chester himself, were ready to plight their faith to him and to follow his fortunes.[3] Odo was just on the point of setting sail for Normandy with a great array, with a view to his further journey southwards. But his schemes by no means fell in with the views of his King and brother. William, who was in Normandy at the time, at once set sail for England, and suddenly met Odo in the Isle of Wight[4] He there gathered together a meeting of the great men of the realm, so

---

[1] Odo, Oddo, or Otto See the Lives of Gregory and Urban in Muratori, iii 347, 352, 355

[2] Ord Vit 646 D "Romam misit, palatium sibi emit, senatores Quiritum magnis muneribus datis sibi amicitiâ copulavit," &c So Will Malm iii 277, "Pene papatum Romanum absens a civibus mercatus fuerat, peras peregrinorum epistolis et nummis infarciens" Both these accounts, whatever we make of the "senatores Quiritum," seem to point to dealings with laymen rather than clergy. The Hyde writer (296) is eloquent on the splendour of Odo's palace. Wace (14310-14321) seems to have fancied that Odo's object was to secure the crown of England after William

[3] Ib 646 D "Illi, quia Normanni leves et extera videre cupidi sunt, protinus præsumptori Episcopo, cui principatus Albionis et Neustriæ non sufficiebat, assenserunt Ingentes quoque fundos quos in occiduis climatibus possidebant deserere decreverunt, ac ut præfato præsuli trans Padum comitarentur per fidem spoponderunt" 

[4] Ib 647 A.

many, we may suppose, as could be got together at a moment's notice.[1] Before them William made his complaint against his brother. Before he crossed the sea, he had entrusted the government of England to the care of Odo.[2] The troubles of his continental dominions, the revolt of Maine, the revolt of his son, had occupied his own attention, while Odo ruled in his name in England. That rule had been a rule of oppression to all; Odo had shown himself a tyrant to the whole realm. He had oppressed the poor, he had spoiled the Church, a thing which specially grieved William's heart when he thought of all the good and pious Kings who had gone before him, and who had enriched the churches of England for purposes far other than those to which their wealth was applied by Odo.[3] Lastly, he had persuaded the King's knights, who were needed at home for the defence of the realm against the Danes and the Irish, to leave their duty and follow him beyond the Alps on vain schemes of winning dominion for himself.[4] How, William asked

CHAP. XXI

He accuses him before the Assembly. 1082

---

[1] Ord Vit 647 A "Congregatis in aulâ regali primoribus regni"

[2] Ib "Antequam transfretâssem in Normanniam regimen Angliæ fratri meo Baiocensi Episcopo commendaveram" The Chronicler (1087) says to the same effect, " He hæfde eorldom on Englelande, and þonne se cyng wæs on Normandige, þonne wæs he mægeste on þisum lande" This, I suppose, refers to a commission later than that held by Lanfranc at the time of Ralph's rebellion, though William of Malmesbury (iii 277) says, " Ille totius Angliæ vicedominus sub Rege fuit post necem Willelmi filii Osberni "

[3] Ib 647 B. " Frater meus Angliam vehementer oppressit . . . violenter opes diripuit, crudeliter pauperes oppressit, frivolâ spe milites mihi surripuit, totumque regnum injustis exactionibus concutiens exagitavit " It is curious to see how Thierry (ii 86) colours all this Odo is accused "d'avoir maltraité les Saxons outre mesure, au grand danger de la cause commune" So he translates " milites qui Angliam tutari debuerant" by "les guerriers sur la foi desquels reposait le salut des conquerants "

[4] Ib. "Contra Danos et Hibernenses et alios hostes mihi nimis infestos " The mention of the Irish should be taken in connexion with the rumour spoken of at an earlier stage

of his Barons, ought he to deal with such a brother as this?

The Assembly remained silent. None dared to pronounce sentence on such a criminal. Then the King himself spoke again. When one man, he said, disturbs the common weal of the whole land, he should not be spared out of any personal favour. He bade his Barons seize Odo and put him in ward. But there was no man there who dared to lay hands on a Bishop. Then William seized his brother with his own hands. "I am a clerk," cried Odo, "and a minister of the Lord. It is not lawful to condemn a Bishop without the sentence of the Pope." Then answered William—the subtle mind of Lanfranc having, it is said, suggested the distinction—"I meddle not with clerks and Prelates. I do not seize the Bishop of Bayeux, but I do seize the Earl of Kent. I seize my Earl whom I set over my Kingdom, and I demand of him an account of the stewardship which I committed to him."[1] While the complaints of the Bishop of Bayeux were thus unheeded, the Earl of Kent was carried off to Normandy and was kept in ward in the castle of Rouen.[2]

His imprisonment was heard of with great indignation by the Pontiff whom he had hoped to succeed. Gregory, in his private correspondence with Hugh Archbishop of Lyons, used very strong language indeed as to the insolence

---

[1] I translate Orderic. The same story is told by William of Malmesbury (iii 277), and in another place (iv. 306) he attributes the distinction to the prompting of Lanfranc.

The same distinction was drawn when the Chancellor Bishop of Ely seized the Bishop of Durham in 1190. See Richard of the Devizes, p 13.

[2] Ord. Vit. 647 C; Ann Wint. 1082 "Fiscatis omnibus quæ habuerat, in carcerem trusit, ubi, si voluit, delicta sua deflevit." Cf. Domesday, 375. "Ipse [Odo] habebat eâ die quâ fuit captus, et postea fuit dissaisitus." This does not imply any general confiscation. See Ellis, i 5. William of Malmesbury (iii 277) has a wonderful story about the treasures of Odo hidden in bags at the bottom of rivers, which seems to come from the same mint as the kindred legends about St·gand.

which the King of the English showed—certainly not for the first time—in putting a priest in prison. To William himself he used milder language, but he had nothing to urge in Odo's favour beyond the stock passages of Scripture which were held to forbid the laying of profane hands upon the Lord's anointed.[1] But William was not to be moved, and Odo remained in prison till William's general release of his prisoners on his death-bed.

The year of Odo's arrest is marked in the English Chronicles as a year of mickle hunger.[2] Next year came the disturbance between Thurstan and his monks at Glastonbury, and the death of Queen Matilda. But the same year or the next saw the beginning of a series of acts touching the internal government of England, acts which were of the highest moment both then and afterwards. These I shall here record simply as events, reserving the discussion of their working and their lasting consequences till we come to consider the last portion of our subject, the results of the Norman Conquest. We first hear of one of those heavy direct impositions in money which were so specially irksome to the minds of our forefathers. The King laid a tax of seventy-two pennies on every hide of land in the Kingdom.[3] The consequences of this taxation

*Famine of 1082, 1083.*

*Legislation of 1083-1086.*

*Tax laid on at Midwinter, 1083-1084.*

---

[1] Ep Greg , Jaffe, 570 "Ad notitiam tuam pervenisse non dubitamus qualiter Anglorum Rex in fratrem et coepiscopum nostrum Baiocensem contra fas et honestam ausus est manum mittere, eumque contra regiam modestiam reverentiamque sacerdotalem impudenter captum et impudentius adhuc in custodiâ . ." The letter is imperfect, as indeed is the longer one to William in p 518 One passage is remarkable, where Gregory says that other Kings complained of the special favour shown to William , "Licet quidam regiæ potestatis non modicum doleant et in nos sæpissime murmurent, se quodammodo contenini, quum querantur se non sic ab apostolicâ sede diligi nec ita factis aut sermonibus per nos honorari."

[2] Chron Petrib 1082. "Her nam se cyng Odan bisceop, and her wæs mycel hunger"

[3] Ib 1083 "And on þes ylcan geares æfter midewinter se cyng let beodan mycel geld and hefelic ofer eall Englaland, þæt wæs æt ælcere hyde twa and hundseofenti peanega" Florence puts the tax of "sex solidi" in

CHAP XXI *showed themselves somewhat later; what we next hear of were measures of which the cause, or at least the occasion, was an immediate military necessity. William's hold on England was now again threatened by the rival power of Denmark. The wise King Swend had now been dead for eight years. His immediate successor was his son Harold, of whom we have already heard as the fellow-soldier of Waltheof when York and Northumberland were for a moment rescued from William's sway. Of this prince the characters given by Danish writers are somewhat contradictory. In some accounts he appears as slothful and contemptible, while in others he bears the name of a wise and beneficent lawgiver.[1] But whatever was the character of his reign in Denmark, it had no importance as regards England. The reign of his brother and successor, Cnut the saint and martyr, was of quite another kind. The conquest or deliverance of England was one of his great objects. He had himself taken part in two English expeditions. Besides that in which he shared with his brother Harold, he had also borne his part in that vain raid on York which had been stirred up by Ralph of Norfolk in the year of his revolt.[2] His ill success on those occasions rankled in his mind;[3] his marriage with Adela of Flanders[4] brought him into close alliance with the bitterest continental enemy of William, and he was further*

State of Denmark. Death of Swend Estrithson 1076

Reign of Harold Hein 1076–1080.

Reign of Saint Cnut 1080–1086

His former expeditions to England 1069, 1075.

---

1084 It was no doubt voted at the Midwinter Gemót of 1083-1084 and levied in the course of 1084 Matthew Paris (i. 27) adds, "unde diatim postea cœpit, maledictionibus super caput suum congestis, corpore manifeste deteriorari" On this tax see vol ii p 574

[1] On Saint Cnut and all that belongs to him the fullest account is to be found in his Life by Æthelnoth, Langebek, iii 325. On Harold's legislation, see c iv p 341, and Saxo, 214. See also Swend Aggesson, Langebek, i 56, who sums up his character; "Haraldus, quem ob benignitatis mollitiem Cotem [Hein] cognominabant, successit in regno. Hic primus leges Danis in regiæ electionis loco jam dicto præscripsit atque rogavit" [2] See above, p 586.

[3] Will. Malm iii 261 "Veteris repulsæ memor"

[4] See above, p 587.

called on to undertake the enterprise by Englishmen who sought his court, and prayed him to come and deliver a kindred people from the bondage in which they were held by men of Roman speech.[1] At last his mind was made up; he would go forth with all the might of Denmark, at once to avenge the blood of his kinsmen who had died on Senlac and to assert his own rights as the successor of his great namesake. The undertaking was planned on a great scale; a thousand Danish ships are said to have been gathered together in the Limfiord, the inlet which in late times has become a strait, and has thus made the northern part of Jutland an island. Six hundred ships were sent or promised by Cnut's father-in-law, the Count of Flanders.[2] Olaf Kyrre too, the pious and peaceful King of Norway, was stirred up to bear his part in a work for which a son of Harold Hardrada might seem to have a special call. Olaf however declined to go in person. He had not Cnut's skill or experience in warfare, nor had the princes of his house found the same luck in their English expeditions as the princes of the house of Cnut. But though he would not go himself, he gladly sent sixty ships to take a share in the enterprise under the command of the Danish King.[3]

[1] The language of Æthelnoth, c xi. (iii 346), is very remarkable, "Anglorum gens nobilissima .. Haroldo Rege fortissimo a Willelmo, *Australium Normannorum* Duce, belli insidiis interempto, ipsoque Willelmo ita demum Anglorum imperium vi arripiente, eorumdem, quos supra commemoravimus, *Romanorum ceu Francigenarum* [he had just before spoken of " Francigenæ qui et Romani dicuntur "] dominatûs jure diutius oppressa, eo tantummodo pristinæ se restituendam libertati præsumebat incipere, si insignissimum principem Kanutum, cum sui exercitûs viris, ad ulciscendam consanguinei necem, Haroldi scilicet quondam Regis, ab eisdem Romanis interempti, Brittanniæ littoribus agnovisset applicare "

[2] See the account of the fleet in Æthelnoth, c xii ; Ord Vit 649 D, Will. Malm iii 261 " Classem, ut accepimus, mille et eo amplius navium in Angliam parat, auxilio ei erat socer Robertus Friso sexcentarum ratium dominus." Our own Chronicle (1085) also bears witness that Cnut "fundade biderward and wolde gewinnan þis land mid Rodbeardes eorles fultume of Flaudran "

[3] See the Saga of Olaf Kyrre, Laing, iii 110.

688    THE LATER DAYS OF WILLIAM.

CHAP. XXI.    England, or at least her King, was thus threatened by a force such as had not set forth from a Northern haven since the great voyage of Harold Hardrada. All the great maritime powers of the North, Denmark, Norway, Flanders, were leagued together to take away the Crown from the head of William. The King who was thus threatened was now in Normandy, engaged in a petty warfare against his vassal of Sainte-Susanne.[1] He was more fortunate in his dealings with the more powerful enemy. William acted with the speed and energy with which he knew how to act whenever speed and energy best served his purposes. He crossed over to England at the head of a vast host of soldiers of all kinds of arms, but among whom native Normans seem to have formed the smallest portion. The more part were mercenaries hired from France and Britanny; the days were gone when William could hope to win battles by the help of Norman and even of English valour. But among those mercenaries a brother of the King of the French himself, Hugh, surnamed the Great, did not disdain to serve[2] These hirelings, brought into England like the Brabançons of the thirteenth century and the Italians of the sixteenth, formed a host both of horse and foot such as had never before sought this land, and men wondered how the land might feed them all.[3] They were quartered

William's return.

His mercenaries.

[1] See above, p. 657.
[2] Will Malm. iii 262.
[3] Chron Petrib 1085. "He ferde into Englalande mid swa mycclan here ridendra manna and gangendra of Francrice and of Brytlande, swa næfre ær þis land ne gesohte, swa þæt menn wundredon hu þis land mihte eall þone here afedan." Cf Hist Ab ii 11  Æthelnoth also (c xii, iii 349) mentions the mercenaries with other details of William's preparations, " Willelmus, arte tuitionis, utpote bellicosus heros, non imperitus, castra et oppida munire, muris et fossâ cum propugnaculis castella circumcingere, urbium muros renovare et eis vigilantiam adhibere, diversosque ad portus nauticas custodias deputare, exercitu vero conducto, tam a Gallis et Brittonibus quam a Cenomannis aggregato, ita urbium ædes replebantur ut vix suis domestici focis assidere viderentur." He adds, " Anglis autem, quibus non minimi desiderii

on all the King's vassals, spiritual and temporal, each man having to feed a certain number of the mercenaries according to the greatness of his estate.[1] That year, the Chronicler tells us, men had great pain and sorrow, for the King caused all the land along the sea coast to be laid waste, that, if his foe came up against him, he might find neither food nor help in the wilderness.[2] Such was the ruthless policy of England's Conqueror, a contrast indeed to the generous heart of her defender, who was ready to risk his life and kingship rather than lay waste a rood of English ground.[3]

But the storm soon passed away. Discontents and dissensions arose in the Danish fleet, discontents which were heightened when Cnut sent the ringleader of the disaffected, his own brother Olaf, as a prisoner to his father-in-law in Flanders.[4] In the course of the next year Cnut died by the hands of his own subjects in the church of Odensee.[5] He was canonized by the Church, and his name was patriarchally lengthened by Papal authority.[6] But, before the former year was out, William knew

Danici exercitûs adventum didicerant, barbas radere, arma et exuvias ad instar Romanorum coaptare et, ad deludendum adventantium visus, per omnia Francigenis, quos et Romanos dici prætulimus, assimilare præcepit, quod perpauci fecere" "Barbas" must at least be translated "whiskers" in the elder sense

[1] Chron Petrib 1085. "Ac se cyng let toscyfton þone here geond all his land to his mannon, and hi fæddon þone here ælc be his land efne"

[2] Ib "And men hæfdon mycel geswinc þæs geares, and se cyng lett awestan þæt land abutan þa sæ, þet gif his feond comen úpp, þæt hi næfdon na on hwam hi fengon swa rædlice."

[3] See vol iii p 435

[4] See Æthelnoth, c xiii, Saxo, 218.

[5] See the accounts of Cnut's death or martyrdom in Æthelnoth, c xxvi-xxviii, Swend Aggesson, c vi, Saxo, 220  Our Chronicle mentions it under a wrong year, 1087, " Þa Dænescan þe wæs ærur geteald eallra folcra getreowust, wurdon awende to þære meste untriwðe and to þam mæsten swicdóme þe æfre mihte gewurðan  Hi gecuron and ábugan to Cnute cynge and him aðas sworon, and syððan hine earhlice ofslogon innan anre cyrcean"  See also Will Malm iii 261

[6] See vol i p 442

VOL. IV.                           Y Y

690    THE LATER DAYS OF WILLIAM.

CHAP XXI
William sends back part of the mercenaries
1085-1086

that the main danger had passed away. Part of his mercenaries he kept in England through the winter, but part he let go to their own homes, and he kept the Midwinter Feast at Gloucester in peace.[1]

Midwinter Gemót of Gloucester 1085-1086.

The Midwinter Assembly of that year was one of the most memorable in our history, and we have a more minute record of its acts than we can often recover of the acts of these ancient Parliaments. The King first held his court for five days with his Witan, discharging no doubt

Lanfranc's Synod

the formal and the judicial business of the occasion. Then, according to the new custom of separating ecclesiastical and temporal assemblies, the Archbishop and his clergy

Ulfcytel of Crowland deposed

held their Synod for three days[2] It was in this Synod that Ulfcytel, the Abbot of Crowland, was deposed; and it was doubtless now that Ingulf, whose name has become so enveloped in legend that it is hard to think of him as a real actor in real scenes, received the pastoral staff from

Election of Bishops

King William.[3] Three Bishops were now chosen, of all of whom we have already heard, Maurice of London, William of Thetford, and Robert of Chester, soon to be of Coventry. All, it is significantly added, were the King's clerks.[4] After this came the great legislative

The King and his Witan

work of the Assembly. "The King had mickle thought and very deep speech with his Witan." The main subject of that mickle thought and deep speech was "about this

---

[1] Chron Petrib 1085 "Ac þa se cyng geaxode to soðan þæt his feond gelætte wæron, and ne mihten na geforðian heora fare, þa lett he sum þone here faren to heora agene lande, and sum he heold on þisum lande ofer winter"

[2] Ib. "Da to þam midwintre wæs se cyng on Gleaweceastre mid his witan, and heold þær his hired v dagas and siððan þe arcebisceop and gehadode men hæfden sinoð þreo dagas" See above, p 393.

[3] See above, p 600

[4] See above, p 393  The Chronicler gives their names and sees, and adds, "hi wæron ealle þæs cynges clerecas" On these Prelates, see above, pp 375, 419, 421.

land, how it was set and by what men." [1] Many things would join together at this time to make William seek for a more full and accurate report of the state of his Kingdom than either he or any other prince of his time had ever before thought of asking for. It had perhaps been found no easy matter to levy fairly and accurately the tax of seventy-two pennies on each hide of land. And the threatened invasion from Denmark, the immediate fear of which had passed away but which might easily come again, might well make William anxious fully to know what were the real resources, military and material, of his Kingdom. It was to this end that the thought and speech of William and his counsellors were directed, and the result was Domesday.

The great record, the work of our foreign King, stands as a national possession side by side with the contemporary Chronicle in our native tongue. Each is unique in its own kind. No other nation has such materials to draw upon for its history. Of the nature of the record itself, of the light which it throws upon the laws and manners of the time, I shall speak fully elsewhere. I have now only to speak of its formation as one of the great events of these memorable legislative years. Commissioners went forth into every shire in England to make the inquiries which the decree of the Assembly had prescribed. The whole work was done in the space of a single year,[2] and

[1] Chron. Petrib 1085 "After þisum hæfde se cyng mycel geðeaht and swiðe deope spæce wið his witan ymbe þis land hu hit wære gesett, oððe mid hwilcon mannon." The "deep speech," the *colloquium*, of our forefathers simply needs translation to become a French *Parlement*

[2] The Chronicle shows that the order for taking the Survey was made at the Midwinter Session of 1085-6 The Colophon of the second volume of Domesday is, "Anno millesimo octogesimo sexto ab Incarnatione Domini, vigesimo vero regni Willelmi, facta est ista descriptio, non solum per hos tres comitatus [Essex, Norfolk, and Suffolk], sed jam per alios" The

692                 THE LATER DAYS OF WILLIAM.

CHAP XXI the way in which it was done was very different in different parts of the country. It would therefore seem that the Kingdom was divided into districts, and that different Commissioners were sent to each. In the case of some of the midland shires the names of the Commissioners have been preserved. Those who took the Survey in Worcestershire were four in number, and three of them are already well known to us. We no longer find among them the names of even renegade Englishmen, as in the earlier commission for the redemption of lands.[1] The four were Remigius Bishop of Lincoln, Walter Giffard the aged Earl of Buckingham, Henry of Ferrers, lord of Tutbury and of Fifhide, and Adam, one of the sons of Hubert of Rye and brother of the *Dapifer* Eudo of Colchester.[2] In each shire the Commissioners made their inquiry by the oaths of the Sheriffs, the parish priests, the reeves, and the men generally, French and English, of each lordship. They were to report who had held the land in the time of King Eadward and who held it then; what had been its value in the time of King Eadward and what was its value then; and—no unimportant matter in William's eyes—whether its value could in any way be raised.[3] These details we learn from official

The Midland Commissioners.

Mode of the inquiry.

---

other alleged dates, which are manifestly wrong, are collected by Ellis, i. 4                    [1] See above, p 25

[2] See the record from Heming's Worcester Cartulary in Ellis, i 20; "Hoc testimonium totius vicecomitatûs Wireceastre, dato sacramento jurisjurandi, firmavit, exhortante et ad id laborante piissimo et prudentissimo patre Domino Wulstano Episcopo, tempore Regis Willelmi senioris, coram principibus ejusdem Regis, Remigio scilicet Lincoloiensi Episcopo et Comite Walterio Giffardo et Henrico de Ferens et Adam fratre Eudonis Dapiferi Regis, qui ad inquirendas et describendas possessiones et consuetudines, tam Regis quam principum suorum, in hâc provinciâ et in pluribus aliis ab ipso Rege destinati sunt eo tempore quo totam Angliam idem Rex describi fecit."

[3] The form is given in the Inquisitio Eliensis, Domesday, iv. 497 (see also Ellis, i 22); "Barones Regis inquirunt videlicet per sacramentum Vicecomitis scirae et omnium Baronum et eorum Francigenarum et totius

records. The national Chronicler lets us know how the popular feeling at the time looked upon such an inquiry. "He sent over all England into ilk shire his men, and let them find out how many hundred hides were in the shire, or what the King himself had of land or cattle in the land, or whilk rights he ought to have to twelve months of the shire. Eke he let write how mickle of land his Archbishops had and his Bishops and his Abbots and his Earls, and though I it longer tell, what or how mickle ilk man had that landholder was in England, in land and in cattle, and how mickle fee it were worth. So very narrowly he let spear it out, that there was not a single hide nor a yard of land, nor so much as—it is shame to tell and it thought him no shame to do—an ox nor a cow nor a swine was left that was not set in his writ. And all the writs were brought to him since."[1]

Such was the spirit—a spirit which has not wholly died out in our own day—with which Englishmen then looked on this narrow spying out of their homes and of their goods. And their discontent found a more vigorous expression than in the mere wail of a chronicler. In some places the inquiries led to open disturbances, and not a few lives were lost.[2] The first results of the Survey

centuriatûs, presbyteri, præpositi, VI villani uniuscujusque villæ" Then follow the subjects for inquiry. The value is to be reckoned "tripliciter, scilicet tempore Regis Æduardi, et quando Rex Willelmus dedit, et quomodo sit modo, et si potest plus haberi quam habeatur." The names of the jurors are a good study of nomenclature. One of the first is "Rodbertus Anglicus."

[1] I translate the well-known passage under the year 1085. The latter part is wonderfully vigorous, "Hit is sceame to tellanne, ac hit ne þuhte him nan sceame to donne, an oxe ne an cû ne an swin næs belyfon, þæt næs gesæt on his gewrite. And calle þa gewrita wæron gebroht to him syððan." The Survey, I need hardly say, is recorded by all writers, good and bad. One of the most curious accounts is in T Rudborne, Angl Sacr. i 257.

[2] Flor. Wig 1086 "Vexata est terra multis cladibus inde procedentibus."

## 694 THE LATER DAYS OF WILLIAM.

<small>CHAP XXI</small>

<small>Whitsun Gemót at Westminster. May 24, 1086</small>

<small>Henry dubbed a knight</small>

<small>The Survey finished. July 1086.</small>

<small>Gemót of Salisbury August 1, 1086</small>

were shown in the next year. While the great inquisition was going on William abode in England. He held his Easter Feast as usual at Winchester, and his Pentecostal Feast at Westminster; and at the last meeting he dubbed his youngest son, the Ætheling Henry, to *rider* or knight.[1] But the greatest Assembly of this year was held at an unusual time and in an unusual place. By Lammastide the Great Survey was made. William now knew how this land was set and by what men. It would seem that the summer months had been passed by him in going to and fro;[2] the process of taking the Survey, and the disturbances to which the inquiries gave rise, may well have called here and there for his personal presence. And now a Mickle Gemót indeed was held, not within or without the walls of any city, but on the great plain where William had once before reviewed his victorious army after the Conquest of England was over.[3] All the Witan, and all the landowners of England who were worth summoning, were gathered together at Salisbury. The royal quarters were doubtless fixed in the castle on the hill where Osmund's minster was rising,[4] while the plain itself was well fitted for the encampment and assembling of a body whose numbers were handed down by tradition as no less than sixty thousand.[5] In this great meeting

---

[1] Chron Petrib 1086. "He dubbade his sunu Henric to ridere þær." We have lost the word *rider* = *Ritter, chevalier*, in this sense, one which was not yet taken by *knight* The religious part of the ceremony was performed by Lanfranc. Ord Vit 665 D, "Hunc Lanfrancus, dum juvenile robur attingere vidit, ad arma pro defensione regni sustulit, eumque loricâ induit et galeam capiti ejus imposuit, eique *ut Regis filio et in regali stemmate nato* militiæ cingulum in nomine Domini cinxit"

[2] Ib "Syððan he ferde abutan swa þæt he com to Lammæssan to Searebyrig."

[3] See above, p 318      [4] See above, p 418.

[5] Chron Petrib. 1086 "þær him comon to his witan and ealle þa landsittende men þe ahtes wæron ofer eall Engleland, wæron þæs mannes men þe hi wæron" The "witan" and the ordinary "landsittende men" are beginning to be distinguished, the germ of Lords and Commons. The

a decree was passed which is one of the most memorable pieces of legislation in the whole history of England. In other lands where military tenures existed it was beginning to be held that he who had plighted his faith to a lord who was the man of the King was the man of that lord only, and did not become the man of the King himself.[1] It was beginning to be held that, if such a man followed his immediate lord to battle against the common sovereign, the lord might draw on himself the guilt of treason, but his men who followed him were guiltless. It was owing to this doctrine, more than to any other one cause, that both France and the Imperial Kingdoms fell in pieces. William himself would have been amazed if any vassal of his had refused to draw his sword in a war with France on the score of duty towards the common overlord. But in England, at all events, William was determined to be full King over the whole land, to be immediate sovereign and immediate lord of every man within it. A statute was passed that every freeman in the realm should take the oath of fealty to King William, the oath that he would be faithful to him within and without England, that he would keep his lands and honours with all faithfulness, and would defend him before all men against all enemies.[2] The statute was passed, and it was at once

*Statute to make all men the men of the King*

*No duty in other countries due from the arrière vassal to the over-lord*

---

number sixty thousand comes from Orderic (649 D), who brings out the connexion with the Survey, "His temporibus militiam Anglici regni Rex Willelmus conscribi fecit, et lx millia militum invenit, quos omnes, dum necesse esset, paratos esse præcepit." He goes on to speak of the preparations of Cnut See also 523 B

[1] See at a somewhat later time the refusal of John of Joinville, as the man of the Count of Champagne, to take any oath to Saint Lewis (Mémoires, p 37, ed Michel, Paris, 1858), "Il le me demanda, mès je ne voz faire point de serement, car je n'estoie pas son home"

[2] Stubbs, Select Charters, 80 "Statuimus ut omnis liber homo fœdere et sacramento affirmet, quod infra et extra Angliam Willelmo Regi fideles esse volunt, terras et honorem illius omni fidelitate cum eo servare, et ante eum contra inimicos defendere"

CHAP XXI

*All take the oath to William*

*Effect on later English history.*

*Another tax laid on.*

carried into effect. The whole Assembly which had been brought together, "whose men soever they were, all bowed to him and were his men, and swore to him faithful oaths that they would be faithful to him against all other men."[1] The great work of William's reign was to make England for ever after an undivided Kingdom. It was on that day that this great work was put into the formal shape of a written law.

William had thus both completed and secured his conquest. He had not only conquered the land, but he had conquered the tendencies to anarchy and division which lurked both in the old institutions of the land and in the new institutions which he had himself brought in and fostered. His work in England was now done, and he left his island Kingdom never to come back to it. But, before he went, he had yet to mark his last days in England by one more act of fiscal oppression. He did after his wont, the Chronicler tells us; he gathered "mickle scot of his men where he might have any charge to bring against them, whether with right or otherwise"[2] Here is another step in the downward course. William had now sunk to wring money from men by false accusations. Different indeed had his rule now become from the rule of that earlier conqueror of England who needed no money raised by unrighteousness.[3] While the money was

---

[1] Chron Petrib. 1086 "Ealle hi bugon to him and wæron his menn, and him hold aðas sworon þæt hi woldon ongean ealle oðre men him holde beon" The direct connexion between the Survey, the Assembly, and the Oath is well brought out by William of Malmesbury (iii 258); "Provinciales adeo nutui suo substraverat, ut sine ullâ contradictione primus censum omnium capitum ageret, omnium prædiorum redditus in totâ Angliâ notitiæ suæ per scriptum adjiceret, omnes liberos homines, cujuscumque essent, suæ fidelitati sacramento adigeret"

[2] Chron Petrib 1086 "And þeah he dyde ærest æfter his gewunan, begeat swiðe mycelne sceatt of his mannan, þær he mihte ænige teale to habban oððe mid rihte oððe elles"

[3] See vol i. p 480

in gathering, William abode in the Isle of Wight; he then crossed over into Normandy with his newly extorted treasure. It was perhaps a sign of the times that the Ætheling Eadgar, discontented, we are told, with the small honour which he received at William's hands, left his court by his leave, and went at the head of two hundred knights to join the Norman warriors in Apulia.[1] His sister Christina about the same time took the veil in the Abbey of Romsey, of which before many years she became the Abbess.[2]

*CHAP. XXI.*

*Eadgar leaves William and goes to Apulia.*

*Christina takes the veil.*

### § 6. *The Last Days of William.*
### *August–September*, 1087.

We now enter on the last year of the reign and life of the Conqueror. And the year in which William died, like the year in which he came into England, was a year of signs and wonders. No comet indeed blazed in the heavens, but men deemed that they saw nearer and darker signs of God's wrath upon the earth. The year of the great gathering at Salisbury had itself been a year of deep sorrow. Besides the tumults which had followed on the taking of the Survey, besides the last and most wrongful extortion of money, it was a year of evil in the physical world. "It was a very heavy year and toilsome and sorrowful in England in murrain of cattle; and corn and fruits were sprouting, and such mickle bad luck was there in weather such as man might not lightly think

*Physical phæno- mena of the years 1086–1087*

---

[1] Chron Petrib 1086 "Eadgar æðeling, Ædwardes mæg cynges, beah þa fram him, forðig he næfde na mycelne wurðscipe of him, ac se ælmihtiga God him gife wurðscipe on þam toweardan" Florence says, "Eo tempore, clito Eadgarus, licentiâ a Rege impetratâ cum cc militibus mare transiit, et Apuliam adiit." William of Malmesbury (iii 251) does not mention this Apulian expedition

[2] Chron Petrib, Flor Wig 1086. Christina's lands are found in Domesday, 160, 244 One estate in Warwickshire had been held by Earl Eadwine, of another it is said distinctly, "Rex dedit Cristinæ"

698    THE LATER DAYS OF WILLIAM.

CHAP XXI. of; such mighty thundering and lightening was there that it slew many men, and ever it grew worse with men more and more."[1] Of the last year itself the picture is yet more fearful. It needs all the strength of our ancient tongue to set forth the full horrors of such a time. "It was a very heavy year and a year of mighty sickness in this land. Such disease came upon men that well nigh every other man was in the worst evil, and that so strongly that many men died of the evil. Then came there through the mickle storms of which we have before told such mickle hunger over all England that many men died sadly through the hunger. Alas, how sad and rueful a tide was that! Then the wretched men lay driven full nigh to death, and then came the sharp hunger and quite slew them. Who is there that may not feel sad for such a tide? or who is so hard of heart that he would not weep over such evil luck?"[2] It was a year too of public misfortunes of other kinds. London and other towns had been burned not many years before,[3] and now Saint Paul's minster was again burned with the most and best part of the city, and many other minsters were burned and well nigh all the head towns in England.[4] But the horrors of storm, fire, pestilence, and hunger were not all; it was a year marked by wars and fightings, by the crimes of men

Fires in London and elsewhere.

---

[1] Chron Petrib 1086  The Chronicler adds, "Gebete hit God elmihtiga þonne his willa sy"  On the words "corn and wæstmas wæron ætstandene," see Mr Earle's note, p. 353.

[2] The year is ushered in by the Chronicler with unusual solemnity; "Æfter ure Drihtnes Hælendes Cristes gebyrtide an þusend wintra and seofan and hundeahtatig wintra on þam án and twentigan geare þæs þe Willelm weolde and stihte Engleland, swa him God uðe, gewearð swiðe hefelic and swiðe woldberendlic gear on þissum lande"  Then follows the description which I have tried to modernize in the text  But our modern speech fails utterly beside that of our fathers

[3] Chron Wig 1078, Petrib 1077

[4] Chron Petrib 1087. The fire in London, besides the minster, burned "þæt mæste dæl and þæt rotteste eall þære burh"  Besides London, "forbarn fullneah ælc heafod port on eallon Englelande."

and by the deaths of men of renown. The wonders of the year seem to have so deeply stamped themselves on men's minds that events were transferred to it in popular belief which a stricter reckoning would have placed under other years. It was held to have been the year of the martyrdom of the holy Cnut in Denmark;[1] it was held to have been the year of the mighty warfare of Alfonso of Castile against the infidels of Seville.[2] Both in England and in Normandy many of the chief men of the land died.[3] Our Chronicler records the death of Bishop Stigand of Chichester, Abbot Scotland of Saint Augustine's, Abbot Thurstan of Pershore, and Ælfsige the last of the Abbots of Bath. And in this year too died the lord of them all, William England's King.[4]

*Supposed contemporary events in other countries*

*Deaths in 1087*

The warfare in which William met his death was one which formed an unworthy and undignified end to such a career as his. The French Vexin, the border land of France and Normandy, had often been a matter of dispute between the Kings of Paris and the Dukes of Rouen. The Norman writers held that it had been ceded by King Henry to Duke Robert as the reward of his restoration to his Kingdom by Norman arms.[5] It was only during the

*Dispute about the French Vexin*
*Its history*
*Ceded to Robert by Henry*

---

[1] See above, p 689, for the real date of Cnut's death in 1086

[2] On this, the only reference to Spanish affairs in our Chronicles, see Mr. Earle's note, p 354  The Chronicler seems to have confounded the conquest of Toledo by Alfonso in 1085 with his defeat in 1086 or 1087

[3] Chron Petrib 1087. " Eac on þisan ilcan lande on þam ilcan geare forðferdon manega rice men " He then counts up the Prelates mentioned in the text  On Stigand, see above, pp 409, 418 , on Scotland, p. 412 , on Thurstan, p 388 , on Ælfsige, p 390  For the like remarkable deaths in Normandy, see below, p 705

[4] Ib  "And þa heora eallra hlaford, Willelm Englælandes cyng, þe we ær beforan embe spæcon "  I think this is the earliest use of the strictly territorial style in English  See vol. i p 84

[5] See Ord Vit 655 B  The homage of the reigning Count Drogo, the son-in law of Æthelred (see vol ii p 130), was transferred to Normandy with his own consent , "Hoc libentissime concessit, hominioque facto dum avixit præfato Duci fideliter servivit"

700                THE LATER DAYS OF WILLIAM.

CHAP. XXI.  confusion of William's childhood that the district had been
Reannexed   again annexed to France, and William had failed to re-
to France
in Wil-     claim it only through his being occupied in such greater
liam's
childhood   matters as the conquests of Maine and England.[1] We can
            well believe that a border warfare often went on along the
Incursions  frontier, but it would seem that just at this time the
of the
French at   incursions of the French commanders in Mantes became of
Mantes.     unusual importance. Two captains, Hugh and Ralph, of
            whom the latter bore the fitting name of *Malvoisin*,
            harried all the neighbouring districts of Normandy, espe-
            cially the lands of William of Bieteuil, the brother of the
            imprisoned Earl of Hereford, and those of Roger of Ivry,
William     the sworn brother of the lord of Oxford.[2] On this, William
demands
the whole   sent to Philip, not merely complaining of the damage done
Vexin       by his officers, but demanding the cession of the whole
            province, with the towns of Pont-Isere, Chaumont, and
            Mantes. Terrible threats were added, unless the disputed
            district were at once given up,[3] but William was at that
            moment not exactly in a condition to carry out his threats
William's   in person. The bulk of his body had so increased that he
medical
treatment.  was driven to seek medical means to lessen it. He was
            therefore keeping quiet at Rouen under a prescribed treat-
Jest of     ment of drink and diet.[4] King Philip was believed to
Philip.
            have made a coarse and silly jest on the condition of his
            mighty neighbour. The King of the English, he said, lay
            in at Rouen, and there would doubtless be a grand display

---

[1] Ord. Vit. 655 D. "Majoribus sibi curis in Cænomannenses vel Anglos crescentibus conticuit, et contra Henricum dominum suum seu Philippum filium ejus pro Vulcassino pago arma levare distulit."

[2] Ord. Vit. 655 A.

[3] Ib. "Nisi jus suum sibi reddatur, terribilibus minis in hostes evehitur."

[4] Will. Malm. iii. 281. "Ventrem potione alleviârat." Wace, 14181,

" A Roem esteit à séjor           Ne sai dire combien le tint
   U il aveit este maint jor,      Ne pout monter sor son destrier,
   Une enferté là li avint,        Armes porter ne guerréier."

of candles at his churching. The wrath of William was kindled, and he swore one of those fearful oaths by which, and by his very look, he was wont to strike terror into men. By the resurrection and splendour of God, he would, when he rose up again and went to mass, light a hundred thousand candles at the expense of King Philip.[1] He kept his word; about the middle of August, when the corn was in the fields, and the grapes in the vineyards, and the apples in the orchards,[2] he led forth his troops to gather in the rich spoil of the fruitful season. All was laid waste; all was overthrown, the thought of mercy passed utterly away from William's mind; the ruin and deaths of multitudes were to pay for the insult offered to him by their King.[3] At last he reached Mantes itself. The defenders of the town had come forth to see at least, if they could not hinder, the harrying of their fields; friends and foes

*CHAP. XXI.*
*William's answer.*

*William enters the Vexin August, 1087.*

*His ravages.*

*William enters Mantes August 15, 1087*

---

[1] Philip's jest, such as it is, is given in two or three forms in William of Malmesbury (iii. 281), Wace (14187), R Wendover (ii 28), M Paris (i. 33). William preserves one very characteristic feature of William's answer, "Talia per resurrectionem et splendorem Dei pronuntians, quod soleret ex industriâ talia sacramenta facere, quæ ipso hiatu oris terrificum quiddam auditorum mentibus insonarent" Wace (14197) makes the answer run,

"Quant jo, dist-il, releverai,      Mille chandeles li oferai,
Dedenz sa terre à messe irai,     Lumeignons de fust i ara,
Riche offrende li porterai,       E fer por feu en som luira"

[2] Will Malm in 282. "Quando et segetes in agris, et botri in vineis, et poma in viridariis" This surely comes from a ballad Orderic, 655 D, gives us the fact in prose, when he speaks of the "conculcatio segetum et exstirpatio vincarum" But, comparing William of Malmesbury and the Chronicles, it would seem that Orderic is wrong in placing the beginning of the expedition in the last week of July.

[3] The reflexion is from William of Malmesbury, iii 282, "Omnia proterit, cuncta populatur, nihil erat quod furentis animum mitigaret, ut injuriam insolenter acceptam multorum dispendio ulcisceretur" Our own Chronicler seems shocked at William's breach of the duty of a vassal, "For Willelm cyng of Normandige into France mid fyrde, and hergode uppan his agenne hlaford Philippe þam cynge, and sloh of his mannon mycelne dæl"

pressed through the gates together,[1] and now the candles of William's churching were lighted in all their brightness. He had reached a spot which had been memorable on two occasions in his earlier life. Mantes had been the town where the hosts of France were gathered for that great invasion of Normandy which had been brought to nought on the day of Mortemer.[2] It was the town whose princes he had been long before suspected of having made away with by the help of the poisoner's bowl.[3] The city of Walter and Biota was now the border fortress of France, and the helpless burghers paid the penalty for the silly jests of their King. To the utter ruin which William's hand wrought that day it is owing that not a trace survives which can be assigned to his age or to the ages before him. The noble church whose two lofty towers of open work attract the eyes of every passer by may have risen slowly from the ground by the help of the posthumous bounty of the repentant destroyer.[4] But there is not a stone in its soaring arcades which can lay claim to a date within a century after William's fatal visit. The other ornaments of the town, the civic palace, the tower of another church which has wholly perished, belong to days later still. On that day all was destroyed; the candles blazed merrily; the houses and goods of the citizens perished; the churches were burned, and holy recluses, who deemed it a crime to leave their cells even at such a moment, were burned with them.[5] William's heart was gladdened by

*Margin: Utter destruction of Mantes.*

---

[1] Ord. Vit. 655 D. "Cum exercitu suo Mandantum ex improviso venit, et cum castrensibus mixtim intravit; milites enim occulte exierant, ut viderent conculcationem segetum suarum et exstirpationem vinearum, quas Ascelinus Goellus pridie quam Rex advenisset cum Normannorum viribus devastaverat. Irruens itaque exercitus Regis cum oppidanis portas pertransivit."

[2] See vol. iii. p. 148.  [3] Ib. 207.  [4] See below, p. 707.

[5] Orderic (655 D) seems to wish to clear William from the guilt of the burning, "Exercitus . . . per rabiem armigerorum immisso igne castrum cum ecclesiis et aedibus combussit;" but the Chronicle and William of

the sight; he rode on, and bade his men heap on fuel to make the flames burn yet more bravely. But at that moment his horse stumbled, some say on the brink of a ditch, some say on the burning embers, the body of the bulky King was thrown forward against the tall iron pummel of his saddle; he kept his seat, but the pain of the blow was such that his eagerness was quenched, and he ordered a retreat to be sounded.[1]

The Conqueror had now received his death-wound. It was an unworthy fate indeed for one who had so often braved death in so many nobler and more awful shapes to fall at last by such an ignoble chance as the stumble of his horse among the burning embers of Mantes. And yet poetical justice itself might well be satisfied when the mighty warrior and ruler, who, with all his crimes, had never before stooped to mere useless and brutal havoc,

---

Malmesbury seem to make it his own work. The Chronicle, followed by Florence, speaks of two male recluses as burned, " And forbearnde þa burh Maþante, and ealle þa halige mynstres þe wæron innon þære burh, and twegen halige menn þe hyrsumedon Gode on ancer settle wuniende þær wæron forbearnde." In William they become " reclusa una, quæ spelæum suum nec in tali necessitate deserendum putavit."

[1] Will. Malm. iii. 232. " Quo successu exhilaratus, dum suos audacius incitat ut igni adjiciant pabula, propius flammas succedens foci calore et auctumnalis æstûs inæqualitate morbum nactus est. Dicunt quidam quod præruptam fossam sonipes transiliens interanea sessoris ruperit, quod in interiori parte sellæ venter protuberabat." The other version comes from Wace, 14213,

" Parmi la vile trespassout          Par grant air avant sailli,
  Sor un cheval ke mult amout,       Li Reis se tint k'il ne chai,
  En un arsiz mist ses dous piez,    Et il por co mult se bleca
  Maist tost les out à sei sachiez,  A son arçon u il hurta."

The tall saddle-bows shown in the Tapestry will be remembered. William of Jumièges (vii. 44) is vaguer, but nearly to the same effect, " Quum Willelmus Rex oppidum Medanta assiliens flammis ultricibus tradidisset, pondere armorum et labore clamoris quo suos exhortabatur, ut fertur, arvinâ intestinorum ejus liquefactâ, infirmari non modice cœpit." Orderic (656 A) is vaguer still, but the epithet which he uses is not without meaning, " Tunc ex nimio æstu ac labore *pinguissimus Rex Guillelmus* infirmatus est."

704                THE LATER DAYS OF WILLIAM.

CHAP XXI.  had to pay his life as the penalty for thus lowering himself
He is      to the level of meaner men.¹  Faint and suffering from
carried to
Rouen      the shock and from the internal wound, William turned
away from his schemes of vengeance, and, instead of
carrying his wasting arms any further within the dominions of his overlord, he was himself borne, a sick or
rather a dying man, to Rouen.  There he first took up
his quarters in the palace, but presently, finding the noise
and bustle of the capital too much for his sinking frame,
William    he caused himself to be moved out of the city to the
moved to
Saint      Priory of Saint Gervase, which stands on the hill
Gervase.   overlooking Rouen from the west.  There a crypt, the
oldest ecclesiastical work to be seen north of the Alps,
a crypt already ancient in William's days, covers the
remains of some of the earliest apostles of northern Gaul.
There was the tomb of the British Mellon, the first
Bishop of the metropolitan see of Normandy, and there
the Norman lord of all Britain, who had so lately received
the submission of Mellon's native land, came to spend
the short span of life which was still left to him on earth.²
There William lay for several weeks of sickness and pain;
but he never to the hour of his death lost either the possession of his senses or his full command of speech.³  We

[1] Chron Petrib 1087 "Reowlic þing he dyde, and reowlicor him
gelamp Hu reowlicor? Him geyfelade, and þæt him stranglice eglade
Hwæt mæg ic teollan? Se scearpa deað þe ne forlet ne rice menn ne
heane, seo hine genam" Men seem almost to have doubted whether the
Conqueror was subject to sickness and death like other men

[2] Ord Vit 656 A "Quia strepitus Rothomagi, quæ populosa civitas
est, intolerabilis erat ægrotanti, extra urbem ipse Rex præcepit se efferri ad
ecclesiam Sancti Gervasii in colle sitam occidentali" I know of no reason
to doubt the vast antiquity of the crypt On Saint Mellon or Melan, see
Orderic, 557, 558, but he seems to make him a Roman  The common
tradition makes him a Briton, and he has a church dedicated to him in
Monmouthshire

[3] Ib. "In ægritudine suâ usque ad horam mortis integrum sensum et
vivacem loquelam habuit" But he could not have lingered six weeks, as
Orderic says

are told that, when the news of the blow which had fallen on him was spread through the land, the enemies of peace rejoiced, deeming that they might now seize on the goods of other men at pleasure, but that those to whom peace was dear looked forward with dread to the death of the man who had so long kept the land in order.[1] Well indeed they might fear, when there was a chance that the rod which had been so long and so mightily wielded by William the Great should pass into the feeble hands of the wayward Robert. But, while men's hearts were thus bowed down, one man, the noblest spirit in all William's Duchy, was taken away from the evil to come. Perhaps while William was harrying the Vexin, perhaps while he lay on his death-bed at Rouen, the soul of Gulbert of Hugleville, the man who had refused to stain his hands with the spoils of England, passed away in peace.[2] Nor did Gulbert die alone; in Normandy as well as in England this year was noted as a year of death among men of note, as if the King of Men who was passing away could not go out of the world without a fitting following.[3] And far away at Bruges, while William was paying the penalty of his deed of wrong at Mantes, Gunhild the daughter of Godwine ended her days in peace.[4]

*Death of Gulbert of Hugleville August 14, 1087?*

*Other deaths in Normandy.*

*Death of Gunhild August 24, 1087*

---

[1] Ord. Vit. 656 A. "Quidam qui paci adversabantur gaudebant, et liberam permissionem furandi seu res alienas rapiendi exspectabant Porro alii qui securitatem pacis exspectabant pacifici patroni mortem multum formidabant."

[2] Ib 664 A. "Dum Rex adhuc ægrotaret, cognatus ejusdem Guilbertus Alfagiensis, filius Ricardi de Huglevillâ, vir bonus et simplex, xix Kal. Sept. defunctus est." This would be August 14, the day before William's hurt at Mantes, according to the reckoning of our own writers. See above, p 701

[3] Orderic gives a list in 664 A. He makes two curious comments, "Moriente Duce suo Normanni multas lacrimas fuderunt, si non pro illo, saltem pro amicis et cognatis suis qui tunc mortui sunt." And again, "Beati qui bene mortui sunt, qui ærumnas desolatæ regionis ac defensore carentis non viderunt"

[4] See above, p 159, and Appendix R.

CHAP XXI

William sends for Anselm, but does not see him.

Meanwhile Bishops and Abbots and other holy men were gathered round the bed of William to prepare their mighty master for his great change.[1] But one was wanting whose words of rebuke or comfort William specially longed for in that hour, one towards whom, stern as he had been towards others, he had ever been meek and lowly.[2] Of all the Prelates of Normandy, the one to whom William's thoughts first turned as the chosen physician of his soul was the holy man who sat in the place of Herlwin. At the bidding of his sovereign Anselm came from Bec to Rouen, but he was himself smitten by sickness, and the confessor and his expectant penitent never met again.[3] But among the assembled Prelates were men able to deal with the diseases of William's body as well as with those of his soul. For among them was Gilbert of Lisieux, skilled in the healing art, and his skill and that of his fellow-leeches told them that there was no longer any hope for William on earth. The death-bed of William was a death-bed of all formal devotion, a death-bed of penitence which we

Verdict of William's physicians.

His repentance.

---

[1] Ord. Vit 656 A. "Circa illum Præsules et Abbates et religiosi viri commorabantur, et morituro Principi salubre consilium perennis vitæ largiebantur"

[2] Eadmer, Vit Ans i 6 47 "Rex ipse Wilhelmus . . quamvis ob magnitudinem sui cunctis fere videretur rigidus ac formidabilis, Anselmo tamen ita erat inclinus et affabilis, ut ipso præsente omnino quam esse solebat, stupentibus aliis, fieret alius"

[3] This is I suppose at least the general meaning of the not very intelligible account of Eadmer (Hist Nov p 13, Selden); "Hic ergo Willielmus quum . . se meritis ac intercessionibus Anselmi omnimodis commendare disposuisset, eum ad se de Becco venire et non longe a se fecit hospitari. Verum quum ei de salute animæ suæ loqui differret, eo quod infirmitatem suam paullum levigari sentiret, contigit ipsius Principis corpus tantâ invalitudine deprimi ut curiæ inquietudines nullo sustinere pacto valeret Transito igitur Sequanâ, decubuit lecto in Ermentrudis villâ, quæ est contra Rotomagum in alterâ fluminis parte. Quidquid tum deliciarum Regi infirmo deferebatur, ab eo illarum medietas Anselmo infirmanti mittebatur, verumtamen nec eum amplius in hac vitâ videre, nec ei, ut proposuerat, quidquam de animâ suâ loqui promeruit. Tanta enim infirmitas occupavit utrumque ut nec Anselmus ad Regem Willielmum nec Willielmus posset pervenire ad Abbatem Anselmum."

may trust was more than formal.[1] The English Chronicler himself, after weighing the good and evil in him, sends him out of the world with a charitable prayer for his soul's rest;[2] and his repentance, late and fearful as it was, at once marks the distinction between the Conqueror on his bed of death and his successor cut off without a thought of penitence in the midst of his crimes. He made his will. The mammon of unrighteousness which he had gathered together amid the groans and tears of England he now strove so to dispose of as to pave his way to an everlasting habitation. All his treasures were distributed among the poor and the churches of his dominions.[3] A special sum was set apart for the rebuilding of the churches which had been burned at Mantes,[4] and gifts in money and books and ornaments of every kind were to be distributed among all the churches of England according to their rank.[5] He then spoke of his own life and of the arrangements which he wished to make for his dominions after his death. The Normans, he said, were a brave and unconquered race; but they needed the curb of a strong and

He distributes his treasure

His last speech

---

[1] Will. Malm. iii. 282. "Consulti medici inspectione urinæ certam mortem prædixere. Quo audito querimoniâ domum replevit, quod eum præoccuparet mors emendationem vitæ jamdudum meditantem. Resumpto animo, quæ Christiani sunt exsecutus est in confessione et viatico." Orderic is fuller on his devotions, and gives us the names of the "archiatri," Bishop Gilbert and Gunthard Abbot of Jumièges.

[2] Chron. Petrib. 1087. "Se ælmihtiga God cyþæ his saule mildheortnisse, and do him his synna forgifenesse." Then comes, "Das þing we habbað be him gewritene, ægðer ge gode ge yfele, þæt þa godan men niman æfter heora godnesse and forfleon mid ealle yfelnesse, and gan on þone weg þe us lætt to heofonan rice."

[3] Ord. Vit. 656 B. "Sapiens heros in futurum sibi multisque commoda facere non distulit, omnesque thesauros suos ecclesiis et pauperibus Deique ministris distribui præcepit. Quantum vero singulis dari voluit callide taxavit, et coram se describi a notariis imperavit." This touch is eminently characteristic. [4] Ord. Vit. ib., Will. Malm. iii. 282.

[5] Florence (1087) gives the details. The different churches got sums ranging from sixty pence to ten marks of gold, besides vessels and ornaments.

CHAP. XXI.
Normandy to go to Robert.

a righteous master to keep them in the path of order.¹ Yet the rule over them must by all law pass to Robert. Robert was his eldest born; he had promised him the Norman succession before he won the Crown of England, and he had received the homage of the Barons of the Duchy. Normandy and Maine must therefore pass to Robert, and for them he must be the man of the French King. Yet he well knew how sad would be the fate of the land which had to be ruled by one so proud and foolish, and for whom a career of shame and sorrow was surely doomed.²

He does not dare to bequeath England.

But what was to be done with England? Now at last the heart of William smote him. To England he dared not appoint a successor; he could only leave the disposal of the Island realm to the Almighty Ruler of the world. The evil deeds of his past life crowded upon his soul.

He confesses his sins towards England.

Now at last his heart confessed that he had won England by no right, by no claim of birth; that he had won the English Crown by wrong, and that what he had won by wrong he had no right to give to another.³ He had won his realm by warfare and bloodshed; he had treated the sons of the English soil with needless harshness; he had cruelly wronged nobles and commons; he had spoiled many men wrongfully of their inheritance;

---

[1] Ord. Vit. 656 D. "Normanni, si *bono rigidoque* dominatu reguntur, strenuissimi sunt," &c. The passage is versified by Wace, 14239.

[2] What Orderic (659 B) gives more fully is summed up in the expressive words of William of Malmesbury (iii. 282), "Normanniam invitus et coactus Roberto delegavit."

[3] The whole passage in Orderic should be read. The particular expressions—which Wace versifies and abridges—are doubtless his own, but we need not doubt that he expresses a genuine tradition as to William's dying state of mind. The words "Non enim tantum decus hæreditario jure possedi" are specially emphatic. But the words of Wace (14267) are stronger still,

"Engleterre cunquis à tort,      E ço ke j'ai a tort toleit,
A tort i out maint hoem mort,     Où jo n'en aveie nul dreit,
Les eirs en ai à tort ocis,     Ne dei mie à mon filz doner,
E à tort ai li regne pris,     Ne à tort nel' deit énter."

he had slain countless multitudes by hunger or by the sword. The harrying of Northumberland now rose up before his eyes in all its blackness. The dying man now told how cruelly he had burned and plundered the land, what thousands of every age and sex among the noble nation which he had conquered had been done to death at his bidding.[1] The sceptre of the realm which he had won by so many crimes he dared not hand over to any but to God alone. Yet he would not hide his wish that his son William, who had been ever dutiful to him, might reign in England after him. He would send him beyond the sea, and he would pray Lanfranc to place the crown upon his head, if the Primate in his wisdom deemed that such an act could be rightly done.[2]

Of the two sons of whom he spoke, Robert was far away, a banished rebel; William was by his bedside. By his bedside also stood his youngest son, the English Ætheling, Henry the Clerk. "And what dost thou give to me, my father?" said the youth. "Five thousand pounds of silver from my hoard," was the Conqueror's answer. "But of what use is a hoard to me," said Henry, "if I have no place to dwell in?" "Be patient, my son, and trust in the Lord, and let thine elders go before thee."

---

[1] He winds up his confession with the words (659 C), "Sic multa millia pulcerrimæ gentis senum juvenumque, proh dolor, funestus trucidavi"

[2] Ord. Vit. u. s. "Guillelmum filium meum, qui mihi a primis annis semper adhæsit et mihi pro posse suo per omnia libenter obedivit, opto in Spiritu Dei diu valere, et in regni solio, si Dei voluntas est, feliciter fulgere." Wace (14275) adds,

"Maiz ultre mer l'enverrai,   S'il le pot fere par raison,
 A l'Archeveske préirai        Jo preie k'il en face le don"
 Ke la corone li otreit,

I do not see that such an expression as that of Florence (1087), "filio suo Willelmo regnum tradidit Angliæ," and that of William of Jumièges (vii. 44), "regno Angliæ concesso Willelmo filio suo," need lead us, with Lord Lyttelton (Henry the Second, i. 396), to set aside the statement of Ordenc. Lyttelton was influenced by the false Ingulf. See the note in Taylor's Wace, 274.

CHAP. XXI.
He foretells Henry's greatness

He sends William to England.

The bystanders intercede for the prisoners.

It is perhaps by the light of later events that our chronicler goes on to make William tell his youngest son that the day would come when he would succeed both his brothers in their dominions, and would be richer and mightier than either of them.[1] The King then dictated a letter to Lanfranc, setting forth his wishes with regard to the Kingdom. He sealed it and gave it to his son William, and bade him, with his blessing and his last kiss, to cross at once into England. William Rufus straightway set forth for Witsand, and there heard of his father's death. Meanwhile Henry too left his father's bedside to take for himself the money that was left to him, to see that nothing was lacking in its weight, to call together his comrades in whom he could trust, and to take measures for stowing the treasure in a place of safety.[2]

And now those who stood around the dying King began to implore his mercy for the captives whom he held in prison. Among them was a long list of the noblest both of England and Normandy. There was Wulfnoth the son of Godwine and Wulf the son of Harold, whose lives had been lives of captivity from their childhood. There were Morkere and Ælfgar and Siward Barn, the

---

[1] Ord. Vit. 659 D. "Tu autem tempore tuo totum honorem quem ego nactus sum habebis, et fratribus tuis divitiis et potestate præstabis." This, I confess, has a legendary sound, and Wace (14282) substitutes something quite different, namely a recommendation of Henry to his brothers;

"Et à Guillalme ci comant   Issi come il n'a en chierté,
Et à Robert l'altre filz mant,   Face Henris riche è manant
Ke chescun en sa poesté,   Plus ke home de li tenant."

Benoît (39521) versifies Orderic. The bequest of money to Henry stands out plainly in the Chronicle, "Se þridda het Heanric, þam se fæder becwæð gersuman unateallendlice." William of Malmesbury (iii. 282) says, "possessiones maternas Henrico delegavit." This agrees with what Orderic said long before (510 D), that Matilda made Henry her heir, "Totius terræ suæ in Angliâ heredem constituit." But it is plain that he did not get her lands.

[2] Ord. Vit. 659 D. "Henricus festinavit . . . munitum gazophylacium sibi procurare."

captives of Ely, Roger the rebel Earl of Hereford, and lastly, William's own brother Odo, once Earl of Kent and still Bishop of Bayeux.[1] He granted the prayer. Let the captives only swear that they would not disturb the peace either of England or Normandy,[2] and all should come forth, save one alone. Odo he would not release. The man whom he had imprisoned for the common weal of his Kingdom, the oppressor of the people, the plunderer of the Church, the man of pride and lust and cruelty, should not be set free by him. He spoke as the father of his people, knowing that, if Odo were once more let loose to trouble the world, the ruin of thousands would follow.[3] Yet once more the men who stood around William's bed, first among them Odo's own brother, Robert of Mortain, prayed for the pardon of his brother. They daringly pledged themselves for Odo's reformation, and William gave orders that Odo should be set free, again protesting that the death and ruin of many would follow.[4]

*He is willing to release all except Odo*

*He is persuaded to release him*

The last earthly acts of the Conqueror were now done. He had striven to make his peace with God and man, and to make such provision as he could for the children

*Death of William September 9, 1087.*

---

[1] Florence (1087) gives the list, Odo, Morkere, Roger, Siward Barn, and Wulfnoth, with the addition, " omnes quos vel in Angliâ vel in Normanniâ custodiæ mancipârat " He afterwards mentions Wulf, and the hostage Donald the son of Malcolm Ordenc strangely fancied that Ralph of Wader was in prison as well as Roger The only way to reconcile his story here (660 A) with his account of the life-long imprisonment of Roger (see above, p 592) is to suppose that he was formally released and imprisoned again, as was certainly the case with Wulfnoth and Morkere

[2] Ord Vit 660 A " Nexi tali tenore de carcere procedant, ut antea jurejurando securitatem reipublicæ ministris faciant, quod pacem in Angliâ et Normanniâ omnibus modis teneant, et pacis adversarus pro posse suo viriliter resistant "

[3] Ib C " Absque dubio, si evaserit, totam regionem turbabit, et multis millibus perniciem subministrabit "

[4] Ib D " Scitote quod multis per eum mors seu grave impedimentum incutietur "

and the subjects whom he left behind him. And now his last hour was come. On a Thursday morning in September, when the sun had already risen upon the earth, the sound of the great bell of the metropolitan minster struck on the ears of the dying King.[1] He asked why it sounded He was told that it rang for prime in the church of Our Lady. William lifted his eyes to heaven, he stretched forth his hands, and spake his last words; "To my Lady Mary, the holy Mother of God, I commend myself, that by her holy prayers she may reconcile me to her dear Son our Lord Jesus Christ." He prayed, and his soul passed away. William, King of the English and Duke of the Normans, the man whose fame has filled the world in his own and in every following age, had gone the way of all flesh. No Kingdom was left him now but his seven feet of ground,[2] and even to that his claim was not to be undisputed.[3]

*Effects of a King's death.*

The death of a King in those days came near to a break-up of all civil society. Till a new King was chosen and crowned, there was no longer a power in the land to protect or to chastise. All bonds were loosed; all public authority was in abeyance; each man had to look to his own as he best might. No sooner was the breath

---

[1] I translate Orderic He fixes the time (660 D), "Quinto idus Septem. feriâ v jam Phœbo per orbem spargente clara radiorum spicula, excitus Rex sonum majoris signi audivit in metropolitanâ basilicâ" So the Chronicle; "He swealt on Normandige on þone nextan dæg æfter Nativitas Sc̄e Marie." William of Jumièges (vii 44) places it a day earlier

[2] Chron Petrib 1087 "Eala hu leas and hu unwrest is þysses middaneardes wela Se þe wæs ærur rice cyng and maniges landes hlaford, *he næfde þa ealles landes buton seofon fot mæl* [see vol iii p 365], and se þe wæs hwilon gescrid mid golde and mid gemmum he læg þa oferwrogen mid moldan." Orderic (661 B) has a lamentation to the same general effect, but far less terse.

[3] Will. Malm iii 283 "Varietatis humanæ tunc fuit videre miseriam, quod homo ille, totius olim Europæ honor, antecessorumque suorum omnium potentior, sedem æternæ requiescionis sine calumniâ impetrare non potuit"

out of William's body than the great company which had patiently watched around him during the night was scattered hither and thither. The great men mounted their horses and rode with all speed to their own homes, to guard their houses and goods against the outburst of lawlessness which was sure to break forth now that the land had no longer a ruler. Their servants and followers, seeing their lords gone, and deeming that there was no longer any fear of punishment, began to make spoil of the royal chamber. Weapons, clothes, vessels, the royal bed and its furniture, were carried off, and for a whole day the body of the Conqueror lay well nigh bare on the floor of the room in which he died.¹ The men of Rouen were struck with fear and amazement, as though a hostile army were coming against their city.² Men took counsel of their wives and their friends what they should do or whither they should flee. They hid their goods or carried them into places of safety. The news of William's death was borne, we are gravely told, the self-same day to banished men in Rome and Calabria. For, so men then deemed, the evil spirit rejoiced, now that the death of the man who had kept the land in peace gave his servants full scope to work their wicked wills ³

Legends like these, which set William before us as the one guardian of law and order in his dominions, are in truth the noblest tribute to his memory. Men who had perhaps cursed his rule while living, now knew what they had lost in him. Their fears did the departed King all

CHAP. XXI.

Confusion on the death of William

Plunder and neglect of his attendants

Fear of the people of Rouen

Witness of legends to William's government.

---

¹ Ord. Vit. 661 A "Arma, vasa, vestes, et linteamina, omnemque regiam supellectilem, rapuerunt, et relicto Regis cadavere pene nudo in areâ domûs aufugerunt" He adds some moral reflexions

² Ib B "Velut ebrii desipuerunt, ac si multitudinem hostium imminere urbi vidissent turbati sunt"

³ Ib "Malignus quippe spiritus oppido tripudiavit, dum clientes suos, qui rapere et *cleperc* vehementer inhiabant, per occasum judicis absolutos vidit" In Calabria they had got nearer to the native soil of κλέφται.

714                    THE LATER DAYS OF WILLIAM.

CHAP. XXI.  honour; but they were too much occupied by those fears
to think of showing him other honours at the moment.
A few clerks and monks, amid the general confusion,
formed a procession, and went with crosses and censers to
the church of Saint Gervase[1] to offer prayers for his soul.

His body to be taken to Caen.  Meanwhile Archbishop William bade that the body of the King should be borne to Caen, there to be buried in the minster of Saint Stephen which he himself had built. But how was the command to be obeyed? The King's sons and kinsfolk had gone, each man to look after his

None of his followers in attendance.  own. His servants and officers had fled away with their spoils. Not a man of his household was ready to do the last duty to his master. At last the honest heart of a plain Norman gentleman was moved by natural piety.

Herlwin undertakes to take him to Caen.  A rustic knight, Herlwin by name, a name which is not found in the roll-call of the despoilers of England, stood forth to do the work which princes and nobles failed to do. For the love of God and for the honour of the Norman name, he was ready to do the last corporal work of mercy to his departed sovereign.[2] His offer was accepted, and the foremost man of all the world, forsaken by his children and servants, was borne to his last home by the voluntary loyalty of a vassal faithful to his lord in life and death.

Zeal and bounty of Herlwin.  The funeral pomp, such as could be provided at such a moment, now set forth. It was at the cost of Herlwin that men were hired to wash and tend, to anoint and to embalm, the royal corpse.[3] It was at his cost that

---

[1] "Georgium" in Orderic, 661 C. I correct "Gervasium" from Camden, Bibliotheca, 34.

[2] Ord. Vit. 661 C. "Herluinus pagensis eques, naturali bonitate compunctus est, et curam exsequiarum pro amore Dei et honore gentis suæ viriliter amplexatus est." Herlwin is mentioned by name by no one else, except Benoît (39740), who here translates Orderic.

[3] Ib. "Pollinctores itaque et vespiliones ac vehiculum mercede de propriis sumptibus conduxit, cadaver Regis ad portum Sequanæ devexit,

a carriage was found to bear the corpse to the haven of Rouen, whence, partly by water, partly by land, his pious care watched over the dead Conqueror, till he reached the haven of Caen, where his faithful bedesmen were ready to receive him. Abbot Gilbert stood at the head of his convent, accompanied by a crowd of clergy and a smaller body of laymen.[1] They met the bier of the great King with all reverence, and began the funeral procession towards the Abbey of Saint Stephen. But the funeral rites of William were to be gone through with as little of order and quiet as his crowning rites. At Westminster his crowning rites had been disturbed by a fire wantonly kindled. At Caen a like misfortune, but seemingly accidental in its origin, disturbed the rites of his burial. As the procession was on its way, flames were seen to burst from a house, and the fire soon spread itself through a large part of the town. The crowd that followed the bier, clergy and laity alike,

impositumque navi usque Cadomum per aquam et aridam perduxit." Benoît (39746) translates Orderic, but Wace's account (14374) is different, which is the more to be noticed, because he so often follows Orderic;

| " Dunc fu la novele espandue | Li cors unt mul bel conree, |
| E la gent fu grant acorue, | Overt est, oint, et embasme. |
| E li Eveske è li Baron | A Caem unt li cors porté, |
| Vinrent o grant procession, | Si com il aveit comandé " |

William of Jumièges (vii. 44) simply says, " Translatum est corpus ejus, sicuti ordinaverat, Cadomum," William of Malmesbury (iii. 283), " Corpus, regio solenni curatum, per Sequanam Cadomum delatum," and the Hyde writer (297), like Wace, says, " Corpus cum debitâ principum pompâ Cadomum est delatum." It is certainly strange if neither the Archbishop nor the Abbot of Saint Ouen's could find the means of doing all that Herlwin is said to have done, yet I cannot bring myself to give up the story of the worthy knight. It is hard to think that any one can have invented it, and something to the same effect had plainly reached Eadmer, when he says (Hist. Nov. 13, Selden), " Ab omni homine, sicut accepimus, derelictum cadaver ejus sine omni pompâ per Sequanam naucellâ delatum."

[1] Ord. Vit. 661 D. " Multitudo clericorum et laicorum adhæsit." William of Malmesbury speaks of " magna frequentia ordinatorum, laicorum pauca."

CHAP XXI were soon scattered abroad to put out the flames and to save their houses and goods. The monks alone kept on their way, singing the office for the dead as they went.[1] Thus, through a scene which might have recalled the awful days of Mortemer and of York, with the smoke of the burning town going up to heaven, the body of William was brought to the minster which he had reared beyond its walls.

The burial of William.

Thus were the candles of William's churching at Mantes in some sort avenged by the candles of his burial at Caen. But the wonders and horrors of the day were not yet over. The rites began. A crowd of Norman Prelates had already made their way to Caen to do the last office to their sovereign. They had doubtless hastened, while the humble procession of Herlwin had been slowly making its way by land and water. The holy Primate was there, and the warrior Bishops, Geoffrey of Coutances and Odo of Bayeux, already set free from his prison.[2] There were the two Gilberts, the learned physician of Lisieux and the eloquent preacher of Evreux.[3] There were a crowd of Abbots, some of whose names are well known to us. Nicolas of Saint Ouen's, the son of the last Duke Richard, was there to do his duty to the kinsman who had in some sort supplanted him.[4] There was Mainer of Saint Evroul, who had received his staff as William was setting forth from England,[5] Gerbert, the learned stranger who had taught Ingulf at Saint Wandrille,[6] William of Ros, whose works

Bishops and Abbots present.

---

[1] Orderic's account of the fire is followed both by Wace and by Benoît. Orderic himself (661 D) deems the occasion worthy of a piece of Greek, and tells us how the monks "*soma* Regis ad coenobialem basilicam psallentes perduxerunt." Cf above, p. 660.

[2] Orderic gives the list, 661 D.

[3] On Gilbert Mammot, see above, pp. 367, 660. Gilbert of Evreux we shall sit under directly

[4] See vol i p 518, ii p. 181; iii p 380.

[5] See vol iii. p 382.  [6] See above, p. 601

may still be seen in the minster of Fécamp,[1] and, best and most righteous of all that great assembly, already recovered from his sickness, stood the Abbot of Bec, the holy Anselm.[2] Of William's children one only was present, the Ætheling Henry, who by this time, we may deem, had safely secured his treasure. Robert was still an exile in France, and William was looking after his own interests in England.[3] By Henry then, his youngest and greatest son, and by the great body of the Norman Prelacy, the body of William was received into his own church, to seek the last home which, even now, he was not to win without a struggle.

*Henry the only son of William present.*

In the eastern limb of Saint Stephen's minster, not yet the vaster and lighter choir of later days, but the single stern apse of Cerisy or Saint Gabriel, a tomb, between the high altar and the choir, had been made ready to receive the Conqueror's body.[4] The procession entered the church, the bier on which all that was left of William lay was borne along the nave, between the stern arches and massive pillars which he himself had reared. They reached the choir, then doubtless filling up

*The tomb.*

*The office begins.*

---

[1] See above, p. 87.

[2] At the head of the list of Abbots comes "Anselmus Beccensis" Eadmer (Hist. Nov 13) tells us, "Et quidem Wilhelmus ita mortuus est non tamen, ut dicitur, inconfessus atque Anselmus evestigio est ab infirmitate relevatus, pristinæque saluti post modicum redonatus."

[3] Will Gem. vii 44 "Solus filiorum suorum Henricus exsequias patris persequutus est, dignus qui paternam hæreditatem aliquando solus obtineret, quam fratres sui particulatim post mortem patris sui possederunt." Will Malm iii 283 "Henricus filius ... solus ex liberis aderat .. nam tunc Robertus primogenitus in Franciâ contra patriam bellabat; Willelmus, antequam plane pater exspiraret, Angliam enavigaverat, utilius ducens suis in posterum commodis prospicere quam obsequiis paterni corporis interesse" So Benoît, 39779,

" De dol pales e descoloriz,     I fu e vint Henris sis fiz"

Orderic and Wace do not mention Henry.

[4] Ord. Vit. 662 A. "In presbyterio inter chorum et altare." Will. Gem vii 44 "Ante majus altare regaliter tumulatum"

CHAP. XXI.

The Bishop of Evreux's sermon.

Ascelin claims the site of the church.

the central space beneath the tower; the stone coffin was placed upon the ground, but the body still lay on the bier before the altar.[1] The mass of the dead was sung, and then the Bishop of Evreux mounted the pulpit[2] to make the formal harangue over the Conqueror of England. He told the tale of William's greatness and William's conquests, how he had enlarged the bounds of the Norman Duchy, and had raised his native land to a height of power and glory beyond all the deeds of his fathers who had gone before him. And he told also of those deeds of the departed Duke which entitled him to truer honour than to have made Maine and England subject to the Norman. He told how William had maintained peace and righteousness in the land, how his rod had smitten down thieves and robbers, how his sword had defended the clerk, the monk, and the unarmed people.[3] He then called on all who heard him to pray for the soul of him whose body lay before them, he bade them crave the forgiveness of his sins at the hands of God, and themselves forgive anything in which William might have sinned against them.[4]

The appeal drew forth an answer. A knight, Ascelin the son of Arthur, arose from the crowd, mounted on a stone, and spoke in the hearing of all; "This ground where ye stand was the site of my father's house, which the man for whom ye pray, while he was yet but Count of Normandy, took away by force from my father, and,

[1] Ord Vit 662 A "Quum jam sarcofagum in terrâ locatum esset, sed corpus adhuc in feretro jaceret." The "sarcofagum" I take to be the stone coffin.

[2] Ib "Magnus Gislebertus Ebroicensis Episcopus in pulpitum ascendit." Perhaps the rood-loft is meant

[3] The Bishop's sermon was a "prolixa loquutio," but it was no more than justice to record how William "justitiam et pacem sub omni ditione suâ tenuerit, fures et prædones virgâ rectitudinis utiliter castigaverit, et clericos ac monachos et inermem populum virtutis ense fortiter munierit"

[4] Ord Vit 662 B "Ei si quid in vobis deliquit benigniter dimittere"

in spite of law and justice, built this church upon it by his might.[1] I therefore claim the land; I challenge it as mine before all men, and in the name of God I forbid that the body of the robber be covered with my mould, or that he be buried within the bounds of mine inheritance."[2] He then came down, and wonder and tumult filled the church as men heard the daring challenge. The office paused; the Bishops and nobles asked of the men of the neighbourhood who stood by as to the truth of what Ascelin had told them. They bore witness that what he had said was true.[3] Yet we should gladly hear what might have been said on William's side, as mere naked wrong, mere plunder, mere robbery for burnt-offering, is not in accordance with William's usual character. At such a moment the facts of the case would not be very accurately looked into. Men who had come together to make prayers and offerings for William's soul would be more ready to admit even a false charge against him than to leave any possible sin of his unatoned for. The Ætheling and the Bishops called Ascelin to them; they spoke friendly to him, and made a bargain with him on the spot. Beneath the roof of Saint Stephen's the covenant was made which first made its soil the lawful property of him who had founded the church and

*The claim allowed to be true.*

*The ground bought of Ascelin*

---

[1] On the appeal of Ascelin see Appendix UU. The most vivid account is given by Wace, from whom I get the detail of Ascelin mounting the stone (14412),

"Sor une pierre en haut monta,
De vers la biere se torna."

[2] Ord. Vit. 662 B. "Hanc igitur terram calumnior et palam reclamo, et ne corpus raptoris operiatur cespite meo nec in hereditate meâ sepeliatur ex parte Dei prohibio." The adjuration in Wace (14418) takes a singular form;

"Jo devée à toz è desfent       E par l'Apostoile de Rome,
De par Jhesu omnipotent        Nel' pois véer par plus haut home."

[3] Ib. "Episcopi et Proceres alii audierunt, et vicinos ejus, qui eumdem vera dixisse contestabantur, intellexerunt."

720       THE LATER DAYS OF WILLIAM.

CHAP XXI of those to whom he had granted it. With the assent of Henry, sixty shillings were at once given to Ascelin as the purchase-money of the seven feet of ground which were to be William's own. The full price of the whole estate which he had lost was promised to him, a promise which was soon after faithfully fulfilled.[1] Ascelin then withdrew his protest; William might now be buried in the ground which had lawfully become his own, and the funeral rites went on.

Last scene of the burial.   A posthumous atonement was thus made for one of the sins which weighed down William's soul; but one misfortune more was still in store for his body. The royal corpse had now to be moved from the bier to the stone coffin which was to be its last resting-place. But by the unskilfulness of the workmen the coffin had been made too small to receive the unwieldy carcase of William. In the

The body bursts  efforts which were made to force it into its narrow room, the body burst; a fearful stench filled the church, which the burning of incense and of all sweet savours could not overcome.[2] The remainder of the office was hurried over; the officiating clergy went back with all speed to their own quarters, and the course of William on earth was brought to an end. He had gone to his

---

[1] Ord Vit. 662 C. "Nam pro loculo solius sepulturæ sexaginta solidos eo protinus adhibuerunt, pro reliquâ vero tellure quam calumniabatur æquipollens mutuum eidem promiserunt et post non multum temporis, pro salute specialis heri quem diligebant, pactum compleverunt" William of Malmesbury (iii. 283) says, "Volente Henrico filio ... centum libræ argenti litigatori persolutæ audacem calumniam compescuere." The hundred pounds must be the price of the whole estate

[2] Ord. Vit u s "Dum corpus in sarcofagum mitteretur, et violenter, quia vas per imprudentiam cæmentariorum breve structum erat, complicaretur, pinguissimus venter crepuit, et intolerabilis fœtor circumadstantes personas et reliquum vulgus implevit Fumus turis aliorumque aromatum de turibulis copiose ascendebat, sed teterrimum putorem excludere non prævalebat Sacerdotes itaque festinabant exsequias perficere et actutum sua cum pavore mapalia repetere" This story seems peculiar to Orderic.

grave amid scenes as stormy and as wonderful as aught that had marked his course from the day when he grasped the straw upon the floor at Falaise to the day when he received his death-wound in the burning streets of Mantes.

The Conqueror had thus at last found his hardly won resting-place. When the first feelings of fear and wonder had passed away, men began to think of doing those honours to his memory which he had failed to receive at the moment of his death and burial. His son William, now crowned King of the English, undertook the duty of raising a fitting monument to the memory of his father. A mass of gold and silver and precious stones was handed over to Otto the goldsmith, a man whose skill in the Teutonic craft had been rewarded by William, when living, with fair estates on English soil.[1] The coffin itself, wrought of a single stone, and supported by three small columns of white marble,[2] was surmounted by a shrine of splendid workmanship, blazing with all the precious materials which had been entrusted to the cunning hands of Otto.[3] On that shrine the epitaph of William was graven in letters of gold. Many poets had striven for the honour of thus commemorating their master, but the verses which were chosen to be placed on William's tomb were the work of Archbishop Thomas of York.[4] The Northumbrian Primate

[1] See above, p 85
[2] The tomb, at its destruction in 1562 (see Hippeau, 181), was described as a " loculle de pierre où estoyent les ossemens du roy duc, sous son sépulchre, lequel loculle estoit d'une forte pierre de Voideryl, couvert de mesme pierre, et soutenu sur trois petits pilastres de pierre blanche "
[3] Ord Vit 663 D  " Hic [Willelmus Rufus] auri et argenti gemmarumque copiam Othoni aurifabro erogavit, et super patris sui mausoleum fieri mirificum memoriale præcepit  Ille vero, regiis jussis parens, insigne opus condidit, quod ex auro et argento et gemmis usque hodie competenter splendescit"  So Will Malm iii 283, but he does not mention Otto
[4] Ib  " Egregii versificatores de tali viro, unde tam copiosum thema

722                THE LATER DAYS OF WILLIAM.

CHAP. XXI.  had put on some of the feelings of an Englishman;
he could not bring himself to sing of the conquest of
England or of the harrying of his own province. From
William's epitaph no one would learn that he had ever
reigned in England, any more than any one would learn
from Domesday that he had won the Crown of England
by the sword. The verses of Thomas told how small a
house was now enough for the great King William, and
how the great King William ruled the fierce Normans, how
he boldly conquered the Bretons, how he overcame the Cenomannian swords and brought the land of Maine into subjection to the laws of his dominion.[1] But on the tomb of
the Conqueror of England the name of England was not
graven. The tomb thus adorned, the tomb rather of the
Norman Duke than of the English King, lived on untouched through the changes which recast the eastern limb
of Saint Stephen's into the form which it now bears.[2] At
last a storm burst upon Caen fiercer even than the storm
which had already burst upon Waltham and Crowland, and
the relics of William were dealt with as the relics of Harold
and Waltheof had already been. In the wars and tumults
of the sixteenth century the church and monastery of Saint
Stephen were plundered and ruined, the minster was
unroofed, the great tower was broken down, the shrine of

England not mentioned in the epitaph

Recasting of Saint Stephen's choir c 1250

The tomb destroyed by the Huguenots. 1562.

versificandi repererunt, multa concinna et præclara poemata protulerunt
Sed solius Thomæ Archiepiscopi Eboracensis versus hujusmodi *pro dignitate
metropolitanâ* ex auro inserti sunt"
[1] Ord Vit 663 D,
"Qui rexit rigidos Normannos, atque Britannos
    Audacter vicit, fortiter obtinuit,
Et Cenomannenses virtute coercuit enses
    Imperiique sui legibus applicuit,
Rex magnus parvâ jacet hic Guillelmus in urnâ,
    Sufficit et magno parva domus domino
Ter septem gradibus se volverat atque duobus
    Virginis in gremio Phœbus, et hic obiit"
"Britanni" may take in the *Bretwealas* on both sides of the sea
[2] See Bouet, Analyse Architecturale, 65-74

William was swept away, the coffin itself was broken open, and the bones, vaster, men deemed, than those of ordinary men, were scattered and lost in the havoc.[1] A single bone, the thigh of William, was kept by the pious care of a monk of the Abbey, and when the church was repaired and restored to religious uses, this one fragment was replaced with sacred rites in a new tomb of less gorgeous workmanship than the first structure of Otto.[2] A hundred years later, this second tomb was deemed inconvenient for the services of the church, and the one remaining bone of William was translated to another part of the choir and covered with a new stone and a new epitaph.[3] Fifty years later, another storm of revolution again broke over the Abbey; the third tomb of William was rifled, and the one remaining fragment of him was lost for ever. And now, after so many changes, while all trace of Harold and Ælfred has vanished from the minsters of their founding, a modern stone, with an inscription in which the words England and Conqueror are not forgotten, marks the place where the bones of William the Great no longer lie.

*CHAP. XXI*

*The church restored 1626*

*The tomb restored. 1642.*

*A new tomb 1742*

*The tomb destroyed. 1793.*

*A new stone 1802.*

I have told my tale, the tale of the Norman Conquest of England. I have traced the earlier events which made it possible for a foreign prince to win and to keep England as his own. I have traced the course of the work of Conquest itself, the work of war and policy and legislation, by which William knew both how to conquer and how to hold down the conquered land, and to hand on the realm which he had won by the sword as the undis-

*Summary.*

---

[1] See the account of the destruction in Hippeau, 181, Bouet, 157. A contemporary, M. de Bras, writes, "Estoient encore inherentes à la teste les machoires et plusieurs dents, les autres ossements, tant des jambes, cuisses que des bras, fort longs." The whole account of the desecration of the Abbey and its restoration by the energetic Prior Jean de Baillehache is most interesting.

[2] See Hippeau, 182, 350, Bouet, 157, 158. Richelieu was nominal Abbot.

[3] See the *procès verbal* in Hippeau, 352, and Bouet, 158.

3 A 2

puted heritage of his house. Those who have followed me have passed through stirring scenes and walked in the company of mighty men. We have tracked the course of the heroes of our own blood; we have fought by the side of Harold and wept over the martyr-block of Waltheof. And we have tracked too, I trust in no carping or ungenerous spirit, the course of the mighty man before whom Harold and Waltheof fell, the man who, even in his crimes, seems raised above the common level of our race. Our tale then, as a tale, is told; but our work is far from being over. As we have traced the causes of the Conquest, we have now to trace its results. We have to look on the land as it is set before us in the picture of the great Survey, in those details, legal, social, and personal, which enable us to call up the England of the days of William as a thing living and breathing before us. We have to trace the lasting results of the Conquest on law and government and religion and art and language. And we have to follow, at least in its broad outline, the general course of our history till the Conquest in some sort undid itself, till the very overthrow of England led to her revival, and her momentary bondage led to her new birth of freedom. We have to pass, however lightly, over those times of silent growth and revolution, those times, as it proved, of salutary chastisement, which part off the earlier freedom of England from the later Our task will be done when the foreign nobles and the foreign King have in truth become our countrymen, when the *wergild* of the heroes of Senlac has been paid in full on the battle-field of Lewes, and when the great Assembly which welcomed the return of Godwine rises again to life in the Parliaments of Earl Simon and King Edward.

# APPENDIX.

## NOTES A, B pp 8, 24

### THE LEGAL FICTIONS AND CONFISCATIONS OF WILLIAM'S REIGN

THE text of this volume having swelled to an unexpected extent, I reserve the substance of these notes, which are mainly founded on Domesday, for the general examination of Domesday in the fifth volume

## NOTE C. p. 26

### THE THREE COMMISSIONERS FOR REDEMPTION OF LANDS

I THINK that, if we put together the passages from the Chronicle and from Domesday quoted in pp 25, 26, we can hardly avoid the conclusion that they all refer to the same transaction, and that Bishop William, Engelric, and Ralph the Staller were joined in such a commission as I have spoken of in the text. Bishop William we already know, a short notice of the other Commissioners may not be out of place

The mention of Engelric shows that the notices must refer to a transaction not very late in William's reign, and that the Bishop intended must be William of London. At first sight, in an entry in East-Anglia, one might have thought that the person meant was William, Bishop of Thetford, who appears in the Survey as the Bishop in possession But he was not consecrated till 1086, and he could only have just taken possession when the Survey was made. But by that time the lands of Engelric had passed, either by death or confiscation, to Count Eustace. The Bishop must therefore be the London William, and the matter referred to must be before his death in 1075. And the comparison of the several passages seems to fix it to this date in 1068.

That Engelric was an Englishman seems plain. He appears as holding T. R. E. in ii. 26 b, 27 b, 32 b, under Harold, under the Bishop of London, and under the Church of Saint Paul In 32, 32 b, 33, we find him holding, seemingly by regular grants from William, lands which had been held by Harold and other Englishmen. But we also find him recorded as guilty of various "occupationes," "invasiones," and other wrongful doings, several of which are distinctly said to have been done in the days of King William See i 137, ii. 5 b, 6 b, 26, 28 b, 29 b, 30, 31, 31 b, 34, 55 b, 102 b, 106 b. One entry (ii. 5) is capable of misconstruction, "Ingelricus abstulit unam feminam Brictevam tenentem xviii acras." This does not imply any personal carrying off of Brihtgifu, but simply that Engelric took possession of her land or of her lord's rights over it Engelric however was a benefactor of the Church. A gift of his to the church of Saint Martin—that is Saint Martin-le-Grand in London —is recorded in ii 14. But even his good works seem to have been tainted with illegality, as it is added that the gift was made, "ut consulatus [='scira' or 'comitatus'] testatur, sine jussu Regis." The reader must judge for himself as to the accounts in the Monasticon, viii 1323–1325, where, on the strength of an alleged charter of William recited in an *inspeximus* of Henry the Sixth, Saint Martin's church is said to have been founded in King Eadward's time by Engelric and his brother *Gerard*. The other places in Domesday where Saint Martin's church is mentioned are ii. 29, 32, where the only benefactors spoken of are "Ailmarus unus teinnus Regis Edwardi" and Count Eustace, who gives some of the lands which had formerly been Engelric's. I suspect that the whole tale, especially that part of it which makes Engelric to have been the first Dean of his own foundation, comes from the same mint as the tale (see vol. iii. p 656) which makes his daughter the mother of William Peverel The charter is said to have been granted at the Christmas Feast of 1068 (evidently meaning 1067), and to have been confirmed at the coronation of the Queen at the following Pentecost It is signed by a crowd of names English and Norman, among whom I doubt about Hugh Bishop of Lisieux, of whose presence in England there is no other mention. And I doubt also about the Cardinal Presbyters John and Peter, who in authentic history do not appear in England till the year 1070.

Of the third Commissioner joined with Engelric and Bishop

William I hoped that I had reached the true account in vol. iii p. 752. I find however by further searching in Domesday that, though the rest of the account there given of the two Ralphs, father and son, will stand, yet I was wrong in inferring that the elder Ralph died before the coming of William. Several passages in the second volume of Domesday, besides the one with which we are now dealing, show that he was alive in William's reign. Thus in ii. 217 b, 218, "In Estunâ tenuit Radulfus Stalra T. R. E. i. carucatam terræ, et dedit eam T R Willelmi cum uxore suâ ad abbatiam concessione Regis." In ii. 87 again, "Benetleiam tenuit Comes Guert T R. E., post eam adjunxit Comes Radulfus Stalra huic manerio pro berewitâ T R. Willelmi." Ralph was therefore alive at William's coming, and he acted under him on this important commission. Here too we get the explanation of his otherwise puzzling title of "Comes." He doubtless held the Earldom for a season after William's coming, and was succeeded by his son. As to the causes which led his son to identify himself with his mother's country, and to serve under William in his invasion of England, we are still left in the dark; but we must suppose some outlawry under either Eadward or Harold, which banished the son without touching the father. There is therefore no reason to suppose that grant of lands to the East-Anglian Bishoprick which I doubtingly inferred in vol. iii. p. 753. We presently read, "Hanc terram habuit A[rfastus] episcopus in tempore utrorumque [Radulforum sc ], et hundret nescit quomodo, et numquam fuit de episcopatu teste hundret." It would seem that Æthelmar and Erfast were tenants successively of the two Ralphs, but that the next Bishop William kept the land as part of the possessions of the see to the prejudice of the Crown. It follows therefore that the elder Ralph was living as late as 1070, in which year the episcopate of Erfast begins.

## NOTES D, E  pp. 32, 36

### The King's Thegns and the Condition of Kent, Surrey, and Sussex.

The substance of these Notes also will be given in the examination of Domesday.

## NOTE F. p. 35.

### THE LANDS AND FAMILY OF GODRIC.

I GAVE some account of Godric and his chief possessions in a note in the Appendix to my third volume, p. 731. The number of details about him which are preserved in Domesday is very remarkable. It is plain that he was, both by office and by extent of property, one of the first men in Berkshire, but it also strikes me that there are other reasons for the prominence given to him in the Survey. His memory seems to be dealt with in somewhat the same way as the memory of Harold. The entries seem to reveal a certain anxiety to represent him as a wrong-doer.

I have already (vol iii. p. 731) stated the evidence for Godric's position as Sheriff of Berkshire. That he was also Sheriff of Buckinghamshire appears from the entry which I have quoted in p. 36 In the same shire (152) we read of "Aluric homo Godric vicecomitis," and he again appears (144) as a landowner in close connexion with various members of the house of Godwine Of Weston, a manor then held by Bishop Odo, we read; "De terrâ hujus manerii tenuit Leuuinus comes ix hidas et dimidiam, et Godric vicecomes iii hidas et dimidiam pro uno manerio, et ii homines ejusdem Godrici iii. hidas et dimidiam, et unus homo Tosti comitis ii. hidas, et ii. homines Leuuini comitis i hidam et dimidiam. Omnes vero vendere potuerunt." Godric's estates in Buckinghamshire were therefore not large, and there are one or two other persons of the same name from whom he seems to be purposely distinguished, such as Godric the brother of Bishop Wulfwig (144), and Godric the man of Esegar the Staller (151) In these latter passages the title of "Vicecomes" might simply be added for distinction, but the grant to the embroideress was clearly an official act, and makes it plain that he was Sheriff of Buckinghamshire. Whether he was not also Sheriff of Bedfordshire is less plain, but a landowner in that shire (213) is described as the man of Godric the Sheriff.

In Buckinghamshire Godric was succeeded in his office by the Norman Ansculf, who was dead at the time of the Survey, but whose son William held large estates. He seems to have acted after the usual manner of Sheriffs, as we find him (148 b) wrongfully dispossessing a Norman holder. As to the succession to the office in Berkshire, the entries bearing on it in Domesday are not very clear. At one of the places called Sparsholt (57 b) lands were held by Henry of Ferrers "quæ, sicut scira testatur, remanserunt in firmâ Regis quando Godricus vicecomitatum perdidit." Of the other Sparsholt we read (60 b) that it was then held by Henry of Ferrers, and that it had been held by "Godricus unus liber homo." But of some of the lands in the same lordship we read, "Hanc terram dicit Henricus fuisse Godrici antecessoris sui, sed, sicut hundreda testatur, Godricus eam occupavit super W Regem post bellum de Hastinges, nec unquam tenuit T E Regis." These passages are difficult. The former of them would certainly at first sight imply that Godric had lived to be deprived of his office by William. But it seems impossible to set aside the distinct statement of the local history that he was killed in the battle. Possibly however "quando vicecomitatum perdidit" may mean "when he was killed," the office being *ipso facto* forfeited by Godric's treason in joining Harold. The death of a man already attainted would, on this view, be a sort of accident accruing to the forfeiture. The entries in the Yorkshire "clamores" with regard to the lands of William Malet supply a parallel. We hear (373) of lands which William held "quamdiu in Euruicscire terram tenuit," and which are claimed by his son. Forfeiture or legal alienation are therefore shut out, and the words "quamdiu terram tenuit" can only mean "as long as he lived." But "Godricus unus liber homo" must be a different man from the Sheriff, from whom he seems to be pointedly distinguished. Henry of Ferrers affirmed that the land had belonged to his "antecessor," that is seemingly to the Sheriff. The Hundred witnessed that the other Godric, "unus liber homo," had taken possession of it since the battle, not having held it in King Eadward's days. But, in Domesday law, the holding, first of Godric and then of Henry of Ferrers, was an "occupatio super Regem W.," and the land ought to have gone to the Crown. What then is meant by this "occupatio post bellum de Hastinges?" It may be that, as we have so many euphemisms and circumlocutions to point out the reign of Harold, we have here, in the words "post bellum de Hastinges," an euphemism or circumlocution to point out the *quasi*-reign of Eadgar. The Ætheling, who, though not crowned

King, confirmed the election of an Abbot of Peterborough (see vol iii p 530), may also have appointed a Sheriff of Berkshire. It is possible then that the Godric who "vicecomitatum perdidit" was "Godricus unus liber homo," and was appointed Sheriff by Eadgar If so, he may probably have been the son of the Sheriff who died at Senlac. But whether Sheriff or not, whether son or not, if Eadgar granted him any lands, if he entered on any lands which, in William's reading of the law, were already forfeited, the act would be held to be null and void, and it would be, in the language of Domesday, an "occupatio super Regem W"

The entries in Domesday with regard to Godric which I have not yet had occasion to quote stand as follows In 57 *b*, "Rex tenet in dominio Eseldeborne Rex E tenuit . . . De isto manerio sunt ii. hidæ et dimidia in manerio Henrici missæ. Una hida fuit de Reue Land, alia de villanis. Et hida et dimidia fuit de firmâ Regis, sed tempore Godrici vicecomitis fuit foris missa. Hoc attestatur tota scira" On the same page, at Sutton, "Henricus de Fereires tenet in hoc manerio de dominicâ terrâ Regis cxx. acras terræ et iii. acras prati, ideo quia Godricus antecessor suus, quum Vicecomes esset, aravit eam terram cum suis carucis sed, ut dicit hundreda, ad curiam Regis pertinet juste, Godricus enim occupavit injuste." On p. 58, at Reading, "Henricus de Fereres habet ibi i. hagam et dimidiam virgatam terræ, in quâ sunt iii. acræ prati. Valet vi solidos. Godricus Vicecomes tenuit hanc terram ad hospitium; ideo Henricus tenet" In 60 *b* there are several entries, "Isdem Henricus tenet Bechesgete, Godric tenuit de Rege E per manerium. Duæ hidæ non geldabant, quia de firmâ Regis erant et ad opus Regis calumniatæ sunt." On the same page come the two Fifhides of which I spoke in vol iii p. 731. Of the one held of the King the entry is, "Isdem Henricus tenet Fivehide; Godricus tenuit de Rege E. et tunc se defendebat pro x. hidis, et modo pro v hidis, quia Rex E sic condonavit, ut hundreda testatur" The next entry is, "Isdem Henricus tenet Henret et alter Henricus de eo, Godricus Vicecomes tenuit de Rege E ; tunc se defendebat pro unâ hidâ, modo pro nichilo. Hæc est illa hida quæ jacuit in firmâ Regis de quâ Aluricus detulit testimonium ;" seemingly the land which William had left to Godric's widow On the same page, "Isdem Henricus tenet Ollavintone, Godricus Vicecomes tenuit de Rege E. . . . hanc terram dedit Rex E. de suâ firmâ Godrico, et inde viderunt sigillum ejus homines de comitatu. Præter istas hidas accepit iste Godricus de firmâ Regis unam virgatam terræ de quâ non viderunt sigillum Regis." These remarkable comments seem to be confined to those lands of Godric which at the time of the Survey were in possession of Henry of Ferrers. The name Godric is so common that it is almost in vain to seek for the Sheriff's possessions in other shires, or even in Berkshire when he is not in some way marked out from his namesakes, but he can hardly fail to be the same Godric who appears in Wiltshire (72) as holding lands which at the Survey were held by Henry of Ferrers.

## NOTE G p 45

### Wigod of Wallingford and Robert of Oily

I MADE some mention of Wigod of Wallingford in the Appendix to my third volume. I have since worked out such notices as I could find in Domesday and elsewhere, and they quite confirm the story there quoted, though it is certainly not to be found in William of Poitiers. Wigod's case is the opposite to that of his neighbour Godric. An Englishman of high rank contrives to make his peace with the Conqueror, to retain wealth and influence, and to hand them on to his descendants in the female line.

The notices of Wigod in the charters I have already spoken of in vol. iii. p. 768. He was, by blood or by courtesy, a kinsman of Eadward, he was his cup-bearer and, as would seem from the charter in Cod Dipl. iv 215, Sheriff of Oxfordshire He is also spoken of in a curious passage in the History of Abingdon (i. 477), where he is described as becoming possessed of the lordship of Whitchurch, belonging to a monk of the Abbey, "Wigodus oppidanorum Walingfordensium dominus possedit, velle monachorum prædictorum hinc et inde de eisdem terris sic se referente"

As Wigod does not appear in Domesday as an actual landowner, he was probably dead before the taking of the Survey. His son also, "Tokig Wiggodes sunu," had died by William's side at Gerberoi (see p. 648) All this falls in with the tradition that his estates passed to his daughter or daughters One daughter is said to have been married to Robert of Oily, probably Ouilly-le-Vicomte, near Lisieux. Now of the large estates of Robert in Oxfordshire it is mentioned in several cases how he came by them. Thus in 158 it is said that one estate was got by exchange with Walter Giffard. Of two places (158 *b*) we read, "Hanc redemit Robertus de Rege," while another (see p. 658) was granted by William before Sainte-Susanne. In one place only is the owner T. R. E. mentioned, and there we read "Wigod tenuit" (158). So of Robert's Berkshire lands (62), part had been held by Wigod of King Eadward. This certainly looks as if Robert had succeeded Wigod in all those lands where the mode of their acquisition is not mentioned. We find also the two names of Robert and Wigod brought together again in a very remarkable entry in Hertfordshire (137 *b*), where Robert seems to be assumed as the natural successor of Wigod; " Hoc manerium tenuerunt v. sochi Horum duo homines Brictici unam hidam et dimidiam habuerunt, et alii ii. homines Osulfi filii Fran unam hidam et dimidiam, et quintus homo Edmer Atule i. hidam tenuit Nullus eorum ad antecessorem Wigot pertinuit, sed unusquisque terram suam vendere potuit. Horum unus terram suam emit a W. Rege novem unciis auri, ut homines de hundredâ testantur, et postea ad Wigotum se vertit pro protectione" (see p 45) This illustrates the process in which Englishmen had to buy back their lands from the new King, and it also shows (see p. 44) how, even after this security, men had sometimes to commend themselves to an inferior lord for protection, and how at least one Englishman remained in a position to afford such protection The passage is strangely dealt with by Thierry (i 277), "Dans la province de Hertford, un Anglais avait racheté sa terre par le paiement de neuf onces d'or, et cependant, pour échapper à une dépossession violente, il fut obligé de se rendre tributaire *d'un soldat appelé Vigot*." King Eadward's kinsman and cup-bearer is thus reduced to the ranks of the Norman army.

Another successor of Wigod was Miles Crispin Of his estates in Wiltshire (71) it is twice said, " Wigot tenuit T R. E.," and of his large estates in Buckinghamshire we read twice in p. 150, " Wigot de Walingeford tenuit," and in 150 *b*, " Hanc terram tenuit Orduui homo Wigot de Walingeford et vendere potuit " Again in 159, 159 *b*, 169 *b*, " Wigot tenuit" is added to lands of Miles in Oxfordshire and Gloucestershire It would seem however, from three entries in the Exeter Domesday (4, 9, 16), that the

Western estates of Wigod did not pass to Miles without King William taking a large toll of them to his own use. The entry in all three cases is, "Rex habet xviii. hidas de terrâ Wigoti, Milo vi hidas." Miles however held many lordships in Oxfordshire which had been held by other owners T. R. E, and in one case at least he seems to have been guilty of an irregular usurpation over the English owner. Of two lordships held under him by Ordgar we read (159 *b*), "Has ii. terras quas tenet Orgar de Milone de Rege deberet tenere. Ipse enim et pater suus et avunculus tenuerunt libere T R E." In three other very remarkable entries we find the names of Wigod and Miles connected in much the same way as those of Wigod and Robert, Miles being taken for granted as Wigod's successor. In Surrey (36 *b*) we read, " Ipse Milo tenet Cisedune. Magno Sueit tenuit T R E . . Quando Rex W. venit in Angliam Wigot non habebat." Here it is plain that Magno (Magnus?) had either commended himself to Wigod or had been dispossessed by him. So in Berkshire (61 *b*), "In Radinges tenet Leuuard in Lonchelei i. hidam de Milone, et non potuit ire quolibet absque licentiâ Wigoti." In Hampshire again (50 *b*), " Alwinus Wit tenet ii hidas. Ipse tenuit T. R. E. . . Hic Alwinus tenuit hanc terram T R E sub Wigoto pro tuitione. Modo tenet eamdem sub Milone, et fuit deliberatus per Hunfridum visde lupo ["visde lupo, visde leuu *Wolf's face.*" Kelham, 363 , see Domesday, 56] in excambio de Bradeuuatre, sicut ipse dicit. Sed Hundreda inde nichil scit." This seems to be Broadwater in Sussex, of which we read in 28 *b*, " Rotbertus tenet de Willelmo [de Braiose] Bradewatre. Wigot tenuit de Rege E."

Our Wigod is also most likely the same as the Wigod who appears four times in Middlesex (129) in the account of lands which at the time of the Survey belonged to Earl Roger, in two of which we get the names of Wigod's men, " Hanc tenuit Aluuinus homo Wigot, et potuit de eâ facere quod voluit ," " T R E Goduinus Alfit tenuit homo Wigoti, et potuit de eo facere quod voluit." The Wigot in Shropshire (252) and Hertfordshire (134 *b*) must have been a different man, as well as " Wigot venator Regis E " in Bedfordshire (217). Of the entries in pp 236 and 239 nothing can be said either way.

These various entries set Wigod before us as one who kept great wealth and power under William, and had opportunities of either protecting or oppressing his less fortunate countrymen. The same evidence also leads us to believe that Robert of Oily and Miles Crispin succeeded Wigod in an orderly way, without any violence or confiscation The only difficulty is as to those lands of Wigod in the West which had passed to the Crown. But the whole evidence falls in with the tradition that Robert and Miles succeeded by marriage The wife of Robert undoubtedly bore the English name of Ealdgyth "Alditha uxor mea" (Mon Angl. viii 1462) consents to his gifts to the college of Saint George in the castle of Oxford. That this Ealdgyth was a daughter of Wigod is the received tradition (see vol iii. p 768) With regard to Miles the case is not so clear Genealogists do not agree as to his wife ' He married the heiress of Wallingford," says Kelham (36), which does not rule whether she was Wigod's daughter or grand-daughter. Sir Henry Ellis (i. 402), after Dugdale (Baronage, i. 413), marries him to "Maud, daughter and heir of Robert de Oilgi, through him he became possessed of the honour and castle of Wallingford." But Robert of Oily never held Wallingford castle (cf. Domesday, 56, 56 b), and it appears (Mon Angl vi 251) that he died without issue. It is therefore almost certain that Miles as well as Robert married a daughter of Wigod. Miles' wife, Matilda by name, is mentioned in the Abingdon History, ii. 106, 110. Most likely, like Eadgyth the daughter of Malcolm, she changed her name. Miles' connexion with Wallingford appears also in Domesday, 56, and in the History of Abingdon (ii. 12) he is expressly called "Milo de Walingaford, cognomento Crispin "

Robert of Oily is a more important person on account of his connexion with Oxford He figures at great length in the local History of Abingdon, where he is described (ii 7) as "ipse praedives, castelli vero Oxenefordensis *oppidanus*," and (ii. 12) as "constabularius Oxoniae, in cujus custodiâ erat illo tempore provincia illa in praeceptis et in factis, adeo ut de ore ejus proferretur illi actio" The character goes on; "Dives enim valde erat, diviti nec pauperi parcebat exigere ab eis pecunias, sibique gazas multiplicari." This may possibly account for the state of the town of Oxford. Robert was for a while an enemy to the monks of Abingdon, and seized on some of their possessions But by dint of prayers, sickness, and visions, he was brought to repentance, he was forced by his wife ("*cogente* eum uxore suâ," ii. 14) to restore the lands of Saint Mary, and he became altogether another man. He not only helped to rebuild the minster of Abingdon, but he restored various ruined parish churches within and without the walls of Oxford ("alias parochianas ecclesias dirutas, videlicet infra muros Oxenfordiæ et extra, ex sumptu suo reparavit") Of his work in this way there is little doubt that we have a specimen in the existing tower of Saint Michael's at Oxford. He was also bountiful to the poor and full of good works of all kinds Among other things we read (ii 15, cf 284) that "pons magnus ad septemtrionalem plagam Oxoniæ per eum factus est." He was buried (ii. 15) with his wife in the chapter-house of Abingdon, but the local writer does not mention her name or parentage He however describes (ii. 12) Miles and Robert as acting together to do honour to the Ætheling Henry, when he visited Abingdon in 1084.

The sworn brotherhood of Robert and Roger of Ivry appears from a manuscript quoted by Sir Henry Ellis (i. 458), "Memorandum quod Robertus de Oleio et Rogerus de Iverio, fratres jurati et per fidem et sacramentum confœderati, venerunt ad Conquestum Angliæ cum Rege Willielmo Bastard" See also Leland, Mon Angl vi 251, where Roger is inaccurately called John The names of the two often come together, as in the Annals of Oseney, 1074 (Ann Mon iv 10), "Fundata est ecclesia Sancti Georgii in Castello Oxenfordensi a Roberto de Oyly primo et Rogero de Iveri" Cf Mon Angl. viii 1461. In Domesday also the two appear as joint owners under Abingdon Abbey (156 b; see the Abingdon History, ii 25), and also (143) as holding certain burgesses of Buckingham, who had been the men of Azor the son of Toti (see vol. ii p 643) I do not see the evidence on which Sir Henry Ellis (i 441) makes him a descendant of Count Rudolf of Ivry, but we know that he married Adeline, daughter of Hugh Grantmesnil (Ord Vit 692 A) She was a benefactress to the Abbey of Abingdon. See the local History, ii. 72-74, 152, and Domesday, 160 His name has appeared in our history as guardian of the castle at Rouen, see p 643.

Robert had two brothers, Nigel and Gilbert, whose consent is recited in his foundation charter of Saint George's College (Mon Angl. viii 1462). Nigel is constantly mentioned in the History of Abingdon He seems to have succeeded his brother Robert on the latter's death without issue He was succeeded by his son, the second Robert of Oily, the nephew of the first. In 1129 (Oseney

Annals; An Mon. iv 19; Mon Angl. vi. 251) he began the foundation of the Priory of Oseney, a house of Austin Canons, in partnership with his wife Eadgyth. She is said (Mon. Ang. vi 251), I know not on what authority, to have been a mistress of Henry the First Her name makes it all but certain that she was of English descent. I do not say absolutely certain, because William of Warren and Gundrada had a daughter so named (Will. Gem viii. 8), who may probably have been a god-daughter of the widow of the Confessor (see vol. ii. p. 347). Robert and Eadgyth left two sons, Henry and Gilbert, who therefore, as well as the descendants of Miles Crispin, were probably of English descent by the mother's side. English names also survived in their foundation of Oseney. The second Prior and the first Abbot (1138-1168) bore the name of Wigod, and must surely have been of the family of Wigod of Wallingford His successor (1168-1183) bore the less distinctive name of Eadward See the Oseney Annals under those years

Ælfred the nephew of Wigod and Wido of Oily appear near together in Domesday, 160

## NOTE H. p. 53
### Robert and Swegen of Essex.

Of Robert the son of Wymarc, Eadward's Staller and favourite, we have already often heard (see vol. iii. pp. 9, 413). He appears as a large landowner in various parts of England under Eadward. He died before the time of the Survey (Domesday, ii. 47 b), and was succeeded by his son, who (cf vol ii pp 417, 663) was Englishman or Dane enough to bear the name of Swegen, "Postquam Rex advenit, dono Regis tenuit Robertus i hidam, et Suenus filius ejus adjunxit iv. hidas cum istâ post mortem patris sui." But nearly the whole of the estates of Robert in other parts of England had before the Survey passed to other owners, while his great estate in the Eastern shires was largely increased Thus his lands in Somerset (92 b), Hertfordshire (134, 137 b), Herefordshire (186 b, 187), Cambridgeshire (193 b, 200 b, 201) had all passed away from the family. So had part of his estate in Huntingdonshire (207), but another part (205 b) was still held by Swegen, as well as lands in Oxfordshire (160) whose owner T R E. is not mentioned. Some parts of his Suffolk and Essex estates (ii 395, 106, 287 *b*, 295 *b*) had also passed from him, but, on the other hand, he had received considerable grants from William in the Eastern shires; see ii 42, 47 *b*, 48 The last entry is worth notice. A tenant of Swegen holds land which had belonged to Brixsi (see vol. ii. p 649, 2nd ed ) , "Hanc terram tenuit iste libere, et quando Rex venit in hanc terram utlagavit, et R accepit terram suam; postea habuit S" A distinction seems to be drawn between Robert's holdings T R E. (ii. 43 *b*, 45 *b*, 46 *b*, 47), his holdings "post mortem R E." (ii. 44, 44 *b*, 45, 45 *b*), and his holdings "post adventum R W." (ii. 46, 46 *b*, 47). Either he received grants from Harold, or else part of his land was lost under Harold and recovered under William. Robert, like other people, was also enriched by irregular means, either by his own act or that of his Reeves. Thus in ii. 23 we read of lands which at the time of the Survey were held by two tenants of Bishop Odo, but which had been held T R E by two freemen ; "Sicut Anglici dicunt, Ravengarius abstulit terram ab uno illorum, et Robertus filius Wimarc alteram terram ab altero, modo vero nesciunt quomodo venerit ad episcopum" And a still more distinct case appears in ii 101 , " Hanc terram invasit Robertus filius Uuimarc T. R. Willelmi, et adhuc tenet Suenus" So in ii 42 we read, "Tenet Osbernus de S quod tenuit Aluuen libera femina T. R E., et nescitur quomodo venerit ad Robertum filium Wicmarc" So in ii 46 *b*, an English tenant of Swegen, Eadmær by name, holds thirty-seven acres, thirty of which had been held by a freeman T. R E , "et illæ vii acræ sunt additæ post adventum Regis Willelmi, quæ fuerunt cujusdam alius liberi hominis." But the most curious entry is in ii 47 *b*, where, out of the lands of a certain Godric, most of which seem to have been granted to Robert, one lordship was granted to Swegen, who gave it to his father , "S. tenet hoc manerium de dono Regis Willelmi, quod dedit patri suo Roberto."

That Robert was Sheriff of Essex under Eadward we have seen in vol. ii p 347. Of his tenure of the office under William we get an incidental notice in the Survey (ii 98) Grim the Reeve holds lands of which is noted ; "Hida est una de hominibus forisfactis erga Regem, quam post adventum Regis addidit G. ad suam aliam terram per Robertum filium Wimarc Vicecomitem, sicut ipse G. dicit." He was probably succeeded in his office by Swegen, of whom we hear as Sheriff in 1 *b*, 2, 6, 7, 19 *b*, but it appears from 2 *b* ("Suen inde abstulit postquam perdidit vicecomitatum") that he had lost the office before the Survey was taken. One curious story of Robert's official life is found in ii. 401 *b*. There was a certain Brungar, a freeman in Suffolk, who was commended to Robert, but over whose lands Saint Eadmund had the rights of sac and soc, "Eodem tempore fuerunt furati equi inventi in domo istius Brungari, ita quod Abbas, cujus fuit soca et saca, et Rodbertus, qui habuit commendationem super istum, venerunt de hoc furto ad placitum et, sicut hundret testatur, discesserunt amicabiliter sine judicio quod vidisset hundret"

Swegen seems, from ii. 401 and other places, to have taken the name of Essex as a sort of surname, and he was father or grandfather of Henry of Essex, whose cowardice in the Welsh war in 1159 is recorded by Gervase (X Scriptt 1380), and his punishment by Roger of Wendover (ii. 296 See also Dugdale's Baronage, 463; Madox, History of the Exchequer, 28, 42, Ellis, i 489) The Eadward son of Swegen in ii. 98 *b* ("tenuit Eduuardus filius Suani dimidiam hidam; modo tenet Edeva uxor ejus") is certainly not a son of Swegen of Essex Swegen built the castle of Rayleigh in Essex (ii 53 *b*) on land which had not belonged to his father. He had also land in the town of Maldon, about which we find the following curious entry (ii. 48), "In hac terrâ habet Rex iii. solidos de consuetudine, et facit adjutorium cum aliis burgensibus invenire caballum in exercitu et ad navem faciendam; ceteras vero consuetudines habet Suenus" Swegen's invasions of ecclesiastical and other property are recorded in 2, 42 *b*, 59 *b*, 101; another of his victims (42 *b*) was "Bricteva libera femina"—doubtless the same Brihtgifu of whose wrongs at another hand we have already heard (see above, p. 726)—" quam Suenus addidit prædictæ terræ."

## NOTE I p 64.

### EADRIC THE WILD

OUR earliest notice of Eadric is in Orderic, 506 B, where he is said to have been one of those who submitted to William at Barking (see p 21). We there get his surname of "Wild," and we are told that he was the nephew or grandson of Eadric Streona; "Edricus quoque cognomento *Guilda*, id est Silvaticus, nepos Edrici pestiferi Ducis cognomento Streone, id est acquisitoris." This statement is one in which Orderic stands by himself and is not copying William of Poitiers. That Eadric submitted to William thus early in his reign seems to me to be distinctly contradicted by the words of Florence which I have quoted in p. 64. The next mention of him in Florence is in 1070, when his submission is recorded (see p. 463). But we learn something of his exploits in the meanwhile from Orderic, 514 A, who records his share in the siege of the Norman garrison at Shrewsbury (see p. 274). The only later mention of him is when he accompanied William to Scotland in 1072 (see p. 514). We cannot tell from any of our narratives when or how he died, or whether he again fell under William's displeasure.

Our other authentic source of information about him is Domesday, where he does not appear as a tenant-in-chief, at least not with his distinctive surname. The entries which are certainly his represent him as a holder of land T. R. E. in Herefordshire and Shropshire. He appears in 183 *b* by the name of Edric *Salvage*, as holding land which had passed to Ralph of Mortemer, and therefore he is doubtless the Eadric intended by four other entries of the same name in the same page. In 256 *b* and 258 *b* we again have Edric Salvage holding lands in Shropshire which had passed to Earl Roger. He may also be the Eadric of 254 *b*, 255 *b*, 256 *b*, 257, 258, 258 *b*, 260, in which last entry the land has passed to Osbern the son of Richard. In 256 *b* we may suppose that he is a different person from the Eadric who is mentioned just above him, with the addition "homo liber fuit," and he may or may not be the same as the Eadric who appears in 257 as a tenant of the Bishop of Hereford, "Edric tenuit de Episcopo de Hereford, et non poterat ab eo divertere, quia de victu suo erat et ei præstiterat tantum in vitâ suâ." (As usual, the reversionary right of the Bishop had not been regarded, and the land had passed to a tenant of Earl Roger.) This is the whole of the evidence of Domesday, and it leaves it uncertain whether Eadric were dead or alive at the time of the Survey, and whether his lands had passed from him by forfeiture or otherwise. All we know is that they had not passed to any descendants of his own.

This is all that is really known about Eadric, a man about whom we should gladly know much more. Some tales about him, which have often been accepted as history, can easily be shown to be fables. In the account of the foundation of Wigmore Priory in the Monasticon (vi. 348), Eadric is represented as defending Wigmore Castle against Ralph of Mortemer, as being at last taken prisoner by him, and as being condemned by William to perpetual imprisonment; "Radulphus, tamquam strenuissimus pugil, in Marchiam, et præsertim contra Edrichum, Salopiæ Comitem et Wygemoriæ ac Melenythiæ cum pertinentiis dominum, conquestui adhuc non parentem, directus, post longam laboris obsidionem ipsum in eodem castro obtentum, dictasque terras et plures alias in Marchiâ, vi gladii et fortunâ, suo quam gloriose mancipavit dominio, quem et perpetuis carceribus mancipandum ad dominum suum Regem adduxit vinctum, dictamque mancipationem castri de Dyneythâ in Melenyth, per eum constructi, tuitione quam bellicose munivit." That this story is wrong may be easily shown from Domesday. Neither Wigmore Castle nor its site ever belonged to Eadric, nor is Eadric called Earl in any authentic record. Of Wigmore Castle the account in Domesday, 183 b, is, "Radulfus de Mortemer tenet castellum Wigemore. Willelmus Comes fecit illud in wastâ terrâ quæ vocatur Merestun, quam tenebat Gunuert T. R. E." I can give no further account of Gunwert except that he is found, with a name spelled in various ways, in several parts of Herefordshire and Shropshire, and generally in the near neighbourhood of Eadric, so that he is not unlikely to have been a sharer in his exploits.

Eadric the Wild of Herefordshire must not be confounded with the East-Anglian Eadric mentioned in p. 121 and in vol. iii. p. 717. On his outlawry Bishop Æthelmar took possession of his lands; "Episcopus Almarus invasit terram" (Domesday, ii. 200). Most likely the land was held by one of the common leases, and, when Eadric's right in it was ended by his outlawry, it legally reverted to the Bishop. But as the Crown was sure to put in some claim, rightful or wrongful, to the lands of an outlaw, the Bishop's occupation was called an "invasio."

## NOTE K. p 66.

### Castles and Destruction in Towns.

The substance of this note also is removed to the examination of Domesday in the fifth volume.


## NOTE L. p. 76.

### The Earldom and Death of Copsige

I have already (see vol ii. p 484) said somewhat about Copsige, the Coxo of the Normans, and his relations to Tostig and to William There is at first sight a chronological difficulty as to the date of his appointment to his Earldom and of the death which so soon followed it William of Poitiers (148, so Orderic, 506 A) distinctly mentions him among the English leaders who submitted to William at Barking (see p 24), " In his erat Comes Coxo, quem singulari et fortitudine et probitate Regi, post et optimo cuique Normanno, placuisse audivimus." Later in his story he tells us of his death, which he evidently puts during William's absence in Normandy in 1067. After telling the story of Eustace and the Kentishmen he adds (158), " Eodem fere tempore Coxo Comes, quem placuisse Normannis diximus, morte occidit immeritâ, et quam deceat propagari " He then goes on with a panegyric on the virtues and loyalty of Copsige, " Hic Regis causam et ipsum favore multo probabat " He then tells us of the many temptations and exhortations by which Copsige's followers and the rest of his countrymen tried to move him from his constancy to William,

" Sui vero satellites ab ipso dissidebant, factionum deterrimi fautores ac socii Proinde cum ab officio transvertere tentabant, sæpe monentes, quasi per amicitiam, de privato honore, ut libertatem a proavis traditam defenderet, nunc obsecrantes atque obtestantes, tamquam gratiâ rerum publicarum, ut, extraneos deserens, optimorum hominum suæ nationis et consanguinitatis voluntatem sequeretur Sane diutinâ variâque calliditate hæc suggerebant, et hujusmodi alia."

742    APPENDIX.

Copsige however withstands all temptations, and dies a martyr to his faith towards William (see p. 107)

We turn from the rhetoric of the Archdeacon of Lisieux to the plainer narrative of our own Simeon, who at least gives us dates, though it is the dates themselves which at first sight raise the difficulty. The story comes in one of Simeon's insertions in the Chronicle of Florence, and, as happens with several of those insertions, it is put out of its place, in that account of the succession of the Northumbrian Earls (see vol i p. 585) which comes in incidentally under the year 1072 (p. 91). He had just mentioned the appointment of Oswulf to the Bernician Earldom by Morkere in 1065 (see vol. ii p 487). He then adds ; " Capto postmodum et custodiæ mancipato Morkaro, Rex Willelmus comitatum Osulfi commisit Copsio, qui erat partis Tostu Comitis, viro consiliario et prudenti." He then goes on to tell the tale of Copsige's death, of which he gives an exact date, fixing it to March 12, five weeks after his appointment to the Earldom, but without mentioning the year. I have quoted the passage in p 107

The difficulty lies in the words " capto postmodum et custodiæ mancipato Morkaro." It is certain that Morkere was not actually put in bonds till after his revolt in 1071 (see p. 476). I was therefore once inclined to think that the whole of these events were to be placed after William's reconquest of Ely in that year But there are several reasons against this date First there is the Norman version, which speaks of Copsige as Earl in 1067 and as being killed in the course of that year. Then Simeon goes on to tell us, in the passages following those which I have just quoted, how Oswulf was himself killed not long after the death of Copsige, and how Gospatric then begged, or rather bought, the Bernician Earldom of William (see p. 134). But Gospatric is called Earl in the Worcester Chronicle under the year 1068, and the account which Simeon gives (see p. 523) of the events of the year 1072 implies that it was in that year that Gospatric finally lost his Earldom I therefore place this account of Copsige, his appointment to his Earldom and his death, in the year 1067. We must therefore suppose a certain laxity of speech on the part of Simeon in the words which speak of an imprisonment of Morkere. In 1067 Morkere was outwardly in the highest favour with William But the character in which he accompanied William to Normandy was practically that of a hostage (see p 75) It was a pardonable exaggeration or confusion to apply to such a state of things language which strictly applied only to his actual imprisonment at a later time.

The account in the Durham Chronicle printed in the Monasticon, i 235, is clearly made up from the narrative of Simeon, from which it differs only in putting the death of Oswulf in the year following the death of Copsige, whereas in Simeon it happens in the same year "sequenti auctumno." But this is no real difference. Copsige was killed on March 12 in the year 1067 Easter fell on April 8. By any one therefore who followed the reckoning which begins the year at Easter, the death of Oswulf would be said to happen in the year following the death of Copsige.

It is curious to see how this story is treated by Thierry. Copsige is killed twice over The first time he dies by his Norman name, or rather by Thierry's wonderful transformation of it (see vol. ii. 484), during William's absence in 1067 He is killed the second time by his own name, or something like it, after William's capture of York in 1069. That is to say, Thierry read the account in William of Poitiers, and also the account in Simeon of Durham, or rather in the Chronicle in the Monasticon founded on it But he did not find out that they both referred to the same person, and that his Kox and his Kopsi (which his English translator brings a degree nearer in the form of Kopsig) were the same man. The history of Kox is told at i. 286, without any hint as to the part of England to which the story belongs,

"Un chef saxon, nommé Kox, reçut de semblables messages, au nom de la vieille liberté anglaise, et n'en tint aucun compte ; irrités de son refus, les conjurés lui envoyèrent des ordres, puis des menaces ; et, comme il persistait toujours dans son amitié pour les vainqueurs, les menaces furent exécutées, et il périt dans une émeute, malgré la protection étrangère. Les historiens normands le célèbrent comme un martyr de la foi jurée, digne d'être cité partout comme exemple, et dont la gloire doit vivre d'âge en âge "

The history of Kopsi (1 326) is more romantic. It is placed in the last days of 1069 or in the first days of 1070, while William is following up his conquests beyond the Tyne I do not know how Thierry got over the difficulty about the imprisonment of

Morkere in Simeon's account, because in his own version Morkere is at this moment in arms against William;

"Quand les Northumbriens, après avoir chassé Tostig, frère de Harold, dans une insurrection nationale, eurent choisi pour chef Morkar, frère d'Edwin, Morkar avait mis, de leur aveu, à la tête du pays situé au-de-là de la Tees, le jeune Osulf, fils d'Edulf. Osulf garda son commandement jusqu'au jour où les Normands eurent passé la Tyne ; alors il fut contraint de fuir comme les autres dans les forêts et les montagnes On mit à sa place un certain Saxon appelé Kopsi, homme que les habitants de la Northumbrie avaient chassé avec Tostig, qui avait à se venger d'eux, et que, pour cette raison même, le nouveau roi leur imposa pour chef. Kopsi s'installa dans son poste sous la protection des étrangers ; mais, après avoir exercé quelque temps son office, il fut assailli dans sa maison par une troupe de déshérités conduite par ce même Osulf dont il avait reçu la dépouille. Il prenait tranquillement son repas, sans s'attendre à rien, quand les Saxons tombèrent sur lui, le tuèrent, et se dispersèrent aussitôt."

With regard to Copsige's earlier life, Geoffrey Gaimar, without much probability, represents him as joining in the first incursions of Tostig in 1066 (see vol. iii. p. 304), and therefore as having shared his banishment;

"En Taneth vont; en cel pais   Il vint de l'isle de Orkeme
Encontre lui Copsi la vint,   Dise seit nefs out en baillie"
Un son baron ki de li tint   (5164-5168 M H B 826)

## NOTE M. p 78.

### The Possessions of the Ætheling Eadgar.

WILLIAM of Poitiers (148) enlarges on the favour which William at this time showed to Eadgar, and on the large estates which he granted him, "Athelinum, quem post Heraldi ruinam Angli Regem statuere conati fuerant, amplis terris ditavit, atque in carissimis habuit eum, quia Regis Edwardi genus contigerat, ad hoc ne puerilis ætas nimium doleret non habere honorem ad quem electus fuerat." The lands now granted would doubtless be confiscated on Eadgar's revolt (see p. 185), and the whole or part would be granted again on his reconciliation (see p 571), but the actual entries in Domesday (142) of Eadgar's possessions hardly agree with the "amplissimæ terræ" spoken of by William of Poitiers, nor yet with the "magnum donativum" spoken of by William of Malmesbury at a later time (see p. 571). Whether Eadgar held anything T R E may be doubted The only entry which looks like it is one in Essex (ii 3 b), where we read, "Cestrefordam tenuit *Comes* Edgarus T. R. E" I know of no other case (see vol. iii p 766) where Eadgar receives the title of Earl; on the other hand, no other Earl of the name is mentioned in the days of Eadward. Of the two lordships in Hertfordshire which he held at the time of the Survey I have spoken in p. 571, and I there mentioned some of their former English owners Besides two socmen of Esegar the Staller, his man "Vluuinus" (Wulfwig), and Stigand's Thegn "Alnod" (probably "Alnod Chentiscus," of whom more anon), there was Ælfward the man of Ælfmær "de Belint," of whom I can give no account, and seven socmen of King Eadward All could sell their land; some of them seem to have been deprived of it late in William's reign, as we read, "Hos vii. sochemannos et Uluuinum et Aluuard apposuit Ilbertus vicecomes huic manerio tempore R W. qui non fuerunt ibi T. R E, ut hundreda testatur"

As Eadgar's departure for Apulia (see p. 697) was later than the taking of the Survey, we know not whether he lost his lands again then.

## NOTE N p 130.

### The Possessions of Count Eustace

The Count Eustace of Domesday is not Eustace the Second of Boulogne, who plays so important a part in our history, but his son Eustace the Third According to the Art de Vérifier les Dates (ii 762), Eustace the Second died, and Eustace the Third succeeded, in 1093, which would make Eustace the Second the landowner at the time of the Survey. But Sir Henry Ellis (1 385, 416) quotes a charter in which his second wife Ida is described as "venerabilis Ida tunc vidua" as early as

1082. And the fact that Ida herself appears as a landowner in Domesday, though it does not of itself prove that her husband was dead, falls in with that belief. But it was doubtless the elder Eustace who was the original grantee of the lands held by his son, and the entries with regard to him throw some light on his history as I have told it in the text.

The first wife of Eustace, Godgifu, the Goda of the Normans, the own sister of King Eadward, appears as a landowner T. R. E. in Sussex (17, 19, 19 *b*, 25), Surrey (34, where she is distinguished as "Goda Comitissa, soror R. E.," 36 *b*), Dorset (75 *b*, 76), Middlesex (130), Buckinghamshire (151 *b*), Gloucestershire (166 *b*, 170), Nottinghamshire (280, where she is distinguished from her namesake "Godeva Comitissa," the wife of Leofric, 287). Not a scrap of these large possessions was kept by Eustace after the death of his wife. Some of the estates of Godgifu were at the time of the Survey in the King's hands; the rest had been granted out to various ecclesiastical and private owners. The date of the death of Godgifu is not exactly known, but it appears to have happened before 1056. (See Art de Vérifier les Dates, ii. 762.) She therefore could not have been a holder "eâ die quâ Rex E. vivus fuit et mortuus." Her appearance in Domesday is therefore a parallel case to those entries where Earl Godwine appears as the owner T. R. E. But her appearance seems to show that her lands passed to her husband. If the lands of Godgifu had from 1056 to 1066 been in the hands of King Eadward or any grantee of his, we should hardly find her name in the Survey. It is a natural conjecture that Eustace succeeded to the lands of his wife, that they were confiscated by William after his treason in 1067, and that the estates which Eustace afterwards held were later grants after his reconciliation. It strengthens this view that three lordships in Dorset (85) were held at the time of the Survey by Ida the second wife of Eustace, which she is also said to have held T. R. E. This looks as if Eadward had made grants to the second wife of his friend, which were not confiscated by William along with the lands of her husband. At the time of Eustace's trial in 1067 the power of William had not yet reached into Dorset.

The Domesday holdings of Eustace were therefore grants later than his reconciliation with William, yet one is tempted to think that some of the lands held by Eustace in the Southern shires must have been earlier grants which were restored. The great bulk of his estates lie in the Eastern shires, especially in Essex (ii. 26-34), and a large part of them could not have been given him in William's first days, as they consist of estates which had been held by Engelric (see above, p 725), and in one case (ii. 27) had belonged to the Lady Eadgyth. But other entries of land which had been held by Harold were most likely either grants which were restored. His estates in Kent (14), Surrey (34), Hampshire (34 *b*), had been mainly held by Godwine, Gytha, and Harold, which looks as if they were early grants of William. And the estates in Somerset, it is plain, could not have been granted till after the conquest of the West in 1068. One lordship in Somerset and one in Surrey (34) are entered in the Survey as belonging to the Countess. That in Somerset is Kenwardston, now corruptly Kingweston, which (91 *b*), as well as Loxton, had been held T. R. E. by Wulfgifu, who was also Ida's predecessor in some of her Dorset lands. Other possessions of Eustace are found in Hertfordshire (137), Oxfordshire (157 *b*), Cambridgeshire (196), Huntingdonshire (205), Bedford (211), Norfolk (ii 151), and Suffolk (ii. 303), where, as also in Hertfordshire, Engelric again appears.

Several of the possessions of Eustace in Cambridgeshire and Bedfordshire were held under him by his follower Arnold or Arnulf of Ardres (see vol iii p 714), whom I should not have confounded, even for a moment, with a man of far larger possessions, Arnulf of Hesdin.

Kenwardston was afterwards given by the Countess Mary, daughter of Malcolm and Margaret, to Bermondsey Abbey. See the Bermondsey Annals, 1114, 1115, 1127, Ann. Mon. iii. 432, 435. I ought to have mentioned the foundation of that monastery in my ecclesiastical chapter, as its founder was plainly an Englishman in favour with William. It was founded in 1082 by one described as "Alwinus [Ælfwine] Child civis Londoniæ" (Ann. Berm in anno) for Cluniac monks who came from La Charité on the Loire, and found a benefactor in William Rufus. But in his charter (Mon. Ang. v. 100) Ælfwine is not mentioned.

## NOTE O. p 135

### THE EARLDOM OF GOSPATRIC.

THE career of Gospatric would have been much clearer, if Simeon of Durham, or whoever is the Northern interpolator of Florence, had given us the events of his life under their proper years, instead of throwing them into a kind of Appendix under the year 1072 (p. 92, Hinde), the date of his deposition (see p 135). He there says distinctly that it was on the death of Oswulf, in the autumn of 1067, that Gospatric begged or bought the Earldom. This fixes the appointment to the first possible moment after the death of Oswulf, that is, to the Midwinter Gemót of 1067–1068; and the next time we hear of him is soon after Pentecost in 1068, when he leaves William's court for Scotland (see p. 185) The difficulty arises from Simeon's incidental way of telling the story. Having mentioned Gospatric's appointment at Christmas, 1067, he goes on to say, "Tenuit comitatum donec Rex causis ex supradictis ei auferret; fugiens ergo ad Malcolmum non multo post Flandriam navigio petit" (see p. 523). This of course refers, not to his first flight in 1068, but to his final flight in 1072. Simeon himself mentions the flight of 1068 under its proper year, and in describing Gospatric's appearance at York in 1069 (p 84) he gives him the title of Earl, which he bears also in the Worcester Chronicle (see p 255); and this is to be noted, because the mention of Gospatric in 1069 is one of Simeon's additions to the text of Florence. Between these two events, in the beginning of 1069, the Worcester Chronicle and Simeon place the grant of the Bernician Earldom to Robert of Comines (see p. 235), which is not mentioned by Florence. It would seem then that William treated Gospatric's Earldom as vacant through his flight to Scotland, Robert was his successor, and William (see p. 523), afterwards at least, looked on Gospatric as having been an accomplice in the rising in which Robert lost his life. Gospatric's reconciliation with William and his restoration to his Earldom in the winter of 1069 are mentioned by Ordenc only Simeon, in recording his acts in the next year, 1070, treats him as if he had been Earl all along He speaks, as we have seen, of his share in the attack on York, and he does not mention him again till he records his attack on Cumberland in 1070 (p 87, see p. 506), when he introduces him afresh, with a reference to his first appointment in 1067, "Gospatricus Comes qui, ut supra dictum est, a Rege Willelmo comitatum Northanhymbrorum pretio assecutus fuerat." He acts again as Earl when he receives Bishop Walcher at Durham in 1071 (see p. 513), he is finally deposed in 1072, but he had been received again into partial favour before the taking of the Survey (see p. 524).

The apparent puzzle arises wholly from the way in which Simeon put his History together, namely by enlarging the chronicle of Florence by such insertions as he thought needful. Gospatric was naturally a much more important person in the eyes of Simeon than he was in the eyes of Florence. Simeon therefore felt called on to speak of him several times when Florence had not mentioned him, and the way in which he made his insertions was a little irregular and incoherent.

The course of events then is something like this;

| | |
|---|---|
| Appointment as Earl | Christmas 1067 |
| Earldom forfeited by flight to Scotland | Summer 1068 |
| Appointment and death of Robert | January 1069 |
| Share in the campaign at York | September 1069 |
| Restoration to the Earldom | December 1069 |
| Final deposition and second flight | Late in 1072 |
| Partial restoration of lands | Before 1086 |

I am glad to find that Mr. Hinde, whose History of Northumberland I had not made use of when I first wrote this note, goes along with me as to the chronology of Copsige and Gospatric, though I have some matters of dispute with him

## NOTE P. p. 136.

### ÆTHELSIGE ABBOT OF RAMSEY.

I HAVE here given the best account which I could put together, from various scattered notices, of the chequered life of a remarkable man. Of Æthelsige's appointment to the Abbey of Saint Augustine (see vol. ii p. 454) there is no doubt, and the local history is explicit as to his being further invested by Eadward with the government of Ramsey. The writer (c 119) describes the sickness of Abbot Ælfwine, and adds words which are equivalent to a resignation; "Crescente indies languore, et spem ei omnem rediturae sanitatis penitus adimente, forinsecae administrationis renuntians officio, omne perfunctoriae potestatis onus, ut secum quietior habitaret, abjecit." He goes on to say that the brethren took good care of him for the rest of his days, and then adds; "Quibus auditis, Rex Edwardus, amicissimi viri adversis condolens casibus et Ecclesiae ipsius provida dispensatione consulens utilitati, cuidam Ailfsio, viro prudenti et industrio, qui tunc temporis monasterio Sancti Augustini Abbatis jure praesidebat, domûs Ramesiensis curam commisit" (The form A*il*fsius in this extract might seem to imply the name Æ*lf*sige rather than Æ*thel*sige, but it clearly should be A*il*sius, A*il* being the usual Latin abbreviation of Æðel) It seems plain then that Æthelsige held the two Abbeys in plurality before the death of Eadward, and that he was appointed Abbot of Ramsey during the lifetime of Ælfwine. But in the Act of 1072 touching the submission of the see of York to Canterbury (Will Malm. ii 298, see p 358) we read among the signatures, "Ego Elfwinus, Abbas coenobii quod Ramesege dicitur, consensi" There is also a charter printed in the Monasticon, ii. 559, and in Cod. Dipl iv 148, but marked as doubtful, the signatures to which seem to speak of Æthelsige and Ælfwine as both Abbots at once. First among the Abbots signs "Ælsius Abbas," as the Abbot concerned, and last among them we read, "Ego Alwinus Abbas hoc meum desiderium ad perfectum adduxi et a Rege hilariter suscepi" On the other hand, it is clear that Æthelsige was Abbot of Ramsey at the time of the Survey, for we read (43 b) of lands in Hampshire, "Hoc sic attestatur Elsi Abbas de Ramesy et totum hundret" From the same source we also learn that he was at one time outlawed, and that he was at the same time or another in Denmark. In 62 b we read of lands in Berkshire, "Elsi Abbas tenuit de veteri monasterio Wintonensis ecclesiae testimonio scirae T. R. E et postea, donec utlage fuit" And again in 208, of lands in Huntingdonshire; "De alterâ hidâ dicunt quod Godricus tenuit eam de Abbate. Sed quum Abbas esset in Danemarkâ, Osmundus pater Radulfi rapuit eam a Sawino accipitrario, cui Abbas eam dederat ob amorem

Regis." Here we plainly see Æthelsige in possession of the Abbey at the time of the Survey, and he is described as having been, at some former time, in high favour with the King, as having been in Denmark for some cause or other, and also as having been at one time outlawed. Further, in the Chronologia Augustinensis in Elmham's History (p 28, ed Hardwick), we read " Egelsinus fugit" under the year 1070, and the story is told more at length in W. Thorn's Chronicle (X Scriptt. 1787) Some of the Normans had unlawfully seized ("violenter occupaverunt") some of the lands of the Abbey, " Egelsinus perpendens se odium incurrisse Regis propter libertates Kancie [this refers to the legend about Stigand and Æthelsige securing the liberties of Kent, see vol. iii p 539] prædia et possessiones monasterii sui Normannis, timore compulsus, invitis suis fratribus, concessit Tandem attendens iram Regis erga se implacabilem, plus suæ saluti quam gregis sibi commissi consulens, exhaustis pretiosis quibuscumque monasterii sui thesauris, in Daciam navigio affugit, nec usquam comparuit."

Putting all this evidence together, there seems hardly room for doubt that Æthelsige of Saint Augustine's and Æthelsige of Ramsey are the same person, that he forsook his preferments in 1070 and fled to Denmark (an act equivalent to outlawry), that, during his absence, the former Abbot Ælfwine resumed his functions, but that at some later time Æthelsige regained William's favour, and was restored to Ramsey, but not to Saint Augustine's The "nec usquam comparuit" of the Canterbury writer is quite accounted for by his not appearing again at Saint Augustine's. But out of all this another question arises, namely as to the embassy of Æthelsige to Swend The direct evidence for this comes only from sources which are greatly mixed up with legendary matter. Langebek (iii 252) has collected three Church legends of the origin of the Feast of the Conception of our Lady, from one of which I copy the part which concerns the history of Æthelsige,

" Eo tempore, quo Wilhelmus Dux Normannorum potentissimus, prostrato Rege Anglorum Haraldo, Angliam sibi subjecisset, contigit ut Danorum Rex, auditâ morte Haraldi consanguinei, venire in Angliam disponeret, ut et mortem ejus vindicaret et terram sibi subigeret, quam dicebat suam esse , quo audito, Wilhelmus omnia castra Angliæ militibus et expensis fortissime munivit, et ad resistendum Danis se, quantum poterat, præparavit Inito autem consilio cum suis optimatibus, Abbatem Helsinum, virum prudentem ac Deo ac beatæ Virgini devotissimum, in Daciam misit, ut et propositum Regis agnosceret et pro pace obtinendâ a Rege Danorum, quantum esset sibi possibile, laboraret.

"Navigans igitur venerabilis Abbas, in Daciam prospere venit, Regique se præsentans, munera ac servitia ex parte Wilhelmi novi Regis Angliæ obtulit, ac proceres terræ muneribus honoravit. Reverenter igitur a Rege Danorum receptus et habitus, non modico tempore apud eum mansit Tandem quum negotia pro quibus missus fuerat ad placitum peregisset, licentiâ redeundi a Rege datâ, iter per mare cum sociis aggressus est." (iii 253.)

The story will also be found at greater length in an English poem of the fourteenth century, quoted by Sir Henry Ellis, ii. 99.

It is of course open to any one to accept the facts that Æthelsige took refuge in Denmark during his outlawry and that he afterwards returned, but to look on the story of the embassy as a legend growing out of these facts, devised to explain his presence in Denmark. But the three lessons given by Langebek, though they run off into an ecclesiastical legend, are yet perfectly probable and consistent in their description of the political state of things There is nothing unlikely, but quite the contrary, in William's sending an embassy to Swend Indeed the singular failure of Swend to send help at the time when it would have been most effectual, his not coming in person at all, might of themselves suggest that William's power of intrigue had been at work. To employ an Englishman and a friend of Harold for such an office would be a matter of obvious policy On the whole the balance of probability seems decidedly in favour of the embassy.

Sir Henry Ellis (ii 105) seems to have confounded Æthelsige with his predecessor Ælfwine See vol. ii pp 372, 621.

## NOTE Q. p. 141

### The Lands of Gytha and her Family in the West.

The Exeter Domesday is full of entries as to the possessions of the house of Godwine in the Western shires They were almost wholly held by the King at the time of the Survey. The greater part of them are entered together in great masses under different titles, which vary somewhat in different shires Of the great heads of Crown lands, the first (75), headed " Dominicatus Regis ad Regnum pertinens in Devenescirâ," contains nothing which had belonged to Godwine's family, and nearly all the estates there entered had been held by King Eadward himself The like is the case with the next head (80), " Dominicatus Regis in Sumersetâ" But the next head, " Dominicatus Regis in Devenescirâ " (84), consists, with the exception of a single lordship, wholly of lands which had belonged to Gytha and her sons. The members of the family who appear under this heading are Gytha herself, Eadgyth, Harold, and Leofwine. The names are spelled in various ways, and in one place (90) Gytha appears simply as " mater Haraldi Comitis." In 90 is the entry, " Terræ Regis dominicæ in Cornu Galliæ," consisting of twelve lordships which had been held by Harold, answering to the entry in the Exchequer Domesday, 120, which has the note at the end, " Has præscriptas xii terras tenuit Heraldus Comes T. R. E." Then (94) follows the heading, " Terræ Regis quas tenuit Godwinus Comes et filii ejus in Sumersetâ." The lands under this head had belonged to Gytha, Harold, Tostig, " Godwinus filius Haroldi Comitis" (96), " Gunnilla filia Comitis Goduini" (96, 99), and Eddeva (97), of whom more anon. In 104 is a distinct entry of " Terra Editdæ Reginæ in Sumersetâ" Also in 26 is the entry, " Dominicatus Regis in Dorsetâ," consisting of seven lordships which had been held by Harold, six which had been held by King Eadward, one by Gytha under the name of " mater Haroldi Comitis," and two churches at Dorchester and elsewhere held by Brihtweard the priest.

It is thus plain that the lands of the house of Godwine formed a large part of the Crown lands kept by William in the Western shires Only very small portions of them were allowed to pass into any other hands, and those chiefly into the hands of William's brother Earl Robert. The conquest of the West was, alone among William's later successes, a distinct triumph over the house of Godwine. He seems to have purposely kept their lands in his own hands as a sort of trophy

Among the members of the house of Godwine who appear in this list, the largest holdings are those of Gytha, Eadgyth, and Harold. Leofwine has several lordships in Devonshire, in Somerset only one for certain, namely, Combe (Exon, 142, Exchequer, 87 *b*), which had passed to Bishop Odo. The Leofwine who appears in Exchequer, 91 *b*, 92, Exon, 252, can hardly be the Earl. Tostig appears as the owner of a single lordship only, that of Winsford in Somerset. Gyrth holds nothing in the West. Wulfnoth does not appear among his brothers, but some of the lands which appear in the Western shires as held T. R. E. by men named Wulfnoth may have been his property (see Dorset, 83 *b*; Somerset, 91 *b*, 95; Devonshire, 103, 106, 109 *b*, 110 *b*, 111, 111 *b*, 113 *b*, 114 *b*, 116, 117, Cornwall, 122 *b*, 123, 123 *b*) But it is perhaps more likely that, like Harold's sons Eadmund and Magnus, he had not received any lands on account of his youth Among the less known members of the family, two Somerset lordships are held by Gunhild the daughter of Godwine, and two by Godwine the son of Harold. There remains only the entry of Eddeva in Exon, 97. She can hardly be the Lady, whose lands in Somerset are entered under a separate head. Is it possible that we have here another trace of Eadgyth Swanneshals?

## NOTE R p. 141.

### The Children of Harold.

Of the sons of Harold, Godwine is recorded in Domesday (see above, p 225), and he and his two brothers Eadmund and Magnus are mentioned in the narrative of Florence (see p. 225, and below, Note DD). Two daughters, Gunhild and Gytha, are known to us from other sources. Sir Henry Ellis (ii. 127) quotes Capgrave for a story of Gunhild, who is said to have been cured by Saint Wulfstan. This may be the Gunhild who held seven hides of land at Kingston in Sussex of Harold. (Domesday, 28 *b*, "Gunnild tenuit de Heraldo.") Of Gytha we hear more According to Snorro (Johnston, 220; Laing, iii 97), " Gyda Haralds-dóttir " married Valdimar King of Holmgard, the son of King Jaroslaf and of Ingigerd the daughter of King Olaf of Sweden. By him she had a son Harold, from whose daughters Malfrid and Ingibiorg most of the Kings of the North seem to have sprung. Saxo (207) tells us how two sons of Harold took shelter along with their sister at the court of their kinsman King Swend, by whom the sister, whose name is not mentioned, was given in marriage to King Waldemar, and a vague account is given of their descendants; "Cujus filii duo confestim in Daniam cum sorore migrârunt Quos Sueno, paterni eorum meriti oblitus, consanguineæ pietatis more excepit, puellamque Rutenorum Regi Waldemaro, qui et ipse Jarizlavus a suis est appellatus, nuptum dedit Eidem postmodum nostri temporis dux, ut sanguinis ita et nominis hæres, ex filiâ nepos obvenit." By Holmgard is meant Novgorod and Northern Russia generally (see Karamsin, Histoire de Russie, ii 411) I cannot pretend to any minute knowledge of Russian history, but, from such light as I can find in Karamsin and the *Art de Vérifier les Dates* (ii 112), I cannot identify these princes Jaroslaf, who reigned from 1019 to 1055, had both a son and a grandson of the name of Vladimir, one of whom is doubtless intended But the son died in 1052 (Karamsin, ii 40), and whether the grandson, Vladimir son of Usevolod, who reigned from 1113 to 1125, married a daughter of our Harold I cannot say. Karamsin (ii 39, 211, 417) accepts the marriage, but seemingly not from any Russian authorities, and he certainly knows of no Russian prince named Harold Vladimir's son and successor was Mstislaf, who reigned at Kief from 1125 to 1132. Lappenberg (557) says, "Die Sohne flohen nach Irland, Gythe zu ihres Vaters Vetter Svend von Danemark und wurde mit Waldemar, Czar von Russland, des Wsewold Sohn, vermahlt, dem sie den Sohn Mistislav-Harold und durch diesen eine fernere erlauchte Nachkommenschaft gab" But I do not know Lappenberg's authority for giving any Russian Prince the double name of Mistislav-Harold.

I have already hinted (see p 142 and vol. iii. p 764) that these three sons and two daughters of Harold were most likely the children of Eadgyth Swanneshals None of the three sons who were grown men in 1068 could have been children of Ealdgyth. Nor is it likely that either of the daughters was hers. Sir Henry Ellis (ii. 80) and Lappenberg (557) assume a former marriage of Harold, of which they make these children the offspring, but they quote no authority for such a marriage, and on the whole it seems easier to make them children of Eadgyth. And their position and that of their mother may have been as good as that of Sprota and "the other Ælfgifu" and their sons.

As to children of Harold and Ealdgyth, it is certain (see Florence,

1087) that Harold had a son Wulf who was imprisoned in Normandy, and was released by William on his death-bed. On the other hand, the genealogy in Florence (i. 276) gives Harold a son by Ealdgyth bearing his own name; " De Reginâ Aldgithâ, Comitis Ælfgari filiâ, habuit filium Haroldum." And again, in William of Malmesbury's (iv. 329) account of the invasion of Anglesey in 1098, we read how Magnus of Norway came " cum Haroldo filio Haroldi Regis quondam Angliæ." The statement about Wulf is so distinct that we cannot reject it, and a son of Harold who had no share in the warfare of his brothers in the West, but who was a captive in the hands of William, can hardly fail to have been a son of Ealdgyth, most likely taken at Chester But the statement which gives Harold a son of his own name is not inconsistent with the other Any child of Harold and Ealdgyth must have been born after his father's death; but Wulf and Harold may have been posthumous twins, like the two sons— twins certainly, though most likely not posthumous—of Eadmund Ironside and the other Ealdgyth. In this case we must suppose that Harold was saved like Lewis from-beyond-Sea (see vol. 1 p. 208), while Wulf was taken.

Gunhild the daughter of Harold must not be confounded with her aunt of the same name, the daughter of Godwine. The latter is recorded in Domesday, and I see no reason to doubt the authenticity of her epitaph. See Ellis, ii. 136, and the fuller account in a small tract on the two Gunhilds, the daughter of Cnut (see vol. i. p. 505) and the daughter of Godwine, published at Ghent in 1833, for a sight of which I have to thank Sir Thomas Hardy.

The inscription is as follows;

"Pater noster: Credo in Deum Patrem, et cetera quæ in Simbolo Apostolorum sunt scripta

" Gunildis nobilissimis orta parentibus, genere Angla, patre Godwino Comite, sub cujus dominio maxima pars militabat Angliæ, matre Githa, illustri prosapia Dacorum oriunda. Hæc dum voveret adhuc puella virginalem castitatem, desiderans spirituale conjugium, sprevit connubia nonnullorum nobilium principum Hæcque dum jam ad nubilem ætatem pervenisset, Anglia devicta a Willelmo Normannorum Comite et ab eodem interfecto fratre suo Rege Anglo- 1um Haroldo, relicta patria, apud sanctum Audomarum aliquot annos exulans in Flandria, Xp'm quem pie amabat, in pectore scilicet semper colebat in opere circa sibi famulantes hilaris et modesta, erga extraneos benivola et justa, pauperibus larga, suo corpori admodum parca; quid dicam, adeo ut omnibus illecebris se abstinendo, per multos annos ante sui diem obitus non vexeretur carnibus, neque quidquam quod sibi dulce visum est gustando, sed vix necessaria vitæ capiendo, cilicio induta, ut nec etiam quibusdam pateret familiaribus, conflictando cum viciis vicit in virtutibus Dehinc transiens Bruggas, et ibi transvolutis quibusdam annis et inde pertransiens in Dacia, huc reversa, virgo transmigravit in Domino, Anno incarnationis domini millesimo LXXXVII, nono kalendas Septembris, luna XXII."

## NOTE S. p. 165.

### EADNOTH THE STALLER

Our slight notices of Eadnoth raise a certain interest in him. There is a temptation to find out as much as we can about a man who was in high place alike under Eadward, Harold, and William. And, if there is reason to believe that he was the forefather of a great English house, the pedigree acquires an interest which does not belong to those pedigrees, real or mythical, which go up only to the sharers of William's spoils That Eadnoth was Staller under Eadward appears from Cod. Dipl. iv. 204, which also shows that he was Sheriff of Hampshire In that writ he is addressed along with Stigand as Archbishop and Harold as Earl. But he does not often sign the charters of Eadward, though his name is attached to the two spurious Westminster charters (Cod Dipl iv. 180, 189) with the title of "Eadnoðus minister" In Domesday he once distinctly appears as "Ednod stalre," in Berkshire, 58 b. (This estate had passed to Abingdon Abbey, and it is added in a significant way, "non erat tunc in Abbatiâ"). The name Eadnoth is a common one, and it is not easy to say which of the various entries under it in Domesday belong to our Eadnoth. He most likely is the "Ednod dapifer" of p. 69, but he cannot be the Ednod (nor yet the Alnod) of p. 124 b Moreover, there can be little doubt that Eadnoth is the person intended by some of the entries of Alnod, Alnodus,

Elnod, in Domesday. Those forms ought to represent, not *Eadnoth*, but *Ælfnoth* Still the case seems clear, and all that we can do is to think of 'Οδυσσεύς and *Ulysses, Ægidius* and *Giles*. Eadnoth undoubtedly had a son Harding, who was living when William of Malmesbury wrote, and of whom he gives (iii. 254) a very curious description; " Vocabatur is Ednodus, domi belloque Anglorum temporibus juxta insignis, pater Herdingi qui adhuc superest, magis consuetus linguam in lites acuere quam arma in bello concutere." We have thus a Harding son of Eadnoth the Staller, and we have further evidence of his connexion with Somerset and Devonshire. "Heardinc Eadnóðes sunu" appears among the witnesses to a Somerset document in Cod Dipl. iv. 234, and we also find him selling a slave at Topsham in Devonshire; "Wulward bohte Leouede æt Hierdinge Eadnoðes sune wið v. scill. to cepe and to tolle" (Thorpe, Dipl. Angl 648). Among the witnesses to the deed we find another "Hierding" not further described Harding the son of Eadnoth can therefore hardly fail to be the same person as "Harding filius Alnod," who appears as a King's Thegn in Somerset in Domesday, 98 *b*, and who is doubtless the same as the Harding who is mentioned in several following entries Besides this, there is a string of entries in Dorset (80) which look very much as if Alnodus, Elnod, Ednod, were used indiscriminately Of one of these, in which Elnod appears as an officer of Harold and an agent in one of his alleged spoliations of the Church, I have spoken in vol. ii. p 548. In another we read, "Unus tainus tenuit T. R. E , et Alnod tulit ab eo T. R. W." These two lead us to a singular entry in Wiltshire (72 *b*) which I have quoted in the second edition of my second volume, p 546 , "Ednodus tenuit T. R. E. . Hanc terram abstulit Godwinus Comes Sanctæ Mariæ Wiltunensi, et *tunc eam recuperavit Ednodus.*" This looks as if "Ednodus" had some claim on the land earlier than the claim of the Abbey, which was asserted on his behalf by Godwine

There can then, I think, be little doubt as to identifying Eadnoth the Staller with the "Alnod," "Elnod," or "Ednod" of the western shires He was in all probability a man who had risen by the favour of Godwine and Harold Of his earlier estate we may perhaps get a glimpse in a Berkshire entry in Domesday, 60; " Ednod tenuit de Heraldo, et non potuit ire quolibet." He rose to high office under Eadward , he kept it under Harold, and he seemingly kept it under William also. And he would also seem, like so many others, to have abused his personal or official influence both under Eadward and under William. He left a son who was alive when William of Malmesbury wrote, and who appears as a landowner in Domesday. But the strange thing is that no part of his estates passed to his son. Harding's property in Somerset, where we are most certain that we are dealing with the right Harding, was held T. R. E. by "Toui," that is doubtless "Touid" or Tofig (a different man of course from Tofig the Proud), who appears as Sheriff of Somerset in two of Eadward's writs in favour of Gisa (Cod Dipl iv. 197, 199). This does not prove that Tofig was dispossessed in favour of Harding, as Harding may have inherited from Tofig. One Wiltshire estate under the name of Harding (74) had been held by the same owner T. R. E. There is a most curious entry in the same shire (67 *b*), how Harding held lands of the Church of Shaftesbury T R. E. which at the Survey were held by "Turstinus," who may be either Thurstan a Dane or Toustain a Frenchman. It is added, "Hanc terram reddidit sponte suâ ecclesiæ Hardingus, quia in vitâ suâ per conventum debebat tenere." But in Gloucestershire (170 *b*) Harding holds lands in pledge ("in vadimonio") of a certain Brihtric, which Brihtric had held T. R E., and the lands held by him in Buckinghamshire (153) had been held T R. E. by Wulfred and others. There were other lands of which a Harding, whether the same or another, had been dispossessed in favour of various foreign owners. Lands in Wiltshire had passed from him to the Count of Mortain (68 *b*) and to Count Alberic (69), and thence to the Crown (see p. 676. This looks like more than an official loss). Others in Warwickshire (239 *b*) and Leicestershire (231 *b*) had also gone to Count Alan and to the Crown, and others in Dorsetshire (82 *b*) to Berenger Giffard. Nowhere does anything of Eadnoth's appear in the hands of Harding. This apparent confiscation of the estate of a man who died in William's service suggests that Harding had given some personal offence which was visited by partial loss of lands. If he be, as is most likely, the "Hardingus Reginæ pincerna" who signs the Waltham charter (Cod. Dipl iv 159), he probably had a friend at court to plead for him.

As to the descendants of Harding, it seems in the highest degree probable that this Harding was the father of Robert Fitz-Harding of Bristol, the forefather of the second line of the Lords of Berkeley. Local antiquaries call Harding of Bristol a son of "the King of Denmark," a follower of William the Conqueror, Mayor of Bristol, and what not. The unlikelihood of a son of Swend Estrithson being in the service of William never strikes them. On the other hand, nothing is more likely than that a Thegn holding lands in Somerset and Gloucestershire, but who clearly held a much smaller amount of land than his father, and who was of the peculiar and unwarlike disposition described by William of Malmesbury, should throw in his lot with the burghers of the great city which lay on the march of the two shires, and should rise to eminence among them.

Another question remains. I was once inclined to identify Eadnoth. under the form of Elnod or Alnod, with another "Alnod" whom we find in other parts of the Kingdom, and who, curiously enough, is charged with deeds of wrong of exactly the same kind as those of the Western Eadnoth This is an Alnod who seems to be specially distinguished as "the Kentishman," and whom I am therefore inclined to identify with the Kentish Æthelnoth whom William took with him on his first voyage to Normandy (see p. 79). In Domesday (2 b) we read of Middleton in Kent, "De silvâ Regis habet Wadardus [our old friend of the Tapestry] tantum quod reddit xvi. denarios per annum et dimidiam, denam tenet; quam T. R. E. quidam villanus tenuit, et Alnod Cild duas partes cuidam villano per vim abstulit." Next we find in Buckinghamshire (144 b, 145), "Alnodus teignus R. E.," "Alnodus Cilt teignus R. E ," and "Alnod Chentiscus teignus R. E ," and in Northamptonshire (220), "Alnod Cantuariensis." To identify this "Alnod" with Æthelnoth is a matter of conjecture, but it seems at least a more probable conjecture than the identification of Alnod Cild with Wulfnoth the son of Godwine. Sir Henry Ellis (ii. 21) takes this from Kelham (174), who seemingly takes it from a Kentish county history, and it is repeated as if there were no doubt about it, but without any reference to Kelham, in Mr. C. H. Pearson's Historical Maps, p. 60. But this notion rests only on the unlucky guess of Kelham's Kentish writer, who seemingly thought that "Cilt" was the same as "Clito," and that Wulfnoth was called "Cild" "from the royalty of his kindred" Now I do not profess to know exactly what this most puzzling title of "Cild" means; it is undoubtedly applied to the Ætheling Eadgar, but it is also applied to people who are clearly not so called from the royalty of their kindred, of whom I have collected instances in vol. i p. 374, and more fully in p. 649 of the second edition. Another case (Domesday, 193 b), "Goduinus Cilt, homo Eddevæ pulchræ, qui non potuit recedere," might almost go some way to justify M. Emile de Bonnechose's explanation (see vol 1 p 375) of "Cild" by "*churl ou chef*" I do not remember that the title of "Cild" is ever given to any of the members of the house of Godwine. Of the possible possessions of Wulfnoth in Somerset and Devonshire I have spoken above, p. 754.

## NOTE T p. 165

### Brihtric and Matilda.

ALL our real knowledge of Brihtric comes from Domesday. His father was named Ælfgar (163 b), and his lands, or the greater part of them, were granted to Queen Matilda. Of many Brihtrics in the Survey the one with whom we are concerned is most likely the same who signs the Waltham charter with the title of "princeps" (Cod. Dipl. iv. 159). We find men of the name in Berkshire (61 b, 62, 63 b), who may be our Brihtric, and others in Somerset (96, 98 b), Cornwall (124 b), Gloucestershire (170 b), who cannot be. But our Brihtric appears distinctly as a great landowner in most of the Western shires. We meet him in Dorset (75 b, Exon, 30) as the former owner of three lordships held by Queen Matilda, with the heading "Has subter scriptas terras tenuit Mathildis Regina," and in Devonshire (101, Exon, 100) we have the still more distinct heading, "Infra scriptas terras tenuit Brictric et post Matildis Regina." The Queen however had not received the whole of Brihtric's lands in Devonshire, as we find (112, 112 b) some of them in possession of William of Clavile, and in one place (Exon 370) our Brihtric is clearly distinguished as "Bristricus filius Algari" from another who is called "Bristicus Ulestanus" It is hopeless to ask to which of these two Brihtrics those entries in the same shire belong to which we have no further clue.

One more Devonshire entry must be mentioned. In 113 we read, "Rogerius de Busli tenet de Rege Sanforde; Brictric tenebat T. R. E," and at the end of the entry is added, "Regina dedit Rogerio cum uxore suâ" In Cornwall (120) we find an entry, "Infra scriptas [terras] Brictric tenebat; post Mathildis Regina." We pass into Gloucestershire, where we find (163 b), "Hoc manerium [Clifort, part of which had also been given by the Queen to Roger of Busli] tenuit Brictric filius Algar T. R. E., et has subscriptas terras aliorum Teinorum ipso tempore in suâ potestate habuit" Then follow six entries with the note at the end, "Qui T R. E has terras tenebant et se et terras suas sub Brictrici potestate submiserunt." One of these the Queen is said to have granted to Reginald the Chaplain and John the Chamberlain. Then follow four more lordships of Brihtric (including Fairford, so well known for its church), among which we again meet with the Queen's name and of her grants to the same John and to one Baldwin. Another Gloucestershire lordship of Brihtric the son of Ælfgar had passed (166 b) to William of Eu. We find him again in those two Gloucestershire entries (one of them being Hanley) which appear in Herefordshire (180 b), and which were in the hands of the King. Immediately follows the Worcestershire entry of Bisley (see also 173), where we find Brihtric buying land on lease from Bishop Lyfing It is needless to go through the countless entries of the same name in various parts of England, in many of which the bearer is distinguished in some way or other from Brihtric the son of Ælfgar

We thus find Brihtric the son of Ælfgar as a powerful Thegn, one to whom lesser Thegns found it expedient to commend themselves, through the whole of the old *Wealhcyn*, and also in the south-western shires of Mercia. We see also that his lands had a special tendency to fall into the hands of Queen Matilda. He stands out in the Survey as a marked man, almost in the same way as the members of the house of Godwine. As for the legend which I have mentioned in the text, it is hard to say whether it grew out of the fact that Matilda received so large a portion of Brihtric's lands, or whether that fact is to be taken as any confirmation of the legend. It is certainly slightly in its favour that it describes Brihtric as being seized at Hanley, which we see from Domesday was really one of his lordships The story comes from the Continuator

of Wace, and will be found in Ellis, ii 55, and Chroniques Anglo-
Normandes, i 73. The story, as far as we are concerned with it,
runs thus,

> " Laquele jadsi, qant fu pucele,     Ke de Brictrich Mau lad graute
> Ama un conte dengleterre     De faire de lui la volente ,
> Brictrich Mau le oi nomer     La reine par tot le fist guerreiet
> Apres le rois ki fu riche ber ,     K'ele li uolt desheriter,
> A lui la pucele enuera messager     Pris fu a haneleye a son maner,
> Pur sa amur a lui procurer,     Le ior ke Saint Wlstan li ber
> Meis Brictrich Maude refusa     Sa chapele auoit dedie ,
> Dunc ele m'lt se coruca,     A Wyncestre fu amene,
> Hastiuement mer passa     Ilokes morut en prison
> E a Willam bastard se maria     Brictrich Mau par treison ,
> Qant Willam fu corune     Qant il fu mort senz heir de sei
> E Malde sa feme a reine leue,     Son heritage seisit le Rei,
> Icele Malde se purpensa     E cum escheit tint en sa main
> Coment vengier se purra     Dekes il feoffa Rob't fiz haim
> De Brictriche Mau kelc ama,     Ki oueke lui de Normandie
> Ki a femme pr'ndre la refusa     Vint od m'lt grant cheualerie
> Tant enchanta son seignor,     La t're ke Brictrich li leissa
> Le rei Willam le Conqueror,     Franchment a Robert dona "

We find the story also in the Chronicle of Tewkesbury, printed in
the Monasticon, ii 60, where we find " Haylwardus [Ælfweard,
Æthelweard, or what?] Snew dictus propter albedinem, ex illustri
prosapiâ Regis Edwardi senioris ortus," who flourishes under
Æthelstan in 930, and who, with his wife Ælfgifu, founds in 980 a
monastery at Cranborne, to which he makes Tewkesbury, of which
he was patron, a cell " Haylwardus " is the father of Ælfgar the
father of Brihtric, a piece of chronology which, as usual, attributes a
wonderfully long life to the persons concerned. The story then
goes on ;

" Postea, versâ vice, scilicet anno Domini mlxvi. Willielmus Dux
Normanniæ Angliam adquisivit, qui duxit secum nobilem virum
atque juvenem, Robertum filium Haymonis, dominum de Astremer-
villâ in Normanniâ Et quum Matildis Regina, uxor Conquestoris,
haberet nobilem virum, scilicet dictum dominum Brictricum Meaw,
et dominum honoris Glocestriæ, exosum, eo quod nollet ei in matrimonium copulari, quum ipse esset in transmarinis partibus circa
negotia regia imbassatoria, et illa erat sola, sed postea maritata
domino Willielmo Conquestori, quæ tempore opportuno reperto,

licentiata a Rege, Regeque jubente, ipsum in manerio suo de Hanleyâ capi fecit et Wyntoniam adduci; qui ibidem mortuus et sepultus sine liberis discessit. Rex vero Willielmus dedit honorem Brictrici Matildi Reginæ, quæ totum honorem Brictrici, scilicet Gloucestriæ, quoad vixit, occupavit; mortuâ vero ipsâ Reginâ anno Domini mlxxxiii. mense Aprili, Rex Willielmus ipsum honorem in manu suâ cœpit. Defuncto igitur Willielmo Conquestore anno Domini mlxxxvii successit sibi Wilhelmus Rufus filius ejus. Iste Willielmus processu temporis dedit honorem Brictrici Roberto filio Haymonis, cum omni libertate et integritate quibus pater suus vel etiam ipse Brictricus umquam tenuerunt, et hoc egit propter magnos labores quos prædictus Robertus sustinuit cum patre suo."

The reader must judge for himself how much of this story he will believe. I cannot go beyond the facts in Domesday. There is nothing there about the Honour of Gloucester, nothing about Robert Fitz-Hamon. But it should be noted that the poem says nothing about Gloucester, while it makes William the Conqueror grant Brihtric's lands to Robert Fitz-Hamon, which is clearly contradicted by Domesday. The chronicle seems to record a real grant of William Rufus to Robert Fitz-Hamon, but to err in making Gloucester a possession of Brihtric's.

## NOTE U. p. 169.

#### THE POSSESSIONS OF ROBERT OF MORTAIN IN THE WEST.

ROBERT of Mortain, the half-brother of William, appears in Domesday as holding a larger share of the conquered land than any other one man in William's following He holds lands in Sussex, Surrey, Hampshire, Berkshire, Wiltshire, Dorset, Middlesex, Hertford, Buckingham, Oxford, Gloucester, Cambridge, Northampton, Nottingham, Norfolk, Suffolk, and especially Yorkshire. But it is in the three Western shires, and above all in that which forms his own Earldom, that his possessions assume a special and systematic character. His estates in Somerset and Devonshire are very large, but in Cornwall they are more than an estate however large. Robert holds a special position along with Hugh the Wolf in Cheshire and Roger of Montgomery in

Shropshire. He holds the whole shire with certain comparatively small exceptions. In Cornwall however there were some Crown lands, though very small. All the rest was Robert's, save the lands of the churches, and two lordships in private lay hands, one in those of Judhel of Totnes, the other in that of Goscelinus, who also appears as a considerable landowner in Devonshire. Robert's wide and reckless spoliation of ecclesiastical bodies strikes us in the Survey almost at a glance. At the head of page 121 is a distinct entry; "Hæ infra scriptæ terræ sunt ablatæ Sancto Petroco, Comes Moritonensis tenet et homines ejus de eo." A number of separate notices of the same kind follow, and they come out still more clearly in the Exeter Domesday (183), where we have a smaller series of entries with the heading "De Ecclesiâ Sancti Germani ablata est." Elsewhere (182, 470) we find a curious entry of an incidental wrong done by the Earl to the see of Exeter. The Bishop had a market on Sundays in his lordship of Saint German's, which was brought to nothing by an opposition market set up by the Earl; "In câ mansione erat i. mercatum eâ die quâ Rex E. fuit vivus et mortuus in Dominicâ die, et modo adnihilatur [ad nihilum redigitur, Exchequer 120 b] propter mercatum quod ibi prope constituit Comes de Moritonio in quodam suo castro in eâdem die." A more direct wrong of the same kind was done to the Canons of Saint Stephen's in their lordship of Lanscavetone (120 b), "De hoc manerio abstulit Comes Moritonensis unum mercatum quod ibi T. R. E. jacebat et valebat xx. solidos." On the opposite page there is a plaintive lament from the Canons of Saint Piran, touching two estates in their manor of Lanpiran, which "reddebant canonicis T. R. E. firmam iv. septimanarum, et decano xx. solidos per consuetudinem." The entry goes on, "Harum unam tenet Bernerus de Comite Moritonensi, et de aliâ hidâ, quam tenet Odo de Sancto Pireano, abstulit Comes totam pecuniam." Complaints of the same sort occur throughout the whole record. One, specially to be noticed, is the alienation of Gytha's gift of Crowcombe in Somerset from the church of Winchester, of which I have spoken in vol. ii. p. 352.

The special objects of Robert's spoliation within his own Earldom were its two head churches, that of Saint German and that of Saint Petroc at Bodmin. The question as to the site of the old Cornish see or sees is examined by Mr. Haddan in the Appendix D. to his

Councils and Ecclesiastical Documents, where he rules that, from 981 to the merging of the Cornish diocese in that of Devonshire, the see was at Saint German's, but with a sort of second cathedral at Bodmin. The church of Bodmin was the scene of many manumissions of slaves (Cod. Dipl iv 308, Haddan, 676) which help us to the fact, which from Domesday we should hardly have guessed, that, though English names were common in Cornwall in the tenth and eleventh centuries, yet Welsh names were common also. Heavy as the hand of Earl Robert fell on the church of Saint Petroc, there seems no reason for accepting the story (see Mon. Angl. ii. 460) that he seized the whole of its lands. Besides the lands which Earl Robert actually seized, there is also (121) a suspicious list of lordships which he, a somewhat too powerful tenant, held of the church But Saint Petroc still held six lordships in his own hands.

As for the two mounts and the two monasteries of Saint Michael, there is no doubt that the lesser one in Cornwall was in after times a cell to the greater one in Normandy, but the relations of the two to one another, and of both to Earl Robert, at the time with which we are concerned, are anything but clear I have elsewhere (ii. 519, 520) spoken of an alleged charter of Eadward (Mon Angl vii. 989) which professes to be a grant to Saint Michael in Normandy "Tradidi Sancto Michaeli Archangelo, in usum fratrum Deo servientium in eodem loco, Sanctum Michaelem qui est juxta mare cum omnibus appenditiis, villis scilicet, castellis, agris, et cæteris attinentibus." Doubtful as this charter is, the spuriousness of that which accompanies it from the same cartulary is still more manifest This also professes to be a grant of the Cornish house to the Norman one, made by Earl Robert; but, to pass by any smaller objections, it is enough that, though it is dated in 1085, it is signed by Queen Matilda who died in 1083, and even by Bishop Leofric who died in 1072, and is followed by an exemption from ecclesiastical jurisdiction granted by the same Prelate "jussione et exhortatione domini mei reverentissimi Gregorii Papæ," who did not become Pope till after Leofric's death In Domesday both the Norman and the Cornish Saint Michael appear, but there is no hint as to any connexion between the two, or as to Earl Robert standing in any relation to either of them, except his usual relation of a spoiler. Saint Michael of Cornwall appears in the Exchequer Domesday (120 b), and more fully in Exon (189), and we read, "Sanctus Michael habet i mansionem quæ vocatur Ticiwal, quam tenuit Brismarus eâ die qua Rex E fuit vivus et mortuus . De hac mansione abstulit Comes de Moretonio i. de prædictis ii. hidis quæ erat de dominicatu beati Michahelis" This is the only mention of the house that I can find, and it would seem to imply a foundation between 1066 and 1085 Brismar was a man of large property in all the three shires, who contrived to keep one Somerset lordship (99, Exon 455, where he is distinguished as "Brismarus Anglicus") He is not unlikely to have been the founder of the Cornish Saint Michael, and, if so, he must have founded it, or at least have given this estate, after Eadward's death At all events we have no trace of Earl Robert in any such character Elsewhere (65) the Norman Saint Michael appears as holding a hide of land and two churches in Wiltshire on lordships held by the King, one of which had belonged to Earl Harold and the other to the Lady Eadgyth. It had also three lordships in Devonshire (104), two of which had belonged to Harold and one to Gytha There is one more entry in Hampshire (43); "Ecclesia Sancti Michaelis de Monte tenet de Rege i. ecclesiam cum i hidâ et decimâ de manerio Basingestoches . . Walterius Episcopus [Herefordensis sc.] tenuit de Rege, sed non erat de episcopatu suo" It seems plain then that whatever possessions in England were held by the Norman Saint Michael were acquired after William's accession, and that, whoever was the founder of the Cornish house, it was not Earl Robert A note in the Monasticon (vii 989) speaks of another tradition as naming Robert's son William as the person who gave the Cornish house to the Norman one Here we most likely have the clue to the mistake

## NOTE W. p 174

### The Condition of Worcestershire under William.

The matter of this note also is transferred to the examination of Domesday in the next volume.

## NOTE X. p 179.

### The Titles of Queen and Lady.

It will be noticed that in the words of the Chronicle quoted in the text the *Lady* Matilda is said to be hallowed to *Queen*. The passage is not unlike an earlier one in 1051, where the Peterborough Chronicler (see vol. ii. p. 156) says of Eadgyth, " þa forlet se cyng þa *hlæfdian*, seo wæs gehalgod him to *cwene* " Otherwise Eadgyth is always spoken of as *Lady* down to the day of her death (see p. 587). With this exception, from the coronation of Matilda onwards " cwen " becomes the usual word ; see the Chronicles in 1083, 1100, 1115, 1118, 1119, 1121, 1123, 1126, besides 1097 and 1100 where it is applied to Margaret of Scotland, and in 1140 to a French Queen. But it must be remembered that, while "Lady" was still the regular title in English, "Regina" had long been familiarly used in Latin. This difference is analogous to that which I mentioned in vol. iii. p. 632 with regard to the wives of Earls, who in English have no title, but whom the Norman writers freely call "Comitissa." In Cod Dipl iv. 72 the words "Leofric eorl and his gebedda" become in the Latin version more reverentially "Leofricus comes et Godgiva comitissa." On the other hand, the style of the Empress Matilda is " Angliæ Normanniæque Domina " (Will. Malm. Hist Nov. iii. 42, 44), and so in a charter in Rymer (i. 14) ; " Matilda Imperatrix, Henrici Regis filia, et Anglorum Domina." But a Queen regnant was something wholly new both in England and in Normandy, and the word " cwen " probably still so far kept its elder meaning of *wife* as to seem hardly suited to one who ruled in her own right. In the Chronicle (1140) Matilda is throughout called " þemperice," while the other Matilda, the wife of Stephen, appears as " þe kinges cuen."

## NOTE Y. p 185.

### The Northern Campaigns of William.

There is a good deal of difficulty about the details of William's campaigns, especially in the North of England. But the difficulty mainly arises, not from actual contradictions in our authorities, but from one writer recording or dwelling on points which another passes by more lightly or leaves out altogether. We have seen exactly the same sort of thing in the narratives of the banishment and of the return of Godwine. Only now we have to compare, not the narratives of Englishmen of different districts or different politics, but the narratives of men of different and hostile nations. But it is due to both English and Norman accounts to say that they are less coloured by national prejudices than we might have looked for. The English writers were too sad for mere abuse of their conquerors, and, though the Normans indulge in plenty of swelling words, I see no reason to charge them with direct perversion of facts. There was not the same motive for falsehood now as when they were dealing with the hated names of Godwine and Harold. The main difference is that the Norman narrative is much fuller than the English one. It is also much more continuous, the English story being in some places quite fragmentary. Still it supplies many important details which are not found in the Norman version.

Our main Norman account is that of Orderic, founded upon William of Poitiers (see 521 C). But from those parts where William's own narrative is preserved we can see that Orderic only followed and did not always servilely copy. On the English side we have the accounts in the Worcester and Peterborough Chronicles, of which, during these years, Worcester is by far the fuller. Florence doubtless had this narrative before him, and it forms the groundwork of his own story, but he is now no longer a mere translator or harmonizer, but a distinct source. He could have heard the story from the lips of Saint Wulfstan. Florence's history again forms the groundwork of that of Simeon, or whatever we are to call the Northern interpolator, who, so far as he copies Florence, copies him far more servilely than Florence himself copies the Chronicler. But he puts in large and most important insertions relating to Northern affairs, of which men at Worcester were contented with a mere sketch. His details are often so full as to make us wish for a Western interpolator to match, but for our details in that part of England we have to go chiefly to the enemy.

The first place where our two sets of authorities seem to diverge is at the very beginning of William's Northern warfare. The

Worcester Chronicler (1067), after recording the fall of Exeter, records the flight of Eadgar to Scotland in these words; "And þæs sumeres Eadgar cild for ut mid his moder Agatha and his twam sweostran Margareta and Christina and Mærlaswegen and fela godra manna mid heom, and comon to Scotlande," &c. Then follows the account of the marriage of Malcolm and Margaret, of which I shall speak in another note Then the Chronicler returns to Exeter and records the flight of Gytha. Then come the King's Easter at Winchester and the Queen's coronation at Pentecost Then William hears of hostile movements in the North, and goes and builds castles at Nottingham, York, Lincoln, and elsewhere Then "Gospatric eorl and þa betstan menn foron into Scotlande" Lastly comes the account of the landing of Harold's son or sons and the death of Eadnoth.

It is plain that in this account there is one great breach of chronological order. The flight of Eadgar, which is said to be in the summer, is put before William's Easter Feast on March 23, to say nothing of the way in which it is thrust in between two events so closely connected as the surrender of Exeter and the flight of Gytha Florence, evidently with this Chronicle before him, corrects the order of events. The flight of Gytha is put in its natural place. The flight of Eadgar is put immediately after the coronation of Matilda, the later passage about the flight of Gospatric and others is left out, and the account (1068) stands thus; "Post hæc Marleswein et Gospatric et quique Northumbranæ gentis nobiliores, Regis austeritatem devitantes, et ne, sicut alii, in custodiam mitterentur formidantes, sumptis secum Clitone Eadgaro et matre suâ Agathâ, duabusque sororibus suis Margaretâ et Christinâ, navigio Scottiam adierunt, ibidemque, Regis Scottorum Malcolmi pace, hiemem exegerunt" Florence also leaves out the account of the Northern movement given in the Chronicle, so that it would seem that it was the flight of Eadgar which led to William's march to Nottingham and York.

The Peterborough Chronicle leaves out all these events except the flight of Eadgar Immediately after the remarkable passage describing William's return which I have quoted in p. 127 come the words, "And þæs sumeres for Eadgar cild út, and Mærleswegen and fela manna mid heom, and foran to Scotlande, and ce cyng Melcolm hi ealle underfeng, and genam þes cildes swuster to wife, Margaretan."

In all this we have no mention of Eadwine and Morkere; the Norman account in Ordelic is, during the present year, equally silent about Eadgar, Mærleswegen, and Gospatric. The Northern movement which began after the Queen's coronation is attributed to the brother Earls, and is described at much greater length (see p. 182). William sets out to quell the revolt, and Eadwine and Morkere submit at Warwick (see p. 192). Then William goes on to Nottingham, York, &c.

Now, in comparing these accounts together, we can have little doubt as to accepting the revolt and submission of Eadwine and Morkere on the strength of the Norman account. It is far more likely that the Chroniclers should, from whatever cause, have left out the doings of the two Earls than that William of Poitiers should have invented an elaborate romance without any obvious motive. On the other hand, we have just as little reason to distrust the English account of the flight of Eadgar and his companions. It is plain that there is no direct contradiction between the two stories. If we take them as two isolated events, happening without any reference to each other, there is not only no contradiction but no difficulty. The real difficulty is that we can hardly fancy the two events taking place without some reference to each other. A flight of the leading Northumbrian Thegns to Scotland is not likely to have taken place just at the same time as a great stir in Northumberland, followed by a submission of Eadwine and Morkere to William, unless the two things had something to do with one another. The obvious explanation would be that all the persons mentioned in the two different accounts had a share in the Northern movement, that Eadwine and Morkere dealt with their comrades as they had dealt both with Harold and with Eadgar, that they submitted to William and were again received to favour, while the more stout-hearted sought shelter in Scotland till the coming of the Danish fleet in the next year. This is in itself a probable and consistent narrative. The only question is whether it can be made to agree with the words of the Chronicles, "And þæs sumeres Eadgar cild for út," &c. At first sight these words would certainly not lead us to think that the going out of Eadgar and his companions was the consequence of something which could be called a campaign. The motive assigned by Florence for their going out looks still less like it. His account would seem to apply only to men who were living in William's court, or at any rate were wholly in his power. Yet the words of the Chronicle, ' for ût" (see p. 256), may be taken as pointing to something like warlike doings on the part of Eadgar and the others, and, if so, we must throw aside Florence's interpretation of their motives as an unsuccessful guess on his part. This is the more likely, as it is not easy to see who, except perhaps Abbot Godric of Winchcombe (see p 177), had been as yet, in any strict sense, imprisoned by William. It would be no great stretch of language to call the actual position of the Ætheling and the Earls at William's court an imprisonment, but Florence clearly conceives them as dreading the fate of some other unknown persons who were imprisoned in a more literal sense Considering then the chronological confusion with which the events of the year are told in the Chronicle, I am inclined to think that the date " þæs sumeres" points to the time when Eadgar and Gospatric left William's court to join the Northern revolters, and that the later account of " Gospatric corL and þa betstan menn" points to their flight to Scotland after the submission of Eadwine and Morkere. If this be allowed, there is no real contradiction in the two narratives; only each fills up gaps in the other

The events of the year 1069 are by some chronological confusion divided in the Peterborough Chronicle into two years, while in Worcester they are wrongly placed under 1068 Mr. Thorpe has further increased the confusion by dividing the Worcester entries between the two years without manuscript authority. See Earle, Parallel Chronicles, 205. If we read them consecutively as the events of a single year, they form a consistent narrative, and one which quite agrees with the account in Orderic The Peterborough Chronicle records much the same events as the Worcester text, only it places the imprisonment of Bishop Æthelric quite out of place, namely before the coming of the Danish fleet in the autumn of 1069, whereas it certainly did not happen till the beginning of 1070 William grants the Northern Earldom to Robert of Comines, who is killed at Durham. This is recorded by both Chroniclers and by Orderic, and we get minuter details of the same event from the Northumbrian writers (see p. 325). Then comes the first revolt of York, which is also told in all three accounts, only Orderic gives details which are not in the Chronicles, especially the death of Robert Fitz-Richard. All agree as to the presence of Eadgar and a large body of Northumbrians, only, while the Chroniclers name no one except Eadgar, Orderic mentions also Gospatric and Mærleswegen. All mention the defeat and retreat of the English ("ceteri sunt fugati"), and the Chroniclers distinctly add that the Ætheling went back to Scotland. Then in Orderic and the Worcester Chronicle comes the second expedition of Harold's sons, the details of which I shall discuss in Note DD. Then comes the Danish capture of York and all that followed it.

In all this there is no contradiction between Orderic and the English Chroniclers. But now comes the singular fact that in the narrative of Florence the coming of Robert of Comines to Durham and the first revolt of York are left out. That is to say, he leaves out all that appears in the Peterborough Chronicle under 1068, all that appears in the Worcester Chronicle under that year, except the Devonshire expedition of Harold's sons. Florence in short records nothing between their two expeditions in 1068 and in 1069.

Now Florence certainly wrote with one or both of the Chronicles before him, and a great part of his work was to arrange under their proper years the events which they record with some chronological confusion. His services in this way I fully accept, and I have taken his chronology as the groundwork of my own narrative. But are we therefore to follow him when he leaves out several important events which, however confused may be the chronology, are told in the Chronicles with perfect distinctness and are confirmed by other authorities? The story of Robert of Comines no one would probably reject, told as it is in both Chronicles, in Orderic, in Simeon's Durham History, and in the Northern interpolations of Florence, whether those come from Simeon or from any one else. The first revolt of York is not quite so clear. A revolt of York in the spring, in which Eadgar appears and which William comes to crush in person, might be easily taken for a mere forestalling of that undoubted revolt of York in the autumn at which also Eadgar appeared, and which also William put down in person. Florence would hardly have struck one of the revolts out of the narrative in the Chronicles unless he had thought that the one was a repetition of the other. And this is the more remarkable, because he keeps both accounts of the two expeditions of Harold's sons, which it is quite as tempting to look on as two accounts of the same event as to look in the same way on the two revolts of York. Florence's judgement accepted the double story in one case and rejected it in the other. But the weight of his judgement is somewhat weakened by his also striking out the story of Robert of Comines, of the truth of which there can be no reasonable doubt. On the other hand his judgement may be held to be somewhat confirmed by the way in which Simeon (if Simeon it be) treated his narrative. He restored the story of Robert of Comines and inserted a notice of the foundation of Selby Abbey; but he did not restore the account of the spring revolt. But the negative authority of Simeon is again weakened by the fact that he has not merely failed to insert, but has positively struck out of the narrative of Florence, a most important piece of Northumbrian history, of which there can be no doubt, and which is indeed necessary to the understanding of his own narrative. This is no other than William's Northern march and occupation of York in 1068, though without it we cannot understand the presence of the Normans at York in the autumn of 1069. And when we look at the narratives of the spring revolt in Orderic, we shall certainly be inclined to think that details like the death of Robert Fitz-Richard, the message of William Malet, the building of the second tower (see p. 241 and the note at p 203) could not be mere inventions or confusions. There is really nothing improbable in the story that Eadgar and the Northumbrians tried their own powers early in the year, and, on being worsted, tried again in the autumn with the help of the Danes I therefore accept the double revolt and double submission of York, reading the entries in the Peterborough Chronicle under 1068 and 1069 as the events of a single year, and that year 1069

The cause of the chronological confusion seems to be this. The entries in the Worcester Chronicle, under the years 1065 and 1066, run over, as they often do, into the next year. That is to say, the year is made to begin at Easter. Thus the coronation of Harold is placed under 1065 and the voyage of William to Normandy under 1066. This left the year 1067 almost void of events, the only things recorded being William's return and the burning of Christ Church, the death of Bishop Wulfwig, and the short account of Eadric's doings in Herefordshire, all told very briefly. But by this way of reckoning the siege of Exeter is thrust back into 1067, and with the siege of Exeter a paragraph ends in Mr.

Earle's edition. Then comes the long passage about Eadgar and Margaret thrust in between the fall of Exeter and the flight of Gytha. This insertion or rhapsody has driven out the proper heading of the year 1068, the annal for which clearly begins with the words, "On þisan Eastron com se kyng to Wincestre." The years 1067 and 1068 having been thus run together, the events of 1069 were assigned to 1068. Then the short account of the early events of 1070, the reconciliation of Waltheof (see p 303), and the plunder of the monasteries (see p 328), which, according to the reckoning followed, should have come into the annal for 1069, has, probably in some attempt at correction, got shoved on to 1071, and the reckoning of this Chronicle remains a year in advance till it breaks off. In Peterborough the confusion is of a different kind. The entry for 1067 stands thus,

"*Her* for se cyng ofer sæ, and hæfde mid him gislas and sceattas, and com *þæs oðres geares* on Scē Nicolaes mæssedæg ... and *þæs sumeres* for Eadgar cild út," &c.

This entry follows two ways of reckoning. William's going into Normandy was "her" or in 1067, if the year began at Christmas or on January 1. But the reckoning which begins at Easter would place it in 1066, and, according to this reckoning, Saint Nicolas' day in 1067 would be "þæs oðres geares." Again, reckoning William's voyage to 1067, the flight of Eadgar in the summer of 1068 would be "þæs oðres geares," though not in the same year as William's return. The Chronicler must have had accounts before him which followed both reckonings. The events of 1067 and 1068 thus got jumbled together. To make matters straight, the events of 1069 were divided into two years, but from the latter part of 1069 the reckoning goes on rightly.

We now come to the great Northern campaign of 1069-1070. The English account here is simply fragmentary. The two Chronicles, Florence, and his Northumbrian editor, confine themselves wholly to the events at York; oddly enough, they take no notice of the movements along the whole western side of England, from Cornwall to Chester. Nor do they take any notice of the earlier course of the Danish fleet and its attempts on south-eastern England (see pp. 251-253); they are content to begin their story when the fleet enters the Humber. They then describe the taking of York by the Danes and English and its recovery by William, and then record the devastation of Northumberland. But the rich and varied details, which show that the campaign was not a mere local warfare, but a warfare spread over the greater part of England, come mainly from Orderic, who doubtless followed William of Poitiers. For the whole western side of England, with the single exception of the Devonshire expedition of Harold's sons, Orderic is our only guide. In the extreme North we can compare him with the Durham writers, who do not always pick out the same facts specially to dwell on, but who certainly confirm the general run of his story.

The accounts given by the two Chroniclers of the events at York seem quite independent of each other. Each supplies some facts which are wanting in the other. For instance, Worcester gives the names of Gospatric and Mærleswegen among the English and Thurkill among the Danes, while Peterborough mentions only Eadgar, Osbeorn, and the sons of Swend—two in Peterborough, three in Worcester. Worcester reckons the fleet at two hundred and forty ships, Peterborough at three hundred Worcester alone mentions the burning of the minster, and Peterborough only mentions that the Norman commanders were among the captives taken ("Þa heafodmen hæfdon on beandon." See p. 269). But the two accounts essentially agree, except in one point where the Worcester writer seems to be led away by a local feeling. The thing which mainly strikes him is the death of Archbishop Ealdred, formerly his own Bishop, which he puts before the Danes came at all (see p 266), whereas they were already in the Humber, but had not yet reached York. Florence corrects this, and gives more exact dates of everything; but his account is clearly an expansion of the Worcester narrative. Simeon inserts one or two things, thus he restores the name of Gospatric, which Florence leaves out. Florence again mentions the captivity of William Malet—one of the "heafodmen" spoken of in the Peterborough Chronicle—and Simeon adds Gilbert of Ghent. The captivity of these men was most likely passed over by William of Poitiers, as there is no mention of it in Orderic, but the fact turns up in Domesday (see p. 270). The single word "fordyde" by which Peterborough describes the great harrying is somewhat expanded in Worcester, somewhat more so in Florence, and naturally most of all in Simeon, who however looks at the matter from a purely Durham point of view. Orderic (see p. 289) adds some remarkable details, but it is from the Evesham writer (see p. 315) and from various entries in Domesday that we learn over how large a part of England William's ravages were spread.

From the Chronicles and Florence however we should hardly have found out that the warfare of 1069–1070 touched any part of the country beyond Yorkshire, and even Simeon would hardly take us beyond Northumberland. For the rest we must go to Orderic, that is to William of Poitiers. It is much to be regretted that in large parts of his narrative we have no means of checking him by any English writer; but I see no reason to doubt the general truth of his story. It is our only detailed narrative of the real Conquest of England; the English writers give us only fragmentary portions of the process. The story is probable and consistent, except in two places. One is the extraordinary confusion which seems to make the same force march at once to Shrewsbury and to Exeter (see p. 279), a confusion the more strange in Orderic, who was born in the neighbourhood of Shrewsbury. Of this I cannot suggest any explanation, but the geographical difficulty in Orderic's account of William's march after Christmas 1069–1070 (see p. 306) is fully explained by Mr. Hinde's correction. William sets forth to chastise certain enemies who are said (515 B) "in angulo quodam regionis latitare, mari vel paludibus undique munito." These enemies he follows as far as the Tees ("ad flumen Tesiam insequitur"), they were therefore somewhere near the mouth of the Tees, on the Yorkshire side. But directly after (515 C) we read, "Haugustaldam revertebatur a Tesiâ," the difficulties of the march are set forth, and as the goal of the journey we read of William as "Eboracum reversus." A march from the mouth of the Tees, or from any part of the course of the Tees, to York by way of Hexham, which must be meant by "Haugustalda," is of course a geographical absurdity. I have somewhere seen it proposed to read "Eboracum" for "Haugustaldam." But no transcriber would put the less known Hexham for the better known York, with the further result of turning sense into nonsense. But if the right reading be, as Mr Hinde suggests, Helmsley or Hamelac, nothing was more likely than that a transcriber might turn it into Hexham, a name less known than York, but incomparably better known than Helmsley.

778    APPENDIX.

William's march was therefore through the Cleveland hills, and the reason why it is during the return march that the difficulties of the road are mainly insisted on is doubtless because in the meanwhile frost had set in—" in acerbissimo hiemis gelu transivit."


NOTE Z. p. 188

THE SUBMISSION OF OXFORD.

THE date of the submission of Oxford to William is very doubtful. One would have been inclined to place it in 1066, when William was so near as Wallingford, and the influence of Wigod and his position as Sheriff of the shire would also make an early date likely There is no undisputed mention of Oxford in any of William's campaigns, nor is it one of the places where castles were built by the King himself. The castle, including the square tower which still remains, was the work of Robert of Oily and was not built till 1071 (Ann. Oseney, in anno, Ann. Mon. iv 9), or 1072 (Mon. Angl vi. 251) On the other hand the prodigious destruction of houses in Oxford which is recorded in Domesday (154) seems to imply a siege, and a most devastating siege Four hundred and seventy-eight houses were so ruined as to be unable to pay taxes, leaving only two hundred and forty-three still taxable. " In ipsâ villâ tam intra murum quam extra sunt cc. et xliii. domus reddentes geldam, et exceptis (his) sunt ibi quingentæ domus, xxii. minus, ita vastæ et destructæ quod geldam non possint reddere." This is far greater destruction than could be involved in the mere building of the castle And it must not be forgotten that, where William of Malmesbury (iii. 248) gives what is commonly taken for a description of the siege of Exeter, one manuscript (see Sir T. D. Hardy's note) for " Exoniam" reads " Oxoniam" This reading is also followed by many manuscripts of Roger of Wendover (ii 4), and again by most of the manuscripts of Matthew Paris (see Sir F. Madden's edition, i 10). Of these, Matthew Paris seems distinctly to connect the siege of "Oxonia" or "Exonia" with William's march to York in 1068. This would of course apply much better to Oxford than to Exeter, and the one incident mentioned in William of Malmesbury's account of the siege is not mentioned in the fuller accounts of the siege of Exeter. On the other hand, it is somewhat strange if the writers who give rather minute details of the campaign of 1068 have wholly left out so important a fact as a siege of Oxford in which more than two-thirds of the town were destroyed. But it would be still more remarkable if such a siege in the campaign of 1066 escaped all notice both in William of Poitiers and Guy of Amiens And it would be nearly as strange if so great a destruction were brought about by any means except a siege Again, while no two names are more likely to be confounded than "Exonia" and "Oxonia," "Oxonia" is not a form used anywhere by William of Malmesbury, who (ii 179 and Hist Nov. ii 20) uses the form "Oxenefordum." "Exonia," on the other hand, he does use, though he also uses "Excestra" (ii. 134, 165, 201). In the Gesta Pontificum also he uses "Execestra" in a formal way as quoting the English name, but he speaks familiarly of "Exonia." But Oxford and Oxfordshire he calls (311, 315) "pagus Oxenfordensis," "Oxenfordensis civitas," "Oxenfordia" This certainly looks as if "Exonia" was the true reading in William of Malmesbury. On the other hand, if Robert of Oily or any one else contrived to make such frightful destruction in a town which was not taken by storm, he must have been a destroyer beyond the ordinary standard of the time.

Thierry (i. 289) tells the history of the siege of Exeter from Orderic. Afterwards (i. 299, 300) he tells the story of the siege of Oxford from Matthew Paris But to this he adds a passage which is mere romance; "Les religieux du convent de Sainte-Frideswide, suivant l'exemple des moines de Hida et de Winchcomb, privent les armes pour défendre leur monastère, et en furent tous expulsés, après la victoire des Normands." For this he sends us to "Monast. anglic t i p 984," that is to say, ii 144 of the new Monasticon. The manuscript from which the passage is quoted is evidently very imperfect, but at all events it shows that Thierry's whole story is a dream, and that there were no monks at Saint Frithswyth's at all at that time. The passage refers to a temporary substitution of monks for secular canons at some unknown date between 1066 and 1122 The words are, " Postea antequam viris Normannorum Angliam subdidisset ab ... cuidam Abbati ecclesia ista cum possessionibus suis a quodam

Rege donata . . spoliati igitur bonis suis et sedibus expulsi suis, canonici sæculares memorati et monachis res addicta per annos aliquot eorum dispositionibus servi . . postea, sicut se habent res mortalium, Regis cujusdam beneficio consilii deliberatione canonicis præfatis sua sunt restituta et usque ad annum MCXXII eidem ecclesiæ præfuerunt" Now whatever is to be made of so lame a story as this, it is certain from Domesday that, at the time of the Survey, the canons of Saint Frithswyth's were in full possession of their property The story of the fighting monks of Oxford would not have been allowable even in an historical novel, as it does not supplement the facts of history, but contradicts them.

## NOTE AA. p. 189.

### THURKILL OF WARWICK.

THERE can be little doubt that Thurkill of Warwick or of Arden was another of those men of English or of Danish descent who, like Wigod of Wallingford, contrived to win the Conqueror's favour, and to retain or even to increase their estates under his government. He stands out more conspicuously in Domesday than any other Englishman, his lands filling more than four columns (240 b-241 b) Two lordships were held of him in pledge by no less a person than Robert of Oily, of one of which we read (241), "Ailmarus tenuit, et licentiâ Regis vendidit Aluuino vicecomiti patri Turchil." In the same page and the next, it is noted of two of Thurkill's lordships, " Aluuinus pater T. tenuit." This gives us a Sheriff Ælfwine as the father of Thurkill, and the Survey helps us to a little more knowledge of Ælfwine himself. He was a benefactor to the Abbey of Coventry in the time of King Eadward, but his benefaction had shared the fate of so many other ecclesiastical lordships and had passed into the hands of a lay stranger We read in Warwickshire (238 b, 239 b) of lands which had been held by Earl Alberic and were now in the hands of the Crown ; "Ipse Comes tenuit Clipstone Aluuinus Vicecomes tenuit T R E. et cum terrâ liber fuit" A marginal note adds, " Hanc terram dedit Aluuin ecclesiæ de Coventreu pro animâ suâ T. R E Comes Albericus abstulit." The earlier entry adds that Ælfwine's grant was made "concessu Regis E et filiorum suorum et testimonio comitatûs," and the act of Alberic is put more strongly, "injuste invasit et ecclesiæ abstulit." We seem to find him again in Oxfordshire (160 b), where we read, "Alwi Vicecomes tenet de Rege ii. hidas et dimidiam. . . . Hanc terram emit ab eo Manasses sine licentiâ Regis." This however may perhaps be a different man, Ælfwig, not Ælfwine, for the entry sounds as if the person spoken of were still alive at the time of the Survey, while the death of Ælfwine is distinctly implied in a notice of the re-marriage of his widow, which is the most curious piece of information which we get about the whole family. It appears from two entries in Gloucestershire (167) that Ælfwine, like other Sheriffs and other officers of all ranks and nations, made free with the King's lands. Of lands and a fishery in the Hundred of Westbury we read, "Aluuinus Vicecomes tenuit et uxori suæ dedit. Hæc tamen fuerunt de firmâ Regis in Westberie." And just above we learn the fate of the widow thus unlawfully jointured. Of other lands it is said, "Rex E tenuit et accommodavit Aluuino Vicecomiti suo, ut in vitâ suâ haberet, non tamen dono dedit, ut comitatus testatur. Rex W. dedit Ricardo cuidam juveni uxorem ejus et terram. Nunc Willelmus successor Ricardi ita tenet hanc terram." Thurkill's mother, or more probably his stepmother, was given away to young Richard. I know not how young Richard became "antecessor" to a certain William Goizenboded, who holds several lordships which had belonged to Ælfwine, but of whom I can give no further account, but they appear again in the same relation in Worcestershire, 177 b, where we get the further information that young Richard, doubtless a Norman favourite, had been in possession in King Eadward's days; "Willelmus Goizenboded tenet Celvestune et Willelmus de eo. Ricardus juvenis tenuit T. R. E." If "Aluui" and "Aluuinus" are two men, we meet with two notices of the former in Gloucestershire (162 b, 163), where we read of one estate, "præstitit Aluui Vicecomes," and of another, "Aluui Vicecomes misit extra firmam."

Thurkill has become a kind of mythical person in local history, and has got mixed up with Warwick Castle and with other things with which authentic records do not bring him into connexion (see Dugdale's Warwickshire, pp 301, 606). His Domesday description is "Turchil de Warwic," but there is nothing in the Survey which connects him in any special way with Warwick Castle, though he holds houses in the borough (241 *b*, 238). In the Abingdon History (ii. 8, 20, 21) he appears as a benefactor of that Abbey. He is described as Thurkill of Arden—"Turkillus de Ardene," "Turkillus quidam de Anglis, valde inter suos nobilis in partibus Ardene mansitans." His connexion with Abingdon is shown also in Domesday (241 *b*), where the Abbey of Abingdon appears as tenant of one of Thurkill's Warwickshire lordships ("de T. tenet Abbas de Abendone"), and where we also read (239), "Abbatia de Abendone habet in Hille ii. hidas quas emit Abbas de feudo Turchilli." Thurkill also appears (160 *b*) as holding a single lordship in Oxfordshire.

The entries of Thurkill's Warwickshire estates are of great importance as illustrating the relation between Norman and English landowners, but I reserve them for examination elsewhere.

Thurkill is said (see Ellis, i. 497) to have had a son Siward, who was dispossessed of the greater part of his lands by William Rufus. The name Siward constantly appears as a surname in the reign of Henry the Third Genealogists might do some service by finding out whether its bearers were descendants of Thurkill and Ælfwine.

## NOTE BB. p. 195

### The Date of the Marriage of Malcolm and Margaret.

There is an apparent contradiction between the Chronicles under the year 1067 and Simeon, or whatever we are to call the Northern interpolator of Florence, under 1070 as to the date of the marriage of Malcolm and Margaret. The Chronicles seem to place the marriage in 1067 or 1068, soon after Eadgar's first flight to Scotland (see p. 195) Simeon distinctly places it at some time not earlier than 1070, when he makes Eadgar and his sisters again seek shelter in Scotland after the final fall of York This contradiction is made the most of by Mr Hinde, both in his History of Northumberland (i. 186) and in his edition of Simeon (86), in order to depreciate the value of the Northumbrian insertions.

The Worcester Chronicle (see above, p. 770) inserts an account of the flight of Eadgar and the marriage of Margaret under the year 1067 (1068) between its entries of the fall of Exeter and the flight of Gytha. This account is manifestly out of place, and I cannot help thinking that the whole passage, whose prolixity and scriptural quotations form a strange contrast to the short entries on each side of it, is an interpolation. It is a sort of little Life of Saint Margaret, setting forth her inclination for a single life, the courtship of Malcolm, the difficulties which he met with, the final consent of Margaret and her kinsfolk, the marriage and its final good results Lastly we get Margaret's pedigree on both sides, and then we go back to Exeter. It is clear that this is not the annalistic way of writing; things are put together which have a connexion of idea, but not of time. The mention of Eadgar's flight to Scotland is followed by an account of all which came of it in the end, but we need not suppose that all happened in the year 1068. The reformation of Malcolm and all Scotland could hardly have been quite so speedy as that. And, as Margaret refused for a long time to marry Malcolm, we can hardly infer that even the marriage happened in 1068, but rather the contrary

The Peterborough Chronicle, in its shorter account, which I have quoted above (see p 770), would be much better evidence in favour of the early date of the marriage than the longer Worcester entry. Our first impression from its words would certainly be that the marriage took place almost immediately on Eadgar's first reaching Scotland, but then we know from the longer Worcester account that this was not so. We are in fact driven to believe that the shorter account, no less than the longer one, follows the order of ideas and not of time; indeed the Peterborough account looks very like an abridgement of that of Worcester. And the chronological confusion of these years must not be forgotten (see above, p 774); the flight and the marriage are in both Chronicles put under 1067, whereas, on any showing, they did not happen till 1068.

Florence records the flight of Eadgar and his sisters and their reception by Malcolm under 1068. He nowhere records the marriage, though he implies it in his narrative of the deaths of Malcolm and Margaret in 1093. But in the entry of 1068 he uses an expression which is of some importance. Eadgar and the rest, including his sisters, "navigio Scottiam adierunt, ibidemque, Regis Scottorum Malcolmi pace, *hiemem exegerunt.*" We know that the stay of Eadgar and the Northumbrian chiefs in Scotland was not long  They stayed there during the winter of 1068, but in 1069 they twice left Scotland and once returned to it (see pp 238, 243, 254, 505). The words of Florence would seem to imply that Margaret and Christina also left Scotland in 1069, they certainly seem quite inconsistent with the notion of Margaret marrying Malcolm in 1068

Margaret's own biographer Turgot gives no date to her marriage  William of Malmesbury mentions the marriage more than once, but he nowhere gives it a date  He speaks of it first when he records the return of the Ætheling Eadward to England (ii. 228), but he says no more than "Margareta, quam Malcolmus Rex Scottorum legitimo matrimonio duxit." In his account of William's reign (iii. 249), where he is grouping together several classes of facts, not by their dates but by their subjects, he says, "Malcolmus omnes Anglorum perfugas libenter recipiebat, tutamentum singulis quantum poterat impendens, Edgarum præcipue, cujus sororem, pro antiquâ memoriâ nobilitatis, jugalem sibi fecerat"  No date can be got out of this, for, if the words were pressed too strictly, they would mean that Malcolm had married Margaret before his reception of her brother. Indeed Orderic (701 B) makes Malcolm himself say as much, "Fateor quod Rex Eduardus, dum mihi Margaritam proneptem suam in conjugium tradidit, Lodonensem comitatum mihi donavit"  One can hardly help connecting these last words with the entry in the Durham Annals quoted in the Corrigenda to the second edition of my second volume (p. xxx). If we take these expressions, not of an actual marriage, but of a mere betrothal, the thing is certainly possible, but no one would guess it from the Worcester Chronicle  And we must not forget the existence of Malcolm's other wife Ingebiorg, the widow of Thorfinn (see vol. iii. p. 344)  Malcolm could not have married her before 1064, the year of Thorfinn's death. Was the betrothal with Margaret earlier than this, and did Malcolm, like our Harold, forsake the betrothed maiden for the widow, and, like Harold Hardrada and the solar heroes (see vol iii p. 341), come back to his first love in the end ? Anyhow we have to dispose of Ingebiorg at some time between 1064 and 1068  And we have to dispose of her in such a way that a saint could consent to take her place  Malcolm may have put away wives as readily as Uhtred, but Margaret would surely be more scrupulous than her great-aunt (see vol. i. p 358). And we can hardly conceive that the widow and mother of Earls of Orkney could have been taken "more Danico."

In all this, as it seems to me, we have nothing to fix the marriage to Eadgar's first stay in Scotland in 1068-1069. And we have another distinct account which puts it in 1070 or 1071 This is in those Northumbrian insertions in the chronicle of Florence which I am still inclined to call by the name of Simeon In this version (pp 86-88) Malcolm is ravaging Northern England, and is in the very act of burning the church of Wearmouth (see p 505), when he sees the ships in which Eadgar and his sisters and other English refugees are again seeking shelter in Scotland. He welcomes them and promises them a friendly reception in his Kingdom (see p. 505) By the time Malcolm has got back to Scotland the English exiles get there also, and the marriage seems to take place pretty soon; " Quo [in Scotiam] etiam Clitonem Eadgarum cum sociis supra nominatis prospero pervexit cursu. Cujus Eadgari sororem Margaretam Rex Malcolmus, consensu propinquorum illius, matrimonio sibi junxit" The account goes on with Margaret's panegyric, setting forth the good effect which she had upon Malcolm, and the number and names of her children.

Now this insertion is one of those passages which Mr Hinde, undoubtedly the best modern writer on Northumbrian matters, picks out specially to assail the authority of the Northumbrian interpolator. "The first thing which startles us," he says (i 186), "is the circumstance of the author placing contemporaneously the flight of Edgar with his mother and sisters to Scotland and the embarkation of Bishop Egelwin for Cologne, and assigning as a common date the year 1070 This date is correct as regards the departure of the Bishop, but all our authorities, including Florence, with whose work the above quotation is interpolated, agree in fixing the flight of Edgar into Scotland, and the marriage of his sister to Malcolm, at all events two years previous"

Mr Hinde forgets that there is no one event which can be called "*the* flight of Edgar into Scotland" The Chronicles record one such flight in 1067 (1068), and another in 1068 (1069) after the second fall of York. What Simeon does is to help us to a third flight at the beginning of 1070 This in no way contradicts the Chronicles, which do not mention Eadgar again till he comes from Flanders into Scotland in 1074 (see p. 568). Nor is it accurate to say that "all our authorities, including Florence, ... agree in fixing ... the marriage of Malcolm at all events two years previous," for Florence does not mention the marriage at all.

For my own part I see no contradiction. I do not see that the Chronicles positively place the marriage in 1068, and the negative evidence of Florence is against so early a date. The Chronicles leave it uncertain what became of Eadgar after the last fall of York. Simeon fills up the gap in the most probable way with a third flight to Scotland, followed by a marriage between Malcolm and Margaret. That marriage may have been, as Orderic says, designed in the time of Eadward; in 1068 it certainly was, whether on account of the matter of Ingebiorg or purely from her own celibate tastes, utterly offensive to Margaret. By all accounts it took some time to overcome her scruples, to me it seems that they were not overcome till 1070.

Of the two last and best writers of Scottish history, Mr. E W. Robertson (i. 135) distinctly accepts the later date for the marriage. Mr Burton (i. 405, 406) is less clear. Speaking of 1068 he says, "one of the sisters, Margaret, was *afterwards* married to Malcolm;" but in the next page he speaks of Malcolm as already Eadgar's brother-in-law in 1069.

## NOTE CC. p. 206.

### The First Submission of Malcolm.

Mr. E W. Robertson (ii. 480) calls this submission of Malcolm in question, mainly because it is recorded only by Orderic, who does not record the homage at Abernethy in 1072. If we weeded out our history on this principle, there would be little left for us to believe; a large part of our narrative has to be made up by piecing together this fact recorded by one writer and that fact recorded by another. The insertions and omissions in all our authorities are singularly capricious; and, if it is reason enough to reject a statement that is found in Orderic only, we must cast away most of the details of the campaigns of 1068–1070, that is, our only connected narrative of the real conquest of England.

Of that narrative this submission of Malcolm is a part, and the story hangs quite well together. Malcolm had engaged to help the Northumbrians in their resistance to William, but, whether through faithlessness or through unavoidable hindrances, he had failed to fulfil his promise. After the fall of York, he makes a nominal submission, which William accepts. Such a course exactly suits the position of the two Kings. Malcolm had no more intention than usual of abiding by his submission, but he staved off any immediate attack on the part of William, and he husbanded his forces for another time. To accept such a nominal submission was of a piece with William's whole policy. He received the formal acknowledgement of his superiority as a means towards establishing a real superiority at some future time. Mr. Robertson argues that, if Malcolm had submitted, the Conqueror would have provided against the reception of Eadgar and his followers by Malcolm. On my view this presents no kind of difficulty. William's object was to obtain from Malcolm a formal submission which he would afterwards be able to use against him. He would not hazard this advantage by insisting on conditions which he had no immediate means of enforcing.

On the other hand, Mr. Robertson is quite successful over Sir Francis Palgrave on another point. Sir Francis (Eng. Comm. ii. cccxxxi) has conjured up an invasion of Scotland in 1068–1069, in which William's son Robert plays the leading part, and the result of which is the submission of Malcolm. This comes, as Mr Robertson truly says, from transferring hither a passage from the Abingdon History which really belongs to the year 1080 (see p. 675). An invasion of Scotland in 1068 is utterly impossible, and young Robert would be a most unlikely commander to be sent on such an errand.

Sir Francis Palgrave does not seem to repeat the story in his History of Normandy and England, but his narrative just at this stage is not very clear.

## NOTE DD. pp 225.

### THE EXPEDITIONS OF HAROLD'S SONS.

IT is, I think, clear that two distinct attempts were made by the sons of Harold in the West of England, in two successive years, 1068 and 1069. As so often happens, there is no contradiction among our authorities, though each fills up omissions in the others. The expedition of 1068 mainly affected Bristol and Somerset, and was repulsed by the citizens of Bristol and the English forces under Eadnoth The expedition of 1069 mainly affected Devonshire, and was repulsed by the Breton Count Brian. It is thus easy to see why the Norman writers speak of the second attempt only

The fullest account of the attempt of 1068 is that given in the Worcester Chronicle, which I have followed in the text. Florence is fuller only in mentioning three sons of Harold and giving their names, Godwine, Eadmund, and Magnus, while the Chronicler simply mentions one son without giving his name Here is no contradiction; Godwine was doubtless the eldest brother and the commander of the force, and Eadmund and Magnus might be mentioned or not Godwine's name appears also in the Winchester Annals (see p. 227), in a version which, whatever we think of it, is at any rate independent, and which fixes, from what source I know not, the number of his ships at fifty-two William of Malmesbury (iii. 254) brings in the story in his usual incidental way, not in its chronological order, but as an illustration of William's policy in setting Englishmen to fight against Englishmen. But he makes no special mention of Harold's sons; the adventurers are simply some Englishmen who had taken shelter in Ireland and Denmark, " Contra quosdam, qui post primam infelicis ominis pugnam Danemarchiam et Hiberniam profugerant, et validâ congregatâ manu tertio anno redierant, Anglıgenam exercitum et ducem objecit." See p 226.

The Worcester Chronicle alone mentions the first harryings at the mouth of the Avon and the unsuccessful attempt on Bristol; the account in Florence begins with the landing in Somerset and the battle with Eadnoth. He however adds the harryings in Devonshire and Cornwall after the battle, which the Chronicle does not record.

The second expedition in 1069 is also recorded by the Worcester Chronicler and by Florence. It is not mentioned by William of Malmesbury or by the Winchester writer, but it is mentioned by Orderic (513 A), and by William of Jumièges (vii 41). It is from these two latter writers that we get the name of King Diarmid as the protector of the exiles. All the accounts agree in speaking of two sons of Harold without mentioning their names, so we are left to guess which of the three were those concerned in this second attempt. The geography of the campaign is worth studying, as the way in which one story fills up another is very curious. All that Florence tells us is that they landed at the mouth of the Taw or the Tavy and were defeated by Count Brian, "De Hibernâ venientes, in ostio fluminis Tavi applicuerunt, et cum Breonâ Brytonico comite grave prœlium commiserunt, quo confecto, unde venerant redierunt." The Chronicler fixes the place of their landing to the mouth of the Taw—"into Táw muðan"—but this at first sight seems only the more contradictory to Orderic's story of their attacking Exeter, "Naves armatâ manu oneratas ducentes Exonio appulerunt. Deinde progredientes a littore terram audacius depopulari cœperunt, et ferro igneque furentes maxima patraie damna conati sunt." Orderic, or William of Poitiers, is clearly so far wrong in his geography as to fancy that the fleet sailed up the Exe instead of the Taw, but his account of an attack on Exeter is not therefore to be cast aside. We have a sort of climax of witnesses to show that the harrying was far more widely spread than any one would think from the words of Florence, and that it stretched over very distant parts of Devonshire. First of all, we get a hint from the Chronicler himself. Harold's sons "coman .. into Táw muðan and þær unwærlice úp codon." Then come Orderic's own words about their leaving the coast and harrying the country, and those of William of Jumièges which are much to the same effect; "More sævissimorum piratarum rapinis et incendiis terræ populum exterminare conati sunt." Lastly, we get a most remarkable entry in the Exeter Domesday which can hardly fail to refer to this expedition, and which goes far to fix its geographical extent. At pp. 300, 301 it is said of nine manors belonging to Judhel of

Totnes, "Hæc ix. prædictæ mansiones sunt vastatæ per Irlandinos homines" The names of the places are given as Torlestan, Bachedona, Coletona, Heuis, Walenintona, Portlamuta, Edetona, Alwinestona, Sura I do not know enough of Devonshire topography to identify every one of these places, but I can recognize several of them which lie in widely distant parts of the shire. "Alwinestona" is probably Alwington near Bideford, in the neighbourhood of their landing-place, while there are two Colytons, both in the south-eastern part of the shire towards Dorset. In the course of a harrying which spread so far as this, an attack on Exeter itself would be anything but unlikely. Huish again and Portlemouth are in the south-western part of the county towards Plymouth, while " Walenintona" would seem to be Walkhampton near Launceston We thus find in Domesday a ravaging of Devonshire "per Irlandinos homines" which touched the whole south and west of the shire We can hardly fail to identify this expedition with the second attempt of the sons of Harold, and we are thus better able to estimate its extent and importance.

## NOTE EE p 228

### The Birth and Education of Henry the First

It is plain from Orderic (510 D) that the birth of Henry the First took place in the course of the year 1068, at some time later than his mother's coronation in May (see pp. 178, 227); " Decorata regio diademate matrona, priusquam annus perficeretur, filium nomine Henricum peperit." As William left Matilda in Normandy early in December 1067 (see p 124), the birth of Henry could not have happened later than August or September. But we need not infer from the words of the Winchester Annalist (1068, Ann Mon ii 27) that Henry's birth followed very soon after Matilda's coronation. He says, " Matildis consecrata est . . . et post non multos dies Henricum filium suum in lucem protulit" The words of Orderic would certainly seem to imply the latest possible time of the year.

As for the place of Henry's birth, I know of nothing to fix it, except the vague Selby tradition which will be found in the Monasticon, iii 485. As usual, a particular building was shown as his birth-place, and, as usual, the building was of far later date. Indeed, however freely we may construe the words of Simeon of Durham under the next year 1069, "Cœnobium Sancti Germani de Selebi sumpsit exordium," it is quite impossible to believe that there was any settled monastery or town at Selby at any time in the year 1068. If therefore Henry was born at Selby, it could only have been through some such accident as I have suggested in the text. The reader must judge whether there is any probability of such being the case I should myself have cast aside the Selby story as utterly unworthy of attention, except for two reasons First, the inherent unlikelihood of the tale itself is really something in its favour, it is hard to believe that the local vanity of Selby could have taken so strange a form, if there had not been some groundwork to go upon. Secondly, though a birth at Selby was a thing not at all to be looked for, a birth at York was a thing by no means unlikely to be deliberately planned But the whole matter is of no great importance, and it must be left in uncertainty.

As to the unusual care bestowed on Henry's education, and the unusual amount of his learning, there seems to be no doubt. The only question is how far his education was an English one. Orderic himself says (510 D), "Hic dum dociles annos attigisset, litterarum scientiam didicit" And in another passage (665 D), "Hic in infantiâ studiis literarum a parentibus traditus est, et tam naturali quam doctrinali scientiâ nobiliter imbutus est." William of Malmesbury enlarges still further on his literary acquirements, and he says plainly that on account of his royal birth he was the only one of William's sons who was looked on as entitled to the English Crown. That this latter argument had a sound foundation in English law I have already shown (see vol. 1. pp 117–291). The whole passage (v. 390) runs thus, "Henricus, junior filius Willelmi magni, natus est in Angliâ anno tertio postquam pater eam adierat, infans jam tum omnium votis conspirantibus educatus egregie, quod solus omnium filiorum Willelmi natus esset regie, et ei regnum videretur competere. Itaque tirocinium rudimentorum in scholis egit literalibus, et librorum mella adeo avidis medullis indidit ut nulli postea bellorum tumultus, nulli curarum motus, eas excutere illustri animo possent" So Will Gem viii 10, "Plurimi sunt lætati, quod modo Regem natum de Rege et Reginâ, natum et nutritum in Angliâ, habere meruissent." It is also worth noticing that Henry was—at least after his mother's death—sometimes left in England while his brothers were in Normandy We find him at Abingdon at Easter 1084 (see above, p 735), when it is specially added (Hist. Mon Ab. ii. 12), " suis in Normanniâ cum patre fratribus constitutis." All these hints look in the same direction. The first sign which I have come across of the traditional name *Beauclerc* is in the Annals of Thomas Wykes (Ann. Mon. iv 11) under the year 1087, where he is described as " Henricus postremus filiorum suorum [Willelmi], quem vulgus *Clericum* nuncupabat "

Henry was thus, unlike either of his brothers, a born Ætheling. I do not remember that he is himself called by that name, but he bears the equivalent title " Clito " in Orderic (689 C), and the English title itself is freely given to his son William (Orderic, 649 B, 702 B, 851 B, 869 B) Was he then, as became an English Ætheling, taught the English tongue from his childhood? Nothing is more likely in itself Henry must have been beginning to speak about the time when his father (see p. 323) was himself trying to learn the language of his new Kingdom William would naturally wish that his English-born son, to whom the learning of the tongue would be no such burthen as it was to himself, should speak and read English from the first Still the evidence is not so strong that I can venture to assert the fact with the same confidence as Sir Francis Palgrave (iv 225, 686) The only direct evidence that I know is the passage of Mary of France (ii 401), of which I have said something in vol iii p 572. The passage in full runs thus,

" Pur amur le cumte Willaume,
Le plus vaillant de cest royaume,
M'entremis de cest livre feire
E de l'Angleiz en Roman treire
Ysopet apeluns ce livre
Qu'il traveilla et fist escrire,

De Griu en Latin le turna
Li rois Henris qui moult l'ama,
Le translata puis en Engleiz;
E jeo l'ai rimé en Françeiz
Si cum gel' truvai premièrement."

Count William is said by M. de Roquefort to mean William Earl of Salisbury, who died in 1257. Mary's own date then belongs to the reign of Henry the Third. If Henry be the right reading, one can hardly doubt that Henry the First is meant. There is no time in the life either of Henry the Second or of Henry the Third when we can fancy him translating Greek fables either into Latin or into English. It depends on the punctuation, which of course is somewhat arbitrary, and which M. de Roquefort and Sir F. Palgrave give differently, whether we take it to mean that the royal translator simply translated from Latin into English or that he translated the Greek, first into Latin and then into English. The latter certainly seems the more obvious meaning. I know of no direct evidence that Henry the First understood Greek; still of all the Kings before Henry the Eighth he was the most likely to have done so. We may, I think, take the witness of Mary as showing that some King of England translated fables into English, certainly from the Latin and probably from the Greek. The very strangeness of the story makes it unlikely that any one would invent it without some ground. If then the translation was made by any King of England after the Conquest, we can hardly doubt as to setting down Henry the First as the translator. In him alone is a knowledge of Greek the least likely, and special care in the study of English exactly suits the circumstance of his birth and position. If the translation was really made by Henry, it would doubtless be, as I suggested in my former volume, a youthful exercise at some stage of his learned education.

There remains however the question whether " Henris " is the true reading, and whether we ought not rather to adopt some of the other shapes in which the King's name appears. For " Henris " other texts read "Amez," "Auvert," "Auvres," " Mires," "Alurez," "Affrus." Whatever we make of " Mires " and "Amez," the other forms seem to be corruptions of *Ælfred* (see vol. 1. p. 519). Now would a transcriber be more likely to put Ælfred instead of Henry or to put Henry instead of Ælfred? There is something to be said both ways. A copyist who was struck with the strangeness of the literary exploit attributed to Henry, especially if he were actually writing under Henry the Third, might be tempted to substitute the name of Ælfred, a name which before the thirteenth century was already surrounded by a thoroughly mythical atmosphere as regards both his literary performances and his other actions. On the other hand, a transcriber meeting with any of the unintelligible forms which I have just quoted might think it a clever hit to substitute some familiar name, Henry or any other. As to the internal probability of the work being Ælfred's, we know pretty well what his attainments were, what he wrote and translated. There is no evidence that he ever translated any fables, and there is nothing to show that he had any knowledge of Greek. There is also the difficulty, a minor difficulty certainly, which is pressed by M. de Roquefort (ii. 37), that the English of Ælfred would hardly have been intelligible to Mary in the thirteenth century. There is still more force in his argument (ii. 37, 39) that the fables are full of ideas and expressions, titles of offices and the like, which suit the time of Henry but do not suit the time of Ælfred.

On the whole then I think that Ælfred cannot have made the English translation of the fables which Mary of France translated from English into French. I am strongly inclined to think that Henry the First was the real translator. The learned education of Henry is certain, and it may probably have gone so far as to take in a knowledge of Greek. His English education is so probable that we may look upon it as all but certain, and the witness to his English education is just the same whether he understood Greek or not. But whether the young Ætheling appeared as a translator of Greek books into English is a point which I think highly probable, but which I cannot, with Sir Francis Palgrave, venture to assume as proved.

## NOTE FF. p 230.

### The Foundation Legend of Selby Abbey

THAT Saint German's Abbey at Selby took its beginning in some shape or another in the year 1069 we may set down for certain on the authority of Simeon of Durham (see p 230). This is the whole of our contemporary knowledge. There is no mention in Domesday of the church or town of Selby, and for details we are left wholly to the "Historia Selbiensis Monasterii" in Labbe, i 594. This account, which is said to have been written in 1184, though containing much legendary matter, contains also several names and incidents which seem to show that there is a kernel of truth in the story. In the heading, as in Simeon, the foundation of the monastery is assigned to the year 1069.

In the early days of William's reign ("eodem ferme tempore quo Angliam Dux Normanniæ Willelmus invaserat potentique dexterâ suo subjugavit imperio," p 596), a brother of the house of Saint

German at Auxerre, Benedict by name, is miraculously bidden by the patron saint to go to a place called Selby in England, which he will find by the banks of the Ouse, not far from the city of York. He is there to found a cell in honour of Saint German on a piece of ground belonging to the King. After some strange adventures, he reaches England with a finger of his patron, and by a confusion of names he is led to Salisbury instead of Selby, for, as the writer truly adds (p. 599), "nomen Salesbyriæ percelebre fuit, Selebiæ vero tunc temporis satis incognitum." At Salisbury he is kindly received by a certain Eadward, of whose merits a glowing description is given (p. 598), "Fuit tunc temporis in Salesbyriâ civis quidam, Eduuardus nomine, vir omni morum honestate præfulgens, et inter secularia vitam et morem diffitens secularem, habitu tamen et specie specimen in eo secularitatis apparebat, qui etiam, non minus censûs quam sensûs locupletatus honore, propter diversarum opum affluentem congeriem Dives cognominabatur." Another friend whom he found was a clerk named Theobald, who acted as his interpreter (p. 600). But being puzzled at not finding the river Ouse and the city of York anywhere in that part of England, and being again further warned by his patron, he set sail at Lyme (Luma) in a merchant ship bound for York. He is landed at the spot called Selby, which we are told means in Latin "marini vituli villa," on the banks of the Ouse, separated from York by about ten miles of wood. Here Benedict made himself a dwelling under a great oak-tree which was called by the natives *Strihac* (p. 600). This, we are distinctly told, happened in the year 1069, in the fourth year of King William, a date which, if it be exact, is fatal to the pretensions of Selby as the birthplace of Henry the First.

The fame of the anchorite was gradually spread abroad, and at last the cross on Benedict's cell was seen by the Sheriff of the shire, Hugh the son of Baldric, who was sailing along the river, accompanied by a large body of soldiers, a way of travelling which was necessary in those times on account of the attacks to which all Frenchmen were liable at the hands of the revolted English. The description is worth quoting (p. 602), "Comitabatur cum [Hugonem] non modica militiæ multitudo, quia bellicæ classis immanitate perdurante non adhuc perfectæ pacis tranquillitas ab armis et acie militem absolverat. Fregit hoc in illis finibus Anglorum indomita ferocitas et invicta constantia, qui semper ad vindictam suam in Gallos insurgentes ultra vires et posse, ubicumque sibi invicem obruebant, quis eorum plus posset in viribus experiri nitebantur. Hac de causâ tantâ militum multitudine prædictus Vicecomes constipatus incedebat." The Sheriff has an interview with Benedict, he leaves him his own tent as a temporary dwelling-place, and directs the building of a chapel for his use.

It next occurs to the friendly Sheriff that Benedict, holy as he is, is after all only a squatter on the King's land He accordingly takes him to William—evidently at York or at least somewhere in those parts—by whom he is favourably received, and obtains a small grant of land, on which he begins to build his monastery. Brethren now flow to him, but he is troubled by a person described (p 603) as "quidam princeps latronum, nomine Suuam filius Sigge, qui in vicinis nemoribus cum adhærentibus sibi complicibus assiduis discursibus vagabatur " In this outlaw we may see a disinherited Englishman of the name of Swegen. Miracles of course follow, one of them being wrought on behalf of Hugh the son of Erneis of Burun (" Ernissius Deburum"), who is described as Sheriff of Yorkshire. Lastly, as far as we are concerned—for the story of Abbot Benedict runs on into the days of William Rufus, and his later history is not specially honourable—we see Benedict blessed as Abbot by Thomas Archbishop of York  The new house was, we are told (p 601), the only monastery in Northern England, except Durham; " per totam Eboraci siriam, exceptâ Dunelmensi congregatione, nec monachus nec monachorum locus aliquis in illis diebus facile valuit reperiri" Here is a clear confusion, as Durham did not become a monastery till several years later (see p 677)  The whole foundation was organized under a charter of William, which appears at p 604 of Labbe and, seemingly from another source, at vol iii. p. 499 of the Monasticon  One hardly knows what to make of its stilted and inflated beginning, which savours rather of Æthelred than of William ;

" Willermus fortissimus, immo potentissimus Rex omnium Regum illorum, a quibus eo tempore sceptra Regalia sub Divino gubernabantur ["sub divo gubernantur" in Monasticon], maximum Imperium Anglicæ terræ regens, quod promissione [" permissione" in Monasticon] atque voluntate Dei primum signis mirabilibusque prodigiis, ac deinde magnis viribus, bellisque debellando Anglos, tandem acquisitum gubernans, viris, tam ecclesiasticis, quam suis Comitibus Baronibusque ac ministris omnibus salutens."

Several other grants of private benefactors appear in the Monasticon, iii. 499, 500. One of them, a grant of Gilbert Tison, is made very suspicious by the signature of Archbishop Ealdred, as well as by its being granted "ad instantiam nobilis Reginæ Angliæ, Matildis nomine, pro animabus Regis Sancti Edwardi et Wilhelmi Bastardi, parentum et successorum meorum" Another grant of the same benefactor is made, in more decent language, "pro animâ domini nostri Wilhelmi Regis," and amongst other things it confirms a grant made by "quidam ex hominibus meis nomine Suanus," who may be the repentant freebooter of the legend

The value of this story lies in the names which it introduces Eadward of Salisbury, Sheriff of Wiltshire, appears in Domesday as a great landowner in Wiltshire and the neighbouring shires. Who he was I do not feel at all certain, whether an Englishman of the school of Wigod and Thurkill or a Norman who bore the name of one of the Æthelings There is indeed a story in the Monasticon (vi. 501), in the account of Lacock Abbey, which makes him the son of a person described as "miles strenuus Normannus, Walterus le Ewrus, Comes de Rosmar," and it is added, "cui propter probitatem suam Rex Guillelmus dedit totum dominium de Saresburiâ et Ambresburiâ." Walter's son Eadward was born after his coming to England, "Walterus le Ewrus genuit Edwardum, natione Anglicum natum, postea Vicecomitem Wiltes." The impossibility of this story has been shown by Mr Nichols in the Salisbury Volume of the Archæological Institute, p 213 So far as it is good for anything, it is in favour of Eadward's English birth, and thereby of the English descent of the Earls of Salisbury who sprang from him. The Selby legend also clearly looks on Eadward as an Englishman, for the Frenchman—at least Ducal-Burgundian—Benedict needs the services of Theobald as an interpreter, and it should also be noticed that Eadward is called "civis" It looks very much as if we had found another great mediæval family, which was really of English descent, but which invented a Norman forefather for itself

Some of the other persons mentioned in the story are also well known. Hugh the son of Baldric and Erneis of Burun are real Yorkshire landowners in Domesday, and Hugh appears in Nottingham (p. 280) as "Hugo filius Baldrici Vicecomes." Hugh therefore was

Sheriff somewhere, and it is very possible that he may have been appointed Sheriff of Yorkshire late in 1069, after the capture of William Malet. All these touches give us confidence in the main outline of the story, but the more we believe it the less we can believe the tradition of Henry the First's birth at Selby.

Matthew Paris (Historia Anglorum, i. 34), or some interpolator of his manuscript, has a strange story about the foundation of Selby. William's two monasteries in England are oddly described as " cœnobia nobilia, videlicet de Bello in partibus Angliæ orientalibus et Selebi occidentalibus" Selby is said to have been founded " pro eo quod quemdam sibi consanguinitate propinquum veneno occiderit, timens ne ipsum de regno Angliæ supplantaret vel ducatu vel utroque, quia strenuissimus fuit." This must be some vague glimmering of the death of Conan, on which see vol. iii. p. 714 The story goes on to say that William on his death-bed was visited by a holy Bishop, his confessor, who asked whether he repented of this crime. William said that he could not repent. Did he repent that he could not repent? William had got thus far in the way of amendment, and with this the Bishop seems to have been satisfied.

## NOTE GG. p 298.

### William's Grants of Holderness.

In the local history of the Abbey of Meaux (i. 89, ed. Bond, and Mon. Angl v. 390) we find a story in which Drogo, a Flemish follower of William (" miles quidam valde probus et in armis probatus, qui cum ipso in Angliam venerat, Drugo de la Bouerer, Flandrensis, qui construxit castellum de Skypse"), receives from William a grant of Holderness ("insulam de Holdernese "). Drogo was married to a kinswoman of the King, whom he killed ("habuit autem idem Drugo uxorem quamdam Regis cognatam, quam omine infausto interemit"). He then goes to the King, he pretends that he is going with his wife to Flanders, and asks for money for the journey. William is deceived and gives him the money, on which Drogo crosses the sea The King, on finding out his mistake, sends to arrest him, but his renowned police was for once ineffectual ; Drogo had crossed the sea and never came back ("ipse denuo non reversurus transfretavit"). William then grants the land to Odo of Champagne, who is, as usual (see vol ii p 587), described as marrying William's sister instead of his niece But Holderness was a barren land and grew nothing but oats, so when Odo's wife had borne him a son, who was named Stephen, he asked the King to give him some land which grew wheat, that he might feed his nephew ("petiit a Rege ut daret ei terram ferentem frumentum, unde alere posset nepotem suum") He therefore gave him the lordship of Bytham and other lands elsewhere. This Stephen was the father of William the Fat, Count of Albemarle, who founded the Abbey of Meaux, at a place so called because it had been held (78) by one Gamel the son of Ketel, who had come in William's train from Meaux in France and gave his new abode the name of the old one "Gamellus filius Ketelli de Melsâ, avus seu pater dicti Johannis de Melsâ, cum Willielmo Notho, Rege et Conquæstore, de prædictâ civitate Galliæ, Meaux Gallice dictâ, exiens, cum aliis, in his partibus Holdernesiæ sortem suæ habitationis est assecutus, et ob memoriam civitatis suæ egressionis, nomen huic loco quem inhabitabat ut Meaux nuncuparetur imponebat"

Now that this story cannot be strictly true is plain from Domesday. There (323 b et seqq) one "Drogo de Bevrere" appears as the owner of a vast estate in the parts of Holderness. He is found also in various other parts of Domesday, especially in Lincolnshire (360 b), where he appears as possessor of Bitham. On the other hand, I cannot find Odo of Champagne or his son Stephen in any part of the Survey. As for Gamel the son of Ketel, a man with such a thoroughly Danish name would be very likely indeed to be a natural Yorkshireman, but very unlikely to have come from France into Yorkshire The only Gamel to be found in Domesday as a tenant *in capite* is the Gamel who had a share in the Northumbrian insurrection (see vol ii p. 483), nor can I find any man of the name even as an under-tenant of the lord of Holderness.

On the other hand, Orderic (522 C) distinctly asserts that William gave what he calls the Earldom of Holderness to Odo of Champagne ("Odoni Campaniensi, nepoti Theobaldi Comitis, qui sororem habebat ejusdem Regis, filiam scilicet Rodberti Ducis, dedit idem comitatum Hildernessæ"), and both Odo and his son

Stephen plays an important, though not a very successful, part in English affairs in the reign of William Rufus. See Florence, 1095, 1096.

I must leave the matter to genealogists and local inquirers. It is of course possible that the story of Drogo, or the facts on which the story is founded, and the grant of Holderness to Odo, may have happened in the very latest days of William, after the Survey was drawn up

## NOTE HH. p 304.

### THE CHURCHES OF JARROW AND MONKWEARMOUTH.

THE history of these churches supplies Mr. Hinde with one of his arguments against the authority of the Northumbrian interpolator of Florence. But, as the arguments are closely connected with the fabrics of the two churches, I reserve their consideration till I examine the effects of the Conquest on architecture in my fifth volume.

## NOTE II p 305.

### RETENTION OF ENGLISH NAMES IN DURHAM.

I RESERVE this also for the examination of the effect of the Conquest on nomenclature which I hope to make in my fifth volume.

## NOTE KK p. 324.

### THE LAWS OF EADWARD AND WILLIAM.

THIS also I keep for a general examination of the effect of the Conquest upon English Law.

## NOTE LL p. 344.

### THE RELATIONS OF THE PROVINCES OF CANTERBURY AND YORK.

THE discussion of this subject also will find a place when I come to examine the effects of the Conquest upon ecclesiastical matters

## NOTE MM. p 345

### THE ALLEGED PENANCE ON WILLIAM'S SOLDIERS.

In Wilkins's Concilia, i. 366, we have a set of canons enjoining certain penances on William's soldiers, which are there described as passed in a council at Winchester, and as printed " ex vetusto libro Saxonico, ad Wigornensem Ecclesiam spectante" They appear also in Bessin's Concilia Rotomagensis Provinciæ, p 50 And it is plain that, if they were ever passed at all, they were passed at a Norman and not an English synod, and the mention of Ermenfrid fixes the date to this synod of the year 1070 The heading stands thus;

"Hæc est pœnitentiæ institutio secundum decreta Normannorum præsulum, auctoritate Summi Pontificis, confirmata per Legatum suum Ermenfredum Episcopum Sedunensem, imponenda illis hominibus, quos Willelmus Normannorum Dux suo jussu armavit, et qui absque jussu suo erant armati et ex debito ei militiam dabant"

I must leave it to the judgement of the reader whether a document can possibly be genuine which imposes penances on all who had taken any share in William's great crusade, and therefore, by implication, on William himself more than on any one else. But the enactments are exceedingly curious They begin by one decree which, according to Guy of Amiens (see vol iii p 509), would have condemned the Conqueror to a penance of two thousand years; "Qui magno prœlio scit se hominem occidisse, secundum numerum hominum pro unoquoque uno anno pœniteat" Provisions follow for those who do not know whether those whom they struck had died, and for those who cannot remember the number of those whom they killed The will is punished as well as the deed; "Qui autem neminem percusserit, si percutere voluerat, triduo pœniteat" Then comes an order seemingly for the special benefit of the Bishop of Bayeux; "De clericis qui pugnaverunt aut pugnandi gratiâ armati fuerunt, quia pugnâsse illis illicitum erat secundum instituta canonum, ac si in patriâ suâ peccâssent, pœniteant Pœnitentiæ monachorum secundum regulam suam et Abbatum judicia statuantur." Special provisions are made for the mercenaries and for the archers; " De sagittariis, qui ignoranter aliquos occiderunt, vel absque homicidio vulneraverunt, tribus quadragesimis pœniteant." Lastly come a series of decrees about acts of violence done after the battle, which have a more genuine sound, and which may be taken in connexion with the accounts which we have of William's strict discipline (see p. 30), and a marked distinction is drawn between acts done before the King's coronation and acts done after;

"Quicumque, excepto hoc prœlio, ante Regis consecrationem, victûs quærendi causâ per regnum discurrerunt, et hostibus repugnantibus aliquos occiderunt, pro singulis uno anno pœniteant.

"Qui autem, non necessitate victûs sed prædandi causâ discurrerunt, et aliquos occiderunt, tres anno pœniteant.

"Qui autem post consecrationem Regis hominem occiderunt, sicut de homicidiis sponte commissis pœniteant, hoc excepto, ut si quis de illis quemque qui adhuc repugnabant Regi occidit vel percussit, sicut supra pœniteat.

"De adulteriis, et raptibus, et fornicationibus quibuscumque, ac si in patriâ suâ peccâssent, pœniteant."

Sir Francis Palgrave (iii 484) accepts the decrees without hesitation, and fixes the synod to the same date as I do

## NOTE NN. p. 398

### FRITHRIC ABBOT OF SAINT ALBAN'S

THIS Prelate fills a great space in the legendary narrative of the Conquest as given by Thierry; but his authentic history will go into a very small compass. I doubt whether it goes beyond the signature which I have quoted in the text and another of "Fredericus Abbas Verolamii" to the decree of the Council of London in 1075 (Wilkins, i. 363). The Life of Frithric by Matthew Paris, in the Gesta Abbatum (i 41), seems mythical in all its details. His origin is thus described, " Iste, ex veteribus Saxonibus claram ducens originem et Dacis, Cnutoni Regi fuit consanguineus, et linealiter descendendo propinquus" He was appointed Abbot in 1064, and was in high favour both with Eadward and with Harold (i. 44). He first appears in Thierry (i. 263) as blocking William's course on his way between Berkhampstead and London before his coronation (see vol iii. p. 555). This seems to come from a mythical story in the Gesta (i. 47), which Thierry himself tells over again in ii 29 William, by Lanfranc's advice, designs or professes to treat the English more gently. William and Lanfranc accordingly meet Frithric at Berkhampstead, and William swears to observe the laws of King Eadward This is of course an echo of the submission at Berkhampstead in 1066 But it does not happen till after a great revolt, in which Eadgar, Stigand, Eadwine, and the Bishops Wulfstan and Walter (see p 379) all take a part, but of which the chiefs are Archbishop Ealdred and Abbot Frithric (i 45); "Aluredum Archiepiscopum Eboracensem omnes Aquilonares elegerunt capitaneum, Australes autem Abbatem Frethericum." They have many of the citizens of London on their side, and they seem to give William a good deal of trouble But he, being "immisericors," "tyrannus inexorabilis," "astutus," and "tyrannus belliger," contrives to divide them and to crush them separately Stigand, an unstable man, "similis arundini ventis agitatæ," fluctuates between the King and the English, till he is deposed and imprisoned, where he shares the fate of Judas or Arius; "in carcere contabuit et visceribus crepuit circumfusis" The new Archbishop Lanfranc wins the Papal sanction for William, and a fierce war goes on between him and the English, headed by Eadgar and Frithric — Ealdred has vanished; "Exercitum numerosum ac fortissimum conflaverunt, præficientes sibi Eadgarum speciosissimum et fortissimum, in cujus sinu tota spes reposita fuit Angligenarum Unde in Angham tale exiit eulogium, 'Eadgar Ethelyng Engelondes derlyng'" (i 47) Frithric also was "inter omnes Anglos dux et promotor efficacissimus" Then comes William's oath at Berkhampstead, notwithstanding which he goes on crushing the English in detail and giving their lands to Normans Eadgar flies to Scotland, others of the chief men to Denmark, Norway, and elsewhere Their loss was great, "Exsularunt ab Angliâ nobiles, tam milites quam prælati, viri sancti, generosi, ac dapsiles, qui more Orientalium, et maxime Trojanorum, barbas et comas nutriebant, armis et fide præclarissimi. Quibus exsulantibus, pristina regni sanctitas ac nobilitas rremeabiliter exsulavit" (i 48). William and Lanfranc now greatly oppress the two patriotic Bishops Wulfstan and Walter. Wulfstan is miraculously delivered in the synod of Westminster, according to the well-known story; Walter seeks shelter in Wales. William himself wonders at his own success, and in full Gemôt ("in quodam conventu ubi cuncti prælati cum nobilioribus regni convenerant" i. 49) expresses his amazement His other hearers, Norman and English, hold their peace, but Frithric tells him that the cause of his success is that the clergy who hold so large a part of the land of the country have so commonly played into his hands Had the laity been less liberal, and kept the lands in their own hands, the country would have been better able to resist him. William answers that, if this be so, the country cannot be in a state to resist the King of Denmark or any other possible enemy. Therefore, for the safety of the Kingdom, he takes part of the lands of the Abbey to distribute among his knights. At last Frithric, fearing that greater evils may come, flees to Ely and dies there, on which the Abbey is granted to Paul.

It is hardly needful to point out the inconsistencies of this story and its utter disregard of chronology. It is chiefly worth noticing because large parts of it have been treated by Thierry as so much authentic history Of his singular treatment of the story of Bishop Walter I have already spoken (see p 379). Still it is remarkable that so elaborate a legend should have grown up, as it evidently did, at Saint Alban's itself, and one would think that there must have been some ground in the traditional character both of Frithric and Walter for the part which they are made to play. But all that certain history has to say about Frithric is that he was Abbot of Saint Alban's, and that he died or was deposed some time between 1075 and 1077.

## NOTE OO p. 455

### The Legend of Hereward

The authentic history of Hereward consists of the notices in the Chronicles which I have mentioned in the text and of the entries relating to him in Domesday. At the time of the Survey he held nothing in chief, but he or some other person of the same name held lands in Warwickshire (Domesday, 240, 240 b) of the Count of Mellent, which he had himself held in the time of King Eadward. He had also held (241) other lands in Warwickshire which had passed to Thurkill, and five hides in Worcestershire (173) held of the Bishop. It is however possible that the Hereward of these entries may be some other person, but there can be no doubt about the entry in 376 b. Among the "Clamores in Chetsteven" we read, "Terram Asford in Bercham hundred dicit wapentak non habuisse Herewardum die quâ aufugit." And again in 377; "Terram Sancti Guthlaci quam tenet Ogerus in Repinghale dicunt fuisse dominicam firmam monachorum, et Ulchel Abbatem commendâsse eam ad firmam Herewardo, sicut inter eos conveniret unoquoque anno, sed Abbas resaisivit eam antequam Herewardus de patriâ fugeret, eo quod conventionem non tenuisset." Lastly, in 364 b Toli and Hereward appear as former owners on the lands of the same Oger the Breton. This is the amount of our positive knowledge. Hereward held lands in Lincolnshire, part of them was held of the Abbey of Crowland, of which Abbot Ulfcytel resumed possession because Hereward did not keep his agreement. At some later time, therefore after 1062, the year of the appointment of Ulfcytel, Hereward fled from the country, but for what cause we are not told. In 1070 and 1071 he appears again as the plunderer of Peterborough and leader of the outlaws at Ely. This is the whole of his undoubted history.

The story in the false Ingulf (pp. 67, 70) is not to be wholly cast aside, as it may contain some genuine Crowland tradition. This story makes Hereward the son of a certain Leofric of Brune or Bourne. This Leofric is described (67) as "cognatus illius magni Comitis Herfordensis Radini, qui Godam Edwardi Regis sororem duxerat in uxorem." This can only mean Ralph the Timid, the son, not the husband, of Eadward's sister Godgifu, so that any English kinsman of Ralph must have been also a kinsman of King Eadward. The mother of Hereward was Eadgyth or Eadgifu (Ediva), a descendant of the famous Earl Oslac in Eadgar's time (see vol i. p. 292). Hereward was banished by King Eadward at the prayer of his father Leofric, on account of his violent bearing towards other lads of his own age. In his exile he visited Northumberland, Cornwall, Ireland and Flanders, but no special adventures are told of him, except that in Flanders he married a wife Turfrida, by whom he had a daughter, who handed on the paternal estate at Bourne to her husband Hugh of Evermouth.  Meanwhile the Conquest of England takes place.  Hereward hears that his father is dead, and that his estates have been granted to a Norman by whom his mother is badly treated.  He comes home with his wife and her mother, the latter of whom before long very considerately takes the veil at the hands of Abbot Ulfcytel  He then receives knighthood at the hands of Abbot Brand of Peterborough, who is said to be his uncle ; he becomes the leader of the outlaws in the Isle, and, when the French Abbot Turold succeeds his uncle, he attacks Peterborough, puts the Abbot to flight, and afterwards takes him prisoner and releases him for a large ransom (see p 485).  We hear nothing of his later life or of his death, but from the mention of his daughter inheriting his estate we may infer that he was restored to his lands and died in peace.

Geoffrey Gaimar first brings Hereward before us as leader of the outlaws at Ely (Chron Ang.-Norm. i. 17) ,

'Des utlaghes mulz i aveit.            Ki Hereward aveit à nun,
Uns gentilz hom lur sire esteit,       Un des meillurs del région."

He records his escape with much detail, and carries him into the Bruneswald  There he withstands the Normans for several years at the head of several companions whose names are given in very corrupt forms, and of whom we are told (21),

" Icil e li altre guerreier             Si un d' els encontrout treis
Guerreièrent issi Franceis ,           Ne s'en alasent sanz asalt"

Then comes the story of Ælfthryth, the share of Hereward in the war of Maine, his reconciliation with the King, and his murder (see p 486).  The tale of his marriage runs thus (22) ;

" Par plusurs anz tant guerroia       Et, s'il la pernoit à muller,
Si qe une dame le manda,              Bien porroit François guerreier
Que de li out oi parler ,             Ceo fut Alftrued qe ço manda
Par meinte foiz l'ad fet mander       A Ereward, qe mult ama ,
Q'a lui vensist, si li plesoit ,      Par plusurs foiz tant le manda
L'onor son père li dorroit ,          Qe Ereward s' apresta "

The *Gesta Herwardi Saxonis* are printed in the second volume of the *Chroniques Anglo-Normandes*.  Mr. Thomas Wright, who seems to have edited the story from a copy without seeing the original, calls it (p. i.) a "precieux document," and adds, "*si nous sommes bien informés,* il a été écrit dans le douzième siècle." The Latin text professes to be a translation of an English book written by Leofric the Deacon, who is described as Hereward's priest at Bourne. This text comes from a common source with a great deal in the Historia Eliensis (ed. Stewart), which is there said (p. 239) to come from the work of a certain Prior Richard who held that office (see Angl. Sac. i. 681) from 1177 to 1189. Hereward's parents in the *Gesta* are the same as in Ingulf—the *Ædina* of one being doubtless the *Ediva* of the other—only one Ralph is changed for another, and Leofric is now (ii. 5) "nepos Radulfi cognominato [sic] *Scalre*," that is, no doubt, *Stalre*—Ralph the Staller. The story of Hereward's banishment is told in the same way as in Ingulf, but we have a much fuller account of his adventures in divers parts of the world. Two points may specially be noticed. First (ii. 7), Gilbert of Ghent was already established at York T R E. and was Hereward's godfather; "Quod ubi quidam Gisebrtus de Gant comperit, scilicet expulsionem ejus, pro illo misit, filiolus enim erat divitis illius. Et profectus ultra Northumberland ad eum pervenit." Secondly, Hereward goes (p. 9) to "quidam regulus Cornubiæ, Alef vocabulo," who, as he was called after the first letter of the Hebrew alphabet, most likely held his court at Marazion. The romance does not venture on any name for the Irish prince whom Hereward visits, but when he is shipwrecked in Flanders, instead of the renowned Baldwin, he comes across "Comes terræ illius, Manasar vocatus nomine" (p. 22). In Flanders he has vehement love made to him by Turfrida, as in the other story by Ælfthryth, and he does many exploits in her honour, somewhat in the style of a hero of Froissart. She is described (p. 26) as "puella nobilis et pulcra, scientiæ liberalitatis multum dedita, in mechanicâque arte etiam peritissima." Elsewhere (p. 49) we read that she "etiam omnem muliebrem jam superexcedebat mollitiem, in omni necessitate perspicui viri compos sæpe probata." At last Hereward comes back to England, and finds his father's house at Bourne in the hands of Frenchmen, one of whom has just killed his brother (p. 41). We get a description of a banquet of the Normans and their female companions, and how "quidam joculator intererat psallendo, exprobans genti Anglorum et in medio domûs incompositos quasi Angligenos fingens saltus"

Hereward of course takes a fitting revenge, and regains possession of his father's house. He is then knighted by Brand, he kills Frederick of Warren (p. 46), goes back to Flanders, and comes back with his wife Turfrida and his two nephews Siward the White and Siward the Red. He gathers a company whose names are given at length. One or two are remarkable (p. 51), as "Godricus de Corbi, nepos Comitis de Warewic, et Tosti de Davenesse, cognatus Comitis ejusdem, cujus et nomen in baptismo accepit"—this Tostig Earl of Warwick should be noticed—" et quidam Turbertinus, pronepos Edwyni Comitis," who, to say nothing of his remarkable name, must have been great-great-grandson of the still living Godgifu. But another name (p. 50) seems to suggest a lost piece of Teutonic song or legend; "Godwinus Gille, qui vocabatur Godwinus, quia non impar Godwino filio Guthlaci, qui in fabulis antiquorum valde prædicatur," which should be taken along with the mention of the Guthlacingas in Orderic (537 C). Then follows a long account of Hereward's exploits in the Island and of his later years and death, to which I have made many references in the text. But one detail of his domestic life must be mentioned. Though Turfrida is still alive, he has proposals of marriage made to him (p. 88) by one who is described as " præpotentissima mulier, quæ fuit uxor Dolfini Comitis," and we are told that "illi formosior nec speciosior fuit in regno, nec opibus pene præclarior." She has made her own peace with the King, and she offers to win the same favour for Hereward. The hero is tempted, and Turfrida makes a way for the new alliance by entering religion at Crowland. But, to keep up the moral of the tale, we are told (p. 89) that, on this account, "multa incommoda ei post evenerunt, quod sapientissima erat et in necessitate magni consilii. Postea enim, sicut ipse sæpe professus est, non ei sicut in tempore ejus sic prospere contigerunt multa."

Now how much of truth is there in this story? There is nothing in Domesday to connect Hereward with Bourne, which appears (364 *b*) as having been held T. R. E. by Earl Morkere, except that Bourne had passed to the same owner, Oger the Breton, as some of the former possessions of Hereward. There is nothing beyond the legend to show whether Hereward's father was or was not called Leofric. There is a Leofric who appears several times in Lincolnshire, and once (369) with the title of "Cilt." But he was not the owner of Bourne. The notion of Sir Henry Ellis (ii. 146) that

Hereward was a younger son of Earl Leofric comes only from the genealogical roll of the fifteenth century (Chron Ang.-Norm. ii. xi), of which I have already spoken in vol. ii p 629 " Fuit tempore Sancti Edwardi Regis quidam Leofricus Comes Cestriæ et Merciorum, cognatus Comitis Herfordiæ, dominus de Brunne, nomine Scarle." The pedigree-maker had the Gesta before him, but he could conceive only one Leofric and only one Ralph, and in his *Scarle* we see the last trace of *Stallere, Stalre, Scalre* The early part of the story in the Gesta is plainly mere romance, but when we get Hereward in the Isle we are on somewhat surer ground The geography at least may be trusted, and one or two of the details, as the death of Frederick and the mention of Warwick, draw incidental confirmation from Domesday. As to Hereward's death, there is nothing to make us choose between the story in the Gesta and the story in Gaimar, except that it is more likely that so elaborate a tale as the latter should have been left out by one writer than that it should have been invented by the other.

As to the wife or wives of Hereward, there can be little doubt that Gaimar and the false Ingulf preserve two independent stories, which have been awkwardly rolled together by the writer of the Gesta. Though independent, they are not necessarily contradictory, as Turfrida may have died before Ælfthryth made her proposals to Hereward But the notion of Turfrida going into a monastery to make way for Ælfthryth is plainly another form of the story in Ingulf which makes, not herself but her mother, do so The description of the "mulier præpotentissima" as wife of Earl Dolfin sounds as if it were a tradition or confusion of something Dolfin, we know, was a great Northumbrian name (see vol. ii p 482), but no Earl so called is recorded

The name of *Wake*, given to Hereward by modern writers, comes from the Chronicle of John of Peterborough, a writer of uncertain date and personality. He has several entries about Hereward, which are to the same effect as the story in the Gesta Under 1068 we read, "Herewardus de partibus transmarinis rediens in Angliam ad hæreditatem suam, et reperiens Regem Normannis eam contulisse, occisis occupantibus, cœpit contra Regem dimicare" Under the next year we read, "Obiit Brando Abbas Burgi, patruus dicti Herewardi le *Wake*, cui ex Regis collatione successit Turoldus" He then goes on to tell the story of Turold being taken by Hereward and ransoming himself. Its appearance at this point shows pretty plainly that it is simply another form of the sacking of Peterborough in 1070. Lastly, under 1071 we read, "Herewardus le *Wake* etiam intra paludes Eliensos, cum multis aliis Anglis exlegatis, Regi restitit."

Another question arises as to Hereward's companions in the defence of the Isle. About Earl Morkere, Bishop Æthelwine, and Siward Barn there is no doubt As to Abbot Frithric I have spoken in the last note, but his legendary coming to the Isle is also mixed up with the legendary coming of Stigand. The tale is found in both the Histories of Ely, that in the Anglia Sacra, i. 609, and more fully in Mr. Stewart's edition, 227 ; " Stigandus interum sæpe dictus Archiepiscopus per loca diffugiens vagus latitabat, nec erat ubi se tute vel sua recederet ; tandem cum summâ thesaurorum ejus in Ely transmigravit." This story is plainly referred to in the passage in the Winchester Annals which I quoted in p 333. It is accepted by Thierry (ii 34), who gives the date 1072, though nothing can be plainer than that Stigand was imprisoned in 1070 But Thierry had already (ii. 15) made Stigand escape in company with an imaginary Bishop of Lincoln, whom he seemingly gets out of R Wendover, ii. 7 (cf. M Paris, i. 13), where the Bishop borrows both his see and his name of Alexander from a well-known Prelate of the next century. This story of Stigand is by the Ely writers mixed up with the story of Frithric, whom they call "Egfridus" (Stewart, 221), and say that he brought with him the relics of Saint Alban, a statement indignantly denied by Matthew Paris (Gesta Abbatum, i. 51). Thierry tells the story of Ecgfrith in ii 12, and that of Frithric in ii 33, without remarking that they are the same story I think it is perfectly plain from the authentic narratives that Stigand was imprisoned at Winchester from his deposition to his death, and did not visit either Scotland or Ely.

The names of Eadwine and Morkere are so closely connected through the greater part of their joint lives that the temptation must have been almost irresistible to carry Eadwine into the Isle as well as Morkere. In the Gesta (p 56) the two Earls come in as it were incidentally. Hereward, on going to Ely, is received "a quodam Comite de Leycestre Adwino, et a fratre ipsius Morkere Comes [sic] de Warwic, et ab alio Comite Tosti nomine, qui ad eos in insulâ confugerant." They appear also with their mythical companion Tostig in the Ely History, 230. In the same account (245), when the island is taken, we read by a singular turning about of the real history, " Capitur Ædwinus et cum eo viri innumeri validi, honoris et potentiæ nominati, et artissime vincti. Condolet exercitus [Normannicus, sc] de effugio Morkardi." Yet in another place (239) the brothers are made to live on to have a share in the rebellion of Ralph of Wader, " Normannorum quoque adeo labefactata est fides et mota ut adversum naturalem dominum suum prœlium procinerent cum collectaneis et cousanguineis, commonente Comite Radulfo de Waher ut ad conspirationem invicem contentiose moverentur, accersito in id Herewardo viro inclito et valido aliisque præpotentibus Angliæ, Ædwino scilicet, Morkaro, Ædelino, Waldevo, Siwardo, et Ædgaro; quorum obstinata studia patriam inquietaverunt seditionibus." The defence of Ely is also connected with Ralph's rebellion in the Gesta (77), where after the story of the pythoness (see p 574) we read, " Isto autem tempore Radulfus Comes cognominato [sic] Waer, clam coacto simul maximo exercitu in quosque de gente Anglorum ad nuptias suas invitaverat et vi eos secum sub sacramento et dolo tenere coegerat, unde totam terram a Norwico usque ad Tedford et ad Sudbiri devastans sibi subjugavit Pro quo tres memorati comites et omnes majores natu qui in insulâ erant ad eum jam confugerant, quasi vindicaturus [sic] sibi regnum et patriam, relicto solo Herewardo cum monachis et cum suis ad custodiendam insulam."

I need not prove that Eadwine and Morkere had nothing to do with the rebellion of Ralph and Roger, any more than I need prove that Eadgar and Ætheling were not, as the Ely writer seems to have thought, two distinct persons, or that, as even William of Malmesbury (iii. 252) thought, the two brother Earls did not perish together. But, more than this, the accounts in the Chronicles, Florence, and Orderic, which I have followed in the text, make it plain that Eadwine was not in the Isle at all. The best argument in support of the belief that he was there was a singular object, probably the boss of a shield, dug up in the Isle of Ely in 1694, with an Old-English inscription, which is given at the very end of the first volume of Hickes' Thesaurus and in Ingram's Saxon Chronicle, 323. It has been thought to be a love-token given to Eadwine by William's daughter. But the name of the owner is not *Eadwine* or its Mercian form *Ædwine*, but *Æduwen*, and *Æduwen* or *Ædwen* is a woman's name. I had suspected for myself that the name had nothing to do with Eadwine, and I am further confirmed in that belief by Mr. Earle, whom I have to thank for referring me to Stephens' Runic Monuments, 290, and to Reginaldus de Vitâ et Miraculis S. Godrici (Surtees Society), p 22

Roger of Wendover (ii 9) preserves the fact of a castle bearing the name of Hereward, "Castrum ligneum in ipsis paludibus construxerunt, quod usque in hodiernum diem castellum Herewardi a comprovincialibus nuncupatur." He of course brings Eadwine thither.

## NOTE PP. p. 477

### Bishops Æthelric and Æthelwine

The account of the two brother Bishops in the Chronicles seems quite clear. Æthelric was imprisoned at Westminster in 1070, and died in 1072 Æthelwine was outlawed at the same time that his brother was imprisoned, but he was not imprisoned till after the taking of Ely in 1071, when he was sent to Abingdon, and died in the winter But it is plain that, not only William of Malmesbury, but even Florence, confounded the two

Under 1070 Florence tells us, "Ægelwinus Dunholmi Episcopus ab hominibus Regis Willelmi capitur et in carcerem truditur, ubi dum ex nimio cordis dolore comedere nollet, fame et dolore moritur" Under the next year we read, "Rex Episcopum Ægelwinum Abbandoniam missum in custodiam posuit, ubi in ipsâ hieme vitam finivit." This latter is the true account of Æthelwine translated from the Chronicles The former entry belongs to Æthelric, though the Chronicles under 1069 carefully distinguish them; "Ægelric bisceop wæs forwreged, þe wæs on Burh, and hine man lædde to Westmynstre and utlagode his broðor Ægelwine bisceop." The Worcester Chronicle puts these events under their proper date, as part of the acts of the Easter Gemót of 1070 (see p 336), while Peterborough puts them out of order before the coming of the Danish fleet in 1069.

Florence's story about Æthelric refusing to eat seems hardly consistent with his vigorous spiritual action against the spoilers of Peterborough (see p. 462). But it appears again in a still more confused account, given by William of Malmesbury (Gest Pont 271), where the succession of the two Bishops is put in a wrong order, and the actions of both are attributed to Æthelric;

"Post Edmundum fuerunt Edred, Egeluuinus, Egelricus Quorum ultimus sub Rege Willelmo rebellionis accusatus, quod turbâsset pacem regiam, piraticam adorsus, perpetuo exsilio Westmonasterium deportatus est. Ibi quantum vixit, voluntaria media et lacrimarum affluentiâ præteritos reatus attenuans et diluens, sanctitatis opinionem apud homines concepit. Denique ab his qui eum viderunt posteris memoriam tradentibus, hodieque tumulus ejus nec votis nec frequentiâ petitorum caret.'

Roger of Wendover (ii. 9) makes the same confusion He gives the right account in ii 6, but he now adds, " Hoc etiam anno Egelwinus Episcopus Dunelmensis, apud Westmonasterium sub custodiâ Regis detentus, obiit, et ibidem in porticu Sancti Nicolai sepultus est" This is translated from the account given by both Chronicles, under 1072, where, in recording the death and burial of Æthelric, they give a little sketch of his life (see vol ii p. 408), including a second mention of his imprisonment. Florence also translates, retaining the right name

NOTE QQ p 577.

THE CONNEXION OF WALTHEOF WITH THE CONSPIRACY OF RALPH

THE story of the Norman monk rebuked by his Abbot for irreverently speaking of the martyred Earl (see p. 602) shows that Normans and English long went on holding different opinions about Waltheof. One might have looked for something from Waltheof's own hagiographer, but the account in the *Vita et Passio*, printed in the *Chroniques Anglo-Normandes*, is simply made up from Florence and Orderic. But William of Malmesbury (iii 253) has a very curious passage in which he balances two accounts, as he so often does. He describes Waltheof's birth and actions down to his reconciliation with William and marriage with Judith, and then goes on ;

"Non permansit in fide, pravum ingenium cohibere impotens : compatriotis enim omnibus, qui existimârant resistendum, cæsis vel subjectis, etiam in Radulfi de Waher perfidiâ se immiscuit, sed conjuratione detectâ, comprehensus diuque in vinculis tentus, ultimo spoliatus capite, Crolando sepultus est , quamvis quidam dicant, necessitate interceptum, non voluntate addictum, infidelitatis sacramentum agitâsse. Anglorum est ista excusatio ; nam cætera Normanni asserunt, Anglorum qui plurimum præstent. Quorum adstipulationi Divinitas suffragari videtur, miracula multa, et ea permaxima, ad tumbam illius ostendens Aiunt enim in catenas conjectum quotidianis singultibus perperam commissa diluisse."

A little way on (iii. 255) he gives an account of the bride-ale, its magnificence, and the drunkenness of the guests, adding, " quod Normannorum gulæ jam Anglorum luxus influxerat " He then says that Roger, Ralph, Waltheof, and many others conspired the King's death (" in necem Regis conjurant"), but the next day, when they were sober, the more part repented (" major pars facti pœnitens a convivio dilapsa ") He then adds, " Unus eorum (Weldeof fertur), qui consilio Lanfranci Archiepiscopi Normanniam ultro navigans, rem Regi, causâ suâ duntaxat celatâ, detulit" There is something singular in this last incidental mention of Waltheof, and in the way in which it is insinuated that Waltheof's confession was not an honest one

Roger of Wendover (ii. 14), who is followed by Matthew Paris (i. 19), distinctly says, " Radulfus, cui Rex Willelmus dederat Est-Angliæ consulatum, consilio Welteofi et Rogeri Comitum, Regem Willelmum a regno expellere moliuntur" He then describes the bride-ale, and adds, " erant hujus factionis complices Rogerus, Weltheofus et Radulfus Comites, plures Episcopi et Abbates, cum baronibus et bellatoribus multis." All these join in the embassy to Denmark, all league with the Welsh (meaning Bretons), all ravage the country. Nothing is said of Waltheof's confession. When William comes back, Roger speaks of him as "subito rediens," which Matthew changes into " ad instar fulminis."

The Hyde writer (294), as usual, has an independent account, and a very curious one. He makes no mention of any but English conspirators;

"Willelmus Rex, quum regnum paci studendo modeste conaretur disponere, quidam principes Anglorum invitæ subjectionis jugum excutere cupientes, rebellare contra cum ad suum interitum non formidavere. *Edmesau Waldeth*, unus ex antiquis et ditissimis Angliæ principibus, staturâ quoque corporis et formâ tam decorus ut alter esse Absalon videretur, tanto iracundiæ igne est accensus ut nullis precibus, nullis muneribus, nec propter consanguineam Regis Juditham, nomine pacis dotæ, ut fertur, sibi conjunctam, nisi simulatam cum Rege potuerit habere concordiam. Denique de conjuratione adversus Regem factâ accusatus, confessus est atque judicatus, *dehinc in pace dimissus*. Item conjuratione factâ et devictâ, secundum leges Anglorum et Dacorum, *apud Londoniam* est damnatus. Mox autem carceri mancipatus totus convertitur ad Dominum, jejuniis, lacrimis, assiduisque orationibus intensis insistens, *oratque suppliciter, sed minime impetrat, quod ipsum Regem postea pœnituit, ut monachus fieri posset*, denique servitio perpetuo mancipari. Itaque capite truncatus, corpus ejus ad quamdam ecclesiam quam maritimis locis construxerat defertur, crebraque ad sepulcrum ejus usque hodie, ut aiunt, fiunt miracula."

Several things may be noticed here. I can give no account of the strange surname or epithet given to Waltheof. The story of Waltheof's dismissal and the second charge against him probably arose out of the fact that Waltheof's case really was discussed in two Assemblies, and the writer is right in making London (Westminster) the place of the actual sentence. Waltheof's prayer to be allowed to live as a monk or to live anyhow, and William's sorrow for not having granted it, are statements well worthy of attention, and by no means unlikely.

My own belief, comparing the account in the Chronicles with that in Orderic, is that Waltheof really did assent to the conspiracy at the bride-ale, but that he drew back, confessed to Lanfranc and William, and had no share in the actual rebellion.

## NOTE RR. p. 637.

### THE SIEGE OF DOL AND THE MARRIAGE OF CONSTANCE.

DID William, in the later years of his life, besiege Dol twice or only once? A siege of Dol, following immediately after the death of Waltheof, is distinctly asserted by all our best authorities But we elsewhere find mention of a siege of Dol by William which is placed several years later. In the note in Bouquet, xii. 566, 596, it is suggested that the accounts refer to two different events I have in my notes to the text referred to the statements in our own Chronicles, in Florence, in Orderic, and in William of Malmesbury. And I have mentioned that neither Orderic nor William speaks of the presence of Philip, which, besides our own authorities, is witnessed to by a charter of Marmoutier quoted by Prevost in his edition of Orderic, ii. 291; "Factum est hoc in anno et in ipsis diebus quando ibat Rex Franciæ Philippus in Britanniam ad pugnandum Regem Anglorum, qui ibi obsidebat Dolum castrum." But the special part of Orderic's evidence is that his words would at first sight imply that the marriage of Alan and Constance took place very soon after the siege of Dol in 1076. He says (544 C);

"Deinde prudens Rex, ut se vincere virtute Britones non posse prospexit, aliud consilium sibi posterisque commodum sollerter præcogitavit. Cum Alanno Fergano fœdus amicitiæ firmavit, eique Constantiam filiam suam in conjugium Cadomi honorifice copulavit. Quæ cum viro suo fere xv. annis venerabiliter vixit."

The fifteen years must be reckoned to the death of Constance in 1090, so that it is plain that Orderic, when he wrote this passage, thought that she was married directly after the siege of 1076. But he himself shows elsewhere (see p. 651) that she was still unmarried in 1081, and the Breton writers put the marriage in 1086 or 1087. See Chron. Brit., Morice, i. 103; Bouquet, xii. 559; "Alanus duxit Constantiam filiam Regis Guillelmi Anglorum in uxorem." So Chron. Kemperlegiense, Bouquet, xii. 562, and Chron. Ruyense, Morice, i. 151; Bouquet, xii. 563. Cf. Chron. Briocense, Bouquet, xii. 566, where however Alan's marriage with Constance is wrongly placed after his marriage with Hermengarde of Anjou (see p. 651). It is impossible to resist this evidence for 1086 as the year of the marriage. Rather than put back the marriage, as Prevost does, to 1077, we must give up Orderic's story altogether. But the two stories may be reconciled, if we suppose a betrothal in 1076 and a marriage ten years later, and that Orderic, when writing the account of the siege of Dol, confounded the two. I do not know that there is any evidence as to the age of Constance.

To speak of Alan as Count before his time is no very wonderful slip, but it does not affect the question as to the two sieges. He did not become Count till after the date given to the second. But, as he was Count at the time of the marriage in 1086, it may be thought to show that Orderic did not simply confound a betrothal and a marriage, but misdated the marriage altogether.

The real difficulty is as to the second siege. Among the Breton and Angevin writers, the Angevin Chronicle of Saint Albinus (Labbe, i. 276; Bouquet, xii. 479) is the only one which mentions our first siege. Under 1076 it records "obsidio Dolensis." In the Chronicle of Raynald of Anjou (Bouquet, xii. 479) we read, "Anno 1086, in mense Septembri, Comes Normannorum, qui et Rex Anglorum, Willelmus obsedit in Britanniis castrum quod dicitur Dolum, quod quum diu obsedisset, nihil profecit, sed etiam machinis suis succensis ab eo infructuose discessit, defendentibus illud fortibus Andegavorum militibus." The Breton writers take care not to mention this valiant Angevin contingent, and they give the siege an earlier date. Thus in the Chronicon Briocense (Bouquet, xii. 567) we read, "Hic autem Hoellus, post mortem Conani fratris Havisæ uxoris suæ, fecit bella adversus Goffridum Comitem cognomento Granonem apud castrum Doli, Guillelmo Comite Normannorum sibi auxiliante per quadraginta dies ingeniis et aliis machinationibus obsedit, quod minime capere potuit. Et anno sequenti, hoc est anno Domini MLXXXIII, Hoellus a suis capitur et eodem anno moritur." And the death of Howel, but without any mention of his capture, appears in other Breton Chronicles in Bouquet, xii. 559, 561.

It seems quite impossible that this description and that of the Norman and English writers can refer to the same event. Besides the difference of date, all the circumstances are different. In the one story William appears the enemy of the Breton Count, in the other as his ally. But this last state of things falls in very well with the suggestion which I have before made as to a betrothal in 1076 and a marriage in 1086. On the other hand, it is hard to join the Breton story on to William's acts in 1083 as recorded by English and Norman writers, and it is quite impossible to give up the siege of 1076 or to move it to any later time The distinct evidence of all our own writers, supported by the one Angevin Chronicle, seems quite conclusive

## NOTE SS. p 648

### The Battle of Gerberoi

The account in Orderic leaves out all mention of the personal encounter between William and his son. I follow the account in the Chronicles. It is recorded in both, and each gives some details of its own. The account in Peterborough, 1079, runs thus;

"And þi ilcan geare se cyng Willelm gefeaht togeanes his sunu Rotbearde wiðutan Normandige be anum castele Gerborneð hatte, and se cyng Willelm wearð þær gewundod and his hors ofslagen þe he on sæt, eac his sunu Willelm wearð þær gewundod and fela manna ofslagene"

Here we get the name of the castle and the wound of William Rufus. In the Worcester version these are not mentioned, but we get the gallant exploit of Tokig instead,

"Her Rotbert feht wið his fæder and hine on þa hand gewundade, and his hors wearð under ofscoten and se þe him oðer tobrohte wearð þærrihte mid ánan arblaste ofscoten, þæt wæs Tokig Wiggodes sunu, and fela þær wurdon ofslægen and eac gefangene."

Then follows the passage which I quoted in p. 649.

Florence this time forsakes both Chronicles, and gives a version which reads like a softening of the genuine story. It might even seem that the exploit of Tokig was transferred to Robert;

"Rex Willelmus filio suo Rotberto, ante castellum Gerbothret, quod ei Rex Philippus præstiterat, dum pugnam intulerit, ab ipso vulneratus in brachio, de suo dejectus est emissario; sed mox ut illum per vocem cognovisset, festinus descendit, ac illum suum caballum ascendere jussit, et sic abire permisit. Ille autem, multis suorum occisis nonnullisque captis, ac filio suo Willelmo cum multis aliis vulnerato, fugam init"

Roger of Wendover (ii. 16) cuts the story short, but adds a new element in a curse pronounced upon Robert by his father; "Rex Willelmus, contra Robertum filium suum bellum agens apud Gerberai castrum Galliæ, equo pulsus est, et Willelmus filius ejus vulneratus, et multi de suâ familiâ interfecti, quapropter Rex maledixit Roberto filio suo, quam maledictionem, antequam obiret, expertus est evidenter"

Matthew Paris (i 21), as usual, follows Roger, but with some improvements. The battle gets the epithet of "cruentissimum" William Rufus is not merely "vulneratus" but "graviter læsus," and the fight is said to happen "apud Archenbrai," on which Sir Frederick Madden remarks, "The spot here indicated appears to be *Auchy en Bray*, situated about six miles south-west of Gerberai." Matthew is also more full about the curse,

"Rex in mentis amaritudine maledixit Roberto filio suo, unde ipse Robertus multipliciter maledictionem paternam ante mortem, quam turpem subiit, in multis agendis evidenter est expertus. Et tunc pater abstulit ei Normanniam, sed moriturus ad instantiam circumstantium, quia cruce signabatur, vel in proximo pro patre signandus erat, eam ei restituit."

There is something specially charming in the notion of Robert having already taken the cross, and of William thinking of taking it, in 1087

Lastly, the Hyde writer (297), as usual, has his own version The wound is transferred from the hand to the foot, and it is clearly not meant to be inflicted by the hand of Robert. A strange story connecting William's death with the war with Robert is also added,

"Accidit quâdam die, ut cum suis in Normanniam ingressus, cædibus et rapinis insisteret, occurritque ei pater cum exercitu, et fugientem prosecutus castrum quoddam intrare compulit. Ubi dum Rex cum suis obstreperet de foris sagittâ in pede ex improviso est percussus. Quumque sanguinem defluere cerneret, terribiliter imprecatus est ne umquam Robertus filius suus hæreditatis suæ jura perciperet. Quæ imprecatio quantum valuit tempora sequentia satis ostendunt. Fertur autem quod, dum eumdem filium suum oppugnaret, valde fatigatus et sudore perfusus potum petierit, aquamque frigidam sibi oblatam bibens, simul cum frigore mortem, pro hoc dolor! nimis cito potaverit."

## NOTE TT p. 655.

### The Betrothal of William's Daughter to Alfonso.

ORDERIC (573 C, D), calling the daughter of William who was betrothed to Alfonso Agatha, and making her the same who had been betrothed to Harold, tells her story thus,

"Agatha Regis filia, quæ prius fuerat Heraldo desponsata, postmodum Amfurcio Regi Galliciæ per procos petenti missa est desponsanda. Sed quæ priori sponso ad votum gavisa non est, secundo sociari valde abominata est Anglum viderat et dilexerat. Sed Hibero conjungi nimis metuit, quem numquam perspexerat. Omnipotenti ergo effudit precem lacrimosam, ne duceretur ipsa in Hispaniam, sed ipse potius susciperet eam. Oravit, et exaudita est; obiterque virgo defuncta est."

William of Malmesbury (iii. 276), distinguishing between the betrothed of Harold and the betrothed of Alfonso, tells nearly the same story of the latter; "Aldefonso Galliciæ Regi per nuntios jurata, virgineam mortem impetravit a Deo. Repertus in defunctæ genibus callus crebrarum ejus orationum index est."

The date of this proposed marriage is by no means easy to fix We must not forget the remarkable passage of William of Poitiers (120) about two brother Kings in Spain disputing for a daughter of William: "Hispaniæ Reges duo germani, auditâ ejus magnitudine, natam ejus in matrimonium cupientissime petierunt, suum et regnum et posteritatem hac magnificaturi affinitate. Nam et lis valde inimica inter ipsos propter eam orta est, minime degenerem sed omnino dignam tali parente, sic moribus ornatam, sic in amore Christi studiosam, ut Reginis et sanctimonialibus exemplo esse posset puella non velata" If the Archdeacon pays the faintest respect to chronology, all this is placed before William came into England. But Alfonso of Leon and Sancho of Castile did not succeed their father Ferdinand till 1065 (Art de Vérifier les Dates, iii 741), and the most stirring time of their warfare was in 1070-1072. But there was an earlier struggle of brothers in the former generation, namely the war between Ferdinand and his brother Garcias,

which is recorded in the Chronicle of Saint Maxentius (Labbe, ii
210) under the year 1058 (see Art de Vérifier les Dates, u. s ).
But this was wonderfully early for any one to be thinking of a
daughter of William, who could hardly have yet displayed the
remarkable excellences of which we hear, and the Kings concerned
are not Alfonso and his brother, but their father and uncle  Again,
in the same Chronicle of Saint Maxentius, 1069, we read that
Alfonso married a daughter of Guy-Geoffrey of Aquitaine, of whom
we have heard before (see vol. iii p. 137)  She is said to have
been divorced and Alfonso to have married again in 1080, so that
the chronology becomes nearly hopeless


NOTE UU. p. 718.

THE CLAIM OF ASCELIN.

THE story of Ascelin appears in Orderic and, with some varieties,
in Wace and Benoit. It appears also in William of Malmesbury (iii.
283), in the Hyde writer (297), in Eadmer (Hist. Nov. 13, Selden),
and in William of Newburgh (i 13), who is copied by Walter of
Hemingburgh (i. 19). But none of them give the name of the
claimant. In William of Newburgh he is simply "quidam," 
Eadmer calls him "quidam rusticus," and the Hyde writer "juvenis satis infimus"  William of Malmesbury's version is, " Miles
quidam, ad cujus patrimonium locus ille pertinuerat, clarâ contestans
voce rapinam, sepulturam inhibuit, dicens avito jure solum suum
esse, nec illum in loco quem violenter invaserat pausare debere "
In Walter of Hemingburgh " terribiliter accedit, omnipotentis Dei
prætento nomine"  He adds much the same comment as William
of Malmesbury ; " Obstupuere omnes qui aderant, transitoriæ dominationis actum considerantes, ut princeps potentissimus, qui tam
late dominatus fuerat vivus, locum corporis sui capacem mortuus
sine querelâ non haberet"  Orderic's story should be compared
with the charter of Henry the Second to Saint Stephen's in
Neustria Pia, 634, referred to by M  Hippeau, Saint-Etienne, 34 ,
"Vendidit Rannulfus filius Anselmi [M  Hippeau seems to read
*Ascelini*] Willelmo Abbati Sancti Stephani omnem terram sui juris

*intra ecclesiam et circa*, et quidquid ecclesia ab eo emerat in omnibus locis, sub eâ conditione ut non liceat vel ipsi vel alicui suo hæredi in rebus prædictis aliquem quandoque clamorem facere In hâc venditione comprehensa est omnino terra quam habuerat *præter domum propriam* et duo jugera prati et unum jugerum terræ cum tribus virgis. Hæc quidem omnia ita diffinivit et firmavit coram altari Sancti Stephani et coram Abbate et magnâ parte conventûs, præsente uxore suâ et præsentibus liberis et concedentibus atque cum patre donantibus." A little way on we read, "Vendidit Lanfranco Rannulfus filius Ascelini quatuor jugera terræ aridæ unde lapides extrahuntur ad opus monasterii" Both these sales belong to an earlier time than the death of William, as the Abbot William of the charter is the William who was now Archbishop of Rouen; see p 661

One can hardly doubt that these passages refer to the same land and the same family as the story in Orderic. To me they certainly suggest the idea that there may have been two sides to the question, and perhaps the more so when we mark the unusual care which the charter seems to take to bar all possible claims, and the equal vehemence with which Ascelin, in Wace's version, is made to deny all sales or transfers We must further remember that the terms "violenter" and "par la force" do not necessarily mean more than an occupation alleged to be illegal, just like "per vim" in Domesday or "mid unlage" in our own charters. And I am inclined to give William the benefit of the same favourable construction which in a somewhat similar case I have asked for Harold; see vol ii p 544

One of the gates of Caen was called Porte Arthur; see Wace, 16407, Hippeau, Saint-Etienne, p. 36.

The objection to burying William in ground not his own may be compared with the scruples of Simon of Valois about his father; see above, p 653

I add a few things which have occurred to me while putting these Notes together.

1 The answer of the men of Exeter to William in p. 146 may be compared with the answer of the Tyrians to Alexander under circumstances not unlike those of William before Exeter. They first promise (Arrian, ii. 15 9) to obey all his commands (πράσσειν ὅ τι ἂν ἐπαγγέλλῃ 'Αλέξανδρος); but when he demands to enter the city, they draw back (ii. 16 11), τὰ μὲν ἄλλα ἔδοξε σφίσι ποιεῖν ὅ τιπερ ἐπαγγέλλῃ 'Αλέξανδρος, εἰς δὲ τὴν πόλιν μήτε τινὰ Περσῶν μήτε Μακεδόνων δέχεσθαι.

2. The story of William's humiliation before Ealdred is also found in William of Newburgh, i 12, "Cujus motum ille (Willelmus) non sustinens, ad pedes ejus (Aldredi) procidit, veniam petiit, satisfactionem spopondit. Quumque optimates qui aderant suaderent, ut regem prostratum erigeret; 'Sinite,' inquit, 'illum jacere ad pedes Petri.' Plane in hoc et quanta fuerit ferocissimi principis præsulis circa principem auctoritas atque fiducia, satis declaratum est." This is copied by Walter of Hemingburgh, i 10

3 In speaking of Battle Abbey (p 409), I ought to have mentioned the legend which says that the blood of the slain is still to be seen, a legend which I found in full force on the spot. The story is told by William of Newburgh, i. 13, where he cites it as a proof of the injustice of William's invasion, "Sane quod idem (Willelmus) Christianos innoxios hostiliter Christianus impetiit, et tanto sibi sanguine Christiano regnum paravit, quantæ apud homines gloriæ, tantæ etiam apud Deum noxæ fuit Cujus rei argumentum est quod a testibus fide dignis accepimus." He then mentions the foundation of the Abbey, and goes on; "Denique in eodem monasterio locus ille ubi Anglorum pro patria dimicantium maxima strages facta est, si forte modico imbre maduerit, verum sanguinem et quasi recentem exsudat· ac si aperte per ipsam rei evidentiam dicatur, quod adhuc vox tanti sanguinis Christiani clamet ad Deum de terra, quæ aperuit os suum et suscepit eundem sanguinem de manibus fratrum, id est Christianorum." This is copied by Walter of Hemingburgh, i. 20

## APPENDIX.

Matthew Paris in the Abbreviatio Chronicorum (iii. 169) strangely makes the consecration of the church of Battle happen within the year after the battle itself, and seemingly before William's coronation; "Ecclesiam, quam Bellum appellavit, anno sequenti sollemniter fecit dedicari, ubi jurans et certissime promittens se dilectissimi Regis Edwardi leges inviolabiliter observaturum, et vestigia ejus sequendo gentem Anglicanam sincero corde conservatam dilecturum, gratanter ob omnibus est susceptus Et Londonias veniens, a civibus cunctis est honoratus et [ab] Aldredo, Archiepiscopo Eboracensi, apud Westmonasterium coronatus est"

4. There is a good deal of confusion as to the dates of the Abbots of Ely, and I seem to have been misled in pp. 482, 483 by following the marginal dates in Stewart's Historia Eliensis. Neither that version nor the version of Thomas of Ely in Anglia Sacra is quite consistent in its chronology. From the Winchester Annals (Ann Mon ii 33) it seems plain that Simeon was appointed, not in 1086, but in 1082 Godfrey administered the church of Ely for seven years (Stewart, 251) This takes us back to 1075, in which year, according to Wharton's note in Anglia Sacra (i. 610), Theodwine died in the month of December, after an incumbency of two years and a half. He could not have died in 1074, as Thomas of Ely says in his text, because he signs the decrees of the Council of London in 1075 It follows therefore that Theodwine's predecessor Thurstan probably died early in 1073. He could not have lived till 1076, nor yet have died, as Thomas of Ely makes him, in 1071, because he signs the decrees of the Council of Windsor in 1072 (Will. Malm. iii. 298) The confusion is probably due to a mistake of the writer of the Historia Eliensis, who mistook the five years assigned to Thurstan's abbacy by Thomas of Ely (Anglia Sacra, i. 610) for five years after the surrender in 1071. But the reckoning of five years must be wrong, because both Thomas of Ely (Anglia Sacra, i 609) and the Ely History (Gale, ii. ch. 44) make Thurstan appointed by Harold in 1066 Thurstan therefore was Abbot just seven years; Thomas of Ely probably got his five years by confounding the surrender in 1071 with Thurstan's death in 1073 The order will therefore stand thus;

|  |  |
|---|---|
| Thurstan . . . | 1066—1073 |
| Theodwine . . | 1073—1075. |
| Administration of Godfrey . | 1075—1082. |
| Simeon | 1082—1094. |

5. The history of Richildis, of which I have said something in page 533, comes out more fully in the Genealogia Comitum Flandriæ (Pertz, ix. 320-322) Some of the details are curious, and Richildis, like some of our other heroines, must have been far from young at the time of William Fitz-Osbern's wooing By her former husband Hermann she had a son Roger, who was conveniently made Bishop of Châlons, "Vitricus ejus Balduinus pro nimiâ simplicitate minus sæculo idoneum clericatu et Catalaunensi episcopio sublimare procuravit, ejus hæreditate ita sibi usurpatâ" She and Baldwin were excommunicated by Engelbert Bishop of Cambray on the ground of kindred between Baldwin and Hermann, but Pope Leo the Ninth, who was uncle of Richildis, partly released them in the Council of Rheims in 1049 (see vol. ii. p. 112), "Hanc meruerunt indulgentiam ut in conjugio quidem, sed absque carnali commixtione manerent." (Yet, according to the same account, their son Arnulf was only fifteen years old in 1070 ) During her regency we hear of her "muliebris insolentia," her "tyrannis," "superbia," and the "nimia crudelitas qua in clerum et populum sæviebat," and especially of her spoliations of the church Her dealings with William Fitz-Osbern are thus described, " Mulier rixosa et callida nec erubescens trigamiam conatur adhuc nubere cuidam Guillelmo subcomiti superbo de Normannia, in hoc quoque commovens amplius contra se quosdam Flandriarum principes et populum." Robert has an interview with Richildis at Ghent and demands the possession of what is oddly called his "paternum *regnum*," but Richildis, "femineo furore exagitata, injuriosis responsionibus protestatur," the "injuriosæ responsiones" taking the form of five hexameters Robert appeals to King Philip, who promises him help, but is bribed by Richildis, who "consilio Regis comperto, animum ejus quattuor millium librarum auri sponsione corrupit et ab incepto negotio fraudulenter revocavit" We then get a minute account of the war and of the battle of Cassel, with the further details that both

Richildis and Robert were taken prisoners, but were afterwards released. But we get no mention of the persons in whom we are specially interested, except so far as they come under the general head of "Normanni." We also hear of the reformation of Richildis, and of the holy life of her later days.

6. I know not how I came, when writing the account of the English Warangians in pp. 628, 633, to pass by the second mention of their exploits in Orderic, 640, 642, where he gives an account of the campaign of Dyrrhachion, but does not mention the exploits of the English in the battle. He has a curious panegyric on Alexios, and tells us (641 B) of his taking the English into his especial favour; "Anglos qui, perempto Heraldo Rege, cum proceribus regni Albionem reliquerant et a facie Willelmi Regis per pontum in Thraciam navigaverant, Alexius in amicitiam sibi ascivit, eisque principale palatium regiosque thesauros palam commendavit, quinetiam eos capitis sui rerumque suarum custodis posuit." This is so far not in favour of my theory of a special migration in 1081.

A great number of passages bearing on the history of the Warangians are collected by Zeuss, *Die Deutschen und die Nachbarstamme*, 560, 561. In the wildness of Byzantine ethnology they are called Germans, Celts, and Britons, but the most remarkable passage is one which does not immediately concern the Warangians, but which shows how thoroughly the notions of axeman and Englishman were identified in Byzantine minds, and how it had not wholly passed out of memory that the land which was then England had once been Britain. This is in Nikêtas, Isaac Angelos, ii. 8 (p. 267, Paris), Philip Augustus and Richard Cœur de Lion appear as ὁ ῥὴξ Φραγγίας καὶ ὁ τῶν πελεκυφόρων κατάρχων Βρετανῶν, οὕς νῦν φασιν Ἰγκλίνους, and directly after Richard is Ἰγγλίων ῥήξ.

7. I do not profess to know with certainty what Florence means by the word "Ytene," which he gives as the English name of the New Forest (see p. 612), but some light is thrown upon it by a passage in the genealogies attached to his Chronicle, i. 276, where we are told that William Rufus "in provinciâ Jutarum in Novâ Forestâ, sagittâ percussus, sine filiis occubuit." I presume that Ytene

has something to do with the Jutes, but I conceive it simply to refer to the old Jutish settlement in Hampshire. Sir Francis Palgrave, in one of the noblest passages of his work, the description of the New Forest in iv. 644, 648, calls it "the Jetten-Wald, the Eotena-Wald, the Giant's-Weald."

8. Æthelnoth's story of the English being bidden to shave their beards, which I mentioned in p. 689, appears again in two passages of Matthew Paris in the Gesta Abbatum, i. 42 (cf. the passage quoted in p. 803). With a grand contempt of fact and chronology, we read, "Conculcabantur spreti et derisi nobiles Angli, jugum servitutis a tempore Bruti nescientes, et more Normannorum barbas radere, cincinnos tondere cogebantur." The other passage in the Historia Anglorum, i. 11, is to the same effect. The same idea comes out in Matthew's account of William of the long beard in 1196 (181, Wats), "Cujus genus avitum ob indignationem Normannorum radere barbam contempsit," in which case it is a little strange that he should have borne the name of William. But how is this doctrine to be reconciled with the Tapestry, where no Englishman of the generation of Harold and William appears with a beard?

END OF VOLUME THE FOURTH.

UNIVERSITY OF CALIFORNIA AT LOS ANGELES
THE UNIVERSITY LIBRARY

REC'D LD-URL UNIVERSITY OF CALIFORNIA LIBRARY
Los Angeles

OCT 23 1975 This book is DUE on the last date stamped below.

REC'D LD-URL
NOV 12 1975

NOV 9 1973

JAN 7 1974

APR 13 1975

JUL 20 '75

REC'D LD-URL
JAN 25 1998

MAR 1998

REC'D LD-URL
MAR 2 1981

MAR 15 1994

Form L9—Series 4939

UNIVERSITY of CALIFORNIA
AT
LOS ANGELES
LIBRARY

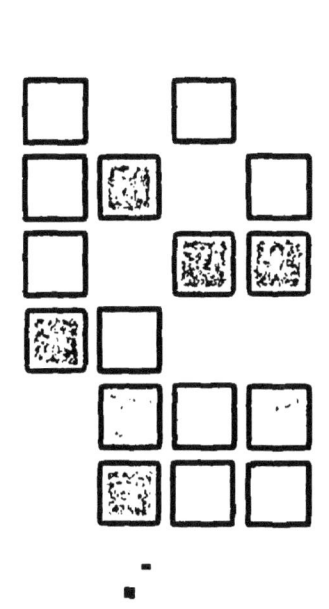

Lightning Source UK Ltd.
Milton Keynes UK
UKHW051253030321
379622UK00022B/532